Contemporary
Literary Criticism

Guide to Gale Literary Criticism Series

For criticism on	Consult these Gale series
Authors now living or who died after December 31, 1959	*CONTEMPORARY LITERARY CRITICISM (CLC)*
Authors who died between 1900 and 1959	*TWENTIETH-CENTURY LITERARY CRITICISM (TCLC)*
Authors who died between 1800 and 1899	*NINETEENTH-CENTURY LITERATURE CRITICISM (NCLC)*
Authors who died between 1400 and 1799	*LITERATURE CRITICISM FROM 1400 TO 1800 (LC)* *SHAKESPEAREAN CRITICISM (SC)*
Authors who died before 1400	*CLASSICAL AND MEDIEVAL LITERATURE CRITICISM (CMLC)*
Black writers of the past two hundred years	*BLACK LITERATURE CRITICISM (BLC) AND BLACK LITERATURE CRITICISM SUPPLEMENT (BLCS)*
Authors of books for children and young adults	*CHILDREN'S LITERATURE REVIEW (CLR)*
Dramatists	*DRAMA CRITICISM (DC)*
Hispanic writers of the late nineteenth and twentieth centuries	*HISPANIC LITERATURE CRITICISM (HLC)*
Native North American writers and orators of the eighteenth, nineteenth, and twentieth centuries	*NATIVE NORTH AMERICAN LITERATURE (NNAL)*
Poets	*POETRY CRITICISM (PC)*
Short story writers	*SHORT STORY CRITICISM (SSC)*
Major authors from the Renaissance to the present	*WORLD LITERATURE CRITICISM, 1500 TO THE PRESENT (WLC)*
Major authors and works from the Bible to the present	*WORLD LITERATURE CRITICISM SUPPLEMENT (WLCS)*

ISSN 0091-3421

Volume 116

Contemporary Literary Criticism

Excerpts from Criticism of the Works
of Today's Novelists, Poets, Playwrights,
Short Story Writers, Scriptwriters, and
Other Creative Writers

Jeffrey W. Hunter
Timothy J. White
EDITORS

Tim Akers
Angela Y. Jones
Daniel Jones
Deborah A. Schmitt
Polly Vedder
Kathleen Wilson
ASSOCIATE EDITORS

The Gale Group

DETROIT • SAN FRANCISCO • LONDON • BOSTON • WOODBRIDGE, CT

Library of Congress Catalog Card Number 76-46132
ISBN 0-7876-3191-4
ISSN 0091-3421

Printed in the United States of America
10 9 8 7 6 5 4 3 2 1

Contents

Preface vii

Acknowledgments xi

Preface

A Comprehensive Information Source
on Contemporary Literature

Named "one of the twenty-five most distinguished reference titles published during the past twenty-five years" by *Reference Quarterly,* the *Contemporary Literary Criticism (CLC)* series provides readers with critical commentary and general information on more than 2,000 authors now living or who died after December 31, 1959. Previous to the publication of the first volume of *CLC* in 1973, there was no ongoing digest monitoring scholarly and popular sources of critical opinion and explication of modern literature. *CLC,* therefore, has fulfilled an essential need, particularly since the complexity and variety of contemporary literature makes the function of criticism especially important to today's reader.

Scope of the Series

CLC presents significant passages from published criticism of works by creative writers. Since many of the authors covered by *CLC* inspire continual critical commentary, writers are often represented in more than one volume. There is, of course, no duplication of reprinted criticism.

Authors are selected for inclusion for a variety of reasons, among them the publication or dramatic production of a critically acclaimed new work, the reception of a major literary award, revival of interest in past writings, or the adaptation of a literary work to film or television.

Attention is also given to several other groups of writers—authors of considerable public interest—about whose work criticism is often difficult to locate. These include mystery and science fiction writers, literary and social critics, foreign writers, and authors who represent particular ethnic groups.

Format of the Book

Each *CLC* volume contains individual essays and reviews taken from hundreds of book review periodicals, general magazines, scholarly journals, monographs, and books. Entries include critical evaluations spanning from the beginning of an author's career to the most current commentary. Interviews, feature articles, and other published writings that offer insight into the author's works are also presented. Students, teachers, librarians, and researchers will find that the generous critical and biographical material in *CLC* provides them with vital information required to write a term paper, analyze a poem, or lead a book discussion group. In addition, complete bibliographical citations note the original source and all of the information necessary for a term paper footnote or bibliography.

Features

A *CLC* author entry consists of the following elements:

- The **Author Heading** cites the author's name in the form under which the author has most commonly published, followed by birth date, and death date when applicable. Uncertainty as to a birth or death date is indicated by a question mark.

- A **Portrait** of the author is included when available.

- A brief **Biographical and Critical Introduction** to the author and his or her work precedes the criticism. The first line of the introduction provides the author's full name, pseudonyms (if applicable), nationality, and a listing of genres in which the author has written. To provide users with easier access to information, the biographical and critical essay included in each author entry is divided into four categories: "Introduction," "Biographical Information," "Major Works," and "Critical Reception." The introductions to single-work entries—entries that focus on well known and frequently studied books, short stories, and poems—are similarly organized to quickly provide readers with information on the plot and major characters of the work being discussed, its major themes, and its critical reception. Previous volumes of *CLC* in which the author has been featured are also listed in the introduction.

- A list of **Principal Works** notes the most important writings by the author. When foreign-language works have been translated into English, the English-language version of the title follows in brackets.

- The **Criticism** represents various kinds of critical writing, ranging in form from the brief review to the scholarly exegesis. Essays are selected by the editors to reflect the spectrum of opinion about a specific work or about an author's literary career in general. The critical and biographical materials are presented chronologically, adding a useful perspective to the entry. All titles by the author featured in the entry are printed in boldface type, which enables the reader to easily identify the works being discussed. Publication information (such as publisher names and book prices) and parenthetical numerical references (such as footnotes or page and line references to specific editions of a work) have been deleted at the editor's discretion to provide smoother reading of the text.

- Critical essays are prefaced by **Explanatory Notes** as an additional aid to readers. These notes may provide several types of valuable information, including: the reputation of the critic, the importance of the work of criticism, the commentator's approach to the author's work, the purpose of the criticism, and changes in critical trends regarding the author.

- A complete **Bibliographical Citation** designed to help the user find the original essay or book precedes each critical piece.

- Whenever possible, a recent **Author Interview** accompanies each entry.

- A concise **Further Reading** section appears at the end of entries on authors for whom a significant amount of criticism exists in addition to the pieces reprinted in *CLC*. Each citation in this section is accompanied by a descriptive annotation describing the content of that article. Materials included in this section are grouped under various headings (e.g., Biography, Bibliography, Criticism, and Interviews) to aid users in their search for additional information. Cross-references to other useful sources published by The Gale Group in which the author has appeared are also included: *Authors in the News, Black Writers, Children's Literature Review, Contemporary Authors, Dictionary of Literary Biography, DISCovering Authors, Drama Criticism, Hispanic Literature Criticism, Hispanic Writers, Native North American Literature, Poetry Criticism, Something about the Author, Short Story Criticism, Contemporary Authors Autobiography Series,* and *Something about the Author Autobiography Series.*

Other Features

CLC also includes the following features:

- An **Acknowledgments** section lists the copyright holders who have granted permission to reprint material in this volume of *CLC*. It does not, however, list every book or periodical reprinted or consulted during the preparation of the volume.

- Each new volume of *CLC* includes a **Cumulative Topic Index,** which lists all literary topics treated in *CLC, NCLC, TCLC,* and *LC 1400-1800.*

- A **Cumulative Author Index** lists all the authors who have appeared in the various literary criticism series published by The Gale Group, with cross-references to Gale's biographical and autobiographical series. A full listing of the series referenced there appears on the first page of the indexes of this volume. Readers will welcome this cumulated author index as a useful tool for locating an author within the various series. The index, which lists birth and death dates when available, will be particularly valuable for those authors who are identified with a certain period but whose death dates cause them to be placed in another, or for those authors whose careers span two periods. For example, Ernest Hemingway is found in *CLC,* yet F. Scott Fitzgerald, a writer often associated with him, is found in *Twentieth-Century Literary Criticism.*

- A **Cumulative Nationality Index** alphabetically lists all authors featured in *CLC* by nationality, followed by numbers corresponding to the volumes in which the authors appear.

- An alphabetical **Title Index** accompanies each volume of *CLC*. Listings are followed by the author's name and the corresponding page numbers where the titles are discussed. English translations of foreign titles and variations of titles are cross-referenced to the title under which a work was originally published. Titles of novels, novellas, dramas, films, record albums, and poetry, short story, and essay collections are printed in italics, while all individual poems, short stories, essays, and songs are printed in roman type within quotation marks; when published separately (e.g., T. S. Eliot's poem *The Waste Land),* the titles of long poems are printed in italics.

- In response to numerous suggestions from librarians, Gale has also produced a **Special Paperbound Edition** of the *CLC* title index. This annual cumulation, which alphabetically lists all titles reviewed in the series, is available to all customers. Additional copies of the index are available upon request. Librarians and patrons will welcome this separate index: it saves shelf space, is easy to use, and is recyclable upon receipt of the next edition.

Citing *Contemporary Literary Criticism*

When writing papers, students who quote directly from any volume in the Literary Criticism Series may use the following general forms to footnote reprinted criticism. The first example pertains to material drawn from periodicals, the second to material reprinted in books:

[1]Alfred Cismaru, "Making the Best of It," *The New Republic,* 207, No. 24, (December 7, 1992), 30, 32; excerpted and reprinted in *Contemporary Literary Criticism,* Vol. 85, ed. Christopher Giroux (Detroit: Gale, 1995), pp. 73-4.

[2]Yvor Winters, *The Post-Symbolist Methods* (Allen Swallow, 1967); excerpted and reprinted in *Contemporary Literary Criticism,* Vol. 85, ed. Christopher Giroux (Detroit: Gale, 1995), pp. 223-26.

Suggestions Are Welcome

The editors hope that readers will find *CLC* a useful reference tool and welcome comments about the work. Send comments and suggestions to: Editors, *Contemporary Literary Criticism,* The Gale Group, 27500 Drake Rd., Farmington Hills, MI 48333-3535.

Acknowledgments

The editors wish to thank the copyright holders of the criticism included in this volume and the permissions managers of many book and magazine publishing companies for assisting us in securing reproduction rights. We are also grateful to the staffs of the Detroit Public Library, the Library of Congress, the University of Detroit Mercy Library, Wayne State University Purdy/Kresge Library Complex, and the University of Michigan Libraries for making their resources available to us. Following is a list of the copyright holders who have granted us permission to reproduce material in this volume of *CLC*. Every effort has been made to trace copyright, but if omissions have been made, please let us know.

COPYRIGHTED MATERIAL IN *CLC*, VOLUME 116, WERE REPRODUCED FROM THE FOLLOWING PERIODICALS:

The American Poetry Review, v. 10, May-June, 1981 for "Edward Hirsch: Poet at the Window" by Edward Hirsch. Copyright © 1981 by World Poetry, Inc. Reproduced by permission of the author.—*The Antioch Review*, v. 52, Winter, 1994; v. 54, Summer, 1996. Copyright © 1994, 1996 by the Antioch Review Inc. Both reproduced by permission of the Editors.—*Ariel: The Israel Review of Arts and Letters*, n. 61, 1985. Reproduced by permission.—*Belles Lettres: A Review of Books by Women*, v. 4, Winter, 1989; v. 8, Fall, 1992. Both Reproduced by permission.—*The Black Scholar*, v. 10, May-June, 1979. Copyright 1979 by *The Black Scholar*. Reproduced by permission.—*The Bloomsbury Review*, v. 15, January-February, 1995 for A review of 'The Gutenberg Elegies' by Wulf D. Rehder. Copyright © by Owaissa Communications Company, Inc. 1995. Reproduced by permission of the author.—*Book World—The Washington Post*, v. 12, September 5, 1982 for a review of Letters from a Father, and Other Poems by Robert Hass; March 12, 1995 for "Vanishing Act" by Walter Abish. © 1982, 1995. Washington Post Book World Service/Washington Post Writers Group. Both reproduced by permission of the respective authors.—*Callaloo*, v. 2, February, 1979. © 1979. Reproduced by permission of The Johns Hopkins University Press.—*Chicago Review*, v. 30, Summer, 1978; v. 41, 1995. Copyright © 1978, 1995 by *Chicago Review*. Both reproduced by permission.—*Chicago Tribune—Books*, April 11, 1993 for "The Collected Mona Van Duyn" by Liz Rosenberg; January 29, 1995 for "Endangered Books?" by Andy Solomon. © copyrighted 1993, 1995 Chicago Tribune Company. All rights reserved. Both reproduced by permission of the respective authors.—*Christian Science Monitor*, v. 84, August 17, 1992. © 1992 The Christian Science Publishing Society. All rights reserved. Reproduced by permission from *The Christian Science Monitor*.—*Colby Library Quarterly*, v. XXIII, December, 1987. Reproduced by permission of the publisher.—*Commentary*, v. 60, September, 1975 for "Trashville" by William S. Pechter; v. 62, October, 1976 for "Altman, Chabrol, and Ray" by William S. Pechter. Copyright © 1975, 1976 by the American Jewish Committee. All rights reserved. Both reproduced by permission of the publisher and the respective authors.—*Commonweal*, v. CXIX, October 23, 1992; v. CXXII, May 19, 1995. Copyright © 1992, 1995 Commonweal Publishing Co., Inc. Both reproduced by permission of Commonweal Foundation.—*The Critic*, Chicago, v. XXV, Winter, 1976. © *The Critic* 1976. Reproduced with the permission of the Thomas More Association, Chicago, IL.—*Critique: Studies in Modern Fiction*, v. XXI, 1979. Copyright © 1979 Helen Dwight Reid Educational Foundation. Reproduced with the permission of the Helen Dwight Reid Educational Foundation, published by Heldref Publications, 1319 18th Street, N.W., Washington, DC 20036-1802.—*Éire-Ireland*, v. XIV, Spring, 1979; v. XXVIII, 1993. Copyright © 1979, 1993 by the Irish American Cultural Institute. Both reproduced by permission of the publisher.—*Film Comment*, v. 10, September-October, 1974 for "Altman: The Empty Staircase and the Chinese Princess" by Michael Dempsey; v. 13, July-August, 1977 for "Floating" by Roger Greenspun; v. 30, March-April, 1994 for "A Lion's Gate: The Cinema According to Robert Altman" by Kathleen Murphy; v. 33, March-April, 1997 for "Kansas City, Kansas City, Kansas City, Kansas City" by Richard Combs. Copyright © 1974, 1977, 1994, 1997 by Film Comment Publishing Corporation. All reproduced by permission of the respective authors.—*Film Quarterly*, v. 48, Summer, 1995 for a review of "Ready to Wear (Prêt-à-Porter)" by Robert Hilferty. © 1995 by the Regents of the University of California. Reproduced by permission of the publisher and the author.—*The Gettysburg Review*, v. 1, Spring, 1988. Reproduced by permission.—*The Hollins Critic*, v. XXX, October, 1993. Copyright © 1993 by Hollins College. Reproduced by permission of the publisher.—*The Hudson Review*, v. 13, Spring, 1960; v. 36,

the respective authors; v. 96, April, 1960 for "The Teeming Catalogue" by John Woods. © 1960 by the Modern Poetry Association. Reproduced by permission of the Editor of *Poetry* and the Literary Estate of John Woods.—*Prooftexts,* v. 4, May, 1984; v. 10, September, 1990. Copyright © 1984, 1990 by The Johns Hopkins University Press. All rights reserved. Both reproduced by permission of The Johns Hopkins University Press.—*The Review of Contemporary Fiction,* v. 13, Spring, 1993; v. 13, Summer, 1993 v. 14, Summer, 1994. Copyright, 1993, 1994, by John O'Brien. All reproduced by permission.—*The Saturday Review,* v. LI, April 13, 1968. © 1968 The Saturday Review Magazine. © 1979, General Media Communications, Inc. Reproduced by permission of *The Saturday Review.*—*Shenandoah,* v. 44, Spring, 1994 for "Life Work" by Robert B. Shaw. Copyright 1994 by Washington and Lee University. Reproduced from *Shenandoah* with the permission of the Editor and the author.—*Sight and Sound,* v. 4, March, 1994; v. 6, December, 1996. Copyright © 1994, 1996 by The British Film Institute. Both reproduced by permission.—*The Southern Review,* Louisiana State University, v. 9, Winter, 1973 for "Deer, Doors, Darks" by Arthur Oberg. Copyright, 1973, by the author. Reproduced by permission of the Literary Estate of Arthur Oberg.—*The Spectator,* v. 269, November 21, 1992. © 1992 by *The Spectator.* Reproduced by permission of *The Spectator.*—*Studies in Short Fiction,* v. 30, Summer, 1993, v. 32, Spring, 1995. Copyright 1993, 1995 by Newberry College. Both reproduced by permission.—*The Times Literary Supplement,* October 7, 1965; October 6, 1972; October 30-November 5, 1987; September 18, 1992; November 27, 1992; March 11, 1994; October 7, 1994. Copyright The Times Supplements Limited 1965, 1972, 1987, 1992, 1994. All reproduced from *The Times Literary Supplement* by permission.—*The Village Voice,* v. 38, July 1, 1993 for "Housekeeping" by Robyn Selman. Copyright © V. V. Publishing Corporation. Reproduced by permission of the author.—*The Wall Street Journal,* v. 204, December 17, 1984; July 15, 1994. Copyright 1984, 1994 Dow Jones & Company, Inc. All rights reserved. Reproduced with permission of *The Wall Street Journal.*—*World Literature Today,* v. 59, Autumn, 1985; v. 60, Winter, 1986; v. 63, Summer, 1988; v. 65, Spring, 1991; v. 68, Spring, 1994; v. 69, Spring, 1995; v. 71, Spring, 1997. Copyright © 1985, 1986, 1988, 1991, 1994, 1995, 1997 by the University of Oklahoma Press. All reproduced by permission.

COPYRIGHTED MATERIAL IN *CLC,* VOLUME 116, WERE REPRODUCED FROM THE FOLLOWING BOOKS:

Alter, Robert. From *After the Tradition: Essays on Modern Jewish Writing.* E. P. Dutton and Co., Inc., 1969. Copyright © 1969, 1968, 1967, 1966, 1965, 1964, 1962, 1961 by Robert Alter. All rights reserved. Reproduced by permission of the author.—Curb, Rosemary K. From "Pre-Feminism in the Black Revolutionary Drama of Sonia Sanchez" in *The Many Forms of Drama.* Edited by Karelisa V. Hartigan. University Press of America, 1985. Copyright © 1985 by University Press of America, Inc. All rights reserved. Reproduced by permission.—De Lancey, Frenzella Elaine. From "Refusing to be Boxed In: Sonia Sanchez's Transformation of the Haiku Form" in *Language and Literature in the African American Imagination.* Edited by Carol Aisha Blackshire-Belay. Greenwood Press, 1992. Copyright © 1992 by Carol Aisha Blackshire-Belay. All rights reserved. Reproduced by permission of Greenwood Publishing Group, Inc., Westport, CT.—Flinker, Noam. From "Saul and David in the Early Poetry of Yehuda Amichai" in *The David Myth in Western Literature.* Edited by Raymond-Jean Frontain and Jan Wojcik. Purdue University Press, 1980. Copyright © 1980 by Purdue Research Foundation, West Lafayette, Indiana. All rights reserved. Reproduced by permission.—Gabbin, Joanne Veal. From "The Southern Imagination of Sonia Sanchez" in *Southern Women Writers: The New Generation.* Edited by Tonette Bond Inge. University of Alabama Press, 1990. Copyright © 1990 by The University of Alabama Press. All rights reserved. Reproduced by permission.—Jennings, Regina B. From "The Blue/Black Poetics of Sonia Sanchez" in *Language and Literature in the African American Imagination.* Edited by Carol Aisha Blackshire-Belay. Greenwood Press, 1992. Copyright © 1992 by Carol Aisha Blackshire-Belay. All rights reserved. Reproduced by permission of Greenwood Publishing Group, Inc., Westport, CT.—Larsen, Max Deen. From "Saints of the Ascendancy: William Trevor's Big-House Novels" in *Ancestral Voices: The Big House in Anglo-Irish Literature.* Edited by Otto Rauchbauer. Lilliput Press and Georg Olms AG, Hildesheim, 1992. © Georg Olms AG, Hildesheim 1992. All rights reserved. Reproduced by permission of the editor.—McCarthy, Todd. From "The Delinquents (Robert Altman) (1974)" in *Kings of The Bs.* Edited by Todd McCarthy and Charles Flynn. E. P. Dutton & Co., Inc., 1975. Copyright © 1975 by Todd McCarthy and Charles Flynn. All rights reserved. Used by permission of E. P. Dutton & Co., Inc., a division of Penguin Putnam Inc. —Morrison, Kristin. From an introduction to *William Trevor.* Twayne Publishers, 1993. Copyright © 1993 by Twayne Publishers. All rights reserved. Reproduced with the permission of Twayne Publishers, Inc., an imprint of Macmillan

Library Reference.—Paulson, Suzanne Morrow. From a preface to *William Trevor: A Study of the Short Fiction.* Twayne Publishers, 1993. Copyright © 1993 by Twayne Publishers. All rights reserved. Reproduced with the permission of Twayne Publishers, Inc., an imprint of Macmillan Library Reference.—Rhodes, Robert E. From "William Trevor's Stories of Trouble" in *Contemporary Irish Writing.* Edited by James D. Brophy and Raymond J. Porter. Iona College Press and Twayne Publishers, 1983. Copyright © 1983 by Iona College Press. All rights reserved. Reproduced by permission of the author.—Roudiez, Leon S. From *French Fiction Revisited.* Dalkey Archive Press, 1972. © 1972, 1991 Leon S. Roudiez. All rights reserved. Reproduced by permission.—Williams, David. From "The Poetry of Sonia Sanchez" in *Black Women Writers (1950-1980): A Critical Evaluation.* Edited by Mari Evans. Anchor Press/Doubleday, 1984. Copyright © 1983 by Mari Evans. All rights reserved. Used by permission of Doubleday, a division of Random House, Inc.

PHOTOGRAPHS AND ILLUSTRATIONS APPEARING IN *CLC,* VOLUME 116, WERE RECEIVED FROM THE FOLLOWING SOURCES:

Altman, Robert, photograph. AP/Wide World Photos. Reproduced by permission.
Amichai, Yehuda, photograph by Jerry Bauer. © Jerry Bauer. Reproduced by permission.
Birkerts, Sven, photograph by Richard Howard. Reproduced by permission of Sven Birkerts.
O'Brien, Edna, photograph. Archive Photos, Inc. Reproduced by permission.
Sanchez, Sonia, photograph by Marion Ettlinger. Reproduced by permission.
Trevor, William, photograph by Jerry Bauer. © by Jerry Bauer. Reproduced by permission.
Van Duyn, Mona, 1971, photograph. AP/Wide World Photos. Reproduced by permission.

Robert Altman

1925-

American filmmaker.

The following entry presents an overview of Altman's career through 1996. For further information on his life and works, see *CLC,* Volume 16.

INTRODUCTION

Robert Altman enjoyed both critical acclaim and commercial success with his film *M*A*S*H* In 1970, but he is known more for his cult following than for his box office smashes. His signature techniques, including multiple voices, meandering plots, and obscure themes, have garnered him critical acclaim for his innovation, but have prevented him from gaining overwhelming popular success.

Biographical Information

Altman was born February 20, 1925, in Kansas City, Missouri, to German immigrant parents. He attended several schools in the Kansas City area, including Wentworth Military Academy, before entering the Air Force to become a co-pilot of B-24 bombers. In the 1940s and 1950s Altman wrote several B-movie screenplays in Los Angeles and then returned to Kansas City to direct documentaries. In the late 1950s Altman tried his luck in Hollywood once again, this time in television. For the rest of the 1950s and much of the 1960s, Altman wrote, produced, or directed episodes of popular shows such as *Bonanza, Alfred Hitchcock Presents,* and *U. S. Marshall.* His first feature film was *Countdown* (1968), but he was not allowed final editing decisions on the film. Although many consider *Countdown* a fine science fiction film, Altman disavows the movie and has insisted on complete artistic control of his subsequent projects. Altman was chosen to direct his breakthrough feature, *M*A*S*H* (1970) after several (according to some reports, as many as fifteen) directors turned the project down. After *M*A*S*H,* Altman made a series of offbeat films that received mixed critical reception and were by no means commercial successes. Altman's *Nashville* (1975) brought the auteur back into Hollywood's good graces for a time, garnering Altman the New York Film Critics Circle awards for best film and best director, as well as multiple Academy Award nominations. Altman experienced a third resurgence in 1992 with *The Player,* another commerical and critical success for which Altman was again nominated for multiple Academy Awards.

Major Works

M*A*S*H is an anti-war film centered on a group of zany army doctors who, though compassionate and skilled surgeons, survive the war through alcohol and humor. Set during the Korean War but released during the Vietnam War, the black comedy contains many of the elements typical of Altman's other films, including improvised lines and scenes, overlapping dialogue and sound effects, light and irreverent humor, no standard plot, and a moving camera which records from a distance. *McCabe and Mrs. Miller* (1971) is a western and love story that subverts many of the conventions of each. In *The Long Goodbye* (1973), based on the Raymond Chandler novel, Altman tackles the detective genre and one of its mythical heroes, the detective Philip Marlowe. Marlowe is out of place in his 1970s surroundings, enabling Altman to make a social commentary on the times. *Nashville* (1975) analyzes the nature of power and opportunism. The story revolves around a cast of 24 characters, mostly singers, aspiring stars, and politicians in the capital of country music. *Buffalo Bill and the Indians, or Sitting Bull's History Lesson* (1976) criticizes commercialism, opportunism, and the making of a celebrity. The title itself sets up a dialectic between two versions of history, and the film makes it difficult to discern historical fiction and historical reality. *Vincent and Theo* (1990) is Altman's only biographical film. Altman takes the unusual approach of making Vincent Van Gogh's art peripheral to the main plot. Instead, the film traces Van Gogh's relationship with his brother Theo and the pain he suffered in his life. *The Player* (1992) is a satiric look at the Hollywood studio system and the role writers play in the system. *Short Cuts* (1993) is another sweeping film with multiple plot lines and a large cast of characters. The film is based on slice-of-life stories by Raymond Carver. *Ready to Wear* (1994) follows another multitude of characters, this time through the fashion world. The film analyzes many topics, including the nature of womanhood, relationships in American society, and the human condition.

Critical Reception

Much disagreement surrounds the critical discussions of many of Altman's films. *M*A*S*H* was Altman's breakout film, becoming both a critical and popular success. Many of the techniques which made *M*A*S*H* popular, however, left critics and audiences uneasy in his subsequent films. Many reviewers criticize Altman's use of sound and overlapping dialogue; others assert that the technique lends a sense of reality to his films. Altman's *The Long Goodbye* created a storm of criticism, but several reviewers attribute this to Altman's alteration of the end of the Raymond Chandler novel, which made Marlowe devotees uncomfortable. *Nashville* was another critical and popular success for Altman, but his style still drew complaints. Some critics felt that despite Altman's finesse in juggling multiple story lines, *Nashville*'s separate plots lacked substance individually. Most reviewers agree that plot is not the central element in Altman's work. Jonathan Baumbach asserted that "Altman generates tension in his film not through plot, which seems to exist as an afterthought . . . , but through movement and image." Despite individual criticisms of some of his techniques, many reviewers appreciate Altman's unique and innovative style. While he has failed to achieve consistent box office success, many critics and fans describe him as one of the best directors of his generation. Todd Boyd asserts that, "Altman remains one of the few independent voices in a sea of repetitive Hollywood mediocrity."

PRINCIPAL WORKS

The Delinquents [writer and director] (screenplay) 1955
The James Dean Story [writer and director] (documentary) 1957
Nightmare in Chicago [director] (film) 1967
Countdown [director] (documentary) 1968
That Cold Day in the Park [director] (film) 1969

M*A*S*H [director; adapted from the novel by Richard Hooker] (screenplay) 1970
Brewster McCloud [writer and director] (screenplay) 1970
McCabe and Mrs. Miller [with Brian McKay; writer and director] (screenplay) 1971
Images [writer and director] (screenplay) 1972
The Long Goodbye [director; adapted from the novel by Raymond Chandler] (screenplay) 1973
Thieves Like Us [with Calder Willingham and Joan Tewkesbury; writer and director] (screenplay) 1974
California Split [writer and director] (screenplay) 1974
Nashville [director] (film) 1975
Buffalo Bill and the Indians, or Sitting Bull's History Lesson [with Alan Rudolph; writer and director] (screenplay) 1976
Three Women [writer and director] (screenplay) 1977
A Wedding [with John Considine, Patricia Resnick, and Allan Nicholls; writer and director] (screenplay) 1978
Quintet [with Frank Barhydt and Resnick; writer and director] (screenplay) 1979
A Perfect Couple [with Nicholls; writer and director] (screenplay) 1979
Popeye [director] (film) 1980
Come Back to the 5 and Dime, Jimmy Dean, Jimmy Dean [director] (film) 1982
Health [with Barhydt and Paul Dooley; writer and director] (screenplay) 1982
Streamers [director] (film) 1983
Fool for Love [director] (film) 1985
Beyond Therapy [with Christopher Durang; writer and director] (screenplay) 1987
Vincent and Theo [director] (film) 1990
The Player [director] (film) 1992
Short Cuts [with Barhydt; writer and director; based on the short stories of Raymond Carver] (screenplay) 1993
Ready to Wear [also known as *Prêt-á-Porter;* writer and director] (screenplay) 1994
Kansas City [with Barhydt; writer and director] (screenplay) 1996
The Gingerbread Man [director; based on an original story by John Grisham] (film) 1998
Cookie's Fortune [director] (film) 1999

CRITICISM

Jonathan Baumbach (review date 1974)

SOURCE: "Show-Offs," in *Partisan Review,* Vol. XLI, No. 2, 1974, pp. 273-74.

[In the following mixed review, Baumbach complains that, "what's finally wrong with The Long Goodbye *is that for all its artistic pretensions, all of them, the film is not quite*

serious, not serious enough to carry the freight of its pretensions."]

Seeing movies, writing about them is a more subjective business than the authoritative voice of most reviews admits. One runs into a good deal of self-deception and cant among reviewers who try to make the fleeting reality on the screen seem unequivocal. There is so much fantasy invested in moviegoing that movie reviews tend to tell us more about the reviewer than the reviewed.

This is prelude to saying that Robert Altman's odd version of Raymond Chandler's *The Long Goodbye,* which has many incidental virtues, disappointed me and that my disappointment may have as much to do with false expectations as with the weaknesses of the film. The movie I witnessed didn't so much demythify the private eye, as reviewers advertised, as offer him to us as something else altogether—a version of the Elliott Gould persona, a wisecracking, crude, and shy New York Jew displaced in a futuristic California. Updating the Chandler novel to the seventies, Altman's ***The Long Goodbye*** is an exercise in self-revealing style, a showcase for the director's impressively eccentric cinematic manner.

Gould's Philip Marlowe is one of those devious schlemiels who fends off vindication by pretending to be less formidable than he is (or secretly thinks he is). Although he seems ineffectual and vulnerable for a man in his profession, Gould's shamus is cool under pressure (as cool as any of his Marlowe predecessors) or, depending on how you want to read him, oblivious to the world outside him. The wisecrack helps him to keep his distance from others and, more importantly, from his own feelings. Living alone with his cat, seemingly uninterested in women, this Philip Marlowe leads a lonely, empty, and violated life. Yet since the Gould character (like the movie as a whole) has an improvised quality, we don't really believe that Marlowe has an existence beyond the moment of the film. Altman makes us aware that we are watching Elliott Gould impersonating an unlikely, mumbling private eye—everyone mumbles in an Altman film—comically out of step with the world he pretends to inhabit. Gould wears a fifties vintage bar mitzvah suit and drives a forties vintage Lincoln. Altman's attitude toward his protagonist as toward his material in general seems to me loosely defined, and what's finally wrong with ***The Long Goodbye*** is that for all its artistic pretensions, *all* of them, the film is not quite serious, not serious enough to carry the freight of its pretensions.

The visual richness of ***The Long Goodbye*** and the exhilarating, tricky ending in which Gould's Marlowe kills his onetime friend, Terry Lennox, leads one to expect more from the work than it actually delivers, which may further explain my dissatisfaction. Most impressive about Altman's distinctive film, even more impressive than its sharply observed

detailing of a dehumanized California, is the work's elaborately sustained rhythm. Altman is a master of a highly controlled frantic pace as if some volcanic nightmare of chaos (or hysteria) were just below the surface of his world, threatening to explode. Altman generates tension in his film not through plot, which seems to exist as an afterthought (you almost feel copies of the Chandler novel ought to be given out to the audience in advance), but through movement and image. ***The Long Goodbye*** is a disturbing and abrasive experience—Altman's best film to date, two hours of variations on his signature, a highly subjective and private work.

Michael Dempsey (essay date September-October 1974)

SOURCE: "Altman: The Empty Staircase and the Chinese Princess," in *Film Comment,* Vol. 10, No. 5, September-October, 1974, pp. 10-17.

[*In the following essay, Dempsey discusses pivotal scenes in Altman's* Thieves Like Us *and* McCabe and Mrs. Miller *which cause the films to fall short of greatness.*]

Two moments in Robert Altman's movies may hold the key to their true nature. In one, the conclusion of ***Thieves Like Us,*** travellers in a railroad station climb a staircase to a train. The film goes into slow motion, and Father Coughlin gives a populist speech on the sound track. Finally, the people disappear, leaving only the stairs. In the other, an episode of ***McCabe and Mrs. Miller,*** a few cardplayers have heard that a contingent of whores on its way to the remote Northwestern town of Presbyterian Church includes one Oriental woman. Some declare that she is an "authentic Chinese princess" who, like all others, is deliriously sexual. Others scoff, but one man clinches it with a story about a friend who paid five dollars to find out, "and it's true."

Most American directors, when they have a multi-megaton hit like ***M*A*S*H,*** try to detonate a series of still bigger blockbusters. Instead, Altman has made a group of offbeat, personal films which explore the genres—fantasy, Western, psychological melodrama, thriller, romance—that they nominally inhabit. ***Brewster McCloud*** throws its bird-boy hero into hard, gleaming Houston instead of yellow-brick Oz. ***McCabe and Mrs. Miller*** turns a straightforward Western into a wispy mirage. ***Images*** makes us lose our bearings inside the mind of a schizophrenic woman. Philip Marlowe is bemused and dreamy in ***The Long Goodbye,*** lost in a city and a crime too labyrinthine for him to understand until too late. ***Thieves Like Us*** almost totally denies us the kiss kiss bang bang that we expect from stories of lovers on the run.

These thumbnail sketches probably explain the commercial

failure of each movie, not to mention the sharply contradictory responses they have aroused in critics, who generally call them mishmashes or masterpieces. Everyone agrees on their *M*A*S*H*-derived techniques: improvised lines and scenes, overlapping dialogue, roving camera, avoidance of standard plots, throwaway humor. But no one has investigated what meanings they convey, or how.

Equally persistent is the figure of the dreamer who, cut off from the community by accident or by design, spins a web of fantasy in which to live. Brewster, Cathryn, the thieves, Marlowe wool-gathering through a stoned reprise of Bogart, Roger Wade suicidally caught up in a parody of Hemingway—all trap themselves in destructive illusions. Even *M*A*S*H* has its dreamers, Hot Lips and the chief surgeon, two pompous hypocrites who play authoritarian games as if they were back in boot camp instead of swamped in blood. *M*A*S*H* and *Thieves Like Us* stand aside stylistically from their fantasizers; visually they are plainer, more depoeticized than the other films, which try to show the world as their beleagured dreamers experience it.

Altman's easygoing, naturalistic techniques, which use realistic details for impressionistic effects, sometimes make people think of him as a tender humanist. . . . Yet Altman has a preoccupation with the destruction of humanity's most vulnerable members, whom he offers little solace.
—Michael Dempsey

The most effective scenes of *Brewster McCloud* center on the Astrodome, from the outside a UFO designed by an interplanetary Bucky Fuller, from the inside a cavernous cage in which Brewster's wings flap pitifully. Every phantasmagoric landscape, every jagged cut in *Images* is filtered through Cathryn's disorientation. The soft, hallucinatory colors, the white nights redolent of smoking joss sticks in *The Long Goodbye* reflect Marlowe's spaced-out confusion as much as they do a recognizable aspect of Los Angeles.

Quite a few of these dreamers—from the chief surgeon freaking out over taunts about laying Hot Lips, to Chickamaw growling manically because Bowie's press is better than his—end up losing their minds. Altman's easygoing, naturalistic techniques, which use realistic details for impressionistic effects, sometimes make people think of him as a tender humanist, much as Jean Renoir's comparable methods have also won this praise. Yet Altman has a preoccupation with the destruction of humanity's most vulnerable members, whom he offers little solace.

Not every Altman character falls into this category; others cast the cold eye of the realist on the delusions of the dreamer. These hardnosed realists—the squabbling flatfoots of *Brewster McCloud* stumbling over corpses and analyzing birdshit for clues, the hoods and plotters who bamboozle Marlowe—swarm around the besieged fantasists. In *M*A*S*H* they take over completely. Hawkeye, Trapper John, and the other madcap medics waste no time disposing of Hot Lips and the chief surgeon; they are too professional to worry about chains of command in the midst of chaos.

The other movies provide secondary characters whose sophistication or mundaneness mocks the quirks and eccentricities of the dreamers. Cathryn's husband, Hugh, patronizes her; Mattie listens scornfully to the gleeful babbling of the robbers; Keechie curses Bowie for not abandoning crime. Her contemporary cousin is Brewster's girlfriend Suzanne, her eyes garishly made up like those of Clockwork Alex with spiky claws of mascara, her tongue wagging with plans for parlaying the wings into a fat fortune and a mansion on River Oaks Boulevard. These realists never lose touch with ordinary life and its day-to-day concerns. They serve as lightning rods for the audience's skepticism about soaring like a bird or wandering in a realm of ghosts.

Although just tracing the themes common to these films will not serve this purpose, it is a necessary starting point. Their characters, in one way or another, are always looking for some kind of community or trying to protect the one that they already have. Many of the best moments in *Thieves Like Us* occur in the hide-outs of its three bank robbers, Bowie, T-Dub, and Chickamaw, where they bide their time after breaking out of prison or plan their next heist. Instead of showing them knocking over the banks or careening off in getaway cars, Altman concentrates on their homey life in between jobs. They catnap, drink, lounge around, chortle and bicker over descriptions of their exploits in the papers, tell corny jokes, join in the family life of T-Dub's sister-in-law Mattie, her obnoxious son James, and her baby-moll sister Lula. Mattie's household oscillates between numbing respectability and quirky outbursts like the robbery that Chickamaw makes them enact.

But beneath everything flows a persistent undercurrent of running men desiring shelter and stability. Affable idiot T-Dub marries dummy Lula, who enjoys parading around in dime store sheaths like a cloning of lean Harlow. Chickamaw, a borderline psychotic, grows restless amid domesticity but still dreams of settling in Mexico. Bowie, the youngest thief who stumbled mindlessly into crime while an impoverished teenager, takes up with placid, unimaginative Keechie out of a yearning for the ordinary romance and home life which his criminal record denies him.

The other films follow parallel routes through settings far from Depression-bound Mississippi. *The Long Goodbye* meanders through the glittering basin of Los Angeles, the classic non-community of major American cities. Yet, unlike the Houston of *Brewster McCloud,* it tantalizes us with the possibility of a new kind of community. By night from on high, its blinking constellation of colors can seem like an enchanted realm capable of making the old lures of sun, wealth, ease, and stardom come true. As the film progresses, characters apparently unrelated to one another—pretty boy Terry Lennox; bellowing blocked novelist Roger Wade; his queen bee wife Eileen; Marty Augustine, the slick-agent show biz thug masterfully updated from Raymond Chandler's slimy "hard boys"; Dr. Verringer, a steely blond runt of a psychiatric quack; even the cops—turn out to be linked, while goofy, dazed gumshoe Marlowe tries in vain to fathom their malignant menage.

In *Brewster McCloud* the cops tracking the hero, who has strangled several expendable bit players for interfering with his scheme to build outsized dove wings and fly away, form a ramshackle group. So does their quarry with his mysterious guardian angel and his two odd girlfriends. The emotionally isolated Cathryn of *Images* works up a dream world for herself of husband, real and imaginary lovers, and a young girl who resembles her. *M*A*S*H* pivots on a community of Army doctors and nurses struggling to save lives in a fragile tent city three miles from the Korean front. Sometimes genuine, sometimes false, always precarious, these communities are the persistent centers of movies that, at first glance, seem bewilderingly varied.

But only *M*A*S*H* allows them a clear-cut victory; alone among Altman's movies, it celebrates the realists unambiguously. Hawkeye and Company are the Good Guys, Hot Lips and the surgeon are creeps, and that's that. *M*A*S*H* remains funny, but its sentimentality about military camaraderie sticks out now that its wisecracks amid spurting arteries no longer seem so startling. Without for one minute going along with Hot Lips and her mania for the rulebook, we can reasonably view Hawkeye and the others as bastards for the way that they expose her naked in the shower. They are quite self-righteous in their determination to reform her, but the movie never questions them as it does the myopic Catholic chaplain, Dago Red. Hot Lips' unconvincing flipflop from martinet to good old broad gives the show away. Nobody connected with the movie seems to have imagined that some people might not fall in love with its cuddly cutups.

The other films have more resonance (without necessarily being better) because their lines of demarcation between dreamer and realist are not so rigid. *Brewster McCloud* satirizes its gang of stumblebum cops, fashion plate sleuths, dimwitted flunkies, and narcissistic politicians. Bubble-brained Suzanne sends the hero to his death by tipping off

the police, yet Altman retains a measure of affection for her saucer-eyed effervescence and her giddy vulgarity.

Keechie comes through similarly, affecting in her wary attraction to Bowie, depressing in her scorn for his attempt to spring Chickamaw from jail, an adventure that leads to his death when Mattie sets him up for an ambush. Their undeceived, illusionless approach to life, untouched by imagination or spirit, seems drab and mean, as limited in its way as the criminals' childish fantasies. In both *Images* and *The Long Goodbye,* the principal realists—fusty, boring Hugh and chrome-plated, cynical Terry—fall to vengeful dreamers, and the audience certainly sheds no tears over them. Realism is not an unalloyed virtue in Altman's films. If fantasy leads to destruction, realism may result in amorality, with hardly a greater guarantee of survival.

Nevertheless, there is no denying that Altman's dreamers generally end up dead or crazy. We leave Brewster and Bowie crumpled on the ground, one splintered amid the wreckage of his wings while a circus swirls around his body, the other hidden in a quilt with his blood leaking through it into the dirt. The others live on but at a murderous cost. Chickamaw brutally destroys a harmless old prison official; Cathryn knocks her husband down a waterfall, derangedly supposing that she has annihilated her alter ego. In the controversial ending of *The Long Goodbye,* Marlowe finally learns how contemptuously Lennox has used him under the guise of friendship and responds by killing his betrayer. This climax may be questionable, yet more harshly than any other Altman conclusion it does deliver his basic message to dreamers: kill or be killed.

These concerns are implicit in Altman's production methods and techniques. An intuitive director, he relies heavily on whims, the chemistry of his casts, sudden inspirations, the unexpected qualities that an actor (or a non-actor) brings to a part. Preconceived concepts, grand designs, tight scripts, and rigid shooting schedules go by the boards as much as possible. Very likely these procedures create a sense of community among the actors, technicians, and aides, one that is heightened by Altman's practice of retaining many assistants (cameraman Vilmos Zsigmond, film editor Louis Lombardo, production designer Leon Ericksen, composer John Williams, assistant director Tommy Thompson) and an irregular stock company of actors (Elliott Gould, Shelley Duvall, Keith Carradine, Sally Kellerman, John Shuck, Bert Remsen, Rene Auberjonois—among others) from film to film.

As happened with Godard before his political phase, making and finding a movie become almost synonymous; you sometimes sense that the process of filmmaking means as much to Altman as the end result. It is as though he were trying to soften the feeling of transience that goes with gathering a company, making a movie, then watching the participants all go their separate ways. At the same time, improvisation, casual comedy, and overlapping dialogue express the free-and-easy give-and-take of a lively, thriving community.

Altman's movies—particularly **McCabe and Mrs. Miller, The Long Goodbye,** and **Images**—are seductive, diaphanous visual slipstreams. But their sound lends them their peculiar distinction. Plenty of directors nowadays have their performers all talk at the same time without bothering to sort out the lines. But for most of them it is only a chic mannerism.

For instance, *Cinderella Liberty* (on which Zsigmond, Ericksen, and Williams worked) uses throwaway lines in the Altman manner (its director, Mark Rydell, having agreed to play Marty Augustine in **The Long Goodbye** to learn Altman's ways), but pointlessly because the throwaways are just ordinary movieish quips. Altman's technique plays a complex role in the creation of his vision. Most obviously, it creates a sense of swarming life, capturing the tetchiness and energy and mulishness of people ricocheting off one another. Loosening the actors' tongues lets them interact more spontaneously; they make us believe that they really are a community instead of a bunch of hired hams reciting memorized dialogue.

A prime example of this occurs in **McCabe and Mrs. Miller** when McCabe gingerly enters Pat Sheehan's ratty saloon for the first time. The gamblers and barflies buzz and mumble all around him; though we can't make out their precise speech, its tone conveys their suspicion of him, as it does the dissolving of their wariness when he stands the house to drinks and breaks out his orange poker-tablecloth.

Meanwhile, we do hear what we need to hear, as when McCabe goes outside to piss and some drinkers discuss his Swedish gun. In an instant, we realize that McCabe's pistol causes comment because no one in this godforsaken hole is armed. This points up the isolation of the town, foretells McCabe's hold on the collective imagination of its citizens, foreshadows their terror at the giant rifle slung on the horse of the hired killer Butler, and undercuts the audience's idea of a traditional Western, in which everybody packs guns. Plot, theme, and mood advance quickly and obliquely, without elaborate dramatic contrivances.

This sequence also indicates how Altman's use of sound gives his comedy a light touch that none of his imitators can match. McCabe's affable manner helps him win over the townspeople, who have heard vague rumors that he is a dangerous gunfighter and would steer clear of him if he stood around hardselling his jokes like a sleazy comic in a night club. His quips, like the one about squaring a circle by shoving a 4x4 up a mule's ass, must have had whiskers even in 1906, but his charm makes them seem witty.

Altman generally avoids milking jokes. Whether it be Painless, the *M*A*S*H* dentist, saying, "Well, big day, got two jaws to rebuild," or Marlowe trying to flimflam his cat into accepting a new brand of food (two examples out of dozens), his actors touch our funnybones deftly and move on. They never slaver and sweat and shout, "Laugh, you schmucks, this is funny!" the way Mel Brooks and his cast do in *Blazing Saddles.* Altman's people never fall into this trap, which is fatal to either comedy or communal sentiments.

Besides this, Altman's sound, especially dialogue, has a more elusive, less pre-plannable effect: reverberation in our minds like a memory. Quite often, particularly in **McCabe** and **The Long Goodbye,** a line will be less important than the way an actor speaks it. The vagueness of much Altman dialogue, the way that the speakers don't worry about well-timed pauses or bell-like enunciation, often gives it a mysterious echoing vividness, even though it may have no literary content.

For instance, in **McCabe and Mrs. Miller** one whore gets sick of another's bitching and cries, "Oh shut up, Eunice, you're always bloody well complaining!" The line, perhaps improvised, does not advance the plot or develop the whore's character; since she is hidden in a crowd, we can't even be sure who speaks it. Yet the sound of her voice leaping suddenly out of the squabbling gives it an impact all out of proportion to its literal meaning.

Or take the moment in **The Long Goodbye** when Marlowe, called "the best neighbor we ever had" when he buys brownie mix for some candle-dipping, yoga-practicing, seminude beauties, mumbles, "Got to be the best neighbor—I'm a private eye." Naturally, this tells us Marlowe's racket, but who needs to be told how Bogey's mutant son earns his living? It's Marlowe's tone of voice, conveying both confusion and zany delight in his own cleverness, that makes it funny and beautiful.

Techniques like these are incredibly risky because they leave the audience unusually free to respond or not. More controlled styles may miss the freedom and spontaneity of Altman's approach, but they also guide the viewer with a firmer hand. Directors as different as Hitchcock, Bresson, Kubrick, and Russell leave practically nothing to chance in their movies, the good ones or the bad ones; Altman leaves just about everything to chance. As a result, if passing moments and details fail to be fresh and exciting in themselves, all we have left is a lifeless skeleton of "themes" or "texture."

The ideas and emotions of Hitchcock, Bresson, Kubrick, or Russell movies can survive local inadequacies that would destroy an Altman movie, which depends more than they do on moment-to-moment life. Lately, Pauline Kael and Norman Mailer, writing on *Last Tango in Paris,* have exalted improvisation as the highest form of filmmaking, and obviously the more controlled approaches can become cold, manipulative, and rigid. But Altman's films, like Bertolucci's, often display the pitfalls of improvisation. As Jay Cocks remarked in his *Time* review of *Thieves Like Us,* they sometimes fall into "a casualness and vagueness about ideas."

Brewster McCloud is an all too obvious example. Thematically, the movie may hang together. Yet it obstinately refuses to work. For one thing, Altman's improvisory touch has clearly deserted him. Most of the performances are mechanical, one-joke cartoons, and awfully tired ones at that. To cite a pair, Michael Murphy and William Windom parody Steve McQueen and Robert Vaughn in *Bullitt,* a waste of time if there ever was one. Worse, the central figure, Brewster, is so nebulous that the film ends up flying apart in all directions, like a centrifuge crumbling as it spins. C. Kirk McClelland's diary of the production reveals that Altman did not seem to know what kind of movie he wanted to make. Evidently he never found out.

This is also partly true of **Thieves Like Us,** even though it is Altman's quietest, most austere movie so far. The film is tender and funny, yet a little flat. It lacks the almost magical resonance of **McCabe and Mrs. Miller, The Long Goodbye,** even bits of **Images,** not to mention the tortuous complexity and brooding power of Faulkner, to whose work Kael inexplicably compared it. Actually, **Thieves** is *Bonnie and Clyde* minus the banjo music, the hopped-up acting, and the mythic overtones. *Paper Moon* also resounds in its sound track, a pastiche of snippets from such radio serials as "Gangbusters" and "Steve Gibson of the International Secret Police." Barring a lapse or two, Altman avoids the machine-tooled gags and the push-button hearttugs that Peter Bogdanovich dotes on, but he still doesn't bring the movie to full life.

The characters, their situations, the observations of quirky Americana, moral atrophy, and rural banality are a trifle shopworn, and not simply because Edward Anderson's novel had already been filmed in 1949 as *They Live By Night.* With simple camerawork and limpid color, Altman undercuts the tenebrous romanticism of Nicholas Ray's *film noir.* But he doesn't find enough to put in its place. Keith Carradine and Shelley Duvall are better actors than Farlay Granger and Cathy O'Donnell, yet their brief idyll is less moving. It never equals *Night*'s tight close-up of O'Donnell as she reads a letter from her dead lover and then turns sorrowfully away from us, her flowing hair filling the screen. Altman's muted style will not allow for lyrical touches like this, yet without

them his characters are too attenuated and his set pieces—especially a blazing nocturnal car crash—too self-contained.

Images, on the other hand, is intensely lyrical. Its throbbing music, its rococo narration, its eerie shots of a blood red lake, an incandescent house glowing in the twilight, an enchanted storybook meadow, a sunstruck valley traversed by cloudshadows in procession are utterly mesmerizing. In fact, their strangeness becomes the movie's true subject when Cathryn's psychology turns out to be barbershop Freud: she wants a baby to save her marriage, simultaneously does not want one, feels guilty over this and her promiscuity, therefore assumes that Hugh must also be involved in extra-marital sex, retreats to reveries of her lost childhood, her "soul."

This schematic characterization recalls Pabst's *Secrets of a Soul;* the film's muddled romanticism of derangement suggests *A Safe Place;* and there are parallels to *Repulsion* (a knifing), *The Whisperers* (bizarre voices), and *The Beguiled* (many lovers in one bed). In *Ms.,* Phyllis Chessler perceptively wrote that Cathryn's confusion of the men in her life certifies her insanity, although many men treat women this way without being thought loony. Beyond this, why does she pick these stiffs? Why did she marry a dolt like Hugh? Wind chimes and colored lights replace the answers to these questions.

Compare this to Kenneth Loach's *Family Life* which, whatever its possible oversimplifications and special pleading, creates a shattering depiction of a woman's slow immersion in madness. Beside the anguish and terror of this film, in which Sandy Ratcliff resembles Susannah York and far surpasses her portrayal of schizophrenia, **Images** is just a fancy finger exercise; intricate psychology, like the botched car chase in **Brewster McCloud,** requires the sort of scripting and planning that wars with Altman's methods.

The Long Goodbye poses a more slippery problem because, however simple-minded its attack on contemporary immorality may be, it is also a mercurial, free-flying, virtuoso performance. Limited space forbids a thorough study of its imagery, which would have to include Roger Wade's death in the nighttime sea while Marlowe and Eileen madly try to reach him from the shore, and the fascinating use of the picture windows in the Wade beach house to create effects oddly similar to certain moments of *Playtime.*

For a long time the film's visual richness made me resist Charles Gregory's criticism of the film's revision of Chandler's Marlowe, particularly in the ending. Gregory feels that Altman has destroyed a hero without understanding him. Yet Marlowe is almost as ineffectual in Chandler's *Long Goodbye* as he is in Altman's. The cops do more to solve the mystery than he does; they even fool him into serving as a decoy so that they can catch some gangsters off guard. Obviously, Chandler had come to see his hero much as Altman sees him, as a pawn and a loser, however admirable. But Marlowe never really finishes last in the book; in the end he does unravel the crime, vindicate his code, get his $25 per day.

Chandler merely dabbles in the romance of being a loser so that Marlowe won't seem slick and phony, like other hard-boiled shamuses. His remark that style "can exist in a savage and dirty age, but it cannot exist in the Coca-Cola age" is glib and sentimental beneath its ersatz social comment. If this were true, then Marlowe's style, such as it is, could not exist either. Gregory praises Chandler for doggedly upholding the virtues embodied in Marlowe, and certainly he was right to do this. But he was wrong in how he did it, through an appealing but basically pulpy figure of fantasy utterly irrelevant to defending these virtues in the real world—of the Fifties or the Seventies.

The movie goes wrong because Altman loses control over the connotations of his conclusion. He seems to intend Marlowe's action as a gesture of rage, one that he shares, against the dehumanizing slickness of people like Lennox, whose manufacture is almost an industry in Los Angeles. Yet it also suggests, not that Marlowe stupidly gave his loyalty to one obviously unworthy of it, but that loyalty to friends is stupid. Perhaps this second implication was accidental; the final "Affectionate remembrance for Dan Blocker," cast as Roger Wade before his death, and the film's generally affectionate treatment of Marlowe both contradict it.

The confusion arises because Altman did not think through one key change that he made in the story. The novel stresses that Marlowe puts himself out for Lennox even though they hardly know each other. Throughout the book, people express astonishment that he would endure three days in jail and risk a murder charge for a virtual stranger; one hood jeers at his "cheap emotions." Chandler's affirmation of his hero's loyalty was linked, it has been suggested, to the McCarthy-HUAC witch hunts; it constituted his tacit rebuke to informers, a point underlined by having Marlowe stand up for a mere acquaintance instead of a longtime friend.

Updating the story to 1973 eliminates this element and thus requires of Altman what he fails (and Chandler had no need) to supply: an explanation of Marlowe's friendship with Lennox. We are clearly not supposed to question their bond in the film, yet right from the start Lennox is so repulsive, so incapable of genuine friendship, that we wonder why Marlowe cannot see through him. (Repressed homosexuality won't do for an answer in this case.) Marlowe may be romantic, but he isn't dumb. As a result, the movie blurs at the outset and, by the time the ending arrives, has grown fundamentally incoherent.

In *McCabe and Mrs. Miller,* Altman pulls all his gifts, themes, and techniques together. More directly than the other movies, it focuses on the possibility of establishing a true community in an indifferent world. Altman sets this up by repeatedly showing isolated individuals forming a group or outsiders joining the town. McCabe's arrival at Sheehan's is the first example. Later, when he leads his first three whores into a clearing in the woods where miners are building up the town, the men gather round uncertainly, afraid to expose their desire. By the time that a similar gathering greets Ida Coyle and Mrs. Miller upon their arrival in Presbyterian Church, the onlookers also include the women of the town.

The film plays variations on this chord at Bart Coyle's funeral, with the second wave of whores helping to sing "Asleep in Jesus"; after their arrival, as they splash and laugh together in a wooden tub; at the end, when a disorganized mob becomes an efficient bucket brigade to put out a fire in the church. These episodes are not unqualified celebrations of the community. The men staring avidly at the three whores also expose the cruelty and exploitation of the arrangement. Ida would not even be in town if she had not been a mail order bride, bought like whores.

Bart's funeral and the ending foreshadow the disintegration of the community. Still, the ideal haunts the movie as more and more strangers arrive, and Presbyterian Church gradually replaces its tents and shacks with the fresh-cut planks of new buildings, particularly the whorehouse, which becomes the heart of the community.

Along with the movie's sound track, its color and camerawork develop its themes almost subliminally. The basic contrast between the snowbound exteriors and the warm, glowing, orange-yellow, honey-brown interiors states the nature of the community: beleaguered people huddled together against an inhospitable landscape. In addition, the colors are so lulling that we experience the sensuality of their life and envy them.

Several camera movements from enclosures to open spaces form a motif too consistent to be entirely accidental. The credit sequence, showing McCabe riding to town through a trackless forest, is a subtly orchestrated series of crane shots which, like the lofty angle that later shows him bringing the three whores to town, works directly on our emotions, makes us feel the exhilaration of finding rest after a harsh journey or clearing out a haven in a desolate wilderness.

Throughout the movie, isolation threatens the community, which never quite embraces everyone. The Chinese mineworkers live in the town but the town will have no part of them. From time to time, we glimpse their placid, opaque faces and their squalid Chinatown. Other strangers the town warmly accepts; these strangers remain outsiders even though they already live in the town—with one ironic exception, the "Chinese princess."

The town's minister, baleful in his black cloth and saturnine scowl, also peers at the life of the community from the fringes of shots; isolation from it is driving him mad. But, unlike the Chinese, he isolates himself, stewing self-righteously because nobody goes to his church. Bart Coyle's death pleases him as the just punishment of another sinner, and he avoids the funeral. He drives McCabe out of the church with a shotgun, pontificating about the "house of God" and vengefully refusing to help defeat the killers. If the community took him seriously, he would poison it with his purism and powerlust. Yet his contorted, lurking figure, reminiscent of the hunched drug addict in *Alice's Restaurant,* expresses an anger that the communal ideal cannot assimilate.

But all of the townspeople are isolated from one another for a deeper reason: their community is based more on business than on fellow feeling. Presbyterian Church would not even exist without its zinc mines; McCabe comes to town to make a killing on whores, gambling, and booze; Mrs. Miller arrives with even more ambitious schemes in mind; and finally the mining company takes over to get control of the zinc.

Money taints every relationship. The whorehouse, even humanized, still sells flesh; McCabe must buy his way into Mrs. Miller's bed; Sheehan plots to take a cut of all new businesses and ends up yielding immediately to the mining cartel, leaving McCabe stranded. The human connections possible among the characters have been curtailed in advance by the premise on which their community is founded.

The townspeople, dimly realizing this, depend on illusions to numb the malaise. The principal one is McCabe's "big rep." Everybody "knows" that McCabe killed Bill Rowntree; some even claim to have known Bill Rowntree, or at least friends of his. Of course, none of them did, any more than any of them personally investigated the sexual magic of Chinese princesses. But somebody somewhere along the line saw both—or something else—and passed the story along. Now, almost like an oral tale of Anglo-Saxon times, it has become a virtual myth, embellished with each repetition.

Even when McCabe proves to be only a pleasant, gabby bumbler, the townspeople's image of him as a top gun persists. They want it to be true. The glamour of it, the possibility that one day McCabe will confirm its truth right before their eyes, adds a pinch of excitement to their bleak lives.

In his offhand way, Altman seeds the movie with other, more individual illusions and teases those that the audience brings to a Western. Some are innocuous, amusing pretensions (a

man solemnly pondering a new style for his beard, a fatuous miner strutting like a master builder); others turn out to be perilous (Butler lording it over the locals, his feral young sidekick waiting to kill someone, a blabbermouth lawyer sucking McCabe into his daydreams of "busting up these trusts and monopolies").

Altman casually violates Western conventions, as when McCabe approaches a horseman for the classic fastdraw show-down only to find a gawky kid looking for the whorehouse. Altman's parodies of clichés like this parallel the ways that, in the movie, life destroys illusions as illusions destroy lives.

But the movie also honors the needs that illusions fulfill, without ever preaching like the O'Neill of *The Iceman Cometh.* The fantasy of the Chinese princess, spoken as they splash and sing in their bath, turns lumpy, bedraggled whores into beguiling creatures. In the same way, the church which the bucket brigade struggles to save from fire may not really be an important part of the community. But the townspeople, although they are unreligious, implicitly *think* that it is, and the force of their belief beautifully affirms the communal dream.

The techniques of ***McCabe and Mrs. Miller***—the qualities of the images, the editing, the camera movements, the sound—suffuse it with the evanescent beauty of illusions. The entire movie is a long reverie and, within it, certain individual shots stand alone as emblems of dreams, transience, pain, loss: a riderless horse galloping softly through deep snow, reflected dancers gracefully misshapen on the glass of a player piano.

Others—a lone man on a footbridge, a horse's hooves piercing the ice of a frozen stream, a shy girl facing some miners—are less overtly dreamlike. They affect us more because the rhythm of the editing takes them away so swiftly; like the sound effects, they resonate in our minds like epiphanies. The movie's concentration on snow, wind, rain, and ice helps give it a softly flowing tempo that gently pulls us into its world, like the strangers drifting in to mingle their dreams with those already present there.

When McCabe enters Presbyterian Church, he immediately becomes the center of attention; we are drawn to him, too, as we never are to Bruce Dern's similar character in *The King of Marvin Gardens.* That movie fails partly because Dern's dreamer is never anything but a cloddish, two-bit hustler. But McCabe charms and intrigues us; he is childish, but also childlike, a pimp but never a scoundrel.

His motormouth is always racing with gnomic sayings about frogs and eagles and money and pain and "butternut muffdivers" and girls trickier than "a goddam monkey on a hundred yards of grapevine." He enjoys playing silly games and putting on airs; with his damsen preserves, his derby, his gold tooth, and the stogie that he twirls in his mouth and wraps a nutty grin around, he is a tinhorn to his bone marrow, yet a stylish prancer-dancer as well. It is completely believable that the townspeople project their fantasies onto him.

But his cockiness barely conceals his fears, and so he also plunges into illusion. He gets caught up in the town's fantasy of his being a fancy dude and a flashy gunslinger, even though he mutters "businessman businessman" when Sheehan probes him about his occupation. He cultivates the town's ideas, plays with them, tries to live up to the big rep, while the town humors him, hopes that the big rep is true, and plays on his vanity.

But his illusions run deeper than the town knows. Even when menaced by the killers, he can swallow the lawyer's pretentious rhetoric. He tries to dazzle Mrs. Miller as he does the town, and again illusion cripples him. He wants her to live up to an adolescent fantasy of dainty femininity, even as he watches her wolf down a meal in a most unladylike manner and then knock him out with her rapid spiel on all that he doesn't know about operating a high class sporting house. He can down a double whiskey and a raw egg in one gulp (drawing gasps of amazement from the audience) but, though he doesn't mind her profession, he cannot get over her matching his etiquette or outdoing him as a "businessman businessman" by unscrambling his ledgers.

Fatally dependent on fantasy, he makes a sad, comic spectacle of himself in his efforts to win fame and love. In one especially moving moment—when he disarms a hysterical whore, his arms twisted brokenly around her, his grin bent into a queasy crinkle as he fastidiously takes a knife away from her—Warren Beatty brilliantly captures the vulnerability and the contradictions of his character, just as he does in *Bonnie and Clyde* when Clyde defends himself against Bonnie's sudden anger at his impotence by weakly raising his arms to his chest.

McCabe and Mrs. Miller are an almost schematically polarized couple; if we warm to him because he is so charmingly foolish, we focus on her because, alone among the townspeople, she seems to have no illusions whatsoever. It is almost an inversion of John Korty's *The Crazy Quilt,* in which "the illusionless man and the visionary maid" form an improbable, unstable alliance.

That is more than McCabe and Mrs. Miller ever do, because she is too tough and intelligent to conform to his sentimental view of womankind. Unlike him, she understands the hard truths of life. She tells him bluntly that "you have to spend money to make money" and assures Ida, upon recruiting her

for the brothel after her husband's funeral, that sex means nothing, that whoredom compares favorably with marriage as a superior business arrangement. Her intelligence and realism, which connect her with contemporary attitudes without making her an anachronism, consistently challenge McCabe's posturing.

Yet they do not render her any more capable of ruling fate than he is. "Take your hat off the bed, it's bad luck," she orders him (like Catherine in *Jules and Jim*), an odd thing for an illusionless person to say. And, in fact, she does have a personal route to comforting fantasy: opium. Only when drugged does she finally sleep with McCabe and share his optimism about worming more money out of the mining company for his property.

At another time, she uses opium to escape a birthday party because she cannot endure its joy; her very toughmindedness gives her an unbearable vision of how transient it is. In one of his subtlest strokes, Altman enriches the movie by gradually associating the soothing browns and oranges of its interiors with opium, as though their warmth and festivity and humanity were illusions seen through the mind's eye of someone deep in a drug-induced daze.

During the concluding sequences, details and motifs that earlier portrayed the birth of the community become ironic witnesses to its death. The three killers are also strangers, but they don't join the community—they shatter it. The townspeople separate apprehensively when the gunmen appear. Even the concluding slow zoom to Mrs. Miller in a dope den reverses previous camera movements. McCabe learns how wrong he was to imagine himself as "businessman businessman"; compared to the killers and the invisible corporation they represent, he is a ridiculous amateur.

Mrs. Miller faces a deeper reckoning. The ruthlessness of the mining company shocks even her, yet it underlies their similarities, for what is "you have to spend money to make money" if not a classic businessman's motto? Like the corporation, she has tried to base all human relations on money, but the sadness of the community and the needs of others pierce her defenses; she cannot escape her ultimate vulnerability to them. What formerly highlighted her cool intelligence now reveals the fear of intense involvement with others that accompanies it. She comforts McCabe on the night before the gunfight, as much to deny how moved she is by his plight as to ease his pain.

This gesture, the central moment of Julie Christie's performance, captures the instant of Mrs. Miller's awakening to her own illusions about herself. One of the things that makes her a compelling character is that we cannot condemn her fear of involvement with others; it is all to justifiable in a world like hers. But we realize, and so does she, that her illusionless realism is as futile as McCabe's romantic dithering. Neither attitude can save them; the dreamer and the realist are one.

McCabe fights for his life, vainly and alone. So it is doubly ironic that he proves to be an inept gunfighter and yet manages to take all three killers with him. He vindicates his big rep when no one is around to see him do it; the townspeople are too busy celebrating the rescue of the church and Mrs. Miller is too far gone on opium.

The concluding gunfight, a messy and protracted affair that debunks the chess-like stalkings and duels of most Westerns, expresses the victory of isolation over community, the film's fundamental illusion. During it, a blizzard begins, and the falling snow makes the images grainier and grainier, as though they were being blown up, as though they were slowly dissolving, disintegrating, drifting away. Soon they, too, come to resemble Mrs. Miller's opium reveries until the boundaries between them blur and, like Franz in Godard's *Band of Outsiders,* we no longer know whether the world is becoming a dream or a dream is becoming the world.

This conclusion is Altman's most open acknowledgment of what his complex of stylistic devices ultimately means: life is only images, beneath whose surfaces lies nothing. Comparison with Renoir only underlies this point. His films resemble Altman's in their rich profusion of images, sounds, events, details, characters. But (however oversimplified this critical standby may be) they evoke the richness and fullness of life. Altman's work evokes its final emptiness, a truth which he tries to disguise by making his images and sounds as mysterious and alluring as possible.

Still, each film has at least one moment when the disguise falls away. In *M*A*S*H,* Dago Red tries to give Extreme Unction to a dead patient; a doctor calls on him to help operate on another casualty; he hesitates, since Catholic dogma teaches that a person dying without last rites risks eternal damnation; the doctor barks, "That man is dead, this man is still alive; now that's fact." In *Brewster McCloud,* a circus pitchman reads off the names of the cast, ending with "Mr. Bud Cort" as the camera zooms to the hero's corpse. Death and water preoccupy *The Long Goodbye* and *McCabe and Mrs. Miller;* we see two characters of each floating lifeless, and water spreads ominously across the screen after the murder of Terry Lennox. *Brewster McCloud* reminds us that its dead hero is only a posing actor; the others emphasize corpses as matter. In either case, they are only "images," which could be the title (or the subtitle) of each Altman movie.

Altman may be trying to disguise this vision of life's hollowness from himself as much as from his audience; it certainly seems to spring from intuition more than thought.

Novels like Camus' *The Stranger* and Gide's *The Immoralist* express this consciousness through characters whose intense awareness of death awakens them to the magnificence of physical reality. But the novels articulate this consciousness intellectually, whereas Altman appears to stumble onto it unconsciously.

Perhaps this is one reason why, despite their measure of common ground, the books are compact and his films are sprawling. When he does try to be comparably spare, as in *Thieves Like Us,* he achieves nowhere near their depth because he has not really thought it out. Similarly, *McCabe and Mrs. Miller* falls short of greatness because McCabe's illusions are not deep enough to touch us as profoundly as the illusions exposed in these novels do. The film's blemishes, especially the overuse of Leonard Cohen's sometimes beautiful but just as often forced songs may be traceable to this "casualness and vagueness about ideas," as though Altman were not sure of his meaning.

Yet his meaning is plain; his films are arabesques around voids, in which (to quote Godard once more) "Life is sad, but it is always beautiful." The slow-motion evocation of "the people" in *Thieves Like Us* is unconvincing, because Altman does not believe in "the people" but in the empty staircase. But he also believes in the Chinese princess.

Todd McCarthy (review date 1975)

SOURCE: *"The Delinquents* (Robert Altman) (1974)," in *Kings of the Bs: Working Within the Hollywood System,* edited by Todd McCarthy and Charles Flynn, E. P. Dutton and Co., Inc., 1975, pp. 215-19.

[*In the following review, McCarthy states that, "Decidedly a minor work by a major artist,"* The Delinquents *proves that Altman can tell a straightforward story without stylistic mannerisms.*]

A reasonable number of people must be aware that Robert Altman directed films before *M*A*S*H,* but most would probably be hard pressed to come up with many titles. Some may have seen *That Cold Day in the Park* and a few watchful airplane passengers and television viewers might have noticed that Altman directed *Countdown* (with some uncalled for assistance from Jack Warner). The elongated *Kraft Suspense Theatre* episode *Nightmare in Chicago,* a definitive documentary of the city's Edens Expressway if nothing else, can claim a few partisans on the underground Chicago-Madison critical axis, and if Altman's and George W. George's distinctive and evocative *The James Dean Story* were rereleased today, the combined Dean and Altman cults might even help Warner Brothers turn a profit on the film (it was a dismal flop when originally released in the summer of 1957, two years after Dean's death).

But the real skeleton in Altman's closet is another film that was released in 1957, but was considerably more successful. It's *The Delinquents,* which Altman, ever the auteur, wrote, produced, and directed in his hometown of Kansas City during the summer of 1955 on a $63,000 budget. As Altman puts it,

> Well, this guy back there said he had the money to make a picture, if I'd make it about delinquents. I said OK and I wrote the thing in five days, cast it, picked the locations, drove the generator truck, got the people together, took no money, and we just did it, that's all. My motives at that time were to make a picture, and if they said I gotta shoot it in green in order to get it done, I'd say, "Well, I can figure out a way to do that." I would have done anything to get the thing done.

Altman may have been glad to get the thing done, but today he doesn't seem all that glad to have people see the film. At the 1973 San Francisco Film Festival tribute to Altman, an enthusiast asked how *The Delinquents* might be seen today. The director replied that he possessed a print, but that, if he had anything to do with it, the young man would never see the film. Although delivered offhandedly, this is quite a severe judgment on a work that, although by no means a great, undiscovered classic, is certainly nothing to be embarrassed about, even for one of the greatest American filmmakers, Altman: "I'm not embarrassed about it. But nobody knew what they were doing. I don't think it has any meaning to anybody."

He probably didn't know what he was doing, but in those five days that he wrote the script, Altman was unobtrusively laying the groundwork for a vast number of the teen problem (or problem teen) pictures that were to follow. By the time *The Delinquents* was finally released, of course, everyone from Sam Katzman to AIP to Jerry Lewis had jumped on the j.d. bandwagon, but in early 1955, *The Wild One* and *The Blackboard Jungle* had only just been released and *Rebel Without a Cause* was still in the shooting stage. (*The Delinquents* was even pre-rock 'n' roll, and part of its score consists of some smooth Kansas City black jazz, with some on-camera work by the late singer Julia Lee.) The youth exploitation field was untested and uncharted and, if he wanted to, Altman could lay claim to having invented, in one picture, many of the conventions (and, soon afterward, clichés) of this subgenre.

The setting is WASPville, U.S.A., that clean-cut community small enough to get by with only one drive-in and one high school, but big enough to have two sides of the tracks. On right side of tracks, good, straight but troubled boy and sweet, innocent but ripe girl are very much in love but her parents stand between them since she's "not ready to go steady" and he "hangs out with the wrong crowd." Forbidden to see his sweetheart, boy implores hot-rodding pal to pick up his girl for him. Pal gets duded up, leads girl out from under noses of suspicious parents, and whole teen crowd meets for party at abandoned mansion outside town. Filter cigarettes and 3.2 beer cause party to get out of hand, reunited lovers leave to be alone, fuzz mysteriously appear and break up drunken free-for-all. Apprehended toughs suspect boy of snitching, kidnap him next day and force him to gulp down whole bottle of Scotch when he won't admit to being informant. Taking besotted boy for ride, toughs bungle gas station holdup and speed off, leaving boy behind with cash and dead attendant. Boy finally staggers home, learns gang has abducted girl, tracks down and beats up toughest tough, learns girl's whereabouts, saves her from clutches of gang, and walks off to confront police, who will surely clear him of gang's crimes.

The Delinquents is framed with sanctimonious narration about how "This story is about violence and immorality," and how "We are all responsible. Citizens must work against the disease of delinquency by working with church groups, community groups," ad infinitum, ad nauseam. Altman claims that this was added by United Artists when the company picked up the film for release (UA paid $150,000 for the film and grossed nearly $1,000,000 with it), but it is curious that a preachy narrative is also the prime weakness of *The James Dean Story.* Aside from this, however, and an occasional line, delivered by the girl friend to her parents, such as, "Why can't you leave him alone?" (perhaps the definitive line of all 1950s teenpix), the film is relatively passive and undidactic in its attitude toward the spectacle of youth led astray. Even then, Altman seemed drawn toward an improvisational approach, and the casual sound of the dialogue reduces the frequency of overblown melodramatic moments. And although not withdrawn to the extent that it is in *Thieves Like Us,* the camera normally records the violence in *The Delinquents* from a distance, often from a high, overhead angle, thereby implicating neither the viewer nor even society-at-large in the misdeeds of the characters (even so, critics at the time felt that *The Delinquents* was an extremely violent film).

The players, who include Altman's daughter and then-wife, were all found in Kansas City, with three major exceptions. The film gave Richard Bakalyan his first stab at playing the greasy punk who makes life miserable for everyone in town, and he did it so well that he was typed forever. Peter Miller, fresh from *The Blackboard Jungle,* was also brought in from California. Tom (Billy Jack) Laughlin, who apparently had a considerable James Dean complex, played the troubled young man and the mere mention of his name makes Altman cringe even today:

> Tommy Laughlin was just an unbelievable pain in the ass. Unbelievable. He's a talented guy, but he's insane. Total egomaniac. He was so angry that he wasn't a priest. Big Catholic hangup. I found out that this Laughlin Kid was doing all the things he'd heard about James Dean doing. Like he'd run around the block when he was supposed to be exhausted and he'd say, "OK, I'll sit down there on the fireplug and when you hear my whistle, you start rolling your cameras." Otherwise, he wouldn't do it. In fact, he did the last half of the picture under protest. He'd say, "OK, tell me what you want me to do." And I'd say, "Well, I want you to . . ." He'd say, "No, tell me exactly what you want. I'll do it just the way you want it. I'm not going to act in this picture. I'm just here because I have to be." And I said, "OK, I want you to fall out of the car like this," and I'd fall out of the car. "Then I want you to take your right hand and move it up and put it on the gravel. Then I want you to look up a minute . . ." He couldn't remember it, but that served his purpose and he'd do it. And he was as good at doing that as when he was really working in the first part of the picture.

Although extremely mannered (he couldn't keep his eyes fixed in one place for more than two seconds), Laughlin gives an adequate performance and manages to make his relatively thankless character somewhat less bland than it might otherwise be. In movies of this sort, the scenes involving the romantic leads are usually so vacuous that, after initial laughter, one begins counting the minutes until the toughs return to liven things up. In *The Delinquents,* there is at least a modicum of concern generated for the admittedly pasty lovers; even in the campiest of moods, one cannot wish total degradation upon them.

In what so far must sound like a perhaps passable but hardly distinguished film, there are two notable features—its technical excellence and its paradoxical relationship with the director's subsequent work. Altman served his apprenticeship making industrial films and documentaries in Kansas City and his know-how in lighting and in photography is impressively evident in his first dramatic film. The quality of the black-and-white image is brilliantly sharp and rich, far better than any produced in similar fare (under studio conditions) by AIP, Allied Artists, or Columbia, and astonishing in a film made independently for so little money.

One need take little more than a casual look at Altman's recent work to realize that the director is fascinated with the conventions of genres. Today, particularly in *McCabe and*

Mrs. Miller and *The Long Goodbye,* he works within established generic frameworks, but subverts and plays upon the conventions, simultaneously expressing his feelings about his characters and the history of the genres' development. In *The Delinquents,* he plays it straight. Foreshadowing, to a remarkable extent, his attitude toward the hoodlum's violence in *The Long Goodbye,* Altman says of his first film, "My main point was to say that kids like this don't plan anything. They don't say, 'Tomorrow we're gonna go knock off the filling station.' They say, 'Hey, there's a filling station, let's go in there and mess around.' And it happens. It's not a premeditated kind of thing. It's just a restlessness kind of thing, I think."

It's this restlessness, principally expressed through the edgy, nervous performances, as well as a fatalistic ambivalence about the plight of the lovers, and a reluctance to implicate society too heavily in the misguided lives of the characters, that sets *The Delinquents* apart from other examples of its genre and reveals that at least some thought went into its creation. Like much of Nicholas Ray's work, it leaves one unsettled and off-balance emotionally. Decidedly a minor work by a major artist, *The Delinquents* could nonetheless furnish proof to those still skeptical of his abilities that Altman can, if he wants to, tell a straightforward story without stylistic mannerisms. Happily, he's doing a lot more than that today.

William S. Pechter (essay date September 1975)

SOURCE: "Trashville," in *Commentary,* Vol. 60, No. 3, September, 1975, pp. 72-5.

[*In the following essay, which was reprinted in* Movie Plus One, Horizon Press, 1982, *Pechter traces Altman's portrayal of America in* Nashville.]

Why make a film about—and full of—country music, if you don't like it? I ask this not as any devotee of country music myself, well over nine-tenths of what I've heard of it striking me as a pile of lachrymose slop. But any film crammed with some 25 country-music original numbers ought, statistically, to hit on one that's better than pathetic. Even a nonentity like *W. W. and the Dixie Dancekings* (whose principal characters are involved with a country-music band) manages to pull one attractive original tune out of its hat for its finale.

Nor do I ask the question rhetorically. There *is* a reason to make a movie about country music when you don't like it (and don't like the people who create it, and don't like the people who like it), and that reason is exemplified in Robert Altman's *Nashville.* It's a reason for which even a knowledge of the country-music milieu isn't required: Altman has himself admitted he wasn't familiar with the Nashville scene before he decided to do this job on it (his method of remedying his ignorance consisting of dispatching a henchperson, Joan Tewkesbury, to Nashville to write the script, and then casting almost all the singing roles with non-musicians who were allowed to compose their own songs). For it's not the music that this country-music epic is after; what it's after is the country that's microcosmically revealed in America's (at least, Middle America's) "music capital." ("You get your hair cut! You don't belong in Nashville!" one of Nashville's leading citizens barks at a young musician early on.) The true locale and subject of this film—which begins with a song declaring, "We must be doing something right / To last 200 years," and ends with a crowd singing, "You may say, I ain't free / It don't worry me" following an assassination—clearly isn't Nashville but nothing less than America itself: America as it really is, stripped of myth and idealization, on this eve of its bicentennial celebration.

The subject is one almost all of Altman's previous films can be seen as leading up to, from the anti-militarist, "anti-war" jibes of *M*A*S*H* through the anti-capitalist ironies of *McCabe & Mrs. Miller* and that film's debunking of romantic myths (and the similar myth-puncturing of *The Long Goodbye* and *Thieves Like Us*) to the depiction of a rootless society in *California Split.* And as befits a work of such vast ambition, Altman's new film seems to draw stylistically as well as thematically on elements of all his films before. A sound truck, broadcasting speeches by a Presidential candidate, wends its way through *Nashville,* and its use as a motif reminds one of the public-address system announcing the showing of war movies in *M*A*S*H,* while that earlier film's closing announcement of itself as the camp's coming attraction is echoed in this one's clever, self-referential, TV-commercial-style opening credits; a *Brewster McCloud*'s many-stranded plot line and cross-section view of the life of a Southern city now seems to adumbrate the use of such things in *Nashville.* From *The Long Goodbye* and *Thieves Like Us* comes the busy detailing of the inundation of American life with the debased currency of our popular culture; from a *California Split, Nashville*'s rapid tempo and subtly garish visual style, and the evocation by such means of its characters' lives of transience and anomie.

Nashville, as its publicity loudly proclaims, portrays the lives of no fewer than 24 characters in the course of a five-day period during which they go their various ways and their fortunes occasionally intertwine within the contours of the city's music industry. Much has been made of the virtuoso accomplishment of the juggling of so many story lines, but, though the purely technical feat of keeping them all in motion without much confusion is impressive, their actual substance is something else again. Tom (of the folk-rock trio Bill, Mary, and Tom) is having an affair with Mary, Bill's wife, while

at the same time trying to seduce Linnea, the gospel-singer wife of Delbert, a lawyer whose clients include some of Nashville's biggest stars, one of whom, Barbara Jean, only just released from her hospitalization for burns from a "fire baton," seems on the verge of a nervous breakdown, and is watched adoringly from afar by Glenn, a young soldier whose mother once saved Barbara Jean's life in a fire, and so forth, and so on, as the Nashville world turns.

One can, of course, synopsize almost any plot to the point of banality; but, in *Nashville,* it's not a case of the transcendence of such banality by the work's imaginative freshness but of a concealment of the banality by the restless and incessant cutting away from one banal plot to another. Zero in on any half-dozen of *Nashville*'s 24 characters' stories, and their impoverishment would be obvious; once again, a bill of goods is being sold on the dubious principle that the losses incurred on each item can be reversed by volume merchandising. And indeed, despite all the ballyhoo about *Nashville*'s audacious originality in featuring 24 leading characters, one could as easily maintain that the film has *no* leading characters, only 24 actors doing their turns (all doing them well, without in the least extending themselves), much as one might say the same of a film like *California Split,* whose leading "characters" number two. In any case, what might be truly audacious would be not this *Grand Hotel*-ish engineering but the kind of freedom in moving from one character to another, following them and then leaving them behind as they enter into the work's development, that one sees in Buñuel's *The Phantom of Liberté. Nashville* may seem refreshingly free of rigid plotting as it's unfolding, but by the time virtually all of its characters have been assembled and their stories converge for the O. Henry-like denouement, one is struck less by the film's freedom of movement than by the ingenuity of its preparation for its payoff.

But for all the noises to be heard about *Nashville*'s Joycean complexities, the extraordinary critical acclaim which has greeted the film has, I think, really very little to do with such things. And the barrage of media hype elicited by *Nashville* (which may well exceed that for any other film since *Last Tango in Paris*) *is* exceptional, even given the semi-hysterical masterpiece-a-month mania with which film reviewing is afflicted. This month, *Nashville;* last month, *Shampoo;* the month before, part two of *The Godfather.* What these widely differing films have in common has nothing to do with a like degree of artistic achievement, or stylistic mastery—but they *do* have something in common. Nor is it *Nashville*'s artistic superiority which accounts for the extravagant heights to which it has been praised (though I could myself argue a preference for the fleet fluidity and lightness of *Nashville*'s style to *Godfather II*'s monumentality). Rather, *Godfather II* wears its heart, a bit too earnestly and exposedly, on its sleeve, while in *Shampoo* one can't entirely shake nagging questions as to whether there's any necessary relation between the personal and the political. But what Altman has constructed in *Nashville* is an all but perfect vehicle—resembling nothing so much as a work of pornography which sanctimoniously (but sincerely) preaches against pornography—for simultaneously feeling superior to "America" and exploiting the appeal of everything he invites us to join him in feeling superior to.

What in fact *Nashville* amounts to specifically, with the spectacle of its horde of hayseed characters seen in all their malice, venality, and scrambling opportunism, is the movies' biggest bout of hick-baiting since *A Face in the Crowd* (a film with which *Nashville* shares such other features as its crude "satire" of commercials—"Goo-goo Candy Clusters," hawked at the Grand Ole Opry—and the way its loathing for the yokels' stars is exceeded by that for the stars' audience, seen, in *Nashville,* to turn angrily on Barbara Jean, its erstwhile favorite, when, obviously distressed, she falters in a performance). Strictly as a depiction of corruption in the country-music business, there's nothing in *Nashville* that wasn't done at least as trenchantly and knowingly (if with less stylistic virtuosity) in *Payday* of a year or two ago, with its portrayal by Rip Torn of an egomaniacal Country and Western singer. But what distinguishes *Nashville* from such a genre study is the later film's scope; and lest one imagine that the corruption of *Nashville's* characters has no larger relevance, a message which issues from the sound truck that weaves through *Nashville* informs us early on that we're all deeply involved with "politics," whether we know it or not, in whatever we do.

That sound truck broadcasts statements by Hal Phillip Walker, a kind of all-purpose third-party (the Replacement party) candidate for President (the truck emerges from a garage whose door bears the cryptic legend, "Walker-Talker-Sleeper"), at a rally for whom the film's climactic assassination takes place. (The rally is held in front of an actual replica of the Parthenon, originally constructed out of plaster of Paris for Nashville's centennial celebration, which has earned the city its appellation of the "Athens of the South.") Though the assassin, an Arthur Bremer-like loner, is presumably gunning for Walker himself, he settles instead for the troubled Barbara Jean, who is entertaining the crowd in preparation for the candidate's appearance. (Why the assassin chooses this target is left unexplained, though those with lively imaginations may speculate on the possible relation between the killer's domineering mother and the singer's just having finished a paean to "My Mommy and My Daddy and My Idaho Home." Or perhaps since, as the candidate's advance man explains, "The thing with these country people is they've got grass-roots appeal; they're the one's who'll elect the next President," one might as well shoot the entertainers as the candidates.) In any case, no sooner do the shots ring out than Nashville's leading star steps forward to forestall panic with assurances that "This isn't Dallas—this is Nashville!" as indeed it is. Nashville is Dallas plus Memphis plus Los Angeles plus Laurel plus . . . By now, that is to say, assassinations have become so routinely woven into the fabric of American life that we can immediately close ranks (as the show goes on, a new star is born, and a *Patton*-like monster flag waves conspicuously) to affirm, "You may say, I ain't free. It don't worry me."

Now whatever my reservations about the version *Nashville* presents of "America," it's not primarily here that my deepest reservations about the film reside. For just as one can appreciate a work of art whose vision of the world one doesn't share, so, too, can I without difficulty conceive of admiring a film whose view of America is different, even radically different, from my own. (I assume, for the sake of argument, that I hold some stable and statesmanly "view" of America rather than the volatile bundle of violent contraries which my feelings actually comprise.) Indeed, the body of work—Sam Peckinpah's—which I find most interesting in the contemporary American film offers a vision of America a good deal blacker, if also more ambiguous, than anything that's implied by *Nashville* or in any of the other films of Altman. Insofar as *Nashville* is engaged in an act of trashing America, I feel no compulsion to defend anything against it. To the extent that America is equitable, as the film would have it, with chauvinistic and pathetic country music, crunched cars, plastic motels, and Kentucky Fried Chicken, the movie's targets can fend for themselves; to the extent that it isn't, such derision as *Nashville's* will hardly undo it.

But when one populates a work of art with numerous characters toward whom one's salient if not sole attitude is a contemptuous condescension, one is involved, I think, in trashing of a different and more deeply offensive sort. To be sure, there are a few of *Nashville's* characters in whose depiction one might discern some warmth of feeling: the much abused Barbara Jean ("I don't tell you how to sing—don't you tell me how to run your life!" her manager-husband snaps at her); a talentless, would-be singer whom we see stuffing tissue paper in her bra as she perfects her stage manner in the mirror amid a clutter of religious figurines, and whose fantasies of a career lead her to having to perform a humiliating striptease at a political smoker; a (white) gospel-singing mother of two deaf children (who presumably gets points also for singing not country music but gospel, with a black back-up chorus, though her voice wouldn't pass muster in the most meager storefront-church choir). Here as elsewhere one sees that streak of morbid sentimentality in Altman's work which allows him to extend compassion only to the damaged and doomed, and which seems related to the ritualistic slaughter of an innocent with which so many of his films end. (To be fair, he didn't specify that *Nashville* end with Barbara Jean's death when he commissioned Joan Tewkesbury's script; he only requested that it end with the death of someone.) The deaf children, in particular, are produced by the film with all the perfunctory piety of Verdoux's family. And as if they didn't in themselves convey pathos enough, they're stuck with a father who, in contrast with their mother, hasn't even bothered to learn the sign language needed to communicate with them.

What was for me the single most affecting moment in *Nashville* drew, I suppose, on a pathos of such sort: the look on Keenan Wynn's face when he's offhandedly informed by a disinterested nurse that his hospitalized wife has "expired" during the night (though it's hard for me to distinguish how much I was moved by Wynn's portrayal of the character's reaction to the situation and how much by the shock of seeing Keenan Wynn himself looking so genuinely old and frail). Wynn begins to utter a cry of grief, when Altman cuts abruptly—the effect is like a slap in the face—to the supercilious laughter of the cast's two "outsiders": an asinine BBC interviewer, in Nashville to gather material for a documentary, and the clean-cut, buttoned-down advance man for the third-party candidate, rounding up local talent for the rally because "this redneck music is very popular now." These two characters are, if anything, portrayed with even more scorn than Nashville's inhabitants, as if to disarm any criticism that Altman's view is, in fact, indistinguishable from theirs. At one point, Altman stages a multi-vehicle freeway pileup, and has the interviewer exclaim of the collision, "I need something like this for my documentary—I need it! It's America—those cars crashing!" At another, she visits an automobile graveyard, and, later, a school-bus parking lot, so that Altman can milk these things for their symbolic worth while at the same time mocking the interviewer's fatuous commentary on them. (The implicit values and level of sophistication from which the film looks down its nose at the Nashville world are more undisguisedly embodied in the figures of Elliott Gould and Julie Christie, who make guest appearances playing themselves as visiting celebrities, with the natives either fawning on them laughably or, what's worse, not knowing for which film the latter won her Oscar.)

But despite the smoke screen with which Altman habitually surrounds his work—his appealingly modest claims that his films aren't "saying anything," their slightly stoned air of "partying," and his letting the individual participants work out their own contribution for themselves—it clearly is no one else, least of all the BBC interviewer or the advance man, who, to score a cheap irony, shunts aside Wynn's grief-stricken outcry; it is Altman himself. And when you thus trash not just your subject but your own characters and their emotions, you lay yourself open to criticism which goes beyond questions of stylistic virtuosity and artistic finesse. What's revealed in such a moment is a coarseness of sensibility, an ugliness, of a kind one glimpses at moments in a number of Altman's films: in the mob's humiliation of the priggish nurse in *M*A*S*H,* the intimidation of the trans-

vestite in *California Split,* the mocking radio adaptation of *Romeo and Juliet* in *Thieves Like Us.* At moments such as these, and others like them, questions of artistic finesse tend to recede before purely human considerations. This isn't to say that such things cancel out the considerable talents which Altman's films display; nor would I want categorically to dismiss his films on the basis of such deficiencies in feeling, though to do so would be, I think, a more honest acknowledgment of what his work is about than to gloss over such things in the stampede to praise its artistry. But if one can hardly hope at this late date to head off the stampede, one can still choose, at least, not to join it. To the extent that one sees everything in *Nashville* as at once cheapened by easy ridicule and rife with a hypocritical exploitation of the "grass-roots appeal" of "these country people" and their "redneck music" for purposes of Altman's own vote-getting campaign, one can choose to turn away and vote, "No."

Aaron Sultanik (essay date December 1975)

SOURCE: "A Merging of Mythologies," in *Midstream,* Vol. XXI, No. 10, December, 1975, pp. 56-9.

[*In the following excerpt, Sultanik compares the view of America presented by Altman in* Nashville *to that presented by E. L. Doctorow in* Ragtime.]

It comes as no surprise, amidst the festivities kicking off the celebration of our bicentennial, that our cultural gurus have focused on two works of art as the definitive summing-up of the way we were and what we are about today.

Though most important books and movies are appreciated only by highbrows and aesthetes who perceive motifs that forever remain obscure to the big public, E. L. Doctorow's *Ragtime* and Robert Altman's *Nashville* have been acclaimed by the critics, and both are selling faster than 59-cent replicas of the Statue of Liberty.

There have been few occasions recently in which an "important" novel or film has met with such approval from all sectors of the American community. *Gravity's Rainbow* and *Something Happened,* probably the two most ambitious novels of the 70s, are not likely to be cuddled up with like Jacqueline Susann's and Agatha Christie's bedwarmers. On the other hand, such box-office hits as *The Exorcist, The Sting,* or *Jaws,* will surely not figure in any museum retrospective of the major artistic successes of the 70s. But *Ragtime-Nashville* has reconciled critics and public in a way rarely achieved by two works from different media.

Ragtime-Nashville explores the way the private, unpublicized lives of our political and intellectual heroes interact with the fantasies of the American public; both Doctorow and Altman emphasize a singular popular from—ragtime and country music—as the variable that brings together our leaders and the public whose subconscious dreams they project.

Ragtime concerns an American family, a black musician, and an immigrant "Tateh" and his daughter, in the opening years of this century, and their interrelatedness with a group of epoch-making figures—Freud, Houdini and Emma Goldman. Though *Nashville* takes place some 70 years later, in a cross-section of its stars, conmen, wastrels, groupies and residents, it gives Doctorow's novel a startling complement. The two works not only explain how we got where we are, but offer poignant insights into the history the bicentennial celebration attempts to exploit on a shabbier, more superficial level.

· · · · ·

Like *Ragtime, Nashville* works best when it remains faithful to the city's raucous surface. While Doctorow worked towards the eventual coming together of the American family—Tateh and his daughter and Coalhouse Walker's child—as symptomatic of the basic historical thrusts that gave *time its march, Nashville,* with its lively, self-conscious, raffish figures, its lumpish, maudlin, saccharine music, becomes the most vital and happily superficial city in present-day America. As in *Ragtime,* Altman and scriptwriter Tewkesbury do not emphasize any one character or diminish the energy and intensity of this pocket of popular culture. They interrelate the lives of 24 people—some famous country-western singers, others aspiring stars, and those groupies, hangers-on, and plain simple folk who like the "unimportant" figures in *Ragtime* contribute a great deal to the myth of their era. Characters like Keenan Wynn's demure melancholic townfolk and his groupie-niece, played by Shelly Duvall provide the emotional chemistry that keeps the Grand Ole Opry hopping.

One of the few negative reviews of *Nashville* (in the *New York Review* by Robert Mazzocco) criticized Altman for banking on the despair and death-wish that seem so chic and logical today. But while Altman's earlier films (*Mash, McCabe and Mrs. Miller*) struck me as too coolly dispassionate to effectively probe the inner realities that produced the chaos in *Mash* and the picturesque, *commedia dell' arte* appeal of the American West in *McCabe and Mrs. Miller,* his fluid camera-eye in *Nashville* has settled on a most resilient community. Here Altman does not have to probe beneath the facade to provide some sublime truth about the city and its inhabitants. Rather, the meaning of Nashville as the mecca of a singular American popular form, as an example of *one part* of the Southern sensibility, is revealed in the artifice, guilelessness and exuberance of the music and moods of the many people whose lives intersect.

This sense of Bergsonian continuity, where there is an overlap of the emotions and experiences of a great many people, is handled with unusual simplicity, exact in detail, yet seeming to play as an unaffected documentary (very strong credit must be given to Altman's entire crew). One is bound to agree (with Pauline Kael and John Simon) that the original eight-hour version be released. But what the film does suggest, in 145-minutes, is the intense, interminable interaction between the naiveté of a would-be star like Barbara Harris, the ignominy of Michael Murphy's political advance man, and the innocuousness of Gwen Wells's daydreaming waitress. A rich, overripe canvas is drawn that gains by having the conversations, emotional clashes and fantasies of these 24 people overlap.

The way the dream imposes on reality is apparent in two scenes, involving Gwen Wells's waitress, who dreams of singing at the Grand Ole Opry, and Keith Carradine's country-western singer, who "needs" to "score" with every woman he meets. While she goes through a strip at a political smoker in order to sing at a concert, her quest remains as true and well-intentioned as the affectionate look that passes between Lily Tomlin and Carradine when, after they have spent a few hours in bed, he calls another girl as Lily prepares to return to her family.

But in the final scene Altman offers the large, profound statement he has avoided throughout the film and thus refutes the experience detailed by the film in such a loving, unbiased way. A young man boarding in Keenan Wynn's house, who has seen how cruelly Wynn has been treated by his groupie-niece, kills country-western star Barbara Jean at a concert held in Nashville's pseudo-Parthenon. With one loud bang Altman attempts to dismiss Nashville as a breeding ground for the violence, past, present, and future(?), that has plagued our country. As a tragic metaphor it is pitifully wrong.

For Nashville itself, like its heroes and self-eulogizing ballads, is a shrill, open town that like Las Vegas must be met on its own terms. One does not compare Las Vegas to Monte Carlo anymore than one would place Nashville alongside Salzburg; both Vegas and Nashville provide a uniquely American experience whose crassness and two-dimensional starry-eyed appeal create their own logic and rhythm.

This warm, unprejudiced point of view is followed until the last scene. Altman has taken us inside the skin of the Grand Ole Opry, its heroes, hillbillies and hustlers, and like a modern Breughel, has invited us into a world that constantly gives new meaning to its fantasies. But in his final, sweeping overhead shot he admits a foreign viewpoint: the logic of a popular form like country music, and the city whose industry and intellect are given over to it, are, finally, completely misunderstood.

Unlike political leaders and their rhetoric, cultural heroes and fantasies are neither created nor destroyed by guns. Barbara Jean falters when the myth she represents no longer works for her audience. At an earlier concert she manifested her emotional instability as those who had dreamed her up booed her off the stage because her myth was shattered and no longer represented the fantasy of Southern purity perpetuated by her presence and songs.

The *Ragtime-Nashville* phenomenon that both the critics and the public cheered not only proves that not much has changed between 1900 and 1975, but that what foreign observers like Dickens and De Tocqueville said more than 100 years ago about the "confraternity" of the American system, of the proximity of the people to their leaders and heroes, remains relevant today. The myths that sustain Americans become our soon-to-be-realized history; we are involved in an inexorable give-and-take between what the people dream and what our leaders perceive as our mythic resources. This certainly constitutes a large part of what we mean by the "American Experience."

It is what makes the two works part of the same phenomenon we are now in the midst of celebrating. It is why the campaign of Hal Phillip Walker in *Nashville,* the man-on-the-horse candidate, which echoes the '72 campaigns of both Wallace and McGovern, parallels not only the songs of the country-western singers but their life styles. . . .

Henry James once noted in despair that America was "all foreground." Our ceaseless urge for experiment and change caused our celebrated aesthete and cultural curator unending grief. Yet if one approaches the American Scene from the other side of the coin, the constant flurry of activity—our undiminishing appetite to gorge ourselves on an uneven but prodigious cultural smorgasbord—can be appreciated for its energy, for the confluence of people and events that interact so furiously across the American landscape. For the most part this is the American Scene celebrated by *Ragtime-Nashville.*

Yet at some moment we question the direction of this constantly changing American experience. Where, one wonders, are the myths that will continue to sustain this glorious and violent dream—the "American experience"? In *Ragtime,* in two or three instances, Doctorow presents an overview:

> What bound them to each other was a fulfilled recognition which they lived and thought within so that their apprehension of each other could not be so distinct and separated as to include admiration for the other's fairness.

The writing is verbose, an attempt at a distilled poetic sentiment as flat and platitudinous as the "theme" of one of

Have Hamilton's songs in *Nashville.* But this freakish, literary novelty, which has attracted readers from *Gone with the Wind* to *Ulysses,* concludes with a classic image, one that ends the most truly cyclical of 20th century novels.

Tateh observes the playing of the three children; this inspires one of the myths that will sustain Americans in the 30s. "The Little Rascals" was a mixed ethnic group of kids whose daily ups and downs paralleled the hard times American democracy was then going through. And if the reader thinks this is not a sufficiently powerful or illuminating myth to see us further along this century, I suggest that Doctorow could have done worse than focus on the most singular and sage of the Little Rascals, Buckwheat.

Buckwheat was the elevator operator in a hotel I once lived in, and I invited him to my room to join a small party on November 7, 1972. While my friends and I were sitting around the TV listening to the latest reports of the Nixon-Agnew landslide, Buckwheat came in after his afternoon shift. Asked what he felt about the election he said: "Don't mean nothing. Things going to keep going on."

Exactly. Doctorow could not have said it better. Mr. B, as he liked to be called, took a clean shot of Chevas Regal and bid us good night.

William S. Pechter (essay date October 1976)

SOURCE: "Altman, Chabrol, and Ray," in *Commentary,* Vol. 62, No. 4, October, 1976, pp. 75-8.

[*In the following excerpt, which was reprinted as "Buffalo Bob and an Indian," in* Movie Plus One, *Horizon Press, 1982, Pechter discusses the ways in which Altman's* Buffalo Bill and the Indians, or Sitting Bull's History Lesson *is similar to his* McCabe and Mrs. Miller, *and he enumerates the ways in which the former film falls short of the latter.*]

There's a sense in which, had Robert Altman's new film been better, I probably would have liked it less. *Nashville* was "better": it dumped a truckload of city-slicker's scorn for "down-home" America at our doorstep, and yet covered its tracks so well that its enthusiasts were able to claim it was actually (if ambivalently) a celebration of the grit and fortitude of our vulgar country cousins. ***Buffalo Bill and the Indians, or Sitting Bull's History Lesson*** comes equipped with no such cagey defenses. The American flag (which figured so prominently in the conclusion of *Nashville*) is raised, and from then on there's not a single shot that isn't bathed in the yellowish, "autumnal" light of decrepitude. (The film does, in fact, seem to have been photographed entirely through yellow filters.) Nor could one easily find two lines together without at least one of them smacking of some point of instruction in the film's own "history lesson." Once again, the doors are thrown open for Robert Altman, your genial host, to give another of his famous parties, but this time it's unmistakably a didactic moralizer who bursts out of the closet to greet you.

And what his lesson consists of is this. Buffalo Bill, prototype of "America's national hero," is a corrupt fraud (we're introduced to him haggling over commercial rights with an associate who assures him, "Everything historical is yours"). As "father of the new show business," Buffalo Bill purveys, via his Wild West show ("America's national family"), a fabricated image of his legendary prowess and derring-do in fighting Indians, palming off this pack of lies (on a receptive and gullible public) as the historical truth. ("The truth?" Buffalo Bill exclaims. "I'll tell you what the truth is! The truth is what gets the most applause.") But when the real Sitting Bull is signed on to enact a role in these charades, he throws a wrench in the myth-making machinery ("History"—i.e., white-man's "history"—"is nothing but disrespect for the dead," he declares), and demonstrates that, far from being the villainous savages that the show has depicted, Indians are actually beings far superior to their victors in nobility and wisdom, and mystically in touch with forces of nature and the realm of dreams. (Sitting Bull joins the show because he's had a dream that, through doing so, he'll meet and be able to make a request of the "Great Father"—Grover Cleveland—who, to everyone else's surprise, does come to see a performance, but, needless to say, flatly rejects the chief's request without even hearing him out.)

Indeed, the innate dignity of Sitting Bull is such that (much to Buffalo Bill's astonishment) the Indian is applauded even by the show's brainwashed audience, when, without any theatrical flamboyance, he merely rides into the arena. But, in the end, the show-business lies prevail. The real Sitting Bull returns to the reservation where he dies, and his place in the show is taken by his former interpreter, another Indian who demeaningly enacts a fictitious version of Sitting Bull's death at the hands of Buffalo Bill. And that such lies only meet the audience's need for them is clearly implicit. ("Is he sitting on that horse right?" an aging Buffalo Bill addresses a portrait of himself during a drunken reverie in which he imagines the dead chief present. "If he's not sitting it right, then how come all of you took him for a king?")

In any case, the show goes on; and, at the end, we see Sitting Bull "killed" by Buffalo Bill, the Indian-fighter's teeth flashing in a smile of manic glee and a look quite as mad as that of *Little Big Man*'s Custer in his eyes—they are, in fact, the perfect teeth and blue eyes of Paul Newman, as America's reigning star portrays its original one. Moreover, the suggestion is plainly made that show business is only a metaphor for business as usual in America, past and present:

that the lies of the Wild West show are continuous with those of the larger society. "Welcome to Buffalo Bill's Wild West," the show's manager greets Sitting Bull. "You'll find it ain't all that different from real life."

Such, then, is the history that the film expounds: the standard demonology of venal white devils trampling noble red men underfoot, envisioned as the paradigm of "America." ("God meant for me to be white," Buffalo Bill declares. "The difference between a white man and an Indian is that an Indian's red, and for a real good reason. So you can tell us apart.") To the general rule of white iniquity, the film offers only two exceptions: Annie Oakley, depicted as a sensitive, "artistic" woman exploited for profit by a manipulative husband (essentially, the Ronee Blakley role in *Nashville*), and Ned Buntline, the writer who "invented" Buffalo Bill, and who functions as a sententious chorus of one ("That's when the show business flourishes, when times is bad," etc.). But in a way, and especially given that a real historical injustice is tangled up with the film's simplistic recasting of bad cowboys against good Indians, it's the treatment of the Indians that is more objectionable. For the portrayal of the red man as Noble Savage is just another way of "not seeing" the Indian (despite his appropriation by radical chic, still the most invisible of America's minorities): of denying him his own identity to serve one's sloganeering. For all the usual Altman-film, revisionist air of seeing through conventional generic stereotypes, there's more real respect paid to Indians in the depiction of their unknowable otherness in such a conventionally "old-fashioned" Western as *Ulzana's Raid* than in all of *Buffalo Bill and the Indians'* facile idealization of them.

And yet, repugnant as the new Altman film may sound when paraphrased on paper, its effect on the screen is, in fact, surprisingly benign, even, despite all its potential for hate-mongering, good-natured. Part of this affability seems attributable to the presence of Paul Newman, who may be a star, but is precisely the wrong kind of star—one indelibly associated with anti-heroic roles and liberal causes—to give the film that extra layer of irony which seems intended; for the film's conception (that of one manufactured image portraying another) to have bite, a John Wayne seems called for, though probably a younger John Wayne than the one now trading shamelessly on his "legend" in *The Shootist*. (The Wild West-Hollywood connection is pressed still further by the character of the show's producer, a figure given to such Goldwynisms as "futurable" and "disimproved," who at one point proclaims his intention to "Cody-fy" the world.) But more important, perhaps because the film's point-making is so emphatic and pervasive, and the points themselves so blunted by familiarity, one can more or less ignore such things (rather as one may automatically filter out the sound of surface noise in listening to some poorly recorded music) and direct one's attention elsewhere: in particular, to several deft comic touches, some nicely turned performances by a typically eccentric Altman cast (one of my favorite funny people, Pat McCormick, plays Grover Cleveland), and, above all, to the recurrent, densely textured scenes of the show people as they mill or rush about in a Saint Vitus's dance of incessant activity.

For all the usual Altman-film, revisionist air of seeing through conventional generic stereotypes, there's more real respect paid to Indians in the depiction of their unknowable otherness in such a conventionally "old-fashioned" Western as *Ulzana's Raid* than in all of *Buffalo Bill and the Indians'* facile idealization of them.
—*William S. Pechter*

Indeed, these latter scenes seem virtually self-sufficient in their hold on one—seem almost to have a rooted life of their own quite apart from the shaky superstructure of statements erected on them. For if, on its surface, *Buffalo Bill and the Indians* is a collection of flimsy ironies about the fraudulent myth-making of American "history," there is also, as in the best of Altman's other films, something far more compelling at work beneath, much as a *McCabe & Mrs. Miller* is "about" capitalist rapacity, but draws its power from some more deeply buried source. *Buffalo Bill and the Indians* expounds its text, but, like Altman's other films, it also has a subtext—and though this new film is among Altman's least substantial ones, it's *McCabe & Mrs. Miller,* his deepest work, of which it most reminds me. (Never more so than when, like the whores in *McCabe & Mrs. Miller,* Sitting Bull stands in wonderment before a prototypical juke box—in which, however, he soon loses interest.) Like *McCabe & Mrs. Miller,* the work's emotional core seems to reside not so much in its action, in what happens, as in its evocation of the life of an isolated community at some outpost of civilization, with the Wild West show's compound resembling less a fairgrounds than a frontier fort. (Both films were, in fact, shot in relatively isolated conditions in Canada.) And though this community's population is composed, is composed, far more exclusively than *McCabe & Mrs. Miller*'s, of buffoons, it's remarkable that, even in the case of Buffalo Bill himself, the characters are no worse than buffoons, and rather gently drawn ones at that. And it's this sense of a communal outpost—of some isolated group banded together to create a refuge from the harshness of the world outside—that underlies almost all of Altman's best films, and radiates a warmth through them despite their overlay of cynical myth-debunking. One may even come to suspect that what these films are about is ultimately the experience of making them: about that fragile, transient, harmonious community that Altman gathers around himself for the making of his

movies. And if his lesser work has the air of a convivial party, the best of it seems more like a celebration of some warmly felt gathering of family.

Yet if *Buffalo Bill and the Indians* is reminiscent of *McCabe & Mrs. Miller,* one is struck no less by the two films' dissimilarities. In *McCabe & Mrs. Miller,* a veneer of irony coats but ultimately doesn't conceal the resonant depth of feeling below; in *Buffalo Bill and the Indians,* a shallow substratum of feeling can intermittently be sensed beneath the top-heavy edifice of meanings on the surface. Nor is this just a case of one film running deeper than another in the way that any artist's work may vary in quality from one creation to the next. Rather, it seems increasingly likely that, with the extravagant overpraise that's been lavished on his work since *McCabe & Mrs. Miller,* Altman is now locked into the role of oracle, committed to telling us, in ever-widening arcs of indictment, that we're living a lie, and all our heroes have feet of clay. And the shame of that is really less that we're likely headed for other Altman films as thin as *Buffalo Bill and the Indians* (or, worse, more *Nashvilles*), than that we may never again be given an Altman film as rich, reverberant, and *mysterious* as *McCabe & Mrs. Miller.* . . .

Roger Greenspun (essay date July-August 1977)

SOURCE: "Floating," in *Film Comment,* Vol. 13, No. 4, July-August, 1977, pp. 55-7.

[*In the following essay, Greenspun asserts that, "3 Women ranks with the best Altman, though it has the pretensions of some of the worst—*Brewster McCloud, Images—*and it divides, as just about everyone has noticed, between a wonderful first half and a highly problematic second."*]

Quite by accident, the day I last saw *3 Women* I also screened John Ford's *7 Women* and the recent *Looking Up.* For the neatness of this introduction, and for lots of other reasons, I could have wished my third film had been, say, *Four Daughters,* or at least *Two Gals and a Guy.* But *Looking Up* offers the symmetry of having been directed and produced by women (Linda Yellen and Karen Rosenberg), and in its abysmal slice-of-pastrami pseudo-realism it offers a sobering corrective for anyone—like me—inclined to lose patience with Robert Altman's desert swimming pools or his well-publicized immersion in the collective unconscious. Ford's last masterpiece, on the other hand, stands almost as a reproach to Altman's loose structures and his indulgence in portents in place of meaning. *7 Women* looked old fashioned when it was released in 1966, and now of course it looks classic, while the fashion of 1966—*A Man For All Seasons? Blow-up?*—grows insignificant by comparison.

Altman has always been a modernist director, and the classical resources—the repeating metaphors and meaningful image patterns, such as the kerosene lamps, the torches, the blazing conflagrations that light up John Ford's long night in Hell—would for him represent access to no such traditional range of significance as that which sustained Ford in the late summit of his career. Perhaps his films embody a pessimism as strong as the late Ford's. But if so, it is less tough and less deep. Where Ford in *7 Women,* keeping his heroine in view, resolutely puts out the lights, Altman only fades or—more likely—tracks or slowly pans away.

3 Women ranks with the best Altman, though it has the pretensions of some of the worst—***Brewster McCloud, Images***—and it divides, as just about everyone has noticed, between a wonderful first half and a highly problematic second. That really isn't anything new. *M*A*S*H* falls down in its conclusion, and so does ***Thieves Like Us,*** while ***California Split*** simply falls apart. The difficulties Altman has in ending his movies sometimes extend pretty far back toward the beginning. Many of his happiest films consist of a succession of new faces and fresh starts. Or else, he will diffuse his energies over a broad spectrum of vignettes (which are meant to come together to make sense) or, rather than actually develop character or situation, he will submit his people to some form of magical transformation.

3 Women belongs with the magical transformations. It is fortunate in its first seventy-odd minutes of, essentially, exposition. But you can't properly accept that and merely reject the changes that come after. The film keeps acting as if it were about something. If, as some critics have suggested, it is really at its most serious about nothing much, then the value of everything you can like about it is called in question.

I assume that anybody reading this will by now know the film's story, how Pinky Rose (Sissy Spacek), fresh from Texas, comes to take over the persona and the place of Millie Lammoreaux (Shelley Duvall) at the Purple Sage Apartments in Desert Springs, California; and how the third woman, Willie Hart (Janice Rule), in the trauma of giving birth to a stillborn baby seems to effect the re-birth of herself and the other two into a self-sufficient pioneer matriarchy that steps back into the style of the old west. Just about everyone and everything has a double or a shadow image: Millie—Pinky, Willie—baby, Willie's husband Edgar and the TV western's star he once stood-in for, even the California desert, which Pinky notes "sure looks a lot like Texas." The geriatric center where Millie and Pinky help exercise the old folks is staffed with twins, or best pals who look amazingly alike, and to watch the old folks themselves wade through their therapy pool, each accompanied and assisted by a young girl, is to sense the theme of replacement that keeps moving (if not exactly motivating) the film. When Millie cheerfully talks to herself, which she frequently does because nobody will listen to her, she is perhaps invoking her own ideal match. Her own ideal match moves in on her soon enough.

Cycles of death and birth—old folks and young folks, the death of Willie's baby and her own rebirth into a new persona, Pinky's swimming-pool suicide and her rebirth out of a fetal dependency on the fluid-carrying tubes of a hospital life-support system into a sluttish parody of Millie (she comes out of her coma just after we see her ancient parents make love in Millie's bedroom)—these must connect somewhere. Perhaps they connect with some other cycles, the motor cycles that circle in apparently endless dirt-bike races behind the Dodge City roadhouse that Edgar and Willie run, and that seem to end up as a too-ominous pile of discarded tires in the final panning shot of the film's conclusion. At least there is the reinvention of "Dodge City" itself, with the ersatz Edgar, the phoney cowboy removed, presumably shot by one of the three women he has wronged, and the investment of Millie as the new proprietress (complete with neat yellow-topped tables and flower arrangements in the bar) and the other women around her as dependents. I'm tempted to see Dodger City as a new recognition of the frontier, though I doubt the film allows any such specific formulation. In any case, we do end with Millie, the pre-packaged, time-tested, processed food girl, boiling whole potatoes for the others in the Dodge City kitchen.

Reviewers of *3 Women* have generally noticed and either cared or not, that they couldn't make much sense out of half the movie. Stanley Kauffmann, who hates the film, attacks Altman for being "middle-class," which I had never thought was a category of film criticism before, and for imitating the manners of his European betters. In the *New Yorker,* Penelope Gilliatt, who seems to like the film, mainly summarizes the plot, getting some of it wrong in the process. And Andrew Sarris, if I read him correctly, comes close to saying that parts he didn't understand are profound because he didn't understand them. However, Sarris has written the best review the film has had, and one of the best general considerations I've ever seen accorded Altman. He acknowledges, interprets, and puts to rest the self-evidence relations between *3 Women* and Fellini and Bergman, and he actually notices what happens on the screen. Thus:

> I could do worse than try to evoke Shelley Duvall's stride as she walks from one social Calvary to another. There is so much spiritual grace in that stride, and so much wisdom in Altman's decision to follow that stride to the ends of his scenario, that one is enobled simply by witnessing the bonds of compassion between the director and his actress. Nothing else in *3 Women* is quite so overwhelming as the cumulative gallantry under stress of Shelley Duvall's Millie. It makes everything Fellini ever did

with Giulietta Masina seem patronizing by comparison.

If I were to isolate what matters most for me in *3 Women,* Sarris' "spiritual grace" would be part of it. And although I am finally more impressed by the dimensions of Sissy Spacek's *performance* than by Shelley Duvall's, the simultaneously idiotic and valiant *presence* of Duvall's Thoroughly Modern Millie from almost the first shot until almost the last is surely the saving buoyancy of the film.

Considering what lies beneath the surface, whether in Bohdi Wind's brutally sexual pool murals or in the underwater visions and dreams with which Altman periodically invests the scene, floating may be the greatest good his world can offer. Pinky shows a real (and disquieting) talent for self-immersion, right from the start when she blows air bubbles into her Coca-Cola glass and then dunks herself completely in the geriatric center's therapy pool. Pinky shows a talent for mimicry too—for picking up Millie's time card (by mistake), her house coat, her Social Security number, her car, her diary, her name, her life. In these terms, cannibalism is the sincerest form of flattery. Indeed, each suggestion of procreation or annexation—from Willie's bloody stillbirth, to the half-reptilian sharp-toothed creatures in the pool murals, to Pinky's slavish attachment, to the symbolic sources of amniotic fluid that seem to abound in this desert landscape—each of these carries a component of nightmare so intense as to make the light stride Sarris admires an expression of the finest, albeit unknowing, heroism.

The first half of *3 Women* celebrates that heroism even while it prepares for something else. Millie descends from a long line of Robert Altman satirical portraits, in which the satire is typically relieved by an understanding so rich and so benevolent as virtually to reshape our awareness of the world it helps us see. That was the special gift of *Nashville* and *California Split,* but it exists as well in *McCabe and Mrs. Miller,* and even in *M*A*S*H.* There is no condescension in this portraiture, and nothing shields Millie from appearing both as ridiculous and as fine as she is. Her marvelous apartment, decorated to the teeth in tones of yellow, rust brown, and white, may be the fullest appreciation ever of how a lonely bachelor girl without much money or real sophistication orders her existence in a world that offers no hint of sympathy from the outside. That women's-magazine dream of perfectibility is not without its poignancy, and Altman, to his credit, never pretends the dream is merely an ignorant lie. Pinky's momentary awe of Millie's far-ranging accomplishments, the rather simple sequence in which she enters Millie's apartment, overwhelmed by the bright decor and perfect convenience, while Millie beams in well-earned satisfaction—may add up to the loveliest passage in all of Altman. It is not so far below that gracious gentle conver-

sation between two beautiful sisters by a Kyoto lake at the center of Ozu's transcendent *End of Summer.*

The power of the sequence derives not only from its benevolence, one of Altman's best qualities as a filmmaker, but also from its fragility, the inevitability with which it must succumb to the passage of time. Pinky will begin to take over the apartment, even before her rebirth through attempted suicide. And no one will come to Millie's dinner party with the store-bought shrimp cocktail and the canned chocolate pudding in the pre-baked sponge-cake shells. The dinner party is a joke, but not the impulse behind it. Millie's pathetic pretenses come as close to true civility—and thus in a sense, to civilization—as any values in the movie. Remember that never far from her, pregnant Willie kneels, painting another nightmare vision on the bottom or the sides of the pools that generate the movement of life in *3 Women.*

Between nightmare and benign delusion, there is nothing much except the background chatter of the Purple Sage swinging singles, the administration of the geriatric center (two perpetually furious disciplinarians), perhaps a few hospital nurses. Where, except to "Dodge City" and along the "Santa Fe Trail" (the derelict miniature golf course next door), the film is finally going, leaves me mostly in the dark. I don't find that an acceptable state of affairs. But *how* it is going, and what it has to work with, I think I somewhat understand, and understand that anyone's "spiritual grace" within it becomes a kind of dancing on the edge of the abyss.

It may be for Altman, as for the late John Ford, that women can face the abyss with greater fortitude than can men. But I doubt that, as in late Ford, they see it more clearly or that they help create it. Nothing in *3 Women* suggests that anyone really sees or comprehends anything. The characters enact, but they don't direct the film's design. It is their destiny but never their decision, and it means little to point out that they lack the element of choice. The Altman films work like great machines tending usually toward some arbitrary dissolution, often through either violent death or outright disappearance. John Ford's abyss—at least in *7 Women*—is a hell. Altman's is a void. This may be why his movies contain so much preliminary exposition and why that exposition will often be the best part of them. Everything that precedes the cataclysm is not only clearer but also infinitely precious. The beautiful encounters and introductions that open *3 Women* are not an accident. Given what he knows must happen, he is being as kind to us as he can.

W. S. Di Piero (essay date Summer 1978)

SOURCE: "Wish and Power: Recent Altman," in *Chicago Review,* Vol. 30, No. 1, Summer, 1978, pp. 34-51.

[*In the following essay, Di Piero discusses Altman's* Nashville, Buffalo Bill and the Indians, or Sitting Bull's History Lesson, *and* 3 Women, *and asserts that, "His career may prove eventually to be the most cogent, and tenacious, of any America director."*]

Public controversy contaminates perceptions, and sudden notoriety often smudges the profile of a newly famous thing. In the past several years Robert Altman, a latecomer in American filmmaking, has become the most conspicuous victim of public misperception. Although his films have inspired lively polemic, they have also drawn forth more opaque, muddled opinion than any other films of the period. Critics and audiences have been dazzled, angered, and frequently baffled by his innovative style, above all by his eccentric narrative strategies. Instead of relying on the centripetal forces of conventional narrative, whereby plot details gravitate toward nuclear characters and events, Altman has exploited a kind of centrifugal style: incidents and characters spin away from the narrative axis, the camera brushes past significant events, the sound track overlaps or truncates "meaningful" dialogue, the editing fragments conventional character exposition. It's a cunning, peripheral style, and one of the few real advances in storytelling method since the innovations of the French New Wave. In his films since *M*A*S*H* Altman has dramatized reality at speeds quite different from those we are used to in narrative cinema, and he has liquified and refashioned traditional fixed point of view. Alan Spiegal describes this new cinema as "a decentralized system in which discrete elements of style and drama float freely in shifting suspension, in which elements confront each other in glancing discord and irresolute debate." Altman casually insists that we train ourselves to see his films in a new way, that we adapt ourselves not merely to a new point of view but to a new method of seeing.

Because of his restless, exploratory methods, Altman has continually undermined and blasted critical expectations. He has moved nimbly from the flashy, jabberwocky profanity of *M*A*S*H* to the dreamy pessimism of *McCabe and Mrs. Miller,* from the looney-tune fable of Brewster McCloud to the puzzle theatrics of *Images,* from the bitter dizziness of *The Long Goodbye* to the lush melancholy of *Thieves Like Us.* Yet he never makes an issue of his own virtuosity. The elliptical cutting, the eight-track sound recording that mimics and revises the babble of reality, the irreal lighting that shapes character, the peripheral events that lunge into the foreground to determine dramatic action: these are Altman's obvious "trademarks," but he is intelligent and vital enough not to have allowed them to harden into mannerism. His versatility, however, has in some quarters undermined his authority. Newspaper critics especially are immediately suspicious of abundance—Altman has made eight films in seven years—assuming that anyone who works quickly must also be brilliantly facile. In this instance, the scaled-down

expectations and attenuated sensibilities of reviewers simply are not equal to Altman's enterprise: his amplitude defeats and embarrasses their reluctant generosity.

> **Like any honorable artist, Altman is a skeptic, never entirely trusting the appearances of things; but he is at the same time celebrative, eager to sing in the presence of what moves him. This tension between skepticism and celebration gives his films their peculiar disarming ambivalence, their brilliant unease.**
> **—W. S. Di Piero**

Nashville was responsible for bringing Altman to the attention of the public at large. Unlike his earlier films, it became a full-fledged media event. Disregarding for the most part the spinning lyric noise of the film, and its fierce ambivalence, critics preferred to seize on what seemed to them an accessible public issue—Altman's vision of America. *Nashville* was discussed in the most unlikely places, from the op-ed page of the *New York Times* to the Johnny Carson Show. The topic of public discussion was not really the film itself but rather the commentators' misperceptions of it. Although Altman denied in interviews any intention of making *Nashville* a critical portrait of America in the seventies, critics inevitably misread the film as a pillorying of America. Yet Altman, in a *Playboy* interview, was quite explicit about his intentions: "When I make films like *Nashville* it's not to say we're the worst country in the world, or what awful people these are. I'm just saying we're *at* this point and it's sad." Instead of fierce, righteous satire, Altman was offering a portrait of American melancholy, a study of personalities under stress, rendered in carrousel narrative. The overheated competitiveness of the country-music industry was an ideal context; the brinksmanship and power struggles that characterize all show business become all the more ambivalent, and poignant, when the music in question sings about Big American Themes. This too was much on Altman's mind: "Another thing *Nashville* signifies is that we don't listen to words anymore. The words of a country song are as predictable as the words of a politician's speech. . . . *Nashville* is merely suggesting that you think about these things, allowing you room to think. Many people, I guess, want to know exactly what it is they're supposed to think. They want to know what your message is. Well, my message is that I am not going to do their work for them." While Altman continues to operate by suggestion and insinuation, many of his critics still hear only soapbox rhetoric, which presumably is what they *want* to hear. Altman's responsibility, as he himself sees it, is to vex his audience into thought and feeling. He prefers revelation to mere explanation. Instead of handing down Polonian criticism of the American way, he was in *Nashville* dramatizing—and often mourning—the vicious operations of chance in a country celebrated as the land of opportunity—political, financial, and sexual opportunity. *Nashville* is abrasive rather than critical, seizing as it does on the dark confusion between opportunity and opportunism.

Altman is certainly curious about the American character and the eccentricities that we have normalized. He wants (and needs) to reveal those things found only in America, the emotional contours and cultural habits that distinguish us from others, the imaginative history that makes us what we are. His attitude is one of curiosity, not pontification; of exploration, not proclamation. Like any honorable artist, Altman is a skeptic, never entirely trusting the appearances of things; but he is at the same time celebrative, eager to sing in the presence of what moves him. This tension between skepticism and celebration gives his films their peculiar disarming ambivalence, their brilliant unease. One of the most unexpected moments in *Nashville* comes when Barbara Jean, arriving at the airport to begin her comeback, is greeted by a high school band and a crowd of scrubbed, chunky baton twirlers. Here surely was a chance for Altman to poke low fun at American hokum, at provincial middle-class culture. But, unexpectedly, Altman has a young peachy twirler, cradling flowers for Barbara Jean, march directly into the admiring and embracing eye of his camera. There is genuine affection and a startling absence of irony in this celebrative image. And at the end of the film, although we are not spared the abrupt horror of the shooting of Barbara Jean, the hysterical lady in white, neither are we spared the cold and accurate irony of American Opportunity: even as the great democratic masses so celebrated in nineteenth-century America offer the young assassin his dramatic opportunity, the tragic event at the same time offers another opportunity, that of instant stardom, to the aspiring singer Albuquerque. In his inspiration and the realization of his vision, Altman is kin to Whitman: his art is ample and inclusive, he wants to see and say everything, to get it all down. The result, as in Whitman, may sometimes have the look of chaos, but this is finally a strategic mask for the symmetries of plenitude, for generosity straining at the tether of common sense.

Nashville is about rituals of power, both public and private. The singers and hangers-on who frequent Nashville all act upon the need to be close to power sources. Most of them seize every opportunity to draw power from the presidential candidate Walker, guided not by serious political loyalties but by career opportunism. The Nashville patriarch Haven Hamilton, the frail convalescent Barbara Jean, the haughty inarticulate trio of Bill and Tom and Mary, all insist they have no interest in politics, yet in the end they all agree to sing at the Walker rally. The sympathetic magic of song might allow them to borrow some of the raw political

power of the event. Within this large context of public power, however, Altman also sets in motion a number of mini-dramas about professional and sexual power struggles, games of brinksmanship that infect personal relationships. Barbara Jean's position as country music queen is threatened by the glamorous hustling of Connie White (Karen Black); Albuquerque's husband chases after her in order to "save" her from Nashville; the young assassin, of all the characters the most isolated and solitary, suffers from his own high-strung wish to draw attention to himself. Each character, in effect, wants an increased sense of self-importance, and the most direct and dramatic way of achieving this is by stepping over the fallen or faltering bodies of others.

Power struggles, whether public or private, thrive on pragmatism: a person may do whatever works best to serve his personal designs. But the most manipulative and ruthless characters turn out to be not Nashville country and western singers but the outsiders, the rock group Bill and Tom and Mary. The Nashville people, especially Haven Hamilton, do indeed believe in the values celebrated in their songs, though their belief is by now blunted by the grinding repetition of sentiment. They are not cynical in believing America to be still a land of milk and honey. Although the lyrics of their songs are often anemic and hokey, they express more or less genuine sentiments. The rock group, on the other hand, are hypocrites in every way. Alienated from each other by sexual drifting and self-servingness, they sing songs that have no real basis in belief; the music is mannered and thin, the lyrics hollow slogans left over from the radical sixties. The mellow truths they celebrate, about loneliness and love, are glamorous instruments that earn them a good living. Tom, the most obnoxious yet most complex of all the characters, is also the most cowardly and self-serving. He is the show business Don Juan, making bedside phone calls to set up his next assignation even while his most recent bed-partner listens on. He is full of canned antiwar sentiments, and his songs are sweet, convincing falsifications of his own feelings. But his arrogance is so apparently self-effacing and understated that it seems almost attractive; he is the perfect rendering of the "sensitive man" so popular in the sixties, soft and pliant manners masking arrogant weakness.

Altman sets the opportunistic rock trio, with their sliding scale of values, against the more sympathetic and conventional character of Haven Hamilton. Hamilton, the gaudy embodiment of Nashville traditions and in his way a smug self-righteous man, bears himself with reserve and dignity. Somehow he ennobles even the flamboyant costumes he wears. Like any hard-eyed businessman he values tradition, yet we learn that he supported both Kennedys. Most importantly, when called upon to act, he makes his choices simply and bravely. When Barbara Jean is shot, it's Hamilton who immediately uses his own body as shield to protect her from further gunfire. Although he himself is wounded, his instincts are to protect another, to preserve Nashville's angel. He is morally outraged that a nearly hallowed place should be profaned by the kind of irrational violence that *should* be foreign to Nashville. His sense of decency, which runs deep, and of traditional values carried on in public rituals, is outraged by the brutal disturbance of communal peace. "This isn't Dallas," he assures the crowd. "This is Nashville." This instinctive defense of his hometown as a locus of value stands out in sharp contrast to the equivocal values voiced not only by the Walker campaigners, but also by most of the other Nashville singers. His courageous gesture transcends pragmatism, cultural sloganism, and brute careerism; transcends, in effect, the most obvious *appearances* which generally are identified with Nashville. Hamilton's action is a selfless, almost self-transcendent gesture, and an instinctive defense of the radical traditions of the town.

Altman's tone, however, and his attitude toward his characters are often ambivalent. Even though Haven Hamilton performs more than one admirable act, we are never allowed to forget that he is also an arrogant businessman. And Tom is allowed some of the cool bemused sympathy we reserve for ruthless Don Juans. Altman's tone, then, can be at once abrasive and affectionate. We have become so accustomed, however, to the generally explicit, flattened tone of American movies that we tend to feel not only uneasy but also defensive when confronted with something more ambiguous and expansive. We do not expect a film so overrun with familiar American images and attitudes to treat them in a new way. Too often our tendency as viewers is to protect our own ritualized responses and to make the darkened theater a place of safety rather than of menace. By embracing a broad range of personalities in his films and by allowing them to pursue their own destinies without the blunt intervening hand of the filmmaker, Altman is close in sensibility to Renoir. And like Renoir, Altman resists making political and moral judgments. *Nashville* offers no explanation of America to itself, but it does render a very singular vision of the complexity of American experience. And I think that Altman's intelligent affection for his characters is tied to his ambiguous affection for American diversity. He is much taken by the peculiar blend of the wild and the forlorn which gives the American character its rough edges, the chattering, expansive, speedy smugness that seems built not only into our behavior but into the environments we surround ourselves with. For instance, everywhere we go there is music—in supermarkets, offices, restaurants, houses, automobiles, factories. The music is meant to be ignored: this is its proper nonpurpose. Altman picks this up as an aural cue to one aspect of the American experience, and he uses it as a unifying element in *Nashville.* The people in the film do not really listen to music, they behave in its presence. Finally, the music does begin to seem like organized noise.

Altman's art, like Whitman's, is first of all revelatory, often interpretive, seldom explanatory. His work is too sensuous to be explanatory, too full of the messy, half-realized, inarticulate experience that gives his films their special numinous quality. Because of its amplitude, *Nashville* yields its own apparent contradictions, its own nonexplanations. For these reasons, the closing sequence deserves its mixed fame. Rather than a neat, summative, programmatic vision of contemporary America, it yields instead a vision of the heterogeneous elements of American experience and of the tensions that bind and enliven them. The pure unreason of the violence against Barbara Jean remains crucially unexplained: the young killer, who has the clenched ascetic look of a young Trotskyite, may be shooting up at the American flag, or at Haven Hamilton. The shooting itself is underplayed, since Altman is more concerned with what happens afterward. We have a moment of unexplained violence followed immediately by Hamilton's act of traditional bravery. The disorder allows Albuquerque her long-awaited opportunity to sing before an audience. Disaster, in effect, creates opportunity and this sudden realization of opportunity, insofar as it reaffirms a crucial American value, is also a provisional restoration of order.

More important than the lyrics of the closing song (with its ambiguous refrain: "You may say that I ain't free / But it don't worry me") is the self-referential incantatory power of song, of organized noise, with its primitive power to soothe and manipulate, to turn benign or malevolent: song as democratic redemption and fascist appeal. While the crowd chants, the camera pulls back slowly. The colorful throng seems shrunken against the hulking modern Parthenon ("made of poured concrete and steel: the Athens of the South"). On stage, isolated from the crowd, are the cheery blond newcomer and a black back-up choir. Above looms the covering presence of the flag, the symbolic organization of all the mixed elements that stand, slightly dazed, beneath it. In this bold context, the theme of the stars and stripes—its tri-color harmonies, its pluralism set against a fixed field—ceases to be ironic. The flag suddenly seems an appropriate metaphor, though certainly at best a *working* metaphor, for the mixed vision the film has offered us. But the film does not, as many critics seemed to think, end here. Intercut into this generalist vision are spastic, isolated close-ups of the crowd: babies, rednecks, freaks, elders, and two conspicuous police officers, one of them female, winding alertly through the crowd. These shots remind us that the generalization "society" exists only by virtue of its discrete parts, its anonymous human units; society is before all else an aggregate of personalities. Once we have absorbed this large, expanding picture, the camera makes another decision. Tilting upward away from the crowd, it leaves both crowd and flag behind and fixes its gaze on the blue and innocent sky. The music finally, mercifully, fades out. Moments later, in silence, the sky too fades. This final progression of images does not resolve the film according to the rather melodramatic conventions of American narrative cinema. Instead of a vision of provisional order and harmony (the standard resolution of Hollywood films), and instead of the false consolation of political or moral platitude, the camera eye *enacts* transcendence, lifting itself above the crowd, above the diversity of the human toward the oneness of sky. It is a powerful enactment of the will to dream, the decision to transcend the appearances of pluralism and emerge into a transcendent, unified reality, an alternate world. It is Altman's instinctive equivalent, I think, of Emerson's aspiration toward the oneness of the Oversoul, a coherent wish for transcendence. Altman of course thinks his way toward this possibility through images, through his round-robin metaphors of plenitude and unity. Like any narrative filmmaker, he tells his story with pictures and sound, but the narrative poetry lies deep within the self-contained metaphoric story. Altman does not so much tell a story as he *tells* metaphors, tells a poetry of deeply related images, and his films after *Nashville* continue to tell this poetry of guarded aspiration and promise.

Buffalo Bill and the Indians, or Sitting Bull's History Lesson, begins precisely where *Nashville* left off, with a vision of sky and mountains and the American flag flying high. The camera eye descends slowly, once again into show business, but this time the show is a dusty historical spectacle of Missouri settlers battling Indians. From the pure presence of Nature we slide down into the staged artifice of entertainment, of Buffalo Bill's Wild West Show, where a revised version of history is being rehearsed so that it may be sold to willing audiences. Altman's vision descends quickly from silence into noise, into the glib speech of commerce, the marketplace of American wish and power. Based as it is on the legends of Buffalo Bill, the Wild West Show is grounded in falsified history, and it uses the American Indian, the fixed center of native culture, as its main ploy; it takes culture and distorts it to serve Bill's ends, to become "civilized" entertainment. In the interests of progress, culture may be falsified, too. Civilization is more important, since it promises greater profits.

The linguist Edward Sapir distinguishes between culture and the civilization which is its vehicle. It is quite possible, he says, for an advanced intelligent civilization to be a very poor culture-bearer. America certainly possesses high civilization, conspicuous material wealth defined almost exclusively by advanced tools, a society where leisure is the highest ideal. Culture, on the other hand, depends not on tools but on a homogeneous mythic truth that must underpin the psychology and actions of an entire people, truth which results from a passionate desire to refine experience, to understand pious communal origins. Culture depends on an understanding of the sky and of man's residence on earth beneath such sky. Civilization places its trust in less permanent things. Moreover, genuine culture is not graduated, is neither high nor low. "It is merely inherently harmonious,

balanced, self-satisfactory. It is the expression of a richly varied and yet somehow unified and consistent attitude toward life, an attitude which sees the significance of any one element of civilization in its relation to all others." The Wild West Show is certainly a mode of advanced civilization; not only is it *efficient* in its entertainment (it even has an "Inventions Department") but it is self-conscious about its materials and impious in the presence of inefficiency. Progress is whatever works. Everything is judged according to its appearance—it is, after all, the show business. What it lacks, however, is what Sapir calls "spiritual essence," a belief in something that is not itself, that stands over and against manmade products. Bill's show may be a success, but it lacks spiritual mastery, lacks the historical abundance and unselfconscious permanence that inhabit the mountains and sky. It is not numinous. Altman's film, perhaps the only truly contemplative American film of the past several years, explores these distinctions, dramatizes the sadness that emerges from supercivilization when it lacks culture, broods on the suppressed envy that lies just beneath the surfaces of American experience, which so often is grief disguised as plenitude.

Show business is high civilization, a world of well-tooled artifice and illusion, the greatest being the illusion of history, a dream of Buffalo Bill as great Indian fighter. The show is indeed well-designed, convincing in its appearances. But it lacks spiritual essence, lacks the one historical truth that might have given it real culture: Bill's identity is not an historical truth but the crude product of Ned Buntline's hack imagination. Far from being a great buffalo hunter and Indian fighter, Bill was above all an illustrious manufacturer of illusions. And the legends that began to cluster around his name were mostly dreamed up by a dime novelist visiting from the East. In order to preserve both his image and the show which markets that image, he must live up to the personality created for him. But in trying to honor his artificial public identity, Bill has become a civilized paranoiac who fears his own legend. He already suspects that his show, his dream, is very dandy waste, but waste nonetheless; it may be civilized entertainment, but it is not culture. It derives not from natural piety or the wisdom of the heart, but from businesslike cynicism and media hype. In Altman's version, Bill is beginning to distrust his own pulp greatness.

Into this hermetic, voluble world comes the threatening stranger, Sitting Bull, silent as a mountain, needing no hype to validate his great spiritual power. Bull really does have visions; he sees what other men do not, because his soul is great. Everything he says or does has its roots in the creation myths of his tribe, the primal piety of man in the presence of his gods, acting out of radical motives. As a man, he *comprises* culture. Unlike Bill, whose world is wildly contaminated by Nate Salsbury's pseudolanguage, Bull needs no words to explain or rationalize his existence. Bill, the civilized creation of literary gossip, feels almost morally obliged to explain himself and to exercise (as flamboyantly as possible) the power of his position; Bull, son of the silent earth, now dispossessed of the means and tools of his own civilization, is pure revelation. From the moment Bull enters, Bill is on his guard, cautious and envious of this unlikely American. Each claims a history drawn from the same historical context, but Bill knows that the Indian is the real thing and hence the only dangerous thing.

Buffalo Bill's main power source is self-esteem. He has assumed the manufactured image of himself; since it is so useful, so profitable, it must be true. Sitting Bull threatens Bill's self-esteem, his control over all aspects of the theatrical production which is himself. Bill thinks he has scored a huge success in acquiring Bull as an attraction in the show, but it turns out that the Indian has come only because of a dream which told him that he would there meet the Great White Father, President Cleveland. To Bill's mind, this is a very spurious "reason," since it has no practical grounding. Bill cannot understand because he does not have such power-dreams. Certain that he is matching Bull's game of brinksmanship, Bill agrees to let him stay, but reminds his nephew Ed that "the difference between a white man and an Injun in a situation like this is that an Injun don't know the difference between a question and an answer. That's why they ain't ever sure when they get what they ask for." Duped by a man of power, Bill can only resort to paleface rhetoric to preserve his self-esteem. Question-and-answer is the most convenient kind of business discourse: the language of exchange and bargaining. Sitting Bull, however, speaks the more direct language of need; his words are impelled by the destiny his dreams dictate. Bull's culture demands that he interpret fantasy, dream-stuff, as one of the power sources behind his spirituality. Buffalo Bill and Salsbury, on the other hand, take the facts of history and rearrange them into palatable illusions; they manufacture historical fantasies as something quite divorced from their own spiritual essences. They deal in titillation, not inspiration. In staging Custer's Last Stand, Bill has Custer scalped by Sitting Bull. When someone objects to the historical inaccuracy, Salsbury justifies it according to show business pragmatism: "We're in the goosebump business." Halsey, Sitting Bull's interpreter, also tries to correct Bill's staging: "Sitting Bull was not present on the battlefield. He was making medicine and dreaming. Sitting Bull will allow you to show his dream. He saw many horses upside down and blue skeletons floating to the promised land." Not only does this not coincide with Bill's idea of the show business, but more importantly Bull's dream exists in a cultural context totally alien to Bill's own. Bill must have big American entertainment, explicit and goosebumping; Bull's oracular dream would not make for good pulp. Moreover, the Wild, West Show is not, as Salsbury says, "in the yesterday business"; the past exists not as radical memory but as raw material for future deals.

Salsbury refers to Bull's contract as "the most futurable act in our history." Historical fact exists in order to be packaged as a future commodity. Thus it is possible for civilization to flourish even while it is culturally impoverished.

All of these materials lend themselves easily to satire, but in *Buffalo Bill* Altman again adopts an unexpected tone. Rather than characterize white men as malicious fools or show business sharks, he allows each character to stand close to the shadow line of grief, to the collapse of self-deception (and hence of self-esteem). If *Buffalo Bill* is a satire, it is elegiac satire, steeped in sadness and uncertainty. Ironically, and painfully, the only person to whom Bill can confide his fears is Sitting Bull. The most seductive scene in the film is the one in which Bill, delirious on whiskey and lack of sleep, hallucinates the presence of Sitting Bull. Provoked by the Indian's astonishing self-containment, he spills out some necessary but disarming truths and reveals some of his own hysterical wisdom. "God meant for me to be white!" he exclaims. The white man's birthright is different in kind and degree from Sitting Bull's; his legacies are different, too, and in their own way terribly burdensome. Bill is aware of the choice he himself has made and the responsibility he has taken on as a paleface showman: "It ain't easy. . . . I got people with no lives living *through me!* Proud people! People to worry about." He knows it's too late to make up for that which was missing in the first place, a sense of piety and of historical memory. The white man's dream is, and always has been, essentially different from the Indian's dream, and white America has had such little time to do so much that we should not, according to Buffalo Bill, be held guilty for cutting corners on history. Civilization, in effect, is a different kind of aspiration than culture; its power must be evident in appearances, the clout of artifice and utilitarian rhetoric. And white America made its choice long ago. Bill goes on to confess his own urge to immortality; like an Indian, he wishes to be remembered by his children's children, but the source of his immortality, unlike an Indian's, will not be rooted in great deeds or spiritual power. "I do what I do for *me*. Because when you do that, you're gonna live a little longer. It makes me true! Because truth is whatever gets the loudest applause." Bill draws his power, his truth, from living for others. Public acclamation of an artificial identity is the soundest confirmation of meaning in his life, and it promises some kind of immortality.

The show business is perhaps the most commonplace ritual of American civilization, and as Ernest Becker says, "ritual is a technique for giving life," conferring the power to outlive oneself. The difference—a tragic one—is that Bill sees himself as the source of his own power. Sitting Bull, too, obeys a set of rituals, but his strategies of immortality depend absolutely on a source of power which is *other*. Bill is a paradigm of American civilization in that he recognizes no numinous power, no spiritual authority beyond his own.

In his impoverished desire, he is a figure of American grief. Here too, Becker's formulation is appropriate: "Man needs self-esteem more than anything; he wants to be a cosmic hero, contributing with his energies to nothing less than the greatness and pleasure of the gods themselves. . . . *Hubris* means forgetting where the real source of power lies and imagining that it is in oneself." When the power source is oneself, and when one's rituals are those of the show business, one must then live not for oneself but for others. This too is a cause of Bill's melancholy. Pointing to a heroic portrait of himself, Bill asks Bull: "Ain't he riding his horse all right? If he ain't, then why did all of you mistake him for a King?" He suffers from the discrepancy between what he knows himself to be and what he knows the crowd expects of him. Whenever he rides into the show ring, mounted heroically on his white charger, Brigham, he barely manages to stay in the saddle. He is, literally and figuratively, slipping, about to lose his image, and he knows it. Obtuse as he may seem, and certainly no visionary like Sitting Bull, Bill still sees enough to suffer. Lacking culture, however, he lacks a spiritual system that might help him organize the disparate perceptions he has of himself and others. Ned Buntline says that Bill "likes to think he's a dreamer, but he's really just a sleeper." Bill's sullen American yearning, cast in the darksome and honky-tonk moods of this film, is directed toward the radical culture he knows he lacks. But his yearning, too, is anxious and uncertain, since he isn't sure he even needs or wants such culture. He has already acquired great material power, but somehow this power has still not satisfied a deeper wish that civilization lacks the language to express, let alone realize. The film, for all its peculiar half-suppressed comedy, is finally a meditation upon lost origins and the histories of power.

The power relations in *Nashville* and *Buffalo Bill* are largely public, practiced by civilized discontents whose anxieties are acted out before large attentive audiences. In both films the protagonists are entertainers, media heroes, fabricators of civilization. In *3 Women,* however, Altman withdraws (once again, unexpectedly) from public to private zones of power. *3 Women* is very much about the anxieties and densities of power, but the drama here is reclusive, and the conflicts are suffered not by public fabricators of civilization but rather by its anonymous consumers. Altman again carefully modulates the American context. Instead of the swarming vitality of American plenitude, he concentrates on a more controlled vocabulary of metaphors, all carefully designed and *placed,* which makes *3 Women* stylistically a more poised and fragile film than the earlier two. If the poetry of *Nashville* and *Buffalo Bill* is public, abundant, open-aired, and utilitarian, the poetry of *3 Women* is cloistered, ascetic, self-referential, aesthetic. In the patterns of emotion dramatized in its (often oneiric) metaphors, *3 Women* is a very clear-minded film about impingement, emotional sabotage, and violation of personality. In the earlier films personality was the battle-front of power, where identities were left battered but intact. In *3 Women,* impingement causes actual changes in personality, normalized monstrosities.

The worst victim of impingement is the woman who at first seems most aggressive. Millie (Shelly Duvall) works at a geriatric health spa. We first see her wading in a heated pool, steering along an old disabled woman. Altman places his metaphors at the very beginning, for Millie walks half immersed in water, half distorted, half "drowned." If the finale of *Nashville* was Altman's expression of Emersonian wish, in Millie he gives us a contemporary misversion of Emerson's self-reliant American. She is a cheery monster of American consumerism, prattling about microwave ovens and new fast-food recipes. Her ferocious sense of self-esteem, aggressive but dull-witted, puts people off. Her self-assertiveness is so obtrusive and overstated that she seems all surface, a tissue of TV and supermarket values. And yet she is fiercely protective of these values, since they do comprise her selfhood. In her rush to be as contemporary and as independent a woman as possible, she estranges herself from her own context: she becomes the author of her own separateness.

Millie's tidy world is invaded by the stranger Pinkie (Sissy Spacek), who comes to work at the spa. Pinkie is a Texas girl (like Millie) and her freckled innocence somehow combines both the cheer and menace of small-town American life. She seems at first Millie's opposite, homely, withdrawn, uninformed, with one pair of panties that she rinses out nightly. The seed of personality-doubling has already been planted, not only because the two women come from Texas, but because Pinkie's real name is Mildred. These coincidences will soon turn into compulsions, and Altman already begins to establish metaphorical symmetries. Pinkie's quick and strategic attachment to Millie is mocked visually by the presence of identical twins who work at the spa and who hold a spooky attraction for Pinkie. They become a model for Pinkie's own behavior; this innocent from the country will patch together her own personality from the scraps and remnants taken from others. If Millie borrows her personality from TV, magazines, and supermarkets, Pinkie takes hers from the personalities that surround her. Millie takes her as a roommate, and soon Pinkie is reading Millie's diary, wearing her clothes, mimicking her speech patterns, and generally insinuating herself into Millie's private world.

The two frequent a desert bar called "Dodge City," a tacky Old West saloon run by Edgar (once a stunt stand-in on the Wyatt Earp Show) and his pregnant wife Willie. Here Altman again reveals his ability to define a special kind of brash American vulgarity. Willie (Janice Rule) is an artist who bears herself with the silent, closed dignity of Sitting Bull, and as in *Buffalo Bill* silence here is a sign of self-containment and hence of personal power. Willie drifts through the desertscape like a wraith, leaving behind power signs, paintings of scale-armoured humanoids. She paints her demons on the walls and floors of swimming pools; her creatures seem ravaged by their own isolation and by their cumbersome sexuality. Some have elastic striated male torsos and flat drooping breasts, others have huge phalli. Their predatory look and sexual menace call to mind Albany's lines from *King Lear:* "Humanity must perforce prey on itself / Like monsters of the deep." Pinkie shows the same attraction to Willie's monstrous doubles as to the twin sisters, and when she later attempts suicide she does it by leaping into a pool, going to meet the monsters whose shapes rhyme just as the names of the three women rhyme.

In *3 Women* style itself is the narrator. Altman builds the movie on a suspended, coherent poetic design, and it cannot be understood without attending to the story as it is narrated in its metaphors. The film's visual coherence depends on two metaphors of place: desert and pool. Each personality is identified with a natural element. Millie is the desert princess, her wardrobe and apartment interior bright with sun colors; the brilliant yellow of her dresses imitates the piercing yellow of the desert cacti and yucca (desert flora is pale and bright, of course, but not the banana yellow we see in the film; Altman is quite consciously designing his metaphors). Pinkie, on the other hand, sees reality most often through watery distortions. Very early in the film, prefiguring her attempted suicide, she dunks herself in the spa pool. When she spies out her apartment window, her gaze passes through a fish tank. Willie, the most self-possessed of the three, passes easily from the dry depths of pools to the cactus landscape: when Pinkie attempts suicide, it is Willie who lunges into the water to rescue her. As the women impinge upon one another, they swing through shifting planes of light, from the slippery greens and blues of the spa to the brittle pastels of the apartment complex to the glaring yellows and browns of the desert. The images to which the characters are drawn also enact the interpenetration of identities, of natural functions. Willie's pool monsters are obviously desert creatures, scaly, saurian. Blurry underwater perceptions and duplications of image are played off against the violent parched clarity of the desert. Altman dramatizes not merely figures in a landscape, but also the landscape itself as an imitative figure of the spiritual contest waged among the three protagonists. As they move through these zones of lucidity and distortion, the zones of self-knowledge and living for others, the three women begin to stake provisional claims on the selfhood of one another. Pinkie takes on Millie's effusiveness, whereas Millie begins to learn from Willie's silences.

When Millie, anxious for the self-esteem that sexual conquest brings, returns home one evening with a drunken Edgar, Pinkie is stunned by her roommate's "borrowing of Edgar," a sexual betrayal of Willie. Suddenly, borrowing is no longer a harmless game; Pinkie feels great sympathy for Willie, and her pleas to Millie not to sleep with Edgar grow out of her fear of harm done to Willie. Rebuffed by Millie, her games now darkened terribly by the subversive reality of sex, Pinkie seeks a way out. In keeping with Altman's poetry of oblivion, she seeks death by water, plummeting into the pool to meet the sexual monsters at the bottom.

When she emerges from the coma induced by her fall, Pinkie is changed. Having surrendered herself to the dark creatures, she now begins her doubling in earnest. While convalescing, she begins to claim more fragments of Millie's personality, even asks to be called by her real name, Mildred. She paints her toenails, appropriates Millie's car (another yellow extension of her personality), picks up Millie's friends, flirts with Willie's husband. Pinkie also suffers from partial amnesia, and here Altman deals with one of his favorite themes: forgetfulness. In *Nashville,* the characters remembered only what they wished to remember, and these were usually memories of power, of the Kennedy campaign and the end of that world in Dallas. Buffalo Bill Cody manages to cope mainly by forgetting his own drab origins, soaking them in whiskey and power dreams. In *3 Women,* Pinkie in her loss of memory is *free to wield power;* she has no memories to define her own personality (which is always shaped by memories and past experience). To be absolved of identity is to be liberated, cleansed for the future. In her presence, Millie becomes unusually timid, deferential, obsequious. The waters of the pool have brought on enforced forgetfulness. Pinkie, like William Cody, thus knows only her wish for power.

The power does not last long, however. One night a dream comes to claim her, a dream filled with images of the past, the hallucinatory reality of doubles, twins, monsters, and Willie, all twisted and warped by the opacity of water, the dream medium. The montage sequence that dramatizes Pinkie's emergence from forgetfulness is, in Altman's rendering, a stunning figuration of the way stored images fuse, collapse, and percolate in the subconscious, as Pinkie makes her bizarre journey from unknowing and mystery into clarity. In effect, she *swims up* into the provisional clarity of self-possessiveness. This change is immediately challenged by yet another. As the stunned Pinkie climbs into bed to be warmed and consoled by Millie, Edgar barges in to announce that Willie is in childbirth, alone, about to bring forth her own double.

Altman uses the childbirth sequence as a poetic fulcrum where the balance of power among the three women is finally tilted and decided. This scene, like Pinkie's suicide attempt, is glazed by the memory of water, of sexual depth and unknowing. Our view is flexed and smeared by the water line that floats so unnaturally up and down the frame of vision while Willie is in labor. Once again Pinkie is being tested by water, and she fails the test, shrinking back from the primal event. Unexpectedly, Millie, who spends her days wading in pools for the aged, is the one who endures the initiation by water into full selfhood. Pinkie's idle games of doubling collapse under the pressure of real circumstances; her fabricated identity cannot survive this traumatic experience in which the fanciful adolescent "freakiness" of doubled images becomes an adult reality. To Pinkie the innocent, the issue of one human from the body of another is the most terrifying event of all. It is finally too real. The scene turns matter-of-factly tragic when the infant emerges from Willie bearing her own chilling silence. Millie, unaided, is left with the stony child on her hands, and her personality is tempered, *fired,* by the experience. Here, Altman suggests, is terminal impingement; after this crib death, this grieving enactment of stillborn selfhood, the lives of the three women can never be the same.

The underkeyed moral and physical bravery revealed in this scene reminds one briefly of Haven Hamilton's moment of instinctive bravery; Millie's courage is also instinctive, but it is intensely private. When Willie plants her feet on Millie's shoulders during the birth, the two seem fused into one embattled, courageous, pained woman. Their dealings with human predators (Millie with Pinkie, Willie with Edgar) lead finally to this encounter with that general predator, death. Altman's tale thus comes full cycle in its poetry; a film about power relations and identity-thievery evolves into—turns a revolution into—a tale about generation. The tale told by the metaphors is finally this: Until it is tested by mortality, all identity is provisional, makeshift, expedient. Once mortality has brushed its cool hand past us, personality hardens, selfhood becomes fixed, and identity drives down permanent roots. We recall the opening scenes of the film, the wrinkled deteriorating elders wading so carefully in the pool at the spa—the aged awaiting death, attended by the young who themselves act as midwives to the yet unborn. In the symmetry of its poetry, the film embodies memories of itself.

The film's closing moments are stern, serene, imperious. The gleaming promise of yellow now belongs to a huge Coca-Cola truck that rears up from the desert to make a delivery to Dodge City, now operated by the three women. Edgar has died of a gunshot wound, clearly the victim of one of the women. Dodge City, in its new version, is a tribal village without men (a bitter inversion of the manly Dodge City of movies). The three women comprise a family. Pinkie, now called Millie, calls Millie "Mom"; she sits at a cashier's desk popping gum and reading fan magazines, the eternal adolescent eternally dependent. Willie, still silent, still paints. But Millie, the poetic center of the film whose "color value" has been the key to the film's figurative tale, is changed utterly. Once the creation of other people, a conflation of popular tastes and vibrant self-esteem, she is now very much her

own woman, self-contained, domineering, unsmiling. Although the three now comprise a household, they are ruthlessly *three,* each an individual possessed of selfhood, each distinct. A new power balance has been achieved, and this time it seems awfully permanent. The permanence is nearly inanimate, locked in the middle of the desert, still brutalized by the insistent yellow sun. There are no pools in sight now, none of the watery opacity and sexual menace that have brought about this final condition. Instead, the most conspicuous element in the landscape, which also is the last vision Altman offers us (so unlike the final transcendent vision of blue sky at the close of *Nashville*), is a heap of worn-out tires, synthetic utilitarian materials finally discarded to bake in the sun in a state of pure inanimate repose, hopelessly earthbound.

Given the deep narrative told in these three recent works, and keeping in mind Altman's previous films, there are at least a few provisional conclusions one can draw about the dynamics of his imagination. He is obviously intent on exploring skyward wish and earthbound power, dramatized alternately in public and private contexts. His style easily accommodates both purity of aspiration and vulgar American reality, both the rarefied world of *3 Women* and the gritty arena of *Buffalo Bill.* He is certainly a self-conscious director, but his sense of his own virtuosity has not yet paralyzed his inspiration. In his middle age he is still full of promise and seems to have a clear vision of his own career, and he is one of the very few American directors capable of surprising intelligent audiences. At this writing, Altman has completed a new feature, *The Wedding,* said to be a spirited treatment of this very public ritual. While *The Wedding* awaits release, Altman is already on location filming his next work, *Quintet,* which promises to be another private film like *3 Women.* He is evidently aware of writing his own history on film, embodying a memory of himself in his work, and of thus filming a future that shall be neatly continuous with his past. The history thus far of his inspiration and achievement is impressive. His career may prove eventually to be the most cogent, and tenacious, of any American director.

Gene M. Bernstein (essay date Summer 1979)

SOURCE: "Robert Altman's *Buffalo Bill and the Indians, or Sitting Bull's History Lesson:* A Self-Portrait in Celluloid," in *Journal of Popular Culture,* Vol. 13, No. 1, Summer, 1979, pp. 17-25.

[*In the following essay, Bernstein analyzes how Altman's* Buffalo Bill and the Indians, or Sitting Bull's History Lesson *examines the film medium itself, including the genre of the western and the making of a superstar.*]

In the last decade there has been a proliferation of films which are reflexive; that is which examine the medium in terms of film making itself or the impact of film on society. Some do it directly, like Francois Truffaut's *Day for Night,* while others do it indirectly, as in Michaelangelo Antonioni's *Blow-Up* and Haskell Wexler's *Medium Cool* (both of which deal with visual media other than film, but do so *on film*). These three directors, as well as several others, display an increasingly apparent and important McLuhanesque sensitivity to and intelligence about the medium with which they work.

So too do a group of directors responsible for films which are reflexive about a particular film genre, The Western. Arthur Penn's *Little Big Man,* for example, is one of the most successful attempts at deflating, sometimes humorously and sometimes grotesquely, the many myths engendered by the very film genre of which it is a type. Others not only expose (and sometimes ridicule) the myths generated by The Western, but actually seek to redress the historical inaccuracies perpetuated by them, as in Ralph Nelson's *Soldier Blue.* As a group these films are concerned with the political consequences of an intrinsic phenomenon of The Western most clearly articulated at the end of John Ford's *The Man Who Shot Liberty Valence:* when a myth becomes a reality through the impact of the media, or as a journalist in the film succinctly expresses it, "when a legend becomes a fact, you print the legend." No single aspect of American history has been more influenced (and distorted) by media than Western history, and no medium has been more influential with regard to popular concepts of Western history than film. These reflexive films are thus significant because they represent a new direction in film making, the self-portrait in celluloid, the picture not only about a given subject matter but also about the very form by which that subject matter is communicated.

The most ambitious self-portrait in celluloid is Robert Altman's **Buffalo Bill and the Indians, or Sitting Bull's History Lesson,** a film which is concurrently reflexive about 1) the film medium, 2) The Western and 3) the creation of a super-star (in this case Buffalo Bill) serving both the medium and history. In this film the subjects are merged in the word "show," which represents both The Wild West *Show* of Buffalo Bill and the movie *show* about Buffalo Bill. What makes this film so difficult to comprehend, yet so brilliant, is that Altman focuses on all three subjects simultaneously where other directors (like those mentioned above) focus on but one or two. Moreover, Altman does so, outrageously at the very time when Americans are so willing to commemorate and glorify those many myths which he seeks to reveal as distortions of history. For lest we forget, 1976 was also the Centennial of the Battle of the Little Big Horn, probably the one episode most symbolic of all that The Western has come to stand for in the popular mind.

Buffalo Bill and the Indians, or Sitting Bull's History Lesson not only examines The Western and Western history, but it develops by a historical dialectic. The "or" in the title, though quaintly reminiscent of the late nineteenth century period which the film depicts, more importantly serves to suggest the opposition between the white man's history and the red man's, as represented by heroes from each culture. The alternative views of Buffalo Bill and Sitting Bull confront us not only with two versions of the same historical phenomena—as in the humorous but troubling exchange between Buffalo Bill on the one hand, and dime novelist Prentiss Ingraham and Indian spokesman Halsey on the other—but also with two interpretations of what actually constitutes history.

In this respect, the film is not unlike John Keats' "Ode on a Grecian Urn"; in both we are teased out of thought by a silent historian, in the former Sitting Bull himself (who never speaks a word throughout the film) and in the latter the urn (the original "silent historian"). Like the speaker of the poem, Buffalo Bill (as well as all white men) seeks to reenact history and in doing so grossly distorts it, turning history into entertainment, both verbal and visual, which makes full use of dramatic license and has but a dubious claim to authenticity. For Sitting Bull, on the other hand, this kind of history is a sham dishonoring the dead, and so he offers instead a silent protest against the theatricality of the Wild West Show. The differences between Buffalo Bill and Sitting Bull result in what might be called an aesthetics of history since the former seeks to commemorate and glorify history at a special time and/or place while the latter reveres and lives it every day, everywhere. These antithetical views give rise only to the tension in the film when, for example, Sitting Bull makes his only appearance in the Wild West Show. Emcee Nate Salsbury introduces him as "the wicked warrior of the western plains, the cold-blooded killer of Custer . . . the untamed scavenger whose chilling and cowardly deeds created nightmares through the West, and made him the most feared, the most murderous, the most colorful redskin alive . . . the battling chief of the Hunkpapa Sioux . . . Sitting Bull." Then, Sitting Bull, attired only in a plain cloth garment and simple beads, rides quietly around the ring to the derisive calls of the audience, calls which rather abruptly change into a thunderous ovation for a man obviously too full of pride and dignity to participate in such a grossly distorted fraud. Like the Grecian urn Sitting Bull's silence speaks a history more convincingly than Buffalo Bill's inflamed words, yet as we shall see, like the urn it too raises many troubling questions.

In a sense Sitting Bull exposes Buffalo Bill as an imposter of what he was, and in a similar sense the film exposes the distortions and untruths perpetrated by other movies about the wild west, as did Altman's **McCabe and Mrs. Miller.** (So too, incidentally, does **M.A.S.H.** parody other war movies, and **Thieves Like Us** other gangster movies.) Yet at the very same time this film is uncovering certain myths and fallacies about the West, it is perpetuating, if not creating others. If Buffalo Bill was too good to be true before the film, Sitting Bull is after it. This may be a brilliant touch of irony by Altman or it may be part of the swing from thesis to antithesis, or it may be a flaw in the film, depending upon your interpretation. In any case, both alternatives are oversimplified: where Buffalo Bill comes across as selfish, vain, pompous and inane, Sitting Bull is equally selfless, altruistic, simple and profound. While neither portrait is convincing, together they offer parameters within which we can struggle with our own sense of history. The film itself attempts to synthesize the two extremes: on the one hand it tries to be as entertaining as Buffalo Bill would have it, and on the other it is as serious and important as Sitting Bull would desire. (So too does Keats' poem synthesize between the hot passion of the speaker and the cool indifference of the urn.)

Were Buffalo Bill and his Wild West Show to limit themselves to entertaining, though, the film would lack the symmetry which provides its very *raison d'etre*. Not content to entertain, producer and emcee Nate Salsbury, star Buffalo Bill and press agent John Burke steadfastly maintain that they are faithfully recounting history, despite their consuming lust for profits and publicity. "We're trying to show things as they really were beyond the Missouri," claims Salsbury near the beginning of the film, "so you can't have anything that isn't authentic, genuine and real. There will be nothing fake about us," he insists.

But the very structure of the film almost defies us to identify the authentic and the real since we are looking at a film about a show: at times characters are playing parts in the Wild West Show, at other times they are playing parts in the movie show. In the end it is impossible to segregate the role from the person. We begin to appreciate more acutely Plato's concern with artistic imitation as a double remove from reality. In the opening sequence, for example, a weary settler and his son trek home only to be attacked and killed by raiding Indians who also kill his wife and carry off his daughter. While the film audience first assumes that this is simply the film itself, they soon realize that this sequence is merely a rehearsal for the show as Salsbury yells "cut," reinforcing the tie between the Wild West Show and the movie show. What we have witnessed is a rehearsal of a reenactment through the film medium.

In addition to this triple remove from reality—the scene in the show being the first, the rehearsal being the second, and the film the third—the last two are also historical events in and of themselves. This point is driven home by the violence attending upon the rehearsal when one of the raiding Indians is accidentally clotheslined off his horse and trampled to death by another. Neither is such a death historical nor is it an act; it is for real. So too is the painful wound suffered by Annie Oakley's husband, dapper Frank Butler, while she is performing increasingly gimmicky trick shots to titillate the audience. Both the Show and the film are recording one history even as they are making another. But as the Show and the film progress, which of course they do concurrently, it becomes increasingly difficult to discern historical fiction and historical reality, which may be precisely the point, as we shall see.

This difficulty does not result from a lack of clarity in the movement of the Show/film, however, which is structured around three major confrontations between the white men and red (much as Keats' poem revolves around three major scenes on the urn). The raid on the homestead is the first such sequence, and represents a fairly "realistic" portrayal of what undoubtedly happened to settlers, though probably not so often as we are wont to think it did. This cannot be said of the second sequence, which takes place near the middle of the show, a reenactment of the Battle of the Little Big Horn. This scene is full of deliberate distortions concocted by none other than Buffalo Bill himself. When Prentiss Ingraham informs him that the battle took place at the Greasy Grass River, not the Little Big Horn, Bill retorts, "I already got the programs printed." And when Prentiss corrects him again by pointing out that the Cavalry ambushed the Sioux, not the other way around as the Wild West Show records it, Buffalo Bill ignores him altogether. Dramatic license even permits Bill to add a cannon to Custer's arsenal, as well as a face-to-face confrontation between the General and Sitting Bull in which the latter kills and scalps the former. All this is rather amusing and serves an important function in the structure of the show, for while Buffalo Bill envies Custer his hair and wears a wig just like it, he will also avenge Custer in the final sequence of the show by fighting Sitting Bull head-to-head, killing and scalping him. But more important is the fact that these details represent deliberate distortions by Buffalo Bill, who at one point claims that "It's about time history took a lesson from us!"

Although the protests of Ingraham against the dramatic liberties are futile, those of Sitting Bull's spokesman, Halsey, are not. He points out that Sitting Bull was not present at the Battle of the Little Big Horn; that instead he was dreaming and making medicine. Thus if the Sioux Chief is to have a part in the reenactment, he will act out his dream rather than participate in the battle. This is but one of the situations in which Sitting Bull defies and humiliates Buffalo Bill, just as his version of history defies and ridicules Bill's. From the very first time they meet, this dialectical opposition is clearly established. As a group of Indians come riding to the village where the Show is housed, all eyes (including those of the film audience) rivet on the biggest, fiercest looking Indian, assuming that he is the Chief. To the stunned surprise of those greeting the party, and especially Buffalo Bill, who has made a gala appearance and has begun a grandiose welcoming speech addressed to the big Indian, we find that he is but the spokesman for Sitting Bull. The Chief, in fact, very small and frail looking, is simply attired in a cloth and some beads.

This scene establishes not only the fatuity of Buffalo Bill and his entourage, all of whom judge things by appearances, but also their defensive posture in dealing with Sitting Bull. When, for instance, they inform the Chief that he is to be housed with the other Indians in the camp, Halsey informs them that Sitting Bull will establish his own camp across the river on a bluff overlooking the Wild West community. This spatial relation becomes, in effect, a metaphor for Sitting Bull's continual dominance over Buffalo Bill. In addition, even as the entourage are laughing at the thought of the old Chief (and the women and children accompanying him) fording the river which has already claimed the lives of six horses and three Blackfoot braves. Sitting Bull's tepees are going up on the other side of it. Amidst the astonishment and incredulity of the men, Buffalo Bill coolly explains, "Boys, on the bluff is *exactly* where I want him. Then I can keep an eye on him, real easy, from this chair, here." (Whatever else he is not, Bill certainly is an accomplished counterpuncher.) But Sitting Bull continues to control Buffalo Bill and retains complete autonomy over his own actions despite the efforts of those who would dictate to him.

On the literal level, then, Sitting Bull's history lesson is composed of two things: setting historical facts such as those about the Battle of the Little Big Horn straight, and setting forth an altogether different interpretation of what constitutes history, namely, a past which lives in the present rather than being reenacted in the present. Annie Oakley is one of the few whites who appreciates these truths, and who understands the precarious position Sitting Bull is in, for if returned to Standing Rock both she and he know that he will be murdered despite his non-violent ways. She quits the show when Buffalo Bill fires the Chief, and protests: "But he wants to show people the truth. You can't allow that just once?" "No," Bill replies, "I got a better sense of history than that." It is this sense of history which makes a travesty of Salsbury's claim that "we're the first people to ever show the red and white without taking sides."

But even more important than the literal lesson is the figurative one taught by Sitting Bull. His silence and simplicity make a sham of everything his counterpart, Buffalo Bill, attempts to do so as to assure his legendary status in history. Where Buffalo Bill wears incredibly garish jackets, Sitting Bull appears in basic cloth; Buffalo Bill rides a strapping mare, Sitting Bull a small pinto; Buffalo Bill carries elaborate guns (which are loaded with buckshot to enhance his marksmanship as one quick, but deft camera shot reveals), Sitting Bull carries only holy beads. In short, Buffalo Bill, constantly primping himself in mirrors and admiring himself in portraits, is so totally caught up in his image that there is no real person beneath the surface, whereas the reality of Buffalo Bill only begins below the surface image in his dreams and visions, all of which come to pass. His sense of history is making the present live up to the future, not, as for Buffalo Bill, the present up to the past. Even when Buffalo Bill has a dream, in which he speaks to Sitting Bull in a Browning-like dramatic monologue, he fails to comprehend what is happening. This contrasts sharply with the dreams of Sitting Bull in which he envisions the President of the U.S.A. visiting the Wild West Show and a massacre of Indian women and children (Wounded Knee?), both of which establish a continuity between present and future.

In the film Buffalo Bill fails to live up to his past and his legendary greatness because they are so hyperbolic. Nowhere during the course of the film do we see him do those things for which he is renowned, except within the Wild West Show, which is more entertainment than history. Much of the film's humor derives from his failure to track down Sitting Bull and his entourage when they abruptly break camp one day and go up into the mountains, his failure to seduce the opera singer Nina Cavalini (who visits the Show with President and Mrs. Cleveland), and perhaps most humorously, his failure to shoot Mrs. Ducharmes' pet canary after returning empty-handed from the search for Sitting Bull.

The canary is another of the overdetermined metaphors in the film, as is the spatial relationship between Sitting Bull's tents and Buffalo Bill's village. Like both opera singing mistresses who own one, the bird symbolizes the alien world in which both it and its owner are caged. But increasingly as the film progresses and in direct proportion to the erosion of Buffalo Bill's legendary status, the birds come to symbolize Bill himself, for he is figuratively trapped in a legend from which he cannot escape. Like the bird he is caged, not by bars but by grand portraits of himself and huge mirrors which hang all about the Mayflower—a name itself rich with historical connotations—constantly entrapping William Cody in the image of Buffalo Bill, superstar. Thus, Cody's inability to shoot Ducharmes' frantic canary despite his close range to it seems to symbolize his growing impotence as man and as legend: he is seen to be as much a failure in the sexual saddle as he has just been in the literal one when tracking Sitting Bull. Understandably, then, he despises the canary that represents both those women with whom he is inadequate and that legendary reputation against which he is equally inadequate.

While it is Annie Oakley who empathizes most closely with Sitting Bull, it is the legend-maker Ned Buntline who seems to best understand what is happening to Buffalo Bill. And after all he should, for Buntline created the legend. "I only brought attention to the man," Ned explains. "*He* supplied the talent. No ordinary man would have had the foresight to take credit for acts of bravery and heroism that he couldn'ta done. And no ordinary man'd realize what tremendous profit could be had by presentin' the truth as if it was just a pack o' lies with witnesses." Comparing him to other directors of the Wild West Show, Ned concludes: "No, Bill Cody can only trust himself and what he picks up with his own senses. And when they fail, he might just see things the way they really are." The humility should not fool us; these are the words of a man who is busy exculpating himself from the monster he has created, much as Victor Frankenstein flees his own creation. And, having established an uneasy truce between his legendary creation and himself, Ned Buntline rides off into the night bound for California; no doubt he is heading for Hollywood!

Buntline's departure for California reinforces the connection between the Wild West Show and the film industry, as does the emphasis on the word *show.* But an even more vital and explicit link between the two is the way in which the cast of characters is introduced at the beginning of the film not by name, but by function—they are not real people but players, actors. Paul Newman is the star, as he is in so many other Hollywood films, and his ineptitude parodies William Cody before he entered "the show business." Similarly, Joel Grey, playing the producer and emcee, parodies his most well-known Hollywood role, the emcee in *Cabaret.* So too does Burt Lancaster, as the legend-maker, parody his roles as the Rainmaker and Elmer Gantry.

But the biggest parody, and the most perplexing, is that of Halsey, played by Will Sampson. Known to audiences as the "Chief" in *One Flew Over the Cuckoo's Nest,* a role in which he did not speak for nearly two-thirds of the film, he is easily mistaken at first for Sitting Bull because of his massive size, a mistake made not only by those in the Wild West show but by the film audience as well. But contrary to his role in *Cuckoo's Nest,* Sampson is neither the chief, nor is he silent; in both instances he parodies his earlier role, and he indicts the viewing audience as well. We are almost as culpable as Buffalo Bill and the others of judging the man by the image. The difference is that the showman creates the image, we simply retain and perpetuate it.

In a sense, then, it is altogether fitting that in the final sequence of the show, Halsey is playing the part of Sitting Bull, since "Halsey looks more like Sitting Bull than Sitting Bull." This sequence represents the third major confrontation between white man and red. Unlike the first, which was a *realistic reenactment* of something which actually took place in which the Indians triumphed, and unlike the second, which was a *deliberate distortion* of something which actually took place in which the white man triumphed as slain heroes, the third sequence is a *complete fabrication* of something which never happened in which the white man is totally triumphant. This completes the structure of the show and reaffirms our

sense of history, but though Buffalo Bill wins the battle—a face-to-face struggle with Sitting Bull in which Bill kills the chief, avenging Custer—Sitting Bull wins the war. Because the sequences have regressed from reenactment to distortion to fabrication, the film audience can no longer abide what is happening, though the Show audience is ecstatic. So too is Buffalo Bill, whose senses have not yet failed him, and who therefore does not yet, see things as they really are. The last action shot in the film is a zoom-in on Buffalo Bill in a triumphant posture, intoxicated by both the roar of the crowd and the booze at which he was nipping before the scene began. His is a total triumph of shorts: the show, the fiction, has first altered and now successfully fabricated history altogether.

As the Show and the film end, the cast of characters is superimposed on a still photograph of the Wild West Show Company. A silent shot, it too is eloquent without words. In this photo Sitting Bull and Halsey are standing next to Annie Oakley. Buffalo Bill had not wanted it this way when the group was posing for the photo, but again Sitting Bull prevailed. Despite Bill's casual rationalization that he will change the picture to suit himself, we now see that he has failed once again, just as in the end, the historical picture he has arranged via the Show has failed. One is tempted to conclude, then, that Buffalo Bill's failure is Sitting Bull's success since the film is structured along a dialectical confrontation. But this will not do.

In the end the film is deliberately ambiguous. A surrogate Sitting Bull has replaced the real one in the arena and is being scalped as news of the real Sitting Bull's assassination arrives over the telegraph. Can we trust Halsey, who throughout has been spokesman for the chief, but has now sold out to the blandishments of "the show business" rather than remaining faithful to the proud vision of his leader? We must not only question Halsey, who first speaks for Sitting Bull and then acts for him in the Show but the film itself as well. As oversimplified as it is in presenting the extremes of Buffalo Bill and Sitting Bull, it does succeed in destroying one myth about the past, even if at the cost of possibly creating another. What are we to make of histories that seek not only to inform, but to entertain as well, histories such as the Wild West Show and this movies show? Where are we to draw the line with dramatic license?

Questions haunt about this film as they do Keats's Grecian urn, and in the end resolution of them escapes us. The film audience, unlike the Show audience, now sides with Sitting Bull, but Buffalo Bill's dream of legendary immortality has triumphed over reality through his creation, the Wild West Show, while Sitting Bull's life has ended ignominiously by savage assassination. The division between show and film audience raises yet another question, this time about the influence of the audience on the historian's work: what kind of audience can he assume he will reach? how will they re-act? can he tell them things they may not want to hear, as I believe is the case with this film? Finally, what possibility is there that a self-portrait born out of reflexive examina-tion—whether it be William Cody's picture of himself as Buffalo Bill, Robert Altman's depiction (and parody) of the Western, or the historians look at his own history—can "set the record straight?" Perhaps the greatest achievement of ***Buffalo Bill and the Indians, or Sitting Bull's History Les-son*** is that it acknowledges what other recorders of history can loathe to admit, that the record can never be set straight, it can only be added to by new portraits of ourselves.

Robert Altman with Frank Beaver (interview date Winter 1983)

SOURCE: "An Interview with Robert Altman," in *Michigan Quarterly Review,* Vol. XXII, No. 1, Winter, 1983, pp. 44-55.

[*In the following interview, Altman discusses the course of his career and his critical reputation.*]

In the Fall of 1982, film director Robert Altman visited the University of Michigan as Howard R. Marsh Professor of Journalism in the Department of Communication. He gave seminars on filmmaking, participated in workshops, and di-rected a stage production of Igor Stravinsky's opera The Rake's Progress *for the School of Music. Frank Beaver, Pro-fessor of Communication at the University of Michigan, in-terviewed Altman for* MQR.

[*Beaver:*] *What attracted you to a career as a motion pic-ture director?*

[Altman:] I was a movie fan when I was a kid. I got pun-ished many times for going into a film and not coming out, seeing it four times consecutively. I remember I had the mumps when *King Kong* first played at my neighborhood theater, in the early 30s. My mother was away and I told the housekeeper not to come into my room, she'd get the mumps for sure. And I snuck down to the theater with the mumps and probably contaminated the entire audience.

When I went into the Army during the second World War, I was trained in Southern California and became more a movie fan than anything else. I had a cousin who was a secretary to Myron Selznick; she said "You should be a screenwriter, your letters are so cute." So I decided I wanted to be in the movie business.

And for a brief time in the 40s and 50s you were a screen-writer.

I started writing short stories when I was overseas and when I came back I stayed in Los Angeles and wrote with another fellow. I sold a treatment called *Christmas Eve* for $750. That was made into a film with George Brent, Ann Harding and Randolph Scott. Then I wrote a treatment of a film called *Bodyguard,* with the same guy, and we sold that for $5000, but they wouldn't let me do the screenplay, even for free, and they wouldn't let me on the lot while they shot it. These were notorious B-films.

So you left Hollywood and for a time in the 50s and 60s directed documentaries in Kansas City, then network tele-vision programs. Did these experiences influence your more recent work as a feature film director?

I think every experience that you have forms you. It gets into your computer and it's there.

I always objected to the way things were done as I saw them being done. I was very rebellious and had no patience in those days. I guess I was arrogant.

Was the immediacy, the spontaneity we see in your films of the 70s due to the experiences of working in television?

Yes, I think it was the experiences with television, some of the early half-hour shows I did like *Whirly Birds* and *U. S. Marshal.* You had two and a half days, no overtime, and at the end of that time—by noon on Wednesday the picture was finished. You couldn't shoot anymore. So we had to get everything in within that time element. There wasn't any preparation time. We had a blueprint and then everything happened spontaneously. I'd see something and say "Quick, let's get it in that way."

How did you get from television to the theatrical motion pic-ture?

I did television for many years and I turned down a lot of motion pictures, because by the time scripts came to me they had been through all the qualified feature directors. They were usually bad scripts and I knew there was just no rea-son for me to do them. I got very comfortable with my fail-ure at achieving the status of feature director. When I was in television, I was considered one of the top directors and I was offered the best assignments. I was mostly doing pilot films for new series and creating series.

The first feature I accepted was called ***Countdown.*** Warner Brothers was making a group of low-budget films in the mil-lion dollar range. They offered me about four of them, but I didn't take them. I took ***Countdown*** because it was from a book by Hank Searls called *The Pilgrim Project,* which I had tried to develop into a screenplay. . . . When I finished shoot-ing *The Pilgrim Project* I was barred from the lot, because

Jack Warner saw the footage and said, "That fool has people talking at the same time."

M*A*S*H, *made in 1969, was the film which suddenly catapulted you to international prominence. How did you come to direct that film?*

I got in with a man named Don Factor and we developed a script called *That Cold Day in the Park,* from a short story. We arranged the financing through Commonwealth United, a small distributor, and went to Vancouver to make the film with Sandy Dennis. When I came back, *M*A*S*H* was offered to me after fifteen or sixteen other directors had all turned it down. The producer, Ingo Preminger, saw *Cold Day* in its rough-cut stage and liked it very much.

I took *M*A*S*H,* because I'd been working on another project for about five years called *The Chicken and the Hawk,* a comedy about World War II fliers—about the ridiculousness of death and war, and containing a large supporting cast. When I read *M*A*S*H,* I realized I could do everything with it I intended to do with *The Chicken and the Hawk.* So I had five years of background preparing for *M*A*S*H.*

M*A*S*H *showed you to be a superb satirist, a black humorist. Would you say that satire and black comedy are interests which have found their way into most of your feature films?*

I think my outlook finds its way into all the work I do. I don't think of myself as a satirist or black humorist. You don't really use those words while you're working. But in retrospect, through my film and TV work, that does come out.

Did you intend **M*A*S*H** *to be a statement with allusions to Vietnam?*

Totally! In fact, I didn't put one reference to Korea in it, and when I finished they said you *have to* put in the titles that it was Korea. That's when we put in the statement of Eisenhower's.

How do you feel about the long-running television series, M*A*S*H?

I hate it! I deplore its existence. I think it's the most insidious propaganda. They've taken the sting out of the original concept. We made people pay for their laughs with the position that nothing could be in worse taste than people with bullets in their bodies and being blown-up. The TV show may be well acted and written and I'm sure the people are all fine craftsmen, but it oversimplifies the emotional and political issues and purports that there's an Asian war going on now and that the Asians are the enemies.

You are well known as a director who likes to approach the filmmaking process in an improvisational manner. It's even been said that once you secure the backing for a motion picture you throw the script—or partial script—away. Is this true?

I don't throw away the script. I feel the script is the sales test; it's the basic artist's rendering in an architect's building. I say, this is the script, the idea, the kind of picture I want to make, and then I try to honor what I've said and if it means deviating from those original words in order to get that effect, I'll do it.

How much of **M*A*S*H** *was created spontaneously?*

I'd say 75 percent.

Can you give an example where actors made contributions to **M*A*S*H?**

In every situation where the characters relate stories that are not important to the plot of the film. For example, when the men talk about committing suicide and come up with the idea of the "black pill." This dialogue was invented by the actors themselves. And this happened throughout *M*A*S*H.*

Were the actors allowed to participate in building their characters?

Oh, sure. Most of the actors, Elliot Gould in particular. I purposely went to San Francisco and got improvisational theater people who could work on their feet: Carl Gottlieb and Corey Fischer and Danny Goldman. People like that who were nearly stand-up comedians.

There have also been many rumors about the spontaneous creation of **Nashville**—*the role played by screenwriter Joan Tewkesbury and the large cast of actors in developing the script. How did* **Nashville** *get made?*

Nashville was a bribe. I wanted to make **Thieves Like Us** and United Artists didn't. They wanted a movie about Nashville, because they had a country music company. They had a script with Tom Jones and they said if I did it, they would finance **Thieves Like Us.** I said I wouldn't do their script, but I would do a film about country western music, so we made the deal and we went down to Mississippi to do **Thieves,** for which Joan Tewkesbury did the screenplay.

I threw the Tom Jones script out and told her to go to Nashville and keep a diary. Neither of us had ever been to Nashville. She went for eleven days. The first thing that happened to her was a traffic jam after leaving the airport; she was stuck for three hours. This appears in the film at about the same time we introduce our characters. It provides an excellent way to introduce people who are in the same proximity, but don't know one another.

Years before I'd had a film idea for a similar story of people whose lives intermingled, but who never knew each other and if they had been back-to-back and turned and met, it could have changed their lives.

I used these elements in **Nashville.** So again, **Nashville** didn't just happen overnight; it came after years and years of thinking out certain kinds of ideas.

It's a structure along the lines of John Schlesinger's adaptation of Day of the Locust, *which to me didn't work as well as your film.*

I think the book *Day of the Locust* is marvelous, but there too you are dealing with specific characters who mingle and jostle in an exotic locale. To pull that off in a film you have to disguise your characters in crowds and hide them, so that they seem to just be passing through, rather than attracting your attention. We tried that with **Nashville,** but United Artists didn't like the final script, so we sold it to ABC which produced it.

Isn't it true that you allow your actors to draw from their personal lives—from events important to them during the making of a film—in order to shape their fictional screen characters?

I try to insist on and encourage that because there are a great deal of truths which come out, that they don't even know about. If I'm trying to show behavior patterns in a certain scene and tell Shelley Duvall, "Here, I've written this marvelous monologue about how you felt the first time you saw the Coliseum in Rome," and she's never seen the Coliseum, it's ridiculous. If these things have nothing to do with the behavior pattern I'm trying to show, I'll try to find out what impressed her and if it turns out it was the first time she flew from Dallas to Houston, I use that.

So, you strive for a kind of credibility of character, even though your films happen in a very spontaneous way?

In order for them to appear spontaneous, you must have credibility and the best way to get this to let the actors use what is natural to them, so they can get into those roles better and express that behavior.

It seems to me that this is one of the strong elements in your films. It's mesmerizing for audiences to see Shelley Duvall in **Three Women** *going through routines that seem so real to her and so real to us.*

That's the idea of it. I try to encourage the actors to become

equal as artists with everyone in the audience, because I believe they are.

Nashville *concludes with the assassination of a celebrity—a country western singer. This was somewhat ominous, wasn't it? And, why that ending to a film about the entertainment world?*

There has been a lot of criticism of that scene. Most people said, "Why did you have him kill the singer rather than the politician?" My answer was, "You've just answered your question." You would accept a political assassination, that is, you condone it as a part of our culture.

I believe that people commit those types of assassinations because by killing someone at that level, they rise to that level themselves. By assassinating a politician they feel there will be a lot of people who will like them for it, because they hear so much against the politician.

The country western singer, or Barbra Streisand or, as it turns out, John Lennon, is the same thing. It did happen, I'm sorry to say.

The coming together of the politician as a celebrity and other types of celebrities—until the two meld into one—was another phenomenon we were trying to deal with in **Nashville.**

How is **Nashville** *representative of your cinematic interests? It seems to me that one characteristic which appears in one Altman film after another is the setting of a familiar American film genre on its ear: the so-called success story in* **Nashville;** *the western and gangster myths in* **McCabe and Mrs. Miller** *and* **Thieves Like Us;** *the romantic film in* **A Wedding** *and* **A Perfect Couple.** *Do you see yourself as a genre revisionist, as many critics have claimed?*

I don't think it would have occurred to me, if I hadn't read it so much. I have never set out and thought, "What haven't I attacked?" It's not calculated. When I see what's happening in life I'm always amazed that everybody's very beautiful in a film. The best corrective to a worn-out formula is a clear vision of how people really live. I think that everybody has the same feelings. In *A Perfect Couple,* Marta Heflin was anorexic at the time and you'd say, "My God, who'd want to get involved with her?" Well, the character that Paul Dooley played wanted to get involved with her. Her sense of love and feeling is certainly as real as Faye Dunaway's or Loni Anderson's or Burt Reynolds'.

One critic has called you a pessimistic modernist. Is this a fair label?

I don't know what a modernist is. I guess I'm an optimistic pessimist or a pessimistic optimist. I think that everybody is pretty much that way. People who advertise what they are, aren't that at all.

People ask why in *A Wedding* I put in the awful car accident, because they hated it. I hated it too. It makes me sick that something like that happens, but it does. The audience reacted in the same way the families in the film did; they were crushed by it, until they found that the bride and groom weren't in the accident. The audience was uplifted and they left the theater and said, "Wait a minute! There were two people dead and we were laughing at the end of the picture." That's the point of the film; life doesn't always work out the way you'd like.

*It's been widely publicized that you dreamed one of your most interesting films—**Three Women**. Is that true?*

I dreamed that I was making the film, but I didn't dream the plot of the film. I dreamed who was in it. I'd been looking for a film for Sissy Spacek ever since she appeared in a film by Alan Rudolph called *Welcome to L.A.,* which I produced. I love Sissy's work and I thought it would be terrific to get her and Shelley Duvall together.

So I dreamed this and the title occurred to me in the dream. I had a hard time trying to find out who the third woman was.

How is it that a film based on a dream can succeed in a country where conservation and escapism—the well-made melodrama—seem to dominate filmmaker and audience interests?

I don't think it did succeed in engaging a wide audience, for all the reasons you mentioned. People want to see the same things over and over again. They desire and get the same experiences and forget the films the minute they've left the theater. It's like doing crossword puzzles.

That's why I keep coming to universities like this and going to film festivals and places where people are interested in film, because I want to expand my audience or at least make people curious enough to want to see some of these films. They find out that it's really exciting.

Whom do you see as your primary audience and what role do you see yourself playing among American filmmakers?

I can tell you who my audience is now: a cult, and a cult isn't even enough for a minority. It's people who have seen films of mine or like mine. They don't necessarily enjoy all of them, but they are stimulated.

I don't think of one particular audience when I make a film. I'll make one film and the gay community says, "Altman's the greatest." Then the next film they say, "You double-crossed us." I don't try to reach any one audience. I feel the audience is as collective as my subject matter. I wish the whole world were my audience.

All of your work seems to generate either great praise or damnation, especially among film critics. How do you feel about the critics?

I think if there are twelve critics, they'd fit on a scale of 1 to 12. I think they're necessary and desirable. Critics give us fill space in newspapers and on television and draw attention to our work. They help communicate that a film is there and that it is playing a particular night.

I can't argue with critics about my films anymore than I can with a member of the audience. They perceive what they perceive. I think they rise and fall with the same tidal properties as the making of a film itself does.

Vincent Canby in the New York Times *recently listed you among the greatest living film directors, placing you beside Akira Kurosawa, François Truffaut, and Ingmar Bergman. When you read a critical comment like that, what do you think?*

I can't help but be pleased by it. No way can it not affect my ego. Stanley Kauffman once said I should be destroyed. It was funny, but I think he meant it. So, I've had equally bad things said.

I find I'm treated the same by people with like or dislike, respect or disrespect for me. I would rather have a little piece like Canby's in the paper than seventeen Academy Awards. It's nice to know you're appreciated.

What is your opinion of contemporary Hollywood?

I don't think it exists. What people perceive as Hollywood. I don't like it at all. I think it's a business; an accounting factory. It's a place that makes comic books.

Do you foresee any future for innovative filmmakers like yourself?

I see a great deal of hope for them, primarily because there are more outlets and avenues opening up all the time. Network television and the major studios in Hollywood have made this kind of art a "closed shop" for many years, and now, because of pay television, cable, art houses and an increasing interest in films in universities, that monopoly is suddenly cracking. Also, the majors and the networks have brought the level of their work so low that the average audience doesn't even follow the films anymore. They're going to lose the audience altogether.

It's been a great seedtime and I think the spirits are coming up out of the ground. It's a great time for artists.

What for you would be the ultimate motion picture experience?

This is theoretical, but I think you must use the intensity of an image and put it before a person, so you engage their attention emotionally rather than intellectually. Not that the latter shouldn't be done also; but divorce the motion picture more—get it away from theater and literature, so you can start dealing with it as an arena of feelings and emotions. . . . The viewer might not even be able to articulate why he felt a certain way about a cinematic experience.

I always wonder how a tiger feels when it looks up through a rain forest and there's a spectacular sunset. I wonder if he calls the other tigers and says, "Hey, look at this." I don't think that happens, but it does with people. For eons, people have been saying, "Wow, look at that sunset." That means they feel something they can't articulate. That's what a film should do.

Recently you've branched out into theater directing and now opera. What have these experiences meant to you?

They've been very challenging, but I think the work is fundamentally the same. You're taking content and through the medium of actors and images and sounds, transmitting it to an audience.

I'm glad I did it and I wish I'd done it earlier. I'm going to continue to bounce back and forth as much as I can. I think the next work I do on film will be greatly influenced by what I've done on stage.

My latest film, **Come Back to the Five and Dime, Jimmy Dean, Jimmy Dean,** was translated from my stage production, so it has a different look than my other films.

How so?

I've never done a film in such a linear, closed-in manner. And this was because I was adapting a stage play. I became aware during the stage production that **Jimmy Dean** is about the inner psychology of the women characters. So I decided to keep the film action in one location—and not open it up to exterior locations. We kept it entirely in the dimestore, as on the stage, and concentrated on the actors' faces—using the camera and closeups to give the women the poignancy that had to come through the dialogue in the theater.

You seem to be at a new juncture in your career—to be moving in new directions, creatively and geographically. At this point in your life and career how do you personally assess the total body of your work?

I've been very happy and I don't consider I've ever had a failure. All the films are what we set out to do. I feel very emotional and warm about the people I've worked with and I think I probably stole a lot more of the spotlight and thunder than I deserved and they less. But, these people realize that too and they seem content. None of us is looking for great recognition. If I had a choice that when a film was released they would put someone else's name on it, I'd jump at the chance to hide my authorship. I don't believe I would have done that twenty years ago, but now I believe the work is the most important thing.

More important than that, is doing the work. When we finish the opera, I'm off to two other things and that's where my energy and ideas will go.

So work is what you live your life for?

Yes, it's the most pleasure that I have. It's the feeling of being worn-out at the end of the day and knowing that you've accomplished what you set out to do. It's back to the sandcastle syndrome. Buying a sandcastle for your kid doesn't mean anything; they have to build it themselves and it washes away. I think that's what's going to happen to all of this.

Robert Merrill (essay date Summer 1990)

SOURCE: "Altman's *McCabe and Mrs. Miller* as a Classic Western," in *New Orleans Review,* Vol. 17, No. 2, Summer, 1990, pp. 79-86.

[*In the following essay, Merrill analyzes Altman's* McCabe and Mrs. Miller *as a classic western, instead of its typical depiction as an anti-western.*]

My title must seem an oddity, for Robert Altman's **McCabe and Mrs. Miller** is almost always taken to be an "anti-western," that is, a film largely devoted to severe satire, even parody, of the classical westerns. Viewed in this fashion, **McCabe and Mrs. Miller** will almost inevitably seem a minor, somewhat quirky example of what other filmmakers were doing in the late 1960s and early 1970s, when the conventions of the John Wayne-type western were sabotaged in such films as George Roy Hill's *Butch Cassidy and the Sundance Kid,* Frank Perry's *Doc,* Philip Kaufman's *The Great Northfield Minnesota Raid,* and Arthur Penn's *Little Big Man* and *The Missouri Breaks.* Viewed instead as that rarest of western subgenres, a genuine love story, **McCabe and Mrs. Miller** comes into proper focus as a film that rejects many classical conventions while refurbishing others. Indeed, I want to argue that Altman reinterprets the social story commonly embodied in the classical western while still managing to tell a moving tragicomic tale of star-crossed (if extremely fallible) lovers.

Judgments about the major westerns obviously vary. The most perceptive recent critic of the form, Philip French, does not include **McCabe and Mrs. Miller** among the *twenty* post-World War II westerns he likes best. My own view is that **McCabe and Mrs. Miller** is one of the best westerns ever made, surpassed only by Sam Peckinpah's *The Wild Bunch,* John Ford's *The Searchers,* and Howard Hawks' *Red River.* To justify such a lofty evaluation, I obviously need to explore Altman's film in some detail. Somewhat ironically, perhaps, my strategy will be to take up the issues addressed by Gary Engle in the most emphatic case for **McCabe and Mrs. Miller** as an anti-western. Engle argues that Altman's film tells two stories: the founding and growth of a frontier town, and McCabe's personal struggle for survival. I do not think these "stories" are discrete plot lines, nor do I believe that McCabe's story can be separated from Mrs. Miller's; but I do agree that Altman's treatment of the frontier community and his handling of McCabe (and Mrs. Miller) should be the major topics in any serious analysis of the film. My aim will be to point out what is overlooked or misrepresented when **McCabe and Mrs. Miller** is read as a film that simply inverts the clichés of the classical western. Having done that, I want to comment briefly on a more general matter: the formal possibilities of the western.

John Cawelti has shown that the classic western is concerned with "social transition—the passing from the old West into modern society." Set in the remote Washington mining town of Presbyterian Church in 1902, **McCabe and Mrs. Miller** tells this story in richer detail than even such famous westerns as Ford's *My Darling Clementine* and George Stevens' *Shane.* Unfortunately, those who see **McCabe and Mrs. Miller** as an anti-western have taken Altman's treatment of his frontier community to be altogether hostile. For example, Engle sees Altman as using Presbyterian Church to dramatize a negative, even truculent view of social progress. Emphasizing the town's refusal to intervene in the killing of first the cowboy and then McCabe, its "sheepish" submission to Jake Butler and the other hired killers who serve the Harrison-Shaugnessy mining company, Engle concludes that Altman portrays his society as "hypocritical, often childish, morally vacuous, insensitive, able to be manipulated and exploited with relative ease by both McCabe and the mining company." There is much in what Engle says, but his reading is finally reductive and illustrates the distortions that result when Altman's film is seen as essentially satiric. Altman's townspeople are in fact a fascinating mixture of the depressing features noted by Engle and qualities much more endearing.

At first it might seem that Engle's reading of Presbyterian Church is the right one, for the town does betray its primitive origins throughout the film. In the opening scenes, as McCabe arrives, the men of Presbyterian Church are presented one by one in isolated shots that stress their extreme slovenliness. Like the town itself, which is no more than a tent camp at this point, the men seem to be vagabonds for whom the concept of community is meaningless. Altman quickly introduces a representative selection of these men, their nominal leaders, the slimy Sheehan and the lachrymose Smalley, and such "average" miners as Bart Coyle, who obtains a wife through a mail-order service, and Jeremy Berg, who constantly echoes McCabe as though the gambler were some kind of absolute authority on life. Indeed, all of the men seem dazzled by McCabe's adolescent humor and the fact that he wears a gun; they treat him as a hero, someone with a "big rep," because he killed Bill Roundtree, a man they have never heard of but somehow understand to be legendary. Later in the film the men band together for economic purposes, but they never lose their initial credulity. In a key scene Jake Butler lectures them about the use of Chinamen in recent mining experiments, in which the Chinese are effectively sacrificed at the cost of $50 a head! The large group surrounding Butler listens respectfully, for the Chinese population in Presbyterian Church means no more to them than it does to Butler or the mining company.

As Engle says, the men follow Butler as sheepishly as they once followed McCabe; they have no moral scruples that might lead them to question either "leader." They are far more interested in McCabe's whorehouse than in Mr. Elliott's church. Perhaps it is to the point that almost everyone calls Elliott "Mister" instead of "Reverend"; that Elliott is not present when the town buries Bart Coyle; that the church is finally revealed as little more than a shabby storage room where no religious services have been held. Even more to the point are the overt acts of violence that belie Robert Meyers' characterization of the townspeople as "innocent"—the stabbing that McCabe must put a stop to soon after he brings his first whores to Presbyterian Church, and the fight in which Bart Coyle is accidentally killed. Presbyterian Church is not the lawless frontier town of so many standard westerns, for no one even carries a gun except McCabe; but it *is* raunchy and amoral, the sort of place that has no lawman and whose leading citizen is a pimp.

The only communal ties that seem to matter in Presbyterian Church are economic, the ties that bind the men to the zinc mines, McCabe to Mrs. Miller, and the town to Harrison-Shaugnessy once McCabe is out of the way. Therefore it might seem ironically fitting that the town's physical and moral center is a whorehouse, first McCabe's flimsy tents and then Mrs. Miller's "proper sportin' house." But Altman presents the whorehouse without such irony. In fact, the house comes to seem "a haven and refuge, an oasis of warmth and cleanliness from the inclement world that rages outside." It is first presented as such when Mrs. Miller's "girls" arrive from Seattle and spend the day playfully cleaning up in the newly-built baths. Soon we see the whores breaking in a huge new music box as they dance in the most genteel fashion with their customers. The dance is followed by a surprise birthday party for one of the whores, Birdie, for whom they have baked a special birthday cake. We see the same civilized camaraderie at Bart Coyle's funeral, where almost half of those present are the whores who sing "Asleep in Jesus" with surprising gusto. When the youthful cowboy comes to visit and stays for several days, the whores take him in as though he were family; when he finally leaves, four of them wave goodbye. And as the church burns at the end of the film, virtually everyone from the whorehouse pitches in to help put out the fire.

Altman's treatment of the whorehouse has encouraged a number of critics to emphasize the division between the rowdy townspeople and the "convivial," "helpful" prostitutes, but this is rather too simple a contrast. Often childish and insensitive, the men also display genuine emotional depths at a number of points. After all, the men also dance to the new music box and participate in Birdie's birthday party, and a fiddler plays at Sheehan's bar well before the whores arrive. Indeed, one of the film's most haunting moments depicts one of the men dancing on the ice to the fiddler's music while the other men encourage him. And of course it is the men as well as the whores who save the church at the end. Whatever we may think of this act, it is truly a common effort.

Altman is sometimes cited for sentimentality in handling the whores and their clientele, but I think he means to honor the human desire for *connection* even in its most primitive manifestations. At the same time, he hardly suggests that the world itself—natural or social—honors such desires. The film's many touching moments are invariably surrounded by scenes that undercut any facile optimism concerning frontier life. When McCabe arrives with his first whores, the men begin to preen in an adolescent but affecting manner; within a few moments, however, they are scuffling with the prostitutes as if engaged in a barroom brawl. Birdie's birthday party is intercut with several events of a very different order: the fight that leads to Bart Coyle's death; McCabe's negotiations with Sears and Hollander, Harrison-Shaugnessy's representatives; McCabe's drunken preparations at the baths; Mrs. Miller's withdrawal to the comforts of her opium pipe. At the end of this sequence Sears and Hollander renew negotiations with McCabe at the whorehouse, and McCabe sleeps with Mrs. Miller after being reminded to pay for her services. By this point Birdie's birthday party seems an extraordinary but quite isolated gesture. The whores' sentimental fervor at Bart Coyle's funeral is engagingly human, but it must also be understood as confirming Mrs. Miller's cyni-

cal advice to McCabe that the girls will turn to religion if allowed to sit around on their "bums." Moreover, it is at the funeral that Mrs. Miller and Ida Coyle make eye contact that eventually leads to Ida's recruitment for the house. Later, the idyllic moment in which the man dances on the ice is broken by the arrival of Butler and his associates carrying rifles; within five minutes of leaving the gaily-waving whores, the cowboy is senselessly murdered by one of Butler's men; and as the townspeople and the whores band together to save a church they never attend, McCabe and his three pursuers track each other through the streets of Presbyterian Church, unattended and unaided.

These juxtaposed scenes dramatize "the paradox of a community founded upon illusions and exploitation." The more positive moments offer an ideal of community that "haunts" the film, as one critic puts it, but this ideal is apparently undermined at every turn. Such is Alan Karp's view when he refers to the film's final sequence: "by intercutting McCabe's struggle with the town's efforts to put out a fire in the church, Altman shrewdly debunks the myth of the frontier society's ability to band together in the face of crisis." For Karp, Engle, and others, this "myth" is exploded throughout a film that cynically depicts the evolution of Presbyterian Church from a tent camp to the sort of town Harrison-Shaugnessy would want to take over. Indeed, Altman's distrust of "social progress" is unmistakable, especially in his relentlessly hostile presentation of Harrison-Shaugnessy. It might even seem that Altman presents the townspeople as somewhat sympathetic—as "lovable clods"—so that we can pity them when they confront their corporate future.

My own view is that Altman's social commentary is far more complex. It is no accident that the townspeople are shown to be almost equally sensitive and obtuse, sympathetic and powerless. In fact, the film is haunted by both the ideal of community *and* the premonition that such ideals are altogether beyond human nature. In this respect **McCabe and Mrs. Miller** is more complex than many major westerns. In *My Darling Clementine*, for example, Ford depicts a desire for community that is obviously exemplary. Symbolized by the community's efforts to build a church, this desire is so pervasive it even transforms the violent Wyatt Earp. The famous Sunday Morning sequence, highlighted by the dance in which Wyatt and Clementine participate, is an unqualified paean to Ford's notion of what true community might be like. At the other extreme we have Fred Zinnemann's bleak perspective on the communal ideal in *High Noon*, a picture in which the townspeople are truly portrayed as cowardly and hypocritical, capable of assisting the hero but unwilling to do so. I would suggest that the world of Altman's film is neither as nostalgic as Ford's nor as dark as Zinnemann's. Altman does not so much debunk the myth of the frontier society as present a world in which Ford's ideals and Zinnemann's ironies are deeply intertwined.

This means that Altman portrays the growth of Presbyterian Church as a thoroughly ambiguous process. The physical signs of this growth are everywhere: the various buildings that are built in the course of the action; the steam engine that comes from Bearpaw; the arrival of Bart Coyle's mail-order bride; the socialization that centers on Mrs. Miller's whorehouse; the invasion by Harrison-Shaugnessy. Notice that this brief list is open to quite differing interpretations. The steam engine may symbolize the undesirable intrusion of "modern" life into a frontier community, but it is also quite useful in saving the church from fire; Bart and Ida's mail-order marriage may seem a parody of courtship, but the marriage appears to be successful; life at a whorehouse is hardly ideal, but life at Mrs. Miller's seems as close to real civilization as the picture ever gets. Even saving the church is a more positive act than Karp suggests, for the men and women of Presbyterian Church are for once shown working together for a common goal. That they cannot achieve greater good simply measures their limitations and the power of such companies as Harrison-Shaugnessy. Indeed, the mining company is presented as the one truly evil presence in Presbyterian Church, the one reality no one can do anything about—thus the scenes involving the cowboy and McCabe, respectively, in which the townspeople do nothing to challenge the company's representatives. The presence of this irreducible evil in modern social life perhaps tips Altman's balance toward the tragic in his tragicomedy, but his film walks the narrowest of lines most of the time. Those of us who like the film no doubt take this line to be something like life itself.

Altman's "line" falls very much within the formal boundaries of the classical western. Altman seems to acknowledge this when he speaks of wanting to take a very standard western story and do it "real." To do the classical western real is to do a less stylized version in which some conventions are qualified or even undermined; most obviously, the part of McCabe is not written for John Wayne, James Stewart, or Gary Cooper, and the social evolution of Presbyterian Church hardly celebrates the western movement. But I have already argued that the story of social transition told in *McCabe and Mrs. Miller* falls between such classical versions as Ford's and Zinnemann's, and I hope to show that Altman takes his hero—and heroine—as seriously as most famous western directors take their protagonists. Altman's purpose is not to mock the western but to offer a "critical" perspective on the optimistic myths embodied in other westerns. To be critical is not to attack a tradition from without but to redefine it from within. It is to present a realistic version of the western community, not a parody of one. Indeed, Altman's achievement in fashioning such a community is almost always overlooked by those who see his film as an anti-western.

I would add that Altman's success depends very much on his repeated use of overlapping dialogue and his reliance on actors who constitute his unofficial repertory company. The dialogue is hard to follow, but it does work to establish a real community, one composed of people rather than actors, as Michael Dempsey first remarked. And the supporting cast is uniformly excellent: René Auberjonois as Sheehan; Bert Remsen as Bart Coyle; Shelley Duvall as Ida Coyle; John Schuck as Smalley; Corey Fischer as Mr. Elliott; Michael Murphy as Sears; Hugh Millais as Jake Butler; Keith Carradine as the cowboy. The sense of reality created by these actors is so great, I must wonder what people can possibly mean when they argue that Altman's film is satire or parody. To be fair, such remarks are usually directed at the principal characters, McCabe and Mrs. Miller, who are often taken to be comic variations on the typical western hero and heroine. Given my claim that *McCabe and Mrs. Miller* is essentially a love story, it is no doubt time that we turned to these primary figures.

"The heroes of *Butch Cassidy and the Sundance Kid* and *McCabe and Mrs. Miller* . . . behave more like characters transported from the pages of a novel by Saul Bellow or Bernard Malamud into the legendary West than they do like the traditional western hero. They win our interest and sympathy not by courage and heroic deeds but by bemused incompetence, genial cowardice, and the ability to face the worst with buoyancy and wit. They are six-gun schlemiels and existentialists in cowboy boots." I quote Cawelti at such length because he expresses so cogently the common view concerning McCabe and Mrs. Miller. But however accurate this passage may be concerning Butch Cassidy and the Sundance Kid, I think it seriously misrepresents Altman's lovers, who are not cowards, who do not face the worst with buoyancy and wit, and who should not be called existentialists even in an age in which almost *everyone* is an existentialist.

It must be admitted that McCabe's bemused incompetence is a major subject in the film. At first it seems that he exercises a kind of comic control over life, as his engaging if boyish humor distracts the men sufficiently for him to raise the stakes in their poker game from 5¢ to 25¢, a move that makes possible his trip to Bearpaw to buy prostitutes. But McCabe's control over life is as fragile as his humor, as we begin to suspect while watching his comical efforts to deal first with his whores and then the more formidable Mrs. Miller. Mrs. Miller quickly diagnoses McCabe as "another frontier wit," someone who wants to be taken for a "fancy dude" but who tries to run a whorehouse with no real knowledge of what is involved. She sees that McCabe is in fact rather "dumb," as Altman once remarked of his own hero. This stupidity is relatively harmless so long as McCabe sticks to his quarter-limit poker games and the easily dominated world of Presbyterian Church; but it is extremely dangerous when McCabe and the town move into bigger financial worlds, signalled by the $5 bets that now occur in no-limit poker games and by the arrival of Harrison-Shaugnessy. We may laugh at McCabe's favorite one-liner, "If a frog had wings he wouldn't bump his ass so much," but the film's major irony is that McCabe himself is such a frog.

Financially speaking, McCabe is the victim of preposterous illusions. He tells Sheehan that he has come to Presbyterian Church to avoid "partners," but it is absurd to suppose that he can build up a profitable enterprise without entangling himself with others, both friends and foes. His struggles to make do with the Bearpaw whores suggest what would have happened if Mrs. Miller had not come to run the business. (The same point is made more comically when McCabe struggles to balance his books without being able to add eight and fourteen.) Later, McCabe's negotiations with Sears and Hollander more or less seal his fate, and it is to the point that here he tries to do without Mrs. Miller's assistance. Even after the negotiations break down and Butler arrives, McCabe persists in insisting that he is in control. He feels sorry for Butler and his men, he tells Mrs. Miller, because they have been sent to deal with a "mule" like himself. This folly is matched only by McCabe's ridiculous repetition of the lawyer's view that McCabe is busting up trusts in his fight with Harrison-Shaugnessy. McCabe's perplexity when one of his whores says she has to go to the "pot" is what he *should* feel whenever business is discussed. "I know what I'm doing," he insists to Mrs. Miller, but the man from whom McCabe buys his first whores knows the truth of the matter: "You don't know what you're doing, McCabe."

The victim of economic forces he neither understands nor controls, McCabe emerges as a lovable fool, if not a lovable clod, so far as his business aspirations are concerned. What makes him more than this is his love for Mrs. Miller. This love is presented in utter seriousness, though McCabe's efforts to "control" Mrs. Miller are almost as comical as his attempts to outmaneuver Harrison-Shaugnessy. By referring to Mrs. Miller as a "chippie," McCabe seeks to assure himself as well as others that she is simply one of his underlings. In fact, however, we see him several times at Mrs. Miller's door, courting her after his fashion (though he must always pay for her favors!). McCabe needs Mrs. Miller to do more than balance his books, for he comes to love her deeply. When he enters the whorehouse to lecture Jeremy Berg about a business matter, McCabe is distracted by the sight of Mrs. Miller going up the stairs with a customer; angered, he turns and leaves the house. Later, McCabe comes to deliver the mail and offers to take Mrs. Miller a package, but he is told that she has "company." Hurt and perplexed, he mutters something and again leaves. These scenes are far more eloquent than McCabe himself. He finally expresses his love in the wonderful soliloquy that follows his interview with Butler. Here McCabe struggles with the fact that he loves a whore, his fear that Mrs. Miller is "freezin'

[his] soul" by dominating their relationship, and his frustration that she will not acknowledge his supreme fiction: that he is master of his own fate. This remarkable monologue precedes McCabe's direct declaration that he has never tried to do anything but put a smile on Mrs. Miller's face, a speech as close as McCabe will ever come to articulating his love.

McCabe's follies perhaps justify one reviewer's assertion that McCabe falls "mawkily" in love, but McCabe's feelings for Mrs. Miller should be respected in the world of Altman's film. As Gerard Plecki notes, McCabe's efforts to win Mrs. Miller are "in the best of western traditions." Indeed, McCabe's decision to stay and face Butler recalls Robert Warshow's definition of what a true western hero fights for: "What he defends, at bottom, is the purity of his own image . . . he fights not for advantage and not for right, but to state what he is, and he must live in a world which permits that statement." The McCabe we first see could not possibly fit this description, but the McCabe who struggles to be worthy of Mrs. Miller's love is a genuine candidate for the role of traditional hero (all limitations noted, by Altman as well as by his critics). I think we should take seriously the fact that McCabe is able to kill all three of his enemies; that he struggles alone, by what lights are available to him; that his motives for staying are more sympathetic than those displayed by the other characters and have nothing to do with busting up trusts, making a fortune, or maintaining his "big rep" amongst the yokels.

Karp suggests that McCabe has "the stature of a tragic hero," but this seems excessive even for those of us who find McCabe's fate poignant. If there is a tragic figure in Altman's film, it is Mrs. Miller rather than McCabe. Intelligent, determined, and apparently unillusioned, Mrs. Miller is fully aware of the world around her as McCabe is not. She recognizes at once the danger McCabe is in from Harrison-Shaugnessy and its envoys ("They get paid for killin'—nothing else"); her efforts to get McCabe away from Presbyterian Church are as realistic as her step-by-step transformation of McCabe's business. Yet Mrs. Miller is more sensitive than McCabe, no less loving, and finally even more painfully the victim of her own dreams. If she cannot learn to trust McCabe, as he asks her to do, she can learn to love him. And loving him, she must suffer the terrible pain of separation and loss when McCabe dies defending his conception of what her lover should be like.

Not everyone has felt that Mrs. Miller loves McCabe or even cares about his fate. She herself denies caring about anything except her share in the business. She advises Ida Coyle that prostitution is more honest than marriage; her arguments with McCabe always turn on maximizing their economic opportunities; and she forces McCabe to pay to sleep with her so that their affair will remain on a firm financial footing. Yet Altman's whole effort with Mrs. Miller is to reveal the sensitive woman beneath the rocklike exterior. On this point Lillian Gerard's feminist reading of Mrs. Miller is exemplary: "she chooses to build up the facade of a cold, detached, unloving woman who is unmoved by McCabe's fumbling attempts to reach her." Mrs. Miller's demeanor is a defense mechanism as profound as McCabe's corny jokes or Marlowe's endlessly repeated "It's okay with me" in Altman's *The Long Goodbye.* Mrs. Miller knows all too well what happens to those who fail to protect themselves against an unfriendly world. She is alone in a world that recognizes only *one* kind of woman, a world to which she will not expose her real self lest she be turned to stone.

As Gerard suggests, however, Mrs. Miller's real feelings are everywhere apparent. The care that goes into her transformation of the whorehouse and her treatment of her "girls" points to Mrs. Miller's true character. Her concern for McCabe is both genuine and deep, as we see most clearly in her almost panicky attempt to get McCabe to flee in a wagon. When McCabe finally declares his love the night before he is to be killed, Mrs. Miller responds with the terse but poignant "You don't need to say nothing" and what is apparently her first invitation to share her bed without payment. She has been accused of deserting McCabe because she exits before he awakes, but her expression as she walks away suggests that she cannot stand to see him killed. Nor can she help him. Mrs. Miller's plight is that she knows what McCabe and the others in Presbyterian Church refuse to acknowledge, yet her feelings are if anything more intense.

Mrs. Miller's stony facade is one response to her situation; the use of opium is another. Her opium habit suggests that she has her dreams like everyone else in Presbyterian Church. Her special desire is for respectability (a boarding house in San Francisco rather than a brothel in the wilderness). If she is a traveling lady, in the words of Leonard Cohen's song, it is because she knows that her dream is hopelessly at odds with life in general and her own life in particular. It is against this bitter knowledge that we must weigh her intense concern for McCabe and her frantic efforts to save him. When she withdraws at the end to an opium den, it is the act of someone who knows the tactics of survival but also the immense pain that will visit the survivor.

Alternately amusing and profoundly moving, childish and thoroughly adult, Warren Beatty and Julie Christie offer remarkable performances that testify to Altman's genius, for neither performer has done anything remotely as good before or since. Moreover, the parts they play are very much Altman's creation, as even a casual reading of the source novel suggests. At the very center of Altman's western, McCabe and Mrs. Miller try to enact the same dreams that haunt their fellow townspeople, but they suffer disproportionately because they carry their dreams through to an end

in which their illusions are shattered either literally (McCabe) or figuratively (Mrs. Miller). The film's somber conclusion is untypical of the classical western but hardly unprecedented. What is most "real" about this film is the sense of life it conveys in every detail, but especially in its lovers, perhaps the most memorable couple in the history of western film.

To remark on the excellence of Altman's direction (as scenarist, director, and guiding spirit) is to reengage the question of what makes *McCabe and Mrs. Miller* a classic western. For one answer is simply that the film is remarkably well done. But the phrase "classic western" also implies that the film in question displays structural and thematic patterns that we identify with Ford, Hawks, Peckinpah, and the other major western filmmakers. Is *McCabe and Mrs. Miller* a classic western in this second sense?

For many viewers Altman's film cannot be grouped with the classic westerns because the gap between its hero and the traditional protagonist is too great. I have shown that McCabe evolves into a far more admirable character than he seems at first, and Mrs. Miller is remarkably resourceful throughout, but these figures hardly embody traditional frontier values. Anyone who *requires* that a classic western focus on a Wayne, Stewart, or Cooper will never be reconciled to Altman's adaptation of the form. I think this point of view defines the classic western as a formula, a single mode that can only be endlessly repeated as again and again the stalwart, incorruptible hero clears the way for that social transition Cawelti identifies as the basic western story. And of course this pattern *has* been repeated endlessly, in such classics as *My Darling Clementine,* in the literally thousands of westerns that can only be defined as pale copies of the original model, and yet again in such recent westerns as Lawrence Kasdan's *Silverado* and Clint Eastwood's *Pale Rider.* But this should not blind us to the virtues of artists such as Altman who reconceive the formula and so demonstrate by example that the form is more flexible than we had thought.

In a very real sense, of course, it does not matter what we call *McCabe and Mrs. Miller* so long as we respond appropriately to it. I have resisted the label of anti-western because I think it distorts Altman's film, which does not debunk or devalue its characters and is far more faithful to the standard western story, as Altman calls it, than such true anti-westerns as *Doc* and *The Great Northfield Minnesota Raid.* Unlike the anti-westerns, *McCabe and Mrs. Miller* presents characters to whom we respond with sympathy if not full approval, people who elicit those comic and tragic responses Altman points to in the comment quoted at the beginning of this essay. As we watch these people discover their fates, the standard western story comes alive for us in new and compelling ways. This has always been true of the best westerns, from *Stagecoach* to *The Wild Bunch,* and is the best evidence that Altman's film is simply the most realistic of the classic westerns.

Richard K. Ferncase (essay date Fall 1991)

SOURCE: "Robert Altman's *The Long Goodbye:* Marlowe in the Me Decade," in *Journal of Popular Culture,* Vol. 25, No. 2, Fall, 1991, pp. 87-90.

[*In the following essay, Ferncase discusses Altman's retelling of the story of Philip Marlowe in his* The Long Goodbye.]

In the popular culture, few artifacts are guarded with the kind of reverence that is commonly reserved for old movies. Defenders of Hollywood's silver screen legacy are frequently vociferous over perceived indignities to which the films are submitted. A figure no less than Martin Scorsese has raged over the fugitive dyes in Eastmancolor prints (which reduced hundreds of 1950s films to faded ghosts of their former selves); strike the practice of colorizing black-and-white movies for video release continues to provoke howls from film academics and movie buffs alike. The brouhaha seems to have less to do with preserving films as art objects than it does with protecting the myths that these motion pictures enshrine.

Perhaps the most popular and enduring myth is that of the detective film genre, which has appeared in endless variations from the *Thin Man* serials to the *Miami Vice* series. It was Raymond Chandler who created the archetypal investigator Philip Marlowe, a cynical but idealistic sleuth who doggedly upholds a code of loyalty, honor, and duty. Chandler's last novel, *The Long Goodbye,* sees Marlowe becoming weary and increasingly, "a man out of his time." Director Robert Altman takes the myth to its logical end and systematically subverts it in his film ***The Long Goodbye,*** wherein his intent is "to put Marlowe to rest for good."

The Long Goodbye was greeted with extremely mixed reviews. New York critics gave the film mostly positive notices, while Los Angeles reviewers and others were generally more critical. Moviegoers were either openly hostile or indifferent; the film was pulled from release after poor attendance in Los Angeles, and did only mediocre business when it was re-released some nine months later.

Marlowe aficionados were not pleased with Altman's vision of Chandler's last novel, mostly because of the altered ending. Screenwriter Leigh Brackett (who also wrote the script for the more orthodox *The Big Sleep*) noted that "the film was greeted, by some critics, with the tone of outrage generally reserved for those who tamper with the Bible." Altman

himself speculated that a possible reason for the film's poor showing was due to the fact that "audiences are disturbed because it raises questions about their own moral hypocrisy."

Much of the film's subversive quality comes from the odd casting: a hulking, disheveled Elliot Gould as Marlowe, former baseball pitcher Jim Bouten as the slippery Terry Lennox, director Mark Rydell as the maniacal Marty Augustine, and Henry Gibson as the sinister Dr. Verringer.

Marlowe, as played by Gould, retains some characteristics of the Bogart archetype, which serves to distance him from his contemporaries. The only character to appear regularly in suit and tie, he drives to his appointments in a late 1940s Lincoln, and lights his unfiltered cigarettes with strike-any-where matches (a la Walter Neff in *Double Indemnity*). Even though Marlowe seems to blunder through much of the film in a daze, he remains true to the fundamental hard-boiled virtues: honor and loyalty. Gould's Marlowe never violates the detective's code of sexual ethics to bed down with a client, as Marlowe does with Eileen Wade in Chandler's original novel. In fact, Marlowe is anything but a lady's man (as Bogart was *par excellence* in *The Big Sleep.*) His motivations lie primarily in exonerating his friend Lennox, and this leads to most of his troubles. His unswerving fidelity earns him the derision of the other characters, including Lennox, who sums him up as "a born loser." This incarnation bears out Chandler's own assessment of Marlowe: "that any man who tried to be honest looks in the end either sentimental or foolish." In the context of the Seventies, Marlowe's anachronistic demeanor is a metaphor for his own outdated code of honor, and his fatal flaw.

The photography by Vilmos Zsigmond is unlike the heavy chiaroscuro of traditional *noir*. Venetian blinds cast no slatted shadows in this detective film. Instead, post-flashing technique creates a diaphanous ozone of pastel hues, blue shadows, and highlights of shimmering gossamer. The effect, rather than one of inscrutable darkness and menace, is more like the insidious glare of a smoggy Los Angeles afternoon. More remarkable is Zsigmond's restless camera, which prowls nervously throughout the film. The camera dollies almost imperceptibly around the characters, often zooming in to seemingly inconsequential details while the main action continues to play offscreen. In contrast to the rock-steady oblique compositions of older *noir* works, this unmotivated camera movement has a subliminal effect on the viewer, one of instability and uncertainty.

An animal motif recurs throughout the film. Unlike the original novel, the film begins with Marlowe attempting to fool his finicky cat into eating an off-brand cat food. Instead, the cat runs away, a loss which haunts him to the film's end (Altman has stated "that the real mystery of ***The Long Goodbye*** is where Marlowe's cat had gotten to"). Dogs, like most of the characters in the film, are either aggressive, in-dolent, or indifferent. Marlowe is repeatedly accosted, chased, and held at bay by the Wade's normally well-be-haved Doberman pinscher, and his forays into Mexico are prefaced by images of sleeping and copulating canines.

Altman debunks not only the myth of the private eye, but the Hollywood myth machinery itself. A number of self-reflexive references allude to classic films of the genre.
—*Richard K. Ferncase*

Altman debunks not only the myth of the private eye, but the Hollywood myth machinery itself. A number of self-re-flexive references allude to classic films of the genre. Marlowe's right-of-way is blocked at one point by a scruffy mongrel, which he addresses as "Asta" (the manicured ter-rier from *The Thin Man*). An eccentric security guard sub-jects visitors to movie star impressions including Barbara Stanwyck (from the Chandler-penned *Double Indemnity*) and Cary Grant (Chandler's original choice to play Marlowe) before he lets them pass. When police interrogate Marlowe, he mocks the old third-degree clichés when he wisecracks "This is where I say 'what's this all about' and you say 'we ask the questions.'" When he sneaks out of his hospital room after recuperating from an accident, Marlowe tells his fully-bandaged roommate, "I've seen all your movies, too."

The traditional Hollywood musical leitmotif is spoofed as the movie theme, a torchy pop ballad, plays throughout in numerous variations. It surfaces as a meandering jazz riff when Marlowe is onscreen, becoming a smoky blues wail for Terry Lennox. When Marlowe journeys to Mexico it ap-pears in Spanish guitar and mariachi versions, is sung by various characters throughout the film, and provides back-ground Muzak in an all-night market. The theme repeats without actually ending, never achieving resolution. The film opens and closes with a scratchy version of "Hooray for Hol-lywood," which further undermines the filmic illusion.

Thus, Altman effectively bids his own farewell to Philip Marlowe and the detective genre in general. His *The Long Goodbye* is "a goodbye to that genre—a genre that's not go-ing to be acceptable anymore." If "lovers of Chandler re-gard it with ontological loathing" as one critic suggests, perhaps they do wish to not see the character the creator en-visioned. Chandler himself acknowledged that ". . . Marlowe is a failure, and he knows it . . ." The film's detractors may also know it, but they might not want to relinquish their cher-ished myth. As Chandler also observed, "to say goodbye is to die a little."

John C. Tibbetts (essay date 1992)

SOURCE: "Robert Altman: After 35 Years, Still the 'Ac-tion Painter' of American Cinema," in *Literature/Film Quar-terly,* Vol. 20, No. 1, 1992, pp. 36-42.

[*In the following essay, Tibbetts discusses Altman's relation-ship to Kansas City, the course of his career, and his films through* Vincent and Theo.]

"They used to lock me up for getting into trouble in this town," quipped filmmaker Robert Altman as he accepted the Key to Kansas City from Mayor Richard Berkeley. "They used to throw away the key. Now, they're *giving* me one!"

Altman lived in his native Kansas City, MO, for his first nineteen years. As a boy he raised quite a ruckus, as he puts it; and he made his first movies there (which is perhaps the same thing). Now, an acclaimed world-class filmmaker, he has returned to receive a Lifetime Achievement Award from the Greater Kansas City Film Commission in the ballroom of the downtown Crown Center Westin Hotel. There is a sense of euphoria in the air that has been growing during the three days of nonstop screenings of sixteen Altman films, press conferences, workshops with area filmmakers and re-unions with family members. Altman and his hometown are both on a roll these days. He is fresh on the heels of his lat-est triumph, **Vincent and Theo;** and Kansas City itself is basking in the glow of the successful completion of two re-cent theatrical films that had been shot in the area—the pres-tigious *Mr. and Mrs. Bridge* and the forthcoming *Article 99.*

"This town and I will have to get together again," he told a press gathering earlier that day. "I haven't shot a film here since **The Delinquents** in 1955—which I'd rather not talk about! But the future of filmmaking is here in communities like this. We help each other. Companies have to figure things now down to the split penny. We go where it's cheap-est and where the artist can get the most return for his time. When I leave here I'll have a whole box of scripts under my arm." He paused with an air of mock drama. He waited a few beats, then—"We'll have to see."

Altman is relaxed, accessible and talkative. His Buffalo Bill beard is neatly trimmed. A white shirt and tie peek out from his zippered navy-blue jacket. He hardly seems the same hard-charging, hard-drinking maverick that barnstormed his way through movie after movie in the early 1970s. With *M*A*S*H, Brewster McCloud, McCabe and Mrs. Miller, The Long Goodbye* and *Nashville,* he was a prime archi-tect—with other young filmmakers like Paul Mazursky, John Cassavetes, Francis Ford Coppola and Martin Scorsese—of what Diane Jacobs has called the "Hollywood Renaissance." He was called a "prairie Buddha" by his associates. He re-ferred to himself as the "action painter" of American films.

Controversies, disputes, awards and brickbats trailed in his wake. College students appointed him their Vietnam-era voice. Critics debated his unorthodox, looping and elliptical style. While Stanley Kauffman called him a pretentious blunderer, Pauline Kael praised his idiosyncracies: "Altman has to introduce an element of risk on top of the risks that all directors take," she wrote in 1981. There was always something protean, even relentless about him. After the failure of *Popeye* in 1980, the big studios rejected him, but he kept going, staging operas at colleges, shooting modest projects like *Come Back to the 5 & Dime Jimmy Dean, Jimmy Dean* in 16mm, and filming plays for cable television. Meanwhile—although Altman wasn't counting—the awards were piling up. There were numerous "Best Film" and "Best Director" awards from the New York Film Critics Circle, the National Society of Film Critics, the National Board of Review and the Venice Film Festival (a Grand Prix for *Streamers*).

"I haven't been back to K. C. in almost 15 years now, I guess; and I come back and don't see the same city." We are talking together in the Presidential Suite on the 17th floor of the Crown Center Westin Hotel. The rooftops, spires and glass ramparts are spread out below us in the late afternoon sun. We have an hour to spend before he greets a sold-out house for a filmmaking workshop. "But I smell it and I feel it," he continues. "This is where I got my 'chips,' my attitudes. I lived on West 68th Street and went to several schools—Rockhurst, Southwest High School, Wentworth Military Academy, and then did a hitch in the Air Force, where I was a co-pilot of B-24 bombers. Restless, I guess." He takes a drink from a tumbler filled with club soda and a slice of lime. That's all he's drinking today.

"Somewhere along in there I saw my first movies at the old Brookside Theater. Those movies just seemed to *happen*—nobody *made* them, you know? And I guess that's the way I still see movies—I want them to be occurrences, to just seem to be happening."

We reminisce for a moment about the fate of the Calvin Film Company, a Kansas City landmark. Established by Altman's grandfather at 15th and Troost, the company had been "home" for every film student and filmmaker in the area for more than 40 years. The building had been razed in 1990. "Actually, I came back to Calvin several times after the war," Altman muses, rubbing his bearded chin. "I'd go to California and try to write scripts, but then return, broke, to Calvin. Each time they'd drop me another notch in salary. Like some kind of punishment. The third time they said it was like the Davis Cup—they were going to keep me!"

In the early 1950s Altman participated in every aspect of filmmaking. "I don't remember actually learning anything," he says; "it was more by a kind of osmosis." For $250 a week he made promotional films for Gulf Oil and safety films for Caterpillar Tractor and International Harvester. "They were training films for me—stuff like "How to Run a Filling Station." They weren't a goal for me, just a process to learn how to do entertainment and dramatic films. It was a school, that's what it was." During these years he met several other young filmmakers who were to form the core of his filmmaking team—writer Fred Barheit and editor Louis Lombardo.

After returning to Hollywood and clicking in the late 1950s and early 1960s on television series like *Alfred Hitchcock Presents, Gallant Men, Bonanza* and *Combat!* (for which he directed fully one-half of the episodes), he was ready to tackle feature films.

"There's always been a sort of division between the feature film business and the television business," he continues. "It's hard to step from one to the other. And that still is the case. But it was a great training ground. I was lucky; it kept me in California. I developed a nice reputation there and learned to stay in budget. But when I did my first movie, *Countdown* (a science fiction thriller) in 1967 for Warner Bros. everything went wrong. Jack Warner fired me. I got a call Sunday night from the studio warning me not to come in because the guard would stop me. I'd been locked out. Warner had looked at the dailies and he said, 'That fool has everybody talking at the same time!' So I went to the studio gate and got my stuff in a box from the guard. Somebody else edited it. 'Since that and another picture, *That Cold Day in the Park,* you've never seen a film of mine that I didn't keep total control over. And that's why I don't work a lot." He laughs outright.

The criticism about Altman's unique use of densely textured sound and dialogue has always aroused controversy. "But, you know, last Saturday night the Audio-Engineers Society—they are the Hollywood sound people—awarded me their own Lifetime Achievement Award." Altman smiles. It's a Cheshire cat smile. If he were to vanish, that knowing grin would still hover there in the air. "This was the first time it's ever gone to a filmmaker instead of some inventor or process, like Dolby. And that very day I had read a review of *Vincent and Theo* complaining of the same thing—that the soundtrack was so muddled you couldn't understand anything. Like all the characters were played by 'Mumbles' in *Dick Tracy.* Look, what I'm trying to do is—" he pauses, groping for the right words. "I don't want you to understand *everything*—not the sound, not the images. What I'm trying to do—and this is what the engineers understood (which pleased me)—I'm trying to present something to an audience where they have to *work* a little bit. They have to invest something. You don't hear everything somebody says in real life, do you? Maybe you're not really listening or distracted or something. That's the illusion I want. It's a way to get the audience involved and participating in the thing." He spreads his hands philosophically. "But some people don't like it." Another pause. "Anyway, I really worked this out the first time in *California Split.* I used 8-track sound. I said, 'They do this in music recording, put a microphone on every different instrument and try to isolate them as much as possible then mix it afterwards. Why don't we do that with the voices on the soundtrack?' So, we developed 8-track tape machines and individual microphones. Which means recording everything and then mixing it later. I can take a person's sound down or push it up. That way, I don't have to go back for post-synching, looping of lines—you know, bringing the actors back in to match their lip movements. When you do that, the acting is gone."

Clearly, Altman still relishes the role of iconoclast. That memorable spurt of movies in the early 1970s took the cherished genres of war story (*M*A*S*H*), western (*McCabe*), detective thriller (*The Long Goodbye*) and the caper film (*California Split*) and turned them inside out. "When I look at a subject and see how it's done, I think, it doesn't necessarily have to be done that way. Like *McCabe.* What a collection of stereotypes! There was the gambler down on his luck, the whore with the heart of gold, the three heavies (the giant, the half-breed and the kid). Everything there you've seen all your life in westerns. The audience can supply most of the story already! That left me free to work on the backgrounds and the atmosphere and the details. The same thing with *The Long Goodbye.* That was a Raymond Chandler story. To this day I've never finished it. I could never figure out what was happening! And I didn't much care. I thought, Raymond Chandler used his plots the way I do— just as an excuse to hang a series of thumbnail sketches on. I had fun dropping the 1940s character of 'Philip Marlowe' into the attitudes of 1973, into a time of marijuana and brownies and health food. He was out of place and that was a great chance for some thumbnail essays of our own of what the culture and society at the time looked like."

Vincent and Theo was offered to me and I didn't even want to read it. I didn't want to make that kind of picture. I don't like those biographical things. I just don't believe them, for one thing. But they kept pressing me to make it and I said, at last, "OK, you let me have artistic control on this and do whatever I want to do and I'll make it."

—Robert Altman

One genre that he tried to avoid—and couldn't—was the bio-pic, or film biography. "*Vincent and Theo* was offered to me and I didn't even want to read it," admits Altman. "I

didn't want to make that kind of picture. I don't like those biographical things. I just don't believe them, for one thing. But they kept pressing me to make it and I said, at last, 'OK, you let me have artistic control on this and do whatever I want to do and I'll make it.'"

The results have been spectacular. As *Variety* reported April 27, 1990, "Seldom has an artist been so convincingly or movingly portrayed on screen." Although it got no Oscar nominations (a grievous sin of omission) it has found the largest, most enthusiastic audience for an Altman film since *Nashville.* For Altman, the movie was a process of avoiding traps. (He frequently describes filmmaking as avoiding hazards and traps.) "For example, at first I didn't want to use any of the Van Gogh paintings at all," he explains. "I wasn't going to show them. And I wasn't going to show him actually painting, either. Finally, I realized I had to show them, but I decided to show them as a kind of 'evidence.' We'll treat them roughly (like he did). We'll have them lying around, people stepping on them. Vincent himself destroys some of them. I wanted the audience to say—'Oh, that's worth $82 million dollars!'—and then somebody steps through the canvas! That's great!"

Our laughter attracts the attention of a young man who has just wandered in from the hallway. He has chiseled features and curly dark hair. He is Altman's son, Stephen, who was the production designer on *Vincent and Theo.* Stephen was born in Kansas City in 1956 and, although he was reared by his mother, Altman's second wife, he began working with his father (he calls him "Bob") on sets and props at age eleven. Stephen claims he can look back upon his father's films and discover his own "fingerprints," evidence of his own presence—like the pay telephone he managed to insinuate into every picture (and which now adorns a wall in his Paris apartment). He describes himself as part scavenger, part prop master and part set dresser. ("Anything an actor touches is a prop," he explains. "If he drives a tank, it's a prop. If he eats cornflakes, it's a prop. If it's something just sitting on the set, then it's set dressing or background.") It was he who arranged for all the reproductions of Van Gogh paintings and sketches seen in the movie.

"They were all done by students at the Beaux-Arts in Paris or in Holland," explains Stephen, whose research into the ateliers and galleries of Van Gogh's time has made him into something of an art historian himself. I ask him where the paintings are now. "Oh," he looks sidelong at his father. "The producer has a lot of them. I know somebody else who keeps some of them in his office." He pauses meaningfully, still grinning at his father. "But I don't have one."

Altman pushes his way into the pause. "Those darned paintings—I'd find the sets would look just like them—the sort of thing you see in the Vincente Minnelli picture, *Lust for*

Life. I didn't want that kind of competition. So, I'd come on the set and I'd say, 'I've seen this before'—and then I'd move the chair and shoot the room differently. I didn't want exact copies, just the—just the *smell* of things." Stephen nods. "On all the Dutch scenes, we wanted a kind of lighting with an 'Old Masters' look—with the light from above, northern light. When we went to Paris, we wanted a gray, impressionistic feel. And when we went to Arles, we had to have a bright shining light."

Altman's eyes twinkle as he leans forward. "Although, if we'd have had to shoot a rainstorm in the sunflower fields, we'd have done that, too. I'd read a lot of stories about David Lean waiting weeks for snow in *Dr. Zhivago;* but in my experience, you're lucky to get the crew together at all. So if you're out there and it's raining, you just change the script from 'sunshine' to 'rain.'"

Robert Altman's laugh fades after a moment. He continues, more seriously. "I wasn't so much interested in showing Van Gogh's creativity as in showing the pain that this guy went through. You have to remember that nobody ever smiled at Vincent Van Gogh. But there was some compulsion to just keep doing what he did, until he finally couldn't stand it anymore and just shot himself. Only in combination with his brother, Theo, was Vincent a complete person. They were connected in some way. That's the story I was trying to tell. You know, people expect movies like this to blow trumpets when a painting is made. But Vincent did not have a great deal of talent. He was not a great draughtsman. It took him a long time to learn how to draw and paint. He taught himself and he worked hard. He copied other people and didn't start any schools. He couldn't paint from his own imagination, just from what was in front of him. He had a lot going against him. If anybody was going to make book and ask which of these painters at the time would sell paintings for millions, like I show at the London auction at the beginning of the movie, nobody would have voted Vincent." He pauses again. His next words come slowly. "I'm sure my film is not factual," he says, "but I hope it's truthful."

I ask about the final sequences in the movie. Rarely has a person's self-destructive impulses been more harrowingly portrayed on film. "I think that when Vincent mutilated his ear, it was a cry for help, for attention," says Altman. "When he went to the asylum for a year, he met the daughter of the man who ran it. But when he rejected her advances, he realized he didn't belong, that he couldn't make it in life, and by that time he abdicated and wanted out."

"There was a dramatic, unexpected moment on the set during the ear mutilation scene," volunteers Stephen. "You know it's a moment that audiences have been waiting for. But when Tim Roth (the actor portraying Van Gogh) cut the ear, suddenly he did something none of us expected. He held on to

the razor and suddenly brought it close to his *tongue.* We just shot it once and Tim surprised everybody with that. I guess he didn't know what to do at that moment, but he felt he needed something else. He didn't tell anybody in advance. It was scary."

"Maybe not so unexpected, though," growls Altman. "I get a lot of credit for having the actors improvise all the time. When we go into rehearsal, I encourage as much improvisation as I can get. And we find out what works and what doesn't work. But by the time we actually shoot the scene, it's very well rehearsed. The secret lies in letting the actor give the good performance. That's what Tim did. I can't teach anybody to act. My job is like a cheerleader's, really—trying to set up an atmosphere and a focus of energies so the actor becomes the most important part of the collaboration. Get them to trust you and take some chances. Get them to know that you won't make them look bad. If they can't say a line in the script, we'll change it."

Our conversation is interrupted by a ringing telephone. It's time for Altman and his son to repair downstairs to the hotel lobby for a workshop with area filmmakers and students. For the next two hours Altman's high spirits continue unabated. As he mounts the platform to the applause of the crowd, he jokes, "I think I forgot my lines!" Peering out at the crowd, he mutters, "You know, the actor's nightmare is to find himself in a play and not know his lines. *Hell, I don't know this play!*" But he fields the questions beautifully. It is obvious that he loves audiences and respects them.

At times the give-and-take is rapid-fire. Examples:

Question: "Are you really a control freak in your movies, like they say?" (The questioner is too young to have seen Altman's first pictures during their first run.)

Altman: "Let's put it this way. Making a movie for me is getting people to work for you who are shooting the same film you are shooting. In ***Fool for Love*** we started with a wonderful cinematographer named Robby Müller. After six days of shooting I fired him. I said, 'I can't do this. I'm sure you're shooting a beautiful movie, but it's not the movie *I'm* making.' So we started over again. Next question!"

Question: "Have you ever tried to make a movie somebody else's way?"

Altman: "I can't do anything but what I do. If I tried to, I'd fail. Next."

Question: "Do you have a particular style?"

Altman: "I don't know what my style is. I'm the last one to say what it is, I think. What I secretly think about myself might be wrong. I didn't know what anybody was talking about when they said my first seven films had 'the Altman signature.' I was just trying to do things totally different from one film to another. Now I look back at them and see my fingerprints all over them. You can't keep your hands clean."

Question: "What do you think of critics?"

Altman: "A lot of people see my films and say, 'I don't get it.' But I've created at least a cult following. That's not quite enough people to make a minority!"

Question: "What is your favorite among your films?"

Altman: "I won't fall into that trap. They are all your children. You can't choose."

Later, while he's surrounded by the crowd for some last questions and pictures, I steal away to the coffee shop with Stephen. I tell him I'm amazed at his father's easy amiability. This is not the same Altman, I tell him, that stormed through critics, press and audiences alike twenty years ago.

"He's mellowing out a little bit," Stephen admits, stirring his coffee. "He used to be a hard drinker. He never drank on the set, but he'd drink a lot and rip into people. Usually they deserved it. But I think it's better now. He's looser. He's not trying so hard. He's had a lot of experience. Hey, he's done more films consecutively now than anybody else working today. I think he's the best director I've ever worked with. He's very tough and very difficult and at the same time can be the easiest and nicest. Anybody can disagree with him on the set, but he'll tell you, 'Anybody can make a suggestion, but only give it once.' He won't easily admit it if he's wrong. He has some funny quirks. People might sit around and talk and it won't seem like he's listening; and then the next day he'll come up and say, 'I had this great idea. We'll do this and that.' And everybody will sit around and say, 'Good idea, Bob!'"

After the ceremonies that night, Altman rejoins me for a wrap-up of our interview. He has to leave early the next morning, he explains, to return to his editing studio in Malibu, CA. He describes the studio as a kind of support environment. "I have lots of people there to help. Primarily, I can get into an environment where I have everything I need. Like being in a submarine. We have a cook who comes in. That way I can keep everybody there. We'll work six days a week, 12-13 hours a day. I like the intensity. I just can't do it leisurely. It's the *process* that's the real reward."

There are many projects in the works. He will begin immediately editing footage, for Japanese television, he has shot backstage during a performance of the Broadway musical, *Black and Blue.* "Like I first wanted to do with *Vincent and Theo,* I decided to ignore the show itself and get the fatigue on the faces of the dancers as they come back offstage. All those smiles and energy would collapse as soon as they hit the black. I'm dealing here with errors and frailties."

Another project is the long-cherished *L. A. Shortcuts,* a script he and Frank Barheit adapted from stories by Raymond Carver. There have been problems lately in getting the financing, but Altman hopes at last the project is in the gate. It sounds like a kind of West Coast version of *Nashville:* "There's a big cast, 27 main actors, who all lead different lives. They don't necessarily affect one another, but their lives all criss-cross. You know, Frank Lloyd Wright said that Los Angeles was made when the continent tipped and all the people without roots slipped into the southwest corner!"

Even more tantalizing are hints at other movies. His highly praised television film, *Tanner '88,* made in collaboration with comic strip guru Gary Trudeau, may have a sequel just in time for the next presidential election. "Let's run Tanner again in 1992," cracks Altman. "Somebody's got to run against those guys!" And he confirms something his son Stephen had told me—that he plans to make a movie called *The Player.* "Oh, yes," he grins, "that's another thing about an artist at work. It's about a studio executive who murders a writer. And gets away with it. We'll get in some shots and make the producers hate us! That's all I'll tell you."

He pauses a moment. The ballroom has almost cleared and some members of the Altman clan still living in Kansas City—a whole contingent of cousins, uncles and nephews—are waiting for him. Doesn't this man ever get tired??? "But with all these projects there are still those that fail, that don't get made," he continues philosophically, apparently in no hurry to leave. "Like *Rossini, Rossini.*" I start in amazement. Robert Altman making a movie about the great Italian opera composer. . .? "Sure," he says, as if reading my thoughts. "This was to be our 'big' film, not *Vincent and Theo. Vincent* was going to be just a warm-up for it. Stephen and I worked on it for over six months, travelling through Italy, scouting locations, dressing sets, hashing out the script. Then, things got very strange. We'd be called back to Rome several times; and finally we were told the movie had shut down. Then I got fired. Somebody else finished it."

Clearly, the aborted project meant a great deal to him. It's the sort of disappointment and pain that tempts me to compare Altman's career with his most recent subject, Vincent Van Gogh. But no. Altman rejects—almost peremptorily—the association. "I can't summon up the fortitude of somebody like Vincent. I've had a good deal of personal adulation in my life and a great deal of success. But I think if I ever made a film and people got up and walked out of a theater before it was over, I'd never make another one. I couldn't change my films to anything else. I don't make mainstream, 'shopping mall' kinds of films, like *Pretty Woman.* I'm not an 'in demand' commodity. If I stepped down off this stage we're on and went straight downhill to the end, I'd have to look back and say, 'I had a great roll.' Some people liked my work—I can at least find a couple. But the minute I don't find *anybody,* then I'm stepping off."

No compromises. No prisoners. After more than 35 years of making films, he still can thumb his nose at the naysayers. He can still say brashly, "There's them and there's us." There's no question that "them" still means the Hollywood establishment, the grownups, the crowd; and that "us" means those who grew up loving his movies—those who felt young and special just watching them.

Robert Altman and Tess Gallagher with Robert Stewart (interview date July 1993)

SOURCE: "Reimagining Raymond Carver on Film: A Talk with Robert Altman and Tess Gallagher," in *The New York Times Book Review,* September 12, 1993, pp. 3, 41-2.

[*In the following interview, which took place in July, 1993, Altman and Gallagher discuss the adaptation of Raymond Carver's short stories in Altman's film* Short Cuts.]

Raymond Carver, who died all too early—at 50—of lung cancer in 1988, left a remarkable legacy of 11 volumes of short stories and poems, among them *Where I'm Calling From, Cathedral, What We Talk About When We Talk About Love, Will You Please Be Quiet, Please?* and *Where Water Comes Together With Other Water.* It is a body of work that brought him international acclaim while he was alive and that has now been translated into more than 20 languages.

It was his stories in particular, with their stark evocation of America's urban and small-town blue-collar world, that made the greatest and, perhaps, the most lasting impact. He'd come from there himself—a world of old factories and sawmills, of truck stops and diners, of bars, of run-down frame houses and the frayed nerves of the families inside; in short, a kind of life in the desperate zone, where the *one* thing one needs is a job, *any* job, but where all one does is stare at the tube and hang on, scramble, come up empty.

The appeal of Carver's stories lies in their raw, spare truthfulness, their grasp of what Freud, in his old age, liked to call "the foul realities," or what Carver himself might have thought of as just plain bad luck Yet it would be an error to dismiss the strains of hope or the theme of surviving against the odds in his work, for these, too are central to his far-reaching popularity.

To the millions of Carver readers here and abroad, one must now add the American film director Robert Altman. His list of films includes *M*A*S*H, Nashville, A Wedding, The Player* and now the soon to be released *Short Cuts,* based on nine stories and a poem by Carver, which will open the New York Film Festival at Lincoln Center on Oct. 1. . . .

In July I met with Robert Altman and Carver's widow, the poet Tess Gallagher, in Los Angeles to talk with them about their thoughts on the transformation of Raymond Carver's work into a film.

[*Stewart:*] *How did the idea for* **Short Cuts** *first get started?*

[Altman:] In the early winter of 1990, I was in Rome planning to make a film there about Rossini. But the situation got very ugly and my life was actually threatened. I told my wife that we were going back to America right away, and I asked my secretary to give me something to read on the plane.

I always keep collections of short stories by various writers around, because they often make good film material. I had heard of Ray Carver, of course, but I had never read him, and now there were four or five of his books in the pile put together by my secretary.

What were your first impressions?

[Altman:] I loved the stories. I read a couple of them during the flight. You have to understand that I was in a fragile state. I was coming from an aborted picture and a big defeat. I got off the plane, and I remember walking down the ramp and thinking, "There's a movie here." I think what I did is I made "Carver soup" out of these stories.

Can you remember what happened next?

[Altman:] I went to Tess Gallagher, who owned the rights, and I made a deal to option the stories. Frank Barhydt, a wonderful writer with whom I had worked before, started working with me. I went to Paramount, sold the idea to them. They gave me money to develop a screenplay. We bought some colored 3-by-5 index cards and put scenes from the stories down on them and pinned them up on a big board. When we finished, Paramount hated the script, turned it down, sent it back to us. But I had sent the Carver script to Tess. I was scared to death about what her reaction would be. I had no idea of what she would think.

What was your initial response, Tess, not only to the script but to the idea of Bob Altman wanting to do a film based on Ray's work?

[Gallagher:] I had seen other scripts based on Ray's stories and they had been very flat-footed. Their approach to his work was to copy Ray's dialogue exactly, copy the character's movements exactly. You couldn't really tell what was going to generate the film's energy in those scripts. But I thought that Bob was really a perfect match for Ray, because he wasn't coming out of literature, in a sense.

Do you mean by that that Ray came out of literature?

[Gallagher:] No, actually, Ray was very awkward in the halls of academe. He was a literary man by virtue of his writing and his reading. He was extremely well read. But the lives of the people he was writing about were the lives of pretty ordinary people and, in fact, that's what everybody was so excited about—that through Ray's stories these people started entering into the literature of the country.

So of all the others, Bob seemed to be the right film maker?

[Gallagher:] I thought if anybody could do it, *he* could. I thought he was doing something very new. He was using the stories as a kind of sourdough, a starter, like yeast. It was generative. It was very interesting to me that he broke the frames of the stories in such a way that the characters began to interact with each other and to glance off each other.

You're known to be careful about Ray's material. Were there reservations?

[Gallagher:] Well, there may have been one thing. I had seen **The Player,** and I knew that one of Bob's great gifts was his irony, that it was a great tool of his. I was very well aware that Ray eschewed irony, that he didn't distance himself from his characters or their dilemmas.

[Altman:] Yes, Tess made me very aware of that. I agree that real art is *without* irony. I think that irony is a product of something. It's not the reason for doing something. Irony is a cheap shot. But I can never get rid of all of it, because that's who I am.

Can you give an example from **Short Cuts?**

[Altman:] After I had cut the picture, Tess made a negative comment about the ending. It's from the story "Tell the Women We're Going." A young girl is brutally assaulted by a sex-starved, violent character named Jerry Kaiser. He beats her to death with a rock. The scene is followed by an earthquake, and it is reported on television that the only known casualty of this earthquake was a teen-age girl—the one he'd killed—caught in a rock slide, which, of course, has its measure of irony. And this was what Tess was responding to. So I immediately went back and recut the picture, the ending of it. I felt I was doing the right thing. Then I had another screening, and it went flat, and I said it's got to go

back. When I took it out, it didn't give the audience an out, a way out of the picture somehow. If you just looked at that one moment, Tess was right. I should have taken it out. But if you looked at the picture as a whole, I needed it.

You said earlier that you had made "Carver soup" out of his stories. What exactly did you mean by that?

[Altman:] I meant that I thought of all of Carver's stories as *one* story. You know, I feel that all of Edgar Allan Poe's stories are really one story. I think of Shakespeare's plays as one big piece. That's the way I look at these things.

[Gallagher:] You saw Ray's *world.*

[Altman:] Yes, I saw his world. It was as if I was inside of an eggshell, *his* eggshell. I was inside of this kind of three-dimensional thing. Even the stories that we fabricated, the ones that didn't come from Carver's work, are *of* his work. Of course Carver is much, much purer. I love the work in the film and I'm not apologizing for any of it—but I don't think it has the power or the truthfulness of Ray's work. I think it has to do with the medium more than anything else.

In what way do you think it has to do with the medium?

[Altman:] When you read these things yourself, you are taking this information, this simple information that Carver is giving you, and you're taking it in and adding it to all the information that already exists in your brain; you are applying it to your own personal experiences, to things that you have seen, done, read, felt, thought before, and it's all judged and filed according to the information you already have.

Now a film audience does exactly the same thing. Except that we're hitting the film audience with visual material; we're hitting them with familiar or unfamiliar material, which is the *actors.* When you look at Tim Robbins on the screen, whether you like it or not, your mind is judging everything you've ever seen him do before. So if you've seen **The Player,** that's rubbing off on you.

So how would you describe what you do when you take one medium and put it into another?

[Altman:] I translate what I saw in Carver's work. I'm trying to use what was written and the effect it had on me. My authorship is shaky and doubtful in this. I'm trying to take an experience that *I* had in reading these stories and use elements and pieces of them to give a similar experience to a film audience.

[Gallagher:] It's a new experience. A fusion of the two consciousnesses, really, and visions—yours and Ray's—to create an entity which didn't exist before. What you do is move Ray's vision into the time in which we are living, the 90's. It's the difference between the vitamins the girl sells in Ray's story "Vitamins" and Jennifer Jason Leigh selling telephone sex in your film. Whereas Ray was considered a realist—and even called a "dirty realist"—you're showing us how much over the fence into fantasy we really live. There are any number of those instances in which fantasy is serving to prop up a reality which is spiritually bankrupt. Ray really had perfect pitch in the soul and the spirit department. He knew what was coming down. And you're saying it *has* come down and this is what we're living now.

[Altman:] I think that he and I see life from a very similar window.

[Gallagher:] A lot of randomness and luck, but striving too. Many of Ray's characters tried to do better, really struggled against chaos and bad luck.

[Altman:] The whole thing about lady luck is that she has to pick a side. You can say it's the toss of a coin, but lady luck has to pick the side of the coin that lands face up. The poem "Lemonade" is the basis of the whole picture for me. I think the film, the whole film, has more to do with the idea of the chain of events—call it luck or fate—in "Lemonade" than it has to do with any of the individual stories.

[Gallagher:] It's a poem about a child's accidental death and about how sequences of actions cause other actions.

[Altman:] Yes, but it's not that those actions cause those actions, it's that, in looking back, we *blame* those actions. And the idea of calling it **Short Cuts.** From the very beginning people kept saying: "Now is that a very good title?" "Why do you call it **Short Cuts?**" "What's it mean?" I couldn't defend it very well at first, but now I can, because when I look at a map, something happens. A child dies and it's devastating to the people who are close to that event. So they say, "Why did that child die?" But instead of retracing the steps that led to the child's death, as in "Lemonade," you can just look at the map and you say, well, there's 16th Street, Mulberry Street, the Pacific Coast Highway, Main Street. It's a kind of sign language that has nothing to do with the cause of the child's death, and yet it's the only thing you can trace.

[Gallagher:] Maps are like an aerial view of blame. It's a short cut to understanding what happened.

Ray said that he was a paid-up-in-full member of the working poor. And in the movie you moved the stories to suburbia, sort of raised them up in terms of class structure. Was that intentional?

[Altman:] In the way that I'm retelling Ray Carver this class

thing is not necessarily an element that is making things happen.

So you didn't try to consciously change from a poor working-class environment to a qualitatively different one?

[Altman:] No, but I probably consciously, and unconsciously, changed it to something that was more familiar to me. To do a whole thing about people who are out of work would give some sort of meaning to this picture that I didn't want to give to it.

You didn't set out to reconfigure the class structure and bring it to Los Angeles, perhaps to appeal to a broader audience?

[Altman:] Oh, no, *au contraire.* My first reason for shooting the picture in Los Angeles was a practical one. I had a limited budget, and I knew I just couldn't go on location. Most of Ray's people were dislocated anyway.

[Gallagher:] Yes, from somewhere else, or going somewhere else.

[Altman:] I was also very conscious of trying to show that this isn't the Los Angeles of Bel Air or of Brentwood. Every house we used in every neighborhood was for sale. Across the street houses were for sale, cars were for sale. So there was an idea of transition, nothing was permanent.

I have a question about a different issue. When I reread the fishing story, "So Much Water So Close to Home," I realized that the woman is telling the story, that Ray used the woman as the narrator. In the film, it's told from the point of view of the men. Did you do that on purpose?

[Altman:] Well, I thought a lot about that story because that story presented a moral dilemma to me. We sat there and I said, I don't want to take sides in this. I don't want to load this thing one way or the other. So Frank Barhydt and I and my son Steve, who was the production manager on the film, would just sit there and we'd talk. And we'd say, "O.K. we are just three guys, now let's really talk about this. Here's where we are. We've walked into these woods. It took us four hours to get there. It's close to nightfall. We find this body. What are we going to do about it? Are we going to fish, or are we going to report the body to the police right away?" Now Barhydt still contends that he would not have gone fishing, that he would have addressed the situation of the body. And I said I would do the same thing if both guys agreed to that. But if they both said, "Oh, we're gonna fish," I wouldn't argue with them. I'd go along with them, which is what happens in the story. I could easily have done what those men did and not feel guilty about it. Now when he gets back and tells his wife about it, there's not a question in *her* mind about the moral irresponsibility of what he did.

[Gallagher:] Yes, and if you had had four women going fishing, it would have been different. It couldn't possibly work out the way it works out here.

[Altman:] You're probably right. And if it's true, Tess, then something of great value has been said in this story.

[Gallagher:] You have told us something we didn't know about the difference in the sexes.

Does that mean that you shifted the narrator from the woman because you didn't want to get into sex differences or feminist issues?

[Altman:] Yes. I didn't want to make any judgment whatsoever. I even had the guy take a leak on the body—and my wife, Kathryn, said, "Why did you have to do that, that's disgusting"—and I said, I know it's disgusting, but the point of it is that all he did was take a leak in the water. There happened to be a body there, and when you see that you think, "Oh, there's something revolting in that, that's a violation, that's a terrible thing." But I kept that in on purpose, because I didn't want to make it easy on anybody.

Do you worry that some critics may find your handling of the story sexist?

[Altman:] I don't care about that. When I made *M*A*S*H* there were a lot of accusations. A woman stood up in a 5,000 seat auditorium in Ann Arbor, Mich., and said, "Why do you treat women the way you treated Hot Lips?" She hated me. She called me a misogynist. "Why do you treat women that way?" I said, "I don't treat women that way. I don't think women should be treated that way. This is the way I see women being treated. You make the moral judgment, I'm not going to make any moral judgment. That's propaganda."

[Gallagher:] I think Ray's story avoids propaganda, but he still manages to show that woman's revulsion at what her husband has done.

[Altman:] I think we did that in the film. And that's why I had Claire and Stuart make love that night when he comes back from the fishing trip. I thought that was a good balance—nice, loving, happy—they made each other happy. She says after they separate in bed, "Oh, you make me so happy." And then he says, "Claire, we found a dead body up there." And two minutes later she's in there and she's saying, "You're making me sick." And she's washing the slime out of her. The next day she gets in her car and she drives 75 miles to be at the funeral service for the dead girl.

[Gallagher:] In the story, Ray made more of a point of the man not telling his wife about the death of the woman until the next morning, until he had his "sexual welcome" so to speak.

[Altman:] I think we did that, too.

[Gallagher:] I guess I mean that you *feel* the delay more in the story. Time somehow collapses in films.

In the story "A Small, Good Thing," in which the child gets hit by the car, Ann asks her husband to pray for the boy. I was just wondering, Tess, if Ray ever thought in religious or spiritual terms, if he believed there was some kind of higher power in the world?

[Gallagher:] Well, Ray was a recovering alcoholic, and I think he did adopt the attitude of a higher power as a help to us. But he never articulated this. And he never preached to anybody, and I don't even know if he believed in a hereafter, really. He pretty much thought you had to do it all here. But he believed in right action.

I'm curious about the element of classical music and jazz that you've added. And you've created this character, Tess Trainer, a faded jazz singer, whose husband has died and whom you've named after Tess.

[Altman:] I did that simply because I wanted to have a reason for the music I didn't want the music to come from a sound studio outside and amplify the emotions. And yet I know that music does that. I knew I couldn't do this picture without music. That's tough for an audience. But I didn't just want to *apply* music.

Whatever the reason, you succeed rather well in creating a story that doesn't disturb the rest of the film.

[Altman:] Actually, it's the least Carveresque of the stories. Most of the people who have criticized the film have said, "Oh, you can do without that story."

What do you think of your namesake, Tess Trainer, Tess?

[Gallagher:] Well, widows don't get much applause in America, and there's a lot of applause built into this film for Tess Trainer. She's a real gift to me. I love her stamina, her wry courage, even her loneliness. "She's seen some things," as Ray would say. I certainly recognize some of the widowhood things from my own life, the painful quality that seeps into things because of how they used to be. I think you even poke fun at her—in the way that you make her so nostalgic. I mean I can even laugh at myself through her in the film, the way she's always looking over her shoulder at the past. Am I wrong?

[Altman:] Well, no, how can you be wrong if you're telling

me what you received? But about the nostalgia. I think that's what music *is*. I think it comes from singing those same songs every day in bars and clubs. My feeling is that the music made her what she was, and the music made her daughter commit suicide. I think it was the sadness of the music.

If you were asked to review this film, Tess, how would you deal with this question of the adaptation of Ray's work?

[Gallagher:] I would be very careful about the comparative, in the way that I'm careful about metaphors. What I mean is that to say that something is like or unlike something else is already a kind of invasion. I would try to protect the integrity of your and Ray's vision. At the same time, I would say that I missed a certain *interiority* of the characters in the film. The suffering in Ray's stories is more palpable; the empathetic qualities in Ray's characters are more present. I also think you're more societal than Ray was in his work. Ray got inside the individual, and any societal ideas that Ray may have had were very much a byproduct. But you actually make that more your terrain.

Do you think one of the things that might come out of this film is that more people will start reading Ray Carver?

[Gallagher:] I hope they are going to discover the great richness in Ray's work. And the interiors are going to stand out a lot more in the stories because so much of the film is action. Now they're going to go inside in a new way. They're going to take a story like "So Much Water So Close to Home" and wonder about those choices.

But despite the differences, Tess, the sense I have of it is that Ray and Bob would have gotten along extremely well.

[Gallagher:] Oh, absolutely.

[Altman:] I kind of think so. I think we would have argued a lot, but a kind of "discussing" arguing, the way I do.

[Gallagher:] I'm sure you would have laughed together, too—and told a lot of stories like the one in a poem of his in which a man goes walking by the river and an eagle drops a huge salmon right at his feet.

Richard P. Sugg (essay date 1994)

SOURCE: "The Role of the Writer in *The Player:* Novel and Film," in *Literature/Film Quarterly,* Vol. 22, No. 1, 1994, pp. 11-5.

[*In the following essay, Sugg traces the role of the writer in Altman's* The Player *as compared to his role in the novel of the same name.*]

Though the novel *The Player* was written first, the film precedes the novel in most of the audience's consciousness, for few who see the film will have read the novel. So let's consider how the writer is presented in the film, and how our understanding of these changes from novel to film helps us see more clearly Robert Altman's ultimate purposes and their achievement in the film. Three sequences are of especial importance to establishing the role of the writer in the film. The first is the opening eight-minute-long shot, which satirizes the Hollywood image production system as well as the marginal role of the writer-author within it. The second sequence is the murder of the writer Kahane by Griffin the producer. And finally, perhaps the most important sequence for understanding the role of the writer is the film's conclusion, presenting a very revealing power dynamic involving the writer, the producer, the audience, and the film's *auteur* which has been revised significantly from the novel. An understanding of each of these three sequences, including an awareness of how each has been revised from the novel, will enable us to understand the importance of the role of the writer in both the novel and film.

The Player'*s** opening declares that understanding the role of the writer is central to understanding the film on all levels—not only the personal conflict between Griffin and the postcard writer, or the socioeconomic conflict between commerce and art, but also the philosophical conflict between image people and word people. The vignettes of writers in the film's opening carry resonances for many important issues of the current critical debate concerning the status and relationship of the three elements of artist, artwork, and audience in the very different processes leading to the production of film's images and literature's words; and prominent among these issues is the concept of authorship and the role of the writer. From the early bang of the clapsticks on the slate board announcing "Le Jeux," ***The Player declares itself a self-reflexive creation and announces its intention to draw power from that stance—not merely from mimetic representation, the traditional source of film's power. Further, the film declares its historic consciousness of the medium's history, for the very first image on the screen is a shot of a painting representing a turn-of-the-century scene with a model posing in front of a painted backdrop for a cameraman, with a writer, pen in hand, sitting beside him; from this "birth-of-cinema" scene, the film then cuts to its famous eight-minute shot detailing the hustle and bustle of the contemporary studio production process at work.

Self-awareness in the service of originality is creative, worthy of an *auteur;* but self-reflexivity alone, without new vision or growth, soon becomes originality's inversion, self-parody. In Altman's ***The Player*** self-parody is the condition of today's Hollywood film industry, and many of the writers who seek to be players in it. This false, parodic self-reflexivity is abundantly evident in the film's opening sequence. Adam Simon, the first writer who buttonholes Griffin on his way in from the parking lot and "pitches" to him, dismisses film's traditional realistic/representational base by declaring that in today's cinema there's "no history, only mythology." Then Buck Henry, scriptwriter of *The Graduate,* seems to prove Simon right when he espouses an anti-historical "timeless star" mythology in his pitch for *The Graduate Two*—all the characters are twenty years older, but when played by the same stars, also twenty years older, as Buck suggests, could they possibly be as interesting as they first were? Then we see two women writers change their story in mid-pitch, chasing after Griffin's whimsical suggestions, only to end up pitching a *Goldie Goes to Africa* script in a spur of the moment sellout so ridiculous that it made the audience in my theater laugh out loud.

Over and over in the film Altman makes the audience become aware of itself, and at least subconsciously, through its laughs or its surprise, acknowledge its own taste for, and complicity in, the zany, self-parodic, sellout mentality that begets studio films and studio people. Sometimes Altman consciously turns the spectators' "laughter at" the satirical picture and deepens it into the surprise of self-recognition, as in the scene where the detectives chant "one of us, one of us," à la Todd Browning's *Freaks,* and then laugh so intensely and loudly at Griffin's squirming discomfort that he panics and looks straight through the camera at the audience—Altman's extreme close-up of this eye-contact shot had a jolting effect on the laughers in my theater. The film's opening vignettes satirically introduce themes to which the film returns often, including several key assumptions of the traditional concept of authorship: In this Hollywood system, film concepts are almost wholly audience-driven, and so the producer can vie with the writer for the claim of authorship; the success, even the very chance to create the artwork (aka "product") doesn't depend so much upon what the artist knows—either his genius or craft—but upon who he knows—it may be more important that he can produce a star like Bruce Willis than that he can write a believable character for Bruce to play (actually the film makes the point that Bruce is one of those stars who can only play himself). Originality of vision is decidedly secondary to ability to imitate previously successful film models (*Ghost* meets *Manchurian Candidate*), to knowledge of how much they grossed ("250 million before video release"), to awareness of possible publicity pitfalls ("does political scare you?"), and most of all to the story's need to mirror the fantasy values of the audience by delivering what the producer-players universally insist is the *sine qua non,* "a happy ending."

But where the film satirizes the writer from the outset, the novel begins explaining the systemic causes of the writer's

sellout early on, thus preparing the reader to accept the postcard writer as a moral scourge and standard-bearer for all writers—not just the eccentric case he seems in the film. Soon after, Tolkin has an independent producer who has made five movies express the general anger of writers and film *auteurs* of all stripes toward the new breed of producer exemplified by Griffin, who is scorned as the studio "executive . . . the corporation man . . . not a moviemaker, not a showman" but rather the misnamed producer who doesn't actually make anything. In the film, on the other hand, it is only near the end that Griffin explains that out of thousands of scripts the studio turns only twelve a year into movies. Thus in the film the plight of the writer and the specific causes of it are less important to the story than the overall Hollywood psychology/mentality within which all would-be Hollywood authors have to operate. This mentality generates the hatred for the system of the player's film-long antagonist—and some would say ultimate conqueror—the postcard writer.

In the film his menacing presence is seen first when Griffin receives a common, drugstore variety picture-postcard of a movie audience, titled "Hollywood." The appropriateness of this first postcard picture is captured best in a quotation from the novel, one which expresses an important theme of the film. Griffin angrily declares that if the Writer "thought himself better than the movies, better than Hollywood, then Griffin wanted the last words the Writer would ever hear to be the player's credo: 'I love the audience, I am the audience.'" The postcard writer knows exactly how much of the producer's power and, from the point of view of the artist, his negative influence in the system comes from this total identification with the money-paying audience; and so the writer knows he can threaten Griffin on many levels by emending the original "Hollywood" postcard to read "Your Hollywood is Dead." Soon after, the postcard writer intensifies his menace with another card, which declares himself "Highly Dangerous." However, while the postcard word-and-image technique works well in the novel, in the film these cards are noticed by the viewing audience primarily for their sender's scribbled messages, not their images. What the film does offer for visual inspection and reflection, instead of Tolkin's postcards, is in fact Altman's pervasive use of cinematic style to present a satirical commentary on the story.

The murder of the writer Kahane is the second sequence important for delineating the role of the writer and Altman's concept of authorship within the film. Griffin's killing of Kahane is best understood as the middle scene of a triptych which begins with Griffin's visit to *The Bicycle Thief* and concludes with Larry Levy's executive meeting to discuss eliminating writers from the movie production process. The relevant facts about *The Bicycle Thief,* the first part of the triptych, are that it is presented here as an icon for all non-commercial art films, it has an unhappy ending, and it is a story about the difficulty of being sure of what one sees; in all these aspects it is the antithesis of, and challenge to, the Hollywood system Griffin represents. It is a scene that makes a subtle comment on the widely held notion that "seeing is believing," as applied to film audiences. Kahane seems to the viewer to be asleep when Griffin stumbles over his feet in the aisle upon entering the dark theater, yet later the writer demonstrates that he saw Griffin come in only ten minutes before the movie's end. On the other hand, the viewer sees that a wide-eyed woman in *The Bicycle Thief* audience, a character who later proves to be crucial to the plot because she declares to the police that she saw Kahane's murderer, actually has Griffin in her sight line several times (including once while he's talking with Kahane); but at the police line-up she fails to pick Griffin out of five men, "swearing" instead that the detective in the line-up was the murderer she saw.

The changes in the character of Kahane from novel to film are instructive as to Altman's intentions for his film. In the novel Tolkin presents Kahane as a wholly innocent victim. The murder scene in the book reveals the depth and pervasiveness of Griffin's sociopathic personality—he kills without obvious passion, and completely without provocation, and afterwards he feels not remorse but an unnatural desire for his victim's mate. Both the murder scene and further events in the novel make the reader see Griffin as a sociopathic personality type whose deviancy is emblematic not just of the film production process he serves, but also of the cool, dispassionate, and detached relationship of the medium's images and the reality they represent (in the film some of this latter theme is picked up in June G's separation of sign from signifier in both mediums of words and images—she, like Griffin, is a manipulator of vision who refuses to acknowledge reality). But in the film's murder scene, the aggressive behavior of a very different kind of Kahane invites Griffin's attack—in fact, Kahane pushes Griffin over a railing before Griffin becomes enraged and strangles him. This crucial change from novel to film, from Kahane as a passive, reflective writer-victim to Kahane as an aggressive and action-oriented writer-challenger, changes the story emphasis, from the novel's analysis of the philosophical nature of the film medium to the film's analysis of the economic nature of the Hollywood production system. In this shift, the writer's role of moral scourge and moral standard dissipates, to be supplanted by the role of the film medium's true *auteur*—here Altman himself—the self-aware, creative, audience-challenging director.

Through these changes in character and story Altman is telling us that it is the maker of the cinematic story who is the *auteur,* the source of its energy—not the writer of a script, nor the executive producer nor the audience. Exceptionally persuasive in this regard are the *auteur*'s demonstrations of purely cinematic technique, such as Altman's use of over-

lapping dialogue as a transitional device linking Kahane's murder with the final, "eliminate the writer" scene of the triptych. As Kahane's strangled corpse lies in the red-tinted water the screen fades to black, while on the soundtrack rises from the scene Larry Levy's voice citing *Fatal Attraction* as an example of the role of the audience in replacing the writer in film making, saying as Kahane's dead body disappears, "who wrote the ending?—the audience." This transition, and the equally subtle use of ironic, *sotto voce* off-screen commentary at the film's conclusion (where children's barely audible voices sing "Na, Na, Na, Na, Na, Na," undercutting the too-perfect film color and content of Griffin's "happy ending" with his new, pregnant wife June), are only two of the many times Altman's film challenges the intelligence and cinematic awareness of the audience (two other oft-cited instances involve the many movie posters Altman uses to both comment upon and, in their obviousness, mock and thus destabilize the film's claim to verisimilitude, and also Altman's pervasive use of film stars as "extras," to demystify and thus reverse the usual star/character relationship thought to be so important to a commercial Hollywood film.

The different endings of novel and film regarding the writer reveal the ultimate intentions of Altman. In the novel's "Epilogue," its concluding two-and-one-half pages set six months after the action of the first 190 pages, the postcard writer sends Griffin a note from Seattle apologizing, and also $1,000 to pay for the car windshield he had shot out (*after* Kahane had been killed). The reader interprets the note one way—as an honest, moral, grown-up understanding of the earlier misdirected anger the writer had felt toward Griffin's Hollywood. At first Griffin himself seems to interpret the note this way, and the reader is ready for him to signal his own corresponding increase of self-awareness, change, and/or growth during the past six months. Instead the novel concludes with Griffin deciding to hide the $1,000 so his new wife won't find it. Only at this point, at the very last word of the novel, do we find out who he married—not Bonnie the story editor (whom he sets up to have fired in the film), but the owner of Kahane's Saab—June. So, as the novel ends, Griffin is an unredeemed sociopath, having been no more affected by the writer's confession than he had been by Kahane's murder. In the novel he remains till the end as the continuing foil to the writer's higher moral vision.

In the film, however, the writer suffers a fall from grace along with Griffin. In a telephone call routed through Levy's office the writer agrees not to reveal that Griffin killed Kahane, and thereby to "rewrite" Griffin's story to ensure a happy ending, if Griffin agrees to produce his story as a movie. That the voice of the never-seen writer sounds like, and uses the same language (to wit, the distinctive adjective "shitbag") as the angry writer who spoke at Kahane's funeral and accused "society" of killing him, makes this change from the novel's realism to the film's "happy ending" all the more a sellout of the writer's role as moral authority in a corrupt Hollywood. One might argue that the writer's exercise of power in the film, albeit through extortion, to force Griffin to produce his script is meant to show that writers, rather than producers or audiences, are or should be the controlling intelligence of a film. But one need only consider that the writer is doing exactly what Griffin does—selling out, changing endings, separating consequences from causes to please a paying customer, rather than staying faithful to the laws of the imagination that require every story to move coherently toward some kind of liberating conjunction of aesthetic pleasure and moral truth—to see the fallacy of that interpretation. But the question remains: why would Altman change the novel this way?

Altman intends his filmic vision to encompass the story writer and move beyond, to celebrate the *auteur*—the film creator who can rise above, and in spite of, the inherent limitations of the film medium in which he works, especially in this case the limitations imposed by the economics of the film production process. The writer who runs away to Seattle can't be the hero in the story of a collaborative medium such as film, though he may still be the hero of literature's tale. In *The Player* Altman creates a rebuttal to the arguments against the *auteur* theory: he makes a film that satirizes but does not run away from the presence of the commercial film system, with its stultifying drive for mass-market products; indeed, Altman has said, "Everyone in *The Player* is as much me as it is someone else. All that shitty behavior is mine as well as theirs." Instead, he sets against the banal *Habeas Corpus,* that oft-revised yet increasingly stereotypical film-within-a-film, his own masterly film *The Player*—a work far more cinematically complex and subtle than *Habeas Corpus.* Further, *The Player* succeeds in being far more attractive and believable than *Habeas Corpus* precisely *because of* such demanding qualities (not in spite of them). Similarly, Altman's film addresses rather than avoids the key question of what should be the role of the audience in the film process. He satirizes the audience's limitations, yet also demonstrates its possibilities by challenging its curiosity and intelligence in *The Player's* tour de force of cinematic techniques, which are designed to make the viewing audience question every one of its conventional assumptions about the relationship of representation and reality—conventions that are formed and routinized through watching thousands of hours of visually unimaginative television and movies. Altman's display of cinematic possibility is the primary weapon of the film, even beyond the satirical content of the story; and it demonstrates the true film *auteur's* power in a way the triumph of the writer in the story never could. Thus the role of the writer in the film *The Player,* unlike the novel, is to allow Altman the *auteur* to transcend it—for only the film medium itself can provide the weapons strong enough to expose and slay Griffin, the

medium's creature and manipulator—and only the medium's true artist and master can wield them.

Jonathan Romney (essay date March 1994)

SOURCE: "In the Time of Earthquakes," in *Sight and Sound,* Vol. 4, No. 3, March, 1994, pp. 8-11.

[*In the following essay, Romney discusses the daredevil nature of Altman's career, including his approach to* Short Cuts.]

The last word spoken in Robert Altman's film *Short Cuts* is "lemonade". We hear it as the camera tracks out over a briefly shaken Los Angeles, as two partying couples toast to survival in the face of a minor apocalypse. As so often happens with Altman, who is famous for his habit of scrambling soundtracks to the limit of comprehensibility, the word is audible but not entirely noticeable, certainly not impressing itself on you as central to the film's meaning. Yet, in an oblique fashion, that is precisely what it is—an operational password for the entire film. For 'Lemonade' is the title of a poem by Raymond Carver, and the poem's subject is also the film's real subject, as well as its structural principle.

Short Cuts is based on nine stories by Carver, who died in 1988 aged 50, having established himself as the poet laureate of small, desolate, claustrophobic middle American lives. 'Lemonade' itself is not directly adapted in the film, although its theme—What if this had happened, rather than that? What then?—is foregrounded in the episode involving Jack Lemmon, and runs throughout the film, both in the narratives themselves and in the way they interlock. In the poem, a man ponders on his son's drowning; he is convinced he would still be alive if only he had not gone to fetch lemonade that day. The lemonade, he reasons, would not have been there if only there had not been lemons in the shops. So he tries to pick his way back causally to a prelapsarian moment: "It all harks back to first causes, back to the first lemon cultivated on earth."

Carver knows there *is* no first lemon, and Altman knows it too. There is no way of untangling the mesh of cause and effect, hence the gloriously unruly tangle of chance that governs *Short Cuts.* The credits divide the cast list conveniently into nine family sets of characters, plus supporting players, but in reality the groups are not separated neatly from one another: rather, they intermingle, meeting, playing, straying with seismic effect into each others' lives. Each group has its own story, but no story belongs solely to one group. Altman plays with an illusion of order by framing the narratives between two urban catastrophes during which all the characters are effectively united simply by virtue of being in the same boat. The sense of unity is illusory, though, imposed as it is by narrative contingency. There is no start or finish, no first or last lemon, only the all-pervasive smell of lemonade. Savour it, or balk at its bitterness, that's all you get in life, and you have to drink it.

There is no first lemon in Robert Altman's career, either. Looking back on the director's exceptionally diverse history, no clear thread is immediately apparent. We can impose an overall narrative on it, but only if we give in to the temptation continually to ask, 'what if?' There is the fact that after the international success of his 1969 film *M*A*S*H,* Altman went on to make a number of movies whose eccentricity wilfully flew in the face of box-office logic—the flight fantasy *Brewster McCloud,* the dreamlike *3 Women,* the bleak science-fiction vision *Quintet.* He also made some that worked over genres in a way that seemed to tap in directly to the sceptical Zeitgeist of the 70s—notably his brutal demystifications of the frontier Western and the Philip Marlowe myth in *McCabe and Mrs Miller* and *The Long Goodbye* respectively.

But *what if* Altman's career had been more coherent? *What if* his 1980 shot at a grandly fanciful comic-book epic, *Popeye,* had been the intended box-office smash? (Indeed, *what if* its star Robin Williams had actually been audible at any point in the film?) And *what if* the administration at Fox had not suddenly changed just in time to scupper the commercial hopes of his 1980 satire *Health?*

Pure speculation, of course, but all these factors contributed to one of the exemplary adventures in American cinema—the strange situation in which the most ambitious, wayward director of his generation (Altman, remember, preceded the Class of Movie Brats) suddenly found himself having to reinvent his career on a shoestring, having blown his luck not only with the major studios but also with his own ill-fated production company Lion's Gate. Hence an extraordinary spate of low-budget ventures into chamber cinema, often drawn from theatre: the remarkable one-hander for Richard Milhous Nixon, *Secret Honor,* which did for Tricky Dicky what Syberberg did for Hitler; *Fool for Love, Come Back to the 5 & Dime Jimmy Dean, Jimmy Dean.* There were other off-the-cuff projects for television, such as the adaptations of Pinter's *The Dumb Waiter* and *The Room,* and a version of that creaky tub-thumper *The Caine Mutiny Court-Martial,* a small miracle of a film which testily jump-started that somnolent genre, the courtroom drama.

It's tempting to consider that had Altman's Hollywood fortunes been more consistent, this whole daredevil chapter might not have happened. Altman himself is sanguine about his whole story and aware of just how random can be the elements that impinge on his progress. Visiting Britain for *Short Cuts'* screening at last November's London Film Fes-

tival, he cited the example of his *Buffalo Bill and the Indians,* co-written with his protégé Alan Rudolph, and after *McCabe and Mrs Miller* his second scathing debunking of the legends of the Wild West.

"*Buffalo Bill* was released on Independence Day 1976, which was the Bicentennial of the country. Nixon had just resigned in disgrace, and the whole country was licking its wounds, and I come out with this picture and say, 'Hi folks, here I am, let me tell you what assholes you are and how America's myths are blah blah blah blah . . .' Nobody wanted it. At a different time in history, that film could have been a big hit."

Short Cuts too falls wonderfully into this schema of apparent randomness. Altman first read Raymond Carver's stories on a plane journey. Inspired by them, he started planning a Carver film, and got as far as selecting the locations and signing up a number of actors, including Tim Robbins, Peter Gallagher and Fred Ward. But finally the finance was not available. While pondering his next move, he was offered a project called *The Player.* Those same actors found their way into that film, which in 1992 turned out to be Altman's first commercial and critical success in years—as well as a modish *succès de scandale* among the Hollywood mandarins, at once outraged and flattered to see their world lampooned. *Short Cuts* was financed on the strength of that film.

The Player was notable for playing an extreme version of a trick that Altman had used before, and fully intends to use again—the interweaving of real and fictional universes. In *The Player,* a host of familiar Hollywood faces played themselves, raising the interesting question of what being 'oneself' might mean in a city predicated entirely on performance. But the most cunning variation on this effect came in Altman's television series *Tanner '88: The Dark Horse,* in which real-life US politicos including Robert Dole and Pat Robertson were drafted in to be encountered by Michael Murphy's fictional Democrat presidential hopeful. Altman intends to push the method further in his next production, *Prêt-à-Porter,* which he is filming this year in the Paris fashion world.

"In *Prêt-à-Porter,* we're using much more reality. There's not much reality in *Short Cuts,* except the presence of the game show host Alex Trebek [who appears early on in a concert scene]. In *Prêt-à-Porter,* I will probably push the mix between reality and fiction as far as I've ever pushed it. I'm dependent on it, because I can't recreate the amount of people in that world—especially when you get into the fashion shows, the press, the photographers. So I have to use a lot of reality."

Unlike *The Player, Short Cuts* plays less on reality *per se* than on the real. Carver's low-key, minimally stylised portrayals of the doldrums and zero moments in blue-collar living led him to be counted as a leading exponent of that amorphous school known as 'Dirty Realism'. He wrote about dead marriages, dead-end jobs, typhoons in teacups, minor misunderstandings that blow up into little household apocalypses—but apocalypses in aspic. What's remarkable about these stories is the way they merge explosiveness with absolute stillness. A typical story, one of those in *Short Cuts,* is 'Jerry and Molly and Sam', in which a fatigued father contrives to lose the family dog, then has to retrieve it. When he finally finds the dog, he simply contemplates it, and the story ends on a suspended moment: "He sat there. He thought he didn't feel so bad, all things considered. The world was full of dogs. There were dogs and there were dogs. Some dogs you just couldn't do anything with."

Altman and his co-writer Frank Barhydt take a very different approach. The episode becomes a source of high farce, the dog a benign comic focus for the chaotic rage of Tim Robbins' blustering cop. There's clearly more meeting the eye—more energy, more incident—in Altman's version than the moments of cold, clear deadness that Carver's original stories are imbued with. Yet Altman claims that he leaves out everything that Carver leaves out—and precisely what *that* is, he says, is "judgment, in most cases. I make a little bit more judgment than Carver made. I have a tougher task in a way. It's very hard to do films as minimalism, because the audience is there and they see every square inch of that screen. They see wallpaper and they see rugs and they see shirts and expressions and weather—until all of the descriptive passages that you have in a book are *there.*

"Carver uses no descriptive passages, so I don't believe a Raymond Carver story can be literally translated to a visual medium. So I just tried to take the feeling from Carver, the type of incident he dealt with, and express that in a way that tells the same story for an audience. I don't think that I could take any *one* of his stories and make a film out of it."

How did Altman and Barhydt decide which stories to use, and which ones would lead into which others?

"They do it themselves automatically. You take one base story, you throw it up on the wall, and it's like vines—they grow where there's space to grow in and out of one another." The image of vines perhaps expresses what's most peculiar to the film. It's certainly true that, as some Carver specialists have pointed out, the film does not strictly adhere to the writer's spirit; it's at once too upbeat and too cynical for that. It only rarely displays the stoic empathy that the stories solicit for their characters; instead, Altman's characters redeem the claustrophobic quality of their lives by the energy and charisma with which they *perform* (to the extent that some of these lives look somewhat glamorous *because* they're incarnated by the likes of Tom Waits or Frances McDormand).

But it is the connections between the episodes that make the film—the sense that they're all bunches of event growing on the same tangled vine. And it's when we become aware of the incongruity of these connections that the film transcends its merely anecdotal base.

There are moments of sublime embarrassment in *Short Cuts,* notably in the sequence where Jack Lemmon, as the estranged father of the son that he hasn't seen for years, turns up at the hospital where his young grandson is in casualty. It's a painful situation in itself, but the film pushes it further by having the father deliver a monologue recounting the banal indiscretion that years ago led to his banishment from the family. Here most of all, the spirit of 'Lemonade' (could Lemmon have been cast purely for a conceptual pun?) makes itself felt. The father's reminiscence represents a crisis in itself, but one that is totally inappropriate to the crisis happening in the hospital ward. It's as if he has wandered from one story into another, suggesting that life's most dramatic moments are the result of inadequate separation between different narratives.

"This is what happens every day of your life," says Altman, "but we don't recognise it so much because we can't take the involvement. Somebody gets hit by a car and you stop and look in the street, and you think, 'I don't want to see that,' so you go the other way. But people who *don't* go the other way see more of that story, and the people who are actually involved in that story have *another* story. These things go on all the time, and it's the juxtaposition of these lives that makes *Short Cuts* interesting."

The Carver stories operate on two levels. Each one is very much like a closed box, a miniature in which a single core of event, or lack of event, is to be contemplated—in the tradition of modernist short story narrative since Chekhov, Joyce, Mansfield. At the same time, however, the stories taken together, and the regularity of the themes and styles, make an overall human comedy made up of small mosaic pieces. *Short Cuts,* though, functions only through the concatenation of parts—the clash of micro-narratives sparking ironic parallels and negations off each other.

It's a technique that has formed the basis of what is probably the most celebrated strand of Altman's work. The idea of sprawling ensemble pieces made of varying, decentred dramas is one he famously perfected in *Nashville.* At one point he planned a follow-up, *Nashville, Nashville,* with some of the same characters, and *Short Cuts* could be seen as the pay-off of that aborted project (Altman plans eventually to make *More Short Cuts*). But there are variations to this approach. *Nashville* derived its unity from having different characters doing different business in one setting—a place that in its iconic status as an anti-Hollywood, America's great *other* dream factory, opened the film up to an allegorical state-of-the-nation reading. *A Wedding* similarly used a single setting, this time to follow the conventions of situation comedy to their extreme conclusion.

Short Cuts differs from *Nashville* in its relation to place—it is not primarily the portrait of a specific city, but simply uses Los Angeles as a convenient, anonymous venue to bring its various protagonists together. (As Frank Barhydt points out, "apart from the palm trees and the weather, there's nothing indigenous to LA, nothing in the characters of the people.") However, the city's anonymity brings its own meaning to the film. Where the city of Nashville forms an arena in which individuals intermingle, with politics and country music as the uniting factor, *Short Cuts* captures the cellular essence of LA, a city in which separate zones, separate homes, are linked by highways. You can imagine each segment to be equivalent to a family cell—and things start happening when characters step out of their own territory into other people's. The theme is seen in undiluted form in the episode based on the story 'Neighbors'. In the film, there is no life-transforming catastrophe as there is in Carver's story. A couple simply make free with the apartment they're caretaking; but our sense of unease is no less powerful, just because we expect the worst—we know they should not be there. As with the Jack Lemmon episode, we receive a sense of *trespass:* lines have been crossed.

Despite the sense of impending chaos that is perhaps inevitable in a film that juggles 22 lead parts, there are plenty of guide rails in *Short Cuts* to ensure that we know where we are. One is the use of familiar faces in the cast. ("I don't have to tell you too much about these people," says Altman. "You do the work for me by recognising them.") Another is the use of a nightclub singer, played by Annie Ross, to act as a chorus, casting a sardonic torch-song commentary throughout the film. And another is the way the diversity of incident is framed between the two minor apocalypses.

At the beginning of the film, the city is sprayed against medfly, a pest which leaves harmless blemishes on fruit (what could be more suggestive of the Californian obsession with cosmetic surfaces?). The end of the film—which, beware, this paragraph reveals in full—is rather more violent. At the very second that Chris Penn's repressed, brooding character Jerry unexpectedly smashes a rock down on a young girl's head, an earthquake erupts. It's a horribly suggestive moment. Perhaps Jerry's pent-up rage is the entire city's; perhaps, because of him, heavenly wrath is being visited on the community. But you could read it more cynically as a self-conscious sleight of hand, a playfully apocalyptic gesture in which Altman plays God and brings all the film's diffuse threads together, packing all his characters back in the narrative toy box.

"That's just coincidence," Altman says of the ending. "I'm

sure that for every earthquake that's ever happened, some very strong, acute dramatic event has happened in somebody's life—I just happened to be there at this particular incident. I needed to polarise the beginning and end of the film—these people's lives never really came together, they just occasionally crossed in a very haphazard way, so that's something that was a common experience. I wouldn't be surprised if in *More Short Cuts* there'll be another two events. One of them might be the California fires."

This closing image of the all-powerful narrative deity suggests a director who likes to keep a tight rein on his creation. But, Altman says, only one type of control interests him: "the control to be able to change and let ideas come in from my collaborators. To have the ability to say 'Yeah' and turn the piece this way or that. *Not* say, 'Wait a minute, you said you were going to do this and you'd better stick to it.'"

Altman's list of recent and future projects may suggest a sense of multi-directional crazy-paving, but there's a flexibility and ambition there that he's always had, and that directors a third his age rarely evidence. Already chalked up: a stage opera version of the novel *McTeague* (the source of Von Stroheim's *Greed*), with composer William Bolcom; a short documentary recording the hoofers' musical *Black and Blue:* producing Alan Rudolph's new film *Dorothy Parker,* itself a multi-character sprawler in the Altman tradition. Planned after *Prêt-à-Porter:* a Mata Hari project; another collaboration with Frank Barhydt about Kansas City's boomtown years during the Depression; a two-film version of playwright Tony Kushner's Aids diptych *Angels in America;* a film called *Cork* with Harry Belafonte, "about blackface and entertainment from the turn of the century". Altman admits, "I'll never do all of those. It's like *pommes frites*—you throw the potatoes in and then whichever one pops to the surface is done first."

Altman also offers another, perhaps more apposite analogy, that applies just as well to his career as a whole—reckless, unruly, wilfully patchy—as it does to particular films like *Short Cuts.* "It comes down to what occurs to me. It's like doing art—I'm not doing Rembrandts or Corots, I'm doing Rauschenbergs. I'm doing collages. If suddenly I want to stick into my painting a photograph of a flat-iron, it just goes in."

Michael Wood (review date 10 March 1994)

SOURCE: "Why the Birthday Party Didn't Happen," in *London Review of Books,* Vol. 16, No. 5, March 10, 1994, p. 19.

[*In the following review, Wood shows how the stories Altman presents in* Short Cuts *differ from the Raymond Carver stories on which the film is based.*]

Robert Altman's **Short Cuts** is a long, loose-looking movie, but the looseness is an effect, carefully worked for. Plenty of themes recur throughout—insecurity, chance, rage, damage, the long, bruising war between men and women—and although there are fourteen or fifteen stories here (based on, extrapolated from ten stories by Raymond Carver—the hand-outs and the introduction solemnly say nine stories and a poem, but the so-called poem is also a prose narrative), they are intricately stitched together, like a miniaturised *Comédie humaine* set in Los Angeles.

A doctor in a story of his own (about his delayed reaction to his wife's ancient infidelity) has dinner with a couple from another story (about the husband discovering the corpse of a young woman), and in yet another story he treats a child who has been hit by a car. The child's parents are the neighbours of an aging jazz singer and her difficult, cello-playing daughter. Both families have their pool cleaned by a character in another story whose wife specialises in talking dirty on the telephone for money. Two of the women in different stories are sisters, and speak to each other regularly. The husband in one story is sleeping with the ex-wife in another. The pool-cleaner is a friend of a joky fellow who is attending horror make-up school, learning how to convert human faces into images of disaster. This fellow in turn is married to a young woman who is the daughter of the couple who . . . You get the picture. There are helicopters at the beginning, borrowed from *Apocalypse Now,* spraying insecticide rather than napalm, flying over all the lives in the film; and everyone is shaken by the earthquake at the end.

The construction is elaborate but not obtrusive in the viewing, and it has an echo in the way Altman moves us from scene to scene—sometimes by sheer jumps, sometimes with cuts which are an elegant mockery of natty editing, from a slow zoom onto a glass of milk, for example, to a shot of a glass of milk being knocked over on television in someone else's house. There are marvellous connections in the soundtrack—a door slams on the beat of the jazz number to be played in the next scene, a song continues over a scene which has no narrative link to the jazz club—and the result is to make *all* the scenes potentially part of each other, however separate they initially seem. The film is casually artful, rather than just casual or just artful. This is something the title suggests too: these are quick takes on the slow messiness of life, but they are also elements of counterpoint, one take commenting quickly or obliquely on another.

Altman, in his introduction to the volume of Carver stories, says his film lifts the roof off different family homes and watches what happens—and it 'could go on for ever'. It

doesn't go on for ever, and the roofs are not lifted off at random. Altman also says he sees 'all of Carver's work as just one story', which is entirely wrong about Carver, but a good way of thinking about this film. It doesn't have *Nashville's* berserk energies, but it is trying for the same kaleidoscopic feel, and it often gets it. It's a more ambitious, if less witty film than **The Player,** and when it goes wrong it's not because Altman loses control or strays too far from Carver; it's because he can't resist a certain sermonising gloom. Tess Gallagher, Carver's companion for the last 11 years of his life, and a great fan of Altman, says in her introduction to the screenplay that the finished film evokes 'a purgatorial world which is probably franker, even more lost than Carver's—and therefore more anguished for its unattended wounds'. That is a way of putting it. It seems to me that Altman has bought the Hollywood mythology he so brilliantly mocks in **The Player.** When he speaks of avoiding Hollywood and Beverley Hills for his setting, going for the 'untapped Los Angeles' of Downey, Watts, Compton, Pomona, Glendale, the very idea has Hollywood written all over it; and he really does think there is a gritty integrity in the very notion of the unhappy end—that unhappiness, unlike happiness or anything else, *is* meaning, you don't have to understand it or interpret it. Carver's hit-and-run driver, for instance, becomes nice Lily Tomlin, who stops her car, and is relieved to see that the boy seems all right. He can walk and talk, and he refuses the lift she offers him. Of course, he's not all right, he soon falls into a coma which lasts for most of the movie, and then he dies. In case we don't get it, there are scenes where Lily Tomlin keeps expressing her relief that the boy wasn't hurt. 'If I'd been going faster I woulda killed him. Imagine. How could you get over that? You couldn't.' In a related story, the only one which has no basis of any kind in Carver's fiction, the cello-playing daughter tries to talk to her jazz-singing mother about the little boy's death, but the mother is too busy rehearsing. The cellist kills herself. Incomprehension everywhere.

The great moments in the film—there are a number of them—have a quite different, far less dogmatic feel. They are all about violence, and often about incomprehension, but they don't have the flattened, that's-the-way-it-is tone that the film slips into when it loses its edge. Perhaps this was Altman's idea of a screen equivalent for Carver's prose deadpan. Tess Gallagher says she suggested to Altman that he restrain his irony, but he may have taken the hint a bit too far. 'Ray never raised himself above the plights of his characters,' Gallagher tells us she told Altman. Well, no, but he never treated the plights of his characters as just one of those things either, and still less as just one of those expected things, the lousiness you're always on the look-out for. Without his irony, Altman just seems morose.

Altman and Gallagher insist quite rightly on the freedom of

the film from the prose fiction. It is 'based on the writings of Raymond Carver', the credit says, it's not the film of the book(s). In some cases—the story of the child and the accident (and the birthday cake that was not picked up), for example—Altman is very close to Carver's material; in others—the story of the couple who look after another couple's apartment is one—he takes the faintest starting clue; in others—say the story of the wife's old infidelity—the basic situation. This is straightforward, but muddled a little by the publications and publicity accompanying the film, which suggest a near-identity between film and fiction, as if we were getting special value here, the film, the book, and a film which is mysteriously the same as the book and different. The film trades on its association with the great dead writer, all the greater for being dead; the publishers get a new book by producing, as a collection, the stories used for the film (they come from four separate Carver works). So it's probably worth saying that Altman's virtues are almost always different from Carver's, and that there is also a sense in which the two men's views and practices are not just different but opposite.

I'm not sure Altman himself quite sees this; there is a Hollywood haze about his vision of Carver. Carver captured, Altman says, 'the wonderful idiosyncrasies of human behaviour'; but Carver's people are not wonderful or idiosyncratic. They are dreadfully ordinary, steady, predictable. Little cracks open up in their lives, bewilderment or pain seeps through, but then the story ends, the cracks close, life goes on. A man who feels his life is falling apart looks at his face in a mirror, and can see nothing of what he feels: 'A face—nothing out of the ordinary.' Carver wants us to see what that face won't show; what Grace Paley calls 'the little disturbances' lurking unseen in the ordinary. Altman, as he says, has always been interested in the 'mystery and inspiration' of human behaviour, and many of his characters in this movie start out pretty exotic: one flies a helicopter, one is a TV news commentator, another is a professional clown; a couple who are schoolteachers in Carver become a doctor and a painter in Altman. There's the cellist and the jazz singer; there's talking dirty on the telephone, the horror make-up school. The implication, also interesting but quite different from Carver's, is that people with strange trades have ordinary hang-ups; that ordinariness creeps up even on the seemingly extraordinary; or that ordinariness doesn't exist. The side-effect of this view, though, is that when the working classes or the unemployed do show up in the film, *they* look remote and exotic, as if they had wandered in from a world beyond the borders of our expectations. Lily Tomlin is a waitress, for example, and Tom Waits is a working and then an out-of-work chauffeur. Altman thinks highly of their performances, which were 'so superb' that he felt the other actors might have trouble in living up to them; but they are actually one of the weak things in the movie, talented people hamming up roles that offer them

nothing but clichés. The actors who *are* superb are all those—Anne Archer, Madeleine Stowe, Julianne Moore, Matthew Modine, Frances McNormand—who get a chance to underact, to play through despair and calamity as if they were just everyday weather.

There is a moment in the film which is pure Altman, as good as anything he has ever done. The man who is learning horror make-up practises on his wife, makes her look like a viciously battered and finally murdered woman, and takes photographs of her in this state. It is a game, but very close to all kinds of things that are not games. When they pick up the photographs, they arrive at the same time as a man who is collecting his fishing photographs, including several shots of the dead young woman he and his friends found floating in the river. The people fetching the photographs bump into each other, drop their bundles, pick up the wrong set. They glance at them and see: a battered woman instead of their own drowned corpse; a real corpse instead of the imagery of their own nasty make-believe. Each person thinks the other is weird beyond belief; experiences his/her own weirdness as normal. No one says anything, although each notes the licence-plate number of the other. None of these people has killed anyone or hit anyone; only found a body and made up an image. But of course someone killed the girl in the river, and many pictures of battered women are pictures of battered women. Altman's very playfulness is eerie here. Of course there's a difference between violence to women and the discovery or the imitation of such violence. But a difference is not a divorce or an unalterable separation, and we can ask how the discoverers of the body feel, and what they do; and about the nature of the pleasure found in imitation. The movie multiplies these questions by its relentless if sometimes comic images of male posturing and female complicity; of wreckage and far from comic sudden murder.

The questions are delicately posed in the film's most indirect and understated story, which concerns the reaction of the wife of one of the men in the fishing party. The men spend about four hours hiking to their fishing spot, find the body before they have even started to fish; decide not to hike back straight away and report their find; leave the body where it is; put in a weekend's fishing, *then* report the discovery. The husband comes home, makes love to his wife. It's more or less the only happy bit of sex we see in the film: 'this is healthy and attractive sex,' the screenplay says rather primly. Afterwards he tells her about the body. She is disturbed, but sympathetic, and then says what seems to me, in the blossoming of its implications, the most haunting line in the movie. 'What'd you do? After you got her out of the water.' She can't imagine they *didn't* get her out of the water, still less that they didn't report the death for a couple of days. She clearly feels an unspeakable outrage was committed in this response to the dead girl, and the fact that her husband is a nice fellow makes it all the worse.

There are dozens of things to think about here, and the movie lets us think. 'She was dead,' the husband says in self-defence in both the story and the film. What was he supposed to do? In the story the wife says: 'That's the point. She was dead. But don't you see? She needed help.' If we can't help the dead, perhaps we can't (or won't) help the living. Altman is close to Carver here, and the story is as amazing as this piece of the movie. But Altman can show us, as the text can't, what the wife's stunned unhappiness, a form of grieving, actually looks like. She drives miles to the funeral of a person she doesn't know. In Carver, her drive indicates to us how vulnerable she feels, at large in a world of men: she could be that girl, any man could be her killer. In Altman, the camera just watches her at the funeral parlour, moving about her house, going out to dinner; it invites us to do what we can with her occluded feelings. The suggestion, I think, is not that even decent men like her husband are potential killers of women, but that no man is likely to have a real idea of what the violent death of a woman means. What it means to women, of course, or even what it means to men, since all we can do, mostly, is fidget in embarrassment and avoidance. Innocent men are not the murderer's accomplices, but they are often his compatriots; they inhabit quite comfortably the gendered mythology he has turned to nightmare. Altman's irony plays a part here too, since the wife is the person who is a professional clown, who on other days wears a coloured wig and funny clothes and make-up, and entertains at children's parties. We catch the clown mourning on her day off, but more important, we see the short cut from clowning as work to mourning as private exorcism, understood by no one. It's shorter than we think, like the path from the birthday party that doesn't happen to the murder we don't see.

Tom Shone (review date 11 March 1994)

SOURCE: "A Fishy Lot, Mankind," in *The Times Literary Supplement,* No. 4745, March 11, 1994, p. 21.

[*In the following review, Shone discusses the relationship between Raymond Carver's short stories and Altman's adaptation of them in his film* Short Cuts, *and asserts that "the union of writer and director is occasionally rocky, may in some cases have needed a little more guidance, but it has a weathered solidity."*]

There is a moment in the first half-hour of **Short Cuts,** Robert Altman's adaptation of Raymond Carver's short stories, when a man on a fishing trip with his buddies, having set up camp by a river, flips down the hinged shades of his glasses with a casual flick of his forefinger. It's a brilliantly mock-heroic gesture—a grey old man is suddenly transformed into something mean, menacing and ready to do

battle with trout. Among American directors, Altman is almost alone in getting such a thrill out of that sort of casual drill, and at moments like this—and there are several studded throughout his film's three hours—Altman and Carver seem a perfect match, a dream ticket.

They certainly appear to have a lot in common—a love of life's haphazard, messy edges and a delightfully come-off-it manner with melodrama. Carver apparently adored Altman's masterpiece, *Nashville,* and saw it several times. But whereas Carver's simplicity was born of a genuine distrust of sophistication, Altman's is born of intellectual nihilism, and the marriage of their sensibilities is a bit like a lunch between a Campbell's soup-can designer and Andy Warhol: you can feel Altman congratulating Carver on things he took for granted.

In the story of the fishermen—one of nine which Altman has chosen to shuffle—the differences between them begin to open up. Carver's original story, "Too Much Water Close to Home", has the fishermen discover a dead girl in a river, and records the domestic waves this causes when one of the men gets back home. Altman, however, has a cast of twenty-two to think of, correspondences to establish, points to make, and so he cuts from his American Ophelia to a shot of some goldfish in a plastic bag. This visual rhyme in turn forms part of a larger rippling of aquatic imagery in the film. Later, a similar cut links a girl floating in a swimming pool to a tankful of exotic fish, which float by to an accompaniment of spaced-out, new age chimes. The effect is one of glazed fascination; Altman seems to be gazing at his characters as if at another species—a fishy lot, mankind—which Carver, for all the iciness of his technique, never did.

Not that this is necessarily a bad thing; and in other instances, the liberties Altman takes with Carver's work are a positive good. In transplanting his characters from the Pacific North West to the suburbs of Los Angeles, Altman has, for instance, administered a healthy check to the febrile mythologizing of books like *Carver Country,* which reduced Carver to a series of aestheticized "dirty realist" trailer-park settings. Washing away a little of the dirtiness from his realism, Altman has spun the globe beneath the feet of Carver's characters, and softened their landing with healthier bank balances and occupations higher up the social ladder: concert cellist, painter, surgeon, TV anchorman.

The setting in LA's suburbs—a place where lives overlap, without connecting as they would do in a small town—has allowed Altman to have characters from different stories interact with one another, and thus make **Short Cuts** more than an exercise in cinematic channel hopping. For instance, the waitress wife from "They're Not Your Husband" is now also the driver who knocks down the young boy in "A Small,

Good Thing", and the boy's resistance to her distraught offers to drive home ("mom told me never to get in cars with strangers") is a touching commentary on the city's capacity for snuffing out kindness. Altman is careful not to let this doubling, sometimes tripling, of a character's dramatic load bend the characterization out of shape, and it is this care that pushes his movie into its third hour.

In its first two, at least, the movie never once sags. Altman cuts back and forth between the stories with a sense of rhythm never less precise for its languidity, and the film mosies along with an unhurried curiosity for small details, reaching an emotional climax with the death of the young boy, Casey—a sequence graced by superb acting from Bruce Davison, Jack Lemmon, and a small miracle of dazed grief from Andie McDowell. Altman can't avoid fiddling, though. It was typical of Carver to stop "A Small Good Thing" just short of melodrama; Altman does the same, but can't help self-consciously congratulating himself on the trick. When Casey first goes into a coma, a glass of milk by his bedside, Altman cuts to a TV advert in which a glass of milk shatters on the floor. Look, he's saying, look what I don't need to rely on to make my film dramatic.

This isn't a heinous sin: at least Altman keeps his irony in the wings. But elsewhere, a mixture of fluffs—both characteristic and wholly uncharacteristic—dot the film.

The last third is less successful partly because Altman's predilection for casting singers, rather than actors—Lyle Lovett, Annie Ross, Tom Waits—begins to wear. In all these cases, Altman seems to be using the singers' ready-made associations as a substitute for on-screen motivation. Ross's torch singer—a character Altman has invented—comes with a prepackaged world-weariness: the songs she sings (and which we hear too much of), "Prisoner of Life" and "To Hell With Love", sound like the titles of bad doctoral theses on Carver. Tom Waits, as the obsessive husband of "They're Not Your Husband", is a rag-and-bone bundle of marionette jerks, drunken rolls across the screen, and B-movie barks. Waits's 3am bleariness is everybody's idea of a Carver parody to begin with, so what you end up with here is a parody of a parody: Carver2.

More surprisingly, Altman's eagerness to empathize with his women characters forces him into needless repetition—"he's a sonofabitch" says one woman of her ex-husband; "he was a prick" says another of hers; "he's such an asshole" still another of hers. But these lapses are isolated, and *Short Cuts* is characterized, on the whole, by a staunch refusal to be tugged into generality. In fact, like the marriages portrayed within the film, the union of writer and director is occasionally rocky, may in some cases have needed a little more guidance, but it has a weathered solidity.

Kathleen Murphy (essay date March-April 1994)

SOURCE: "A Lion's Gate: The Cinema According to Robert Altman," in *Film Comment*, Vol. 30, No. 2, March-April, 1994, pp. 20-1, 24, 26, 28.

[*In the following essay, Murphy discusses some prevailing images from Altman's films.*]

In Provence, Vincent Van Gogh centers his easel in a field of glorious sunflowers. Robert Altman's camera darts about frantically, catching closeups of golden novas and overviews of entire restless constellations. Neither the director nor the painter can settle on framespace; like some sorcerer's apprentice, nature has generated a vertiginous profusion of forms, each potentially unique flower a momentary stop in a grid of pulsing yellow light. Finally, Van Gogh surrenders to chaos, smearing black pigment over his empty white canvas with a maddened hand, then tears a clutch of sunflowers out of the earth. Vased but still potent, these selected shoots become rich loci of thickly layered yellow-to-ochre pigment in painting after painting.

This extraordinary sequence in Altman's *Vincent and Theo* at once terrifies and intoxicates. Our vision is assaulted almost to delirium by the natural world's hot flux and largesse. Overcome and outcast by the sheer plethora of external phenomena, the artist-hero according to Altman must find some access to the heart of the matter. Racking focus, riding a slow zoom, framing a crowded, multiplaned field of vision, Altman's hungry eye can never get enough to contain the whole mystery. That unsatisfied appetite can feel like an abyss inside, dissociation or death.

The christs, madonnas, holy ghosts, magdalenes, and judases of Altman's mythology are all looking to take communion in some kind of company of saints. Though they fall far short of finding definitive food, family, and shelter—even in dreams and art—the director's high-flyers, private eyes, soul-snatchers, lovers and other strangers pattern a cinematic nervous system unparalleled in its complex vitality. Like some of his real and imagined communities (Lion's Gate, Presbyterian Church, *Popeye's* Sweethaven, Philip Marlowe's apartment building, La-La Land), this collection of eccentric synapses hangs on the edge of things, connected only by suspension bridges.

Altman's images work like poetic metaphors, each one webbing outward within and beyond its home-film, an ever-widening gyre that takes in his whole oeuvre. Tease out for a moment that thread of gold from *Vincent and Theo:* thirteen ways of looking at a field of sunflowers. In *McCabe and Mrs. Miller,* islands of golden light signal a whole range of sanctuary for the eye, from McCabe's striking the match that starts a movie/town, to the proliferating lamps and fires that glow against wilderness gloom, to a cold-comfort church in flames that unites a community, freezing out the maverick soul who dreamed up Presbyterian Church in the first place.

Mrs. Miller's plates of scrambled eggs shimmer like soul food, but she's no fertile Van Gogh, whose blackened teeth ally him in taste to gold-crowned McCabe (Warren Beatty), done in by a restless scrim of sunlit snow-motes. Constance Miller (Julie Christie) is a conspicuous, tidily corrupt consumer who knows the value of food and keeps it locked up in her heart. Paul Gauguin's her crueler kin, a judas who deliberately designs his food into aesthetic forms that are meant to kiss off and madden his better half. When Vincent Van Gogh (Tim Roth) lets wine flow out of his slack mouth, he is assenting to his degenerating mental health, but also flaunting the holy appetite that drives the way he takes in and passionately transubstantiates the world.

McCabe's an expendable auteur of lucrative mise-en-scène; Presbyterian Church's payoff will accrue to real moneymen after he's gone, just as, in modern-day auction, Van Gogh's sunflowers pan out in the millions. Mrs. Miller, McCabe's art director and accountant, focuses in on the brown bowl of an opium pipe until its curve becomes the molten edge of a sun. The poetry that McCabe had in him speaks out largely in warm shelters built of rich yellow lumber and his symbiotic attachment to his "Beautiful Dreamer," the whore with a heart of gold (literally), who sucks solar heat and sustenance into her very pupil as snow swallows him up. McCabe's crouched shape prefigures Theo Van Gogh's (Paul Rhys) naked form in a dark cell, his body bent, his face and arm upraised to moonlight, Constance made constant to the point of lunacy.

Van Gogh's struggle to find a way to look at his field of sunflowers falls on the same spectrum that carries BBC Opal's (Geraldine Chaplin in *Nashville*) skirmish with a screenful of yellow school buses she reduces to journalistic banalities. Further down the line, *Three Women's* Millie Lammoreaux (Shelley Duvall) uses a little imagination to color-coordinate her apartment, clothes, and car in shades of yellow, as though symbolic sun might fill and warm the void of her ghostly existence—though it's Sissy Spacek's Pinky Rose who will grow large with Millie's personality: an embryonic stage in the evolution of a trinity of women into self-sufficient matriarchy.

"We are all alone . . . on parallel lines," raves Mrs. Hellstrom (Viveca Lindfors) during *A Wedding,* the ritual that is supposed to "merge the interests of community and nature." Presiding spirit over yet another flawed union, matriarch of family and the movies alike, Lillian Gish lies dead upstairs throughout the festivities. When one of Altman's Miltonian storms drives the members of his teeming anti-family down

into the basement, a born-again Baptist leads them in a comforting chorus or two of "Heavenly Sunlight." Altman's camera eventually rises to the sky, as blue and noncommittal as *Nashville's* ending.

Gish is on the same wavelength with *Nashville's* country-music queen Barbara Jean (Ronee Blakley)—they share sweet smiles, dreams of what "My Old Idaho Home" once was, and death. Neither can be sustaining angels; as with Louise (Sally Kellerman), explicitly angelic mentor to *Brewster McCloud,* scars are where their wings were. The antithesis to these sweet-faced patron saints is *Three Women's* Dirty Gerty, the witchy head that, spitting in the face of humankind, screeches a mocking death-rattle laugh. The only angel in *A Wedding* is a black, blank-eyed *penates* at the door of Gish's home—its frozen posture and lack of affect an echo of Barbara Jean-wannabe Sueleen Gay (Gwen Welles) and her paralyzed stance against a fake Parthenon pillar in the aftermath of a kind of ritual murder.

Let the sun go for awhile, and track blackbirds. Brewster's fairy godmother carries a raven as familiar; presumably its shit adorns the dead faces of those who would ground her protégé—and it must share in Louise's terrible birdcry of bereavement signaling Brewster's fall, his flesh now too much with him for flying. Her white witchery is no match for Dirty Gerty's miring of all human endeavor. In *The Player,* moviemaker Griffin Mill (Tim Robbins) never aspires to flying; his white-robed *gudmundsdottir* (Greta Scacchi) makes him at home in her blue cave of unfinished, self-reflexive paintings; and both of these beautiful dream-stealers rest comfortably in mud baths. Leaning back arrogantly on an ebon couch, black-clad arms spread wide, Mill judases his jilted girlfriend and acutest critic (Cynthia Stevenson): "You'll land on your feet. You always do."

Louise's birdcry of awful loss and incipient madness is echoed by Brewster (Bud Cort), who doesn't land on his feet, and the crows in Van Gogh's wheatfield, the violent black lines that slash his Provence sky. Self-wounded, Vincent disappears into the landscape he would have painted, loosing a coven of crows into the air, as though his soul had flown up in agony.

In *Short Cuts,* where Dirty Gerty mostly reigns, Dr. Wyman (Matthew Modine), just one among many cuckolds, turns his white-painted clownface to the camera, opens his mouth wider than a mouth should go, and shrieks an *Invasion of the Body Snatchers* version of Louise's heartbroken caw. He might be one of his wife's canvases, hyperrealistic variations on Munch's "The Scream." When faultlines finally fracture under and within pool cleaner Chris Penn and he beats down the hateful flesh that so unmans him, a flock of birds explodes out of the underbrush, madness on the wing. At the beginning of *M*A*S*H,* wartime whirlybirds transported bloodied souls for healing; by *Short Cuts,* the blackbirds (camouflaged in patriotic red, white, and blue) spray America's City of Angels with a pesticide in the "war against the medfly." Maybe medflies are what we become after we've fallen so far from grace.

What refuge is there from blackbirds? Altman wheelers-and-dealers such as *M*A*S*H'*s Hawkeye and Trapper John (Donald Sutherland, Elliott Gould) and *California Split's* Bill and Charlie (George Segal, Gould) work desperately to be insiders, their cooler-than-thou shticks thin insurance against getting frozen out, disappearing, breaking down. Altman's eye so powerfully authenticates the illusion of community—among hotshot medics or gamblers on a winning streak—that when the house of cards collapses we're left with nowhere to go.

In the profoundly elegiac *California Split,* Bill and Charlie trip off to Reno's Land of Oz to rake in what they're missing—money and meaning. After Altman's rich movies take us in by offering food and shelter, they often conclude by striking the set and drifting off toward nothing. In the aftermath of his exhilarating run of play, during the final moments of *California Split,* George Segal's naked, utterly emptied expression reprises that of the tired boxer who much earlier gazed blank-eyed out at his energized audience: "It don't mean a fuckin thing." Altman's no warm-hearted wizard: When Segal, shattered, announces that he has to go home, fellow-player Gould nails him—and us as audience: "Oh yeah? Where do you live?"

Altman's isolatos partner at their peril; their projections and symbionts may be sanctuary or the death of them. McCabe's a "dealer . . . who wants to trade the game he plays for shelter" (a line from one of several Leonard Cohen songs that "narrate" *McCabe and Mrs. Miller*), but he's evicted from his House of Fortune—and every other refuge—by the efficiently business-minded whore and man-killer his less focused character cannot contain. *Three Women* dreams a fluid world in which twinning can anchor hollow men and women in increased visibility and co-dependent sanity. The murals painted by Willie (Janice Rule)—cannibalistic, lizard-like aliens, red of tongue and claw, poised outside an urban maze of sterile concrete boxes—are the nightmare aspect of McCabe's civilizing vision. They also preview the mute laughers? screamers? Marian (Julianne Moore) paints in *Short Cuts,* which ends with a pan from a party on the artist's patio out over a polluted city constructed on potential abyss.

*Three Women'*s Millie Lammoreaux begins as an invisible soul who babbles self-aggrandizing formulas for living that no one listens to. Cast out of even the fragile shelter of personality, she takes final shape as mother superior of a convent house that might be the last standing structure in Altman's dissolving world. In the film's finale, this angular,

American Gothic antithesis of a fairy godmother matter-of-factly warns her progeny—Pinky the tabula rasa and Willie the aborted artist—that "it's time to come inside."

There's comfort in that invitation, but also chilling cadences. At the beginning of *McCabe,* a long lateral pan follows the first coming inside of the postlapsarian poker-player, and Altman's promising trajectory draws us into his movie like any brand-new, privileged "Once upon a time. . . ." By contrast, the six-minute-long shot that opens *The Player* gleefully touts itself as tour-de-force, piggy-backing on *Touch of Evil,* promiscuously attaching itself to anything that moves, and playing postmodernist peeping Tom at a studio window—framing insider Griffin Mill as he receives pitches for sequels, remakes, and rip-offs.

Mill—half Mrs. Miller—won't be frozen out of any picture that matters. Eventually masterminding the takeover of his Hollywood House of Fortune, he lives happily ever after in a blandly edenic movie, his celluloid dreamgirl by his side. This is heaven as imagined by those who would buy into the satanic recipe for art benignly recommended by the doctor-"angel" (Jean-Pierre Cassel) who tries to make a pet of Van Gogh: "People need shelter even in paradise."

What's inside can be as "deceiving to the eye" as movies, as empty or as pregnant. The shack at the end of *Three Women* might be only a false front, like the James Dean Disciples' cherished Riata, or as deserted and debris-filled as the last Woolworth's in *Come Back to the 5 and Dime, Jimmy Dean Jimmy Dean.* "Sincerely" is the song that finally unites and celebrates *Jimmy Dean'*s trinity of 5-and-Dime dreamers: the de-breasted sex goddess (Cher), the deluded mother of a god's son (Sandy Dennis), and a Janus-gendered transsexual (Karen Black).

"If I could just walk into the painting, shut the door, and stay there forever," yearns Theo Van Gogh, just before the daughter of his brother's whore appears to try just that, squatting to take a pee in a panoramic, trompe-l'oeil beach scene that presages a wraparound Imax movie. Cut out of dead Vincent's imagination, blocked Theo can't make water—and is shut up first behind the door of his bathroom and then that of a madhouse cell, the fatally constricted space of a self divided from nourishing ideal. Much earlier, Vincent sketched like a man possessed when his prostitute-model settled down on a chamber pot, and lifted her lived-in face up to windowlight. All of Altman's froggy souls slide that line between shit and a fantasy of flying. (McCabe's metaphysic is the last word: "If a frog had wings he wouldn't bump his ass so much.")

Often Altman's shattering souls sojourn in glass houses, where epiphany seems as accessible as light: *Images'* Green Cove, where doors open and shutter like lenses; the much-windowed Wade beachhouse in *The Long Goodbye;* the 5 and Dime split by a Cocteauvian mirror; *Laundromat's* garishly neon-runed picture-window; the video-screened confessional in *Secret Honor.* Such Altman interiors are kaleidoscopes filled with bright shards of a past coterminous with the present, the most private and irreducible parts of ego and experience.

No other working director measures such depth in surfaces. Altman's movies are one, a round-table banquet and mystery play celebrating the persistent aspirations of his low-down knights and unfaithful ladies. His vision does not finally diminish us, though this is a Swiftian artist who can document our every smallness. Altman's greatest gift is his genius for images that can be critically framed, but resist being frozen into stop-motion significance. They lodge in memory like land-mines that never stop detonating.

Short Cuts' Lady in the Lake is one of those images. Altman's male triumvirate (Fred Ward, Buck Henry, Huey Lewis) fishes around, pisses on, and Kodaks her submerged and violated flesh. Her cold corpse is no catch for their larder; it's just the shell of a downcast muse who will never gift an artist-Arthur with sword or wings. And yet in the pesticide-drenched City of Angles, a poolman has assured us from the start that "water's the safest place to be." Robert Altman's golden eye has never stopped reflecting on this and other mysteries in the lifecycle of the medfly.

Robert Hilferty (review date Summer 1995)

SOURCE: A review of *Ready to Wear (Prêt-à-Porter),* in *Film Quarterly,* Vol. 48, No. 4, Summer, 1995, pp. 35-8.

[*In the following review, Hilferty states that, "Less about fab fabric than the tenuous fabric of society,* Ready to Wear *is an elaborate striptease of the human condition."*]

First, the facts.

Robert Altman's new film is not a "behind-the-scenes" look at the fashion world. Nor is it a particularly *fashionable* treatment of that world. Nor is it a conventional narrative complete with audience-identification protagonist and tidy plot. Nor is it much like *Nashville,* despite its many characters and multiple vignettes.

That's why it disappointed so many. The movie flew in the face of all expectation.

Altman's new cinematic panorama should be seen on its own terms first—then you can throw knives at the screen if you see fit. *Ready to Wear* is an idiosyncratic odyssey, an odd

essay film with its own peculiar pattern and design. Far from being "unfocused," "flimsy," or "vapid" (recent critical put-downs), every element in the film—even down to the dogshit everyone's stepping in—has a rhyme and reason, and builds up carefully to the sublime finale: designer Simone Lo's naked *défilé.*

Although the movie juggles about three dozen characters and their overlapping situations, there emerges, amid the hustle and bustle of the splintered narrative, a dominant story line—that of Simone Lo (Anouk Aimée)—around which all others revolve like illuminating satellites.

What gets things rolling is Sergei Oblomov (Marcello Mastroianni), a 70-something master tailor who leaves Russia after the collapse of Soviet Communism and heads west in search of the love of his youth, his abandoned wife Isabella de la Fontaine (Sophia Loren). To get to her, he has secretly contacted her present husband, Olivier de la Fontaine, who is head of the French Fashion Council. Olivier meets Sergei at the airport and brings him back to Paris, but during a traffic jam on Pont Alexandre III, Olivier unexpectedly dies a déclassé death: he chokes on a piece of ham. Panicked, Sergei hops out of the limousine, and the chauffeur screams murder. Sergei jumps into the Seine. Although he's been falsely accused, he's safe: the authorities can't identify him because the only evidence they have are photos of what he was wearing.

Everyone in the fashion world seems more pleased than saddened by Olivier's sudden demise. Apparently he wasn't such a nice guy, and despite several claims by TV reporters that his death has eclipsed Paris's most important fashion week, *prêt-à-porter* proceeds as usual without a morsel of mourning—not even from his wife. Isabella thinks her husband is no more than the dog turd she steps in at the beginning of the film.

Simone Lo (changed from the original Lowenthal) acts more the widow, and everyone treats her as one—it's no secret she was Olivier's lover. Although she readily admits that she didn't like Olivier either, Simone seems to have some depth, unlike the other designers, who come off as frivolous, trendy, and self-important. Simone stands out as a genuine artist. Simone's son, Jack (Rupert Everett), makes a witty remark to characterize his mother: "You know, my mother makes dresses for herself. Dressing for men has never particularly interested her, although she's certainly undressed for a few of them. The main difference between men and women in fashion is this: women make dresses for themselves and for other women . . . a man makes clothes for the woman he wants to be with, or in most cases, the woman he wants to be." This not-so-innocent comment, situating fashion on the gender battleground, inadvertently provides the key to the entire film.

These divergent—and possibly antagonistic—attitudes about fashion and its relation to women are played out on the body of supermodel Albertine (Ute Lemper). On the eve of the biggest show in Paris, she shows up pregnant. Albertine can't fit into the clothes earmarked for her, but on a deeper level, she now presents an image of womanhood totally unfit for the runway. Simone, however, is the only one who adjusts quickly and calls her pregnancy "wonderful"; someone like Cy Bianco (Forest Whitaker) thoughtlessly explodes at her because she's ruining his show. Albertine calls him "woman-hater."

Albertine's bursting belly raises two interesting questions which are at the crux of the movie: "What is the essence of womanhood?" and "Who's the father?" The first question is implicit in women's fashion. But clothing intended to enhance womanhood is usually in the service of some idea of "beauty," and the clothes may actually conceal, alter, or exaggerate the true woman underneath them. Women become fashion victims: they are trapped in an image of themselves that's not quite true, an image generated by male fantasy and anxiety over female sexuality. As Cher, who plays herself in the movie, says, "Fashion is about women trying to be beautiful, but none of us is going to look like Naomi Campbell . . . so in a way I think it's kind of sad . . . I'm a victim as well as a perpetrator." Albertine's pregnancy brazenly confronts and complicates the issue, as framed by the high fashion industry, and will ultimately be taken up in the final *défilé*.

The second question is, of course, the fundamental issue of paternity. When Jack Lowenthal asks Albertine, "Who's the lucky man?" she blithely answers, "Well, maybe it's you, darling." It sounds tongue-in-cheek, but the charge is a distinct possibility; Jack is a notorious philanderer (he's cheating with his own wife's sister). In fact, Altman creates an atmosphere of uncertain paternity: Jack doesn't even know who his own father is.

Altman's world is peopled with fatherless children and abandoned wives/mothers. The masculine penchant to flee the situation may be the basis of the warfare Altman sees being waged between the sexes not only in this film but in others as well (*Images, 3 Women, Short Cuts*). We eventually learn that Sergei abandoned Isabella on their wedding night to leave for Moscow.

"We were Communists," he says.

"*You* were a Communist," responds Isabella, "I was only fourteen."

Communism wasn't what it was cracked up to be, and Sergei ended up living in fear and poverty, making uniforms for Soviet officials. After Communism went out of fashion—

Altman cleverly hints at the fad quality of political ideologies—Sergei tries to regain his lost youth. In trying to recapture their youthful passion, Isabella plays a sensuous Salome to Sergei's faltering Faust (in fact, "Salome" and "Faust" are the names of mirror hotel suites in the film). Isabella reveals a body that's scandalously well preserved—she's the spitting image of ageless Eternal Feminine—and does a tantalizing striptease only to discover that her first husband has fallen asleep. (This magnificent scene is ingeniously reproduced from a film Loren and Mastroianni made together over 30 years ago, *Yesterday Today and Tomorrow*.) She leaves a note on his chest: "Two husbands, two corpses."

Twice abandoned, twice betrayed.

Which brings us back again to the main story line. Simone Lowenthal, like Isabella, was probably abandoned in some way too—that's why her son has no father. Betrayal rears its ugly head again, in the form of another male close to home. Jack, without the approval of his mother, sells his mother's logo ("Lo") to a Texan manufacturer of cowboy boots, Clint Lammeraux (Lyle Lovett).

"You know, you're worse than your father," says Simone.

"Whoever that was," replies Jack.

"You sell and buy everything," Simone responds, "even your own mother."

In spite of Simone's protest, Jack sabotages his mother even further. Behind her back, he arranges a photo session featuring the boots. Imprinted prominently and gaudily with the "Lo" logo, these boots eclipse Simone's spring collection ("These Boots Are Made for Walkin'" plays on the sound track). Simone has been stepped on, not only as an artist but also as a woman (since her art celebrated the female body). She is powerless.

Or is she?

By sending her models down the runway totally nude, Simone is revolting. She is making an explosive statement, not only in defiance of her traitorous son, but also, symbolically, against the entire male order. To pull off such a coup, the solidarity of her models is necessary. Preceding Simone's final showdown, a confluence of new feminine alliances is forged in different corners of the movie but indirectly connected to Simone's plight. For instance, the three fashion editors, who have been fierce competitors throughout the film, eventually join forces against star photographer Milo O'Brannigan (Stephen Rea). Throughout the film, he has humiliated these women by taking photos of them in compromising positions with a spy camera. They gain the upper hand after seizing his negatives, which include, not insignificantly, the treacherous boot shoot. At the same time, Jack's power starts to wane when his estranged wife and her sister, with whom he had been cheating, reunite against him. They call him a rat to his face.

Accompanied by the haunting song "You Are So Pretty the Way You Are," Simone's models take the runway. This defiant *défilé* doesn't end up defiling the female body with eroticization or desexualization. Rather, Simone presents Mother Nature's getup: the naked female body. This anticlimactic gesture might be considered ridiculous, even mildly pornographic, if it weren't for the presence of Simone's daring centerpiece, her pièce de résistance: Albertine's pregnant body, an impregnable fortress. Formerly banned from the runway, Albertine now rules it as a nude queen-bride, a fabulous figure right out of Botticelli's *Primavera*. Literally bursting with life, Albertine represents the feminine essence. With her, Simone unveils the primal beauty, power, and mystery of the female body: its ability to bear life—which all the (male-dominated) fashion in the world can't contain or control. Simone liberates the female body from fashion fascism, the mechanism which dictates, regulates, and disseminates images of women. (Altman laces his film with subtle and subliminal references to the Holocaust.)

The effect of Simone's *défilé* is not shocking. It's sublime.

Simone goes beyond making a feminist statement: the Eternal Feminine (think again of Sophia Loren's vibrant 60-year-old body), the origins of the species, the very beginnings of culture are put on display. As the new announcer of FAD-TV says, "Simone has spoken to women the world over, telling them not what to wear, but how to think about what they want and need from fashion."

(Altman creates an intriguing cross-reference by crosscutting a crossdressers' ball across town. As Simone's women undress, these men dress up. This juxtaposition visualizes metaphorically what Altman feels is really going on in fashion: men are not really making clothes for "real" women but for themselves. Or, to paraphrase Jack, they make clothes for the "ideal" woman they want to be with or the woman they want to be. A gigantic ice sea horse sits in the middle of the transvestites' banquet table. Why a sea horse? It's the only example in nature in which the *male* carries the fertilized eggs, a fact which underlines the central mystery of gender. In the case of men, no amount of dressing up as a woman makes a woman.)

Ready to Wear is mythic narrative in the guise of satiric spoof. What Altman envisions here is women's revolt, a *Trojan Women* for post-modern times. Less interested in high fashion than in why humans, who are born naked, cover their

bodies in the first place, Altman provides us with a menu of the uses of fashion—in concealing, revealing, or fabricating identity (ethnic, class, occupational, ideological, sexual, gender). And as one designer says, "Fashion is about looking good . . . it's about getting a great fuck." Therein lies the paradox: we dress up in order to undress (for sex). Joe Flynn (Tim Robbins) and Anne Eisenhower (Julia Roberts) certainly have no use for fashion: they spend the entire time under bed sheets.

In revealing the ironies and absurdities that result from the age-old conflict between culture and nature, *Ready to Wear* resembles *A Wedding* more than *Nashville*. Here, the omnipotence of nature asserts itself in two areas: sex and death. In *A Wedding*, Altman shows how a socially constructed ritual comes apart at the seams when realities which run counter to the order-defining myths associated with marriage constantly intrude on the party (infidelity, homosexuality, interracial desire, etc.). In *Ready to Wear*, it's also the body's desires and function which are at odds with the aims of high fashion.

Death frames both films. In *A Wedding*, it's the controlling family matriarch played by Lillian Gish; in *Ready to Wear*, it's the head of the Fashion Council. In both cases, death is presented as an embarrassment, an inconvenience, an obscenity, a reality that's not dealt with, ignored. That's the way of human culture. But the show goes on.

In the face of chaotic Eros and dead-end Thanatos, what the hell does fashion amount to anyway? This is a question Altman keeps on posing as he exposes the color-blind phonies, the glamour hounds, and the trend-trotting ignoramuses who dominate that world. Everyone has a fake name, nobody wants to be who they are, nobody knows who they are. Altman's world of fashion is ultimately as drab and unfab as what Cher (of all people) says: "It's not what you put on your body, but who you are inside."

In the last scene of *Ready to Wear*, Altman comes full circle and creates an ironic picture of the human life cycle. Seven naked newborns playing in the grass fill the screen. The camera pulls back to reveal that the toddlers are being photographed for a fashion ad. The campaign appears to be ripping off Simone Lo's "naked look." The slogan: "Get Real." As the fashion shoot takes place, Oliver de la Fontaine's funeral procession goes by. Isabella does not wear traditional black, but bright red. Perhaps this funeral is a cause for celebration: her liberation.

While Isabella may be making a fashion statement, Altman is not. Less about fab fabric than the tenuous fabric of society, *Ready to Wear* is an elaborate striptease of the human condition.

Todd Boyd (review date December 1996)

SOURCE: A review of *Kansas City,* in *Sight and Sound,* Vol. 6, No. 12, December, 1996, pp. 49-50.

[*In the following excerpt, Boyd calls Altman's* Kansas City *"aimless film-making."*]

"Kansas City here I come!" These are the words of Big Joe Turner's classic rhythm and blues song 'Going to Kansas City', and it's also the mission of film-making elder statesman Robert Altman in this homage to his hometown. Set in a colourful 30s world, in which the city is an oasis for the political party bosses, gangsters and jazz musicians who ran the show, *Kansas City* is trademark Altman, a series of interconnected episodes all linked to one central theme: the uses and abuses of power.

The film centres on the evolving relationship between two social opposites, telegraph operator Blondie O'Hara (Jennifer Jason Leigh) and her rich, laudanum-soaked hostage Carolyn Stilton (Miranda Richardson). They wander in and out of situations: the after-hours telegraph office at the railway station from which Blondie wires Carolyn's politically powerful husband, a bar where vote-rigging is being organised by Blondie's sister's husband (Steve Buscemi), a home for unmarried African-American mothers, and a cinema featuring Blondie's role-model Jean Harlow in *Hold Your Man.* But the only point to this somewhat aimless journey—other than for the two women to discover they have a lot in common once they get past their surface antagonism—seems to be to spin out the suspense as to whether Blondie's ploy will save her captive husband Johnny (Dermot Mulroney) from the vengeance of black gangster Seldom Seen (Harry Belafonte).

Yet the mundanity of the Blondie-Carolyn relationship by contrast at least elevates our awareness of the film's real virtue: its outstanding music. In 1934, Kansas City was a conservatory for jazz, especially the big band's of Count Basie, Jay McShann, and Bennie Moten. From these groups come many of the figures who would later become jazz legends including Lester Young, Coleman Hawkins and Charlie Parker (each of whom appears as a character in the film). It was the pervasive wide-open lawlessness of this town that supported the creative environment, and it is this larger environment that Altman's film tries so hard to capture. Using many of today's top young jazz musicians—Joshua Redman, Christian McBride, Nicholas Payton, Cyrus Chestnut—as some of the original jazz greats, the many musical scenes jump with a rhythm that leaves the rest of the film searching for a pulse. Because here, the multiple stories that Altman is so famous for weaving, are curiously uninvolving. In fact it would not be a calumny to say that *Kansas City* seems like an elaborately constructed excuse for some great musical performances.

Hollywood has long maintained a sub-genre of film that uses jazz as a cipher with which to explore America's racial politics. Films like *Young Man With a Horn, All the Fine Young Cannibals, Paris Blues,* and *A Man Called Adam* recreated the jazz milieu to engage, directly or indirectly, with the racial undertones of the idiom. More recently, films like *'Round Midnight, Bird,* and *Mo' Better Blues,* have likewise foregrounded race and culture in American society, but more overtly. Altman's *Kansas City* easily fits into this latter attitude. The racial politics of the 30s are mostly explored through the gangster character Seldom Seen. His Hey-Hey Club is a nexus which suggests that the city's colourful flavour is rooted in a perverted racial co-existence. Harry Belafonte is excellent as Seldom Seen ("but often heard"). He is a menacing presence who circles the room, smoking cigars, carrying his money around in a cigar box, and dropping words of wisdom in long lectures about the political situation. "White people are consumed with greed," he says to his captured white criminal Johnny O'Hara, who has tried to rob one of Seen's best gambling customers. He goes on to explain to Johnny that the Great Depression was because, "Y'all couldn't get enough."

Seldom's embrace of black political leader Marcus Garvey and his critique of the establishment are powerfully conveyed, especially with the music of a 'Coleman Hawkins' versus 'Lester Young' cutting contest playing behind him. But Altman does not seem to know what to do with him, spinning out the one basic scenario of him lecturing Johnny as to the white man's follies so that it lasts for almost the whole movie. The action is elsewhere, in gangster and election-rigging subplots, but whenever Seldom or the music is absent you feel the loss. At one point Seldom tells Johnny that the music of "Bill Basie's one of the reasons you ain't dead yet." This line could be modified to comment on the film. It is indeed the music that keeps *Kansas City* alive.

When Altman's *The Player* was released in 1992 many thought that this 70s Hollywood maverick had finally returned to form after a long hiatus. *The Player* was a provocatively satirical look at Hollywood's underbelly made from Michael Tolkin's wry script that made us realise how much we missed Altman's light touch with acerbic material. With *Short Cuts* in 1993, his ability to juggle multiple narratives and many characters was again transfixing, and seemed to suit the mood of the Raymond Carver stories it was based on. Yet the more ad-hoc *Pret-a-Porter* in 1994 lacked any real insight and *Kansas City* continues that film's pattern of aimless film-making.

This is highlighted by the grating performance of Jennifer Jason Leigh in the film's central role as the Jean Harlow-obsessed Blondie O'Hara, (she's a behatted brunette recovering from peroxide-induced baldness). Her trawl across the city with the equally irritating Miranda Richardson is pointless, a transparent excuse for showing off snapshots of the time and place. Out of the corrupt party politics of the Democratic bosses, the predictable self-indulgence of the wealthy liberals, and the blonde ambitions of O'Hara and her pathetic husband Johnny, fed by Hollywood. Altman weaves the tapestry of a city life that is long gone. But unlike *McCabe & Mrs. Miller, MASH,* or *Nashville,* Altman's finest movies, *Kansas City* never gathers its threads together. Nevertheless, Altman remains one of the few independent voices in a sea of repetitive Hollywood mediocrity. Films such as *Kansas City* at least attempt to focus on real people rather than computer-generated fantasies. And besides, any film that uses jazz as its source—America's highest art form—can never be given too much attention. For these things only, Altman and *Kansas City* are to be praised.

Richard Combs (review date March-April 1997)

SOURCE: "Kansas City, Kansas City, Kansas City, Kansas City," in *Film Comment,* Vol. 33, No. 2, March-April, 1997, pp. 68, 70-1.

[*In the following review, Combs discusses the lack of personal references in Altman's films, noting the exception of* Kansas City, *which is set in Altman's home town.*]

In his biography of Robert Altman, *Jumping Off the Cliff,* Patrick McGilligan charts some lost territory in the Altman story—lost in the sense that there are whole areas of the director's life that haven't shown up in his work. Altman was born in Kansas City, Missouri, in 1925, of German immigrant stock. The family name was originally Altmann, the loss of the second *n* prompting Altman on occasion to refer to himself as a "closet German." But unlike others of his filmmaking generation—say, Martin Scorsese and Francis Coppola, who are of different stock but have their Catholicism in common with Altman—he has excluded his personal, cultural, and historical roots.

McGilligan has counted the ways: "It is next to impossible to find Helen or B. C. [Altman's parents] explicitly evoked by a character in one of his movies." . . . "If Altman was touched at all by the mass despair, the unemployment, the protests, the riots and the Hoovervilles of the Depression era, that vivid backdrop is absent from his movies." . . . "In the one hour drive of some fifty miles from Kansas City to Lexington, one comes across markers for the Santa Fe Trail, the Lewis and Clark Trail, the old overland stagecoach lines, and for Indian burial mounds. And one passes over land that Daniel Boone explored and Quantrill's raiders raided . . . all

of it—with the exceptions of *McCabe* and *Buffalo Bill and the Indians*—curiously ignored in Altman's films."

With the release of *Kansas City* in 1996, some of that lost territory has been filled in. Altman has come out of at least one of his closets. This is cultural autobiography, a story set in the jazz milieu of Kansas City in the Thirties, eloquently pictured in a background article in *Time Out* magazine: "The Count Basie band came out of this regional style, taking the Blues uptown and jumping 'em. Those beefy Blues riffs and driving 4/4 beats came on like herding cattle across the plains . . . the city boasted the greatest conglomeration of clubs and sin since Storyville." Altman has said that by his mid-teens he was an habitué of the clubs: "I knew everybody, I felt welcome. I listened to Julia Lee, Baby Lovett, Bill Nolan, Jay McShann." He would have been 9 when the central event of the film took place—a cutting contest, during an all-night jamming session, between local boy Lester Young and the visiting Coleman Hawkins. Young was still on hand, though, to play at hops when Altman was in high school.

And *Kansas City* reflects more than cultural history. There are evidently personal memories woven into its texture. Altman has talked about the politician Henry Stilton, the vaguely presidential adviser played by Michael Murphy, as being in some ways a reflection of his father, B. C. Altman. Stilton's laudanum-addicted wife, Carolyn (Miranda Richardson), is "patterned after the mother of a kid I grew up with. I knew that she was on something, but I didn't know what it was." There may even be an explanation of why Altman's mother, Helen, has never been evoked in his films. "We had a black maid called Glendora Majors—I use her name in the film—who was responsible for my introduction to jazz. All my life, Glendora was more important than my mother to me. My mother was some other figure."

What is surprising, in fact, is that none of this background and these allegiances show up in *Jumping Off the Cliff,* although McGilligan devotes separate chapters to Kansas City, to Altman's family tree, his schooling, and his friends and lovers. In all matters of work, love, and play, McGilligan goes into detail on Altman's "whirling dervish" lifestyle. But this is not really to fault his book for missing out biographical elements he claims Altman has missed in his films. It might just suggest that there is more than one kind of biography—and more than one kind of biographical art that can be made from it.

A different Altman story could begin from different geographical and historical points. There is, for instance, the fact that there is not just Kansas City, Missouri, but Kansas City, Kansas—one city bifurcated. During the Civil War, this doubleness, or division, was a particular and turbulent feature of the region. McGilligan records, "Altman liked to point out that Missouri had supplied both sides in the conflict." Maybe Kansas City has to face two ways at once because, as Altman has also observed, it enjoys a special geographical status, which is what makes it so important in jazz history: "It had to do with the city being the center of the country. To go anywhere from East to West, you had to go through Kansas City, so it became a depot for trains and a stopover for planes. For musicians, it was the crossroads."

And from here we might take off into his movies. Doubleness, of course, is a fairly common movie trope, and doppelgängers and mirror images are the signature of more than one director—Joseph Losey, for instance, whom Altman has explicitly said he was trying to emulate in his first film to go into mirrors in a big way, *Images.* But Altman's looking-two-ways-at-once is something else, something both more fantastic and more concrete. In a sense, it's a mistake to think of it in terms of 'images' because it's not really a matter of reflecting surfaces. It's the basis of the real in Altman's world, a principle of dramatic construction and an effect as detonative as splitting the atom.

Think of the two halves of *Come Back to the 5 & Dime, Jimmy Dean Jimmy Dean:* two time zones back to back; two identical sets, one the reverse of the other, separated by a two-way mirror. It's a movie trick but not an optical one; it's done really, mechanically. Then there's the two families of *Fool for Love,* produced by one father, and also, as he puts it, out of one love: "It just got split in half." Twins proliferate, of course: within the mirages of *3 Women,* but also in the conspicuously real-life Hollywood of *The Player,* whose screenwriter Michael Tolkin plays one half of a writing duo within the film with his identical-looking sibling Stephen.

In *Kansas City,* Carolyn Stilton is roused from her laudanum stupor at one point by something she notices about her abductor, Blondie (Jennifer Jason Leigh), and the latter's sister Babe: "What I find fascinating is that both you ladies are married to men named Johnny." Blondie and Babe aren't twins, but then they don't need to be. In Altman, sisterhood alone, whether real or metaphorical, is itself a powerful matrix for the uncanny connections in life, and for generating new life. Again, this can run the gamut from the mixing and matching of personalities in *3 Women*—around the still, silent center of Janice Rule, pregnant and an artist with a mission—to the more prosaic sisters of *Short Cuts* played by Madeleine Stowe and Julianne Moore (though the latter, too, is an artist).

Which is where Altman's treatment of doubleness, doppelgängers, and mirror images separates itself from cinematic tradition. His fracturing centers on female rather than male protagonists, and even where the stories come close to the obsessive, haunted, self-repeating conventions of the

doppelgänger—in *Images,* say—they're not couched in expressionist or noirish imagery. There's scarcely a noirish shot in all of Altman. The mood is more one of drift and dream, the floating, drowned-world feeling of *3 Women.* That film is set in a desert, but its medium is aqueous, an amniotic fluid in which new lifeforms, or transformations of the old, are waiting to sprout. The fracturing in Altman is also a giving-birth. It's what saves the self-repeating from being an expressionist doom.

Even in *Kansas City,* a tale of jazz clubs and gangsters, of violent scams and corrupt politicians stage-managing an election, a tale centered on a double abduction, the medium is somehow a female one. Pregnancy is again an issue: the baby that Blondie had and lost; the baby that another character, a black girl, Pearl Cummings, has come to the city to deliver under the aegis of the do-gooding ladies of the Little League (whose leader, Nettie Bolt, is named after Altman's grandmother). They misplace Pearl and she is taken under the wing of the young Charlie Parker (Albert J. Burnes). And for all that the story hinges on the contest between Coleman Hawkins and Lester Young at the Hey-Hey Club, its mood is shaped by a succession of domestic interiors, a cross-section of Kansas City's interior life, as Blondie peregrinates about the city with her hostage, whom she dubs "Red."

This tale of two women is even broached in Altman's dream mode. The opening credits are broken up by Blondie's arrival at the Stilton home. In her gangster moll persona—a tough-talking snarling out of the corner of her mouth that she has modeled on Jean Harlow, even though she is temporarily bereft of the peroxided hair—she has decided on her own desperate scam. Her Johnny (Dermot Mulroney), a small-time hoodlum, has robbed an out-of-town gambler on his way to spend lavishly at the craps table run by the owner of the Hey-Hey, gangster Seldom Seen (Harry Belafonte). Johnny's accomplice is Seldom's black driver, "Blue" Green (these color-doubling names go back to *3 Women*'s Pinky Rose). But Seldom figures out the plot and grabs Johnny, to toy with him through most of the film.

Which inspires the bereft, lovelorn Blondie—a woman who will do anything to hold her man, as the title of a Jean Harlow-Clark Gable movie tells her—to try to get him released by grabbing the wife of Henry Stilton. In this town, it's politicians who can deal best with gangsters. But all this is explained only later. For the moment, Carolyn Stilton is merely confronted with the nightmare vision of Blondie waving a gun while a thunderstorm builds outside. This storm never seems to be delivered, but then the self-contained melodrama of the scene might just be part—as it is in *Images*—of the womanly medium. *Something* is about to be delivered.

The scene ends with a slow zoom into Carolyn as she gratefully reaches for the laudanum bottle being held out by Blondie, and then a fade to black. The rest of the film is a product, in a way, of that blacked-out consciousness. It's an effect that seems to signal an end rather than a beginning— as it does with Mrs. Miller's retreat into an opium nirvana at the end of *McCabe.* But then, the slow zoom in with accompanying loss of focus is Altman's most characteristic camera move. It suggests a letting-go, a slipping-away, the blurring into an altered state. And it can be traced right back to the beginning of this Altman genre in 1969's *That Cold Day in the Park,* whose heroine was prone to it without apparent narcotic assistance.

Altman's fondness for telling his stories through his female characters has often been noted. Patrick McGilligan relates that even as a raconteur Altman would take the point of view of a distaff member of his family—one of his sisters or his mother. *Jumping Off the Cliff* contains a photograph of the 12-year-old Altman bracketed by his mother Helen and his two sisters, not twins but dressed identically. There's said to be little of his mother in Altman, but the descriptions of her—"like an angel . . . on another planet, an astral sphere"—and one thing she is quoted as saying, "I am just drowned. It's like I am a nobody," suggest that she is not absent from his films.

Altman is apparently more like his father, B. C.: a demon salesman and great charmer, socializer, and womanizer. This, of course, is just the kind of male figure who is caricatured. treated as a sideline buffoon, in films like *3 Women.* But it shouldn't be assumed from this that the dream films, the women's subjects, are some sort of crypto-feminist making-amends. It's the double structure coming into play again, the yin and yang sets bolted together. Altman the partygoer, the seducer, the organizer of elaborate meals and entertainments, the social animal who, as all his collaborators attest, just wants to have fun, is also the personality who directs jamborees like *Nashville* and *Short Cuts.* Even if these, in the end, might not be his most profound films.

Kansas City is the Altman dream film that occasionally resembles—in its social canvas, its treatment of the jazz sessions, and the background of party machine politics—one of the jamborees. Or it may be that this is Altman's subjective cinema given historical meaning and form. It adds one important dimension to his double structure, or another kind of doubling: the presence of blacks. Perhaps this, as much as the municipal twinning of Kansas City, was the original doubling in Altman's life. There's that elision of his own mother with the black maid who introduced him to jazz via Duke Ellington's "Solitude," which is the final extended number in *Kansas City,* when Altman turns the film over to his musicians. Through the story wanders Charlie Parker's mother, Addie, who reassures Blondie that she won't tell anyone what is going on, because no one will ask her anyway.

There's a more sinister conjunction here, a bonding of doubles. Altman has referred to the territorial tactics of the different gangs in the Thirties, and how the blacks only had access to knives as weapons, just as slavery had shaped their music by denying them musical instruments. It's chilling, then, when he places the contest of the two jazzmen so close to another "cutting contest," when Seldom Seen's henchmen vie with each other in slashing "Blue" Green to death. And how much should this language and weaponry put us in mind of other Altman scenes—those played by his cutting heroines, Susannah York in *Images* or Sandy Dennis in *That Cold Day in the Park?*

In this respect, there's one powerful, unmissable connection. In the penultimate scene of *Kansas City,* Johnny is restored to Blondie, but dying on his feet, with his abdomen slashed open and emptied, like a mangled abortion, a terrible stillbirth. Blondie frantically tries to stuff her Jean Harlow gown into the wound, while calling for help to Carolyn Stilton, who is too laudanum-stoned to do anything until the moment she puts a bullet in the back of Blondie's now perfectly peroxided head.

In the penultimate scene of *3 Women,* Shelley Duvall attends at the messy still-birth of Janice Rule's child, while appealing to a traumatized, immobile Sissy Spacek. That scene was capped by the dream finale, the transmutation of all three personalities. All that is left for Carolyn Stilton is to emerge in the cool light of evening, to her waiting husband and no prospect of change at all. "You know what I didn't do today—I didn't vote."

FURTHER READING

Criticism

Bush, Lyall. Review of *Short Cuts: The Screenplay. Studies in Short Fiction* 33, No. 1 (Winter 1996): 145-48.
    Briefly discusses how the script of *Short Cuts* by Altman and Frank Barhydt differs from the short stories by Raymond Carver.

Dick, Bernard F. "Film Editing." In his *Anatomy of Film,* pp. 48-51. St. Martin's Press, 1978.
    Discusses the editing in Altman's Nashville.

Edgerton, Gary. "Capra and Altman: Mythmaker and Mythologist." *Literature Film Quarterly* XI, No. 1 (1983): 28-35.

Compares the different mythologies of America created
by Frank Capra and Robert Altman.

Additional coverage of Altman's life and career is contained in the following sources published by Gale: *Contemporary Authors,* Vol. 73-76; and *Contemporary Authors New Revision Series,* Vol. 43.

Yehuda Amichai

1924-

German-born Israeli poet, novelist, short story writer, and dramatist.

The following entry presents an overview of Amichai's career through 1997. For further information on his life and works, see *CLC,* Volumes 9, 22, and 57.

INTRODUCTION

An influential member of Israel's first literary generation, Amichai synthesizes in his poetry the biblical rhythms and imagery of ancient Hebrew with modern Hebraic colloquialisms to try to make sense of the dislocation and alienation experienced by many Jews living in war-torn Israel. Many critics describe Amichai's early work as intensely intellectual and reminiscent of the metaphysical verse of John Donne, George Herbert, and W. H. Auden. In his later work Amichai incorporates sensual imagery and vernacular cadences in poems whose simplicity and wry humor belies their existential, often tragic, undertones.

Biographical Information

Amichai was born in Würzburg, Germany, in 1924. When he was twelve, he emigrated with his parents to Israel. His family avoided the horrors of Nazi Germany, but Amichai lost many friends and relatives in concentration camps, a loss that has haunted him ever since. He served in the British Army in World War II and later with Israeli defense forces during the Arab-Israeli war of 1948. These experiences, along with witnessing Israel's other wars of the mid-twentieth century, strongly influenced Amichai's work; many of his poems and short stories revolve around themes associated with war and its aftermath.

Major Works

The turbulence of living in a society that is frequently at war has had a major impact on Amichai's world-view. In his poems dealing with sexual love, as well those dealing with war, he depicts human beings as ultimately separate and alienated from each other, unable to connect except for the briefest periods of time. Often he uses ironic humor both to distance himself from his serious themes of emotional and societal loneliness, and to emphasize in a subtle manner the mundane tragedies of the human experience. His poetry is frequently mistaken as lacking a comprehensive philosophical system because of his seemingly simple observations and syntax. But it is his ability to infuse ordinary moments of

daily life with extraordinary metaphysical meaning that first drew international attention to his work. Amichai first gained the notice of British and American audiences with the English translations of *Amen* (1977) and *Time* (1978), two volumes of poetry Amichai translated with the English poet Ted Hughes. Both books address the spiritual and political concerns of the Jewish people. Amichai's preoccupation with history and its impact on individual lives is evident in much of his poetry and in his novel, *Lo me-'akhshav, Lo mi-kan* (1963; *Not of This Time, Not of This Place*), in which a Jewish archeologist is torn between returning to the German town where he grew up and staying in Jerusalem to carry out his extramarital affair. The novel is generally considered a seminal work of Israeli Holocaust literature, investigating two options for living with the knowledge of Nazi genocide: with the past or denying it. In *Great Tranquillity: Questions and Answers* (1983), Amichai addressed Israel's troubled political history and its paradoxical desert landscape, which is both arid and rich with promise. "Travels of the Last Benjamin of Tudela" is a sequence of fifty-seven poems in which Amichai analyzes his Jewish identity by comparing his life story with legends of a wandering medieval rabbi. Published separately in book-length form as *Travels* in 1986, this work also appears in *The Selected Poetry of Yehuda Amichai* (1986), a compilation of verse from ten volumes published over a thirty-year period. Amichai's short story collection, *The World Is a Room, and Other Stories* (1985), expands upon many of his verse themes. While some critics contend that the stories are unstructured and overburdened with poetic diction, others admire Amichai's startling metaphors and sensuous imagery. In *Even a Fist Was Once an Open Palm with Fingers* (1991), Amichai again drew from biblical stories to illustrate the individual's struggle with history. *Yehuda Amichai, A Life of Poetry: 1948-1994* (1994) is a comprehensive collection containing representative verse from the time of the Arab-Israeli war through contemporary works translated by Benjamin and Barbara Harshov.

Critical Reception

Amichai is generally considered one of the most important poets of his generation of Israeli writers, focusing as he does on Israelis' painful and often ambivalent feelings about their post-Holocaust and post-liberation existence. His poetry is widely praised by an international audience for its spare, honest exploration of emotions many people find too painful to face. But Amichai is not without his detractors. Some critics find his work simplistic and missing a crucial core philosophy, since Amichai, like many of his peers, does not adhere to an orthodox ideology. Nonetheless, Amichai's work is admired overall for the strong, if sometimes sorrowful and confused, passion it displays.

PRINCIPAL WORKS

Akhshav uba-yamin na-aherim [*Now and In Other Days*] (poetry) 1955
Ba-ginah ha-tsiburit (poetry) 1958
Be-merhak shete tikrot (poetry) 1958
Be-ruah ha-nora'ah ha-zot (short stories) 1961
Masa' le-Ninveh (drama) 1962
Shirim, 1948-1962 (poetry) 1962
Lo me-'akhshav, Lo mi-kan [*Not of This Time, Not of This Place*] (novel) 1963
Selected Poems (poetry) 1968
Selected Poems of Yehuda Amichai (poetry) 1971
Songs of Jerusalem and Myself (poetry) 1973
Amen (poetry) 1977
Time (poetry) 1978
Love Poems (poetry) 1981
Great Tranquillity: Questions and Answers (poetry) 1983
The World Is a Room, and Other Stories (short stories) 1984
The Selected Poetry of Yehudah Amichai (poetry) 1986
Travels (poetry) 1986

Poems of Jerusalem (poetry) 1988
Even a Fist Was Once an Open Palm with Fingers: Recent Poems (poetry) 1991
Yehuda Amichai, A Life of Poetry: 1948-1994 (poetry) 1994

CRITICISM

Robert Alter (essay date 1969)

SOURCE: "Confronting the Holocaust," in *After the Tradition: Essays on Modern Jewish Writing,* E. P. Dutton and Co., 1969, pp. 163-80.

[*In the following essay, Alter discusses three novels of the post-Holocaust period –including Amichai's* Not of This Time, Not of This Place*—that attempt to reconcile survivors of modern Judaism with the horrors of the Holocaust.*]

Most people in our time have the face of Lot's wife, turned toward the Holocaust and yet always escaping.—Yehuda Amichai

With all the restless probing into the implications of the Holocaust that continues to go on in Jewish intellectual forums in this country, and at a time when there has been such an abundance of novels—even some good novels by American Jews, it gives one pause to note how rarely American-Jewish fiction has attempted to come to terms in any serious way with the European catastrophe. Alfred Kazin, among others, has argued that no one can really write an imaginative work about the Nazi terror because art implies meaning, and Hitler's whole regime represented an organized annihilation of meaning. It would in any case be an act of spiritual presumption for someone other than a survivor to try to reconstruct the hideousness of the experience from within. But, even standing outside what actually happened, we all have to live with this irruption of utter meaninglessness into history, which implies, finally, that we have to make some kind of sense of it. This is what historians, social commentators, literary intellectuals, and others over the past two decades have tried to do in introspective or even argumentative essays; it is just this that the more serious American-Jewish novelists have been unwilling or unable to do in their creative work. Two possible explanations for this disparity in response suggest themselves. It may be easier to reason discursively about the inconceivable, to box it in with words, than to assimilate it imaginatively; and, for a variety of reasons, American writers in recent years often seem to have found that the essay, not the novel, has offered the most dependable and penetrating kind of illumination into the dark areas of their inner life and the deepest perplexities of their moral world.

Although in Israel the reflective essay does not have this kind of ascendancy over the imaginative genres, there have been other reasons why Hebrew fiction, at least until fairly recently, has done almost as little as American fiction in the way of looking into the wound of consciousness left by the destruction of European Jewry. (Survivors of the Holocaust living in Israel and writing in Hebrew must of course be excepted from this and all that follows.) Israeli writers, to begin with, have all been participants in a very different kind of major historical event—the rebirth through armed struggle of an independent Jewish state. It was not only that this latter event was more immediate, more palpable, more humanly comprehensible than the grim events in Europe that preceded it, but also that those terrible events raised certain disturbing questions about the values and the very existence of the Jewish state which, at least for a time, Israeli writers were not prepared to confront. During the fifties, Hebrew fiction came to be more and more a medium for wrestling with problems, both personal and cultural, but not this particular problem. In a purely descriptive sense, I would say that there is something strikingly adolescent about Israeli fiction of the fifties. In a number of the important Hebrew novels of this period, the major characters are all, in fact, adolescents; plot and dialogue serve as means for the characters (and the writer) to work out identity crises in a sustained effort consciously to come of age. As one might expect, these adolescent heroes and their retrospectively adolescent authors have little interest in anything that is outside the immediate circumambience of a self struggling for definition, anything beyond the youth movement, the army, the party, Papa and Mama's bourgeois staidness or old-fashioned Zionism, sweet Dalia or Shula and that moonlit night of first nakedness on the shore of Lake Tiberias.

I am not completely sure whether Israeli fiction of the sixties is getting significantly better (though I suspect that it is), but it has clearly gone beyond this stage. Israeli writers now more typically turn to the adult society in which they actually live, where the problems of self-definition are set in the complicating context of urban existence, professional responsibilities, and married life, where the characters have lived through enough to realize that what is most profoundly relevant to them is not always identical with what immediately impinges on them. Even the retrospective novel of adolescence, as we shall see, is now able to imagine its subject in circumstances that more firmly engage it in a complex historical reality.

As the Israeli writer in recent years has been better able to see his own condition entangled in a broad network of social, cultural, historical particulars, both the passage of time and the pressure of public events have pushed the European experience more toward the center of his awareness. The Israeli-Arab war seems to have been a kind of collective trauma for many sensitive young Israelis. Several of the most serious Hebrew novels of the fifties tried to work out the terror of an experience in which the sons of the pioneer-conquerors of desert and swamp were called upon to fight people, to kill in the name of the state. But as the sharpness of this experience now gradually fades, the raw edges of the deeper, darker trauma that preceded it begin to be exposed. At the same time, the events of the past four or five years have repeatedly focused attention on Israel's morally problematic relationship with Germany. The imminent end of reparations made many people in Israel aware of the extent to which the country's economy was dependent on these payments from Germany for the horrors inflicted upon European Jews. The arms deal with Bonn pointed to an even more grimly ironic dependence of Jew on German for instruments of destruction. The prospect of diplomatic relations with Germany, finally realized in 1965, introduced a note of inescapable conclusiveness to the official acceptance by the Jewish state of postwar Germany. And looming behind all these events in the early sixties is the figure of the mass murderer in his glass cage in Jerusalem, with all the storm of worldwide debate, moral and legal, about him, about his being there, about what he represented.

> **The Jerusalem sections of [*Not of This Time, Not of This Place*] also reflect Amichai's fondness for symbols, but in this case the unique city he knows so intimately affords him a very natural symbolic landscape. No one else has caught with such sharpness the bizarre, slightly mad life of the intelligentsia in Jerusalem. . . .**
> **—Robert Alter**

It is against this general background that, in 1963, the first important novel by an Israeli dealing with the Holocaust appeared, Yehuda Amichai's *Not of This Time, Not of This Place.* For the sake of accuracy, I should say that Amichai was born in Germany, from where he was brought to Palestine in 1936 at the age of twelve. The fact of his German childhood, his awareness of kin and earliest friends murdered by the Nazis, clearly determines the broad direction of the sections of his novel set in Germany, and yet the general attempt of the book to make moral contact with the destruction and its perpetrators is eminently that of an Israeli beyond the experience, not of a European Jew actually torn by it. Indeed, the peculiar structure of the novel—a brilliant but not fully worked out invention of Amichai's—provides a kind of diagrammatic illustration of the difficulties Israeli writers have in trying to imagine this ultimate catastrophe and how one can live with the knowledge of it.

The hero of Amichai's novel is a young archaeologist at the Hebrew University—quite obviously, a man dedicated to digging up buried layers of the past. Like the protagonist of virtually every Hebrew novel of consequence over the last ten years, he has gradually fallen into an unsettling sense of aimless drift after the challenging years immediately before and after Israel's independence. At the beginning of the book, we find him wondering whether he ought to stay in Jerusalem for the vacation and perhaps find some great, intoxicating love (he is married and vaguely loyal to his wife), or spend the summer in Germany confronting the murderers of his childhood companion, Ruth. The wife of a friend— we afterward discover that she is about to be committed to an asylum—tells him that he must do both these things at once. And so he does. That is, the novel splits into two alternating narratives, one continuing in the third person to report a summer of sensual abandon in Jerusalem with an American woman named Patricia, the other switching to the first person to tell the story of the same character's return to his native city of Weinberg for the purpose of "wreaking vengeance," as he dimly and grandiosely puts it, on the Nazi murderers. The hero of the novel, to cite a mythic parallel that Amichai alludes to obliquely, is a kind of bifurcated Odysseus: he descends into the underworld in hope of encountering the spirits of the dead and learning from them his own future, and, simultaneously, he lolls in the paradisiac bed of Calypso, the alien goddess who keeps him from the responsibilities of home and people.

Amichai clearly means to suggest that both experiences— eros in the city of Jerusalem, thanatos in the town of Weinberg—must be exhausted to enable his hero to find some new point of anchorage for his life. But what actually happens in the novel is that the Jerusalem sequence is vividly and convincingly realized, while the German episodes, despite many arresting moments, occur in a hazy twilight region between memory and fantasy, history and self-dramatization. This attempt of the novelistic imagination to immerse itself in the aftermath of the horror ends up being a kind of earnest exercise in synthesizing the literature of nightmare—dramatic situations from Kafka; motifs from Rilke; and from Agnon, style (the aphorisms of the abyss), narrative technique (the expressionism of Agnon's *Book of Deeds*), and even symbolic plot outline (Agnon's *A Guest for the Night,* also about a man from Jerusalem who returns to a destroyed European hometown in a futile search for the world of his childhood). Amichai intends his protagonist to discover both the old and the new Germany, but in fact his archaeologist of the self wanders about in a Germany compounded of symbols through which historical actualities are only intermittently glimpsed. One gets the uneasy sense that events happen only in order to be available as symbols: there is a roller-skating competition in Weinberg, to serve as the occasion for reflections on the pointless way our lives go round and round in the postwar era; a little German girl is named Sybil, to trigger a meditation on pagan prophecy and apocalypse; a cynical Indian appears in Weinberg solely to gather material for a book about Despair, and to pronounce bleak epigrams on that subject.

The Jerusalem sections of the novel also reflect Amichai's fondness for symbols, but in this case the unique city he knows so intimately affords him a very natural symbolic landscape. No one else has caught with such sharpness the bizarre, slightly mad life of the intelligentsia in Jerusalem, with its serious academic types, its bohemian poets and artists, its drifting cultists from home and abroad, sundry amateurs of Yoga, Zen, vegetarianism, and the Kabbalah. No one else has been so imaginatively alive to the uncanny suggestiveness of Jerusalem's stark location at the borders of the desert, the sky, and the enemy.

> Joel walked along, carrying the bundle of Patricia's dress under his arm. With great happiness he felt the dress and with great happiness he felt the city, its houses and empty lots, and the no-man's land beyond them. He felt the shards and rubble, the rusting oil drums, and the barbed-wire fences in which flying pieces of paper were caught as the wind shifted. No-man's land served as a kind of strainer. A strainer of hatred, of the past, of distant history. It was also the place of mines, the maps for which had been lost, so that no one knew where they were buried. And behind all the hubbub, the buildings and the walls, with no transition, the desert stretched out. All at once a desert of many hills rising in heavy, silent folds all the way to the mountains of Moab.

In passages like this, Amichai does not have to "work up" his symbols because they are already there in his city: the freight of meaning in landscape and objects is as immediately *felt* as the palpable burden of clothing imbued with Patricia's physical presence. But it is significant that the sense of reality radiates out from an object associated with sensuality; this explains much of the disparity between the two halves of the novel and, as I shall try to show, is an orientation explicitly shared by other Israeli writers in attempting to create a credible world against the unthinkable background of the Holocaust. Where horror has deadened the nerve of response to reality, made it difficult to believe in the real world, it seems as though there is a natural movement toward the primal act through which the body affirms life, in an effort to recapture the sheer sense of being alive. "They wanted to stretch out over reality," Amichai writes of his lovers, fusing the act of love with Elisha's miraculous resuscitation of the dead child in the biblical story, "eye to eye, mouth to mouth, and to give it life again with their own breath." But the miracle is not achieved, and Amichai's hero comes at some points to feel that the only fully credible reality is a purely sexual one: "The whole world seemed to Joel to be emptied, and covered over with canvas and tin and flimsy boards, like the world of stalls and stands in a fair. The last and only thing actual to him was Patricia's body. Not even her speech, but the sinking into her."

This sexual submergence, however, means forgetting both personal and collective history. Early in the novel, we are introduced to one of the protagonist's friends, a survivor of the death camps who has had the tattoo of a mermaid super-imposed upon the tattooed number on his arm—not in order to obliterate the grim blue figures but to leave them just barely perceptible through the lines of the mythological female form. As the image of the ambiguous tattoo floats in and out like an apparition through both halves of the narrative, Patricia is associated with the mermaid and the sea: she is seen as a bowsprit figure on an old ship, her favorite skirt is made of sailcloth, the pitch of ecstatic fulfillment to which she brings her lover makes him think of "waves, waves." Amichai finally turns her into a mythic embodiment of all the allurements of otherness for his protagonist (with a redeeming touch of playfulness, since he seems aware of the comic aspects of our modern penchant for mythicizing experience). Patricia is American and Christian, she is imagined by her lover as a sort of female Davy Crockett, a creature of the Wild West, half lizard and half mare; she is Venice, the sea-city that is the antithesis of mountainous Jerusalem, or, alternately, she is the Jerusalem of no-man's-land (the Hebrew equivalent literally means "area of abandonment"). The sea, however, remains the chief mythic sphere with which Patricia is associated, a sea at once attractive and potentially destructive to the man whose calling is to delve into the parched earth covering the dead past. As a physician friend dabbling in Kabbalah pointedly tells Joel, "Lilith comes from the sea."

The thematic complement to this absorption of life by erotic experience in Jerusalem is the fantasy of sexlessness in the German half of the novel. The narrator dreams of becoming an "angel" (the Hebrew *malakh* also suggests "messenger," a being with a single, appointed purpose) in order to carry out unswervingly his schemes of revenge. He looks at the display in a toy-shop window and compares the hesitancy of flesh and blood with the implacable fixity of the manufactured object: "All dolls, even the most perfect ones, have no sexual organs; they are angels." The opposition between this fantasy in the town of Weinberg and the sexual actuality in Jerusalem sets up a dilemma that the resolution of the novel cannot cope with. Amichai's attempt at a denouement is to arrange for the destruction of the Jerusalem-Joel while the Weinberg-Joel comes home, having undergone some undefined catharsis, ready to resume his life, though tentative about himself and unsure of the future. The thematic development of the novel, however, suggests that there is no way out for this self divided by love and death. The only means by which Amichai's protagonist can enter into active relation with the European past, that grisly realm of mass-pro-

duced death, is to divest himself of his humanity, and this is no more possible for him than it is really desirable. But the other self, the one that revives its humanity by obliterating past and future in the sweet intensity of the sexual present, is also living a lie. The dark revelations of history from 1933 to 1945 are too radical in implication to be forgotten with impunity. This, in any case, would seem to be what is suggested by the incident with which the Jerusalem plot concludes: the dangerous buried residue of the past—an unmarked mine from another war—explodes beneath the neglectful archaeologist as he tries to untangle the knot of conflicts in his love for his mistress and his love for his wife.

During the year 1965, two more Israeli novels of unusual interest that attempt to deal with the Holocaust appeared, Haim Gouri's *The Chocolate Deal* and Hanoch Bartov's *Wounds of Maturity*. Each of the two novels is remarkably different from Amichai's, neither could be said to be "influenced" by the earlier book, but the extent to which Gouri and Bartov share Amichai's moral problematics is equally remarkable. The authors of the two more recent novels are both native Israelis about the same age as Amichai: Bartov served in Europe with the Palestinian unit of the British Army at the end of World War II; Gouri is the author of a book-length account of the Eichmann trial and has translated Elie Wiesel into Hebrew. Of the two, Gouri is closer to Amichai in his technical handling of the European experience, possibly because he, like Amichai, is a poet writing his first novel; the strategies he adopts to get a hold on his intractable subject are more typically poetic than novelistic.

The Chocolate Deal is set in the rubble of a large German city (Berlin?) in the months immediately following the war. Rubi Kraus and Mordi Neuberg, two old friends who in their separate paths of flight have managed to survive the Nazis, meet by chance in a dreary railroad station. Rubi has schemes of establishing himself through the help of a rich uncle, one of the prominent lawyers of the city; Mordi, knowing that the uncle and his family were sent to the death camps, tries to dissuade his friend from going in search of his relatives. It does not take us long to realize that the sketchy action of the novel constitutes a parable about the moral ambiguities of survival. Of the two returned refugees, Mordi is unfluctuating in his loyalty to his slaughtered fellow Jews, but this loyalty proves to be, necessarily, a relationship impregnated with death. "There is no future in me," says Mordi (whose name may even unconsciously pun on the French *mort*). Living for him means the necessity for joining hands with the murderers and their accomplices—nature itself, the birds in the sky and the spring rain, seem to him silent collaborators with the planners of the Final Solution. Mordi dies mysteriously and symbolically about halfway through the book, just at the moment when Rubi is in bed with a German woman, the first woman he has had since the war. When the lights come on and the plot unfolds, she turns out to be his old mistress and former servant of his uncle's; during the war she had apparently been a kind of Gestapo camp follower, and she is now doubling as a street-walker and as a servant to the German doctor who has usurped the house of Rubi's uncle.

Because Rubi wants money, he conceives a plan of black-mailing this German doctor into issuing false medical statements to influence the price of surplus chocolate that the American occupation forces have been dumping on the local market. His course of action clearly illustrates the other half of the dilemma of survival raised by his friend Mordi. The only way to keep one's loyalty to the dead uncontaminated is to die. A Jew who wants to go on living in a world of murderers must end up cashing in somehow on the murderers' guilt—one thinks of Israel and the reparations issue—and thus must become implicated in the guilt himself. The weakness of Gouri's formulation of the moral quandary generated by the Holocaust is apparent: like most parabolic fiction, his novel states moral alternatives too sharply, not leaving a sufficient middle ground of possibilities between the extremes.

The Chocolate Deal does, however, handle its subject with an imaginative richness scarcely suggested by this abstract of its moral argument. Gouri has used his resources as a poet—in a more calculated fashion, I think, than Amichai—to create a world in which the metaphysical implications of the Holocaust will be everywhere manifest. The sense of time, after the breakdown of history, is dulled, confused; time speeds up, skids along erratically, stops dead, allowing no meaningful progression. Action itself then becomes arbitrary: one act will do as well as another; fantasy, accident, and choice are indifferent alternatives; the narrated event becomes (as in Amichai) the sketching out of mere possibility, not the report of accomplished fictional fact. In this *univers concentrationnaire,* place, too, is emptied of its distinctiveness so that one gray setting is almost interchangeable with another; and, finally, individuality is blurred, a character may have several, simultaneous identities (like Rubi's mistress) or may be a mere counter to which some future identity could be assigned. The bleakly elegiac prose and the disorienting generality of descriptive viewpoint in the following passage typify much of the novel:

> Slowly, slowly, the ways turn to meet. Time passes, false healer, giving to the suffering the potion of forgetfulness to quiet them, to take them further away. Sending the lost to sleep the very extended sleep, till the last trumpet. A gap yawns wider and wider between the rememberers and those who are remembered, and there the rivers flow, and there are the seasons of the year, and there the cities dark-gray in the snows, cities of marble and gold in the sun. In the purple conflagrations. And there the

> privilege of those who move to demur to the silence, to dream, to go onward.

In this world of flattened dimensions where roads, rivers, seasons, and time all run together on the same plane of occurrence, even a hint of affirmation—"those who move to demur to the silence"—is partly withheld through a kind of syntactic reticence. A more precise syntax would imply an explicit and coherent ordering of existence in which Gouri is unable to believe. His most distinctive stylistic trait is the verb followed directly by an infinitive, with the logical connection between the two suppressed, as at the beginning and end of this passage, or in sentences like "This time is dying away to be finished." The disjuncture here between the process and the end product of the process, between the happening in time marked by the temporal verb and the absolute state marked by the infinite verb, is the quintessential expression of Gouri's post-Holocaust world—a present which scarcely dares think of the past or hope for the future, where one empty now crumbles into another, ceaselessly, to the unimaginable end of time, "the last trumpet."

The Chocolate Deal suggests two ways out of this bleak prison of the present. The first, and more convincingly realized, avenue of escape is sexuality. Gouri's protagonist, like Amichai's, plunges into the sphere of sensual otherness of an alien woman in order to revive the sense of life in himself, though the symbolic retreat from Jewish selfhood involved in the act is stated more extremely here than in Amichai because the woman in this case is directly connected with the murderers. But where Amichai imagines the act of love contracting life into the present, Gouri sees in it a moment that partakes of past and even future—always, however, in a personal or mythic sense, never historically: "On the other side of the emptied space [between their bodies] is his own private messianic era. . . . And now he is about to perform an act ancient as death, surviving beyond him." It is significant that the one moment in the novel when memory comes fully alive is Rubi's recollection of a distant night of pleasure with his uncle's maid. At other points the past is caught obliquely in confusing fragments, or, in the one case of Mordi's account of his war years, it is rehearsed consecutively in the deadened, somnambulistic voice of the present. By contrast, the details of Rubi's sensual memory are unaffected by the passage of time: the glint of the August moon through the blinds, the chill touch of the brass doorknob that turned to the left, the suntanned body against the white sheets—through these sensuous particulars the past for once becomes present.

The other gateway from the present, but this time to a historical, not merely personal, past, is through an acceptance of the terrible paradoxes of survival while actively engaging heart and mind in the fate of those who were murdered and also of those who managed to escape. It is here that

Gouri is most reticent of all, perhaps because, with the kind of integrity he has, he is afraid that any affirmation of "the tragic necessity for commitment" may quickly degenerate into a slogan. This is clearly the alternative that it is most important to imagine and most difficult to imagine honestly. Though Gouri concludes his novel on a note of commitment to the martyred ones, he manages no more than a thinly symbolic gesture. Earlier in the book, Mordi had told of meeting a certain Mr. Schecter at the end of the war. Mr. Schecter, a watchsmith (obviously, the man who is to remind his fellow Jews of time and history), was genuinely concerned for Mordi, acted vaguely to tie him to his prewar past. At the end of the novel, as Rubi stands over Mordi's grave—the whole Chocolate Deal, we suddenly realize, has been a projected possibility, not an action carried out—someone calls to him, portentously, "Reuben Kraus? Mr. Schecter is looking for you." The intention here is surely admirable, but Mr. Schecter has been only a shadowy figure in the book, and I do not think this is one of those moments of achieved art that help us see into the dark places of our existential quandaries.

Hanoch Bartov's *Wounds of Maturity* is less original in technique than the other two novels, but it succeeds in throwing into sharper focus the perplexed problems of national values involved in an Israeli's attempt to relate to the grim past. Bartov's first-person narrator, the eighteen-year-old Elisha Kruk, begins his story with the words, "About the surrender." He has enlisted in the Palestinian Regiment of the British Army in hopes of redeeming his self-respect as a Jew by participating actively in the battle against his people's enemy. But his unit has not yet made contact with the German forces in Italy when the Nazi surrender is announced. This pattern of frustrated intention recurs in a series of memorable variations through the remainder of the novel. The company of Palestinian soldiers goes rolling north toward Germany, with the chalk-scrawled menace of *Die Juden Kommen!* on the tarpaulin sides of their transport trucks—only to be halted at the border, where they are stationed in a small Italian town. After a delay of almost two months, the Palestinians get orders to move into Germany, but on the last night in Italy, their campsite is inundated by a flashflood, and when the self-styled avengers cross the German border, this is the figure they cut: "Along the sides of our vehicles we had stretched out lines and belts and had hung up our clothes to dry, and our bodies we covered with whatever had been rescued from the water. We looked like a traveling camp of gypsies."

This is, of course, an old story in war fiction: it goes all the way back to the farcical frustrations of Fabrice del Dongo, Stendhal's aspirant to heroism at the tail end of the Napoleonic Wars. But the familiar antiheroic theme assumes a special gravity and morally problematic nature when it is associated with an Israeli's relation to the destruction of European Jewry. Bartov's novel makes one point particularly clear: the Holocaust raises larger questions for an Israeli than for an American Jew because it casts a long shadow of doubt on the new vision of Jewish identity implicit in the creation of a modern Jewish state. If the new Jew is, ideally, a kind of reincarnation of the rebuilder of Jerusalem in Nehemiah, "one hand performing the work, the other holding his weapon," what is such a figure to make of six million of his people allowing themselves to be led off to the slaughter, and what good is his own brave posture of armed self-assertion as a response to Nazi monstrosities, for which any conceivable retribution through violence could be only the nightmare of a maniac? The point of the novel's vaguely melodramatic title (which puns ironically on an Israeli idiom for "acne") is that the young Palestinian begins to discover through his encounter with both the survivors and the perpetrators of the Holocaust who he is—that whoever he may be, he is not the man on the Zionist poster out of Nehemiah, and not so different, perhaps, from Jews in other lands.

Bartov has an extraordinary gift for inventing dramatic situations that bring into high relief the contrast between what his Palestinian soldiers really can be and what they are expected to be, by others and also by themselves. The first of these scenes takes place in a pizzeria in Bologna, where Elisha Kruk finds himself hauled into the victory celebration of a group of wildly drunken Negro soldiers. When they finally understand that he comes from Palestine, one of them hails him in the style of an evangelist preacher as "the youth from the city of Bethlehem, the birthplace of Lord Jesus our Savior." Kruk, drunk himself, is prodded into a dizzying speech on the miraculous splendors of the holy city of Bethlehem, in fact a dirty little Arab town. The tipsy hallelujah cries that punctuate Kruk's fantastic oration set the keynote for the role of the Jewish soldiers as spurious redeemers. Later, Kruk and three of his friends will come upon their first actual refugees from the camps—a group of pious Hungarian tailors sitting in a basement at their Sabbath meal, singing the traditional table-hymns about the coming of the Messiah. At the entrance of the soldiers, the tailors leap up from their places, clutch the young men to make sure of their reality; they are ready to pack, in the middle of the Sabbath, and to be led by these Jewish men of war across the sea to the Promised Land. The Palestinians, of course, can only respond lamely—the authorities will arrange these matters, one must be patient and wait for official procedures—and so the tailors' cries of enthusiasm die in their throats.

Still more disturbing for the soldiers are the encounters in which their own image of themselves as a bold new breed of Jews is threatened. Kruk and his friends meet a handful of deported Ukrainian women, sitting by the roadside cooking their morning *kasha*. The soldiers are unable to convince the women that they are members of the "Jewish Army." The women, in a kind of obscene coquetry, take this claim as some obscurely ribald joke and answer with a knowing wink: "We've seen the Jewish armies; in chariots of flame they went up to heaven, in columns of smoke." The ambiguous question of kinship with European Jewry becomes most agonizing when Kruk discovers an actual cousin in a refugee camp. His initial eagerness is dissipated in a moment as his cousin tells him nonchalantly, almost proudly, how he managed to survive by working in a crematorium. "More than anything else," Kruk says of himself, "I was filled with the terror of belonging to him. More than the shock, more than the disgust." Such inability to face the survivor, twisted as he may be by his experience, is clearly a more immediate problem for the Israeli than for the American because in Israel the survivor is everywhere.

The most crucial inadequacy, however, in the Hebrew soldiers' attempt to take hold of this unmanageable historical reality, is revealed in the fantasies of revenge to which a few of them give voice. The logical consequence of a Jew's learning to fight for himself, as others do, would seem to be that he should take bloody vengeance for himself, as others do. What will we say, wonder the angrier of the young men, when our children ask us someday why we failed to use this one possible moment of history to pay back a little for all the horrors that were done to us? "We are here as blood-redeemers. For one wild Jewish vengeance. Just once like the Tartars, like the Ukrainians, like the Germans." Or, as the chief advocate for the course of revenge puts the case with more intellectual subtlety, possibly thinking in the Nietzschean idiom of Jabotinsky's Revisionist Zionist ideology, "One can free oneself from the fear of the bestial crime only by means of bestial retribution."

But any retribution the young soldiers try to take is hesitant, bungling, and, of course, grotesquely inadequate. The one attempt at vengeance, moreover, almost carried out in the novel, provides the culmination to that series of revelatory scenes begun in the pizzeria through which the Palestinians are forced to face their own inner weakness, the uncertainty of their ideals. Elisha Kruk and his cynical (European-born) friend Brotsky have billeted themselves in the home of an SS officer who has fled, leaving behind his wife and grown daughter. From their room upstairs, Kruk and Brotsky hear two other Jewish soldiers break into the kitchen and attack the women. Brotsky sits listening intently to the struggle below with a "glassy smile." Kruk, frightened by the reflection of himself that he sees in Brotsky's expression and unnerved by the women's shrieks, seizes his rifle, rushes downstairs, and angrily orders the would-be rapists out of the house. Bartov makes it clear that Kruk's deliverance of the German women is not a moral act—it proceeds from weakness, just as to join the rapists would have confessed to a different kind of weakness. Kruk, like Isaac Babel's Jewish soldier, might well dream of having "the simplest of

proficiencies—the ability to kill my fellow-men"; but he knows, perhaps better than the Babel character, that he is compelled by his nature and upbringing to remain achingly human in a world that is for the most part callously inhuman. "In a single moment," he comments on his response to the quaking vulnerability of the assaulted women, "all the anthems of hate were wiped away and I was once more Papa's son. Wallowing in purity. A human being. A crapped up human being. Now I know, that's what we are, condemned to go around with the divine image on our forehead like the mark of Cain."

Bartov's protagonist, like Amichai's and Gouri's, is at least temporarily pulled away from the world of harsh moral confrontations by an alien woman, in his case a sensually generous, high-class Venetian whore, appropriately named Felicia. She nearly succeeds in keeping him with her in Venice just when his company is receiving orders to move into Germany; and, later, when he tries to focus his hatred for the Germans, the memory of her vivid body intervenes and confuses him. It is clear that to luxuriate with Felicia and to violate the women of Germany are simply two different alternatives of alienation from self for the young Palestinian: he literally flees from Felicia's sun-drenched bedroom as he psychologically flees from the bestial darkness of the rape. In the end, Elisha Kruk has no choice but to go on with his old Jewish self, understanding now its terrible inadequacies, its confusions and cowardice—and, just possibly, its potential for moral sensitivity. Bartov concludes his novel by recalling, as does Amichai, the image of Lot's wife in order to suggest his protagonist's relationship with the Holocaust: "'I will never turn my face back there,' I whisper like an incantation over the bleeding memory, but my thoughts turn into pillars of salt."

All these novels, Bartov's most explicitly, suggest the moral purpose that Hebrew fiction on the Holocaust is trying to fulfill: the writers do not seek to scare themselves or their readers with horror stories, but, recognizing the necessity to exist now in the presence of the ultimate horror, they want to see by its baleful light what a Jew can discover about himself, how he can go on with the difficult business of living unillusioned and yet responsible. The novel is an ambiguously potent means to this end. Because it creates its own world, it can place us at the nexus of time, place, and event where a dilemma raised by history is totally felt, in this way overcoming the distance of abstraction and analysis inherent in discursive treatments of the same dilemma. But because the novel necessarily manipulates the elements of its own world, it may inadvertently contrive reality, reducing it to an overly simple scheme. Both the inherent advantage in the novelistic approach to moral issues and its potential weakness are present in the three novels we have been considering, but the general effect of each of the books is clearly to bring us a little closer to the imponderable realities of recent history and to the problems of identity raised by that history. It is not easy to think of another area of contemporary Jewish culture, either in Israel or in America, where the written word and the imagined act have been used with such self-critical intentness, such freedom from moral posturing and institutional cant, or where such an unflinching effort has been made to look into the abysses flung open by the Holocaust in both the individual and the collective lives of Jews.

Nancy Sullivan (review date May 1970)

SOURCE: "Snap Judgments," in *Poetry,* Vol. CXVI, No. 2, May 1970, pp. 120-25.

[*In the following review, Sullivan praises Assia Gutmann's translations of Amichai's work.*]

The poems by Yehuda Amichai in *Poems* have been translated from the Hebrew by Assia Gutmann. Since I do not know Hebrew and since, even if I did, the text is not bilingual, my reactions to Amichai's poems are based solely on these often brilliant translations. Michael Hamburger admits to a similar problem in his *Introduction:*

> Poems are made of words, and I cannot read the words of which Yehuda Amichai's poems are made, cannot follow—let alone judge—his way with the Hebrew language, what he does with its ancient and modern, literary and vernacular components, how he combines and contrasts them to make them talk or sing as they have never talked or sung before.

I wonder why someone who knows Hebrew wasn't asked to do the introduction. Anyway and in addition, German, not Hebrew, was Amichai's first language; his family did not emigrate to Palestine until 1936 when he was twelve. It is obvious, even from the translations, that Amichai has read both contemporary German and English poets.

> Sometimes pus
> Sometimes a poem.
>
> Something always bursts out.
> And always pain.

says Amichai/Gutmann in **"Ibn Gabirol."** There is very little pus in this book; instead, there are many *poems* burst in fruitful pain from Amichai's confrontation with the vagaries of the human condition. Most of the poems are short, just one page long, occupying space frugally but no less importantly for that. Take, for instance, this poem called **"A Pity. We Were Such a Good Invention."**

> They amputated
> Your thighs off my hips.
> As far as I'm concerned
> They are all surgeons. All of them.
> They dismantled us
> Each from the other.
> As far as I'm concerned
> They are all engineers. All of them.
>
> A pity. We were such a good
> And loving invention.
> An airplane made from a man and a wife.
> Wings and everything.
> We hovered a little above the earth.
>
> We even flew a little.

In such poems, often in single lines—"I stroked your hair in the direction of your journey" or "Like the cry of paper tearing / Across the forty-two years of my life"—Amichai says it right, right *there.* This book is almost incentive enough to make me learn Hebrew.

John Pickford (review date 28 December 1973)

SOURCE: "Hard and Soft," in *New Statesman,* Vol. 86, No. 2232, December 28, 1973, p. 978.

[*In the following review of* Not of This Time, Not of This Place, *Pickford praises Amichai's evocation of "survivor's guilt" and his protagonist's ambiguous response to post-war Germany but, finds the novel somewhat disjointed and meandering.*]

There is . . . a strong vein of autobiography in Yehuda Amichai's novel, newly translated, from the Hebrew by Shlomo Katz. But its impact is less urgent and direct than that of [Wolfgang] Borchert's stories, partly perhaps because Amichai was the luckier of the two—he left Germany before the war started. *Not of This Time, Not of This Place* is, in a sense, two novels running parallel with each other. One is a first-person account of a Jew's return from Israel to the German town where he was brought up. The other, in the third person, describes the same man's love affair in Jerusalem with an American doctor. In Germany we see the man—Joel—brooding, introverted and intent on a revenge in his head which he finds impossible to practice in his heart. In Jerusalem we meet a spry, sensual Joel, whose identity crisis is being washed away by love.

Joel's response to what happened to the Jews who remained in his home town is, of course, a response to the past. So Amichai's account of Nazi oppression is, oddly enough, much less tortured, much more reflective than anything we find in Borchert. Joel discovers it difficult to hate when once again there are race-horses in the yard of Mr Klein, who had been the richest Jew in the district before the war. And when he conjures up in his mind the face of Ruth, his childhood sweetheart burnt by the Nazis, it only has 'a calming effect on me and fills me with wild melody and happiness and sadness, instead of driving me to acts of vengeance'. Joel only begins to feel violent towards Germans when he sees trains going east and once when he stumbles onto an American film crew's reconstruction of SS atrocities.

The novel is striking for its awareness of history, its study of the complexity of human motive, its Old Testament lyricism and its generous sense of shared guilt for what happened in the concentration camps. At the same time, it seems a somewhat diffuse and protracted work for one of Israel's leading poets to have written. The book is too much a sequence of 'strange meetings' connected only by the personality of Joel.

Noam Flinker (essay date 1980)

SOURCE: "Saul and David in the Early Poetry of Yehuda Amichai," in *The David Myth in Western Literature,* edited by Raymond-Jean Frontain and Jan Wojcik, Purdue University Press, 1980, pp. 170-78.

[*In the following essay, Flinker examines Amichai's use of the biblical figures of Saul and David in his poetry.*]

In a series of poems first published in 1958, a modern Israeli poet, Yehuda Amichai, revised the traditional stories of Saul and David to make these public, national heroes figures in the private world of an introspective speaker. His myths contrast markedly to the popular folk traditions about Saul and David that abound in the Israeli cultural landscape, extending from names of streets and hotels to the many folk songs and associated dances that sound the praises of these biblical heroes. Amichai focuses on their individual human qualities, while making only passing reference to the various traditions about Saul and David that the reader must keep in mind. The poems articulate a complex attitude toward the past by means of ironic tensions that neither embrace nor entirely reject the traditional details to which they allude.

"King Saul & I," "Young David," and **"Mt. Zion"** preserve the original historical continuity of selected biblical details from poem to poem, but the sequence presents a modernized view of them and thus elicits a contemporary identification with the ancient past. The David poem, at the center of the sequence, forms its focus. The longer Saul poem sets up a series of comparisons implicitly applicable

to the Davidic focus. Young David's perceptions qualify those of **"King Saul & I,"** just as they hover in the background of **"Mt Zion."** All the poems sound echoes in the author's mind. Together they are a poetic portrait of an inner landscape.

Amichai's sequence begins with a comparison between Saul and a contemporary first-person speaker (**"King Saul & I"**). The speaker uses Saul's career as a means of measuring and understanding himself. In the first stanza the speaker compares himself to Saul through three consecutive images, followed by a statement of their brotherly connection:

> They gave him a finger, but he took the whole
> hand
> They gave me the whole hand: I didn't even take
> the little finger.
>
> While my heart
> Was weightlifting its first feelings
> He rehearsed the tearing of oxen.
>
> My pulse-beats were like
> Drips from a tap
> His pulse-beats
> Pounded like hammers on a new building.
>
> He was my big brother
> I got his used clothes.

Amichai's initial presentation of Saul contrasts with the biblical story where the future king's shy, retiring personality has him hiding "himself among the stuff" when Samuel wanted to make him king. The modern poet stresses Saul's strength in the images which move from the physical power associated with "hand," to a gymnastic workout (or "rehearsal" in this translation), and finally to pulsebeats. The "tearing of oxen" appears as an example of apparently random violence. The biblical context for this particular detail is simply ignored in the poem. In general, Saul's appearance in the first stanza projects a sense of power with ambition, aggression, and seething in qualified violence.

The contemporary first-person speaker contrasts himself pointedly with Saul. Although offered an entire hand, he refuses even a little finger. In the gym, he works out his primal feelings while his blood pressure remains low. But while these lines seem to suggest the total opposition between Saul and the speaker, the stanza concludes by making them brothers. The reader is left puzzled about the nature of those "used clothes." Implicit is a sense of connection with Saul's power and activity. If these qualities are his clothes, perhaps their being "used" conveys a lessening in the violence underlying his taking "the whole hand," or "tearing of oxen," or pounding "like hammers on a new building," but the basic nature of Saul's power and activity is not changed by use. The stanza thus ends with a contradictory sense of conflict and harmony between King Saul and "I."

Stanza two is entirely devoted to Saul. Here the seething violence of the first stanza is seen under greater control:

> His head, like a compass, will always bring him
> To the sure north of his future.
>
> His heart is set, like an alarm clock
> For the hour of his reign.
> When everyone's asleep, he will cry out
> Until all the quarries are hoarse.
> Nobody will stop him!
>
> Only the asses bare their yellow teeth
> At the end.

Saul's head is attuned to the future, much as the compass is in accord with the earth's magnetic field. There is something mechanical about Saul's attitude to the world, but with it comes the ability to deal with the realistic political situation in a firm, purposeful way. The next image, more mechanical still, compares Saul's heart to an alarm clock. There is not an immediate cosmic connection here between device and nature, such as that between compass and earth; clocks artificially measure time while compasses point direction by conforming to natural forces. Like an alarm clock, Saul has set his heart on being king, so that at the right time he can cry out to awaken the nation. Almost like God, who occasionally threatens to do something "at which both the ears of every one that heareth it shall tingle" (I Samuel 3:11), Saul's shouting, by echoing back and forth, makes the quarries hoarse. This sort of power and drive is not to be stopped. Nevertheless, the stanza concludes with a proleptic hint of Saul's tragic end. When the asses "bare their yellow teeth" at the end of his path, Saul's control over fate and destiny will be gone. The lost asses, which once brought Saul to Samuel, become, in Amichai's poem, a reminder of the final destruction of a formerly exalted leader.

Stanza three returns to Saul's rise to power, after a few apparent digressions into the speaker's present:

> Dead prophets turned time-wheels
> When he went out searching for asses
> Which I, now, have found.
> But I don't know how to handle them.
> They kick me.
>
> I was raised with the straw,
> I fell with heavy seeds.
> But he breathed the winds of his histories.
> He was anointed with the royal oil

> As with the wrestler's grease.
> He battled with olive-trees
> Forcing them to kneel.
> Roots bulged on the earth's foreheads
> With the strain.
> The prophets escaped from the arena;
> Only God remained, counting:
> Seven . . . eight . . . nine . . . ten . . .
> The people, from his shoulders downwards,
>   rejoiced.
> Not a man stood up.
> He had won.

The first-person references at the outset of the stanza are central to the poem, since they remind the reader of the relation between Saul's biblical past and the reality of contemporary existence. This relation is quite complicated and is presented here in terms of biblical images that unexpectedly reappear in a modern Israeli landscape. Like so many archaeological artifacts, the "asses," the "straw," and the "seeds" present an ambivalent attitude toward the past.

The lost asses are first mentioned in the Bible when Saul's father sends him to look for them (I Samuel 9:3). Later, Samuel predicts that two men will meet Saul and tell him: "The asses which thou wentest to seek are found" (10:2). In the previous stanza of the poem, the asses are a premonition of Saul's failure, and here he has "time-wheels" bring them to the contemporary speaker. The herd has had offspring. The inability of the speaker to handle them may at first appear as an indication of contemporary ineptitude in contrast to a past heroic age; yet, at the end of his path, Saul himself does not seem to be much more adept at handling the asses than the modern speaker, who gets kicked.

At this point Amichai adds another kind of biblical image in order to balance the comparison. "Straw" and "heavy seeds" are biblical metaphors, charged with traditional meaning and values. Separating wheat from chaff by winnowing on a hill takes on spiritual significance in Isaiah: "They shall flee far off, and shall be chased as the chaff of the mountains before the wind, and like a rolling thing before the whirlwind" (17:13). For the prophet, God's enemies are likened to the worthless chaff (the same Hebrew word that is translated "straw" in the poem) that is blown to the winds. The metaphor implies that the speaker's inability to deal with the kicking asses is not as derogatory as first appeared. Having found the asses, he is raised with the chaff but falls with the wheat, while Saul, "like the portion of them that spoil us, and the lot of them that rob us" (Isaiah 17:14), is blown away. On one level, Amichai reverses the biblical metaphor, with falling as negative and blowing in the "winds of his histories" as positive, but on another level it is Saul who is found wanting in this traditional trope for distinguishing the good from the worthless. Thus, before describing Saul's rise to power, Amichai compares him with the modern speaker in rather ambivalent terms that present them almost as equals, with Saul's superiority less clear after the reversal of the wheat-chaff image.

The rest of the stanza treats Saul's anointment in images that recall the physical power and violence of stanza one. Anointment oil, probably an olive product, is associated with wrestler's grease ("oil" in Hebrew), which leads to a wrestling match with olives. Saul forces the olive trees to bow down, but then his opponent, Proteus-like, seems to change shape. The strain of the struggle, seen on the earth's forehead, is on the one hand a realistic impression of the soil of an olive grove, where the thick roots of the trees bulge within the soil much like blood vessels on a forehead. On a more metaphorical level, this struggle expands Saul's conflict into a Herculean wrestling match with the Antaeus-like olive grove, taking on some of the characteristics of a mythic personification of nature. With the flight of all the referees but God (the Hebrew *shoftim*, rendered "prophets" in the translation, literally means "judges" and is used for "referee" in contemporary sports events), the struggle is faintly reminiscent of Jacob's wrestling with the angel (Genesis 32). Although his victory is more complete than Jacob's, the rejoicing of the inferior crowds and the absence of a real opponent places Saul in a less heroic light. He is victorious, but it remains unclear just whom he has defeated.

The fourth stanza places all this in a contemporary perspective. Saul's kingdom, justice, and ultimate historical verdict are juxtaposed against the day-to-day weariness of the speaker:

> I am tired,
> My bed is my kingdom.
>
> My sleep is just
> My dream is my verdict.
>
> I hung my clothes on a chair
> For tomorrow.
>
> He hung his kingdom
> In a frame of golden wrath
> On the sky's wall.
>
> My arms are short, like string too short
> To tie a parcel.
>
> His arms are like the chains in a harbour
> For cargo to be carried across time.
>
> He is a dead king.
> I am tired man.

Here it is clear that Saul's energy and violence in the first stanza were not included in the "used clothes." Nevertheless, the tired speaker is not dead, like Saul. Saul's hanging "his kingdom / In a frame of golden wrath / On the sky's wall," as opposed to the Philistines, who "fastened his body to the wall of Beth-Shan" (I Samuel 31:10), is Amichai's version of the end first intimated by the bared yellow teeth of the asses. He thus avoids the interests of an earlier poet, Shaul Tchernichovsky, who interpreted Saul's last moments on Mt. Gilboa in heroic, nationalistic tones. Saul's glory is manifest in Amichai's image, but it is juxtaposed against the speaker's prosaic hanging of clothes on a chair. Amichai's interest here is primarily in the speaker. Saul's final act is envisioned with ambiguous grandeur (whose wrath—Saul's? God's? David's?), but with a definite tone of finality. "He is a dead king" whose arms reach out across time to the tired speaker. The latter, despite his weariness and short arms, is in a position to wear his older brother's used clothes, and by using the harbor chains to lengthen the string, can participate in carrying the cargo of Saul's history into his own life.

"King Saul & I" thus articulates a view of biblical myth that makes a connection with contemporary consciousness possible. Despite his power, control of destiny, and initial victories, Saul was reduced to windblown chaff, at least in his final defeat, while the weary contemporary speaker, heavy like the wheat, is still capable of germination. The tired speaker, asleep and dreaming on his bed, sees himself as reliving, in miniature, Saul's regal career. The justice of the modern kingdom is achieved as a dream that acts as an imaginative leap beyond the realism of clothing and chains. Brotherly connection with Saul provides the speaker inspiration for imaginative activity that enlarges the significance of contemporary daily existence.

Once Amichai has reduced Saul's heroic stature to terms that make him relevant to his contemporary speaker, he moves on to **"Young David,"** the giant killer, in a poem that probes the conquering hero's feelings upon returning to Saul's army with Goliath's head:

> David came back to the boys
> (Cheers still in his ears)
> And the noisy ones in armor
> Were terribly mature.
>
> They slapped him on the back, they laughed,
> Hoarse, and one cursed and a couple
> Spat. But David was lonely and felt,
> For the first time, that there were no more Davids.
>
> And suddenly he didn't know what to do with
> Goliath's head, he'd forgotten it, still
> Held by the curls.

It was heavy. Who needed it, now?
And like the birds of blood, flying far, he
No longer heard the crowd roar.

The octave describes David's return in colloquial language that imitates the talk of the young soldiers and then suddenly registers the hero's loneliness and sense of superiority. The sestet presents David as stunned before the roaring crowd, uncomfortably aware of the pointlessness of carrying his enemy's head. His loneliness at the conclusion of the octave is matched by the ambiguity of the final line of the sestet, where it is unclear in the Hebrew whether it is David or Goliath who, like the birds of prey, doesn't hear the crowd. In a sense, David is like his victim for an instant; and he is like Saul before the inferior crowd that rejoiced in their king's victory. The common people are merely able to shout, whereas their heroic kings feel both their own superiority and the near absurdity of the crowd's raucous noise.

There was a disparity in Saul's poem between the images of glory attendant on his rise to power and the ironic retrospective on the end of his story—"only the asses bare their yellow teeth / At the end"—which the modern Israeli, knowing the whole story of Saul and the subsequent history of his own Israeli, cannot escape: "He is a dead king. / I am a tired man." David thus stands in contrast to both Saul and the speaker. In his poem, we glance into his mind to see that he, unlike Saul, is aware of the distance between the popular response to his dead and the real, almost embarrassing significance; it's just a dead head in his hand. And unlike the speaker, David was truly great. His irony was the irony of the strong man who could see in his hands the little (if real) value of real, brave deeds. The speaker's arms, we recall, "are short, like string too short / To tie a parcel." The irony that David commands is the center of the sequence.

The crowd's noise shifts to confusion with the beginning of **"Mt. Zion,"** the final poem of the sequence:

> As confusion tosses things up
> Suddenly, facing the closed wall,
> The psalms, the stairs, the cemetery stones
> And the barbed wire and the dark cypresses—they
>   also
>
> Knew everything, but said nothing as
> They shot wailing rounds from
> Their prayer posts. And then the rams' horns
> Broke the silence past
>
> Repair. The wall stood, only the wall,
> And monks sang in Mary's Church,
> And the mosque tower pointed into
>
> The sky until it got cut off.

But they covered their David with warm carpets
Even though he wasn't there.

The confusion is everywhere. The Jewish worship with psalms, weeping, and rams' horns is mixed with the chanting of the Christian monks and the palpable silence of the Moslem mosque. The ungrounded spiritualities weave in and out of the windings of wire and patterns of bullets, which their conflict with one another somewhat resembles. The cacophony of sound and purpose reaches a climax as the mosque tower is "cut off" in the sky. This failure to reach heaven seems characteristic of the organized efforts of all three religions at the site. The final sentence strikes a blow at the national myth that made David's supposed tomb into a Jewish and Israeli holy place, charged with representing the national ethos. His absence adds a degree of absurdity to the confusion.

Some things to make one hopeful do survive, however. There is an implicit longing for the time when the old city was open. And if David is gone and the three religions similarly ignore this in their worship, still there is among them a common groping toward some more universal myth. (All three shrines are actually on Mt. Zion.) The poem offers no plan for composing such a myth, but its tone perhaps softens the denial of David's presence into an expression of longing and loss. This might be the necessary preamble to an agreed upon opening of hearts and gates in the future, when David's clear understanding of the precise worth of things might be more universally enjoyed.

Amichai's treatment of biblical heroes reduces their traditional stature somewhat, to refashion a new, more acceptable view that can lend meaning and spiritual substance to the emptiness of daily existence.

—*Nancy Sullivan*

Amichai's sequence is primarily concerned with the contemporary relevance of biblical heroes such as Saul and David. His version of the biblical myth focuses attention on a few highly selected details in order to stress the ways in which Saul and David can help direct present thinking. In this way, in T. S. Eliot's terms, Amichai has "the past . . . altered by the present as much as the present is directed by the past." The biblical materials are reshaped, with Saul as ambivalent hero against whose reduced public personality a private modern can view his own inner life. David's more extended popular reputation is reviewed through the musings of a quiet introvert who presents a very different image than the mythic king of Jewish tradition. Paradoxically, David's absence at the conclusion of the sequence helps to register a longing for Old Jerusalem, the city of David. Amichai's treatment of these biblical heroes reduces their traditional stature somewhat, to refashion a new, more acceptable view that can lend meaning and spiritual substance to the emptiness of daily existence. Saul, young David, and Mt. Zion must all be purged of certain traditions that blur their contemporary relevance. Then the alienated Israeli can attempt to see himself, both individually and collectively, in terms of the new tradition, which is itself a collage of ambivalently mixed details and feelings.

Edward Hirsch (essay date May-June 1981)

SOURCE: "Edward Hirsch: Poet at the Window," in *The American Poetry Review,* May-June 1981, pp. 44-7.

[*In the following essay, Hirsch praises Amichai's book of poems* Amen, *in particular his love poems and his ability to evoke major metaphysical issues through microcosmic images.*]

1

Yehuda Amichai has thus far published three books of poetry in English—*Songs of Jerusalem and Myself, Poems,* and *Amen.* These books are the work of an imaginative writer with a unique ability to render and enact the complex fate of the modern Israeli, the individual man locked in and responding to history. Amichai is a historical poet of the first order, a political writer in the deepest sense of that term. At the same time he is a writer who always speaks of his own concerns, his private love pangs and personal questions, his parents' history and his own intimate secrets. Part of the achievement of Amichai's work has been the conjoining of these two spheres, always speaking of one in terms of the other. Indeed, one of the central themes of his work has been the way the personal is implicated in the historical, the private impinged upon by the public. Always his poems register the human implications of the political event, in Lorca's phrase, the drop of blood that stands behind the statistics. He is, like Wordsworth, a passionate man trying to speak to other men and, as a modern Hebrew poet his work is appropriately steeped in the common imagery of the Prayer Book and the Psalms, the communal imagery and mythology of the Old Testament, the underground stream of Jewish mysticism.

Most often Amichai speaks without the mask of a fictive persona, as an individual witness, a quiet man who is always standing at the window. The poem **"Out Of Three Or Four In A Room"** (from *Poems,* translated by Assia Gutmann) captures and enacts precisely what it means to be a witness, a writer trying to bridge the speechless and enormous dis-

tance between the inadequate and false words (cut loose and "wandering without luggage") and the terrible event. It is a poem that, in the example of its making transcends its own pessimism, but it shows too that, as Williams said, "There is nothing sacred about literature, it is damned from one end to the other."

"Out Of Three Or Four In A Room"

Out of three or four in a room
One is always standing at the window.
Forced to see the injustice amongst the thorns,
The fires on the hill

And people who left whole
Are brought home in the evening, like small change

Out of three or four in a room
One is always standing at the window
Hair dark above his thoughts.
Behind him, the words.
And in front of him the words, wandering, without luggage.
Hearts without provision, prophecies without water
And big stones put there
And staying, closed, like letters
With no address; and no one to receive them.

Amichai is a poet who may say truthfully that "I go out to all my wars." He was born in Germany in 1924 and emigrated to Israel in 1936. The poem **"Like the Inner Wall Of A House"** reports that

I found myself
Suddenly, and too early in life
Like the inner wall of a house
Which has becomes an outer wall after wars and devastations.

Wars and devastations are behind all of Amichai's work; sometimes they are implicit and in the background, more often they are explicit and imminent, violently impinging on his life. And the place where they impinge most is on his own love life, for Amichai is perhaps first and foremost a love poet, a writer preeminently concerned with the tenderness and ironies of sexual love. And he is continually waking to find that love engulfed by the external historical world. He writes that "In the middle of this century we turned to each other," thus specifying the personal moment in terms of the larger epoch, and he announces wryly that:

Even my loves are measured by wars:
I am saying this happened after the Second

World War. We met a day before the
Six-Day War. I'll never say
before the peace '45-'48 or during
the peace '56-'67.

In his perceptive introduction to *Amen* Ted Hughes comments on the way in which Amichai's imagery ramifies both outwards and inwards, wedding the private to the public. Hughes writes:

> Writing about his most private love pangs in terms of war, politics, and religion he is inevitably writing about war, politics, and religion in terms of his most private love pangs. And the large issues are in no wise diminished in this exchange... Each poem is like a telephone switchboard—the images operate lightning confrontations between waiting realities, a comic or terrible conversation between the heavy political and spiritual matters and the lovers.

Perhaps the finest example of Amichai's conjunction of love and politics (or love and war, or love and religion), his imagistic tangle of supposedly separate but inevitably tangled realms, is the poem **"A Pity. We Were Such A Good Invention"** (also from *Poems*). This poem is remarkable for its directness and profound simplicity, its unique mixture of the erotic and the political, its subtle tone of outrage and nostalgia. As a love poem it is worthy to stand beside "The River Merchant's Wife: A Letter" or, more appropriately, "The Good-Morrow" and "Canonization." Donne was an early influence on Amichai and this poem has some of the qualities, though presented retrospectively, of "For God's sake hold your tongue, and let me love . . ." It reads:

"A Pity. We Were Such A Good Invention"

They amputated
Your thighs off my hips.
A far as I'm concerned
They are all surgeons. All of them.

They dismantled us
Each from the other.
As far as I'm concerned
They are all engineers. All of them.

A pity. We were such a good
And loving invention.
An airplane made from a man and wife.
Wings and everything.
We hovered a little above the earth.

We even flew a little.

The final memory of this poem, understated and passionate, may be effectively placed against the violent and surgical destruction of the unspecified "them." Here the lovers are not "stiff twin compasses" as in Donne's famous image, but appropriate to their century, "an airplane made from a man and wife." There is a sad, ironic, outraged, bitter, and wistful tone in the homely invention of this little hovering aircraft. And though it is true that there is an enormous burden in this act of remembering, there is also a vehement anger and determination. This is the same poet who will convincingly title another poem **"To Remember Is A Kind Of Hope."** Because to remember *is* a kind of hope, particularly as those hopes are embodied in poems.

2

Amen begins not at the window but in the street, and it starts out not with the poet but with Mr. Beringer "whose son / fell by the Canal." Mr. Beringer is the first of many in this book who has lost a son or a husband or a father or a lover. He is grief-stricken and responsible to his dead son and because of the weight of that responsibility (or rather because of the weight he is losing) the poet becomes responsible to him.

"Seven Laments For The Fallen In The War"

1

Mr. Beringer, whose son
fell by the Canal, which
was dug by strangers
for ships to pass through the desert,
is passing me at the Jaffa gate:

He has become very thin; has lost
his son's weight.
Therefore he is floating lightly
through the alleys,
getting entangled in my heart
like driftwood.

The poem goes on to speak of the monument to the unknown soldier which, ironically and because it is on the enemy's side, will become "a good target marker for the gunners / of future wars." It remembers Dicky who was hit "like the water tower at Yad Mordecai"; there "everything poured out of him." It speaks of "Bitter salt dressed up / as a little girl with flowers" and a dead soldier who "swims above little heads / with the swimming movements of the dead." These laments come from a country where "everything (is) in three languages: Hebrew, Arabic, and Death." And in this world even an old textbook, faulty but tenderhearted, becomes an emblem of a friend who died "in my arms and in his blood."

4

I found an old textbook of animals,
Brehm, second volume, birds:
Description, in sweet language, of the lives
of crows, swallows and jays. A lot of mistakes
in Gothic printing, but a lot of love: "Our
feathered friends," "emigrate to warmer
countries," "nest, dotted egg, soft plumage,
the nightingale," "prophets of spring."
The Red-Breasted Robin.

Year of printing 1913, Germany
on the eve of the war which became
the eve of all my wars.

My good friend, who died in my arms and in his
    blood
in the sands of Ashdod, 1948, in June.

Oh, my friend,
red-breasted.

One of the remarkable and metaphysical aspects of this sly and sad poem is the way the feelings for the textbook imply, without becoming sentimental, the tender feelings for the friend. The connection is made with lightning-like precision, the name of the robin transformed and infused with new meaning as it comes to represent the dead soldier, frozen in time, red-breasted. And by speaking about this outdated textbook of animals ("year of printing 1913") the poet lines the poem not only with sorrow but with warmth and affection too. Indeed, the sixth lament makes this distinction important: "Yes, all this is sorrow" . . . but "leave / a little love burning, always / as in a sleeping baby's room a little bulb." The lightbulb gives off a "feeling of security and silent love" that keeps us from giving ourselves wholly to grief. It is true that sometimes, as on Memorial Day in the seventh lament, the poem itself gives way, mixing grief with grief, sorrow with sorrow, until the poet (in "camouflage clothes of the living") cries out, much as one imagines Job crying out:

Oh, sweet world soaked, like bread,
in sweet milk for the terrible toothless God.

But against this, and with a terrible irony infusing a kind of tender hopefulness, the poem juxtaposes its final line: "Behind all this some great happiness is hiding."

Amichai's war poems are unique in that they are informed by a strong sense of personal responsibility—the self simultaneously implicated in, and victimized by the war—or as one poem puts it "the hunter and hunted in one body." No poem demonstrates this sense of personal responsibility, the individual voice assuming the weight and burden of these collective deaths (and what is that collective but a sum of individuals?) better than the fourth poem of **"Poems From A Cycle Called 'Patriotic Songs.'"** The poem begins, typically, with a disclaimer about itself ("I have nothing to say about the war") and it ends, also typically, with a complex and sweet voiced affirmation.

4

I have nothing to say about the war,
nothing to add. I'm ashamed.

All the knowledge I have absorbed in my life
I give up, like a desert
which has given up all water.
Names I never thought I would forget
I'm forgetting.

And because of the war I saw again,
for the sake of a last and simple sweetness:
The sun is circling round the earth. Yes.
The earth is flat, like a lost, floating board. Yes.
God is in heaven. Yes.

This final affirmation, in a language that is itself a kind of last and simple sweetness, is particularly poignant in that it is an affirmation of a world that has long been lost, a world that has been initiated into another kind of knowledge. That extraordinary sense of a world which has a flat wooden surface and a calm God can only predate 1913, that dark eve of all our wars, when the west put on its helmet of fire and, like the Hebrew poet, "crossed the borders of being an orphan." It is now a blood-stained, red-breasted world for adults and, as an early poem of Amichai makes clear, "God takes pity on kindergarten children . . . but adults he pities not at all."

He abandons them,
And sometimes they have to crawl on all fours
In the roasting sand
To reach the dressing station,
And they are streaming with blood.

It is with this knowledge and through these eyes that one must consider Amichai's final affirmation. Somehow and all at once that affirmation is simultaneously sincere and ironic, terribly honest and tender, deceptively simple and impossible. Perhaps most of all it is impossible. And yet, like Rilke in his self-portrait, the poem does make its affirmation, "it says its yes."

Reading Amichai's poems is a harrowing experience. The sheer accumulated weight of these losses is enormous. I find it nearly impossible to read these poems, however successful, as a merely literary performance. Their human presence is too close. Even the weakest poems, and some of the little love poems towards the end of the book seem tossed off and merely cute, bear a particular human stamp. Ultimately these poems may not have the stature of, say, Whitman's poems but, as in Whitman, one cannot read them without simultaneously touching the man who stands behind him. And at times, in their deepest moments, in their naked splendor, the simple recital of losses may take on the quality of a sacred litany. Here is Amichai's eleventh **"Patriotic Song."**

> The town I was born in was destroyed by shells.
> The ship in which I sailed to the land of Israel was
>   drowned later in the war.
> The born at Hammadia where I had loved was
>   burned out,
> The sweet shop at Ein-Gedi was blown up by the
>   enemy.
> The bridge at Ismailia, which I crossed to and fro
>   on
> the eve of my loves,
> has been torn to pieces.
>
> Thus my life is wiped out behind me according to
>   an exact map:
>
> How much longer can my memories hold out?
>
> The girl from my childhood was killed and my
>   father is dead.
>
> That's why you should never choose me
> to be a lover or a son, or a bridge-crosser
> or a citizen or a tenant.

It is no wonder, given the accumulated burden of these losses that the thirty-fourth poem goes on to move in three ascending sentences from "Let the memorial hill remember, instead of me / that's his job" to

> let dust remember, let dung remember
> at the gate, let afterbirth remember.
>
> Let the wild beasts and the sky's birds eat and
>   remember.
> Let all of them remember, so that I can rest.

Amen is a book of faith and doubt, sorrow and sweetness, astonishment and recognition. But mostly it is a book of memory, a book that continues to remember even as it refuses that very act, even as it longs to rest. But there is no rest. Out of three or four in a room, one is always standing at the window.

3

With the aid of Ted Hughes, Yehuda Amichai has translated

his poems from Hebrew into English with surprising immediacy and effect. Many of the poems are written in a style that is disarmingly playful and direct, deceptively simple; they are so artful that at times they appear artless and naked, utterly spontaneous. What a long apprenticeship must precede such simplicity! Much of Amichai's strength rests in the tone and temper of that style, the way in which he strikes the exact registers of feeling, the sympathy that is always flowing outwards in his work. Almost always his poems move on the wings of a rich and nearly surreal imagery, somehow both personal and anonymous, absolutely contemporary and yet very ancient. In a way the poems seem like one of the women they describe: "With a very short dress, in fashion, / But weeping and laughter from ancient times."

> Amichai's war poems are unique in that they are informed by a strong sense of personal responsibility—the self simultaneously implicated in, and victimized by the war—or as one poem puts it "the hunter and hunted in one body."
>
> —*Edward Hirsch*

Unlike most books of contemporary poems *Amen* is filled with other people. These poems speak with a natural and real tenderness of a village Jew ("God fearing and heavy eyed"), a tired gym teacher ("I never realized gym teachers could be sad"), a Czech refugee in London ("She behaves here as in a schoolbook for foreign languages"), and a bride without dowry ("What a terrible blood bath is she preparing for herself"). In a country filled with "all this false tourism" he speaks, comically but also with a certain amount of warmth of "a Jewish girl / Who has American hope / In her eyes and whose nostrils are still / Very sensitive to anti-semitism." And there is a heart-rending poem about a school teacher who travelled all the way to New York to commit suicide.

> People travel far away to say:
> this reminds me of some other place.
> That's like it was, it's similar. But
> I knew a man who travelled to New York
> to commit suicide. He argued that the houses
> in Jerusalem are not high enough and that
>   everyone knows him.
>
> I remember him with love, because once
> he called me out of class in the middle of a lesson:
> "There's a beautiful woman waiting for you
>   outside in the garden,"
> and he quieted the noisy children.
>
> When I think about the woman and about the

garden
I remember him on that high rooftop,
the loneliness of his death and the death of his
    loneliness.

Amichai's poems, as in this elegy for his school teacher, always try to keep "the route to childhood open." Often they speak with warmth, nostalgia, and reverence for his dead father. There are so many lovely lines about Amichai's father here (and "All those buried with him in one row / His life's graduation class") that it is hard to resist quoting them all. One poem begins "My father's cheeks when he was my age were soft / Like the velvet bag which held his praying shawl." And in **"Letter of Recommendation"** the son inside the lover breaks loose and he cries out

Oh, touch me, touch me, you good woman!
This is not a scar you feel under my shirt.
It's a letter of recommendation, folded,
from my father:
"He is still a good boy and full of love."

I remember my father waking me up
for early prayers. He did it caressing
my forehead, not tearing the blanket away.

Since then I love him even more.
And because of this
let him be woken up
gently and with love
on the Day of Resurrection.

When Amichai speaks of childhood he does so with a sly and wistful sadness, a tender hopefulness, a longing to cross the barriers of that other. Cocteau tells us, rightly I think that "there are poets and grownups." But at times Amichai almost takes Cocteau one step further as if to say "there is no such thing as a grownup" and, simultaneously, "we are all in exile from childhood." Lit up by a dry interior weeping, we are always recalling our lives, lugging around worn out letters of recommendation from the past, our futile hearts, our endless queries for affection.

In Amichai's poems those queries are most often sent out as a lover. Sometimes his love songs (**"Love Song," "Menthol Sweets," "Sometimes I Am Very Happy and Desperate"**) seem to be too short and unrealized, too imagistically interchangeable. But his finest love poems are filled with a bittersweet tenderness, an ancient mine of wisdom. He tells us that "He who put / masculine and feminine into the language put / into it also departing." Amichai is best however, not when he laments a lost love but when he praises: simply, wildly, without restraint **"A Majestic Love Song,"** for example, begins majestically

You are beautiful, like prophecies,
And sad, like those which come true,
Calm, with the calmness afterward.
Black in the white loneliness of jasmine,
With sharpened fangs: she-wolf and queen.

He is a poet able to speak of the royal scar and the blind golden scepter; he names a woman's rings as "the sacred leprosy of your fingers." It is only when the erotic poems move at the speed of such marvelous images that they earn their delicate vulnerability, their deep heart-breaking voices. And from "You are beautiful, like the interpretation of ancient books" they move successfully into

To live is to build a ship and a harbor
at the same time. And to complete the harbor
long after the ship was drowned.

And to finish: I remember only
that there was mist. And whoever
remembers only mist—
what does he remember?

Robert Lowell once called Randall Jarrell "the most heart-breaking poet of his generation." Amichai, too is a heart-breaking and heart-rending poet and, in an odd way, in a different incarnation, speaking in a different language of a different people moving through a different landscape, his poems sometimes remind me of Jarrell's finest and most luminous poems. Artfully simple, direct, and absolutely honest, simultaneously sweet and sorrowful, tender and unsentimental, both poets continually remember the enormous burden and mystery of ordinary adults shouldering their memories, carrying around the secret of their childhoods, the weight of their losses, the endless rituals of their daily lives which are so utterly original, so utterly "commonplace and solitary." I would not push the connection, but I cannot shake the feeling that, however different they are, Jarell's housewives, secretaries, and ball turret gunners are part of the same human band as Amichai's gym teachers, tourists, refugees, and Jewish soldiers. Both poets speak naturally of orphans, warriors, parents, children, and citizens.

Yehuda Amichai is a poet with a genuine talent for rendering the complex interior lives of other people. Human sympathy flows generously out of his work like a great river. He is, in his own small way, part of a tradition that dates at least as far back as the ancient Hebrew prophets. *Amen* is the book of a representative man with unusual gifts telling the tale of his tribe.

Nikki Stiller (review date Fall-Winter 1983 and Spring-Summer 1984)

SOURCE: "In the Great Wilderness," in *Parnassus: Poetry in Review*, Vol. 11, No. 2, Fall-Winter 1983 and Spring-Summer 1984, pp. 155-68.

[*In the following review, Stiller praises Amichai as a poet who is representative of the Israeli spirit and tradition, but who also adds an air of modernity to the historical consciousness of his poems.*]

We recognize the speaker in the poem. His skin is leathery from long hours in the sun; he is rugged, muscular. He might be a farmer, but then again, he appears to have been doing something more abstract, going over accounts, say, someone else's as well as his own. In his mid-thirties, he has been through a couple of wars, many alarms. Though history is continuously knocking at his door, he has taken on a private life. He has a wife, three kids, an affair from time to time. He prefers to dress in a comfortable coat that keeps his form, but he is not a comfortable man: his clenched jaw makes his head ache, and he probably grinds his teeth at night. He handles tradition familiarly—he has known it from childhood—and is accustomed to the desert where he spent a good part of his adolescence with his friends, the *chevrah*. Yet here in adulthood for one long moment he loses his confidence. "Obsolete maps" in hand, he stands alone, "without recommendations," in the great wilderness.

So Yehuda Amichai, Israeli poet, represented himself some twenty years ago. From the sun-squint of his eyes to the protective coloration of his skepticism, we recognize ourselves. And this desert he posits, whether the Judean or the Negev, reminds us of our own. But there is a major difference. The *midbar ha gadol* of Amichai's poem does not stretch forever like Frost's desert places. Nor is the great wilderness, to an ancient Hebrew or a modern Israeli, only sandy waste. It is also the source of comfort and enrichment; at the very least, it is what he must traverse on his way to the Promised Land.

The Israeli sets out well equipped. Yet a plethora of directions—call them traditions or recommendations—may confuse the poet as well as the common man. Israeli identity encompasses 1) the Bible and the land, Eretz Israel 2) two thousand years of dispersion 3) the values of Western Jewry 4) a Levantine country on the edge of the Mediterranean 5) the twentieth century in its technological chaos 6) a war-torn and politically inhibited nation forced to define itself by artificial boundaries. Modern Israel is a place—or a state of mind—which accommodates the gasworks on the road to Hedera as well as the oasis of Ein Gedi. It has planted the Diaspora's longings in the stoic garden of reality. Arab music winds through the indolence of a Tel Aviv street in its sabbath nap, stucco crumbles in middle eastern *laisser aller,* but the German Jews have erected shrines to industry in Haifa, and the wrath of the people whom Amichai calls the

"black crows" of Mea Shearim underlines the fact that the Messiah has not arrived. Where the diaspora Jew is inclined to cry "Oy!" and to express his feelings lavishly, the Israeli is taught from kindergarten to tighten his emotional belt, to keep a glinty eye on the horizon, to contain himself and his utterances. Under such circumstances, wilderness can indeed become bewilderment.

Amichai successfully fuses these disparate elements of self in his work, which includes prose as well as poetry. His early pose has not paralyzed him; he has not turned to stone. Going out into the wilderness has not led him to hear strange voices in that extraordinary landscape. Nor does Amichai dance around a calf in his poetry, although from time to time he remembers the fleshpots of Egypt and even pines after them. But to crave what you have left behind is only natural. Amichai has proven himself: he has not refused to take Jericho or to inhabit the cities of the plain. He leaves the pure, clean air of the desert for the clutter of Dizengoff Square and the claustrophobia of the kibbutz steering committee. More than any other Israeli poet, he has consistently brought together different sets of images and vocabularies.

Amichai's linguistic task was not small. One of the greatest problems for an Israeli poet is to keep Biblical echoes out, since the rhythms and diction of the prophets threaten to drown the individual voice. Some very beautiful Israeli poetry, in an exalted diction more possible in Hebrew than in English, retains the chiselled purity of desert speech, seems to be composed of the elements themselves. In Amir Gilboa's "Against the Wind," for example, the speaker, striking a rock with a sledgehammer "Preserved here from a generation past," pauses to hear the wind answer, "Amen, Selah." This elevated diction, however, excludes the incidents of daily life.

Poets such as Avoth Yeshurun, on the other hand, abandon classical Hebrew for cadences that reflect a transposed and quirky *Yiddishkeit.* Yeshurun's work is full of "*alte sochen*": the tight little stores of the pursemender or keymaker, with their rags and remnants, their dark interiors; the words themselves like refugees from ghetto life. Amichai avoids both extremes in his phrasing and diction; moving towards greater and freer use of prose or colloquial rhythms, his lexicon, like that of the state, meshes incongruities, polarities. He has an assured stride, an extraordinary—and sometimes overbearing—sense of self:

> Once I escaped, but I do not remember why or
> from which God,
> I shall therefore travel through my life, like Jonah
> in his dark fish,
> We've settled it between us, I and the fish, we're
> both in the world's bowels,
> I shall not come out, he will not digest me.

("**Two Quatrains**")

We recognize the pitch of his voice; it is familiar speech.
His father's moments of peace, he tells us, have been so few

      that he could pick
Between the bombs and smoke
And put them in his tattered sack
With the remains of mother's hardening cake.

("**Here We Loved**")

He makes learned allusions:

My deeds grow fewer,
Progressively fewer,
But commentaries about them have increased:
Just as the Talmud grows difficult
concentrated on a page,
And Rashi and the Tosaphists
Enclose it on every side.

("**On My Birthday**")

He ranges from the Biblical and prophetic in tone—

The earth must be cured
Of history
And the stones need to sleep
Even that one
That which killed Goliath must sleep, dark.

("**Leaves Without Trees**")

to the soiled quotidian:

But I
Like a garage
Turned into a synagogue,
And again abandoned.

("**Leaves Without Trees**")

These vocabularies coalesce:

And now for the thirty-second time,
After the thirty-second year,
I am still a parable
With no chance of a moral.
I stand without camouflage before enemy eyes,
With obsolete maps in my hands,
With growing opposition and amidst towers,
Alone without recommendations
In the great wilderness.

("**On My Birthday**")

Amichai the man has nonetheless managed to orient himself and therefore the poet has not remained mute. By what means has he found his direction? Through human relationships, for one thing, the pull of emotion between father and son, man and woman. His poems about his father are extremely moving, unsullied by the bitterness which sometimes accompanies the topic of sex. At times, addressing his father, Amichai's voice assumes the intimacy of a man addressing his God, and with great tenderness.

Mothers are another matter. For Amichai, childhood represents the part of us that refuses the knowledge of adults; mothers are its guardians. The mothers in these poems supply sweets, i.e., the stale cake in his father's knapsack, and cautions (**"My Mother Once Told Me,"** *Poems*). They also supply a continuous reminder to the poet of an innocence he can neither return to nor reject:

The bannister I clung to
When they dragged me off to school
Is long since burned.
But my hands, clinging,
Remain
Clinging.

("**My Mother Once Told Me**")

The Ur-mother of Jewish tradition thus appears ringed with ironies:

Sons of warm wombs join the army.
Those with feet kissed by mothers and aunts
and with shoes decorated with buckles and
    beautiful buttons
will have to pass through minefields.

(**No. 23**)

She cannot keep his childhood and protect her son forever. Amichai has therefore created an alter ego for her, the "man-eating evil" woman (**No. 14**, *Time*).

Yiddish, *mamalushen,* is the language of childhood; Hebrew was and symbolically remains the language of grown men. It is the father who initiates Amichai into the rites and responsibilities of his inheritance. At times, the past as represented by his father and forefathers is a burden:

So many tombstones are scattered behind me—
Names, engraved like the names of long-
    abandoned railway stations,
How shall I cover all these distances,
How shall I keep them connected?
I can't afford such an intricate network.
It's such a luxury.

("**Luxury**")

More often, however, the past is carried proudly; the poet has been entrusted with it as a sign of loving approval. The figure we recognized earlier is not a boy-poet but a grown man. While the father in Amichai is more tender than forbidding, the speaker has arrived at his understanding, at his adulthood, through conflict. In **"King Saul and I"** (*Poems*), Amichai evokes the struggle between the old king, the man of action, and the young David, the man of words; "He is a dead king," Amichai relates at the conclusion, and "I am a tired man." In other poems, more frequently, resolution comes through identification rather than replacement; the poet sees himself in an entire series of genetic mirror images:

> The figure of a Jewish father I am
> with a sack on my back returning
> home from the market. I have a rifle hidden
> among soft woman-things in the closet in the scent
>   of lingerie.
> A man hit by the past and ill with the future I am.

(No. 21)

To be the son of a Jewish father, the father of a Jewish son, is to know both strength and sweetness. At night, in the poem above, the speaker "lonely and slowly" cooks jam:

> stirring round and round till it grows pulpy and
>   dense
> with thick bubbles like thick Jewish eyes
> and froth, white and sweet for coming generations.

Perhaps half of his poems are addressed to a woman. There is a collection entitled *Love Poems.* Amichai must feel with Pasternak that the mystery of attraction is tantamount to the mystery of life. Some of these poems descend directly from the Song of Songs:

> Your eyes are still as warm as beds—
> time slept in them.

("Six Songs for Tamar")

Many are playful, expressive of the romantic teasing that is almost a national characteristic:

> When you smile
> serious ideas suddenly get drowsy
>
> all night the mountains keep silent at your side—
> at morning, the sand goes out with you, to sea
>
> when you do nice things to me
> all heavy industry shuts down

("Songs for a Woman")

Many more remind us of the transient nature of love, its fleeting presence before death:

> I think these days of the wind in your hair,
> and of my years in the world which preceded your
>   coming,
> and of the eternity to which I proceed before you;

("Savage Memories")

Sometimes, as in the poems of Wilfred Owen, romantic love pales in the face of war's reality:

> and I think of the bullets that did not kill me,
> but killed my friends—
> they who were better than me because
> they did not go on living;

("Savage Memories")

Thinking of love makes the poet aware of separation and loss:

> We came back to our empty room already let to
>   others,
> On the floor a torn mattress and orange peels
> and a sock, a newspaper and other knives for the
>   heart.

("Return from Ein Gedi")

The lovers in this poem, grown apart, are aware of themselves as distinct and separate entities:

> Once more we looked out of the arched window.
> Together we saw the same valley, but each of us
> saw a different future, like two fortunetellers
> who disagree with each other in a serious and
>   silent encounter.

The poet laments the lovers' lost sense of wholeness:

> And as we stray further from love
> we multiply the words
> words and sentences so long and orderly.
> Had we remained together
> we could have become a silence.

Yet lovemaking, for the poet, is often an attempt to stem thought and feeling:

> People here live inside prophecies that came true
> as inside a thick cloud after an explosion
> that did not disperse.
> And so in their lonely blindness they

touch each other between the legs in the twilight.

(No. 1)

The reader senses an undercurrent of resentment towards the women whom the poet loves. No woman is the mother to whom the speaker wishes to cling. None of his lovers can protect him, and thus some of the poems reveal an ancient grudge (**"An attempt to hold back history,"** *Great Tranquillity*). Love hurts:

> I'm like an old-fashioned firearm,
> But accurate: when I love
> The recoil is fierce, back to childhood, and
> painful.

("When I have a stomachache")

Amichai the poet experiences women as Other:

> What's it like to be a woman?
> What's it like to feel
> a vacancy between the legs, curiosity
> under the skirt. . .?
>
> . . . .
>
> What's it like to have a whole voice,
> that never broke?

And finally, tellingly, he asks:

> What's it like to "feel a woman"?
> And your body dreams you.
> What's it like to love me?

(from *The Achziv Poems, Love Poems*)

A painful sense of betrayal pervades the poems Amichai addresses to his city, his country, as if city or country were a woman also. "Jerusalem is a cradle city rocking me," the poet relates (**No. 52,** *Time*), but he finds himself "always on the run"

> from blows and from pain,
> from sweaty hands and from hard hits.
> Most of my life in Jerusalem, a bad place
> to evade all these. All my wars took
> place in deserts among hard stones and sharp
>   wounding gravel.

(No. 74)

Amichai, a twentieth-century poet, cannot travel by the old routes. All his "prophets died long ago," and his country's fate, to be in a perpetual state of siege, has been a tragic one. Though humanity protests, the very trees point him in the direction of death. Since the battle at Ashdod in the War of Independence,

> all the cypresses and all the orange trees
> Between Negbah and Yad Mordechai
> Walk in a slow funeral procession
> Since then all my children and all my fathers
> Are orphaned and bereaved
> Since then all my children and all my fathers
> Walk together with linked hands
> In a demonstration against death.

The ideals of his youth, too, have been defeated, "fell in the war / In the soft sands of Ashdod" (**"Since then,"** *Great Tranquillity*). This landscape, this wilderness, nature itself, erodes our history; while the poet replaces forgetting with remembering, he articulates the often unspoken grief of his countrymen in a place which bespeaks mutability:

> Everything here is busy with the task of remem
>   bering:
> the ruin remembers, the garden remembers,
> the cistern remembers its water and the memorial
>   grave
> remembers on a marble plaque a distant holocaust
> or perhaps just the name of a dead donor
> so that it will survive a little longer than the names
>   of others.

("In the mountains of Jerusalem")

Amichai also articulates the terror of his countrymen at being hedged in, circumscribed, debilitated by living in fear and denying it. "You mustn't show weakness," the speaker reports in one poem, "And you have to be tanned":

> But sometimes I feel like the white veils
> Of Jewish women who faint
> At weddings and on the Day of Atonement.
> You mustn't show weakness
> And you have to make a list
> Of all the things you can pile
> On a child's stroller empty of children.

("You mustn't show weakness")

This hidden fear becomes, to the man so inhibited, a cosmic one:

> This is the situation:
> If I take the plug out of the tub
> After a pleasant and luxurious bath,

I feel that all Jerusalem and with it the whole
  world
Will empty out into the great darkness.

The inner self, the speaker intimates, is irreparably damaged
and its capacity for speech impaired, though its listeners cannot perceive the distortion:

And you mustn't show weakness,
Sometimes I collapse inside myself
Without people noticing. I'm like an ambulance
On two legs carrying the patient
Inside myself to a no-aid station
With sirens blaring.
People think it's normal speech.

This straitened condition of the soul leads to a compensa-
tory swagger. Sometimes Amichai accepts the constraints.
The tough guy does not cry but makes a wisecrack. Contemplating his children in one poem, the speaker compares
their eyes to different kinds of fruit; he concludes:

And the eyes of the Lord roam the earth
And my eyes are always looking round my house

God's in the eye business and the fruit business
I'm in the worry business.

(**"Eyes"**)

Sometimes this tough guy relaxes and reveals his longings
for a moment. These he must immediately qualify or playfully mock:

I lay in the dry grass, on my back,
I saw high summer clouds in the sky,
motionless, like me below.
Rain in another land, peace in my heart.
And from my penis white seeds will fly
as from a dandelion tuft.
(Come, blow: poof, poof.)

(**No. 2,** *Time*)

Sometimes the persona overdoes it. He boasts, for example:

I feel good in my trousers
In which my victory is hidden
Even though I know I'll die
And even though I know the Messiah won't come,
I feel good.

(**"I feel good in my trousers"**)

Daring imagery, refreshingly bold, a kind of poetic Entebbe,
is sometimes dismissive:

I'm made from remnants of flesh and blood
And leftovers of philosophies. I'm the generation
Of the pot-bottom; sometimes at night
When I can't sleep,
I hear the hard spoon scratching
And scraping the bottom of the pot.

(**"I feel good in my trousers"**)

Like many of his countrymen, Amichai's persona prides himself on his rudeness, which trait can lead to inappropriate
metaphor, or a downright boorish analogy. He watches his
child sleeping and asks,

Will he get soft or harder and harder
Like an egg?
That's the thing about cooking.

(**"The parents left the child"**)

He is at his best, I think, when his manners are improvisational, born of the necessity of finding his way beyond the
conventional. In **"Things that have been lost,"** for example,
"From newspapers and notice boards" he finds out "what
people had / And what they love." Once, letting his head fall
on his chest, he finds his "father's smell / Again, after many
years"; altogether, he tells us, his memories

. . . are like someone
Who can't go back to Czechoslovakia
Or who is afraid to return to Chile.

He dares to take the last barriers by storm. In the final poem
of his most recent collection, Amichai records that "People
in the painfully bright hall / Spoke about religion" as it is
manifested in modern life. They spoke, he notes, "in excited
voices / Like at airports." The speaker leaves them:

I opened an iron door over which was written
"Emergency" and I entered into
A great tranquillity: questions and answers.

(*Great Tranquillity*)

Amichai's poems translate well. His greatest strength lies in
his resourcefulness in reading the world. No event is too
trivial, no analogy too homely, for his eye:

A clean washed board is saved
from the fate of becoming furniture.
Half an apple and half a footprint
in the sand try to become together
a whole new thing.

(**No. 80,** *Time*)

Amichai's prose rhythms are compatible with English or American poetic speech while Biblical cadences lend depth and breadth:

> The salt eats everything and I eat
> salt, till it eats me too.
> And what was given to me was again taken
> from me and given again, and what was thirsty
> has since quenched its thirst,
> and what was quenched has found rest in death.

(**No. 80**, *Time*)

His versification is organic, and he uses Hebrew's native tendency to compress expressively. The original language of the poems is often more terse and clipped than the translations. The absence of the indefinite article or the present tense of the verb "to be" in Hebrew tightens the tone further. Deeply sonorous, the poems make effective use of the Hebrew phenomenon of echoing constructions; in Hebrew, much more than in English, since different forms of the word stem from the same root, repetition is not only desirable but inevitable. But Amichai does not carry this too far. As in Italian poetry, harmonious endings can become tedious. We find him varying the kinds of verbs he uses, choosing from various classes (*binyanim*), and making sure that his line endings do not perpetually ring with "ah," "im," and "ot," the most common endings for nouns. An abundant concatenation of sounds marks true poetic association: "I am still a parable / With no chance of a moral" is in Hebrew "Ani adayin *masal*, / Bli sikooyim lihiot *nimsal*" (**"On My Birthday"**).

Yehuda Amichai's strengths are the strengths of his country; he manifests a freshness, even a brashness, yet he is rooted in history and tradition. Like a desert plant, he has flowered in what might appear adverse circumstances. What is missing here may be the outcome of historical forces beyond the poet's power or reckoning. It is said that when the People of Israel went into Exile, the Shekinah, the female emanation of the godhead, went along in order to comfort and console them. It may be that her spirit with its gentleness and grace still has not returned from the Diaspora.

Naomi B. Sokoloff (essay date May 1984)

SOURCE: "On Amichai's *El male rahamin*," in *Prooftexts*, Vol. 4, No. 2, May 1984, pp. 127-40.

[*In the following essay, Sokoloff examines the significance and use of language in* El male rahamin *as well as how the work fits into the modern Hebrew literary canon.*]

In an essay that outlines some major trends in recent Israeli poetry and prose, Shimon Sandbank shrewdly assesses the unusual relationship to language that distinguishes modern Hebrew literature from other contemporary writing. Israeli literature comes only belatedly—with the New Wave writers of the 1950s and 60s—to a dismay at the inadequacy of words such as was typical of a variety of modernist movements at the start of the century. Hebrew fiction and lyric have undergone this special development, Sandbank argues, because they have had to grapple so strenuously with the "inbuilt sacred meanings" of the language itself.

> For thousands of years Hebrew existed only as a written language, steeped in religious tradition and permeated with biblical and talmudic associations. Its revival as a spoken language, with the rise of Zionism, required an adaptation to secular needs—a rejuvenated or newly created vocabulary for modern everyday life and a syntax to match the carelessness and fluidity of living speech. This has been a painful process, perhaps not yet completed to this very day. The creative energy that has gone into the process has left little initiative for a "modernistic" questioning of communication itself. To opt for silence, one must despair of language; to despair of language perhaps one must first exhaust its possibilities. Hebrew literature, it seems, has not yet exhausted the possibilities of the Hebrew language.

In short, its idiosyncratic history as a language has invested modern Hebrew with both an overload of allusive power and an awkward, though promising newness. The challenge of reconciling these two qualities in a flexible new idiom has diverted interest from the kind of experimentalism so characteristic of other twentieth century literatures.

Even so, with the work of Amichai, Zach, Carmi, Avidan and others of the post-1948 period, there figures prominently in Israeli poetry a new element of doubt about language. Marked by an impatience with the still incomplete revitalization of Hebrew, this poetry signals a moment of linguistic reevaluation and literary self-consciousness. If, previously, the modernization of the holy tongue absorbed too much energy to leave room for despair, now the slow progress of that renewal became in itself an irritant and cause for reexamining artistic values. As the younger poets shunned the grand certainties, collective focus and ideological stances of the older writers, they reacted also against grandiose language. This group of poets had a strong sense that the writing of the preceding generation was inauthentic—verbose, mechanical, out of touch with the living world of the present, and incapable of capturing contemporary experience with any kind of immediacy. Searching for a mode of expression more aptly suited to convey their own individual experience and inner lives, the New Wave poets made

1

a concentrated effort to divest their Hebrew of traditional meanings. In their struggle to forge a new style they turned sharply to colloquial (heretofore unliterary) diction, to ironic understatement and to parody of liturgical allusion.

The discontents which helped motivate this new artistic sensibility involved more than a critique of poetic fashion directed by rebellious writers against established ones. At issue is a pervasive questioning of the nature of language which frequently thematizes itself in the poetry and which thereby adds a deliberate metalinguistic dimension to this writing. As Shimon Levy has remarked in an article called "Elements of Poetic Self-Awareness in Modern Hebrew Poetry," there are far more poems about poetry in the work of Amichai, Zach, and Carmi than in that of their predecessors, Bialik, Alterman, Shlonsky, Rachel and Steinberg. Among the interesting poems of this sort there is lyric which, like many another modernist text, dwells on problems of communication and on a rift, perceived as inevitable, between words and feeling. In addition, too, there is verse which specifically laments the difficulty of adapting an ancient tongue to modern expressive needs.

This intellectual climate goes a long way toward explicating one of Amichai's most well-known and finest poems, *El male rahamim.* The poem is worthy of close analysis, in part, precisely because it encapsulates so many of the central tensions of the generation's work. It presents an inadvertent poetics for Amichai's own writing and exemplifies in condensed form his contemporaries' major accomplishments as well.

The poem revolves about a rejection of tradition and a complementary openness to linguistic innovation. The two attitudes are intimately linked in a crumbling of collective values, both religious and nationalistic. Like the other New Wave writers, Amichai turns away from public concerns to a focus on the individual and the inner self; the elevated diction of allusion disappears as the system of values to which it refers can no longer validate it, and the shift of interest to the individual leads naturally to a new placing of importance on creativity, on private frames of reference, and on personal freedom and inventiveness. The metapoetic element in *El male rahamim* emerges as a byproduct of this process. Most directly this happens as a concern with self results in a concern with the self as poet and, eventually, with the role of the poet in renovating language. Less directly, the breakdown of referentiality here draws attention to language itself. When words no longer signify effectively within the context of external frames of reference, they may come to produce meaning primarily with relation to one another as elements of discourse within a text. Such a case, which brings language itself to the fore, prevents the reader from perceiving words simply as a medium to larger, shared understandings. This is what

comes about in Amichai's *El male rahamim.* A close reading of the poem illustrates how, by bringing the focus of signification back inside the text, the poet insists that we notice the medium, the words themselves, in their capacity for semantic renewal.

2

"God Full of Mercy"

God full of mercy,
were it not for the God full of mercy
there would be mercy in the world and not
   only in Him.
I, who picked flowers on the mountains
and I looked into all the valleys,
I, who brought corpses from the hills,
know to say that the world is devoid of mercy.

I, who was the king of salt by the sea,
who stood without decision by my window,
who counted the footsteps of angels,
whose heart lifted weights of pain
in the awesome contests.

I, who use only a small portion
of the words in the dictionary.

I, who must solve riddles against my will,
know that were it not for the God full of mercy
there would be mercy in the world
and not only in Him.

The first three lines of *El male rahamim,* which also constitute the first full sentence, proffer an assertion and define the basic premise of the entire poem: were it not for God, a God of compassion, there would be more compassion in the world. The rest of the poem serves as an elaboration on this statement and a justification for the poet's irreverence.

The hypothesis postulated here depends at several levels on a reversal of expectations. The logical supposition—that a God of compassion will foster compassion in the world—is challenged by a simultaneous over-turning of literary convention, a parody of liturgical language. The parody, in turn, hinges on a wordplay, that is, on phonetically similar words that engender a semantic inversion. Beginning in the first line with the opening from the prayer for the dead, the first sentence makes an abrupt about-face in line 2. Through the word *ilmale,* which consists of the same consonants as *el male,* the poem barely departs from the letter of the prayer, but renders its spirit completely alien. Thanks to the slightest of shifts in division between almost identical letters, this repetition entails a radical revision of meaning. Consequently, rather than the supplication to God that one would expect from line 1, the poem presents a protest and makes a plea not for the priority of divine will, but of man's well-being.

A tiny displacement of linguistic components thus turns the vocative of prayer to a disavowal of faith, delimiting a shift of emphasis from the divine to the human realm and so undermining a whole world view. The reversal of expectations here also dramatizes a reorientation toward the self and so helps enact the shift to the human realm advocated in lines 2 and 3. How does this dramatization come about? First of all, the word-play, the inventiveness of an individual poet, subverts the allusive power of the opening line and so mocks the traditional frame of reference on which it depends. Secondly, to call on God blasphemously is to heighten one's own rebelliousness. As Jonathan Culler notes in an essay on apostrophe, the vocative attributes responsiveness to the one invoked. If the being addressed in a poem is not one who can react, the whole convention then serves to call attention to the voice that does the addressing. Hence, a man standing in the rain cursing buses does not make the bus come faster; he merely makes a spectacle of himself. By the same token, the Romantic poet who calls out to inanimate objects most effectively draws attention back to himself and his own action. For this reason Culler surmises, "One who successfully invokes nature is one to whom nature might, in its turn, speak. He makes himself poet, visionary. Thus, invocation is a figure of vocation." If Amichai's God is removed from mankind and unresponsive to its needs, then the poet's ability to engage in some kind of discourse with the deity magnifies his own stature, emphasizing his own spiritual capacities and initiative.

The pivotal wordplay of lines 1 and 2 alerts us, however, not only to the distance between reverence and blasphemy, but also to their inherent proximity. Just as the words *el male* and *ilmale* resemble one another yet remain opposite in intention and implication, so the poet maintains a stance simultaneously close yet far from tradition. The very use of a vocative testifies to a recognition of God and reminds us that loss of faith is predicated on having had faith in the first place. The parody acknowledges that the poet's understanding of the world derives from the past, grows out of Jewish religion, and cannot deny the formative importance of that heritage. It could even be argued that perhaps the man would not know compassion had he not known religion; what remains entirely without doubt is that religious tradition and language no longer suffice to sustain him.

The next full sentence of the poem (lines 4-7) leaves the past behind and reconfirms the importance of the poetic self. A speaker is only implicitly active in lines 1-3, but the next sentence clearly identifies the poetic voice as *I*. Repeating the word *ani* at the beginning of line 4 and the beginning of line 6, the poem most emphatically introduces an individual

as source of the contention that the world is empty of mercy. Together, the first two sentences of the poem comprise the first verse, and this stanzaic separation highlights the central contrast, divine/human. The focus on God in 1-3 stands in direct contradistinction to the focus on the individual in 4-7.

The second verse (lines 8-14) defines in more detail the nature of the self and the individual's knowledge of the world. There are no complete sentences in this verse, and this fact acquires significance by contrast with the careful division of focus between the two complete sentences of verse 1. Here we have merely a listing of relative clauses that describe the self. (Note that *she* appears five times here with reference to *ani,* just as it has twice in the preceding verse.) These lines are clearly to be understood as a continuation of 4-7: that is, not as an addition of fundamentally new information, but, instead, as a filling-in of details. This elaboration, in its insistent attention to the self, further advances the shift of importance to the individual which began in the opening verse. The word *ani* itself assumes special prominence, since it stands in the initial position of lines 8 and 13, as it does, too, in 4, 6, and 15. This location, moreover, makes the description reminiscent of liturgy. Many prayers in Jewish and Christian tradition likewise follow an enumerative structure, providing long lists of attributes or epithets that serve to imply the immensity of God, the multifacetedness of that which is unlimited. In this way the poem again satirizes traditional literature as it replaces God with a human being.

The last verse of Amichai's poem (lines 15-18) summarizes and recapitulates the first three lines. Repeating the exact words used previously (*ilmale ha'el male rahamim / hayu harahamim ba'olam / velo rak bo*), this verse introduces two variations over the preceding treatment of God's disregard for human beings.

To begin with, these lines combine *ani* and *el* in the same sentence and in this manner, for the first time, forge a direct link between the two words. (Before we had only an implied contrast between them, along with the tacit understanding that an *I* is addressing God in line 1.) Significantly, in this sentence *ani* is the subject of the main clause and *el* that of the subordinate clause. Man claims to have the upper hand here, to encompass God to a certain extent in his own knowledge. Moreover, we realize here that this man's knowledge led to the conclusion with which we began. This means that the intervening lines have served a primarily epistemological function, explaining how the self came to an understanding of God. While the opening assertion presents itself as an abstraction, the final lines, with their emphasis on the insights of the person, reinforce yet again the reorientation from the divine to the human realm developed throughout the poem.

The second departure of this refrain from the earlier statement both strengthens and counterbalances the effect of this first variation. The last line ends with the phrase *lo rak bo,* separated, as it was not before, from the rest of the sentence. In this way the final line reflects the isolation of God, but reminds us once more that blasphemy depends on a faith once held and then questioned: *El male rahamim* begins and ends with God, and though the closing remark is a rejection, awareness of God remains the frame around the celebration of self in the middle segment of the poem. This insistent return to God suggests the poet's lingering nostalgia for belief, a longing for a kinder world transmuted now into an angry sense of injustice at God's indifference.

Within this general organization of the poem, how does the poetic *I* portray itself? Within this world neglected by God, how does the self view its own function and the meaning of its own existence? Immediately striking is the fact that all the verbs in the poem are governed by *ani* (save for *hayu rahamim,* lines 3 and 17). God is associated only with the predicate adjective *male,* that is, an attribute and not an action. There is no indication of past, present or future here. This God full of mercy remains at a remove from the world of fulfillment, of efforts, disappointments, realizations and change. Underscoring the difference between God and man, most of the verbs linked with *ani* appear in the past (*katafti, histakalti, heveti, 'amadti, hayiti, safarti, [libi] herim*). It is experience that defines man's nature and shapes his character. While God has stayed apart from the world, the poet deals directly with it and, indeed, with a very concrete, physical world. He has extended contact with nature: valleys and mountains, hills and sea, flowers, salt and death in its most palpable form (*heveti geviot min hageva'ot,* line 6). His, moreover, is a very specific reality. The proliferation of definite articles (*bahar, ha'amakim, hageva'ot, ha'olam, melekh hamelah, hayam, bataharuyot hanora'of, hamilim, bamilon*) roots us in a here and now imbued with particularity. Though not an identifiable social setting familiar to the poem's readers, this world of personal perceptions and the imagination nonetheless values its own inherent worth. It does not defer to any other, more transcendental realm, and in this here and now things in themselves matter; people, as individuals, matter. (It is worth noting, too, that the phrase *el male rahamim* uses *rahamim* in indefinite form. This is not specific compassion, not mercy directed toward a particular end. The definite article does attach itself though to the noun *rahamim* when the poet associates compassion, albeit only as wishful thinking, not with God but with the world [*hayu harahamim,* lines 3 and 17].)

The general motion away from the spiritual and toward the material in verses 1 and 2 entails more than just the poet's allegiance to earth-bound concerns. The change in outlook depends as well on a rapprochement between the lowly and the lofty, which ends by curtailing the sacred or divine and, concomitantly, attributing new spiritual importance to the individual.

The motif of limitation begins as the *I* brings corpses out from the hills. Here it is important to read this poem specifically as an Israeli text, and not as a universal one, for nature, not traditionally the sustenance of the Jewish people, in Zionism establishes itself as a praiseworthy new ideal. This new embodiment of the sacral, however, cannot divorce itself from the cruelty of the human world. To realize an ideal in this case is literally to bring it down to earth. Contact with the land of Israel, the materialization of Jewish longing and dreams, has inevitably meant acceptance of violence and bloodshed. As the poet juxtaposes images of death and of mountains, he vivifies the notion that out of the exalted heights comes compelling proof that the world is empty of compassion.

The phrase *melekh hamelah* (line 8) furthers the idea of a leveling process occurring between two opposite realms. Rather than extolling the supreme being (*elohenu melekh ha'olam*), the poet joins the superior with the humble to ironize the idea of sovereignty and supremacy. He does so in order to insist simultaneously on his own importance and his own boundaries; this is a paradoxical self-aggrandizement of humility. In similarly ambivalent fashion the poet asserts in line 16 that he counts the steps of angels. The human here has access to heavenly creatures, but only in order to quantify them, to assign them an earthly measure. A comparable leveling emerges furthermore in line 11, *libi herim mishkalot ke'ev.* In this inescapably concrete world, pain and feeling are perceived as phenomena with tangible weight. This pain struggles with the heart, which, conversely, is a physical entity associated by convention with the emotions. Neither contestant clearly overpowers the other (though *herim* suggests at least an element of success in the fight against gravity), and so the confrontations between the two are designated as *taharuyot nora'ot.* The word *nora',* indicating tremendous conflict, a battle of equals, in addition has strong religious connotations. In the poet's world, we should note, qualities of awe and terror do not belong to a special, identifiably religious domain. They are part and parcel of everyday life on man's earth, in a realm of feeling that does not admit differentiation between the physical and the spiritual.

The reciprocal transfer of qualities in lines 11-12 prepares us for the ambivalence of 13-14 as well: *ani shemishtamesh rak behelek katan min hamilim shebamilon.* Up to this point the attention to limitations has been aimed at exalted things, and as an extension of this pattern, writing or speech, too, now become something lofty. The limitations of language here come from the man who uses words, and not from the act of writing itself. The poet in this manner again stresses his own humility, even while insisting on the high purpose of the activity in which he engages.

The statement in 13-14 then creates a transitional link to the motif of limitation in the final verse, which begins with a direct parallel in line 15: *ani shemukhrah liftor hidot be'al korhi.* The limitation in question here is one of enthusiasm. The poet solves riddles, and therefore is one who confronts mystery, the unknown, things beyond his grasp, but he does so against his will. His attitude reveals both a longing for a faith bigger than himself, and a conviction that he has nowhere else to turn but to himself.

Reconfirming this reading of his outlook as an existentialist kind of self-reliance in an indifferent universe, the poem as a whole highlights the idea that he cannot rely on absolutes nor on inherited teaching, but must find wisdom only in his own perspective and in what he learns from a series of painful personal events. In contrast to the other verbs in the poem, the verbs in 13-16 appear in the present tense (*mishtamesh, mukhrah* [*liftor*], and *yode'a* as a refrain to line 7). This fact indicates that the poet's arrival at knowledge has depended on a temporal process, a progression from past action to present realizations. He bases his conclusions, moreover, on a wide variety of data. The mention of extremes (mountains and valleys) and opposite perspectives (inside and out: *leyad hayam, leyad haloni*) implies a breadth of empirical evidence as does the repeated use of plurals (*taharuyot, milim, prahim, geviot, geva'ot, mishkalot, malakhim,* etc.). Images of multiplicity again recall the enumeration of prayer, replacing hints of God's immensity with the implication that, in this case, comprehensiveness of experiences leads to comprehension.

In short, it is the individual who formulates supreme values, and he does so by drawing on his own experiences and senses rather than on a system of beliefs emanating from divine law. The entire motion of leveling between the human and the divine, which culminates in this state of affairs, expresses itself most clearly in that final verse which subordinates God's action (or inactivity) to man's knowledge. The same process culminates as well, we might say, in the very act of writing the poem, in replacing the *El male rahamim* of the prayer book with the poet's. The poet glorifies his own responses to the world, and his writing certainly counts as one of the most important among those responses.

Supporting this argument, lines 13-14 in a relatively overt metapoetic statement, have already called our attention to the elevated nature the poet imputes to writing. In addition, literary self-consciousness, which calls attention to the poet's ingenuity and invention, manifests itself in the conspicuous wordplay of the poem. This process comes about as the wordplay illustrates Roman Jakobson's definition of poetic language as self-referential. This is language that doubles

back on itself as a primary point of reference. The words *el male* and *ilmale,* for instance, signify not so much due to their denotation of an extratextual reality, as due to their relation with one another: their similar sounds, their parallel positions in lines 1 and 2, their contrasting vocative and declarative functions. By the same token, the phrase *melekh hamelah* derives much of its meaning from the phonetic closeness of the two nouns, rather than from inherent definitions of these words. These two nouns ordinarily share no semantic similarity, but the sameness of sound puts into relief that they do indeed have something in common. In the poet's view the high and the low, the supreme and the base, are not far apart; they are inseparable elements of everyday life. In this way the poem creates a focus internal to itself and so directs the reader again to the poetic self who produces meaning by bringing disparate realms together, inventing new sense out of the resulting synthesis.

The resemblance of the words *geviyot* and *geva'ot* plays a comparable role in line 6, reminding us that when we think of nature, we must also think of death. The line *heveti geviyot min hageva'ot* works particularly well, because the poet seems to have drawn one word out of the other, precisely as he has drawn corpses out from the hills. The act described and the poetic act of describing therefore reflect one another, and the mutual reinforcement of sound and sense increases our awareness of the active role of the poet. Just as the *ani* draws conclusions about the world from his own experience, without relying more on his own authority than on that of conventional definitions and reference. This means that as the poet turns in on himself, his language also turns in on itself. Having begun with a parody of prayer that depended on a play on words, *El male rahamim* takes us quickly from a disillusionment with the language of tradition to a celebration of self and of linguistic invention.

3

The kind of playfulness that characterizes *El male rahamim* is not unique to this one poem, of course. It is, in fact, one of the hallmarks of Amichai's style, though at times it functions very effectively and at other times less so. Critics have on occasion taken Amichai to task for the over-ingeniousness of his writing, for being glib, or simply for overwhelming the reader with an unassimilable amount of wordplay and metaphor. Is this the case with *El male rahamim*? To be sure, the quality of play raises disturbing questions, for it jolts the reader in its prominence and in its incongruity with the seriousness of the poem. What is the place of punning and wit in such a text? What does it contribute?

Gershon Shaked has appraised this aspect of Amichai's writing most perceptively as resulting from pressure to escape the cruelties of the external world. Attempting to shake himself of historical, political, metaphysical and personal anguish, the poet rejoices in the free play of language. Such an explanation could well apply to the text at hand, in which the poet recoils from the misery around him. To an important degree *El male rahamim* is "about" language; that is, it is "about" the poet's own cleverness, since this is an outstanding aspect of his self and the poem returns time and again to the self as source of wisdom and supreme values. To say this, however, is not to dismiss the human feeling in the poem, nor to call this work superficial. The poet's evasion does not represent irresponsibility nor lack of concern and compassion so much as a creative response to a crisis of belief. Having rejected the language of prayer which implies an entire network of significance and values, the poet attempts to invent a personal world, an inner world, through language of his own. His wordplay represents an impulse to create a refuge from the hardness of life, to maintain a sense of order and personal integrity when external harmony and inherited understandings are called into question. He writes to express anguish, certainly, but he also writes to forge a network of values in which his anguish will acquire meaning, despite the meaninglessness of a universe abandoned by God.

George Steiner, in *After Babel,* is perhaps the most eloquent spokesman for the counterfactual genius of language as just such a territorial defence of the self. He argues that the communication of verifiable fact, of ostensible information, is a secondary part of human discourse. By contrast, the ability to manipulate the future tense or the subjunctive, to imagine worlds beyond ourselves, is a basic way of gaining freedom over death and over our terrible limitations of time in this world.

> Ambiguity, polysemy, opaqueness, the violation of grammatical and logical sequences, reciprocal incomprehension, the capacity to lie—these are not pathologies of language but the roots of its genius. Without them the individual and the species would have withered.

El male rahamim, in its polyvalence, ambiguity and wordplay, in its pivoting around the word *ilmale* and in its conditional statements (*hayu rahamim,* lines 3 and 17), is a poem that very deliberately focuses on man's ability to envision alternative worlds. The entire poem is not only about the self, but about what that self can envisage as a better world. And, implicit in the very act of writing the poem is hope in the redemptive capacity of language, that is, the capacity to help conceive of new worlds when old worlds fall apart.

El male rahamim does not necessarily exhibit self-consciousness more than do many others of Amichai's work which likewise bristle with wordplay and ingenuity. This poem does, however, distinguish itself in this regard for rea-

sons already explicated but which bear recapitulation. First, as a text that explicitly addresses loss of faith, *El male rahamim* also cultivates an awareness of language by rejecting the vocabulary of prayer. Second, through the word *ilmale* and conditional constructions, this poem alerts us directly to the possibility of fashioning new worlds out of words. In addition, the seriousness of the poem gives us pause to think about its wittiness; if wordplay is not entirely out of place here, then it, as well, must have a serious function. The examples of wordplay in question do, furthermore, add dimensions of subtlety and meaning to the poem and are far from being superfluous or frivolous. Finally, lines 13-14 call attention to the poet as someone, who, writing, wrestles with exalted matters. Every poem can be said to have a metapoetic element, but these lines in this particular piece encourage us to consider that aspect of the poem as an essential, and not as a secondary concern. All these points force us to keep our sights on language and to tie linguistic questions in with the central ethical and theological problem *El male rahamim* poses: how to live and act in a merciless world, abandoned by God. Throughout Amichai's work there is an inextricable link between building faith only on the individual, without benefit of divine guidance, and an emphasis on individuality in language. This poem, though, illustrates in a particularly effective and concentrated way this assumption which underlies so much of the poet's writing.

Whether or not we sympathize with Amichai's existential values, his poetry nonetheless brings us in this way to a fundamental problem which plagues twentieth-century literature. When a system of beliefs no longer holds up, what happens to language? Faced with incomprehensible disaster or a failure of conviction, is silence or incoherence all that remains for the individual? How do words mean, and how can we continue to make them signify in a world bereft of meaning?

These are far more than merely aesthetic questions, as *El male rahamim* demonstrates. At the same time, though, at issue here is a problem of referentiality which helps explain the aestheticism that permeates so much modernist poetry and prose. The breakdown of traditional understandings, the threat of disintegration and a sense of the absurd leads again and again in literature of this century to introspection, to the mind that turns in upon itself, and so also to the isolated imagination in precarious touch with the external world. The reasons for hermeticism in modern art are many, to be sure: not only a sense of horror at the world (as in Kafka or Celan), nor a profound interest in private time, dream vision and hallucination (e.g., Proust, Stevens or Vallejo), but also an anxiety of influence, a compulsion to find ever new modes of expression (such as in portions of Joyce, Gertrude Stein, the Dadaists), as well as a basic loss of faith in language itself (witness the Symbolist realization that there is no essential mimetic link between signifier and signified). What all these tendencies have in common is that they bring the writers to the very edge of language, to an awareness of its limits and to questions of what it can and can't do. An aesthetic of fragmentation and discontinuity that lends itself to conveying inner worlds, worlds inaccessible to logic, may resemble the wrenching syntax and neologisms of experimentation for the sake of novelty, and it may also resemble the faltering, stammering incoherence of an Ionesco or a Beckett which suggests that the important things cannot or ought not be expressed. All of these self-referential kinds of discourse call attention to the internal dynamics of the text itself. From there it is only a short leap to a new critical, metalinguistic focus or to a rejoicing in the creative energy of language itself. Deemphasis on the external world therefore frequently leads to fiction about fiction and poetry about poetry. The language of breakdown then becomes the basis for new strategies of reading and writing.

The isolated imagination, the collapse of consensus and the self-absorbed text all remained alien concerns to the Israeli writers of the '48 generation, deeply engaged as they were in the struggle for national, cultural rebirth and political independence. It is only with the questioning of collective values that the New Wave writers leave Israeli literature open to a modernist orientation. Then they, too, develop a certain degree of literary self-consciousness. As do other modernist poets, Amichai as well takes refuge in introspection as he turns from the horrors of the world, and as he flees the heavy burdens of the past and the language of tradition, he attempts to invest private energy in Hebrew semantics through wordplay.

All the same, this introspective and individualistic poetry does not border on the hermetic by any means. True, it may be self-contained, self-referential and self-centered, but it is not hermetic. For one thing, the language is too accessible and the syntax too orderly. And, more important than the simplicity of the language itself, but working fully in connection with it, the poet's deep concern for the world still binds him to others about him. In his commitment to compassion we see that the poet of *El male rahamim* has not lost a sense of identity within community.

Here the discrepancy between Hebrew and other modernist traditions makes itself felt. In Amichai's generation the challenge of the Hebrew language seems to have created a pressure against the esoteric or solipsistic. For these writers experiment with colloquial diction represented innovation and an expression of individualistic artistic impulses. This means that these poets, in their individualism, come naturally but ironically back to the language of shared understandings and so closer to the popular audience. This turn of events, this odd combination of the individualistic and antihermetic, explains itself in terms of the literary history

of the previous generation. While Greenberg and Alterman, for example, stayed in line with other modernisms and delved much deeper than their successors did into extravagant metaphor, expressionistic imagery, and a personalized idiom marked by neologisms, they did so nevertheless in the service of a pronounced nationalism and without the alienation so widespread elsewhere. The New Wave poets subsequently gained precisely that kind of modernist alienation absent before, but at the same time they moved in reaction against outdated styles toward "fluency, immediacy and localism." Their efforts consequently resulted in a curious blend of distrust in language, literary self-consciousness, and a contradictory reaffirmation of communication.

Gila Ramras-Rauch (review date Autumn 1985)

SOURCE: A review of *The World Is a Room and Other Stories,* in *World Literature Today,* Vol. 59, No. 4, Autumn 1985, pp. 652-53.

[*In the following review, Ramras-Rauch offers a favorable impression of Amichai's volume of short stories, noting Amichai's ability to suffuse ordinary experiences with extraordinary insights.*]

Amichai's prose is suffused with simile and metaphor, not unlike his poetry. Indeed, some of the present stories can be regarded as poetic presentations in prose. Amichai often breaks the narrative line, defying temporal succession with the immediacy of Homeric simile. One may even question whether the selections in *The World Is a Room* are "stories"; many of the episodes are without an axis of causality or sequence. The stream-of-consciousness technique and synoptic view allow the narrator to function at various layers of memory and figurative language. Despite the poetic looseness, however, there is a strong sense of place (e.g., Jerusalem) and of time (e.g., 1948, the War of Independence).

Amichai's fiction is essentially spatial; his narrators and characters are incessantly on the move, as are their moods and voices. His strength lies in endowing the mundane with a quality of phosphorescence. Still, the war is an ineluctable background for the lovers in the title story, even if delineations are so blurred that the narrated moment and the moment of narration are fused in the consciousness of the speaker. In **"The Snow"** he achieves a mythopoeic quality, making daily events timeless. The Romans, through archeological remains, are as alive in Ashkelon as are the modern-day guests at the hotel in this Mediterranean city, where time and artifacts merge.

Through poetic imagery, Amichai intensifies his hold on reality, yet he transforms that reality and makes it a part of a wider framework, a poeticized autobiography. His friend (in **"Dicky's Death"**) and father (in **"The Times My Father Died"**) are alive and changing in these stories, despite the irreversibility of their deaths. It is a family album Amichai presents, but also his observations of war, friends, Jerusalem, the landscape—with the result that a benign irony emerges about people, events, and the mystery of everyday existence.

Hillel Halkin (essay date 1985)

SOURCE: "Yehuda Amichai: The Poet as Prose Writer," in *Ariel: A Review of Arts and Letters in Israel,* No. 61, 1985, pp. 20-4.

[*In the following essay, which was originally presented as an address in February 1985 in Mishkenot Sha'ananim, Jerusalem, to celebrate the English translation of Amichai's volume of short stories,* The World Is a Room, *Halkin explains the differences between a poet and a prose writer and speculates on Amichai's decision to turn to prose to express himself.*]

Yehuda Amichai, one of the finest Hebrew poets of our time, requires no introduction from me. On the contrary, since those gathered here, I am sure, know Yehuda and his work far better than me or mine, it would have been more fitting for him to have introduced me. Nevertheless, there is one reason it is appropriate for me to present Yehuda tonight: I have a special relationship to the book for which he is being honoured, one story of which I translated; not only because I translated it, but because when I did so, nearly 25 years ago to the day, it was the first translation I had ever done—or rather, the first for which anyone paid me. It was—as they say in the world of athletics—the translation that cost me my amateur status and for which I was for the first time fully accountable as only a professional can be. For better or for worse, Yehuda is responsible for the fact that ever since then I have been earning a good part of my living as a translator, and it is a pleasure to repay him in part tonight.

Out of curiosity I looked this week at the translation in question—it is of a story called **"The Battle for the Hill"**—and in all honesty I believe I could do it better today. Indeed, if I may be permitted a brief aside on the subject of translation, while reading **"The Battle for the Hill"** I was struck by the fact that I had not yet begun to learn at the time what today seems to me (assuming, that is, a modicum of aptitude to begin with) the secret of all good translation, namely, the readiness to put aside the original as quickly as possible (once you have got down a rough first draft of it, of course), get it out of your mind, and concentrate on your own recre-

ation of it. That was something I did not know then, being too much in awe of the text (as most beginning translators are) and the result was a good deal of stiffness, as happens in translation when the language translated into is not wearing its own clothes as it were, but is still going about dressed in the borrowed ones of the original language.

A very fine translator, Ralph Mannheim, who has been translating from German and French into English for more years than I have been alive, once wrote that every translator has to be an actor. That was not a thought to which I paid much attention when I read his article. I simply took it to mean that when you translate fiction in which there is usually a good deal of dialogue, you have to act the part of the characters, pretending you are them and asking how you would say what they would if they were speaking your own language. Today it seems to me that this is only part of what Mannheim meant. The rest is that when you translate *you have to act the author himself.* In other words, every good translator must also be a bit of an impersonator. If I am translating a story of Yehuda Amichai's into English, for example, I have to become Yehuda Amichai writing that story in English because Yehuda Amichai is now an English writer. That is the only way I can do a proper job. It is something I did not know 25 years ago.

On the subject of impersonation, it seems to me that Yehuda Amichai also appears here in the guise of an impersonator. That is, he is a poet impersonating a prose writer and although he does it very skillfully, his impersonation is not so impeccable that anyone reading him carefully does not realize that he is really a poet in disguise. In fact, I rather think that if we prose writers were better organized and had the kind of union regulations other professions do, this sort of thing would not be allowed. There would be strict rules against poets writing prose, just as there are injunctions against electricians doing the plumbing on a building site. You may ask: but why should prose writers care? It's true that poets sometimes write prose, but what is there to keep prose writers from writing poetry in retaliation? That may sound fair, but it's really about as equitable as the remark once made by Emile Zola that the rich and the poor are perfectly equal, since the rich have the same right as the poor to sleep in the streets. For though a poet can go slumming in the streets of prose whenever he wants, the reverse is simply not the case. It is a fact that although poets who have written good or excellent prose are not uncommon in the history of literature, prose writers who have written good poems are few indeed. Many may have wanted to dwell in the mansion of poetry but did not possess the price of admission.

If we ask why it seems so much easier for poets to write good prose than for prose writers to write good poetry, the first answer—that writing good poetry must be harder work than writing good prose—is not, I believe, true. Not only is writing good prose very hard work but writing poetry is not really work at all. It is something of an entirely different nature. Prose is something that, with a certain amount of talent and a lot of sheer grit, you can create; poetry is not. There is no way to will or to sweat poetry into existence. There is something magical in its creation, which may one day be discovered to be merely some special electro-magnetic tremor of the brain, but about which all we know in the meantime is that it either comes to you or it does not— if it does not, as the Song of Solomon says about love, it can be neither stirred up nor awakened until it pleaseth. Permit me to read a small section of a Socratic dialogue in which Socrates is having some fun with Ion, a young performer who has been awarded first prize at the Athenian festival for his reading of Homer, accompanying himself on the lyre. In it Socrates goes about proving to Ion that Ion himself does not understand the first thing about poetry, not because he is particularly dim-witted, but because no one can.

> For all good poets, says Socrates, compose their beautiful poems not as works of art, but because they are inspired and possessed. And as the Corybantian revellers when they dance are not in their right mind, so the lyric poets are not in their right mind when they are composing their beautiful strains. For they tell us that they gather their strains from honeyed fountains out of the gardens and dells of the Muses; thither, like the bees, they wing their way. And this is true. For the poet is a light and winged and holy thing, and there is no invention in him until he has been inspired and is out of his senses, and the mind is no longer in him: when he has not attained to this state, he is powerless and unable to utter his oracles.

Those of us who, though not poets ourselves, have had the temerity to try writing poetry, know too well how painfully true are these words. Prose is a human endeavour, but poetry, as Socrates says, comes from the gods. And I must say that when a true poet writes prose it is as if someone a bit godlike were walking among men. What is it that gives him away in the end? Perhaps the very effortlessness of his performance; he never seems to exert himself at precisely those moments when even the best prose writers must pack all the literary muscle that they possess. True, he may sometimes write sentences like the rest of us; sooner or later he will make a too light or graceful movement, something gravity-defying from the point of view of prose, and make us realize suddenly that we are in the presence of a poet as the biblical Manoah realized he had seen an angel when the man he was talking to rose skyward before his eyes in a tongue of flame.

It is this almost acrobatic ease in Yehuda Amichai's stories

that strikes me most when I read them. Prose has its own laws of gravity, its own laws of space and time that must be obeyed. We are told—and it is on the whole good advice—that a story must have a beginning, a middle and an end. We are told that it must have a plot to impart to it the movement that will carry it from one point to another. We are told that it must have credible characters to give the plot mass. Yet when one reads the stories in *The World is a Room,* one sees that it is possible, although perhaps only if one is a poet, to thumb one's nose at all of these rules and write wonderful prose all the same. In this book there are stories that have beginnings and no ends. There are others that have ends and no beginnings. Some are all middles. One, **"Love in Reverse"**, begins with its end and ends with its beginning. None has what might be called a plot. None has any characters worth speaking of. Nothing happens in the stories. Many of them even seem to be about that. In **"The Battle for the Hill"**, a company of soldiers prepares for an imminent war that never breaks out. In **"The Orgy"** some friends plan and plan an orgy that never takes place. In **"The Class Reunion"**, that reunion is never held. There is a story called **"My Father's Deaths"** in which a man dies and dies, and then dies again, and then really dies, and then dies and dies and dies and keeps on dying. If Auden was correct when he said that "poetry makes nothing happen," that description alone clearly labels these stories those of a poet.

Yet, if poetry makes nothing happen, what the stories in this book tell us is that there is one thing that truly and constantly does happen in this world, and that is poetry itself. The rest is illusion. We may think that it happens but it never does. We cannot even say what "it" is, for everything in these pages is a metaphor for something else, every event is an evocation of another, every situation is a correspondence or symbol that points away from itself. The world in Yehuda Amichai's stories is written in a code to which the poetic imagination alone has the key and the eye to discern the secret meanings and hidden relationships. Although the publisher has named this volume *The World is a Room* (after one of the stories in it), it might more accurately have been called "The World is a Poem."

Why then say it in prose? Because while the world may be a poem, a poem is not a world. A lyric poem is too much of a fragment for that task. It takes the stretch and breadth of prose to make a world—that is, to create a self-enclosed reality in which there is enough space, time, and extension to make us feel that we are within it and not just on the outside looking in. But it takes a poet writing prose to show us that such a reality is itself unending poetry. That is my sense of these stories. If any of you wish to take issue with it, allow me to defend myself by calling once more on the greatest and slyest of all philosophers. At the end of his dialogue with Ion, having thoroughly befuddled the young man and made him realize that he has little idea what his beloved

Homer is all about, Socrates says: "And if, as I was saying, you have art, then I should say that in falsifying your promise to me that you would exhibit Homer, you are not dealing fairly with me. But if, as I believe, you have no art but speak all these words about Homer unconsciously and under his inspiring influence, then I acquit you of dishonesty and shall only say that you are inspired. Which do you prefer to be thought, dishonest or inspired?" To which, Ion, being no fool, answers, "There is a great difference, Socrates, between them, and inspiration is the far nobler alternative." "Then, Ion," Socrates generously concludes, "I shall assume the nobler alternative and attribute to you in your praises of Homer inspiration and not art."

Yair Mazor (essay date Winter 1986)

SOURCE: "Farewell to Arms and Sentimentality: Reflections of Israel's Wars in Yehuda Amichai's Poetry," in *World Literature Today,* Vol. 60, No. 1, Winter 1986, pp. 12-17.

[*In the following essay, Mazor examines Amichai's unsentimental approach to the brutality of Israel's wars.*]

> War's a brain-spattering, windpipe-slitting art,
> Unless her cause by right be sanctified.
>
> Byron, *Don Juan,* 9.4

One may convincingly argue that all art is enduringly besieged by an intriguing paradox. A considerable part of any work of art is founded upon emotion. Even the most ambitiously intellectual, logical, artistic creation that aspires only to analytical insight is not completely devoid of emotion. Such a lack would undoubtedly devitalize the piece, leading to shallowness. Thus emotion is not only laudable but crucial to any work of art. When feeling deteriorates into over-emotionality, however, when the delicate balance between depicted object and artistic depiction is upset or destroyed, the work suffers. The artistic paradox is therefore enticing and potentially devastating at the same time; the creative work's vitality and its deterioration spring from the same source, and the dividing line between the two may be hazy. In most cases, though, readers seem to possess a reliable capacity to distinguish correctly between well-monitored sentiment and exaggerated sentimentality.

Perhaps it is easier to demonstrate a methodology for avoiding sentimentality than it is to define the difference between delicate sentiment and coarse sentimentality. Although all art develops its own means of preventing a stumbling metamorphosis from the former to the latter, one may plausibly discern a common denominator among all the techniques and devices: the enduring effort to cultivate an equilibrium between the emotional resonance evoked by the material and that earned by the artistic depiction. This goal may be adroitly achieved by a deftly calibrated process of restraining emotions, distilling sentiments, dimming the eroding emotional potential, and damming the potentially inordinate effect.

Amichai's poetry displays a flexible and sensitive capacity to modify literary means according to alternating emotional resonances emerging from different wars.
—*Yair Mazor*

One might contend that distancing is easier to establish in literature, the verbal art, than in the other arts. This argument is based on the fact that the distance between the artistically molded reality and the molding medium is greater in literature than in, say, painting, sculpture, music, or dance. Color, form, sound, movement are all physical phenomena; words are the only creative materials not found in nature. This unique character of the verbal arts is acknowledged by the Psalmist, who lauds: "The heavens declare the glory of God; and the firmament sheweth his handiwork. Day unto day uttereth speech, and night unto night sheweth knowledge. *There* is no speech nor language, *where* their voice is not heard" (Psalms 19:1-4). The verbal personification which the Psalmist bestows upon nature maintains the only thing it does not possess: words.

More than fiction or drama, poetry seems to shrink literature's inherent distance between depicted object and depicting medium because poetry more strongly prefers emotional to rational expression. Fiction, especially the novel, is the most conscious and intellectual literary form: it doubts, examines, muses, inquires, suspects, expounds, probes, and analyzes. Poetry appears to engrave the importance of being emotional on its ideological ban. The need to curb emotions and block sentimentality in poetry therefore becomes an urgent one.

This need increases when the poetic subject itself is highly emotional, such as war—particularly the protracted, lacerating Israeli wars in which poets have participated and continue to participate. The historical proximity of these wars, especially the War for Independence (1947-49), to the Holocaust, the perpetually besieged position of the state of Israel, the knowledge that defeat would lead to national calamity, the haunting sense of David compelled to face Goliath—all these factors give Israeli wars a remarkably condensed emotionality and consequently increase the hazard of an oversentimental poetic response.

Since it is beyond the capacity of a single paper to discuss the quantity of techniques mobilized by Israeli poets for taming emotionality in war-related verse, it seems preferable to concentrate on one poet whose ars poetica may represent major tendencies shared by many. Yehuda Amichai (b. 1924) is one of the most distinguished and prolific of contemporary Israeli poets. Although war is certainly not a predominant component in his work, his poetry does embrace all Israeli wars from the struggle for independence through the recent conflict in Lebanon. Furthermore, Amichai's poetry displays a flexible and sensitive capacity to modify literary means according to alternating emotional resonances emerging from different wars. The unique feelings generated by the Six-Day War and the Lebanon war in comparison to the War for Independence are prudently mirrored in his verse, and his work may be considered a poetically historical account as well as a sensitive moral barometer of Israel's conflicts.

Nathan Zach, another contemporary Israeli poet, states, "When sentiments fade away, the correct poem speaks out." Zach does not recommend the purging of emotions from poetry but suggests dealing with emotions in an unemotional way. Amichai's poetry differs markedly from Zach's yet ardently exemplifies Zach's axiom. Amichai uses a repetitive technique in his poetry, adopted for disarming sentiments of their undesirable potential for sentimentality. Although a poem's focus is war and its agonizing outcome, the subject is treated not directly but obliquely. Thus war is evasively depicted through themes and topics which are relatively or even exclusively divorced from war itself. Consequently, war is uprooted from its highly emotional immediacy and anchored in a distant context, which meliorates the emotional resonance, serving to dilute it. In other words, a deflection of attention from a given war insulates its emotional potential and thereby establishes esthetic distance.

This technique is proficiently displayed in the following sonnet, which opens a cluster of sonnets titled **"Ahavnu Kan"** (**"We Loved Here"**):

> My father spent four years in their war
> And neither hated his enemies nor loved them;
> But I know that already there
> He built me day by day from his tranquillities
>
> Which have been so few, collected by him
> Between bombs and smoke,
> And he put them in his worn bag
> With the rest of his mother's drying cake.
>
> And he collected in his eyes nameless dead
> Many dead he collected for me,
> For I will recognize them in his looks and will know them,

And I will not die like them in the atrocity—
He filled his eyes with them and he was wrong:
I continue going to all my wars.

The poem's major theme is the narrator's own forced participation in war (despite his father's hopes), but it is suspended by the poem's end and consequently is considerably blurred. One may also discern a rhetorical device we might call thematic swindling. The reader assumes that the father's wars are the poem's focus, only to realize at the poem's conclusion that he has been misled. The swindle that yields frustrated expectations, however, grants the poem an enigmatic tinge, making necessary an intellectual deciphering process. The reader must extricate the poem from the emotional level to the rational one, and therefore the emotional potential is weakened.

Furthermore, the majority of the poem is devoted to the father's wars. Despite their horrors, they deflect attention from the narrator's wars and thus blunt their impact in the poem. A similar thematic deflection is demonstrated in **"Shir al hakravot harishonim"** (**"A Poem on the First Battles"**).

> On the way to the front we stayed overnight in a
>   kindergarten,
> Under my head I put a woolen Teddy bear
> Upon my tired face dreidels descended
> And trumpets and dolls—
> Not angels,
> My feet, in the heavy boots
> Let fall a tower of colorful dice
> Which have been put each on the other,
> Each die smaller than the one under it
> And in my head big and small memories
>   confusingly mingled
> And made dreams.
>
> And beyond the window there were fires. . .
> And also in my eyes under my eyelashes.

Here thematic deflection seems to reach a level of extreme elaboration. Though war is again the poet's center of interest, it is left to a relatively marginal part of the poem and alluded to only hastily. In **"We Loved Here"** the narrator's war is suspended until the end, whereas in the present example the war is inlaid from the very beginning and then blatantly abandoned. The dilution of war's emotional potential is achieved through a diversion of attention from war to a kindergarten. The naïve and peaceful connotations thus evoked soften the harsh, devastating impact of armed conflict. On the other hand, the encounter emphasizes the horrors of war when contrasted to the tranquil background of the kindergarten. The shift mutes the emotional response generated by war but does not let emotionality completely dissipate. Consequently, the poem's emotional tone is balanced.

Another example of Amichai's skillful use of thematic deflection to control inordinate emotionality is found in **"Bet hakravot hatsva'i habriti behar hatsofim" ("The British Military Cemetery on Tsofim Mountain")**.

> Forgetfulness in the valleys. More remembrance
>   on the mountain.
> A diligent prudency constructed
> On the mountain slopes. How can one die
> At a great distance for
> A country that does not exist? And I
> Was not born then, yet.
>
> Sometimes in summer
> When the terrestrial globe is transparent,
> The grandchildren of those who died watch
> Their dead grandfathers calmly floating
> As on the floor of the ocean
> Of the land of Jerusalem.

The British wars in Israel took place many decades ago, and their selection as the poem's theme already establishes a certain historical distance. Still, since British rule in Israel is historically bound to the Israeli struggle for independence, the emotions aroused by the war have not completely faded. Thus, the War for Independence saliently echoes between the poem's lines, but its emotional resonance is muted. Moreover, the narrator's reference to the soldiers killed by the British as grandfathers serves as a cunning device of temporal displacement and cultivates the illusion that they continued to live after death, as young men, and eventually became grandfathers. The temporal remove and the illusion of survival together function to lessen the sorrow of the soldier's death and consequently reduce its emotional impact.

The same technique is well demonstrated in one of a group of poems titled **"Kinot al hametim bamilkhama" ("Lamentations on the War Dead")**.

> The memorial of the unknown soldier is
> On the other side. The enemy's side.
> A good reference point for the artillery men
> Of the future.
>
> Or the war memorial in London
> Hyde Park corner, decorated as a cake
> Fancy and rich: one more soldier raises his head
>
> And a gun, one more cannon, one more eagle, one
>   more
> Stone angel.
>
> And a big marble flag like whipped cream.
> Poured from above
>
> Artistically
>
> The oversweet cherries
> Too red
> Already have been gluttonized by the glutton of
> hearts.
>
>   Amen.

Although the poem begins with reference to what was probably an Israeli unknown-soldier's memorial, erected in haste during the battles and now beyond the border, on the enemy's side, the focus shifts rapidly to a British war memorial in the heart of London. That depiction of the British monument, so different from the Israeli one, occupies most of the poem's text and closes the piece. The coquettish richness of the foreign memorial confronts the meekness of the Israeli monument. Whereas the latter is bleakly besieged on the enemy's side, the former is proudly located in the center of the capital, declaring its arrogant artistry. Furthermore, the foreign memorial is made of stone, symbolically announcing that the war and its horrors are also now petrified, never to return. In contrast, the Israeli marker is described as a good target for artillerymen in future conflicts. The foreign war came to an end; the Israeli one did not and is augured to continue, as bloody as ever.

Imagining the Israeli memorial as a convenient target for future marksmen is also bitingly ironic: the soldiers who were shot and killed are doomed to repeated shellings after their death. Even the tomb cannot provide the repose they never found while alive. Another ironic barb is directed at the foreign monument. The British role in Israel during the years prior to the War for Independence was certainly not laudable, despite lofty pretensions of bringing order and peace to the region. Now British rulers have erected a grandiose memorial to commemorate their army's service, while the war they pretended to end goes on. Such irony is not only ideological, but also acts as a tool to curb sentimentality by establishing an emotional distance, leading to clear-eyed rationality.

Amichai also restrains sentimentality with verbal simplicity, a sort of rhetorical meekness, as in **"Geshem bisdeh hakrav" ("Rain on the Battlefield")**: "Rain falls on the faces of my friends: / On the faces of my living friends, who / Cover their heads with a blanket— / And on the faces of my dead friends, who / do not cover any more." The simple, ordinary language and the modest tone of this short poem create a considerable distance between emotional essence and rhetorical utterance. A cry becomes a whisper; weeping all but vanishes. Potential sentimentality therefore fades, and a very correct poem (following Zach's prescription) results. The dead and the living are equal because the rain soaks everyone. That horrible equality is again shown as the live soldiers cover their faces with blankets and look like dead comrades—who are customarily covered with a blanket on the battlefield. The enormous emotional impact born of such statements demands drastic restraints. Monitoring the language and tone seems an appropriate rhetorical technique for the poem's esthetic needs.

The same verbal monitoring is applied to the metaphorical texture of another poem from **"Lamentations on the War Dead."**

> Dikki was hit
> Like the watertower in Yad Mordechay.
> Hit. A hole in the belly. Everything
> Streamed out of him.
>
> But he remained standing like that
> In the landscape of my memory,
> Like the watertower in Yad Mordechay.
>
> Not far from there, he fell
> A bit northward, near Chulekat.

Poetry's exalted, celebrated verbal characteristics are missing here, replaced by a surprising simplicity in which a dying soldier is compared to a collapsing watertower. The customary elevation of the figurative level is not completely abandoned, however, for a dryly reported simile that could have been taken from an informative newspaper account attains its rhetorical purpose. The holy becomes secular, the divine becomes earthly, and the emotionally laden poem escapes sentimentality.

Elsewhere, simile gives way to metaphor, and the hierarchic relationship between the metaphorically related elements acts as a cornerstone for rhetorical restraint, as in the fourth poem of **"Lamentations on the War Dead."**

> I found an old book about animals,
> Brehm, second volume, birds:
> In a sweet language, depiction of a starling's life,
> A thrush and a swallow. Many errors in an old
>
> Gothic script, but a lot of love. "Our winged
> Friends," "Wandering from us to the warm
>   countries,"
> A nest, a spotted egg, soft down, the nightingale,
> The stork, "The spring harbingers."
> The red chest.
>
> Year of publication, 1913, Germany,
> The eve of the war which was the eve of my wars:
> My good friend who died in my arms and his
>   blood
> In the dunes of Ashbod, 1948, June.

> Oh, my friend
> The red chest.

The metaphorical bond between the robin's red breast and the blood-covered chest of the speaker's friend is cleverly wrought and meaningfully baffling. The poem's first two stanzas lead the reader to assume the poem's focus is an old, alluring German bird book. The third stanza then connects the book's date of publication to World War I, provoking the reader's curiosity, and further links that war to the Israeli War for Independence. The German defeat in World War I prodded Germany to start World War II; the Jews who escaped that war and reached Israel were later forced to fight for independence. Only the poem's closing stanza fully reveals the true focus, however, and the reader's frustrated assumptions compel him to reread and reconsider the poem. The bird descriptions, especially the red breast, are not the thematic nucleus, as previously believed, but only a vehicle for the metaphorical equation within which the narrator's dead friend is the tenor.

This zigzag process of literary comprehension is certainly not unique. Many literary texts deliberately dictate a reading-comprehension process whereby later information casts new light upon previously rendered information and consequently alters the initial perception of meaning. As Iser says, "The act of reaction is not a smooth or continuous process, but one which, in its essence, relies on *interruptions* of the flow to render it efficacious. We look forward, we look back, we decide, we change our decisions, we form expectations, we question, we muse, we accept, we reject; this is the dynamic process of reaction." However, in Amichai's poem the reading process is prudently mobilized toward the rhetorical goal of preventing sentimentality: its baffling characteristics condition a drastically rational reaction which eliminates its emotional potential. In other words, the reader's reaction to the poem is extricated from the emotional level and "exiled" to the rational level, enabling sentiment without sentimentality.

Another effective use of poetry's figurative tissues to block sentimentality is evident in Amichai's poem **"Elohim merakhem al yaldey hagan" ("God Pities the Kindergarten Children").**

> God pities the kindergarten children
> He pities the schoolchildren less
> And He does not pity the adults at all.
> He leaves them alone
> And sometimes they are forced to crawl on all
>   fours
>
> In the burning sand,
> To get to the first-aid station
> And they are bleeding.

Perhaps He will pity the true lovers,
Will bestow mercy and will shade
Like the tree that shades the homeless
Who sleep on a bench on the boulevard.

Perhaps we also shall give them
The last coins of grace
Which mother left us
So their happiness will protect us
Now and in the days to come.

Although the war theme is concealed in the poem's embroidery as a seemingly marginal metaphor, its presence significantly affects the overall meaning. The narrator's blatant accusation against God, who wrongly and stintingly distributes His mercy, takes on a singular meaning as the castigated adults are portrayed as wounded soldiers, crawling in the burning sand, bleeding and in grave pain. The phrase "crawling on all fours" also likens the adults to helpless infants and consequently emphasizes their miserable condition. It is ironic, moreover, that whereas true infants are well protected by God, adults who are as helpless as infants are indifferently deserted by the same Lord. However, once God's injustice toward the chastised adults is configured in metaphorical terms of bleeding, wounded soldiers, the impact of war's atrocities permeates the poem's fabric and dominates its ideological features. The impact of war's horrors is in no way diminished, yet the emotional resonance is successfully restrained. The precarious border between sentiment and sentimentality has once again been avoided.

The thematic structure of the poem, I might add, is founded upon a pervasive critical irony. The speaker's contention that divine pity for kindergarten children is coupled with a disturbing injustice toward adults offers a stark contrast to the traditional image of a merciful God. This fundamental irony prevails throughout, but it is not the most striking ironic aspect. In fact, it serves as a foundation upon which an even more intricate irony is developed at the poem's conclusion. The speaker, bitterly disappointed by a God whose generosity does not even match that of a tree, decides to replace this pitiless Lord. He bestows upon the agonized adults the last coins of grace from his mother's inheritance. The final two lines of the last stanza shed a surprisingly ironic light on this generous initiative: "So their happiness will protect us / Now and in the days to come." Accordingly, the speaker's magnanimity is nothing but a selfish investment: he aspires to support the castigated adults because it may be beneficial. Consequently, the ironic accusation leveled at God boomerangs and hits the speaker himself. Furthermore, to his allegations of divine indifference toward human misfortune, he adds the charges of selfishness and hypocrisy, thereby only widening the abyss between his pretentious self-portrait and his true nature.

Irony and sentimentality cannot coexist. The rational critical consideration dictated by irony does not admit of superfluous emotionality. Excess emotionality is based on a lapse of critical distance; irony springs form that distance. The attainment of such distance becomes more problematic as Amichai's thematic focus shifts from the independence struggles (1947-49) and the Yom Kippur War (1973) to the recent conflict in Lebanon, the most confusing and most heatedly debated war Israel has ever known. This war is painfully different from and far worse than previous ones; it aspired to bring peace, yet it still continues. Some argue that although the conflict erupted in 1982, its roots can be traced to the laudable Six-Day War (1967), whose consequences were dramatic and even spectacular. The haunting sense of a besieged country threatened constantly by murderous animosity was drastically alleviated. The stifling perpetual fear of destruction was suddenly replaced by glorious self-confidence. The starkly constricted borders, exposed to vicious attacks, were expanded through stupendous conquests from horizon to horizon. Victory was not easily digestible, however. The sharp transition from a state of siege to sweeping conquest also invoked a sense of modesty. High pride, excessive self-confidence, and vain haughtiness arose. David not only smote Goliath but also succeeded him.

The traumatic Yom Kippur War was the bitter result of those perilous developments. Still, the lesson was not learned. Grief and blatant rage surfaced during the summer of 1982. Hostile foes of yesterday turned into fervent peace-seekers, whom Israel spurned. Even the absence of Egypt did not radically alter the vicious calculus of enmity in which Israel is still the threatened component. Israel's basic struggle for survival was no less right than before, but the protracted Lebanon conflict raised more questions than answers. The painful nature of Israel's most recent war is piously mirrored in the poem "**Hagibor ha'amiti shel ha'aqedah**" ("**The Real Hero of the Aqedah**").

The real hero of the *aqedah* was the ram
Who did not know about the conspiracy among the
  others
As if he volunteered to die instead of Isaac.

I want to sing him a memorial poem,
About the curly wool and his human eyes
About the horns which were so quiet on his
  vibrant head
And after he was slaughtered they made of them
  shofarot
For the cheering of their war
Or for the cheering of their vulgar happiness.

I want to remember the last scene
Like a handsome photograph in a refined fashion
  journal:

The tanned young man, indulged in coquettish
   clothes
And next to him the angel dressed in a long silk
   garment
For a celebrated reception.
And they both stare with empty eyes
At two empty seats

And behind them, like a colorful background, the
   ram
Held in the thicket before slaughter.
And the thicket is his last friend.

The angel left for home
Isaac left for home
And Abraham and God left long ago

But the real hero of the *aqedah*
Is the ram.

Though the *aqedah* story has inspired numerous variations, both in Hebrew and non-Hebrew literature, Amichai's approach to this ancient yet fresh and tantalizing motif is striking: all the traditional participants in the sacrificial drama are bypassed, and the ram, the real victim, is elevated to a leading role. This surprisingly innovative interpretation is not superficial manipulation or vain literary provocation, but a useful vehicle to render a critical message. The specific nature of this message is clarified in the last three lines of the first stanza: "And after he was slaughtered they made of them *shofarot* / For the cheering of their war / Or for the cheering of their vulgar happiness." These lines refer to the euphoria that flowed from the intoxicating victory of the Six-Day War. Associating the *shofarot* with that "vulgar happiness" expressly recalls the sounding of the ram horns after the conquest of the Wailing Wall during the Six-Day War, a celebration that the poet interprets as a disturbing sign of presumptuousness. The phrases "*their* war" and "*their* vulgar happiness" manifest his recoil from such conceited behavior, in which he wishes no part.

A common denominator between Amichai's critical elucidation of the *aqedah* and his denunciation of the Six-Day War's unfortunate consequences is clear, however: there are always forsaken victims who pay for others' happiness with their lives. In this sense, the slaughtered ram and the young soldiers who fell during the war are analogous sacrifices sharing analogous altars. In this vein, the word *volunteered (lehitnadev)* is particularly significant, since volunteerism is a key concept in regard to the Israeli army. The term may thus be considered an integrative element that binds past and present, the fable to its moral. An identical expressive connection springs from the change in verb tense between the opening and closing lines of the poem: "The real hero of the *aqedah* was the ram . . . the real hero of the *aqedah* is the

ram." The biblical ram was sacrificed in the distant past; its young human successors are being continually sacrificed today. Past and present are bound in bloody redundancy.

As in previously discussed poems, thematic deflection is evident here, for the war in Lebanon is indirectly presented through the isolating screen of the *aqedah* fable. Consequently, an esthetic distance is achieved and the poem is redeemed from potential sentimentality. **"The Real Hero"** is ironical, hyperbolic, and critically piercing. Shakespeare cleverly stated in *1 Henry IV,* "The arms are fair / When the intent of bearing them is just" (5.2.88-89). Indeed, despite the questionable nature of the Lebanon conflict, Israel did not say farewell to fair arms. Long years of haunting terrorism have certainly produced a just intent for bearing arms, yet too many aspects of this continuing war are not fair. This change in the nature of war has dictated a change in Amichai's literary response to the subject. Though lamentation for the dead is undiminished, it is joined with biting irony and exaggerated criticism. In Amichai's verse, historical dynamics are faithfully shadowed by poetic dynamics. In this regard, his poetry aspired not only to mirror history but to judge it as well. Amichai's "war poem" is a "correct poem" not only because it extinguishes sentimentality and prefers a whisper to a cry, but also because it is a farewell to arms as much as it is a farewell to sentimentality.

Mark Irwin (review date Winter 1988)

SOURCE: "Toward a Tragic Wisdom and Beyond," in *Kenyon Review,* Vol. X, No. 1, Winter 1988, pp. 132-39.

[*In the following review, Irwin praises the poems in* Selected Poetry of Yehuda Amichai *but questions the publisher's decision to have the poems retranslated.*]

Toward the end of Camus' novel *La Chute* (*The Fall*), in which the narrator Clamence rambles on in a drunken soliloquy, we are told: "Pour que la statue soit nue, les beaux discours doivent s'envoler" (For the statue to stand bare, the fine speeches must take flight). The narrator's plight, one in which speech embellished with exaggeration and lies prolongs a hypocritical life, becomes a metaphor for the predicament of language in a postmodern era. One might argue that there are two types of language: one which attempts through excess to conceal emptiness, and the other which through reduction attempts to embrace all that is absent, and which finally leads into the mysteries of silence and the most profound poetry.

In modern poetry, Yehuda Amichai has accomplished an act as significant, yet perhaps even more far-reaching, as that accomplished by William Carlos Williams. He has created a poetry whose purposeful lack of stylistic ornamentation is merely a further extension of its irony, which suggests that if language is to become truly inevitable, no artifice must stand between speaker and object. Amichai has reduced poetry to its most powerful common denominator—truth.

"Spy"

Many years ago
I was sent
to spy out the land
beyond the age of thirty.

And I stayed there
and didn't go back to my senders,
so as not to be made
to tell
about this land

and made
to lie.

Adjectiveless as it is universal, this funereal song on the loss of innocence sears into the heart. It is a faint voice, spiritually exhausted yet noble, for it is the voice of both survivor and rebel. What more could one ask in art? It stands mock-heroic and stubborn, faithlessly sustained and stripped-down as a Giacometti sculpture—a memorial to our *posteverything* era.

Amichai has created a poetry whose purposeful lack of stylistic ornamentation is merely a further extension of its irony, which suggests that if language is to become truly inevitable, no artifice must stand between speaker and object. Amichai has reduced poetry to its most powerful common denominator—truth.
—Mark Irwin

Amichai's work, despite its deeply biblical and historical roots, remains ultimately postmodern, for often he succeeds in expressing what escapes language, the ineffable (such as personal and political fate) through concrete images and unadorned metaphor:

Flags
make the wind.
The wind doesn't
make the wind.

The earth makes
our death.

Not us.

Your face turned west
makes the wandering in me,
not my feet.

The voice in Amichai's best work echoes the disillusioned characters created by some of this century's most significant writers: Kafka, Joyce, Beckett. It is the voice of the exile who errs endlessly and realizes the impossibility of permanence; a voice that finally accepts wandering and exile as truth.

Unfortunately, [*Selected Poetry of Yehuda Amichai*], the most comprehensive so far, does not contain the two previously quoted poems translated by Harold Schimmel. In fact, only one poem from Amichai's splendid volume published in 1973 appears here: *Songs of Jerusalem and Myself.* My major quarrel with these poems has to do with "re-translation"—not that these translations are inadequate; in fact, many are quite good. Why, however, did Harper & Row enlist two new translators when superb versions by Yehuda Amichai, Robert Friend, Assia Gutmann, Ted Hughes, and Harold Schimmel already existed? I suspect that the answer is the attractive sales of a major poet. Compare the slang ("we even got off") and prosaic, awkward rhythms ("As far as I'm concerned, they're always") in the Mitchell version with the speed and facility of the more regularly metered lines in the Gutmann version:

"A Pity. We Were Such a Good Invention"

They amputated
your thighs off my hips.
As far as I'm concerned
they are all surgeons. All of them.

They dismantled us
each from the other.
As far as I'm concerned
they are all engineers. All of them.

A pity. We were such a good
and loving invention.
An airplane made from a man and wife.
Wings and everything.
We hovered a little above the earth.

We even flew a little.

—Translated by Assia Gutmann

"A Pity. We Were Such a Good Invention"

They amputated

your thighs from my hips.
As far as I'm concerned, they're always
doctors. All of them.
They dismantled us
from each other. As far as I'm concerned,
they're engineers.
A pity. We were such a good and loving
invention: an airplane made of a man and a
woman,
wings and all:
we even got off
the ground a little.
We even flew.

—Translated by Stephen Mitchell

The tedium of the more regular rhythm is crucial here, for it mimics the collapse of humanity, in this case man and wife, through the methodical and inhumane progress of science and technology. The dissolution of marriage in society is reduced to a mechanical cross: "an airplane made from a man and wife." Eden still provides its exile in a technological era. They "even flew a little." This is the genius of simplicity. Again, consider these three lines (Mitchell translation) from another poem:

Of three or four in a room
there is always one who stands beside the window,
his dark hair above his thoughts.

The third line in a previous version by Assia Gutmann reads: "Hair dark above his thoughts." The Mitchell version remains entirely literal, almost cosmetic, while the placement of the adjective "dark" after the noun allows both a literal and metaphorical range which coincides with the poem's theme of exile, wandering, and the ineffectuality of language. By not risking "drama" (a small amount) Mitchell has lost a great deal. Enough said. It only becomes embarrassing when a superb translator of Rilke inadequately renders one of Amichai's most memorable poems, **"A Pity. We Were Such a Good Invention."**

The notion of memorability in Amichai's poetry should be discussed, for it is the profound and elemental starkness of his images coupled with the terse incantation of his rhythms that allow his poems to sculpt their often horrid truths.

Dicky was hit.
Like the water tower at Yad Mordekhai.
Hit. A hole in the belly. Everything
came flooding out.

But he has remained standing like that
in the landscape of my memory
like the water tower at Yad Mordekhai.

("**Seven Laments for the War-Dead,**"
trans. Chana Bloch)

The juxtaposition of man with tower (living vessel with non-living yet life-sustaining), blood with water, and mortality with steel, sears an indelible image into the mind, an image that remains standing like the ghostly outline of a water tower on the horizon. As Ted Hughes has so aptly commented on the honed-down effect of Amichai's poems: "As they grow more open, simpler, and apparently more artless, they also grow more nakedly present, more close-up alive. They begin to impart the shock of actual events."

Heidegger defines truth as *a-letheia,* "out of forgetfulness," and he argues that pain is what flushes being out of concealment into consciousness. The often brutal truths in Amichai's poetry are distilled from experience. He carries his dead like eggs within him, and often carries them back across "the river Lethe" (forgetfulness) so that they might be born again into the light of this world where we might learn from them. The first section from the same poem illustrates this point:

Mr. Beringer, whose son
fell at the Canal that strangers dug
so ships could cross the desert,
crosses my path at Jaffa Gate.

He has grown very thin, has lost
the weight of his son.
That's why he floats so lightly in the alleys
and gets caught in my heart like little twigs
that drift away.

Again, the personal loss is transposed to the universal and mythic through the uncanny senselessness of war in which a man falls by a canal originally constructed in good faith. But that canal crosses the desert (exile, estrangement) and was dug by strangers, and now, ironically, becomes the mythic vessel for transportation of the soul estranged from its body. Later, in section two, it is again an elemental simplicity coupled with the ironic notion of the earth (dirt and sand that clean) that raises the poem to a mythic level.

A living child must be cleaned
when he comes home from playing.
But for a dead man
earth and sand are clear water, in which
his body goes on being bathed and purified
forever.

Finally, in section seven, the poem's tragic overtone is slowly, yet hesitantly, transposed to the joy of acceptance.

Oh sweet world, soaked like bread
in sweet milk for the terrible

toothless God. "Behind all this,
some great happiness is hiding." No use
crying inside and screaming outside.
Behind all this, some great happiness may
be hiding.

Let me quote sections from a more recent Amichai poem
(Bloch translation) in order to give a sense of how deftly
the poet moves through ranges of emotion:

"When I Have a Stomachache"

When I have a stomachache, I feel like
the whole round globe.
When I have a headache, laughter
bursts out in the wrong place in my body.
And when I cry, they're putting my father in the
    ground
in a grave that's too big for him, and he won't
grow to fit it.

And later we are told:

And if I'm the prophet Ezekiel, I see
in the Vision of the Chariot
only the dung-spattered feet of oxen and the
    muddy wheels.

I'm like a porter carrying a heavy armchair
on his back to some faraway place
without knowing he can put it down and sit in it.

I'm like a rifle that's a little out of date
but very accurate: when I love,
there's a strong recoil, back to childhood, and it
    hurts.

It's all here, Nietzsche's appraisal of a godless world: man,
having quested absolute knowledge, is sentenced to the burden of his own exile and wandering until finally all that remains is the fragile dependence upon personal love, that god
within us all.

Chana Kronfeld (essay date September 1990)

SOURCE: "'The Wisdom of Camouflage': Between Rhetoric and Philosophy in Amichai's Poetic System," in
Prooftexts, Vol. 10, No. 3, September 1990, pp. 469-91.

[*In the following essay, Kronfeld argues that, despite the
opinion of his detractors to the contrary, Amichai demonstrates in his poetry a clearly defined philosophical and ontological system of thought and belief.*]

Amichai's system? This playful, "easy" poet has a system?
The poet for whom ideas are game pieces and objects in the
world are "color blocks you can . . . rearrange at will, without too much concern for broadening our knowledge"? Ever
since the first reviews of Amichai's poetry appeared in the
early fifties, the predominant opinion in the critical literature has been, with few exceptions, that Amichai's poetry is
not only devoid of any philosophical system but that as a
poet, he has no reflective bent at all (*hu eyno hogeh
mahshavot klal*).

This common view is shared by fans and foes alike. Indeed,
sometimes Amichai's greatest admirers are in the biggest
rush to accept the playful ease of his poetry at face value:
Here, at last, is a great modernist poet who does not subject
the reader to the rigors of philosophical systematicity and
hermeneutic seriousness. Glenda Abramson, who regards
Amichai as "one of [Israel's] most sensitive and perceptive
literary observers," a "master poet" with "a poetic finger
firmly on the twentieth-century pulse," writes in the conclusion to her book-length study of Amichai: "His writing presents no world-view, nor does he proceed from an
identifiable system of thought." It is a fascinating question,
from the perspective of literary dynamics and canon formation, whether this *descriptive* critical commonplace is related
in any way to the important role that *prescriptive* or normative criticism (especially in the genre of the *retsenzya,* the
journalistic review but also in works of a more scholarly nature) has played in the critical reconstruction of Amichai's
poetics. Thus, it may be significant that the belief that
Amichai's poetry presents no world-view first came into
vogue in the fifties and sixties, during the Statehood Poets'
bitter ideological and aesthetic struggle for dominance. The
critical establishment, affiliated with either Palmach Generation poets (*dor ba'arets*) or the older guard of the Russian
inspired *moderna,* perceived Amichai as a representative of
the "valueless," "westernizing" neo-imagist group, with their
"empty spirit that shows off its emptiness and lacks any
world-view."

An examination of the language and rhetoric of the early reviews of Amichai's poetry reveals time and again that in the
context of the period, to "lack a world-view" meant something quite specific. The phrase becomes a coded reference
to works which challenged—or simply refrained from giving poetic expression to—one of the (literarily) dominant
ideological trends and the aesthetics that through convention came to be associated with it: nationalist nativism, so-
cialist Zionism, or traditionalist Judaism. The *anti-
ideological* stance of Amichai's poetry was often described
as a lack of *idealism* or, ultimately, as the absence of *ideas.*

In the seventies and eighties, with the rise of a new generation of postmodern poets, some wishing to return to a Jewish nationalist or nativist literary philosophy, younger critics

(many poets themselves) adopted much of the early critics' stance against Amichai, accusing him, as the poet Menachem Ben charged, of creating "an anti-intellectual, anti-metaphysical" "flattening of the world," or of being trapped in a "small, unbrilliant egotism," which leads quite easily to "contempt . . . for the whole history of Israeli heroism." Even more reminiscent of the Shlomo Tzemachs and Yosef Lichtenboyms of the fifties and sixties is Ortzion Bartana's long series of attacks on Amichai claiming that "by his nature, which reflects the nature of his period, he is incapable of reaching any metaphysical thinking," and that his poetry is the central marker of the philosophical void, the "absence of ideation (*hoser ha'ide'iyut*) of Israeli poetry, of Israeli culture."

The puzzling thing is not that Amichai should at once become one of the most canonical and most attacked of Israeli poets. After all, tensions between marginalization and canonization are essential to the very life of the literary system; and these tensions often center around the reception of a generational paragon. What is remarkable, however, is that descriptively and prescriptively, the view has persisted that Amichai is not a poet of thought and that his being a *poeta ludens* somehow precludes his being a *poeta sapiens*. How could this have come about when, as Boaz Arpali points out, "almost every poem by Amichai [is a statement about the] general human condition, . . . [and] Amichai, in a certain sense, is always a philosophical poet." Moreover, how could the impression that Amichai's poetry expresses no philosophy have been maintained even in the face of Amichai's later poetry in which he spells out the major terms of his conceptual system with increasing directness, taking care to describe the ways in which ontological and rhetorical principles match and motivate each other?

A solution to the puzzle of this persistent impression holds the key to Amichai's system. The popularity of the (mis)conception that Amichai has no poetic world-view reveals, quite paradoxically, the working of the rhetorical and philosophical systems whose very existence this conception denies. Amichai has simply been successful in producing a new prototype of mundane poet, "an 'everyman,'" "'the man with the shopping bags,' the 'square.'" As Hayyim Nagid has shrewdly observed:

> A middle-aged Jerusalem poet puts on a mask of a middle-aged Jerusalem poet, acts [in the poems] in familiar everyday circumstances and writes poetry whose explicit poetics is the abolishment of partitions between the mundane and the poetic. Should we wonder, then, if a critic who has lost respect for the poetic world-view, tries to correct the poet's own impressions and rate his experiences for him according to a value system that belongs to a different world? Paradoxically, this situation isn't just part of

the lynching spirit [*avirat hakasalt*] of our society at large, but is also an immanent consequence of the new poetics, heralded by the central figure of Yehuda Amichai.

In Hebrew literary history, this central issue of the stature of the poet and his or her relation to the reading public often differentiates poetic world-views from each other, and marks various periods or trends. Amichai's construct of the populist poet reacts against both Bialik's premodernist image of the poet as a prophet who castigates his people, and Shlonsky's early modernist conception of the poet as a linguistic wizard who charms and transforms his audience. As Amichai himself has described it, his is a reaction against any form of "aristocratization of art." Yet because of the minimized role of the poet *qua* poet, Amichai cannot take on his literary forebears directly, as Zach does Alterman, and Shlonsky, in his day, took on Bialik. To do so would require him to transform himself too dramatically and self-consciously into one of "art's generals." Instead, Amichai stresses—in typically autobiographical terms—his transitional stance *in between* two generations. In a lecture entitled **Dorot ba'arets,** Amichai says:

> My divided fate [*gorali hamefulag*] has willed it so that I should be planted in between two generations, a sort of "double agent," for "biographically" I belong to that generation—British Army, struggle, smuggling in weapons and immigrants, Palmach, three or four wars—whereas "literarily" I belong to the generation of writers [*dor hakotvim*] which came later in the fifties. I identified with the trend toward a different kind of writing: a feel for everyday language, for concrete experiences.

Amichai shrewdly uses a plural form of the conventional name for the Palmach Generation (*dor ba'rets*) in the title of the lecture (*dorot ba'rets*), and instead of the customary *sofrim,* "writers," or *meshorerim,* "poets," he has *kotvim,* "those who write." Amichai's simple shift from *dor* to *dorot* questions the literary hegemony of Palmach Generation social realism, and points out the plurality of generational voices "in the land." At the same time his use of *dor hakotvim* deflates the *moderna's* maximalist view of the poet as linguistic wizard, and promotes an orientation toward writing as an ordinary, "physical" act.

What Amichai describes here simply as an accident of his "divided fate," becomes a central ontological and rhetorical principle of his poetics: the state of *beynayim,* or in between. At once deflating and engaging in the process of changing the model of the poet, Amichai's poetry and his explicit statements about poetry construct an alternative system whose simplest—and most deceptive—component is a series of equivalences between the poet and the ordinary person; between poetic language and ordinary language; and, between the reading public and the poet's immediate or intimate community (family, friends, fellow soldiers, lovers). This is why, as Warren Bargad has observed, while "reading Amichai's poems one often has the feeling of reading a diary without days, a record of someone's personal impressions or intellectual musings, set down at random." Bargad correctly relates this general effect to four of Amichai's central rhetorical strategies: "the quasi-autobiographical voice," "the aphoristic nature of many of his lines," "the patently casual, candid tone," and finally the creation of "sequence through seemingly disjuncted images or metaphors." The poetry reveals a conceptual interdependence between these and other principles, an interdependence that is responsible for both the consistency of Amichai's system and its self-effacing nature.

In its untraditional perception of the poet as everyman, Amichai's poetry is globally motivated by a general *rhetoric of autobiography* which blurs the traditional distinctions between poetic and prosaic, fictional and nonfictional, written word and oral discourse. Many of the poems appear to be composed in this problematized, often contradictory "meta-genre," using autobiography to veil and realistically motivate any philosophical generalization or ars-poetic thematization. Genre and tone both suggest the poems are nothing but the attempts of one ordinary man to come to terms with his experiences. The famous aphorisms in Amichai's **El male rahamim** which characterize the world as devoid of compassion or mercy, and describe the usability of only a few of the words in the dictionary, emerge as the personal conclusions of a citizen-soldier who has brought back the corpses from the hills (line 6) and has stood indecisively by the window (line 9). The philosopher-poet in search of a post-theological humanism, or a postromantic poetic idiom has no place here. Clearly, many poems deviate from this quasi-autobiographical mode. Still, there are good reasons why this type of poem has become the prototypical example of Amichai's treatment of philosophical and rhetorical issues. Furthermore, when the poems are explicitly nonautobiographical, their sustained meditative feel is often veiled through other means, especially those associated with the concept of "play."

"To write not as a poet, but as a person," Amichai told me in a 1984 interview, "that's the whole business." The self-marginalization of the poet, and of poetry as a calling or profession, are matched by the corresponding foregrounding of the ordinary human voice, and of traditionally unpoetic occupations: "Writing poetry is the most amateurish of all arts. And . . . I mean this as praise," Amichai tells his interviewers time and again. By contrast, direct ars-poetic messages, rare as they are, are more likely to be voiced in the poems by soldiers, lovers and children or archaeologists, geologists and gardeners than by the "professionally" *poetic* "I." When

Amichai's poetry does focus explicitly on poets, as in the poems **"Yehuda Halevi, Ibn Gabirol, Leah Goldberg meta,"** ("Leah Goldberg Died"), **"Mota shel Assia G."** (**"The Death of Assia G."**), or **"Moto shel Celan"** (**"The Death of Celan"**), the concrete poet's life or death and the poetic "I"'s ordinary human response to it, occupy center stage. As Hillel Barzel has pointed out, while Amichai's poetry cannot focus explicitly on poetry as an object of direct contemplation, "for this might magnify the topic under discussion and restore to it the metaphysical aura," no such danger exists if the poem focuses on a particular poet, "identified by name, to whom the words are addressed naturally," since he or she is "an admired, close or deceased poet, who deserves a eulogy like any other friend." For Barzel, Amichai's revolutionary perception of the poet derives from "a rejection of the infinite as a source of poetry," a reversal which puts "the finite before the infinite" [*hipukh hamaqdim et hasof la'eynsof*], and the human before the divine. I believe Amichai goes even beyond this simple existentialist posture, so trendy in the literature of his generation. Within his model of the poet this step beyond existentialism is expressed in the deliberate and systematic tensions between the poems' official "deflation" of the poet and the implicit insistence on his indispensability (albeit in new, anti-prophetic terms).

The poet's ambivalent "self-marginalization" is consistently evident not only in the tone of the poetry but also in the choices that Amichai—in his public persona—has repeatedly made over the years. Although a founding member of the modernist group whose journals, *Liqrat* and later *'Akhshav* first published the works of the Israeli neo-imagists in the fifties and sixties, Amichai maintained, quite self-consciously, a marginal role in the group's explicit poetics and politics. Unlike Zach and the Anglo-American paragons who influenced *Liqrat* (Eliot and Pound, especially), Amichai has never *written* an artistic manifesto or credo. His only credo, as he often repeats in interviews as well as in a poem of the same title, is *ha'ani halo ma'amin sheli* ("my non-credo"), a brilliantly simple ambiguity of parsing that allows the simultaneous rejection of religious orthodoxy and aesthetic positivism ("my [theologically] non-believing self," and "my artistic 'I don't believe'" or "anti-manifesto"). The prototypically modernist genre of the manifesto is replaced by the pre- and post-modernist genre of the "diary," the poetic essay—by the oral interview or poetry reading. Most importantly, the self-conscious thematization of poetry and poetic technique is replaced by or disguised as poems on the nature of ordinary language, especially the kinds of language that are traditionally considered unpoetic. Grammatical patterns, idioms and fixed expressions, familiar quotations, and word etymologies not only show up in new ways that make them perceptible in the poems' rhetorical make-up; quite often they become the very focus of the speaker's (non-systematic, philosophically unpretentious, and ever so informal) thoughts. For the poet, as for the reader, poetry should be easy. "I write poetry," Amichai always tells his audiences, "because I'm lazy. It's the only thing I can do effortlessly." It is ordinary language that is magical, inexhaustible, and more creative than any poet can ever hope to be.

But clearly, this is not the whole story. After all, this easy, effortless poetry has also produced some extraordinarily complex and difficult works, like **"Mas'ot Binyamin ha'aharon mitudela" ("The Travels of the Last Benjamin of Tudela")** or the elegies, to name just a couple of examples. And, as far as the thematization of poetry is concerned, the very reduction of poetic language to nonpoetic and ordinary usage allows poems to be implicitly metapoetic even while discussing legal, scientific, commercial or religious discourse. While Amichai's construct of "the poet as every-man" foregrounds the accessibility and directness of his poetry and the ordinariness of his language, other aspects of his rhetorical and philosophical system, such as his conception of time, order, and play often mandate elusiveness, strong metaphoricity, and defamiliarization. How then can Amichai's poetry be both things at once, easy and difficult, direct and highly figurative, colloquial and richly allusive? How, to return to our initial topic, can a poet who consistently demystifies the poetic process, and who declares that he uses only a small part of the words in the dictionary, get away with placing that same poetic process at the center of richly allusive and figurative junctures? Amichai's work develops numerous strategies for doing exactly that: abstaining from the elitist, self-conscious "poetry for poets," and at the same time— indirectly, surreptitiously—making poetry the covert subject of the poem. While a full exploration of these strategies is beyond the scope of this paper, a closer look at a few poems may help illustrate some of the most central principles of Amichai's philosophical and rhetorical systems in action.

"Lo kabrosh" ("Not Like a Cypress") is a seminal early poem which has come to represent for many readers the antiheroic and unassuming position so typical of Amichai's poetic persona:

"Not Like a Cypress"

Not like a cypress,
not all at once, not all of me,
but like the grass, in thousands of cautious green
exits
to be hiding like many children
while one of them seeks.

And not like the single man,
like Saul, whom the multitude found
and made king.
But like the rain in many places
from many clouds, to be absorbed, to be drunk

by many mouths, to be breathed in like the air all
year long
and scattered like blossoming in springtime.

Not the sharp ring that wakes up
the doctor on call,
but with tapping, on many small windows
at side entrances, with many heartbeats.

And afterwards the quiet exit, like smoke
without shofar-blasts, a statesman resigning,
children tired from play,
a stone as it almost stops rolling
down the steep hill, in the place
where the plain of great renunciation begins,
from which, like prayers that are answered,
dust rises in many myriads of grains.

Whether the poem is taken to present a critique of accepted norms or a series of personal wishes, whether it expresses the poet's perception of his art or remains completely without a concrete referent, **"Lo kabrosh"** is a dazzling example of Amichai's rhetorical-philosophical sleight of hand: it is a sustained meditative poem about the need to be both inconspicuous and indispensable, whose subject is (semantically and syntactically) both absent and perfectly clear, and whose speaker makes his wishes appear quite personal, even though he almost never uses the first person point of view.

Through what Arpali describes as an open-ended catalogue technique, the poem presents, in apparent free association, a series of negated and affirmed similes, analogies and metaphors, whose topics or tenors—which are also the subjects and predicates of the poem's elliptical sentences—are never explicitly stated. Most importantly for our concerns, this rhetorical strategy allows Amichai to describe "the manner in which he would like to be accepted as poet and person in the world" without ever mentioning poetry or the poet. The clusters of similes (stanzas 1 and 2) and predications (stanzas 3 and 4) appear to lack any linear or narrative unity. But, in fact, the sequence is held together roughly by the logical form of an argument:

Not as a but as b (stanza 1),
and not as c but as d (stanza 2),
not e but f (stanza 3),
and then g, h, i, j (stanza 4).

The concluding stanza is thus the only component that does not have an antithetical structure.

Amichai has often been criticized for the loose structure of his poems, a looseness which would allow, as Nissim Kalderon has argued, for the shifting of lines and stanzas without a concomitant change in the meaning of the poem.

This, I believe, describes the surface impression many poems are meant to create. More specifically, in this poem, the impression of a casual composition serves as a correlative for the very inconspicuousness that the poetic "I" seeks. Because of the flaunted unstructured sequence, it is harder to notice—as it is in many other Amichai poems—how tight and symmetrical the "spatial form" tends to be. As I show elsewhere, this poem and others—especially those that employ four stanzas and sonnet-like forms—display exactly the same types of systematic relations of equivalence among their four strophic units that Roman Jakobson has revealed in his analysis of Shakespeare's Sonnet 129: (1) alternation (abab), (2) framing (abba), (3) neighborhood (aabb), and in addition—the relationship which Jakobson conceived of as peculiar to the Shakespearian sonnet—(4) contrast between terminal and nonterminal strophes (aaab). As the outline of the argument in **"Lo kabrosh"** indicates, the last relationship may be the most important for the poem because the speaker finally emerges from the cloak of antithesis and litotes—the description of his wishes by the negation of their opposites—and allows the heterogeneous catalogue to come to rest in the extended metaphor of *mishor havitur hagadol* ("the plain of great renunciation"). Thus, through the very tension between the poem's linear and spatial structure Amichai's poem can be taken to both embody and describe the role of the poet.

The rhetorical tension between the impressions of the linear and spatial composition is paralleled by a thematic oscillation between deflation and valorization of the poet's ontological status and social role. The speaker in **"Lo kabrosh"** who never even says "I," much less describes himself as a poet, nevertheless expresses his wish to leave a mark on the world. But his wish is not simply to be inconspicuous, as the title suggests, just as the persona of the great Hebrew acmeist poet Rachel does not simply endorse the ant's point of view of poetry when she declares *Raq 'al 'atsmi lesaper yada'ti / tsar olami ke'olam nemala* ("Only of myself do I know how to tell / Narrow is my world like the world of an ant"). On the one hand, the speaker wants to remain unnoticed, hidden, almost passive. On the other, he wishes to make his presence all-encompassing, comingling with and reaching out to as many people as possible. Desired inconspicuousness and secrecy in the mode of existence are paralleled, antithetically, by a desired comprehensiveness and communality in the *scope* of existence. Only when taken together do these thematic features motivate the tensions between pervasive symmetry and overt looseness in the composition of the text, and between elliptical, concealing syntax and a detailed, innovative figurative language. Thus, the course of the poem may be the occasion for the fulfillment—or the frustration—of the very wishes that are its topic.

In the first set of images, the poetic "I" describes himself not as a salient, singular vertical presence but as hidden, multiple horizontal emergences. The progression of the poem and its catalogues of indirect descriptions are thematized almost geometrically in these opening similes. We do not find out about the poet's self-perception through one neatly defined model (like the cypress), but rather through a series of numerous half-articulated and seemingly unconnected images (the blades of grass). Only by implication can we then infer that like blades of grass, drops of rain, air breathed by people over a year, and blossoms scattered in springtime, the poet's work also aims wide rather than high, and wishes to be absorbed by all, like simple and necessary nourishment. His aesthetic—as that of the poem's own structure and figurative language—is modelled after the disorganized and scattered (*mefuzar*) blossoms of the brief Israeli spring, rather than on any classic ideals of eternal, permanent beauty.

Alternating between the natural and the social realm, Amichai's similes of child play and kingship are picked up again in the metaphors of a medical emergency in the third stanza. Once more, the poet's work (to risk again inferring the same tenor for the entire catalogue of vehicles in a poem where no tenor is ever mentioned) is deflated and stripped of all heroism or glamor; yet for that very reason the poet is also integrated into life and community. Rather than fashioning himself after the first Israelite king, the chosen one, who—as we recall—was head and shoulders above his people (like a cypress), the poet-speaker likens himself to children in a game of hide and seek. It is, however, the children at play who enjoy and always ultimately find what they are seeking. Saul, by contrast, went looking for his father's asses, and before he knew it was uprooted from both family and community by the unwanted, isolating role of king imposed upon him. Similarly, in a blatantly antipoetic comparison between two blatantly antipoetic sounds, the poetic process is not like a single sharp ring at the door of the doctor on call, but like the tedious process of securing some medical care from a faceless institution by repetitive knocking on many bureaucratic windows and side doors. At the same time that the poetic process is thus deflated through the bureaucratic imagery, the context of the medical emergency serves to do just the opposite, imbuing it with the critical importance of a life or death situation. Thus, the poet's social mode of existence touches human lives *beharbe defiqot lev,* which can be taken here both idiomatically to mean "with a lot of anxiety" or "with trepidation," and literally—"with many heart beats."

Lacking the antithetical structure of the first three stanzas—"not [as] a but [as] b"—the fourth seems at first to present a complete collapse of all linear order. Within the inverse logical relation between "the poem's theme and its mode of presentation," it is quite consistent that the poem's theme, which so far had to be reconstructed exclusively by the reader, will be expressed more directly at the very point where the poem's order seems to collapse into an open catalogue of freely associated items (the quiet exit, smoke without a blast [*tru'ah*], a government minister resigning, children tired of their play). At this very moment, in the middle of the last stanza, appears the philosophically most explicit, and figuratively most developed image: "*bamaqom shemathil / mishor havitur hagadol, asher mimenu, / katfilot hamitqablot, / 'oleh avaq beharbeh riba gargerim*" ("where the plain of great renunciation begins, / from which, like prayers that are answered, / dust rises in many myriads of grains"). Gad Keynar's interpretation, stressing the *biographical* sense of an end, also sees "the plain of great renunciation" as a frustration of the poet's wishes. The poet's prayers are just like dust; his wish "to be absorbed by many" is ironically and cruelly frustrated in the image of "the many myriads of grains" of fruitless dust. In a very different vein, Rachel Tzukerman-Teres identifies the resignation with giving up both extremes, abrogating all poetic wishes and offering oneself up to nature. Shlomo Yaniv points out the ways that this stanza reinterprets the poet's creative wishes from earlier sections of the poem as indicators of his imminent death: the "cautious green exits" become a "quiet exit," "the single man" becomes "the statesman resigning," etc. Like the other critics, Yaniv also argues that the fulfillment of the poet's wish is already within "the plain of great resignation" and that "it too is nothing but dust." "The movement in the last stanza," Yaniv concludes, "of the rising smoke, the descending stone and again of the rising dust matches the ups and downs of human life, and ultimately forms a cycle with no way out."

These readings fail to grasp the extent of the radicalism of Amichai's critique of accepted norms—aesthetic and other— and fall back on the monologic autobiographical model, in which resignation and dust represent personal failure, meaninglessness, and death. Note, however, that it is the dust which is rising up like "prayers that are answered" (and not the reverse, as Keynar suggests: prayers that are rising like dust). Note also that *mishor havitur hagadol* reads not only as "the plain of great renunciation" but also as "the great plain of renunciation"; and, finally, that the biblical resonances of *harbe ribo gargerim* (many myriads of grains) are not only closer to poetic diction and traditional euphony than anything else in the poem, they also echo two contradictory—but traditionally linked—biblical themes: God's promise to make Abraham's offspring as numerous and uncountable as grains of sand, and the specific use of *harbe ribo* in the threat of destruction of Nineveh in the last verse of the Book of Jonah. The special force of this final sustained image derives, I believe, precisely from the contradictory, and therefore profoundly unsettling, import of its components. Within a metapoetic perspective, the poem's ending both describes and constitutes the—always modified, self-ironical, and not very substantial—fulfillment of the poet's wishes. (Interestingly, the readings I cite all hasten to aban

don any metapoetic perspective once death is implied in this final image.) Comparing the dust rising from the plain to the answered (literally, "accepted") prayers only emphasizes the gap between the two: the poet's aesthetics of dust do not rise up into any poetic heaven. But even this "poorhouse apotheosis"—simply because it undoes any delusions of grandeur and permanence—paradoxically overcomes the finiteness of the death it connotes. Instead, it points to a new beginning; *bamaqom shemathil* (the word "begins" significantly *ends* the line) toys with our biographical expectations for an end-of-the-road despair. It suggests that with the abdication of all transcendental poetic expectations, with the resignation even from the struggle against what the poet cannot or does not want to be (structurally, the end of the antithetical argument), comes a new beginning, the initiation of the poet into a world he has given up fighting for rather than a world he sets out to conquer.

Amichai's most recent book of poems, titled ***Gam ha'egrof haya pa'am yad ptuba ve'etsba'ot (Even the Fist Once Was an Open Hand and Fingers)***, which is perhaps an entire volume of covert *ars poetica*, provides counterpart poems to many early seminal works, including **"Lo kabrosh."** In ***Gam ha'egrof*** the poem titled **"Ma lamadti bamilhamot"** (**"What Have I Learned in the Wars"**) ties the poet's mode of existence to a central facet of Amichai's rhetorical and philosophical system. In the second half of the poem, the speaker, having learned in the wars "*lits'oq 'ima' beli shehi shoma'at / velits'oq 'elohim' beli leha'amin bo*" ("to cry out 'mommy' without her hearing / and to cry out 'God' without believing in him"), relates the poet's desire to remain inconspicuous to the veteran's *hokhmat hahasva'ah*— his "wisdom"—and—"art of camouflage":

From: "What Have I Learned in the Wars"

But above all I have learned the wisdom of
  camouflage
so that I won't stand out, so that they won't
  recognize me,
so that they won't be able to tell me from my
  surroundings
[not] even from my love,
so that they may think I am a bush or a sheep,
I am a tree, or the shade of a tree
I am a doubt, the shadow of a doubt,
a hedge, a dead stone
a house, the corner of a house.

If I were a prophet I'd dim the splendor of vision
and darken my faith with black paper
and cover the Divine Chariots with nets.

And when the time comes I'll wear the
  camouflage clothes of my end:

White of clouds and lots of sky blue
and stars that have no end.

In order to avoid becoming a target, the veteran-poet has learned to take on the appearance of his surroundings, not in a pantheistic or nativist union with the land, as in Tchernichowsky or Shlonsky, but in a gesture of poetic and existential self-defense; flaunting the splendor of a poet's vision is as dangerous as leaving the lights on during an air-raid. Yet, the poet's retreat into the shade of a tree and the shadow of a doubt is not only a comment on a self-imposed marginality. These actions also define a more general principle of Amichai's rhetorical ontology: the principle of *inter-categorical existence.* At this point the camouflaged artist, soldier, and lover of his poetry merge and, in effect, systematically challenge our tendency to reduce rhetorical and philosophical distinctions to neatly discrete binary oppositions. Rather, Amichai's poetry defines its place in between these oppositions, in the "narrow interims" (*babeynayim hatsarim*) that both bridge and penetrate all bipolarities.

From: **"Interims"**

Where will we be when these flowers turn into
   fruit
in the narrow interims, when flower is no longer
   flower
and fruit not yet fruit. And what a wonderful
   interim we made
for each other between body and body. Interim
   eyes between waking
      and sleep.
Interim dusk, neither day, nor night.

This narrow and makeshift *beynayim* (also described in the earlier poetry temporally as *beterem,* "before") used in its dual grammatical form, as well as in its biblical sense of a "duel" (*milhemet beynayim*), or "duelist" (*ish beynayim*), marks the existence of—and inevitable connection between—both love and war. In another famous early poem, **"Shneynu beyahad vekhol ehad lehud" ("The Two of Us Together and Each of Us Alone"),** Amichai first develops the concept of *ahavat-beynayim,* a highly ambiguous, simultaneous description of love's transience, and of the lovers as duelists performing their love before and in between the warring armies. Thus, in trying to stop the armies, they also paradoxically become, like David and Goliath, token opponents who do battle with each other. This interpenetration of love and war, foregrounded in the ambiguous concept of *beynayim,* is typical of all actively opposed categories as well as their linguistic and rhetorical corollaries. The need of opposite concepts to switch places, to be camouflaged as each other, or ultimately to be revealed as the same, is the philosophical and rhetorical principle that underlies the function of *beynayim.* Thematically, it accounts for concerns as diverse as the indistinguishability of memory and forgetting, self and other, hope and danger, God and human being. Rhetorically, it motivates the interpenetrations of opposing genres (sonnet and ode; elegy and joke), of literal and figurative, and, ultimately, of poetry and non-poetry.

Again, Amichai's latest volume provides some of the most crystallized statements (which are, of course, non-statements) of this principle, as in the poems **"'Atsvut vesimha" ("Sadness and Joy"), "Hanefesh" ("The Soul"),** and **"Eyze min adam" ("What Kind of Man").** In the special botanical imagery which this volume perfects, the co-existence of *"ahava uvilti ahava, shney tsva'im / bevered ehad"* ("love and unlove, two colors / in one rose") is not some wild mutation but *"zan nifla / heseg limegadel havradim sheshmo nish'ar bavered"* ("a wonderful species / an accomplishment for the rose grower, whose name remains in the rose"). The poet as gardener gives way to the familiar trope of the poet as traveler who passes *in between* the blessing and the curse, justice and injustice. Finally, it is the very proximity of death which gives the speaker the freedom to abolish the opposition between the human and the divine, claiming for himself both the apotheosis of the human and the deflation of the divine: *"ani adam / ani adam-elohim, ani elohim-adam / sheyamav sfurim. Haleluya"* ("I am a man / a man-god, a god-man / whose days are numbered. Hallelujah").

But how does Amichai's union of opposites differ from other dialectical systems? I believe the answer lies in the least understood aspect of Amichai's poetic world-view, and perhaps its most revolutionary one: "the rage for chaos," to use Morse Peckham's controversial term. "There must be . . . some human activity which serves to break up orientations, to weaken and frustrate the tyrannous drive to order. . . . This activity, I believe, is the activity of artistic perception." Certainly Amichai doesn't subscribe to Peckham's peculiar mixture of postmodernism and psychobiology, but he does maintain on all levels of his poetics an active or passive resistance to *clohey haseder,* "the God(s) of order" (and of the seder ritual). Let me once more illustrate this point briefly with a poem from Amichai's most recent volume:

"The Sea and the Shore"

The sea and the shore always next to each other.
   Both
wanting to learn to speak, learn to say
just one word. The sea wants to say "shore,"
and the shore wants to say "sea." They have been
   getting closer,
for millions of years, to speaking, to saying
the one word. When the sea says "shore,"
and when the shore says "sea,"
salvation will come to the world,
the world will return to chaos.

This parabolic poem defines its own code, which in retrospect makes sense of a consistent trend in Amichai's poetic world-view. Salvation is described as a release from the bonds of any superimposed or institutionalized (theological, political, aesthetic) order. The biblical story of creation set up, through the powers of *dibur* (speech), an artificial border between the fluid and contradictory categories of existence, as a form of control over elemental, chaotic forces (the sea and the shore). It is this enforced dualism, this separateness that is for Amichai the source of all stagnation, conflict, and, ultimately, death. Running against the imposed order, confusing the periods, or mixing up the Bible are therefore necessary activities for staying alive as human being and as poet. The decreation of the categorical borders is also to be achieved *bedibur* (by speech), as in the original biblical account of creation, hence the powerful valorization of ordinary language. Evolution is redefined as the gradual acquisition of the language of the other, the sea gradually learning over millions of years to say "shore," the shore—to say "sea." Ultimately, equating *ge'ula*, "salvation," with its apocalyptic opposite *tohu*, "chaos," is itself a manifestation of Amichai's unique version of rhetorical anarchism.

If there is one work within Amichai's corpus that combines and embodies all the rhetorical and philosophical aspects of this complex system it is, without doubt, **"Mas'ot Binyamin ha'aharon mitudela" ("The Travels of the Last Benjamin of Tudela")**. I discuss this work in great detail elsewhere. Here I will use a small section of this long poem to illustrate some ways in which the various components of Amichai's rhetorical and philosophical systems come together:

> Sometimes I want to go back
> to everything I had, as in a museum,
> when you go back not in the order
> of the eras, but in the opposite direction, against
>   the arrow,
> to look for the woman you loved.
> Where is she? The Egyptian Room,
> the Far East, the Twentieth Century, Cave Art,
> everything jumbled together, and the worried
> guards calling after you:
> You can't go against the eras! You won't learn
>   from this,
> you know you won't. You're searching, you're
>   forgetting.

This "declaration of intent," in its indirect and figurative rhetoric of autobiography embodies one of the major trends in this central work and in Amichai's poetry as a whole: the poem as an achronological, discontinuous, and disruptive reconstruction of the various layers of the speaker's experience. Although his quest always has a specific goal, e.g., to find the lost beloved woman, or the (equally lost) God of his childhood, these disruptions of personal and communal chronology cannot bring the speaker back to "everything (he) had." Still, by retrieving arbitrary (or seemingly arbitrary) images from his personal and historical museum, and engaging them in interdependent and interpenetrating juxtapositions, the speaker can at least protest actively against the deadening effects of divine, social, and aesthetic order.

The poem as a whole, Amichai's longest, engages only a partial and tenuous simultaneity of personal and communal history, and only a blurred and fragmentary focalization of the spatial-geographic panorama. The speaker, himself split into first, second and third person, leaves his here (Jerusalem) and now (age 43) to set out on his confusing and impossible simultaneous travels through time and space. But the trip is from the start modelled on a fictional genre, the travelogue, with a long history of parody and satire, whose most recent precedent—Abramovitsh's satirical *Travels of Benjamin the Third*—involves circular motion which can never reach the goal. Thus, even when the traveler attempts to disrupt linear order and effect simultaneity, it is not the geographical Egypt, Far East, the historical twentieth century, or the actual Stone Age but their conventionalized semiotic and artistic representations that he can grasp: the Egyptian Room, the Far East wing in the museum, etc.

The poem's main thematic materials nevertheless flaunt their autobiographical and historical veracity. The rhetoric of autobiography is reinforced through the inclusion of many concrete details from Amichai's personal biography, especially those dealing with time and place. We find out exactly how old he is while writing the poem, at what age he emigrated to Palestine, when he went to a Montessori Kindergarten, where he lives, etc. However, the expectations for a continuous narrative of chronological and spatial development, which such materials raise, are subverted from the start. Instead of providing a chronological and panoramic composition which takes the speaker from childhood to middle age and from Würzburg to Jerusalem, the poet constructs a multilayered cross-section of tumbling images of then and now, there and here, autobiography and historiography. This tenuous and shaky "stratification of the self" (for Amichai's archaeological layers and geological plates always seem to be moving in opposite directions, as in an earthquake; his 1968 book, *'Akhshav bara'ash* means both "now in the noise" and "now in the tremor") also causes a simultaneous refraction of all three thematic centers of the poem: religion, love, and war. Love in this poem, as elsewhere, is seen as the *beynayim* state, wedged between the wheels of war and institutional religion, but also switching places with them, and all three undermine each other in a breathtaking barrage of apocalyptic images.

It may be more apparent now how the ways in which the

poetic "I" conceives of himself form crucial rhetorical and philosophical links in Amichai's system; the poet's persona, always self-described as a transitional figure, embodies the inter-categorical existence, or the *beynayim* state, which his philosophy and rhetoric expound. When the poetic "I" looks inside his "self," he encounters the simultaneous layering of opposing personal and collective forces. The volatility and tenuousness of this archaeology of the self can only be mitigated by a brutally honest recognition of the fragmentary and borrowed nature of these layers of the poetic persona. Still, as in **"Lo Kabrosh,"** this recognition itself is redemptive and deeply liberating. For paradoxically, once the process of resignation has begun, and the speaker claims no ownership, no uniqueness for his notions of self and of poetry, then the cosmic reaches of his world become embodied within him, and he can create a symbiotic ethno-cosmic circulation, the blood flowing from the heart of stars, through the great artery of the milky way, through his and his country's body cosmic to the *hamsin* of the Great Lungs:

> I'm sitting here now with my father's eyes
> and with my mother's graying hair on my head, in
> a house
> that belonged to an Arab, who bought it
> from an Englishman, who took it from a German,
> who hewed it out of the stones of Jerusalem,
> which is my city;
> I look at the world of the god of others
> who received it from others. I've been patched
> together
> from many things, I've been gathered in different
> times,
> I've been assembled from spare parts, from
> disintegrating
> materials, from decomposing words. And already
> now,
> in the middle of my life, I'm beginning to return
> them, gradually,
> because I want to be a good and orderly person
> at the border, when they ask me: "Do you have
> anything to declare?"
> So that there won't be too much pressure at the
> end,
> so that I won't arrive sweating and breathless and
> confused.
> So that I won't have anything left to declare.
> The red stars are my heart, the distant Milky Way
> is the blood in it, in me. The hot
> *hamsin* breathes in huge lungs,
> my life is close to a huge heart, always inside.

Ezra Spicehandler (review date Winter 1992)

SOURCE: "An Analysis of Yehuda Amichai," in *Judaism*, Vol. 41, No. 1, Winter 1992, pp. 97-104.

[*In the following review, Spicehandler finds Glenda Abramson's* The Writings of Yehuda Amichai: A Thematic Approach *to be a valuable contribution to Amichai criticism.*]

Yehuda Amichai has enjoyed international acclaim beyond any of Israel's poets. His works have been translated into many languages, particularly into English. He has taught as a poet-in-residence or lecturer at numerous universities. Although at least a hundred articles dealing with his poetry and prose (including fifteen in English alone) have been published, until recently, only one Hebrew book has appeared which treats Amichai comprehensively, *Haprahim Vehaargtal* by Boaz Arpaly (Tel Aviv, 1986). Glenda Abramson's new study in English, *The Writings of Yehuda Amichai,* is an important, first-rate, scholarly exploration of Amichai's literary achievement. It differs from Arpaly's work in several ways. Arpaly confines himself to Amichai's poetry, while Dr. Abramson covers both his poetry and prose. Abramson's is almost exclusively a thematic approach; Arpaly's also explores Amichai's structure and poetics. Moreover, the audience which each addresses is different. Arpaly aims at the literary specialist, and his language is heavily freighted with the professional jargon of the Tel Aviv School of Criticism; Abramson, while thoroughly acquainted with contemporary criticism, writes for a more general reader. Her work is far more readable than Arpaly's.

Both Arpaly and Abramson disagree with the wide-spread negative critical appraisal of Amichai's current writing as being "tired" and a "regurgitation of themes and techniques" which were once his unique contribution to Hebrew letters. Both divide his career into two phases: the younger Amichai of the 1950s and 1960s, and the "maturer poet" of the last two decades. Undoubtedly, the earlier Amichai was more exciting and innovative, and became one of the fathers of Israel's "new poetry." The later Amichai's mature line, while reflecting a more sedate imagery and the adult skepticism which modifies his youthful certainties, nevertheless reconfirms his position as one of Israel's major poets.

I shall confine myself to Dr. Abramson's discussion of Amichai's poetry, and deal with the six themes discussed by our author: (1) Biography and Autobiography, (2) Allusion and Irony, (3) The Father and God, (4) Alienation and Fragmentation, (5) Love poetry, and (6) Jerusalem.

1. BIOGRAPHY AND AUTOBIOGRAPHY

No one can argue with Dr. Abramson's assertion that "Yehuda Amichai's personality as a poet is, in many respects, a reflection and distillation of the poetic personality of his generation, and conclusions about his poetic 'I' are relevant to the generation as a whole."

Born in Bavaria in 1924 to Orthodox Jewish parents, Amichai was brought by them to Israel in 1936, where he studied in religious schools at Petach Tikvah and Jerusalem, to which latter city the family moved before the outbreak of World War II. Following his graduation from secondary school, he enlisted in the Jewish Brigade and, when the war ended, joined the *Palmach,* the striking force of the *Haganah,* participating, first in its clandestine operations of smuggling Jewish refugees through the British blockade and, later, as a combatant in Israel's War of Independence. In the early 1950s, he studied at the Hebrew University and he published his first volume of verse in 1956 (***Akhshav Uveyamim Ha'aherim,*** [***Now and In Other Days***]).

These biographical facts, with some variation, constituted the common experience of an entire generation of his literary colleagues. Many, like him, were born abroad, either in Central or Eastern Europe; others were native born to parents who themselves were immigrants. Most were affected directly and indirectly by the experience of the Holocaust. Almost all served as soldiers in either the *Palmach* or the Jewish Brigade or in both, and attended the Hebrew University in the 1950s. Many came from an Orthodox background, which they rejected during their adolescence.

They constituted the first generation of Israeli writers, whose primary childhood language was, or became, Hebrew (although Amichai was twelve years old when he arrived in Eretz Yisrael, Hebrew rapidly became his vernacular). The incursion of spoken Hebrew into poetry was primarily due to this fact, but was also caused by the general trend in European and American poetry not only to write in a "conversational style" but also to permit commonplace words (including slang and blatant sexual terms and phrases) to enter the hitherto "aesthetic" domain of poetry.

A common characteristic of Amichai's literary generation was their fierce disillusionment with the ideologies upon which they had been nurtured in their youth. In his case, this disillusionment was two-tiered. First, was the loss of his transcendental Orthodox faith, a tragedy which is frequently connected with the image of his father (often his dead father), who had remained steadfast in his faith, and the feelings of guilt toward him and the tradition which Amichai had forsaken. Second, was his abandonment of his utopian Zionist dreams, which were shattered against the rock-hard realities of grimy, bloody wars and the grey, bureaucratized society which emerged as the new state developed and was swamped with the mass immigration of the 1950s.

2. ALLUSION AND IRONY

Amichai uses his biography as a symbolic lexicon rather than as a record of personal history. His war years usually serve as the great divide between his childhood world of faith and wholeness and his adult's hell of alienation, loneliness and fragmentation. At times, this dividing line is rolled back to the period of his departure from Germany, pre-Hitlerian Bavaria representing a childhood world of Orthodox wholeness and tranquility, while Erez Yisrael represents a kind of exile in reverse, a chaotic, war-torn immigrant society. But, paradoxically, Erez Yisrael is seen as the real world to which one must desperately cling, since there is no returning to the vanished dream-world of the past.

The Hebrew poet is compelled to express the disjunctive secular world which he inhabits through the medium of Hebrew, a language which, but a century ago, was the holy tongue. Amichai manipulates the religious resonance of the Hebrew language as an ironic device by which to express the *angst* of a generation which had lost its faith in utopias. In Dr. Abramson's words:

> The central figure of this poetry is its intertextuality and its reliance on the Bible, Rabbinic literature and the liturgy. Amichai employs a more subtle subtext, composed of an attitude towards the texts, not only his ironic response to their message but also his tacit agreement to relinquish their canonic value and consequently their entrenched holiness. . . The poet is . . . able to supply the texts with his own value; one not validated by tradition, but open to a new testing in his own time. Richard Ellmen's assessment of Joyce may exactly be applied to Amichai: ". . . Joyce left the Catholic Church not so much by denying it as transmuting its language for his own uses. Christianity had subtly evolved in his mind from a religion into a system of metaphors which as metaphors could claim a fierce allegiance. He converted a temple to new uses instead of trying to knock it down."

One may add, parenthetically, that Amichai's lexicon of such symbols is usually drawn from Jewish religious practice, the Bible, the *Siddur* and the High Holiday *Mahzorim,* and only to a limited extent from Rabbinic and Medieval literature.

Hillel Barzel has suggested that "transposing" is a more apt term for this technique! "The taking of words, sentences, parts of biblical verses, proverbs, similes etc. out of their normative context and inserting them into a new frame with an imaginative sweep." Barzel broadens the scope of this technique beyond the Jewish vocabulary to include everyday cliches and even common contractual phrases such as "both parties as one and each one individually," which Amichai uses to allude to the ambivalence of the relationship between lovers. In dealing with traditional texts, Dr.

Abramson contends that Amichai resorts to three techniques: (1) parodies of the original, (2) verbatim quotations followed by the poet's commentary, and (3) allusions to the text but misquoting, disturbing and engaging in word-play. These "transpositions" become a vehicle for what Russian critics call "surprise"—an ingenious, unexpected freshening of the familiar. This tool was used, if only occasionally, by Bialik, but undoubtedly Amichai also learned it from the English metaphysical poets, either directly or via Auden and Eliot, two poets whom he greatly admires.

3. GOD AND FATHER

Amichai's "presentation of God as one of the central themes of his poetry" is more a transpositional technique than it is an expression of faith. Dr. Abramson avers that "the Jewish God of his childhood becomes, through a series of permutations, a psychological interjection." I would suggest that Amichai's view is agnostic, and that when he asserts that God has pity on kindergarten children, less on school children and none at all on adults, he is contending that for many (including himself) God is a reality only for the immature and that one outgrows the belief in Him. Yet, Dr. Abramson hesitatingly suggests that Amichai does retain a belief in God as a cosmic force whose ways are incomprehensible to human beings. "It is necessary to decide whether . . . God . . . throughout Amichai's early verse (1948-1964) refers consistently to the kind of arbitrary destiny defined in Hellenistic literature as *Tyche* or to some unspecified power." After 1962, she suggests, he no longer inveighs against "a primitive anthropomorphic deity and now invokes the Lord of the Universe worshipped by the Jews throughout their dispersal . . . a transition from a concretized God to the God . . . who no longer dabbles capriciously in human affairs." In the early poetry, Amichai's father appears as an embodiment of traditional Jewish values, historicity, and spiritual morality, in contrast to a capricious God, while, in the later poetry, both images fuse into one.

The diversity of the God/Father relationship seems to be eclectic, dependent on how the poet chooses to "play" with these symbols, rather than on his later developing a new concept of deity. Amichai's cry

> O my father, Chariot of my life, I want
> to go with you, take me a little way,
> Set me down next to my house
> And then continue on your way

("A Second Meeting With My Father")

is nothing more than an anguished, nostalgic wish for a return to the God/Father, a wish that the poet finds impossible to fulfill.

4. ALIENATION AND FRAGMENTATION

Loss of faith breaks the circle of coherence, and without a center one's world-view is shattered into fragments. The speaker becomes alienated from family and society. Dr. Abramson avers that, although Amichai's early poetry is a "chronicle of futility, frustration, sadness and worthlessness," his

> alienation is never entirely convincing and he is able to break out of his self-absorbed passivity and attempt . . . a confrontation with the external world, [and that the] "I" in the major body of Amichai's poetry is never wholly isolated but is concerned with relationships: father-son, lovers, friends, husband-wife and tender pupil.

However, these are but rare and very ephemeral gleams of light, soon turned into darkness. Indeed, "Amichai's poetry is peppered with images of isolation, helplessness, passivity, and impotence." His frustrated efforts to find "wholeness may not always result in the negation or rejection of value," but is not this very failure the cause of his alienation?

> the city in which I was born was destroyed by
>   cannon
> The ship on which I emigrated was later destroyed
>   in the war
> The barn in Hamadia where I lived was burned
>   down
> The kiosk in Ein Gedi was blow up by the
>   enemy . . .
> My life is being wiped out behind me
> According to a precise map.

5. LOVE POETRY

Alienated, devoid of religious faith or social idealism, man turns again and again to human love to fill the void, only to find that human relationships are ephemeral. A child's fantasy about an ideal love: Ruth, a little girl he once knew in his native Würzburg and who was killed in the *Shoah* represents an ideal love which can never be retrieved.

> What remains. The crisscross marks
> of a raffia chair in the thigh of a woman
> who sat by the sea and then went away
> Or, writing on a celebratory cake
> The words "I love"
> Already cut away from "you."

Again Dr. Abramson divides Amichai's love poetry into two periods, 1948-1968 and 1968-1984. In the first period the speaker explores the manipulation of love by forces beyond the lover's control, even when these emanate from the lover because of guilt and conflict. "The goal of fulfillment with a romanticized and unrealistic illusion as the guide" is never attained even against the puritanical tradition represented by God and father. Sexual love is at once an assertion of liberation and a source of guilt. Religious allusions are used to contradict the old moral code, yet the choice of physical love, and the correlated rejection of religious and spiritual love, is not easily made, for underlying it is a sense of sin, of stealing the exultation meant for God and offering it to a woman.

In the second period, the speaker resigns himself to failure. Love "did neither content the lover nor become a replacement for lost spirituality." Love is a human phenomenon and not a metaphysical state, and the love experience is now recorded with greater physical explicitness. It is viewed "in relation to the banality of life, not its promised or imaginary glory." The speaker's aging also becomes a recurrent *motif.* "Amichai's love poetry . . . [may not] at this stage be about love at all, but about the problems of youth and maturation. . . Love becomes a conceptual synonym for the shock of aging, physical change and the shifting roles in family and society. The solder becomes a good citizen; the young lover, a responsible husband. The son becomes the father."

6. JERUSALEM

My remarks about the Jerusalem theme in Amichai's poetry will include my reaction to the recent republication of the bi-lingual *Poems of Jerusalem* (Harper & Row, 1988). Amichai has lived in Jerusalem for more than forty years, and his poetry expresses the ambivalence of residents of ancient cities to their history. On the one hand there is a rather matter of fact relationship to one's domicile, no different, for example, than the one which Hawthorne, in *The Marble Faun,* ascribes to 19th century Romans toward their external city. On the other hand, there is an awareness that one is living in the sacred capital of Jewish history. Thus, in the poem **"Tourists"** the speaker wryly remarks:

> Visits of condolence is (sic) all we get from them.
> They squeal at the Holocaust Memorial
> They put on grave faces at the Wailing Wall
> And they laugh behind heavy curtains
> In their hotels. . .
> They weep over our sweet boys
> And lust over our tough girls
> And hang their underwear
> To dry quickly
> In cool, blue bathrooms. . .

This poem concludes with a deliberate *prose* paragraph which tells of an experience that the speaker had, as he paused at the Tower of David on his way home from the vegetable market and rested his two heavy baskets on its steps.

A guide leading a group of tourists uses the resting speaker as a target marker.

> "You see that man with the baskets. Just right of his head there's an arch from the Roman period. . ." I said to myself redemption will come only if their guide tells them. "You see that arch from the Roman period? It's not important; but next to it left and down a bit, . . . sits a man who's bought fruit and vegetables for his family." (the translation is by Drs. Abramson and Parfitt)

In contrast, in the poem **"All Generations Before Me,"** written in 1967, the speaker is animated by a sense of the continuum of Jewish history.

> All the generations before me donated me
> bit by bit, so that I'd be
> erected all at once
> here in Jerusalem, like a house of prayer. . .
> it binds. . .
> I have to change my life and my death
> daily to fulfill all the prophecies
> prophesied for me. . .
> it binds.
> But, he sees more:
> I've passed forty
> There are jobs I cannot get
> . . . Were I in Auschwitz
> they would not send me out to work
> but gassed me straightaway. . .
> it binds

This double vision of Jerusalem goes beyond its particularistic Jewish relevance. The speaker, climbing the Tower of David in another poem, tells of rising

> a little higher than the highest prayer
> Halfway to heaven. A few ancients
> managed: Mohammed, Jesus
> and others. . .

Yet his agnosticism intercedes:

> But they didn't find peace in heaven,
> only the excitement of heights.
> Yet the acclaim hasn't stopped.

And Jerusalem remains a divided city, seething with animosities. Its fluttering laundry lines bear

> a white sheet of a woman who is my enemy
>   woman
> the towel of a man who is my enemy
> to wipe off the sweat of his brow

and concludes with the ironic coda:

> We have put up many flags,
> and they. . .
> to make us think they're happy
> To make them think that we're happy.

The divided city becomes a metaphor for the poet's divided self: old vs. new, tradition vs. modernity, union and ideal love vs. the inevitable separation of earthly love. Dr. Abramson claims that, in the poetry after 1967, Amichai's speaker abandons his role as prophet and chastiser and becomes "a mellowed and fond Jerusalemite. . . [N]o longer the observer of a spoiled woman's depredations, he has become rather like a loving although not critical husband." Yet I find little evidence for such a change. Jerusalem remains, for him

> a place where everyone remembers
> That they have forgotten something there
> But don't remember what it is

And although the speaker declares in order to remember

> I wear my father's face
> on mine

his reference to his father's mask (tradition) fails to alter his alienated state.

A word about *Poems of Jerusalem* and its translators. The sparse, conversational style of Amichai usually lends itself to successful translation—like, for example, the highly textured styles of poets like Pagis and Gilboa. This has much to do with Amichai's international reception. Yet, when his lines are freighted with puns and allusions to Jewish texts, the translators fail. Poems like **"If I forget Thee Jerusalem,"** because of its Hebrew texture, are untranslatable. One cannot render into English the double-entendres implicit in such verbs as *shakhah* meaning both to forget and to turn lame, puns like *tizkor* (remember) > *tisgor* (close), or the rhymes *tishkhah* > *yipatah* < *tislah.* Much of the poem's musicality cannot be transmitted, and the Hebrew reader wonders why anyone troubled to translate a poem whose texture and tone are primary and, therefore, untranslatable.

Admirers of Amichai's will find Dr. Abramson's work an invaluable companion as they explore the deeper regions of the poet's literary world. They will, like myself, hope that she will produce a second volume, which will deal with his poetics, a task which, judging from this fine book, she is certainly well-equipped to undertake.

Gila Ramras-Rauch (review date Spring 1995)

SOURCE: A review of *A Life of Poetry: 1948-1994,* in *World Literature Today,* Vol. 69, No. 2, Spring 1995, p. 426.

[*In the following review, Ramras-Rauch presents a brief overview of Amichai's career and praises his collected volume* A Life of Poetry: 1948-1994.]

"Life is lived forward and understood backward." This dictum of Soren Kierkegaard can, in certain cases, be applied to an extensive work of a creative artist. Yehuda Amichai (b. 1924) has been writing for over fifty years; he is still a prolific poet. In his early years he wrote fiction (***Not of This Time, Not of This Place,*** a novel, and ***The World Is a Room,*** a collection of short stories). In recent decades he has published his unique and seemingly simple poetic diction. Throughout his poetry the centrality of the speaker is manifested in self- and world-definition in an ever-moving constellation of binary relationships. His quasi-autobiographical speaker records the multiple and intricate relationships between the fleeting experience and the self. In one of his early poems, **"God Full of Mercy,"** he writes: "I who use only a small part / of the words in the dictionary. . . . I who must decipher riddles / I don't want to decipher."

The mystery of language and the mystery of the universe do not create an August, bombastic, and euphemistic poetry. As a careful builder of poems made of what seems to be a spoken language, Amichai uses canonic Hebrew in a unique way. Biblical stories and symbols, together with Jewish liturgy, are employed to shatter preconceived conventions. His negative dialogue with ancient texts is performed in the arena of personal statement. Demythicization of the accepted mode is embedded in his verse. In the opening line of one of his later poems he writes, "The real hero of the sacrifice was the ram." This ironic treatment of one of the most sacred myths in Judaism, the sacrifice of Isaac and the substitution of the ram for the intended Isaac, gives the reader the sense of reaching for the basic story stripped of an unchallenged narrative. Here again, the centrality of the first-person voice serves as a prism and a crucible in the interpretation of text and experience.

Amichai historically belongs to the 1948 generation in Israeli literature, but in effect he belongs to the Statehood Generation of the 1960s. This generation severed its ties with prescribed national expectations and focused on personal perceptions. The personal voice and the unadorned language created a silent revolution in modes of expression. The irony is that, at the same time a giant visionary poet like Uri Zvi Greenberg composed his mystical-nationalistic-prophetic poetry, several miles away the young emerging generation was forging a new voice. Classical Russian and German poetry no longer served the Israeli writers in the 1960s as it had served Hebrew poetry for generations before. Amichai and other Israeli poets discovered T. S. Eliot, Ezra Pound, and W. H. Auden. Succinct expression and the search for the right word captured their imagination. Stripping the language of its heavy historical gear and enhancing its accessibility to contemporary readers made Amichai's poetry favored by a large readership in Israel (where one still offers a poetry book as a birthday present).

Amichai's verse is a curious mix of an active dialogue with the surrounding world mingled with a contemplative mood. He does not bare his breast against pressing elements; neither does he expect the world to reveal its secrets to its speaker. His ironic tone, alluding to the basic incongruity inherent in everyday existence, also maintains a certain serenity. He is a poet of prolonged implosion that reverberates around his deceptively simple poems.

Amichai loves the direct statement, anchoring it in the personal album of his family. He tries to create familiarity in the world, like a buttress against the absurd embedded in the facticity of human life. Can one point to "periods" in Amichai's poetry, from 1948 to 1994? From its inception it was not the poetry of a young man. His daring images, his subtle irony, his subdued tone have been his hallmarks for decades. Occasionally he will refine and hone earlier images. The speaker continues to conduct his ever-present dialogue with the inventory of his life.

This handsome volume, with its careful and sensitive translations, serves as a fitting gift for Amichai's seventieth birthday.

David R. Slavitt (review date Summer 1995)

SOURCE: "Two Jewish Ironists," in *New England Review*, Vol. 17, No. 3, Summer 1995, pp. 187-92.

[*In the following review, Slavitt examines Amichai's characteristic use of irony.*]

The language of Jews, the real mother tongue, is not Yiddish or Hebrew, as it certainly is not Russian, or Polish, or English, but . . . irony. The complicated experiences of five millennia have elicited a series of emotional and linguistic postures by which we Jews express ourselves, and it is these double messages that American Jews have always found particularly interesting as well as demanding. Until Korea, the United States had never lost a war, and there was a sappy optimism, part positive thinking, part togetherness, part Chamber of Commerce boosterism, that seemed unrecognizable to us and, with a particular force, made us aware of our foreignness. Only the Southerners, who had lost the Civil War, had any notion of the mysterious ways of history and destiny, or understood that there can be an aristocracy of suf-

fering. Young Jewish men and women reading William Faulkner and Eudora Welty and Flannery O'Connor were reassured by the discovery of these un-American, recognizably sane, and unimpeachably grown-up voices.

Yehuda Amichai's popularity, in Israel and here as well, owes much, I think, to his reliance on irony. His poems have that authentic ring of the words of some wise-ass uncle who is always joking around but whose jokes, we come to learn as we grow up, are more often than not in deadly earnest. Amichai's voice, even in translation from the Hebrew, has that unmistakable edge to it. He seems to make light of what is serious and terrible, but his remarks are scalpel-sharp so that the quick scratch we hardly felt is suddenly gushing with our blood.

> **Amichai's poems have that authentic ring of the words of some wise-ass uncle who is always joking around but whose jokes, we come to learn as we grow up, are more often than not in deadly earnest.**
> **—*David R. Slavitt***

Here, for instance, is one of his "**Seven Laments for the War-Dead**":

Dicky was hit.
Like the water tower at Yad Mordekhai.
Hit. A hole in the belly. Everything
came flooding out.

But he has remained standing like that
in the landscape of my memory
like the water tower at Yad Mordekhai.

He fell not far from there,
a little to the north, near Houlayquat.

This is as funny as a lament gets. The bizarre comparison between Dicky's gore pouring out of him and the water tower's water spilling down is unseemly, but then any such death is unseemly, and the only way to be faithful to it is to hold onto it, clutching its absurdity all the more tightly, holding onto its homely truth. The specificity ("not far from there, / a little to the north, near Houlayquat") hangs there, tight-lipped and eloquent. Even though Houlayquat is now Heletz, for Dicky, and for Amichai's memory of his death, time stopped.

This translation, alas, is not from the new generous selection of Amichai's verse that Benjamin and Barbara Harshav have just published (*Yehuda Amichai: A Life of Poetry*) but from a smaller volume that Harper brought out eight years ago and is still in print, *Selected Poetry of Yehuda Amichai,* edited and translated by Chana Bloch and Stephen Mitchell. The Harshav version of the same poem is rather less fortunate:

> Dicky was hurt
> Like the water tower in Yad Mordekhay.
> Hurt. A hole in his belly. Everything
> Flowed out of him.
>
> But he remained standing like that
> In the landscape of my memory.
> Like the water tower in Yad Mordekhay.
>
> He fell not far from there,
> A bit to the north, near Huleikat.

Hurt? Killed is more like it. "Hit" is better because it is so much worse than "hurt" and doesn't hold out any false hopes. The tense of the Mitchell version's second stanza, suggesting that he has *even up to the present moment* remained standing is better than the imperfect which, in English, is indistinguishable from the passé simple. The Harshavs' verb implies that the action may be completed, while the whole point of the poem is its demonstration that the macabre and dreadful scene won't go away.

In one of his famous pieces, **"The Real Hero,"** Amichai demonstrates something of the appeal he has always had for those who, like me, are more certain of their Jewishness than of their religious faith or even their politics. He tells the difficult story of Abraham's sacrifice in this way:

> The real hero of the Isaac story was the ram,
> who didn't know about the conspiracy between the
>   others.
> As if he had volunteered to die instead of Isaac.
> I want to sing a song in his memory—
> about his curly wool and his human eyes,
> about the horns that were so silent on his living
>   head,
> and how they made those horns into shofars when
>   he was
> slaughtered
> to sound their battle cries
> or to blare out their obscene joy.
>
> I want to remember the last frame
> like a photo in an elegant fashion magazine:
> the young man tanned and manicured in his jazzy
>   suit
> and beside him the angel, dressed for a party
> in a long silk gown,
> both of them empty-eyed, looking
> at two empty places,

> and behind them, like a colored backdrop, the ram,
> caught in the thicket before the slaughter.
> The thicket was his last friend.
>
> The angel went home.
> Isaac went home.
> Abraham and God had gone long before.
>
> But the real hero of the Isaac story
> was the ram.

The subversive suggestion about how "they" made those horns into shofars for battle cries and the sounding of obscene joy is particularly welcome to me. "They" are the official spokesmen, whether governments or rabbis. In its imaginative expression, Judaism is somewhere else, and its wise guys are often closer to the complicated truth of things than its ostensible wise men.

Writing in *The Nation* some years ago, Mark Rudman called Amichai "one of the half-dozen leading poets in the world," saying that he "has found a voice that speaks across cultural boundaries and a vision so sure that he can make the conflicts of the citizen soldier in modern Israel stand for those of humankind." One of the half-dozen leading poets in the world? But it isn't hyperbole. Try to think of a sextet to outshine him. Czeslaw Milosz? Geoffrey Hill? Richard Wilbur? Derek Walcott? Zbigniew Herbert, maybe? And who else?

Here is **"Huleikat—the Third Poem about Dicky"** in the Harshavs' version (it is a piece Amichai wrote after the *Selected Poetry* volume):

> In the hills, even the towers of oil wells
> Are a mere memory. Here Dicky fell,
> Four years older than me, like a father to me
> In times of trouble and distress. Now I am older
>   than him
> By forty years and I remember him
> Like a young son, and I am his father, old and
>   grieving.
>
> And you, who remember only faces,
> Do not forget the hands stretched out,
> The feet running lightly,
> The words.
> Remember: even the departure to terrible battles
> Passes by gardens and windows
> And children playing, a dog barking.
>
> Remind the fallen fruit
> Of its leaves and branches,
> Remind the sharp thorns
> How soft and green they were in springtime,
> And do not forget,

Even a fist
Was once an open palm and fingers.

The Biblical tonality is not an accident. Amichai is a psalmist of our time, and the Bible haunts him with its presence—inescapable and often inconvenient, like the rubble of Jerusalem in which it is all but impossible to dig without making archeological finds. It may be interesting to scholars, but it makes life difficult for the people who are trying to put up buildings or improve roadways.

Amichai's reputation in Israel and among Jews in the United States is well established, and I confess I opened this new collection of his work with a slight narrowing of my eyes, a slightly skeptical attitude prompted by my belief that, for poets at least, too much popularity is a danger sign. Amichai has a persona—the soldier poet, the cynical lover, the tender tough-guy—that comes through in a cumulative way and is suspiciously cozy. But one realizes that he is not at all a naif, that he is quite aware of this mask, and that he enjoys wearing it and working it for rhetorical purposes. It is not unlike Frost's pose of the craggy Vermont farmer, which he used as much as a disguise as anything else. Amichai is like Frost and Cavafy, too, perhaps, coming on in an aggressively parochial way but knowing that by the strategies of metaphor and metonymy we will refract what he is saying until it is more or less what he meant in the first place. In other words, in his poems he enlists us as his collaborators, and we have the giddy feeling of having had some small share in their creation.

Chana Kronfeld (essay date Summer 1996)

SOURCE: "Reading Amichai Reading," in *Judaism,* Vol. 45, No. 179, Summer 1996, pp. 311-23.

[In the following essay, Kronfeld explores the ways in which Amichai retains accessibility while also using complex intertextuality in his poetry.]

Yehuda Amichai is the most distinguished Hebrew poet of our time and an internationally prominent literary figure. His poetry is part of the literature curriculum that new generations of readers are raised on, from Israeli school children to college and graduate students in Israel and the United States. His work is the subject of academic conferences and increasingly—though still insufficiently—of serious scholarship. In the hands of any other poet this poetry's steady diet of allusions, parodic midrashim, pseudo-commentary, and other forms of intertextuality would result in a dauntingly difficult body of work. Yet Amichai continues to be a phenomenally popular poet, accepted and admired as the crafter of the "easy poem."

In this essay I try to explore how, and perhaps why, Amichai's poetry maintains an accessible, transparent quality even while engaging in involved dialogues with numerous precursor texts, from the Hebrew Bible to the classics of European literature; and to outline some of the ways in which Amichai's poetic egalitarianism relates to his life-long struggle—and love affair—with textual traditions. I discuss elsewhere in some detail the philosophical and rhetorical aspects of this surface simplicity in terms of what Amichai himself describes in one of his later poems as "the wisdom of camouflage":

> But above all I learned the wisdom of camouflage,
> Not to stand out, not to be recognized,
> Not to be apart from what's around me,
> Even not from my beloved.
> Let them think I am a bush or a lamb,
> A tree, a shadow of a tree,
> A doubt, a shadow of a doubt,
> A living hedge, a dead stone,
> A house, a corner of a house.
> If I were a prophet I would have dimmed the glow
>   of vision
> And darkened my faith with black paper
> And covered the magic with nets.

Veiling the poet's intricate artistry under the camouflage net of artlessness is as necessary as covering the windows with black paper during an air-raid or as dimming the brilliance of prophetic vision during the precarious moments of divine revelation. Yet the evocative density of "*ma'asey merkava*" in the last line above (an untranslatable expression interestingly rendered here by the Harshavs as the common but multivalent "magic") affords a glimpse of the allusive depths, indeed the plenitude, beneath the poet's (literally) self-effacing rhetoric ("A tree, a shadow of a tree, / A doubt, a shadow of a doubt"). Amichai's self-imposed minimalism, his project of "dimming the glow" which tradition associates with poetic/prophetic vision is articulated in terms which are anything but minimalist: they go to the center of the complex and often arcane intertextual web that constitutes the rabbinic genre of *merkaba* literature, a genre whose originary moment and *locus classicus* is Ezekiel's uninhibited depiction of "the lineaments of the divine chariot-throne and its angelic bearers," in Joel Rosenberg's vivid terms. Idiomatically, the expression "*ma'asey merkava*" invokes the secrets of both divine and artistic wisdom. Yet at the same time it can be taken literally here as an implicit elaboration of the image of war, which—given a role of mock-teacher throughout—deflates and demystifies the traditional discourse of poetic and divine wisdom. The concrete experiences of war are described in the poem's title and first half as hands-on tutorials in the art, theory, or wisdom of camouflage, for "*chokhmat hahasva'a*" could mean all three; and the mock-divine chariots (*merkavot*) of our time may simply be tanks hidden under camouflage nets.

In a poem from the late fifties, **"La'em" ["To the Mother"]**, Amichai provides one of the earliest thematizations of the tensions inherent in his intertextual camouflage, a thematization that is itself carefully camouflaged, as we see in this section of the poem.

> Like an old windmill,
> Always two arms raised to yell at the heavens
> And two lowered to make sandwiches.
>
> Her eyes clean and polished
> Like Passover eve.
>
> At night she lines up all the letters
> And the photographs in a row,
>
> To measure with them
> The length of God's finger.

The mother of the title is never directly addressed by the speaker. Though it is clear from later sections of the poem that she is the speaker's mother, she is never referred to as *ima* or *imi* but addressed in the title with the formal and universal *la-em,* "to/for the mother." It is indeed only in the title that she is identified explicitly as the mother. The text itself introduces her through the mediation of the speaker's highly unconventional expanded simile: "Like an old windmill, / always two arms raised to yell at the heavens / and two lowered to make sandwiches." [*kemo tachanat ru'ach yeshana, / tamid shtey yadayim muramot lits'ok el raki'a / u-shtayim muradot le-hakhin prusot*]. With her body as reference point, the mother becomes the dialogic site of cross-cultural linguistic and visual puns. The initial simile of the old windmill grafts the Hebrew and Yiddish colloquial hyperbole, "a mother needs four hands" (both "hand" and "arm" are *yad* in Hebrew), onto the literary cliché of fighting with windmills taken from the western canon. The quixotic human struggle is rewritten as the protest of a feisty and combative feminine windmill who does not give up her right to raise a voice—and a hand—against the heavens, even as she continues to care for her family. The windmill, and the mother along with her, turn from object to subject and become the focus of redoubled agency—two and two—fighting and care giving. Amichai's simile divides the textual image-schema so that the upward, heaven-bound orientation is identified with protest and the lower, earth-bound one with nurturing. In the process he also radically humanizes the theological emblem of "yad" (hand, arm), a lexicalized metaphor in biblical Hebrew for divine power, providence, or inspiration.

The mother, like Amichai's critically engaged human agent, occupies the privileged crossings of cultural categories, be-

tween the sacred and the secular, the Judaic and the western. By placing her between heaven and earth, and between the ironic pathos of Jewish slang and the parodic bathos of Cervantes, Amichai both undercuts and redoubles her empowerment. While God's power in the Bible is always described as a singular *yad* (hand), Amichai's version of the proverbial Jewish mother is a mock-heroic yet powerful four-armed heroine. And in Cervantes it is the windmills who in the most direct sense win.

This figure of the mother (and elsewhere the wife or lover) becomes the metonymy in Amichai's poetry for the human and poetic subject, a metonymy that is not accidentally female. Amichai is the only mainstream Hebrew poet to present repeatedly his own poetic lineage, at least in part, as a matrilineage. He acknowledges his poetry's debt both to the German Expressionist poet Else Lasker-Schüler and to the Hebrew poet of modernism Leah Goldberg. What the speaker inherits from his biological mother in the poem is also what Amichai as poet adopts from the tradition of women's writing: the right, indeed the necessity, to personalize, domesticate, and transpose to the first person singular both history and theology, and to use overtly simple, concrete and familiar modes of discourse to confront the most universal and anonymous formations of authority.

Thus, the mother in the third stanza of the poem lines up all the letters and photographs in a row, "to measure with them / the length of God's finger." The larger context of this series of poems suggests that these might be letters and pictures of loved ones who died, perhaps "in one of the wars," in the words of the last line. In her silent act of protest, the mother uses the photos and letters, these personal traces of visual and textual memory as a homemade yardstick to measure the length of God's finger. The biblically and rabbinically privileged notion of *etsba elohim* (miraculous divine intervention or providence; see, for example Exodus 8:15) is itself a derivation by synecdoche from *yad elohim* (God's hand) in a Judaic context, or *yad ha-goral* (the hand of fate) in a western cultural context. In the course of this maternal anatomy of the divine it becomes merely a literalized single finger of divine power, as opposed to the mother's four hands or arms. In the process of her personal assessment of God's achievements in the world, the mother—and Amichai with her—call into question both the Judaic notion of justified fate (*tsiduk ha'din*) which is associated with *etsba elohim,* and the western visual emblematics of a life-giving, healing divine finger, from Michelangelo to E.T. The mother appropriates the clichés of transcendent justification for human suffering, and in the process calls to task both the Jewish God and western humanism: when lined up against the row of family pictures and letters, God's finger may not measure up.

A Jewish mother who measures the length of God's finger

is not exactly the paradigmatic example of intertextuality in current critical theory. I would like to suggest that it may be a mistake to ignore such examples and the type of personal intertextual engagement which they model.

In his discussion of *Casablanca* as a cinematic archetype, Umberto Eco articulates with almost poetic sensitivity a model for a postmodernist conception of intertextuality (as well as for his own novelistic practice): "Two clichés make us laugh but a hundred clichés move us because we sense dimly that the clichés are talking among themselves, celebrating a reunion." When in later films the dialogue of cinematic clichés becomes a self-conscious act of quotation, it creates an aesthetic marked by what Eco has aptly termed *intertextual collage:* "what *Casablanca* does unconsciously, later movies will do with extreme intertextual awareness." These, he concludes, "are 'postmodern' movies, where the quotation of the topos is recognized as the only way to cope with the burden of our filmic encyclopedic expertise."

Whether Yehuda Amichai's poetry is construed as post-modernist, modernist, or anti-modernist—and I have argued elsewhere, within a model of partial yet plural literary affiliations, for all three—it provides one of the most sustained examples of intertextual collage in contemporary poetry. Yet it does this while rejecting— ideologically and rhetorically— the alienated, elitist view of intertextuality as the burden of encyclopedic expertise. Amichai's intertextual practice and his meta-poetic thematization of this practice serves me then to call into question current postmodern conceptions of intertextual relations as totalizing conditions.

What seems to be behind Eco's position is the trivially correct view that anonymous tissues of citations encompass all textuality. The extra step which Eco, and other post-structuralist critics before him have taken, though, is that the general intertextuality of all texts renders meaningless any selective, purposeful and critical engagement with any particular one. It is interesting that Israeli theories of allusion and intertextuality developed by Ziva Ben-Porat on the model of modern Hebrew poetry and by Daniel Boyarin on the model of midrash avoid—each in its own way—this totalizing trap. That they can do so is made possible to a large extent by what the late Amos Funkenstein described as a text-oriented, interpretive Jewish tradition in which engaging in intertextual activities such as exegesis and commentary constitutes "a primary religious command and value." In Eco's account, by contrast, a generalized "we"—the universal consumers of the cinematic text—are presented as agentless by-standers, eavesdropping as the reified, personified clichés are having their reunion, even with respect to a cult movie like *Casablanca.*

In focusing on Amichai's critical-interpretive subject I argue tendentiously and directly—and I believe it's important

to state one's own assumptions as clearly as possible—for the need to reinscribe agency into our understanding of intertextuality. In the process I also wish to underscore the need for a historicized, culturally specific view of the ways poets and readers activate not only allusions but also parodies, pastiches, quotations, etc., and to describe these not as closed encounters between fragments but as the cultural and ideological practices of human beings. What I am advocating is not a simplistic return to the biographical poetic "I" as was common in traditional influence studies but a new understanding of what it means for a human agent, be it a reader, a poet, or a poetic persona within a text, to activate, interpret, critique, and rewrite the collective clichés and stereotypes of a culture.

The intertextual reunion Amichai's poetry celebrates is infinitely more complex than Eco's model suggests, and not because it isn't cinematic clichés but sacred texts that typically talk among themselves in the pages of his poetry. In fact, Amichai often applies the same strategies which he uses for critiquing the topos of the Binding of Isaac or the Yom Kippur liturgy to quotations from popular songs or, indeed, to the intertextual practices of old movies. What makes things complex, and yet forces them to appear rhetorically simple is, instead, Amichai's commitment to reinvest intertextuality with *agency,* rejecting its authority as an "impersonal field of crossing texts." He does this in a literary age when, for a variety of reasons, both the dominant Hebrew trends and the western modernist/postmodernist models typically advocate an agentless and ahistorical view of the appropriation of textual traditions. Amichai's reinscription of intertextuality as the practice of a historicized, *ordinary human subject* focuses around this subject's doubly critical—yet overtly naive—engagement with "the words that accompany [his] life." (See the poem "**Summer Rest and Words**," below.) His is a personal, critical gesture aimed both inward, toward the Hebraic intertextual traditions of a mosaic of quotations (*shibbutz*) or ornate stock phrases (*melitza*), textual commentary, and midrash, and outward, toward Euro-American views of the poetic text as a fragmented, unharmonized tissue of citations. Both Judaic and Western intertextual practices are experienced as vital layers in the unstable geology or archaeology of the self, the verbal spare parts (Amichai's pun is *chelkey chalof*) which the poet needs to keep fixing and changing in order to survive.

Amichai's claims for agency over inherited or imported "tissues of citations" often take the form of a deliberate deflation by the speaker—and by critics who take him at his word—of intertextual practice. Rendered as the ordinary verbal baggage of a non-poetic "I," his citations aim to create the rhetorical impression of popular or intimate discourse or of a playful fiddling with words even when—or perhaps precisely when—they involve a rewriting of the most sacred texts of cultural memory. Iconoclastic biblical allusions, critical reversals of liturgy, parodies of midrash and rabbinical commentary are normalized and explained away by the speaker's state of mind, his biography, and/or the history of his personal involvement with the texts they evoke. These radical reinterpretations of the *mekorot,* of "the sources," are inserted alongside sub-canonical, blatantly non-literary or non-Judaic intertexts, which are subjected by the speaker to the same scrutiny as the most canonical allusions. Just as Amichai begins some poems with a biblical quotation on which the rest of the poem offers a pseudo-commentary, so does he often cite the text on bulletin boards and plaques, or quotes snippets of personal conversation as the starting point for an intertextual meditation.

I shouldn't have been surprised, therefore (but I was!), to find in his latest book of poetry (1989), a poem titled Hadera which starts out with a self-quotation from a phone conversation we had a few years earlier: "'*me-olam lo hayiti bachadera' ze kmo / psak din memit mi-tsa'ar ve-kove'a uvda, kmo mavet. / rak avarti darka ve-lo shahiti ba*" ("'I never was in Hadera,' is like / a verdict killing by sorrow and establishing a fact, like death. 'I just passed through and didn't stay'"). At the time I had of course no way of knowing that this innocuous phone call in which I gave Amichai directions how to get to my in-laws' house in Hadera for a weekend visit ("'near the water tower you turn left, to Heroes St.'") would end up as the subject for exegetical meditation in a poem. I cannot tell you for sure therefore whether these are the exact words Amichai used. But I think it's safe to assume that he probably said something like "*af pa'am*" rather than the literary "*me-olam,*" that he didn't pronounce it *ba-chaderá,* but *be-chaderá,* and that in all likelihood he didn't actually use the verb *shahiti* with the high-falutin' inflected prepositional *ba.* But of course these stylizations are needed if this phone call is to get us thinking in terms of the philosophical discourse of life and death, love and war while preserving the lexical facade of subcanonical intertextuality (as contrasted with biblical or literary allusion, for example). In fact, however, a highly canonical intertextual dialogue is concealed by this mundane phone call, a dialogue which many other poems conduct more directly, with the great medieval Hebrew poet Shmuel Ha-Nagid.

In a recent article titled "'As in a Poem by Shmuel Ha-Nagid': Between Shmuel Ha-Nagid and Yehuda Amichai," Tova Rosen describes the discourse-structure unique to Ha-Nagid where the starting point for a meditation is in a self-quotation and in "the articulation in the first person of a personal experience (biographic or pseudo-biographic)." The stylistic elevation of self-quotation in the first two lines is therefore not merely a way to make mundane materials more literary but the first step in a carefully structured meditative discourse, modeled, as Rosen astutely observes, on Ha-

Nagid's self-quoting personal meditations. Thus, for example, when *be-chadéra* becomes *ba-chaderá,* the change may enable a pseudo-etymologic midrash on *chadirá* (penetration), just like *darka* (through it/her; literally, her way or road; the femininity of place terms in Hebrew really helps here) is associated by the self-exegetical speaker with the question of how one's way or route in life is determined. The biographical background, which Amichai has since expanded on in several interviews with me, clarifies the connection between a literal passing through Hadera, the mention of love and war in the poem, and the metaphorical meditation on the ways of life. In the summer of 1942 Amichai passed through Hadera en route to enlisting in the Jewish Brigade in the British army. He had there a brief encounter with a woman. Had he "stayed in" Hadera and not just "passed through" it—his life would have been different. What we must grasp is that the effect created by this internal translation from colloquial Hebrew is precisely the same—and carries the same ideological message—as that created by Amichai's poetics as a whole: that everyday, personal conversation, even a phone call asking for directions, is every bit as important a source of intertextual engagement as any canonical cultural text.

The poem **"Menuchat kayits u-milim"** ("**Summer Rest and Words**") is a recent example of the anti-elitist impact of Amichai's reinscription of personal agency into intertextual practice; it is also a carefully wrought thematization of this practice, a meta-poetics of intertextuality that, like the other meta-poetic poems in Amichai's latest volume carefully veils its own radical artfulness.

> The sprinklers calm summer's wrath.
> The sound of the sprinkler twirling
> And the swish of the water on leaves and grass
> Are enough for me. My wrath
> Spent and calm and my melancholy full and quiet.
> The newspaper drops from my hand and turns
>   back into
> Passing times and paper wings.
> I shut my eyes.
> And return to the words of the rabbi in my
>   childhood
> On the bimah of the synagogue: "And give eternal
>   salvation
> To those who go off to their world." He changed
> The words of the prayer a little, he did not
> Sing and did not trill and did not sob
> And did not flatter his God like a cantor
> But said his words with quiet confidence,
>   demanded of God
> In a calm voice that accompanied me all my life.
> What did he mean by these words,
> Is there salvation only for those who go to their
>   rest?

And what about our world and what about mine?
Is rest salvation or is there any other?
And why did he add eternity to salvation?
Words accompany me. Words accompany my life
Like a melody. Words accompany my life
As at the bottom of a movie screen, subtitles
Translating their language into mine.

I remember, in my youth the translation sometimes
Lagged behind the words, or came before them,
The face on the screen was sad, or even crying,
And words below were joyful, or things lit up
And laughed and the words spelled great sadness.
Words accompany my life.
But the words I say myself
Are now like stones I fling
Into a well in the field, to test
If it is full or empty,
And its depth.

In a series of deliberate self-referential deflations which mimic the secularization of the sacred in Amichai's earlier allusive poetry, the poem reduces the intertextual heritage with which the speaker struggles to a bunch of words that follow him around throughout his life, or to verbal associations that pass through his mind as he dozes off on a summer day. Radical reversals of liturgical texts are subversively presented as pseudo-tradition, as the sleepy nostalgic return to "the words of my childhood rabbi," a rabbi who liked to change the text of the prayer just a little bit, and who modeled for the speaker both an aesthetic and a theology of change through valorized simplicity: his calm voice and unadorned style as well as his practice of changing "ever so slightly" the words of the prayer, have accompanied the speaker throughout his life.

Towards the end of the poem, the rupture which the poet reveals within the intertextual baggage of the culture, the anachronistic inappropriateness of the sacred intertexts to his personal modern condition, is deliberately trivialized through a simile, which is itself presented as drawn from personal memory and not from the stock of literary figures: the words which accompany the speaker lag behind their referents just like the handwritten subtitles in old movies in Israel in the 1940s and 50s, which could never keep up with the picture. The intertextual baggage that follows him around is hopelessly out of synch with the expressive needs of his reality, the sad or happy human faces on the screen. Yet the speaker "forgives" or "excuses" this as the malfunctioning of an old subtitles projector, most likely of the kind that had the translation "from their language into mine" on the side, *bashulayim,* "in the margins," as the original Hebrew has it. Only after the speaker has asserted his agency over the mistranslations and misquotations which he has inherited can the words reach beyond soporific nostalgia, background

music or mere verbal accompaniment. In the final lines of the poem they become, instead, personal touchstones, projectiles that actively, aggressively test the waters, question the plenitude or depth of tradition, and appropriate for the agent the right to assess for himself whether there is anything in it for him, any water left in the well to quench his thirst. It is, therefore, precisely into the well of traditional sources from which he has been drinking all his life that the speaker now assertively throws stones.

It is almost as if in late poems such as **"Summer Rest and Words,"** in the space between summer siesta (*menuchat kayits*) and final rest (*menuchat olamim,* or *menuchat ha-kets*), Amichai feels compelled to insert an accounting of his intertextual practices, to claim them as his own—the first six lines are a collage of internal allusions to earlier poems of Amichai—and in the process to take personal responsibility for their success or failure, meaningfulness or emptiness.

Reinscribing human agency into the impersonal tissue of citations doesn't allow for much authority to remain, either in "the sources" or in their contemporary iconoclastic appropriation. But that, Amichai ventures to suggest, can only be for the better.

Chana Bloch (essay date Summer 1996)

SOURCE: "Wrestling with the Angel of History: The Poetry of Yehuda Amichai," in *Judaism,* Vol. 45, No. 3, Summer 1996, pp. 298-300.

[*In the following essay, which is part of the Foreword to* The Selected Poetry of Yehuda Amichai, *Bloch explains Amichai's significance as a contemporary poet.*]

A friend of mine tells a story about some Israeli students who were called up in the 1973 Yom Kippur War. As soon as they were notified, they went back to their rooms at the University, and each packed his gear, a rifle, and a book of Yehuda Amichai's poems. It is a little hard to envision this scene: these days we don't think of soldiers as resorting to poetry under fire, and Amichai's poetry is not standard government issue. It isn't patriotic in the ordinary sense of the word, it doesn't cry death to the enemy, and it offers no simple consolation for killing and dying.

Still, I know what these young soldiers were after, because I have often found myself turning to Amichai's poetry as a kind of restorative. Pungent, ironic, tender, playful and despairing by turns, it draws me by the energy of its language, the exuberant inventiveness and startling leaps that freshen the world, making it seem a place where anything is possible. And by the humor, too—a briny Jewish humor that can set the teeth on edge. And I am attracted by a certain astringent quality of mind, a skeptical intelligence that is impatient with camouflage and pathos and self-deceit, that insists on questioning even what it loves.

Love is at the center of Amichai's world, but he is quick to grant that his mistress's eyes are nothing like the sun, that sex is at once an enticing scent and a sticky business. And Jerusalem, the beloved city, he contemplates with a mixture of love and exasperation. No one has written more intimately about this landscape—the dust and stones and the ghosts of barbed-wire fences; the Old City with its Wailing Wall and mosques and churches, its Solomon and Herod and Suleiman the Magnificent, all under a cloud of prophecy; the foreign consulates and the housing projects; the Jews and the Arabs; the zealous black-coated Hasidim and the tourists; the brooding presence of the dead.

Amichai's way of seeing this place—and most things he writes about—from both the inside and outside, balancing tenderness against irony, reflects his experience of two very different worlds. Born in Würzberg, Germany, in 1924, he grew up in an Orthodox Jewish home with its strict religious observance and its protective God, as inescapable as family. His father was a shopkeeper, his grandfather a farmer, and his memories of childhood (the political situation notwithstanding) idyllic. In 1936 he came to Palestine with his parents, and his adult life has been lived in the midst of the convulsive struggle of Israel to become a state, and then to survive and define itself. Amichai made his living as a teacher while studying war—as a soldier with the British army in World War II, with the Palmach in the Israeli War of Independence in 1948, and with the Israeli army in 1956 and 1973. He was formed half by the ethics of his father and half by the cruelties of war.

Throughout his career, he has written about memory and the burdens of memory; about the lingering sweetness and simplicity of his parents' lives set against the perplexities of his own; about war as loss and love as a hedge against loss. The most troubling loss is that of his childhood, left behind in the normal course of life and then destroyed by war. "My childhood of blessed memory," he calls it, borrowing an expression commonly used when speaking of the dead.

Amichai holds on tightly to whatever he has lost. "What I will never see again I must love forever" is his first article of faith. That is why there are so many elegies of love here. And that is why the God in these poems, who at times seems no more than a figure of speech, deeply embedded in the language, makes his presence strongly felt even in his absence. Amichai's quarrel with God is what stamps this poetry as so unmistakably Jewish. That quarrel carries on the venerable tradition of Abraham, Jeremiah, and Job—though the object of his irony is the Bible as well, not least the vi-

sionary fervor of the prophets. As he writes in **"When I Banged My Head on the Door,"** a poem that may be taken as his *ars poetica:*

> When I banged my head on the door, I screamed,
> "My head, my head," and I screamed, "Door,
>   door,"
> and I didn't scream "Mama" and I didn't scream
>   "God."
> And I didn't prophesy a world at the End of Days
> where there will be no more heads and doors.

What Amichai loves best is the ordinary human being with his pain and his joy, a museum in his heart and shopping baskets at his side. In **"Tourists"** it's not the Roman arch he wants us to care about, but the man sitting nearby with the fruit and vegetables he has just bought for his family. . . .

Amichai began to write in 1948; his first collection of poetry appeared in 1955. Since then he has published eleven volumes of poetry, many of them best sellers, as well as novels, short stories, and plays. His poems enjoy an enormous popularity in Israel. They are recited at weddings and funerals, taught in the schools, and set to music. And for a poet so rooted in his own place, his work is remarkably well known outside of Israel, having been translated into some thirty-three languages, including Chinese, Japanese, and Albanian.

These poems, chosen from Amichai's best work over a productive career of nearly half a century, should give some notion of his stylistic range: long poems and short, rhymed and unrhymed, in formal meters and in free verse; poem cycles; prose poems and poems hovering at the borders of prose; poems of an overflowing abundance and poems of a tightly coiled concision. All the translations are our own: Stephen Mitchell translated the poems written before 1969, and I translated the later ones.

The poems lend themselves to translation because they speak clearly and directly, and because Amichai's striking metaphors carry the burden of his meaning. But his language is far more dense and inventive than this may suggest. Reading these poems in Hebrew, one encounters allusions to biblical and liturgical texts on every page. The Israeli reader, even one who has not had Amichai's formal religious education, will have studied the Bible from grade school through college, and is also likely to recognize the kind of liturgical texts that Amichai refers to, such as the Mourner's Kaddish or the Yom Kippur service. Because this is obviously not true of most readers of English, we have often borrowed from or imitated the King James Bible as a way of pointing up allusions that might otherwise have gone unnoticed. On the other hand, modern Hebrew, revived as a spoken language only a hundred years ago, is much closer to the Hebrew of the Old Testament than our own language is to seventeenth-century English, and Amichai's allusions never have a "literary" air. So when we felt that the archaisms of the King James Version intruded awkwardly on the naturalness and ease of Amichai's diction, we found other equivalents. And when an allusion would have required too much explanation, we sometimes chose to disregard it.

To write poetry in Hebrew is to be confronted with the meaning of Jewish experience in all its strangeness and complexity. Amichai's provocative allusions—ranging from the witty and mischievous ("The man under his fig tree telephoned the man under his vine") to the subversive and iconoclastic ("The army jet makes peace in the heavens")—are one way of wrestling with the angel of history. The necessity of confronting the past is imposed by the language itself; it is Amichai's achievement to have found in that wrestling his distinctive identity as a poet:

> to speak now in this weary language,
> a language that was torn from its sleep in the
>   Bible: dazzled,
> it wobbles from mouth to mouth. In a language
>   that once described
> miracles and God, to say car, bomb, God.

Gila Ramras-Rauch (review date Spring 1997)

SOURCE: A review of *The Selected Poetry of Yehuda Amichai,* in *World Literature Today,* Vol. 71, No. 2, Spring 1997, p. 448.

[*In the following review, Ramras-Rauch presents a brief overview of Amichai's major themes and praises* The Selected Poetry of Yehuda Amichai *as "another occasion to enjoy the work of a poet whose complex simplicity continues to challenge lovers of poetry."*]

Yehuda Amichai's simple, beguiling, and challenging poetry continues to fascinate readers and translators alike. He is recognized in Israel and abroad for his seeming simplicity of tone, image, and syntax. The centrality of a speaker in Amichai's poetry inevitable reflects the man himself: a gentle, often self-effacing man whose soft voice is frequently in contrast with the bold statements his poems make.

Amichai uses known and familiar materials for his poetry: the images of Jerusalem, his parents, his loves, his children, the marketplace—all act as a storehouse of raw materials for his verse. These familiar materials however, are often left behind when his poetry, without warning, soars into a new verbal reality where paradox, irony, and a certain wonder coexist. In a way, Amichai seduces his reader with his bla-

tant declarative simplicity. The almost prosaic opening allows for a way into a more complex world. His world of analogies, metaphysical conceits, images, and paradoxes changes proportions while still using everyday imagery.

Among other things, is Amichai a political poet? Is there a hidden agenda under his well-turned verse? Are political issues alluded to in his innocent apolitical poems? Amichai's antiwar sentiment has been there from the inception of his writing. On a personal level, for instance, his basic experience in the 1948 war and the death of his close friend Dicky mark Amichai's strong antiwar feeling. In the short cycle **"Seven Laments for the War Dead"** from *Behind All This a Great Happiness Is Hiding* he writes: "Dicky was hit. . . . But he remained standing like that / in the landscape of my memory." The landscape of memory is but one resource for Amichai's warehouse inventory of images. Memory, time, history, people, smells—all float in his poetic orbit. Amichai is a perennial observer. As he says, his verse is haunted by hollow memories.

Amichai's poetry rejects his work as a guide to the perplexed. Love, a constant presence in his lyric work, touches on intimacy and his familiarity with the man-woman bond. At the same time, love is a concept tied to the Platonic idea of Love: Love that overcomes the physical, Love that transcends time, space, and causality. Amichai is bounded by the physicality of experience. Simultaneously, he aches to break away from the very matter that gives him his voice.

In this vein, in the attempt to transcend the expected and the causal, Amichai rejects a continuity of idea or stanza and opts for contiguity as a liberating mode. Simple words and complex notions merge. His poetry is strewn with road signs. The reader who is traversing the lines will, like a child in a drawing book, connect the dotted lines and thus create his or her own poetic map.

Amichai is fortunate to have had excellent translators into English—from Asia Gutman, to Chana Bloch, to Stephen Mitchell, to Benjamin and Barbara Harshav and others. The comprehensive selection *A Life of Poetry: 1948-1994* appeared three years ago (1994). The current volume was first published in 1986 by Harper & Row. Updating that original, the present edition adds several excellent translations from Amichai's 1989 book *The Fist Too Was Once the Palm of an Open Hand and Fingers,* giving the reader another occasion to enjoy the work of a poet whose complex simplicity continues to challenge lovers of poetry.

John Haines (review date Summer 1997)

SOURCE: "Poetry Chronicle," in *The Hudson Review,* Vol. 50, No. 2, Summer 1997, pp. 323-24.

[*In the following review, Haines discusses the contemporary relevance of Amichai's work in* The Selected Poetry of Yehuda Amichai.]

I should perhaps defer speaking of poems in a language I do not know and cannot read, but the poems of the Hebrew poet, Yehuda Amichai, as translated by Chana Bloch and Stephen Mitchell, have offered a useful means of comparison with the work of a few of our more immediate American contemporaries. . . . I must . . . refer briefly to the poetry of a place and a situation all too representative of our present world, and which in these poems has been written of with so much insight and passion.

> And so farewell to you, who will not slumber,
> for all was in our words, a world of sand.
> From this day forth, you turn into the dreamer
> of everything: the world within your hand.
>
> Farewell, death's bundles, suitcase packed with
>   waiting.
> Threads, feathers, holy chaos. Hair held fast.
> For look, what will not be, no hand is writing;
> and what was not the body's will not last.

"Farewell"

Here, subtly imprinted, is the unmistakable tone and historical burden, of which one can say: this is our time, this speaks for all. "Beautiful is the world that wakes up early for evil . . ." ("**In the Middle of This Century**"). It is not the only world we know, but it is one of which we must somehow speak, hold in conscience—or, it may be, remain silent before it. And the silence so common among us, in spite of our books and our talk, is heavy, dense with memory and premonition.

> And silently, like a doctor or mother, the days
>   bent over me
> and started to whisper to one another, while the
>   grass
> already was laid flat by the bitter wind
> on the slope of hills I will never walk again.

"Travels of the Last Benjamin of Tudela"

A poetry quietly eloquent with the pain, the losses and displacements of our time, in which one writes with the only instrument at hand.

While considering the books for this review I have had in mind a recent newspaper photograph of a street in Grozny, in Chechnya, a scene of almost total ruin: buildings shattered and gaping, trolley lines torn up, streets clogged with debris, a few trees still standing in leaf. A solitary couple, a man and woman, plastic bags in hand, with a child in a buggy, are making their way as if returning from market. But in that bleak setting there is nothing else alive or moving. Set beside this chilling scene, the poems of a Dave Smith may appear as an extreme of frivolity. Anthony Hecht's assembly of poems on Death are rather like a deck of playing cards, skillfully made to be sure; but the death and devastation revealed in this picture are another matter altogether. And one thinks: might this one day be Peoria, Trenton, or Denver? In our shifting and volatile world it seems a not unlikely possibility. And where then will our poets be?

The poems of Yehuda Amichai are proof that despite adversity, or perhaps because of it, a redeeming vitality is latent in the dialogue between society and the poet. In our case at present one half of that dialogue is largely missing.

FURTHER READING

Criticism

Bar-yaacov, Lois. Review of *Selected Poetry of Yehuda Amichai. Southern Humanities Review* XXII, No. 4 (Fall 1988): 402-05.
> Praises the translations of Amichai's works in *Selected Poetry of Yehuda Amichai* and presents Amichai as an Israeli writer observing Jewish history from the outside, disillusioned by historical experiences he did not witness first-hand.

Corn, Alfred. Review of *Even a Fist Was Once an Open Palm with Fingers. Poetry* CLIX, No. 3 (December 1991): 163-66.
> Admires Amichai's ability to infuse ordinary images and scenes with extraordinary metaphysical meaning.

Gold, Nili Rachel Scharf. "Flowers, Fragrances, and Memories: The Different Functions of Plant Imagery in Amichai's Later Poetry." *Hebrew Studies* XXXIII (1992): 71-92.
> Argues that "images of vegetation serve as a kind of prism through which to observe changes in [Amichai's] poetics."

Review of *Amen. Virginia Quarterly Review* 54, No. 2 (Spring 1978): 58.
> Calls Amichai "one of the essential poets of our day."

Review of *Time. Virginia Quarterly Review* 55, No. 3 (Summer 1979): 108.
> Praises Amichai's honest portrayal of his emotions in *Time.*

Siggins, Clara M. Review of *Not of This Time, Not of This Place*. *Best Sellers* 28, No. 7 (July 1, 1968): 137-38.
Finds the novel difficult and "strange" but ultimately rewarding in its examination of identity and reality.

Additional coverage of Amichai's life and works is available in the following sources published by Gale: *Contemporary Authors,* **Vol. 85-88;** *Contemporary Authors New Revision Series,* **Vol.46, and 60; and** *Major Twentieth-Century Writers.*

Sven Birkerts
1951-

American essayist and critic.

The following entry presents an overview of Birkerts's career through 1996.

INTRODUCTION

The author of *An Artificial Wilderness* (1987) and *The Gutenberg Elegies* (1994), Birkerts is a self-described "amateur" literary critic, who received a citation in excellence in book reviewing from the National Book Critics Circle in 1986. Though not formally trained in criticism nor espousing any particular academic theory in his approach to literature, Birkerts has established a reputation for arguing his positions with passion, clarity, and eloquence, both provoking and welcoming debate about his ideas. His extensive reading (usually in English translation) has qualified him to critique European, Russian, and Latin American literature, producing a critical discourse that not only acknowledges the talents of such literary luminaries as Heinrich Böll, Marguerite Yourcenar, and Jorge Luis Borges, but also recommends the merits of such lesser-known writers as Robert Musil and Erich Heller. Birkerts's critical purview also has extended to matters dealing with the relationship between society and technology in late-twentieth century civilization, specifically in terms of the art of reading, the printed word, and the proliferation of electronic media. Intrigued by the freshness and range of Birkerts's thought, critics generally have admired the simple, quotidian language and style of his essays, although a few have claimed that his literary exegeses neglect problems germane to translated texts and that his cautionary essays about "the fate of the book" often betray profound nostalgia.

Biographical Information

Born in Pontiac, Michigan, Birkerts attended the University of Michigan, where he earned a bachelor's degree in English in 1973. Upon graduating, he stayed in Ann Arbor and worked as a clerk in bookstores there, and later, at Cambridge, Massachusetts, until 1983; he has credited his bookstore experiences for prompting his voracious reading habit, remarking that "I chewed my sandwich with an open book in my lap." Meanwhile, Birkerts contributed book reviews and critical essays on world literature to such periodicals as *New Republic, Mirabella,* and the *Boston Review,* serving the latter publication as contributing editor since 1988. In 1984, Birkerts accepted an invitation to join the faculty at Harvard University as a lecturer in expository writing, a po-

sition he held until 1991. Following his National Book Critics Circle award, he published his first book, *An Artificial Wilderness* (1987), a collection comprised mostly of book reviews first published over a seven-year period during the 1980s. For his second book, *The Electric Life* (1989), Birkerts won the P.E.N. Award for Distinguished Essays in 1990. A prolific contributor of articles and book reviews to numerous periodicals, he collected some of these in *American Energies* (1992), which deals exclusively with American fiction and writers. A defining moment of Birkerts's reputation came with the publication of his controversial essays in *The Gutenberg Elegies.* Subsequently, he assembled the essay collection *Tolstoy's Dictaphone* (1996), which presents opinions on the social effects of technological media. Birkerts, who has lectured extensively both in person and on-line, has taught writing part time at Emerson College in Boston since 1992.

Major Works

Birkerts's writings display a genuine fondness for literature as books (opposed to texts), an abiding respect for the printed word (opposed to electronic formats), and a minute attention to the act of reading words on paper (as opposed to on a screen). The thirty-nine essays collected in *An Artificial Wilderness* draw attention to the works of some of the world's notable twentieth-century writers whose works are available in English translation, including Joseph Roth, Osip Mandelstam, Marguerite Duras, Michel Tournier, Primo Levi, Lars Gustafsson, V. S. Naipaul, Salman Rushdie, and Julio Cortázar, among many others, notably excepting any contemporary American authors. The other essays in *An Artificial Wilderness* concern general cultural topics; for instance, the function of television in the creation of the "mass age." The title of *The Electric Life* alludes to a phrase found in Percy Bysshe Shelley's *A Defence of Poetry* (1821), which describes poetic language as "electric life that burns." The essays comprising *The Electric Life* concern the influence of electronic media on contemporary literacy and describe the contemporary social context for the art of poetry. Among the themes contemplated are the ways television informs late twentieth-century poetic language, the idea of poetic inspiration, the politics and aesthetics of poetry, and analyses of some individual poems and poets. *American Energies*, Birkerts's third collection of book reviews and critical essays, offers a general assessment of the contemporary American novel genre, which he finds weakened or "lightweight"— lacking depth and historical resonance of vision in comparison to previous generations of American novels—due to its coincidence with the technological boom in communications media. Divided into three parts, *The Gutenberg Elegies,* a collection of fifteen essays, concerns the place of reading in society, centering on changes occurring in print and electronic media and the threat to the act of reading occasioned by these changes. The essays comprising the first section, "The Reading Self," are largely autobiographical, dealing with Birkerts's own reading experiences that illuminate the dynamics of reading. In the second section, "The Electronic Millennium," the essays examine the question of how reading, or the interpretation of texts, changes in an electronic environment. The last section, "Critical Mass: Three Meditations," addresses changes in the culture at large with respect to the quality of literary or intellectual life, the so-called "death of literature," and the ways in which technology has affected the role of the serious writer. *Tolstoy's Dictaphone,* an essay collection edited by Birkerts, features twenty articles by "writers who use and have been used by today's electronic machinery," as Cliff Stoll has described them, each one reflecting the tension that frequently exists when technology impinges upon social intercourse.

Critical Reception

Birkerts generally has impressed critics with his breadth of knowledge of world literature as well as with his common language and cogent, direct style as an essayist and literary critic. As David Holmstrom put it, "Birkerts brokers his analysis on the reader with a sharply reasoned but calm style." Birkerts's critical acumen, though esteemed as it is in most literary circles, has prompted a vigorous debate about the demise of print-oriented culture in the face of explosive developments in electronic modes of communication. Although many commentators frequently have pointed out Birkerts's evident bias for the printed word and often have cited what Wulf D. Rehder has called "falling in love with our own nostalgia" as the principal defect of the tone of his thought, the majority also have responded to the inherent value of Birkerts's insights, particularly those expressed in *The Gutenberg Elegies.* "There is no denying that Birkerts' quiver of arguments contains many sharp arrows that are, like Cupid's, dipped in such a sweet poison of persuasion and passion and appeal that, once hit, we might want to give in to their narcotic effect," Rehder has stated. "That Birkerts proves so open to attack," Andy Solomon has observed, "is far more a testament to the courageously vast sweep of his polemic than to the disputable validity of his argument," suggesting that Birkerts's way of thinking and style of writing invites the reader "to synthesize a new, deepened understanding of our own relationships to the printed and electronically transmitted word." Gesturing toward the significance of Birkerts's contribution of *The Gutenberg Elegies* "to our ongoing discussion of the nature of the continuing electronic revolution and its impact on the nature of the process by which we 'read' and acquire information, knowledge, and wisdom," Norman D. Stevens has asserted that "in the long run, we will all be the poorer if we fail to take [Birkerts's] insights into account as we design and implement electronic alternatives to the book."

PRINCIPAL WORKS

An Artificial Wilderness: Essays on Twentieth-Century Literature (essays) 1987

The Electric Life: Essays on Modern Poetry (essays) 1989

Writing Well [with Donald Hall] (criticism) 1991

American Energies: Contemporary Fiction (essays) 1992

The Gutenberg Elegies: The Fate of Reading in an Electronic Age (essays) 1994

Tolstoy's Dictaphone: Technology and the Muse [editor] (criticism) 1996

CRITICISM

Sven Birkerts (essay date Fall 1983)

SOURCE: "Television: The Medium in the Mass Age," in *Michigan Quarterly Review,* Vol. XXII, No. 4, Fall, 1983, pp. 619-32.

[*In the following essay, Birkerts ponders the role of television in contemporary society, describing its "consciousness" with respect to the social implications of "watching" it.*]

No one who has walked through the excavations at Herculaneum and Pompeii is likely to forget the oppressiveness of the experience, far outweighing its historical fascination or its cachet as future table talk. The dreariness of a George Segal sculpture has been multiplied a thousandfold: the heavy seal of Time has been impressed upon the ordinariness of daily life. We are suddenly able to imagine our lives embalmed at a casual moment. Indeed, I sometimes wonder what hypothetical aliens might find if our planet were surprised by an avalanche of ash—especially if their craft landed, years hence, somewhere on our shores. I try to imagine their exclamations, their cries of puzzlement, as they go from house to house. I envision through their eyes the petrified, white-washed figures, their arrangement—singly, in groups—some four to eight feet from a prominent up-ended box. There would be boxes with horns, boxes without. Gender markings? The more enlightened among them would shake their heads. "These are clearly religious objects, domestic shrines. We have found the remains of a very spiritual race."

Television. The truth of it is too much to grasp, too various. Seen synoptically, from an imagined altitude, all these blue lights look like a radiant roe, or a swarm of cells in a tissue culture. But from another place, from the ease of a chair in a room, they seem like nothing much, a breather from the assaults of the day, a few laughs, a shine of fantasy. Both views are true; neither view is true. Who is going to say? And how? Stalk it with language and it cackles at you, formulate a concept and it sprays you with dots. It is as tricky as mercury. You shiver it to pieces and it hugs itself back together. Mercury is apt. If you could do the impossible, if you could contrive some kind of barometric instrument for which television and its contents would be a mercury, you would be able to read the spiritual air-pressure of a time and place. But in fact you can do little more than play, break it into blobs, stare at their sheen, watch as they hurry back into a single imponderable lump.

At one time, twenty years ago, say, to write about television was a more feasible undertaking. Twenty years ago television had not yet seeped as deeply into the culture; it was not so co-extensive with the social fabric. There were still free zones, places to stand, Archimedean points from which to work the lever. This is no longer the case. Where television could once be considered apart from reality, as a toy, an "entertainment," it has now greatly expanded its reach and impact: it has become, by way of massive social participation, a significant portion of the reality itself. So much so, in fact, that the interface between society and television can no longer be clearly described. Television programs increas-

ingly comprise the content of private lives; shows and situations are discussed as if the personalities and events were real and in the world; the information and opinion purveyed determine, to a large extent, the public perception of historical and political events. To discuss the phenomenon, therefore, with some hope of grasping its essential nature, its *quidditas,* is to embark on one of those classic fool's errands—to quest for fleece. Though in this case the fleece takes the form, in Norman Mailer's words, of "a pullulation of electrons."

Tele-vision. Quite literally "vision at a distance" or "over a distance"; also, the instrument or appliance whereby this is accomplished. When not in use it is a strange enough object, an opaque window fronting a box, the box studded with dials and connected, by way of wire and plug, to the sorcery of an electrical system. Its function, by all accounts, is to provide entertainment and information. Like the automobile and the telephone, it has become nearly indispensable. Like the automobile and the telephone, it is one of our guarantors of equality: anyone can drive anywhere, call anywhere—any American can watch any show.

Television watching, this vast and ramified ritual, this mass phenomenon, is scarcely served by the word "entertainment." It wears the guise of being a relaxant—like softball, dancing or drinking—but it is so much more, or less, than that. If it were simply entertainment or relaxation that people sought, they would soon be driven to other expedients: the fare is passing poor. No, there is very little correlation between the available entertainment content and the 800 or so million man-hours that are put in—every day—in front of 200 million television sets.

Television represents the "outside world" to the individual. This is one of its services. To own a television is to have a seat in the arena where the world is visually presented. Of course, television is by no means co-extensive with the world, nor do its visual contents in any way encompass the world; but it is part of the nature of the medium to convey this impression subliminally. By simply pressing a button, the viewer makes contact with what is, in his imagination, an international information empire. The assurance is patent that if anything of urgent importance happens anywhere in the world, the information will be promptly conveyed. In this one sense television is no different from the radio. The fact that it is a visual medium, however, greatly magnifies the unconscious impact of this function.

But this is basic, obvious. There is another function that is far more important and worrisome: television acts upon the unconscious of the viewer not as an appliance or a plaything, but as a consciousness. It fosters and encourages the most bizarre sort of identification. The implications are staggering. But before we consider them we must question some of the mechanics of this phenomenon.

The identification is not really attributable to the fact that the medium delivers human voices and images. Those are contents. Prior to contents are the impacts of the form itself, the medium. Consider, first of all, the seamlessness: the impression derived from the absence of holes and gaps, coupled with its electronic nature, coupled further with its insistent uniformity. The visual possibilities of the medium are, potentially speaking, inexhaustible. But what has in fact happened is that the corporation-owned networks have narrowed the range and content of presentation to such an extent that it is impossible to distinguish one channel from another. The idea of channels as separate bands is further negated by constant switching. Not only is the medium seamless, its contents are as well. The result is that the images, sequences and structures are so much alike that they become, for the viewer, different simultaneous utterances by the same entity, and, in the last analysis, one utterance. And this entity, television, thereby takes on the lineaments of consciousness.

This ersatz consciousness is, so far as its contents are concerned, rudimentary enough. It scarcely reflects the complexities of the human mental operation. Its form, however, is unconsciously most persuasive. It depends upon—and itself creates—lack of resistance. There are no obstacles. The visual and audial materials are ingested directly with no need for translation. They are calculated thus: to resemble reality while being simpler than reality. The fluidity of the medium conditions us to passive absorption. There is nothing to engage the conscious faculty. A broad, one-way "channel" is opened between the medium and the unconscious. As we suspend our supervisory powers, the medium sets itself up as a surrogate. It is with our consent that a generally flat, banal configuration of materials is alchemized into a ghostly dimensionality.

What is the nature of the medium that can effect so subtle an interchange? Norman Mailer, in his essay "Of a Small and Modest Malignancy, Wicked and Bristling with Dots," writes:

> Often, when the stations would go off the air and no programs were left to watch, he would still leave the set on. The audio would hum in a tuneless pullulation, and the dots would hiss in an agitation of what forces he did not know. This hiss and the hum would fill the room and then his ears. There was, of course, no clamor—it was nearer to anti-noise dancing in eternity with noise. And watching the empty video, he would recognize it was hardly empty. Bands of grey and lighter grey swam across

the set, rollovers swept away the dots, and something like sunspots crackled forth.

The primeval echo of the passage is not fortuitous—the grey, tuneless hum represents nothing so much as our idea of undifferentiated consciousness. We know these sputtering voids because we produce something very like them in ourselves. Eyes closed, emptied of thought, hovering near sleep, we fill up with a similar pullulation. This is the primary level of identification: that our consciousness generates images and thoughts—contents—out of an agitated void just as television does. The medium has a psychic likeness. And we project upon that likeness something of our own sense of psychic dimension. It is this dimensionality—which does not actually exist—which welds into a disquieting unity the various differentiated emanations.

Identification and projection, both subliminal, secure a reality status for what is, in essence, a play of illusion. It could even be argued that we attribute a higher reality status to television than we do to life itself. I say this only half in jest. I suspect that there is a certain by no means small percentage of chronic viewers in whom the organized materials of television programming have effectively replaced any active, discriminating consciousness they might have once possessed. But can it be that the two—consciousness and television—are similar enough to be interchangeable? Or, to put the question differently, can it be that life as seen on television is effectively interchangeable with life as the individual experiences it? These are by no means idle questions.

> **The processes that strip modern experience of uniqueness and resonance, that make possible the shopping mall, the housing project, the uniformity of the suburb, the bland interiors of the work place—the list could go on and on—these prepare us for television.**
>
> **—Sven Birkerts**

It is not television that is conforming to modern life so much as it is modern life that is taking on the hues of the medium. The processes that strip modern experience of uniqueness and resonance, that make possible the shopping mall, the housing project, the uniformity of the suburb, the bland interiors of the work place—the list could go on and on—these prepare us for television. Since television cannot transmit uniqueness or resonance by its very nature (I will discuss this later with reference to the concept of "aura"), it is admirably suited to mirror modern experience. To television belongs all the persuasiveness of the ordinary. Its flatness, banality, the ambient feel it confers to time, all conform closely to our experience. What is more, it presents us with that experience in distilled and organized shape. We experience ordinariness in condensation; it is more real to us than the ordinariness of our lives. The fact that it is electronically "bedded" impresses upon it the stamp of authority.

Television as consciousness. This impression comes, in part, from a simple, potent illusion: that we perceive the medium as layered, and therefore deep. The illusion is created by constant alternation of contents. The hero is, say, trapped inside a burning building; a sudden—but expected—elision brings us the imagery of a tropic isle, a voice enticing us to sample something unique; another elision brings us the face of our local news anchorman, the pulsing sound of a ticker, a quickly-pitched summary of the hour's headline. And then we are back in the burning building. The impression is not one of segmentation, but of layering. With our partial suspension of disbelief, we imagine that our hero was battling flames while we were hearing the latest on the border war. The illusion reinforces in yet another way the idea that we are in contact with a complex, superintendent, perhaps even profound, entity.

Walter Benjamin was one of the first thinkers to investigate seriously the impacts of technology upon the sphere of art. He did not live to see the invention of television, but the structure of his analysis is such that the subsequent technological advance has not altered it significantly. The ideas about "aura" which he articulated and elaborated in his essay "The Work of Art in the Age of Mechanical Reproduction" are perfectly applicable to the problem of television.

Briefly, aura can be conceived as the invisible envelope of presence or context that surrounds and, in effect, guarantees the uniqueness and reality of a work of art. It is by nature impenetrable and intransmissible. Though Benjamin defines the concept primarily with reference to art, he recognizes its generality. Aura is the essential attribute of any individual, location, situation or object that has not been compromised by displacement or reproduction. He writes:

> We define the aura . . . as the unique phenomenon of a distance, however close it [the object] may be. If, while resting on a summer afternoon, you follow with your eyes a mountain range on the horizon or a branch which casts its shadow over you, you experience the aura of those mountains, of that branch.

Aura forms, in other words, the basis of subjective experience; it cannot be objectively isolated. To take anything from its natural context is to destroy its aura. Anything stripped of its aura is no longer that thing—its certificate of uniqueness is gone. Insofar as it then presents itself in the guise of the original, it is false.

This fairly simple recognition—though, of course, much ramified by Benjamin's prismatic intelligence—was one of the bases for his critique of modern life, a critique which centered itself upon the disintegration of meaning and the radical disharmony between the individual and his world.

A few sentences later, Benjamin claims:

> Every day the urge grows stronger to get hold of an object at very close range by way of its likeness, its reproduction. Unmistakably, reproduction as offered by picture magazines and newsreels differs from the image as seen by the unarmed eye. Uniqueness and permanence are as closely linked in the latter as are transitoriness and reproducibility in the former. To pry an object from its shell, to destroy its aura, is a mark of a perception whose "sense of the universal equality of things" has increased to such a degree that it extracts it even from a unique object by means of reproduction.

If we consider not just objects, but the fragile, context-bound webbing of all human interchange—which television undertakes to mimic and reproduce—then the concept of aura is immensely useful.

We must take care, however, to avoid the direct substitution of terms. The situation is somewhat more complicated. For television does not set out to reproduce the actual world. Nor, with few exceptions, does it pretend to transmit genuine human interaction in context. No, what television does is to manufacture situations and interactions among created, scripted personalities. What it delivers, therefore, is essentially a caricature of social reality, the simulacra of human exchange. There is no question of aura being destroyed— what is captured by the television cameras has no aura to begin with. Instead, subtly and insidiously, reality, the genuine human interaction, is being steadily sponged, divested of authority. The aura is robbed, not directly, but by proxy. All human exchange—travestied, replicated, absorbed by 200 million watchers—is progressively, and perhaps permanently, diminished.

Television and aura are incompatible. Anything filmed directly—an animal, a landscape, an embrace—is promptly dispossessed of presence. The image preserves certain accuracies while the essence is flattened out and caricatured. What we receive through the picture tube has the outer lineaments of the actual with none of the pith or savor. The viewer, of course, is not unaware of this. The problem is that after a while—after sufficient exposure—he starts to forget. The more he watches, the more the tension between the thing and its image is vitiated.

Television, I have said, provides a psychic likeness and is

received by the unconscious as a consciousness. But it is not a consciousness. It is a hybrid, a collage possessing some of the rudimentary attributes of consciousness. It is utterly bereft of aura. And consciousness without aura, without context or uniqueness, is a monstrosity, a no-presence that matches up with nothing in the natural world. It is something that is not alive that is trying to impersonate life: it is travesty. Possibly Mailer has something like this in mind when he writes:

> So, in those early mornings when television was his only friend, he knew already that he detested his habit. There was not enough to learn from watching TV. Some indispensable pieces of experience were missing. Except it was worse than that. Something not in existence was also present, some malignancy to burn against his own malignancy, some onslaught of dots into the full pressure of his own strangled vision.

That "something not in existence" is the Frankenstein of a consciousness pieced together like a quilt from a thousand heteroclite fragments.

To turn on the television set is to make the flight from three dimensions into two. It is an escape, an effort to kill self-reflective consciousness, at least for a time. Two dimensions are easier to reconnoiter in than three. But it is not only while watching that one participates in two-dimensionality. After enough exposure to the medium, the world itself—which we may here define as everything that is *not* television—loses some of its thickness and complexity. The eye of the beholder is altered. Television has the same power of alteration as art, except that it works in the opposite direction. The reality content of the world is diminished rather than augmented. But why? That is, why would consciousness, the supreme distinguishing feature of the species, its evolutionary trademark, wish to obliterate itself? It must, to some extent, be due to the quality of life available to the individual. That life consists, for too many people, of meaningless work and prolonged exposure to the concentrated ordinariness of television. A self-perpetuating tautology sits near the heart of the issue.

Television-watching also represents a diffusely-enacted participation in ritual. The viewer is, to a certain extent, looking past the content, engaging the form itself, the sentient global mesh which gives the medium much of its authority. This participation is passive and abstract. The viewer interacts with the medium; the medium, in turn, interacts with the whole world of viewers. One makes oneself a part of the circuitry and thereby extends and deepens the circuitry. It is participation in the life of the times—insofar as television-watching is itself a significant part of the life of our times. Another tautology. The same impulses that were once discharged actively—in public assembly—are now expressed from the armchair. The medium thus becomes the abstraction of community itself. It is a touchstone, a point of reference. A common mental property attains a powerful pseudo-reality through cross-referencing. The coffee-break ritual—"Did you see *Dynasty* last night?"—is not so much an expression of interest in the show as it is an act of self-substantiation.

Most discussions and analyses of the effects of television occupy themselves with the contents of programming. I would contend that the effects of the medium itself, the fact of it, its form, the structure through which the contents are presented, is of far greater importance. It is the medium that forges the connection with the unconscious, enables the contents to pass directly by all conscious monitoring. It is the form that gradually conditions the psyche of the viewer.

Television establishes a path of least resistance—visually, psychologically—indeed, it *is* that path. It is a prism that refracts the rays of attentiveness. The attention faculty itself is gradually altered. For one thing, new time-expectancies are created. The viewer becomes accustomed not only to 30 and 60-minute units, but to mini-units as well, two and three minute blocks of commercial interruption coming every five to seven minutes. The effects of this are not easily gauged, except in the realm of television-viewing. Here we find that people come to expect—and need—side-tracking every few minutes. Uninterrupted programming generates anxiety and boredom. The fact is that the commercial interruptions are a welcome distraction from the banality of most programming. Night after night, month after month, the mind is made to be a shuttle-cock. How can we believe that this leaves its focus and tenacity unimpaired?

In the same way, the structure of programming promotes the idea of resolvability. The container shapes the content, and not vice-versa. Thus, every thirty minutes there has to be a wrap-up, a conclusion. Can it be that the constant repetition of this expectation does not begin to affect the viewer's psyche? That it cannot be proven to do so is no assurance. There are other questions. For example: if television does function as a surrogate consciousness, does this in any way undermine the viewer's existential base, his awareness of himself as a creature suffering time? No one will disagree with the assertion that television makes time more palatable. But what does it mean that time is made more palatable? What painful encounters with the voids in the self are thereby short-circuited?

We cannot very well pursue these questions without bringing will into the discussion. Will, the capacity or power whereby the self consciously acts upon itself. It is will that we call upon in order to persevere in an action, to endure difficulty without relinquishing our intention. Any movement against the natural grain of a situation requires some amount of will. But what are the effects upon the will of prolonged passivity, of putting the self repeatedly into a state of suspended animation, of replacing obstacles by a path of least resistance? Is the faculty of will analogous to a muscle—does it atrophy from lack of use? If it is, then the whole issue of television is tremendously important. For the world will not change its nature to conform to the laws of television. If the will is indeed eroded by television-watching, then what is affected is the public as well as private domain. The obvious consequence is political passivity, a passivity that readily translates into susceptibility to power. Nature abhors a vacuum; so does the social sphere. Where there is passivity there will flourish, in some form, the will to power. This is not to say that watching television is paving the way for the demagogue. It is to say, however, that the arena of impact may be larger than we at first imagine.

I have avoided almost entirely the discussion of the contents of television. This is not to say that the contents are negligible. They are not. But I don't believe that their effects can be properly taken into account until certain features of the medium have been examined. Secondly—and this is a more elusive reason—I believe that the contents cannot be discussed independently. They are too much influenced and shaped by the nature of the medium. For this reason a substantial amount of what is "on" television exists below the threshold of language. It is too diffuse, too ambient, too random. It generates a liquid near-emptiness that defies words or concepts.

This randomness is an attribute of the medium more than of the contents. It is a direct consequence of the inability of the electron tube to transmit aura. There is a permanent shortage of legitimate material, of visual elements that will effectively "play." The contents, therefore, are always inadequate to the container; they cannot fill it up enough. What happens as a result is that there are, cumulatively speaking, long minutes of visual vacuum—eternal-seeming car-chase sequences, desolate facial pans, etc. Visual muzak. A network must fill up all of its allotted time, daily, weekly, yearly. There is not enough quality to go around. What little there is must be diluted into the solution of available time. Television maneuvers, therefore, in a field of extremely narrow options. And the options grow fewer as repetition exhausts the basic repertoire of scenarios. Networks are forced to use the same formulaic high-tension sequences over and over. The stock sit-com imbroglio has not changed from the times of Terence. There is no possibility for visual beauty—nothing beautiful has ever survived passage through the electron tube. For beauty is the apotheosis of aura—it dies running the electronic gauntlet. Instead, there is ambiance—not "ambiance"—dead-time in which the viewer is brought face to face with the medium itself, its grey, crackling, fundamentally alien presentness.

The case of John Hinckley Jr. invites a few observations on television content. We are informed that the would-be assassin was a misfit and a loner—the usual epithets—and that prior to his attempt on the president he put in hundreds of hours in motels across the country watching game shows, soap operas, and crime shows. Now, I would not dare to be so simplistic as to assert any actual causal connection. Hinckley did not become the kind of person he was by watching television—if he had there would be 50 million Hinckleys in the streets. No, he watched as much television as he did because he was the kind of person he was. The question that emerges is whether or not there was some small but vital area of overlap, some way in which watching exacerbated something in his psyche and rendered certain previously passive traits volatile.

In any case, the issue raised—as murky as it is important—is that of the impact of television, form and content, upon the unconscious. Not just the unconscious of John Hinckley Jr., but of millions of children and adolescents who have not yet integrated their unconscious into their ego structure. The more hours put in before the pullulating tube, the fewer are the hours spent in contact with the stubborn grain of the world. In other words, the materials absorbed into the unconscious include proportionately more illusion. The unformed, atomized ego structure absorbs the form, the violence, the caricature of relations, and shapes itself to those in the way that it should be shaping itself to actual experience. Again, consider the extreme case—Hinckley. He turned to fantasies of violence, I would argue, not because he had been made violent, but because he did not comprehend what violence really is. Shooting the president was a garish fantasy that took up obvious, available imagery without any understanding of its real nature. Not only is the will subject to erosion; the reality sense is as well.

It has been argued that television, along with certain other developments in modern technology—computerization, information processing—is opening the way for a new social evolution, that the time-honored view of the self—as a solitary, suffering being—is giving way to another. Maybe there is a new socially-integrated species of "mass man" waiting in the wings. If so, this passive acceptance of circuitry, this collective participation in suspended animation, is to be regarded as highly advantageous.

If this turns out to be the case, I, for one, would surround the word "evolution" with a thicket of quotation marks.

I don't believe that transformations like this take place without profound upheaval. I hold with the Freudian model enough to think that repressed instincts return in altered form. The species is not yet at a point where the instincts have atrophied entirely. I pray that it is not one of the secret offices of television to insure that atrophy.

I come back, finally, to my epiphanic moments on neighborhood streets, to my shock at seeing so many separate patches of blue light. I cannot shake the feeling that these form in their aggregate some new terrestrial constellation. Like all constellations, this one will have to be named and charted. And we will have to determine whether its occult influences are finally benign or not. I would be surprised if they were.

Jack Miles (review date 30 August 1987)

SOURCE: A review of *An Artificial Wilderness,* in *Los Angeles Times Book Review,* August 30, 1987, p. 4.

[*In the following review of* An Artificial Wilderness, *Miles admires the range of Birkerts's literary knowledge.*]

This is too cruel, but I will do it. One of the books reviewed in this collection of Sven Birkerts's book reviews and other short essays is a similar collection by George Steiner, of which Birkerts writes: "When I heard that Oxford University Press was issuing *George Steiner: A Reader* (1984), I was distressed to see that venerable old house giving in to the bonbon sampler trend—and shocked to find Steiner a party to the deed." Obviously, Birkerts has been party to just such a deed at Morrow; but readers who have been reading and enjoying his work here and there without knowing anything about him will not be distressed.

Birkerts, we learn in the introduction to the collection, fell in love with literature in an Ann Arbor bookstore, not in the classroom. He worked in that and other bookstores for years, defining his "field" as he went. And where he went, before too long, was to contemporary literature written outside the United States. The result, as the years passed, was that he became an unofficial or informal authority on European, Russian and Latin American literature, widely published and eventually invited to teach at Harvard University.

World Literature is not really the name of any academic field, but so much the better for the unpretentious, undefensive style of a critic who can admit what he does not know because there is nothing that—according to some diploma or catalogue title—he *must* know. Birkerts' motto, as spoken of literature, might be the bookstore clerk's: "I just work here." But of course he has worked there long enough and with such a happy freedom that by now he knows not just how to answer your question but how to correct it.

I think of Birkerts, who won the National Book Critics Circle criticism prize in 1986, as some combination of critic laureate and patron saint for booksellers. For reviewers, his range is such that [*An Artificial Wilderness*] might claim a spot on the shelf almost as a reference work. But for those

in the trade, his book is a proof of how high their calling truly is. It should be stocked and displayed accordingly.

Donald Hall (review date 8 November 1987)

SOURCE: "Truth in Transit," in *The New York Times Book Review,* November 8, 1987, p. 16.

[*In the following review of* An Artificial Wilderness, *Hall praises Birkerts's "urgent, serious, energetic voice" for celebrating non-American writers and books.*]

Sven Birkerts shakes us by the shoulders, telling us what to read and how to read it. He urges Robert Musil on us, comparing him to Nietzsche: "We find in both the same impatience, the same determination to stay in motion, and the understanding that the truth is itself a process, its seeker forever embattled. We turn to Musil because he never lies to us and because he never hides from the unsightly implications of a particular thought." In *An Artificial Wilderness,* his first book, Mr. Birkerts's urgent, serious, energetic voice ranges over the world of modern letters—with passionate intelligence discovering, praising and recommending books and writers: many German-language novelists, Marguerite Yourcenar, Malcolm Lowry, Cyril Connolly, V. S. Naipaul and Derek Walcott together, Borges, Walter Benjamin.

This critic is above all a reader, even a book lover, without the props of pipe and tweed that once characterized these roles. Just now he teaches composition at Harvard but he is not an academic; he has spent a third of his life —I take him for 35 or so—working in bookstores: "I chewed my sandwich with an open book in my lap." Another critical bookstore clerk was R. P. Blackmur, whom Mr. Birkerts quotes to define their art as "the formal discourse of an amateur."

An Artificial Wilderness collects essays written out of love for literature and concern over the condition of our culture. Mr. Birkerts is best when he is most ambitious, taking account of a great writer's vision and voice in conjunction with the history of our times. His awareness of "the brutalities of history," especially as observed by European writers, removes any suggestion of cozy connoisseurship from this critic's essays. Mr. Birkerts is meliorist only in respect to literature: as he demonstrates for us German, Russian, French and Italian authors, he says, "Transportation *is* civilization. . . . Every exchange across cultures between writer and reader betters our chances."

Which of course brings up difficulties inherent in this transportation. Correctly Mr. Birkerts mocks readers who pass up great writers because they refuse to read translations; but he seldom addresses himself to the losses.

We know that he is aware of the problem because he will talk about foreign poets only when they write prose. Two essays on Osip Mandelstam form the center of this book. Mr. Birkerts understands that it is "the very nature of lyric poetry that its idea inheres in the prosody, that you cannot detach it and lift it out in the way you might lift out the backbone from a well-cooked fish." Therefore he celebrates a poet by way of the poet's prose, without recourse to prosody or syntax, developing ideas from translated images, from abstractions, and from summaries—from a relentless assault that uses whatever seems transportable.

It is strange but effective, this homage to poetry and poet by way of prose. (Later he does something similar with Joseph Brodsky and Eugenio Montale.) As he enacts and embodies the great Mandelstam, martyred by Stalin, Mr. Birkerts continually rehearses literary embodiments of moral thought in circumstances of historical brutality. Mandelstam refused to lie to us and died of the refusal.

An Artificial Wilderness ranges from useful praise of European novelists and Russian poets to **"Critics and Thinkers"** like Erich Heller and Walter Benjamin. When he touches on contemporary American literature—**"The School of Gordon Lish," "Docu-Fiction"**—Mr. Birkerts celebrates less and criticizes more. Reading him, we celebrate the arrival of a new critic prepared to direct us and to argue with us.

Sanford Pinsker (review date Spring 1988)

SOURCE: "Collecting Cultural Evidence," in *The Gettysburg Review,* Vol. 1, No. 2, Spring, 1988, pp. 351-9.

[*In the following excerpt, Pinsker evaluates Birkerts's style, range, and method in* An Artificial Wilderness.]

Sven Birkerts, a voracious reader and reviewer, is "burdened" neither by the venerable reputations that Professors Marx and Brooks enjoy nor by the tortured jargon that infects so many of his contemporaries. He writes with independence and with *style* and surely deserves the citation he recently won from the National Book Critics Circle for excellence in reviewing.

An Artificial Wilderness is a collection of some thirty-nine pieces written over the last seven years. Birkerts is, above all else, a wide-ranging, extraordinarily catholic reader. Indeed, his table of contents reads like an international *Who's Who* of the most interesting twentieth-century writers: Robert Musil, Joseph Roth, Osip Mandelstam, Marguerite Duras, Michel Tournier, Primo Levy, Lars Gustafsson, V. S. Naipaul, Salman Rushdie, Julio Cortazar. Conspicuously

absent, of course, are any contemporary American writers, but as Birkerts explains,

> Though I had grown up on a steady diet of American moderns—Salinger, Heller, Mailer, Bellow, Percy, and others—I found that I was growing more and more dissatisfied with the local product. In this most frightening epoch, American writers seemed to have retreated into a perverse kind of hibernation. Self-consuming metafiction (Coover, Barth, Barthelme), genre subversion (Vonnegut, Doctorow, Vidal), docu-fiction (Mailer, Capote), numb affectlessness (Carver, Beattie)—none of these trends connected me with the larger picture, the world beyond words.

The writers who came to interest Birkerts "offered perspectives that allowed me to make some sense of my own disquiet." They were, in a word, more *serious,* more engaged with the problematical:

> Maybe because the authors had known more directly the brutalities of history—had suffered—they were able to break that terrible membrane of *self.* Their sentences seemed to lead me toward things, places, and events. Many—most—were bleak in outlook, but somehow the very fact of their writing assured me that we still moved within the realm of meaning.

Birkerts makes no apology for his admittedly eclectic method: "I write about what has moved or affected me as a reader." Nonetheless, there is every bit as much *vision* in *An Artificial Wilderness* as there is in *The Pilot and the Passenger* or *On the Prejudices, Predilections, and Firm Beliefs of William.* The difference, of course, is that Birkerts is grappling more directly than the others with our post-Holocaust condition and what it means to somebody formed by reading books. As he puts it:

> I see now that my choice of subjects has everything to do with the life we have all been living in the last decades. The essays are a kind of thinking by proxy, a way of testing perspectives. The recurrent questions are simple in the asking, but they are no less daunting for that. How did humanism—the faith in an ongoing human enterprise—fail? What has come in the wake of that failure? What are the grounds for hope, if any?

In one way or another Birkerts's essays pose these questions, and search for instances of moral courage, examples of artistic integrity, hedges against our collective ruin. To read *An Artificial Wilderness* is to feel the delicate balance within which we exist.

The same refusal to blink in the face of unpleasantness that we see on the general level in this book is present as well on more specific—and more exclusively literary—matters. For example, this is what Birkerts has to say about "minimalism" in a piece about Marguerite Duras:

> Minimalism is, for the practitioner, one of the more seductive literary modes. Like abstract painting, it looks easy, and as most of the action takes place in the realm of the unstated, the writer need not be bothered with the messy mechanics of plot or character development. Hemingway bewitched several generations of prose stylists with his primer-simple narratives and his aesthetic of exclusion: the unstated emotion, he maintained, can pack as much of a wallop as the stated one. In his hands the technique often worked—the early stories and novels, especially, quiver with repressed materials; but his legion of imitators the world over have given understatement a bad name. Few of them have bothered to learn the all-important distinction to that aesthetic—that the emotion, though not declared, must nevertheless exist. Most of us, I suspect, now balk when confronted with a page of fashionably lean prose. Dress it up how you will, I say it's spinach and I say to hell with it.

Birkerts's last remark can, of course, be applied as well to a good many collections of critical essays: dress them up in dust jackets and they're still so much spinach. But this is decidedly *not* the case with the books under consideration here. Marx, Brooks, and Birkerts do much more than merely demonstrate that the literary essay is alive and well; indeed, they suggest the complicated ways in which an individual piece becomes part of a larger, more significant pattern.

Jay Parini (review date Summer 1988)

SOURCE: "Reading Sven Birkerts," in *The Kenyon Review*, Vol. 10, No. 3, Summer, 1988, pp. 124-27.

[*In the following review of* An Artificial Wilderness, *Parini illuminates Birkerts's critical technique with respect to contemporary, academic criticism.*]

"The arrow of modern life and the arrow of private sensibility have passed in opposite directions," writes Sven Birkerts, one of the most independent critics now writing in America, in his first collection of essays, ***An Artificial Wilderness.*** This remark is made in the course of an "appreciation" of Cyril Connolly, a critic who in many ways Birkerts himself recalls. Connolly is praised for his awareness of literature as part of a larger historical process: "Implicit in his

valuations, supporting and authorizing them, was an active recognition of historical process. This awareness was at once particular—he grasped the dynamic interactions of person, place, and milieu—and relativistic." He sets this concern for context against the "prevailing thrust of critical theory," by which he presumably means the formalist strategies subsumed under the title of post-structuralism.

The flight from history to "language"—that is, to a disembodied system of signs, a resonating void wherein meaning flickers, tenuously, and fades into an infinitely recessive dark—clearly obsesses Birkerts, as well it should, though one wishes he defined his objections more precisely and named deconstruction and formalism as the culprits. (In other words, his sweeping judgments do not take into account the neo-Marxist and feminist schools, both of which have refused the "flight from history.") One has seen the formalist tendencies of criticism—from the New Critics and structuralists of an earlier era through deconstruction—driving a wedge further and further between word and object, between text and world. It is no wonder that, especially in America, the critical climate has worked *against* literature, against its very possibility. What gets singled out for praise is prose and poetry that exemplify the sense of exhaustion, of passivity, presupposed by critics. Thus, in his introduction to ***An Artificial Wilderness,*** Birkerts writes: "Postmodernism contends that everything has been done, that all artistic modes and genres have been exhausted. Innovation is no longer seen as possible. Style, therefore, is no longer bound to historical context . . . Art is to be viewed more as an arena for ingenuity than as an expressive necessity."

Birkerts laments what he considers the sorry state of contemporary fiction (pointing a finger directly at the so-called school of Gordon Lish, who remains a major figure only in the mind of Gordon Lish), concluding that literature is elsewhere. Though he admits to liking Thomas Pynchon, Saul Bellow and Walker Percy—major figures (except middle-aged Pynchon) of an older generation—his preferences are for Continental and South American writers. Indeed, he is like a radar station, scanning the horizon for major and minor figures: Robert Musil, Osip Mandelstam, Jorge Luis Borges and Eugenio Montale as well as Gregor von Rezzori, Eva Demski, Lars Gustafsson, and Blaise Cendrars. He notes that most of these writers are from countries where one cannot or could not hope to avoid "the sharp pressure of history." Writing of Mandelstam's "Fourth Prose," for instance, he observes: "'Fourth Prose' represents his decision to speak his mind and accept the consequences, and as such it is as courageous and historically loaded a document as has ever been written. Any one of its sixteen sections would have sufficed for his arrest. It is Mandelstam's credo, his moral integrity affirmed at a time when no one dared affirm anything." He continues, analyzing the prose—its "beautiful fury and invective"—with due regard for its place in time, its sense of audience, its *rhetoric* in the older, nobler sense of that term.

In each of the essays, most of which were published as reviews, Birkerts takes great pains to describe the object before him. He is never less than adroit, and his descriptions occasionally rise to wonderful heights of suggestiveness and precision, as in his piece on Julio Cortázar:

> Entering Cortázar's would, we leave behind our ordinary time perceptions. Sequence and succession, the lockstep of ticking seconds—these have almost no place in the fiction. The time of a glance or a caress is elastic: the psyche dilates and opens onto expanses of experience. And in the face of the experience, the sweep of the clock hands is irrelevant, if not absurd.

He is equally strong on the subject of Walter Benjamin, the German critic:

> Benjamin's appropriation of the image of the flâneur for himself was to some extent an ironic gesture. He knew that the harmony between man and his world had been all but irreparably violated. But it was precisely this knowledge—this hopelessness—that forced him to effect a major transformation. Moving from the objective to the subjective, he brought the flâneur sensibility to bear upon the inside life.

Again and again, reading Birkerts, one sits up and says, "Yes, that's it exactly!" This is a rare experience for readers of professional "Lit Crit," which tends to be jargon bound and nervous, wary of what somebody at Yale or Johns Hopkins might think or, worse, say when they read this or that. Birkerts cites R. P. Blackmur's famous definition of criticism as "the formal discourse of an amateur," thus (quietly) describing his own view of his critical project. He is unabashedly belletristic (though, of course, most theorists would say that Birkerts is naive in assuming this role, which is not as free of bias as it presupposes).

Critics quite often betray their own positions when describing other critics; in fact, they ought to. Birkerts does not hide his admiration for Connolly or Benjamin, for George Steiner or Roger Shattuck—all of whom he discusses here—but he carefully shows where his own ideal reader (every critic's Platonic self) goes beyond the critic under discussion. Thus, writing of Shattuck, he concludes: "Shattuck's stance at the end of *The Innocent Eye* leaves no doubt about his profound antipathy for the so-called postmodern developments. I would like to see him roll up his sleeves and engage in some real polemics—we may not be able to change history, but we can certainly argue with it."

Oddly enough, Birkerts rarely engages in polemics except on a fairly quiet level, by implication. The most explicit gestures in the direction of polemics occur in the last section of *An Artificial Wilderness,* which contains six lucid essays on general cultural topics, such as the function of television in the creation of the "mass age." His argument is not original. He thinks, quite logically, that the more hours we spend "before the pullulating tube, the fewer are the hours spent in contact with the stubborn grain of the world." The intellectual pyrotechnics of a Marshall McLuhan are blessedly absent from this essay, which is nevertheless full of subtle observations about the development of modern technology—television, the computer, information processing—and its consequences, which (he suspects) will not be benign.

Where Birkerts most obviously parts company with theoretically oriented critics is in his enthusiasm for reading itself.
—Jay Parini

Where Birkerts most obviously parts company with theoretically oriented critics is in his enthusiasm for reading itself. Here the amateurism is engaging. In **"Notes from a Confession,"** for instance, he writes:

> The world is covered with words, and I go about reading them. The urban surface. Signs, billboards, graffiti. I read and reread the same idiotic slogans on the cereal box morning after morning. If I require more variety, I study the jam jars, breaking apart and recomposing the letters in the lists of ingredients.

Going beyond this ephemera, he comments: "Gustave Flaubert, Graham Greene, Henry James, Virginia Woolf, Robertson Davies, Thomas Hardy—each author allows me to experience sensations that I find nowhere else. Each novel is a differently cut and differently tinted lens that I turn upon myself." The voice behind this prose recalls an earlier time, when the act of reading was not plagued by an obsession with intertextuality, when critics could be blissfully ignorant of their prejudices and presuppositions. (On the other hand, there is something frightening about the notion of a return to male-biased, elitist readings of the kind generated by three decades of New Critics.)

The theme of reading as self-discovery surfaces repeatedly throughout the book. Reading, for Birkerts, has much to do with the location of self in time: a theme rarely sounded in the pages of *Diacritics* or *Glyph.* Nevertheless, contemporary criticism is poorer for its loss. Criticism—at its best—remains an act of moral comprehension, an effort to locate the place of a text in the world, to identify its leverage, to calculate its angle of approach. By locating the self in history, the critic (however tacitly) admits the necessarily flawed, partial view of any stance. The flight from history to language can only result in moral deadness and political lethargy. It is symptomatic of a culture on the run, on the wane. This is true enough of imperial America, which seems to have run out of excuses. It seems equally true of academic criticism, which serves the society at large by remaining elitist, self-referential, and dull.

One hopes that criticism such as Birkerts's—outside the academic mainstream, hit-and-run, "belletristic," and rashly personal—can find its place and readership. It is promising that his essays have acquired a major publisher. In general, the high quality of writing in *An Artificial Wilderness* is a testament to its genre, which is too often spoken of in derogation as "literary journalism." I grant that the Sven Birkerts of the journalistic world are rare. Nevertheless, with the abdication of academic critics from the culture at large, with their withdrawal into coteries and schools, the everyday work of "appreciating" books has to fall on someone's shoulders. These shoulders, at least, are strong.

John L. Brown (review date Summer 1988)

SOURCE: A review of *An Artificial Wilderness,* in *World Literature Today,* Vol. 63, No. 3, Summer, 1988, p. 515.

[*In the following review, Brown appreciates the way Birkerts treats "literature as literature" in* An Artificial Wilderness, *outlining the contents of the book.*]

Sven Birkerts began his career as a member of that menaced species, the bookseller whose passion is "the unpunished vice of reading," the bookseller who is also a talented man (or woman, like Sylvia Beach) of letters and whose shop is no Walden or Crown supermarket of perishable print but the equivalent of a literary salon. He carries on the tradition of an Edmund Wilson and writes, not for the specialist, but for the cultivated general reader. He deplores the jargon, the unreadability of much academic criticism. He insists that "literature is worth nothing if it can not help us make sense of our historical circumstance." He regrets that so many contemporary American writers have failed to do this and "have retreated . . . into the dumb affectlessness" of a Carver, of a Beattie. So he sought guidance elsewhere, in the work of Europeans like Milosz, Frisch, Kundera; and they, in their turn, led him back to their great predecessors, Musil, Benjamin, Mandelstam.

Like Larbaud before him, Birkerts proclaims himself "an amateur": "These essays are finally the arguments and enthusiasms of a reader. An amateur. They advance no strict program, no theoretical fortifications." Not that he is indifferent to all the competing modern esthetic theories. It's simply that he refuses to "make peace with any discipline that promotes its own interests over those of the text in question." He is convinced that many of the most significant authors of our time "are from cultures that feel the sharp pressure of history." Combinatory exercises, not to mention "indeterminacies" and "sliding signifiers," "can't matter much to the writer who would speak of hunger, terror, or the ongoing incidence of evil." Within the area of twentieth-century literature, his range is very wide and inevitably somewhat superficial. The section on German writing includes pieces on Musil (one of the most important), Walser, Roth, Frisch, Gregor von Rezzori, Böll, Bernhard. Only two Russians, Mandelstam and Brodsky, are commented upon. The section, "XXth Century Constellations" is an omnium gatherum of French (Cendrars, Yourcenar, Duras, Tournier), Italian (Umberto Eco, Primo Levi), and Latin American (Borges, Cortázar) authors and touches in passing on Naipaul, Walcott, Yaakov Shabtai, Rushdie. Perhaps the most interesting essay in this group, **"The School of Gordon Lish"** (Lish is an influential editor with Knopf), throws an unflattering light on a type of fiction currently in vogue, which "represents an abrogation of literary responsibility": "If fiction is to survive as something more than a coterie sport, it must venture something greater than a passive reflection of fragmentation and unease."

Among the "critics and thinkers" grouped in part 4, Birkerts expresses his greatest enthusiasm for Walter Benjamin, "a flâneur" who practiced "the esthetics of indirection," and discusses Erich Heller, Montale, Roger Shattuck, George Steiner, and Cyril Connolly—who, we are somewhat surprised to learn, "was, by the time he died, England's, and perhaps the world's, leading critic." The volume concludes with a miscellaneous group of essays on television, on literary biography, on Flaubert's *Madame Bovary* and leaves the reader with the sense of pleasure which comes from sharing the enthusiasm of a discerning critic who takes an infectious delight in literature as literature.

Helen Benedict (review date 16 April 1989)

SOURCE: A review of *The Electric Life,* in *The New York Times Book Review,* April 16, 1989, p. 2.

[*In the following review, Benedict describes Birkerts's attitude toward poetry in* The Electric Life *as intellectually challenging yet provocatively open to debate.*]

Sven Birkerts—who won considerable acclaim for his first book of literary criticism, *An Artificial Wilderness,* and who won the 1966 National Book Critics Circle award for criticism—writes in a voice that veers between passionate harangue and smart-aleck banter. He is not too arrogant to engage the reader in debate, for even when he sounds contemptuous he leaves open a back door for disagreement, but he does tend to be annoyingly, though wittily, snide. "Poetry is now largely a face-saving operation, with poets pulling their bitterness inside out and preening themselves on their own uselessness," he writes in *The Electric Life.* Mr. Birkerts, who teaches at Harvard University, contemplates the declining state of literacy in our television-addicted age and tries to discover how, and if, poetry fits into our world. He discusses the ruinous effect of the electronic media on our minds, offers a reverential study of inspiration and conducts a rather precious debate on what makes poetry political. Mr. Birkerts then explores why he loves certain poems and, in brave defiance of academic tradition, attempts to find out what makes a poem beautiful. He proceeds to more conventional criticism, some in the form of analyses of the poetry itself, some in the form of attempts to analyze the poets. Mr. Birkerts clearly loves the stuff of which he writes, and his love is catching. This is a book for poetry readers who wish to be awakened by fresh arguments—intelligent enough to challenge yet provocative enough to be open to question and debate.

Sven Birkerts with David Holmstrom (interview date 17 August 1992)

SOURCE: "A Call to Authors: Explore Culture," in *The Christian Science Monitor,* Vol. 84, August 17, 1992, p. 14.

[*In the following interview, Birkerts expresses his attitude toward contemporary novelistic fiction and reading habits of the public.*]

To stretch a comparison here, critic Sven Birkerts has approached what he sees as the weak cathedral of the American novel, and like Martin Luther with his 95 theses, has nailed a protest to the door.

In this case, the protest (really a summons) is directed at American novelists writing in the fields of minimalism, nostalgia, and the other sweet-smelling soaps of Post-Modernism. Mr. Birkerts wants them to return to the novel form that explores culture with depth and historical resonance.

His engaging new book, *American Energies,* contains his "summons" on page 150. It is a list of the attributes to be found in the works of "elder writers," followed by the "lite" attributes of younger writers.

Younger novelists fall short, says Birkerts, because their books are morally neutral, without depth, fragmented, and conceived ahistorically with everything taking place in the

present. Character is implied without much social dimension, and the books end with insignificant resolutions.

Birkerts brokers his analysis on the reader with a sharply reasoned but calm style. No urgent shouting here; no doomsday lurking for the novel (yet), but a somewhat raised voice of concern by a critic who still likes to "stumble onto a novel and have my breath taken away." He recognizes talented writers today, but sees their fiction as a "flutter at the margins of the culture."

His first book, *An Artificial Wilderness: Essays on Twentieth Century Literature* (1987), won the National Book Critics Award for Criticism. A second book on modern poetry, *The Electric Life* (1989), won the PEN Award for Distinguished Essays.

For seven years, Birkerts taught expository writing at Harvard University. Now he teaches writing part time at Emerson College in Boston, and is working on his next book about the place of reading in society. From his home in Arlington, Massachusetts, Birkerts was interviewed by phone.

[Holmstrom:] *If the novel of substance and resonance is fading, could it be that nonfictional forms of writing—literary travel books, personal-experience books, even literate food books—are becoming more compelling to this age?*

[Birkerts:] As far as my sense of human nature goes, we have an absolute and fundamental appetite for narrative. What I think is happening is that we are getting our narrative much more expeditiously elsewhere these days. I think the idea of the novel as being the carrier of extended and complex narrative that shows us our world used to be its reason for being. That has been taken over and eclipsed by the narratives everyone gets by going to movies or turning on TV at night. The price of entry for a reasonably demanding novel is a certain willingness on the part of the reader to make a sacrifice, to say, "I believe this narrative is going to be worth my time." This has to be seen within the larger context of reading itself, which is moving a little bit to the margins. It's a sad thing because it speaks to a change in our culture away from certain habits of being.

Fifty years from now, you might be proved to have been wrong.

I imagine in 50 years there will be a small, self-perpetuating kind of elite squadron of people who still read for the reasons that one reads, just as people go to the opera. For me, and this is the point I argue in my book, the biggest challenge the novel has to face is to find a form and a series of approaches that can deal with a reality that has so radically changed around us in the last 30 or 40 years. What the novel is doing is scurrying in retreat into minimalism or looking back at scenarios that are 20th-century timeless in small towns or domestic circles. I see few works trying to serve up life as a great many of us are now living it, which is simultaneously on many levels.

I think in the pre-TV world, things were more opaque; there was more of a sense of true obstacle and distance and otherness. . . . The nature of what TV does, no matter what you watch, is that it gives you a kind of fluid and transparent sense of the world's nature, almost unconsciously, and I think it begins to structure your own attitude toward reality . . .

Perhaps what we are seeing is the loss of power of male novels, just as male power in our culture is changing, and we are seeing the inevitable rise of feminine sensibilities in novels.

In the beginning of the 1970s, there was a kind of explosion of the woman's novel. That process is now being duplicated on other fronts in the sense that women had been held back from expression. Now there has been a great efflorescence, for instance, of gay novels and African-American writing. These are upon us with the pent-up energy which seeks to right a lot of wrongs.

With more novels written from the woman's perspective now, won't this writing give us an enriched understanding of the human condition?

Over the last two decades that is what has happened. My complaint is that I'm finding a little bit of the law of diminishing returns kicking in. This kind of subtle and sustained domestic exploration, which was a new thing 20 years ago when women began exploring the untold story of the family, I think, has run its course. I think families have been archaeologized possibly too far. I would like to see some of these extremely talented writers plunge into the larger social [arena], one that would require a kind of structural frame, which in the past, at least, we associated with male writers.

Earlier, you mentioned a squadron of people who love to read.

If you are a true reader, and you love books, then there is something you have in the world that nobody can really take from you. . . . It's a world you can reoccupy, not that every book is a different world; it's a world that various books define, and you can enter that world. . . . You know you can hoard it, that after you brush your teeth, you've still got three chapters left, and it's something waiting for you.

David Holmstrom (review date 17 August 1992)

SOURCE: "Today's Novels Are Lightweight, Says Critic," in *The Christian Science Monitor,* Vol. 84, August 17, 1992, p. 14.

[*In the following review, Holmstrom concentrates on a question of excellence that he believes is implied by Birkerts's arguments in* American Energies.]

After a reader turns the last page of Sven Birkerts's ***American Energies,*** a question comes quickly to thought: Is there any effort left in the United States to be excellent? Not to win, not to have the most, or be the biggest, or the quickest, but to be excellent?

Birkerts's collection of essays on what he sees as the weakened condition of American novels is not directly about excellence.

It's the lack of depth and resonance in novels that worries him. As a reflection of an American culture spun into confection by technology, he argues, mostly lightweight novels are being written now. While my guess is that he would validate the pursuit of excellence as worthy even in novels, the desire for excellence is a characteristic, not a vision.

But inadvertently, Birkerts suggests that excellence and vision are intertwined. He wants novels to return to encompassing visions, to the kind of stories that "gather what we are" and become unforgettable.

He offers a partial lineup of novelists who "reached artistic maturity" just before technology and the sonic boom of media communications swept the globe—Saul Bellow, Eudora Welty, Robert Penn Warren, Peter Taylor, and John Updike. He compares them with a current list of novelists he calls "children of the media culture": Jay McInerney, Tama Janowitz, David Leavitt, Amy Hempel, Mary Robison, Deborah Eisenberg, Bret Easton Ellis, Ann Beattie, and Bobbie Ann Mason.

Is the latter group a purveyor of lightweight excellence?

Yes, if you apply Birkerts's criteria loosely and call them minimalists.

No, if you are a member of that generation, and accept the world of sudden pulses, quick images, and "circuit processes," as Birkerts calls it. Excellence is not any point at all; experiencing the NOW is the point.

You want real excellence and vision? Birkerts offers reviews of books, and comments about at least 40 American writers in the second part of the book. Here are some of the big themes and bedrock members of American fiction; three of the most important novelists are Don DeLillo, Thomas Pynchon, and Robert Stone.

Birkerts says, "The work of these three novelists is the thread of sanity that we will need if we are to escape from the labyrinth" of a society filled with "distraction, spectacle, and the bromides of public relations."

Excellent.

Bernard Sharratt (review date 18 December 1994)

SOURCE: "Are There Books in Our Future?," in *The New York Times Book Review,* December 18, 1994, p. 14.

[*In the following review, Sharratt exposes several assumptions that inform Birkerts's analysis of reading in* The Gutenberg Elegies.]

Major historical transformations can be imagined most poignantly as parental anxieties. Any book-loving parent today contemplating a 5-year-old daughter absorbed in the first magic of solo reading can whisk forward to her teen and college years, vicariously re-anticipating that first full encounter with Austen, Dostoyevsky, Thomas Mann—only to halt this nostalgic rerun in sudden recognition of an alternative possible scenario: of a generation by then so enmeshed in electronic information, so tuned in not just to television but to pervasive interactive multimedia, so besotted by on-line data services, as to have grown up barely acquainted with printed books at all, except as museum exhibits or as unwelcome inherited wallpaper.

This worry is the starting point for Sven Birkerts's collection of essays *The Gutenberg Elegies,* which focuses on the epochal shift he sees occurring between print and electronic media. He imagined his daughter graduating into a post-book world already partly inhabited by college freshmen so attuned to the rapid rhythms of MTV as to be wholly unresponsive to the patient patterns of Henry James's prose, so seduced by the flickeringly powerful identifications of the screen as to be deaf to the inner voicings of print.

Several times Mr. Birkerts sketches the opposing poles of the transformation he sees awaiting our children: from books to electronic circuits, from print-based linearity and logic to the semi-arbitrary serendipity of hypertexts. The global inrush of digital data across a screen is to replace that remembered cozy curl in the armchair, coiled into expectation, exploration and adventure. Never again, even, that quick oblivious dip into the paperback thriller, until the subway stop enforces a jerky re-entry into reality.

Mr. Birkerts has a palpable emotional investment in the richly evoked book world he fears we are about to lose. A candid and engaging autobiographical account sketches his own almost obsessive trajectory through avid childhood reading, adolescent bookshop browsing and amateur book collecting, culminating in that common dream of book lovers: managing a secondhand bookstore. Then the final, predictable failure of his novel-writing efforts twists the story into a modestly happy ending, with his late discovery of a talent for criticism and his subsequent career as respected reviewer and freelance essayist.

Unfortunately, as his warmly elegiac essay on Lionel Trilling recognises, the profession of critic opened its doors for Mr. Birkerts some decades after its apogee: the ethos of those "last intellectuals" of the 1930s has long dissolved, their print-based cultural influence barely conceivable to today's aspiring freelancers. Here Mr. Birkerts's diagnosis seems unfocused, uncertain whether the emergence of a narrowly academic literary profession his driven a wedge between a general reading public and the best of literature, or whether the commercialization of publishing has brutally reduced available work to the lowest bottom-line denominator. This sense of unspecific analysis arises partly because Mr. Birkerts's own book echoes the form he commemorates in Trilling, the republication of loosely linked occasional pieces as an essay collection.

That genial mode falls short of the claims he makes for the book form as such: linearity, sustained narrative, cohesive argument. There are individually rather slight pieces on a CD-ROM collection of classical Greek literature, on the experience of driving while listening to audio "books" and on the limited appeal of current hypertext fiction. Yet each piece only makes opening moves, without building collectively into an overall case.

The core, and persuasive achievement, of the book is Mr. Birkerts's attempt to capture the central experience of reading he fears may soon be lost. He acknowledges that "I value the state a book puts me in more than I value the specific contents." That state is "other than thinking," a peculiar process of immersion, of filtered double-consciousness of both the book's world and our own, a two-way involution of self into character and of text into voice. This state underpins, for Mr. Birkerts, our very capacity for complex language, for self-formation, for historical awareness.

Yet though this profoundly reflective process is skillfully described, Mr. Birkerts's formulations of his wider position seem, under scrutiny, dubious as a basis for grasping any truly epochal change. "The complexity and distinctiveness of spoken and written expression," he writes, "are deeply bound to traditions of print literacy"—yet Cicero had never seen a printed book. "The depth of field that is our sense of the past . . . is in some essential way represented by the book and the physical accumulation of books in library spaces"—but did the archivists of Alexandria therefore have that same "depth of field," and is an adequately archeological sense of the past primarily a matter of books or of sensitivity to sites, stones and sediments? "We may even now be in the first stages of a process of social collectivization that will . . . vanquish the ideal of the isolated individual"—but was the "isolated individual" ever an ideal or rather an image of exile and alienation?

One summarizing passage suggests a deeper flaw, bias or limitation of horizon. Mr. Birkerts writes: "Consider the difference. Text A, old-style, composed by a single author on a typewriter, edited, typeset, published, distributed through bookstores, where it was purchased by the reader, who ingests it in the old way, turning pages, front to back, assembling a structure of sense deemed to be the necessary structure because from among the myriad existing possibilities the author selected it. Now look at Text B, the hypertext product composed by one writer, or several, on a computer, using a software program that facilitates options. The work can be read in linear fashion . . . but . . . the reader can choose to follow any number of subnarrative paths, can call up photographic supplements to certain key descriptions, can select . . . possible endings. What is it that we do with B? Do we still call it reading? Or would we do better to coin a new term, something like 'texting' or 'word-piloting'?"

This writing has, in Lawrence's phrase, its thumb on the balance. We should think also of Text C: the Duc de Berry's *Book of Hours* or William Blake's *Songs*—luscious illumination, resplendent multimedia, hyperlinked entwinings of text and image. No typewriter could produce a single page of either. Or Text D: Peter Greenaway's *TV Dante* or Andrei Tarkovsky's film *Andrei Rublev*—compelling re-imaginings of one medium into another.

It is not a new term for reading that we need, but rather the imagination to devise new creative forms, appropriately innovative genres, beyond the dispiriting design clichés of business "presentations," the flat fantasies of video games, the essential inertness of interactive information kiosks. The new Limbourgs (the medieval artists who illuminated the *Book of Hours*) and the Blakes of the electronic era will one day learn to think beyond bulletin boards, digital encyclopedias and multimedia versions of 19th century novels. Mr. Birkerts complains, with sweeping pessimism, that "electricity and inwardness are fundamentally discordant." Does he really read by candlelight?

In Henry James's Manhattan of carriage mews and horse droppings, no one could have judged the future of the horseless carriage without the capacity to imagine both reeking exhaust fumes and the purring sleekness of a Rolls-Royce Silver Cloud. Our granddaughters may one day treasure their multimedia disks as much as Yeats once relished those "beloved books that famous hands have bound." In the 1480's a conscientious bishop paid a printer to proofread, against the original manuscript, each individual copy of the whole print run of a liturgical text. Some anxieties can, eventually, become merely historical. After 500 years, though, it's sad to still be saying goodbye to Gutenberg.

Andy Solomon (review date 29 January 1995)

SOURCE: "Endangered Books?," in *Chicago Tribune,* January 29, 1995, pp. 4-9.

[*In the following review, Solomon discusses the pros and cons of Birkerts's thesis in* The Gutenberg Elegies.]

Deeply imprinted in both our racial and individual psyches is the image of a lost golden age, paradisiacal in its virtue and brilliance. Nothing, it seems, can recall that Edenic hour of splendor in the grass or glory in the womb except lamentation that the good old days have yielded to coarser, brasher times.

So those of us who love the spell and sensuous delight of books come with predisposed sympathy to Sven Birkerts' mournful elegy for the printed page [*The Gutenberg Elegies*]. Writing on an antiquated typewriter a mere floppy disk's throw from MIT, the justly acclaimed literary critic has peered into the technological future of letters and found, to his horror, that it moves at the speed of light.

Speaking as "an unregenerate reader, one who still believes that language and not technology is the true evolutionary miracle," Birkerts argues with passion and dismay that modern electronic communication and information technologies have brought our culture to "what promises to be a total metamorphosis . . . What is roaring by, destined for imminent historical oblivion, is the whole familiar tradition of the book."

That many are reading these words on America Online rather than newsprint makes credible Birkerts' point.

His case, though, is no mere curmudgeonly refusal to keep running with the accelerating pace of change. He sees the dawning era of reading on glass screens as a time of "dissolution" that will cripple our souls. He notes: "Our entire collective subjective history (the soul of our societal body) is encoded in print . . . We have been stripped not only of familiar habits and ways, but of familiar points of moral and psychological reference."

Herded by electronic impulses and fiber optics into a global mass, what we most disastrously risk losing, Birkerts fears, is what books provided: the opportunity to read, pause, reflect, reread, memorize, reflect some more. We risk the part of our minds and hearts capable of depth, meditation, inner expansion. Progressively, Birkerts implies and constantly reiterates, each embrace of newer, faster technology becomes another step away from the individualized self, the inner space of tranquillity where we find aesthetic and spiritual centeredness.

Given its full weight, then, this book prophesies the end of intellectual privacy, individual depth and the clarifying silence in which creativity occurs, the moment in which we conceive a "Divine Comedy," a law of thermodynamics or even a computer chip. Short of global nuclear or viral destruction, it would be hard to imagine a future more grave.

Not surprisingly, then, parts of this book have already appeared in forums ranging from *Harper's* to the *Associated Writing Programs Chronicle.* And, not surprisingly, Birkerts is being vehemently refuted, for his argument is open to attack at virtually every turn.

The idea of reading on the ephemeral screen even has some humane attractions; as one of the nation's preeminent book reviewers, Birkerts himself must recall numerous volumes for which trees should never have died.
                    —Andy Solomon

That electronic communication threatens the primacy of the book does not, after all, promise to render books obsolete, much less threaten silent reflection. Was not Gutenberg's (disputable) discovery of movable type a threat to the handcrafted artistry of the illuminated book? Did writing itself eradicate the sung Homeric epic or did it make the *Iliad* tangible, portable and capable of wide distribution?

When Birkerts writes despairingly of the modern worker who rises to an electronic clock, shaves with "Good Morning America" droning in the background, starts his day with email and voice mail and goes home to collapse watching "NYPD Blue," he knows he risks seeming less an intellectual patrician than a hopeless reactionary. For he knows, and frequently admits, that the good old days were not necessarily all that good. And those days before Internet, penicillin and flushing toilets were less good than he admits. Were we a more spiritual race when instead of breaking up the work week with "NYPD Blue" or pro football we broke it up with gladiatorial combat or bear baiting? For that matter, was there ever a time when most people read books, much less good books?

The idea of reading on the ephemeral screen even has some humane attractions; as one of the nation's preeminent book reviewers, Birkerts himself must recall numerous volumes for which trees should never have died. Moreover, our interconnected computer society, with its thousands of discussion forums, can hardly be accused of robbing us of the chance to conduct dialogues about ideas. Far more guilty, no doubt, is the publish-or-get-denied-tenure academic morality that crowds out stimulating polemic (such as Birkerts' own) and replaces it with timid trivia and faddish sophistry.

Birkerts' scope here is so large that it lures him into numerous inconsistencies. He decries even the telephone for eliminating the printed postal letter, yet the letter itself was once a dehumanizing modernism rendering old-fashioned the face-to-face personal encounter.

While reading Birkerts' long autobiographical chapter, a paean to his boyhood days with *Tom Sawyer* and student days working in a bookstore, I sensed and identified with something between his lines that seemed less prophetic than wistful. Just as I often suspect in middle-age insistence on political correctness an unvoiced longing to recapture one's bead-wearing salad days of marching behind Dr. King, I sensed Birkerts' nostalgia for a youth that was personally magical.

Were times really as good then as they now seem? In some ways, no doubt. Yet, as I look, as Birkerts also does, with mystified distance on my Nintendo playing, on-line lovemaking students, I recall that when I wore my cap backwards it was because I wanted to be Yogi Berra. And when Birkerts contends, "No one thinks any longer about writing the Great American Novel," I must note that each semester I see a dozen young people who wish to do exactly that. When Birkerts blows "Taps" for individualism and echoes Don DeLillo's "The future belongs to the crowds," I suspect I'm hearing what was moaned also by those who saw the storming of the Bastille or heard, "Not this man, but Barabbas."

That Birkerts proves so open to attack, however, is far more a testament to the courageously vast sweep of his polemic than to the disputable validity of his argument. For it quickly becomes clear that the enormous value of [*The Gutenberg Elegies*] hinges not at all on how much readers will agree or disagree with Birkerts but on his unspoken invitation to reflect on his thesis, offer a rebuttal and then synthesize a new, deepened understanding of our own relationships to the printed and electronically transmitted word.

And, at that, I'm not sure it would have proved as engaging on a computer screen.

Wulf D. Rehder (review date January-February 1995)

SOURCE: A review of *The Gutenberg Elegies,* in *The Bloomsbury Review,* Vol. 15, No. 1, January-February, 1995, pp. 3, 8.

[*In the following review, Rehder praises Birkerts's powers of persuasion in* The Gutenberg Elegies, *heeding the emphasis on the personal aspect of his thought.*]

Second only to sex, the human mind seems concerned about books. Both can be all-consuming, and their decline has been seen as a sure sign that Western culture is coming to an end. What the nether areas of pornography are to sex, the new media of TV, hypertext, CDs, and the Internet are to books. According to Sven Birkerts, they are "masturbation aids" for the mind, except that these outcroppings of high technology don't make us think dirty thoughts; they just get us thinking. They also get Sven Birkerts writing, and what terrific writing it is! Yet it won't do just to call Birkerts a stylist of the highest order, steeped in the tradition of Lionel Trilling's liberal imagination. He does reach the depth of intellect and the height of sensibility that Trilling wrote about so eloquently. But Birkerts is not as indirect or "Jamesian" about his convictions, because he has seen the devil at the crossroads more clearly than Trilling could 50 years ago. A vow to refuse the devil's temptations rather than a call for exorcism, these *Elegies* are about thinking and about ideas.

> Ideas are not the sum and substance of thought; rather, thought is as much about the motion across the water as it is about the stepping stones that allow it. It is an intricate choreography of movement, transition, and repose, a revelation of the musculature of mind.

Birkerts is the author of *American Energies* (Morrow, 1992), *The Electric Life* (Morrow, 1989), and *An Artificial Wilderness* (Nonpareil Books, 1987), for which he received a National Book Critics Circle Award. These books show him as a sympathetic reviewer of poetry and fiction from the 19th and 20th centuries, some avant-garde, and many modern classics. He writes under the axiom that the best vehicle for thinking is our natural language, not the artifacts of technology. When our thinking condenses into ideas, there has been, for 500 years, an unsurpassed receptacle: the book. Now, though, Gutenberg's invention is suffering from neglect. A book is a lazy machine that requires a lot of collaboration. It doesn't do the thinking for us. As the Nintendo

and MTV generation is asserting itself against Henry James, indications are, writes Birkerts, that James has lost already.

Birkerts states his case in loosely coupled essays that are held together by the theme of "reading and meaning." He begins with a highly personal ecology of reading. Moving on many paths toward the conclusion that a millennial transformation of society is upon us, he also celebrates the private joys of reading, of living with and out of books. Symptoms of this transformation, which he describes as a flattening, or trivialization, of intellectual life, are to be found in the rise of electronic communication with its promise of a fast, global, lateral connectedness, its emphasis on the "now." To collaborate properly with books, on the other hand, requires a slow and vertical immersion, a readiness for the experience of other worlds and of deeper time, of Bergson's "duration." Subsequent essays highlight the concrete dangers of the electronic age. Loss of a historical perspective, language erosion, and the waning of individuality seem to be the price we, the heirs of McLuhan, are ready to pay.

A coda, entitled **"The Faustian Pact,"** epitomizes Birkerts' point. We are at a crossroads, he claims, and our tragedy lies in the fact that the decision has already been made. We are going down the road of the devil, the way of the "sorcerer of the binary order." What for Henry Adams was still an honest conflict between the forces of the mechanical machine and the virtues of faith and inwardness, a division of the world under the two metaphors of the Dynamo and the Virgin, has degenerated into a clear victory, without a fight, for the can-do boosterism of a hard-wired, computerized America over self-reflectiveness, privacy, solitude, and soul.

The Gutenberg Elegies are more authentic than Neil Postman's depressing threnodies (e.g., *Amusing Ourselves to Death* [Penguin, 1985] or *Technopoly* [Knopf, 1992]) and less self-righteous than Alvin Kernan's dirge about *The Death of Literature* (Yale, 1990). Not that Birkerts has newer data than Postman about the detrimental impact of TV on our attention span; nor does he subscribe to Kernan's miserly suspicion that leftist radicals are undermining the ivory tower. Birkerts' arguments are more convincing simply because they are so seductively personal. *Personal* does not mean merely subjective. The way Birkerts describes the reading experience—the "shadow life of reading," the existence of "the dreamy fellow with an open book on his lap" while surrounded by the never-ending hum of circuits processing trivial information through an invisible web—all this must be uncannily familiar to every committed reader. And yet I feel a residue of dissent. There is no denying that Birkerts' quiver of arguments contains many sharp arrows that are, like Cupid's, dipped in such a sweet poison of persuasion and passion and appeal that, once hit, we might want to give in to their narcotic effect. But we must resist falling in love with our own nostalgia. To paraphrase writer Robert Musil, it is a matter of mental hygiene to put the novel aside once in a while and solve a difficult integral. The number of rooms in our interior castle (where the soul reigns supreme) is larger than one. It is not enough to feed the soul an optimal dose of its recommended daily allowance of novels and poems. Such one-sided nutrition leads to hypertrophy of the fiction muscles. A more balanced diet does not, however, come from injections of the so-called reality or from ingesting the junk food of the mind that technological progress advertises and administers. More delicious mind-food is available in those other rooms in the interior castle. Their doors are labeled Music, Mathematics, Dancing, Playing, perhaps even Solving-Hard-Problems-in-Quantum-Mechanics. The human faculty that Henry James once called "the beautiful circuit of thought and desire" need not be restricted to fiction. His poles of "reality" and "romance" span a larger terrain than that of computers and novels, and Trilling's intellect and sensibility describe a wider realm in heaven and earth than is dreamt of in most lit majors' philosophy.

Thus speaks the rational skeptic in me. But in my more melancholy mood I hear deeper in *The Gutenberg Elegies* a most mesmeric music, and I shudder from the resonance these essays generate in my heart.

Jay Tolson (review date 22 May 1995)

SOURCE: "Afterwords," in *The New Republic,* Vol. 212, No. 21, May 22, 1995, pp. 40-1.

[*In the following review, Tolson describes the principal themes of* The Gutenberg Elegies, *explaining the deficiencies of Birkerts's arguments yet admiring his passion for reading.*]

It's not easy to pick up a book about the impending death of a practice once thought to be at the heart of the well-lived life. I mean the practice of reading, especially the kind of serious reading we were taught was not only the means to an education, but its self-delighting end. And though it may be comforting to hear one's twilight fears echoed and elaborated by someone so steadily persuasive as Sven Birkerts, it's hard to shake the feeling that his book would more profitably sit in the hands of those who are least likely to turn to it: the growing number of "wired" citizens who consider books, and book-reading, quaint atavisms in the evolution of information technology. This book's message is apt to seem to them as distant as its medium.

The medium in this case is the old-fashioned discursive essay—personal, reflective, edifying and (true to the title of the collection) elegiac. Through the fifteen essays gathered

here, two themes march solemnly, purposefully and often hand in hand. The first is that the reading of good books is an essential, and essentializing, activity: that it deepens and individualizes us, cultivates our inwardness and even our souls. The second is that the act of reading—specifically, the serious and solitary engagement with works of great literature—is endangered by the rise and expansion of the modern technology of electronic "interactivity."

Few readers will have difficulty embracing the first theme. Indeed, as readers, they will have a harder time believing that anyone who doesn't engage with great books can possess a soul worth wondering about. This readerly species of hubris in fact merits consideration, not least because it persists despite the efforts of some of the more canny modernist writers to challenge its blinkered arrogance. Joyce's Leopold Bloom is a perfect case in point. This supreme creature of the Dublin middle class, this urban stroller and relisher of the everyday, is not a reader in the sense Birkerts would understand. That is, Bloom would never sit down to an evening with a novel by Flaubert; a line from Yeats would probably baffle him. Yet Joyce makes it abundantly clear—it is practically the point of his novel—that Bloom, in another sense, is a profoundly discerning reader of the world's manifold and seemingly random signs, whether they be details from ephemeral newspaper stories or advertising slogans, the muttered words of his fellow citizens, or the shifting moods of his wife. That a writer of such exquisitely mandarin learning could have arrived at so democratic an appreciation of the interior life of an extraordinary ordinary man is one of the marvels of *Ulysses.*

The matter of Bloom is not tangential to Birkerts's larger argument, as Birkerts well knows. One of his essays explicitly takes on the charge that literary sensibility (or what Birkerts calls "coherent inwardness") is no more than an elitist affectation. To some extent, though, all of the essays here force one to ask whether "people of the book" are indeed guardians of the sacred and the true, or just well-intentioned but ultimately misguided idolaters who mistake the vessel for the contents in their efforts to perpetuate a cult of esotericism, high learning, difficulty.

Birkerts makes a good case against the second conclusion and in favor of the broadest, most democratic claims of a literary education. He does so partly through a sympathetic *autobiographia literaria* that tells how he came to books and how his life has been shaped in service to them. Birkerts's literary education had a very unstuffy, American quality— after college, he supported himself by working in bookstores, fighting off depression and self-doubt with voracious reading—and the self-mocking candor with which he describes himself is winning. "I saw my role," he writes of his bookstore years, "as quasi-priestly: I was channeling the nourishing word to the people who wanted it most. I had to feel that because, otherwise, I was just putting in time at a low-paying retail job, not at all ministering to the life of the culture or moving along a worthy career path."

But even while the priestly metaphor is ironic here, it hints at a somewhat less democratic notion of the literary life. Simply put, Birkerts believes that literature has a salvific purpose, though salvation, to him, is very much a worldly matter: its other name is individuality. We go to serious reading, Birkerts suggests, out of a sense of self-insufficiency (a secular variant, one might say, of Original Sin): "To open a book voluntarily is at some level to remark the insufficiency either of one's life or of one's orientation toward it." And what do readers accomplish in reading? Typically, Birkerts explains, they establish their "inwardness, the more reflective component of their self, in the space that reading opened up." That space is more temporal than physical—not the time of sequential, measurable units but time beyond time, in which the reader can see that, "God or no God, life has a unitary pattern inscribed within it, a pattern that we could discern for ourselves if we could somehow lay the whole of our experience out like a map."

If such arguments have a familiar ring, it is because Birkerts embraces the Arnoldian ideal of art as the last stay against anarchy, the noble stand-in for the lost established creeds. He is an epigone among the literary intellectuals, critical and creative, who self-consciously defined their labors in priestly terms. According to the high modernist tradition elaborated by this clerisy, the artist creates the works whose unity, clarity and integrity the critic then identifies and sets forth before the Common Reader.

Over the years, the critical terminology—objective correlative, negative capability, dissociation of sensibility, irony, authenticity, the anxiety of influence—has come to form a kind of catechism for initiates into the literary culture. The terms have become precepts not only for reading well but also for living well. They constitute an ethos and a doctrine, at whose center is an act of submission. One submits, Birkerts makes clear, to the authority of the author:

> This "domination" by the author has been, at least until now, the *point* of reading and writing. The author masters the resources of language to create a vision that will engage and in some way overpower the reader, the reader goes to the work to be subjected to the creative will of another.

Although there is much that is appealing about this metaphysics of reading as "self-making," it is a doctrine grounded in specific historical conditions, with problematic origins and an equally problematic demise. Birkerts, however, scants the historical question, and thus exposes his defense of the reading culture to easy attack. When, exactly, does he see the

emergence of those practices of reading that nurtured the modern ideal of the individual? Does he find them in the stirrings of the Renaissance, in the efforts of the humanists to extend and expand the educational uses of reading? What is the significance of the fact that the kind of reading Birkerts values emerged precisely as revealed religion was beginning to lose its absolute and universal hold? Was it, at least at first, an alternative mode of the religious life, with Protestantism being the church of self-justification through the unmediated encounter with the Word?

Some acknowledgement of the historical dimension might have led Birkerts to see that the demise of literary culture is no more the death of reading than the collapse of Christendom was the end of Christianity. What we may be seeing in this "reading reformation" is the end of a certain institutionalized, hieratic approach to reading, one that subtly reified itself as a sacred thing. Reading, as it literally escapes the confines of the book—and the authority of the clerisy that instructs in the correct ways of reading—may lose much of its mystique, but it's possible, at least arguable, that there was something far too rarefied and precious about that mystique.

It's possible, too, that there was something terribly confused about the confidence that the Romantics and their Modernist successors placed in the moral and spiritual adequacy of art. There were hints early on—in Pound, in Yeats, in Eliot and indeed throughout post-Romantic European culture—that the literary ethos comported quite easily with self-delusion, moral vacuity and barbarism. Art can produce monsters, just as it can be made by monsters. Then, too, to force art into the role of moral or spiritual guide is in some ways to trivialize and overdomesticate it. As Lionel Trilling suggested, great books can lead to the abyss as well as to the Grail.

It may be for the good, then, that reading is turning renegade in our time. As reading resituates itself under less strongly institutionalized conditions, we may need fewer Jeremiahs of the literary culture and more critics who accept the variety of ways in which people find a "coherent inwardness." Birkerts is surely right to say that reading teaches us how to cultivate our solitude. But he forgets the lesson of Leopold Bloom by suggesting that reading is the only way to cultivate such inwardness. The dire either/or arguments about reading won't work. The wired generation has heard them too many times, from the likes of Neil Postman and Theodore Roszak and others who bemoan the incursions of the buzzing electronic media upon the quieter, more solitary business of "self-making." Such admonitions, often delivered with Sunday school solemnity, now provoke titters from the pews, if not indifference.

Similarly, to Birkerts's assertions that electronic interactivity spells the end of "a society of isolated individuals," the wired generation will have a ready retort: "What was so great about that splendid isolation? And aren't we building communities through the Net, truly democratic communities in which authority—derived from knowledge—is dissolved or at least spread among more people?" For that matter, I'm not sure they'll be convinced by Birkerts's claim that readers are the last of the heroic individualists. Under the new dispensation, Birkerts says, we "no longer prize the loner, the dreamer, the disaffected protester, or the tormented misfit." As poorly as I understand the world of the Internet, I do know that the very idea of the hacker is bound up with renegade individualism.

A more nuanced argument is called for, one that includes greater sympathy for the wired world and its human complexities, and perhaps a little more honesty about the failures of literary culture. In the world of electronic interactivity, for example, there has been, and will continue to be, a struggle to protect the freedom, spontaneity and individuality of the early Net (personified, again, by the hacker) against great public and commercial interests that want to dominate, control and profit from the expanding network. The politics of this struggle have been widely reported upon in the press. But the human dimensions of the conflict have been largely ignored by high literature, possibly to its peril.

The reasons for such neglect are not hard to find. Literary people are famously impatient with technology. It vexes them when it doesn't bore them; technophiles seem juvenile in their fascination with gadgets and tinkering. Birkerts, to his credit, chides writers for such genteel disdain and calls on contemporary novelists to attempt to make sense of the new consciousness now being created by the emerging media. He even suggests that this might be the great theme of our time, and mentions briefly—too briefly for the purposes of his book—some of the better writers who have ventured into the new territory. Yet from what Birkerts says elsewhere, one would have a hard time understanding why this new consciousness would be anything worth exploring.

Birkerts should insist on more from the literary culture he so passionately defends: more daring on the part of our best writers in confronting the electronic culture, and (simplistic as it may sound) more confidence among our teachers in the value of pleasurable engagements with great literary work. Birkerts would like to update the arguments of Trilling, to extend the defense of the liberal uses of a literary imagination into our electronic age. This is a worthy goal, and he has taken a step toward it. The next step would be to acknowledge more bravely the darker side of literary experience, its power to disorder the senses as well as to order them. Literature's window onto chaos and unpredictability may even be what keeps serious reading alive in the uncentered virtual worlds that are now emerging.

Wen Stephenson (review date 1995)

SOURCE: "The Message Is the Medium: A Reply to Sven Birkerts and *The Gutenberg Elegies*," in *The Chicago Review*, Vol. 41, No. 4, 1995, pp. 116-30.

[*In the following review, Stephenson challenges Birkerts's thesis in* The Gutenberg Elegies, *addressing the impact of electronic media on the literary arts.*]

"Where am I when I am involved in a book?"
—Sven Birkerts, *The Gutenberg Elegies*

"You're in cyberspace."
—Kevin Kelly, executive editor of *Wired* magazine, responding to Birkerts in the *Harper's Magazine* Forum.

I have before my eyes a page, and on the page, typewritten in a serif font, is a poem. It is an ode written in 1819 by John Keats. I read the first words aloud to myself, slowly, pronouncing each syllable as though it were a musical note or a percussive beat: "Thou still unravish'd bride of quietness, / Thou foster-child of silence and slow time." As I continue down the page, I linger over certain phrases and rhymes; I go back and re-read, taking the stanzas apart and putting them back together again in my mind. The words fall into their order, and I feel their rhythm somewhere in my chest, the resonance of language uttered by a human voice in solitude. I am forced back into myself by the words on the page, my mind pushed deeper and deeper into a realm of images and associations, and emotion that did not exist a moment before is conjured from some mysterious wellspring.

I repeat the last lines of the poem—an indecipherable pronouncement on the relation of art to life—and then a noise from outside draws my attention to the open window; the spell is broken. It is a sultry Sunday afternoon over the rooftops of Boston's Back Bay, and through the window of my office a humid breeze rustles the papers strewn across my desk. I notice the clock: nearly five hours have elapsed since I sat down to read, and in that time I've wandered through a collection of British poetry. It seemed like no time at all. As I stand up to stretch, there's the sensation of floating that I often experience after long immersion in literature. But the pressure of the world returns, and its gravity pulls me back. The shock of reentering the temporal zone leaves me a little dazed, disoriented. I am still inside that Keats poem. Or it is inside me—the experience proved upon my pulse, which, by the way, is beating somewhat more rapidly than normal.

Where have I been? What has happened to the sense of time and space that governed my consciousness before I came upon that text? Something has happened, something connecting me across space and time to another human being, perhaps untold others—some experience of language that is ageless, primal, and indefinable. Perhaps I have had what some would call an authentic aesthetic experience of the art of poetry. If so, then I have experienced it directly through the digital channels of the Internet, on "pages" of the World Wide Web, through the circuitry of an Apple computer and the cathodes of a Sony monitor, at some 28,000 bytes per second.

If imitation is the sincerest form of flattery, then I hope Sven Birkerts will take the preceding paragraphs not only as a rebuttal but as a compliment. His most recent collection of essays, ***The Gutenberg Elegies: The Fate of Reading in an Electronic Age,*** is one of the most engrossing, engaging, provocative, and frustrating books I've come across in a long while. Published in December, 1994, on the cusp of the millennial hype surrounding the so-called "online revolution," it has become one of the most talked about literary events of the past year. There should be nothing mysterious about its notoriety. At a time when the subject of the Internet and the new media it has spawned is everywhere you look— not just in the pages of *Wired* magazine but on the covers and in the headlines of the very print publications these new media are said to be replacing—Birkerts strikes deeply and often convincingly to the core of an anxiety felt by many in our postmodern literary culture. The strategy is simple and rather brilliant: to explore the relationship between a reader and an imaginative text at a time when serious literature is increasingly marginalized by the communications technologies that are transforming mass media and mass culture.

> **It isn't just that Birkerts is less than optimistic about the prospects for serious literature in cyberspace—his misgivings go well beyond a reasoned critical skepticism toward new forms of literary activity springing up on the World Wide Web and in other multimedia applications.**
> **—Wen Stephenson**

And yet, as one of a growing number of people with a foot in both the worlds of traditional literary publishing and the emerging online media, I can't help wondering how Birkerts could be so closed-minded to the possibilities the new media present for serious literary activity. Reading the book, especially his descriptions of the reading experience itself, I often felt as though Birkerts and I should be allies; but time and again I found myself fundamentally at odds with him, baffled by his condescension toward all forms of electronic media. Here's typical statement in ***The Gutenberg Elegies:*** "[circuit and screen] are entirely inhospitable to the more subjective materials that have always been the stuff of art. That is to say, they are antithetical to inwardness." Elsewhere he has elaborated on the idea that the Internet is barren of serious thought and writing. "What the wires carry is not the stuff of the soul," he said in the August, 1995, Forum in *Harper's.* Afraid of what he calls a "creeping shallowness," Birkerts complained in another context, "If I could be convinced that the Net and its users had a genuine purchase on depth, on the pursuit of things which are best pursued in stillness, in dread, and by way of patiently articulated language, then I would open wide my heart. I just don't see it." The fact that this last comment was made in the course of a live *online* conference hosted by *The Atlantic Monthly* on the America Online network (in which, I must confess, I participated as an editor), complicates things and adds perhaps more than just a touch of irony. I can only ask, as a worker in the "shallow" domain of cyberspace: should I be concerned, or merely insulted?

It isn't just that Birkerts is less than optimistic about the prospects for serious literature in cyberspace—his misgivings go well beyond a reasoned critical skepticism toward new forms of literary activity springing up on the World Wide Web and in other multimedia applications. The magnitude of his subject is spelled out in the opening pages of ***The Gutenberg Elegies.*** While Birkerts is hardly the first in recent years to see a "total metamorphosis" of our culture brought on by the revolution in communications technology, his stance in regard to the effects on literature and the consequences for Western culture is, I believe, radical. "Suddenly," he says,

> it feels like everything is poised for change. . . . The stable hierarchies of the printed page . . . are being superseded by the rush of impulses through freshly minted circuits. The displacement of the page by the screen is not yet total. . . . But, living as we do in the midst of innumerable affiliated webs, we can say that changes in the immediate sphere of print refer outward to the totality; they map on a smaller scale the riot of societal forces.

At the vortex of this transformative riot is for Birkerts the printed page. Not only is the "formerly stable system" of literary publishing being undermined and eroded, but as "the printed book, and the ways of the book—of writing and reading—are modified, as electronic communications assert dominance, the 'feel' of the literary engagement is altered. Reading and writing come to mean differently; they acquire new significations." Pondering what he calls the "elegiac exercise" of reading a serious book, Birkerts concludes that "profound questions must arise about our avowedly humanistic values, about spiritual versus material concerns, and about subjectivity itself." Clearly, there's more at stake here than the fate of the traditional publishing industry. For Birkerts, it is never merely a question of whether we get our reading material via the Internet or from a bookstore; what matters is how we experience what we read: "I speak as an unregenerate reader, one who still believes that language and not technology is the true evolutionary miracle . . . that there is profundity in the verbal encounter itself . . . and that for a host of reasons the bound book is the ideal vehicle for the written word." I follow along fine until his insistence on the bound book and the primacy of print stops me cold. Birkerts raises his devotion to the printed word to a nearly religious level: the book as holy relic, the page a fetish embodying everything he holds sacred.

Nowhere does Birkerts provide better insight into the underlying reasons for this devotion to print than, of all places, the inaugural issue of the electronic magazine *FEED*. As one of four participants in *FEED's* first hypertext roundtable "Dialog," called "Page versus Pixel" (June 1995), Birkerts gets top billing and is allowed to fire off the first shot. Thus, with the kind of irony that has come to characterize so much of the self-reflexive discourse on media, Birkerts offers the crux of his argument in favor of print in the context of a hip new e-zine on the World Wide Web:

> I do not accept the argument that a word is a word is a word is a word no matter where it appears. There is no pure 'word' that does not inhabit context inextricably. I don't think the medium is absolutely the message, but I do think that the medium conditions the message considerably. A word incised in stone (to be extreme) asks to be read as a word incised; a word skywritten (to be extreme again) asks to be looked at as such. A word on the page at some level partakes of—participates in—the whole history of words on pages, plays in that arena. Reading it, we accept certain implicit notions: of fixity, of hierarchy, of opacity. By 'opacity' I mean that the physical word dead-ends on the page and any sense of larger resonance must be established in the reader and by the reader.

Inexplicably, for the same words to be displayed on a computer screen, in Birkerts's reasoning, causes their presence to disintegrate, and with that loss so goes the entire hierarchy they represent: the whole culture disintegrates into random bits of digital information as soon as the words disappear from the screen, as if irretrievably. The image strikes me as an apt metaphor for the chaos that has been unleashed in literary studies by deconstruction and the linguistic indeterminacy associated with postmodernism. It's as though Birkerts fears for the stability and efficacy of language itself, and I begin to imagine him as Dr. Johnson's hapless lexicographer, who in the preface to his dictionary laments the vanity of the wish that language "might be less apt to decay, and that signs might be permanent, like the things which they denote." Like Johnson, Birkerts appears to suffer an acute discomfort over the mutabilities of meaning and the transience of cultural values.

It is not surprising, then, that the fixity of words printed on a page, and bound in a book, becomes Birkerts's last best hope for Western civilization. What's at stake for Birkerts is nothing less than the tradition of Western humanism dating back to the Renaissance and rooted in Hellenic civilization. Books are the repository of that tradition. It all rests on the stability of print. "For, in fact," he says in *The Gutenberg Elegies,* "our entire collective subjective history—the soul of our societal body—is encoded in print. . . . If a person turns from print . . . then what happens to that person's sense of culture and continuity?" Birkerts observes how the narrative and syntactical structures afforded by print are for the most part linear, whereas in electronic media everything from the jump-cut in film and video to the lateral and tangential movements of hypertext works against our traditional notions of time and historical progression. That Western culture is threatened both by these technologies and by the intellectual and artistic movements associated with postmodernity is to Birkerts no mere coincidence:

> Transitions like the one from print to electronic media do not take place without rippling or, more likely, reweaving the entire social and cultural web. . . . One could argue, for instance, that the entire movement of postmodernism in the arts is a consequence of this same macroscopic shift. For what is postmodernism at root but an aesthetic that rebukes the idea of an historical time line, as well as previously uncontested assumptions of cultural hierarchy. The postmodern artifact manipulates its stylistic signature like Lego blocks and makes free with combinations from the formerly sequestered spheres of high and popular art. Its combinatory momentum and relentless referencing of the surrounding culture mirror perfectly the associative dynamics of electronic media.

Postmodernism's "relentless referencing" of mass culture and its rebuke of the historical time line are closely related, in Birkerts's picture, to the electronic media that are undermining the "stable hierarchies" upon which both narrative history and the novel are based. In the midst of these rioting forces, can there be any doubt that Birkerts would prefer for the spheres of high and popular art to remain sequestered? It would seem that the fate of literature in the electronic age depends upon the extent to which they do.

Accordingly, Birkerts feels the decline of print most acutely in the accompanying eclipse of the "serious" or "literary" novel as a form wielding cultural authority. Its eclipse, the direct result of the rise of electronic culture at the expense of print, represents for Birkerts no less than the death of literature itself, or at least the possibility of its death. We realize soon enough that Birkerts would defend the literary novel (and his heroes Flaubert, Joyce, and Woolf) from the destabilizing forces of postmodern intellectual and artistic culture—from the various manifestations of post-structuralism in the humanities, particularly deconstruction, and from the politics of multiculturalism as manifested in the growth of cultural studies—as well as from mass-cultural art forms that threaten the authority, if not the very existence, of the novel. It is here that Birkerts's position begins to come into clearer focus, and we see a nostalgic modernist overwhelmed by the currents of postmodernism carried on the tide of electronic media. In response, Birkerts erects the physical certainty and materiality of the printed word as a levy against the flood.

Knowing as he does that the levy cannot hold—or, more likely, that it has long since broken—at least Birkerts shows a sense of humor (if a somewhat perverse one) as he takes his stand. In the final essay of *The Gutenberg Elegies,* an eerie coda titled **"The Faustian Pact,"** we find our champion of high-modernist print culture resisting the temptations of a cyber-pop Mephistopheles decked out in the "bold colors, sans serif type fonts, [and] unexpected layouts" of *Wired* magazine. Appropriately, one of Birkerts's rare bows to popular art takes the form of the blues refrain he intones from the chapter's first sentence onward: "I've been to the crossroads and I've seen the devil there." He pauses. "Or is that putting it too dramatically? What I'm really saying is that I've been to the newsstand, again, to plunk down my money for *Wired.* You must have seen it—that big, squarish, beautifully produced item, that travel guide to the digital future." Evidently it's not too dramatic for Birkerts; he develops the theme thoroughly before returning to it on the climactic last page. The image would be more humorous if not for the distinct impression that Birkerts is only half joking:

> Yes, I've been to the crossroads and I've met the devil, and he's sleek and confident, ever so much more 'with it' than the nearest archangel. He is casual and irreverent, wears jeans and running shoes and maybe even an earring, and the pointed prong of his tail is artfully concealed. Slippery fellow. He is the sorcerer of the binary order, jacking in and out of terminals, booting up, flaming, commanding vast systems and networks with an ease that steals my breath away.

You can almost hear Birkerts pronouncing these (to him) exotic terms of the digital present, distrusting them, not quite sure what to make of them, superstitious of the mystical powers they seem to hold, as though they're poised to steal our souls—or, as Birkerts would say, "our subjective individualism."

He goes on to lament the inevitable loss of this individualism in the midst of an increasing "electronic tribalism," or "hive life," and he identifies the consequences of our Faustian contract in the realization of his "core fear"—"that we are, as a culture, as a species, becoming shallower." In our embrace of technology and its transformation of our culture we have sacrificed depth, "adapting ourselves to the ersatz security of a vast lateral connectedness." Woven into this expanding web—pervading our academic institutions and trickling down into the mass media by way of highbrow journalism, film, and now, he fears, the Internet—is a nihilistic "postmodern culture" with its "vast fabric of competing isms," chief among them a terrorizing "absolute relativism." Birkerts's answer is to resist the reflex response that all is "business as usual," and to see through the illusions that our wired Mephisto would weave seductively before our eyes. Birkerts won't be fooled: "The devil no longer moves about on cloven hooves, reeking of brimstone. He is an affable, efficient fellow. He claims to want to help us all along to a brighter, easier future, and his sales pitch is very smooth. I was, as the old song goes, almost persuaded." From somewhere deep in his "subjective self," Birkerts summons his courage and with his final words heeds the inner voice that says, "Refuse it."

It's a dramatic ending, to be sure—the work of a skilled evangelist. Yet, as it turns out, in his rhetorical flourish Birkerts has inverted the meaning of the "old song," the traditional evangelical hymn in which the speaker is, as the title says, "Almost Persuaded" to respond to the call of salvation but is ultimately too late. The hymn is supposed to strike fear and contrition into the hearts of sinful listeners, and using it the way he does is a telling maneuver on Birkerts's part, turning it around so that it's the voice of an electronic-age Devil rather than the voice of God that nearly persuades him. To be honest, he almost persuades me that my soul is in danger, nearly convinces me of my shallowness—almost, but not quite.

The truth is that, like many in Birkerts's target audience, I'm susceptible to the alarm. Like the fretful soul in the revival tent I am vulnerable to the message, and the heightened passion of its delivery makes inroads where reason cannot. I recognize myself in his portrait of the "unregenerate reader." Here's my confession, my creed. Yes, I believe. I believe in aesthetic experience and in the need for literature to communicate something otherwise unknowable—and in that communication to achieve some connection with other human beings, however slight and fleeting, and however compromised by the indeterminacies of signs and the structures of meaning and power imposed by our cultural contexts. I make my own refusal: a refusal to accept that such communication is impossible. I take the very existence of this literary journal and the hundreds (thousands?) like it around the planet as evidence that others share a need for this kind of communication, within and across personal and cultural boundaries. A postmodern pilgrim, I struggle to maintain my faith in the ability of language to transmit not just what one culture calls beauty (though that, too, is an important function) but more so, to communicate what people recognize across time and space as human experience. If I truly believed that any of this is threatened with extinction by the new electronic media, I would gladly cast my modem down the sea's throat and never look back. But, in fact, the picture I see looks considerably different, considerably less frightening.

To be fair, there are glimpses of hope even in the midst of Birkerts's apocalyptic visions, though they are rarely pursued. These are the occasions. usually at the end of a chapter, upon which he rises to affirm the possibility that language itself, even literary language, might survive despite the decline of print. "We may discover, too," he concedes, "that language is a hardier thing than I have allowed. It may flourish among the beep and the click and the monitor as readily as it ever did on the printed page." Yet these moments are few and far between. The conclusion forever reached is that our literary culture and our civilization rest on print, and that the fate of our individual and collective souls depends upon the solidity of ink and paper.

It is hard to believe, despite his statements about words incised in stone versus words written in the sky, that Birkerts really accepts the McLuhanesque determinism embodied in the ubiquitous cliché about the medium being the message. What if the medium in question is language? Then what does the message become? At the end of his chapter called **"Close Listening,"** in which he describes his experiences with books on tape, Birkerts confesses to having had an epiphanic moment, one that may suggest an answer. He recalls driving down a stretch of open road after visiting Walden Pond, near Concord, Massachusetts—a good place for a transcendental experience—and popping in a cassette of Thoreau's *Walden,* spoken by Michael O'Keefe. The effect is that Birkerts seems momentarily transformed into an all-encompassing, all-hearing ear:

> The words streamed in unmediated, shot like some kind of whiskey into my soul. I had a parenthesis of open country, then came the sentence of the highway. But the state held long enough to allow a thought: In the beginning was the Word—not the written or printed or processed word, but the spoken word. And though it changes its aspect faster than any Proteus, hiding now in letter shapes and now in magnetic emulsion, it remains. It still has the power to lay us bare.

I remember first encountering that passage and putting down the book, thinking, "Precisely! I rest my case!" I can only hope that Birkerts has more experiences like this one. For he as much as admits that the essence of literature might ac-

tually survive in the valley of its saying, even outside the precincts of print.

Given such a revelation, the absence of poetry from Birkerts's discussion of literature's fate becomes all the more conspicuous. In *The Gutenberg Elegies,* he has given us a moving paean to the achievements of great prose stylists, such as Flaubert, whose *mots justes* represent the essence of what Birkerts fears we are losing. But what of the poets? How is it that they do not figure into his scheme of things? After all, sound as much as sense is the essence of poetry, and verse may bring us closer than any other use of language to that primal "Word" Birkerts communed with on the road from Walden. And that is just the point. Poetry does not fit into the design of his argument. For unlike prose, and especially the kind of prose narrative Birkerts is so keen to salvage, poetry has long been comfortable outside of print. Poetry, in many of its forms, comes much closer to the kind of aesthetic Birkerts describes as characterizing postmodern, electronic culture. And where much is made of the non-linear, cinematic techniques employed in prose narrative, so we would do well to remind ourselves that poets have been using those techniques since the first invocation of the Muse.

Whether Birkerts misses the significance of his epiphany, or whether he represses it for the sake of argument, perhaps the most telling moment occurs when he takes up the well-known essay by Walter Benjamin, "The Work of Art in the Age of Mechanical Reproduction," in his concluding chapter. There, Birkerts invokes Benjamin's notion of the "aura" of a work of art—"its presence in time and space, its unique existence at the place where it happens to be." But whereas Benjamin refers to the withering of the original artwork's aura in the age of mechanical reproduction, and develops his thesis on the transformation of art and its social function at the hands of technology, Birkerts borrows the term, stretching it beyond recognition, and applies it to his notion of the subjective self. He writes:

> To put it in simple terms: Do we each, as individuals, have an aura, a unique presence that is only manifest on site, in our immediate space-time location? And if we do, how is this aura affected by our myriad communications media, all of which play havoc with our space-time orientation? . . . I am taking it as a given that every person is blessed with an aura, that he or she gives off the immediate emanation, or 'vibes,' of living.

If poetry is what is lost in translation, then Birkerts's idea is that an individual's "aura" is what gets lost in the transmission through layer upon medicated layer of electronic communication. Groovy. I appreciate Birkerts granting me my own unique vibes. And, yes, he may have hit upon something important here; perhaps changes in communications media do somehow affect our sense of subjectivity. But Benjamin is concerned with the status of things that are made and reproduced as art objects, and with the way technology transforms the function of art from that of sacred object in the secular cult of beauty (*l'art pour l'art*) to that of a mass-cultural phenomenon, with a new social and political function, that is part of a larger dialectic in which bourgeois capitalism gives way to socialism. Birkerts, on another plane altogether, is concerned with the status of individual souls and how technology is transforming the self.

As he adapts Benjamin's term in this way, Birkerts avoids having to acknowledge that the good old-fashioned book is itself a mechanical reproduction. And at this point I find myself wondering, where is the "aura" in a work of literature? If it is merely that of the author, of some elusive authorial subjectivity, then isn't that "aura" diminished as much by the printed page as by the pixels of a computer screen? But Benjamin does not speak of aura in regard to literary works. Written works of language would seem to fall into a separate category. For no matter how the words of a literary work are reproduced and transmitted, the essential qualities of the language, the sounds and meanings, survive. If anything, Benjamin's thesis of the aura of an original artwork only points up the fact that works of language are inherently different. Language is more than content; it is itself a medium—the medium of literature—and it transcends print, paper, silicon, electricity, even the human voice.

So, where does this leave literature—or, more to the point, literary language and the kind of communication it allows—in the computer age, and in a future of rapidly expanding online networks? One place to look is the emergence of literary publishing on the Internet. If we venture beyond the too-easy opposition of print and pixel, we might find that literature will take to the digital environment more naturally than many would expect. For one thing, computers themselves, and the experience of cyberspace, can appeal to our imaginations in ways similar to the aesthetic experience of literary language. As Robert Pinsky wrote in *The New York Times Book Review* this past spring, in an essay titled "The Muse in the Machine: Or, the Poetics of Zork," poetry and computers may have something uniquely in common, sharing what he identifies as "a great human myth or trope, an image that could be called the secret passage: the discovery of large, manifold channels through a small, ordinary-looking or all but invisible aperture." Pinsky appears to be tantalized, rather than threatened, by the possibilities implied in the comparison. "This opening up," he continues in the same essay, "the discovery of much in little, seems to be a fundamental resonance of human intelligence. Perhaps more than the interactive or text-shuffling capacity of the machine, this passage to vast complexities is at the essence of what writing through the machine might become. The computer, like everything else we make, is in part a self-portrait; it

smells of our human souls." From hypertext and archival databases, to advanced language experimentation, to the increasingly sophisticated descendants of early computer text-adventure games such as Zork, the "peculiar terrain of literature-for-the-monitor" offers a vision of what the digital future may hold for the literary imagination.

Not long after that essay appeared I had the opportunity, as the moderator of another online conference for *The Atlantic Monthly,* to ask Pinsky if he would elaborate on his thoughts about poetry and its potential life in cyberspace. He confirmed a qualified optimism, emphasizing certain practical advantages of the new medium over the old, while leaving no doubt as to where, he believes, the message is to be found. "The medium of poetry—real poetry, for me—is ultimately breath," he typed (broadcasting the words to a live audience), "one person's breath shaped into meaning by our larynx and mouth. So like print, the computer is still a servant or a conduit—not the ultimate scene of poetry, which is in the ear." He then declined to predict what might be the most promising applications of computer technology to literature, opting instead to point out perhaps the most significant aspect of electronic publishing, not only for poetry but for literary activity in general: "the capacity to download what used to require a publisher, a bookstore, etc. . . . that compression and availability have amazing potential for freeing individuals from control, from the treatment of people as masses. In that, poetry (an ancient technology) and new technologies are potential allies in the service of individual creativity, orneriness, imagination." A few hours browsing on the World Wide Web will more than bear Pinsky out. What he tentatively projects is in fact taking shape, albeit in an infantile form, on the Internet, especially across the multimedia landscape of the Web.

Yahoo, one of the most popular directories on the World Wide Web, lists at the time of this writing more than 290 individual Web sites under the heading "Poetry." It lists more than a hundred sites under "Literary E-zines" and another 217 under "Authors" (from Edward Abbey to Virginia Woolf). I've barely scratched the surface of the literary scene emerging on the Web, so any attempt to list my favorite places would be highly arbitrary. Nevertheless, I've recently come across two sites that represent what I hope is a direction literary publishing on the Web will take. The first of these, *Switched-On Gutenberg,* based at the University of Washington, calls itself "A Global Poetry Journal on the World Wide Web." Fortunately, the poetry is much better than the name, including work by some of this country's most accomplished and acclaimed poets (Galway Kinnell and Maxine Kumin for example). The editor notes in an introductory message that the main reason for starting the electronic journal is the demoralizing structure of literary publishing for poets today, and the opportunity offered by the Internet to expand access to poetry to a potential audience of twenty million (a very generous estimate at this date), all at very little cost, while doing away with the old limitations of processing and production time, the problems of storage, shipping, and handling, not to mention saving a few trees. The other is a site developed jointly by the University of North Carolina Press and the UNC Office of Information Technology. They've created the fledgling Internet Poetry Archive, with the stated goal "to make poetry accessible to new audiences (at little or no cost) and to give teachers and students of poetry new ways of presenting and studying the poets and their texts. Noting that the Internet is becoming "more inclusive and more public" they've recognized the need to provide first-rate literary content, of which there is still relatively little (quantity, alas, does not compensate for quality). Their first "unit," or edition, will feature eight poets, providing sound and graphics as well as text: poets reading and commenting on their work, along with biographical and bibliographical information. The first two poets featured are Czeslaw Milosz and Seamus Heaney.

It is becoming clearer that the Internet has vast potential to expand the audience for works of the literary imagination; and not only to expand access but also opportunities for interactivity, and for building communities of creative minds that could not exist otherwise. It's a lovely picture, one I'd like to believe in. But I know it is more likely that the Internet will become a vast cyberspace mall, every bit as commercialized as any other mass medium in a free-market society. And yet, if it's true, as Auden put it, that "poetry makes nothing happen"—at least not within the realm of an expanding and virtually untapped marketplace—it is nevertheless also true that individuals do make things happen. And I will maintain—surely Birkerts would agree with me here— that literature, as a means of communication, has the power to make something happen within individuals. For this reason, it is all the more important that we do not surrender cyberspace and the new media to the purely market-driven forces of late-twentieth-century multinational capitalism. There are other values—values which cannot be measured in monetary units—that will survive only if we vigilantly carve out a space for them to breathe.

At the end of another long day of work in the cyberfields, I watch from my office as a late-summer dusk darkens the sky over the rooftops of Back Bay and the skyline of Cambridge across the Charles River. Most of my colleagues have gone, and I'm left in the semi-darkness of my office with the glow of a lamp and my computer monitor before me. Emanating from the screen is a poem by Jane Hirshfield that is featured in the first issue of *Switched-On Gutenberg*. The poem is titled "Studying Wu Wei, Muir Beach," and I can't help thinking that somehow Hirshfield is speaking to me, and to Birkerts, as if to point out the futility of our engagement in what Birkerts calls **"The Reading Wars."** Hirshfield describes the difficulty of bringing in a horse that is grazing

in "bright spring fields," where the grass is a little too ripe, and the "wild-anise breeze" wanders in and out of his mane, a mare "jutting her body between his and yours":

> It is hard not to want to coerce a world that
> takes what it pleases and walks away, but *Do not-doing,*
> proposed Lao-tsu—and this horse. Today the
> world is tired.
> It wants to lie down in green grass and stain its
> grey shoulders.
> It wants to be left to study the non-human field,
> to hold its own hungers, not yours, between its
> teeth.
> Not words, but the sweetness of fennel. Not
> thought,
> but the placid rituals of horse-dung and flies.

I know Hirshfield's poem has nothing to do with Birkerts and me—but the tired world of which she speaks evokes a pang of recognition, and I'm drawn to her images. She is practicing the kind of communication I know can and must endure in the midst of our over-mediated lives. And after another day in which I've contributed my share of the noise and the hype, it's hard not to feel the fatigue she describes, or the desire for placid ritual, or the impulse to lie down and surrender words to the non-human world, letting them fall silently back into their mute materiality.

But I resist, wisely or not, and I jump to another page that I've "bookmarked," where I find the poem that's been going through my head for the last few days, ever since I discovered it here on the Internet Poetry Archive site. I open the sound file I've saved on my hard disk, and the soft Irish voice of Seamus Heaney comes over the speakers of my computer. I follow his voice through the eight concentrated lines of "Song":

> A rowan like a lipsticked girl.
> Between the by-road and the main road
> Alder trees at a wet and dripping distance
> Stand off among the rushes.
>
> There are the mud-flowers of dialect
> And the immortelles of perfect pitch
> And that moment when the bird sings very close
> To the music of what happens.

What does happen when I am reading or listening to a poem? And does it matter that it is transmitted to me, voice and word, through a computer? The second part of the question is beginning to bore me by now. The first part I doubt I'll ever answer. And so I print out both Hirshfield's and Heaney's poems and take them with me to pore over on the train-ride home.

Norman D. Stevens (review date January 1996)

SOURCE: A review of *The Gutenberg Elegies,* in *Library Quarterly,* Vol. 66, No. 1, January, 1996, pp. 105-06.

[*In the following review of* The Gutenberg Elegies, *Stevens evaluates Birkerts's insights on the act of reading in an electronic environment.*]

Technocrats are likely simply to reject the views expressed by Sven Birkerts in these fourteen challenging essays as being a Luddite love of the way things are. Old-fashioned librarians are likely simply to accept those views at face value or, worse, to quote excerpts that they may have read in a review to justify their continuing reluctance to deal with technology. That would be unfortunate, for in *The Gutenberg Elegies* he presents a carefully reasoned point of view of various aspects of reading, and not necessarily other forms' of communication, and how the skills and techniques of reading are altered and changed in an electronic environment. All of us, and especially librarians, can learn a great deal from a thoughtful reading of these essays regardless of whether we disagree or agree with what he has to say.

As Birkerts is careful to point out in his brief introduction, **"The Reading Wars,"** much of what he has to say is derived largely from his own personal experiences as a reader. That is especially true of the seven essays in the first section, "The Reading Self," of his book. Much of the content of those first essays is predominantly autobiographical and carries us from his attendance as a college student at a lecture by Anthony Burgess, through his career at Borders when it was simply an Ann Arbor bookstore, to his battles to keep his daughter from being overwhelmed by the entertainment environment that surrounds the release of a film like *Beauty and the Beast.* Those initial essays give the reader a sense of how he has developed the views he will express in the concluding essays in a way that we seldom are given by other writers dealing with the complex issues of technological change. Along the way, he also uses those essays to begin to develop his major theme, which is that reading is a dynamic, subjective, analytical, experience that enables us, as individuals, to develop our own sense of meaning to the world. In the best of those initial essays, **"The Shadow Life of Reading,"** he talks in an analytical way about how he approaches the experience of reading, including not only the physical aspects of that experience but the important intellectual aspects of what he carries away from that experience. By the end of those first essays, he has provided some important insights on the process and meaning of reading as we have known it.

In the second section, "The Electronic Millennium," Birkerts offers four essays in which he examines the question of how reading, or, perhaps more realistically, our interpretation of texts, changes in an electronic environment. In those essays he examines carefully the significant differences between reading in a print and an electronic environment initially by largely summarizing the commonly understood differences between the linear, private, static, layered, permanent nature of a printed text and the free-flowing, public, dynamic, incremental, and temporal nature of an electronic text. If that was all that he had to offer, his essays would be entertaining but of somewhat limited value. Fortunately, his analysis continues into a more thoughtful philosophical consideration of how we view and interpret words as they are presented to us in various ways. While almost an aside, his essay **"Close Listening"** that deals with the experience of listening, or "reading," audio books is especially charming but also especially valuable for its analytical insights into the distinctions between reading and listening to the same works.

In an attempt to place his experiences and his views into a broader context, Birkerts's three main concluding essays, in the section "Critical Mass: Three Meditations," deal with the larger cultural context of the changes that are taking place by examining what he sees as a decline in the quality of our literary or intellectual life, the substantial decline or death of literature, and the unfortunate ways in which our culture and technology have changed the life and role of the serious writer. Oddly enough, while clearly more analytical and certainly less personal, those essays, which are built around his analysis of other works, seem more superficial and, in some measure, distract from the important things that he has to say about the nature of the reading experience.

> *The Gutenberg Elegies* **is an important contribution to our ongoing discussion of the nature of the continuing electronic revolution and its impact on the nature of the process by which we "read" and acquire information, knowledge, and wisdom.**
> **—*Norman D. Stevens***

All of what Birkerts has to say is finally neatly summed up in a concluding brief essay, **"Coda: The Faustian Pact."** There he admits that the process of electronic transformation is well under way and is not likely to stop. He ponders the meaning of that transformation in terms of "giving up on wisdom, the struggle for which has for millennia been central to the very idea of culture" in favor of a quest for information by "pledging instead to a faith in the web." He concludes that we should refuse to partake of that transformation although it is difficult to see how that is truly possible at this stage of the game.

On balance, *The Gutenberg Elegies* is an important contribution to our ongoing discussion of the nature of the continuing electronic revolution and its impact on the nature of the process by which we "read" and acquire information, knowledge, and wisdom. Its immediate value may lay in its strong challenge to accepting the electronic age, as futile as that may be, but its long-term value lies in the valuable insights that Birkerts offers into the nature and process of reading as we have known it. In the long run, we will all be the poorer if we fail to take those insights into account as we design and implement electronic alternatives to the book.

Sven Birkerts (essay date Summer 1996)

SOURCE: "'The Fate of the Book,'" in *The Antioch Review,* Vol. 54, No. 3, Summer, 1996, pp. 261-72 .

[*In the following essay, Birkerts speculates about the implications of the transition from page-centered (book) to screen-centered (on-line) communication in contemporary society.*]

I would need the fingers of both hands to track how many times this past year I have been asked to give my thoughts on something called "the fate of the book." I have sat on symposia, perched on panels, opined on-line, and rattled away on the radio—not once, it seems, addressing the fate of reading, or literacy, or imagination, but always that other thing: the fate of the book. Which would be fine, really, except that the host or moderator never really wants to talk about the book—the artifact, the bundle of bound pages— or even much about the class of things to which it belongs. That class of things is of interest to people mainly insofar as it is bound up with innumerable cultural institutions and practices. In asking about the fate of the book, most askers really want to talk about the fate of a way of life. But no one ever just comes out and says so. This confirms my general intuition about Americans, even—or especially—American intellectuals. We want to talk about the big things but we just can't let ourselves admit it.

I begin with this observation because I am, paradoxically, always encountering intelligent people who argue that if we were to leave the book behind, replacing pages with screen displays, we would not be changing very much finally; that people would still read and write, only more efficiently; and that the outlook for education would very likely be improved. There are many people out there who don't make a strong connection between the book and the idea, or culture, of the book. I would say that this connection is everything.

My position in the matter is fairly simple. The fate of the book must be considered side by side with the fate of electronic chip and screen-based technologies. It is only by ask-

ing about both that we can see what is happening around us, and to us. Which is, I insist, a total redrawing of the map. Here are changes so fundamental as to force us to redraft our hitherto sacred articles of faith about public and private life.

We make a mistake if we view books and screen technologies as competing for popularity or acknowledged superiority. These are not two approaches to the same thing, but two different things. Books cannot—and should not have to—compete with chip-powered implements.

Nor is there a war going on. It is not as if we are waiting to see what the battlefield will look like once the musket smoke has blown off. No, screens and circuits are here to stay— their empery is growing daily—and the only real question is whether the book will remain, and in what form, and to what end? And: what will it mean when the functions of the book have been superseded, or rewritten as new functions that no longer require paged things, only databases and screen displays?

New functions. That is, in a way, what it all comes down to. The book will disappear, if it does, because the functions and habits for which it is ideally suited will themselves disappear. And what will the world be like then? How will people act toward one another?

Many questions—and here is another: is technology driving the change of functions and habits, or is it the other way around? Could it be that we are changing, evolving, and beckoning that future toward us? The lightbulb was invented, it has been said, when the world was clamoring, like the dying Goethe, for more light. Inventions don't just initiate change—they are themselves responses to changed needs and circumstances.

Maybe we are ready to embrace the pain of leaving the book behind; maybe we are shedding a skin; maybe the meaning and purpose of being human is itself undergoing metamorphosis. I fully accept that my grandchildren will hear me tell of people sitting in rooms quietly turning the pages of books with the same disbelief with which I listened to my grandfather tell of riding in carriages or pitching hay. These images trigger a deep nostalgia in many of us, and we will have a similar nostalgia for the idea of solitary reading and everything it represents.

But evolution is evolution, and no amount of nostalgia can temper its inexorability. We need to look past the accrued associations and longings to see the book in a historical light, as a technology. A need was felt, and the ingenuity arose to meet the need. And so happy was the result that we have great difficulty in letting it go, in facing the fact that the new imperatives now dictate new solutions. These new imperatives do not yet define us, but they may come to. To understand what they are, we need to look closely at both the old technology and the new. For the technology takes the print of our needs and our desires.

How *do* books and screen technologies differ? Or—and—how will a dominantly electronic culture differ from the print-centered culture we have known these past few centuries? The basic oppositions, we will find, give lie to the claim that screen technologies are only modifications and improvements of the pre-existing.

Closure versus Open-endedness

Whether scholarly or non-, the book has always represented the ideal of completion. The printed text has strived to be standardized, authorized, a summa. Indeed, we may notice that when new materials are added, requiring a "new" or "expanded" edition, the effect is often to compromise the original edition, suggesting retrospectively that its original appearance of authoritativeness was ill founded, its completion spurious, and making us wonder if all such appearances should not be considered skeptically. Similarly, an erratum is like a pimple on an otherwise creamy complexion. The fixity of the word imprinted on the page, and our awareness of the enormous editorial and institutional pressure behind that fixity, send the message that here is a formulation, an expression, that must be attended to. The array of bound volumes on the library shelves communicates that knowledge and understanding are themselves a kind of structure assembled from these parts. The societal imprimatur is manifest in the physical characteristics: the lettering on the spine, the publisher's colophon embossed on the title page.

Screen technologies undo these cultural assumptions implicitly. Stripping the work of its proud material trappings, its solid three-dimensionality, they further subject it to fragmentation. That a work comes to us by way of a circuit means that we think of it as being open—available—in various ways, whether or not we avail ourselves of those ways. We can enter cleanly and strategically at any number of points; we can elide passages or chapters with an elastic ease that allows us to forget the surrounding textual tissue. With a book, the pages we thumb past are a palpable reproach. Whereas the new texts, or texts of the future, those that come via screen, already advertise (many of them) features that fly in the face of definitive closure. The medium not only allows—it all but cries out for—links, glosses, supplements, and the like.

Suddenly it appears that the deconstructionists were the hierophants of the new dispensation. Their questioning of closure, of authority, of the univocal nature of texts, heralded the arrival of a new kind of text—a text made possible by a technology that was only beginning to unfold its possibili-

ties when the first deconstructionist writings were published. How odd, then, to see that the temper of the academy is turning against the theoreticians of the decentered, the polysemous, just as what was indirectly prophesied is coming to pass.

Already we find the idea of boundlessness encapsulated in the technically finite CD-ROM packages that are coming on the market. The structure—the referentiality—is such that one never reads or uses them with the totality in view. One uses them open-endedly, always with the awareness that the options have scarcely been exhausted. This would be true, in a sense, of a print encyclopedia—except, of course, that the material orientation is such that, as a user, you never forget exactly where you have landed and where that situates you with reference to the whole body of text. Fittingly, encyclopedias and compendious reference works have been first in line for transfer onto CD-ROM

Hierarchy versus the Leveling of Hierarchy

With finality, with closure, there follows ineluctably the idea of canonicity, that great bugbear of the deconstructionists. Where texts are deemed closed and where expressions are seen to strive for finality, it is unavoidable that vertical ranking systems will result. The push to finality, to closure, is also the push for the last word, which is another term for the struggle for vertical ascendancy. If intellectual culture is seen as the product, or benefit, of book learning, then it is the marketplace of ideas that decides which books will shape our thinking and our values. The battle of the books.

But now substitute circuit-driven screen textuality, put mutability and open-endedness in the place of definitiveness, and it's easy to see that notions of hierarchy will be very hard to sustain. In the theoretically infinite database, all work is present and available—and, in a way, equal. Where discourse is seen to be woven and, technologically speaking, collective, the idea of ranking dissipates. New systems of search and access will eventually render the notion of the enclosed work antiquated. Without a system of rigorously closed and definitive authored works the whole concept of hierarchy is useless.

Historical Layering versus Simultaneity

The system of print textuality has always promoted the idea of culture as a matter of tradition and succession, with printed works leading back into time like so many footprints. The library or special collections department gives this notion concrete embodiment. Tracking an idea, an influence, we literally go from newer to older physical texts. The scholar's finger brushes the actual molecules of bygone eras. And historical depth is one of our most powerful metaphors—for centuries it has been our way of figuring the idea of time, of past receding from recent to ancient.

Screen technologies, circuited to their truly mind-boggling databases, work implicitly against the sedimentary paradigm. To plunder the analogy, they are metamorphic: they have the power to transpose the layered recession of texts into a single, vast collection of cross-referenced materials; they change the standard diachronic approach to history to one that is—in the absence of the material markers that are books—synchronic. And in this they further promote the postmodern suspicion of the historical time line or the notion of narrative. The picture of history that data base and screen unscroll is of webs and "trees," a field of relations and connections that eluded earlier historical projections, and that submerges any notion of story (and recall that the etymological root of history is "storia," meaning story), submerges it in vast informational complexity.

But the impact of such a paradigm change is less upon scholars and historians, who certainly don't need to be reminded that historical time is a kind of depth; rather, it will be the generations of students who learn about the past from these connection-rich databases who will, over time, internalize a very different understanding of the past than was held by the many generations preceding them. Is this good, bad, or neither? I naturally incline to the view that while we can never really *know* the past, or grasp history except fleetingly in the comprehended detail, time past is a powerful Other, a mystery that we never stop trying to solve, one that is closely bound up with our somewhat poetic conception of depth.

The Private Sphere versus the Public Space

Although the technology of the book originally evolved to preserve and transmit information outside the intimate space of the geographical community—a fact that can be understood as giving the word a much larger public—it is also true that book reading is essentially private. This is not only because of the need for self-possessed concentration on the part of the reader, but also because the medium itself—the book—is opaque. The word signifies against the dead-endedness of the paper it is printed on, and in the process of signifying it incessantly enforces the awareness that that word is a missive from an individual sensibility, that its inscription originated in a privacy. Whatever one reads, the act is understood to be a one-to-one communication: Henry David Thoreau or Roland Barthes to myself. In this, reading has always been the verso of writing; the two acts are more intimately bound than we usually imagine them to be.

Reading from a screen invokes, automatically, the circuit system that underwrites all screen transmissions. Again, on a subliminal level the traditional assumptions are modified, undone. The words on the screen, although very possibly the

same as the words on the page, are not felt to dead-end in their transmitting element. Rather, they keep us actively aware of the quasi-public transparency out of which they emerge. These words are not *found* in the way that one can thumb forward in a printed text and locate the words one will be reading. No, they emerge; they are arriving, and from a place, moreover, that carries complex collective associations. To read from a screen—even if one *is* simply scrolling *Walden*—is to occupy a cognitive environment that is very different from that which you occupy when reading a book. On a small scale this does not amount to much. But when the majority of reading acts take place at the screen, then we might argue that a blow of some sort has been dealt to solitary subjectivity. Especially as the book has always been more than a carrier of information or entertainment— it has traditionally represented a redoubt against the pressures of public life, a retreat wherein one can regroup the scattered elements of the self.

> **To read from a screen—even if one *is* simply scrolling *Walden*—is to occupy a cognitive environment that is very different from that which you occupy when reading a book.**
> **—*Sven Birkerts***

The other obvious difference between printed and screen-delivered text derives from the fact that chip-driven systems not only allow but encourage collaborative and interactive operations. Texts programmed for CD-ROM are the obvious instance of this, but there is little doubt that we will see more and more of these applications, especially in classroom settings. Which suggests once again that the developments that may strike those of us who are children of the book as exotic will seem perfectly natural to the generation now carrying out its first exploratory mouse clicks. And who will doubt that when reading CD-ROM is normal, reading the linear, missionary-position way will seem just a little bit strange. Moreover, as more and more texts get written on the computer, we will probably see writers experimenting with the new presentation options that the medium accommodates. Though conservatively minded critics may question the aesthetic validity of collaborative hypertext ventures, these ventures will certainly flourish and further undercut the old paradigm of the lone reader turning the pages of some one author's book. Again, this is not just a change in reading modes; it is at the same time a major alteration of our cognitive environment. By degrees we will see much of our intellectual and artistic enterprise move away from strictly private exchange and in the direction of the collective. Maybe the day will come when most of our thought—and its expression—is carried out by teams. The lone creator or thinker will be a figure in our nostalgia banks, a memory preserved on commemorative postage stamps—although the odds are that postage stamps, too, will have vanished into that museum of images that will be the past.

We are moving, then, toward Roland Barthes's "Death of the Author," and toward his idea that texts are not bounded entities, but weavings ("textus" means weaving). The idea that the individual can be a carrier of some relevant vision or message will give way to a suspicion of the individual producer as atavistic romantic. Indeed, the "romantic," bound up as it is with notions about the symbolic agon of the solitary self, is already something of a category of derision. To call somebody a "romantic" nowadays is like calling him a "hippie"—a term that signifies as unambiguously in the cultural sphere as Edsel does in the automotive.

This may seem like a wild extrapolation—and I hope it is—but if one spends some time factoring tendencies, it's hard to get a significantly different outcome. The point is that subjective individualism is on the wane, and that, given the larger dynamics of a circuit-driven mass society, the tendency is more likely to intensify than to abate. Of course, the transition from book to screen that I've been speculating about is not the driving force behind the change—there is no one culprit to finger—but it is certainly part of the system of changes; it stands as yet another instance of what in the larger view has begun to assume an evolutionary character.

Expressive versus Functional Uses of Language

Hand in hand with the shifts noted above—and abetting the move toward the collective/collaborative configuration of our intellectual culture—will be the redefinition of our expressive ideals. That is, our very usage of language will change—as it is already changing—and literary style will be the obvious casualty. This makes perfect sense. Style has always been predicated upon absence and distance. A writer refines a style in order to compensate for the fact that she has nothing but words on the page with which to transmit her thoughts and emotions. Style is, in a sense, the injection of personality into communication, the attempt to leap the gap of time and space using the wings of expressiveness. But as any habitué of the Internet or e-mail user will tell you, style is not of the essence in screen-to-screen communication. For the very premise of this communication is near immediacy. The more we are linked up, the more available we are to each other, the less we need to ponder what Flaubert called the "mot juste." We don't slave over our sentences when we are face-to-face—don't because we can use gesture and inflection, and because we are present to supplement or amend our point if we detect that our listener has not got it right. In this respect, screen communications are closer to conversation than to, say, letters, even though they use the written word as their means of delivery.

So long as we take the view that style is merely an adornment—a superfluous extra—this may not seem like a great loss. There is even a bias in certain quarters that style is some kind of corruption or affectation, that we should prefer Hemingway to Fitzgerald, or Orwell to Nabokov, because less is more and plain speaking is both a virtue and the high road to truth. But this is a narrow and reductive perspective. For not all truths can be sent through the telegraph, and not all insights find a home in the declarative sentence. To represent experience as a shaded spectrum, we need the subtle shading instruments of language—which is to say that we need the myriad refinements of verbal style. This is my fear: that if the screen becomes the dominant mode of communication, and if the effective use of that mode requires a banishing of whatever is not plain or direct, then we may condition ourselves into a kind of low-definition consciousness. There may result an atrophy, a gradual loss of expressions that are provisional, poetic, or subjectively nuanced. We should worry, then, not just about the "dumbing down" that is fast becoming the buzzword for this possibility, but also about the loss of subjective reach. If there is one line of defense against the coming of the herd mentality, it is the private intransigence of individuals, and that intransigence feeds on particularity as a plant feeds on sunlight.

If I am right about these tendencies, about the shift from page-centered to screen-centered communication, then we will be driven either to acquiesce in or to resist what amounts to a significant modification of our patterns of living. Those who assent will either do so passively, because it is easier to move with what appears to be the current of the times, or else they will forge on with zeal because they believe in the promise of the new. Resisters will have to take an active stance—to go against the current, you must use paddles. In both contingents, upstreamers and downstreamers, we will find a small number of people who recognize what is truly at stake, who understand that page and screen are really just an arena where a larger contest of forces is being played out.

Though I class myself as one of the resisters, I think I can see how certain tendencies that I deplore might seem seductive to others. Is there anything intrinsically *wrong* with viewing the work of culture as fundamentally collaborative rather than as an individual-based enterprise? Have we not made too great a fetish of the book, and too large a cult of the author? Aren't we ready for a change, a new set of possibilities?

Mired as I am in the romance of subjective individualism, in the Emersonian mythos of self-reliance, I cannot concede it. I have my reasons.

Let me begin by appropriating Nicholas Negroponte's now familiar distinction between *atoms* and *bits*. A simple definition should suffice. Atoms, though invisible to the naked eye, exist in space; they are the foundation stones of the material order. Bits, by contrast, are digits; they are coded information—arrangements of zeros and ones—and while they pass through appliances made of atoms, they do not themselves have any materiality. They weigh literally nothing. Atoms are like bodies and bits are like the thoughts and impulses that instruct them in their motions. Indeed, we can assert that ideas and the language that expresses them are bits; books are atoms, the bodies that sustain them.

Mr. Negroponte and I agree that we are but in the first flushes of the much-ballyhooed Information Age, and that by the time the gathering momentum has expended itself—a decade or two hence—the world will look and feel and *be* utterly different from the more slowly evolving place we all grew up in. Atoms will, of course, still exist—after all, we are significantly atoms, and computers themselves are atoms. But the determining transactions in our lives will happen mainly by way of bits. Images, impulses, codes, and data. Screen events and exchanges that will, except for those who refuse—and some will—comprise an incessant agitation through one whole layer of the implicated self. For many this will bring a comforting sense of connectedness—they will be saying good-bye to the primal solitude that all but defined selfhood down through the millennia. The citizen of the not-so-distant future will always be, in sense, on-line; she will live inside an envelope of impulses. And to be on-line thus is to no longer be alone. This will be less and less a world hospitable to old-style individualism; that will be seen to have been an evolutionary phase, not a human given.

The relevance of this admittedly grand projection to the fate of the book should be starting to come clear. The book as we know it now—the printed artifact that holds in its pages the writer's unique vision of the world, or some aspect of it—is the emblem par excellence of our threatened subjectivity. The book represents the efforts of the private self both at the point of origin, in the writer, and at the point of arrival, in the reader. That these are words on a page and not a screen has enormous symbolic significance. As I have suggested, the opaque silence of the page is the habitat, the nesting place, of the deeper self.

This is a bit abstract, and I will have to get more abstract still before coming around full circle. The book, you see, the tangible paper item, the very ink shapes of the words on the page—these are things. Atoms. But what the atoms are configured to convey—what gives value to the book—is the intangible element. The bit. In this way alone the book is a primitive computer, or an analogue to brain and mind. Visions and thoughts and their expression in language have never been atomic. They are *about* the atomic, the material, at least in very large part. Though they are without dimension or gravity, bits refer mainly to entities that have both.

Well, you might say, if this is true, then what is all the fuss about? What's the difference whether the content of these bits comes across on the page or on the screen? How can I argue that the digital future threatens anything that really matters?

I have two thoughts on this.

On a micro scale, I would propose that a significant, if highly elusive, part of the reading operation is marked by the transfer from atom to bit. The eye motion converts the former to the latter. The printed word becomes a figment in the mind much as water becomes vapor. There is a change of state, one that is a subthreshold part of the reading transaction. Words on a screen, already part of the order of bits, are not made to undergo this same fundamental translation. There is a difference in process. When we read from a screen, or write directly onto a screen (without printing out), we in fact never cross the border from atom to bit, or bit to atom. There is a slight, but somehow consequential, loss of gravity; the word is denied its landing place in the order of material things, and its impact on the reader is subtly lessened.

"Ridiculous!" you say. To which I can only reply that outwardly nothing about our fiscal processes changed when we went off the gold standard (nobody but tourists ever saw the vaults at Fort Knox), but that an untethered dollar feels different, spends differently, than one secured by its minim of bullion.

On a macro scale, I am also preoccupied with the shifting of the ground of value. By moving increasingly from A to B—from atom toward bit—we are severing the ancient connection between things and their value. Or if not that, then we are certainly tipping the sacred ontological scales. Bits are steadily supplanting atoms. Meaning what? Meaning that our living has gradually less to do with things, places, and human presence, and more to do with messages, mediated exchanges, ersatz environments, and virtual engagements of all descriptions. It is hard to catch hold of this by looking only at the present. But try a different focal adjustment. Think about life in America in the 1950s in terms of these fundamentals and then project forward to the millennium, now less than five years away.

You cannot fail to note how that balance has shifted—from the thing to its representation, from presence to mediation. And if this is the case, then life, the age-old subject matter of all art, cannot be rendered in the same way anymore. The ground premises of literature—indeed of all written content—are altered, or need to be, for everything is altered. Instead of bits referring simply to atoms, we find more and more that bits refer to other bits. If the book is a mirror moving alongside our common reality, then the future of the book—and of writer and reader—is tied to that reality.

When we ask about the future—the fate—of the book, I interpret this to mean not just the artifact, but a whole kind of sensibility. Questions about that future are, really, larger questions about ourselves. How will we live? Who will we be? What will be the place of the private self in the emergent new scheme of things?

Myself, I see no shame in the label "romantic" and I will not accept that it is now unfashionable to be tilting at windmills. The idea that the book has a "fate" implies, in some way, the *fait accompli.* And while I believe that there is a strong evolutionary tendency underlying our moment-to-moment dealings and decisions, I don't believe that it is pointless to counter or protest that tendency. My instinct, signaling from some vestigial part of the psyche, tells me to avoid placing all my faith in the coming of the chip-driven future. It bids me to question the consequences of the myriad promised simplifications and streamlinings and to stall somehow the rush to interconnectivity, that comes—as all interconnectivity must—at the expense of the here and now. Certainly the survival of that archaic entity called the soul depends on resistance. And soul or not, our remaining individuals depends on our keeping the atom-to-bit ratio weighted, as it ever has been, toward the atom. Otherwise we are in danger of falling into a dream that is not ours or anybody else's, that spreads inexorably on the legs of its ones and zeroes.

Lisa Jardine (review date 13 September 1996)

SOURCE: "Pulling the Plug," in *New Statesman,* Vol. 125, No. 4300, September 13, 1996, pp. 46-7.

[*In the following review, Jardine faults the integrity of Birkerts's polemic in* The Gutenberg Elegies, *dismissing his prediction of cultural doom from technological advances.*]

Sven Birkerts composes his literary essays on an old IBM Selectrix typewriter. He is proud to admit that he understands little about new technology. But he is absolutely sure that the advent of the personal computer marks the end of reading, and that the headlong expansion of the Internet sounds the death knell for the book as we know it.

Enthusiastic reviews of the U.S. edition of *The Gutenberg Elegies* eloquently testify that plenty of cultivated people will welcome Birkerts's lament, full of foreboding, because it resonates deeply with their own sense of the end of culture. The *Bloomsbury Review* is quoted: "In my more melancholy mood I hear deeper in *The Gutenberg Elegies* a most mesmeric music, and I shudder from the resonance these essays generate in my heart."

What is Birkerts so afraid of? Broadly speaking, that the days when we could ask adolescents to read the exquisitely intricate prose of Henry James and William Faulkner with unselfconscious ease and delight may be over. As a teacher I can confirm that he is right, but is he also right to insist (to the point of dogmatism) that nothing culturally enriching has taken, or will ever take, their place? Ask that question of *The Gutenberg Elegies* and you've tumbled Birkerts. He already knows that the answer is yes.

Birkerts is already sure that the individual reader communing with "great books" (classic fiction down to the turn-of-the-century novel) is the eternal type of the truly cultivated person—the person in touch with "reality", the person with sensitivity and a soul. He knows without looking that all of us who compose on word processors are doing a bad job, that hypertext writing is intrinsically ugly and boring, and that the possibilities for experimenting with written form and content offered by new technology are, of necessity, creatively diminishing.

The Gutenberg Elegies has nothing at all to say about the electronic age, beyond the fact that it is a very bad thing. Birkerts does not bother to consult anyone beyond the 1960s' guru Marshall MacLuhan ("the medium is the message") on the complex implications of the explosion in communication forms. He is happy not to have read those whose writing celebrates new possibilities and expanded horizons. He looks at the graphics in *Wired* and tut-tuts at its visual seductiveness, but avowedly has no interest in reading the articles in it, which try to explore new creativity.

Instead Birkerts devotes himself to honing his elegant sentences into a shimmering celebration of solitary, introspective writers and readers: "The writing process begins in the writer, the life; it branches off on to paper, into artifice; but the final restless resting place of every written thing is the solitary life of the reader. There it hibernates, a cluster of stray images, forgotten incitements and conversational asides, a mass of shadow wrapping itself around the thoughts and gestures of the self."

The tones are those of Harold Bloom, sometimes plangently reflective, sometimes hectoringly apocalyptic. The message is the same. The man (definitely a man) alone with his book is the guardian of civilisation as we know it. But Birkerts' civilisation is a very particular thing. It is a world of privilege and prejudice that looks nostalgically back to a time when only elite initiates had access to art and literature, when a few mandarins claimed the right to legislate for all of our tastes.

The Gutenberg Elegies is a fundamentally dishonest polemic. Like all champions of the past, Birkerts smugly distorts the arguments of others, because he is without respect for those who make the contrary case. He doesn't mind that his "real" world leaves out anyone who doesn't wish to join the Ivy League club he so cherishes. He doesn't notice how essentially ill-mannered he is as he determinedly refuses to listen to or engage with any arguments outside his own frame of reference. He is curiously comfortable to tell us that he hasn't bothered to read them, while reproaching each one of us for not having read and reread obscure short stories by authors he recognises and respects.

It's odd how the prophets of cultural doom always exempt their personal dependence on progress from their condemnation. I remember vividly when I acquired an IBM Selectrix typewriter in the early 1970s, passed on to me by my father to help me finish writing up my Ph.D. It was the most hi-tech piece of writing equipment I had ever seen. I was awe-struck by its capacity to ease the pains of cutting and pasting text, and to aid my production of flawless pages of limpid prose. I knew that my relationship to writing had changed for ever. I was thrilled. The miracles of technology seemed to me to promise wondrous possibilities for the future. Seated today in front of my Apple Mac, I haven't changed my mind.

Cliff Stoll (review date 1 December 1996)

SOURCE: "Wired Thing, You Make My Heart Sing," in *Los Angeles Times Book Review*, December 1, 1996, p. 4.

[*In the following review, Stoll highlights the degree of ambiguity surrounding the relationship between society and technology, explaining the titular allusion of* Tolstoy's Dictaphone.]

Slowly, our blind infatuation with digital technology is giving way to some obvious questions: How do we treat computers? How do computers affect us? Might we be involved in an electronic Faustian bargain?

My online friends immediately respond: "Don't worry, the computer is just a tool." But in *The Media Equation*, Stanford University professors Byron Reeves and Clifford Nass show that we don't treat computers as tools. Rather, we relate to computers as if they were real people and places. Suddenly, this rationale explains plenty: the yearning for simple, user-friendly systems; the spread of Internet addiction; viewers' hypnotic attachment to multimedia games.

The authors work in mass communications and sociology: They study computing using psychological means. In one experiment, they programmed one computer system to present a dominant style of answers, another to be more submissive. The first machine made assertions and answered

questions with great confidence. The other responded with timid suggestions and a bit of wavering. Sure enough, subjects using the two systems saw the first as dominant, the second as passive. From such tests, the authors claim computers have personalities.

Computers with personalities? Indeed—we treat computers with a politeness undeserved by mere tools. The authors ran the following nifty test. After people used computer A, it asked them how it did. Computer B also asked them about computer A's performance. The people scored computer A more highly when they were directly answering its question. They didn't want to hurt computer A's feelings! Reeves and Nass see this as more than simple anthropomorphism: We view computers as people, deserving of courtesy and emotional investment.

In trying to impress the importance of their conclusion, the authors stretch themselves way too far. "It's possible to take a psychology research paper about how people respond to other people, replace the word 'human' with the word 'computer' and get the same results," they argue. Oh? In other words, media experiences are actual human experiences. Pretty soon, you start relating to them as though they were real things. But is a video of a forest anything like a walk through the woods?

Nass and Reeves mix an academic style with an italicized breathiness that is off-putting. Missing are references to classical psychological testing—after all, isn't a computer the ideal Skinner box for testing the effects of different stimuli? Haven't psychologists showed that we're far more likely to use cruelty when a person is concealed behind a machine than when he or she is visible? Marshall McLuhan isn't mentioned either—perhaps his comments on media no longer matter? According to Reeves and Nass, "what seems true is more important than what is true."

Taking the opposing view is *Tolstoy's Dictaphone: Technology and the Muse.* Sven Birkerts has collected essays from 20 writers who use and have been used by today's electronic machinery. This showcase of jewels glistens with insight into our social and technological worlds. Throughout these reflections, a simpler life calls—a life without the numbing glut of a thousand World Wide Web sites and 500 television channels.

Paul West's essay, "The End of an Elite," alone justifies this book. A prolific writer without a word processor, West sees writing as "my mystery, not computing." He has no use for electronic crutches: Against the mediocrity of today's literacy standards, the only reasonable response is to go down with all guns firing. West takes no prisoners: "Decadence achieves its consummation in the self-righteous banalities of

National Public Radio" or "Do-gooders debate the place of prayer in schools, but who cares about the place of reading?"

Novelist Jonathan Franzen describes the warm feelings and low costs of rotary phones in "Scavenging." Those art deco style telephones not only look proud, they last. Taiwanese touch-tones lack stamina and character. Franzen touches on a rarely spoken truth: While phones and computers may seem cheap, they're not free. High-paid programmers don't blink at dropping a few thousand dollars for techno-gizmos, but young artists and novelists sure do. Lynne Sharon Schwartz explores how we treat telephones and answering machines in "Only Connect?" For many, a disembodied shadow of a voice means as much as the physical presence of the actual person they're trying to reach.

In "Nerds, Technocrats, and Enlightened Spirits," poet Robert Pinsky recognizes the melancholy of the technocrat. With pathos and wit, he tells the story of a tinkering gadgeteer who couldn't see around his nerd-like blinders. Despite the techie's background, he's more bewildered than most by the undesired consequences of highway development and television—decaying cities and lousy shows.

Much ambiguity remains in the relationship between people and technology. This circumstance is best captured by the title of Birkerts' book, which is borrowed from Askold Melnyczuk's essay. Thomas Alva Edison sent Tolstoy a dictaphone, but the great writer didn't use it much. This wasn't because he opposed technology but because he found it "too dreadfully exciting," so it offered a distraction to him as he tried to write. Tolstoy knew his relationship to new technology; today, many are still trying to figure theirs out.

Additional coverage of Birkerts's life and career is contained in the following sources published by Gale: *Contemporary Authors,* Vols. 128, and 133.

Edna O'Brien
1936-

Irish novelist, short story writer, playwright, nonfiction writer, poet, and screenwriter.

The following entry presents an overview of O'Brien's career through 1997. For further information on her life and works, see *CLC,* Volumes 3, 5, 8, 13, 36, and 65.

INTRODUCTION

O'Brien's works focus on the lives of women, portraying their yearning for love and acceptance and their inevitable disappointment. O'Brien, who was born and raised in western Ireland, has spent most of her adult life in London. Both Irish village life during the 1940s and 1950s and contemporary urban settings are depicted in O'Brien's fiction. The influence of her Catholic upbringing is apparent in much of her work, even when it is furthest removed from the Irish Catholic milieu of her youth. The pleasure that O'Brien's heroines find in sex, for instance, is often mixed with guilt and shame. Her frank portrayal of female sexuality has drawn both praise and criticism and has caused her books to be banned in her native country. O'Brien's women are often presented as martyrs whose dependence on men leads to unhappiness and tragedy; her male characters are typically drunken, callous, and irresponsible.

Biographical Information

O'Brien was born December 15, 1936, in Taumgraney, County Clare, a small, rural, devoutly Catholic village in western Ireland. O'Brien first attended a local national school before continuing her education in a convent. She escaped rural life by attending the Pharmaceutical College of Ireland in Dublin. In 1952, she eloped with Czech-Irish writer Ernest Gebler, with whom she had two sons. They divorced after twelve years of marriage. O'Brien currently lives in London.

Major Works

O'Brien's first novel, *The Country Girls* (1960), was an immediate success and begins a trilogy that continues with *The Lonely Girl* (1962) and *Girls in Their Married Bliss* (1964). These books follow two young girls from a convent school in rural Ireland to Dublin and finally to married life in London. Like many of O'Brien's heroines, the girls are thwarted in their search for love, and the last novel ends on a bitter note. *August Is a Wicked Month* (1965) is similarly desolate. It concerns a vacationing divorced woman who seeks meaning and union with a variety of sexual partners. At the

end of the novel, her young son dies during a camping trip, and she is further than ever from finding fulfillment. In *Casualties of Peace* (1966) O'Brien introduces an element of violence, as the protagonist is killed by her best friend's husband. O'Brien returned to a rural Irish setting for *A Pagan Place* (1970), and wrote directly about her own youth and Ireland's continuing influence on her in *Mother Ireland* (1976). *The High Road* (1988) concerns Anna, a middle-aged, successful Irish writer who is recovering from the ending of a romantic relationship; she travels to a Spanish island, seeking solitude and time for introspection and healing. However, instead of remaining isolated, Anna becomes involved with others on the island, ultimately becoming romantically involved with another woman who then dies. In *House of Splendid Isolation* (1994), O'Brien departs from her usual subject matter and presents the story of an IRA terrorist who takes as his hostage an elderly woman; the narrative is driven both by the actions of the terrorist and by the personal remembrances of the hostage. O'Brien's short story collections present many of the same settings and themes as her novels. Her stories located in the Irish countryside are narrated by young girls observing their mothers, fathers, and neighbors. The narrators are often confused by the ties and conflicting passions that connect these people. As Lorna Sage observed in a review of *Returning* (1982): "The tales belong to an era of austerity, intensified by Irish puritanism." O'Brien has also written stories which, like her urban-centered novels, involve older, sophisticated women whose experiences with love and sex have left them disappointed. Praised for their sensitivity and universality, the short stories in *Lantern Slides* (1990) focus on O'Brien's familiar theme of victimized women who grieve for lost love or struggle to overcome their pasts. Her story "Storm" is frequently cited for its poignant depiction of the quiet suffering experienced by a middle-aged woman recently abandoned by her lover. While vacationing with her son and his girlfriend, the woman grows resentful of the young couple's exclusivity, but only further alienates herself when she vents her anger.

Critical Reception

When assessing O'Brien's work, most critics focus on her female characters. Her portrayal of women struggling to escape the role society has assigned them has drawn praise for evoking a full range of emotion in the reader. Due perhaps to her convincing portrayal of rural Ireland in so many of her works, O'Brien has been faulted by critics when she moves away from the influence of her upbringing. Oliver Conant noted: "When O'Brien turns from constrained, personalist Western Ireland to an urban culture of drifting hedonists, in which no one is known to anyone else . . . , something of her sureness of touch is lost." Many critics have maintained that her writing is most effective when it recreates the Ireland of her childhood. During her prolific literary career, O'Brien has been widely regarded as an artist dedicated to evoking emotions, rather than one who experiments with fictional form. Nevertheless, numerous critics have contended that the distinct style of *Lantern Slides* is influenced by the Irish Gothic tradition of fable, as well as O'Brien's own childhood in rural Ireland. Thomas Cahill asserted: "[O'Brien] is a storyteller, an Irish storyteller, one of an ancient tradition of storytellers, people who tell the truth. In old Ireland, the words of a truthful poet were both sought and feared: They could kill. Her best work has the sound of something prehistoric—palpable, thrilling, incantatory—about it. It should be read aloud, like poetry. It is, indeed, not prose, at least not in any modern manner."

August Is a Wicked Month (novel) 1965
Casualties of Peace (novel) 1966
The Love Object (novel) 1968
Three into Two Won't Go (screenplay) 1969
A Pagan Place (novel) 1970
Zee and Company (novel) 1971
Night (novel) 1972
A Pagan Place (drama) 1972
The Gathering (drama) 1974
A Scandalous Woman, and Other Stories (short stories) 1974
Mother Ireland (nonfiction) 1976
Arabian Days (nonfiction) 1977
Johnny I Hardly Knew You (novel) 1977; also published as *I Hardly Knew You*, 1978
Mrs. Reinhardt, and Other Stories (short stories) 1978
Seven Novels and Other Short Stories (novels and short stories) 1978
I Was Happy Here (screenplay) 1979
A Rose in the Heart (short stories) 1979
The Wicked Lady (screenplay) 1979
A Woman at the Seaside (screenplay) 1979
The Dazzle (juvenilia) 1981
James and Nora: A Portrait of Joyce's Marriage (nonfiction) 1981
Virginia (drama) 1981
A Christmas Treat (juvenilia) 1982
The Expedition (juvenilia) 1982
Returning: Tales (short stories) 1982
The Country Girls (screenplay) 1983
The Rescue (juvenilia) 1983
A Fanatic Heart: Selected Stories of Edna O'Brien (short stories) 1984
The Keys of the Cafe (drama) 1984
Stories of Joan of Arc (short stories) 1984
Vanishing Ireland (nonfiction) 1986
Madame Bovary [adaptor; based on the novel by Gustave Flaubert] (drama) 1987
Flesh and Blood (drama) 1987
The High Road (novel) 1988
On the Bone (poetry) 1989
Lantern Slides (short stories) 1990
Time and Tide (novel) 1992
House of Splendid Isolation (novel) 1994
Down by the River (novel) 1996

PRINCIPAL WORKS

The Country Girls (novel) 1960
A Cheap Bunch of Nice Flowers (drama) 1962
The Lonely Girl (novel) 1962; also published as *The Girl with Green Eyes*, 1964
Girls in Their Married Bliss (novel) 1964

CRITICISM

The Times Literary Supplement (review date 7 October 1965)

SOURCE: "Girl Meets Men," in *Times Literary Supplement*, No. 3,319, October 7, 1965, p. 893.

[*The following is a mixed assessment of* August Is a Wicked Month.]

A great deal of nonsense has been written in gossip columns and glossy magazines about Miss O'Brien as a militant spokesman of her sex, voicing in her new novel all the perplexity and private savagery said to be felt by women today. *August is a Wicked Month* seems, for this if no other reason, all set for a *succès de scandale*; and it would be foolish to pretend that the author's personality, or the topical titillation of her subject-matter, ought not to influence any so-called literary judgment of the book. Miss O'Brien is a naturally subjective writer, and the fact that her sense of the ridiculous, which in previous novels she allowed to prick the bubble of sentimentalism and soften the bitterness, is this time subdued almost out of sight, means that many readers—probably men more than women—will find the uninhibited exposure of sexual emotion and guilt quite uncomfortable, if not shocking. Ellen, who is an older and sadder Kate, may not be the kind of woman any stable society could content or cushion against the turmoil of her emotions, but her pragmatic honesty and vulnerability do make her peculiarly characteristic of her sex today.

Here, however, the trend comment must stop. To see this novel as part of the sex-war, with Miss O'Brien waving some kind of feminist banner inscribed "Men may be necessary but let us humiliate them", or to regard Ellen as a determined scalp-collector enjoying sexual emancipation even when it leaves her feeling leprous and hard of heart, is to misjudge Miss O'Brien's intention, which was surely not to add fuel to the fire of fake social problems or salacious arguments on sex and marriage.

A year convalescing from a broken marriage has been for Ellen an effortful, lonely but reassuring experience. When her child goes off camping with his father, and a skilled and tender lover appears for one night, the spell breaks—to be in love again, anxious and apprehensive and purposeful, is to see the "spacious calm" so carefully acquired simply as time wasted. Now, to be alone in stifling London becomes unbearable, and Ellen heads blindly for the South of France, to be dazzled by bright colours and charming decadent strangers. Her solitude and hunger for excitement provoke a disastrous escapade with the hotel violinist and she is picked up by a collection of immensely rich and fast-living theatrical layabouts staying in a luxurious villa. Everything about them, from the tough drink-sodden women with their beautifully manicured hands, to the elegant ageing men grateful for a little understanding in bed, disgusts and fascinates her. When the unthinkable horror of guilt about what is happening at home, in the real world, actually takes shape, Ellen cannot leave, can only cling numbly to the pity of these dreadful new friends and allow Bobby, the well-known philandering actor with his bloodshot eyes and fierce, bullying

kindness, to coax her back to laughter. It seems a triumph to have surprised even him with the intensity of her love-making, but her hatred, when she finds he has left her with a venereal infection, is as much for herself as for him and the whole nightmarish place. Alone again, the autumn beginning in London, Ellen wonders whether the purging has been, perhaps, a way of learning to live at peace—"if the days were never to be quite so lustrous-bright again, equally so the nights would not be as black. Or so she liked to think".

The irony of Ellen's predicament is poignantly exposed—Miss O'Brien has never been more self-critical or paradoxical, while admitting much more openly than in her former novels that the predicament is in fact what makes the majority of women feel they are alive and necessary to others—because the more love is needed and the more sacrificial it becomes the more quickly and hurtfully others retreat. The special guilt, so noticeably felt by all Miss O'Brien's heroines, because there seems no way of sharing it, is part of the Irish Catholic environment she is determined to reject, but the kind of hell—here terrifyingly typified in the glittering despair of the Riviera world—into which Ellen blunders is not very different from that threatened from the pulpit in the bog. To make it as glaringly wicked and loveless as she had to, Miss O'Brien has perhaps overdone the squalor of riches—Mammon does not need to be obviously maggot-ridden for us to recognize him.

There is also an over-insistence on actual physical atonement for guilt; one suspects an almost masochistic self-indulgence in forcing Ellen to be quite so completely bereft and degraded, because retribution in a world as real in detail as hers does not follow so swiftly on such comparatively heedless sin.

The danger for Miss O'Brien, as with all writers whose tremendous natural talent has been exposed to the spotlight of success, is that spontaneity and openness become an end in themselves; if the subject imposes no limits, then the writer himself must begin to select and withdraw, or there may seem to be nothing left in reserve. *August is a Wicked Month* does not, as some extraneous publicity has suggested, mark a new departure for Miss O'Brien; it is a sadder and wiser exploration of happiness and guilt, but one which comes dangerously near exploiting emotion without the professional discipline which sees that life, in fiction, cannot be entirely subjectively presented.

Eleanor Dienstag (review date 26 March 1967)

SOURCE: "Deadly Chain of Events," in *New York Times Book Review*, March 26, 1967, pp. 24-5.

RIEN

and analogies. These are charmingly intricate, and they
te a life of forms and rituals, local superstition, lore,
hymes and reasons of place. The book begins with a
ne and ends with a howl, the first a village notation, the
a cry of parting. From first to last the girl sees her young
in terms of anniversaries, but she does not claim that the
ial and religious forms define a vivid life of personal feel-
. Indeed, the novel implies that the forms and customs
ve lost nearly all the feeling that gave them their original
stance. Substance persists only as a remembered shadow.
cept for the heroine's mother, the figures in this landscape
e shadows too, names affixed to few characteristics. The
nsumptive Della is torn between her lovers, Clark Gable
d Robert Donat. Miss Davitt, the crazy teacher, composes
own epitaph. "Hail life, sweetness and hope and the
ner the better, to thee do we cry poor banished children
ir." The heroine, no Proust, recalls each moment in a
sentence, the feeling congealed in the reported facts,
ints of intersection between routine and romance.

thod is associative. The nun communes with herself,
erself as the second person, now more substantial
first: "The sun looked to be near. The sun was gold.
was silver. Silver and gold you had none. Gold
dug for in the mountains, and on the isle of Capri
ld a woman with a plain golden ring on her fin-
n had two wives, and still sang to his Mammy,
y, Mammy. The songs exploded in your head."

k explodes in her head, facts and events be-
alchemical reactions, village constriction
ong, Hollywood a child's Heaven. One thing
the dearest associations are loose, and the
not strained. One of the merits of the book
ile seeing everything through the veil of
ask the reader to connive with her senti-

of Miss O'Brien's minor pieces, after
pleasant thing to read, but it dawdles
es not go deep. Near the end, Miss
ing grand, but it is too late for pro-
a seduction. To put some heat into
s to have the heroine seduced by a
merely an emigrant Irish novelist
land; it should not be taken too
e, it should not be taken at all.
re paragraphs of a child's sen-
crossed by fact and time. There
O'Brien has been reading her
ging schools, *Dubliners* and
ng Man. Several pages sound
nslated into rural terms, the
Clare. But a serious criti-
ssume that Miss O'Brien's

book is offered as an agreeable diversion, good while the
reading lasts.

The Times Literary Supplement (review date 6 October 1972)

SOURCE: "Hooligan's Wake," in *Times Literary Supplement*, No. 3,683, October 6, 1972, p. 1184.

[*In the following review, the critic provides a largely negative assessment of* Night, *in which O'Brien is faulted for failing to sustain and build on the "strength and honesty" in her writing.*]

A grievance and an exasperation to critics they are, those writers who are as bad as possible and yet never let us quite out of their pockets. (Their style is so catching too.) By about page 10 of **Night** a series of useful phrases were already beginning to line themselves up: . . . self-indulgent whimsy . . . formless preciosity . . . mixture of narcissism and Irishry as before, but with stylistic knobs (or balls) on . . . gift-wrapped porn for NW1 people . . . earlier books better . . . sense of feeling and fun lost . . . one long act of public literary masturbation.

And yet. "The silences are unnerving. I can hear my own hair splitting." "There is a substance called glutamate added, which casts aspersions on the whole thing." "The artificial tea roses were still there, thick with dust, it was as if they had been plunged in molten dust and were coated in it rather than in some silver or golden dip." In hell "I could see the poor souls rotomating like chickens, as I've seen and watched them in the take-away 'Nosh' place". And in particular whenever Mary Hooligan, the "I" who ruminates through the night over her life and non-loves, goes back in thought to Ireland, feyness and self-regard drop away with the smell of damp, the hawthorn, the clothes flapping on the line. Where the growing of rhubarb, the drying out o cowpats, the lighting of a primus are concerned, the writir gets some strength and honesty in it.

Edna O'Brien must have heard all this before. But why that she can draw sustenance only from that one scene? from it, the rest is a drift of streaming memory that often tends towards pretentious prose than to those verbal flashes. One has only to compare Virginia handling of the drifting of time and thought to see ference when apparent formlessness has strong r perhaps the comparison is unfair.

And there is the semi-pornographic element. As raphy, the central character Mary is incessantl criminately randy, but never was less joy con

[In the following review of Casualties of Peace, Dienstag asserts that O'Brien's "old-fashioned" and clichéd structuring of her novel destroys the effectiveness of her "extraordinary style."]

Willa McCord is dreaming. She is walking down a dark street toward her house when a car with two men in it stops flush beside her. One of the men asks the way to a theater. She gives a quick answer, a lie. They drive off. She rushes to her door, but can't find it. The men return. It is now daylight, and there are witnesses, but it doesn't seem to matter. The men get out of the car, closing in for the kill.

So begins *Casualties of Peace,* a novel about the violence of ordinary life and the victims of that violence, sometimes innocent strangers, sometimes not. Willa McCord is one of those victims—yet this is not a murder story in the conventional sense. It is about two women, Willa and her resident housekeeper Patsy, their love affairs, disparate lives and desires, and the chance crossing of their paths which leads to the kind of bizarre tragedy one reads about in the tabloids.

Though Patsy and Willa experience extremes of brutality and sex, in other respects they are exact opposites. Willa, a sculptor of glass figures, is neurotic, frail, and fleeing from the after effects of marriage to an impotent Svengali. A virgin, "though tampered with," she is terrified by sex. Patsy, on the other hand, is a Molly Bloom—simple, sensual, unhappily wed but thigh-high in a torrid affair. She has, in fact, determined to leave her husband—and, when we first meet her, she is packing her things and writing her crude good-by note.

Inexplicably, while doing a few last-minute chores, she blurts out her plans to Willa, who persuades her to put off her departure and inform her unsuspecting husband of what is about to happen. Willa's meddling sets off a deadly chain of events it would be unfair to reveal here. When Patsy finally escapes, it is too late.

Though *Casualties of Peace* is a grim tale, the book itself is anything but depressing. Edna O'Brien has an extraordinary style. The novel pulsates with her racy, exuberant, nervous prose, a prose that often achieves the intensity of unique shorthand. Her robust humor dependably infring upon an acute Catholic sense of sin; and along with the female writers of our age, she is unblushingly candid her own sex. Why, then, doesn't it all add up?

What is most contradictory in Miss O'Brien's fic tterly modern voice echoing in an old-fashione e present book, this conflict between style and tween what she is saying and the techniques she u nvey it, is especially damaging. As in an earlier nove

August Is a Wicked Month, one is puzzled to find a hibited view of life coupled with the tidy and somewh real form of the well-made novel, with all the small falling into place, working up to tragic inevitabilities th they might in a detective story.

In *Casualties of Peace,* for example, the opening scer a dream of murder neatly mirrors the closing one (in of plot) of an actual murder. This is an irritatingly device for framing a novel, the slick stuff of wh drama is made. It has nothing to do with the no tone of the rest of the book, or with the disord solved quality of modern life of which the much aware. Such a device (and others spr out the story) only diminishes the novel's

One feels a large and important w O'Brien's grasp. *Casualties of Peac that work.

Denis Donoghue (review

SOURCE: A review of A Book Review, May 3, 19

[In the following revi Place is an "interes "go deep" enoug work of literatur

[*A Pagan Pl Irish girl, n family, th tral in th of an e a nur the cv

and
he
soo
of L
short
the p

The me
taking
than the
The moo
was being
a man behe
ger. Al Jols
sang Mamm

The whole bo
come agents i
transformed by
leads to another
quality of desire i
is that the nun, w
memory, does not
ment.

But the novel is one
all. It is interesting, a
upon the surface, a
O'Brien tries for somet
fundity, so she settles fo
the occasion, she arrange
priest. But it is nothing,
taking a swipe at Holy Ir
seriously. As a social ima
The best parts of the book
sory life, the lyric evocation
is some evidence that Miss
Joyce again, especially the si
A Portrait of the Artist as a Yo
like Stephen Dedalus's idiom tr
novelist on a trip from Dublin t
cal comparison is not intended. I a

[*In the following review of* Casualties of Peace, *Dienstag asserts that O'Brien's "old-fashioned" and clichéd structuring of her novel destroys the effectiveness of her "extraordinary style."*]

Willa McCord is dreaming. She is walking down a dark street toward her house when a car with two men in it stops flush beside her. One of the men asks the way to a theater. She gives a quick answer, a lie. They drive off. She rushes to her door, but can't find it. The men return. It is now daylight, and there are witnesses, but it doesn't seem to matter. The men get out of the car, closing in for the kill. ·

So begins *Casualties of Peace,* a novel about the violence of ordinary life and the victims of that violence, sometimes innocent strangers, sometimes not. Willa McCord is one of those victims—yet this is not a murder story in the conventional sense. It is about two women, Willa and her resident housekeeper Patsy, their love affairs, disparate lives and desires, and the chance crossing of their paths which leads to the kind of bizarre tragedy one reads about in the tabloids.

Though Patsy and Willa experience extremes of brutality and sex, in other respects they are exact opposites. Willa, a sculptor of glass figures, is neurotic, frail, and fleeing from the after effects of marriage to an impotent Svengali. A virgin, "though tampered with," she is terrified by sex. Patsy, on the other hand, is a Molly Bloom—simple, sensual, unhappily wed but thigh-high in a torrid affair. She has, in fact, determined to leave her husband—and, when we first meet her, she is packing her things and writing her crude good-by note.

Inexplicably, while doing a few last-minute chores, she blurts out her plans to Willa, who persuades her to put off her departure and inform her unsuspecting husband of what is about to happen. Willa's meddling sets off a deadly chain of events it would be unfair to reveal here. When Patsy finally escapes, it is too late.

Though *Casualties of Peace* is a grim tale, the book itself is anything but depressing. Edna O'Brien has an extraordinary style. The novel pulsates with her racy, exuberant, nervous prose, a prose that often achieves the intensity of a unique shorthand. Her robust humor dependably infringes upon an acute Catholic sense of sin; and along with the best female writers of our age, she is unblushingly candid about her own sex. Why, then, doesn't it all add up?

What is most contradictory in Miss O'Brien's fiction is her utterly modern voice echoing in an old-fashioned house. In the present book, this conflict between style and structure, between what she is saying and the techniques she uses to convey it, is especially damaging. As in an earlier novel,

August Is a Wicked Month, one is puzzled to find an uninhibited view of life coupled with the tidy and somewhat unreal form of the well-made novel, with all the small details falling into place, working up to tragic inevitabilities the way they might in a detective story.

In *Casualties of Peace,* for example, the opening scene of a dream of murder neatly mirrors the closing one (in terms of plot) of an actual murder. This is an irritatingly clichéd device for framing a novel, the slick stuff of which melodrama is made. It has nothing to do with the noncommittal tone of the rest of the book, or with the disorder and unresolved quality of modern life of which the author is very much aware. Such a device (and others sprinkled throughout the story) only diminishes the novel's impact.

One feels a large and important work is within Miss O'Brien's grasp. *Casualties of Peace,* unfortunately, is not that work.

Denis Donoghue (review date 3 May 1970)

SOURCE: A review of *A Pagan Place,* in *New York Times Book Review,* May 3, 1970, pp. 5, 31.

[*In the following review, Donoghue maintains that* A Pagan Place *is an "interesting" and "pleasant" novel, but does not "go deep" enough to merit consideration as a significant work of literature.*]

[*A Pagan Place*] is a novel in the guise of a memoir. An Irish girl, now a nun in Brussels, recalls her childhood, her family, the neighbors, holy and pagan Ireland officially neutral in the years of World War II, a trip to Dublin in search of an erring sister. No occasion is too trivial to be invoked, a nun's dedication to God being apparently compatible with the exercise of an emigrant's total recall. The degree of accuracy is presumably high, though Portarlington is remembered as Port Darlington, and Kinnegad as Kenigad. The heroine is a country girl, but not a peasant. Her parents have some of the marks of decayed gentry, notably an internal lavatory, a social point somewhat confused, however, by the fact that the father relieves himself in the open air. The mother earns some money by selling eggs, but on the other hand the father owns a few horses in training. There are 30 pubs in the village, if a nun's recollections are to be taken literally. As for the plot: the erring sister Emma gets pregnant, the father gets drunk and the intending nun gets seduced.

These events are represented as happening in a village in the West of Ireland. The characters are rudimentary, and the only form of development is given as a network of rural customs and analogies. These are charmingly intricate, and they denote a life of forms and rituals, local superstition, lore, the rhymes and reasons of place. The book begins with a rhyme and ends with a howl, the first a village notation, the last a cry of parting. From first to last the girl sees her young life in terms of anniversaries, but she does not claim that the social and religious forms define a vivid life of personal feeling. Indeed, the novel implies that the forms and customs have lost nearly all the feeling that gave them their original substance. Substance persists only as a remembered shadow. Except for the heroine's mother, the figures in this landscape are shadows too, names affixed to few characteristics. The consumptive Della is torn between her lovers, Clark Gable and Robert Donat. Miss Davitt, the crazy teacher, composes her own epitaph: "Hail life, sweetness and hope and the sooner the better, to thee do we cry poor banished children of Lir." The heroine, no Proust, recalls each moment in a short sentence, the feeling congealed in the reported facts, the points of intersection between routine and romance.

The method is associative. The nun communes with herself, taking herself as the second person, now more substantial than the first: "The sun looked to be near. The sun was gold. The moon was silver. Silver and gold you had none. Gold was being dug for in the mountains, and on the isle of Capri a man beheld a woman with a plain golden ring on her finger. Al Jolson had two wives, and still sang to his Mammy, sang Mammy, Mammy. The songs exploded in your head."

The whole book explodes in her head, facts and events become agents in alchemical reactions, village constriction transformed by song, Hollywood a child's Heaven. One thing leads to another, the dearest associations are loose, and the quality of desire is not strained. One of the merits of the book is that the nun, while seeing everything through the veil of memory, does not ask the reader to connive with her sentiment.

But the novel is one of Miss O'Brien's minor pieces, after all. It is interesting, a pleasant thing to read, but it dawdles upon the surface, it does not go deep. Near the end, Miss O'Brien tries for something grand, but it is too late for profundity, so she settles for a seduction. To put some heat into the occasion, she arranges to have the heroine seduced by a priest. But it is nothing, merely an emigrant Irish novelist taking a swipe at Holy Ireland; it should not be taken too seriously. As a social image, it should not be taken at all. The best parts of the book are paragraphs of a child's sensory life, the lyric evocation crossed by fact and time. There is some evidence that Miss O'Brien has been reading her Joyce again, especially the singing schools, *Dubliners* and *A Portrait of the Artist as a Young Man.* Several pages sound like Stephen Dedalus's idiom translated into rural terms, the novelist on a trip from Dublin to Clare. But a serious critical comparison is not intended. I assume that Miss O'Brien's

book is offered as an agreeable diversion, good while the reading lasts.

The Times Literary Supplement (review date 6 October 1972)

SOURCE: "Hooligan's Wake," in *Times Literary Supplement,* No. 3,683, October 6, 1972, p. 1184.

[*In the following review, the critic provides a largely negative assessment of* Night, *in which O'Brien is faulted for failing to sustain and build on the "strength and honesty" in her writing.*]

A grievance and an exasperation to critics they are, those writers who are as bad as possible and yet never let us quite out of their pockets. (Their style is so catching too.) By about page 10 of *Night* a series of useful phrases were already beginning to line themselves up: . . . self-indulgent whimsy . . . formless preciosity . . . mixture of narcissism and Irishry as before, but with stylistic knobs (or balls) on . . . gift-wrapped porn for NW1 people . . . earlier books better . . . sense of feeling and fun lost . . . one long act of public literary masturbation.

And yet. "The silences are unnerving. I can hear my own hair splitting." "There is a substance called glutamate added, which casts aspersions on the whole thing." "The artificial tea roses were still there, thick with dust, it was as if they had been plunged in molten dust and were coated in it rather than in some silver or golden dip." In hell "I could see the poor souls rotomating like chickens, as I've seen and watched them in the take-away 'Nosh' place". And in particular whenever Mary Hooligan, the "I" who ruminates through the night over her life and non-loves, goes back in thought to Ireland, feyness and self-regard drop away with the smell of damp, the hawthorn, the clothes flapping on the line. Where the growing of rhubarb, the drying out of cowpats, the lighting of a primus are concerned, the writing gets some strength and honesty in it.

Edna O'Brien must have heard all this before. But why is it that she can draw sustenance only from that one scene? Away from it, the rest is a drift of streaming memory that more often tends towards pretentious prose than to those bright verbal flashes. One has only to compare Virginia Woolf's handling of the drifting of time and thought to see the difference when apparent formlessness has strong roots; but perhaps the comparison is unfair.

And there is the semi-pornographic element. As in pornography, the central character Mary is incessantly and indiscriminately randy, but never was less joy conveyed by the description of sex. One of the author's novels is called *Casualties of Peace.* Might a future historian of twentieth-century literature see her as herself a casualty of current literary permissiveness, like those gifted Victorian painters now seen to be victims of their period's demand for detail at the expense of form and restraint? Licensed by profitable current fashion, a writer may be deluded into thinking that personal sexual kinks are substantiating rather than detracting from literary value.

The Hooligan (hooligan, literally) side of the book is weak: to look back on a series of joyous, mad encounters, of life really lived, is obviously part of the intention, but it sounds more like a scream of postcoital horror. Pseuds Corner crops up most often when things are being ever so larky and gay; the real feeling is all for darkness and loss and disgust. The sad, Mary, side of the book is therefore the realest; the most moving passage is the nursing of her mother through a final illness.

In short: a writer who can play with words like coloured marbles, who sometimes looks out at what was lost and true, but who prefers, far too often, to pose in fascination before the mirror, tempted by insidious dishonesty.

John Broderick (review date Winter 1976)

SOURCE: A review of *Mother Ireland,* in *The Critic,* Vol. XXV, No. 2, Winter, 1976, pp. 72-3.

[*In the following review, Broderick offers a highly unfavorable assessment of* Mother Ireland.]

It is surely no coincidence that most of the Irish writers who have lived out of the country have felt the urge to write about their relationship with the land of their birth. One thinks of Lady Morgan, a trashy novelist and the Edna O'Brien of her day; Thomas Moore, whose Memoirs in the form of letters and correspondence were edited by Lord John Russell; Sean O'Casey, George Moore, Kate O'Brien, Mary Colum and Oliver Gogarty. I seem to remember that Shaw wrote some pages of autobiography in extreme old age; while Elizabeth Bowen published a history of the Shelbourne Hotel, which was part of her youth. Yeats, who spent a far greater amount of time in England than he liked to admit, reconstructed his childhood and youth in *Autobiographies,* published in 1926. Joyce was the exception to this rule, as he was to so many others. But then he used everything that happened to him in his books, which are all self-portraits.

One would think that Miss Edna O'Brien would be content with telling her experience in childhood and youth over and over again in her novels. But no such luck. Here she comes again with her version of Ireland, and the effect it had on her development. She tells us in the last paragraph that she wants to retrace the same route again and again, "that trenchant childhood route" in the hope of finding some clue "that would make possible the leap that would restore one to one's original place and state of consciousness, to the radical innocence of the moment just before birth." This is an ominous threat. Not content with boring everybody with the very ordinary experience of poor little me, she is evidently now preparing to regale us with her pre-natal experiences also. She is a silly and sloppy writer, the darling of the semi-literates; but is it possible that even they are prepared to believe such a ridiculous statement?

Mother Ireland begins with a potted history of our unfortunate country which is obviously aimed at a foreign readership. To give her her due I don't think that even Miss O'Brien really believes the mad Kerry nun who in 1860 proved to her own satisfaction that we are all descended from a Jewish lady who was a niece of Noah. That should go down well in America, where the tradition of *Abie's Irish Rose* still lingers.

There is a hilarious passage about my own town of Athlone which got its name, according to Miss O'Brien, from a battle between a couple of bulls. One of them left his loins in the place: hence Ath Luaine, the ford of the loins. Naturally, she would pick on that particular fairytale. It never seems to have occurred to her that the original name of the place was Atha Mor, the big ford. And she describes Clonmacnoise as "a land of roses fair." "Fair" is not mentioned in Rolleston's poem. In many ways this is a sad book. It is obviously a pot-boiler; and even on that level it is not good.

After knocking off the history of Ireland in her not-too-elegant prose, Miss O'Brien goes on to repeat all she has told us before about the village in Clare where she was born and brought up. It sounds a pretty dreadful place. And will we ever hear the end of the man who was in the habit of opening his trousers as the little girls passed by and inviting them to "come here till I do Pooley in you"? Apparently not.

Then we get the boarding-school days in a convent. These were pretty awful too. And unconsciously, I imagine, Miss O'Brien presents herself as a thoroughly sly little girl. But that is already apparent in her other books. Never was such a television career made on so slender a talent.

After the convent comes Dublin, where she glimpses the great big world, or so she thinks. This includes walking out with a breadman from the firm of "Johnson, Kennedy and O'Brien": an unlikely combination. But perhaps this is deliberate. Even Miss O'Brien could not have such a defective ear as that. Or could she? It may be the reason why her writing is so execrable.

Eventually of course she escapes to England, with no regrets. Would to God that she had the ability to match her ambition. As it is, all one can say about this deplorable production is that the photographs are wonderful. It is a thousand pities that they are accompanied by such a text.

Lotus Snow (essay date Spring 1979)

SOURCE: "'That Trenchant Childhood Route'?: Quest in Edna O'Brien's Novels," in *Éire-Ireland,* Vol. XIV, No. 1, Spring, 1979, pp. 74-83.

[*In the following essay, Snow explores the "journey" O'Brien's heroines make "to reclaimed innocence" in her novels.*]

At the close of **Mother Ireland,** Edna O'Brien defines her aim both as a writer and as a woman:

> Ireland for me is moments of its history and geography, a few people who embody its strange quality, the features of a face, a holler, a line from a Synge play, the whiff of night air, but Ireland insubstantial like the goddesses poet dream of, who lead them down into strange circles. I live out of Ireland because something in me warns me that I might stop if I lived there, that I might cease to feel what it means to have such a heritage, might grow placid when in fact I want yet again and for indefinable reasons to trace that same route, that trenchant childhood route, in the hope of finding some clue that will, or would, or could, make possible the leap that would restore one to one's original place and state of consciousness, to the radical innocence of the moment just before birth.

Eleven years before the publication in 1976 of **Mother Ireland,** Miss O'Brien expressed the same desire—less poetically, it is true—in an interview with Nell Dunn [in *Talking to Women*]:

> ... the reason I think on the whole that women are more discontent than men is not just that they get old sooner or that they have the vote, or that they haven't the vote, or that they bleed, but that there is, there must be, in every man and every woman the desire, the deep primeval desire, to go back to the womb. Now physically and technically really ... a man partly and symbolically achieves this when he goes into a woman. He goes in and becomes sunken and lost in her. A woman never, ever approaches that kind of security.

The journey back to the state of being before knowledge, to reclaimed innocence, is one Edna O'Brien's heroines have tried to make in each of her eight novels. That the journey is a perilous one, as earlier pilgrims attest. Christian struggles from the City of Destruction through the Slough of Despond, By-Path Meadow, Doubting Castle, and Vanity Fair to the Heavenly Gates of the Celestial City. Though the madness of his sinful love attends his knightly quest, Lancelot glimpses the Holy Grail. Faust experiences the heights and depths of life to discover in a vision of charity the moment to which he can say, "Stay, thou art so fair." Henry James's Isabel Archers and William Faulkner's Ike McCaslins earn a lost innocence through suffering and endurance. But Miss O'Brien's heroines, pursuing an even course in the early novels, appear to have lost their way.

Reviewing the early novels in the pages of *Éire-Ireland* [Spring, 1967, pp. 79-80], Seán McMahon noted that the first novel, **The Country Girls** (1960), established Miss O'Brien "as an important new Irish writer with a fresh, unselfconscious charm, an acute observation of life, and a fine, ribald sense of humor"; the second novel, **Girl with Green Eyes** (1962), affirmed this reputation; and the third, **Girls in Their Married Bliss** (1964), proved startlingly disappointing. The trilogy, it is true, carries a pair of innocents, Caithleen Brady and Baba Brennan, from their school days in County Clare to divorce and adultery in London. Because the note of ironic disillusion first sounded in **Girls in Their Married Bliss** grows more strident with each succeeding novel, the reader asks why the journey, the quest for good love, so regularly fails for Miss O'Brien's heroines.

In the first novel of the trilogy, **The Country Girls,** Caithleen tells the poignant story of the drowning of her adored mother, the brutal rages of her alcoholic father, the stifling conventions of the convent school to which she and Baba are sent. As tender and vulnerable as Baba is malicious and full of swagger, Caithleen seeks the love her mother had provided in a neighbor, the elderly and married Mr. Gentleman, whose qualifications are his sad, chiseled face and his genteel manners. Once Baba has contrived their escape from the convent school to Dublin, Mr. Gentleman proposes a holiday in Vienna with Caithleen. But her first experience of romantic love, as well as **The Country Girls,** ends with his failure to resist the threats of his wife and Caithleen's father. Wounded but still game, Caithleen in **Girl with Green Eyes** becomes the mistress of Eugene Gaillard, a director of documentary film, who, like Mr. Gentleman, has a melancholy, sculptured face. Try as she does to be all-in-all to Eugene, she realizes that "Eugene and I were all right alone. But when anyone else came I lost him to them.... I had nothing to talk about really except things about my childhood, and he had heard all of that." The liaison ends less because of the bludgeoning attacks of her father than because of Eugene's contempt for her:

. . . even in loving him, I remembered . . . the separated, different worlds that each came from; he controlled, full of reasons and brain, knowing everyone, knowing everything about everything—me swayed or frightened by every wind, light-headed . . . bred in (as he said. . .) 'Stone Age ignorance and religious savagery.'

It is Baba, disillusioned with her bar-hopping conquests in Dublin, who engineers the country girls' flight to London.

With *Girls in Their Married Bliss* the reader, accustomed to Caithleen's lyrical innocence, is jarred to find Baba speaking in her slangy, obscene patois. Sourly she recounts that Caithleen has married the sadistic Eugene; had a son, Cash, whom she cherishes; and despairing of her inadequacy, is being divorced. Baba herself has married a wealthy businessman—stupid, crass, and impotent. The unhappy close to the country girls' siege of London is Baba's pregnancy by a faddist drummer and Caithleen's sterilization to prevent the conception of children with future lovers. "Romantic Ireland's dead and gone"; hereafter, Miss O'Brien's heroines will not look for fulfillment in marriage. As Peter Wolfe comments [in "Husbands and Lovers," *Saturday Review,* February 17, 1968], Miss O'Brien's subject has become "sex, its dynamics and ethics, and she treats it as a many-sided problem."

And "a jaunt into iniquity" is the phrase Ellen Sage uses to describe her sexual orgy on the French Riviera in *August Is a Wicked Month* (1965). She is separated from her husband, who, as in Caithleen's experience with Eugene, had taken her "into the fresh pastures of ideas and collective thought and flute music" and lost patience "when she hankered after the proverbs and accordion music and a statute of the virgin hewn from blackthorn wood." Again like Caithleen, she has an adored son of eight, Mark, whose holiday in Wales with his father enables Ellen to emplane for Cannes.

Here, however, the resemblance ends. As Grace Eckley observes in her highly sympathetic monograph *Edna O'Brien,* "*August* marks a transition between the heroine's earlier quest for self-development through marriage with a hero and the later knowledge that such is impossible. That dream was almost relinquished in *Girls* and was retained only in the ideal of a lover in *August.*" A tone of self-pitying rancor replaces Caithleen's Irish rhythms as Ellen acts out her conflict between the Roman Catholic teachings of her youth and her rebellious libertinism. On the one hand, she is "a great believer in punishment"; "people," she says, "get what they deserve." On the other hand, she clings to her defiant conviction that "slipped in between the catechism advocating chastity for women was the secret message that a man and a man's body was the true and absolute propitiation." When, during her debauches, word comes from her husband that Mark has been killed by a speeding motorist, Ellen feels that she has killed her son. If she had not left her husband, she would have been holidaying with him and Mark and would have prevented the accident. Numb with guilt, bored and disappointed in her lovers, she finds she has contracted a venereal infection from Bobby, a Hollywood actor. Returning to London and nothing, she regards her "punishment" as just. "You know what I want," she tells an earlier lover, "To cease to be me. . . I want to love someone other than myself." "It is your Roman Catholicity," he responds.

Like *August Is a Wicked Month, Casualties of Peace* (1966) appears to be a transition between the artless candor of the early novels and the overt sensuality of the later ones. The most appealing of Miss O'Brien's heroines, Willa McCord is not only a disillusioned victim of male sadism, like Caithleen and Ellen, but also a terrified one. Twenty-six and virginal, she has escaped her husband, Herod—Herod of the "long-suffering icon face, his forehead high and pale, lineaments fixed in thought, an expression of pity that turned out to be merely self-pity." Her escape is dual. First, it is a profession, work in glass, for "glass is not human . . . does not endure," like her horror-ridden dreams and memories. Second, it is the peace of a home with a young Irish housekeeper, Patsy, whose speech and exploits are very like Baba's, and her husband, Tom, a factory-worker and handyman.

What Willa forgets, both in her studio and at home, is that she and Patsy are women and thus in need of love. She has permitted herself to love only a neighbor's nine-year-old son. Then Auro, a direct lineal descendant of Bobby in the previous novel, comes to purchase one of Willa's glass works for his wife. Patiently and tenderly he cracks her glass image of herself. At home, Patsy becomes pregnant by Ron, a fellow she met at a bar, and determines to leave Tom for him. The plot, as contrived as the symbolism of glass and color is clogged, centers about a white fur coat with irregular black patches. Auro, a Jamaican Negro, gives it to Willa, who lends it to Patsy as consolation for Ron's disappearance and Tom's murderous rage at his wife's infidelity. Agreeing to go to a hotel until Willa has dismissed Tom, Patsy returns the coat to Willa. Wearing it, Willa goes to her assignation with Auro. But Tom does not leave; instead, he plots Patsy's murder by strangulation. It is, of course, Willa who returns home at dusk in the coat and is strangled. Willa's recurrent nightmare of her murder and her belief that she is fit only for a coffin have been realized. At the close of the novel, Patsy gives Auro the letters Willa had written and not sent him. Reading Willa's account of Herod's impotence and masochism, Auro comes to understand how Willa saw herself as distorted, like the sheets of colored glass in which she worked.

Of her next novel, *A Pagan Place* (1970), Edna O'Brien told

David Heycock [in "Edna O'Brien Talks to David Heycock about Her New Novel, *A Pagan Place,*" *The Listener,* May 7, 1970]:

> I wanted this time . . . to get into the kingdom of childhood. I wanted to get the minute-to-minute essence of what it is when you're very young, when you're both meticulously aware of everything that's going on around you and totally uncritical. . . . And of course the only place I could set it is in Ireland where all my associations, all my dreams and all my experience is. . . . I was brought up very much on mythology and folk-tales, and on verse, and I wanted, as I always do, to write an extremely non-literary book.

A Pagan Place is told by an Irish child—called only "you"—who records the impressions of her youth and who tells the story of her parents' shame at her sister Emma's easy virtue and illegitimate pregnancy. Seen from a little sister's point of view, Emma becomes a dull wanton, lacking the touching bravado that redeemed Caithleen's Baba and Willa's Patsy. Since her plight fails to interest, except as it partially motivates the child narrator to elect the vocation of nun, the reader turns to the child's impressions and her sensibility. Here the novel is not "extremely non-literary," for it resembles an unstructured, diluted *Portrait of the Artist As a Young Man.* There are the violent politics of the father, who "burnt the house rather than let the Black and Tans occupy it as a barracks"; the peace-making of the mother, whose suffering stabs the heart of the child; the quarrel on Christmas Day; the bewilderment of the child that a single word can mean more than one thing; the experience of sex; the vision of hell, "the tongues of flame touching every part of you"; and the mortification of all the senses as penance. With such Joycean echoes are the familiar O'Brien characters, anecdotes, and phrases. There are the father given to bouts of drinking; the dearly loved mother; the faithful hired hand, this time named "Ambie," not "Hickey," as in the trilogy; the adored young priest; the school mistress of flaming temper. There are the incidents of the horse the father bet on, which "stood up to shit and is shitting still," and the bus-driver who got out to "pay-pay, getting the word for pee-pee wrong." And there is the lyrical rhythm of the child narrator's yearning for home with the "crushed stone in a field, and the wind, and the way it touched you on the face and the cattle too, an accompaniment to everything," as well as the usual comment of the girl's seducer: "I could go through you like butter."

Like *A Pagan Place, Night* (1972) derives from Joyce: from the long soliloquy of Molly Bloom in the final pages of *Ulysses.* It is the repetitious and bawdy reminiscence of an aging Irish floozy, Mary Hooligan, hired as caretaker by a couple during their absence from London. During one long night in their fourposter, she reveals a personal history already familiar to O'Brien's reader. Only the names are new: the beloved mother and the deeply feared father, here Lil and Boss; the malicious best friend, here Madge rather than Baba or Patsy; the sadistic husband, here Dr. Flaggler, not Eugene or Herod; a son, Tutsie, about whom, as with Caithleen's Cash, Ellen's Mark, and Willa's nine-year-old, Miss O'Brien writes her most winningly; the Irish tinker woman who stole a pair of shoes; and the series of lovers whose sexual preferences are graphically described.

Consequently, critical opinion of *Night* and Mary Hooligan varies sharply. Stanley Kauffman remarks tolerantly [in "Women of Worlds Apart," *World,* January 30, 1973]:

> There seems little reason to doubt that O'Brien is still producing (largely) confessional fiction, tricked out with a deliberately transparent persona. The style has changed from impudent charm and wide-eyed mischief to lyrics of the loins, laced with a warmly cherished sense of disillusion. . . It would have been false and precious for her heroines to have remained the Caithleen of the first book; that is not the argument. But it would have been tedious by now to follow her bed stands except that she has some humor and some insight . . . and she is subject to fits of really good writing.

Dr. Eckley also regards the seven novels as conveying a personal odyssey, but she finds in Mary Hooligan "the creation of a fully integrated personality." The clash between ego, represented by the sensitive and inadequate Caithleen-character, and alter ego, depicted in the extroverted and aggressive Baba-character, is resolved into a harmonious whole in Mary. "This," writes Dr. Eckley, "is the achievement of Mary Hooligan in *Night,* where the country past impinges on the city present, and religion, the ex-husband and the near friend converge through dramatic rumination." The O'Brien heroine, now mature, faces independence and the consequent loneliness with integrity. Conversely, Charles Lam Markmann takes a harsh view of *Night* [in "Nothing Above the Belt?," *The Nation,* May 14, 1973]:

> If a lesser author had written *Night,* one would never have bothered to read it through. But Miss O'Brien is a novelist of many gifts, including poetry and comedy and compassion: that is why the reader keeps the presumption of innocence alive by forced feeding to the very end, and why he then feels so frustrated and cheated. . . . The reasons for the book's failure may be indeed more interesting than the book. Is it conceivable that the vein has been mined out? Is it possible that virtually nothing new can be thought or said about the emptiness of lives that are just plain empty? Is it thinkable that

there are really subjects that not even the finest writer can bring to life because there is simply nothing there? Apparently, yes.

Conceivably, Miss O'Brien would say, "Apparently, no," for she sees her subjects as inherent in an Irish heritage, not peculiar to her individual experience:

> Loneliness, the longing for adventure, the Roman Catholic Church, or the family tie that is more umbilical than among any other race on earth? The martyred Irish mother and the raving rollicking father is not peculiar to the works of exorcised writers but common in families throughout the land. The children inherit a trinity of guilt (a Shamrock): the guilt for Christ's Passion and Crucifixion, the guilt for the plundered land, and the furtive guilt for the mother frequently defiled by the insatiable father. [*Mother Ireland*]

Though she does not include the husband or lover of the pensive, delicately carved features, she does admit to attraction to a "Peter Abelard face." Reflecting upon the many descriptions in the novels and in *Mother Ireland* of the Christ of the Sacred Heart, the reader can but speculate that He is the physical archetype of the men with whom the O'Brien heroines relentlessly fall in love. Miss O'Brien's reply to Suzanne Lowry's question about the genesis of *Johnny I Hardly Knew You* (1977) lends support to the conjecture. "The idea came," Miss Lowry reports [in "Edna We Hardly Knew You," *Limerick Evening Press,* July 20, 1977], "from seeing a friend of her son in a play who seemed the stuff from which saints are made." Nora, the narrator, likens Hart, who is a college friend of her son and her lover, to a saint, to St. John of the Cross, to Michelangelo's *David,* and to Christ.

In prison, awaiting sentence for the murder of Hart, Nora, the middle-aged monologist, ponders her motives for suffocating the boy when, during their lovemaking, he suffered an epileptic fit and cried wordlessly for help. One reason, she realizes, was to revenge herself on her mad, drunken father, "scion of all fathers, who soiled my mother's bed, tore her apart, crushed her and made her vassal" on the brutal husband who "had threatened that if I did leave I would find myself committed to an asylum"; on her son toward whom she feels "incest raising its little tonsured head"; and on her lovers, whose faithless promises were "the real villains of affection." It was also to avenge all "us Gerties, us Nancies, us Delias, us Kittys, us Kathleens" upon "men the stampeders of our dreams." These reasons are not inclusive for Nora. True, in Hart she killed the image of all men, but why Hart, mere surrogate for her son? Why had she not killed her father, her husband, her earlier lovers? The answer comes with her recall of the actual murder:

He begged for help, with the worst, the most humiliating, the most craven, the needful beg, and undoubtedly I saw my own begging famished self-reflected in him, and I took the pillow from under the bed cover, placed it across his contorted face, pressed with all my might, and held it there until he went quiet as a baby, whose breath is almost inaudible.

In Hart, then, she tried to murder her self-image: the image of a middle aged woman so lonely and so lacking in resources as to consider sensitive-looking boy half her age as her last chance at life.

Of *Johnny I Hardly Knew You,* Anatole Broyard wryly comments [in "One Critic's Fiction: *I Hardly Knew You,*" *New York Times Book Review,* January 1, 1978]: "The title of the novel is intended as a rueful irony, addressed to the young man who is its love object; but I'm afraid that I hardly knew him either and I see no reason to regret his demise. I'm more perplexed by the fact that the heroine could get worked up enough to kill him." Nor is Hart's the only minimal characterization; the other persons about whom Nora soliloquizes—mother, father, husband, son, lover—are those of the previous novels thinly apostrophized. Equally disappointing is Nora's characteristic style of expression, even more slipshod than Mary Hooligan's, as in such errors as "pertaining to be" for "purporting to be," "origined" for "originated," "like" for "as if," and "but blood nor water carry no issue." Such flaws, however, are insignificant beside the despairing, and distorted, focus of the novel: the search for self-fulfillment ends in self-destruction.

The quest for "radical innocence" has taken a tortuous route for Miss O'Brien's heroines. Caithleen and Baba of the early trilogy looked for and failed to discover it in marriage. Disillusioned with marriage, Ellen of *August Is a Wicked Month* sought it in a festival of sex and found only boredom and despair. In *Casualties of Peace,* Willa's efforts to overcome her dread of sex, marital and extramarital, resulted in her death. And Mary Hooligan of *Night,* divorcée and many times mistress? Surely the murderess Nora of *Johnny I Hardly Knew You,* a novel written after Dr. Eckley published her monograph, dissipates the theory that, in Mary Hooligan, the O'Brien heroine attained to maturity. In undertaking the journey to earned innocence, Miss O'Brien's heroines select one route only: sex. They never consider the professions, social service, art and music, politics, travel. Willa, it is true, works in glass, but less as a craft or art than as a defense; and Nora, who restores paintings, does so only for a livelihood. A monomaniacal lot, these women reject all of life but sex. Indeed, in greedily defying an incest taboo, Nora rejects life. Unless a future heroine plots the journey afresh, she must continue to record not "that renchant childhood route . . . to one's original place," but a tedious sojourn in decadence and despair.

Margaret Peters (review date 17 December 1984)

SOURCE: "Irish Passions: Women Under the Spell," in *The Wall Street Journal,* Vol. 204, December 17, 1984, p. 32.

[*In the following review, Peters surveys the stories in* The Fanatic Heart.]

Reading Edna O'Brien's **The Fanatic Heart,** an anthology of nearly 20 years of short stories, one sees the same story born again and again, built up into new configurations although the root is the same.

Ms. O'Brien writes from the different turns her passion takes for her native Ireland, the innocence of her Catholic girlhood, and the deep magnetism of sex. They drive the artist back, in memory—force her to return to people and houses and voices she was once overjoyed to quit. Often in adulthood, the female character is an exile—wed to a Protestant, living in England, without custody of her children if divorced. And often she is alone; in the ruins of a love affair.

The stories of abandoned women who try to fend for themselves (**"Mrs. Reinhardt"** or the brilliantly queasy **"Paradise"**) or who scavenge adulterously on the leavings of other women's marriages (**"The Love Object"**) have the compulsive edge of a woman top much alone, with no purpose except to feel love returned. They are not perhaps the author's best stories; the ones of girlhood where everything is felt with such biting keenness and humor are more pleasing to read. And yet, the various portraits of the older, exiled women linger in the mind like warnings, with their emotional fatigue, their soreness, their hysteria.

Sometimes, the worlds come together, perfectly, as in the first story, **"The Connor Girls,"** where an insatiably curious country girl is hypnotized by the love lives and oddities of two British sisters. The sisters held themselves apart from everyone in the village and, consequently, loomed large in the girl's childish imagination.

Years later, when she returns to the village with her own child and her husband, the pair of withered old ladies are ingratiating and less haughty. They are about to reward her ancient curiosity with an invitation to tea, when her English husband nastily preserves himself and their child from contact with their kindness. Cutting both ways, slashing against her husband and against the homecoming, she writes, ". . . at that moment I realized that by choosing his world I had said goodbye to my own and to those in it. By such choices we gradually become exiles, until at last we are quite alone."

In many stories, nevertheless, Ms. O'Brien is driven back, to her country and her family; driven back to see with an impassioned eye, still girlish in her dread, still Catholic in her sense of evil, and Irish in her piercing, flaying language.

In **"A Rose in the Heart of New York"** a self-made, sophisticated young woman takes her mother on holiday to see if they can share their secrets, as two grown women. The daughter is so hungry for mother love she tramples her mother's delicacy when the elderly woman timorously confesses to an old romance that could have led to a different life. Then, furious at having her own life called "unsettled" by her mother, she blames her parent, and the moment's intimacy is shattered. The daughter is left to endure her own choices, which seem no better than her mother's before her. Ms. O'Brien is especially fine at showing this yearning for the past by one who has broken with it, a yearning that co-exists with revulsion at the power the past has to bind one.

In these stories, childhood in the country is bright with promise and joy and mystery. Horses stamp the ground, there is butter to churn and tinkers spark her with fear. And seeping into that clever girl's childhood are an unwanted suitor who drops to fees down her jumper (**"The Bachelor"**), and a young nun to whom she develops a forbidden attachment (**"Sister Imelda"**).

In **"Courtship,"** a girl years for the attention of a particular young man, and is invited to a dance with a clod instead. "His hands were the most revolting, being very white, and his fingers were like long white slugs."

Having endured the boy's flabby attempts on her, she returns home to a dreamlike encounter with the boy she loves: "There was nothing for it but to be glad; that wild and frightened gladness that comes from breaking out of one's lonely crust, and just as with the swimmer who first braves the depths, the fear is secondary to the sense of prodigal adventure."

Sex can move girls and women from their humdrum round of chores to some thing briefly sublime. The thwarting of it, too, can lead to horror, as in **"Savages,"** where a woman named Mabel scandalizes everyone by flourishing a pregnancy that turns out to be false.

These stories are not so much in fashion now, when fatal attraction between men and women seems almost antiquated and the idea that marriage is a girl's best prospect has lost its force. It is not that Ms. O'Brien recommends either of these destinies, but she is gifted in describing girls and women who are in thrall to them, and have found the cup bitter. ". . . I thought that ours indeed was a land of shame," she writes in **"A Scandalous Woman,"** "a land of murder, and a land of strange, throttled, sacrificial women."

Maeve Binchy (review date 1 March 1987)

SOURCE: A review of *Tales for the Telling: Irish Folk and Fairy Stories,* in *New York Times,* March 1, 1987, p. 31.

[*In the following review, Binchy offers a favorable assessment of* Tales for the Telling.]

Edna O'Brien can tell a good story and she has a great ear for the way people talk.

Up to now the people who have talked in her books have been complicated women, anguished because their expectations were so ill fulfilled, or happy girls, carefree because they didn't yet know what disappointments lay ahead.

Now she has found a new voice, and a whole new range of characters, in the peopled tapestries of Irish folklore, a world where nothing stays the same and where the action is as fast as the waterfalls and rivers that cascade from the hills, and the quick thinking of heroes who are momentarily outsmarted is like mercury.

There are 12 stories in [*Tales for the Telling: Irish Folk and Fairy Stories,*] this children's collection. Some are of heroes already known to children even in the United States and to the adults who will read the tales aloud only too willingly. Some are about the famous Finn, leader of the Fianna, some are of beggars, pipers and tricksters not known by name but familiar in their antics. Some of them are moral tales where good is rewarded in a very satisfying way. Take, for example, **"The Magic Apples,"** the story of Marteen, whose mother used to collect manna but got greedy and ate all that fell on the fields and so is reduced to begging at the church gates. Marteen, the son and heir, is a bit more ambitious and has heard of a lord in the city of Limerick "who had a beautiful house in its own grounds, who kept a capital table, served fine wines and victuals, had his carriage and equipage and a daughter that had no equal for sauciness." This is all music to Marteen's ears, so off he goes to find the lord near Limerick, and though he has only six pennies he kindly gives them away to three beggars he meets who seem in worse shape than he is.

But those beggars are not three separate beggars, oh no, they are the same beggar three times over, and he is testing Marteen. The lad comes out with an A in kindness and so he gets a magic ring that turns things into gold. Life looks up then and the lord's daughter thinks him a fine fellow, but

there are setbacks—as when he falls asleep rather intoxicated and the ring is stolen and disgrace descends on him. But Marteen is still in favor, and is given magic apples that make people develop antlers on their heads and start to butt each other, so a great mayhem ensues in the lord's house in its own grounds near Limerick until Marteen gets his lovely magic ring back. Then he solves the antler problem and everyone except the bad stepsister who stole the ring is rewarded and they all live ecstatically ever after.

Some stories are less clear about right and wrong. In **"Two Giants"** Finn pretends to be a baby in order to fool a rival giant who has come over to do battle with him; Finn sits in a cradle and in between bellows claims to eat stones that are really cakes, and to squeeze water from rocks that are really curds, and psychs the other giant, who had played fair, completely out of the contest.

Michael Foreman, already an award-winning illustrator, has entered into the fey and whimsical spirit of the tales and the way they are told. His pictures are in a variety of styles, some of them simplistically comic, some mystical and others downright terrifying.

With the one reservation that some of them are ill-advisedly written in an Oirish-style dialect, I would warmly recommend these stories, told so well that they could become classics.

Peggy O'Brien (essay date Autumn 1987)

SOURCE: "The Silly and the Serious: An Assessment of Edna O'Brien," in *The Massachusetts Review,* Vol. XXVIII, No. 3, Autumn, 1987, pp. 474-88.

[*In the following essay, Peggy O'Brien explores the psychology behind Edna O'Brien's literary choices and examines the negative critical commentary on her works.*]

An intriguing fact about the past reception of Edna O'Brien's work is that American and Irish audiences have been largely at odds, her compatriots tending to be harsh while critics here have lavished praise. She is receiving a great deal of attention now in America, where two collections of her work have been published within the last three years. Her short stories came out in 1984 as **The Fanatic Heart** and last year the three early novels were gathered together under the title **The Country Girls Trilogy,** with an epilogue added to tell the fates of her continuous central characters, Kate and Baba. Even if these new editions hadn't prompted fresh attention, O'Brien would be due a retrospective assessment of her writing simply because it now amounts to so much: eight novels, four books of short stories, several plays and screenplays and a work of non-fiction. Much of the disapproval from home has been directed at O'Brien's persona, an outrageous concoction of what foreigners expect an Irish person to be—mellifluous, volatile, wanton, irrational. But more serious artistic reservations underlie this carping. The American criticism now emerging discloses many of the deep reasons why discerning readers of whatever nationality might find O'Brien flawed. Some American critics repeat the error of endorsing O'Brien's stage-Irishness, but many incisive observations about her art push the process of just evaluation further along. Using these readings as a starting point, I will explore the ways in which the inadequacies of her prose are bound to less visible strengths. My interest is double: to understand rather than judge an author's psychology that avoids certain opportunities and embraces others, and to broach those questions of literary evaluation which these choices raise.

Mary Gordon's review of *A Fanatic Heart* [in *The New York Times Book Review,* November 18, 1984] epitomizes the rapt response one has come to expect outside of Ireland. Gordon is seduced by O'Brien's voice, enthralled by the Irish writer's use of language: "All the words are fitting; none of them shocks. . . . It is the emblem of her genius: the genuinely surprising word, not in itself exotic but conjuring in the reader a response inexorably physical." This leads Gordon to praise O'Brien's undoubted descriptive powers, the way she evokes the physical world through sensuous language. Recalling O'Brien's description of a young woman, Gordon comments, "The physical detail burrows into the mind; how clearly one sees Eily." What limits Gordon's judgment is the way she elevates linguistic richness and vividness over other qualities of good prose, such as narrative control. Moreover, Gordon invites suspicion, if not derision, from Irish skeptics when she betrays that she views O'Brien through green-tinted glasses. She is beguiled quite simply by the author's Irishness. This, along with her gender, goes a long way toward establishing O'Brien's credentials with Gordon: "Edna O'Brien tells the Irish woman's inside story . . . she speaks with a voice identifiably and only hers. No voice could be less androgynous or more rooted in a land." It is worrying to the Irish, especially Irish women, that O'Brien is viewed as their representative and voice. But there is a contradiction in Gordon's statement that must be noted. Does O'Brien present herself as an individual, speaking "with a voice identifiably and only hers," or as a type of her sex and nationality? O'Brien herself is only too willing to exploit the potential for universal acceptance in such confusion.

Whereas sometimes she puts herself forward as the essential woman and other times as the voice of Ireland, in the short essay, **"Why Irish Heroines Don't Have to be Good Anymore"** [in *The New York Times Book Review,* May 11, 1986], she conflates the two stereotypes to define Irish womanhood. In a transparent effort at pandering to transatlantic taste, she assumes a susceptibility on the part of Americans for Celtic charm and trades blatantly on her origins. So open and roguish is she in weaving her obvious spell, however, that it is not so much this manipulation which seems reprehensible as her misappropriation of a native tradition. Hers are sins of presumption and reduction. Sprinkling tidbits of Yeats and Synge and snippets from legend and history throughout the essay, unabashed, she aligns her own persona with the great women of Ireland's past. Her egoism robs other characters and events of their individuality and usually their stature. She transforms the searing story of Deirdre into a maudlin, melodramatic tale of woman's woe. No self-ironic tone indicates an authorial awareness of how her penny-romance summary robs a great tragedy of passion. Characteristically, she touts intensity but presents risible soap opera: "When Deirdre of the Sorrows saw her husband slain, she tore her golden hair out, became distraught, uttered the most rending lament and then fell down beside him and died." The busy syntax, piling verb upon verb, creates a flurry of excitement rather than a solemn procession toward death. An austere heroine becomes an hysterical exhibitionist.

The essay, however, contains a clue to the serious shortcoming of O'Brien's imagination and, ironically, its interest. After she gives a cursory and specious account of two types of Irish heroine, robust and meek, she places her own Baba and Kate in this double line: "Realizing that the earlier heroines were bawdy and the later ones lyrical I decided to have two, one who would conform to both my own and my country's view of what an Irish woman should be and one who would undermine every piece of protocol and religion and hypocrisy that there was." She places calculating Baba in line with heroines such as Deirdre and the Old Woman of Beare who have been justly celebrated for their passion and spontaneity. The telling and dangerous opinion divulged as the basis for her thinking is that being strong means having no emotion. Defending her decision to kill off vulnerable Kate in the epilogue and allow crass Baba to survive she explains, "lyricism had to go, just as emotion had to be purged." The equation of vigor and invulnerability is alarming, for this repudiation of emotion points to an evasion in O'Brien's work, which is nearly disguised by sexual and ethnic antics. It is the paradoxical birthplace of both the silly and the serious in her. More, it is the source from which her imagination springs and continues to be generated.

In an interview with her [in *The New York Times Book Review,* November 18, 1984], Philip Roth asks some penetrating questions which, overall, demonstrate an enviable balance between indicating the impressive and hinting at the defective in her. Paying tribute to her prodigious memory and the part it plays in her descriptive ability—"the ability to reconstruct with passionate exactness an Irish world"—

he also wonders if a tenacious clinging to the past, especially an obsession with her mother and father, hasn't blocked O'Brien emotionally. He asks, "I wonder if you haven't chosen the way you live—living by yourself—to prevent anything emotionally too powerful from separating you from that past?" O'Brien answers, "I'm sure I have. I rail against my loneliness but it is as dear to me as the thought of unity with a man." In this same interview O'Brien speaks of a continuing battle with her father that has only abated slightly with his death but that still would make it intolerable to be reincarnated as his daughter. The dream of unity, therefore, is in direct proportion to the reality of alienation. A stalemate exists because the emotion which creates this tension hasn't been released. In the same interview she also speaks of loving her mother overmuch and having "a sense of her over my shoulder judging." Then, in another section she talks of what seems at first an unrelated subject, her need to leave Ireland: "I do not think I would have written anything if I had stayed. I feel I would have been watched, would have been judged (even more) and would have lost that priceless commodity called freedom." It seems that the need to recover Ireland imaginatively and from a distance is more deeply a need for union with her mother. The great poignancy and artistic success of a story like **"A Rose in the Heart"** is that it meets this estrangement head-on and records with unflinching honesty an emotional ambivalence that doesn't take recourse in any of the diverting extremes of sex or country which are so common in O'Brien and are nothing but red herrings for the critic.

In his interview Roth also makes the important connection between O'Brien's descriptive acumen and these unresolved emotions, seeing description as a strategy to contain what are otherwise anarchic feelings: "You seem to remember the shape, texture, color and dimension of every object your eye may have landed upon while you were growing up—not to mention the human significance of all you saw, heard, smelled, tasted and touched. The result is prose like a fine piece of meshwork, a net of perfectly observed sensuous details that enables you to contain all the longing and pain and remorse that surge through the fiction." O'Brien's descriptive skill does, indeed, enable her to deal with emotional tumult, but it also encourages an avoidance of emotional honesty that places the value of her work in question. Her psychology as an author is revealed more by certain decisions she makes, especially with regard to how much she will indulge a narrator. There is a peril in using an interview, however, as evidence for this argument, since doing so can imply that my appeal is to certain biographical truths about Edna O'Brien, but, given her irrepressible, perverse humanity, the voice that we hear in her interviews is even more fictional than that of her fiction.

One could be forgiven for seeing O'Brien's work as autobiographical, for she is a writer who sounds most affected speaking in ordinary life and most candid narrating prose fiction. It is understandable why Anatole Broyard, in a quite contemptuous review of **The Country Girls Trilogy** [in *The New York Times Book Review,* May 11, 1986], identifies the author with her chief character: "Like Kate, Miss O'Brien too sees the world through 'wronged eyes' and the success of her career suggests that, in literature at least, two wrongs may make a right." For most of the review Broyard's complaint is the futile one that O'Brien doesn't succeed at being someone else, the sort of woman he would like. His comments, however, lead in a more useful direction when he points to a collusion between author and character which his "two wrongs" implies. "Like Kate's, Baba's extramarital choices are conspicuously odd, and if Miss O'Brien means these men to stand for women's fate, she has certainly stacked the deck. . . . The women in the later books are attractive, intelligent, witty—surely they could do better if the author let them." Stacking the deck and permitting characters particular destinies are authorial choices, matters for artistic control.

> **The abiding problem for critics of O'Brien's work is to explain the constant blend of powerful and weak writing in her. So often she creates chilling evocations of confused and chaotic existence by means of an art which fails to distance itself from this cogent material.**
> —*Peggy O'Brien*

The abiding problem for critics of O'Brien's work is to explain the constant blend of powerful and weak writing in her. So often she creates chilling evocations of confused and chaotic existence by means of an art which fails to distance itself from this cogent material. More often than not it enacts the same confusions. Her practice as a fiction writer raises proverbial questions about the craft, such as whether authorial detachment and objectivity are necessary virtues or whether to demand them is to be outmoded and unfair. A perfect example of this dilemma is raised by the story **"Paradise,"** a terrifying representation of a needy woman's insecurity and self-loathing in a loveless relationship. The prose itself is brittle with the anxiety and panic felt by the protagonist; however, she is also a relentlessly whining, self-pitying person who is never thrown into ironic relief by authorial interpositions. The author seems complicitous in the self-destructive behavior, and this can prompt reader disapproval as much as intense reader identification. If we disapprove, the problem arises of whether we reject the personality of the author, that of the character or some elusive entity that we call the art itself. The fact remains, however, that the story leaves an indelible impression as the recreation of an extreme mental state.

Mary Jo Salter reviews *The Country Girls* [in *The New Republic,* June 30, 1986] in a more probing, engaged manner than Broyard. Her response, puzzled rather than disdainful, seems more appropriate, given the genuinely mixed quality of O'Brien's work. Salter's position also may reflect how the women's movement has played a role in prompting American critics to question O'Brien's representation of women just as the Irish question her portrayal of them. Salter, in relation to Kate, refers to "all that dreaming of men, and no thinking about her own plans regardless of them." She speaks too in a concerned tone of the catastrophic consequences of such an attitude: "In time the alternatives for such a woman reduce to death—either her own, as in Kate's probably suicidal drowning, or her lover's, as occurs in O'Brien's 1977 novel, *I Hardly Knew You.*" But Salter makes a statement which suggests her own suspicions of a complicity between author and material, thereby calling O'Brien's detachment into question. Commenting on the dramatic transformation of a husband-figure from one book to the next, Salter observes, "It seems at least as much O'Brien's failure as Eugene's that he has changed from a complex man—charming, but with some serious faults—into a villain." This is a problem of accuracy and restraint, of lapsing from proportionate representation into stereotyping. Salter sees this degeneration occurring over time, with later books and stories more prone to generalized, blurred portraits than the lucid, extremely life-like *Country Girls.* Salter puts this difference down to the artist's special skill in portraying adolescence, which, she says, is the same for most people, as opposed to middle-age where more telling, individual distinctions surface. It could just as easily be, however, that the authorial identity is arrested in its development and has difficulty imagining mature adults with clarity. O'Brien's characters, projections of a turbulent authorial psyche, participate in a dialectical relationship with that center, and the dynamic created promotes personal development. Aiding the discovery of authorial identity, these fictions serve a serious purpose.

If a characteristic of the late authorial persona and characters is that they chronically seek affirmation from others, the refreshing and reassuring attribute of Kate, as she first appears, is a radiant self-containment. We trust her precisely because she doesn't ask us to. Perhaps the adolescent tendency toward self-absorption makes her refer to no other tribunal than herself; but, because she has no interest in manipulation, she is utterly reliable as a narrator. As a result, the author disappears as a mediating presence. Salter rightly isolates the opening to *Country Girls* as an example of this transparency, but also, ironically, as an announcement of a major authorial obsession, her father: "I wakened quickly and sat up in bed abruptly. It is only when I am anxious that I waken easily and for a minute I did not know why my heart was beating faster than usual. Then I remembered. The old reason. He had not come home." As the passage un-

folds, what distinguishes it from later, similar moments is the narrator's refusal to disguise or displace feeling. For instance, Kate laments, "There was a smell of frying bacon in the kitchen, but it didn't cheer me." The temptation for indulging her senses doesn't divert her from the main feeling; she doesn't pretend that vapors from the kitchen fill the hole of dread in her stomach.

At the same time, immediate sensations save her from being sucked under by another whirlpool of feeling, associated with her mother:

> Getting out, I rested for a moment on the edge of the bed, smoothing the green satin bedspread with my hand. We had forgotten to fold it the previous night, Mama and me. Slowly I slid on to the floor and the linoleum was cold on the soles of my feet. My toes curled up instinctively. I owned slippers but Mama made me save them for when I was visiting my aunts and cousins; and we had rugs but they were rolled up and kept in drawers until visitors came in the summer-time from Dublin.

The prose lets us know that the mother has been internalized as a repressive force dictating every movement within her domain, where the gratification of simple pleasures is delayed and there are rules for the smallest operations. The reader senses clearly the mother's controlling personality and its toll on the child but is not enlisted to be on the daughter's side or to blame the mother, for there is nothing wheedling in the tone. Kate's healthy sensuality naturally and without defiance asserts itself against the rectitude of the mother. Smoothing the "green satin bedspread," she soaks in color and texture as psychic sustenance. It is as though the instinctive curling of her toes from the cold of the linoleum is a metaphor for the recoiling of her sturdy young nature from the pathology of her parents. Kate's autonomy guarantees our own, so we don't require an implied author to save us from fusion with a narrator's subjectivity.

This opening passage, O'Brien's first published words, is prophetic in many respects, not just for the considerations about narration which it raises, but for the place description occupies within it. It contains one of the best illustrations of O'Brien's capacity to observe nature minutely, with a painter's eye, and reproduce what she sees in language. She provides Kate with an exquisite evocation of early morning, as much a projection of a fanciful, feminine spirit as a description of mist and verdure:

> The sun was not yet up, and the lawn was speckled with daisies that were fast asleep. There was dew everywhere. The grass below my window, the hedge around it, the rust and paling wire beyond that, and the big outer field were each touched with a deli-

cate, wandering mist. And the leaves and the trees were bathed in the mist, and the trees looked unreal, like trees in a dream. Around the forget-me-nots that sprouted out of the side of the hedge were haloes of water. Water that glistened like silver. It was quiet, it was perfectly still. There was smoke rising from the blue mountain in the distance. It would be a hot day.

This is an ingenuous deflection of feeling onto the outside world. There is honesty too in not confusing the subjective descriptive process with objective reality: the romantic passage comes to the empirical conclusion, "It would be a hot day." The child feels free to project onto nature innate and valid longings for peace and perfection, the utter stasis of the scene showing her need to escape family turmoil. Through the personification of the "daisies that were fast asleep" she expresses a desire for an undisturbed innocence belied in real life by her waking abruptly in an anxious state. The dew as it touches and bathes the landscape becomes an ethereal medium which transforms the ordinary into the extraordinary. "Haloes" alerts us to the transcendent aim of this imagination. All this evanescence, however, is in balance with concrete fact: "The sun was not yet up." We don't feel that the narrator mistakes her hopes and needs for their actual fulfillment. The act of projecting feeling onto nature and describing the composite scene which results serves a healthier purpose than escape. It affirms a human vitality manifested by this creative power.

The exact place where the narrator is launched into this fantasy is important. It doesn't follow a further stab of anxiety about the father, but rather another subliminal reminder of the mother's censorious ubiquity. The window blind has shot up and the cord tangled itself when the girl reflects, "It was lucky that Mama had gone downstairs, as she was always lecturing me on how to let up the blinds properly, gently." These last two words succinctly communicate the ambiguous impression the mother makes, as forbidding and attractive. By describing a beautiful world which is entirely her own, the daughter creates both a defense against maternal control and a means of imitating the mother's winning romanticism, which insists that even mundane tasks be imbued with grace. Both of these functions for the descriptive act, self-affirmation and emulation of another, come out in a key passage from *Johnny, I Hardly Knew You.* At this late stage, however, there is an enormous split between unbearable feeling and the solace of the physical world. During a session with a psychiatrist the narrator experiences a gothic, fantasized reentry of the womb followed by an escape into apparent ordinariness.

> I was hurtled down, down down into the denizens of horror, with the devils to direct and make mock of my flight. The walls purred with blood and the

spheres through which I had to pass were lit by flame. There were no doors or no way out. Yet I had to get out, or die, or choke, and out I did get only to be dragged back again, back into the swirling sphere, and again and again, with no respite. . . . As helpless as spermatozoa . . . the world that I came back to was indeed unswerving, almost exquisite. I was glad to feel the tableness of a table, to trot down a little path towards a garden seat and know that I wouldn't be swept away.

The inanimate object world is identified as an anchor for a psyche otherwise driven mad by vertiginous feelings. The author wants us to believe that the salvation found is objective reality, but the narrator's oasis, in its quiddity, is even less material than the wonderland Kate conjured from her window. A platonic table is less than material, and "to trot down a little garden path towards a garden seat" is to romanticize the landscape. There is a definite push from within to idealize. It is as though the acceptable face of the mother, her gentle, romantic side, is projected outward, leaving the controlling, punitive part inside, repressed.

The balanced creature in *Country Girls,* who preserves a paradoxical response to her mother and knows the difference between raw nature and her transmutation of it, is replaced by someone who splits and polarizes emotion. Moreover, her emotional life is encased in fantasy and the physical world is rendered abstract, an insidious inversion which is caused by sustained stress. *Country Girls,* with its unembellished frankness, contains this important disclosure by Kate: "Always on the brink of trouble I look at something, like a tree or a flower or an old shoe, to keep me from palpitating." Much of O'Brien's descriptive writing is not the product of deliberate looking at something but distracted movement away from one thing, usually an acute feeling, toward another, an object, a transition essentially from emotion to sensation. A moment in the story **"Paradise"** demonstrates this involuntary response. When a conversation among people she fears comes to a subject that provokes anxiety in the protagonist, the dialogue abruptly stops and the next words are, "The sun, filtered by the green needles, fell and made play on the dense clusters of brown nuts. They never ridicule nature, she thought, they never dare." This is more than description and a more radical outcome is intended than finding self-affirmation through recreating nature imaginatively. Here we witness an empathic flow into the object itself. Invulnerability from excruciating pain comes from a Keatsian entry into an object which the senses have intensely perceived. This particular imaginative act blurs the boundaries of genre and we enter the territory of lyric poetry. We also come to the crux where strength and weakness combine in O'Brien, for at such moments she fails to distance herself from the narrator to enable us to see the gesture of escape for what it is. We fail to receive an emotional profile of the character, achieved through irony, gaining instead, through our own unaided extrapolations, a profile of the author, who participates in both the romanticism and escapism.

> **The collusion between author and character is essentially a blurring of the boundaries between individual and parental identities; and the unresolved nature of these primary relationships accounts for O'Brien's overall obsessiveness.**
> —*Peggy O'Brien*

O'Brien's penchant and capacity for descriptive writing does more for her prose than lend it texture and warmth. Even Roth's image of containment, the fine meshwork through which feeling surges, doesn't do justice to the subtle interaction of emotion and description that takes place. A passage from *Johnny* illustrates the psychological complexity such instances involve when the descriptive strategy is a paradoxical effort to control and avoid reality. When rape is imminent the speaker tells us, "I knew for certain there would be a scuffle within minutes. It was nearly dark. Strange to say I was able to notice the countryside." She then constructs a stylized view of the scene which is more like a description of a Sienese painting than an actual landscape. Our suspicions are confirmed when she casually remarks, "I thought down there [Siena] were the paintings I had seen." This literary moment is similar to the famous scene in *The Ambassadors* when Strether is on the brink of discovering the truth about a sexual liaison he has regarded as innocent, as much a crisis for James' fastidious hero as rape is for O'Brien's worldly heroine. In his crisis Strether frames the French country side where the truth will be imminently revealed in the terms of a painting he previously saw in Boston. Both figures project an ideal, static image from memory onto an inanimate object world in order to control a dynamic, threatening human situation. They manage by the tactic to place themselves at least two removes from the source of their anxiety. James' particular genius is that he interjects just enough irony for us to perceive Strether's evasion, to know that his picturesque projections differ wildly from the facts. O'Brien's prose does not generate irony because the narrator's tactic for survival is shared by the author. A benefit for the reader, however, is that the absence of mediating cerebration brings the unsettling mixture of fear and rationalization immediately before us.

The preeminent attraction of descriptive writing for O'Brien is that its overt focus is the non-human world, one safely outside the emotional melee of human relationships. The descriptive act becomes anodyne when it mingles the unbearable feelings produced by intimacy with the innocence and inertness of objects. If one reads O'Brien for the extreme effect those first intimates, mother and father, have had on her authorial psyche, then various aspects of her fictional practice become comprehensible, indeed seems necessary in the light of these psychological exigencies. The collusion between author and character is essentially a blurring of the boundaries between individual and parental identities; and the unresolved nature of these primary relationships accounts for O'Brien's overall obsessiveness. It is this quality of her imagination which provides the energy both to explore unfamiliar psychological recesses and to repeat the same hackneyed experiences over and over again, without apparent control. The former makes reading her works exciting, the latter makes it wearying. The reader is torn between interest and impatience.

O'Brien admits baldly to Roth, "I am obsessive, also I am industrious. Besides, the time when you are most alive and most aware is in childhood and one is trying to recapture that heightened awareness." A telescopic look down the length of her works reveals this quality of obsessiveness in a simple, direct way: the repetition of the same characters in only slightly different guises. Kate and Baba appear in the three early novels, then become Willa and Patsy in *Casualties of Peace,* Stella and Zee in *Zee & Co.,* Emma and Caithleen in *A Pagan Place.* The procession of pairs within the stories is too long to relate. The passive-aggressive husband figure enjoys minor mutations in the different fictional embodiments of Eugene in the trilogy, Robert in *Zee,* a malevolent presence in *August is a Wicked Month,* Dr. Flaggler in *Night,* Herod in *Casualties.* The recurrence of stock characters and incidents articulates the psychological law that early crises dictate the content, in the form of psychological projection, of later experience. No wonder adult life seems tepid compared to childhood, when the only immediate experiences, if they are not subsequently relinquished, take place. It is intriguing to ask why evidence of obsessiveness mounts in the works directly after *Country Girls.*

The answer may be that sex comes into her fiction after this point and physical intimacy unleashes primitive feelings that induce a regression back into the triangle of the parent-child relationship. Kate in *Country Girls* gains steadily in autonomy because she is constantly affirming parts of herself that lie beyond parental control. Sex and the atavistic emotions it uncovers disturbs this progress and leaves identity in fragments. In the preface to the Collins selection O'Brien describes herself as a "searching, somewhat fractured adult." The creation of fictions is part of an effort to redeem herself, become whole.

The Kate/Baba division is fundamentally one between the sides of the author's character dictated by mother and by father. All the morbid Kates yearn for romantic fulfillment and transcendent, sublime experience; the Babas are hard realists—sensual, opportunistic but decent. The father's roistering fecklessness affects the author's psychology and artistic development by informing all the Baba characters who prod the introspective, meek Kates into adventure and fun. It is crucial that the personality traits of Baba's fictional parents reverse those of Kate's: Mr. Brennan is the sober, nurturing parent, while Martha is the alcoholic extrovert. It is important to see this reversal as meeting an authorial need.

The reversal expresses the fantasy, with its own inner logic, that if her father were more feminine, then she and her mother might be less so, might enjoy more crude Baba-buoyancy. As matters stand, the father with his patent, relentless flaws forces a realism on the author so extreme that it can mean the extinction of finer feelings in the face of brute physical force. The result can be a self-conscious toughness which seeks to eliminate feeling rather than express it with exuberance. This defensive imitation of the father's indifference to feeling results in a personal loss of the resilience which emotional fluency provides. The positive face of the anti-romantic author is that endearing rogue who endorses in her characters a rude capacity for survival. Its darker face is the adolescent who persistently generates in her plots an acting-out rather than a considered judgment, superficial busyness rather than purposeful activity, endless stimulation rather than emotional satisfaction. The glacial nihilism of these middle novels, heavy with casual sex and philistinism, in contrast to the ebullient *Country Girls,* is caused largely by suppression of a sensitive Kate (modelled on her martyred mother but with a generous leavening of the father) in favor of a more radical split between Kate and Baba types, with a preference for the latter. The sensualist manqué of *August* thinks she can expunge painful feeling through merely desperate acts, chiefly sexual. The appropriation of first-person narrating space to Baba in *Married Bliss* (where Kate anomalously receives third-person handling) heralds this phase of emulating paternal callousness rather than exquisite maternal suffering.

O'Brien also told Roth, "I am a creature of conflicts. . . . I am often rather at odds with myself and others." While the dialectic set up between narrators and author stimulates growth, one shouldn't underestimate the value in the creative conflict of Kate and Baba as opposing but interacting projections. The father, perceived as sexually rapacious and perpetually absent, is also the model who urges a breaking away from the mother's stranglehold into the autonomy of sex and the outside world. If the mother's influence on the author's descriptive ability is to promote romantic projections onto landscape, the father bends those powers toward realism, sometimes with a very hard edge.

The story **"Forgetting,"** a chronicle of the bland, recuperative days after the end of an affair, contains instances of an extreme, in fact bogus, realism prevalent in the later works,

where Baba's cynicism eclipses Kate's naïveté. The truth is more that the two converge but with the hard, protective armor of Baba on the surface. The realism is only apparent. A soft center lies within the stark perimeters a jaded eye perceives. It is apt, therefore, that the scene is a Mediterranean resort where a glaring sun gives objects their clinical outline and the heavy scent of holiday sex provides the required, lurid aura. The opening words contain an unsettling blend of apparent naturalism and obvious metaphor. It begins with a studied neutrality—"Then the foliage is wet, the sun shining on it, while all the umbrellas and parasols are already dry and people hurrying down on their pop-pop bicycles or on foot, down to the sea"—but quickly abandons this antiseptic vision to observe, "By evening the yellow flower of the marrow tops will have wilted to an unrecognizable shred, holiday couples will have quarrelled, will have made love and half-built castles will be like forlorn forts on the vistas of dark sands." Once the metaphorical intention has been made explicit, we endow retrospectively what has come before with an implicit content. The initial coldness is seen with hindsight as a pitiable denial of feelings that seem crushed by circumstance. The flat surface of images is a barrier to keep down a pain derived through sexual involvement with men. O'Brien gives us no pointers by which to perceive this irony.

The feelings associated with the father are so engulfing they make distancing impossible. It is his introjected image which makes O'Brien ceaselessly portray sexually insatiable women, like the father, in disastrous relationships with hurtful men, also like the father. When one of her protagonists complains that "one man is the same as another," we read a profound truth beneath the cliché: when each man is a projection of an original father figure and each romance a replaying of an original trauma, sameness is the result. The promiscuity which has become a hall-mark of O'Brien's writing is the result of a serious authorial need to realize the full content of the intense feelings associated with a father figure. As though still relying on an unreliable father to validate their relationship as an intimate one, she seeks one male spectre after another in futile quest of this elusive conclusion to years of waiting. The sexual partners become more apparitional and allegorical as her fiction evolves because they become mere representatives of an inherently remote figure from the past. However painful and inaccessible the father has been, however, he is idealized in direct proportion to the degree he has removed himself and caused hurt.

Mother Ireland, which may with justification be read as a series of psychological projections onto Irish history and landscape, contains a tendentious account of patriarchal culture which reveals a relishing of the violence associated with her father. Referring to ancient warriors she exclaims, "Their chess pieces could pierce a man's brain and often did. Warriors sat down with their opponents' slain heads under their belts and guts falling about their feet." Mary Hooligan in *Night* luxuriates in such gore and the author offers not a single caveat to the blood-lust. This is the author who propels the Kate of *Lonely Girls* to derive more sexual excitement from a brawl between country rowdies than from sex with her civilized partner. This same Kate endures an inordinately protracted term of imprisonment with a drunken, distracted father, from whom escape would be easy. It appears that if Kate's sights were not obscured by idealization she would see her father's limits and bolt, but it is her author's bondage to a paternal image that determines Kate's paralysis.

This powerlessness, which expresses itself most in a fixation with rape, could only be reduced by an objective distancing from the explosive emotions associated with the father. The obstacle to achieving this self-control, however, is the introjected image of an excessively controlling mother. The quandary is that assuming responsibility for one's own feeling seems like acceding to her tyranny. If relationships with men for O'Brien's characters commonly culminate in the eruption of psychotic violence (the ending to *Johnny,* for example, where a young man is actually murdered), confrontation with the mother's influence leads to a much more insidious effect, an ineffable implosion of the psyche. Much of the tedium that comes with reading O'Brien is the result of the melodramas constructed around men, while the struggle with female identity produces a hidden content which is more subtle—so too the artistic rendering of it. If the lack of objectivity about the father results in a lack of ironic distance from her female characters; masochism in relation to men, the basic collusion between the author and these characters, the continuous nature of their composite identity, is the consequence of a failure in differentiation from the mother. An unhealthy fusion is responsible for that blurring of boundaries between author and protagonists which creates so many evaluative doubts. But the search for identity involved also creates an interaction between author and characters which is the essential but covert story O'Brien is telling. A dimension beyond conventionally defined content, this struggle for self-objectification gained through the process of narrating gives a psychological immediacy and urgency to the prose that compels our attention and respect.

Much of her best writing occurs when O'Brien confronts directly the implications of fusion with the mother. The sustained honesty of **"A Rose in the Heart"** stems from her finding the courage to admit and articulate a paradoxical truth, one half of which is alienation from the mother, the other half an intense fusion:

> The food was what united them, eating off the same plate, using the same spoon, watching one another's chews, feeling the food as it went down the other's gullet . . . when it ate blancmange or junket it was

eating part of the lovely substance of its mother. . . . Her mother's veins were her veins, her mother's lap was a second heaven . . . her mother's body was a recess that she would wander inside forever and ever . . . a sepulchre growing deeper and deeper. . . . She would not budge, would not be lured out.

O'Brien as an author remains embedded in the flesh of her female protagonists in order to avoid depicting, and perhaps experiencing, the terrors of separation, emergence and action on the surface of a world stripped of the mythological projections rampant in *Mother Ireland.*

In **"Rose,"** the speaker refers to her mother as a "gigantic sponge, a habitation in which she longed to sink and disappear forever and ever." As O'Brien's fiction advances it becomes apparent how strong the impulse is to "sink," how increasingly reluctant she is to be "lured out." This spectacle of fusion may frighten and repel the reader, and it does hinder artistic qualities of detachment and control, but it also makes reading what might be considered the worst of O'Brien a powerful encounter with the messy and unresolved in human experience. More lifelike than any art of lapidary perfection, its impact on the reader is visceral and personal. This sort of art fails to mitigate pain and confusion just as the mind often fails to dispel the anxieties of actual living. Many of O'Brien's narrators become haunting figures for the reader precisely because no implied author has pinpointed and filed away their misconceptions. Their neuroses aren't magically corrected by an ulterior voice of psychological normality. For example, in **"A Scandalous Woman"** an unreliable narrator, disappointed in marriage and deeply repressed, follows with pathological doggedness the career of a sexually precocious childhood friend, who eventually suffers and recovers from a mental breakdown. The parasitic motives of the frustrated narrator are not exposed through irony, but, if they were, it might lessen the uncomfortable effect the prose has on us. This self-deluded narration possesses a resonance not unlike that created by Fitzgerald's Nick Carraway, whose homo-erotic obsession with Jay Gatsby is also left throbbing under the surface of the text as an unconscious sexual drive.

O'Brien's most revealing disclosure in the Roth interview concerns a female compulsion to merge with the mother: "If you want to know what I regard as the principal crux of female despair, it is this: in the Greek myth of Oedipus and in Freud's exploration of it, the son's desire for his mother is admitted; the infant daughter also desires its mother but it is unthinkable either in myth, in fantasy or in fact, that the desire be consummated." O'Brien's most authentic writing centers around this secret wish, either demonstrating the catastrophic consequences of trying to realize the fusion, as in **"A House of My Dreams,"** or in presenting the growth that separation from a fantasized fusion promotes, the subject of

"Sister Imelda." It is no coincidence that this story of a schoolgirl's moving beyond a reciprocated crush on a repressed and febrile nun is one of O'Brien's most finely crafted works, artistic control working hand-in-hand with autonomy. So much is the primal unity a fugitive ideal, the more it's sought the more it disperses, and the ego that chases the phantom is fragmented in the process. The speaker of **"House of My Dreams,"** who ends in mental breakdown, begins to caress another woman and says, "It was a strange sensation, as if touching gauze or some substance that was about to vanish into thin air." So too, those works in which the author fails to differentiate herself from her material, **"Night"** being the outstanding instance, tend to fragment for the reader and "vanish into thin air."

When the center of a work doesn't hold, we are presented with a troublesome problem of response. The rapidly disintegrating story seems to beg us for help to erect boundaries, and bestow integration. Or perhaps to be complicitous in the breakdown and suffer it too. Even the hint of such an invitation can leave some readers disgusted and cold, dismissing the work as an artistic failure. A detached but secure reader may regard even the manipulation as part of an appalling but convincing enactment of a real psychological condition. The prose unquestionably makes this powerful gesture of appeal to us, demanding reaction, either to affirm or reject the author. O'Brien's search for the innocence of recovered unity ends with this bid to merge with the reader which appears to replay some very old drama. We become the idealized other, pursued by a seductive rhetoric that intends to ensnare but may fly past us on the scent of more willing prey.

James M. Haule (essay date December 1987)

SOURCE: "Tough Luck: The Unfortunate Birth of Edna O'Brien," in *Colby Library Quarterly,* Vol. XXIII, No. 4, December, 1987, pp. 216-23.

[*In the following essay, Haule examines O'Brien's treatment of birth, infancy, childhood, and motherhood in her works.*]

Edna O'Brien's *Mother Ireland* is a book filled with memories that move starkly between terror and pity as it explains, with the help of the haunting photographs of Fergus Bourke, why Ireland must be left and why Ireland can never be escaped. Her last statement is a remarkable admission of an entrapment at once willing and unwilling, a confession of both victory and defeat:

> I live out of Ireland because something in me warns
> me that I might stop there, that I might cease to feel
> what it has meant to have such a heritage, might

grow placid when in fact I want yet again and for indefinable reasons to trace the same route, the trenchant childhood route, in the hope of finding some clue that will, or would, or could, make the leap that would restore one to one's original place and state of consciousness, to the radical innocence of the moment just before birth.

The entire book, short as it is, clearly demonstrates the extent to which O'Brien's own life has been transformed into the early novels (especially *The Country Girls Trilogy*) and a number of her short stories (many collected recently in *A Fanatic Heart*). What makes this autobiographical statement so unusual is that it is an admission that the only escape from the oppressive heritage of moral obligation and social responsibility lies not in death or in unconsciousness, but in *pre*-consciousness: a state prior to knowledge that can only be lost at birth, befuddled by life, and fixed forever in death. Her work is an attempt to return to this condition of stasis, of innumerable possibilities unencumbered by the mothering that is their ruin.

This, of course, does not make O'Brien wholly unique. The stories of Elizabeth Bowen often center on children of profound moral and intellectual power who come to learn that life narrows rather than expands possibilities. "The Tommy Crans" and "Maria" are especially good examples of this. In a unique exploration of this same idea, Muriel Spark reveals in her story "The First Year of My Life" that all babies possess at birth a cosmic awareness that life is designed to destroy. At birth the child knows everything:

> Babies, in their waking hours, know everything that
> is going on everywhere in the world; they can tune
> in to any conversation they choose, switch on to any
> scene. We have all experienced this power. It is only
> after that it is brainwashed out of us . . . .

Because the narrator is as yet "unable . . . to raise my head from the pillow and as yet only twenty inches long," she must observe the activities of the adults without comment. The First World War is raging and even the most brilliant authors, she discovers with disgust, miss the mark: "'I only wish I were a fox or a bird,' D.H. Lawrence was writing to somebody. Dreary old creeping Jesus. I fell asleep."

It soon becomes clear, however, that Spark's narrator does not lapse into unconsciousness just to gain the strength necessary to participate in the world. Her human inheritance, intact at birth, makes the world seem dull and vicious. Sleep is escape. Life will be long, and there is much to unlearn. She begins life in a condition of intellectual superiority and physical dependance. This is an encumbrance that cannot be maintained, since it would make life with humanity impossible.

It is an analogous condition that O'Brien describes in nearly all her published work. While the child for her is not the awfully empowered infant of Bowen or Spark, it is a morally and intellectually superior being nonetheless who begins, as it encounters the world, to construct fictions in an effort to ward off the terrible depravity of adults. While Spark's narrator describes a ridiculous nursery routine in an arid and satiric way, O'Brien's child finds in the dependancy of infancy and childhood a betrayal that is too dark to afford more than a slender moment of relief. The child instinctively desires what the adult, in Ireland or in exile, more fully understands to be a useless longing: the desire to be her own mother, at once to embrace and to betray the single compelling figure that represents the beginning and the end of life. It is mothering that will require Spark's infant to relinquish its intelligence, and it is mothering throughout O'Brien's work that condemns the women of Ireland to the support of a social and moral order that is hopelessly destructive.

In O'Brien's Ireland, this order is the product of a mediaeval repression that focuses on reproduction in general and motherhood in particular. Divorce, contraception and abortion are all proscribed, leaving women with no choice but to be "good." Thus Irish women fear men who will not care for them and whose dominance is supported by Church and State; they conceive new life long before they have even an elementary understanding of their own; they deliver children into a world that denies natural emotion and desire. The result is successive generations of women who associate the misery of life, not with the oppressor, but with the oppressed who support with resignation this obliteration of intelligence and identity. Mothers are, therefore, more feared and hated than loved by their daughters. The prospect of motherhood itself is so horrible to O'Brien's young women that it leads to emotional and physical deformity. Clearly, a woman's own birth and its replication in the birth of her daughter is, in Ireland, a tragedy of impossible proportions. This is the thematic center of O'Brien's stories and her novels.

"A Scandalous Woman" is a good example. The narrator claims that she participates in the events of the story only slightly. It is not her own, but "another's destiny that is . . . exciting." This other is Eily who had the "face of a madonna," but the energy and desires of "a colt." Much is made throughout the story of her similarity to an animal, and once her downfall is confirmed, she is treated like a wild and dangerous beast much in need of "breaking." The success of the conspiracy of church and family to reduce Eily to compliance with moral and social orthodoxy results, at the end of the story, in the narrator's realization that "ours indeed was a land of shame, a land of murder, and a land of strange, throttled, sacrificial women."

Innocence is reserved for childhood. Even then, however, the games most often played mimic adult situations. The most telling of these was "hospital." Eily's sister "Nuala was happiest when someone was upset" and it was then that she liked to play at being a surgeon:

> Nuala liked to operate with a big black carving knife, and long before she commenced, she gloated over the method and over what tumors she was going to remove. She used to say that there would be nothing but a shell by the time she had finished, and that one wouldn't be able to have babies, or women's complaints ever. She had names for the female parts of one, Susies for the breasts, Florries for the stomach, and Matilda for the lower down.

Eily was the nurse. The narrator, invariably the patient, was disconcerted with the necessary preparations for surgery, since "Nuala would be sharpening the knife and humming 'Waltzing Matilda' . . . ."

This "woeful event" is more than comic relief, since it prepares us for the reduction of Eily, and finally of the narrator herself, to a mere shell. Eily is betrayed by her own physical desires. This results in an unwanted pregnancy and a loveless marriage with a forbidden Protestant boy who wishes for nothing more than escape. Ironically his first name is "Romeo," but his middle name, "Jack," is also the name of Eily's father from whom, as a small child, she used to hide under the table in order to "escape . . . thrashings." Eily meets the boy at a dance organized for the "aid of the new mosaic altar" for the local church. It is her "debut," and it leads to a series of surreptitious meetings "Sunday after Sunday, with one holy day, Ascension Thursday, thrown in."

The narrator agrees to help, but is beset with guilt "over the number of commandments we were both breaking" and so gargles with salt water and refuses proper food as "forms of atonement to God." Eily was asking her to do "the two hardest things on earth—to disobey God and my own mother." When this Romeo seems to lose interest in Eily after she sacrifices moral conviction and family responsibility for his company, both girls consult a "witch" who reluctantly tells the truth: Eily will see a "J" return twice. The girls assume that this means that her lover will always be hers. The truth of the matter is, however, that her lover will become another "Jack" like her father, and that he has sired within her a child who, after the shotgun wedding that morality and decency require, will in turn be called "Jack." It is a bitter fate that reproduces the tragedy of domestic Ireland, making endless repetition unavoidable.

Once her condition is known, the narrator laments that Eily's "most precious thing was gone, her jewel. The inside of one was like a little watch, and once that jewel or jewels were gone, the outside was nothing but a sham." Ironically, Eily has been reduced by pregnancy to the hollow shell of the childhood operation. Her punishment is to be kept like an untrustworthy animal, "hemmed in by her mother and some other old women" at church, and locked up all day with the animal feed. The parents discussed her like "a beast that had had some ailment." When she is let out, she is seen trying "to dart into the back of the car, tried it more than once, just like an animal trying to get back to its lair." At one point Eily's father "wanted to put a halter around her, but my mother said it wasn't the Middle Ages."

Most telling of all is the fear that all this engenders in the young narrator. As she washes dishes, she finds that she is "unable to move because of a dreadful pain that gripped the lower part of my back and stomach. I was convinced that I, too, was having a baby and that if I were to move or part my legs, some freakish thing would come tumbling out." These fearful pains are not sympathetic but symptomatic. Mindless mothering offers only loneliness and rejection and is the cause of her grief. Her mother responds to the scandal, not with openness and love, but with the enjoiner "to go home in pairs, to speak Irish, and not to walk with any sense of provocation." The narrator is praised for her goodness, though she knows how much she has shared in Eily's sin. She is warned to cut her hair and look as unattractive as possible, since "'Fine feathers make fine birds.'" Like Eily, she too is treated like an animal worth watching with alarm. Internally, the narrator is consumed not just with her "pains" but with parasites. After the grim wedding, she reports, I "passed a big tapeworm, and that was a talking point for a week or so . . . ." Both physically and emotionally, she is slowly being reduced to the lifeless shell demanded by conformity to moral and social requirements.

Eily gradually loses her hair and her sanity and cannot remember her best friend without effort. Her "recovery" is effected only when she accedes to the demands of parents and church, ignoring her wayward husband and the dreams of her youth. The "restored" Eily is a mother herself many times over when she is finally confronted by the narrator, who is herself pregnant for the second time. Neither of them can talk convincingly about themselves and center their attentions instead on a child. The narrator's "first thought" when she sees her old friend is that the enemy, "they," must have changed Eily by drugging "the feelings out of her, they must have given her strange brews, and along with quelling her madness, they had taken her spark away." As a final gesture, Eily anoints the narrator with "a little holy water on my forehead," a telling reminder of the curse that they both must bear for a lifetime.

The reduction of Eily and the narrator to moral and social stereotypes is clearly linked throughout the story to their mothers and their own mothering. They both become increasingly concerned with forgetfulness and order, yearning for a state of stasis associated mysteriously with womb and womankind. The powerful imagination of youth is lost as they desire to conform to a social conscience that allows them no individual moral or mental life. As O'Brien says in *Mother Ireland,* they gradually awaken to "a world where help and pity did not forthcome." It is their own birth that they desire, this second time without the mothering that was their ruin. O'Brien herself understands, but allows few of her characters to realize, that "to be on an island makes you realize that it is going to be harder to escape and that it will involve another birth, a further breach of waters." More awful still is the realization that to be born again, even at your own prompting, will ultimately make little difference. The "radical innocence of the moment just before birth" cannot ever be recovered.

This yearning for another birth outside the womb is even more powerfully dramatized in O'Brien's novels, most especially in *The Country Girls Trilogy.* The recent publication of a one-volume edition of these novels provided an opportunity to conclude the sad story of Kate and Baba. Twenty years after the events that concluded *Girls in Their Married Bliss,* Baba relates in her own voice the terrible fate that opened beneath them both.

O'Brien herself described the purpose of this unusual conclusion in a brief article published in *The New York Times Book Review.* Entitled **"Why Irish Heroines Don't Have to Be Good Anymore,"** it approaches directly the center of Edna O'Brien's quarrel with the world—her warfare with the destructive role that Ireland demands of her women. She describes "the glorious tradition of fanatic Irish writing which flourished before sanctity and propriety took over" and admits that

> it was with this jumble of association and dream and hope that I first sat down to write. Realizing that the earlier heroines were bawdy and the later ones lyrical I decided to have two, one who would conform to both my own and my country's view of what an Irish woman should be and one who would understand every piece of protocol and religion and hypocrisy that there was. As well as that, their rather meager lives would be made bearable by the company of each other. Kate was looking for love. Baba was looking for money. Kate was timid, yearning and elegiac. Baba took up the cudgel against life and married an Irish builder who was as likely to clout her as to do anything else. That was 20 years ago. The characters remained with me as ghosts, but without the catharsis of death. I had never finished their story, I had left them suspended, thinking perhaps that they could stay young indefinitely or that their mistakes might be canceled out or they would achieve that much touted fallacy—a rebirth.

Without youth or hope of rebirth, Kate and Baba face death and bewilderment. We learn in the "Epilogue" that Kate has "gashed her wrists, thinking daftly that someone might come to her rescue, a male Florence Nightingale might kneel and bandage and swoop her off to a life of certainty and bliss." Baba sees that Kate's desire for mothering has blinded her to life and led inevitably to death, for she could not realize that

> we're lonely buggers, we need a bit of a romp so as not to feel that we're walking, talking skeletons. Kids don't do really; at least not when they grow up, and that was Kate's mistake, the old umbilical love. She wanted to twine fingers with her son, Cash, throughout eternity.

It was to avoid "the rupture" that Kate experienced that Baba isolates herself from tenderness and love. Sex is purely physical; it carries no spiritual significance or danger. She refuses to accept the responsibility of mothering most especially, perhaps, because her illegitimate child is female. Baba does not abort it, but instead severs all emotional connections. Thus, her daughter rejects her from birth, for the girl had

> a will of her own and a mind of her own from the day she was born. Vomited the milk I gave her, rejected me, from day one, preferred cow's milk, solids, anything. She left home before she was thirteen, couldn't stand us. . . . I'm not a mother like Kate, drooling and holding out the old metaphorical breast, like a warm scone or griddle bread. She stood up to me, my little daughter, Tracy. At five years of age she walked into my bedroom and said, "You better love me or I'll be a mess."

Ironically, when her brutal husband Durack suffers a stroke, Baba must forego recreational sex on "one of those tropical islands" and come home to play nurse. His illness has turned him into an enormous child who insists on seeing *A Thousand and One Dalmatians* and who writes pathetic little notes, like "I love you, do you hear. Answer me now.'" Baba is not moved; she would not mother a child, and she will not mother an afflicted husband. She is repelled by his desire to

> to be with me all the time, nestling. He'd think that I had gone and he'd tell me that Baba had gone when I was there in the kitchen making fucking potato cakes and barley soup to remind him of his martyred mother and all that mavourneen mush. I was full up to the gills with guilt and pity and frustration.

Hardened to the demands of life, Baba is able to survive, however unhappily, because she recognizes no claims upon her. She sees no purpose, only survival. Because Kate cannot relinquish claims, she is doomed to as much unhappiness and, finally, to death by suffocation. Her drowning is ruled accidental, but Baba knows better: "Death is death, whether it's by accident or design." She knows Kate swam after dark on purpose. It was all a "blind really, so that no one would know, so that her son wouldn't know, self-emulation to the fucking end."

What most irritates Baba is that Kate's normal condition was, after all, much like Durack's final predicament. What's more, Kate chose to live in darkness and unreason. Baba is infuriated that her friend has died in a fit of irrational devotion to all that betrayed her, to motherhood and duty:

> Why couldn't she see reason, why couldn't she see that people are brigands, what made her think that there was such a thing as twin-star perpetuity, when all around her people were scraping for bits of happiness and not getting anywhere?

During her last days, Kate writes and talks in a kind of code that not even Baba attempts to interpret, for "you'd need a brain transfusion to understand them." Everything she writes or speaks has, in one way or another, to do with the betrayal of desire and mother love. Kate's notebook records an almost Blakean aphorism worthy of "The Marriage of Heaven and Hell": "The flushes of youth are nothing to the flushes of age, the one is rose leaf, the other the hemorrhage of death." More telling still is Kate's inability to pray, a condition that leads to her "mumbled petitions to St. Anthony" (Patron of the Lost) and her questions about "infinity, if there was something more to life." What she dreads most is the fearful condition of the narrator of **"A Scandalous Woman"** who, by story's end, has become a shell. Kate fears "the emptiness . . . the void." She experiences strange physical pains and hallucinations, as does the teller of Eily's story. She sees herself, by turns, "stitched to the sky with daggers or pins," or feels that her teeth were too large for her head and "were crushing her."

> **O'Brien's complaint, then, is that Irish women cannot hope for life from their mothers, and they cannot hope to give life, in turn, to their daughters.**
> **—*James M. Haule***

The anguish of birth trauma haunts Kate's final weeks. The departure of her son is the "last breach" that proves too much for her. Kate knows that her heart is her great affliction and, along with the female organs that have betrayed her, she wants to "tear it out, stamp on it, squash it to death, her heart being her undoing." She has become a shell as surely as the conspirators of **"A Scandalous Woman."** Baba will not forgive her, because she cannot tolerate "people like her" who are "always looking for meaning." Baba knows there is no meaning, not at least where Kate would find it. She knows that Kate's first problem was with "father—the crux of her dilemma." Her second was an acceptance of the role she had learned from her mother—to suffer and to die. In Baba's view, this makes her worthy, finally, of compassion:

> I don't blame her. I realize she was in the fucking wilderness. Born there. Hadn't the reins to haul herself out. Should have gone to night school, learned a few things, a few mottos such as "Put thy trust in no man."

Baba's monologue ends, unexpectedly, not in anger but in longing. She too, it seems, cannot completely deny that "much touted fallacy." She wants to be the true mother, the progenitor that Kate could not be for herself. She wants rebirth, this time without mother or father to bring it to a bad end:

> Jesus, is there no end to what people expect? Even now I expect a courier to whiz in on a scooter to say it's been a mistake; I'm crazy, I'm even thinking of the Resurrection and the stone pushed away, I want to lift her up and see the life and the blood coming back into her cheeks, I want time to be put back, I want it to be yesterday, to undo the unwanted crime that has been done. Useless. Nothing for it but fucking hymns.

Baba's graphic language here is all the more poignant because she realizes its futility. She has demonstrated that she "understands every piece of protocol and religion and hypocrisy that there was." Yet, though she has taken "up the cudgel against life," she is still unable to dismiss entirely the hope of salvation from "a world where help and pity did not forthcome." Kate is no different. She knows all too well that it is mothering and motherhood that have betrayed her. Twenty years ago she sought a physical remedy to the problem, choosing to be sterilized rather than face mothering again. At the end of *Girls in Their Married Bliss,* an alarmed and confused Baba visits the hospital after the surgery. It is a grim tableau:

> "Well," Baba said after some time, meaning, "What does it feel like?"

> "Well," Kate said, "at least I've eliminated the risk of making the same mistake again," and for some reason the words sent a chill through Baba's heart.

> "You've eliminated something," Baba said. Kate did

not stir, not flinch; she was motionless as the white bedpost. What was she thinking? What words were going on in her head? For what had she prepared herself? Evidently she did not know, for at that moment she was quite content, without a qualm in the world. It was odd for Baba to see Kate like that, all the expected responses were missing, the guilt and doubt and sadnesses, she was looking at someone of whom too much had been cut away, some important region that they both knew nothing about.

In a violent act close to self-mutilation, Kate has attempted to cut away all resemblance to the great betrayer. Sadly, however, the "Epilogue" dramatically demonstrates that Kate has not "eliminated" any of the "risk." After twenty years more of life and after the most extraordinary efforts to release or deny the effects and obligations of mothering, neither she nor Baba are able to reject entirely the claims of Irish maternity. Kate's operation is a real-life version of the playful surgeries of **"A Scandalous Woman,"** but the results are the same: "there would be nothing left but a shell . . . and one wouldn't be able to have babies or women's complaints ever."

O'Brien's complaint, then, is that Irish women cannot hope for life from their mothers, and they cannot hope to give life, in turn, to their daughters. Perhaps the solution to the problem of birth, to follow the author's own example, is exile—to seek "that further breach of waters" she discusses in **Mother Ireland.** But even this "rebirth" is not free from the ruinous effects of fathering and mothering. As Edna O'Brien admits, freedom is partial because the "leaving is conditional. The person you are, is anathema to the person you would like to be." Perhaps the truth, then, is that there is no safe place for women born to a country that offers no chance for health or happiness. If so, to be born in Ireland at all is the worst of luck.

Marilynne Robinson (review date 20 November 1988)

SOURCE: "A Colony of the Disgruntled," in *New York Times Book Review,* November 20, 1988, p. 11.

[*In the following review, Robinson offers a mixed assessment of* The High Road.]

Edna O'Brien is a prolific writer of short stories and novels, noted for the elegance of her prose. **The High Road,** her second novel in over a decade, is a series of more or less free-standing narratives, framed by opening and concluding scenes that declare certain large themes only developed by contrast or indirection in the intervening narratives.

The language here is often infused with an intense energy, but the form of the novel makes it difficult to know what these energies arise from or tend toward. Most of the stories concern expatriate and vacationing northern Europeans on a Spanish island, while the framing events invoke the earthy primitivity of the island itself, at least as the narrator perceives it.

The narrator, Anna, is a middle-aged, Anglicized Irishwoman, a writer or a scholar who has toured America lecturing on the sorrows of Irish history. She is the sort of person who finds the horses in Central Park more human than the people in the streets of New York. Emotionally destitute, she has sought out this island as a refuge. It is an artists' colony and resort, a place to which the civilized have brought their discontents for so long that the locals, while practiced at accommodating their expectations, are also a bit weary, a bit jaded, as any community colonized by the drunken, querulous and disgruntled of other nations must no doubt be. The nonconsecutive form of the novel puts usual notions of meaning in question, a strategy appropriate to disrupting conditioned responses to an entrenched convention. Anna is one among the legions who have for generations quartered themselves upon those they consider simple with the thought of being comforted and enlightened. *The High Road* describes how and why the consequences of this unarmed occupation are so notoriously sad.

Ms. O'Brien's rich prose is laid on the surface of her narrative like the flourishes of technical brilliance that fade last when the vision of an age begins to slide away. The emptiness at the core of this tale is not the Romantic isolation from which it borrows phrases and gestures, but a circumscribed, thoroughly contemporary malaise preoccupied with the muted deaths of minor and guarded hopes, comfortably endured in a landscape which, however beautiful, is not visionary but decorative.

Early in the novel Anna meets an Irish painter, in his cups, who gossips, expostulates, alliterates and alludes, until the character of the island and of the fiction itself is established. He mentions the name of the young island woman on whom the story will finally turn, Catalina, in religious and legendary contexts. He tells Anna that the church is built on the site where an Iberian moon goddess once had her shrine. He establishes the significance of the narrative's beginning on Easter morning by reciting a phrase from the Mass, "Resurrexi, et adhuc tecum sum." The story will be about regeneration through death.

He tells us, too, about members of the expatriate community—an American would-be Hemingway, seduced by his own powers of seduction and unable to set aside time to write, painters who produce landscapes of "untortured banality" to sell to American matrons. He himself paints an imitation Van Gogh, and copies his imitation. The level of aspiration is notably depressed among these artists. Their situation recalls the Romantics in Italy, Hemingway in Spain, Gauguin in Tahiti. Yet for these latter-day artists the properties of the creative life bear the same relation to real productivity that Miss Havisham's wedding cake bears to the joys of married life. Self-exile is a solution that has lost its marrow of problem, and has grown small and brittle.

Anna's interactions with other expatriates establish the narrator as one who transforms the honorable role of perceiver into intrusion or violation. For a while she shares a house with Charlotte, a morbidly private woman who nevertheless gives Anna a place to stay on the condition that her privacy should be respected. Anna thinks she recognizes in Charlotte a girl once prominent in London society, who suffered two disastrous marriages. She breaks into Charlotte's locked room, finds proof, is caught and sent packing. Staying at the home of an acquaintance, she accidentally starts a tape made by the woman's son as he committed suicide. She hears it out. Once again she is confronted and sent packing. Anna goes to the home of Catalina, the peasant girl by whom she has become fascinated, and finds her exposed in the embarrassments of her poverty, disheveled and fighting raucously with her father. Catalina forgives her failure of tact, more gracious than the others.

To Anna, Moorish Catalina suggests abandon and release. But she, it turns out, is modern, too, with a broken marriage, a dismal affair and a child whose paternity has been established by blood tests. She has read enough to have discovered an earth goddess, Gaia, and with her perhaps a willingness to be seduced by Anna, to be "eclipsed inside the womb of the world." It is characteristic of urban Western culture to consider its newest tolerance a recovery of the primordial, appropriately acted out among the earthy folk at the cultural margins. But their tryst causes outrage in her village, as Anna had reason to expect it would. The lavish respect accorded to the pretty gravity of peasant life vanishes when it is found to be severe at its heart. The Irish Van Gogh defaces village walls with the word "lesbos," in retaliation for its being painted on Catalina's family house. So much for unspoiled beauty.

Disaster comes of Anna's inability to let things be. While she rummages through experience for a salve to cure her own hurt soul, she never thinks what injuries she might inflict. The fetish, or trophy she carries away at the end is Catalina's bloody hair, "so vibrant, so alive it was as if her face still adhered to it." Her gloss on the text "resurrexi" would seem to be that her own angst is ended by the death of a young, generous, interesting woman. The concept of rebirth is as diminished as the concepts of art and of self-discovery.

There is a glancing allusion to the effect of Chernobyl on

the island. The book suggests a profound erosion under the flowery appearances of things, a more sinister intrusion into the world we profess to love. The old woman who makes Anna the gift of the bloody hair tells her, "to love one must learn to part with everything." The book suggests this is a lesson we may have learned too willingly and too well.

Kitti Carriker (essay date Spring 1989)

SOURCE: "Edna O'Brien's 'The Doll': A Narrative of Abjection," in *Notes on Modern Irish Literature,* Vol. 1, Spring, 1989, pp. 6-11.

[*In the following essay, Carriker analyzes O'Brien's "The Doll," in terms of the author's use of the doll as a means of communicating the abjection of the narrator of the story.*]

In Edna O'Brien's short story **"The Doll,"** the narrator and the doll stand in an uneasy juxtaposition which is exemplary of Freud's notion of "The Uncanny." The conflict of **"The Doll"** is centered in the question of the doll's subjectivity, and the story contains what Freud has called "a particularly favorable condition for awakening uncanny feelings." He discusses dolls as a significant element of childhood life, describing how children—like O'Brien's narrator—frequently maintain that their dolls are alive or that they themselves can make the inanimate dolls come to life. In conjunction with Freud's "Uncanny," [Julia] Kristeva's concepts of abjection, dejection, and displacement illuminate the narrator's crisis in **"The Doll."**

The narrator of **"The Doll"** is a woman who as a child received a doll each year for Christmas. The behavior of this unnamed child is like that of the children observed by Freud in "The Uncanny" who treat their dolls as living people, making no distinction between the living and the inanimate. For example not only do her dolls have names and living quarters but each has "special conversations . . . endearments, and . . . chastisements" as well. Her favorite is "the living representation of a princess . . . . a sizable one," and her description of it as "uncanny" is consistent in every detail with the characteristics named by Freud as specific to the sensation of uncanniness: "She was uncanny. We all agreed that she was almost lifelike and that with coaxing she might speak . . . the gaze in her eyes [was] so fetching that we often thought she was not an inanimate creature, that she had a soul and a sense of us. Conversations with her were the most intense and the most incriminating of all."

After several of her classmates see the splendid doll, lying in state in its silver box, it becomes "the cynosure of all," and the children beg that it may be used to represent the Virgin Mary in the Nativity scene which is being assembled for the school's Christmas pageant. The child has mixed feelings about volunteering her doll for the event, yet she is pleased by the doll's popularity and success. At the program, the doll outshines the faltering pupils; they are subject to the human failing of forgetting their lines while the inanimate doll is protected by the composure of the ideal.

Representing the Virgin Mary, the lovely doll is like the ornate and finely finished figures described by Susan Stewart in her comparison of the modern dollhouse to the crèche of the Middle Ages [in *On Longing: Narratives of the Miniature, the Gigantic, the Souvenir, the Collection,* Johns Hopkins University Press, 1984]. She explains the tradition of "locating the sacred within the secular landscape. At the heart of such crèches are the abstract mythologized figures of the Nativity, but as one moves out from that location, the landscape becomes more familiar." The doll in O'Brien's story is unusual in her sacred role because she was initially created to be a child's toy or an object of decorative display—not to represent one of the mythologized Nativity figures. Her placement at "the heart" of the Nativity provides an interesting example of the juxtaposition of secular and sacred, an inversion of the movement described by Stewart. Here the secular is located within the sacred landscape.

In **"The Doll,"** this inversion signifies the displacement of abjection. The doll, the secular representative standing in for the sacred, exemplifies what Kristeva calls [in *Powers of Horror: An Essay on Abjection,* translated by Leon S. Roudiez, Columbia University Press, 1982] the purified abject. She says that the history of religious catharsis is likewise a history of purifying the abject and that the artistic experience is rooted in the abject. Posing as the Virgin Mary, the finely crafted doll is both an art object and a religious symbol. In exchange for the doll's privileged treatment, however, the girl is "dejected" and separated. She is the one who "strays instead of getting [her] bearings, desiring, belonging, or refusing." She suffers loss and displacement at every level. In her family, for example, she is the only one of her sisters to receive these "miraculous" dolls each year from an eccentric friend of the family who has whimsically chosen the narrator as her favorite. The child is victimized by her own good fortune; for her older sisters "of course, were jealous and riled against the unfairness."

At school, too, the girl is outcast. She remembers that the teacher "harbored a dislike for me" and, rather inexplicably, "referred to me as 'It.'" Perversely, the teacher, who like everyone else is enamored of the doll, objectifies the child. The doll and the child change places—the doll becoming a subject, the child an object. After the Christmas pageant, the strangely tyrannical teacher refuses to return the child's doll, a loss which makes the girl feel "berserk." After requesting the doll's return several times to no avail, the child must resign herself to the teacher's unkindness. When she finally leaves the narrow life of the village for boarding school in the city, she hopes to forget the schoolteacher, to "be free of her forever . . . forget the doll, forget most of what happened, or at least remember it without a quiver." She believes that she can leave behind her anguish over her stolen doppelganger, the lost doll. Having decided to leave home and develop a new identity, she is once more separated from her environment, the third level at which she is displaced. She says to herself, "I am on the run from them. I have fled. I live in a city. I am cosmopolitan."

Feeling "far from those I am with, and far from those I have left," the narrator is the stray, the figure without bearings. She is without a sense of belonging in her new situation as much as she was in the old. Yet she is, to use Kristeva's description of the abject, "not without laughter—since laughing is a way of placing or displacing abjection." The dinners and parties hosted by the narrator of O'Brien's story are filled with this sort of laughter. Musing on the wary detachment of her new friends, she observes that their talk takes the form of pleasant, drifting wandering hallucinations. She does not share with these new acquaintances the intense and special conversations which she once shared with her doll. Instead, their desultory chatter resembles the distracted and detached speech of what Kristeva calls the blank subject, the non-object, "he through whom the abject exists." This subject moves about in a daze of fear that "permeates all words of the language with nonexistence, and with a hallucinatory ghostly glimmer." The language of abjection does not retain the property of naming and describing experience. If language itself has been permeated by nonexistence, then it is no surprise that the subjects who utter such a language stray in their search for significance and meaningful existence. This eerie mode of communication is missing one crucial factor, the capacity to "ceaselessly confront that otherness, a burden both repellent and repelled, a deep well of memory that is unapproachable and intimate: the abject."

The narrator realizes that her discourse and that of her friends does not address the self and does not confront otherness. Issues of identity and personal history have no place in their lively meandering conversations but remain submerged in the "deep well of memory," camouflaged by the laughter that conceals abjection: "None of us ever says where we come from or what haunts us. Perhaps we are bewildered or ashamed." She herself, for example, is still haunted and bewildered by the unforgotten princess doll, which is for her the repelled and neglected other, the absent body that now maintains an existence entirely separate from hers, stuck away somewhere among the schoolteacher's belongings. She is ashamed of the jealousy which this miniature representation of her own fate evoked in her childhood acquaintances, and she has consigned this emotion to the unapproachable regions of her consciousness.

When she returns home for a relative's funeral, she is forced to confront her own intimate history. The familial responsibility of making the funeral arrangements falls to her; and she must visit the village undertaker, named Denis, who is the son of the once hated teacher. When she goes to pay her aunt's final debt, the dead body that she sees in Denis' care is not that of her aunt—it is her own. She encounters the metaphorical interment of a small part of herself, her own abandoned double, with whom she comes face to face at last; and what is "fixed up," paid off, fully dealt with at this final reckoning is her lingering emotional aversion to its existence. When she spies the confiscated doll in the overstuffed china cabinet, she is shocked to see that it has defied the immutability of its idealized body by aging. It now resembles that most extreme and abhorrent form of the abject, the corpse: ". . . if dolls can age, it certainly had. Gray and moldy, the dress and cloak are as a shroud, and I thought, If I was to pick her up she would disintegrate." The doll has retained her distinctive status for old times' sake but lost her initial luster and all the stimulating attributes which had made her seem like a living subject.

When Denis sees that she has noticed the artifact, he tells her how much his mother, who has since died, admired the doll; and he boasts that he does not let his children play with it ("thereby implying that she was a sacred object, a treasured souvenir"). But the very thought of how both she and her doll were misused by the older woman gives the narrator a chill. Even from an adult perspective, she feels certain that the woman "kept the doll out of perversity, out of pique and jealousy. In some ways she had divined that I would have a life far away from them and adventures such as she herself would never taste." This envy informs the son's behavior toward her as well as the mother's. She senses that Denis is filled with curious notions of what her life is now like, and she knows that the reality of her experiences must differ widely from his expectations. Their encounter ends awkwardly because she is not what "he imagined me to be."

After her visit to the undertaker's, she feels reduced to "wretchedness." The sight of the captive, shrouded, corpse-like doll gives her the sudden "conviction of not having yet lived," of dying the same slow death that the doll has. Stewart says that, as a mirror of the world, the miniature "is the antithesis of the 'self-reflecting' mirror, for the mirror's image exists only at the moment the subject projects it." The miniature, on the other hand, "projects an eternalized future-past" and "consoles in its status as an 'always there.'" For O'Brien's narrator, however, the image of the doll fails to give any consolation. Instead of projecting the past and the future as "always there," it represents the narrator's past and future—times that are *never* there. It has responded to the passage of time and has existed in the reality of the present. Rather than feeling consoled by her miniature self-image, the narrator recognizes the doll's loss of vibrancy and fears that such early potential may be forever unrealized in her own life as well.

Far from the days when her favorite doll was "the cynosure of all," the narrator has become cynical and wary of the contradictions of life. More like a mortal than an idealized object, the doll comes to represent only her abjection.

She overcomes the sensation of nausea by admiring the "singular and wondrous" stars, which symbolize to her some hope against the "currently and stupidity" of the world. They seem to her "an enticement to the great heavens . . . one day I would reach them and be absorbed into their glory." The element of euphoria in her vision is analogous to the correlation between the sublime and the abject identified by Kristeva: the sublime "expands us, overstrains us, and causes us to be both *here,* as dejects, and *there,* as others and sparkling." Kristeva's here/there formula of abjection/sublimation can be used to explain the narrator's dichotomous stance. Standing on the sidewalk (i.e., here), she is a deject, made nauseous and frustrated by her memories and by the world's abjection. Looking to the sky (i.e., there), the anguish caused by her brief distasteful reunion with the doll and the teacher (in the form of the undertaker) is alleviated. The unpalatable otherness of the doll is sublimated by the sparkling otherness of the stars.

Kristeva says that "The abject is edged with the sublime" and describes this relation in a descriptive passage which approaches the visionary. For her the abject, as a non-object, is closely related to the sublime: "For the sublime has no object either. When the starry sky, a vista of open seas or a stained glass window shedding purple beams fascinate me, there is a cluster of meaning, of colors, of words, of caresses, there are light touches, scents, sighs, cadences that arise, shroud me, carry me away, and sweep me beyond the things that I see, hear, or think." She then finds herself removed from the location of the "I" to what she calls a "secondary universe." In this secondary universe, delight sublimates loss. It is appropriate that the subject of abjection turn to an experience of transport as an alternate to the complexity of lived reality, for Kristeva emphasizes that the deject is more concerned with questions of place than with questions of being: "'*Where* am I?' instead of '*Who* am I?'" In accordance with this priority, the narrator, at the conclusion of **"The Doll,"** thinks only of leaving the small oppressive town for somewhere else: "Tomorrow I shall be gone. . . I had not lost the desire to escape or the strenuous habit of hoping."

Having endured an unnerving confrontation with the abject, she seeks to escape from the "here" of her childhood home into the "secondary universe" of the stars or the "there" of the city. She expresses the need of the abject, the tireless straying "in order to be" by which she is saved. Even though she realizes her own lack of groundedness, she is still compelled, in the true mode of the deject, to "constantly question [her] solidity." A positive result of this questioning is that the abject may become the sublime; the "deep well of memory" which contains the shunned and hidden history of abjection may be transformed into the "raptures of bottomless memory" where the sublime object is finally dissolved. Thus O'Brien's narrator, having relinquished her hold over the abjected doll, is herself finally liberated from its uncanny power.

José Lanters (review date Spring 1991)

SOURCE: A review of *Lantern Slides,* in *World Literature Today,* Vol. 65, No. 2, Spring, 1991, pp. 303-4.

[*In the following review,* Lanters *provides an unfavorable assessment of* Lantern Slides.]

Edna O'Brien's outspokenness on the subject of women and sexuality gained her a certain notoriety in Ireland in the early 1960s, when such matters were still considered taboo. Since then, Irish writing has come a long way, although one would hardly gather as much from O'Brien's latest collection of stories. The title **Lantern Slides** itself is suggestive of former times, although the stories are not overtly set in the past, and the themes are familiar from O'Brien's earlier work: loneliness, madness brought on by jealousy and sexual repression, guilt over strained relations between parents and children, women coping with ending love affairs. At least half the stories, mostly set in rural villages, seem positively nostalgic for the bad old repressive days out of which Irish writers used to get so much mileage, but even those set in modern Dublin have a whiff of mothballs about them, as if the characters in them had somehow mentally remained stuck in an earlier time.

The book's epigraph from Thomas Mann implies that it was O'Brien's intention to depict the human condition rather than specific people in specific places, something which is also suggested in the first story, **"'Oft in the Stilly Night,'"** which portrays what goes on behind the sleepy façades of an Irish backwater: "Perhaps your own village is much the same, perhaps everywhere is." Somehow, in relation to these stories, the generalization fails to be convincing.

In this light, some of the selections are even slightly embarrassing; they might almost be parodic, except that there is no hint that they are to be taken that way. The destructive gossip in **"The Widow"** is like something out of Brinsley MacNamara's *Valley of the Squinting Windows*; in **"A Demon"** the reader is asked to believe that both the nuns in a girl's convent school and the parents who take her home because she is "poorly" can ignore or deny a pregnancy which is so advanced that she goes into labor the same night; and if we are to be made to feel sympathy for the plight of a gay village shopkeeper, it is not clear why he should have to be quite such a pathetically stereotypical homosexual who cooks and sews, goes in for amateur dramatics ("He was very convincing when he acted the women or the girls"), and ends up getting drunk with a famous actor and his friend from Dublin, the three of them dressing up in pantomime drag before being arrested by the village police. For a variety of reasons, these stories do not quite ring true.

A few of the pieces are notable for their language, especially **"Brother,"** a rambling monologue in which a woman reveals the sordid intimacy of her relationship with her brother and her murderous intentions toward his wife-to-be. Unfortunately, *Lantern Slides* provides all too few such memorable instances.

Gale Harris (review date Fall 1992)

SOURCE: "Bearing the Burden of Love," in *Belles Lettres,* Fall, 1992, pp. 2-3.

[*In the following review, Harris offers a laudatory appraisal of* Time and Tide.]

In the prologue of **Time and Tide,** we learn that the protagonist, Nell, has lost one son to a "watery" death and is terrified that her hastily spoken words have forced a permanent breach with her surviving son. Throughout the rest of Edna O'Brien's latest novel, Nell is dominated by her parents, husband, lovers, and children. She moves from a degrading marriage through a series of damaging love affairs, experiences a terrifying acid trip, suffers a nervous breakdown, loses her mother and her home, and watches her eldest son succumb to drug abuse. Although Nell struggles' through each of these situations, she is never prepared for the next catastrophe, which is all too likely to occur. In the hands of an ordinary writer, this scenario might produce nothing more than a depiction of yet another woman victimized by people, fate, and her own paralysis.

But Edna O'Brien is not an ordinary writer. She is as rare as the exquisite possessions that Nell, at one stage in her life, collects from market stalls and antique shops: "velvet cushions, goblets threaded with gold, cranberry glasses that seemed to have the essence of the fruits secreted within." O'Brien transforms what could have been a depressing or, at best, maudlin tale into a revelation. I have found no other writer who so precisely and sensitively describes the harrowing burden borne by people who need to love deeply.

For Nell, who craves more intimacy than her parents or husband would allow, love has become virtually synonymous with the fear of loss. She is afraid to ask her abusive husband what has gone wrong with their marriage. She is reluctant to take lovers after her divorce because she is "afraid of being inadequate to the situation, the room somehow too shabby and she herself too emotional." She is afraid to express her feelings to her mother, who might say something that Nell could never forget or bear without mortification. She is "dangerously enchanted" with her sons, and her greatest fears are of being separated from them.

O'Brien exposes the anxiety that underlies love and weighs tentative happiness with sorrow. She describes how it drives a person to live automatically without even tasting one's food or to walk the streets in hope that one can leave pain behind in a park or launderette. The power of that fear also can intensify moments when the imminent chasm of separation is temporarily avoided.

> They laughed then, the pent-up laughter of anxiety, the laughter of people who have been estranged, and glad of this abandon, they laughed loudly, shrilly, exuberantly—eddies of laughter everywhere, issuing out like burps of water; laughter on the mirror's front, on the hairy underlay which needs cheering, along the bannister sheer from their sliding; laughter in the old fire grate and lurking in the corner where the new occupants, whoever they were, might catch some hint of it, like a whinny; laughter that was loud, oh yes, loud and feverish, but not quite friendly, laughter that said, "How bitter life is . . . how bitter life is"; but laughter all the same.

It requires courage to dissect a character's weaknesses thoroughly and a penetrating humanity to make us care about someone who becomes utterly appeasing in order to retain love. O'Brien succeeds because she allows us to discover with Nell the tenacious force with which human beings hold onto their lives, a force that can become something courageous and illuminating. Even as Nell stands on the brink of greater, unforseen tragedy, she faces her future with the hope of a survivor.

> Far from being downcast at having lost everything, she felt elated, felt that these clouds and this [statue of a] rising woman were a sign to her, a challenge and a reminder that she was a woman, too, that her hopes had not died, had merely been put to sleep and were waiting to be ignited by some new, some magic intervention. Yes, a chapter had just begun.

O'Brien has the gift that Nell, as a successful editor for a publishing firm, seeks in the manuscripts that she reads, the "sacred breath of otherness that she believed to be essential." O'Brien has breathed an uncanny life into the story of one woman's struggles through the kind of intense creative process that Nell describes to a prospective novelist.

> You have to be near to [your story] to tell it, and then you have to go very far away from it to give it that enchantment that distance bestows . . . take the little motif from under your pillow, or from under the linen that you keep in your oak chest, where the wood-lice scramble, and give it away, then sit with your story, your rich, raw, bleak, relentless story, the one you are so near to, too near to, and moisten it with every drop of pain and suppuration that you have, until in the end it glistens with the exquisite glow of a freshly dredged pearl.

It is not only O'Brien's acute depiction of Nell's inner life that burnishes the glow of this story. Rich portraits of Nell's outer world also grace page after page of the book. Her experiences are interwoven with descriptions of crammed market stalls in London, the fading golden light of Italian evenings, and the traffic of tugboats along the river Thames. Some passages add a fresh luster to familiar scenes of charmed domesticity, whereas others have a hallucinatory quality that reflects Nell's perilous emotional state. O'Brien's prose is full of images that affect one like the memory of chiming bells—bright, resonant echoes that veil even the most bitter pain with enchantment.

O'Brien compares certain words to a baptism, "a presence within absence, and, yes, within pain, within death." Through the power of her words in *Time and Tide,* we are privileged to see a life transformed, to witness a woman gathering the unbearable burden of love and carrying it to a sanctuary devoid of consolation. When I read the last lines of this book, I found myself raising a hand in an involuntary, wordless salute. It was a salute to Nell, to Edna O'Brien, and to all the women who guide us on this painful passage from birth to death, who consecrate the struggles that we meet along the way, and who teach us to cherish whatever reminds us that we are alive.

Patricia Craig (review date 18 September 1992)

SOURCE: "Against Ample Adversities," in *Times Literary Supplement,* September 18, 1992, p. 23.

[*In the following review, Craig provides a mixed evaluation of* Time and Tide.]

"Fear death by water." This injunction from *The Waste Land* must strike a chord with Edna O'Brien, whose earliest heroine—in *The Country Girls*—lost her mother in a boating ac-

cident; now, eleven novels on, it's the heroine's son who goes down with the Marchioness (as we read on the opening page of *Time and Tide*). This central disaster is prefaced by a lot of subsidiary disasters; the whole drift, of *Time and Tide,* is to show what a star-crossed Irishwoman can endure, without going under.

What is wrong with Nell, a one-time Irish country girl and mother-of-two? She has many resources, yet seems impelled to get the maximum poignancy out of life. She suffers to the full. Some kind of ancestral acrimony seems to have warped her prospects. At the start of *Time and Tide,* she is living on the outskirts of London, with two small sons and a terrible husband, the kind of spouse who specializes in mental cruelty, cold as any Casaubon and deeply unhinged. The family farm in Ireland isn't a refuge, containing as it does a virulent old couple—chickens' innards in the kitchen and a sour and restrictive Catholicism pervading the place. Presently Nell is separated from her husband, then divorced; the children stay with her, but only after a bitter struggle to gain custody of them. She goes to work for a publisher and rents a small Victorian house. The boys grow older and attend a boarding school. A holiday abroad proves unsatisfactory. Being far too tremulous and open-hearted for her own good, Nell is soon in the throes of an infatuation—once again, with a man as insufferable as her husband, though in a different way. This one says things like, "Transubstantiate, Sister", and leaves pretentious jottings about the place: "Life is a habit of walking and talking, I have a habit of walking towards death." Such pseudo-profundity has a period flavour, it's true, and it may be used to evoke a particular decade (the 1960s); however, in the hands of Edna O'Brien, these embarrassing utterances seem to come without a satiric, or indeed any kind of critical, undertone. One could wish to be sure that she understands their awfulness.

The problem with O'Brien's writing has always been one of excess baggage, all the heartfelt or sorrowful or fanciful trappings with which she sees fit to lumber herself. They are back again in *Time and Tide.* All of which obscures, but doesn't obliterate, the charm and robustness which marked her earliest novels; parts of *Time and Tide* are wonderfully clear-toned and powerfully imagined—for example, the section towards the end, when the pleasure-boat has sunk and relatives have been summoned, achieves a genuinely harrowing intensity. And the opening chapters, in which the wife's wrongs are recounted more or less dispassionately, recall the picturesque adversities articulated by another specialist in woman's vicissitudes, Barbara Comyns (though Comyns is more luminous, less fraught). But throughout the bulk of O'Brien's narrative, clarity gets lost in a fuzz of emotions.

Nell's story continues: in a moment of lust, she throws herself at a Russian named Boris, and shortly afterwards finds Boris and his girlfriend installed in her house, where they inadvertently cause a gas explosion which puts Nell in hospital with burns. Being in hospital renders her unable to earn money, and she loses the house when she can't pay the rent. So it goes on. No one comes to the aid of Nell. Bouts of madness, brushes with drugs, all kinds of guilt and agitation: these are among the troubles we find afflicting a heroine who isn't deficient in acumen or allure—just luckless. Her life falls into no particular shape—it merely continues, as most lives do. And, as a kind of back-up to the novelist's sense of things being asked, innumerable passers-by are allotted a single appearance in the book, to expose the bees in their bonnets and promptly fade out. Nell is constantly beset by strangers, or semi-strangers, all bent on disclosing fragments of their past. "How she gloated, how she warmed to it, pressing closer to Nell at each saucy admission. . . . Had smacked her, oh yes, made her black and blue. . .". It isn't a satisfactory means of eking out a rather meager storyline. You are irked by the abundance of arbitrary encounters. Less embellishment, or a more rigorous approach, wouldn't have gone amiss. At one point Nell, in her capacity as publishers' editor, is advising a would-be author on how to proceed, "sit with your story", she writes, "your rich, raw, bleak, relentless story . . . and moisten it with every drop of pain and suppuration that you have, until in the end it glistens with the exquisite glow of a freshly dredged pearl". You can see how Edna O'Brien, for all her undoubted gifts, perceptiveness, imagination, alertness and so forth, has been led astray; and you want to chime in with some contrary advice, such as: "Then tone it down."

Robert E. Hosmer, Jr. (review date 23 October 1992)

SOURCE: "Down & Out in Life," in *Commonweal,* October 23, 1992, pp. 25-6.

[In the following review, Hosmer offers a commendatory assessment of Time and Tide.*]*

Like Milton's elegy "Lycidas," Edna O'Brien's latest novel, ***Time and Tide,*** is a haunting water poem, a heartfelt elegy engendered by the two most powerful human emotions: love and loss. Only here the waters swirl not just in a mighty river but also within the human amnion, for this is a book about what is likely the most dangerous of human activities: mothering. O'Brien's achievement in ***Time and Tide*** is so extraordinary that this eleventh novel may well eclipse the previous ten, even her first, ***The Country Girls*** (1960).

Time and Tide is the story of Nell Steadman, a middle-aged woman from the west of Ireland, long resident in London. Nell first appears musing as she tries frantically to prevent her second son's departure from home: "What could she do

now to retrieve things. She thought of rushing down the stairs to his bedroom with as normal a manner as artifice can manage and asking, 'Would you like a cup of tea?'" His departure, which she cannot forestall, is the last in a series of painful, unresolved separations. In the course of the narrative, which moves with effortless inferiority from past to present, we learn Nell's story: an early marriage to Walter, an older, tyrannical, and abusive man whose idea of a Christmas gift is a postcard inscribed "Happy Nothing"; her separation from him and the brutal battle for custody of their two sons, Paddy and Tristan; her chaotic life as a single mother caring for two children with no support from their father; and finally the story of her losing both sons, one to the Thames, the other to a young, pregnant woman.

Nell is a classically divided consciousness, torn between restraint and reckless abandon, between self-immolation and self-indulgence, between death and life. At her very center lies a most acute absence: Nell has never had the kind of vital, osmotic, and nurturing connection with her mother that characterizes the original, amniotic bonding between mother and child. Her dealings with her mother are bruising battles: with extraordinary aptness, Nell converts experience to resonant metaphor when she selects an egg, "shell-less, soft as any placenta, its bruisedness a resemblance of us," as emblematic of their relationship. The two women agree about nothing, and the level of their compact is mortal. When Nell finally summons the courage to tell her mother how she feels, the results are catastrophic for both.

Nell longs for a man to rescue her: she is ever vulnerable, sometimes ludicrously so, as when she falls for a man who inscribes "Let us see the Northern lights together" on a matchbook cover. One man—whether actor, director, greengrocer, shopkeeper, or son—will do it, must do it, she feels. She thinks "in secret of a man who would come and whisk her to altitudes of happiness." Yet, though men continually fail her, she clings to a sacral-romantic vision ("it was as if she had learned nothing and still believed in transubstantiation through another"), until she suffers a complete nervous collapse. That illness marks the beginning of a painful shift in consciousness as Nell begins to learn the lesson Anita Brookner has discerned in O'Brien's fiction, "no compensation for the loss of the mother is possible . . . all the men in the world could not replace the original closeness." Nell Steadman's pain is exacerbated by the absence of that original closeness: she seeks what she has never had, and the results, at least in the short term, are disastrous. Marriage fails. Lovers fail. Children fail. God fails. What's left?

Time and Tide is a fiction of female development. Nell Steadman comes to perceive more about her mother as she plumbs the depths of her own experience; her own lately held conclusion about the nature of motherhood shocks both Nell and the reader: "What pretty names we give to the carnivorousness that is called mother." Near the end of the novel, as Nell begins to pull things together, she articulates the great questions she now knows have preoccupied her: "What does one do with grief? What does one do with hate?" At the very end, Nell experiences a Joycean moment: "Everything radiant for a moment, as if she reached, or was reached, beyond the boundaries of herself." The pain and the pleasure of the text reside in our intimate access not only to Nell Steadman's suffering but to her final affirmation:

> "'I can bear it,' she said, and looked around at the air so harmless, so flaccid, and so still, a stillness such as she had not known since it had happened, or maybe ever. In the stillness there was silence, but there was no word for that yet because it was so new; pale sanctuary devoid at last of all consolations.

> "'You can bear it,' the silence said, because that is all there is, this now that then, this present that past, this life this death, and the involuntary shudder that keeps reminding us we are alive."

This novel could only have been written by a woman, and one feels that O'Brien has more than a speaking acquaintance with the surging forces that shape this story. After assuming custody of her children, Nell works for a publisher, often taking manuscripts home with her; one evening, as she plows through a pile she happens on one of particular interest. To the writer, Nell offers advice that O'Brien herself seems to have taken to heart: "You have to be near to it to tell it, and then you have to go very far away from it to give it that enchantment that distance bestows, the infallibility of the gods . . . no one else can do it but you . . . Think only of big things, Millie, big, sad, lonely, glorious, archetypal things."

James Joyce described his play *Exiles* as "an extravagant excursion into forbidden territory"; Edna O'Brien's latest novel is that and more. Read *Time and Tide* and know what it is to surrender to a courageous and honest writer of fiction.

Kiera O'Hara (essay date Summer 1993)

SOURCE: "Love Objects: Love and Obsession in the Stories and Edna O'Brien," in *Studies in Short Fiction,* Vol. 30, No. 3, Summer, 1993, pp. 317-25.

[*In the following essay, O'Hara surveys O'Brien's handling of obsessive love in her short stories.*]

I am obsessed quite irrationally by the notion of love . . . ,"

writes Edna O'Brien. "It's an obsession and I know it's very limiting. At the same time it's what I feel truest and most persistently about, and therefore it's the thing that I have to write about" [Patrick Rafroidi and Maurice Harmon, editors, *The Irish Novel in Our Time,* Publications de L'Université de Lille III, 1975-76]. And write about it she does—the obsession, that is, perhaps more than the love.

A reading of O'Brien's stories, beginning with the 1969 collection, *The Love Object,* reveals that several of her characters share their author's obsession with "the notion of love." Yet between these women and their love objects there is so little real connection, so little love. For them, obsession with love seems to stand in the way of its attainment.

That O'Brien's protagonists should find themselves in this bind is perhaps not surprising. Obsession—a "persistent or inescapable preoccupation with an idea or emotion"—seems to involve not only compulsion but insatiability. A person obsessed, whether with an *idée fixe* or a person, seems disinclined, or perhaps unable, to feed her obsession to the point of satiation. Obsession, like addiction, sets in motion a self-fueling and potentially endless cycle. Love and obsession are, in a sense, opposites. Obsession feeds on itself, is self-absorbed, while love reaches beyond the self toward authentic contact with another. In the stories considered here there *are* moments of genuine love and compassion. But these occur only as their protagonists free themselves, or are torn, from the grip of their obsession.

"Irish Revel," one of O'Brien's early stories from *The Love Object,* pictures what might be called the birth of the obsession. It opens with a young country girl, Mary, making her way by bicycle to town. She has been invited to a party at the home of Mrs. Rogers, one of her "betters," and welcomes the ride as an opportunity to entertain in solitude her treasured memories of John Roland, the young painter she met two years earlier, also while visiting Mrs. Rogers's house. Perhaps, magically, he will be there again.

Soon after her arrival at the party, she realizes not only that her dream of seeing John is a groundless fantasy, but also that she has only been invited to serve guests, clean up, and add color to the affair. She takes shelter in daydreaming again of John and remembers a ride she took with him on his bicycle: "They did not talk for miles; she had his stomach encased in the delicate and frantic grasp of a girl in love and no matter how far they rode they seemed always to be riding into a golden haze" [*Love Objects*]. She then recalls his calling her "Sweet Mary" and remembers his explanation that "he could not love her, because he already loved his wife and children. . . ."

At the close of **"Irish Revel,"** Mary returns home burdened with her fruitless hopes and crushed by the ordinariness and crudity of the party. She stops briefly for a view of the countryside from a hill above her home and surveys it in a way that clearly echoes Joyce's language in "The Dead" [Grace Eckley, *Edna O'Brien,* Bucknell University Press, 1974]. However, instead of the falling snow that Gabriel Conroy views from his hotel window, a snow that softens the harsh outlines of the physical world and suggests gentle acceptance, Mary witnesses an unforgiving frost:

> The poor birds could get no food, as the ground was frozen hard. Frost was general all over Ireland; frost like a weird blossom on the branches, on the riverbank from which Long John Salmon leaped in his great, hairy nakedness, on the plough left out all winter; frost on the stony fields, and on all the slime and ugliness of the world. [*Love Object*]

Despair surrounds her on all sides, from the frozen, unyielding landscape to the equally grim vista of her family's cottage, evoking as it does the specter of a dead-end life: "She was at the top of the hill now, and could see her own house, like a little white box at the end of the world, waiting to receive her."

In her response to the despair of her situation, Mary prefigures numerous O'Brien protagonists: "If only I had a sweetheart, something to hold on to, she thought, as she cracked some ice with her high heel and watched the crazy splintered pattern it made." This clutching to a sweetheart as an escape from a desperate situation forms one strand of a "crazy splintered pattern" of obsessional dramas into which subsequent O'Brien protagonists weave themselves. Pia Mellody defines addiction, a condition that, like obsession, involves "a persistent or inescapable preoccupation," as "any process used to avoid or take away intolerable reality" [John Bradshaw, *Healing the Shame that Binds You,* Health Communications, 1988]. In Mary's search for relief from intolerable pain, the addiction to a love object is born. And, as with other O'Brien women, the object chosen is one who is both bathed in "a golden haze" and beyond the protagonist's reach.

The title of O'Brien's story, **"The Love Object,"** seems to suggest awareness on the part of its author that there is something inherently contradictory or at least problematic in the notion of a "love object"—perhaps an acknowledgment that love objects are more often the objects of obsession or addiction than of love. But the narrator evinces no irony in her account. She describes the man who will become her lover— "The love object. Elderly. Blue eyes. Khaki hair. . ."—and the progress of their affair, straightforwardly [*Love Object*].

There is little discernible love in the affair but a good deal of passionate sex. The narrator's obsessiveness comes into view when her lover ends the relationship with the explanation, "I adore you, but I'm not in love with you. . . ." She

relates a period following the breakup in which she drinks heavily, doesn't sleep, hatches plots of vengeance, and considers suicide. Then a change somehow occurs. She has, it seems, forgiven him: "I thought of him and my children in the same instant, their little foibles became his: my children telling me elaborate lies about their sporting feats, his slight puffing when we climbed steps and his trying to conceal it." Perhaps, thinks the reader, this signals the narrator's release of her love object. But her next words rule out this possibility: "It was then I think that I really fell in love with him . . . It rose like sap within me, it often made me cry, the fact that he could not benefit from it!"

When her former lover proposes meeting again from time to time as friends, the narrator says that she "neither welcomed nor dreaded the thought. It would not make any difference to how I felt." What becomes clear is that whatever change her feelings for the man have undergone, there has been no real letting go. The narrator describes lying in bed at night waiting for her lover to return: "I mean the real he, not the man who confronts me from time to time across a cafe table, but the man that dwells somewhere within me."

Like Mary in **"Irish Revel,"** this woman seeks a prop against the void, against the threat of a life with no meaning and no future. Like Mary, she chooses a painful something over a more painful nothing. While Mary dwells in recollections of a long-departed visitor, the narrator of **"The Love Object"** clutches to her former lover through apparent forgiveness: "I suppose you wonder," she concludes,

> why I torment myself like this with details of his presence but I need it, I cannot let go of him now, because if I did all our happiness and my subsequent pain—I cannot vouch for his—will all have been nothing, and a nothing is a dreadful thing to hold on to.

Eleanor, in **"Baby Blue,"** a story from O'Brien's 1978 collection, *The Fanatic Heart,* is left with a nothing to hold on to when her anguished-over love object kills himself. The bulk of the story has Eleanor suspended in the tortuous and almost violent hope that Jay, her lover, will leave his wife, while he repeatedly promises to do so, and repeatedly falls into vacillation. Eleanor refuses to recognize that, in all probability, Jay's ambivalence will never be resolved and she gives her all to a ferocious competition with his wife. When she finally does realize that Jay will probably not end his marriage, she writes him a burning letter of condemnation. It is shortly after receiving the letter that he commits suicide.

As the story ends, Eleanor takes a walk near the graveyard where he is buried. A carnival is setting up its tents, and she tries to take in the scene and the life it holds. She notes how "schoolchildren with no thought of death" pursue their adventures at the edge of the death place where she will take her final parting from her deceased lover. Eleanor feels a moment of tenderness for the unknown people who occupy the tents, for the temporariness of their (and all) existence: "The caravans had arrived, the women were getting out their artificial flowers, their china plates, and their bits of net curtain, to set up yet again their temporary dwellings." This tenderness stays with her as she stands at Jay's grave site. It is not a grandiose feeling; in fact she barely recognizes that she is feeling it. Perhaps because the finality of death forces a more profound experience of absence, Eleanor's tenderness here does not cloak a deeper obsessional strategy for continued possession of a lover figure, as did that of the narrator in **"The Love Object."** She experiences a compassion that is not *particular* to him or to their involvement, but that *encompasses* him and his imperfections:

> It will pass, she thought, going from grave to grave, and unconsciously and almost mundanely she prayed for the living, prayed for the dead, then prayed for the living again, went back to find the tomb where his name was, and prayed for all those who were in boxes alone or together above or below ground, all those unable to escape their afflicted selves.

Eleanor is one of those who dwell "in boxes alone" while Mary in **"Irish Revel"** shares her "little white box at the end of the world" with her family. Both contemplate the seeming inevitability of an afflicted life. Consolation, for Eleanor, comes as obsession gives way to compassion for the afflictions of others.

Concern for the well-being of another is also the means by which Nell, the protagonist of **"Ways"** (also from *The Fanatic Heart*) derails a familiar obsessive pattern. Nell is a touring poet from Ireland who stops in Vermont to do a reading. There she strikes up an immediate friendship with Jane, the woman at whose home she stays during her visit. Jane is attentive to Nell's needs—she keeps "a beautiful silence on the way to the reading, allowing Nell to do her deep breathing and memorize her poems"—and strikes Nell as a gentle, unassuming, and generous person.

The day after Nell's reading, as she and Jane take a walk, Jane shows Nell a picture of her husband, which she keeps in a locket around her neck. He is "gaunt and pensive, very much the type Nell is drawn toward. At once she feels in herself some premonition of a betrayal." When Jane tells Nell that she would like Dan, her husband, Nell becomes uneasy:

> "Why would I like him?" Nell says, picturing the face of the man that started out of the locket. All

of a sudden Nell has a longing not to leave as planned, at six o'clock, for New York, but to stay and meet him.

> "Why don't I stay till tomorrow?" she says as casually as she can.

Nell has identified Dan as a love object—someone who can electrify the atmosphere of life with magic. After her conversation with Jane, Nell goes to a general store in town: "She goes inside and buys rashly. Yes, she is curious. Already she has decided on her wardrobe for tonight, and resolves to be timid, in her best sky-blue georgette dress." She leaves the store having purchased gifts for Dan and Jane's children.

When she meets Dan in person, Nell's intuition of possible electricity is confirmed. Jane introduces them and "he nods. There is something in that nod that is significant. It is too offhand. Nell sees him look at her with his lids lowered, and she sees him stiffen when his wife says that their guest will stay overnight. . . ." Into this charged atmosphere Jane volunteers a simple story, delivered somewhat shyly, about taking a trip to London with a blind aunt, "and remarking to Nell how she saw everything so much more clearly simply by having had to describe it to her aunt." Nell suddenly excuses herself and hurries to her room where she confronts herself and her longstanding pattern in relation to her love objects:

> "I can't," she says later as she lays coiled on her bed. . . . She foresees the evening, a replica of other evenings—a look, then ignoring him, then a longer look, a signal, an intuition, a hand maybe, pouring wine, brushing lightly against a wrist, the hair on his knuckles, her chaste cuffs, innocent chatter stoked with something else.

She decides to leave that night instead of waiting till morning.

On the way to the airport there is between her and Jane the weight of things unsaid: "Does Jane know? Nell wonders. Does Jane guess? Behind that lovely exterior is Jane a woman who knows all the ways, all the wiles, all the heart's crooked actions?" They talk briefly, Nell asking Jane about whether Dan has ever given her cause to be jealous. Jane answers directly, describing her response to Dan's first infidelity and to subsequent ones. "Nell knows then that Jane has perceived it all and has been willing to let the night and its drama occur. She feels such a tenderness, a current not unlike love, but she does not say a word." The women say an awkward goodbye, uncomfortable with the unspoken knowledge and intimacy between them. As she leaves, Nell "thanks the small voice of instinct that has sent her away without doing the slightest damage to one who meets life's little treacheries with a smile and dissembles them simply by pretending that they are not meant."

The closing of **"Ways"** offers a moment of what Mark Schorer calls moral revelation, an instance of love triumphing over obsession. Nell's real and present love for her friend proves stronger than her temptation to repeat an obsessive pattern of flirtation and brief liaison. O'Brien is very powerful in her capturing of that moment of allurement, of electric attraction, that so entices Nell. This was no small sacrifice for her.

O'Brien has spoken of her happiest moments in life as being those during which someone she is about to fall in love with is about to fall in love with her [Nell Dunn, *Talking to Women,* MacGibbon and Kee, 1965]. This seems also to be true of her characters. It is, in fact, this moment of allurement, the *possibility* of union, to which O'Brien's characters seem addicted. Perhaps it is a prolongation of that sense of exciting uncertainty that they attempt to duplicate by their attachments to lovers who can promise them nothing. Their search for the eternally pregnant moment seems to draw these women into what might be called a cycle of unattainability. One pole of the cycle—the "high" of contemplated but uncertain union—contrasts sharply with the other—the grinding uncertainty of pursuing an unwinnable love object. Two recent O'Brien stories reveal the two poles of this "unattainability cycle."

In **"Lantern Slides,"** from O'Brien's 1990 collection of the same name, the author gives one of her most enticing evocations of the "up" phase of the cycle—a magical moment of mutual attraction raised to mythic proportions. Here we witness a large dinner party to which a gentleman named Mr. Conroy brings his old friend, Miss Lawless. Like Mary in **"The Revel"** (and like the wife of Joyce's Mr. Conroy in "The Dead"), Miss Lawless is reminiscing about a past love—a man she calls Abelard because she imagines him to resemble the medieval scholar and lover. As Mr. Conroy contemplates the possibility that the embers of his friendship with Miss Lawless might flame into passion, Miss Lawless notices a guest at the gathering who bears an uncanny resemblance to her Abelard.

O'Brien has spoken of her happiest moments in life as being those during which someone she is about to fall in love with is about to fall in love with her.
—Kiera O'Hara

Against the background of the Mr. Conroy/Miss Lawless/Abelard triangle and of other reciprocated and spurned at-

tractions among the various guests, the narrator introduces Betty, the woman in whose honor the party has been given. As the story swells toward its climax, Betty arrives from another event that she has attended with her husband, John, who, as all the guests know, is in the midst of an affair with another woman. Everyone's unspoken question is, will John appear at the party?

At this point Miss Lawless's hopes for a liaison with the new Abelard, along with the hopes of Betty and all the other guests for a reunion between Betty and John, are seen by the narrator as culminating in one deliciously charmed moment of possibility. When they hear someone enter the house, all wait in breathless expectation of an apotheosis:

> . . . everyone hoped that it was John, the wandering Odysseus returned home in search of his Penelope. You could feel the longing in the room, you could touch it—a hundred lantern slides ran through their minds; their longing united them, each rendered innocent by this moment of supreme suspense. It seemed that if the wishes of one were granted, the wishes of others would be fulfilled in rapid succession. It was like a spell. Miss Lawless felt it, too—felt prey to a surge of happiness, with Abelard watching her with his lowered eyes, his long fawn eyelashes soft and sleek as a camel's. It was as if life were just beginning—tender, spectacular, all-embracing life—and she, like everyone, were jumping up to catch it. Catch it.

In another of O'Brien's recent stories, this one from the *New Yorker,* we plummet from this exquisite moment to the "down" pole in the cycle of unattainability. In **"No Place,"** the narrator pursues a Moroccan tryst with a man who quite evidently has nothing to give her. Early in the story, Duncan, the narrator's lover, issues a warning familiar to readers of O'Brien's stories: "We mustn't fall in love. . . ." Nonetheless, the lovers arrange a fairy tale meeting in Morocco: "Sand and silence and us." The narrator arrives first and waits for Duncan, who is supposed to arrive the next day. However, the following morning he telegrams that he won't be coming. She frantically packs her things and gets on a bus for the airport to return home. Like Eleanor in **"Baby Blue,"** she tries to see her pain at the loss of her lover in the larger context of all human suffering. How can she be mourning a lost love, the narrator asks herself, when there are those whose fate is so much bleaker, like the women she views from her bus window—"women bent over their weeding as if they had dropped from their mothers' wombs onto the every parched stretches of land that all their lives they would be tied to." She also shows a high degree of awareness about her addiction to her love object, and about the connection between that addiction and her own long-standing pain: "She felt, and hated herself for feeling, a wound, a great childish gape within her; it was as if she had learned nothing and still believed in transubstantiation through another." O'Brien has described herself [in *The Irish Novel in Our Time*] as "very committed" to her "mythology, which is Roman Catholic . . ." Here the idea of transubstantiation—the transmutation of one substance into another (a term employed in Catholic doctrine to refer to Christ's bodily presence in the Eucharist)—conveys the narrator's desperate desire to be *transformed* by her connection to her lover, to be made into someone else, someone without "a great childish gape within her."

When the protagonist of **"No Place"** arrives back in the city where she lives, she looks up Duncan: "'I was just passing,' she said, knowing she shouldn't have come." Her self-knowledge, her awareness about the probable outcome of her exchange with the lover who has abandoned her, are not sufficient to overcome her compulsion to see him again.

With the end of **"No Place,"** we have come full circle, back to the close of **"Irish Revel."** The protagonists of both stories look with dread on the homes that await them; they feel that they have *no place,* no true home at all. Only the setting—from rural to urban—has changed: "She did not want to go back to her house. She did not know where she wanted to go, but it was not home. Cold city. Black city." And from the ecstasy that closes **"Lantern Slides,"** we have moved to deep despair, the other pole of the cycle formed by obsession with the unattainable.

Critics have puzzled about why O'Brien's characters are obsessed with unattainable love objects. "Why haven't her women wised up?" asks Richard Woodward [in "Reveling in Heartbreak," *The New York Times Magazine,* March, 1989]. In an interview with Nell Dunn, O'Brien speaks of herself as having been "very wounded" in her life. Perhaps this is a reference to her childhood with an abusive alcoholic father. It seems likely that this is at least one of the wounds to which she refers. It is a sad fact that sometimes the unattainability of love in childhood causes a person to seek, in fact to eroticize, the same kind of unattainability in later life. The obsession of the adult is a haunted shadow of that which absorbed the child; that which is most unattainable is most sought.

Writers on addiction have pointed out that a behavior that turns addictive is initially established as a way to escape pain. The twist is that this behavior eventually becomes itself the *source* of pain. The original wound remains unhealed as frantic repetitions on the obsessive treadmill continue. The obsession of O'Brien's characters with "the notion of love" fits this pattern as clearly as does a substance addiction.

People in the grip of an obsession, an addiction, seldom simply "wise up." The road away from obsession (which is also

the road home) is one on which the wounded child, rather than fleeing her wounds, begins to accept "the great childish gape within her." It is also a road on which the wounded soul comes to believe that infinite resources for her healing are available for the asking. O'Brien's characters seem unable to envision such a road; self-love and faith elude them. The cycle of obsession—endless repetitions of yearning and despair—seems bound to continue.

Hermione Lee (review date 13 June 1994)

SOURCE: "The Terror and the Pity," in *The New Republic,* June 13, 1994, pp. 52-3.

[*In the following review, Lee offers a mixed evaluation of* House of Splendid Isolation.]

"The Ireland you're chasing is a dream . . . doesn't exist anymore. . . . It's gone. *It's with O'Leary in the grave.*" That's what we're told. The heroes have become terrorists, Queen Maeve is a battered wife, the big house is derelict. As Mary Hooligan says at the end of Edna O'Brien's novel *Night* (1972), "The harp that once through Tara's halls is silenced, mute." Baba, one of the original "country girls" from the fine Irish trilogy that made O'Brien's name in the 1960s, looks back on the past, twenty-five years later, in a bitter "Epilogue" written in 1987. She savages anything that will tear at her heartstrings as "pure slop": "Too fucking elegiac." Yet Baba ends her retrospect lamenting. "I want time to be put back, I want it to be yesterday." And even Mary Hooligan, long exiled from the "glorified bog" of her birth, calls out, "O Connemara, oh sweet mauve forgotten hills." In *House of Splendid Isolation,* too, "Romantic Ireland" is far from dead and gone. It's lurking all over the place. Cuchulain rides again, blue eyes blaze once more, legends and ghosts return to haunt us. The past is execrated, but the past is yearned for. The grim realities all have soft centers.

The plot itself makes you feel you have been here before. A notorious escaped terrorist from the North, McGreevy, known as "the Beast," breaks into a house in the west of Ireland. He's heard about it from an IRA sympathizer who used to work there, and it's well-placed for the job he has to do, the killing of a retired British judge (an echo of the assassination of Mountbatten in 1979) who takes his holidays boating on the lake nearby. (This is a return to O'Brienland, the boggy and mountainous country near Limerick, around the Shannon and Lough Derg, the part of Ireland, it is said, that holds "the powers of darkness in it.")

McGreevy first terrifies, then builds up a relationship with, the elderly widow, Josie, who is living in the house alone after a period in a nursing home. Their confrontation requires him to justify his life to her, and requires her to recall her past. Meanwhile a net closes around him. The local guard, Rory (who goes deer hunting in his spare time, laments his lost athletic youth and has a personal obsession with catching "the Beast"), is on his trail. He picks up the clues he needs from Josie, and from the girl who loves McGreevy and believes in his cause—her mother still calls the police the Black and Tans. Yes, thinks the mother, it is going to be "a fateful night on the mountain." And so it proves.

This strong but familiar story, revolving around the tense relationship between the terrorist and his unwilling host, is something like Brian Moore's *Lies of Silence,* but without his spare, driving pace; or like *Cal,* but without the sex. There *is* sex in the novel, of course, but it's in Josie's past, and all of it is bad. Her relationships follow the usual course of women's lives in O'Brien's fiction. Her kind of heroine is summed up by this sentence in *Time and Tide* (1992), which describes a woman victimized by a grotesquely hateful husband: "Her emotions were all tangled and she yearned now for a massive love." What an O'Brien heroine mostly gets instead is a massive martyrdom, especially if (as in one of her best stories, **"A Scandalous Woman"**) she is living in Ireland, "a land of shame, a land of murder and a land of strange, throttled, sacrificial women."

Josie is no exception. Driven away from her home by a jealous mother into years of servitude as a maid in Brooklyn, she returned to Ireland as the bride of "a man she scarcely knew," to find herself captive to a sad, violent drunkard who abuses and rapes her (or in O'Brien-speak, "mounts her with a lingual gusto"), and who has always in his eyes "a vacancy, like a lost stunned animal, far from home." The local men are all the same, either loathing her, like her husband's brother, or lusting after her, like the doctor who thinks of her as "a woman asking to be broken in," or worshipping her from afar, like Paud, who has two simple passions, his mistress and a united Ireland. There's only one exception, the gorgeous cultured priest ("his eyes were dark," "his smile was utter") who drives her into a frenzy of fantasized romance. ("In a silence they will couple, their shadow selves going beyond the gates of propriety to the deeper hungers within. . . . They are meant, like tubers under winter bedding.") But he turns out to be as terrified of women as the rest of them. She aborts her child, the priest humiliates her, her husband is killed in a messy accident, she goes mad.

All this is laid on so thick because Josie has to stand in for Ireland's troubles. Her "isolation" in the old house is like the island's, claustrophobic and cut off from the rest of the world in its own bitter commitment to the past. Like those who long to unite the country, she longs to die "whole." Like her, Ireland has been abused and raped and has killed its own children. The child she has killed makes an appearance at the start and the end of the novel (like the ghost-child in Toni Morrison's *Beloved*), speaking of the deaths and the weeping and the blood of the country and the need for enemies to understand each other.

A feminist message intermittently makes itself heard through this analogy between the woman and the country. The cruelty of terrorism has its sources, it is suggested, in the way men treat women in this land of shame and murder. "If women ran your organization there would be no shooting," Josie tells McGreevy. (He is not convinced.) Stronger than any protest, though, is the sense of fatalism and helplessness, always present in O'Brien's treatment of women's lives, but here reaching outward from the domestic to the political. All are at the mercy of "something fateful that is to be," which will re-enact yet once more the fatefulness of the past. Like Josie, "soaked in the yeast" of her terrible memories, so Ireland is held to ransom by what are variously and predictably described as the chains, the grip and the dark threads of history.

To make this plain, Irish myth and legend, song and story, infiltrate the present-day story. The legends of Guaire and Diarmait, St. Caimin and St. Calum, Queen Maeve and Cuchulain, the story of the Colleen Bawn, the songs commemorating Michael Collins and Kevin Barry, fill the air. Everyone knows the stories and the songs. So the interesting question is raised of who can claim to be the more truly Irish, who is entitled to inherit these myths. Is it the terrorist from the North, spouting Gaelic to show that he is "a far better keeper of the country's soul and the country's heritage," or the young Catholic policemen who capture him, their heads also full of their country's history? "We're all Irish under the skin," says one of them. Who is the more Irish—politicians, men of violence, women? Mutual inheritance and mutual responsibility is argued—that no one, North or South, can escape this war; and that it is only the ordinary people (the argument, also, of *Lies of Silence*) who can bring it to an end.

But the novel's Celtic sentiment fatally softens and blurs its treatment of harsh realities. "The songs get to one," thinks one of the policemen, revealingly. Josie sings a song of the Fenian heroes and had an uncle who was killed by the Black and Tans. That was all different, we're repeatedly told. This is not 1916: "These guys are without conscience, without ideals and with only one proclamation, money and guns and murder, guns and money." McGreevy is one of "these guys." But, bound by an oath to the liberation of his country, amber-eyed, redheaded, famously cunning, he begins to look suspiciously like a reincarnation of Cuchulain. He's a somewhat shadowy, over-romanticized character, with "a sort of radiance" emanating from him, "something stubborn and young and alone and tender about him." Josie, too, with her blue eyes and deep passions and cruel past, has a riskily folkloric air. Certain mysterious events at the book's tragic end suggest that she may herself become a legend, another Queen Maeve.

And Irish stereotypes are as ubiquitous as Irish myths. There's the lecherous eccentric neighbor, there's Brid the servant-girl who dreams of meeting her lover "in the soft unruly underlay of bog and bogland, everything seeping into her, his instrument in tooraloora fettle," there's the lovely young girl devoted to her revolutionary hero. Only in the brief sightings of the local townspeople, peevish and gossipy, something sharper and funnier comes through. More of this satire, and less keening, would have been welcome.

And more pace, too. In spite of the drama of the plot, the writing feels ponderous and slow, even flabby. There is not enough self-editing: "He stands above McGreevy, possessed of a cold and furious determination to smash through that lashing radius of hate and fanaticism to get to him"; "There are moments in life when a great softness is coupled with a great hardness." One particular mannerism, of turning verbs and adjectives into nouns—meant perhaps to sound vaguely Irish—makes everything feel passive and inert: "There was a jealousy in her"; "A fecklessness had taken root in him"; "There was something animal within the stillness of him"; "An urgency in her limbs, a precognition of what was to be"; "A great lunatic fork of longing rose up in her"; "A loneliness in it, the ache of a man hoping"; "In every jawline, a setness, a gravity betokening this appointment with morality"; "a terrible gravity to him." No one sets his or her jaw or feels feckless, everyone endures the condition of jaw-setness or fecklessness. It makes no difference if we are reading the child's voice, or the main narrative, or Josie's diary or the journal of Josie's uncle, an Irish Volunteer fighting against British rule: it all sounds the same, solemn, portentous and clichéd. It comes as no surprise to hear that the moans of an Irish cow in labor had "something primeval in them." After a while you begin to wait for someone to say that this was a beautiful and tragic land. And sure enough someone does: "What beautiful countryside, what serenity, what a beautiful tragic country to be born into," thinks the policeman. The policeman? In O'Brien's country, that's how policemen talk.

John L'Heureux (review date 26 June 1994)

SOURCE: "The Terrorist and the Lady," in *New York Times Book Review,* June 26, 1994, p. 7.

[*The following is L'Heureux's generally laudatory review of* House of Splendid Isolation, *in which he notes some faults in the novel but asserts that O'Brien's "attempt nonetheless merits praise."*]

This is a fascinating and disturbing novel—fascinating because it marks a dramatic departure for Edna O'Brien in both subject matter and in style, disturbing because for the first time we see her audacity fall and her elegant prose run badly out of control. Still, where she succeeds, she succeeds handsomely.

In *House of Splendid Isolation* Ms. O'Brien attempts to isolate and anatomize the human aspects of Irish history. She succeeds, poignantly, when she explores the relationship between an Irish Republican Army terrorist and the elderly Irish woman who is his hostage. They taunt each other, they fight and in time they achieve a tentative equilibrium. We come to know the mixed motives, the blind passions and the inability of terrorist and bystander alike to understand where these passions lead and how they can be controlled. As we observe their struggle, hear the old arguments that justify their positions, see them—in their new proximity—accommodate to each other for convenience's sake and then for charity, we feel that for the moment we are looking deep into the conflicted mind and heart of contemporary Ireland. This is the book's great strength.

After a brief invocatory prologue—in overwrought prose, a bad mistake—the novel opens like a political thriller. McGreevy, an I.R.A. terrorist known as the Beast, has leaped from a moving car, fled across an open field and is holed up in a hollow tree outside an Irish village. One of his own men has betrayed him and the chase is on. A police helicopter circles overhead, searchlights flood the field, there is "war in the sky and war on the ground and war in his heart." The formula works; we are caught up at once in the terror of the hunt. McGreevy escaped. He holds a rendezvous with a ragged gang of sympathizers. He hijacks a catering truck and heads for Limerick. His flight ends, finally, at the crumbling mansion of Josie O'Meara, an elderly, embittered Roman Catholic widow living out her last days in the house of splendid isolation. In Josie, McGreevy has found the perfect antagonist.

Ms. O'Brien does not write thrillers, and so what we expect now from the struggle of these two powerful and determined characters is a deepening of the novel, psychologically and philosophically. Instead, we are taken on a detour into old and familiar O'Brien territory: the life and lovers of Josie O'Meara up to the present moment. We see her damaged childhood, her three years as a maid in Brooklyn, her return to Limerick and her disastrous marriage to James O'Meara, a horse-breeding aristocrat who brings the house of O'Meara to ruin.

The author is comfortable here. She understands the blindness and desperation of these characters and she gets inside them with devastating effect. We see the hideous marriage up close, with drink as the necessary prelude to sex and sex itself as a weapon and a punishment. Josie's abortion confirms the sterility and hopelessness of their union. The story is engrossing, the prose highly charged, and the harsh emotions rise up from the page. Emboldened by her success, Ms. O'Brien takes us on a second detour: an account of Josie's passion for the local priest. Josie is obsessed with him, she pursues him, and though the affair comes to nothing, in the end she is disgraced, whipped to blood by her drunken husband, held in contempt by the surrounding villagers.

All this is interesting, but irrelevant. It has almost nothing to do with the principal story of an I.R.A. terrorist who moves into and takes over an aging widow's house. Ms. O'Brien attempts to bind the two stories together with a minor character. Paud, who for the most part exists offstage. He is the dramatic link between the past of the novel and its present.

Paud is a boy when Josie, newly married, hires him to do occasional work about the house. He is dazzled by her beauty and her style: "He could not look at the missus. He wanted to kneel down at her feet and adore." When she asks him about himself, if he can add and subtract, if he knows anything of his country's history, "at once he burst into a recitation of what Miss McCloud, his teacher, had dinned into him and others day after day: how their country, their beloved country, had been sacked, plundered and raped by the sister country." When he was very small, he says, he thought he would be a priest, but now in his teens he has taken an oath to save his country. "He had two loves, two women to die for, Ireland and the missus."

Paud, with his blind devotion to Ireland and the missus, is the cause of Josie's ruin and the mainspring of the novel's action. By accident, he exposes her to public disgrace and private whipping. By accident, he brings about her husband's death. By accident too, and out of his long devotion, "blathering about the house and the woman, like a lady on a coin with a leash of hounds, her husband and herself martyrs for Ireland," he sends McGreevy to her and quite literally completes the destruction of the house of splendid isolation. It is not by accident that Ms. O'Brien has made Paud a halfwit.

The house is symbolic, the priest is symbolic, Josie's marriage and her sex life and her abortion are symbolic. And so is Paud: a half-wit Fenian changeling who, with the best intentions, creates havoc and heartbreak wherever he goes. He is the child of history and of fanatic devotion. Like the Irish terrorist, he destroys what he worships. The symbolism is obvious and this, alas, is the novel's weakness.

The house is Ireland, Josie is Ireland, Paud in his innocently destructive way is Ireland. Uncomfortable with her story of the terrorist and the lady, Ms. O'Brien seeks refuge in easy

symbolism, and her art is swallowed up in rhetoric. There is an inflation of prose, of character, of incident, even of dialogue. Josie demands that McGreevy explain himself. "Why did you come here . . . why here?" she asks. And he replies, without irony or sarcasm. "The anvil of circumstances." This is Edna O'Brien speaking, not the character. Nor does it help that she describes a murdered I.R.A. soldier lying in a ditch, "his outsides at least being washed clean in an extreme unction of rain." The prose is overblown in a needless attempt to lend importance and drama to a story that by its nature has both. But she does not trust the power of her story to work its own spell.

Ms. O'Brien begins and ends the novel with sections called "The Child." "History is everywhere," she writes "It seeps into the soil, the subsoil. Like rain, or hail or snow, or blood. A house remembers." And she concludes, "It weeps, the land does, and small wonder. But the land cannot be taken. History has proved that. The land will never be taken. It is there." Symbolically, this may be effective, but as rhetoric it is less than effective, and as fiction writing it is not only ineffective, it is downright bad.

In the end, however, what the novel does accomplish is both impressive and worthy. *House of Splendid Isolation* leaves us with a vivid image of Ireland today. Here is a study of the nature of war: the sorry operations of love and hate that unite husband and wife, the police and protester, the civilian and the I.R.A. And behind the story, in the lives of minor characters, we glimpse the Republic's ambivalent attitude to Ulster, the south's memory of its own bloody revolution, the unremitting horror and injustice of British occupation. Ms. O'Brien has gone behind the newspaper headlines of bombings, atrocities and midnight murders and finds there only good intentions, blind devotions, stalemate and ruin. All of it unnecessary, all of it sadly human.

This is a brave book, and if it does not altogether succeed, the attempt nonetheless merits praise. Edna O'Brien has shown that all wars begin at home.

Bruce Bawer (review date 15 July 1994)

SOURCE: "The Widow and the Terrorist," in *The Wall Street Journal*, July 15, 1994, p. A11.

[*In the following review, Bawer offers a largely positive assessment of* House of Splendid Isolation, *but notes some stylistic weaknesses.*]

Since the appearance of her first novel, *The Country Girls,* in 1960. Edna O'Brien has won fame as a passionate, lyrical prose stylist and a sensitive observer of long-suffering

Irishwomen and their barbaric husbands. Her 13th novel, *House of Splendid Isolation,* centers on a paradigmatic O'Brien heroine a reclusive old widow named Josie O'Meara who lives among "listless fields" on the outskirts of a village.

Yet this book marks a departure for Ms. O'Brien. For she's taken this "women's novel" protagonist and placed her in a story right out of a high-concept male-targeted movie thriller. McGreevy, an Irish Republican Army terrorist who's wanted for murders and bombings and tagged by police as a "madman," moves in on Josie, using her house as a hideout.

Yes, it's that old Hollywood gimmick, the plot about the stressful relationship between a fugitive and the person or persons whose home he's invaded. If you were pitching the story to a studio executive, you'd describe it as *The Desperate Hours* meets *The Crying Game*—or maybe *The Petrified Forest* meets *In the Name of the Father.*

At first McGreevy not only repels but baffles Josie. What difference, she asks, would it make if the British *were* driven from Northern Ireland? She muses about "the words he had used—Justice . . . Identity . . . Community. What did these words mean? What value had they against the horrors of a crime?" She's a pragmatist, more attuned to real-world particulars than to high-flown abstractions. For his part, of course, McGreevy is a throwback to the "romantic Ireland" that Yeats pronounced "dead and gone" in his poem "September 1913."

But in fact romantic Ireland isn't dead and gone. The novel's two epigraphs quote illustrious English officials—Sir John Davies in the 17th century and Lloyd George in the early 20th—both predicting the imminent end of the Irish Troubles. If the Troubles persist, Ms. O'Brien implies, it's because Ireland is a land haunted by deathless memories and irrational dreams. "History is everywhere," reads the novel's opening sentence. "It seeps into the soil, the subsoil. Like rain, or hail, or snow, or blood. A house remembers. An outhouse remembers. A people ruminate."

Heir to this oppressive legacy of heroism; McGreevy is a dangerous man driven by ideals. And, one might add, by grievances, patriotic as well as personal—for, we learn, both his wife and child are dead, the former murdered. As it turns out, moreover, Josie has much in common with him: Long ago, her uncle was killed while engaged in an IRA operation. Though her yearning to avenge that death has long since abated, McGreevy's entrance into her life causes her memory of that almost for gotten passion for vengeance to resurface and turns her relationship with him into something far more complex and troubling.

The book's strongest moments, indeed, are those in which Ms. O'Brien delineates the difficult, nuanced, highly credible bond between Josie and her captor. There's something impressive, too, about the elegant way in which Ms. O'Brien turns Josie's remote cottage, a house divided, into a metaphor for Ireland itself.

Despite these merits, however, *House of Splendid Isolation* suffers from some serious stylistic handicaps. There are scenes here that you'd swear you've seen in a hundred bad crime movies and TV cop shows, complete with all the hackneyed melodramatic dialogue. In one familiar scene, the hostage taker is accused by one of his tougher cohorts of going soft and getting too chummy with the hostage. "A journeyman like you." McGreevy's accomplice threatens him heavyhandedly, "wouldn't like to be lost to the under taker." Then there's the arresting officer's high minded speech to the felon: "You could have done a lot for your cause and your country, McGreevy . . . but all you done was death upon death upon death." To read this book is to be aghast at its corny B-movie dialogue.

Nearly as irksome is the languid, self-consciously poetic narrative style. Though well-suited to the torpid pace of Josie's pre-McGreevy widowhood, it misses the mark in the book's more intensely dramatic moments. Even when (in one of many flash-back scenes) Josie's husband learns she's been unfaithful and flies into a brutal rage. Ms. O'Brien's prose remains maddeningly lugubrious.

Then there are the overwrought symbolic passages. Harking back to Josie's brief fling with a priest named Father John. Ms. O'Brien writes: "Spring. Thaw. The wildest impulses that befell one, the almost irrepressible longing to run back and grasp his arm and convey something— gentian stars wrung from a wintery cusp." It's all quite numbing.

Yet even with its failings. *House of Splendid Isolation* demonstrates that Ms. O'Brien—an Irishwoman who has lived in London for many years—has not entirely lost her impressive gift for offering up sympathetic and illuminating glimpses beneath the surface of Irish life. One hopes that in future novels she will return to what she does best.

Jeanette Roberts Shumaker (essay date Spring 1995)

SOURCE: "Sacrificial Women in Short Stories by Mary Lavin and Edna O'Brien," in *Studies in Short Fiction,* Vol. 32, No. 2, Spring, 1995, pp. 185-97.

[*In the following essay, Shumaker explores O'Brien's and Mary Lavin's use of martyred, Madonna-inspired women characters in their stories.*]

Edna O'Brien's **"A Scandalous Woman"** (1972) ends with the statement that Ireland is "a land of strange, sacrificial women." Like O'Brien, Mary Lavin features sacrificial women in her short stories. The disturbing martyrdoms of the heroines created by both writers stem, in part, from Catholic notions of the Madonna. The two writers criticize their heroines' emulations of the suffering Virgin. Julia Kristeva's "Stabat Mater" (1977) and Marina Warner's *Alone of All Her Sex: The Myth and Cult of the Virgin Mary* (1976) scrutinize the impact of the Madonna myth on western European women. Their feminist scholarship illuminates short stories such as Lavin's "A Nun's Mother" (1944) and "Sarah" (1943), as well as O'Brien's **"Sister Imelda"** (1981) and **"A Scandalous Woman."** In each story, female martyrdom (en)gendered by the Madonna myth takes different forms, from becoming a nun to becoming a wife, mother, or "fallen woman."

Kristeva comments upon the fluidity of the Madonna, who encompasses diverse female roles, as do the Irish female characters who emulate her. Discussing the dimensions of the Madonna—Virgin, mother, wife—Warner describes the primary effect of the Madonna myth: "By setting up an impossible ideal the cult of the Virgin does drive the adherent into a position of acknowledged and hopeless yearning and inferiority." The heroines of Lavin's and O'Brien's stories fit the pattern of self-hatred that Warner describes. Their varieties of sacrifice stem from self-disgust fostered by failing to reach the standards of the Madonna myth.

In O'Brien's **"Sister Imelda,"** the teenage narrator falls in love with her teacher, the beautiful young nun of the title. The joys of their love are the Foucauldian pleasures of self-denial—a passion never to be realized but fanned by both teacher and student through notes, whispered confidences, devotional gifts, and an occasional hug or kiss. This story fits the pattern of O'Brien's novels that Thomas F. Staley calls [in his book *Twentieth-Century Women Novelists,* 1982] confessional, "crying out for absolution." Imelda's and the narrator's romance makes life in the cold nunnery tolerable, even enjoyable. The romance stands, in miniature, for the unrealizable passion that Sister Imelda holds for Christ. Thus it becomes an enlistment tool for the nunnery, as Sister Imelda lures the narrator into a permanent sisterhood of sublimated passion. The narrator abandons her plan to become a nun after she leaves the convent, instead taking up the worldly solaces of makeup and nylons to attract the attention of men. Her best friend, Baba, outdoes her at dressing like a mature woman, becoming the narrator's model as Imelda once was. Baba's name suggests trite babytalk among lovers, as well as the magic of the Arabian Nights—here the transformations of puberty that are supposed to lead to marital joy.

The narrator's struggle to sublimate her sexuality into a pure

love for Sister Imelda may come from her wish to emulate the Virgin. Warner writes that "the foundations of the ethic of sexual chastity are laid in fear and loathing of the female body's functions in identification of evil with the flesh and flesh with woman." The nuns' routine mortifications, which the schoolgirls are expected to imitate, reveal their sense that the female body is an inherently evil possession for which they must compensate. Sister Imelda gets a sty that suggests both her neglect of her body and her distorted view of it. Meanwhile, "Most girls had sore throats and were told to suffer this inconvenience to mortify themselves. . . ." Sore throats are a metaphor for the voicelessness of the girls and the nuns under the convent's regimen. Both the nuns and the girls are often hungry because the convent habitually underfeeds them. Delicacies, such as the narrator's comically suggestive gift of bananas for Imelda, are saved for visiting bishops. The semi-starvation of both nuns and girls by a wealthy church forces their bodies into thin and spiritualized shapes that avoid the lush fecundity stereotypically associated with woman as sexual body. Weakened from hunger and other mortifications, the women are to look as undesirable and feel as undesiring as possible; however, the story shows that neither goal is actually met.

The narrator feels the loathing for her body that underlies the convent's ascetic practices when, at the end of the story, she wants to jump out of the bus window to escape the gaze of Sister Imelda after two years of living outside of the convent. The narrator now sees Imelda as a judge who might condemn her for adhering to her culture's vision of woman as a sexual commodity. To the narrator, Imelda stands for the virgin identity that the narrator has decided to shun despite its high status when held by nuns. As Warner writes, "Thus the nun's state is a typical Christian conundrum, oppressive and liberating at once, founded in contempt for, yet inspiring respect for, the female sex. . . But the very conditions which make the Virgin sublime are beyond the powers of women to fulfill unless they deny their sex." That denial of sexuality is not easy for Imelda is suggested by the narrator's describing the nun's lips as those of "a woman who might sing in a cabaret." When Sister Imelda reads Cardinal Newman to her class, "she looked almost profane." Imelda's sensuality surfaced during a fling with a boy on the night before she became a postulant; it reappears during her inappropriate friendship with the narrator. In the convent's context of preserving a nun's or a schoolgirl's virginity, a mental lesbian liaison is more acceptable than a consummated heterosexual relationship. Within the context of current sexual scandals within the Church, the reader may wonder if the narrator's and Imelda's liaison was ever consummated, and if that consummation was beyond representation when the story was written. For the story's purposes, however, the desire itself is what matters. As Kiera O'Hara writes [in "Love Objects: Love and Obsession in the Stories of Edna O'Brien," *Studies in Short Fiction,* Summer,

1993] of O'Brien's characters, it is "the possibility of union," however unlikely, that obsesses the narrator of **"Sister Imelda."** That transcendent union with Imelda would have both spiritual and physical dimensions.

In presenting a lesbian relationship from the point of view of the immature, enraptured narrator, O'Brien shows its appeal in a patriarchal world in which becoming like the hedonistic Baba seems more debased than becoming like the idealistic Imelda. Defying the restrictions of the nunnery, Imelda seems free and daring—"how peerless and how brave"—to the narrator. The narrator is drawn not only to love Imelda, but to want to imitate her. As Imelda the nun emulates the Madonna, the narrator models herself upon her beautiful teacher, suggesting the erotic dimensions that female worship of the Madonna may take. Imelda's erotic dimension includes maternal self-sacrifice, for Imelda enjoys feeding the narrator jam tarts which she herself refuses to eat. The tarts stand for forbidden sexuality that is tied up with the maternal: "Had we been caught, she, no doubt, would have had to make a massive sacrifice." As a sexualized stand-in for both the narrator's mother and the Madonna, Imelda eroticizes stereotypical female selflessness while she models it for the narrator.

> **"Sister Imelda" suggests that girls want to become nuns to experience the high drama of religious renunciation rather than the low comedy of becoming a sexual commodity.**
> —*Jeanette Roberts Shumaker*

The appeal of Imelda's asceticism is its drama: "Each nun, even the Mother Superior—flung herself in total submission, saying prayers in Latin and offering up the moment to God. . . It was not difficult to imagine Sister Imelda face downward, arms outstretched, prostrate on the tile floor." Imelda's gesture suggests [Julia] Kristeva's *jouissance* of the mystic and Foucault's notion that repression can be more fun than indulgence. The nuns' pleasure in prostration may come from ceasing to fight their awareness of their inferiority to the ideal wife and mother of God, the Madonna.

The irony is that the narrator does not know that a woman's life outside the convent may also require humiliating renunciations for her children or for a domineering husband; both sides of the Madonna ideal—Virgin and mother—are identically submissive. At the convent, the narrator does not try to grasp her mother's lot, although she visualizes her father darkly as "losing his temper perhaps and stamping on the kitchen floor with nailed boots." Certainly the narrator, like her mother, is a follower—first of Imelda and then of Baba, with the latter's makeup rites becoming so sacred that the narrator never removes her paint. Like Baba, Imelda prepares the narrator to be devoutly feminine; Imelda teaches the narrator a masochistic style of loving that the narrator will be able to use with men: "It was clear to me then that my version of pleasure was inextricable from pain." Kristeva [in "Stabat mater," *The Kristeva Reader,* 1986] might call this "A suffering lined with jubilation" characteristic of the woman who lives suffused by the image of the sacrificial Madonna. Grace Eckley argues [in *Edna O'Brien,* 1974] that O'Brien always defines love as sadomasochistic. That seems to be true. However, I believe that in **"Sister Imelda"** O'Brien is critical of sadomasochism as a feminine style of loving. The nuns' gestures of willing prostration are emblematic of the suffering Irish female condition in general. That the story ends with the narrator's pity for Imelda and her fellow nun suggests the narrator's coming awareness of the commonality of women's lot: "They [the two nuns] looked so cold and lost as they hurried along the pavement that I wanted to run after them." This commonality results from the sacrifices that the Madonna ideal requires of Irish women. It leaves O'Brien labeling herself, according to Eckley, as "only a guilt-ridden Irish woman." The excessive humility of the "only" is what O'Brien challenges her readers to escape through avoiding the self-abnegation that restricts Imelda, the narrator, and herself.

"Sister Imelda" suggests that girls want to become nuns to experience the high drama of religious renunciation rather than the low comedy of becoming a sexual commodity. Lavin's "The Nun's Mother" presents a related explanation for why girls want to become nuns—to avoid male predation. More painfully than O'Brien, Lavin exposes the inescapability of patriarchal power, whether in the home or the convent. The story concerns a nun's mother's meditations after leaving her daughter, Angela, at a convent. Angela's mother, Mrs. Latimer, never dared to ask Angela why she chose such a career, when all of Angela's life she appeared to dislike going to mass. The girl's father, Luke, is horrified that his daughter is renouncing the physical joys of marriage without realizing what they mean. Like Mrs. Latimer he does not dare to question Angela. Mrs. Latimer reflects on her happiness in marriage, noting its rarity. She is both glad that her daughter will not have to risk a marriage failure, and sorry that she won't know intimate love. Although the parents do not realize it, a reason for Angela's choice is given at the end of the story, when the father notices a flasher who has been operating near their home for months.

Angela apparently wishes to escape a world of invasive male sexuality for a sexless world in which wearing a swimsuit into the bathtub will safeguard her. The daughter's acceptance of such prudish defenses can be explained by "the terrible reticence about the body between mothers and daughters, a reticence based on revulsion, and not, as with mothers and sons, upon respect and mystery." Shame over their bodies keeps Angela and Mrs. Latimer emotionally distant. Hence, Mrs. Latimer cannot ask Angela why she is becoming a nun: "She [Mrs. Latimer] was conscious of this revulsion [about the body] every time she was alone with her daughter during the last month." As a result, Mrs. Latimer says nothing to Angela about her decision. Mrs. Latimer pretends to her husband that she has spoken to Angela, for Mrs. Latimer feels humiliated by her inability to be as intimate with her daughter as Luke expects. Mrs. Latimer knows that if Luke had a son, Luke would talk to him easily, since men lack women's shame about sexuality. At the story's end, Mrs. Latimer can't even imagine Angela being disturbed by the flasher near their home, because she never thinks of Angela as a sexual being capable of noticing a nude man. Mrs. Latimer's and Angela's revulsion against their bodies comes from the self-hatred engendered by a religion that regards female sexuality as evil. It is the same self-disgust that causes the narrator of **"Sister Imelda"** to hide from her once-beloved nun, and that perhaps caused Imelda to join her order. Only by denying her body as a nun can a woman preserve it from becoming that of a temptress.

Angela's fear of violation by the flasher or other men can be linked, through Warner, to the Church's "historical fear of contamination by outside influences, and its repugnance to change" that is symbolized by the Virgin's (and nun's) chastity. It is a fear of contamination that Angela's mother shares. Mrs. Latimer believes that the appeal of becoming a nun is gaining sexual independence from men. "And so, for most women, when they heard that a young girl was entering a convent, there was a strange triumph in their hearts . . . they felt a temporary hostility to their husbands." However, Mrs. Latimer denies that she herself ever felt the allure of sexual emancipation. She would not give up her memories of passion with Luke for anything. Luke is gentle; both Angela and her mother seem to see him as an exception to typical male aggressiveness. Despite the presence of Luke, the story countenances Angela's fear of men in that the flasher epitomizes all the varieties of perverts who do in fact hurt women; that flashers themselves usually don't rape women physically, however, suggests Angela's naïveté about men. Angela's other naïve belief is that nuns are immune from sexual attacks.

The story ends with Mrs. Latimer's fantasy of Angela as a water lily about to be picked by the flasher. That Mrs. Latimer associates Angela with water lilies shows that Mrs. Latimer sees the female experience as a conflict between beautiful nature and a degraded civilization that endangers it. Mrs. Latimer's essentialism appears in her aligning of woman with nature. The danger for the female flower is not just one of being picked, but of withering in a self-protective, ossifying ideology of asceticism that the Irish Catholic Church endorses for women. Angela avoids the physical threat of rape but not the mental one of ossification, choosing her own form of sacrifice. Angela will be a water lily in a bowl on the convent's altar, her life a slow withering. With Angela's sexual independence from men comes intellectual dependence on the male-dominated Church. Angela's payoff will be the high status which Warner and Kristeva agree that emulating the Virgin earns.

Angela's mother will get that high status too. Mrs. Latimer realizes this upon arriving home, when her housekeeper treats her with a new deference. Yet this status is seen satirically by Mrs. Latimer, who abhors the pretentious acts of piety she may be expected to perform now that she is the mother of a nun. Mrs. Latimer fantasizes, "'Meet Mrs. Latimer, who has a daughter in the convent.' She would be quite an exhibit at church bazaars and charity whist drives. She might even have to assume an attitude." The pathetic requests for prayers that Angela receives from her dressmaker, plus the stereotypical gifts of rosary beads, quartz angels, and holy pictures, fill, Mrs. Latimer with dismay. By association, Angela's mother is supposed to be aligned with the Madonna as a holy mother of a sacrificial child. But because the circumstances of Angela entering a convent in twentieth-century Ireland are portrayed with mundane humor, they contradict any glorified image of nuns and their mothers. Such images of transcendence are sold to girls by bestsellers like *The White Sister,* according to Mrs. Latimer. Transcendence of what? Of being a Mrs. Latimer—the reader knows her only by her married name, as though marriage had consumed her identity. Yet the story portrays Mrs. Latimer's marriage as a happy one in which the husband is the subordinate party if anyone is, whereas Angela's nunnery is seen not as a refuge from male dominance but as a museum.

For any mother, the ultimate price of bearing a nun might be knowing that her line ends with her daughter, as Christ ended Mary's. Mrs. Latimer will not have the pleasure of having grandchildren to love. In her odd relief at this apparent misfortune, her likeness to her daughter appears: both fear contamination above all else. At the birth of Angela, Mrs. Latimer had imagined her descendants falling into lurid varieties of wickedness that she can only observe, but not interrupt. "For the lives they led had suddenly seemed evil in every case. Some were prising open drawers and looking over their shoulders. Some were stealthily crossing the 'ts' of letters that were forged." Mrs. Latimer's relief comes from knowing that her daughter's pure choice will eliminate any responsibility for future generations. Her relief at Angela's chastity vows outweighs her regret that she will no longer need to stay young for Angela.

The story's initial image of Mrs. Latimer is telling: her eyes are closed as she leaves Angela at the nunnery, as though Mrs. Latimer is afraid to face reality. This image reveals Mrs.

Latimer's compulsion to control what she knows and experiences, as well as the actions of her descendants. Perhaps Mrs. Latimer chooses not to see the pathetic reason for Angela's vocation, as that vocation allays Mrs. Latimer's anxieties about her posterity. Mrs. Latimer would have been a good mother but for her fear of the future that she unconsciously passed onto her daughter. Mrs. Latimer's obsessive desire to control the future contradicts the healthy side of the Madonna myth that Kristeva describes as its connectedness to past and future through "a flow of unending germinations, an eternal cosmos." Fertility is lost to the paranoid nun and her mother, as the virginal side of the Madonna excludes the maternal side. Whereas Angela imagines herself a victim of male predators, Mrs. Latimer dreams of being their ancestor. This is a dark turn to the story that makes Angela's desire to become a nun seem a result of her mother's pathology, not of an actual vocation.

As if to validate Angela's fear of sexual predation in "A Nun's Mother," O'Brien's **"A Scandalous Woman"** shows that childbirth may doom a mother rather than being Kristeva's mystic experience. In O'Brien's story, female imprisonment and madness are caused by the fertility that nuns renounce, perhaps wisely given the story's context. Eily—unmarried, pregnant and Catholic—is locked up by her parents after being caught sleeping with a Protestant bank clerk. The clerk is forced to marry Eily, with the enticement of a substantial dowry and with the threat of being murdered by her father if he refuses. Of course the clerk is not a loving husband, and Eily goes mad after bearing several children. Later, her recovery into a mindless contentment despite her husband's affairs is portrayed as even more disturbing than her madness. The story is told by a girlfriend of Eily's who is a few years younger than Eily. The narrator begins by describing events from their childhood and proceeds chronologically.

What is most pertinent to the Madonna myth is Eily's and the female narrator's ambivalence about their pubescent bodies. Their distrust of their womanhood is learned from Eily's elder sister, Nuala. Lavin's Angela learns a similar fear of becoming a nature woman from her mother. When Eily and the narrator are little girls, Nuala pretends that she is a doctor. Every Tuesday Nuala plays that she is cutting out the young narrator's female parts, gesticulating above the narrator's body. As Nuala sharpens the knife with Eily assisting as nurse, Nuala sings "Waltzing Matilda"—Matilda being their code word for female reproductive organs. This ritual operation is accompanied by the narrator's confession, since the "elastic marks [of her underpants are] a sign of debauchery." James M. Haule writes [in "Tough Luck: The Unfortunate Birth of Edna O'Brien," *Colby Library Quarterly,* December, 1987] that the surgery game "prepares us for the reduction of Eily, and finally of the narrator herself, to a mere shell." The self-hatred of these little girls is already profound; they have been taught, perhaps through proscriptions against masturbation, that woman as a sexual being is a monster needing maiming to correct her inborn flaws. The narrator's guilt over helping Eily conceal her affair leads the narrator to gargle with salt and water, and to reject food: "These were forms of atonement to God." The narrator feels not only her guilt as Eily's accomplice, but anticipatory guilt over her coming womanhood. The child narrator is put in the position of a latent werewolf dreading the full moon that must come no matter whether or not she wants the transformation into womanhood. The hell that descends upon Eily after her romps with the clerk shows a further significance to Nuala's Gothic operation. If only Eily's female parts had never developed, her life would have remained tolerable.

Warner argues that the Magdalen myth suggests that sexual crimes are the only significant ones a woman can commit. Eily's so-called "fall" thus makes her a criminal; whereas if she had stolen something or gambled her savings away, her family might have forgiven her more readily. The mistrust of female sexuality that Warner links to the Madonna myth is seen when Eily's parents jail Eily in their oat room. On the day of her wedding, Eily "kept whitening and rewhitening her buckskin shoes," as though hoping her marriage might restore the virgin purity her parents prize. Eily's relief from pain comes not through wifehood, but through a madness that allows her to express her rage towards the family and friends who were supposed to protect her, not reject her. Finally, her relief comes through a supposed cure, possibly a lobotomy, a numbed sanity that represents oblivion.

Several of Eily's actions pitifully enact the impoverished vision of romance that leads to her liaison. Eily gives the narrator a bottle of cheap perfume in appreciation for her help with hiding Eily's affair. Like Baba's makeup rites, Eily's perfume symbolizes the young woman's obsession with making herself attractive to men; through her gift of perfume, Eily tries to pass on her obsession to the narrator. Eily's passion for her fickle clerk takes her and the narrator to a witch's pub to have Eily's fortune told. The narrator acts as a guard while Eily and her lover make love furtively, outdoors. This is not the sublimated lesbian romance of **"Sister Imelda,"** but a consummated heterosexual affair that the naïve narrator describes in humorous detail. Instead of reading *The White Sister* mentioned in Lavin's story, Eily seems never to read at all, but merely to gather tabloid notions about romance from her friends. Hence, Eily believes that "the god Cupid was on our side." Eily has replaced Kristeva's *jouissance* of the mystic who loves God with the passion of heterosexual romance. The pathos of Eily's affair is that it is not worth the price that Eily's family and friends force her to pay for it.

The narrator suggests that the sane Eily at the end of the

story has "half-dead eyes," because "along with removing her cares they [her psychiatrists] had taken her spirit away." That Eily has lost her memories alarms the narrator. Yet Eily is apparently content without the past that had driven her mad in the first place. The narrator writes that not only is Ireland "a land of strange, sacrificial women," but it is also "a land of murder." To be happy as an unloved wife, Eily must have her thoughts, memories, and dreams killed. That the narrator may soon share Eily's fate is implied when she meets Eily while pregnant "under not very happy circumstances," and in the company of her mother. When the narrator again meets Eily years later, a husband as resentful as Eily's waits impatiently for the narrator and her son. Is it the narrator who is really the scandalous woman of the story's title? If so, the narrator exorcises her memories not through a nervous breakdown but by transforming her memories into fiction. Was the narrator, like Eily, sacrificed to the Irish ideal of virginity? Through not answering that question, O'Brien suggests that numerous women can be labeled by her story's title. Generation after generation, scandalous women are made to pay for their rebelliousness with a lifetime of submission to their husbands and parents.

As in nineteenth-century British fiction, the "fallen" twentieth-century Irish mother can only redeem herself through dedication to her children. Eily, the modern Magdalen, sacrifices herself for her parents' reputation, as well. As Lavin's Angela and O'Brien's Imelda die one kind of slow death in the convent, Eily dies another kind of slow death as a wife and mother. Eily is so numbed after her lobotomy that she cannot act affectionate toward her children. Each living death represents a different, murdering facet of the Madonna myth—the Virgin and the Magdalen mother.

Whereas a spiritually dead woman is the heroine of O'Brien's **"A Scandalous Woman,"** an actual murder victim is the heroine of Lavin's "Sarah." As a widow who struggled to raise her children and eventually remarried a man who left the priesthood for her, Lavin can confront the paralyzing Irish middle-class conformity that Joyce critiqued. But Lavin presents a female point of view. As Zack Bowen writes, "Given Mary Lavin's lifelong concern with practicalities, money problems, responsibilities, and the effects of death, her vision of reality is harsh and closely circumscribed by an acute awareness of social class, and society's sanctions and rules." "Sarah" is one of Lavin's most hard-hitting pieces of social criticism. In her village, unmarried Sarah is respected for her piety and for her diligence as a cleaning lady. Yet Sarah dies from exposure while bearing her baby in a ditch during a rainstorm. The baby also dies. Sarah's angry brothers had kicked her out of their home, after depending on her cleverly efficient housekeeping for years. Although Sarah was already raising three sons whom she bore out of wedlock, this is apparently the first time Sarah had informed the father of his

paternity. Sarah is no longer willing to claim sole responsibility for her children, or to pretend that she was honored by virgin births. As a result, Sarah's brothers can no longer hide behind their previous myth that the men who slept with Sarah were "blackguards" who took advantage of her. Her "fall" thus becomes a public shame that her brothers must acknowledge.

Sarah's brothers' violence is only a step beyond that of Eily's family. Since Sarah's paramour is a married man, her brothers cannot force a marriage as Eily's did. Sarah inflames her eldest brother by reminding him that her lovers are none of his business. What bothers him more than Sarah's affair is her defiance of his authority. But he hides his irritation at not being able to control his sister behind worry over their family's honor that is more socially acceptable. He regards Sarah's adultery as much more dishonorable than her previous affairs with single men, as he tells his younger brother: "No one is going to say I put up with that kind of thing." Concern for their reputation motivates the cruelty of Sarah's brothers and Eily's family. O'Brien and Lavin suggest that Irish families punish scandalous women without compunction. Eily's and Sarah's scandalousness comes from their insubordination to their families as much as from the premarital sex that is the proof of their defiance.

The wife of the man Sarah slept with, Mrs. Kedrigan, writes to Sarah's brothers to protest Sarah's letter to Mr. Kedrigan informing him of her pregnancy. Mrs. Kedrigan is angry in part because her neighbors had warned her not to hire Sarah, but Mrs. Kedrigan had wanted to show them that her husband was entirely trustworthy. Sharing a belief in the double standard with Sarah's brothers, Mrs. Kedrigan does not blame her husband for his affair; nor does she believe his denial of it, or she would have ignored Sarah's letter. The illusion that Sarah is the sole culprit lets Mrs. Kedrigan avoid fighting with her husband about his affair. As Mrs. Kedrigan relies on him for physical and psychological support, it is in her interest to keep the peace. Without a job to support their baby who will soon be born, Mrs. Kedrigan can't leave her husband. But she gets back at him indirectly by telling him the news of Sarah's death with vengeful relish, saying that the ditch is the place where Sarah belongs. Mrs. Kedrigan can be seen as a victim of patriarchal restrictions that are whitewashed by the Madonna myth, to the point that she becomes a caricature of the wronged wife. Warner notes that the Virgin myth's influence is greatest in countries where women are primarily wives and mothers; Ireland would certainly qualify. Janet Egleson Dunleavy says that Lavin's stories from the 1940s focus on "the universal truth of restricted vision"; petty, vindictive vision is clearly Mrs. Kedrigan's flaw, as much as it is Sarah's brothers'. Mrs. Kedrigan condemns Sarah because, as Warner writes of the Madonna myth, "There is no place in the conceptual architecture of

Christian society for a single woman who is neither a virgin nor a whore."

Lavin questions the ideology that allows Mrs. Kedrigan and Sarah's brothers to label Sarah a whore, much as O'Brien does in **"A Scandalous Woman."** As Richard F. Peterson writes, Sarah's tragic death represents "the triumph of the unnatural over the natural." Oliver Kedrigan kindles Sarah's animal attraction to him by complimenting her red cheeks; he laughingly asks her whether she rubs them with sheep-raddle. At the end of the story, when Mrs. Kedrigan tells Oliver of Sarah's death, he yells at her to give him the sheep-raddle, cursing it. Oliver is cursing the instinctive lust which led him to cause Sarah's and his baby's death. He also curses the unnaturalness of those deaths, which were fostered by an unforgiving man-made morality that is supported by Mrs. Kedrigan's jealousy and Sarah's brothers' shame. And Oliver is cursing his cowardice for denying his natural family outside of wedlock. Lavin suggests that Sarah is destined by nature for motherhood by contrasting her healthy pregnancy with that of the sickly Mrs. Kedrigan. The village women had predicted that Mrs. Kedrigan could never become a mother, and had wondered why the earthy farmer had married her. Her hysterical illnesses during pregnancy cause her to rely on her husband's ministrations even though she calls him "a cruel brute" for making her pregnant, whereas Sarah cheerfully works as hard as usual during pregnancy, without the help of any man. Perhaps Sarah's natural fitness for motherhood explains why upright matrons had delivered all of her previous births, and why they continued to hire her to clean their houses. Yet when the protection of her brothers and lover is withdrawn, self-reliant Sarah and her baby die; unnatural patriarchy triumphs over the natural mother.

Trying to show their disgust with Sarah, her brothers exceed her sin of lust with one of violence. Mrs. Kedrigan also tries to prove that her value is beyond Sarah's, but fails for the same reasons that Sarah's brothers do. Lavin exposes how respectable women such as Mrs. Kedrigan reconcile themselves to the low status of their gender by seeing themselves as worthy like the Virgin, whereas "fallen women" are despicable. Kristeva might call this regarding oneself as unique among women like the Virgin herself. For Mrs. Kedrigan, it is a self-delusion of superiority with horrible consequences for Sarah, Sarah's baby, and herself.

Sarah's martyrdom draws attention to the malice and artifice latent within the virginity ideal. However unconsciously, the village priest acts in accord with the cruelty of that ideal by nagging Sarah and her brothers about her affairs. The priest tells Sarah's brothers that their sister should be put into a Home. This idea encourages them to view Sarah as less than human—as criminal trash that should be thrown away. The brothers exile Sarah from their home to prevent their priest from continuing to blame them for Sarah's behavior. The priest also helps to cause Sarah's death through having repeatedly chastised her for not revealing the names of the fathers of her older children. Like Sarah's brothers, the priest hates Sarah's lack of submissiveness as much as her so-called fallenness. For although Sarah is pious, she will not accept the repentant Magdalen role that the priest dictates. Instead, Sarah gets pregnant out of wedlock again and again. To the priest, Sarah is an embarrassment—a rebel against the notions of proper womanhood that the Madonna myth promotes. Writing Kedrigan about his upcoming fatherhood may be Sarah's half-compliant, half-defiant response to the priest's exhortations. The priest's role as an underlying cause of Sarah's death suggests that the Church teaches Irish families to murder their own "fallen women."

For Lavin and O'Brien, the demand for virginity enforces the punishment of the rebellious "fallen woman," whereas it restricts the life experience of the well-disciplined nun. Although critics have noted that the alternatives to marriage for women in Ireland rarely go beyond the brothel or the convent, nuns and "fallen women" in O'Brien's and Lavin's stories don't recognize the economic factors that shape their choices; instead, they act masochistically to pay for the evil they perceive as inherent to their female bodies. The high status of the nun is achieved through the low status of the "fallen woman," through contrasting the hard-bought virtue of one with the so-called sinfulness of the other. The nun's convent may seem imprisoning, but so may the home of the respectable wife or the ditch of the "fallen woman."

Whereas O'Brien's heroines are captivated by two forms of romance—the religious and the sexual—Lavin's heroines seem impervious to both. The Madonna myth may be regarded as a source for both the religious and the sexual romances critiqued by O'Brien's stories. As the central model for the Irish woman, the Virgin fosters the ideal of chastity to which the nun aspires and from which the "fallen woman" falls short. O'Brien's Eily is led to a lobotomy through sexual passion. Lacking Eily's heterosexual fantasies of romance, Imelda and her admirer mingle religious and sexual romance in ways that question the standard formulations of both. In contrast with O'Brien's yearning heroines, Lavin's Angela becomes a nun out of fear of the romantic side of men, Sarah has affairs without expecting courtship, and Mrs. Kedrigan places revenge above both love and religion. Whereas O'Brien deconstructs religious and sexual romance by merging the two, Lavin shows the paucity of experience that lacks any form of romance. Lavin focuses upon the least glamorous effects of the Madonna myth—killing rivalries between women and ossifying chastity. Lavin and O'Brien share an awareness of the unrealistic desires—whether for superiority or sacrifice—that the Madonna myth fosters in Irish women, along with the women's guilt at never reaching their ideal of purity and selflessness.

Sandra Manoogian Pearce (essay date Summer 1995)

SOURCE: "Edna O'Brien's 'Lantern Slides' and Joyce's 'The Dead': Shadows of a Bygone Era," in *Studies in Short Fiction,* Vol. 32, No. 3, Summer, 1995, pp. 437-46.

[*In the following essay, Pearce examines similarities between the works of O'Brien and James Joyce, in particular focusing upon O'Brien's "Lantern Slides," which Pearce characterizes as a "feminist rewriting" of Joyce's "The Dead."*]

In 1974, Grace Eckley noted [in her *Edna O'Brien*] the similarities between James Joyce and then-emerging Irish talent, Edna O'Brien. Eckley specifically cites O'Brien's **"Irish Revel"** as "a West of Ireland version of Joyce's classic, 'The Dead,'" comparing the blanketing snow of Joyce's metaphoric ending to the frost that comes "like the descent of winter on Mary's heart" at the end of the O'Brien story. O'Brien's diction and rhythm clearly bestow homage on Joyce: "Frost was general all over Ireland: frost like a weird blossom on the branches, on the river-bank from which Long John Salmon leaped in his great, hairy nakedness, on the ploughs left out all winter; frost on the stony fields, on all the slime and ugliness of the world" (in *The Love Object*). The title story of O'Brien's latest collection *Lantern Slides* places O'Brien even more securely within the Joycean sphere, for now setting has moved east to Dublin. Gone is the lush Irish countryside; gone are the proper Connor girls; gone are Cait and Baba. Gone, too, are the erotic but innocent prelapsarian longings of those protagonists reminiscent of Joyce's two West country women, Gretta and Bertha. In their stead is a dazzling display of Dublin's dinner "nobs." While richly resonant of Joyce's "The Dead," this party is not consumed with talk of politics, music, or lost loves, but rather with Gucci ties, tacky poetry, and lost lusts. O'Brien's feminist rewriting of "The Dead" is delightfully, searingly ironic, but the subtext is even more so, revealing a satiric pen that blots male and female alike with the same scathing ink, delivering an indictment that goes far beyond Joyce's.

From the opening paragraph of **"Lantern Slides,"** O'Brien's extension of Joyce's story is glaringly apparent. Gabriel Conroy has become Mr. Conroy, hotel worker, whatever that means. Mr. Conroy's stories suggest that he is working in a brothel rather than a hotel. While "The Dead" evokes lyrical images of faintly falling snow, **"Lantern Slides"** opens with imagery more reminiscent of "Circe," in a "big hall" where in "a big limestone grate, a turf fire blazes." The next few sentences confirm the story's setting: "The surround was a bit lugubrious, like a grotto, but this impression was forgotten as the flames spread and swagged into brazen orange banners. In the sitting room, a further galaxy of people. . . . Here too was a fire . . . ." We are in Hell, the hell of Dante's

Inferno, where not only flames assail the body, but also noise (remember the din of Satan flapping his wings?). Waiters move "like altar boys among the panting throngs," while people ask "from time to time how this racket could be quelled, because quelled it would have to be when the moment came, when the summons for silence came." But no silence comes, unlike the beautifully haunting silence that ends "The Dead". Here, openly flirtatious Dr. Fitz will not shut up; outrageously sexist Mr. Gogarty keeps on joking. Even the chandeliers "seem[ed] to be chattering, so dense and busy and clustered were the shining pendants of glass." These "chattering" chandeliers set the tone of the story: we will judge and be judged by gossip, rumor, innuendo, and association.

O'Brien replaces Gretta's impassioned weeping for a lost Michael Furey with Miss Lawless's lustful desires for the newly resurrected appearance of a second Peter Abelard, her lost lover of 25 years earlier (and of course, invoking the original Abelard—twelfth century scholar, monk, and lover of Heloise). The Dantesque vision of Gretta/Beatrice enshrouded in the "dusty fanlight" (evoked more fully in John Huston's movie version, in which Gretta stands earlier in the stained-glass stairwell) gives way in O'Brien's story to "patches of sea like diagonals of stained glass," reminding us that the lantern slides are not infused with Dantean light, but clouded with mists of the sea, or shrouded in distant and disjointed memories. Instead of this vision conjuring up Gretta's heart-rending story of the young, rain-soaked Furey's stand beneath her window and its fatal consequences, O'Brien treats us to a panoply of twentieth-century soap operas. Miss Lawless's lost love is married, an adulterous bastard (a highly ironic allusion, considering the medieval Abelard's castration) who would "embrace her but did not want to know anything about her," who would "introduce her to his wife at some party," who would even allow his wife to invite her to their home, where O'Brien gives us a glimpse of his garden, complete with "tiny shrunken apples that looked as if they had some sort of disease, some blight." Whatever prelapsarian longings Joyce evokes with his story, O'Brien totally undercuts with hers. Indeed, even the Edenic moment of *Ulysses*—Molly and Bloom on Howth—is undermined in O'Brien's story. Mr. Conroy fantasizes stealing a kiss from Miss Lawless on the "Hill of Howth, with its rhododendrons about to burgeon," thinking she would not go "the whole hog," while she fantasizes about the old Abelard and how this new stranger is "enough for her," brilliantly exposing the totally separate lives of these two protagonists.

This interesting overlay of the Molly/Leopold relationship with the Gretta/Gabriel and Lawless/Conroy (and likewise Heloise/Abelard) one is reinforced by two earlier vignettes. The first, Mr. Conroy's public retelling of their early morning's "glorious walk," is undermined by his private recollection of his need to stop for breath and to speak of his varicose veins. The second, Miss Lawless's private reverie of first meeting Abelard in a newspaper office where she delivered a paper for competition, winning first prize but having her name misspelled, recalls the misspelling of Bloom's name at Paddy Dignam's funeral in the "Hades" chapter, reminding us once more where we are—in hell. Perhaps, the most telling remark of the evening is Miss Lawless's comparison of the sand on Dollymount Strand "being white as saltpetre," identifying clearly the sterility of this couple (of this whole dinner party) when compared to the fertility (and conventionality by these new standards) of Molly and Bloom and to the potential for renewed understanding with Gretta and Gabriel.

O'Brien's story explodes the moment of silence in "The Dead," destroying any notion of the epiphany. While Gabriel Conroy's feelings transform from sexual desire to self-pity, to, perhaps, understanding and empathy, Mr. Conroy's feelings remain rooted in a haze of unstated, but nonetheless lurid sexuality. He thinks not only of Miss Lawless, but also of his other "pinup," Nicola. His sexist musings allow him this dubious insight about himself—that his unhappy marriage had had "an excess of emotions . . . at the root of it. 'Too much love' . . . ." Mr. Conroy "knew that emotions often blur pleasure, especially for a man." And what manly pleasure is Mr. Conroy seeking? A ludicrously adolescent revelation that his "lifelong dream" has been to kiss Miss Lawless. Not only is the Joycean epiphanic moment missing, but so, too, the biscuits and tea, the shortcakes and wine of Joyce's multilayered eucharistic imagery. Here, the bread of communion is replaced by "plates of sugared biscuits that were shaped like thumbs and caramelized at the edges"—a mutilated, paralyzed image more darkly evocative of the other stories of *Dubliners*.

This twisted/perverted eucharistic image is introduced earlier in one of Miss Lawlessness's "flood of childhood evocations," another potentially powerful image lacking epiphanic significance:

> . . . A painted-cardboard doll's house with a little swivelled insert for a front door, which could be flicked open with a thumbnail; a biscuit barrel impregnated with the smell of ratafia essence; and a spoon with an enamelled picture of the Pope.

To us, her memory is foolish and inappropriate, foreshadowing not only the carmelized thumbs, but the ending image of the lantern slides. Instead of a cozy birthday gathering of friends, reviewing mutual memories, we have an odd assortment of transparently empty people with disconnected private musings—spoiled, rich people—"coiffured and bejewelled" nobs waiting to be seen. All the images are disturbing. Even the name Miss Lawless is hardly reminiscent

of gracious, graceful Gretta or law-abiding, careful, dutiful Gabriel. The instances of O'Brien's scathing irony abound on every page.

O'Brien's story presents the natural extension of Joyce's, a Dublin party of the latter half of the twentieth century rather than the first half, a Dublin party of the "new generation." Gabriel Conroy, in his yearly address at his aunts' Christmas dinner, remarks on the "hospitable roof" under which they are gathered around the "hospitable board," recipients of the "hospitality of certain good ladies." Lest we miss the irony, Joyce has his verbose/modest speaker ("I am afraid my poor powers as a speaker are all too inadequate"), mention hospitality twice more, reminding the guests that Ireland "has no tradition which does it so much honor and which it should guard so jealously as that of its hospitality" and reminding the three hostesses of "the tradition of genuine warm-hearted courteous Irish hospitality." These five references to "hospitality" are succeeded by a sixth:

> A new generation is growing up in our midst, a generation actuated by new ideas and new principles . . . . and sometimes I fear that this new generation, educated or hypereducated as it is, will lack those qualities of humanity, of hospitality, of kindly humor which belonged to an older day.

While others have discussed Gabriel's character, particularly its epiphanic nature, my concern is with O'Brien's story where Gabriel's prophecy comes to fruition in the inhospitable behavior of O'Brien's dinner "nobs."

Say what we will about the drunken antics of Freddy, the sudden departure of Miss Ivors, or the cosmopolitan snobbery of Gabriel's dismissal of the Irish West, there is a genuine warmth of human camaraderie at Gabriel's aunts' house. The "new generation" (or two or three) celebrating Betty's birthday in O'Brien's story display an alarming paucity of humanity, hospitality, and kindly humor. Humanity is utterly lacking in this room charged with blatantly sexist remarks. O'Brien is writing no feminist defense of Irish womanhood, however; she condemns both her male and female characters. Not a single character elicits her sympathy, nor ours. Sinead's nearly hysterical description of her abusive husband hardly prompts a compassionate response from anyone in the story. And when we learn of her secret pregnancy as a ploy to trap Dr. Fitz in marriage, we, too, feel no compassion for her. Yet we feel little pity for Dr. Fitz either. His sexist views and those of all the male characters are constantly annoying, especially his winks at Miss Lawless about his good friend the "widda," identified knowingly by Mr. Conroy as "the floozie with the Jacuzzi." The female characters fare no better. Dot the Florist in a tightly-fitting, pink cat suit schemes to find a man to pay her bills before the bank's foreclosure, willing to dance with any man who "didn't have his wife with him." Sinead points to the "blown-up snapshots of Betty in a bathing suit and a choker" plastered all over the walls and wonders aloud how Betty's husband could leave her, "Why would any man leave a beautiful woman like that for a slut!" "Why indeed?" queries O'Brien's ironic narrator.

To return to the concerns of Gabriel's speech, there is no humanity and very little hospitality. Certainly, little hospitality exists for the "strange girl" who enters the party, prompting Dot the Florist's outburst, "Jesus, there's the queer one." Miss Lawless's "pity" and Mr. Conroy's lack of "worry" are the closest sentiments to hospitality. More vocal though is Dr. Fitz's castigation of those "who had let her in"; his angry, ugly retort, "It's a damn shame" is hardly indicative of the hospitality of Gabriel's bygone era. The only hospitable action toward the girl is the waiter's gift of a balloon, but any kindness seems undercut by the strange description of the balloon—"big silver kidney-shaped" and "clutched . . . as if it were a baby." Even the "hospitable board" of Gabriel's aunts is replaced by a ridiculous argument over whether the fish is trout or salmon.

And humor? Humor permeates nearly every line of O'Brien's dinner party. But of "kindly humor," again, there is none. While Joyce's story sparkles with multiple examples, the humor of O'Brien's "nobs" degenerates into coarse, sexist jokes by Mr. Gogarty (another Joycean allusion—the Dublin physician and writer who served as a model for Buck Mulligan):

> With a glint in his eye, Mr. Gogarty brought it to the attention of the two other men that the city they lived in was a very dirty city indeed. They did not blanch, knowing this was a preamble to some joke.
>
> "Haven't we Ballsbridge?" he said, waiting for the gleam on their faces. "And haven't we Dollymount?" he said, with further relish, hesitating before throwing in Sandymount and Stillorgan.

and

> "Now, what is the difference between Northside girls and Southside girls?" Mr. Gogarty asked with pride.
>
> Answers were proffered, but in the end Mr. Gogarty was pleased to tell them they were all dullards. "Northside girls have real jewellery and fake orgasms," he said, and laughed loudly, while Eileen Vaughan repeatedly blessed herself and, as if it were a maggot, lifted the streamer that joined her to Mr. Gogarty.

Self-righteous, puritanical Eileen Vaughan "thump[ing] her husband" as she wages her one-woman fight against smut is hilariously funny, but we laugh at her, never with her. Dot's mention of her "half" a florist shop nudges a laugh, but her intentions are hardly kindly. Perhaps, the funniest instance in the story is Mrs Vaughan's copying and distributing of the letter Mr. Vaughan's English mistress sends, detailing his sexual exploits, neatly paralleled by Sinead's flourishing of Dr. Fitz's love letter among the crowd of the party. Funny? Definitely. Kindly? Clearly not. The single kindness O'Brien allows her creations is demonstrated in Bill the Barrow Boy, whose innocence, whose cliches, whose malapropisms amuse us: "'Ah, it's the hors d'oeuvres that's at her,' Bill the Barrow Boy said, meaning the nerves." Of course, simply his name is humorous. But again, as kind as he may be, even he has his marital problems. He wants children; his wife does not—it will ruin her figure.

At the story's end, O'Brien takes the dinner nobs' collective longings for fulfillment and likens them to the "rapid succession" of lantern slides. As they all wait in mocked suspense to discover who is coming, suspecting that it is John, Betty's "vagrant husband, "hoping that it is John, "the wandering Odysseus returned home in search of his Penelope" (while Betty stands poised with knife in hand—to cut the birthday cake), a spell floods the room:

> You could feel the longing in the room, you could touch it—a hundred lantern slides ran through their minds; their longing united them, each rendered innocent by this moment of supreme suspense. It seemed that if the wishes of one were granted, then the wishes of others would be fulfilled in rapid succession.

These two-dimensional people, transparent as glass in their mundane, selfish wishes, project no mythic connective, only a distant, diffused, disjointed collection of meaningless slides, evoking no pleasant nostalgic moments, no warm family or friendly portraits, no poignantly human memories, emitting no light of any real sort, only shadows of a bygone era, of another Dublin dinner party.

As the "spell" circles the room, O'Brien's ironic pen darkens, blackens the scene. Life is not "just beginning," is not "tender, spectacular, all embracing." These nobs cannot jump up to "catch it"; they are incapable of catching life; they have denied life. The story ends, the projector dims, and this dinner party is left in darkness.

Ironically enough, while winter talk abounds—"a turf fire blazing" and "a nippy evening"—it is nearly spring in O'Brien's story: "Yet by looking through the window Miss Lawless could see that lilac was just beginning to sprout, and small white eggcups of blossom shivered on jet-black magnolia branches." It may be the commencement of spring, but O'Brien's Dublin is more dead than the snow-covered, winter-world of Joyce's Dublin.

Hilary Mantel (review date 25 May 1997)

SOURCE: "Saved from Drowning," in *New York Times Book Review,* May 25, 1997, p. 11.

[*In the following review, Mantel offers a favorable assessment of* Down by the River, *but faults O'Brien for what she perceives as overly pedantic, elaborate prose and a tendency to exhaustively reiterate issues.*]

Out in the country things get very murky," says Mary, the protagonist of *Down by the River,* Edna O'Brien's forlorn, unsparing and consciously exquisite novel of rural despair. Ireland is Ms. O'Brien's mother country, and mothers, as we know, are often capricious, often rejecting, often unwilling to mother at all. Mary is about to be a mother and unwilling to be so: because she is not quite 14 years old, and because the baby is the product of incest with her father.

Mary's own mother has died a premature and painful death; the child has nowhere to turn. She is unable to tell anyone of her plight, though she tries to signal it. She also tries to drown herself, but is prevented by a neighbor out walking her dog. The neighbor, Betty, arranges for them to travel to England, where she can obtain a legal abortion. Before it can take place, Mary is pressured into returning to Ireland. There she is passed from hand to hand. Opponents of abortion offer compassion for the child but little for the mother. She receives the conscience-dogged sympathy of quivering liberals, the quizzical and qualified aid of lawyers who fight for her right to travel freely. The weeks go by, the little prisoner inside her flourishes. Then nature solves her problem, in its own ghastly fashion.

The novel's clearest link to real life is to the 1992 case of a 14-year-old Irish girl, said to have been a rape victim, whose struggles with the legal system wrung hearts on both sides of the Irish Sea and caused in Ireland itself a nation wide examination of conscience. But behind the story lies a significant swath of women's history: years of winking and connivance, of deceit and fear and pain—concealment of pregnancy, unattended births, infant corpses. The retired midwife of Mary's district recalls "the silenced creatures she had found in drawers and wardrobes and in bolster cases, like sleeping dolls: a little baby boy in a lavatory bowl, twins with binding twine around their necks."

This is powerful material, and Ms. O'Brien has apparently decided her prose must rise to it. The reader may feel some initial queasiness. "O sun O brazen egg-yolk albatross." Unripe blackberries are "little excrescenses purposing to come forth in a pained fruition." In this novel, all fruition is pained. There is a harrowing description of a mare struggling to give birth to a foal presenting feet first. The mare's life is saved, and the foal safely delivered —by Mary's father. It is one of Ms. O'Brien's subtleties that he is not a brute, through his actions are often brutal. Witnessing his tenderness to the creatures, Mary thinks "that if she could be a child, maybe if she can be truly a child and make her needs known, he can feel as a father."

There is no lack of human sympathy in *Down by the River,* and a powerful perception of loneliness runs through it. Mary is surrounded by people who want to control her and own her, rather than people who want to help her. In her own district, she attracts odium merely for existing, merely because controversy has soiled "our beautiful, wholesome happy parish." For a short time it is believed that the father of her baby is a street musician she met in Galway, and when the police talk about this kindly, hapless man, Ms. O'Brien captures all the scorn and rage of people who believe they have never put a foot wrong: "I work my butt off, seven days a week, I work overtime to buy shoes for my kids. . . . I grow my own vegetables. . . . I don't permit myself a drink, I don't go to the dogs, I don't go to the bookmakers while he and his ilk sponge off the nation, beget children. . . . Holy Christ, I'd send the lot of them down the mine and dynamite it."

The wider community won't help Mary either. A radio phone-in program is choked with evil banalities; some callers abuse Mary and some assert her right to travel to England, but the show's host assures them, "You're all one hundred and ten percent right." And God is of no use, no matter how many times He is invoked. Before her pregnancy, desperate to escape from the abuse, Mary visits a shrine, but she can do no more than leave a coded message: "Please cure my father's epilepsy." Later, she finds a statue of the Sacred Heart with its head detached. She becomes, with reason, "ashamed of the habit of hoping."

Ms. O'Brien's best moments are a heady blend of insight, intellect and poetry. Four vases of flowers in a hospital ward are "carnations lined along the windowsills in opaque hospital vases, a little flourish of white gypsophila over each one, like nurses' caps." Mary watches her cousin Veronica— one of her unofficial warders, one of the suicide watch— work with a crochet needle "so that a piece of straight thread was converted into a tight and unrippable little conundrum."

That is what encloses Mary: a tight and unrippable conundrum, legal, moral physical. Why, then, despite the sensuous, violent prose, is the reader able to detach from her and think so hard about the problems of the novel itself? Perhaps because Mary as a three-dimensional human being is hardly present in her own story. She is featureless, like some scarred, depopulated battleground. Our anxiety on her behalf remains impersonal; our outrage is aimed at her society rather than her circumstances. She is as innocent as Mary, Mother of God; she passes from Virgin to Mother, her physical condition an interesting one, but her moral travail hidden from us.

Then again, Ms. O'Brien writes orgy prose, dripping and rich and fantastic. Her ironies are crushing, not piercing, and the seriousness and dignity of her undertaking is marred by a solemnity that sometimes trips her. Mary's mother, besotted with her farmyard flocks of fowl, will die of ovarian cancer, images are stretched, themes are beaten. When Mary escapes briefly to a convent boarding school, the first night's supper is "egg salad and single slices of cheese." A paragraph later, Mary's mother writes to her to say they miss her: "Your father is not hard-boiled." Ms. O'Brien also suffers from a lack of flexibility in tone. A report in a "rag of a newspaper" sounds more like Edna O'Brien. Mary's diary sounds like her too.

How should Mary sound? What is the best manner for her story? That the problems of the poor, the powerless and the deprived have their own moral grandeur, no one denies. But in what manner to address them—in the grand manner? That is what Ms. O'Brien has chosen. "Nearly everything reminded her of blood. Her father's, her mother's, her ancestors', her own." When poetry and polemic mix, the sublime may happen; what results here is a kind of rococo indignation, clean lines obscured by language that is often ornate and sometimes florid. A novel, of course, is not a how-to book for legislators or a manual of moral etiquette. Yet Ms. O'Brien, whose early books were censored, has no doubt played her own part in changing the climate of her native country. Earlier in her career, she wrote with a wit and ferocity that were enhanced by the sweetness and simplicity of her style. Her old weapons were sharp and effective; perhaps she comes too late to this particular fight.

Charlotte Innes (review date 8 June 1997)

SOURCE: "Obsession," in *Los Angeles Times Book Review*, June 8, 1997, p. 6.

[*In the following review, Innes offers a positive appraisal of* Down by the River.]

When I was asked to review Edna O'Brien's latest novel, *Down by the River,* I called my sister in London. I wanted to know if she was still reading this prolific and seminal Irish writer who was so important to us 20 years ago. Newly arrived in London from a small town, we related heavily to

Kate and Baba, the mismatched Irish friends of *The Country Girls* trilogy, O'Brien's first fictional work, for whom England's capital represented freedom from the bigotry of rural Irish life. Now, my sister confessed, she's come to reject O'Brien's deep fatalism about intimacy as "unbelievably depressing." And she hates the way O'Brien's women see themselves: "They're always victims."

Some things never change: The women in *Down by the River* are still victims. But I'm going to have to tell my sister that our old favorite is venturing into new literary territory—realist fiction rooted in contemporary Irish affairs.

Ireland's troubles are not totally absent from O'Brien's work. *House of Splendid Isolation* features an Irish Republican Army terrorist hiding out in a widow's house. But in most of her work, political strife tends to be more the background music to her characters' personal musings. In *Down by the River,* which is based on the famous "X" case of 1992 involving a 14-year-old girl made pregnant by her best-friend's father, politics is inescapable.

O'Brien sticks closely to the main facts of the case. When the girl was prevented by the Irish High Court from going to England for an abortion (illegal in Ireland), the ensuing international outcry led to a reversal by the Irish Supreme Court of the lower court decision, forcing a public referendum in which the Irish people voted overwhelmingly for girls in her situation to be allowed to go abroad for abortions. The girl had a miscarriage before she could take advantage of the court decision. Her abuser was jailed for 14 years.

If this had been an earlier work, O'Brien might have explored the inner life of her pregnant 14-year-old heroine, Mary. Instead, she is more interested in the politics of abortion and all its public players—abortion rights foes and advocates, lawyers, doctors—until Mary seems almost to have no voice at all.

And yet, astute readers will catch the familiar images and themes that weave through all of O'Brien's 20 books and innumerable short stories (many of which have been published in the *New Yorker*), which have prompted some critics to remark that O'Brien has only one story to tell. (Although what author doesn't braid and rebraid the same obsession in an effort to pin down some perpetually elusive personal demon?)

Down by the River is in some ways yet another reframing of O'Brien's continuing obsession with not simply Ireland but, the Ireland she left as a young woman. Though she has lived in London for 30 years, O'Brien can never leave the Ireland of her imagination behind.

In *Down by the River,* as in all her works, the Irish countryside, soaked in bloodshed and myth, is inevitably a dreary symbol of death, cruelty and stagnation, epitomized by an image repeated here from earlier fiction, the image of a dark copse where a donkey died and decayed.

There are also the abusive father and self-sacrificing mother. Even the details reflect earlier works. The father likes horses, the mother raises hens, while the perennial dog lingers at the gate, needing caresses and hoping, like previous O'Brien dogs and many of her characters, that despite continual kicks, he will be loved.

Mary is the typical O'Brien overly sensitive girl: She has a Kate-like convent crush on a nun and a Baba-like friend. And like all O'Brien's heroines, however far they might be from their rural origins and however sophisticated their current milieu, Mary is haunted by the oppressive, joy-denying, guilt-laden religious dogma of her childhood, the superstitious bigotry of village life forever an evil stamp upon her soul. (Not surprisingly, until 1972, O'Brien's first seven works of fiction were banned in Ireland and were even publicly burned by the priest in her native village.)

If O'Brien's older stories also dwell on Ireland's awesome beauty as a symbol of purity and simplicity for those mired in urban life—if they emphasize the double-edged nature of life, swinging between death and beauty, between joyous, steamy sex and despair (for taking one solitary vacation, the heroine in *August Is a Wicked Month* pays with the death of her child)—there is little of that joy here. Country scenes in *Down by the River* pulse with a sinister sexuality, from the stark coupling of a stallion and mare to the suggestive "dark coils" of the river where Mary considers drowning herself.

A number of British reviewers (always hard on O'Brien) have criticized her for the uneasy mix of old images with current affairs. And it's true that a kind of authorial documentary voice occasionally bumps up against the novel's overall lyric tone. There's an awkward chapter in which the daughter of a judge makes feminist speeches at her father. This novel also lacks the assured, richly textured language that makes *The Country Girls* trilogy and her short stories so remarkable. And yet it works.

The key is to see *Down by the River* not as realistic fiction (despite having the outrage of an old-fashioned protest novel) but as the Irish equivalent of a Faulkner novel, a reimagined, more deeply colored, symbolic version of the real thing. (Faulkner, Joyce and Chekhov are O'Brien's acknowledged literary idols.)

For example, O'Brien makes some significant changes to the reality of the "X" case. The fictional sexual abuser is Mary's own father, James, a wonderful portrait of self-pitying self-absorption, who pursues Mary with increasing violence after her mother, his wife, dies of cancer. In an especially shocking scene, James tries to abort Mary's pregnancy with a broomstick. What happens to the father in the final pages of the novel is more dramatic, more appalling, than the fate of his real-life counterpart and pushes the drama almost to the point of gothic melodrama, certainly to a level of overwrought, emotional excess.

O'Brien has always enjoyed playing with different styles in an effort to pull new insights out of familiar material. *Casualties of Peace* has parallel stories with heroines from different classes. *A Pagan Place* is told in the second-person singular. *Night* is the monologue of a woman lying in bed. The narrative in *Down by the River* is quite different from, say, the measured, seamless prose of O'Brien's *New Yorker* stories. Tugging the reader along at suspense thriller speed, it bounces among short scenes, flashing the story at the reader in jagged glimpses of horror comparable to the shifting photography of television news, even as the fervent language transforms each scene into a small story or lyric poem.

Out of these broken, over-wrought, pared-down pieces, out of the tension between documentary and poem, O'Brien surely intended an archetypal story, a sort of Irish epic, that takes all her old themes and intensifies them to the point of impersonal tragedy, distilling the grief of all traumatized women who don't make news headlines. From the first chapter, Mary (and surely the choice of name is deliberate, the Virgin impregnated willy-nilly by the God-like father) is every woman who has ever been hurt by a man. The road she and her father are walking along seems to speak of history, "of the old mutinies and a fresh crime mounting in the blood." When he molests her for the first time, "she thought she had always known that it would happen, or that it had happened, this, a reenactment of a petrified time."

Thus, *Down by the River* is more than O'Brien's typical reiteration of male-female torment and offers instead a greater story about power—the power wielded by fathers, states, institutions, anyone with an agenda (there are a couple of terrifying scenes featuring abortion foes)—the kind of power that crushes individual happiness. On the run from her father, saved from drowning by a neighbor who later tries to get her an abortion in England, Mary looks at her face in the neighbor's mirror and sees not the terror of a little girl but of "an animal, animal eyes staring out from the prongs of an iron trap." It's a viscerally terrifying moment.

What's also new here is O'Brien's attitude toward victimhood. Like other O'Brien heroines who haul themselves up from the depths, Mary has a fine thread of resilience at her core that wears but never snaps. But she is also boosted throughout her terrible journey by individuals who offer her genuine kindness without an ulterior motive. There's Luke, the gentle musician, a kind of fairytale prince who gives her shelter, and Mona, another pregnant girl, who offers lively female companionship. If, in other works, O'Brien was concerned with the essential loneliness of the human state, here she offers a glimpse of community.

And with all the gloom in this dark and desperate book, there are hints of O'Brien's old life-affirming humor. Her voice has always been double-edged, as if she herself were split down the middle. On the one hand, she is a passive, dreamy Kate, but she is also a wise-cracking Baba who shrugs and says, "Yeah, life sucks, but I'm going to get the most I can out of it." In **Down by the River,** a disc jockey's patter is both disgusting and delightfully absurd, an upbeat note of presentation at odds with the downbeat of the subject matter.

Yes, I must definitely call my sister. For in this moving addition to O'Brien's impressive body of work, fatalism is edged with genuine glimmers of hope, and the reader discovers, despite evidence to the contrary, that there is goodness in the world.

FURTHER READING

Criticism

Craig, Patricia. Review of *Tales for the Telling,* by Edna O'Brien. *Times Literary Supplement,* No. 4,371 (9 January 1987): 46.

> Provides a synopsis of the stories in *Tales for the Telling,* which Craig calls "a lively collection."

Jaffee, Annette Williams. Review of *The High Road,* by Edna O'Brien. *Ms.* XVII, No. 5 (November 1988): 76-8.

> Highly laudatory assessment of *The High Road.*

Osborne, Linda Barrett. "Two Hostages to An Ancient Feud." *Washington Post Book World* XXIV, No. 34 (21 August 1994): 3.

> Positive review of *House of Splendid Isolation,* which Osborne characterizes as "a moving portrait of the continuing drama that is Ireland."

Additional coverage of O'Brien's life and career is contained in the following sources published by Gale: *Contemporary Authors,* **Vols. 1-4R;** *Contemporary Authors New Revision Series,* **Vols. 6, 41, and 65;** *Concise Dictionary of British Literary Biography,* **1960 to Present;** *Dictionary of Literary Biography,* **Vol. 14;** *DISCovering Authors Modules: Novelists; Major Twentieth-Century Writers;* **and** *Short Story Criticism,* **Vol. 10.**

Georges Perec
1936-1982

French novelist, playwright, poet, scriptwriter, translator, and nonfiction writer.

The following entry presents an overview of Perec's career through 1996. For further information on his life and works, see *CLC,* Volume 56.

INTRODUCTION

Although regarded by many critics and contemporary writers as one of the most distinctive and versatile writers of the twentieth century, Perec described himself as totally without creativity. Several critics, while acknowledging that Perec's work shows the influences of other authors, insist it cannot be described in terms of any other author, that it is truly unique. Italo Calvino, an Italian novelist, regarded Perec as "one of the most singular literary personalities in the world, a writer who resembles absolutely no one else." Perec is perhaps the best known, and certainly one of the most innovative members of the Ouvroir de Littérature Potentielle (OuLiPo), or Workshop of Potential Literature, a Parisian literary society founded in 1960 by novelist Raymond Queneau and mathematician François LeLionnais. The objective of OuLiPo was to create a synthesis of mathematics and literature, and to stimulate creativity through the application of rigorous and arbitrary constraints. This suited Perec, who was driven to literary discovery. In an interview with Kaye Mortley he said, "I would like to write science-fiction and detective novels and *bandes dessinees* [comic strips], cartoons, and music for operas—not music, libretto, and I want to do dramas and comedy and film scripts. I would like to work in all fields of literature. . . . I would like to have used all the words of the dictionary. That's impossible. That's my ambition." This desire to do everything encompassed style as well as genre. The critic Leon S. Roudiez observed that Perec's first four novels each seemed "like the first book of different writers."

Biographical Information

Perec's parents were from families of Polish Jews who emigrated to France in the 1920's. Perec's parents were married in 1934, and he, their only child, was born in 1936. At the onset of World War II, Perec's father joined the French army and was killed in June of 1940. In 1942, Perec was evacuated to a Catholic orphanage in Grenoble. His mother remained in Paris where, in 1943, she and her sister were picked up in a raid and deported to the Auschwitz death camp. Raised by relatives, Perec studied sociology in college and began publishing literary reviews at the age of twenty. Even before joining OuLiPo, Perec showed an affinity for experiment in his writing. His first novel, *Les choses: une history des annes soixante* (1965; *Things: A Story of the Sixties*) is described as having a style similar to a sociological case study. The book was a runaway success. His next two novels enjoyed similar success, but then Perec, according to Gabriel Josipovici, "found himself at a dead end, unable to see any way forward. It was at this point, in 1967, that he was invited to join OuLiPo, and it changed his life." The rigorous linguistic constraints of the group—the incorporation of anagrams, acrostics, mathematical algorithms, as well as the revival of classical forms such as palindromes and lipograms, into the writing—provided fuel for the fire of Perec's creativity. In his first OuLiPian novel, *La disparition* (1969; *A Void*), Perec wrote a lipogram without using the letter "e." The execution was so masterful that several of the first critics failed to note this constraint. A subsequent lipogram, *Les revenentes* (1972; *The Ghosts*), used only the vowel "e." His next major novel, *W, ou, le souvenir d'enfance* (1975; *W, or, The Memory of Childhood*), used a style of alternating storylines in a manner that has inspired a wide variety of interpretations. *La vie, mode d'emploi* (1978; *Life, a User's Manual*), is regarded by most reviewers as his finest work, developing themes that reappeared in *Je me souviens* (1978; *I Remember*) and *Un cabinet d'amateur* (1979; *An Art Lover's Collection.*) He was working on a mystery novel, *53 jours* (1989; *53 Days*), at the time of his death in 1982.

Major Works

Perec's first novel, *Things,* won the French Prix Renaudot and sold over 100,000 copies in France. It is the story of Jérôme and Sylvie, a young couple working as market researchers, who become obsessed with things, with the material possessions they hope will define their lives. But their obsession with the tangible trappings of the good life (which they cannot afford) emphasizes their spiritual emptiness . *La disparition* was translated under the title *A Void* to maintain the lipogramatic avoidance of "e" in the original French, although a more accurate translation would be *The Disappearance* or, more morbidly, *The Death.* Both would be correct, as disappearance and death figure prominently in the plot and theme of the story. In addition to the disappearance of the letter "e", a main character Anton Voyl (A. Voyl— "voyelle" is French for "vowel") also disappears. The group of friends who search for him each die at the moment when they are about to speak a word with the banished letter "e" in it. In *W, or, The Memory of Childhood* Perec, in alternating chapters, tells two stories. In the first narrative, often described as allegorical, W is an island off the coast of Tierra del Fuego, which is at first described as utopian, but progressively appears sinister and totalitarian. The second narrative is presented as an autobiographical tale of Perec's own childhood; yet early in the narrative Perec states "I have no childhood memories." This statement, and other similar ones, lead some reviewers to conclude that Perec is telling the reader that both stories are fiction and that all memories are allegorical attempts to make sense of the chaos of history and memory. Perec expands on the themes of history and mystery in *Life, A User's Manual.* The plot moves physically through a one-hundred apartment building in a mathematically determined manner and through the lives and histories of its residents, past and present, in a wild, disjointed fashion. A central metaphor of the novel is found in the story of Percival Bartlebooth, a resident who has constructed an elaborate but meaningless scheme to occupy fifty years of his life, yet dies unable to complete his plan, thwarted by the unknown vengeance of another resident. In a clear reference to Perec's earlier novel, Bartlebooth is trying to finish a jigsaw puzzle as he dies. The remaining space is shaped like an X (a letter who's metaphoric significance Perec has explored in other writing), but the only remaining piece is in the shape of a W.

Critical Reception

Perec has been favorably received by the critics, although the focus of their praise has been as varied as the styles and subjects of his works. Many critics have been dazzled by Perec's gifted use of language. Justifiably so. The creation of a palindrome (a work that, letter for letter, reads the same backwards as forwards) 5,000 words long is an achievement nearly incomprehensible to most people. And, although several writers before and after Perec created novel length lipograms (works which do not use words containing a specific letter), it is a testimony to his masterful command of the language that several of the early reviewers of *A Void* heaped praise on the novel without even realizing that the letter "e" was never used in it. His incorporation of anagrams and acrostics into poetry, his bi-lingual poetry (poems created with carefully chosen words, so that they would be meaningful in more than one language), are further examples of his linguistic abilities. But many critics see beneath the surface flash of Perec's works a powerful merging of style and content. The sparse, restrained style of *Things* is regarded as a central metaphor for the empty lives of the main characters. The alternating, then merging, story lines in *W, or, The Memory of Childhood* is seen as a refutation of the defining of the present through history and memory. Karen R. Smith suggests Perec's meaning in *W* is that history is an attempt to apply allegory to events, to retroactively structure the chaotic past into a meaningful story that helps define the present. She observes that, in merging past and present, fiction and fact, Perec "collapses the boundaries that separate past from present. Without such boundaries, the past cannot be represented as a coherent whole, fixed in its relationship to the present and offering that present stable meaning." Other critics also see *W* as an attempt to deal with the loss of both parents to the Nazis. In *Life, A User's Manual,* Perec's most popular and acclaimed work, the complex but meaningless work to which the character Bartlebooth has devoted his life is seen as an attempt to superimpose meaning on life, an attempt which is doomed to failure by forces outside the character's control. *53 Days,* Perec's unfinished mystery novel, received the most mixed review. Francis King felt that the novel was insufficiently completed to be worthy of publication, but "the trouble with genius is similar to the trouble with royalty: whatever it does is considered worthy of note." Other critics have praised *53 Days,* suggesting that Perec, aware of his cancer and his limited time, planned this into the execution of the story. John Taylor said that "Perec, notorious for leaving little to chance, seems to have organized his novel in a way that would permit him, once he had completed several chapters and sketched out the others, to abandon it, at any subsequent stage, without unduly weakening its effect."

PRINCIPAL WORKS

Les choses; une histoire des annes soixante [*Things; a Story of the Sixties*] (novel) 1965

Quel petit velo a guidon chrome au fond de la cour? [*What Small Bike with a Chrome-plated Handlebar Standing in the Courtyard?*] (novel) 1966

Alphabets (poetry) 1969

La disparition [*A Void*] (novel) 1969

Les revenentes [*The Ghosts*] (novel) 1972

La boutique obscure [*The Dark Store*] (novel) 1973

W, ou, Le souvenir d'enfance [*W, or, The Memory of Childhood*] (novel) 1975

La vie, mode d'emploi [*Life, a User's Manual*] (novel) 1978

Je me souviens [*I Remember*] (novel) 1978

Un cabinet d'amateur [*An Art Lover's Collection*] (novel) 1979

53 jours [*53 Days*] (unfinished novel) 1989

CRITICISM

Elizabeth Easton (review date 13 April 1968)

SOURCE: "All or Nothing," in *Saturday Review,* Vol. LI, No. 15, April 13, 1968, pp. 46-7.

[In the following short review, Easton discusses the plot and style of Les choses.*]*

This seems to be the era of the non-fiction novel—first Truman Capote's, then Norman Mailer's, and now, on a much smaller scale, one by Georges Perec. For while **Les choses** is subtitled "A Story of the Sixties," it is closer to a case history than to fiction. Jérôme and Sylvie, the young Parisian couple on whom the account centers, remain two-dimensional. Never once in the book's 125 pages do they speak for themselves; there is no dialogue. M. Perec tells the reader rather than shows him; one is not allowed to draw his own conclusions.

And yet the idea that M. Perec is exploring is fascinating and probably explains why **Les choses** won the French Prix Renaudot and, according to the publisher, sold 100,000 copies in France. The author is a sociologist who became interested in why young people are so avid for money. Jérôme and Sylvie are obsessed by a desire for material things, and this greed makes their lives sterile. "They succumbed to the signs of wealth; they loved wealth before they loved life."

Jérôme and Sylvie have been students. However, possessing no real scholarly motivation, they have given up their studies for relatively well-paying jobs as psycho-sociologists, doing motivational research for advertising companies. "Why do tank-type vacuum cleaners sell so badly? What opinion do people in modest circumstances have of chicory? Is prepared puree liked, and why?" Such questions fill their days.

Their passion to live better, to have the finest, is so intense that they have nothing. If the library cannot be redone in light oak, there will be no library at all, and the books will be piled up on two shelves of dirty wood. The charming potentials of their apartment remain unrealized, only dreamed about.

M. Perec allows his cardboard characters no escape. In trying to flee the world of their *petit bourgeois* parents they and their friends embrace the values preached in magazine advertisements, in show windows, in the movies. (The book is, by the way, very French in its connotations. The subtleties of their preferring *Le Monde* to *L'Express* mean little to most Americans.)

M. Perec views the struggles of the young couple with no emotion, not even pity. But if this does not make for an exciting book, the ideas put forth are at least sufficiently stimulating to prompt the thoughtful reader take another look at his own world—which is undoubtedly what the author intended.

Leon S. Roudiez (essay date 1972)

SOURCE: "Georges Perec," in *French Fiction Revisited,* Dalkey Archive Press, 1972, pp. 290-305.

[In the following essay, Roudiez analyses the subject and style of Perec's major works. He shows the emphasis of the author's early life and his association with the OuLiPo in the recurring theme of identity.]

By 1972, Perec was known for having produced four variegated works of fiction, each one seeming like the first book of different writers. **Les Choses** (1965; **Things**) is subtitled "Une histoire des années 60," a narrative that could make one think of Stendhal and his chronicle of the 1830s. If the reference was intentional, however, it could only have been ironical, for the two main characters (there is of course no "hero"), Jérôme and Sylvie, have no real ambition aside from acquiring the material "things" of the title. They are petty bourgeois who aspire to the comforts and pleasures of the upper bourgeoisie, and the narrative that describes their activities comes close to being sociological. Actually, Jérôme and Sylvie are both psycho-sociologists who go about polling people as to their desires, habits, preferences, and reactions to this or that advertisement. They neither like their job nor dislike it; it pays for the "things" they want and leaves them enough free time to look for them. They are moderately happy, although realizing that their happiness hangs by a thread. They have no real political conscience even though they read the proper newspapers and magazines; they long for the days of the Spanish Civil War or the Resistance when, as they see it, choices were clear and inescapable. Somewhat hypocritically they do not acknowledge the existence of the Algerian war, which actually presents them with a choice. Only at the end do they join in a street demonstration or two—an exercise in frightened futility, and they know it. Their material ambitions, likewise, are not based on practical strategies but on dreams; they imagine themselves winning fantastic sums from the lottery or inheriting them from a forgotten rich uncle. They then decide to flee: they go to Tunisia where Sylvie has been offered a teaching job, and both manage to survive on her salary in mediocre fashion. Not long after they spend a weekend in the beautiful home of a wealthy English couple, they realize that such a home would always be beyond their reach and decide to go back to Paris and live as before. But it is also too late for that; through friends, they find a "responsible" position in Bordeaux. The book ends as they enter the dining car of the train that takes them to a life of relative ease, admiring the table settings "where the thick, escutcheoned plates will seem like the prelude to a sumptuous feast. But the meal they will be served will be utterly insipid". One will have noted the future tense in this quotation: in fact, it dominates the last seven pages, giving them an aura of irrevocable destiny, in contrast with the first six pages that are permeated with the conditional of dreams.

What prevents *Les Choses* from being a mere cautionary tale is the writing itself. The economy of means, the variety of style, the irony not only keep the reader interested, amused, and alert, they also involve him or her in the sense that one realizes that the story is not just about Jérôme and Sylvie but about readers of their age, that is, approaching thirty—as Perec himself was when he wrote it.

This was followed by a narrative with a preposterous title, *Quel petit vélo à guidon chromé au fond de la cour? (1966; What Small Bike with a Chrome-plated Handlebar Standing in the Courtyard?).* It is a short piece of fiction that seems to be about a soldier who suddenly discovers that he might be shipped to North Africa during the Algerian war (obviously an inescapable presence in Perec's early texts). He begs his first sergeant to do something about it, such as running over him with a jeep so he can be hospitalized. The first sergeant, Henri Pollak, who could be called the main character and is the friend of the anonymous narrator, consults with other friends who think up a number of hare-brained schemes to keep the soldier out of the war. The one they try to carry out fails, but in the end no one knows what happened to the soldier. That matters only to the extent that he could be termed a deserter, an act that would be echoed in the lives of several other characters in later fiction. At first sight, however, the plot is of no consequence: what matters is the telling of it. It is told by Perec in what appears to be a transcription of spoken French. One soon realizes, however, that it is a very contrived version of oral French and that Perec enjoys playing with language: he has fun, and so does the reader, who may be forgiven for thinking of Raymond Queneau. The soldier, whose fear of war is the pretext for the whole thing, bears an undecidable name. Queneau, in *Le Dimanche de la vie,* managed to provide about forty different spellings for the name of one of his characters; twelve years after *Quel petit vélo,* in *La Vie mode d'emploi,* twenty different pronunciations are given for one character's name, and there are also a number of possible spellings for that same name ranging from Kleinhof to Cinoc (as he is known in the text). The latter is identical in pronunciation to "*sinoc*" or "*sinoque,*" a colloquialism for "crazy." Such undecidability is related to Cinoc's Jewishness, since officials "needed little encouragement to seem somewhat illiterate and rather hard of hearing when it came to giving identification papers to a Jew." Perec's soldier, who is branded not as a Jew but as different is given more than sixty different spellings for his, all beginning with "Kara," going from Karaphon to Karabibine. But what about the bike with chrome-plated handlebars? What bike?

Un Homme qui dort **(1967;** *A Man Asleep***)** is, like Michel Butor's *La Modification,* written in the second person—al-though in the more familiar "*tu*" form rather than the formal "*vous.*" While it seems, at first, quite different from the two preceding books, it actually hovers somewhere in between. It is not composed in a variant of spoken French, but there are sections that benefit from being read aloud. The main character, who is nameless, is not intent on acquiring "things," quite the contrary—his dream is to withdraw from the world, detach himself from all earthly considerations. The result, however, is that even though his path is the opposite of that of Jérôme and Sylvie his life is eventually bound to be the same as theirs, and there is nothing either one of them could have done about it. On the penultimate page of the text whoever speaks gives a quotation from Sophocles (who is not identified as the source), unless it be from the epigraph to Robbe-Grillet's *Les Gommes:* "Time who sees all has found you out against your will."

That kind of subdued echo from another writer can be detected a number of times. After the initial brief remark, "As soon as you shut your eyes, the adventure of sleep commences" (a negative echo or perhaps a contradictory response to the first sentence of Maurice Roche's *Compact,* published the previous year), there follows a forty-seven-line sentence that has a Proustian aura about it. Later one thinks of Maurice Blanchot's title when encountering the phrase "l'attente et l'oubli"; a line by Lamartine appears at the bottom of page 44, Rimbaud is invoked on page 48 through the mention of a "*bateau ivre*" and Harrar; a section begins on page 79 with the same words that initiate Diderot's *Neveu de Rameau.* The bells that toll the hours from the church of Saint Roch recall those that are heard throughout the night from a nearby convent in Butor's *Passage de Milan.* There are also reverberations of Baudelaire, Raymond Queneau, Albert Camus, and Claude Simon. On pages 152-53 Perec has inserted a brief summary of Melville's "Bartleby the Scrivener" (without mentioning writer or title) and half a dozen pages before the end he suggests that no wandering *Rachel* will rescue the anonymous main character from the *Pequod*'s wreck.

In several respects *Une Homme qui dort* marks a turning point in Perec's work. The assimilation of lines by other writers is developed in extraordinary fashion in his masterpiece. *La Vie mode d'emploi* (1978), the title of which reads like a response to this early work's statement, "You are not surprised to discover that there is something wrong, that, to speak bluntly, you don't know how to live, you never will"—and I shall discuss that text presently. References to crossword puzzles emphasize his concern with linguistic play, practicing a particular version of solitaire reveals an interest in complex riddles, both of which are illustrated in subsequent works. All that is related to the Ouvroir de Littérature Potentielle, better known as Oulipo, a "research" group whose conception harks back to the Raymond Queneau colloquium at Cerisy-la-Salle in 1960; its actual birth, signified by the first meeting of the group, took place on November 24 of the same year. The better-known members were Queneau and Marcel Duchamp and the group has included one American, Harry Mathews, since 1973. The cofounder of Oulipo was a mathematician, François Le Lionnais; the combination Queneau—Le Lionnais might possibly account for the mixture of rigor and playfulness (sometimes verging on black humor) that characterizes the activities of the group. Perhaps less obviously comical, Jacques Roubaud, a mathematician, poet, and more recently novelist (whom I mentioned with reference to Jean Pierre Faye and the *Change* collective, and in whose fiction humor does come to the surface) joined the Oulipo in 1966; he has specifically mentioned the troubadours as models (he has written about them and the legends of King Arthur and the Grail) and the sonnet as a privileged form.

Queneau's own *Cent mille milliards de poèmes* (1961), although elaborated earlier, appeared a year after the birth of Oulipo; it is a collection of ten sonnets, each line of which is printed on an individual strip of the page and bound to the spine on its left side. Any first line may thus be followed by any second line, and so forth, and as a result the number of different sonnets that can be read is ten to the fourteenth power; the time required for reading the complete set, devoting eight hours a day and two hundred days a year to the book, would amount to more than one million centuries. So much for combinatory literature, potentiality, and long-term fun. Italo Calvino, who became a member in 1972, said that the Oulipo sailed "under the banner of hoaxing and practical joking."

While members of the Oulipo do not indeed care to become victims of what Sartre called "*l'esprit de sérieux*" there is, nevertheless, a serious background to their activities, and this may be seen through the imposition of constraints. "Writing under constraints" is how Roubaud defines their method. As most everyone realizes, that has been nearly inseparable from the practice of literature but usually not emphasized as such. Called rules or definitions, constraints were part of the accepted canon, like the definition of the sonnet, for instance. When new, more visible constraints are added critics take notice and react—often unfavorably. The French *rhétoriqueurs* of the fifteenth century have not fared well at the hands of traditional literary historians; Gongorism and preciosity have fared even worse. But as Claude-Edmonde Magny noted with reference to Jean Giraudoux's *préciosité* (and I have alluded to this in connection with Maurice Blanchot and Jean Pierre Faye), preciosity is the outcome "of a secret despair facing the irremediable imperfection of the world." It is a protest against evil—even though such a stance might not be fully conscious. The difference with the Oulipo and the reason for the latter's playfulness—at least, I should think, in the mind of Raymond Queneau—is that in the long run, no matter what we do in the world it is of no real consequence, for the world will eventually come to its inevitable end—beyond which there is nothing.

One of the activities related to the Oulipo is known as PALF, that is, "Production Automatique de Littérature Française." The idea is to take a text and replace each word with its dictionary definition; if the result is unsatisfactory, one does the same thing again and again. A variation on this is to replace each noun with the seventh (or any other numeral) noun following it in a given dictionary, or each verb, or both, and so forth. A refusal of the given text, or the world it stands for, is quite clear.

Perec joined the group in 1967 as an associate member. *La Disparition* (1969) would seem to be directly influenced by his interest in the Oulipo; it is a lipogram, which Webster defines as "a writing composed of words not having a certain letter or letters." This book is a fascinating tour de force in that it is written without making use of the vowel *e*, the one most frequently used in French as in English. The narrative is prefaced with a sonnet by Roubaud, from which, in addition to other constraints germane to the sonnet form, the letter *e* is also missing. The writing of *La Disparition* constituted quite a challenge, an exalted form of play, and its surprising aspect is that Perec managed to make it readable. The book relates a series of burlesque, preposterous adventures that are more or less disconnected and in which a number of "characters" disappear (including one named Voyl, who might have been called "*voyelle*" [vowel], if the vowel *e* had not been banned) and also features the device I emphasized in connection with *Un Homme qui dort*—drawing on names, characters, parodic episodes or summaries, and other references to well-known writers (Proust, Kafka, Lowry, Roussel, Wilde, Melville, and so forth), in this instance in order to enhance the knowledgeable reader's amusement. Scholars will no doubt busy themselves unraveling that multitude of threads. A few years later *Les Revenentes* (1972; *The Ghosts*) marked the return of that vowel and the elimination of others (resulting in the unavoidable misspelling of the title)—something like the return of the repressed, and this indeed would seem to invite a thematic, psychoanalytic interpretation.

The suggestion that beneath the superficial, commonplace occurrences of life, "Another thread had always run, forever present, always kept at a distance", as if it were repressed, is also conveyed in a later work, *W ou le souvenir d'enfance* (1975; *W, or The Memory of Childhood*). The thread may be related to Perec's Jewishness, of which he seems not to have been overly conscious at first but which keeps cropping up in various, puzzling fashions beginning with *Un Homme qui dort*. The last fourth of this book is marked by a tone that is bitter, even violent, beginning with the exclamation that begins a section: "Free like a cow, like an oyster, like a rat!" The rat, as a metaphor, initiates a nine-page development, after which the notion of "monster" creeps in and fills the following pages with a litany that insults practically all categories of human beings, "your fellow creatures, your brothers". They include "the exiles, the outcasts, those who have been excluded, the bearers of invisible stars". The allusion to the stars Jews were forced to wear during the Nazi occupation of France is obvious, and the statement that begins the next paragraph is disturbing: "You follow them, you watch them closely, you hate them". The Jewishness and cruelty of Georges Perec have posed problems for critics.

A man who sleeps is bound to dream. *La Boutique obscure* **(1973; The Dark Store)** is a collection of 124 dreams, or rather what can be remembered of them, sometimes in the shape of a narrative, sometimes less than that. The dreams supposedly took place between May 1968 and August 1972, a relatively short period of time, but one during which, assuming Perec had only one dream per night (a very conservative assumption), he should have had well over fifteen hundred dreams. One supposes that less than 10 percent were remembered or worth noting; over 90 percent have disappeared, like the letter *e* in *La Disparition.* While this is intriguing it is mainly a problem for psychoanalysts to worry about. I cannot help noting, however, that a number of the dreams that are recorded (or invented—but is there really a difference?), including the first and the last, involve scenes of concentration camps, police actions, and arrests of civilians by the Nazi SS. Now Georges Perec was born in 1936 and his father, who enlisted in 1939, died at the front in 1940, the day the armistice between France and Nazi Germany was signed, when Georges was four years old. The boy was evacuated to Grenoble (he had relatives nearby) through the offices of the Red Cross in 1942; his mother was arrested in 1943 and never heard of since. My point is that Georges Perec as a child could have had no immediate, conscious experience of concentration camps, arrests, or deportations. These were part of a dark aura that surrounded his childhood; it affected his personality and unsettled his identity in a way that he could not immediately comprehend. If one is tempted, with respect to some of the dreams related in *La Boutique obscure* and other writings as well, to speak of the return of the repressed, one might point out that what was involved was more like a collective repression.

Espèces d'espaces **(1974; Species of Spaces)** could be viewed as an illustration of such a repression in that it is a description of the spaces in which we live or move about, as they are now, without historical or ideological considerations. There is the space of the page on which one writes, the bed in which one-third of life is spent (the suggestion that it is also the space of dreams, fears, and desires is not enlarged upon), the room, the apartment, and so forth, until one reaches the world and space itself, in the abstract. The constraints are not strong enough, however, and there are two pages on unlivable space that include instructions for planting trees and bushes around the gas chambers at Auschwitz.

With *W ou le souvenir d'enfance* one is confronted with Perec's life as a child during the occupation and with the experience of a totalitarian state, although the latter is presented in allegorical form. The composition of the book is intriguing. It is made up of two seemingly distinct narratives, told in alternating chapters—on the one hand a kind of adventure story leading to the description of the island called W and its people devoted to Olympic-like sports, and an autobiography on the other. In other words, fiction versus reality. The fictional tale, however, begins in the most realistic fashion; the reality of the autobiography is challenged at the outset of the second chapter: "I have no childhood memories". The narrator added at the bottom of the same page that he challenged anyone to question him about his childhood, for History (with a capital H and a large ax—"H" and "ax," as I pointed out in connection with one of Sollers's texts, are pronounced the same in French) had already answered in his stead: war and camps have replaced childhood memories. Indeed, as he tries to tell about his childhood he finds he must ask relatives what happened; he also discovers that his own memories are often contradicted by what other people recall. He remembers injuries that no one else does, and false accusations involving actions of which he says he was innocent. Following one such instance, a bee stung him on the thigh and his leg immediately began to swell alarmingly: "For all my schoolmates, and above all for myself, that sting was *evidence*" of guilt. Somehow, the Jewish experience of persecution followed by self-deprecation seeps through those pages and produces a tension between the actual life of Georges Perec between the ages of four and eight and his reshaping of it in his midthirties. On one level, this tension is mirrored in the contrast between an "autobiographical" text he wrote when he was in his late teens and reproduced here, followed by many corrections that represent the "truth" as he saw it in 1970-74 when *W* was being written.

Going back to the fictional narrative, one notices a few telling correspondences. For instance, identical turns of phrase give the (different) month, day, and hour of birth for Georges Perec and Gaspard Winckler (the fictional narrator). Both actual and fictional narrators trace the decision to write and publish *W*, which is described by one as "a" (not "the") story of his childhood, by the other as the account by "the only guardian, the only living memory, the only remnant" of a given world, to an incident that took place in Venice some years before. The latter fictional statement should be tied to what Perec says concerning his scription: "I write: I write because we have lived together, because I was one of them, a shadow among their shadows, a body among their bodies; I write because they have left within me their indelible imprint, the trace of which lies in its scription: their memory is dead to scription; scription is the memory of their death and the affirmation of my life". The fictional Gaspard Winckler explains that he deserted from the army, was taken in charge by an organization of conscientious objectors who provided him with a new identity (his present one) and a passport. The passport was a real one, and the original Gaspard was a deaf-mute child who subsequently disappeared after (or perhaps before) a shipwreck in the vicinity of the Tierra del Fuego islands. The false Gaspard Winckler is urged to go and find out what happened to the real one. The parallel with the autobiography is obvious: the six-year-old Perec "deserted" occupied Paris and his Jewishness (of which he was hardly aware), was taken in charge by the International Red Cross and sent to the nonoccupied Grenoble area, where he was given a new identity as a pupil in a Catholic school. When he wrote *W ou le souvenir d'enfance* he tried to find out who the "real" Georges Perec was.

With *W ou le souvenir d'enfance* one is confronted with Perec's life as a child during the occupation and with the experience of a totalitarian state, although the latter is presented in allegorical form.
—*Leon S. Roudiez*

The book is divided into two parts. While the "autobiographical" narrative continues more or less chronologically and still somewhat spasmodically, the "fictional" narrative breaks off without saying anything about the narrator's decision, how he reached the southern tip of South America and was able to land on a nearly inaccessible island. It begins the second part in a make-believe manner that presages its allegorical nature: "There would be, over there, at the other end of the world, an island. It is called W". It was settled in the nineteenth century by a man named Wilson, about whose identity contradictory stories are told (identity is a leitmotiv in *W*). At first the narrative continues by providing a favorable, although seemingly detached description of life on W(ilson) island. It is a country devoted to sport and the glorification of the body. Gradually, though, one is reminded of the Nazi's attitude toward physical prowess and their contempt for the human individual, and in the end, after describing how children enjoy a pampered life before being suddenly thrust into the brutal atmosphere of adult life, the tone changes: "Very few attempt suicide, very few become truly insane. Some never stop howling, but most remain silent, relentlessly so". This last sentence could remind one of Bartleby's stance and justify enlarging the scope of the satire beyond the obvious condemnation of fascist totalitarian regimes (Pinochet is mentioned on the book's last page) to a commentary on life in our Western society as well as its intense competitive spirit.

If one is to believe Perec's "autobiographical" narrative, his fictional counterpart, Gaspard Winckler, had already been the main character of his first unpublished novel, "Le Condottiere"; Winckler then permeated the text of the monumental *La Vie mode d'emploi* (1978; *Life: A User's Manual*), in which his wife Marguerite dies in 1943, the year Perec's mother disappeared, bound for Auschwitz. It is intriguing to think of Winckler as a sort of mirror image of Perec as it is to muse on the initial letter of his name, which is the same as that of the Tierra del Fuego island and has been, in the book and in the title, reduced to that initial. Perec, perhaps as a consequence of his activities in the Oulipo, was fascinated by the material qualities of the letters of the alphabet. In *W ou le souvenir d'enfance* he commented on the only French substantive to be represented by a single letter, *x*, referring to a sawbuck table, on the importance of the symbol in mathematics, where it stands for the unknown, on the geometric transformations that change an *x* into a swastika as well as into the Star of David. There is also the one that, by rotating the lower half of the *x*, transforms it into a *w*. It all entailed a phantasmatic geometry of which "the basic figure was the double *v*, whose multiple entanglements delineate the major symbols of my childhood history." (One might add that *w* is not a French letter, just as Perec's parents were originally Polish.) The final chapter of *La Vie mode d'emploi* shows the dead Bartlebooth seated before an almost completed jigsaw puzzle, and "the black hole for the piece that still needs to be fitted in is in the nearly perfect shape of an *x*. But the piece that the dead man holds between his fingers has the shape, long foreseeable in its very irony, of a *w*."

There are basically two ways of approaching *La Vie mode d'emploi*, according to one's bent. If one is a scholar and/or a devotee of puzzles of various kinds, mathematical, linguistic, or literary, the text will be analyzed in order to discover the rules and constraints that presided over its composition. If one is an amateur, in the best sense of the term, one will seek the pleasure of the text, whether it be ethical or aesthetic, and describe the emotions that are experienced. Either approach is valid, and although I favor the latter I believe some information about the former will enhance one's pleasure. In this instance there has been (and still is) such critical emphasis on the composition of the work that I need only sum up what scholars have discovered without repeating the details.

After a preamble (to be repeated word for word at the outset of chapter 44), in which the nature and practice of the more complex, sophisticated jigsaw puzzles are examined, the first chapter then takes the reader to a Paris apartment building where a woman from a real-estate agency is climbing the stairs, looking carefully at everything, on her way to a small apartment that has just been put on the market. Upon completing the second or third chapter, the reader realizes that the lives of tenants and former tenants of the building will be accounted for—but in what order? Perec decided to rely on the solution to a chess problem: what path must the knight follow in order to touch every square of the board; he then adapted that solution to his imaginary building's architecture. Next came the major constraint. Essentially, it required that in making up the stories that would involve his tenants Perec, by means of mathematical permutations (Queneau had a passion for mathematics, which was also the basis for the architecture of such works as Ollier's *La Mise en scène* and Butor's *Degrés*), arrive at a list of forty-two objects (some of which might be quotations) or themes that must be included in each chapter. As he himself explained: "Thus, in chapter 23, I had to use a quotation from Jules Verne and one from Joyce. The one, or rather the several quotations from Verne pertained to the library, which is Captain Nemo's, and the list of tools that reproduces that of the magic chest in *The Mysterious Island.* The house Leopold Bloom dreams about at the end of *Ulysses* has become the dollhouse on page 135." One will recall that quoting the texts of other writers is a practice that began with **Un Homme qui dort.** The question that logically follows, for which it might not be possible to provide an answer, is, why those particular writers, why those specific themes, why those precise objects?

On page 695 of **La Vie mode d'emploi** there is a postscript that lists thirty writers (including Perec himself) whose texts, "sometimes slightly modified," have been inserted into his own. Among the half-dozen projects he enumerated in 1976 and which his premature death in 1982 prevented from completing, there is that of "Le Roman du XIXe siecle": starting from a standard anthology of nineteenth-century French literature he planned "to unify its components in order to end up with a narrative whose chapters would contain fragments out of *Adolphe, Attala,* and so forth, down to Zola." Michel Butor had already practiced this form of unemphasized quotations in *Portrait de l'artiste en jeune singe* (1967) and *Illustrations II* (1969) and asserted in the issue of *L'Arc* featuring his work (also in 1969) "A [literary] work is *always* a collective work." He has not, however, generalized the process of incorporating other texts into his own to the extent that Perec has. **La Vie mode d'emploi** includes Butor among those he has borrowed from, and quotations from seven books have been identified, thus suggesting a certain affinity in the two writers' stance as to the act of scription. Also, the reader who begins the book is almost bound to notice the similarity, superficial as it may be, with Butor's *Passage de Milan.*

As was the case with Raymond Queneau's *Le Chiendent* (1933), it is quite possible that few if any critics would have noticed such architectural features if the writer himself had not called attention to them. Sources are the just-mentioned postscript to **La Vie mode d'emploi,** a number of interviews,

and contributions to literary reviews. Once readers have become acquainted with those compositional secrets, they can go back to the text and discover (or imagine) a number of clues they had overlooked. It thus seems possible that descriptions in the present tense might be those of a painting—the one that Serge Valène, a painter who was a tenant in the building, had contemplated doing but never did. Another painter, Hutting, also a tenant, had planned a series of twenty-four paintings, to be executed at the rate of one per month in a predetermined order. They were to be portraits, whose subjects, while playing a determining part, were merely one of their basic elements; the first and last names of the subjects together with their profession were to be the starting point of each picture: "Subjected to various linguistic and numerical processings, the buyer's identity and profession would successively determine the painting's size, the number of figures, the predominant colors, the 'semantic field' . . . the central theme of the anecdote, the secondary details (historical and geographic allusions, clothing, accessories, and so forth), and finally the price". Valène's project, detailed in chapter 51, which was to include 179 topics, all of which can be identified as being part of *La Vie mode d'emploi,* did not materialize; Perec is the one who completed it in words, following a method similar to Hutting's.

> **The street, an imaginary one, can nevertheless be precisely located on a map of Paris. . . . It is impregnated by the surrounding reality and thus quite emblematic of Perec's books.**
> **—Leon S. Roudiez**

Putting aside such complex matters dealing with the composition of the book, one can now resume one's reading of the first chapter and learn that the vacant apartment was that of Gaspard Winckler who died two years earlier (the "chronological indications" at the end of the volume disclose that it was in 1973). Perhaps one has noticed that the chapter begins in a very tentative manner, with verbs in the conditional, like the beginning of **Les Choses,** "Yes, it could begin this way, right here, just like that, in a somewhat slow and ponderous fashion, in this neutral space that belongs to everyone and to no one," before firming up on the second page with verbs in the future tense, like the end of **Les Choses:** "Yes, it shall begin here: between the fourth and the fifth floor, 11 rue Simon-Crubellier." The street, an imaginary one, can nevertheless be precisely located on a map of Paris, for it is surrounded by actual streets, and its "history" is given on pages 570-71. It is impregnated by the surrounding reality and thus quite emblematic of Perec's books—and not only his: the fictitious lycée of Butor's *Degrés* is similarly implanted in the reality of Paris. While other tenants' names are mentioned, this first chapter focuses on Winckler's name and apartment, for it is his death that has belatedly caused the real-estate agent's visit, and it ends with a tantalizing statement: "Gaspard Winckler is dead, but the slow vengeance that he has so patiently, so meticulously contrived has not yet been fully sated". A few minutes and 578 pages later, Percival Bartlebooth, a wealthy Englishman who bought an apartment in the building in 1929, dies as he is about to complete a jigsaw puzzle; he dies, unable to figure out how to fit a *w* into the unknown—the space shaped like an *x*.

The generic subtitle of *La Vie mode d'emploi* is "*romans,*" in the plural. There are indeed many independent narratives in the book; they emerge in associative fashion, much the way secondary narratives do in some of Raymond Roussel's works. What links them is that their protagonists have at one time or other lived in the apartment building or are related to someone who does or has. Nevertheless, it is the story of Bartlebooth and that of the Bartlebooth-Winckler relationship that helps in bringing it all together. Bartlebooth's name is a compound of Melville's Bartleby, who first showed up in *Un Homme qui dort,* and Valery Larbaud's millionaire, A. O. Barnabooth. Bartlebooth's wealth was matched only by the indifference to what wealth generally allows one to do. He "decided one day that his entire life would be organized around a single project, the arbitrary necessity of which would have no other end but itself". He planned to spend ten years learning how to do watercolors (he knew it would take that long because he had no aptitude) and twenty years to travel around the earth painting five hundred watercolors of seaports; each one was to be sent back to Paris where Winckler would transform them into jigsaw puzzles. Back in the rue Simon-Crubellier, Bartlebooth would finally spend twenty years putting the puzzles together again; permanently glued, they would be sent to the place where they had been painted, the watercolor dissolved, and the paper, in its original whiteness, returned to Paris. Another metaphorical circle in contemporary French fiction has once more been completed.

Fifty years of his life would thus be fully occupied by an undertaking as complex and difficult as it was futile. In the end, all trace of his activity would have been eradicated. In contrast to the many who aspire to leave a record, a monument testifying to their presence on earth, and fail, Bartlebooth wished that there be nothing left—and he, too, failed. The agent of his undoing was Gaspard Winckler, for solving a jigsaw puzzle is not a solitary activity: "Every gesture made by the puzzle solver, the puzzle maker had made before; every piece he takes and picks up again, examines, fondles, every combination he tries and tries again, every trial and error, every intuition, every hope, every discouragement, have been determined, calculated, studied by the other."

What the book does not tell the reader, however, is what prompted Winckler to seek revenge, what Bartlebooth had done to arouse such deep, slow-burning passion. The question's importance is attested by the recurrence of the theme throughout *La Vie mode d'emploi.* It crops up in the story of Elizabeth de Beaumont, who lived with her mother on rue Simon-Crubellier for only one year, as a teenager, and ran away; she then turned up in England working as an au pair and taking care of the five-year-old son of a Swedish diplomat; she accidentally, carelessly, or intentionally let the boy drown in the bathtub and fled. The mother, who arrived shortly afterward, committed suicide. The father, who only returned home two days later, vowed to find Elizabeth: he "swore to devote [his] life, wealth, and wit" to avenging his wife and son. After six years of a relentless search, three-quarters of his wealth having been spent, and on the verge of insanity, he finds out where she is and kills her and her husband. Elizabeth, for her part, had soon realized that he was pursuing her and did her best to elude him; in the end, however, she gave up. She wrote him to say that she would stay in one place, that it was hopeless trying to escape, because (and this is a significant detail) "luck and money have been, and will always be, on your side." She did not mention obstinacy, although that is a theme often present in the narratives of *La Vie mode d'emploi,* not necessarily connected with revenge, not necessarily leading to success. Bartlebooth's life might be cited as an example of obstinacy leading nowhere.

A second story of an avenging quest is that involving Oswald Zeitgeber, who murdered the forty-nine inhabitants of an African village in order to gain access to a graveyard of elephants whose ivory made him fabulously rich. Another man had "incessantly tracked him down for twenty years, unremittingly searching for the evidence of his guilt: now he had found it." It would be hard to forget Hélène Gratiolet, whose father owned the apartment building. After he died in 1917 she sold her share of the inheritance, got married, and emigrated to the United States where her husband was killed by three thugs. She found out who they were, where they were, followed them until she could methodically kill them one by one. It all started, in a way, because she had felt slighted in her father's will.

Bartlebooth was a millionaire, of course, but money as a motive for revenge is, in Winckler's case, never mentioned. At this point we should probably keep in mind what Perec himself told one of his interviewers: "It is once again necessary to start from the metaphor of the jigsaw puzzle or, if one prefers, that of an unfinished book, of an unfinished 'oeuvre' within a literature that will never be completed." Each book is like the individual pieces of the puzzle, which have no meaning in themselves but must be related to the whole. The various narratives of *La Vie mode d'emploi* do not yield their full meaning when considered individually;

each "roman" relates to the entire set of "romans." Likewise, that book considered alone does not yield its full meaning, for it must be considered in the context of all the other books written by Perec.

The characters, or rather the words that bring forth characters in the reader's mind, are one of the more obvious links. Perec, in the novel he was working on at the time of his death, *53 Jours* (posthumously published, in fragmentary fashion, in 1989), suggested that the various transformations that are effected between one novel and the next "do not have the same effect on the progress of the story as, for instance, having a major character circulate from one book to another." One recalls that Gaspard Winckler is the distorted mirror image of Perec himself in *W ou le souvenir d'enfance,* that he is connected with the unknown, the lack of identity, the *x.* He is the one who bears witness to the atrocities that characterize life on W(ilson) island. There is nothing in the text of *La Vie mode d'emploi* that might allow one to state that Gaspard is Jewish or that he is not; he has no relatives that anyone knew about, and after his death it takes a lawyer several months to dig up a distant cousin; he is connected with the darker side of life, as evidenced by his making what was known as "the Devil's rings" and "Witches' mirrors." Bartlebooth, on the other hand, is related to Melville's Bartleby, hence to Perec's *Un Homme qui dort,* the man who sleeps while the holocaust takes place. Bartlebooth himself, protected, like Barnabooth, by his wealth, seems completely unaffected by the Second World War during which he continues to travel, paint his watercolors, and send them to Winckler (sometimes through the good offices of the Swedish diplomatic services). The plight of the Jews is illustrated in one of the *romans,* the one telling the story of Appenzzell, the anthropologist who left for Sumatra in 1932 in order to study an isolated tribe by becoming a part of it. He soon discovered that they would not accept him. After that traumatic experience of rejection, he found he could not return home in Austria because he was a Jew and the Anschluss had been accomplished. He disappeared, and his mother who refused to wear the star identifying Jews during the German occupation managed to escape to the unoccupied zone, only to be killed in 1944 in the Vercors.

As I see it, Jewishness in Perec's work seems to function as a catalytic agent bringing together and exacerbating a sense of otherness, of injustice, prompting a desire for revenge. At first, the otherness could not be rationally accounted for. As he noted in *W ou le souvenir d'enfance,* "How could it have happened that . . . during Christmas night, I was the only child left in a school that was practically filled, not with sick children, as originally intended, but with refugee children." He did not realize it at the time, but the reason was that he was Jewish and had no immediate family. On the whole, in the light of some of the stories told in *Le Vie mode*

d'emploi and the one subsequently related in *Un Cabinet d'amateur (1979; An Art Lover's Collection),* it would seem that it is injustice that matters, whether suffered by a Jew or a non-Jew.

That 1979 fiction is about a German immigrant to the United States who made a fortune in the brewery business in the latter part of the nineteenth century and decided he would rival or better the art collections of people like Duveen in England or Mellon in America. He soon discovered, however, that the paintings he had begun to collect were either worthless or fakes. With the help of his nephew who had studied art in Boston and a couple of experts he then put together a complex machinery to provide authentication for the initial items in his collection as well as for all the subsequent fakes that he purchased or manufactured afterwards. His revenge was posthumous, as his paintings were auctioned off after his death and very profitably sold to wealthy individuals, foundations, and museums; later, the nephew wrote a letter to all buyers explaining what had happened. A double irony is in evidence here. First, the title of the book refers to a painting representing the brewer, Hermann Raffke, in the midst of his collection, a painting in which all the "original" works were imitated; it turns out that this is the only original painting of the lot—now unavailable as it was placed in a sealed vault facing Raffke's mummified body. Second, Raffke was full of "patriotic" feelings for his old country and an admirer of the emperor William II; providentially, he died before the First World War was begun and in all likelihood he was not Jewish. The final lines of *Un Cabinet d'amateur* point out that, like the paintings of Raffke's collection, "most of the details of this fictional narrative are false, and it was conceived for the sole pleasure, and the sole thrill, of pretending." Such is sublimated revenge.

A fondness for puzzles, including crossword puzzles (of which he contributed quite a few to periodicals), mathematics, playing with language merged with the theme of revenge in *La Vie mode d'emploi* and were perhaps intended to be fused together in *53 Jours.* As this work is unfinished, there is no way of knowing in what shape Perec would eventually have published it had he lived long enough to do so. The themes can be identified, and all those I just mentioned are present. The architecture would appear to be less associational, more integrated, drawing the reader into the narrative's fabric. Indeed, while the epigraph to *La Vie mode d'emploi,* taken from Jules Verne's *Michel Strogoff,* "Keep your eyes open, keep them fully open," suggests the position of a spectator, the reader of *53 Jours* (supposedly the time it took Stendhal to write *La Chartreuse de Parme*) is taken in hand by a narrator who, through an intermediary, the local consul (this takes place in a former French African colony), has been given a manuscript drafted by a mystery-novel writer named Serval who claimed his life was in danger and if anything happened to him the explanation could be found in the manuscript. Serval has disappeared, the manuscript is the unfinished text of a mystery entitled "The Crypt"; we read it, only to find that references to other mystery novels are embedded in it, making the problem more difficult to solve.

By the end of the first part, we understand that Serval was implicating the consul in a scandal and, to protect himself, the consul kills Serval and arranges things so that the narrator will seem guilty of the murder. At the outset of the second part we learn that what we have just read is an unfinished manuscript entitled "53 Jours," found in Grenoble (Stendhal country, in addition to being Perec's temporary country as a child) in the abandoned car of a man called Serval, a businessman and former Resistance hero. This manuscript is supposed to contain clues that will solve the mystery of Serval's disappearance. Thanks to Stendhal, Balzac, and others, the reader may decide that the man who disappeared was not Serval but an impostor who took his place after he was killed a few weeks before the liberation of Grenoble. The text becomes a sort of avenging machine that sets in motion a number of complex, dizzying devices that enable one to arrive at the truth. *La Vie mode d'emploi* played on the reader's emotions as well as his mathematical, puzzle-solving imagination; *Un Cabinet d'amateur* emphasized the pleasure of putting together a complex fiction. In spite of echoes from the French colonial wars of this century and of the deadly underground struggles during the occupation, what evidence there is points to a novel more in the spirit of *Un Cabinet d'amateur*. As Robert Pinget might have said, Perec, in polishing and rewriting *53 Jours* (perhaps under another title), would have done his best to produce an object of art, one that pleased him emotionally and thrilled him intellectually. It is a pity he was not given the chance.

Kaye Mortley (interview date August 1981)

SOURCE: "The Doing of Fiction," in *Review of Contemporary Fiction*, Spring 1993, pp. 23-9.

[*In the following interview from 1981, conducted in English, Mortley questions Perec about his theories of fiction.*]

[Perec:] I began writing, I was twenty about. I am now forty-five and I think I learn how to write. I know how to write stories and even poetry and dramas, I could say, and it's my way of living in a sense. I can't imagine a life in which I won't spend some hours every day writing. I can't say exactly why I started writing. I can say now that I am in great familiarity with language and it's a kind of, I could say, struggle. I began with French language and fiction in which I try to do what I told you about the boy child with the alarm

clock when I try to undo the letters and sentences and paragraphs and chapters and books and to reorganize the game.

When I was twenty about, there was some twenty authors I loved, I liked very much, and they drew a kind of puzzle between them. They were Michel Leiris and Jules Verne and Roussel and Flaubert and Stendhal and all of them were different but all of them had something in common—some *frontières*, borders, and I could draw a puzzle with them and somewhere in the puzzle there was a space in which I will myself move and then when I take my books, I think that all my books are different one from each other and all have something in common and again they draw a kind of puzzle in which there is a blank space which is the new book I am going to prepare. And of course, the blank spaces, the white spaces, blanks will always . . . it has to stay there. And what I can hope for readers and people who will write after me, that I will take the place of one of these pieces of puzzle and give way to somebody to write again after my death. I mean, of course, if there is a temporal thing in all that, that is, that I will live from 1936 to, I don't know, and then my work will be, sometime, will be both unfinished and finished. Unfinished because what I have to say is everything. I mean, as every writer, I would like to say everything in every way possible. I like to write stories for children of six when they begin to read and I would like to write science-fiction and detective novels and *bandes dessinees*, cartoons, and music for operas—not music, libretto, and I want to do dramas and comedy and film scripts. I would like to work in all fields of literature and to, I would like to use, at the end of my life. I would like to have used all the words of the dictionary. That's impossible. That's my ambition. That's why I write and how I write at the same time.

[*Mortley:*] *Perhaps one way to situate your work might be in the context of the group of writers "OuLiPo."*

Yes. *OuLiPo* means *Ouvroir de littérature potentielle. Ouvroir* is a kind of workshop and "potential literature," we have to define what is potential. The first name of the group was "experimental literature," then we find that the word *experimental* was too heavy to carry and we chose another term, "potential," which means to try to decipher what is in writing. We mean, by which way a writer can govern what he's trying to do. There is a play by Molière, a man who is called M. Jourdain and he makes poetry without knowing he is doing so—*il fait de la poésie sans le savoir. Il fait de la prose sans le savoir*—without knowing it. We want to know, the Oulipian writer makes prose knowing it. We want to know what we are doing and want to experiment what we are doing and we want to choose pattern and models and structure and *contraintes*. I don't know exactly what the name for *contraintes* is.

We are in front of writing like a little child who is playing with a clock, a *réveil-matin,* an alarm clock, and he will undo it in order to know how it works. And in a way we are like mathematicians. For instance, we put things like that: suppose there is no *e* in the language. How would we write a story without *e*? And the result of that is a book I wrote which was **La Disparition.** And suppose we want to do a text in which vowels would be introduced one by one. First *a,* then *e, i, o, u,* and again, *a, e, i, o, u.* A kind of sequence. We work a little like musicians. We do permutations, we do lipograms and all, there is a tradition which goes very far away. Oulipian began with Greek literature and then in the Middle Ages there was a great *ouvrage* called the "rhetoration"— "great rhetorics"—and in a lot of literary fields—in Arabic poetry—and Japanese poetry—and in novels too. At many times in the history of writing there were people who wanted to try to understand what they were doing when they did it. We like to function as a group, not as a movement.

It's like when we try to decipher our own unconscious—through the conscious patterning.
—Georges Perec

We could say at first, that an Oulipian is a man who doesn't take literature seriously but who takes it as a play, as a game, but we think that play and game are serious things and in fact we were a little bored by people like the old Hugolian image of the god-shaped writer and we want to insist on the *art* of fiction. The doing of writing. We insist that, for instance, a form like tanka has great importance in Japanese poetry for about ten centuries and a form in European poetry like the sonnet has been preponderant for about the same length of time and we wonder *why* there are such structures and for a lot of time, from, in French literature, for instance, from Renaissance to Victor Hugo, there was no question about writing. You could learn at school how to write and write well and you can learn to write poetry. You have to count to twelve. The twelve, the alexandrine—that was a really great shape, a great pattern for poetry. Then it began with Victor Hugo and Baudelaire and then Mallarme and then Rimbaud and it was broken. Now we are obliged to find new forms, new ways of tracing our way through that thing which is so opaque. The writer, his first purpose is to say something to somebody else—and he has to find his way and his voice. He had to find something which will completely seduce the reader. We have to, first, to examine the old, old patterns that were at work in all novels and poetry and all things, and then we try to find new, new ways of, how we could say, to stimulate.

[*Perec was then asked about his attitude to surrealism.*]

You know, surrealism was a group very important in the

twenties but at the level of text production of fiction, of poetry it was limited by (*comment dire: le hasard?*) chance. It shows chance as a way of writing, like automatic writing and which used to be most, as most as possible, out of chance. We want to predict what we are doing and Raymond Queneau once said anybody can push the people, characters, like if it were a flock of sheep, and he pushed them and pushed them and through the pages he will arrive at something, something that people will read as a novel. And he said he couldn't support with something which was only like that. He wanted that the number of characters and the relation of the characters to be governed by a structure. He tried to program his inspiration. He tried to build the labyrinth through which he will have the best access to what he was trying to do.

We were, sometimes we were astonished by the way that through this apparently conscious process, the unconscious appears more likely and it's very obvious in some of our works. It's like when we try to decipher our own unconscious—through the conscious patterning. I think it, for instance, it reinforces it, for instance, when I was working without the letter *e* in my novel, the missing of the *e* was like a pump for me. All I had to invent was opening a lot of doors. *Ça levait des barrières.*

Myself, I entered the OuLiPo in 1966, after my second novel exactly. And it was the end—the sixties were the end of what was called "Existentialism," *littérature engagée*—and Queneau was at that time a very particular figure in literature. He was related to another kind of tradition which was not very well known. He has been through surrealism but he was not—he has been only a very short time in the surrealistic movement and he was in a kind of border of experimental novel and poetry which was not recognized as itself. And through OuLiPo, through the existence of OuLiPo, there was now a kind of sensibility which is aware of what we could, of how to write, in a sense, is to take the dictionary, I mean *réservoir* of the language and syntax and all the tradition of novels and poetry and to try to do something else. Something which is a little different to what was before. Of course it's always the same kind of stories and the same kind of descriptions and the same kind of action and fiction and we only tried to strengthen again what happens between the writer and the reader and which is the text. I mean the text functions only if a reader will read it and so we have to, I put it, to seduce him.

You mention the relationship for the first time, I think, between the writer and the reader and the text which is the relationship between them. How do you situate yourself in relationship to your readers, for instance?

I represent myself as something like a chess player and playing a chess play with the reader and I must convince him, or her, to read what I wrote and he must begin the book and go until the end. If he doesn't, I miss my aim. And do you mean what happens when he did it? I don't know, I try, I only imagine that he can take as much pleasure and pain as I expended when I was writing.

So you regard him as a sort of alter ego, who reads, who is reading?

Not exactly—yes, at the end. But I mean during the process of reading, I consider him like a chess mate—somebody who is playing a part with me. The model for that kind of thing is the detective novel, all detective novels. And when you read a detective novel, you don't care really about who kills the victim and who is the murderer and you care only about, you wonder why you don't find. And it's very interesting because in a novel you try to play with what is true, what is false, what to think, what to—just to keep an aura of suspense in a sense—like Roland Barthes uses it. Something is *suspendu*—hanging—and it's a way of dreaming, of going elsewhere through the process of fiction. What is most important in a novel, it's, I could say it's not written. It's something which is behind the words and which is never said.

Yes, I consider that the most defined area is that of the novel, that of fiction.

I think I am. I could generalize a little, that in almost everything I am producing there is, we could say, a story and the story of the story. A fiction and a fiction about the fiction and like, it's like mirrors, and it doesn't end with the fiction and the fiction about the fiction—there'll be speculation about the fiction of the fiction and so on. And there is, I could say there is several levels.

Have you, then, a personal definition of what you consider to be fiction?

I don't think so. I can't—*surtout en anglais*—I can't think about it in a clear way. It's something which goes with dream and with construction of something who takes its part in what we are doing and seeing and hearing and living and a part which is completely made of substance of words and who depends so closely on what words are—how they function and language and even in writing—even in the physical act of writing. But I can't know exactly what the fiction is. It's like a mayonnaise, I should say.

In fiction there is a narrative self, or there is some itinerary?

I begin just now, from until a few weeks, to have something who could become later, very later, a theory about narration. And I only can give you an example. You know in linguistic theory people speak about *morpheme* and *lexeme* and so

I think there is something which could be called the *narrateme.* That is a very tiny element that is, is like a pearl in a mother of pearl which will gradually become the fiction, become the narration. At the beginning there is almost nothing. I think Balzac does exactly this. You see, he began to write a book, two books, three books, then a character came back in another book and at the end the mass of the books looks like the description of the entire nineteenth century. And at the beginning it's only the linking characters from one book to another or inside a book the linking of details with their backgrounds which could be true or false. . . .

I am, I was a great pedestrian. I like to walk in my town, in Paris, and I chose some years ago, 1969, twelve places in Paris and I decide I will go then every month and describe one of them and then I will try to write another text about the memories I have concerning that place. I do that program, not, I didn't do it all that long time and it was, I suppose it would be very interesting because I would get, when I finish, I would get three kinds of *vieillissement*—aging. The aging of the places, the aging of my writing, and the aging of my memories. And it was very difficult. It was a hard discipline. The interest was to try to get a very close view of what is to be seen in the street, or in the street scene. Most of the time we don't pay attention to what I call the *quotidiennete,* the everyday. For instance, we are not aware of how many cars are in our scenery and once I did a radio piece about Carrefour Mabillon where I enumerate all the cars and what I have was very terrifying, because we don't see them. We don't pay attention to what exactly is in front of our eyes. So when I do those texts, I try to be the most precise and flat, I could say, like if I was a Martian going through a city, going through something he doesn't know what it is and describes only by little pieces what's going on. I don't try to interfere and I don't try to put myself in the position other than an eye looking, but afterwards I think it will nourish some kind of fiction, some kind of details of some kind of everyday which I like to speak aloud.

I did another kind of thing which was called *Je me souviens,* "I Remember," in which I try to remember very tiny facts. Movies, or songs, or a way of dressing, or food we used to eat at certain times and it was like if I was working on a diary that could have been written by everybody of my generation in France. I mean it's not, it's very difficult to translate. And I think it's not fiction in itself but it's like a trampoline to fiction. For instance, it's like a trampoline to a kind of nostalgia, to a kind of sympathy. Sympathy between people who remember that some years ago when you took the underground in Paris they do a hole in your ticket.

It's another type of petite madeleine.

Yes, it's a kind of *petite madeleine* but it's a game that can be played with a lot of people. And I was astonished when

I wrote the book in the beginning of 1978, I received a lot of letters from people who said I was wrong in my "souvenirs," in my memories. But it doesn't matter if I was wrong or right. And people send me their own memories of the same "I Remember." We think we remember very important facts and of course we have lived through very unimportant facts but which speak to us more strongly. Maybe the most important is that, this awareness of everyday. When I try to describe it, first I try to describe what I see. I mean reality. And when I try to remember, I try to remember reality but gradually reality is only transmitted through language, through writing. What is around the reality through the language is fiction and it's through fiction and language that people can communicate.

A work of yours which is very closely linked to this area of language-reality is Tagstimmen, *the piece which was done by the German radio which exists only in German.*

Tagstimmen was a work which was a *commande.* I was asked to do it with a musician whose name was Philippe Drogoz and with my German translator which is Eugen Helmle. What I was asked to do was to explore systematically the potentialities of human voice. That is to produce an *Hörspiel* in which the voices would be organized in all their manifestations. For instance, whispering, shouting, singing, different ways of singing, children counting in school—human voice environment in everyday—and it was to be done in German. When I started to work with it I tried to choose a non-narrative line to incorporate two things that seem important to me: first was the length of life, that is from birth to death, then the length of day, that is from morning to evening, and then to transform the narrative elements. That means what happened to a man from his morning to evening in everybody's language—that is proverb. And so I chose a lot of proverbs, a lot of proverbs and I try to move them from line to line, from letters to letters until they become noise, which was a problem, for instance: *l'avenir appartient à celui qui se lève tôt.* For instance if we choose "the early bird gets the worm," we would change one letter and "worm" will become "warm," for instance, and then from "warm" we could go to *se lève tôt* and we change one letter and it's *rêve, l'avenir appartient à celui qui se rêve tôt*—"who dreams soon." And then we go forward and then we do a kind of programming with all the elements. The problem was to translate them into German, so we worked with bilingual dictionaries and we chose proverbs and ready-made expressions and we worked on them until the work was achieved.

The translating process, then, which you did for this work, or any translation, approximates fairly closely the sort of experiments we were talking about with OuLiPo. Translation is something like that. It's a schema.

Yes. Translating is to impose oneself, to produce a text

through a constraint which is represented by the original text. And for me, in a utopian way of thinking, there is no difference between languages. I would like to know a lot of languages, but unfortunately it takes too long to practice so I just am able to balbutiate in English. But it's very interesting to try to produce the same text when you start from a different one.

Gabriel Josipovici (review date 30 October-5 November 1987)

SOURCE: "Celebrations In a House of Fiction" in *Times Literary Supplement,* No. 4413, October 30-November 5, 1987, pp. 1191-92.

[*In the following review, Josipovici favorably reviews* Life: A User's Manual, *but finds fault with the English translation by David Bellows.*]

As with most major artists there is an exemplary quality about the life of Georges Perec: the contingent and the arbitrary have been transmuted into the resonant and meaningful. He was born in France in 1936 of immigrant Polish Jewish parents and was an orphan by the age of six, his father killed in 1940 fighting for his adopted country and his mother deported by the Nazis in 1943. Brought up by an aunt, he became in some ways more French than the French, as evidenced by the chord his first, rather modest novel, *Les Choses* (1965) seemed to strike in the public and critics alike. But after two further novels, one in the manner of Raymond Queneau and the other in that of the young Sartre, he found himself at a dead end, unable to see any way forward. It was at this point, in 1967, that he was invited to join OuLiPo, and it changed his life. Suddenly he had a purpose, and his art blossomed. Its finest fruit, and what seems to me likely to remain one of the great novels of the century, was *La Vie mode d'emploi,* written between 1969 and 1978. He died of cancer in 1982, just short of his forty-sixth birthday.

What then is OuLiPo and why was it so important to Perec? Four volumes of Oulipian writings have so far been published, including manifestos, exercises, and tributes to two of the members who died, Queneau and Perec. It is thus possible for an outsider to grasp something of what it stands for. The group was founded in 1961 by the mathematician François le Lionnais and by Queneau, himself a mathematician and the editor of the Pléiade Encyclopedia as well as a novelist and poet. The abbreviation stands for "Ouvroir de Littérature Potentielle", and other members have included the poet, novelist (and mathematician) Jacques Roubaud, Italo Calvino and the American writer Harry Mathews. The group's task; as it sees it, lies in two related but distinct areas: to explore the history of the use of constraints in literature (lipograms, acrostics, palindromes, sestinas, etc) and thus in the process rehabilitate artists and periods dismissed by a literary history still dominated by mimetic and expressionist models; and (the more important task) to devise new constraints for poets and writers of fiction alike, and see what results from their rigorous application.

What is immediately striking about OuLiPo, and perhaps explains its longevity, is its good humour. It is not, like most artistic movements, embattled; besides, the presence in its midst of the likes of Queneau and Perec has ensured that the emphasis would fall on wit and enjoyment rather than on polemics. One of the pieces reprinted in Volume One of the *Bibliothèque Oulipienne* is the outcome of a visit to Lyon made by several members of the group at the invitation of a local bookshop. Bored by the long motorway journey and rendered pleasantly drowsy by a light meal of *hors-d'oeuvres*, ham and cream cheese, washed down with a pleasing variety of local wines, and someone having mentioned the singer Montserrat Caballé, there descended on the company what Perec in his preface calls a "fièvre symphonique", which did not abandon them till long after they had reached Lyon, much to the bewilderment of their hosts, who had hoped to hear them talk about Art. One hundred homophonic variants on the singer's name are printed here (under the title "La cantatrice sauve"), ranging from "Un faf exasperé entra un jour dans la librairie Maspéro en criant: 'MAO SERA ECRABOUILLE!'", to "La mère chatte devina que son petit avait commencé a manger un rongeur dont la chair était bien trop corsée pour son encore jeune estomac: 'MONTRE CE RAT QUTAVALAIS!'"

There are two aspects of OuLiPo which need to be grasped, one obvious and superficial, the other never alluded to by its members but always present at a deeper level. The first is that it turns all art into a game. There is nothing wrong with this, but those who believe that art consists of more than play will tend to dismiss it as merely frivolous. That would be a pity, because at the heart of OuLiPo's endeavours lies the central post-Romantic issue of the meaning of art and its place in society, and the related problem of the arbitrariness of the artistic process and the sorts of measures the artist can take to overcome it. That is the question which drives both Prufrock and Eliot, both Marcel and Proust, both Leverkühn and Thomas Mann. Indeed, what else is *Doktor Faustus* but at once a meditation on the nature of artistic constraints, and an embodiment of such constraints in the manner of Schoenberg's serialism (itself the product of a search for strong enough constraints to allow the honest composer to work again in the wake of the chaos left by Beethoven and Wagner)? And to those who argue that to concentrate on purely formal matters is to deny the personality of the artist, two replies are necessary: the first and obvious one is that we have no difficulty in distinguishing Schoenberg from

Berg, early Boulez from early Stockhausen, or Queneau from Calvino and both from Perec. The second and more interesting one is that it is precisely those who imagine that they need only rely on their personal genius and inspiration who produce works which very quickly turn out to resemble all the other works in their culture. Here of course the criticism of inspiration and individuality implicit in the OuLiPo project joins hands with that of their more solemn and polemical contemporaries, Barthes, Foucault and Derrida.

> *La Vie mode d'emploi* is something completely different. To move from one of Perec's earlier novels to this one is like moving from *A Portrait of the Artist as a Young Man* to *Ulysses*, from "Prufrock" to *The Waste Land.*
> —Gabriel Josipovici

There is nevertheless a modicum of truth in the criticism that might be levelled at OuLiPo procedures and at those of their forebears, such as Raymond Roussel. Literature is not music and poetry is not prose fiction. Too often the result of imposing conscious playful constraints on narrative is the production of a text which is both fantastic and whimsical. As we read Calvino's *If on a Winter's Night a Traveller* (Calvino has an essay in the second Oulipian volume on the constraints he employed in writing parts of that book) or Harry Mathews's *The Sinking of the Odradek Stadium*, we may be amused but we quickly cease to feel any compelling reason to read on. The author may be exceedingly clever but neither the characters nor the narrative ever really engages our interest. To some extent this is true of Perec's first Oulipian work, *La Disparition,* a long novel written entirely without the letter *e,* a task even harder in French than it is in English. One can admire it, laugh with it, but only as one admires and laughs at a juggler. However, for Perec himself the book was of the utmost importance, for it showed him that, at a moment when he thought he had nothing more to say, the fiercest of constraints opened up a whole new world of possibilities: the adrenalin and the invention started to flow again. And there is a further point, made (after his death) by Robert Bober, the film-maker who worked with Perec on *Return to Ellis Island,* that this, like all his later books, was an attempt, hardly realized even by himself, to come to terms with a real-life disappearance: that of his mother, deported to the camps when he was still too young to understand at a conscious level what was going on.

La Vie mode d'emploi is something completely different. To move from one of Perec's earlier novels to this one is like moving from *A Portrait of the Artist as a Young Man* to *Ulysses,* from "Prufrock" to *The Waste Land.* It began as three separate projects. One was a novel based on a drawing by Saul Steinberg, showing a large apartment block with the front missing; it would be a celebration of the ordinary, of hot-water bottles, sleeping cats, cards pinned on walls, all those things which mean so much to us but which novels, in their hurry to get on with the story, overlook. One was a novel whose constraints would be dictated by the Graeco-Latin magic square of ten (such squares, like the simple one depicted in Dürer's "Melancolia I", are simply aids to permutational processes, and as such have been used, for example, by the composer Peter Maxwell Davies). And the third was the story of a millionaire who would plan a life for himself which would be at once totally absorbing and completely useless. Suddenly Perec realized that these three were really one single project: the magic square would be the building with its hundred rooms; and in the building would live Percival Bartlebooth, an English millionaire, who, at the age of twenty-five, decides to spend the next fifty years of his life in the following way: for ten years he takes lessons in water-colour painting (from Valène, who lives in a bed-sitter at the top of the building); for twenty years he and his manservant travel the globe, while he paints watercolours of ports and seaside towns at the rate of one a fortnight, sending them back as they are completed to Gaspard Winckler, whom he has installed in the building, and whose task it is to turn them into wooden jigsaw puzzles of seven hundred and fifty pieces each; the next twenty years will be spent in his flat, reconstituting the puzzles, also at the rate of one a fortnight, and, as each is finished, dispatching them to another craftsman, who has the job of detaching the original watercolour from the completed puzzle; this is then sent back to the spot where it was painted and a chemical solution is applied to it which removes the paint; the pristine sheet of What-man paper is then returned to Bartlebooth.

Always it is the users who triumph, and among them, of course, is the reader, peering behind locked doors into the privacy of room and lives.
—*Gabriel Josipovici*

Each chapter consists of the description of a single room. Sometimes an object leads into an account of the occupant of the room or some other anecdote connected with it, and sometimes an earlier occupant is invoked. The tone remains neutral throughout, whether an elaborate piece of furniture is being described or a story of triple murder, suicide or accidental death is being recounted. Since it would be tedious to start at the top right hand corner and work across and down, Perec has devised a further set of rules for the transition from room to room and chapter to chapter, but devised it so cunningly that the last chapter brings us to the room in which sits Bartlebooth himself, bent over his jigsaw, and to the single shocking event which actually occurs in the course

of this huge novel, an event, though, which has been prepared for from the very opening chapter.

The neutral tone and the abrupt transitions from room to room, life to life, far from flattening out character, enhance it, in line with the good Brechtian principle that interruption reveals far more than continuity. Our experience of the novel is in some ways akin to our experience of a great stained-glass window, at Chartres, say, or Canterbury: we are overwhelmed by colour and detail, yet we bask in the assurance that though we cannot quite make out all that is going on there are excellent reasons for every element being just as and where it is. That is why the effect of Perec's book is in some ways closer to that of the great medieval encyclopeadic narratives of Dante and Chaucer than to that of the anxious masterpieces of Sterne and Joyce.

And yet of course it is a book very much of our own time, and what makes it, in the end, a great book rather than a mere brilliant one, is that it is a book about failure. Bartlebooth's attempt to find a use for his life ends in failure and despair, and the same is true of Winckler, Morellet, Appenzzell, and of many others. Life cannot be *used*. As each finds age creeping up on him or is struck down by a blow from life—the death of a beloved wife, the discovery that talent does not match up to ambitions—he withdraws deeper and deeper into silence. In this crowded book, so full of lives and objects and word-games that it makes Rabelais seem almost anaemic, what affects one in the end is the sense that the only important things cannot be said or described. And this is where the novel's subject-matter and its form come together so remarkably. For all those rules developed by Perec over the years with OuLiPo are themselves ultimately seen, like Bartlebooth's project, to be merely ways of staving off the ultimate silence, the ultimate triumphs of life (time, death) over the plans men have for using and mastering it. Yet—such is the paradox of art—it is only by the almost manic deployment of such rules that this can be made manifest. Thus the book is ultimately a celebration of life itself, that which can never be used or mastered.

Like all great works of art, it grows in relevance the longer it exists among us. It arrives in England with nice timing as we enter a third stretch of Thatcherite government. For at one level it is about the uneven contest between those who respect life and the limits it imposes on us, and those who are governed by nothing but naked greed to seek to enlarge the space they occupy at the expense of others, or to discover the secrets of others in order to use them. It begins with the arrival of an estate agent come to work out how best to modernize Winckler's flat now that the puzzle-maker is dead, and it ends with a television impresario trying to force Bartlebooth out of his anonymity. Always it is the users who triumph, and among them, of course, is the reader, peering behind locked doors into the privacy of room and lives. But the reader is made to recognize his role and to see that no matter how much you know about a person, you never fully know that person; that no matter how many shares you acquire, time will not spare you. The terrible vision Valène has of the entire block of which the building forms a part razed to the ground, not by nuclear holocaust (Perec would see such apocalypses too as forms of false consolation) but simply by the greed of acquisitive builders planning some monstrous profit-making dream city in which all our wishes would be immediately catered for, is one of the bleakest in modern literature, all the more so for forming part of a wonderfully tender and funny novel.

It is a novel that present a mighty challenge to any translator, so full is it of puns, secret games, allusions to other works and other styles. David Bellos, who has written some remarkably illuminating essays on the book, and the publishers, are to be congratulated on at long last making it available in English (German and Italian translations came out five years ago). How sad then to have to say that the book has been translated and edited extremely carelessly.

To begin with, key decisions have not been taken. Some book titles and quotations (or mock-quotations) have been translated or given English equivalents, while others have been left in French. On page 186 one of the many mock-reproductions in the book shows us an advert for an india-rubber; Bellos has cleverly substituted the name "Kansell" for Perec's "Héphas", but then has ruined it by giving the address of the shop as "85 Dame Street, Brussels". The French has "rue de Dames, Bruxelles", which is what we would expect; surely if you are going to anglicize the name of the product and the street, though, you need to alter the location to an English town. This might seem a trivial objection, but hundreds of such details combine to give the impression of something slightly clumsy and unfocused, which is the precise opposite of the effect of the book in French. And could not someone at Collins have noted that there is no such church as Santa Maria Maggiora, or asked the translator to look again at the French on page 106, where the English reads, incongruously: "In the middle, beneath a chandelier with an opaline bowl hanging on three gilded cast-iron chains, stands a table made of a cylindrical block of lava from Pompeii, on which sits a six-sided smoked glass table laden with little saucers. . ."? By contrast chapters twenty-seven and seventy-four, which were translated by Harry Mathews and had already been published, read as though Perec had written in English. Let us hope the book will be enough of a success even as it stands for the publishers to commission Bellos to make a thorough revision. Perec deserves no less.

Mark Ford (review date 2 February 1989)

SOURCE: "Pretzel," in *London Review of Books,* Vol. 11, No. 3, February 2, 1989, pp. 15-17.

[*In the following review, Ford briefly summarizes several of Perec's works. He then provides a comparison of Perec's personal history to the events in* W, or, the Memory of Childhood.]

These are the first of Georges Perec's wonderful and extraordinary writings to be translated into English. Perec has been a household name in France since the runaway success of his first and most popular novel, ***Les Choses*** (1965), which still sells twenty thousand copies a year. ***Les Choses*** describes, with a sociological exactitude justified in the novel's concluding quotation from Marx, the motivations and disappointments of an utterly ordinary middle-class couple in a consumerist culture. Sylvie and Jérôme are both public opinion analysts, as indeed was Perec at the time; they emerge as a kind of generically rootless Parisian couple of the Sixties, whose experiences and emotions are such that no one of that generation could help but identify with them. The book ties in neatly with, indeed was partly inspired by, Barthes's theories on the language of publicity, which were appearing around the same time; its precision and syntactical ingenuity aspire to Flaubert, a major figure in Perec's pantheon of favourite authors.

Until recently in England Perec was simply known as the crazy writer who first wrote a book without any e's in it, ***La Disparition*** (1969), and then one with e's but no other vowels, ***Les Revenentes*** (1971). (One's heart goes out to the translators of those two.) Both books certainly establish benchmarks in the virtuosity with which they sustain themselves within the most severe of Oulipian constraints. OuLiPo (Ouvroir de Littérature Potentielle) was a literary association founded by Raymond Queneau and François Le Lionnais in 1960 and dedicated to the search for new forms of writing, mainly through the application of mathematical structures, gratuitous forms of word play, and bizarre constrictions on content. The Oulipian text aims for a state of absolute paradox, at once wilfully arbitrary in the rules imposed at its conception, and slavishly obedient to the internal logic arising from their fulfillment. Italo Calvino's *If on a winter's night a traveller,* Harry Mathews's *Tlooth* and *The Sinking of the Odradek Stadium* (both translated into French by Perec), Queneau's *Exercises in Style* are striking examples of what may be achieved in the mode. Perec joined in 1967 as the group's youngest member, but one of its most inventive. He excelled in composing bilingual poems, palindromes (his longest is five thousand letters long), *exercises d'homosyntaxisme* (in which a text must be written to a formula that predetermines the number of its words and the order of its verbs, substantives and adjectives), and in heterogrammatic poetry. 'Ulcérations' is a good instance of the latter, a poem written using only the letters of its title, which also happen to be the 11 most frequently used letters in the alphabet. 'Alphabets' is an even more prodigious feat; each of its 16 sections of 11 poems is written using only the ten most frequent letters—that is, a, e, i, l, n, o, r, s, t, u—plus one variable letter. In the first 11 poems the variable letter is b, the next c, and so on through to z. In other poems the vowels used are not allowed to deviate from the strict order of a, e, i, o, u-*A demi-mot un art chétif nous parle,* and so on. In an interview with *L'Arc* magazine Perec revealed he treated such exercises as a wordsmith's equivalent of a pianist's scales, and found in their intense difficulty nothing compared to the horrors attendant upon any attempt to write poetry freely.

Practically all of Perec's texts are constructed, with varying degrees of extremity, in this kind of pre-programmed way. *Un Homme qui dort* is written entirely in the second person. *Je me souviens* is fabricated out of sentences all beginning *Je me souviens,* followed by some randomly chosen remembrance. *La Boutique obscure* relates 124 dreams Perec had over a period of years. (In a particularly harrowing one he dreams he finds first one e, and then two, then 20, then 1000 in the text of *La Disparition.*) *Life: A User's Manual* describes the contents and inhabitants of a Parisian apartment block at 11 Rue Simon-Crubellier. The block is ten stories high and ten units wide, and the order in which the apartments are treated is determined by the route a knight at chess would have to take to cover all the squares on a ten x ten chessboard without alighting on the same square twice. Perec decided on the 42 constituent elements of each chapter, including references in each to three of the 30 authors systematically alluded to throughout the book, via a particularly complex mathematical algorithm. It's in *Life* in particular that Perec most exhaustively exploits the eccentric compositional techniques invented by another of his great heroes, Raymond Roussel.

Perec's obsession with autistic, self-propagating literary forms of this kind, which implicitly reject all preconceptions of depth and significance, is wholly compatible with Post-Modernism's ideal of literature as a self-reflexive surface, a field of clues that reveal nothing beyond their internal chance coherences. *La Boutique obscure* ends with a quote from his close friend Harry Mathews's *Tlooth:* 'for the labyrinth leads nowhere but out of itself.' *La Disparition* more bleakly talks of an enigma that will destroy us whether it is solved or not. But Perec's own adherence to this idea of literature as a self-sustaining puzzle, a teasing game between writer and reader, developed also, as he most clearly explains in the autobiographical chapters of *W,* in response to the circumstances of his own childhood.

Both sides of Perec's family were Polish Jews who emigrated to Paris during the Twenties. His father's name was Icek Judko Peretz; but in France he became known as Andre

Perec. (Peretz in Hungarian means 'pretzel'; in a typical cross-reference Gaspard Winckler, in the other half of *W*'s narrative, reveals that he never eats pretzels.) While his father's family was originally quite prosperous, his mother grew up in the Warsaw ghetto; from there they moved to Paris during her teens. Perec's parents married in 1934, and he was their only child, born in 1936. His father enlisted when war broke out and was killed by a stray shell the day after the armistice, bleeding to death in a church converted into a hospital. Perec was evacuated by the Red Cross as a war orphan in 1942. His mother remained in Paris. She made one failed attempt to reach the free zone. In January of 1943 she was picked up in a raid with her sister and deported to Auschwitz. Perec comments: 'She saw the country of her birth again before she died. She died without understanding.'

Perec's evocation of his childhood in *W*—through chance memories, closely argued hypotheses and wishful speculation—is achieved with exhilarating clarity. The few surviving photographs are minutely analysed for clues, remembered details sifted for evidence, contradictions carefully weighed. Perec, deprived not only of his parents but of all traces of his Jewish inheritance, confronts the bewildering absences of his childhood identity. (Derrida wrote: *Juif serait l'autre nom de cette impossibilité d'être soi.*) In this context writing itself, any kind of writing, becomes the psyche's ultimate defence against nothingness, though Perec is as clear-sighted as Beckett about its final ineffectiveness:

> I do not know whether I have anything to say, I know that I am saying nothing; I do not know if what I might have to say is unsaid because it is unsayable (the unsayable is not buried inside writing, it is what prompted it in the first place); I know that what I say is blank, is neutral, is a sign, once and for all, of a once-and-for-all annihilation. . . I write because we lived together, because I was one amongst them, a shadow amongst their shadows, a body close to their bodies. I write because they left in me their indelible mark, whose trace is writing. Their memory is dead in writing; writing is the memory of their death and the assertion of my life.

The autobiographical chapters alternate with a fictional story Perec originally invented when he was 13, centered on 'W', an island off the coast of Tierra del Fuego which is wholly in thrall to the Olympic ideal. In Part One Gaspard Winckler—a name Perec used for himself in his first unpublished autobiographical novel, and which turns up in *Life* as well—receives a mysterious summons from a certain Otto Apfelstahl, MD. They meet in a hotel. Gaspard Winckler is not Gaspard Winckler's real name, it turns out, but one accorded him with appropriate papers by a relief agency when he deserted from the Army. The original Gaspard Winckler is the deaf and dumb son of a fabulously wealthy opera singer. In an attempt to cure him she takes him on a round-the-world cruise on a yacht. Their ship is sunk in a hurricane off Tierra del Fuego. Only Gaspard Winckler's body is never found. . . .

The story breaks off abruptly here, and in Part Two an omniscient narrator tells us about the sports-dominated life of the inhabitants of W. The four Olympic villages on W compete against each other almost continually, under a system of penalties as well as rewards: while the day's winners are toasted and feasted, the losers are deprived of food, and forfeits often imposed on them. A losing athlete may have to run around the track with his shoes on back to front, or between rows of officials who beat him with sticks and cudgels. As in Borges's lottery in Babylon, the ultimate penalty is death. The athletes' diets are deliberately deficient in sugar and vitamins. In addition, the rules of the sports are often changed arbitrarily It may be decided that the athlete who crosses the line last is the winner, or an official may suddenly shout 'stop,' and the athlete who keeps still the longest is then declared the victor. The athletes' names also depend on their performance on track or field, as the winners and runners-up of each event inherit the names of the original winners of the event, for as long as they hold their title. The current holder of the 100 metres Olympiad title would be simply known as the Jones, of the 400 the Gustafson, of the high jump the Andrews, and so on: names are added or lost as the athlete wins or loses. The most horrendous event on W takes place at the Atlantiads. Women are severely culled on W, only one in five being allowed to survive. On reaching child-bearing age, women are taken in batches of around fifty to the stadium, their clothes are removed, and they are released onto the track, where they start to run. When they are half a lap ahead, 176 of W's best athletes, also naked except for keenly spiked running shoes, are released in pursuit of them; the women are of course soon caught and raped by the fifty fittest and most cunning sportsmen.

The double narratives of *W* surreptitiously allude to each other: their juxtaposition is at once startling and seemingly inevitable. In their 'fragile overlapping', to use Perec's words, they complete each other. As the Olympic community becomes more and more like a concentration camp, the gaps and links between Perec's imagination and his experience become ever clearer. In a further twist to the tale, Perec concludes the book by remarking that several of the islands off Tierra del Fuego are, at the time of writing (1974), deportation camps run by Pinochet's fascists. The fiction, which must have originated in the young Perec's imagination as a form of consoling escapism, not only reflects political reality but also anticipates it.

W's split between the opposite worlds of carefully documented reality and total imaginative freedom is typical of much of Perec's writing. Perec took the Nouveau Roman's concern with everyday living to new heights, martyring himself with minute enumerations of the infra-ordinaire, as he called it. We may be thankful some of his projects in this field never reached fruition—for instance, his plan to list all the food and drink he consumed in the course of 1974. Perec had a prodigious memory—indeed, like Joyce, he saw literary composition s largely a question of memory and problem-solving, and in the epilogue to La Disparition he rubbishes the idea of inspiration. Another scheme he never realised was to describe all the rooms he had ever slept in, excluding only those of earliest childhood. Perec liked the idea of cataloguing in neutral, objective terms the physical facts of external reality. For a half-achieved project called Les Lieux he chose 12 places of personal significance to him in Paris and set out to visit and describe each one once a year in a different month over 12 years. These careful documentary pieces would be played off against 12 evocations of each place generated solely by memory. At other times Perec finds a form to blend the two opposites. *Un Cabinet d'amateur* describes a series of paintings in meticulously precise detail, as if for an auction catalogue. It's with a shock that you learn at the end of the book that none of the pictures actually exist. Absolute fixity and absolute freedom are fused in the illusion.

In a short introduction to *W* Perec explains how the book's meaning begins in the hiatus between the Gaspard Winckler story and the depiction of *W*. 'In this break, in this split suspending the story on an unidentifiable expectation, can be found the point of departure for the whole of this book: the *points de suspension* on which the broken threads of childhood and the web of writing are caught.' The image of suspension is important in the book. Twice—once when saying goodbye to his mother for the last time at the train station, and once during his stay at Villard-de-Lans—Perec remembers himself clearly with an arm in a sling. In fact, he later works out, neither memory is true: these fractures occurred only within his imagination. They must have served psychically both to give an external expression to his inner suffering, and to suggest that that suffering, after a period of suspension, would eventually heal. Most of Perec's's fiction hangs in a similar void, deliberately indifferent to the sensible aims with which we try to justify our lives. *Un Homme qui dort* is about a student who one day gives up, for no particular reason. He lies on his bed, staring at the cracks in the ceiling, refuses to answer the door, and wanders haphazardly around Paris at night. The story alludes frequently to Sartre, but is more an undoing of Existentialism—as *Les Choses* also was of the Nouveau Roman—than an addition to its literature. Perec's dead-pan style leads absolutely nowhere. The story is picked up again in Chapter 52 of *Life*. Here the student is called Grégoire Simpson, after the insect man in Kafka. In the end he simply disappears, but the chapter concludes movingly with an incident from Simpson's childhood in which the young boy dresses up in traditional costume to join in a mid-Lent procession, 'as proud as Punch and as grave as a judge'. Later he rushes about excitedly, pausing only 'to stuff himself with juniper-roast ham and to slake his thirst with great gulps of Ripaille, that white wine as light as glacier water, as dry as gunflint'. The more flexible medium of *Life* can both include and transcend Perec's earlier style.

The emptiness of *Un homme qui dort* becomes positive emasculation in *La Disparition.* The absent e broods like a vengeful god over the text. As e is the fifth letter of the alphabet, the fifth of the novel's 26 chapters is missing, as is the second of its six books, e being the second of the vowels. The fifth of the 26 boxes containing Anton Voyl's manuscripts is also missing; Anton Voyl's name itself seems heartlessly truncated. Indeed, contact with e in the book means death. In a famous scene a bartender drops dead when asked to make a Porto-flip because it requires eufs, and they have an e in them. The absence of by far the most popular letter in the French alphabet is a self-imposed handicap similar to the young Perec's imaginary slings, and indicative of a similarly fundamental lack. *La Disparition* adopts the plot of the detective novel with a few epistemological knobs on; the characters who solve its enigma automatically die, or rather disappear. A finished crossword or jigsaw puzzle might be seen as an analogue to these fictional vanishings. More sinisterly, they suggest the limitless powers of modern techniques of annihilation, capable of extinguishing all traces of a disappeared person.

Perec's games parody our instinctive willingness to believe in language's absolute authority, and release language into a neutral space where words fulfil their own random, intrinsic connections. One of the most appealing features of Perec's writing is its lack of self-righteousness, its wholehearted enjoyment of its own fictive procedures. *Life: A User's Manual* is very much the consummation of his achievement, bringing together stories and characters from much of his previous writing, and continually alluding to those writers who define the fictional space in which Perec's texts also aspire to move. In a short pieced in *L'Arc* on his borrowings from Flaubert, he explained that he saw these references as being like indications of land-measuring or the nodes of a network, establishing the contexts and parameters of his own literary sensibility: but they can be seen as even more than this. In the disembodied world of his childhood, as described in *W,* he finds in reading almost a substitute for his lost parents. 'I reread, and each time it is the same enjoyment, whether I reread twenty pages, three chapters, or the whole book: an enjoyment of complicity, of collusion, or more especially, and in addition, of having in the end found kin again.' Intertextuality is built into the very structure of *Life,* but in highly unmodernist fashion. The references argue for no unified cultural tradition, and noticing them adds nothing to the text's meaning: they simply furnish Perec with elements of material requiring to be worked into each chapter.

Life: A User's Manual follows the poetry of Roussel in approaching its location—the apartment block—from the vantage-point of an instant frozen in time. Perec first got the idea for the book from a painting of Saul Steinberg's called *The Art of Living,* which shows an apartment block with part of its facade removed, revealing the interiors of twenty or so rooms. (Within the novel the painter Valène is embarked on, but will never complete, a similar project.) Each of the book's 99 chapters describes a room, or section of the stairs, or lift, itemising its contents, and filling in the often wildly improbable backgrounds of its present and previous inhabitants. The most important of the book's multifarious narratives concerns Percival Bartlebooth, an eccentric Harrow-educated millionaire.

Strung between the extreme asceticism of Melville's Bartleby and the prodigal generosity of Valéry Larbaud's A. O. Barnabooth, Bartlebooth organises his life into a single massively self-contradictory project. Though absolutely talentless, he spends ten years having himself taught to paint water-colours by Valène. The next twenty years, accompanied by his servant Smautf, he spends tracking around the globe, indifferent to political upheavals, painting water-colours in 500 arbitrarily chosen ports. These are dispatched every fortnight or so back to 11 Rue Simon-Crubellier, where Gaspard Winckler glues them onto plywood and then cuts them into ever more difficult jigsaw puzzles of 750 pieces each. On his return Bartlebooth completes the puzzles in chronological order. When solved, the joins of the puzzles are recomposed by a special machine, separated from their backing and glaze, and returned to the spot where they were originally painted, to be dipped in the sea until the colours dissolve and the paper is its original white again. Bartlebooth's self-cancelling scheme is a typically Perecian one: 'his aim was for nothing, nothing at all, to subsist, for nothing but the void to emerge from it, of only the immaculate whiteness of a bland to remain, only the gratuitous perfection of a project entirely devoid of utility.'

The image of the puzzle dominates *Life: A User's Manual.* Each of every chapter's 42 constitutive elements are fitted together like parts of a puzzle, and the chapters themselves fit together like pieces in the overall jigsaw of the book. The fictions with which Perec links his given elements reveal him at his most inventive and playful. The book teems with startling characters and fictions, and seems as endless in its narrative resources as even the greatest of Victorian three-deckers. There is the ethnologist Marcel Appenzzell who pursues for five years and 11 months an unknown tribe of Sumatrans without getting them once to acknowledge his existence; there is Cinoc, the word-killer, who is hired by Larrousse to diagnose obsolete words and eliminate them from the dictionary but who, on leaving his job, sets about compiling a dictionary of all the forgotten words that still appeal to him; there is James Sherwood, collector of *unica* (one-of-a-kinds), who pays a million dollars in counterfeit currency for the vase in which Joseph of Arimathaea supposedly gathered the blood of the dying Jesus; there is Monsieur Jérôme who left Paris in the diplomatic service as culture attaché in Lahore and returned home penniless years later, but will never talk of his Eastern experiences; there is Hutting the artist, famous for his 'haze period', which places him on a par with his famous quasi-namesake Huffing, the New York pioneer of *Arte brutta* who first appears in Harry Mathews's *The Conversions.*

Perec, like Bartlebooth, was haunted by ideas of incompletion, despite his manic productiveness. In an interview a couple of years before his death of lung cancer in 1982, he pictured his achievement as *l'image d'un livre inachevé, d'une 'oeuvre' inachevée à l'intérieur d'une littérature jamais achevée.* Though each of his books is an element in an overall ensemble, the only thing about that ensemble he can ever know is that he will never finish it. Bartlebooth's project is similarly doomed. Time is frozen in **Life: A User's Manual** at a little before eight on the evening of 23 June 1975. Bartlebooth has just died in the middle of his 439th puzzle. His efforts to complete his arbitrarily self-imposed scheme have been complicated both by the fiendish cunning of Gaspard Winckler and by the loss of his eyesight. The 439th puzzle is almost finished except for a space in the perfect shape of an X: but the piece the dead Bartlebooth holds is shaped like a W.

In *W* also the young Perec sees in an X the story of his childhood: by extending its branches you get a swastika, by unjoining and rotating it you get an SS sign. Two X's joined horizontally can be easily made into the Star of David. Bartlebooth's defeat at the hands of the already dead Winckler is both poignant and uplifting; all the systems of life, from Nazism to the Olympics, must leak at the seams, and only through the encroachments of chaos does existence transcend the absolutes it craves and become livable.

Mereille Ribière (essay date March 1989)

SOURCE: "Doing Theory," in *Paragraph*, Vol. 12, No. 1, March 1989, pp. 56-64.

[In the following essay, Ribière questions the effectiveness and appropriateness of some of Perec's self-imposed literary constraints. Ribière suggests that, by not making clear what constraints were in effect in various works, Perec was working counter to the bond he wished to forge with the reader.]

Georges Perec stressed his concern for the practice rather than the theory of literature as witness two statements separated by an interval of eleven years:

> La fonction de l'écrivain est d'écrire et non de penser; et même si l'on peut accorder quelque crédit aux réflexions qu'il lui arrive d'émettre sur sa production, elles ne sauraient en aucun cas constituer une théorie.

> (The writer's function is to write and not to think; and even if one can give some credence to the comments he may happen to make on what he produces, these in no way can constitute a theory.)

> Je n'ai jamais été à l'aise pour parler d'une manière abstraite, théorique de mon travail: même si ce que je produis semble venir d'un programme depuis longtemps élaboré, d'un projet de longue date, je crois plutôt trouver—et prouver—mon mouvement en marchant: (. . .) je sens confusément que les livres que j'ai écrits s'inscrivent, prennent leur sens dans une image globale que je me fais de la littérature, mais il me semble que je ne pourrai jamais saisir précisément cette image, qu'elle est pour moi un au-delà de l'écriture, un 'pourquoi j'écris' auquel je ne peux répondre qu'en écrivant, différant sans cesse l'instant où, cessant d'écrire, cette image deviendrait visible, comme un puzzle inexorablement achevé.

> (I have never been at ease speaking about my work in an abstract, theoretical way: even if what I produce seems to derive from a programme worked out long ago, a long-term project, I think rather that I find—and prove—my movement as I proceed: [. . .] I feel in a vague sort of way that the books I have written find their place and their meaning within the overall image I have of literature, but it does seem to me that I shan't ever be able to grasp that image exactly, because for me it is something that exists outside writing, a 'why do I write' to which I cannot give an answer except by writing, by putting off endlessly that moment when, by my stopping writing, that image would become visible, like a jigsaw puzzle that inexorably gets completed.)

In the first statement, the plural of 'réflexions' (thoughts, comments) is in marked contrast with the singular of 'une théorie' (a theory) and in the second one, theory is associated not only with abstraction but with unity of purpose. In both instances, the distinction between the practice of writing and the theory of literature is coupled with a further distinction between thinking about or planning one's work, on the one hand, and theorizing, on the other. The decision-making process, which represents the intellectual part of his—and any—art is therefore considered by Perec as an integral part of the practice; its function is to provide a practical solution to a practical problem, and it is not, as a result, perceived as belonging to the realm of theory.

Perec's position reflects both his natural modesty and his inability to account in general or abstract terms for the various directions in which his work is engaged. He has no desire to 'pontificate', as he puts it in his Warwick lecture, and finds himself unable to construct the framework that would reconcile intellectually, as opposed to intuitively, all aspects of his production. Although he postulates a unity, a coherence always in the making, which he describes in characteristic fashion through a comparison with the jigsaw puzzle, the unity of purpose both being shaped by and shaping his work remains even to Perec himself problematic. It is not surprising therefore that the question of coherence both within individual works and within Perec's *œuvre* at large has been raised time and time again by both critics and theoreticians and has received conflicting answers.

The debate has focused, in particular, on the use of predetermined formal constraints and the related issue of their perception by the reader. While scholars come to terms with the paradoxes of Perec's strategy through sheer familiarity with the texts, the issue remains a stumbling block for nonspecialist readers as witness the recurring discussions on the subject at seminars and conferences.

At Cerisy, in 1984, it was Benoît Peeters who raised the issue by pointing out the ambivalence of the strategy adopted by Perec in *La Vie mode d'emploi* and *Un Cabinet d'amateur,* in which the widespread use of formal pre-composition and the role of borrowings from a whole range of literary texts are deliberately obscured. The conclusions drawn from this forceful analysis were as follows:

> Cette dissimulation des contraintes, (. . .) loin d'ouvrir à la lecture de nouveaux horizons, arrête triplement son cheminement.

> Elle l'arrête une première fois lorsque l'ignorance des contraintes rend opaques un grand nombre de fonctionnements du texte: interdisant au lecteur non informé de mesurer ce que peuvent être les 'machines à inspiration' de l'écrivain, elle l'amène à envisager les récits comme le produit d'une imagination rare et miraculeuse. (. . .)

> Elle l'arrête une seconde fois lorsque le méthodique débuscage des contraintes incite à chercher hors du

texte les informations les plus décisives: reprenant la formule de Klee citée en exergue de *La Vie mode d'emploi,* 'l'œil suit les chemins qui lui ont été ménagés dans l'œuvre', on peut en effet lui apporter ce corollaire inattendu: 'l'œil ne peut suivre les chemins qui ne lui ont pas été ménagés dans l'œuvre' (. . .)

> Elle l'arrête une troisième fois lorsque l'euphorie de la découverte conduit le décrypteur à se satisfaire de ce qu'il a trouvé, négligeant des pistes plus simples peut-être mais guère moins importantes. La lecture, on le sait, ne doit nullement se confondre avec une reconstitution de ce qui fut le périple de l'écrivain. Pour qu'elle puisse éviter cet écueil, il est non moins indispensable que l'ignorance de ce trajet ne conduise pas le décrypteur à se laisser fasciner par les méandres de la genèse.

(This concealing of constraints, [. . .] far from opening up new horizons for reading, arrests its progress in three distinct ways.

It arrests it for the first time when being unaware of constraints means that a number of levels of textual functioning are simply not apparent: by preventing the uninformed reader from gauging what the writer's 'machines of inspiration' might be, this leads to the narratives being regarded as the product of an uncommon and miraculous imagination.

It arrests it for the second time when the methodical tracking down of constraints leads one to search for the key information outside the text: adapting the formula by Klee that is quoted as an epigraph to *Life A User's Manual,* 'the eye follows the paths that have been cleared for it in the work', one could add to it the unexpected corollary: 'the eye cannot follow the paths which have not been cleared for it in the work' [. . .]

It arrests it for the third time when the euphoria of discovery leads whoever is deciphering the text to be satisfied with what they have found, neglecting simpler but hardly less important approaches. Reading, as is well known, is not to be confused with a reconstituting of the itinerary followed by the writer. In order to avoid this pitfall, it is no less indispensable that ignorance of that itinerary should not induce the reader to be fascinated by the meanderings of the work's genesis.)

What covering up the generative process has achieved is in direct contradiction with Perec's conception of the writer as producer and his emphasis on the interaction between writer and reader. One cannot but wonder at the reasons why a writer of Perec's stature came to adopt this logically untenable position. It seems to be the result of the step by step approach that he describes as his own: the solution to one problem creating at times more problems that it solves. Hence the sense of confusion which is created by readjustments within a work such as *Alphabets* and the more disconcerting effects, in *La Vie mode d'emploi,* of some of the conclusions Perec draws from his experimentation with formal composition.

At the London Perec Colloquium held in March 1988, the issue of coherence was raised by Jan Baetens in connection with the three different types of formal permutation at work in *Alphabets.* First he pointed out the contradiction inherent in the fact that one formal rule is made clearly visible while another, which is complementary, is imperceptible; the generative constraint is visualized on each page by the presentation side by side of a square of 11×11 letters and its 'poetic' transcription whereas the rule which governs the exact position of the lettric pattern and the transcription on each page is obscured. Secondly, he expressed surprise at the fact that the three types of formal rules shaping *Alphabets* are not closely related and that one of them at least, the one which defines the order of the poems in the volume, is far from being consistent within itself. When it comes to analyzing the reasons why such discrepancies appear, there is room for debate, but one cannot help thinking that they might be an indication of Perec's dissatisfaction with certain types of formal pre-composition and his awareness, at the time when the volume was put together, of the lack of dynamism of the constraint adopted in *Alphabets.* Hence the introduction of new kinds of operations and the creation of anomalies. The fact that these additions fail adequately to challenge the rigidity of the constraint may help us to understand why anomalies become an integral part of the framework adopted in *La Vie mode d'emploi,* and why within *Alphabets* they can appear superfluous.

Should we necessarily mourn the fact that there is an element of inconsistency in *La Vie mode d'emploi* when it is in so many respects an outstanding book?
—Mireille Ribière

When Perec later draws the lessons from his experimentation with formal pre-composition, he lumps together *Alphabets* and *La Disparition* on account of the response of the reading public and literary critics in particular, who were 'blinded' by the system and never talked about the book: he concludes from it: 'c'est trop systématique' (it's too systematic). But however spectacular the procedures adopted in both books may be, they are not altogether comparable and

Perec must have known it: there is a marked difference between the heterogrammatic constraint used in *Alphabets* and the lipogrammatic form of *La Disparition.* In the collection of poems, writing is a way of exploring and exhausting the potential of the constraint with very little scope for development even at the semantic level. In *La Disparition,* on the contrary, the disappearance of the letter 'e' is but the first step towards an increasing number of complex operations and outlines the two movements first analyzed by John Lee: contraction and expansion. This is not only true of the lexical and syntactical choices which, when restricted, provide a strong stimulus for verbal invention, it is also true of the development of the fiction. In a text which never ceases to point out what has prompted its writing—the omission of the letter 'e'—and whose argument is therefore tautological, the risk of atrophy is high: Perec avoids the trap he has set himself by using a second type of generator, literary borrowings. By providing new materials to be transferred and integrated, borrowings offer indeed numerous narrative and fictional developments. Because in *La Disparition* the origin of many of these borrowings is indicated either by direct references or by marked allusions, borrowings both strengthen and introduce an element of diversity in the self-referential framework: they momentarily divert the reader's attention from the linear development of the novel by tapping the resources of our cultural memory. Unsuspected new implications are bestowed on individual borrowings—often to great comic effect—and bonds forged between texts which seemed hitherto to have little in common. Previous literary symbols and obsessions are read in more materialistic or literal terms while the significance of the missing sign is gradually enriched. Ultimately when one has become accustomed to a language always at variance with linguistic norms and the effect of Perec's remarkable verbal invention wears off, borrowings have an increasing role to play in stimulating the process of reading. Thus the formal device is equally prohibitive in the first instance and equally stimulating thereafter for both writer and reader. Although the spectacular character of the lipogrammatic constraint favours simplistic approaches, *La Disparition* will undoubtedly be vindicated by posterity since it is precisely one of those books that repeated close readings do not exhaust.

The limitations of the non-evolving constraint adopted in *Alphabets,* as well as the fact that the all-pervading first generator—the omission of the letter 'e'—and the emphasis on a self-referential system in *La Disparition* seemed in the first instance to inhibit the process of reading, lead Perec to alter his approach to formal pre-composition: in *La Vie mode d'emploi,* he diversifies his procedures through even more complex systems, in which a principle of self-contradiction is included from the start, and plays down self-reference to the point where generators such as borrowings can only be traced by scholars. In so doing Perec lost in *La Vie mode d'emploi* one of the crucial elements which in *La*

Disparition actively contributed to the 'game' between writer and reader.

One may be tempted to ask: should we necessarily mourn the fact that there is an element of inconsistency in *La Vie mode d'emploi* when it is in so many respects an outstanding book? But this may not be the right question: the fact that it is endowed with what Benoît Peeters calls 'densité romanesque' (novelistic density)—something which formal theory finds extremely difficult to define, let alone analyze— has not been denied. However, when literary criticism uses formal analysis, not to describe a practice or envisage new areas for experimentation, but to justify *a posteriori* a work of art on the grounds that it is clever or rigorous—an attitude which we all tend to adopt particularly when dealing, as is the case here, with works experimenting with form— theoreticians will inevitably come up with examples of even more clever and consistent uses of form, which is what Jan Baetens did in his analysis of the palindromic form at the London Perec Colloquium.

This does not necessarily mean that the formal choices and experiments made by Perec are not interesting *per se*— equally for what they did not and for what they did achieve— and that they cannot act as a stimulus and a challenge for further practical and theoretical developments. The fact that he was not working within a cohesive intellectual or theoretical framework, keeping the decision-making process step by step in check, may well have prevented Perec from thoroughly exploiting some of his findings. But in other respects, the fact that he did not have a precise overall image of what literature is, or should be, enabled him to experiment freely with different types of discourse.

Perec's writings are stamped with a highly personal hallmark and recurring patterns are beginning to emerge which offer more precise answers as to why he wrote as he did. But his writing continues to raise more theoretical and practical questions than it actually solves, and perhaps it is this lack of resolution that will ultimately be considered his particular contribution to contemporary literature.

Partrick Parrinder (review date 10 January 1991)

SOURCE: "Funny Old Fame," in *London Review of Books,* Vol. 13, No. 1, January 10, 1991, p. 18.

[*In the following excerpt, Parrinder reviews a recent translation of* Things *and* A Man Asleep.]

Once upon a time, before the Channel Tunnel was built, there were two contemporary French novelists. Georges Perec died in 1982 at the age of 45, and nobody in England who was not a French specialist had ever heard of him. With Philippe Sollers it was different. Editor of the avant-garde theoretical journal *Tel Quel,* and associate of literary and psychoanalytic thinkers such as Barthes, Kristeva and Lacan, his was a name of which no self-respecting British intellectual could afford to remain entirely ignorant—though his novels, so far as I can discover, were neither translated nor read. But as Sollers grew older he abandoned his youthful Maoism to become a worshipper of American capitalism and, finally, some sort of Catholic mystic. *Tel Quel* changed its name to *L'Infini.* And, since fame is capricious, in the last years of Mrs Thatcher's reign it was Perec, not Sollers, who—with the publication of David Bellos's translation of *Life: A User's Manual*—found a keen British audience.

There were logics in these things, as we shall see. Perec's reputation might easily have crossed the Channel two decades earlier. His first novel *Les Choses* was published in 1965 to immediate acclaim, and it was soon to be found on French literature syllabuses, if unfortunately nowhere else, in the Anglo-Saxon countries. In 1967 Perec lectured at Warwick University on the situation of the contemporary French novelist. This lecture, given before he joined the experimental group OuLiPo and started to produce fiction saturated in linguistic puzzles, lipograms, cryptograms and mathematical figures, was not quite the heady stuff those days demanded. In it, Perec offered the sort of candid and complex account of his literary influences usually permitted only to the already famous. When it came to situating himself on the French literary scene, he all too sensibly advocated a middle course between the extremes of Sartreian *engagement,* on the one hand, and *Tel Quel*'s brew of nihilism and linguistic experiment, on the other.

The Warwick lecture is printed for the first time in *Parcours Perec,* a collection of papers given in French at a conference in London in 1988. Now that we have *Things* in David Bellos's translation, Perec's acknowledgment in the lecture of the impact of Flaubert, Barthes, Kafka and Melville, together with his citations of the literary theories of Brecht and Lukacs, can be seen to provide an essential commentary on the early fiction. *Things* and its successor *A Man Asleep* handle with a piercing irony material that is essentially autobiographical. *Things* has, so to speak, a joint protagonist in Jérôme and Sylvie, a pair of young market researchers whose story is narrated almost entirely in the third person plural. Obsessed with a colour-supplement fantasy of gracious and fashionable living, Jérôme and Sylvie start out in hope but gradually sink into the mire as the story progresses.

Things portrays a brittle, photogenic world, a two-dimensional Paris framed by images from advertising, fashion photography, interior design and film-sets. Jérôme and Sylvie start out like browsers through some immense mail-order catalogue, whose pages they have only just begun to turn.

But, like Jay Gatsby's green light, their artificial paradise is destined to remain a promise of the future, a narcissistic fantasy. For all Perec's stylistic sang-froid one can detect in this prose the shadow of a master whom he did not mention in his Warwick lecture: the inventor of an overheated romantic fiction founded on the dreams of consumerism. *Things* speaks for the bourgeois, mass-market Sixties just as, eighty years earlier, Huysmans's *A Rebours* became the Bible of the Decadents. To move from Huysmans to Perec is to go from the gaslit naughtiness of a Late Victorian brothel to the antiseptic pages of a soft-porn magazine. Yet Huysmans's arch-Decadent des Esseintes was also the consumer of an imaginary lifestyle, a designer world of objects embodying and surfeiting his eccentric desires.

Colour photography, the cinema and mass production are essential constituents of Perec's version of commodity fetishism. Jérôme and Sylvie roam through Paris, wide-eyed, like characters from one of the New Wave films of the period, nursing a perpetual hunger and a secret dissatisfaction. They go to all the new releases, but the cinema, like the city they inhabit, can never fulfil their expectations. They are just penniless students, and later freelance professionals, with no antecedents; and the 'film they would have liked to live' remains only in the mind.

In Huysmans's novel it was quite different. Des Esseintes, fabulously wealthy, had the means of realising the ultimate movie from the beginning. He holds precocious dinner-parties at which the guests eat black puddings served by naked negresses while a hidden orchestra plays funeral marches. Tiring of these excesses, he sells his ancestral mansion and becomes the reclusive owner of a country villa stocked with the choicest furnishings and pictures that money can buy. Des Esseintes may have joined the bourgeoisie, but Jérôme and Sylvie have to work for their living. Though they start out like yuppies, they prefer flâneurism to the bureaucratic rat-race and are soon left behind by their contemporaries. How to escape? In one of the wittiest episodes of *A Rebours*, des Esseintes decides on a complete break with his previous life, and prepares to take a holiday in England. His Anglophile instincts are so quickly satiated that he never gets beyond the Gare du Nord. Jérôme and Sylvie, like Sixties neo-romantics, throw up their market-research jobs and go to live for a time in a small town in Tunisia. Here, faced with Third World actuality, they experience a 'life sans everything' in which, like the most traditional of expatriates, their main compensation is to go to the café and read the Paris newspapers.

Things is without dialogue and, in the melodramatic sense, virtually devoid of incident: no wonder the project of filming it came to nothing. Despite its autobiographical basis (Perec himself worked in market research and spent a year in the Tunisian town named in the narrative), the main characters are deliberately transparent figures, cyphers without individual features or personal quirks. They think and feel as an undifferentiated couple. *Things* ends with the image of life as a feast, where 'the meal they will be served will be quite simply tasteless.' This is a fine inversion of the so-they-lived-happily-ever-after convention, and Perec's precision and control in this lucidly translated masterpiece is everywhere apparent.

Things is followed in this edition by *A Man Asleep* (1967), where the protagonist begins by failing to get out of bed on the day of his examinations. He becomes a hermit, shunning all direct human contact though he rambles through Paris at night reading the signs of metropolitan life as if scanning the runes of some dead civilisation. The narrative is, again, based on one of Perec's own experiences, and it is later echoed in the story of the student Grégoire Simpson in Chapter 52 of *Life: A User's Manual*. Grégoire's story barely hints at the intense sollpsism of *A Man Asleep*, however; the later and much briefer version is broadly humorous, with some outrageous puns. In *A Man Asleep* we take the full weight of the student's self-pitying view of himself as a 'missing piece in the human jigsaw', a motif that anticipates Perec's majestic obsession with games and puzzles. Yet the novel is also a monologue (spoken, in the film version that Perec directed, by means of a female voice-over) in which every sentence is cast in the second person singular. Like *Things,* it must be read at one level as the virtuoso elaboration of a simple grammatical figure. . . .

Francis King (review date 21 November 1992)

SOURCE: "Held by the Dead Hand of a Dictator," in *The Spectator,* Vol. 269, No. 8576, November 21, 1992, p. 49.

[*In the following review, King suggests that the posthumous publication of Perec's unfinished mystery novel,* 52 Days, *was the result of Perec's reputation as a genius, and that the work is without significant literary merit.*]

Some people in this country and many people in France ascribe genius to Georges Perec. On the basis of his *Life, A User's Manual* ('a transcendent achievement' we were assured by the *Daily Telegraph,* 'one of the great novels of the century' by the *Times Literary Supplement*), they may well be right.

The trouble with genius is similar to the trouble with royalty: whatever it does is considered worthy of note. The result is that just as, say, Queen Victoria's knickers are regarded as collectable, so such things as Graham Greene's inconsequential dreams, Philip Larkin's life-hating and self-hating letters and a juvenile novel by Samuel Beckett are regarded as publishable. The latest and most dire consequence of this attitude is the appearance, nowhere near its conclusion and wholly unrevised, of the literary thriller on which Perec was working at the time of his premature death in 1982 at the age of 46.

Perec resembled Anthony Burgess in his fecundity, his versatility and—the consequence of these two things—his determination to excel in every kind of writing. From autobiography to crossword puzzles, from novels to radio plays, from essays to palindromes, from poetry to an essay on the Japanese game of Go, he was restlessly indefatigable. One kind of writing in which his determination to excel was likely to encounter no competitors was the novel composed without any use of the letter 'e'. The result was *La Disparition.*

The Caribbean novelist Edgar Mittelholtzer once embarked on a novel without any use of the letter 's'. This bizarre and never to be completed undertaking was regarded by his friends as one of the first indications of the insanity which was eventually to drive him to the atrocious act of suicide by dousing his clothes with petrol and setting light to himself on Wimbledon Common. That Perec was similarly insane, there is no evidence. At all events, we are promised a translation of *La Disparition* by Gilbert Adair.

The more conventional challenge which Perec set himself in *53 Days* was to outdo all the masters of the detective story whom he so much admired by producing an example of the genre even more elaborate, even more crammed with surprises, even more ludic in its snook-cocking at probability and even possibility. What he was clearly attempting was the literary equivalent of the triple somersault: superficially everything points to X as the culprit, careful ratiocination then points to Y, but finally, on the last page, it is Z who, a lightning flash of divine intuition reveals, can only have been guilty.

The setting is an imaginary African state, a Senegal or Chad, once a French possession. The French narrator, sucked against his will into the alternating roles of fall-guy and amateur detective, is a well-read, prissy, fortyish teacher at a lycée. To him the French consul entrusts the task of discovering what has happened to a famous crime-writer, Robert Serval, who for many years has held himself totally aloof from his compatriots, while occupying a suite in the sole luxury hotel in the run-down, poverty-stricken country. Before disappearing, Serval, as though foreseeing his fate, entrusted to the consul the typescript of his latest novel, *The Crypt,* with the instructions to hand it on to the teacher, should anything untoward befall him. 'But why to me?' the teacher in effect asks; to be told that Serval claimed that the two of them had been school-fellows in France. But the teacher has no recollection of this. Hoping that in *The Crypt*

he will find some encoded message, he devours it. He then searches out the woman who typed it at Serval's dictation. Serval's book-within-a-book is full of literary allusions, most notably to Stendhal's *La Chartreuse de Parme.* The fact that Stendhal took 53 days to dictate that novel provides Perec with his title.

The cruel, corrupt third-world country, with its dictator and its equivalent of the Tontons Macoute, is familiar from the novels of Graham Greene and Eric Ambler. So, too, is the unworldly, unsuccessful innocent, who becomes first a pawn and then a crucial piece in a game of which he is constantly struggling to master the arcane rules. Perec himself shows a familiarity with the rules of the Greene-Ambler game; but sadly he lacks their easy mastery in spinning plot and establishing place and character. One is held for the 92 pages which make up what he left completed at the time of his death; but the hold, it must be said, is rather a limp and clammy one.

There follow 162 pages comprising, under such headings as 'Rhodia Notepad', 'White Exercise Book', 'Black Ring-file', notes left behind by Perec. Readers who share Perec's taste for crossword puzzles may be fascinated by teasing out such a jotting (to take but one example) as:

> THIRTEENTH
> I suppose that even
> the choice of typewriter
> was dictated
> by the fact that I knew
> the supplier well

Such enigmas are for the same sort of people who read *Finnegans Wake* not so much as a supreme literary masterpiece but as a supreme puzzle. I am not one of them.

No doubt someone will also be attracted to this book in the way in which people are from time to time attracted to *The Mystery of Edwin Drood:* in the determination to discover and then carry out the dead author's intentions. For such a person Perec's devoted friends and fellow members of the writers' circle OuLiPo (*Ouvroir de Littérature Potentielle*), Harry Mathews and Jacques Roubaud, have assembled all the extant building-blocks for the task. But whether, if and when the book is completed, it will turn out to be a literary masterpiece, who can say? My own suspicion is that, had Perec himself lived to complete it, what would have been found in the last of a series of Chinese boxes fitted ingeniously one into another would have been merely a void.

John Taylor (review date 27 November 1992)

SOURCE: "The Sense of An Ending," in *Times Literary Supplement,* No. 4678, November 27, 1992, p. 25.

[*In the following review, Taylor notes the influences of Stendhal and his novel* La Chartreuse de Parma, *on Perec's unfinished mystery* 53 Days.]

There is something poignant about the elaborate narrative structure of *53 Days,* the novel on which Georges Perec was working at the time of his death from lung cancer in 1982. Racing against time (the title refers to the fifty-three days it took Stendhal to dictate *La Chartreuse de Parme*), Perec builds this increasingly paranoiac literary thriller into an intricate labyrinth of "nested narratives". Indeed, one of the seemingly insoluble murder stories making up the maze of tales involves a manuscript entitled *The Crypt,* which, like Perec's master novel, has been left unfinished; in any case, it mysteriously concludes with a blank page. Perec was able to draft only eleven of twenty-eight planned chapters, but Harry Mathews and Jacques Roubaud's reconstruction of the plot—from notes, outlines and sundry completed passages—suggests that inconclusiveness and indeterminacy are in fact the subjects of this fiction. Perec, notorious for leaving little to chance, seems to have organized his novel in a way that would permit him, once he had completed several chapters and sketched out the others, to abandon it, at any subsequent stage, without unduly weakening its effect. As the primary narrator remarks in his initial role as detective (before becoming, like all the other characters, a potential victim and a plausible culprit), "every time some piece of the puzzle begins to come into focus, it fades away in a blur, evaporates in a wisp of thin and dubious haze". A similar elusiveness would conceivably have characterized the finished novel.

53 Days is, moreover, replete with observations applying as much to presumed authorial intentions as to *The Crypt* and to the several other books (including Balzac's *Le Colonel Chabert* and Agatha Christie's *And Then There Were None*) that participate, almost as full-fledged characters, in the plots-within-plots-within-plots. Perec's primary narrator describes his sleuthing—and our reading?—as an "endless pernickety *explication de texte* which purports to pierce the story's obscurity but which in fact only sets its wheels in motion". A mind-whirling pace is indeed maintained by means of a "vertigo of explanations without end". "The book contains no hidden truth", admits a fragment which is indicative of both *The Crypt's* and the master novel's qualities, at once teasing and grim. "It was just a decoy, a pretext."

Stendhal's ghost haunts the disparate settings: a politically corrupt post-colonial African nation, an arctic country, and occupied France. Klaus Barbie, Paul Touvier and Jean Moulin eventually appear when a shift in perspective discloses that a key character, the whodunit novelist, Robert Serval,

the author of *The Crypt* and a famous *résistant,* was perhaps a traitor to his comrades during the war. The reader now perceives that the real mystery, all along, probably concerns an unelucidated dark deed committed during the Occupation.

Appropriately enough, Serval's pseudonym is Stéphane Réal, a name which, after a series of Oulipian permutations, later recurs as Saint Réal, Sanréal and, somehow, Stendhal. Emphasizing further this obsession with "an ever absent reality", the latter's intriguing aphorism—"Un roman est un miroir qui se promène le long de la route"—recur often as a cryptic code. Each character in turn (as well as each reader) must discern whether the text he is perusing is a mirror—or an inverted mirror—of reality. Or could it be, as Perec implies in a note, that none of the texts "really 'meant' anything"? "The truth", he concludes, "barely touched upon, recedes into the distance."

Veracity and Illusion preoccupied Perec at the very beginning of his career. *L.G.,* a collection of essays destined for a review that never got off the ground, *La Ligne générale,* shows the aspiring writer charting a path between the *roman engagé* and the *nouveau roman.* It is enlightening to compare *53 Days* with Perec's precocious endeavours to lay the theoretical groundwork of a narrative art that would express "la plus totale des réalités concrètes". In the novelist's view, a veritable realism "ordonne le monde . . . le fait apparaitre dans sa cohérence . . . le dévoile, au-delà de son anarchie quotidienne, en intégrant et en dépassant les contingences qui en forment la trame immédiate". Designed to expose the dangers of such contingencies, *53 Days,* in this truncated yet, none the less, readable (and sprightlily translated) form, movingly reminds us of Perec's lifelong engagement with the complex problem of justifying, as he puts it in one essay, a "mise en ordre du monde".

Irving Malin (review date Summer 1993)

SOURCE: "Georges Perec. A Void," in *Review of Contemporary Fiction,* Vol. 15, No. 2, Summer 1993, pp. 200-01.

[*In the following review, Malin suggests that the missing "e" in the lipogram* A Void *is symbolic of the loss of loved ones.*]

It is impossible to convey the oddities and beauties of this text. There are plots within plots, mysteries within mysteries, times within times, shadows within shadows. The text is, in a sense, a whirlpool. Perec, in effect, wants to suggest that language (is there a world *within* a word?) is an attempt to convey consciousness; it is the "bond" that connects us (even though we take words for granted). By compelling us to understand that our very existence as social creatures depends on language, he forces us to hear and say and write with concentrated (consecrated?) understanding. As one "character" puts it: "dumb-struck, as I say you and I, although not totally grasping at this point what its [inscription] is saying to us, call at last boast of proving its validity as a signal, as a communication." But Perec also understands that we often deliberately *deform* communication. We use words as white lies, as political slogans. We construct to deconstruct crimes.

I assume that readers of this review know that Perec's text does not contain the vowel *e*. Why should he even attempt to make it *disappear*? Why is he so *obsessive* about absence, loss, rupture? By stressing absence, he suggests that it ultimately refers to the lives of *those we once knew,* to the *times we once treasured.* And, of course, he knows that in a paradoxical way, we often grant greater presence to absence than to presence. We don't take into account present life; we yearn for a "golden past."

Perec is, of course, using the "formula" to mourn the missing relatives who were sent to the death camps. Thus it would be foolish to consider this text as a *mere puzzle.* It is a moral statement that masks itself; it makes us *participate* in the search for meaning (linguistic, political, religious).

The novel concerns Anton *Vowl,* an incurable insomniac who cannot understand his surroundings. "Far off, a church clock starts chiming—a chiming as mournful as a last post, as an air-raid alarm, as an SOS signal from a sinking ship." Time is described metaphorically as an SOS of loss, alarm, sinking—perhaps of death itself. Vowl cannot sleep because he is afraid of "the big sleep." His companions, with their absurd names, occupations, grotesque and amusing words, are perhaps his "occult shadows," his "secret sharers."

Although there is a "last" chapter, there is another "last" (lost?) chapter after that. It appears that the author—or the book itself—doesn't *want closure.* Finally, we are given passages that appear as "metagraphs." A quotation from "E. Baron": "The language of the Papuans is very impoverished; each tribe has its own language and its vocabulary is ceaselessly diminishing because, after every death, a few words are eliminated as a sign of mourning." Perec's text "ceaselessly diminishes." We readers *diminish* as we move—or are moved?—through its labyrinthine trails (trials?). But we don't mourn because we perceive an oddity there, an amulet here. We are, in fact, laughing as we are crying.

Karen R. Smith (review date Fall 1993)

SOURCE: "Allegory and Autobiography: Georges Perec's Narrative Resistance to Nostalgia," in *The Journal of Narrative Technique,* Vol. 23, No. 3, Fall 1993, pp. 201-10.

[*In the following review of* W ou Le Souvenir d'Enfance, *Smith focuses on the novel's allegorical structure. She suggests that Perec's intention is to show that the creation of a narrative is an attempt to give coherent meaning to the chaos of the past.*]

In the context of Georges Perec's postmodern *œuvre,* which consists of novels that demonstrate through playful manipulation the pliability of language and narrative as media of communication, his autobiographical *W ou Le Souvenir d'Enfance* poses problems. Because it purports to reconstruct factual events of the past, it appears to draw upon a referentiality that is undermined by Perec's other, hyperfictional, works. The form of *W ou Le Souvenir d'Enfance,* nevertheless, signals its departure from the conventions of the autobiographical genre. Its juxtaposition of apparent fiction and fact, of sincere and ironic discourses, of narrative and anti-narrative structures, revises the general premises of autobiography.

The book is made up of two texts that alternate chapter by chapter. The first, which describes the imaginary land of "W" (a boy's utopia of athlete-citizens perpetually engaged in Olympian games) is obviously a fiction. The second, which charts Perec's apparently sincere attempt to reconstruct his life as a French Jewish child during the Second World War, may be seen as a collection of facts. The duality of these two alternating texts, of fiction and fact—or of what may be called allegorical and literal modes of representation—poses a problem for the reader. For in the process of determining the nature of the relationship between the two texts, each text affects the other, and thus the reader is unable to assume that any given moment in the text is real, or truly "autobiographical".

As readers, we first encounter this problem when we read the title: *W ou Le Souvenir d'Enfance.* If we read "*W*" as the main title of the work, and "*le souvenir d'enfance*" as the subtitle, we are led to see the depiction of the land of W as the fiction of which the autobiographical text, the "memory of childhood," is factual commentary, context, or explanation. Put another way, we read "*W*" and "*souvenir d'enfance,*" as interchangeable names, the first as an allegorical version of the second.

Another, perhaps less immediate possibility, however, is to read the title as presenting us with a choice: either "W" *or* "the memory of childhood." In this instance, the two texts are anticipated as separate stories, with the relationship between them no longer that of fiction and fact but rather that of one fiction and another.

At the heart of the problem posed by the unconventional form of Perec's autobiography, then, is a questioning of the way in which we distinguish fiction from fact and, consequently, how we understand the relationship between allegory and history. While it may be easy at first to designate the story of W (corresponding to the "*W*" in the title) as the allegory in this work, and the reconstruction of Perec's childhood (corresponding to the *souvenir d'enfance* of the title) as the history, a close reading of the texts reveals elements of the other in each. Rather than two different renderings—figurative and literal—of the same reality, the allegory and the history become two separate realities, as well as two separate fictions, that work together to form a larger, if still incomplete, narrative of the past.

Ordinarily an autobiographical work by Georges Perec may interest us for two reasons. We may expect it to offer us a key to understanding Perec and his creative work. We may also expect it to help us understand his "era"—the larger, collective history of the Second World War and the Holocaust. These expectations, like those that we usually bring to narratives of history, are shaped by our desire to understand the past, to locate within it a meaning that, ultimately, will stabilize our experience of the present. We look to the genre of autobiography for a construction of a past that disguises its status as a construction, offering us meaning that we can perceive as trustworthy, absolute, and real.

Such a view of the past, which could be called nostalgic in that it responds to the desires of the present, is never fully realized in Perec's autobiography. Striking us in its apparent failure to achieve narrative coherence, the unfolding of **W ou Le Souvenir d'Enfance** works to highlight the process through which its history is constructed. In particular, the self-conscious and even ironic use of allegory in the work serves to remind us that our understanding of the past is necessarily based upon an arbitrary—and in that sense allegorical—representation of reality. Perec's autobiographical novel, then, thwarts the nostalgia that motivates our desire to recreate history—"reality"—through narrative.

I will argue here that Perec's anti-nostalgia responds to a problem particular to post-war twentieth century literature. It is the problem that Shoshana Felman, in her essay "Narrative as Testimony," identifies in terms of a disruption in the conventionally interactive relationship between history and narrative. Arguing that the incomprehensible event of the Holocaust severs the relationship through which narrative serves history, Felman focuses upon the possibly recuperative role of the witness whose testimony enables us to begin to imagine a history that eludes our established "frames of reference." In **W ou Le Souvenir d'Enfance,** the autobiographical narrator's position as a *non-witness*—as someone whose experience of the Holocaust is shaped by his absence from its immediate and concrete institutions—generates the irony of his attempts to tell the story of a personal past so inevitably pervaded by a larger history that defies narration. The connection that Perec's work thus im-

plicitly draws between the positions of witnessing and narrating points to the limits of our capacity to create sincere, authentic narratives of history. In its alternating texts Perec's memoir highlights the gaps produced by a narrative mediation of memory.

The narration of W, the fictional text, begins as a pseudo-autobiography. The protagonist, Gaspard Winckler, speaks in the first person and includes in his narrative specific autobiographical details: place and date of birth, occupations and deaths of parents. These details are irrelevant to the story of his discovery of W. However, within the genre of autobiography, which is expected to provide a complete and untempered version of the past without regard for aesthetic concerns, they may be read as necessary information. In a sense, then, we are given clues that help us read "W" as a factual, autobiographical account.

The authenticity that these details suggest, however, is complicated in Winckler's story by intertextual references. The narrator compares himself to another fictional protagonist—Ishmael of Melville's *Moby Dick.* The comparison is ostensibly based upon the status of these two protagonists as witnesses to, rather than heroes in, the adventures of their stories. But it is significant that, in choosing a literary protagonist, Winckler takes one from a novel that is most commonly read as an allegory, and which borrows—in the choice of this name alone—from another text which is allegorically read, the Old Testament. It is also important to note that this allusion may refer not only to Melville's work, but also to Perec's use of that work in one of his earlier novels. The layered textuality of this reference, i.e., the reliance not on literal reality but on literary constructions of it, of course, heightens the fictional status of Winckler's story.

While the story of W thus opens as a fiction with autobiographical elements, the text of the literal autobiography begins with a statement that may be read as a fiction. In this text Perec speaks in first person. His voice, which is recognized as that of the "real" author, highlights the fictionality of Gaspard Winckler's narrative, making ironic that narrative's semblance of authenticity. At the same time, however, the sincerity of Perec's own voice must be called into question. His first words are "*Je n'ai pas de souvenirs d'enfance*"; all he can remember of his childhood, he tells us, amounts but to a few lines. Because of their confessional tone, these words seem sincere. But their context renders them ironic: they are written within a work partly titled, "*souvenir d'enfance,*" and they are followed by more than "a few lines" of autobiographical writing. Indeed, the text that follows these opening words reveals their status as strategy rather than fact. Perec tells us that his denial of memory allowed him to take comfort in the "*absence d'histoire*" it created . Thus, instead of serving the truth, the sentence "*je n'ai pas de souvenir d'enfance*" in fact serves the ideological function of protecting its speaker from the burden of truth. By the third paragraph of this confessional text, we read the statement again, but this time it is surrounded by quotation marks. Its status as strategy, as an ideological *and* literary construction of reality rather than a statement of fact, is thus textually marked.

At this very early stage in the book, then, the desire for authenticity, for a sincere account of reality, has already been thwarted. In place of authenticity, we are given alternating modes of representing reality, each of which renders the other ironic by revealing its strategies. In their interplay, these texts go further to cast doubt upon the already known, already narrated, canonized history generally used to explain the larger, collectively experienced events of Perec's childhood. Perec speaks of *"une autre histoire, la Grande, l'Histoire avec sa grande hache"* which he has, strategically, allowed to tell his story. That Perec is able to summon this History with two synecdoches, *"la guerre, les camps,"* makes clear the assumption that the reader already "knows" it. However, the distinction that Perec makes between his *"histoire"* and *"une autre histoire . . . l'Histoire"* suggests that both are arbitrary and incomplete. By extension, the reader's knowledge is also suddenly incomplete. For if we see this larger history, which we may have already incorporated into our understanding of Perec's era, as perhaps itself strategic, we might doubt the capacity of "History with a capital H" fully to explain the past. That history can be modified both by the article *"une"* and by the article *"la"* in itself undermines its trustworthiness.

The book *W ou le souvenir d'enfance* is, of course, a testimony to Perec's sincere effort finally to come to terms with his personal history and commence the task of reconstructing it through narrative. From the beginning, however, the "reality" of this history is qualified. Consequently, what begins as sincerity is necessarily transformed into self-conscious irony. We are led to find the truth in what is apparently a fiction, and we are made aware of the lapses in what passes for fact. We are reminded that the world of W, which we recognize as a fiction, has its roots in Perec's actual past. As a reconstruction of his boyhood fantasy, it is, Perec tells us, the closest he can come to giving us a real history of his childhood: *"sinon l'histoire, du moins une histoire de mon enfance"*).

The actual autobiography, on the other hand, is obviously incomplete; it lacks a coherent structure, and is marked by gaps and lapses of memory. Ultimately, this autobiography revolves around absence: the mystery of Perec's mother's disappearance, which may have ended in her death at Auschwitz, and, in general, the murders of his family and people by the Nazis. Ironically, then, Perec's attempt to overcome through writing a self-imposed "absence of history" results in a history of absence. At the center of Perec's per-

sonal history is total annihilation: *"aneantissement une fois pour toutes"*. To render an accurate portrayal of the past is thus, Perec writes, pointless. At the bottom of the story there is absence instead of concrete reality, and silence instead of an authentic personal voice: *"je ne retrouverai jamais, dans mon ressassement même, que l'ultime reflet d'une parole absente à l'écriture, le scandale de leur silence et de mon silence"*.

If Perec's autobiography is a history of absence, then his story of W might be seen as an allegory of this absence. More precisely, the fiction of W may be seen as a replacement or substitution for the factual absences of Perec's childhood memory. The story of W, in this way, serves to demonstrate how fictional narrative can be used to explain or comment upon the silences, and the absurdities, of reality.

At first, the narrative of W develops as an adventure. Winckler is asked to assist a shipwreck victim's relief society in recovering the boy whose name he illegally assumed in order to escape conscription years earlier. The search for the boy takes us to the islands of Tierra del Fuego, upon whose surrounding rocks the ship carrying the young Winckler was supposed to have wrecked. Abruptly, however, the narrative shifts from charting this search to a description of W, a completely enclosed society existing on one of the islands. At this point, the voice and identity of Winckler clearly changes from a participant in an adventure of discovery into a commentator, documentary-style, upon the social organization of W.

In the narration of the adventure story, correspondences between Winckler and Perec are noticeable. Both are brought suddenly to remember a forgotten and horrible past while in the city of Venice; both tell of their fruitless searching through archives in an attempt to recover this past; both experienced at an early age the deaths of their parents. The reader may, then, read Winckler as a fictional counterpart, an allegorical double, of Perec. We may also see the young, authentic Winckler, a deaf and dumb child lost at sea, as a representation of Perec's uncomprehending childhood self, whose identity the adult Perec hopes to recover through his journey of memory.

As this interaction between allegory and reality is established, with Winkler's fiction becoming a concrete and imaginative illustration of Perec's efforts to remember, we are led to read the discovered land of W as an image of Perec's recovered past. At first, this image is utopian. W is set off from historical time and space, and represents an idealized version of Perec's imperfect childhood reality. Although W is set in an actual place, an island in Tierra del Fuego, it takes on the aura of myth. The island's impenetrable natural boundaries separate it spatially from the rest of the human world, including the European community to which Perec belongs. The temporality of W has similar mythic qualities, as it cannot be located along the progression of European history. Although the narrator touches upon W's original links with Europe—its founders are of Dutch and German descent—he does not trace its historical development. Rather, we are presented with a static world in which little has changed since the time of its origins.

Thus spatially and temporally removed from reality, W is not a part of the world community of Perec's childhood. It represents that community in its ideal, utopian, form. While Europe at the time of Perec's childhood was in reality torn by war, society in W is shaped by the ideals of the Olympic games, an institution resurrected in this century in order to create unity among nations. The contrast is clear: the W of Gaspard Winckler's description is, at least initially, a utopian inversion of the reality that the child Georges Perec experienced.

With this fixed, utopian image of the past, Perec comments upon the nostalgic construction of history assumed within the genre of autobiographical texts. At least one scholar of Perec has noted implicit references in *W ou Le Souvenir d'Enfance* to Proust's *A la Recherche du Temps Perdu*, calling Perec "Proust without a madeleine". The image is an apt one. Perec, like Proust, seeks an affirmation of identity through the recollection of childhood. Unlike Proust, however, Perec is not effectively served by memory. He does not have access to a device that would, like Proust's madeleine, retrieve the past in whole, coherent form. Indeed, in Perec's autobiography, memory does not retrieve the past; rather, it creates a past that is marked by evidence of its construction. By encouraging a comparison between his work and that of Proust, then, Perec comments ironically upon the nostalgic view of the past that Proust's novel assumes. Perec offers a utopian, or nostalgic, image of the past only to demonstrate its inadequacies in representing—in his case—the truth. *L'enfance*, he tells us, "*n'est ni nostalgie, ni terreur, ni paradis perdu, ni Toison d'or, mais peut-être horizon, point de départ. . . .*"

Significantly, Perec groups "nostalgia" with specific mythical and utopian allegories: "*paradis perdu*," "*Toison d'or.*" Nostalgia, he suggests, creates a fiction from history—an allegory through which the meaning of the past affirms that of the present. That nostalgia is closer to fiction than fact is made clear in at least two autobiographical passages in Perec's work. In the one Perec reconstructs his mother's childhood, peopling it with a kind and tender family amidst harsh circumstances. The sentimental picture of her childhood hardship, which includes a vision of her as "*une petite chose*" bundled up against the cold, turns out to be based upon Perec's memory of a fairytale, Anderson's "Little Match Girl," rather than on reality. At another point in the autobiography Perec describes a pleasant scene of childhood, perfectly framed, in which he helps his mother clear the table and then settles down to do his homework. The scene is told, however, in the conditional past. At the end of the paragraph, we learn that it comes from a book: "*C'est comme ça que ça se passait dans mes livres de classe*". In both of these instances the connection between nostalgia and fiction is clear. Nostalgia creates a fiction from history to serve the needs of the motherless adult. In other words, nostalgic constructions of the past substitute for the primary loss, and lapse of meaning, in Perec's childhood.

Including "terror" as a companion to "nostalgia," Perec implies that the painful childhood can be mythologized as easily as the comfortable one. A dystopian image of the past may serve the same function as a utopian one: both represent the past in coherent, temporally static and thus a historical form. As the concrete embodiment of either terror or desire, the nostalgic image of the past closes off "horizons" and prevents "departures" from a fixed version of reality.

The metamorphosis of W from utopia to dystopia articulates a resistance to the nostalgic scheme of fixed reality. As the fairness and order of W turns in the middle of the work into a nightmare of arbitrary and sadistic cruelty, the seemingly benign details of its utopian description take on ominous meaning. The striped uniforms, the triangular Novice patches, and the W badges that unite the athletes of the island become symbols of the stars, triangles, and striped uniforms used to classify and dehumanize concentration camp victims. The peculiarly emphasized roles of hairdresser and shower-operator, the rituals of punishment and privilege, the impersonal and arbitrary system of naming—all suggest aspects of the concentration camp order. Thus new meanings are produced as the description of W shifts into dystopia. Rather than an allegory of what the world might have been, W becomes an allegory of what the world was. The implied shift in reference from the conditional to the actual past brings W, as an allegory, closer to real, historical time.

That move toward history is completed in the book's last chapter, where Perec as autobiographer turns to the pages of another work, Rousset's *L'Univers Concentrationnaire*, in order to make explicit the connections between his boyhood fantasy and the reality of the Nazi death camps. At this point the story of W and the memory of childhood merge: the allegory points to memory's site of repressed trauma. For W can be seen as a figurative representation of Auschwitz, the presumed place of Perec's mother's death, and the most well-known of the camps in which Perec's family and people as a whole were almost entirely annihilated. Paradoxically, then, the annihilation or absence at the center of Perec's history becomes the concrete referent of the allegory produced by his fictional narrative.

However, to read the story of W simply as an allegory, with Auschwitz as its fixed referent, is to miss the point it makes about the very nature of allegory. For at the same time that this final chapter marks a convergence of allegorical and literal modes of writing, it prevents us from holding on to a fixed correspondence between them. When Perec remarks upon the coincidence that the islands of Tierra del Fuego, mythologized by his boyhood fantasy, are presently used by Pinochet for punishment camps similar to Hitler's, he completes the move of W from fictional into real time and space. In doing this, he collapses the boundaries that separate past from present. Without such boundaries, the past cannot be represented as a coherent whole, fixed in its relationship to the present and offering that present stable meaning. Thus, the past can no longer exist in a conventionally allegorical relationship with the present; it no longer points to one absolute meaning for the present.

Once the coherence of the allegory collapses, we recognize coherence as a strategy rather than a reality in the making of history. Unlike "reality," a strategy or fiction can take many possible forms. W can "mean" both Auschwitz and Pinochet's punishment camps. As it breaks the fixed relationship between W and the specific historical reality of Auschwitz, the second referent, that of Pinochet's camps, starts a chain of other possible meanings.

If Perec's autobiographical work ironizes allegory, in the sense of a fixed sign referring "to one specific meaning" and exhausting "its suggestive potentials once it has been discovered", it does so by destabilizing its "specific meaning." Perec's work reveals the idea of fixed meaning to be a strategy serving an ideological need for the semblance of absolute and authentic reality. Biblical Christian allegory, of course, provides the most obvious example of such ideological allegory. As Dante explained in his *Letter to Can Grande,* it is through the allegorical meaning of historical events that we are able to understand the mysteries of the divine. Thus allegory, especially in its canonical Christian form, is primarily an instrument of understanding.

The paradox confronted in Perec's work, and perhaps in any work attempting to reconstruct events of the Holocaust or of similar atrocities, is that it uses this structure of understanding to give meaning, or presence, to an absence. In the sense that the absurdities of the Second World War are mysterious, incomprehensible, and hence "absent," we may seek a substitution for the gaps and lapses in our literal understanding and represent the reality of that war allegorically. Indeed, it can be argued that a discourse of allegory, specifically Biblical and often Christian allegory, has arisen in response to the Holocaust. As psychologist and concentration camp survivor Bruno Bettelheim points out, the very term "holocaust," with its

biblical roots and its inference that its victims are martyrs, participates in this discourse by giving religious meaning to senseless murder. This strategy is also at work, for perhaps different ideological purposes, when a recent travel brochure issued by Poland's touristry bureau calls the site of the concentration camp at Auschwitz a "State Museum of Martyrology". Such euphemisms produce an allegory of the Holocaust in which the senseless murders of its victims are given divine meaning through an implicit comparison to Christ, as well as to other victims in both the Jewish and Christian biblical texts. The irony inherent in such discourse is that it affirms the presence of what is finally, as Perec's text asserts, an absence. The horror of systematic murder and the absurdity of genocide are given, through the structure of a fixed allegory, the status of "mystical meaning." By giving the Holocaust meaning, even a name, we begin the work of constructing its presence, and of making fictions or stories of its reality.

Such fiction-making is, perhaps, unavoidable and in some cases even regenerative. Indeed, Felman argues that the "holocaust of history" requires the imaginative function of narrative not to recreate what happened, but to enable us to imagine how it could and that it did happen. She explains that the allegory of the plague in Camus' *La Peste* creates a frame of reference through which we can understand the Holocaust: "It is precisely because history as holocaust proceeds from a *failure to imagine,* that it takes an *imaginative* medium like the Plague to gain insight into its historical *reality*". Perec's work shows us, however, that in its purest form the imagining of history that is absence produces nostalgia, i.e., an image of the past that is removed from the time and space of history, and thus a fixed reality that represents the fulfillment of a desire for complete understanding.

History, then, lies between an assertion of absence and a totality of presence. It lies between Perec's statement "I have no childhood memories" and the projected utopia that he begins to give us as a representation of childhood memory. Between Perec's denial and his unworldly utopia is the self-conscious reality of his writing. We may recognize its fallibility, its status as a fictional narrative, as one of many possible histories. But we may also glean from it some historical knowledge and insights.

At the end of Perec's autobiographical work we are not rewarded with a coherent and complete understanding of the past. We are, however, given a greater understanding of what we can expect from our readings of history. Perec's work points out the extent to which our knowledge is based upon an interplay of past and present experience, two incomplete narratives of reality that together produce a meaning we can use for the moment.

Harvy Pekar (review date Summer 1994)

SOURCE: "George Perec. *Things: A Story of the Sixties/A Man Asleep,*" in *Review of Contemporary Fiction,* Vol. 11, No. 2, Summer 1994, pp. 233-34.

[*In the following review, Pekar summarizes the plots of* Things *and* A Man Asleep. *He is particularly impressed by Perec's descriptions of the sleeping state.*]

In looking over Perec's longer literary projects it's amazing how little each of them has in common with the others. *Things,* previously issued by Grove Press in a different translation as *Les choses,* is almost a sociological study centering on a deliberately gentricized, dilettante Parisian couple, Jerome and Sylvie, their constant search for consumer goods and quest to avoid dull, routine duties. They work at market research jobs during a boom in the 1960s, interviewing people about things they buy. Market research positions are not too secure, which our couple realizes; nevertheless they don't want to commit to more drudgery and consequently remain researchers for as long as possible.

What Perec shows them and their friends mainly doing is shopping. There is, in fact, so much description of material products that it's tempting to call *Things* a *nouveau roman*-type work. But there is too much explicit social commentary here for that. Perec is hard on the trendiness and bad taste of his young characters. In fact they even seem somewhat reminiscent of the commodity-hungry Babbitt; it's conceivable that the old Sinclair Lewis novel might've had an influence on *Things.* Perec knew his American literature (he was really into Melville).

Anyway, Jerome and Sylvie finally decide to take a chance and move to Tunisia, where Perec intimates they could've built a rich life with some effort: "Jerome would've got a job for himself. They would not have been short of money . . . they would have had a fine detached house, a big garden."

Instead, what Perec predicts for them is a quick return to France and, through the intercession of some of their more influential friends, jobs running an "agency" in Bordeaux. Thus the rat race catches up to them.

Perec's accomplishment in *Things* is obvious if modest. He's done a solid job, described what he wanted to describe, criticized what he wanted to criticize. . . . The work does lack a certain amount of emotional impact since it reads so much like a case study, but I assume Perec realized what he was doing.

A Man Asleep, written in the second person, is on the contrary emotionally charged. The protagonist, a university student, tries to drop out of what he thinks is "life," "to want nothing, just to wait until there is nothing left to wait for. Just to wander and sleep." To exist "as a blessed parenthesis." For a while this works. The young man haunts the night, going into and out of theaters, bars, pinball parlors, gets lost in crowds and apparently feels an enjoyable loss of responsibility or restraint. After months, though, the routine begins to wear. The student realizes he's just moving in circles, not accomplishing anything. And so, at the end, our hero is chastened and appears headed back toward a more or less normal existence—winding up, interestingly, pretty much like Jerome and Sylvie.

One of the most unique and interesting features of *A Man Asleep* is Perec's effort to describe sleeping and near sleeping states, which are highly unusual, reminding me of very little other fiction. Robert Musil sometimes did try to paint a portrait of the mind's eye, but descriptive passages like theirs are exceedingly rare.

To really appreciate the range of Perec's skills and interests it's necessary to be familiar with several of his works. This volume is as good a place as any to begin.

John Sturrock (review date 10 November 1994)

SOURCE: "E-less in Gaza," in *The London Review of Books,* Vol. 16, No. 21, November 10, 1994, p. 6.

[*In the following review, Sturrock favorably compares Gilbert Adair's lipogrammatical translation of* La Disparition *to Perec's original French text.*]

We hear a lot about floating signifiers and how they bob anchorless around on the deep waters of meaning; we hear too little about sinking signifiers, or language items that have stopped bobbing and been sent silently to the bottom, if not for the duration then at least provisionally, while we see how well we can do without them. To scuttle a signifier in this way is to play at lipograms, an elementary language game that has been around for two and a half millennia. This *lipo* has nothing to do with fat, or with the world of the liposuctionist's hoover: it comes from a Greek verb meaning to 'leave out'. The lipogram is a piece of writing from which one or more letters of the alphabet have been excluded, preferably common ones if the game is to be worth playing. There is in theory no reason why there shouldn't also be spoken lipograms, or lipophones—indeed, I can imagine that, the bit once between their teeth, composers of lipograms find themselves talking lipogrammatically, either because they can't stop or because they think it will help them to keep their eye in.

The earliest lipograms are thought to have been composed in the sixth century BC, but none of them has survived; maybe they were never actually written down, only imagined, to circulate among the clerisy as instant legends of verbal skill. One Greek lipogrammatist is said to have written poems from which he left out the letter sigma because he didn't like the hissing sound it made when spoken; a more ambitious fellow Greek rewrote the *Iliad* excluding a different character from each of its 24 books: no alphas in Book One, no betas in Book Two and so on—odd that the number of books in the *Iliad* and of characters in the Greek alphabet should be the same, unless, perish the Perecquian thought, that is *why* the poem is divided into 24 books. The sigmaphobe with his ulterior aim was in fact missing the point of the lipogram, which is not designed for the writer's convenience. The *Iliad* man was the purist of the two, he had grasped that the lipogram should be a purposeless ordeal undertaken voluntarily, a gratuitous taxing of the brain, and the severer the better. It should make the business of writing not pleasanter but harder.

Harder or, if you think like Georges Perec, easier. Perec has to have been the most talented and entertaining player of word-games in the long history of Homo ludens, and he gave as his reason for taking to them so whole-heartedly that had he not been bound to observe tough formal constraints when writing, he would have been unable to write anything at all. He needed to have the possibilities narrowed down for him in advance, to be made to feel less free in respect of language. He had, he said, not 'one carat of inspiration', didn't believe indeed that there was any such thing: there is a bracingly cool theory of preplanning and calculation behind all the writing that Perec did. He was the star performer among the similarly uninspired members of the OuLiPo, or OUvroir de LIttérature POtentielle, a formidably ingenious group of poets, mathematicians and others who met together regularly in Paris from the late Fifties and set themselves to reactivate long obsolete forms of prosodic constraint as well as to work out ferocious new ones.

The lipograms composed and published in the past—in those nicely decadent moments of cultural history when putting the signifier before the signified has been seen as the enlightened pastime that it is—were, with rare exceptions such as the lipogrammatised Homer, of modest, parlour-game size: a neat quatrain leaving out a particular vowel or consonant perhaps, or a page or two of similarly deprived prose. Perec, however, had gone into the bibliography of these things, and found examples where the lipogrammatist had kept going and produced a text aspiring to gigantism. Notably, there was a lipogrammatic novel written earlier this century by 'an American sailor' called Ernest Vincent Wright. It was published in Los Angeles in 1939 and declared its achievement in its subtitle: *Gadsby: A Story of Over 50,000 Words Without Using the*

Letter E—can this have been a lipogrammatical *Grat Gatsby*?

Perec was denied the use of some invaluable linguistic forms: *je, se, le, ce, elle, de, les, des, avec, après, quel, que, est:* **the list is potentially very long, and frightening.**

—John Sturrock

American sailors nothing: word-game players are competitive to the core, and with this imposing predecessor in his sights Perec undertook to write the mother of all lipograms, an ultimate OuLiPogram. It came out in the late Sixties, a king-sized *e*-less novel with a suggestive though by no means giveaway title, **La Disparition** ('The Disappearance' or, more morbidly, 'The Death')—Perec was not one to flaunt his cleverness on the title-page, à la Ernest Vincent Wright. This was several thousand words longer than *Gadsby,* whose title and author-minus the Ernest, of course—are fraternally evoked a number of times by Perec in his own text, Wright being at one point awarded the degree of Auctor Honoris Causa at Oxford and later ennobled as Lord Gadsby.

Perec having kept mum about the nature of the constraint under which **La Disparition** had been written, there were those at the time by all accounts who read the book without noticing that it was *e*-less and that its author was without question the new *recordman du monde* among lipogrammatists. This is just about credible. **La Disparition** is a wonderfully amusing book to read, deliriously full of stories, objects, allusions, characters and bizarre incidents: a learned display of what in an afterword (still *e*-less) Perec called 'his passion for accumulation, for saturation, for imitation, for quotation, for translation, for automatisation'. A plot so hyperactive, even by Perec's unusually robust standards of plotting—see **Life A User's Manual**—might have aroused suspicion, as might his glaring and often hilarious refusal throughout the book to limit himself to one permissible word when the sentence allows of another ten such to be introduced in close conjunction with it. Yet even with the title there to help you, it wouldn't be so easy to tell that its paradoxical verbal opulence had originated in the absence of a certain letter of the alphabet. You can either *see* that a text has no *e*s in it or you can't.

It wasn't long before the word went round: **La Disparition** hadn't a single *e* anywhere in its 300-odd pages. Knowing this, readers could begin to spot and so to enjoy the many clues that it contains as to its own ludic nature. The name of the main protagonist for a start, Anton Voyl, decryptible without too much difficulty as the suitably devocalised form of *voyelle*, the French word for 'vowel'—the more accurate but weird-looking Voyll would no doubt have made the whole thing too obvious. And then there are the many stories, and the many stories within the many stories, to which *La Disparition* is the ample host: they have all to do with sudden disappearances, with violent deaths, with pursuit, with the revealing, or not, of secrets. The book is a sort of parody of the Lacanian theme of the 'lack', or that painful, permanent but creative absence that Lacan has it is the source of our endlessly renewable human desires.

Perec presumably enjoyed knowing that not everyone who read *La Disparition* at the outset had rumbled him, that for all its eccentricities of wording and syntax it had seemed near enough to linguistic orthodoxy to be read as if it had been written by someone able to call on all the elements of his native alphabet. On the other hand, he could hardly have wanted those who didn't realise it was a lipogram to go on not realising it, since whatever admiration they had felt for the book would then rest on the wrong, insufficient premises. This is a situation that Gilbert Adair will be glad not to have had to face. His astonishing adaptation of Perec's novel makes no secret of its lipogrammatic status: the front-cover blurb proceeds loyally enough without any *es*, only to blow the gaff in the final few words and tell those who read blurbs at least that this is a book written under a peculiarly taxing constraint.

To do without the letter *e* in English may be marginally more difficult than to do without it in French. Perec was denied the use of some invaluable linguistic forms: *je, se, le, ce, elle, de, les, des, avec, après, quel, que, est:* the list is potentially very long, and frightening. Written French, on the other hand, allows of elision, so that some of these banned substances can be invited back in by the lipogrammatist in the form of *j', s', d', qu'* and so on. Adair was not so lucky. For him there can be no *he, she, we, they, the, be, see, before, after, then* . . . an even more frightening thought when you are setting out to 'translate' a book of three hundred pages. Nor is elision a legitimate way out in English: short of shifting Perec's action to Yorkshire, and introducing a lot of *t* apostrophes of the *trouble at t'mill* variety, Adair was faced with doing without the definite article; and short of cheating in a rather different direction, and going in for quasi-poetical apostrophe *d*s, he was faced with doing without a great many English past participles.

Handicaps indeed, and ones that Adair has overcome with a vigour and inventiveness that verge on the heroic. Some years ago, there was talk of *La Disparition* being translated into English as an ordinary novel, ignoring the fact that it was a lipogram. That might have been some kind of backhanded compliment to Perec, suggesting that the book read so well that it wouldn't greatly matter if the tabooed letter were allowed back into the translation. But it was a miserable, a philistine, idea and thank goodness it died. It might

have seemed at that time that no anglophone lipogrammatist would ever come forward with the time, the vocabulary and the will-power to achieve a full *e*-less version, though at least one hopeful addict was known to have been at work on it for years. Gilbert Adair has now shown quite brilliantly that a lipogrammatic text in one language can be more than adequately done into another, retaining not only the alphabetical constraint but much of the virtuosity of the original. The two languages need to be reasonably close in terms of letter frequency for the achievement of one writer to be measured against that of the other. French and English are close enough, and *A Void* will stand henceforth as the longest and most glorious lipogram that our language possesses, just as *La Disparition* has long stood as that in French.

Whether or not Adair's work should count as a 'translation' of Perec is an interesting question. *A Void* certainly sticks closer to *La Disparition* than one might have expected. All the very many personal and place names in the original can of course be reproduced as is, though Adair has rightly altered the name of the hero to Anton Vowl. And the multiple plots and subplots follow much the same erratic course, except where a detour has been made necessary for Adair by the shortage of suitable vocally challenged words in English. Since Perec's text might be said to be all detours anyway, this is no great hindrance. If anything, it is the reverse. On those many occasions when an exact correspondence of one lipogrammatic text to the other becomes impossible, the translator is out on his own, free to revel in the rare pleasures of periphrasis just as Perec was before him, and showing himself in Adair's case to be a dab hand at visiting some of the remoter attics and cellars of our local word-hoard. It is doubtful whether *A Void* has quite the extraordinary lexical richness of the French, but it comes commendably close and provides enjoyable evidence of how carried away it is possible to become when playing the game of circumventing a letter ban:

> But whilst a goatishly rutting Albin was ravishing Anastasia just as (if you know your classical mythology) Apollo had had his way with Iris, Adonis with Calypso, and Antinous with Aurora, his gang, complying with his wish, was attacking that studio adjoining Anastasia's caravan, blowing it sky-high with a ton of TNT, illuminating a pitch-dark night with its conflagration and making an almighty Doomsday din. It was a sort of Walpurgisnacht. Its poor occupants . . . ran this way and that, shouting and howling in panic. Most got it instantly, struck by a burning plank, by a scorching whirlwind, by a boiling rock torn out of its soil, by a spray of stinging-hot, skin-riddling coals, or by a smoking brand whooshing up as if from out of a volcano.

In its tipsy verbosity, this paragraph from *A Void* gives just the right hectic impression of the paragraph of *La Disparition* from which it has taken off. It's arguable that translation is in fact made easier when certain words are forbidden to you as a translator, on the same OuLiPesque principle that writing in general is made easier by being obliged to conform to rigorous constraints. It would be comforting when translating to know that you need no longer aim exclusively at achieving a semantic equivalence. The translator engaged on translating a lipogram has the best of both worlds: a text to work from that will keep him from getting lost; and the freedom to stray and indulge himself whenever some chicane is placed in his way by the original wording.

As a pair of closely related lipograms, *La Disparition* and *A Void* make an odd but desirable couple: in terms of artistry, *this* Gilbert and Georges could teach their vapidly cavorting namesakes a thing or two.

The Los Angeles Times (review date 12 February 1995)

SOURCE: "Tricky, Tricky," in *The Los Angeles Times,* February 12, 1995, p. 3.

[*The following review discusses the effect of the e-less lipograms of Perec and his translator, Gilbert Adair.*]

Snails. You'd want Gallic or Italian cooking to fix such a dish. You wouldn't call for it at lunch in Oslo, Omsk, Cardiff or Stuttgart; nor as an Alabama snail-fry with grits, nor smoking atop Oklahoma fatwood, nor in Cajun gumbo. And only a light hand such as that of this particular tricky and knotty Parisian author could bring off *A Void:* a total snail of a book in its spiral contortions, so that prying out its pith is both difficult and savory and (pry as you may) bits will always stay stuck within.

Eeeeeeeeek. One paragraph is all I want to do of this. *A Void* does it from beginning to end, and much better (once the names of Perec and his translator, Gilbert Adair, are declared on the title page). Does what? Does entirely without the letter *e.* You didn't spot it just now? Neither did the critic for "Les Nouvelles Litteraires" when the novel was published in France in 1969. He judged it to be a political-existential mystery in the best contemporary style; he rated it "captivating and dramatic" though a bit artificial.

It was a review with a void in it, just like the novel. Unlike the novel, its void was embarrassingly involuntary. To assist English-speaking readers, not to mention reviewers, in avoiding the void, the dust jacket hints discreetly at the complete absence of *e*'s throughout the novel's 285 pages.

Perec, who died in 1982, was the son of French Jews, both of whom perished during World War II: his father in the French Army, his mother at Auschwitz. In his greatest work, *Life: A User's Manual*—a landmark of contemporary literature—and in several lesser but remarkable novels, he used a seemingly arbitrary and abstract series of experiments with language and narrative to come up with an astonishingly humane rendering of tragedy, comedy, absurdity and tenderness. Perec's novels are games, each different. They are played for real stakes and in some cases breathtakingly large ones. As games should be, and as literary games often are not, they are fun.

A Void is an extreme game. It is more than that, as well. If it is not one of Perec's major works—though its vowel-suppression does make it a major tour de force—it shares with them two qualities that Perec apparently never lost. First, as to the game: It is perhaps too much to say it is irresistible, but it is very hard to resist playing it. Like a rare gifted child, Perec inveigles you into mischief you would never get into on your own. Second, even while the game of "look: no *e*'s" is played out—the translator is Perec's devilish equal in playing it—there are perceptible overtones of something more serious and more enchanting.

Perec sets out his game as a mock mystery; or perhaps I should say, as the performance of a mystery in which players and author occasionally drop their comic masks to reveal grief and horror, but only for a split second and with the sinister elusiveness of a subliminal message. Anton Vowl, a writer, disappears; his friends search for him and are killed off one by one. Each death occurs just where the character is on the point of enunciating the mystery or "damnation" that has them all in its grip. Or, to put it differently—it is the link between Perec's alphabet gimmick and his story—just as they are about to speak a word containing the letter *e.*

Putting aside for a moment the story and the use it makes of its void, what happens when we read *e*-less prose? It is considerably odd and effortful. For one thing, there are the roundabouts in thought and expression that Perec is obliged to take: it is like someone making deliberately mannered use of a stutter. Then there is what happens to our eyeballs. We read not word-by-word but by scanning lines or half-lines. The lack of *e*'s—the most common vowel—is like getting a splinter in the eyeball; we become aware of our eyes limping effortfully from left to right.

On the other hand, there is a joyful comedy to the game, even when it irritates. This is the place to praise the other player. Adair has accomplished more than a translator's *tour de force;* he has added a dexterous verbal lunacy of his own. At one point, Vowl's friends receive a clue in the form of a packet of well-known poems. Perec chose several French warhorses, and Adair has chosen English equivalents. We get Hamlet's soliloquy rendered as "Living or not living; that is what I ask," and thus *e*-lessly through the remaining 32 lines. We get Milton's sonnet "On His Glaucoma." And most brilliantly and hilariously we get Poe's entire "The Raven" rendered as "Black Bird" and instead of "nevermore," intoning "not again."

The story divagates, exfoliates, crumbles and reconstitutes itself. It can move simultaneously in two or three different time-frames, so that we get someone recounting a story in which someone recounts another story. Among the characters are Gifford, who owns the chateau where everyone gathers and perishes; his son Haig, an opera singer who was struck dead just as he was about to go on as the Statue (watch that "e") in "Don Giovanni." There is Olga, Haig's wife and the descendant of a line of ferocious Albanian bandits. There is Ibn Abou, who is stabbed just as he is about to reveal something; a comically bumbling police detective and his sinister boss; and two other friends of Vowl's Conson and his long-lost brother Savorgnan.

The writing goes from purple melodrama, to wry, to reflexive, to dryly didactic (one character spouts a garbled version of Critical Theory) to haunting. The reader, forewarned (unlike the hapless French reviewer), will have no trouble picking up Perec's frequent hints about his suppressed vowel, nor in surmising the nature of the void that swallows up the characters one by one.

What stalks them then? It gives nothing away to say that the author does. It is he who has decided that they may exist only without e's and will exist no longer when they, like Pirandello's characters, rebel. Who killed Roger Ackroyd? Agatha Christie, of course. Whodunnit? Dashiell Hammett, Rex Stout, John Macdonald, Ngaio Marsh and so on and so on.

Is it a game? Only partly. *A Void* has its problems. We can get tired of the bumpy hike along Perec's paradox-littered road. But he is like the juggler who knew no other way to pray than by juggling before an image of the Virgin. His humanity operates through his paradoxes. The characters, helpless in the lexicographic fate that their author has devised, are not much unlike ourselves, submitted to the fates that write us while we are trying to write them.

Walter Abish (review date 12 March 1995)

SOURCE: "Vanishing Act," in *Washington Post Book World,* Vol. XXV, No. 11, March 12, 1995, p. 11.

[*Walter Abish is an author and critic. In the following re-*

view, he suggests that the lipogram format of A Void *is more than just an arbitrary constraint. It is, rather, an integral part of the meaning of the story.*]

Georges Perec's preferred representation of life was the elusive, artfully constructed conundrum—an unlimited mystery that engages the reader as much as it animates, in several of his books, the very characters. The customary, the everyday is subsumed by the question, why, how and to what end? Questions that never receive a satisfactory response. In *Life A Users Manual,* a tantalizing labyrinthine novel for which Perec received the prestigious Medicis Prize in 1978, Bartlebooth, an eccentric millionaire, masters watercolor painting to paint, over the next 10 years, 550 seascapes, which he then has made into jigsaw puzzles. Finally, once each picture is reassembled, "the seascape would be 'retexturised' so that it could be removed from its backing, returned to the place where it had been painted . and dipped into a detergent solution whence would emerge a clean and unmarked sheet of Whatman paper."

This intent, this effort to return to a former pristine state, exemplifies the machination of repression at work—for in Perec's books everything ultimately leads to obfuscation and concealment. In an earlier book, *W, or the Memory of Childhood,* two parallel stories—one, a Delphian allegorical tale, the other various autobiographical fragments including finely drawn descriptions of Perec's early childhood in the French Alps, where he was hidden during the German occupation—are recounted with a formal constraint that disallows any display of emotions. What we have instead is a chilling clarity, as structure is made to carry the full weight of Perec's emotional communication, including the fractional mention of the death of his parents, both Jewish (his father, a soldier was killed during the German on-slaught in 1940, and in 1942 his mother, despite her being a war widow, was shipped to Auschwitz, from where she never returned).

When in 1967, in what was to be a significant step in his career, Georges Perec became a member of OuLiPo, which stands for Ouvroir de Litterature Potentielle or "Workshop for Potential Literature," that group was a small organization of writers, poets, literary historians and mathematicians, intent on investigating the many stratagems and constrictive devices, such as the palindrome and the lipogram, that have been applied over the centuries by writers seeking to expand textual possibilities. OuLiPo, under the forbearing leadership of Raymond Queneau, was an intellectual haven and provided an ideal audience for the verbally adroit and inventive Perec. It not only generated ideas, it led Perec to the lipogram—the art of writing a text with one or more letters of the alphabet missing—and the following year it enabled him to write *La disparition,* now translated as *A Void.* He may have chosen the constrictive form of the lipogram for any number of reasons, not least of which was that it enables the writer, in the words of Rimbaud, whose lipogram-poem appears in the novel, "to express the inexpressible." It is also, it should be noted, an ideal vehicle for concealment, for hiding the inexpressible.

The history of the lipogram dates back to the ancient Greeks. Its many more recent practitioners include Mallarmé, Rimbaud, Thomas Hood and an American, Ernest Vincent Wright, who omitted the letter "e" from his novel *Gadsby,* published in 1939. Indeed, Wright may have served as a model for Perec, for he is referred to a number of times in *A Void* as "The Boss" to highlight his significance.

On reading *A Void,* which is distinguished by the noticeable omission of all words containing the letter "e," the question arises: Can this be a serious undertaking or is it just plain tomfoolery, balderdash, drivel? For, given the constraints, language is severely mangled, and a certain silliness becomes unavoidable. The book opens with the novel's anti-hero, fittingly named Vowl, consulting an otoiaryngologist for a cure to his chronic insomnia, and being talked into a questionable sinus operation. For six months, as Vowl recovers, he keeps a diary in which he enters the trivial everyday events of his life, omitting nothing. Then, once he has mailed the 26 books of the diary to an acquaintance, Vowl disappears on All Saints Day. His friends, who suspect foul play or, at the very least a kidnapping, search his apartment. Clues abound in the form of postcards, mystifying lists, a cryptic diary; there are also endless digressions and mocking references to the numbers 25 and 26, to empty spaces, to obscurity, to language, to literature. Along with a description of himself, the presence of the author hangs over the novel as a constant reminder, as much of a clue as he is the answer to its enigma. While the police maintain that the disappearance bears all the signs of a suicide, Vowl's many friends, convinced that he is alive, proceed to search for him in earnest. Then, one by one, these searchers for Vowl are eliminated in what appear to be random and unrelated homicides.

The events take place in France, yet the characters and even the terrain are set in a kind of spurious Flatland that, with a stroke of the pen, could be transformed into an equally credible Romania or Belgium and no one would be the wiser. Only the clues, such as the missing Zahir, a historic ring swallowed by Jonah, the pet carp, are made specific, as Perec invests his boundless energy in all manner of devices and strategies to establish a universe of his own. Paradoxically, Perec did not seek to escape from this world or to negate reality—rather, with the power of divination, he created plausible alternatives, as if these would provide a key to his own relentless probing for signification.

One could say that *A Void* is a text that is camouflaged to resemble a novel: It possesses a requisite beginning and ending; it offers a multitude of characters, albeit all bearing out-

landish, mostly non-French names; it has a protagonist of sorts; it purports to tell a story, though within the story there are numerous other stories and literary references to lead one astray. *A Void* is parodic and farcical, and at the same time, as it underscores the difficulties of proceeding in this e-less landscape, it encourages the reader to unravel the many false leads to this absurd quest, for a quest it is.

But a quest to what end? Surely not Vowl, whose disappearance provides the pretext for the quest, for *A Void* is a construct, a deliberate artifice, a mystification in search of a decoder. In it the eccentric and the improbable are countenanced, as much as the mishaps, the accidental encounters, the many puzzles and riddles that are the lifeblood of Georges Perec's writings. Nothing is what it truly appears to be. There is not so much a subtext to interpret as there is a buried text, something the author is at pains to conceal from the reader and, quite possibly, even from himself.

Lines such as, "And didn't Anton Vowl claim long ago that a work of fiction would contain a solution to his plight?" and "By rights, your surviving such a holocaust is illogical" cry out to be interpreted. For concealed between the lines of *A Void* is an untold account of decimation and survival. This painful history, buried so effectively, so deeply, is only now, since the publication of David Bellos's biography of the late Georges Perec, who died in 1982 at the age of 46, laid bare, waiting to be deciphered. *A Void,* in Gilbert Adair's masterly translation, may be an invitation to a misreading, but it is decidedly worth the journey for the intrepid reader.

James R. Kincaid (review date 12 March 1995)

SOURCE: "Read My Lipograms," in *New York Times Book Review,* March 12, 1995, pp. 3, 30.

[*In the following review, Kincaid focuses on the playfull nature of the lipogram form, and offers several examples.*]

"OAF! Pinbrain! Numskull! Big fat ninny! Nincompoop! Half-wit! . . . Moron! Lazy good-for-nothing!" That's a passage from our novel. Notice anything odd about it? Read it aloud—but don't yell it at somebody. Then sing this song (karaoke background helps). It's the opening of the well-known and affecting "You-Can't-Attain-It Fantasy":

> *To fancy that unavailing apparition!*
> *To fight that dirt-tough bad guy!*
> *To put up with that aggravating sorrow!*
> *To run in many risky spots!*

That stops before we hit the best line—"To just march right

into Satan's pit in support of a good policy"—but you get the idea. The idea is to write without using an E.

The real idea is: "Only within severe, almost crippling restraint do we find freedom." (I'm sure that was said by Schoenberg, Joyce or another just as unlikely; but I can't find it in Bartlett's, so I'll attribute it to Madonna.) Georges Perec published *La Disparition* in 1969, and now it's been translated by Gilbert Adair as *A Void,* with no E anywhere in either, although it's a novel of nearly 300 pages. There's restriction for you, E being by far the most common letter in both languages, as you already knew.

But the paradox of liberating fetters is not one that will puzzle us, not when we think of the way we all narrow our options in order to expand our horizons in everyday life. Think of the new possibilities you have found in denying yourself, no matter what, the use of the far right lane; in never humming a tune whose lyrics employ "baby" or "girl" or "doncha know"; in going one day at a time without using the P-word (pr*bl*m*t*c).

> **When he turned to a commonplace thing like a palindrome, Perec wasn't satisfied with some piddling "Madam, I'm Adam," but did one 5,000 letters long. . . .**
> **—*James R. Kincaid***

This early novel by Perec, best known here for *Life: A User's Manual* (published in France in 1978, in America almost a decade later), is an example of a lipogram, a form in which one or more letters of the alphabet are voluntarily suppressed. It dates from the sixth century B.C., according to Perec, no mean scholar and one of the most dazzling and entertaining game-playing writers of this century. (He later used all the E's saved from *La Disparition,* pouring those E's, and only those E's, into *Les Revenentes.*) Perec, who died in 1982 just short of his 46th birthday, was a longtime member of Oulipo, the Ouvroir de Littérature Potentielle, which you can translate as well as I, once you know that *ouvroir* means "workshop." Oulipo, a group of deliriously brilliant mathematicians, theorists and writers, devoted itself to extraordinary linguistic experiments, designed to test the limits of received esthetics and to drive traditional critics and readers to drink.

Perec himself participated in writing S-7 poems (redoing famous poems by replacing every word with the seventh word following it in the dictionary), snowball verses (start with one word, add a word each line, up to 11, and then go back down), bilingual poetry (easily comprehensible in two or more languages), acrostics, anagrams and various heterogrammatic forms (too complicated to describe, but not for

me and you to try, take my word for it). When he turned to a commonplace thing like a palindrome, Perec wasn't satisfied with some piddling "Madam, I'm Adam," but did one 5,000 letters long, a record, he felt. From 1976 until his death he concocted weekly crossword puzzles for the magazine *Le Point* that I'm told are "difficult." I'll bet.

A Void is a rollicking story, wildly amusing and easily accessible to all of us who don't mind slipping, sliding and being tripped. It's a novel about voids, accidental and murderous, about body snatching and snatching 40 winks, about abduction and seduction. Unless I'm mistaken, it's a detective novel or at least a whodunit, with this twist: E done it, but we mustn't ever say that. We can't. When the characters get close to E, they get written out of the plot (maimed, shredded, fed to carp). The plot, which I can be counted on to have mastered or I wouldn't be writing this review, concerns (probably) the disappearance of one Anton Vowl (A. Vowl) and the attempts of an irregular group of friends to discover what's what. The Sphinx is consulted, and the white whale, and clues start to glimmer dangerously: there are 26 cartons, but the fifth one is missing; and so it is with the 26 (now 25) folios and the number of cousins as well. We may ourselves notice (to our peril) that of the 26 chapters there is no Chapter 5. But I don't want to give too much away.

Understand too much of this book and you die: "Any full and final form of illumination is blinking at us, winking at us, just out of our sight, just out of our grasp." That's the frolic in it—we never get there, which means that the fun never ends, not really, not unless we yearn too much for the secret of E.

But that's a mundane wish, a wish for closure that the translator has blocked as effectively as Perec himself. Allowing himself some sweet liberties (introducing, for instance, Miss Piggy and her "*Moi*"), Mr. Adair must have found here the same heady linguistic tripping available to the author. Of course, the restrictions are preposterous: imagine having virtually no past tense; no definite article; few personal pronouns; no here, there, where, when; no be; no elephant; no eye, ear, nose, elbow; no yes; no love; no sex!

Who would want to read the starved wee thing that could be squeezed out of what remains? Well, I think anybody who gives this a try will roar along with it, and not just its flashier parts, though those set pieces are first-water bamboozles, certainly. Not only do we have sonnets by Milton and Shelley, but Hamlet's celebrated soliloquy (a sample: "And thus our natural trait of fixity/Is sickli'd through with ashy rumination"). Even finer is Poe's "Black Bird," of which you deserve here at least two stanzas:

> *Wondrous was it this ungainly fowl could thus*
> *hold forth so plainly,*

> *Though, alas, it discours'd vainly—as its point*
>   *was far from plain;*
> *And I think it worth admitting that, whilst in my*
>   *study sitting,*
> *I shall stop Black Birds from flitting thusly*
>   *through my door again—*
> *Black or not, I'll stop birds flitting through my*
>   *study door again—*
>   *What I'll say is, "Not Again!"*
>
> *But that Black Bird, posing grimly on its placid*
>   *bust, said primly*
> *"Not Again," and I thought dimly what purport it*
>   *might contain.*
> *Not a third word did it throw off—not a third word*
>   *did it know of—*
> *Till, afraid that it would go off, I thought only to*
>   *complain—*
> *"By tomorrow it will go off," did I tristfully*
>   *complain.*
>   *It again said, "Not Again."*

But such excerptible parts do not give a good sense of the pleasures available in this book, in its parodies and borrowings, its allusions and puzzles, its good-natured games and fiendish traps. The characterization is startling in its blissful refusal to psychologize: "Parfait was . . . simply mad about fighting. If you hit him, Parfait hit you back, again and again and again: it was as basic as that." Communication among these characters proceeds with the lunatic confidence available only to those who haven't the slightest idea what they're doing:

> A poltroon if not a coward, anyway a bit of a milksop, your son saw a distinct possibility of his also rotting in jail, a possibility that wasn't at all to his liking. So, moving out of that casbah of corrupt cops and cutthroat crooks, Douglas took a maid's room on Boul'Mich. It didn't boast all mod. cons. but it had a kind of comfort that was, shall I say, succinct.

This Nabokovian and thrilling book is also, of course, self-reflexive and jagged, talking to other books, including the author's own, to critics, to itself and, most of all, to readers (even those who move their lips). The characters jabber about the book they're in and consult friends like "Dmitri of Karamazov Bros Inc." Perhaps it is such whirligig exhibitionism that has kept Perec from doing very well, up to now, in America. But I suspect the problem is rather that we have identified him too readily (and falsely) with Alain Robbe-Grillet, Michel Butor and other New Novelists, whose brand of rhinocerine frolic has not been to our taste. But Perec's formal experiments and exquisite comedy are

so much lighter, more inviting and self-mockingly hip than anything his pedantic cousins ever manage.

Still, you say: "But so what? What's the point of no E? Why do it at all, this silliness?" In a postscript, Perec mentions that in being forced down so many "intriguing linguistic highways and byways" he discovered unexpected and tickling things that he figured might offer "a stimulant" for "fiction writing today." By abandoning "rampant psychologization" and "mawkish moralizing," by breaking the rules and extending the game, he gives us a glimpse of the rules themselves and how tied to them we have always been. Perec has a firm and courageous allegiance to amusement, to its profound and gleeful ability not simply to solve problems (though that's no small delight) but to find in the game an energy that keeps going outward and onward.

Another, perhaps less inviting, way to view Perec's project is in terms of esthetics, unmediated art. According to Perec, writers write to write and readers read to read, not to promote or restlessly to seek out some activity other than writing and reading. As with Parfait, it's as basic as that. Perec, like the Sterne and Rabelais he cites as models, works within a tradition of pure invention, putting his money on our willingness to play along, participate, get it.

Not that "getting it" means sweating over another's completed masterpiece, trying not to be obtuse, worrying that someone will blow the whistle on our failure to know what's really going on. I was told (or rather, my wife let fall) that certain British reviews in highbrow publications had made fun of amusingly mangled references to "A Void" in the daily papers; my wife also said that two British reviews were themselves written (faultlessly, masterfully) as lipograms. I forgot her valentine, which is why she torments me, I think. Anyhow, Perec (unlike my wife) does not make one defensive, but rather inspires one to invent, to come along and play.

The British may have done these lipogram reviews (sounds very dull to me), but I can actually do lipogrammatic songs and poems, and so can you, if you try. The following will get you started. I included the originals for you to compare.

From *The Pirates of Penzance* (Gilbert and Sullivan), with the original first and then the lipogram:

> Here's a first-rate opportunity
> To get married with impunity,
> and indulge in the felicity
> Of unbounded domesticity.
> You shall quickly be parsonified,
> Conjugally matrimonified,
> By a doctor of divinity,
> Who resides in this vicinity.

What a damn good opportunity
Ho! To marry with impunity,
And to wallow in the jollity
Of suburbanist frivolity!
Think about a happy you and I,
Matrimonially sharing our own sty,
Thanks to a doctor of divinity,
Who hangs out in this vicinity.
Ho!

(The fifth and sixth lines would be better as "Think about a happy you and dad/Matrimonially sharing our own pad"; but it wouldn't fit the sense that way. No poem is altogether perfect, as Coleridge observed.)

From Matthew Arnold's "Dover Beach":

Ah, love, let us be true
To one another! for the world, which seems
To lie before us like a land of dreams,
So various, so beautiful, so new,
Hath really neither joy, nor love, nor light,
Nor certitude, nor peace, nor help for pain;
And we are here as on a darkling plain
Swept with confused alarms of struggle and flight,
Where ignorant armies clash by night.

Ah, hon, how about you and I cling tight
And crouch! for this world, which might
Pass for a goodly gift from God,
So various, so alluring, so awfully mod,
Hath in fact no joy, no amour, no light,
No indisputability, no tranquillity, no succor for
   pain;
And you and I lurch dizzily as on a darkling plain,
All about us whirling alarms of tussling and flight,
As many ignorant troops clash by night.

As I needn't tell anyone as quick as you, that last item even has rhyme. Top that, British reviewers! But I don't want to discourage you or wear out my welcome. You'll have more fun with your own lipograms and with *A Void,* which, like me—and unlike British reviewers and my wife—displays the knack Perec calls "knowing just how far to go too far."

Daniel Gunn (review date 7 October 1996)

SOURCE: "E-free," in *Times Literary Supplement,* No. 4475, October 7, 1996, p. 28.

[*Gunn favorably reviews Gilbert Adair's translation of* A Void.]

Reviewers of Gilbert Adair's splendid translation of Georges Perec's *La Disparition* find themselves—appropriately enough before a novel so concerned with contradiction and paradox, with "masking and unmasking"—at both an advantage and a disadvantage. They have an advantage over the reviewers of the 1969 French original, because they are spared the possible embarrassment of reading and then reviewing the book without noticing its structuring principle and implicit subject: the lack, throughout its 285 pages, of the letter *e.* They are at a disadvantage, however, because such embarrassment, and an accompanying fear or panic at the loss of face, leads to the heart of the novel—for such nagging anxieties are the characters' daily bread.

Yet even for forewarned readers—and the British publisher is making such forewarning a selling-point—there are still feelings of loss. For it is impossible to read more than a sentence or two of the novel without strangeness insinuating itself. And knowing its ostensible location does not dispense with it. The breathlessness, the bristling at the back of the neck—both of the characters and of the reader—do not disappear. Strangulation, actual and metaphoric, abounds.

A violence is being committed here against language, a throttling which yields a perilous jubilation. Committed once by Perec, it is then repeated by Adair, with the pain, the peril, and even the jubilation all potentially redoubled. *La Disparition* is all about what it cannot translate. Reading *A Void,* not least because of Adair's successes, is a doubly unnerving experience. For not only does the attention flit from actual sentences to a general amazement at Perec's self-enforced rationing, but now also we can admire his translator's devotion. "How did he manage that one?", and "Why did he bother?" become: How did *they* manage; why did *they* bother?"

Perec's answer to these questions is sketched in his Postscript, where he claims a total lack of inspiration, and a resulting dependence on "accumulation, saturation, imitation, quotation, translation and automatization"; all of which, he suggests, become enticing when subjected to the noose of constraint. For a fuller picture, one would have to doubt whether the constraint was really self-imposed. For, while entirely compatible with OuLiPo strategies, Perec's extirpation of that letter which is by far the most frequently occurring in French (it is somewhat less so in English) testifies to a burning commitment to loss, a compulsion indeed, and one whose terms were surely not of his choosing.

We know from his later novel, *W,* and from David Bellos's biography, that Perec's constraints are a means of broaching the unbroachable loss of his parents, and the systematic attempt to annihilate the Jewish people—an annihilation which was to be achieved in secrecy. *A Void* never mentions this, yet everywhere hints at it, right from its Introduction, where apocalyptic chaos and violence reign, and terror, hatred and suspicion are universal. Into this valueless universe steps Anton Vowl, whose search for the missing element which might relieve his psychic and physical torment occupies the first four chapters. Until Vowl himself disappears, as does the whole of Chapter Five (fifth out of twenty-six).

The following twenty-one chapters develop a confusing series of implausible plots, in which about the only thing that is certain is that Vowl's disappearance is linked to a curse which is destined to destroy him and his entire clan. Vowl's friends congregate to track him down. Only to find themselves disappearing too—the majority brutally murdered. The closer they come to the "mad and morbid whim" on which their existence is predicated, the closer they come to their own extermination. Olga Mavrokhordatos dies with the word "Maldiction" on her lips: Ottavio Ottavini dies speaking of a lipogram in which the letter *a* has been spotted as missing: "Nor has it got a solitary. . . ." The other lack is the letter *e,* which he fails to pronounce.

By the end, virtually everyone is revealed to be related, and the curse hangs over them all. It has no clear origin, but there is a tyrant determined to enact its cruel edict: the father or grandfather of them all, who is committed to slaying each last one of them, and who has as his henchman one Aloysius Swann. A solitary photograph exists of the terrifying primal father. And it closely resembles that progenitor the characters cannot see, the bearded and besmocked Georges Perec.

Stories proliferate, each taller than the next, making this novel an anticipation not just of *W* but of *Life a User's Manual* as well. But, whereas in the later novels, exuberance and violence are perfectly balanced, here the tension between masking and unmasking, between knowingness and ignorance, becomes almost intolerable. The reader risks being overwhelmed in the deluge of bravura, implausibility and proper names.

The proper names, one imagines, must have been oases for Adair. Take the example of numerals. Perec writes them out, but of the first ten, seven in French lack the *e* whereas only three do in English. And so Adair has on occasion to print figures, on others to change a "three" to a "four", a "twenty" to a "thirty", or, more surprisingly, an "eighteen" to a "six". The passing of "a year" becomes "six months" or a "spring" or "autumn". And this is just the start. The past tense in English is so replete with *e*s that the present is required, and the third person pronoun is untouchable; while as a gain there

is "and", which gives fluency to Adair's sentences, and of course "I".

Adair's energy and ingenuity are almost bottomless. His *e*-less version of Hamlet's "To be or not to be" soliloquy is wonderful, his "Ozymandias" hilarious. And smaller gems abound. "Un Anglais" is welcome as "a brilliant Scotsman", while, in a horse-racing context, "un mauvais roman" becomes "a Dick Francis", and elsewhere "paradis" becomes "Arcadia", "la mort". "Thanatos", and "par trois fois", "again and again and again". And just as important, the novel's flippancy of tone, fluctuations of register, and eerie precision have all been maintained, along with the excess and the exuberance.

A few waverings detract little from Adair achievement. If *A Void* sketches an answer to why Perec bothered, it does not answer the same for his translator. And there must be more to it than his surname. A "book of the translation" would open to us a mine of Adair experience, as well as something of the richness and deficiencies of the French and English languages—indeed of language *tout court.*

FURTHER READING

Criticism

Bellos, David. "Literary Quotations in Perec's *La Vie mode d'emploi,*" *French Studies* XLI, No. 2 (April 1987): 181-94.

     Provides a detailed analysis of the mathematical constraits which governed Perec's use of quotatons from other authors in the structure of this novel.

Josipovici, Gabriel. "Georges Perec's Homage to Joyce and Tradition," *The Yearbook of English Studies* 15 (1985): 179-200.

     Josipovici argues that *La Vie mode d'emploi* is the finest novel in French since Becket. He compares its encyclopaedic structure to Joyce's *Ulysses,* Dante's *Commedia,* and Chaucer's *Canterbury Tales.*

Mathews, Harry. "Georges Perec," *Grand Street* 3, No. 1 (Autumn 1983): 136-45.

     Discusses the plot and themes of Perec's works, and argues that his contribution to literature is unique, indescribable in terms of comparison to other authors.

Additional coverage of Perec's life and career is contained in the following sources published by Gale: *Contemporary Authors,* Vol. 141; and *Dictionary of Literary Biography,* Vol. 83.

Sonia Sanchez

1934-

(Born Wilsonia Benita Driver) American poet, playwright, short story writer, essayist, and editor.

The following entry presents an overview of Sanchez's career. For further information on her life and works, see *CLC*, Volume 5.

INTRODUCTION

Sonia Sanchez is considered by many to be the leading female voice of the Black Revolution. Her poetry contains a visionary quality and a strong sense of the past. She typically presents positive role models and often harshly realistic situations in an effort to inspire her readers to improve their lives. Regina B. Jennings says, "Creating a protective matriarchal persona, she has through versification, plays, and children's books inscribed the humanity of black people."

Biographical Information

Sanchez was born in Birmingham, Alabama, on September 9, 1934, to Wilson and Lena Driver. Her mother died when Sanchez was only one year old, and she spent the next eight years with various relatives. At the age of nine she moved with her father and stepmother to New York City. Sanchez began writing poetry as a child to battle the alienation and loneliness she felt as a shy stutterer, which she did not overcome until she was 16. Although not spoken in their home, Sanchez consciously learned the black dialect spoken on the streets. She would later base the rhythm of her poetry on the rhythm of this speech. She received a Bachelor of Arts degree from Hunter College in 1955, then studied with poet Louise Bogan at New York University. Bogan was an important influence on Sanchez's poetry, especially with regard to her use of traditional structures and form. After completing her graduate work at NYU, Sanchez taught at several colleges, including San Francisco State, the University of Pittsburgh, Rutgers University, Manhattan Community College, Amherst College, and Temple University. She cofounded the Black Studies Program at San Francisco State and was the first to develop and teach a course on black women in literature. Sanchez has also travelled extensively, including a trip to China, where she wrote many of the haikus in her collection *Love Poems* (1973).

Major Works

Sanchez's first collection of poetry, *Homecoming* (1969), focuses on embracing black identity. The poems in *We a*

BaddDDD People (1970) have a political thrust and show the influence of jazz in Sanchez's work in the improvisation of the rhythm and in the attempt to imitate the sounds of different instruments. While *Homecoming* and *We a BaddDDD People* have urban landscapes, however, Sanchez began to use natural landscapes in *Love Poems,* but not the idyllic presentation usually found in poetry. Her poetry became much more lyrical in this volume and focuses on love, loss, and relationships. *A Blues Book for Blue Black Magic Women* (1973) relies on history as a liberating device. The poet acts as guide and teacher and urges readers to embrace their blackness and turn away from the falsity of Western values. The poems in this volume are very ritualistic and religious. Sanchez's *I've Been a Woman* (1978) follows the journey of one woman as she comes into being as a woman and as a human being. The poems in this collection speak to and for women and provide a more personal look at the themes which have consumed her work thus far, including oppression, exploitation, and loss. *Homegirls & handgrenades* (1984) is an autobiographical collection, in which the poet acts as a character in the work. In this volume, Sanchez employs techniques similar to those used by Jean Toomer in

Cane, including the use of narration, dialogue, and poetry to create sketches. In addition to her poetry, Sanchez has also written several plays. *Sister Son/ji* (1969) presents five periods in the life of a black revolutionary shown through flashbacks. Son/ji moves from a first act of resisting racism, to a sense of betrayal by the male revolutionaries who abandon women, and finally to a maturity arising out of loss and survival.

Critical Reception

Some critics accuse Sanchez of repetition and a lack of originality in her work because many of her themes reappear numerous times. Others praise the continuity this repetition brings to the body of her work. Andrew Salkey says, "Altogether, the iron truthfulness in her work emerges out of her deep need to thwart existential gloom, to support her embattled self-esteem, and to renew her faith in herself in order to keep on keeping on." Some reviewers criticize Sanchez for falling into sixties rhetoric in *We a BaddDDD People.* Many critics preferred her more personal poems to her politically oriented ones, which they found shrill and harsh. Several critics praise Sanchez for her use of traditional forms and her ability to make them her own. David Williams says, "The haiku in her hands is the ultimate in activist poetry, as abrupt and as final as a fist." Many critics have noted that Sanchez has failed to garner much attention for her accomplishments as a vital member of the Black Revolutionary Movement. Kamili Anderson asserts, "Relative to her merits as both prolific poet . . . and social activist, widespread critical acknowledgment of Sanchez's talents has been remiss."

PRINCIPAL WORKS

The Bronx is Next (drama) 1968; published in periodical *The Drama Review;* also published in *Cavalcade: Negro American Writing from 1760 to the Present,* 1971
Homecoming (poetry) 1969
Sister Son/ji (drama) 1969; published in *New Plays from the Black Theatre,* 1969
We a BaddDDD People (poetry) 1970
It's a New Day (poems for young brothas and sistuhs) (poetry) 1971
A Blues Book for Blue Black Magical Women (poetry) 1973
Dirty Hearts (drama) 1973; published in *Breakout: In Search of New Theatrical Environments*
Love Poems (poetry) 1973
Uh Huh: But How Do It Free Us? (drama) 1974; published in *The New Lafayette Theatre Presents: Plays with Aesthetic Comments by Six Black Poets*
I've Been a Woman: New and Selected Poems (poetry) 1978

Malcolm Man/Don't Live Here No More (drama) 1982
Crisis in Culture: Two Speeches by Sonia Sanchez (speeches) 1983
homegirls & handgrenades (poetry and prose) 1984
Under a Soprano Sky (poetry) 1987
Black Cats Back and Uneasy Landings (drama) 1995
Wounded in the House of a Friend (poetry) 1995
Does Your House Have Lions (poetry) 1997

CRITICISM

John D. Williams (review date February 1979)

SOURCE: "The Pain of Women, The Joy of Women, The Sadness and Depth of Women," in *Callaloo,* Vol. 2, No. 5, February, 1979, pp. 147-49.

[*In the following review, Williams asserts that the poems in Sanchez's* I've Been a Woman *speak for and to all women.*]

The Black Scholar Press has recently published a new book from Sonia Sanchez, and a powerful book it is indeed. A collection which includes a fine cross-section of Sanchez's earlier work as well as some of her latest poems, *I've Been a Woman* recounts the journey of one woman from the early stages of herself into the meaningfulness of herself as a woman and as a human being. One hears in the voice of this woman-poet the pain of women, the joy of women, the sadness and depth of women. The voice of this woman is pregnant with the voices of women, and all readers of the collection are advised to listen closely.

I've Been a Woman is divided into six sections. The first four sections are comprised of poems and passages drawn from Sanchez's earlier volumes. In these four sections, there are many of those poems, as readers familiar with her work will recognize, that have come to safeguard our ears and our steps: from *Homecoming:* "Poem at Thirty," "Malcolm," and "Personal Letter No. 2"; from *We a Baddddd People:* "Blk/Rhetoric" and "Indianapolis/Summer/1969/Poem"; from *Love Poems:* "Poem No. 7" and "Old Words"; and from *Blues Book for Blue Black Magical Women:* those indispensable passages which describe growing up in America and the fundamental transformation which occurs in the necessary reaching back to oneself. However, it is the final two sections of *I've Been a Woman* that we are concerned with here, because they are the new works of the poet, and, more importantly, because they are the celebration and praise of life that the transformed self, facing the death constantly masquerading before our eyes, must engage in daily.

Each of the short poems in "Haikus/Tankas & Other Love Syllables," the fifth section of the volume, is a re-energization of many of the words we have come to take for granted: love, responsibility, concern, pain. These poems line the world up with the immediacy and accuracy of our moment to moment feelings and sensations:

> never may my thirst
> for freedom be appeased by
> modern urinals.

> my body waiting
>   for the sound of yo/hands is loud
>   as a prairie song.

> these autumn trees sit
> cruel as we pretend to eat
> this morning goodbye.

> these words stained with red
> twirl on my tongue like autumn
>   rainbows from the sea.

Sanchez's fingers are nimble here as she catches moments, hours and sometimes days in seventeen syllables:

> the rain tastes lovely
> like yo/sweat draping my body
> after lovemaking.

> who are you/   iden./
> tify yourself. tell me your
> worth amid women.

> i listen for yo/
> sounds prepare my nostrils for
> yo/smell that has detoured.

> you have pierced me so
> deeply i can not turn a
> round without bleeding.

These poems/these words are like a cutting flame burning deeply to the inside, welding together again/somehow reuniting a divided flesh.

The final section of this book, "Generations," is the poems of praise. They speak sufficiently for themselves. In a poem for Sterling Brown, Sanchez writes:

> how shall i call your name
> sitting priest/like on mountains
> raining incense
> scented dancer of the sun?
>   . . . .
> you. griot of fire.
> harnessing ancient warriors.

> . . . .
> you. griot of the wind
> glorifying red gums smiling tom-tom teeth.

and in the poem for a young brother named Gerald Penny:

> At first you do not speak
> and your legs are like orphans
> at first your two eyes cross
> themselves in confusion
> at first your mouth knows only
> the full breasts of milk
> a sweet taste of this world.

>   . . . .
> Silently to life
> you spoke
> young male child.

> You praised life
> coming as a river between hills
> and your laughter
> was like red berries in summer
> and your shouting like giant eagles

and in the last piece in the book, **"kwa mama zetu waliotuzaa,"** (for our mothers who gave us birth):

> call her back for me
> bells. call back this memory
> still fresh with cactus pain.

> call her name again. bells.
> shirley. graham. du bois
> has died in china
> and her death demands a capsizing of tides.
> olokun.
>   she is passing yo/way while
>   pilgrim waves whistle complaints to man
> olokun.
>   a bearer of roots is walking inside
>   of you.
>   prepare the morning nets to receive her.

In these words we are able to see ourselves/to hear ourselves, emerging into our own vision of life. Sonia Sanchez's poems in this book are commendable and we thank her.

Andrew Salkey (review date May-June 1979)

SOURCE: "In Appreciation of Sonia Sanchez," in *The Black Scholar,* Vol. 10, Nos. 8 and 9, May-June, 1979, pp. 84-5.

[*In the following review, Salkey discusses the poems from*

Sanchez's I've Been a Woman *and describes her poetry "as songs of difficult truth and harsh beauty."*]

The title of this new collection of poems by Sonia Sanchez reads as if it were the poet's answer to the question, "What have you been doing since the '60s?" And so it may be construed.

Even a cursory reading of the text would yield evidence enough that the poet has been quintessentially *herself,* all the way throughout the emblematic '60s into the even more sign-confusing and numbing '70s.

And incidentally, for . . . *A Woman,* in the title, the equivalent, "radically compassionate," is amply suggested in the poems.

Indeed, ***I've Been a Woman*** is a richly layered and lucid statement of radicalism and compassion in which Sonia Sanchez has chosen the response of hard-edged truth over the rhetoric of hopelessness, in spite of her continuing experience of oppression, exploitation and personal loss.

The answer to the imagined question, therefore, is: "I've been radically compassionate."

While her earlier poems raised hopes of public liberation, her recent ones confront and penetrate the anguish of internal inequities which are the thorns at the heart of her concerns as a woman and a poet.

Altogether, the iron truthfulness in her work emerges out of her deep need to thwart existential gloom, to support her embattled self-esteem, and to renew her faith in herself in order to keep on keeping on.

The selected poems, here, provide a rewarding retrospective view of the highlights of the poet's way-forward over the last ten years. The new poems lock neatly into the on-going process. I admire and respect the choices; and the old favorites certainly tug at the memory.

I'll long remember the cautionary blast at the treachery of the intellectuals, when Sonia Sanchez reminded us of Malcolm's excellence (in **"Malcolm,"** from *Homecoming*):

> he was the sun that tagged
> the western sky and
> melted tiger-scholars
> while they searched for stripes.

Then, there was her admission of the inevitable fighter's-pause in the struggle (in **"Personal Letter No. 3,"** from *We a Baddddd People*), which caused some of her admirers, themselves, to take pause, at the time:

> it is a hard thing
> to admit that
> sometimes after midnight
> i am tired
> of it all.

And the excoriating truth-saying (in **"Poem No. 7,"** from *Love Poems*):

> when he came home
> from her
> he poured me on
> the bed and slid
>
> into me like glass
> and there was
> the sound of splinters.

And this equally truthful look-back at her childhood trusting innocence (in **"Sequences,"** also from *Love Poems*):

> in my father's time
> I fished in ponds
> without fishes.
> arching my throat,
> I gargled amid nerves
> and sang of redeemers.

Still another moment of owning up truthfully to the pain of her growth and development as a person making a strong bid for completeness (in **"Past,"** from ***A Blues Book For Blue Black Magic Women***):

> i sang unbending
> songs and gathered gods
> convenient as christ.

And in the new poems, "Haikus/Tankas & other Love Syllables," from ***I've Been A Woman,*** this revolutionary advice:

> familiarize your
> self with strength. hold each other
>   up against silence.

And finally, this summary of the life's credo which Sonia Sanchez holds dear, and acts on, courageously (in **"Kwa mama zetu waliotuzaa,"** in "Generations," also from *I've Been A Woman*):

> no longer full of pain, may she walk
> bright with orange smiles, may she walk
> as it was long ago, may she walk
> abundant with lightning steps, may she walk
> abundant with green trails, may she walk

abundant with rainbows, may she walk
as it was long ago, may she walk

at the center of death is birth.

Among the precious few true poets of revolution and recla
mation, in our time, Sonia Sanchez stands out, not only for
her belief in achievable "green trails" and "rainbows," but
also for her gritty understanding that they are glimpsed only
on a long walk of renewal through the living death we are
plunged into immediately after birth.

That alone will always make me think of her poetry as songs
of difficult truth and harsh beauty.

David Williams (essay date 1984)

SOURCE: "The Poetry of Sonia Sanchez," in *Black Women
Writers (1950-1980): A Critical Evaluation,* edited by Mari
Evans, Anchor Press, 1984, pp. 433-48.

[*In the following essay, Williams analyzes the changes that
have occurred in Sanchez's poetry from her first collection,*
Homecoming, *to her* I've Been a Woman, *including a new
sense of rootedness.*]

The title of Sonia Sanchez's first collection, **Homecoming,**
marks with delicate irony the departure point of a journey
whose direction and destination can now be considered. *I've
Been a Woman,* her most recent book, invites such an appraisal, including as it does a retrospective of her earlier
work as well as an articulation of a newly won sense of
peace:

shedding my years and
earthbound now. midnite trees are
more to my liking.

These lines contain an explicit reworking of images that
dominate **"Poem at Thirty,"** one of the most personal statements in **Homecoming.** That early poem pulses with a terror rooted in a consciousness of age as debilitating. Midnight
and traveling, images of perpetual transition, bracket the
poem's fear:

it is midnight
no magical bewitching
hour for me
i know only that
i am here waiting
remembering that
once as a child
i walked two

miles in my sleep . . .
travelling. i'm
always travelling.
i want to tell
you about me
about nights on a
brown couch when
i wrapped my
bones in lint and
refused to move.
no one touches
me anymore . . .

In the new poems of *I've Been a Woman* Sanchez revokes
these images in order to establish her new sense of assurance. Midnight no longer terrifies; rootedness has succeeded
sleepwalking as an emblematic image.

Correlating these poems in this way allows a useful perspective on the work of a poet whose development has been as
much a matter of craft as it has been a widening and deepening of concerns. **Homecoming** largely satisfies Baraka's
demand in "Black Art" for "assassin poems, Poems that
shoot / guns"; but there is from the beginning an ironic vision in Sanchez's work that ensures that she differentiate between activist poetry and what she herself has labeled, in *We
a BaddDDD People,* "black rhetoric." The difference is that
between substance and shadow, between "straight / revolutionary / lines" and "catch / phrases." And it is clear from
Sanchez's work in **Homecoming** that she believes that the
ideal poetry demands the practice of a stringent discipline.
The poems in that collection are characterized by an
economy of utterance that is essentially dramatic, like language subordinated to the rhythms of action. The verse of
Homecoming is speech heightened by a consciousness of
the ironies implicit in every aspect of Black existence. The
poems read like terse statements intended to interrupt the silence that lies between perception and action.

In the title poem of the volume, Sanchez presents the act of
returning home as a rejection of fantasy and an acceptance
of involvement:

i have returned
leaving behind me
all those hide and
seek faces peeling
with freudian dreams.
this is for real.

The opposition set up is enriched by her perception of other
dichotomies: between youth and maturity, between Blackness and "niggerness." And Sanchez also knows that for a
while earlier she had chosen Blackness over "niggerness":

once after college
i returned tourist
style to catch all
the niggers killing
themselves with
three-for-oners
with
needles
that cd
not support
their stutters.

She had been one of those "hide and seek faces" on the outside, looking in at the niggers; in the real world she is now a nigger:

        black
niggers
        my beauty.

This, the climax of the poem, is the real homecoming; and the opening lines, reread, acquire a new resonance:

        i have been a
        way so long . . .

The division of "away" by the line break turns the second line into an extraordinarily weighted phrase; it rings like the refrain of a spiritual. This is a homecoming from very far away. The poem's closing lines, following the natural climax, provide an amplification of the earlier "now woman":

        i have learned it
        ain't like they say
        in the newspapers.

This truth, not learned in college, is at the core of a whole complex of meanings contained in the almost offhand casualness of the verse, which reads like transcribed speech.

"Homecoming" is a meditation meant to be overheard; the sense of an audience is a necessary part of the poem's meaning. Much of Sanchez's poetry in her first two collections is even more overtly dramatic, designed to be spoken as part of a larger performance in which silences and an implied choreography say as much as the actual words. **"Summary,"** another focal point of the first collection, quickly abandons the initial pretense of being inner-directed:

        this is
        a poem for the world
        for the slow suicides
        in seclusion.
        somewhere on 130th st.
        a woman, frail as a

child's ghost, sings.

The sibilances here are deliberately accusatory, and the simile is as generalized as it can be without becoming a cliché. The snatch of song that follows transforms the poem fully into what it is, a plaint for all the women (Cassandra, Penelope, Billie Holiday, Bessie Smith) who have been victims. Spoken in the accents of this specific Black woman, **"Summary"** is rooted in a sisterhood of angry pain. As the poem's rhythm begins to stutter, its linear form disintegrates into a scattershot catalogue in which numerous lives and experiences are summarized:

        life
    is no more than
        gents
            and
            gigolos
            (99% american)
        liars
            and
        killers (199% american) dreamers
        and drunks (299%
            american)
            i say
    is everybody happy / . . .

The emotion crests and breaks at this point, driven against a wall of futility. The voice falls back into the monotone with which the poem started—except that now it has been reduced to the barest of statements:

        this is a poem for me.
        i am alone.
        one night of words
        will not change
        all that.

The point, of course, is that these lines are more than just "a poem for me," and we are intended to perceive this. **"Summary"** is a performance in which an unobtrusive intelligence has acknowledged the presence of an audience.

The imagined response of this audience is occasionally crucial to the poems in *Homecoming,* some of which are, in essence, communal chant performances in which Sanchez, as poet, provides the necessary language for the performance. The perceptions in such poems are deliberately generalized, filtered through the shared consciousness of the urban Black. **"Nigger"** is the heard half of a dialogue with someone who can almost be visualized; his response seems to fill the gaps between the surges of speech, which gather confidence until the word "nigger" has been exorcised and the poem's initial claim has been made good:

that word
ain't shit to me
man . . .

The coupled poems **"Black Magic"** and **"To a Jealous Cat"** pick up the "my man" refrain from **"Nigger"** and transform it. In that poem it has the weight of a public epithet, a designation for someone whose relationship with the voice in the poem could only be that of an adversary. In **"Black Magic,"** on the other hand, it has the warmth of a private endearment, a whisper in which both words are equally stressed (*"my man"*) and therefore become an assertion of possession as well as of pride. In the process the phrase "black magic" is itself transformed:

> magic
>   my man
> is you
>   turning
> my body into
> a thousand
> smiles . . .

In **"To a Jealous Cat"** the appellation remains private, but it is now the privacy of anger and disappointment. The poem is the second act in the drama of a human relationship, and it makes bitter and ironic play with the same elements that make **"Black Magic"** so celebratory:

> no one never told
> you that jealousy's
> a form of homo
> sexuality?

The lineation transforms "homosexuality" into an ironic shadow of the ideal sexuality earlier gloried in. At the same time the word is used as a bitter taunt:

> in other
> words my man
> you faggot bound
> when you imagine
> me going in and out
> out some other cat.
>   yeah.

In retrospect, the earlier question ("don't you / know where you / at?") acquires a new and savage significance, and when "my man" recurs it is cruelly ironic. As a consequence, the deceptively ordinary lines with which the poem closes are really an indictment:

> perhaps you ain't
> the man we thought.

It is significant that the pronoun here is "we" and not "I." The lines are meant to underscore the ambiguity with which "my man" has been invested; sexual identity becomes, by extension, a metaphor for self-awareness.

Poems such as **"Nigger"** and **"To a Jealous Cat"** demonstrate that, in one sense, Sanchez has been "earthbound" from the beginning. Her use of Black speech as the bedrock of her poetic language ensures that her imagery remain sparse and wholly functional, even when it is most striking, as in the final lines of **"For Unborn Malcolms"**:

> git the word
> out that us blk/niggers
>   are out to lunch
> and the main course
> is gonna be his white meat.

Even here, the spirit of this extended image remains true to its origins; it accords with the poem's characteristic tone of dramatized anger. Sanchez can break open the routine hipness of street talk with a single word that allows a glimpse into the complexities of some area of the Black experience:

> some will say out
> right
>   baby i want
>   to ball you
> while smoother
> ones will in
> tegrate your
> blackness . . .

"Integrate" is such a word; as used here, it sums up a whole history of betrayal and anger with a sharp wit that is itself characteristic of much of Sanchez's work. In **"Short Poem"** she recounts her man's praise of her sexiness; then, with impeccable timing, she delivers her assessment:

> maybe
>   i
>   shd
>   bottle
>   it
>   and
> sell it
> when he goes.

The ironic twist in the final line is reminiscent of such poems as "Widow Woman" and "Hard Daddy," where Langston Hughes uses the same device. Sanchez's wit is generally more cutting than Hughes', however. **"Small Comment"** is a deadly parody of the academic style of discourse; after successive restatements of the initial thesis have mired the poem in verbiage, the final "you dig" is devastatingly mocking. **"To Chuck"** is a different sort of parody; Sanchez offers a caricature of e. e. cummings, but the tone of the mockery is gentle. The poem, like **"Black Magic,"** is ultimately celebratory:

        i'm gonna write me
          a poem like
            e.e.
            cum
              mings to
            day. a
        bout you
              mov
        ing iNsIDE
              me touc
        hing my vis
              cera un
            til i turn
        in
          side out. i'
                m
        go
          n n
            a sc
              rew
        u on   pap   er

There is also something of self-parody here: Sanchez is obviously aware of the parallels between cummings' approach to poetic form and that favored by the militant young poets of the sixties. The feeling celebrated by the poem is genuine, however. Beneath their deliberate anarchy, the lines suggest that sexual commitment is a species of revolutionary act.

The poems in **Homecoming** and **We a BadddDDD People** lie along a spectrum bounded by two extremes. At one pole there are those poems that almost seem to have exploded from the force of the raw anger at their center; for **"The Final Solution"** and **"Indianapolis/Summer/1969/Poem,"** for instance, the visual shape on the page is the equivalent of a stutter:

        like.
          i mean.
            don't it all come down
        to e/co/no/mics.
            like. it is fo
        money that those young brothas on
        illinois &
          ohio sts
            allow they selves to
        be picked up
          cruised around . . .

Poems like these appear to be still in the process of being composed; words seem to have not yet settled into place. The poem in flux is given to the reader, and the act of reading becomes an act of composition. At the other pole are those poems where Sanchez creates the sense of a monotone by presenting a stream of meditation in which the individual semantic units flow into each other without any single word or image breaking the aural surface of the rhythm. In **"Poem at Thirty," "Personal Letter No. 2,"** and **"Personal Letter No. 3"** the audience is relegated to insignificance. These poems are entries in a personal diary which is the extension, not the converse, of the communal scrapbook of being Black in America. The weariness of spirit they reveal finds its verbal counterpart in a vocabulary cadenced to a slower rhythm, one very different from the streetwise staccato of a poem like **"Indianapolis. . . ." "Personal Letter No. 3"** is typical in this regard:

        no more wild geo
        graphies of the
        flesh. echoes. that
        we move in tune
        to slower smells.
        it is a hard thing
        to admit that
        sometimes after midnight
        i am tired
        of it all.

Midnight and travel: the emblems recur. They are mythic images that summon up vistas of Black history, even as they fix the particular anguish of an individual soul.

The most striking difference between **Love Poems** and Sanchez's earlier work lies in the widening of the range of her imagery. The world evoked in **Homecoming** and **We a BadddDDD People** is that of the urban nighttime, bereft of any glimpse of the natural landscape. From **Love Poems** on, images of trees, flowers, earth, birds, sea, and sky dot the verse. Sanchez, however, is very far from using them to suggest an idyllic universe; in fact, the natural world enters the verse of **Love Poems,** in particular, as part of a vision of an external reality in which things are out of kilter:

            this earth
        turns old
        and rivers grow lunatic
        with rain. how i wish
        i could lean in your cave
        and creak with the winds.

There are occasional instances of such images being used in a more upbeat fashion ("he / moved in me like rain"), but by and large they function as elements in an astringent lyricism that is a development of the mood of early poems such as **"Personal Letter No. 3"** and **"Poem at Thirty." "Fa-**

ney backward from woman
ment is measured in terms
darkness of the South, of
games of adolescence:

her

ve finally arrested
es purpose of dis-

scent
ghten-
poem,
ence be-
. Ocean,
ecome the
spark that

partakes of the
d her earlier po-
ather and Daugh-
emotion within a
pt even further in
e surge of the verse
of the triplet used
se of this tension:

t that aunts the
monsated *how*
pointe move-
oves through
t whe is pro-
h reb *n:*

alking.

as replaced
e blues cre-
real in **"Re-**

mpression to its ultimate
ve Poems. In these, emo-
illed into moments which
immediacy of an action
ge. Sometimes the act of
the poem is pared down
ce left:

ion here, no sense of an
however, Sanchez pulls off
rity, impaling a single per-
te and as inevitable as the
graphed dance:

en.

nse of his-
resent and
as the nar-

---

go from day to day like an
ordained stutterer.

Unlike imagist poetry, this does not depend for its meaning on the ripples set off by a static image. The simile generates its own energy, compelling us to partake in the emotion. The haiku represents for Sanchez the point at which the irreducible statement of personal assertion ("still. i am. / i am.") converges with the ideal of "straight / revolutionary / lines." The haiku in her hands is the ultimate in activist poetry, as abrupt and as final as a fist.

> **The haiku in Sanchez's hands is the ultimate in activist poetry, as abrupt and as final as a fist.**
> **—David Williams**

But Sanchez is also concerned with experience as process, with the accumulation of small adjustments that constitute the data of individual and communal life. This concern involves more than just the juxtaposing of past and present; in **"Sequences"** and **"Old Words,"** Sanchez struggles to divine the almost insensible shifts that result in our present dilemmas. The latter poem, in particular, attempts no less than an exploration of the growth of the malaise that Sanchez believes to be endemic in modern life:

we are the dis
enfranchised ones
the buyers of bread
one day removed
from mold
we are maimed
in our posture . . .

Following this initial evocation of despair, Sanchez chronicles the race's (and humanity's) emotional history through a series of images that all connote a failure to communicate. Against these she places the iconic figures of Billie Holiday and Prez, both of whom tried to reach out through their music. They become, for Sanchez, part of a process of human history that has moved us from "herding songs" to "mass produced faces." In the penultimate section of the poem she summarizes the gradations in that process in a way that suggests a movement from life to death:

Are we ever what we should be?
seated in our circle of agonies
we do not try to tune our breaths
since we cannot sing together
since we cannot waltz our eyes
since we cannot love,
since we have wooed this world

too long with separate arias of revolution
mysticism hatred and submission
since we have rehearsed our
deaths apart . . .

Each of these failures has contributed to our "maimed posture." The poem's facsimile of narrative catalogues the history of the human experience, then adds a somber coda:

we have come to
believe that we are
not. to be we
must be loved or
touched and proved
to be . . .

How we come to "believe that we are not" is the object of
Sanchez's concern in her next collection, *A Blues Book for
Blue Black Magic Women.* The principles and techniques
of narrative dominate this volume. The poems, developing
on the style of **"Sequences"** and **"Old Words,"** represent
the fulfillment of a truth and a form that Sanchez had
touched much earlier in such works as **"Summary," "Poem
at Thirty,"** and **"Summer Words of a Sistuh Addict."**
These early poems all turn upon the image of woman as
ghost, as mummy:

i want to tell
you about me
about nights on a
brown couch when
i wrapped my
bones in lint and
refused to move . . .

The music that twines around her is a dirge whose nursery-
rhyme lyrics mockingly underline her impotence; it is as if
her anguish, ultimately inexpressible, has to be contained in
formulas. In *Blues Book* Sanchez, submerging her personal
self in a persona that is deliberately generalized, undertakes
a ritual of acceptance, confession, cleansing, and rebirth.

In **"Past"** that ritual begins with a prayer for cleansing:

Come ride my birth, earth mother
tell me how i have become, became
this woman with razor blades between
her teeth.
      sing me my history O earth mother . . .
for i want to rediscover me, the secret of me
the river of me, the morning ease of me . . .

The narrative is at the starting point of a movement back
into the womb of memory, where the traumas of youth and
adolescence can be relived. The verse leans heavily on rep-

etition and incantation as the jou[r]
to young girl is made. The move
of a descent into darkness—the
remembered cruelty, of the savag

remember parties
where we'd grindddddDDDD
and grindddddDDDDD
but not too close
cuz if you gave it up
everybody would know. and tell
then walking across the room
where young girls watched each o[f]
like black vultures . . .

The backward movement of the narrati[ve]
when this ritual of cleansing accomplish
covering how it all started:

i walked into young
womanhood. Could not hear
my footsteps in the streets
could not hear the rhythm of
young Black womanhood.

This image is that of a ghost, the same ghos[t]
lines of the early poems. The narrative has d[e]
this state of nonbeing was reached. From thi[s]
ment is in the other direction. **"Present"** m[
a redefining of the now, up to the momen[t]
cess conceives the possibility of the woma[n]

    and my singing
becomes the only sound of a
blue/black/magical/woman. walking.
womb ripe. walking. loud with morni[ng]
making pilgrimage to herself. walkin[g]

The deadened senses are alive again; sing[ing]
silence. The spirit of affirmation inheren[t] in th[e]
ates the possibilities that are finally to b[ec]ome
birth," with its images of gestation:

whatever is truth becomes know[n] nine
months passed touching a botto[m]less sea.
nine months i wandered amid waves
that washed away thirty yea[r]s of denial . . .
nine months passed and my body
heavy with the knowledge of gods
turned landward. came to rest . . .
i became the mother of sun. moon. star child[ren]

What Sanchez does in *Blues Book* is to use a s[
tory as a liberating device. The wasteland of the
the immediate past is transformed and renewe[d]

rative takes us back to an awareness of beginnings, a green world whose innocence can redeem our sense of sin. It is no accident that the poetry of **Blues Book** is both ritualistic and religious. To sing the blues is to affirm a racial truth. Lyricism here has the special purpose of achieving a communal sense of worship, and Sanchez is the shaman, the "blue black magic woman" whose words initiate that process. The weight of meaning in **Blues Book** thus rests on the narrative, on the actual sequence of the ritual, for it is only in this way that the experience of change can be concretized.

The new poems in *I've Been a Woman* benefit from the sense of continuity and evolution conferred by the earlier work. The impact of the section entitled "Haikus/Tankas & Other Love Syllables" is immeasurably enhanced by *Love Poems,* for instance; the new poems, drawing on a relatively limited stock of images (water in various forms, trees, morning, sun, different smells), are an accumulation of moments that define love, age, sorrow, and pride in terms of action. Particular configurations recur: the rhythms of sex, the bent silhouettes of old age, the stillness of intense emotion. But taken together, these poems are like the spontaneous eruptions that punctuate, geyserlike, the flow of experience.

The other new poems in *I've Been a Woman* consist of a series of eulogies, collectively titled "Generations," in which Sanchez explicitly claims her place among those who speak of and for Black people. There is a schematic balance operating here: the individual poems respectively eulogize Sterling Brown (age), Gerald Penny (youth), Sanchez's father, and the idea and reality of mothers. The synthesis implied in this design is enacted in the poetry itself; the imagery and rhythms of the verse in this section convey an overwhelming sense of resolution and serenity. The poems dedicated to Sterling Brown, however, seem overloaded with busy imagery. This is especially true of the first of the two. Cast in the form of a praise song, it presents Brown as a priest-poet and simultaneously implies Sanchez's awareness of her own membership in the tradition which Brown has so honorably helped to maintain. But the effect of the poem is to dilute our sense of Brown's significance; the succession of carefully wrought images, along with the overly schematic structure, gives the poem the feeling of an exercise.

The same cannot be said of the other poems in this section. The Gerald Penny eulogy, built around its song-prayer refrain, is a convincing celebration of a life. Its images—rainbow, yellow corn, summer berries—are felt metaphors of fulfillment, and its diction manages to avoid naïveté while maintaining an appropriate simplicity:

> I am going to walk far to the East
> i hope to find a good morning
> somewhere.

> I am going to race my own voice
> i hope to have peace
> somewhere . . .

By the time the poem arrives at its final refrain, its language has enacted a measured movement to a point of calm:

> I do not cry
> for i am man
> no longer
> a child of your
> womb.

> There is nothing which does not
>   come to an end
> And to live seventeen years is good
>   in the sight of God.

This calm carries over into **"Father and Daughter,"** the final entry in a diary which began, in *We a BaddDDD People,* with **"A Poem for My Father."** In this early work the anger is open and raw:

> when i remember your
> deformity   i want to
> do something about your
> makeshift manhood.

The vengeful rhythms of these lines allow no dialogue; but **"Father and Daughter,"** deliberately repeating the title of an earlier poem which ends in a vision of destruction, moves quietly into a portrayal of family. The grandchild who frolics between father and daughter is an emblem of generation and reconciliation, as is the image of snow melting into a river. The final lines, slowing the graceful rhythm of the poem, pointedly return to the image of the cross with which **"A Poem for My Father"** closes. **"Father and Daughter,"** which begins with the act of talking, concludes with a rejection of the gesture made in the earlier poem and an acceptance of a shared human frailty:

> your land is in the ashes of the South.
> perhaps the color of our losses:
> perhaps the memory that dreams nurse:
> old man, we do not speak of crosses.

The sense of reconciliation here evoked has its corollary in **"Kwa Mamu Zetu Waliotuzaa."** Alternating discursive, image-filled passages of verse with rhythmic, incantatory refrains, this poem enacts a ritual quest for peace that is finally attained through the hypnotic mantras of the closing lines:

> the day is singing
> the day is singing

he is singing in the mountains
the nite is singing
the nite is singing
she is singing in the earth . . .

This poem, as much as anything else in *I've Been a Woman,* actualizes the condition of being earthbound. The journey begun with *Homecoming* ends here, in a vision of earth and roots and parenting.

Rosemary K. Curb (essay date 1985)

SOURCE: "Pre-Feminism in the Black Revolutionary Drama of Sonia Sanchez," in *The Many Forms of Drama,* edited by Karelisa V. Hartigan, University Press of America, 1985, pp. 19-29.

[*In the following essay, Curb discusses Sanchez's revolutionary plays and states that the plays "dramatize the need for active cooperation among black women in political struggle for sexual as well as racial justice."*]

In 1960 when the first sparks of Black racial discontent were igniting the roaring conflagration of the Black Revolution, Sonia Sanchez was twenty-five. At twenty she graduated from Hunter College with a Bachelor of Arts and continued graduate study at New York University. She had been writing poetry since her childhood in Birmingham, Alabama. By the mid-sixties, Sanchez was raising two sons as a single mother and declaiming her poetry at Black Power Conferences in northern cities across the country. She was generally regarded as the leading female literary voice of Black Revolution.

In the now classic collection of the period titled *Black Fire,* edited by LeRoi Jones and Larry Neal, published in 1968, only four of the fifty-six poets included are women. Barbara Simmons has one poem, Lethonia Gee two, Carol Freeman three, and Sonia Sanchez four. **"To All Sisters"** by Sanchez succinctly presents the movement's orthodox position regarding the obligation of Black women to bolster Black male ego by reassuring Black men about their superior sexual power: "there ain't / no MAN like a Black man."

In most of her poetry and drama in the sixties, Sanchez promotes racial separatism, but she also hints at sexist oppression within the Black movement. Her recurring sub-motif, less popular with male revolutionaries than separatism, is the loneliness and sense of betrayal of Black women, loyal to the hope of a future Black nation, deserted by the men to whom they have given an almost religious allegiance. The lonely bitter female speaker in the more emotionally and rhetorically complex poem **"summary,"** [sic] published in

Black Fire, apparently represents many Black women in America, even though she has not recognized the collective nature of her oppression nor the collective male benefit of keeping women separated from each other in their private anguish.

Most of the Black revolutionary plays by women and men in the sixties present a majority of male characters. When unrelated women are presented together, they are usually portrayed competing for male attention. Among the ten plays is only one by a woman. "The Suicide" by Carol Freeman encourages woman-hating by portraying women abusing each other. A character called The Cop shouts: "Hey, Come in here, you gotta see this! Nigger bitches fighting over a dead man."

In Black revolutionary drama in the sixties female characters are rarely portrayed cooperating on a project which primarily aids women. Rarely do we see women educating each other about male oppression and offering strategies for independence and autonomy. Bell Hooks analyzes the motives of the sexist male revolutionaries:

> Black leaders, male and female, have been unwilling to acknowledge Black male sexist oppression of Black women because they do not want to acknowledge that racism is not the only oppressive force in our lives. Nor do they wish to complicate efforts to resist racism by acknowledging that Black men can be victimized by racism but at the same time act as sexist oppressors of Black women.

About the same time that *Black Fire* appeared, Sonia Sanchez started writing plays because the longer dramatic form was useful when a poem could not contain her political message. The first published play by Sanchez appeared in *The Drama Review* special issue on Black Theatre, edited by Ed Bullins. The short play **The Bronx Is Next** is set in Harlem in the midst of a racial revolution. Revolutionaries are burning all the buildings in a poor section to force the construction of livable housing units. A character called Old Sister, who is judged by the male leaders to be too attached to her oppressive past in Birmingham, is sent back to her apartment to go up in smoke with her possessions.

The play's other female character, called Black Bitch, projects the strident Sapphire stereotype so despised by male leaders of the movement as a threat to male superiority. The woman is devalued as both promiscuous, if not actually a professional prostitute, and non-separatist. Not only is she caught in a compromising intimacy with a white policeman, but she spews forth condemnation of Black men's abuse of Black women, to which the male leader responds, "Oh shit. Another Black matriarch on our hands." The leader immediately punishes and humiliates her with a brutal sexual asther and Daughter" is typical in this regard. The poem, which consists of paired sonnets whose formal structure acts as a brake on the emotional immediacy of the experience, closes with these lines:

> don't cry. late grief is not enough. the motion of
> your tides still flows within: the ocean of deep
> blood that drowns the land. we die: while young
> moons rage and wander in the sky.

This is a glimpse of apocalypse. The lines are reminiscent of Derek Walcott's "The Gulf," which ends with a frightening vision of America's future, and like Walcott's poem, Sanchez's turns upon the sense of a personal experience being magnified into a perception of an entire society. Ocean, earth, and moon, with their mythic associations, become the moving forces in this process. The imagery is the spark that ignites the poem.

The intensified lyricism of Sanchez's work partakes of the same economy of utterance that had marked her earlier poetry. If her use of the sonnet form in **"Father and Daughter"** represents an effort to compress emotion within a restraining mold, she carries that attempt even further in works such as **"Poem No. 4."** The supple surge of the verse strains against the compact, even form of the triplet used here; the poem succeeds precisely because of this tension:

> i am not a
>
> face of my
> own choosing.
> still. i am.
>
> i am . . .

Sanchez takes this principle of compression to its ultimate form in the haiku that punctuate *Love Poems.* In these, emotion has been concentrated and distilled into moments which capture the now and the then, the immediacy of an action as well as its intimations of change. Sometimes the act of compression is almost too drastic; the poem is pared down until there is little of real significance left:

> did ya ever cry
> Black man, did ya ever cry
> til you knocked all over?

There is no moment of intersection here, no sense of an abrupt discovery. At other times, however, Sanchez pulls off the haiku with tremendous authority, impaling a single perception with an image as definite and as inevitable as the climactic movement in a choreographed dance:

> O i am so sad, i

go from day to day like an
ordained stutterer.

Unlike imagist poetry, this does not depend for its meaning on the ripples set off by a static image. The simile generates its own energy, compelling us to partake in the emotion. The haiku represents for Sanchez the point at which the irreducible statement of personal assertion ("still. i am. / i am.") converges with the ideal of "straight / revolutionary / lines." The haiku in her hands is the ultimate in activist poetry, as abrupt and as final as a fist.

> **The haiku in Sanchez's hands is the ultimate in activist poetry, as abrupt and as final as a fist.**
> —*David Williams*

But Sanchez is also concerned with experience as process, with the accumulation of small adjustments that constitute the data of individual and communal life. This concern involves more than just the juxtaposing of past and present; in **"Sequences"** and **"Old Words,"** Sanchez struggles to divine the almost insensible shifts that result in our present dilemmas. The latter poem, in particular, attempts no less than an exploration of the growth of the malaise that Sanchez believes to be endemic in modern life:

> we are the dis
> enfranchised ones
> the buyers of bread
> one day removed
> from mold
> we are maimed
> in our posture . . .

Following this initial evocation of despair, Sanchez chronicles the race's (and humanity's) emotional history through a series of images that all connote a failure to communicate. Against these she places the iconic figures of Billie Holiday and Prez, both of whom tried to reach out through their music. They become, for Sanchez, part of a process of human history that has moved us from "herding songs" to "mass produced faces." In the penultimate section of the poem she summarizes the gradations in that process in a way that suggests a movement from life to death:

> Are we ever what we should be?
> seated in our circle of agonies
> we do not try to tune our breaths
> since we cannot sing together
> since we cannot waltz our eyes
> since we cannot love,
> since we have wooed this world

too long with separate arias of revolution
mysticism hatred and submission
since we have rehearsed our
deaths apart . . .

Each of these failures has contributed to our "maimed posture." The poem's facsimile of narrative catalogues the history of the human experience, then adds a somber coda:

we have come to
believe that we are
not. to be we
must be loved or
touched and proved
to be . . .

How we come to "believe that we are not" is the object of Sanchez's concern in her next collection, *A Blues Book for Blue Black Magic Women.* The principles and techniques of narrative dominate this volume. The poems, developing on the style of **"Sequences"** and **"Old Words,"** represent the fulfillment of a truth and a form that Sanchez had touched much earlier in such works as **"Summary," "Poem at Thirty,"** and **"Summer Words of a Sistuh Addict."** These early poems all turn upon the image of woman as ghost, as mummy:

i want to tell
you about me
about nights on a
brown couch when
i wrapped my
bones in lint and
refused to move . . .

The music that twines around her is a dirge whose nursery-rhyme lyrics mockingly underline her impotence; it is as if her anguish, ultimately inexpressible, has to be contained in formulas. In *Blues Book* Sanchez, submerging her personal self in a persona that is deliberately generalized, undertakes a ritual of acceptance, confession, cleansing, and rebirth.

In **"Past"** that ritual begins with a prayer for cleansing:

Come ride my birth, earth mother
tell me how i have become, became
this woman with razor blades between
her teeth.
        sing me my history O earth mother . . .
for i want to rediscover me, the secret of me
the river of me, the morning ease of me . . .

The narrative is at the starting point of a movement back into the womb of memory, where the traumas of youth and adolescence can be relived. The verse leans heavily on rep-

etition and incantation as the journey backward from woman to young girl is made. The movement is measured in terms of a descent into darkness—the darkness of the South, of remembered cruelty, of the savage games of adolescence:

remember parties
where we'd grindddddDDDD
and grindddddDDDDD
but not too close
cuz if you gave it up
everybody would know. and tell . . .
then walking across the room
where young girls watched each other
like black vultures . . .

The backward movement of the narrative is finally arrested when this ritual of cleansing accomplishes its purpose of discovering how it all started:

i walked into young
womanhood. Could not hear
my footsteps in the streets
could not hear the rhythm of
young Black womanhood.

This image is that of a ghost, the same ghost that haunts the lines of the early poems. The narrative has demonstrated *how* this state of nonbeing was reached. From this point the movement is in the other direction. **"Present"** moves us through a redefining of the now, up to the moment when this process conceives the possibility of the woman reborn:

and my singing
becomes the only sound of a
blue/black/magical/woman. walking.
womb ripe. walking. loud with mornings. walking.
making pilgrimage to herself. walking.

The deadened senses are alive again; singing has replaced silence. The spirit of affirmation inherent in the blues creates the possibilities that are finally to become real in **"Rebirth,"** with its images of gestation:

whatever is truth becomes known. nine
months passed touching a bottomless sea.
nine months i wandered amid waves
that washed away thirty years of denial . . .
nine months passed and my body
heavy with the knowledge of gods
turned landward. came to rest . . .
i became the mother of sun. moon. star children.

What Sanchez does in *Blues Book* is to use a sense of history as a liberating device. The wasteland of the present and the immediate past is transformed and renewed as the narrative takes us back to an awareness of beginnings, a green world whose innocence can redeem our sense of sin. It is no accident that the poetry of **Blues Book** is both ritualistic and religious. To sing the blues is to affirm a racial truth. Lyricism here has the special purpose of achieving a communal sense of worship, and Sanchez is the shaman, the "blue black magic woman" whose words initiate that process. The weight of meaning in **Blues Book** thus rests on the narrative, on the actual sequence of the ritual, for it is only in this way that the experience of change can be concretized.

The new poems in *I've Been a Woman* benefit from the sense of continuity and evolution conferred by the earlier work. The impact of the section entitled "Haikus/Tankas & Other Love Syllables" is immeasurably enhanced by *Love Poems,* for instance; the new poems, drawing on a relatively limited stock of images (water in various forms, trees, morning, sun, different smells), are an accumulation of moments that define love, age, sorrow, and pride in terms of action. Particular configurations recur: the rhythms of sex, the bent silhouettes of old age, the stillness of intense emotion. But taken together, these poems are like the spontaneous eruptions that punctuate, geyserlike, the flow of experience.

The other new poems in *I've Been a Woman* consist of a series of eulogies, collectively titled "Generations," in which Sanchez explicitly claims her place among those who speak of and for Black people. There is a schematic balance operating here: the individual poems respectively eulogize Sterling Brown (age), Gerald Penny (youth), Sanchez's father, and the idea and reality of mothers. The synthesis implied in this design is enacted in the poetry itself; the imagery and rhythms of the verse in this section convey an overwhelming sense of resolution and serenity. The poems dedicated to Sterling Brown, however, seem overloaded with busy imagery. This is especially true of the first of the two. Cast in the form of a praise song, it presents Brown as a priest-poet and simultaneously implies Sanchez's awareness of her own membership in the tradition which Brown has so honorably helped to maintain. But the effect of the poem is to dilute our sense of Brown's significance; the succession of carefully wrought images, along with the overly schematic structure, gives the poem the feeling of an exercise.

The same cannot be said of the other poems in this section. The Gerald Penny eulogy, built around its song-prayer refrain, is a convincing celebration of a life. Its images—rainbow, yellow corn, summer berries—are felt metaphors of fulfillment, and its diction manages to avoid naïveté while maintaining an appropriate simplicity:

> I am going to walk far to the East
> i hope to find a good morning
> somewhere.

> I am going to race my own voice
> i hope to have peace
> somewhere . . .

By the time the poem arrives at its final refrain, its language has enacted a measured movement to a point of calm:

> I do not cry
> for i am man
> no longer
> a child of your
> womb.

> There is nothing which does not
>   come to an end
> And to live seventeen years is good
>   in the sight of God.

This calm carries over into **"Father and Daughter,"** the final entry in a diary which began, in *We a BaddDDD People,* with **"A Poem for My Father."** In this early work the anger is open and raw:

> when i remember your
> deformity   i want to
> do something about your
> makeshift manhood.

The vengeful rhythms of these lines allow no dialogue; but **"Father and Daughter,"** deliberately repeating the title of an earlier poem which ends in a vision of destruction, moves quietly into a portrayal of family. The grandchild who frolics between father and daughter is an emblem of generation and reconciliation, as is the image of snow melting into a river. The final lines, slowing the graceful rhythm of the poem, pointedly return to the image of the cross with which **"A Poem for My Father"** closes. **"Father and Daughter,"** which begins with the act of talking, concludes with a rejection of the gesture made in the earlier poem and an acceptance of a shared human frailty:

> your land is in the ashes of the South.
> perhaps the color of our losses:
> perhaps the memory that dreams nurse:
> old man, we do not speak of crosses.

The sense of reconciliation here evoked has its corollary in **"Kwa Mamu Zetu Waliotuzaa."** Alternating discursive, image-filled passages of verse with rhythmic, incantatory refrains, this poem enacts a ritual quest for peace that is finally attained through the hypnotic mantras of the closing lines:

> the day is singing
> the day is singing

he is singing in the mountains
the nite is singing
the nite is singing
she is singing in the earth . . .

This poem, as much as anything else in *I've Been a Woman,* actualizes the condition of being earthbound. The journey begun with *Homecoming* ends here, in a vision of earth and roots and parenting.

Rosemary K. Curb (essay date 1985)

SOURCE: "Pre-Feminism in the Black Revolutionary Drama of Sonia Sanchez," in *The Many Forms of Drama,* edited by Karelisa V. Hartigan, University Press of America, 1985, pp. 19-29.

[*In the following essay, Curb discusses Sanchez's revolutionary plays and states that the plays "dramatize the need for active cooperation among black women in political struggle for sexual as well as racial justice."*]

In 1960 when the first sparks of Black racial discontent were igniting the roaring conflagration of the Black Revolution, Sonia Sanchez was twenty-five. At twenty she graduated from Hunter College with a Bachelor of Arts and continued graduate study at New York University. She had been writing poetry since her childhood in Birmingham, Alabama. By the mid-sixties, Sanchez was raising two sons as a single mother and declaiming her poetry at Black Power Conferences in northern cities across the country. She was generally regarded as the leading female literary voice of Black Revolution.

In the now classic collection of the period titled *Black Fire,* edited by LeRoi Jones and Larry Neal, published in 1968, only four of the fifty-six poets included are women. Barbara Simmons has one poem, Lethonia Gee two, Carol Freeman three, and Sonia Sanchez four. **"To All Sisters"** by Sanchez succinctly presents the movement's orthodox position regarding the obligation of Black women to bolster Black male ego by reassuring Black men about their superior sexual power: "there ain't / no MAN like a Black man."

In most of her poetry and drama in the sixties, Sanchez promotes racial separatism, but she also hints at sexist oppression within the Black movement. Her recurring sub-motif, less popular with male revolutionaries than separatism, is the loneliness and sense of betrayal of Black women, loyal to the hope of a future Black nation, deserted by the men to whom they have given an almost religious allegiance. The lonely bitter female speaker in the more emotionally and rhetorically complex poem **"summary,"** [sic] published in

Black Fire, apparently represents many Black women in America, even though she has not recognized the collective nature of her oppression nor the collective male benefit of keeping women separated from each other in their private anguish.

Most of the Black revolutionary plays by women and men in the sixties present a majority of male characters. When unrelated women are presented together, they are usually portrayed competing for male attention. Among the ten plays is only one by a woman. "The Suicide" by Carol Freeman encourages woman-hating by portraying women abusing each other. A character called The Cop shouts: "Hey, Come in here, you gotta see this! Nigger bitches fighting over a dead man."

In Black revolutionary drama in the sixties female characters are rarely portrayed cooperating on a project which primarily aids women. Rarely do we see women educating each other about male oppression and offering strategies for independence and autonomy. Bell Hooks analyzes the motives of the sexist male revolutionaries:

> Black leaders, male and female, have been unwilling to acknowledge Black male sexist oppression of Black women because they do not want to acknowledge that racism is not the only oppressive force in our lives. Nor do they wish to complicate efforts to resist racism by acknowledging that Black men can be victimized by racism but at the same time act as sexist oppressors of Black women.

About the same time that *Black Fire* appeared, Sonia Sanchez started writing plays because the longer dramatic form was useful when a poem could not contain her political message. The first published play by Sanchez appeared in *The Drama Review* special issue on Black Theatre, edited by Ed Bullins. The short play *The Bronx Is Next* is set in Harlem in the midst of a racial revolution. Revolutionaries are burning all the buildings in a poor section to force the construction of livable housing units. A character called Old Sister, who is judged by the male leaders to be too attached to her oppressive past in Birmingham, is sent back to her apartment to go up in smoke with her possessions.

The play's other female character, called Black Bitch, projects the strident Sapphire stereotype so despised by male leaders of the movement as a threat to male superiority. The woman is devalued as both promiscuous, if not actually a professional prostitute, and non-separatist. Not only is she caught in a compromising intimacy with a white policeman, but she spews forth condemnation of Black men's abuse of Black women, to which the male leader responds, "Oh shit. Another Black matriarch on our hands." The leader immediately punishes and humiliates her with a brutal sexual assault and then sends her back to her apartment to burn in the holocaust. Although the Black Bitch character criticizes abusive men, she is portrayed as an enemy of the revolution who must be sacrificed for the future purity of the Black nation. In the context of the dramatic piece her complaints sound trivial and irrelevant if not downright Black-hating.

Sanchez created her second play *Sister Son/ji* for *New Plays From the Black Theatre,* edited by Ed Bullins. This dramatic monologue presents in flashbacks five periods in the life of a Black revolutionary woman. Although the single speaking character does not present herself as a feminist, she acknowledges woman's frequent devaluation by abusive men intoxicated with self-importance. As Son/ji grows from her first act of resisting racism to a sense of betrayal by male revolutionaries who seduce and abandon women to maturity borne of loss and survival, the reader/audience watches the character grow into solitary strength.

At the opening, the title character appears to be an old woman collecting her memories. With grey hair, bowed head, dragging feet, she turns and addresses the audience from her dressing table: "i ain't young no mo. My young days have gone, they passed me by so fast that i didn't even have a chance to see them. What did i do with them? What did i say to them? Do i still remember them? Shd i remember them?" She recalls sadly that all four of her sons are buried there in Mississippi, and she decides to "bring back yesterday as it can never be today." With costume and makeup transformations, she changes into a successively older character, while lighting changes punctuate each flashback.

As a young Negro woman of eighteen or nineteen in the first flashback, Son/ji breathlessly tells her boyfriend Nesbitt, who has come up for the weekend from Howard University, how she raged out of her political theory class at Hunter College because the "ole/bitch" professor could not distinguish her from the other two Black women in a class of twelve students. Son/ji's first assertion of Black pride and rebellion against passive white racism is tinged with woman-hating:

> she became that flustered red/whiteness that ofays become, and said but u see it's just that—and i finished it for her—i sd it's just that we all look alike. yeah. well damn this class

When the more conventional Nesbitt, fearful of offending white authority, apparently chides Son/ji for her impulsiveness, she replies: "it might have been foolish but it was right. after all at some point a person's got to stand up for herself just a little." Ironically Son/ji submits to Nesbitt's will to seduce her in the well-baited trap of his father's car and reluctantly loses her virginity. Aware of his insensitivity to Son/ji's loss and her desperate desire for his approval, she asks:

"nesbitt do u think after a first love each succeeding love is a repetition?"

In the next flashback Son/ji remembers learning at a Black Power Conference "about blk/women supporting their blk/men, listening to their men, sacrificing, working while blk/men take care of bizness, having warriors and young sisters." Although Sister Son/ji calls the asymmetry of the sexes within the movement "blk/love/respect between blk/men and women," the subtext of the orthodoxy demands female subservience to the male will to power.

While the ostensible purpose of asserting increased male dominance within the Black movement was to strengthen the race by glorifying Black masculinity and destroying the supposed Black matriarchy, Bell Hooks regards the promotion of patriarchy as a racist devaluation of Black women.

> By shifting the responsibility for the unemployment of Black men onto Black women and away from themselves, white racist oppressors were able to establish a bond of solidarity with Black men based on mutual sexism. White men preyed upon sexist feelings impressed upon the Black male psyche from birth to socialize Black men so that they would regard not all women, but specifically Black women as the enemies of their masculinity.

Sanchez illustrates Son/ji's growing consciousness of the selfish hypocrisy of male leaders by juxtaposing the public rhetoric of the meeting with Son/ji's private lament to the particular man whose power she is supporting:

> Is there time for all this drinking—going from bar to bar. Shouldn't we be getting ourselves together—strengthening our minds, bodies and souls away from drugs, weed, whiskey and going out on Saturday nites. alone. what is it all about or is the rhetoric apart from the actual being/doing? What is it all about if the doings do not match the words?

Just as she effectively counterpoints Sonji's first act of rebellion against white racism with her submission to seduction, "the mutual love and respect" that Sanchez believes essential for the growth of Black families seems out of Son/ji's reach. She finds herself trapped: assertive behavior wins her the label "bitch," but continued passive behavior reaps only further abuse and desertion.

In the next brief scene, which begins softly and builds to a crescendo, Sister Son/ji seems to be breaking down. In her mania, she weaves Black Power slogans with fragments from radio shows and childhood games, personal pleas to the man in her life with public shouts against white racism.

THE CRACKERS ARE COMING TO TOWN TO-DAY. TODAY TODAY. HOORAY. where are u man? hee. hee. hee. the shadow knows. we must have an undying love for each other. it's 5 AM in the morning. i am scared of voices moving in my head. ring-around-the-honkies-a pocketful-of-gunskerboomkerboomwehavenopains. the child is moving inside me. where are you? Man yr/son moves against this silence. he kicks against my si-lence. Aaaaaah. Aaaaaah. Aaaaaah. oh. i must keep walking. man, come fast. come faster than the speed of bullets—faster than the speed of lightning and when u come we'll see it's SUPER-BLOOD. HEE. HEE. HAA. FOOLED U DIDN'T IT? Ahhh- go way. go way voices that send me spinning into noth-ingness.

The absent but imagined deserting husband has become transformed in Sister Son/ji's fantasy into a Black macho superman. Her hollow laughter, which acknowledges the empty facade of masculinity, becomes increasingly chilling.

In the next scene Son/ji is an emotionally cool revolution-ary warrior wearing a gunbelt and a baby carrier. She is pre-paring for an attack by the white forces by sending her younger children away from the battlefield with lunches, while her thirteen year old son Mungu fights and dies in the war. Son/ji resists accepting white people who have come to aid the Black revolutionary cause. In accord with Black Muslim tradition, she calls them "devils." Son/ji says that she does not "mind the male/devils here but the female/devils who have followed them." After grieving for her son, she calls for the expulsion of a "devil/woman" who has appar-ently attached herself to one of the Black warriors:

> have we forgotten so soon that we hate devils. that
> we are in a death struggle with the beasts. if she's
> so good. so liberal. send her back to her own kind.
> Let her liberalize them. Let her become a camp fol-
> lower to the hatred that chokes white/america.

Sister Son/ji suggests executing the man if he tries to keep his white female lover in the camp. Michele Wallace, ana-lyzing the sudden increase of northern middle class white women going down South to battle for civil rights and be-coming involved with Black men, conjectures that the women were eager to avoid being called racist. Inevitably Black women despised the influx of white women who were attracting Black male attention.

The third revolutionary play published by Sanchez in the six-ties, *Uh, Uh; But How Do It Free Us?* presents three scenes which have no narrative connection but which illustrate the oppression created by power imbalance implicit in sexual polarity. The oppressed women in each scene suffer as a di-rect result of male selfishness and vanity. The male antago-nists in the first and third scenes are portrayed as less per-nicious than the female competitors for male attention.

The absurdist middle scene throws light on the power struggles in relationships dramatized more realistically in the framing first and third scenes. In the absurdist scene four (Black) brothers and one white man ride rocking horses as a theatrical metaphor for their narcotic addictions. A Black woman and a white woman, both called whores and cos-tumed appropriately, cater to the sado-masochistic fantasies of the men by whipping them and bringing them cocaine upon demand. The scene concludes with a bizarre "queen contest" between the Black whore and the character now called "white dude" prancing around the stage in drag and shouting, "See, I'm the real queen. I am the universe." Fi-nally the white dude punches his opponent to the floor de-claring, "Don't look at her. She's Black. I'm white. The rightful queen." The scene suggests that all women are ser-vants and caretakers for all men, regardless of race, but that only Black men possess the true macho qualities inherent in the American masculine stereotype. White men easily de-generate into women.

The first and third scenes both centrally portray Black revo-lutionary leaders whose vanity requires the sexual and nur-turing attention of several women. Malik's two wives, both pregnant, are not sufficient to feed his insecurity. The reas-surance of conquest is luring him on to pursue other women. The conservative homebody Waleesha contrasts with younger revolutionary activist wife Nefertia. Despite his past attentions, Malik has apparently tired of both of them by the time the play opens. Michele Wallace notes that the inordi-nate value placed on Black masculinity tended to devalue Black women's humanity to such an extent that young Black women were dropping out of school because their boyfriends had convinced them that doing anything other than having babies and performing domestic chores was "counterrevo-lutionary."

The longer, more fully developed third scene dramatizes the dilemma of an unnamed Black man. Both costume and stage set illustrate the split allegiance of the revolutionary leader. His costume is half African dashiki and half white Ameri-can business suit. One side of the stage is the apartment of a white woman, the Black man's weakness/addiction but also his source of material wealth. The other half is the apart-ment he shares with a Black woman who has come to Cali-fornia from New York to live and work for the revolution with him. As the Black woman becomes more well known in the movement, the Black man's interest in her and devo-tion to her decline:

> It's just hard for me, you know, to see you up there
> on stage gittin' all that applause. Makes me won-

der why you chose me. After all, I'm not really famous yet. I'm working on it. But you, everybody knows you.

The frantic oscillation of the man called Brother between Black and white women finally reaches a climax on the evening he tries to be with both of them simultaneously. Although Brother refuses to accompany Sister to her reading, he promises to wait at their apartment for her return. Meanwhile he rushes over to his white woman lover, who is drowning her grief at her anticipation of losing Brother to Sister with Scotch and sleeping pills. Brother frantically tries to wake her.

> I am committed to you, lady. Don't nobody mean to me what you mean to me. C'mon, baby, you gonna be all right. I'm you mannnn. Nothing can change that, you know. So what if she's having a baby. It's something she wanted. I guess it fulfills her as a Black woman, but it didn't bother you and me, baby. Not us. We were together before she came and we'll stay together.

Brother thanks the unconscious white woman for the money that put him through school, money that enables him to travel and dress well. He even says, "I'm a man because you've allowed me to be a man."

Although Brother seems to need the white woman's affection and approval as much as he needs her money, other Black men justified their involvement with white women not only as a means of gaining money to support themselves and the movement (a curious blend of masculine and political prostitution) but also used the sexual availability and willingness of white women, who "didn't put them down and made them feel like men" as a means of controlling or devaluing Black women. According to Michele Wallace, some Black men regarded a white woman as "a piece of the white man's property that he might actually obtain."

In the final confrontation with Brother, Sister unleashes her fury: "To you being a Black woman means I should take all the crap you can think of and any extra crap just hanging loose. That ain't right, man, and you know it too." Like Son/ji, Sister urges Brother to follow the puritan code of abstinence from alcohol, drugs, and tobacco that the revolution preaches. After the man makes his final exit, Sister decides not to leave him because she believes that he will change.

> He'll understand why a Black man must be faithful to his woman, so she'll stop the madness of our mothers repeating itself out loud. . . . I am the new Black woman. I will help the change to come. Just gots to rock myself in Blackness in the knowledge of womanly Blackness and I shall be.

All three Black revolutionary plays by Sonia Sanchez produced or published in the sixties portray Black women being abused by Black men. The two female characters in the first play are verbally condemned by the male revolutionaries and rewarded for their self-assertion of counterrevolutionary views with the "poetic justice" of extermination. The play does not present them as strong or even sympathetic characters.

Sister Son/ji, however, is portrayed as heroic in her solitary strength. Nevertheless, the man or men who abuse her are not presented as representatives of the oppressive system of patriarchy but as isolated flawed men. Thus Son/ji's struggle against masculine vanity is seen as an isolated dilemma. At no point does she acknowledge that any portion of her suffering results from a system of male domination which separates women from mutual struggle. Despite her name, Sister Son/ji seems bereft of loving and supportive sisters. She exhibits no hint of feminist consciousness or sense of solidarity with other women battling against patriarchy. Both Sister Son/ji and Sister in the third section of *Uh, Uh; But How Do It Free Us?* survive alone. Even though the women are admirable, such dramatic portraits do not promote the liberation of Black women.

Bell Hooks explains how sexism within the male Black revolution camouflaged the need to struggle against women's oppression and silenced Black women from speaking out in their own behalf:

> Without a doubt, the false sense of power Black women are encouraged to feel allows us to think that we are not in need of social movements like a women's movement that would liberate us from sexist oppression. The sad irony is of course that Black women are often most victimized by the very sexism we refuse to collectively identify as an oppressive force.

Although none of the three revolutionary plays by Sonia Sanchez asserts a conscious feminist position, their portrayals of the victimization of strong women constitute a preliminary raising of consciousness. They dramatize the need for active cooperation among Black women in political struggle for sexual as well as racial justice. Chronologically the plays progress toward feminism.

Sonia Sanchez with Herbert Leibowitz (interview date Spring/Summer/Fall/Winter 1985)

SOURCE: "Exploding Myths: An Interview with Sonia Sanchez," in *Parnassus,* Vol. 12, No. 2, and Vol. 13, No. 1, Spring/Summer/Fall/Winter, 1985, pp. 357-68.

[In the following interview, Sanchez discusses her poetry and the development of her career.]

[Leibowitz:] Do you think there is a feminine sensibility which differs conspicuously from that of the male?

[Sanchez:] Yes. Women are quite different from men in what they feel and think and how they view the world. I use feminine imagery which is drawn from ancient cultures. I use words like Olokun—she is the goddess of the sea—so that people understand when we're talking about the sea that we're talking about women. I use Oshun and Yémaya who are the female riverain goddesses. Some of these goddesses use bells to announce, resoundingly, their teachings. From the pine tree to water reflecting water, a lot of my poetry expresses what it means to let people taste and feel sweetness and power running together, hate and love running together, beauty and ugliness also running together. My poetry has talked about what it means to be a woman ironically, too, in portraits of women who have been violated, as the earth has been violated. I try to focus attention on injustices, on wrongs, but I try to do it in a way that is both sharp and loving. Black poetry often incorporates "playing the dozens," that bawdy and tough talk about family and love and race. Americans never had people talk to them in this fashion, at least not out loud. What some of us women poets did was come out with a sprinkling of curse words to needle the finicky.

Do you think there's a language which belongs to women, to black women poets?

Sometimes. Sometimes. It depends on the subject matter, on whether the poem happened to be cerebral, political, lyrical, or just moving somewhere else.

A lot of my poetry expresses what it means to let people taste and feel sweetness and power running together, hate and love running together, beauty and ugliness also running together.
—Sonia Sanchez

Do the young women on the street play the dozens in the same way that the young males do?

I think it's less violent with women. We hear it and understand it but we play it less, of course. It was a way of getting attention, of bringing black culture into poetry. You can't criticize the poetry unless you understand the culture. And if you don't understand the culture, you don't understand Sterling Brown or Gwendolyn Brooks or Margaret Walker, their use of blues, poetry, and folk poetry, and black lan-

guage. In the same way, I can't criticize the poetry of other ethnic groups in this country, not unless I first study their histories. Just because people are what I call "American-made" does not necessarily mean that they can be quickly analyzed. My generation and perhaps the generation coming after me did not play the dozens in such a violent way, but young women in the schools today are as "bad" as some of the young men. (I mean "bad" in the good sense.) They have no compunctions against saying and doing what they damn well please.

How does black dialect and the vitality and humor of street talk get into your poems?

That happens from listening and talking and speaking, not just as an adult but as a little girl. Not, interestingly enough, as an Alabamian, not those eight years in Alabama. My memory is very quick on that because when we came to New York City I remember we didn't have a southern accent—you know how people expect you to have a southern accent? Well, we didn't—and we had not even eaten chitterlings. We spoke very tactfully, very properly, no street talk. My father was a schoolteacher in Alabama. But we learned street talk because everyone else outside the house spoke it. I learned it consciously. I made mistakes initially and people would laugh. And it was hard for me because I was a stutterer as a young girl. And I didn't stop stuttering until I came out of high school at sixteen; I would memorize how I was going to say things, so when the words came out they came out right. I'd listen very carefully and I'd never say anything unless I repeated it twenty times in the sanctity of my room, in the sanctity of my head, and going down the hallway; then I would come outside and burst right out with it.

You have a very good ear for street talk.

My stepmother, who was a very interesting woman, spoke what I call black English. I remember coming home from school and carrying on dual conversations with her. In school, they were pulling us to get beyond ourselves, beyond our "defects." But I used to listen to the students who would not conform in class, the hip kids. I would walk with them sometimes and think, "that's really a great way of saying it." But above all, I remember my grandmother, who also spoke in black English. She was not an educated woman but I remember listening to her imagery. I didn't stutter when my grandmother was alive, only after she died (I was about six). It was a kind of self-protection, I think. No one bothered me once I began to stutter; people would say, "oh, she's strange, a quiet one. Give her food and leave her alone." So I sat and read and wrote and no one really intruded. But when my grandmother was alive and spoke, I remember taking her words sometimes and repeating them. "Why?" she would ask. "Because I like to float into words," I answered. Now that was a child's way of saying that her words were beautiful and couched in interesting similes and images. I could really see them floating. And she was so permissive and loving that she allowed the imitations. She knew I wasn't mocking her. She gave me that language. Now I hear some little kid out in the street acting tough and sassy and speaking black English, and I'll stop and talk to him and say, "isn't that pretty?"

Black kids invent metaphors with ease?

Their metaphors are unbelievable. I taught one of the first courses in black English at San Francisco State. The English Department was wondering what in the hell I was going to do. I shrugged. "I know how the students will greet me, how nervous they'll be in the classroom. I'm going to let them understand that black English exists alongside standard English and that it's fascinating." I didn't know how to teach it initially. I had to fight through it, to come home and even battle myself, but that was a very exciting class. My students were able to release a part of themselves without shame or guilt.

When did you write your first poem?

In Alabama, after Momma died. I must have been seven. I was sitting in the corner and I had a real "Live" stepmother—I had three of them—who was really classic, mean like in the fairy tales. She came over and grabbed what I was doing and read it to someone (I believe it was her sister) who said, "that's a poem!" My first real poem as such, if you can call a ten-year-old's scribblings poems, was about my grandmother, memories of her that began to come back in a very sharp fashion in New York. We were not accustomed to living in a small apartment, or to a bedroom window that faced a blank wall. I began to suffer from claustrophobia. The poem was about Mama and how she let me run; I ran with the boys instead of playing with dolls. She allowed that. I could come home with my dresses torn and she'd say, "Don't put those on her, she's not a fancy girl." I've never worn frilly things; I've kept my style to this day. If I see little girls dressed in pinafores, I collapse. So the first piece I wrote was about that. I don't have it anymore. You get older, and see that it's terrible and throw it out. But the Schomburg—I'm giving my papers to the Schomburg Collection—they get upset about things like that. The first poem I ever published, in the *New England Review,* was again about the South. Once an aunt and I were on a segregated bus on which blacks could only sit at the back and whites up front. When it got very crowded, blacks had to move to the last seat and when it got jammed, they had to stand up. That day the driver stopped it and said, "Get the hell off." Well, she wouldn't get off. You know how tall I am now, you can imagine at that age how little I was. I was also very thin. I was holding on to her. This bus driver came towards her and she spit on him. There was an uproar and so she was rushed out of town under cover of darkness.

Why did you choose poetry instead of prose?

I don't know. Perhaps because of the fun with words I had with Momma. I've always been trying to recreate that. I did it in a streetwise manner in New York City where I spent all my years from nine on. We spent time playing dozens, and tripping people out. The poems were my way of protesting: how could you let me grow up in this country and not tell me about black history? How could you make me feel so inferior? Playing with words, as I used to, was like going outside and running and jumping over walls and getting cuts that are still with me. I was running into words because I thought they were so inventive and beautiful. My grandmother was a deaconness, and the Sisters would have meetings on Saturdays at our house. I'd go behind the couch or sit under a table and listen. That's where I learned how to watch people. My grandmother would become very emphatic about a particular kind of woman she respected or despised and to this day I identify people from what she said to me.

In **Homegirls and Handgrenades** *you do have several long pieces that are not exactly short stories, not prose, but prose poems. You seem to have moved quite comfortably into vignettes that remain poetic. Everybody's favorite seems to be* **"Just Don't Never Give Up on Love."**

That's one of my favorites also.

How did it come to be written?

It really is unbelievable. One morning I went out to the playground with my twins. I saw this old woman who was not eighty-four, but ninety-four; no one would believe that someone ninety-four could be that lucid. I'd come outside to read a book and write a review for a journal. When I got up on her, she was nodding in the sun, and she opened one jaundiced eye. My whole body movement said, "Don't bother me, old woman; I have work to do." I sat with my back to her and opened the book I'd been assigned to review. Anyway, as I watched the twins go back and forth, I suddenly felt this nudge and it was she. She actually had slid across from her end of the bench to the middle. I turned and began to stutter—I reverted—because I didn't know what she wanted or what she was saying. Looking at me, she said her first words in black English, and I responded: "Look, woman, please don't talk to me, I have work to do, I'm so far behind that people are screaming and it's my fault." But she was very persistent, as older people are, and kept talking. When I said something abrupt like, "yeah, that's nice," she laughed. I stopped, then put my book down, and looked at her because this old woman really laughed, and she said, "you've got some kind of spunk about you, after all. Come on, sit close to me." She had been married five times, though she talked about two marriages. The first man was beautiful, but he would have killed her if she hadn't left him. Afterwards I hugged her and the next day there she was and we talked again.

Which writers were the important influences on your work?

When I first started to write in school I had to read the usual people—Longfellow, Whittier, Scott—and I knew I didn't write poetry like them. I never read any real modern poets until I was in college. And then I found a black woman in the library on 145th St. who gave me Langston Hughes and Pushkin, which was fascinating. I'd come in and she'd say, "you're always in the poetry section. You should read this man because he was a black man." And then she said, "Have you read Robert Browning?" She began to redirect me, handing me, interestingly enough, some of the Latin poets I'd never touched, and though I didn't quite understand some of their imagery, I still read the poems. I didn't understand Pushkin completely but I read him.

Louise Bogan was a very important influence. I studied with her at NYU. One of the first things she said was: If you're going to write poetry, you must read it aloud. None of us believed that. I was one of the first people who had to read aloud in that class, and as I read the damn poem, Bogan, in her droll, distant fashion, remarked, "Did you read that poem aloud, Miss Sanchez?" The rest of the students looked at me as if to say: I'm glad it's you. I was literally caught, and I started to fake it. Bogan just looked away and commented, "Well, I hear some problems in the poems." But she never rewrote any of the content, and I felt safe on that point.

At that time of course I didn't write anything that really said anything about being black or being a woman because no one wanted to bring her face or sex to anyone's attention; that was naughty, especially if you were a woman who declared "I'm a woman." People would say, "Please, you shouldn't be writing poetry if you're a woman. Or if you're black, by god, you shouldn't be writing poetry at all." So I never referred to it. But every now and then something would creep in. Usually I'd write a mild little poem about something that was happening in the south; the civil rights struggle was intense. And a poet in the workshop said: "We don't want to hear that at all." It was really rough.

How did Bogan respond to your poems?

I never came out and asked: "Do you think I can write?" She remarked dryly, "There are some people who can write and others who can't. I would say that you can write if you work and study form." Then I began to read her work and I saw her structures. This classical woman poet was shaping

a lot of us. Though some resisted form as too rigorous, I did not because I thought that my sprawling work needed form. To this day, I teach my students the villanelle, the sonnet: I preach all the exercises and discipline that Bogan gave to me. I began to move, to see how form can work, can demand a certain kind of response. That was very important for me. I realize now that she was not necessarily interested in her students. She was not a woman who'd open up to you, but she was honest and fair. That was what I needed.

It sounds fortunate to have had so rigorous a mentor at the foundation of your career rather than somebody who was permissive. What other poets exerted an influence on you?

Neruda and Lorca for their imagery, their showing that you could pile image on image and still make people understand. Langston Hughes, Gwendolyn Brooks, Margaret Walker. At the Schomburg Collection, I met Jean Hutson, the curator, who told me that the library was devoted to books about black folk. My reaction was, "You must be kidding." I had just gotten out of Hunter College and hadn't read anything by blacks. She gave me an entire library; that's where I first read W. E. B. Dubois, Claude McKay, and Zora Neale Hurston. One day I turned to Jean Hutson and said: "I'm going to have my books in here," and she looked at me as though thinking that I was a rash young woman, but now she tells my students, "This is the young woman who vowed that one day she'd have her books in here," and she hugged me. After I read these black writers, I knew I was on the right track. They nurtured me. Later on I greedily read a lot of women poets: Atwood and Piercy, Brooks and Walker, Dickinson and Bogan. Then I began to buy books of poetry—that's the one thing I would spend money on—and write in the margin, to indicate the things I liked and disliked. I also read aloud. Bogan really insisted that a poet must read her work aloud. She said, "You will not always have people with you who will tell you whether something's good or bad, but your ear will."

Could you talk about Neruda's importance to your writing of political poems?

My early poetry was introspective, poetry that probably denied or ignored I was black. I wrote about trees, and birds, and whatever, and that was hard, living in Harlem, since we didn't see too many trees, though I did draw on my residual memories of the South. People kept saying to me, if you write a political poem, it will be considered propaganda—an ineffective and poor poem—but I read Neruda and saw that he didn't deny the personal. In the early Sixties I became aware that the personal was the political. Even my loneliness was never just my own but a much larger loneliness that came out of a society that did not encourage blacks to learn for the sheer joy of it, to expand beyond drinking a bottle of beer at the end of the day and watching the idiot box. I may show you a picture of an alienated and hostile person, but there are reasons for it, and lessons to learn, too.

You call your latest book **Homegirls and Handgrenades.** *A hand grenade is very explosive, destructive. Do you intend us to think that poetry is in some way like a grenade?*

The hand grenade can also explode myths. Take the poem about the Amtrak ride. It really happened. A young/old/black man bopped on at Newark; he had a mobster's look. I immediately put my shopping bag on the seat, warning him that I didn't want to be bothered. He looked away but sure enough, he sat right behind me and began to talk to a middle-class white man. I heard this man inhale, from unease, you know, and I felt that the young old man heard it also. They had a conversation that I had to record because myths exploded there. It finally ended with the man not taking in those uneasy breaths and the black man saying simply, "I've been trying to deal with the problem of how non-work makes you less of a man in this country" and then they said goodbye and smiled at each other. That's what I mean: hand grenades are the words I use to explode myths about people, about ourselves, about how we live and what we think, because this is really the last chance we have in this country.

Were you stereotyped as a political poet?

Writing has been a long, tense road of saying what I wanted and needed to say. When I gave my book *Love Poems* to a friend, she said, "god, I didn't know you wrote love poems." But in every book of mine there's been a section of lyrical pieces. If you describe me, as some critics do, as a lyrical poet, I say yes, I am, but I'm also a hard-hitting poet and a political poet because this is a lyrical world and a terrible world, too, and I have to talk about that.

I have also been deeply involved in Philadelphia with what they call the literacy campaign. I go to older men and women who are learning how to read and read the poems aloud and discuss them. Once someone said to me, "I read that because it was about me, and I read it well." This person actually said good, I read it good, and I felt that she did read it good. "If this is poetry," they say, "I like poetry." And the whole point is to bring poetry to a larger audience, something I've tried to do for a long, long time.

Are you conscious of writing for a particular audience?

No—but I know my audience, if that makes sense. From the beginning I've had a black audience, women, and students, black and white. Now because of what's happening in this country, that audience has widened. I get letters from people saying "I understand what you're doing because I feel the same thing." What I felt as a woman, as a black woman, had to get translated to other women, too.

Ishmael Reed made a comment recently that he wished Alice Walker had written about strong black men rather than unreliable males in The Color Purple. *Is there a conflict between black male and female writers?*

America doesn't allow two or three major black writers to exist at the same time. You know the business: when Baldwin came along he had to kill off Wright, and when Ellison came along he had to kill off Wright, also, because Wright had maintained that position of power. Whether you have genius or not, if what you're saying sells, then by golly, by gee, they'll elevate you. Alice Walker is a talented woman. She's one of the nurtured, so therefore black success could happen.

Nurtured by?

By the establishment, by her publishers, purposely, so the flowering happens. Ishmael and some of the other writers are perhaps announcing: we, too, have something to say and it's not necessarily getting the play it deserves.

Not reaching the same wide audience?

Ish should understand that there's a different movement happening: a special interest in what women are saying, a lot of support of women writers now. Some black women writers are creating characters that reflect the negative aspects of some black men. The problem is that there's no balance in the marketplace. For that we shouldn't fault the writer; instead we should understand the need to provide progressive images. But black writers, male and female, have to maintain a sense of themselves, politically and as writers. I never look up to see who's better or worse. When I finish a reading and people come up and hug me, not because I've been sassy and smart but because I've prodded them and insisted that they think, and they say, "You've made me go another step." I know why I write.

My work, really, has always been motivated by love. In the Sixties, the country had to be shocked with the horror of how it had raised Negroes who hated themselves, who were bent on wiping themselves out, intent on not seeing themselves, on being invisible. So I have a poem about Norma, who had a genius for language. I saw her on 145th St. years later, with tracks on her damn legs. What in the hell could she have done? Can you imagine what her four little girls, involved in that drug scene, see and know? She said they're going to be different, but of course I knew they weren't going to be different. This is what, finally, I'm talking about in my poems.

What is your argument when somebody, not only a conservative, says that poetry transcends gender, that ultimately a poet has to be judged on the variety and brilliance of the language rather than on the question of being male or female, black or white?

That time has not arrived. So the poet must educate people, which is what a lot of us are doing. If someone says, I am this, because my hair curls when it gets in water, there can still be beauty in the work. There can still be brilliance in the language that informs. Exhorts.

Isn't there an implicit bias that such a poem favors content over style?

For many of us our change in style was synonymous with a change in content. This forged a new and exciting creation, movement.

Mallarmé's comment to Degas that poems are not made out of ideas but out of words is a favorite piety of modernism. Perhaps the twentieth century has gone too far in the direction of purity of language and we need the pendulum to swing back more toward substance.

Good poets write all kinds of poems. Women poets today might make a political statement about what it is to be Hispanic or black or Jewish, whatever; their poems give me an understanding of their pain, their joy, their determination to be what they are, what they want to be. This amplifies poetry as opposed to narrowing it.

What are your criteria for deciding whether poems are good?

Is it well structured? Is the imagery vivid? Is there beauty in it? I might say something smartly, but the poem must have another leap and another bound to it so that style and content can walk together, can become fused. When a poet relies only on the crutch of "I'm this or I'm that" and does not bring us the sharpened tools of craft, we have to look up and protest. Some people think that the poem should not have a race or gender; it should be weightless. Whether you're Wallace Stevens or Audre Lorde, you bring what you are to the poem.

Where does the criticism of your work come from? From black critics?

Mostly black critics. Black women critics have done some of the best work to date. But every audience I read to becomes a profound group of critics. Their reactions affect the work, affect me. When I write, I tune in to the collective unconscious, and there I hear voices, lines, words, I hear music. For a long time I rejected the music because I felt I couldn't sing, I'm not a singer, but now in some of my pieces, I do sing. In the Martin Luther King poem, I chant. When the chant first came out, I literally shook, I said what

the hell, how can I do this? But I wrote it out. When Biko was killed in South Africa, the women had come out singing *ke wa rona, ke wa rona,* so I wrote that down, with some other words around it, to chant. It was frightening to me but I just did it. I wrote that poem for the University of Pennsylvania's celebration of King's forty-sixth birthday. As I stood up to recite it, I said, I will just say *ke wa rona:* Malcolm, *ke wa rona:* Mandela, *ke wa rona:* Martin, you know, and they will know what that's about. Forces had come to me while I wrote it and I did exactly what they wanted me to do.

When did the African influence enter your poetry? I take it you're fascinated by African religions.

There were some phenomena I could not explain, like the collective unconscious, but I wanted to. When I read *Flash of the Spirit,* the Egyptian Book of the Dead, I laughed. That's the person I talked to, that was Yémaya. I was born on the ninth month and the ninth day and one of the numbers for Yémaya is nine. I was bringing into the arena of poetry the sense of another sensibility, another way of looking at the world, another life force. If I touch you, I give you a life force, also. To those who record desolation and say you can't do anything about it, I'm affirming that a person can do something, I'm saying yes. In other words, I'm taking what might be considered a metaphysical concept, this collective unconscious, and using my relationship to it to change real things.

Sonia Sanchez with D. H. Melhem (interview date Fall 1985)

SOURCE: "Sonia Sanchez: Will and Spirit," in *MELUS,* Vol. 12, No. 3, Fall, 1985, pp. 73-98.

[*In the following interview, Melhem provides an introduction to Sanchez's career, which is followed by an interview in which Sanchez discusses the influences, themes, and forms of her work.*]

Dynamic: the word immediately describes Sonia Sanchez and her art. Petite, attractive, her diminutive size, like that of actress Vinie Burrows, seems to acquire physical volume on stage. Born to Wilson L. and the late Lena (Jones) Driver on September 9, 1934, in Birmingham, Alabama, Sanchez was named Wilsonia after her father who had wanted a boy. She has an older sister, Patricia. Her half-brother, Wilson S. Driver, Jr., about whom she is writing, died in 1981.

At the age of nine, Sanchez moved to New York, where she attended elementary school, junior high, and George Washington High School. She was graduated from Hunter College in 1955. Selected for a poetry workshop, she studied at New York University with Louise Bogan, for whom she has the highest respect. Her daughter, Anita Sanchez, product of an early marriage, was born on May 24, 1957. The twin sons, Morani Meusi ("Black Warrior" in Swahili) and Mungu Meusi ("Black God") were born on January 26, 1968.

Sanchez has taught at several colleges, including San Francisco State (1967-69); University of Pittsburgh (1969-70); Rutgers University (1970-71); Manhattan Community College (1971-73); and Amherst College (1973-76). At Temple University, where she has been teaching since 1977, currently as Associate Professor, her courses include creative writing, Black Literature, and Women's Studies. She has taught at Graterford Prison as part of a community writing program since fall 1980. In our interview, April 1, 1981, at the Statler Hilton, New York, where she was staying for the Fifth Annual Conference of the National Council for Black Studies, she discussed her love of teaching:

> I get a lot of joy out of teaching. I think it is important for those who have vision to be around students and make them see what this country is about and have them see their relationship to their parents. . . . A teacher can give them a sense of reality, a sense of the future, of what can be, what they can be. It makes them take chances, bring new ideas and new possibilities into the curriculum.

Sanchez speaks rapidly, fluently with conviction. One finds it difficult to believe she ever had a speech problem. The following exchange gives remarkable testimony to her will in overcoming the impediment and in determining early to write poetry.

. . . . .

[*Melhem:*] *What was the first art form that interested you? When did you start writing, and was poetry your first genre of expression?*

[Sanchez:] I think the first art form was poetry. I first started to write poetry when I was a little girl in Alabama. As a child I stuttered, and I was what Black people call "tongue-tied," too. It was a hell of a combination (laughs). So I would go, "Det-det-det-uhm"; I would go "Ah-ah-ah-ah-ah-ah-ah-I." I was a very introspective kind of child as a consequence of that, and I started to write these little things on paper, and someone finally told me, "That's a poem," and I said "Oh!" And I just kept writing.

When we moved to New York, I continued to write; didn't show it to anyone, actually. One day my stepmother called me into the kitchen. You know how children wash dishes sometimes. I mean the dishes aren't clean, and she had, the way mothers do, she had decided to fill up that sink with hot water again, and she proceeded to put the dishes—all the dishes—back into the sink. She said they were greasy, what a terrible job I had done. And so when I heard her call, I ran, because the kind of call she actually sent into that bedroom was like, "You'd better get here in one minute, Sonia." So, I was writing a poem, and I left the poem on the bed, something I never did. No one knew that I wrote poetry in that house or had continued to write poetry. And I ran in there and I said, "Just a minute." She says, "Right now, young lady." So I was, sort of like, I had to do it at that point. Well, while I was washing dishes, out comes my sister with the poem in her hand, and I reached for it with my soapy hands, and she pulled away, and the whole family was in the kitchen, and she started to read this poem that I had written—I don't have a copy of it, I wish I did, about George Washington crossing the Delaware—(Laughter) you can imagine, right? Because we were home on holiday that day; it was George Washington's birthday, when it was celebrated on the twenty-second. And she read this poem, "Da-da, da-da, da-da, da-da, da-da, da-da, da-da, da-da." Well, I was utterly mortified. I was utterly hurt, and I felt so betrayed. So I grabbed—I finally grabbed it and took it into the bedroom and hid it someplace, and I came back, and they were all laughing at this poem I had written, and I was very much upset. So, from that point on, no one actually knew that I was still writing, because they never found anything. . . .

You said that you stuttered. Now you are a beautifully articulate person. How did you get over it? Was it the poetry that helped you?

When I was in high school—you know in high school when you have to give all these damn speeches—

Yes.

We were in a speech class, and the most terrible time for me was to get up and give a speech, or to open my mouth and say anything. I just very seldom talked to anyone, period. As I was studying this speech, oh, almost day in and day—every night. And I would read this speech for my sister—she says, "Oh, it's fine, it's fine." But what she meant by that was that she understood what I said, and so she had no difficulty with the way I presented it. But I was determined that I was going to give this speech without one stutter, because everybody, I was sure, was just laying for me to get up and make this speech and then to try and speak very fast at the same time and just wreck this whole thing. So when I got up to give my speech—and I was about the last person to give a speech, too—I took my nails and literally dug my nails into my hand like this. (Gestures.) And when I finished, I saw blood. And every time I heard a stutter begin, I would just go—(gestures).

That's amazing. You taught yourself, really, to stop. You conditioned yourself.

That's exactly what it was all about. Every time I felt pain I would just—(gesture). It wouldn't come out. When I finished, I said to my sister—we were in the same class—I said, "How was I? How was I?" She said, "It was o.k." I said, "No, but how *was* I?" What I was really asking her was had I stuttered. And she really hadn't paid any attention to it at all, because she was accustomed to the way I spoke, et cetera, but the difficult part about a stutterer is that he or she always hears the stutters, you see, in the back of the head. So for years, even though I didn't stutter, I always heard the stuttering. So it didn't make me all of a sudden, since I had "conquered" that, in quotes, o.k., that I was then going to jump up and just be a fantastic speaker. (Laughing.) I was still quiet in school.

(Laughs) Yes. It's like a fat person losing weight and still seeing that fat person in the mirror.

Yes. I still heard—in fact, that was even to the point the first time I had a reading in New York. I was going to chicken out and not read, because I figured I would get up there and just, you know, go out, stutter, whatever. And finally I said, "I'm not going to read." And they said, "Of course, you're going to read! Other people are reading, so you just go on out." So I went out and read a couple of poems, and I came back and I said, "How was it?" And they said, "Fine, Sonia," and I said, "I mean, really, how was I?" I went to another person, and he said, "O.k., Sonia." They thought I was getting a big head! What I was really afraid to ask was had I stuttered, because I still heard the stutters.

And it took me years, I mean throughout college days I always would be talking and still would hear the stutters. I mean for *years,* years, years. It's almost ironical that I decided to go into something which required talk, speech, whatever. And I don't know why I chose that. The interesting thing, when I was in school, when I was in college, I would say I wanted to be a lawyer. I wanted to go to law school, and again, the choice of speaking. It's almost really sadistic, I thought—(laughs).

Sort of an act of will.

Probably. Well, you know, my name is *Wil*sonia. My father's name is Wilson—

Yes—

W-i-l-s-o-n. So they expected a boy and, as the custom sometimes in the South, sometimes they have relatives naming you, and I guess he was so disgusted with having another girl that he called someone in the family and said, "Well, I

have another girl. I have no name. We were going to call this boy coming 'Wilson,' and now I have another girl." So she said, "Don't worry, I'll help you out." So she called back, my father tells the story, a couple of hours later. She said, "Well, name her 'Wilsonia,' after you. Benita. Wilsonia Benita." (Laughing.) So I had a tag called "Wilsonia Benita." And I always think that people do name you, on some levels, in some ways.

And you're right. I have always made use of the will as if it's a muscle, which needed to be exercised and trained and disciplined. And as a consequence, the only way I have ever been able to do anything is via disciplining myself, sometimes very harshly, I think. But otherwise I couldn't have done twelve books if I hadn't. I mean, working the way I've had to work, in my time, without that discipline.

Who and what were some important influences on your work? Haki Madhubuti, with whom your work has been compared, feels there have been only Black influences on his poetry. How would you view your own art in this respect?

I would say, when I first started to write, I read everything, and I still do, to this day. I read all poets, and when I teach in the classroom, I make my students read all poets. Period. Because they don't get much Black poetry, I would quite often read a lot of Black poets to them. Or because they don't get a lot of Latin poets or African poets, whatever, I will read a lot of that, also. I begin a class, always, with a poem that's not in the textbook that we have, and in that way, I'm always able to share other kinds of poets with them, which I think is important.

When I first started to write, I was reading—there's a librarian in my neighborhood—not actually my neighborhood but in the library, and she used to see me. I used to *live* in the library; I was in the library all the time. And finally she said, "Well, you read a lot." And I said, "Yes." And she says, "Do you like everything?" And I said, "Yes." Well, the next time I came she had Langston Hughes, for me, and she had Gwen Brooks, also, and someone else . . . Pushkin, also. I never forgot this Black woman who worked in that library, the first Black woman I found in the library. She said, "This man, you should read, because he was a Black man who lived in Russia." And my head just kind of swirled with that information, and I remember reading some of his poetry, not understanding it all, but being very much involved with the imagery, and just the sheer words, the power of the words, et cetera.

But I would just go in at will and pick up a poet's work. It didn't matter, really, who it was, and would read. In that manner, I stumbled across a man by the name of Lorca, and it was really wild, just roaming through that library. And to this day I love Lorca, you know, for the passion that's involved with his work, et cetera. And I remember reading his plays and also some of the things he had done at that time....

It was also my smutty period. One of the reasons why I was going to the library so often was because I was reading novels—(Laughter) and I was reading all the good parts of the novels. I had to go through the whole book to get to the good parts, sometimes. And so I always maintain that like you leave people alone, even when they're going through a smutty period, because if they're reading, it really doesn't matter what they read, as long as they continue to read.

[Sanchez also mentioned Zora Neale Hurston, Countee Cullen, and Sterling Brown as positive figures and influences. Paul Laurence Dunbar she found "coy": "One always felt that Dunbar was dealing with minstrels."]

You've written some fine tributes to Brown in **I've Been a Woman.** *Beautiful tributes. Your reading, as well as your poetry, is both dramatic and musical. How did you develop your compelling style of presentation?*

... It occurred to me at some point, and I tend to think that was in San Francisco, because in San Francisco we really, many of us really got out, began to get our teeth into that whole reading bit. And, you must remember, when we were reading poetry at that time, there was not that interest in poetry. Period. People had their ears tuned to radios and whatever, et cetera, and you know, something with a beat. So you had to engage people in a dialogue to draw them into what you were going to do. So I began to, when I got an audience that was like really rough or loud, or perhaps saying, "Well, what is this?" before someone comes on the scene, or "Where is this pot coming from?" before the dance or whatever, I began to talk about what the poem was about, or something about the poem which would lead right into the poem. And then you had people, they'd listen to what you said, and then, when you had their ear, you'd take them into a poem.

This was in the early sixties.

This was in the early sixties. This was also when the poetry began to change and move towards Black themes much more. We're talking about '65, '66. And what that meant simply is that, for some reason, I began to understand the need to integrate the talk with the poem—

The rapping with the reading—

Yes. Right. And as a consequence, you didn't know where one began and where the other one left off, et cetera. It was

such an integration of the two, which I think is quite often important.

. . . . .

After the sixties, her reputation grown as a figure in the new Black poetry and in the drive to establish college-level Black studies programs, Sanchez gave a year-long workshop at the Countee Cullen Library in Harlem. **three hundred and sixty degrees of blackness comin at you,** her anthology culled from the student writings, includes poetry, short stories, and plays. In 1972, as part of a cultural tour, Sanchez traveled to Guyana, Bermuda, and Jamaica; the following year to the People's Republic of China. She visited Cuba in the summer of 1979, on a tour sponsored by the Venceremos Brigade.

Introducing her first book, **Homecoming,** published by Broadside Press, Haki Madhubuti (then Don L. Lee) notes: "Black people's reality is controlled by alien forces. This is why Sonia Sanchez is so beautiful & needed; this is also why she is dangerous." He sees her poetry as love poetry, "the love of self & people," negating negative influences, inspiring pride and hope. The first poem, **"home-coming,"** tells of her return home from college:

> i returned tourist
> style to watch all
> the niggers killing themselves with
> 3 for oners
> with
> needles
> that
> cd
> not support
> their stutters.

The poet returns home as teacher. Her return to Black identity is a "home-coming." Stuttering becomes a metaphor of weakness. A practical moralist, she sees the self-destructive anger in her people and seeks to reverse its path. In **"nigger,"** she scores use of the word among Black people and points the way to pride: "i know i am black. / beautiful. / with meaning. / nigger. u say. / my man / you way behind the set." The last phrase conveys being behind the times, not keeping up with the "set" or music being played; the term has come into general use at poetry readings. (Sanchez also favors the word *gig,* originally a jazz musician's job, in referring to her reading engagements.) There is a sense of colloquial, up-to-the-minute speech, the quickness of speed-writing ("cd" for "could," frequently), unconventional, attention-getting devices: words fully capitalized; words scattered on the page in relation to breath and emphasis; change of pace. Responding to my questions on technique, regarding her lowercasing Sanchez noted:

It has a lot to do with the ego on many levels; having to deal and control it and move in such a way that moving into work, moving into a realm that is important, but also making the writer be less important.

While her technique may be experimental, Sanchez's moral canon is a stern one, issuing from her own self-discipline. Like Madhubuti, she is a vegetarian who neither smokes nor drinks alcoholic beverages. She, too, views love as strictly heterosexual, ideally family-oriented, and shares his impatience with homosexuality. In **"to a jealous cat"** she warns her man "that jealousy's / a form of homosexuality." In **"black magic,"** blackness proves essential to the power of love: "black / magic is your / touch." In **"short poem,"** the intense lover says "he can / smell me coming," the gerund ambiguously connoting orgasm and approach. The poet wryly asks whether she should bottle the scent "and / sell it / when he goes," skeptically anticipating his departure. **"to Chuck"** parodies the style of e e cummings ("i'm gonna write me / a poem like / e.e. / cum / mings to / day."). It shows to advantage Sanchez's humor, admits of self-parody, and defends her lyricism while it acknowledges cummings' liberating features.

The personal poems in *Homecoming* are self-revelatory, full of anger and compassion for her sisters, edged with loneliness and melancholy introspection. The touching lyric, **"poem at thirty,"** reflects upon her childhood when "i walked two / miles in my sleep," and depicts a poet who is still "traveling. i'm / always traveling." In a powerful image of isolation, the speaker describes how she spent "nights on a / brown couch when / i wrapped my / bones in lint and / refused to move." Then, in a gesture to another isolated being, she calls:

> you you black man
> stretching scraping
> the mold from your body.
> here is my hand.
> i am not afraid
> of the night.

The poem, begun in solitude, at midnight, a time of decision, at thirty, looks past early youth, struggles out of the self that "no one touches" anymore, toward a mature confrontation. Mounting its images toward growth, it culminates in a brave offering of love.

Again in first person, **"summary,"** "a poem for the world / for the slow suicides / in seclusion," describes an unhappy "stuttering self" that projects its misery onto a perfidious American culture. Poems "to all brothers" and "to all sisters" attack Black stereotypes of white women, in the former, as desirable, in the latter, as exemplary. Sanchez assures her

Black sisters that the white woman has no advantage, except her whiteness; that Black men are superior and worth loving, even though love may bring pain: "hurt ain't the bag u / shd be in. / loving is / the bag, man." The poet seeks to elevate the pride of both sexes, thus turning them to each other.

Of the political pieces, some address heroic figures: Malcolm X, Bobby Hutton of the Black Panthers, saxophonist Pharaoh Sanders. Others are general, like "small comment," a lesson in compulsive inquiry:

> the nature of the beast is the
> man or to be more specific
> the nature of the man is his
> bestial nature or to
> bring it to its elemental terms
> the nature of nature is
> The bestial survival of the
> fittest the strongest the richest . . .

The "man" is, of course, the white man. The poem instructs in both language and politics. As a sentence unpunctuated until the last words—"you dig?"—its rhetorical structure defines white capitalist American society. Like motifs or themes with variations, the words "man," "beast," and "nature" recur in new configurations and semantic contexts. Finally, the clear simple language has communicated both basic and complex issues.

Like many elegies by Black poets for the slain leader, **"malcolm"** elicits some of Sanchez's most moving lines and images. Its anger reflects Malcolm's own ("he said, 'fuck you white / man. we have been / curled too long. nothing / is sacred now.'"), yet it articulates an overwhelming sorrow. The poet, who will "breathe / his breath and mourn / my gun-filled nights," knows she, too, will die, and with delicacy asserts that "violets like castanets / will echo me." As she merges with the fallen Malcolm, "what could have been / floods the womb until i drown." But the womb connotes procreation and continuity. Though the grieving poet maintains "death is my pulse," she has assured us from the beginning that she rejects martyrdom: "i don't believe in dying."

Another political poem, **"the final solution,"** asserts that America's version of genocide is sending Black men to fight in Vietnam. Sanchez speaks ironically from the leaders' viewpoint. **"for unborn malcolms"** splutters rage over the assassination, warns that revenge ("an eye for an eye") will be taken. Her triptych, **"Memorial,"** comprises **"1. the supremes—cuz they dead,"** a rebuke to a singing group as "bleached"; **"2. bobby hutton,"** an angry elegy that ranks the Black Panther leader, martyred by policemen's bullets, with Denmark Vesey, Malcolm X, Marcus Garvey; and **"3. rev pinps,"** a poem that mocks translation of Black revolutionary fervor into sensuality. "ain't nothing political / bout fucking," she admonishes.

The two children's poems, **"definition for blk/children"** ("a policeman / is a pig / and he shd be in / a zoo") and "poem (for dcs 8th graders—1966-67)," the latter exhorting the capital's children to consider their proud history and blackness, target the thinking of Black children. **"personal letter no. 2"** ends the volume with another personal cry of loneliness that ends, nevertheless, with courage. "but i am what i am what i / am. woman. alone / amid all this noise." Amid disorder, chaos, a world of transience and disobedient children, the mature poet looks back wistfully at youth, remains stalwart, aware of realities and willing to face them.

We a BaddDDD People, published in 1970, was criticized for its "noisy exhortation." Haki Madhubuti found fault with its shrill sixties rhetoric and, like Dudley Randall, who wrote its Introduction, preferred Sanchez's more personal poems Randall notes in the Introduction:

> Some of her poems are political, but I think the most moving are those in which she talks of man and woman, of women and of drug addiction. It is apparent that she has suffered during the writing of this book. Her suffering has moved her to song, sometimes to inarticulate screams.

Suffering, much of it related to her marriage (Etheridge Knight had a drug problem), and political fervor mark this volume. It is dedicated to "blk/wooomen: the only queens of this universe." A breathless racing to uplift reveals most of the poems as rescue attempts. At times the emergencies override delays of shaping, grasp quickly at facile rhetoric. **"221-1424 (San/francisco/suicide/number),"** which, for this reason, Madhubuti suggests may be "a minor disaster," opens the volume and the first section, "Survival Poems." Yet its monologue dramatizes the ironic situation: a Black expressing rage, then feeling better and advising the "honky" at the suicide prevention number to "hang it up." **"a poem for my father,"** the most personal, exposes a young woman's chagrin at the love affairs and six marriages of her father.

The main thrust of the book, however, is political. In **"blk/ rhetoric,"** she asks:

> who's gonna give our young
> blk/people new heroes
>   (instead of catch / phrases)
>   (instead of cad / ill / acs)
>   (instead of pimps)

pointedly marking the syllables and words with a solidus. **"catch"** invokes "slavecatcher;" "cad," "ill," and "acs," negative images ("acs" suggests "aces," gambling, "acts,"

"axe"), join as Cadillac, automobile symbol of luxury and American capitalism. The poem is frankly "an S O S."

In the first section, personal poems commingle with public ones. The lyrical **"personal letter no. 3"** muses on time and aging, confessing that "sometimes after midnight / i am tired / of it all." **"hospital / poem (for etheridge 9/29/69)"** expresses the poet's feelings about her husband's immortality, despite medical predictions that he will die of drug abuse. Poems on television, like **"summer/time T.V. / (is witer than ever),"** attack white cultural values imposed on Blacks "in the yr/of/ tele/vised ass/asi/nations. 1968." In **"blk/ chant"** ("we programmed fo death/") and "in the courtroom," Sanchez continues to attack the falsity of white justice for Blacks. **"on watching a world series game"** suffers from the same excess as **"221-1424,"** but "summer words of a sistuh addict" movingly interprets the history of a young drug addict. Shifting dramatically from the girl's voice, the poet ("someone") asks, "sistuh. / did u / finally / learn how to hold yo / mother?"

The second section, "Love/Songs/Chants," reveals Sanchez's ample lyric gifts; her personal struggle with the man she loves, who is "on shit" (heroin). She mourns, tries to retrieve his spirit, fails, and identifies with Billie Holiday, also a drug victim, in **"for our lady."** Having uttered her love in **"poem for etheridge,"** she turns to **"a chant for young/brothas/ & sistuhs,"** using her own tragedy of the man "who went out one day & died." The section ends with **"blk / wooooomen / chant,"** a demand that Black men appreciate their women who have been

> waiten. waiten. WAITEN, WAITENNNNNN
>   A long AMURICAN wait.
> hurrrrreeehurrrrreeehurrrrreeeeeeeeee

In this section, so passionately expressive, typography clearly registers intensity, shifts in emphasis, rhythmical beats and breaks.

The last section, "TCB/en Poems," carries the acronym for "Taking Care of Business" or meeting one's commitments efficiently. The business here is "blk/nation/hood builden." In **"listenen to big black at s.f. state,"** Sanchez calls for constructive action at San Francisco State, where she had taught, and praises Malcolm, Elijah Muhammad, and Amiri Baraka ("Imamu") as "chiefs." In a poem like **"TCB"** she reveals her humor, even while seriously criticizing the substitution of rhetoric for action. She repeats "white/motha/ fucka" with alternate endings of "whitey," "ofay," "devil," "pig," etc., and ends with, "now. that it's all sed.   let's get to work."

Two of the strongest poems in the section, **"we a baddDDD people (for gwendolyn brooks / a fo real bad one),"** and the closing, **"a/coltrane/poem,"** together with the Nina Simone tribute, reveal a vital jazz influence. Using an improvisational flux of rhythms, they sometimes attempt to imitate sounds of the instruments. The poem to John Coltrane, the great tenor saxophonist, is difficult to perform, as the poet notes in the next interview fragment. Despite occasional excesses of rhetorical zeal, its musicality leaps at the reader, confronting with possibly baffling passages of words and sounds to be sung, to be chanted.

. . . . .

[Melhem:] **We a BaddDDD People,** *especially, reflects the influence of jazz improvisation. Do you want the reader to improvise interpretation of some of the musical passages, or do you prefer an attempt to achieve a uniform rendition?*

[Sanchez:] I think that sometimes when people hear me read from *We a BaddDDD People,* they say to me, "I didn't read it that way," and I say, "That's o.k." I think poetry works on many levels. One level is to come hear the poet read her/his work. Another level is to take the poem home and then read it to yourself, quietly, silently. And then, at other times, for you to read it loud and then, whatever. And it doesn't really matter what that's all about. . . .

One of the first poems that I did where I actually said "to be sung," it was in *We a BaddDDD People.* It was **"a coltrane poem,"** but I never read it aloud. I would read it at home. . . . Well, to make a long story short, I was going to a gig at Brown University, and we had bad weather, and we were late coming into that place. And by the time I got there it was like nine thirty, ten o'clock, and the reading was supposed to be at eight, and people actually had stayed; they had gone to get something to eat and come back, and so I said, I'll have to give a good reading—these people have waited all this time. So I gave a long reading, about an hour and a half; I was really tired when I had finished. And one little hand went up in the audience and said (laughs): "Would you read the Coltrane poem?" Right? And I looked down, as if to say, "I'm tired; we've been circling this damn place for hours, and thinking we were going to run out of gas and have to go back to New York;" I mean it was really that kind of terrible kind of set. And then I said, "Well, since you've been such a good audience, I will."

So I read that poem. And I did the whole thing, from like banging on my thighs to singing and tapping my foot at the same time, and it was really interesting, the response. People actually started to stamp their feet and cheer. And, I don't know, wherever it was I was working—sometimes they send the things back to the universities when you're working, like "Professor So-and-So was here, and I thought you might want to hear"—and it seems that someone an editor or a

newspaperman was in the audience, and when I finished reading that poem which talks a lot about Rockefellers—

Yes—

and very graphic things—

Right.

that need to be done, he said that I was there instigating students, you know, to stretch people's necks, and (laughing) whatever whatever whatever. Because what they had done was they responded—not only response but a loud, standing up, going "Yeah" that kind of thing, and people actually were doing that, and I had never read that poem before.

When I started off I was so nervous, but the section that says, "are u sleepen / brotha john   brotha john," which is the coltrane section in there, and then when I actually got to the part where I literally had to do the sounds that he had done, I kept thinking, I was like looking down in advance at it saying, "How the hell are you going to do this?" And I didn't really remember it. But the crowd was with me. It's amazing what a crowd will do, also. They were just that friendly and just such a good crowd, that by the time I got to it, people were making sounds in the audience at the same time. It was just like kind of a very interesting set.

And so it just flowed, until the time I got to "are u sleepen / brotha john," to the tune of "My Favorite Things," I literally had tears in my eyes, because I remember seeing Coltrane for the last time, here in New York when he was playing with Alice [Coltrane], and the whole group had left the stage and left the two of them on stage when she was playing the piano and he was playing, and they were playing back "My Favorite Things," which became very apparent that each one was the other one's "favorite thing."

And did you sing part of that?

Yes, I did. I sang it, I sang. I did the actual "Woo oo oo da" on down to the singing part, and I think I haven't read that poem no more than maybe ten times in my life, because it is an exhausting set, to do it. Period. But I think the times might demand that a poem like that come back, because it says a lot about capitalism and whatever. . . .

Yes, I think it's an amazing poem, too. I know that you use slash marks in that, and in **We a BaddDDD People** *you use slash marks a lot. Were they sometimes just arbitrary, or did you think of them in terms of breath or—*

I thought of them sometimes in terms of emphasis, sometimes in stoppage—

Different reasons, different functions—

Um-hum.

Yes. O.k. Were there musical and dramatic influences in your childhood environment?

Oh, yes, yes. My father, you see, is an ex-musician, and today, after I had finished talking, and he had come to hear me talk, a woman had come up, and I introduced my father to her, Queen Mother Moore, and he was talking about people like musicians were always around us in the South, and even in the North.

I was raised on Art Tatum; the music that we heard—I would walk in someone's house and hear Art Tatum playing, and people would say, "Art Tatum—well, how did you know Art Tatum?" My father would let us hear Art Tatum and, you know, Count Basie, and he took us down to Fifty-Second Street to meet people like Billie Holiday and introduce us to them.

Oh—you met Billie Holiday—

Yes, Sid Catlett, people who used to work those clubs on Fifty-Second Street, you know, you would shake the hands, and whatever. He took us to the Paramount to meet Billy Eckstine, Count Basie, Art Tatum, Sid Catlett, the big drummer, people like that, but then at the same time, I remember in Alabama, when they had parties at night they would play songs by Billie and people like that, and I remember Bessie [Smith], but they wouldn't play them during the day, interestingly enough, but during the day the radio would go on to a Doris Day singing "Que Será Será" (laughs).

Did your father play an instrument?

Drums. He played drums. And so those are the people that we were involved with, and then, of course, living in New York, being involved with growing up on Symphony Sid, on many levels, which had a lot to do with a whole lot of jazz things, et cetera. And then later on, always beginning to turn on the jazz stations here in New York; there's always been that kind of influence. I am not here to say that I was always a person who fully understood all the ramifications. I always know what I like. I don't always know the reasons why, if you know what I mean. The reasons why you like certain things, but you do know you like them, you know what I'm saying?

That's why I'm saying I would go and listen to Coltrane and other people. But I'm not a mixer. It takes a lot for me to get up and go out some place. . . . So a lot of things I hear and enjoy—it does come via records that, you know, people get to me. One of the records I was stricken by, however, years ago, was Max Roach's and Abbey Lincoln's *Freedom Suite.* I will never forget hearing that for the first time, which for the first time made me hear some people talk about freedom on a record in such a—I guess it was almost a belligerent manner. And then there's a part that Abbey does on that record that is like a series of moans and groans. Have you ever heard *Freedom Suite?* It's a fantastic suite. I sat down and wrote from that piece because of what was happening there. . . .

[Despite Sanchez's deep concern with music and craft, it is their political meaning and usage that lie at the root of her art, determining her view of the contemporary scene.]

In 1971, you stated in a Black World *interview with Sebastian Clarke, "I think the prime thing with art, or being a writer, be it a playwright, a poet or even a musician, etc., is to really show people what is happening in this country. And then show them how they can change it." Does this substantially represent your position now?*

I think so. And by that I meant that at the same time you show what is wrong you show what can be or what could be. At the same time you show the horror, you show some beauty. You know, you always need that; you always need the movement of one and the other. You need the beauty, whatever that beauty is, if it's self, children, or ideas, whatever, to keep people moving. Otherwise, people will not move; if all they see is horror, they say, "The hell with it. I'm not going to involve myself anymore with any of this." So I think, yes, that's about true. I think it's important that artists not just involve themselves with themselves, and almost like an egotistical thing, I think we have, we do involve ourselves with ourselves. You can't help but do it on some levels. But, at the same time, I think we must always be aware of what is happening in the world, and I think we've got to make statements about what is happening in the world. . . .

You've spoken, in the Black Collegian, *of the 1970s as "ushering in an Age of Reason." How do you view the 1980s?*

I view the '80s as a very dangerous time for Black people, or anyone who intends to survive. I think it is a time of the humanitarians vs. the inhumanitarians. I think that is very important for us to understand. I think it is time for us to recognize that we are now in the midst of a struggle to save Black people, political white people, people who have actually seen what America is about, and recognize the fact that it must be changed; Third World people, all over the planet Earth who also must understand what this is about, that we're in a world struggle at this particular point to wrest control from the inhumanitarians who are in power at this point, and who could very well succeed in blowing up this whole damn world. You see, you can't keep on polluting the minds and bodies of one segment of your community or of your country, and then not expect for it also to seep among other segments of your community or country. . . .

. . . . .

Three years after *We a BaddDDD People,* Sanchez entered a new creative phase. Remarried and having moved to Massachusetts (Amherst College), her lyricism flourished. *Love Poems* abounds in haiku, several of which were written in China. There are poems of love and loss, of father/daughter (two sonnets), parent/child, and of man/woman relationships, mostly difficult, at times ecstatic. Marked by simplicity and delicacy, the poems move in clear images that swirl about the reader. As the author notes on the dust jacket:

> These poems are the sun stretching
> like red yellow butterflies across
> the sea,
> these poems are you and me running
> toward each other hands reaching
> out to hold the morning,
> These poems are yesterday, today
> evaporating with fireworks of touch
> These poems are love

I've Been a Woman: New and Selected Poems garners from four volumes of adult poetry; a fifth section is called "Haiku(s)/Tankas & Other Love Syllables"; the concluding sixth, "Generations." The sampling enables us to sort the strands of development.

. . . . .

[*Melhem:*] *Your early books of poetry are written mainly in free verse, with the influence of blues and jazz. Then, in* **Love Poems,** *there are haiku and sonnet forms; haiku, the sonnet, and African rhythms in your new work in* **I've Been a Woman.** *What is your attitude toward the study and use of conventional forms?*

I tell someone they have three lines, and sometimes seventeen syllables or thirty-one syllables. They've got to choose the right word to make a certain motion come across. That's word choice there; that is work. Period.
—Sonia Sanchez

If you notice, in **I've Been a Woman** I have haiku, tankas, and again, the movement towards what I call "African" ideas and feelings, and also the movement towards a Black ethic and a feminine one, too. If you really read the poem that I

did to Shirley Graham Du Bois and my mother, **"Kwa mama zetu waliotuzaa"** (for our mothers who gave us birth), that has a lot of feminine kinds of energy in there, woman kinds of things. Repeat the question; that's the tiredness, now. I still have that headache, so you'll have to forgive me, from that blow. [The poet was referring to her fall in a supermarket.]

All right. What is your attitude toward the study and use of conventional forms?

I teach poetry. And people are always stricken—sometimes, when they first come into my class, I teach form. I teach form on purpose. I do it in a way where we start off with something called "Free Association Exercises." I do that from taste and smell, whatever, to, in a sense, release them from a lot of things that they might have, et cetera. And then I also move into the haiku. Someone said to me, "Sonia, you shouldn't be teaching college students haiku or the tanka form, because they'll never give you any great haiku or great tankas." I say, "That might be so, but I use the haiku and tanka form for discipline and for what I call 'word choice.'" I tell someone they have three lines, and sometimes seventeen syllables or thirty-one syllables. They've got to choose the right word to make a certain motion come across. That's word choice there; that is work. Period. And so I make use of the haiku and tanka in terms of making them look up and recognize the fact that whether the poem is a haiku, a tanka, a sonnet, whatever, that you are involved with choosing words, and quite often the best word that you can find in a poem, and once you get into that habit of choosing the best word, or then you understand why, when you deal with free verse, the free verse also has discipline, and also the need and necessity for choosing the correct words for that, and not just go and sprawl.

When students first come to me they sprawl everything all over the page. What I do is I compress them. I start with something, the smallest form you can possibly do, the haiku, tanka, cinquain, whatever. Then, after I compress them for about three or four forms of haiku, tanka, cinquain, and perhaps their own syllabic verse, I say, "Here, you can do a free verse," and all of a sudden they look up and they say, "Oh, I don't know. I had difficulty doing a free verse." And I do that on purpose, because I said, "I know; then you really recognize what a free verse is all about. It is *not* free. It is not sprawling all over that damn page. There's a reason for having one word on one line, not just because you feel like it, but there is also—you must begin to hear that reason, and understand that reason, also." And that's how and why I do form. And then we do ballads and blues. . . .

Now the sonnet interested you in your earlier—

Well, yes, I had done sonnets. Bogan also gave us form—I

studied with her—which like used to bore the hell out of me. I had to write a villanelle with Bogan, and I teach the villanelle, also—(Laughter) and the first time my students— I gave them a villanelle, and they said, "Are you kidding?" But when they started dealing with the rhyme, an interesting thing happened. They learned that if you are going to repeat or if you are going to use rhyme, you really must, one, get a rhyming dictionary; two, you're not talking about "you" and "blue" for the rest of your life, the way some of us just hear easy rhymes; and third, you're talking about repetition. That means you've got to have strong lines. Any time you repeat something, you cannot have weak lines. It just teaches all that. . . .

Are you a reviser? Do you revise—

Oh, sure, sure. I write in notebooks, so I have all my poems that, as it moved towards a second, third, fourth, fifth revision, et cetera.

I make use of the haiku and tanka in terms of making [students] look up and recognize the fact that whether the poem is a haiku, a tanka, a sonnet, whatever, that you are involved with choosing words, and quite often the best word that you can find
                                                    —*Sonia Sanchez*

Do you wait for inspiration or do you write regularly?

I write regularly. If I waited for inspiration, I'd be finished. (Laughter.)

Right!

So I'm a regular writer of poetry—of not just poetry—of many things. I keep a diary, for one, so usually I write in the diary impressions and thoughts and ideas. And it's something that I always go back on at night, sometimes, some days, and just really remembering what I was doing in 1974 someplace.

. . . . .

Sanchez's finest poetry, perhaps her strongest artistic achievement until *homegirls & handgrenades,* is represented by *A Blues Book for Blue Black Magical Women.* Of this "mountain-top poem," George E. Kent writes that it

> possesses an extraordinary culmination of spiritual and poetic powers. It is in part an exhortation to move the rhythms of black life to a high peak through deep and deeper self-possession; in part, an

address to all, with specific emphasis upon women; in part, a spiritual autobiography.

Dedicated to the poet's father and to Elijah Muhammad "who has labored forty-two years to deliver us up from this western Babylon," the book carries an epigraph from the Quran. In five parts, it begins with **"Introduction (Queens of the Universe),"** addressed to Black women, urging them to "embrace / Blackness as a religion/husband," turning away from acquired, false Western values. The voice is that of the poet as Teacher, a guide at one with her audience yet standing a little apart in order to gain and share perspective.

The longest section, Part Two, "Past," details the poet's physical and spiritual growth, beginning with an address to the "earth mother," whose voice responds. Birth, adolescence, the move from South to North, painful childhood experiences with a stepmother, confusion of identity with white culture, and then the rejecting, "vomiting up the past" until

> i gave birth to myself,
> twice, in one hour.
> i became like M t,
> unalterable in my
> love of Black self and
> righteousness.
> and i heard the
> trumpets of a new age
> and i fell down
> upon the earth
> and became myself.

Part Three, "Present," lyrically affirms her position. She accepts the Nation of Islam as her faith. In Part Four, "Rebirth," the poet returns to an ancestral home, one imaginatively inspired by Sanchez's travels in the Caribbean (Bermuda, Jamaica, Guyana). She also traveled to the People's Republic of China before finishing the book. In "Rebirth," her plane trip becomes a metaphor for her spiritual odyssey, "roaming the cold climate of my mind where / winter and summer hold the same temperature of need." The poet states that she has destroyed her imperfection, has "become like a temple," made her form from the form of Allah, and is "trying to be worthy."

Part Five, "Future," begins with a Blakean kind of vision.

> When the sun spins and rises in the West
> when the stars lose their boundaries
> when ancient animals walk together
> when the oceans recede . . .

describes the "day of accounting" and continues with a series of five visions. **"We Are Muslim Women"** asserts the faith. **"in the beginning,"** the fourth and concluding subsection of Part Five, utters a hypnotic chant of continual creation: "in the beginning / there was no end." This is repeated twice, with the poet's note: "(to be sung)." **"let us begin again the / circle of Blackness"** introduces the closing lines:

> me and you
> me and you
> you and me
> me and you
> you and me
> me, me, meeeeEEE
> & have no beginning
> or endddDDDDD!

The emphatic spelling and capitalization are used judiciously in the book. Discussing the work, Sanchez revealed some interesting facts about its nature and composition.

. . . . .

[Sanchez:] I had visions during the time I was writing that poem, which was very interesting. And so people have asked me a great deal about what books, what was I reading during that time, and I always give some off-handed comment. But the point of that book is that during the time I was writing that book, I used to wake up in sweats and with visions. I pictured a lot of this. The first part was a very obvious part in terms of being almost—it was a section I had written in Pittsburgh when some women had asked me to write something for them, to keep them holding together. So that's how I did **"Queens of the Universe."** And then I sent it to *Black Scholar* and they published it, from Pittsburgh, about '68, I guess, around that time. So that seemed like a logical, introductory theme to the book.

But when I went into the second part, "Part Two," which is called "Past," I wanted to show people the movement of me in America, and what that meant in the South and in New York City, and during junior high, high school, college days, and the movement as a young Black woman, and then the movement as a woman, and then the ending of "Past" with the present, being a woman who was then involved with Africa and Africanisms as such, and reclaiming of the past. That's what that whole "Present" section is about. Then, after I went from "Present" I figured that that was the end of the book, because I had struggled through a lot of the writing of that book. It was just not very easy on many levels, you know, to do that whole book. I said, "That's it. Forty-two pages is enough for me." (Laughter) Then I started—you know how you write a book, and you know that you're not finished, although you say you're finished. Well, I knew this book was not finished, and I'd start waking up in the middle of the night, and I had these visions of destruction in this country. I also—I went to China; I was in Guyana, then into China. Guyana reminded me—the Caribbean re-

minded me a great deal of the Continent. Although I had never been to the Continent, I could see it. So the "Rebirth" section came next. Being that I had seen all those Black people there, and it was the first time being in America and not really being around a lot of Black folk was something else again. You don't live in Black towns or see Black people running things in America. So that's what "Rebirth" is all about. That motion. You know, "when i stepped off the plane i knew i was home," that's what I'm saying. You knew what that was about. That whole section, which is very much part of nature and water and birth; walking out on the sea.

One line I like a great deal—"i rowed out from boulevards / balancing my veins on sails"—it was moving from the cities, you know. Being there, amid the water, the water that was blue. The first time I saw water that was blue-green, as opposed to the Hudson River dirt. The ocean—I saw the ocean—seas—the way they should have looked before pollution hit them. . . .

[She mentioned Baraka's influence on **"in the beginning."**]

In *Black Mass,* Baraka discusses the Jacoub myth. But what had stricken me about it was the idea of inventing just for the sake of inventing, and what I did in **"in the beginning"** at that time—I wrote this after I saw that play, that's what it was. It had come from having seen something. Quite often I do that, I come in so full. And that's what that was about. The way they talked about being first man on the planet, you know, an original man on the planet, too. And then the idea of inventing or making people who would kill other people, because in the play *Black Mass,* the scientist invents, makes what he calls a beast, and the beast turns around and kills all the people that are there. And I took that whole Jacoub myth and put it into that poem. The reason why I remember that poem so well is because I knew I had done it before this book. It's a poem that I chant; it's not just read, it's a poem that is chanted altogether.

It's a wonderful poem. I was wondering whether there was any thought of Eliot's "East Coker": "In my beginning is my end."

No, I didn't—I hear what you're saying.

Or even in the beginning of the Gospel of John, "In the beginning was the Word."

Right. No, that came just on the level of—basically, I don't know where it came from. I walked into that house after I had seen that play, and literally it poured out almost just as it is. . . .

. . . . .

Although Sanchez has left the Nation of Islam, she sees the

period and her work in historical perspective. In her discussion she observed:

> At some point you had to see something that resembled you, or something that was positive, besides the very negative stuff. I don't consider any of that time a wasted time, especially not when one looks, views **Blues Book,** and you see the work you've done.

I've Been a Woman: New and Selected Poems presents work from *Homecoming, We a BaddDDD People, Love Poems, A Blues Book for Blue Black Magical Women,* "Haikus/Tankas & Other Love Syllables," and "Generations," its sixth and last section, which importantly celebrates a heroic heritage. **"A Poem for Sterling Brown,"** one of two tributes to him, reveres him as a "griot of fire / harnessing ancient warriors . . . griot of the wind . . ." with language and imagery suggestive of Africa and its music. There is a sonnet, **"Father and Daughter,"** in which the poet comes to terms with the relationship. And the final eulogy, the stirring **"Kwa mama zetu waliotuzaa,"** proclaims that Shirley Graham Du Bois "has died in china / and her death demands a capsizing of tides." By coincidence, the poet's stepmother died the same year.

Sanchez's closeness to her own children sparks her affinity for children's literature, an interest reminiscent of Gwendolyn Brooks. *It's a New Day (poems for young brothas and sistuhs),* published in 1971, is filled with inspirational poems like **"It's a New Day," "don't wanna be," "We're not learnen to be paper boys (for the young brothas who sell Muhammad Speaks),"** poems that are "teachen new songs to our children . . . cuz we be a new people in a new land / and it will be ours" (from epigraphs to Sets 2 and 4). *The Adventures of Fathead, Smallhead and Squarehead,* an illustrated story about three friends on a pilgrimage to Mecca, teaches that "Slow is not always dumb / and fast is not always smart . . . / Just as a lion is never dangerous without a head / so a people never progress without a leader." *A Sound Investment,* short stories for young readers, offers moral tales followed by discussion questions.

Sanchez is also drawn toward writing plays. While there is a strong dramatic tendency in her other work, it is interesting to observe her flexibility and to see how she began as response to a challenge. *The Bronx Is Next; The Death of Malcolm X; Sister Son/ji; Uh Huh, But How Do It Free Us;* and *Dirty Hearts* deal with the world as it is for Black people and seek to change it. The form of the one-acters is flexible, ranging from personal monologue (*Sister Son/ji*) to plays with a broad range of characters.

. . . . .

[*Melhem:*] *What is the special appeal for you of writing plays?*

I don't know—I started to write plays—I think I still have to tell you, because I had written a first play for *Black Fire.* Someone asked me, "If you write poetry, do you also write plays? And I said, "Sure."

(Laughs) And you'd never written one.

Never written a play, except I had done plays in college, when I was pledging a sorority, I did a takeoff on *1984.* It was a funny play that I had done, you know, I had done this play that was really with commercials and everything, et cetera, and also in teaching, I'd have students always do plays. It was always comedy, never serious plays. And so I said, "Sure, I do," and I literally sat down in my apartment again, one or two days, and wrote, *The Bronx Is Next,* without saying, "What should I write about?" And I wrote *The Bronx* and typed it up myself like this (gestures)—I'm a lousy typist—and sent that. Luckily enough, I had a carbon in there. Anyway, it got lost. Ed Bullins used it in *Tulane Drama Review,* the *Black Drama Review of Tulane Drama Review.* Then the next time I was in California and Ed called me and said, "Sonia, I'm doing a collection called *New Plays from Black Theatre,* and will you do a play?" I said, "Oh, sure, I'll do a play!" (laughing). So, I guess what happens is that the head begins to work on it. I had the twins, and then Ed called me one day and said, "Where is that play?" All the plays were in, except mine. So I said to Ed, "Oh, but you must understand, I just had these babies." He said, "Look, don't tell me your problems, I want the play!" (Laughter)

. . . . .

In both poetry and drama, Sanchez maintains she is trying to reach all kinds of audiences. She sees no real change in Black life since the sixties, and says, "I couldn't write *Homecoming* and *We a BaddDDD People* now." While the point of Black Pride has been made, it is time to progress from there toward concrete gains, by organizing well and powerfully through—and here she differs radically from Madhubuti—interracial coalitions. "Organize in terms of particular issues?" I asked her. "Always, always, always," she replied.

Sanchez offers this advice to beginning writers:

> Read and read and read and read everything you can get your hands on. One of the things Louise Bogan told me was, "Whatever you write, read aloud. Your ear will be the best friend you will ever have." And join a workshop at some point when you really feel

you want to work more and/or apprentice yourself to a poet or writer and study with her or him.

Only near the conclusion of the Wednesday evening interview, which followed a heavy schedule of Conference activities, did Sanchez refer to her fall in a supermarket the previous Sunday. The accident had left her with an almost constant headache, one she had endured without complaint throughout the interview. Grace and good humor bespoke not only her professionalism but also her strict, personal discipline, put to the service of social commitment. For such writers, categorical imperatives are understood; morality is life. And life is common purposes, goals that far exceed the boundaries of self-expression. The Lucretia Mott Award Sanchez received in 1984 attests to her humanity as much as to her distinguished writing.

In a recent telephone conversation, I discussed with the poet her latest book, *homegirls & handgrenades.* "I enjoyed doing that book because I was able to celebrate some homegirls and homeboys, like '**Bubba**' and '**Norma,**' who needed to be celebrated but never came through the Harlems of the world."

The fiction and poetry of *homegirls & handgrenades*—its *I* becoming—*eye*—fully commands the poet's range of private and public concerns. Back cover tributes by Margaret Walker and Amiri Baraka are joined by Andrew Salkey, who commends "her poetry as songs of difficult truth and harsh beauty." Lyricism, the gift of her love poetry, moves the first two sections, "The Power of Love" and "Blues is Bullets"; animates the humanitarian poems of "Beyond the Fallout"; and splashes the public poems of "Grenades Are Not Free."

In stories like **"Just Don't Never Give Up on Love,"** relating an encounter with an old woman on a park bench, and **"Bluebirdbluebirdthrumywindow,"** about a chance encounter with a homeless Black woman ("This beached black whale.") in a Pennsylvania Station restroom; **"Bubba"** and **"Norma,"** bright friends from her childhood and school, who stayed behind in Harlem among the rubble of their thwarted dreams, Sanchez reveals the compassionate immediacy with which she relates to the lost ones of earth, and her felt responsibility as an artist to voice their inarticulate despair.

Richness of that voice culminates in public poems of the last section. As she writes to Ezekiel Mphahlele, the exile returning to South Africa after twenty years; addresses Dr. Martin Luther King, Margaret Walker, Jesse Jackson; reflects on the June 12, 1983 March for Disarmament; and exhorts Third World working-class people in **"MIA's (missing in action and other atlantas)";** visionary hopefulness transforms her anger and pain into a call for action. **"MIA's,"** the concluding poem, interspersed with Spanish and Zulu,

explodes its real and surreal images to light a landscape of suffering from Atlanta to Johannesburg, South Africa. It invites:

> plant yourself in the eyes of the
> children who have died carving out their
> own childhood.
> plant yourself in the dreams of the people
> scattered by morning bullets.

Sanchez's **"Haiku,"** written from Peking to her children, epitomizes the dedication of this extraordinary poet.

> let me wear the day
> well so when it reaches you
> you will enjoy it.

James Robert Saunders (essay date Spring 1988)

SOURCE: "Sonia Sanchez's *Homegirls and Handgrenades:* Recalling Toomer's *Cane,*" in *MELUS,* Vol. 15, No. 1, Spring, 1988, pp. 73-82.

[*In the following essay, Saunders analyzes the techniques Sanchez employed in* Homegirls and Handgrenades *which are reminiscent of those Jean Toomer used in* Cane.]

It is appropriate when analyzing a work such as *Homegirls and Handgrenades* to wonder about what might have been the motivation for its subject matter and form. It might be declared by some that this is just another in a long line of Sonia Sanchez's books of poems. Her very first volume, *Homecoming,* was an impressive display of staggered-lined poems with word-splitting diagonals. *We a BaddDDD People* and *It's a New Day* contained even more of the same stylistic devices. Part of Sanchez's early effort was to experiment with words in verse to create a new perspective on how blacks should perceive themselves within the context of a nation struggling to admit them into the fold of social equality. Although that task remains incomplete, one can nevertheless sense a development on the part of the poet as she advances her work to include the mystical *A Blues Book for Blue Black Magical Women* as well as *Love Poems* where there can be seen an attempt to reconcile all the various aspects of black culture for the benefit of progress. *I've Been a Woman* and *Under a Soprano Sky* are further examples of how the author has examined, in particular, the plight of black women as they strive toward freedom in a world not always conducive to that undertaking.

Nonetheless, it is in *Homegirls* where Sanchez delivers what Henry Louis Gates has characterized as "the revising text

... written in the language of the tradition, employing its tropes, its rhetorical strategies, and its ostensible subject matter, the so-called Black Experience." Gates further explains how many black writers have either consciously or subconsciously "signified" on previous authors' works so as to explore their own impressions while yet remaining faithful to certain literary strategies used by their predecessors. The former slave, Olaudah Equiano, wrote his narrative based to a large extent on what a previous slave narrator, James Gronniosaw, did. Ralph Ellison's *Invisible Man* is largely a response to the literary work of Richard Wright. And recently, Alice Walker has drawn on the basic themes and dialect style of Zora Neale Hurston to render her prize-winning novel, *The Color Purple.* This tradition of signifying on what other writers have done is a deep-rooted feature of black writing that has as its origin the culture of blacks as a whole. It is, interestingly enough, the mark of black culture in its most creative posture, that of being able to play upon what is available, in terms of form and substance, and convert it into something new and unique.

Such is the achievement of Sanchez who, in *Homegirls,* has rendered a marvelous collage of thirty-two short stories, poems, letters, and sketches that often ring loudly with the truth of an autobiographical fervor. In one short story, entitled **"Norma,"** the narrator describes:

> I was rushing to the library. The library had become my refuge during the Summer of '55. As I turned the corner of 145th Street, I heard her hello. Her voice was like stale music in barrooms. There she stood. Norma. Eyelids heavy. Woman of four children, with tracks running on her legs and arms.
>
> "How you be doing Norma? You're looking good, girl."
>
> "I'm making it Sonia. You really do look good, girl. Heard you went to Hunter College."

We observe the author as also a personality in the literary work. Both the autobiographical character, Sonia, and the author, Sanchez, attended Hunter College in New York, and to a large extent the writer is engaged in self-analysis even as she evaluates Norma. Similarly, Jean Toomer's *Cane* is as much a study of the author as it is the presentation of various characters and scenes aimed at depicting black life. Moreover, in *Homegirls,* Sanchez has exploited the Toomer technique of using narration, dialogue, and poetry to render her own portrayals most efficiently.

It is of great significance that the two poems Sanchez has positioned just before **"Norma"** are **"Poem Written After Reading Wright's 'American Hunger'"** and **"Blues,"** for they provide an effective introduction to a major theme in

the following vignette that shows Sonia's friend, Norma, as the quintessential victim, once a mathematical genius while in high school, now the mother "of four children, with tracks running on her legs and arms." Both of the poems are symbolic of how relationships between black men and black women have deteriorated to a level of immorality that corresponds with society's reaction to the black masses in general. In the poem about Wright, Sanchez condemns insensitivity on the part of that great black author who could not understand why a poverty-stricken girl from Chicago's South Side would want to go see a circus. Noting, in the second part of his original autobiography, how insurance agents often accepted sex in exchange for the otherwise required ten-cent premium, he callously expressed, "I stared at her and wondered just what a life like hers meant in the scheme of things, and I came to the conclusion that it meant absolutely nothing." Sanchez's response is worth repeating in its entirety:

> such a simple desire
> wanting to go to the circus
> wanting to see the animals
> orange with laughter.
> such a simple need
> amid yo/easy desire
> to ride her
> while clowns waited offstage
> and children tugged at her young legs.
>
> did you tell her man that we're
> all acrobats tumbling out of
> our separate arenas?
> you. peeling her
> skin while dreams turned
> somersaults in her eyes.
>
> such a simple woman
> illiterate with juices
> in a city where hunger
> is passed around for seconds.

Sanchez calls the late author to task, asking why he declined to tell that sex partner how we are all "acrobats," that absurdity is one of life's conditions, and that the wish to see a circus has just as much meaning as his need for sexual diversion. Instead of possessing the sort of forthrightness one might imagine Sanchez admiring, Wright took on a persona that is shared by many who would similarly manipulate a woman for selfish advantage.

One sees, in **"Blues,"** the private Sanchez again expanding her perspective to such an extent that it encompasses many black women. The third stanza conveys the poem's main message:

what do you do when you need
a man so much it hurt?
i say where do you go when you
need a man so much it hurt?
you make it down to the corner
and start digging in the dirt.

By "digging in the dirt" that narrator specifically means that her loneliness has driven her into the arms of a twenty-year-old man-child who now substitutes for the maturity she had expected from a former lover. This act of desperation is reflected in the final lines:

you see what my needing you
has done gone and made me try.

Unfortunately, the loneliness remains and though the narrator of **"Blues"** fares better than what we could ever hope for Norma, there is the same emptiness that results from failed relationships.

An important issue in the construction of **Homegirls** must have been, for Sanchez, one of determining the best means to conduct her search for meaning in the midst of such social chaos. Gates notes, "in general, black authors do not admit to a line of literary descent within their own literary tradition." Much of that phenomenon is a consequence of certain kinds of jealousies that have occurred within the black literary community due to a tendency among quite a few publishers to be satisfied with one great black writer at a time. How many black authors can afford to give too much acknowledgment in light of such a circumstance? Notwithstanding, Sanchez, in a 1983 interview, has offered insight: "You don't come out of a vacuum. We're not like Topsy; we don't just grow." Further analyzing what she perceived to be a definite connection between earlier black writers and those of a later time, she added, "Each generation builds on a higher level. They were supposed to produce us in spite of themselves."

Such remarks become even more fitting as we consider the circumstances of Toomer who, in the words of Darwin Turner, used *Cane* as "perhaps merely an interlude in his search for understanding." Toomer alternatively passed for black and white depending on where he was and what he was trying to accomplish at the time. Turner further informs us that Toomer, in 1923, met Georges Gurdjieff, a spiritual leader who "professed to have the ability to help people fuse their fragmented selves into a new and perfect whole—a harmony of mind, body, and soul—through a system of mental and physical exercise emphasizing introspection, meditation, concentration, discipline, and self-liberation." Toomer himself became a disciple, adhering for ten years to strictures of the Gurdjieffian cult. Clearly, as Turner has suggested, the search was on for Toomer far into his post-*Cane* years.

Experiments with Jungian psychology, psychoanalysis, and Eastern mysticism would follow virtually up until the time of his death in 1967.

Still, regardless of Toomer's lengthy introspection, in the final analysis we are left with *Cane* as a primary source for investigating the author's literary purpose. Consisting of twenty-nine short stories, poems, and sketches, this work is largely the result of a brief visit Toomer made to Sparta, Georgia, in 1921, to fill in as the head of an industrial and agricultural school for blacks whose principal had left temporarily on a fund-raising drive. Just as Sanchez would do sixty-one years later in **Homegirls,** Toomer supplied *Cane* with an autobiographical essence that varies from section to section. Within the context of his first three stories, he assumes the pose of an omniscient narrator who has in some ambiguous sense been touched by the circumstances of Karintha, Becky, and Carma. However, once we get to Fern's story, the author places himself as a character among the many other men who have been filled with uncontrollable desire. Toomer writes:

I first saw her on her porch. I was passing with a fellow whose crusty numbness (I was from the North and suspected of being prejudiced and stuck-up) was melting as he found me warm. I asked him who she was. "That's Fern," was all that I could get from him. Some folks already thought that I was given to nosing around; I let it go at that, so far as questions were concerned. But at first sight of her I felt as if I heard a Jewish cantor sing. As if his singing rose above the unheard chorus of a folk-song. And I felt bound to her. I too had my dreams: something I would do for her.

But no matter how much men do for Fern, she is ultimately unfulfilled, and realizing this, men "leave her, baffled and ashamed, yet vowing to themselves that some day they would do some fine thing for her: send her candy every week and not let her know whom it came from, watch out for her wedding-day and give her a magnificent something with no name on it, buy a house and deed it to her." The tragedy comes with the lack of realization on the parts of those men that material possessions and sexual relations add little to the development of the unique Fern who, like many of the other women in *Cane,* had been cast adrift in a world where women in general had yet to be thought of as individualistic human beings. They had too far to go before the notion of equality would be considered their birthright.

It can easily be said that Toomer was a man before his time as he considered the "dilemma" of women's equality in the 1920s. However, *Cane* leaves us with no happy ending. As we move from the South to settings in the North and then back to the South, in the three basic parts of this so-called novel, we are made to be constantly aware of at least one thing, and this is that men and women, particularly black men and black women, have fallen prey to society's limitations and allowed a chasm to develop, preventing the very understanding that Toomer had sought with such diligence. Taking on the forms of "Professor" Kabnis and the "queer feller," Lewis, in the final section of *Cane,* Toomer makes one more attempt at ascertaining the proper direction, but both alter egos succumb to the urge to partake of "corn licker, love th girls, an listen t th old man mumblin sin," that old man being the gray-haired Father John who can barely fend for himself in this underground world where both men and women fumble on in the darkness.

Comparing *Cane* to such works as W. E. B. Du Bois' *The Souls of Black Folk* and James Weldon Johnson's *The Autobiography of an Ex-Coloured Man,* Alan Golding maintains that "*Cane* advanced on these works by pursuing such modernist prose techniques as the breakdown of continuous narrative into juxtaposed fragments, an emphasis on psychological over narrative realism, snatches of plot more symbolic than literal, and the elevation of governing metaphors to almost mythic status." Furthermore, Golding notes that quite a few of the parts making up *Cane* were originally published as separate pieces, specifically in such periodicals as *Crisis, Broom, Double Dealer, Liberator,* and *The Little Review.* Similarly, various items that went into the making of **Homegirls** had already been published in *Callaloo, Essence, The American Poetry Review,* and *Confirmation.* Still, the important point to remember when analyzing *Cane* and **Homegirls** is that Toomer and Sanchez, in their separate literary arenas, did finally involve themselves in the exercise of accumulating those various parts, among others, in the effort to create a single product. Commenting on how *Cane's* form puzzles readers, Turner informs, "Some have identified it as a novel—perhaps because it has a thematic and structural unity, or because it faintly resembles Sherwood Anderson's *Winesburg, Ohio,* or because a few literary critics—for reasons of their own—have labeled it a novel, or merely because they have not known what else to call it." Golding defines *Cane* as a modernist work, perhaps due as much to the era in which it was produced as anything else. Nevertheless, it can just as easily be called postmodern as it conducts searches for individuality, employs language to reflect a certain absurdity, and reflects a world that might already have extinguished the means to resolve some of our crucial issues.

In *Cane's* final section, Kabnis sulks and contemplates "these clammy floors . . . just like th place they used t stow away th wornout, no-count niggers in th days of slavery . . . that was long ago; not so long ago . . . no windows." From visions of American slavery and its consequences, in *Cane,* we move to a different and yet similar type of slavery in South Africa elaborated upon by Sanchez in her final poem,

"MIA's," where she assumes the voice of an oppressor, reporting:

> i regret to announce that stephen
> biko is dead. he has refused
> food since sept. 5th. we did
> all we could for the man.
> he has hanged himself while sleeping
> we did all we could for him.
> he fell while answering our questions
> we did all we could for him.
> he drowned while drinking his supper
> we did all we could for the man.
> he fell
>   hanged himself   starved
> drowned himself

There are key differences, in terms of speaker and context, between what Toomer has presented and Sanchez's postmodern depiction, but a basic thrust remains the same. There is an element of self-hatred, explicit in "Kabnis" and implied in **"MIA's,"** that is based on assumptions about how blacks should react to their condition, symbolized by the prison without windows in Kabnis' mind and the bars seen by Biko from day to day.

Social restrictions are at the heart of both *Cane* and **Homegirls,** and just as it cannot simply be stated that *Cane* is a novel, it should not be concluded that **Homegirls** is just another of Sanchez's volumes of poems. What both writers sought was an adequate means to investigate a most intricate situation, and the literary collages exemplified in those two works are more indicative of what is taking place in black society than has ever been accomplished through any one genre. Black life in America involves such a high degree of complexity that the multiple genres—the sketches, short stories, and poems in each book—are crucial to the rendering of a proper perspective. And even in the stories the poetic aspect is so powerful that what is rendered is more than just prose. At the very beginning of *Cane* we see this in "Karintha carrying beauty, perfect as dusk when the sun goes down." While that phraseology is somewhat vague it does convey the almost mystical beauty this girl has possessed since her early youth. Moreover it provides reinforcement for the actual poem that also serves as a prologue:

> Her skin is like dusk on the eastern horizon,
> O cant you see it, O cant you see it,
> Her skin is like dusk on the eastern horizon
> . . . When the sun goes down.

Three more times in the tale of Karintha we are provided with poetic refrains, and though we might still wonder what Karintha looks like exactly, we do feel the intensity of what it was that attracted men while she was yet a child.

We will be reminded here of what Sanchez has done with her **"Norma"** who:

> would sometimes shake off her friends and sit down with the "pip-squeaks" and talk about the South. She was from Mississippi. She ordained us all with her red clay Mississippi talk. Her voice thawed us out from the merciless cold studding the hallways. Most of the time though, she laughed only with her teeth.

It was apropos for Toomer to have made Karintha possessed with great beauty. During the time he was writing *Cane,* being pretty was often all that a black girl could hope for; it at least allowed for some options within the realm of black womanhood. Norma, on the other hand, has in her early development become a mathematical whiz. She "pirouetted problem after problem on the blackboard." She could, as Sanchez poeticizes, "shake off" friends, "thaw . . . out" classmates; she "ordained" them with her southern talk. Just as was the case with Karintha, Norma has awesome power only to have it depleted far before her prime.

The movement north that is evidenced in both *Cane* and *Homegirls* does little to diminish the suffering that continues to be experienced by blacks whose lives are consumed in a vicious pattern. Even in the tragic tale of "Bona and Paul," with its Chicago setting, Toomer directs us back toward the South with language that evokes nature. The source of the problem, with regard to what might have been a successful interracial union, can be traced to another place in time as:

> Paul follows the sun, over the stock-yards where a fresh stench is just arising, across wheat lands that are still waving above their stubble, into the sun. Paul follows the sun to a pine-matted hillock in Georgia. He sees the slanting roofs of gray unpainted cabins tinted lavender. A Negress chants a lullaby beneath the mate-eyes of a southern planter. Her breasts are ample for the suckling of a song. She weans it, and sends it, curiously weaving, among lush melodies of cane and corn.

We sense there is a power to be attained through Paul's connection with the sun; it allows him to transcend time and space. Yet, what he discovers among those "slanting roofs of gray unpainted cabins" is something over which he has no control even as it causes pain.

In Sanchez's story of **"Bubba"** it is the moon that enables him to transcend time and space. He ponders:

> "When I was real small . . . I used to think that the moon belonged to me, that it came out only for me,

that it followed me everywhere I went. And I used to, when it got dark there in North Carolina, I used to run around to the backyard and wait for the moon to appear.

Transported from Harlem to the southern locale where he formerly lived, Bubba reminisces "about seeing behind trees and walking over seas with flowers growing out of my head." Again we are made privy to the potential for power in nature. But as Bubba's father, also a feature of that faraway past, hollers, "Stop that foolishness boy," we are snapped back to reality.

Golding had pointed to the use of "juxtaposed fragments" as an innovative prose technique in *Cane,* and the same writing strategy is employed by Sanchez. Moreover the use of poetic prose continues as a device as in *Cane* we move to Esther who, realizing that she and the well-traveled Barlo can never have a life together, feels that there "is no air, no street, and the town has completely disappeared" although many of the townsfolk are there, jeering at what was her failed attempt. The psychological absence of air, the street, and the town best conveys Esther's alienation.

Likewise, Sanchez is ever the poet, even while writing prose. Hoping, in **"After Saturday Night Comes Sunday,"** that she and her well-traveled man can attain a satisfactory union, Sandy awakens one morning to find:

> The bed wuz empty. She ran down the stairs and turned on the lights. He was gone. She saw her purse on the couch. Her wallet wuz empty. Nothing was left. She opened the door and went out on the porch, and she remembered the lights were on and that she wuz naked. But she stood fo a moment looking out at the flat/Indianapolis/street and she stood and let the late/nite/air touch her body and she went inside.

The narrator's assertion that "nothing was left" is reminiscent of Toomer's Esther for whom there is no air or street or town. Esther "wheels around and walks stiffly to the stairs"; Sandy similarly goes inside. The going inside is symbolic in both situations, for it signifies not only a return inside from the outdoors but also a going back into the self for solace in spite of the gloom.

It is in the final section of *Cane,* the "Kabnis" segment, that Toomer makes his most ardent attempt to investigate the deepest recesses of his own psyche as he also seeks to reconcile tragedies that have befallen black Americans. What we are left with, however, are the babblings of a false prophet, Father John, who can offer very little in the way of direction. At the end of *Homegirls,* Sanchez likewise can offer no final solution. But in broadening the scope of concern to include places such as South Africa and El Salvador, we can see how the dilemma goes straight to the core of all human existence. Unchecked power can wreak tortuous consequences, whether in the midst of just two individuals or as used to subjugate an entire people. Sanchez's advice is for the masses to take a long hard look at their lives and then undertake the challenge to generate change.

Kamili Anderson (review date Winter 1989)

SOURCE: "Giving Our Souls Ears," in *Belles Lettres,* Vol. 4, No. 2, Winter, 1989, p. 14.

[*In the following review, Anderson asserts that "the poems in [*Sanchez's* Under a Soprano Sky] are tempered and configured to scorching extremes, they are, simultaneously, her most introspective and intricate."*]

The name Sonia Sanchez may be the most undeservedly underspoken of contemporary women poets in America. Relative to her merits as both prolific poet (she has authored thirteen books) and social activist, widespread critical acknowledgment of Sanchez's talents has been remiss. No doubt this is a result of the boldly rhetorical nature of her work and her involvement with so-called "radical" Black literary and cultural factions. But her poetry, for its precision and insightfulness, warrants far broader recognition, no matter how belated.

Sanchez was a leading spokessister for the women's side of things in the defiant Black Arts literary upsweep of the 1960s and 1970s. It was often she who, even as a female follower of the Honorable Elijah Muhammed and the Nation of Islam, was the strongest feminist poetic voice in a cultural movement with strong sexist leanings. Noted for her dramatic and moving articulations of her own work, Sanchez now (she is in her fifties) presents an intriguing study in juxtapositioned extremes. Her poetry has burned consistently with a fierce but expertly controlled intensity. With each collection, that fire has burned hotter and cleaner.

Her latest and finest work, **Under a Soprano Sky,** is hot enough to melt rock, and it comes hard on the trail blazed by her previous book, **Homegirls & Hand Grenades.** Although the poems in this collection are tempered and configured to scorching extremes, they are, simultaneously, her most introspective and intricate. They deal with age, AIDS, alienation awareness, Africa, and all of us, men and women.

Sanchez has a penchant for enlisting words to imagery. She can mesmerize with scenarios that require readers to transfuse all of their senses, so much so that the ability to dis-

cern whether one is reading with the soul or with the eyes, or listening with the heart or the ears, is lost.

This is deep, deep stuff that conjures and commingles the senses in a potpourri of images. "i shall spread out my veins," she writes, "and beat the dust into noise." "i hear the wind of graves moving the sky"; "hands breathing"; "my eyes put on more flesh" and "i hear the bricks pacing my window" are more of the same. "Under a soprano sky / a woman sings / lovely as chandeliers," sings the refrain from her title poem. Lovely and fiercely, she should add.

Under a Soprano Sky offers a full dose of a mature woman-poet rising to the height of her powers, a woman very much like the older Black women Sanchez writes respectfully of in **"Dear Mama"**: "women rooted in themselves, raising themselves in dark America, discharging their pain without ever stopping." This collection poses the "full moon of sonia/ shining down on ya" to anyone who might take her or her sisters' visions lightly. With it comes the warning: "you gon known you been touched by me / this time."

Few poets write with more succinctness or intensity. Sanchez's expansive poems can incorporate guttural sounds insistent upon vocal rendition or be terse, taut haikus. Haikus such as those **"for domestic workers in the african diaspora,"** "i works hard but treated / bad man. i'se telling you de / truth i full of it." and **"for a black prostitute,"** "redlips open wide / like a wound winding down on / the city / clotting." provide searing examples.

From **"fragment 3"** echoes the call:

> come all you late twenty
> year olds you young thirties
> and forties and fifties.
> O lacquered revolutionists!
> all you followers of vowelled
> ghosts painted on neon signs.
> O noise of red bones cascading dreams.
>
> come to conscripted black
> mounted on a cell of revelation
> come and salute death
> while the rust of tombs
> murmur old sonnets
> and my grave sinks with
> the pleasure of insects

who wear no diadem.

Sonia Sanchez is a poet not to be disavowed further. Her work is high reality transformed into high rhetoric, transformed into high art. *Under a Soprano Sky* and the corpus of her work deserves a thorough reading that is worthy of her substantial and finely honed literary talents.

Joanne Veal Gabbin (essay date 1990)

SOURCE: "The Southern Imagination of Sonia Sanchez," in *Southern Women Writers: The New Generation,* edited by Tonette Bond Inge, The University of Alabama Press, 1990, pp. 180-202.

[*In the following essay, Garbin discusses the themes of Sanchez's works in terms of what she calls "Sanchez's strong Southern imagination, one that was born in the impressionable times of her youth in Alabama, where the tensions of struggle were fed with mama's milk."*]

> Death is a five o'clock door forever changing time. And wars end. Sometimes too late. I am here. Still in Mississippi. Near the graves of my past. We are at peace . . . I have my sweet/astringent memories because we dared to pick up the day and shake its tail until it became evening. A time for us. Blackness, Black people. Anybody can grab the day and make it stop. Can you my friends? Or maybe it's better if I ask:
>
> Will you?

The woman who utters this challenge at the end of Sonia Sanchez's play *Sister Son/ji* has the gift of second sight: she is a visionary, a prophet, a revealer of truths. She has touched love, births, deaths, danger, tumult, upheaval, and change and has distilled from these experiences "sweet/astringent memories." Willing to pick up the day and "shake its tail until it became evening," she helped to bring into being an order that transformed time and defied death itself.

In many ways, *Sister Son/ji* becomes a metaphor for the poet herself and the visionary quality and sense of the past that pervade much of her poetry. Like *Sister Son/ji* Sonia Sanchez has been a singer during turbulent times, a translator of the needs and dreams of black people. Sanchez has written to challenge black people—all people—to change the world, "to make people understand . . . that we are here to perpetuate humanity, to figure out what it means to be a human being," "to show what is wrong with the way that we are living and what is wrong with this country . . . to cor-

rect misinterpretation and bring love, understanding, and information to those who need it." If this all sounds idealistic, it is. For Sanchez matured as a writer in an era in which ideas took on an elasticity heretofore unheard of. It was a time when a visionary president challenged the nation to land a man on the moon before the end of the decade; when a black power movement, led by such political thinkers as Malcolm X, Stokely Carmichael, H. Rap Brown, Angela Davis, Huey P. Newton, and Elijah Muhammad, ushered in a change in race relations in America; when 250,000 people, culminating several difficult years of boycotts, sit-ins, voter registration drives, marches, and riots, marched on Washington to make America accountable to black and poor people. It was a time when Americans protested an undeclared war in Vietnam, and the country mourned and immortalized its fallen heroes: John F. Kennedy, Robert Kennedy, and Martin Luther King, Jr. This era shaped the mettle of the poet, and like the Mississippi woman, Sanchez has become an armed prophet whose voice is at once a prod and a sword.

In her eight volumes of poetry, which appeared between 1969 and 1987, Sanchez's voice is sometimes abrasive but never as profane as the conditions she knows must be eradicated; her tone ranges from gentle to derisive, yet the message is one of redeeming realism. Also undergirding her poetic expression is a deep concern for heritage; for the sovereignty of time with all its ramifications of birth, change, rebirth, and death; for the impress of the past and memories; and for nurture, nature, and God. Moreover, these themes reveal Sanchez's strong Southern imagination, one that was born in the impressionable times of her youth in Alabama, where the tensions of struggle were fed with mama's milk.

Homecoming, Sanchez's first book of poems, is her pledge of allegiance to blackness, to black love, to black heroes, and to her own realization as a woman, an artist, and a revolutionary. The language and the typography are experimental; they are aberrations of standard middle-class Americanese and traditional Western literary forms. As such, they reflect her view of American society, which perceives blacks as aberrations and exploits them through commercialism, drugs, brutality, and institutionalized racism. In this book and the poetry that follows, the vernacular and the forms are clear indications of her fierce determination to redefine her art and rail against Western aesthetics. *Homecoming* also introduces us to a poet who is saturated with the sound and sense of black speech and black music, learned at the knees of Birmingham women discovering themselves full voiced and full spirited. The rhythm and color of black speech—the rapping, reeling, explosive syllables—are her domain, for she is steeped in the tradition of linguistic virtuosity that Stephen Henderson talks about in *Understanding the New Black Poetry.* Black music, especially the jazz sounds of John

Coltrane, Ornette Coleman, and Pharoah Sanders, pulse, riff, and slide through her poetry.

Sanchez's voice is sometimes abrasive but never as profane as the conditions she knows must be eradicated; her tone ranges from gentle to derisive, yet the message is one of redeeming realism.
—*Joanne Veal Gabbin*

In her second volume, *We a BadddDDD People,* Sanchez is wielding a survival sword that rips away the enemy's disguise and shears through the facade of black ignorance and reactionism. Arranged in three groups, "Survival Poems," "Love/Songs/Chants," and "TCB/EN Poems," the poems extend the attack begun in *Homecoming* and tell black people how to survive in a country of death traps (drugs, suicide, sexual exploitation, psychological slaughter via the mass media) and televised assassination. Her message, however, is not one of unrelieved gloom, for it is rooted in optimism and faith: "know and love yourself." Like Sterling A. Brown's "Strong Men" and Margaret Walker's "For My People," **"We A BadddDDD People,"** the title poem of the volume, is a praise song that celebrates black love, talent, courage, and continuity. The poems appear rooted in a courage learned early from aunts who spit in the face of Southern racism and sisters who refused to be abused by white men or black men. In this volume, Sanchez reveals her unmistakable signature, the singing/chanting voice. Inflections, idiom, intonations—skillfully represented by slashes, capitalization (or the lack of it), and radical and rhythmic spelling—emphasize her link with the community and her role as ritual singer.

In *It's a New Day,* a collection of poems "for young brothas and sistuhs," Sanchez nurtures young minds, minds that must know their beauty and worth if the nation is to be truly free. Her belief in the seed-force of the young led her to write the children's story *The Adventures of Small Head, Square Head and Fat Head.*

In 1973, her fourth volume, *Love Poems,* appeared. Haki Madhubuti calls this "a book of laughter and hurt, smiles and missed moments." The poems are collages of the images, sounds, aromas, and textures of woman-love. With the clarity and precision of Japanese ink sketches, Sanchez skillfully uses the haiku to evoke emotion:

> did ya ever cry
> Black man, did ya ever cry
> til you knocked all over?

Using the haiku, the ballad, and other traditional forms that

advance her preference for tightness, brevity, and gemlike intensity, she fingers the raw edges of a woman's hurt and betrayal:

> When he came home
> from her
> he poured me on
> the bed and slid
> into me like glass.
> And there was
> the sound of splinters.

The poet also celebrates the magic that love has to transform and transcend:

> i gather up
> each sound
> you left behind
> and stretch them
> on our bed.
>   each nite
> i breathe you
> and become high . . .

A Blues Book for Blue Black Magical Women is a dramatic departure from the poetry of earlier volumes. The scope here is large and sweeping. The language is no longer the raw vernacular of *Homecoming,* though, as in *We A BadddDDD People,* it is possessed by the rhythms of the chants and rituals. At its most prosaic, it is laden with the doctrine of the Nation of Islam and ideologically correct images. At its best, it is intimate, luminous, and apocalyptic. Tucked inside *A Blues Book* is a striking spiritual odyssey that reveals the poet's growing awareness of the psychological and spiritual features of her face.

In 1978, Sanchez culled some of her best poetry from earlier volumes in *I've Been a Woman: New and Selected Poems.* To these she adds a collection of haiku and tankas that is dominated by the theme of love: the sensual love of a man, the love of old people and young, the love for a father and spiritual mothers. She brings to this theme a style that is replete with irony, wit, and understatement. And in most of her poetry, her feelings are intensified and her symbols, those of nurturing, birth, growth, freedom, civilization, are deeply feminine. Here, as Margaret Walker Alexander states, is poetry of "consistently high artistry that reflects her womanliness—her passion, power, perfume, and prescience."

In *homegirls & handgrenades,* Sanchez shows the further deepening of the poet's consciousness, for it is a sterling example of her going inside herself, inside the past, to pull out of her residual memory deeply personal experience. From the past, she draws images that explode the autobiographical into universal truths. The predominant genre in this volume is the sketch, much like those that stud Jean Toomer's *Cane.* Bubba, "the black panther of Harlem," lost in a sea of drugs and unfulfilled dreams; Norma, black genius that lay unmined; or the old "bamboo-creased" woman in **"Just Don't Never Give Up on Love"** all live again and vividly show Sanchez distilling "sweet/astringent memories" from her own experience.

Distinguishing much of her poetry is a prophetic voice that brings the weight of her experience to articulating the significant truths about liberation and love, self-actualization and being, spiritual growth and continuity, heroes, and the cycles of life. Her vision is original because it is both new (a fresh rearrangement of knowledge) and faithful to the "origins" of its inspiration. Therefore, it is not surprising that in her most recent volume of poetry, **Under a Soprano Sky,** the mature voice of the poet is giving expression to the sources of her spiritual strength, establishing and reestablishing connections that recognize the family-hood of man/womankind, and singing, as another Lady did, of society's strange fruit sacrificed on the altars of political megalomania, economic greed, and social misunderstanding.

Throughout her poetry, which will be the focus of this study, Sanchez demonstrates the complexity of her Southern imagination. Though she spent a relatively short period of her life in the South, her way of looking at the world is generously soaked in the values she learned during her childhood in Birmingham, Alabama. The importance of the family and love relationships, her fascination with the past and her ancestry, her search for identity amid the chaos and deracination of the North, her communion with nature, her exploration of the folk culture, her response to an evangelical religious experience, and her embracing of a militancy nurtured in fear and rage are Southern attitudes that inform her poetry. Especially in **A Blues Book, I've Been a Woman,** and **Under a Soprano Sky,** Sanchez's fascination with the concept of time, her faith in the lessons of the past, and her deep notion of continuity firmly root her in the tradition of Southern imagination.

In *The Immoderate Past: The Southern Writer and History,* Hugh Holman explores the relationship between the concept of time and the Southern writer:

> The imagination of the Southerner for over one hundred and seventy-five years has been historical. The imagination of the Puritans was essentially typological, catching fire as it saw men and events as types of Christian principles. The imagination of the New England romantics was fundamentally symbolic, translating material objects into ideal forms and ideas. The Southerner has always had his imaginative faculties excited by events in time and has

found the most profound truths of the present and the future in the interpretation of the past.

In part two of *A Blues Book,* the poet invites her readers to:

> Come into Black geography
> you, seated like Manzu's cardinal,
> come up through tongues
> multiplying memories
> and to avoid descent
> among wounds
> cruising like ships,
> climb into these sockets
> golden with brine.

Describing history as the spiritual landscape of events and images, she invites the reader to travel back in time, through what George Kent calls her "spiritual autobiography," her "own psychological and spiritual evolution in the past." Sanchez has the past define the features of her identity and uncover her origins. Calling on the earth mother as the inspiration and guide on the journey, she implores her to reveal the truths locked in time:

> Come ride my birth, earth mother
> tell me how i have become, became
> this woman with razor blades between
> her teeth.
>
>   sing me my history O earth mother
> about tongues multiplying memories
> about breaths contained in straw.

The poet realizes that the essential clues to who she is are there in the dusty corners of history, in the myths and tales preserved by "tongues multiplying memories," in the seemingly inconsequential bits that can be gleaned from those who live in the spirit and in the flesh. Because she is in tune with her oral tradition, she shares with other Southern black writers, such as Ralph Ellison, Richard Wright, Margaret Walker, Ernest Gaines, Maya Angelou, and Alice Walker, what Ellison calls some of the advantages of the South:

> I believe that a black Southern writer who does know his traditions has some of the advantages which William Faulkner or other white Southern writers have had: the advantage of contact with a long accumulation of history in a given place; an experience which has been projected in other forms of artistic expression, which has traditional values and variants, and which has been refined by being defined by generations of people who have told what it seemed to be: "This is the life of black men here. . . ."

This is one of the advantages of the South. In the stories you get the texture of an experience and the projection of values, and the distillation of a kind of wisdom.

For Sanchez, who she is and who she is to become have much to do with the texture of experience, the values, and the wisdom alive in the folk community of Birmingham, Alabama.

Sonia Sanchez was born in Birmingham on September 9, 1934. Her parents, Wilson L. Driver and Lena Jones Driver, faced with naming a second girl (the first daughter was named Patricia), gladly turned over the task to relatives, who returned quickly enough with the name Wilsonia Benita. The communal name turned out to be a portent of the role relatives would play in her upbringing, for when she was one year old, her mother died in childbirth, and she thus began a series of moves from one relative's home to another during the next nine years.

After her mother's death, Wilsonia and her sister were cared for by her father's mother. Elizabeth "Mama" Driver, whom Sanchez describes as a "heavy-set, dark-complected woman," was the head deaconess in the African Methodist Episcopal Church. In an interview, Sanchez remembers her grandmother: "My grandmother spoiled my sister and me outrageously. She loved us to death . . . she loved us so much that she used to walk us to Tuggle Elementary School. This old, old woman used to walk very slowly up that hill. . . ." Mama Driver brought the girls into the circle of the rituals of the A. M. E. Church. They experienced the sonorous roar of the minister, who strode across the pulpit of the wood frame church; the buzz of the congregation when a sister got "happy" and threw her pocketbook "clean across the aisle"; and the wonderment of the spirituals when all those choir members, dressed in white, sounded like the angels at the gates of the city.

Sanchez remembers the many occasions her grandmother had allowed them to sit quietly at her knees while she talked with the women who visited their modest house in a Birmingham housing development. In **"Dear Mama"** in her most recent book, *Under a Soprano Sky,* she recalls vividly the Saturday afternoons when she "crawled behind the couch" and listened to the old deaconesses as they told of their lives "spent on so many things":

And history began once again. I received it and let it circulate in my blood. I learned on those Saturday afternoons about women rooted in themselves, raising themselves in dark America, discharging their pain without ever stopping. I learned about women fighting men back when they hit them: "Don't never let no mens hit you mo than once

girl." I learned about "womens waking up they mens" in the nite with pans of hot grease and the compromises reached after the smell of hot grease had penetrated their sleepy brains. I learned about loose women walking their abandoned walk down front in church, crossing their legs instead of their hands to God. And I crept into my eyes. Alone with my daydreams of being woman. Adult. Powerful. Loving. Like them. Allowing nobody to rule me if I didn't want to be.

And when they left. When those old bodies had gathered up their sovereign smells. After they had kissed and packed up beans snapped and cakes cooked and laughter bagged. After they had called out their last goodbyes, I crawled out of my place. Surveyed the room. Then walked over to the couch where some had sat for hours and bent my head and smelled their evening smells. I screamed out loud, "oooweeee! Ain't that stinky!" and I laughed laughter from a thousand corridors. And you turned Mama, closed the door, chased me round the room until I crawled into a corner where your large body could not reach me. But your laughter pierced the little alcove where I sat laughing at the night. And your humming sprinkled my small space. Your humming about you Jesus and how one day he was gonna take you home. . . .

Mama Driver also gave the children a sense of continuity as she acquainted them with the long line of aunts, uncles, and cousins who made up their extended family. She acquainted them with a community that held dear the notion of family ties and took for granted the willingness of family members to take another member in: "My life flows from you Mama. My style comes from a long line of Louises who picked me up in the nite to keep me from wetting the bed. A long line of Sarahs who fed me and my sister and fourteen other children from watery soups and beans and a lot of imagination. A long line of Lizzies who made me understand love. Sharing. Holding a child up to the stars. Holding your tribe in a grip of love. A long line of Black people holding each other up against silence."

When Mama Driver died, the small frail child of five experienced the manufactured adult mystery of death and the insensitivity of relatives who shut children out of this fact of nature. As a way of managing the loss and the pain, she withdrew behind a veil of stuttering that remained with her for the next twelve years. When she and her sister lived with her father and his second wife, the stuttering protected her from the brunt of her stepmother's cruelty. In part two of *A Blues Book,* she raises the specter of this woman:

And YOU U U U U U U step/mother.

woman of my father's youth
who stands at a mirror
elaborate with smells
all shiny like my new copper penny.
telling me through a parade of smiles
you are to be my new mother. and your painted
  lips
outlined against time become time
and i look on time and hear you
who threw me in angry afternoon closets
till i slipped beneath the cracks
like light, and time stopped.
and i turned into myself
a young girl breathing in crusts
and listened to those calling me.

to/	*no matter what they do*
be/	*they won't find me*
chanted/	*no matter what they say*
	i won't come out.

The collective images of the woman—her stepmother's resentment, her rages, her neglect, and her authoritarianism that weighed heavily on the two girls—had the effect of distorting time itself ("and your painted lips / outlined against time"). The mature sensibility records the prominence of the cruel punishment that loomed prodigiously in the child's mind ("and time stopped / and i turned into myself") and indelibly marks her personality. She, the youngest, had hidden behind her "black braids and stutters"; she, the strange one, the quiet one, would not come out. When her father learned of his second wife's treatment of the children, he sent them to live with relatives, and they remained with relatives or friends until their father married again and took them to New York, reenacting the solemn ceremony that many thousands of black people performed as they migrated to Northern cities.

Reflecting on her childhood, Sanchez said that, despite the unhappy experiences, she had "a good Southern girlhood." Her grandmother had initiated her into the rituals of black life; aunts and uncles and cousins had given connections, continuity to her sense of self, and Birmingham, Alabama, had rooted her in a history of black struggle, with its lessons of fear, segregation, rebellion, and an awareness of her place. Years later, in her first published poem, she urges from her subconscious the memory of a cousin who, when made to move from her seat on the bus, spits in the white driver's face.

From 1944 until she graduated from Hunter College, Wilsonia Driver lived in Harlem at 152d and St. Nicholas Place, where there was "no space." In the small apartment she shared with her sister, her father, and his third wife, she felt hemmed in. Her tiny bedroom, whose window faced a redbrick wall, further mocked her sense of loss, now far from the greener, open space of the South. She also felt hemmed in by the kind, yet restrictive, care of her new stepmother and by the unwritten expectation placed on a young girl growing up in an environment that did not offer its girl-women protection but demanded that they protect themselves or run the risk of scorn and censure:

coming out from alabama
to the island city of perpetual adolescence
where i drink my young breasts
and stay thirsty
always hungry for more than the
georgewashingtonhighschoolhuntercollegedays
of america.
    remember parties
    where we'd grindddddDDDD
    and grindddddDDDD
    but not too close
    cuz if you gave it up
    everybody would know. and tell.

In those early Harlem days, the young girl was hungry for more than the restrictions of the island city, so she daydreamed and began to write. In an *Essence* magazine article, Sanchez recalls that she started writing because it was a way to express herself without the annoying stuttering. She remembers writing a poem about George Washington's crossing of the Delaware. The poem, which was left out while she rushed to rewash dishes, was found by her sister, who began reading the poem to their parents in a singsong rhyme. "I reached for the poem, but she pulled it away and finished reading it to everybody in the kitchen. They all laughed. I don't really remember it as cruel laughter, but I was a very sensitive little girl. So I was very much upset and after that I began hiding my poems. I doubt if anyone knew I was still writing."

This incident recalls a similar experience related by Richard Wright in his book *Black Boy.* After he read one of his stories to a woman in his neighborhood, he realizes that she cannot possibly understand his desire to write: "God only knows what she thought. My environment contained nothing more alien than writing or the desire to express one's self in writing." According to Ladell Payne in *Black Novelists and the Southern Literary Tradition,* Richard Wright's life of imagination sustained him in his estrangement but also served to isolate him further from his family and community. Similarly for Sanchez, from the very beginning, writing was a solitary endeavor that simultaneously isolated her from others and gave her the distance that she needed to see herself, her family, and community reconstituted in a new light.

As the young woman matured, her estrangement extended

into most areas of her life. At Hunter College, she wanted more than the benign indifference that left her sense of self unnourished. She was not only alienated from those at school, but she was also separated from those on her block. They left the serious-eyed, quiet, college girl alone. However, in **"Bubba"** in *homegirls & handgrenades,* the poet remembers one who saw more in her than she was prepared to acknowledge: "One summer day, I remember Bubba and I banging the ball against the filling station. Handball champs we were. The king and queen of handball we were. And we talked as we played. He asked me if I ever talked to trees or rivers or things like that. And I who walked with voices for years denied the different tongues populating my mouth. I stood still denying the commonplace things of my private childhood. And his eyes pinned me against the filling station wall and my eyes became small and lost their color."

And the alienation reached her in her home. She had not really known her father. Though she lived with him from the time she was ten until she left college, on many levels, they remained strangers. **"A Poem for My Father"** in *We A BadddDDD People* and **"Poem at Thirty"** in *Homecoming* tell poignantly of this relationship.

But more significantly, the young poet felt alienated from herself and her roots. In *A Blues Book,* she recalls those times when she "moved in liquid dreams":

> and i dressed myself
> in foreign words
>   became a proper painted
>   european Black faced american
>   going to theatre parties and bars
>   and cocktail parties and bars
>   and downtown village apartments
>   and bars and ate good cheese
>   and caviar with wine that
> made my stomach stretch for artificial
>   warmth.
>
>   danced with white friends who
>   included me because that was
>   the nice thing to do in the late
>   fifties and early sixties
>
> and i lost myself
> down roads
> i had never walked.
>
> and my name was
> without honor
> and i became a
> stranger at my birthright.

Perhaps it was this sense that she had lost her birthright that

turned her thoughts to her past. And the South became the place where the mysteries of her past could be discovered. There too was the knowledge of her mother.

It was not until she graduated from college that she learned anything about her mother. When her father showed her a photograph of Lena Jones Driver, a beautiful Latin-looking woman with fair skin and dark eyes, she became aware of the void that existed in her life. On a pilgrimage to the South in 1980, she found a wizened old man who held the knowledge that had long since been lost in county records. He told her that her mother was the daughter of a black plantation worker and her white boss by the name of Jones. The revelation convinced the poet of her intimacy with historical events and finds its way into her upcoming novel, *After Saturday Night Comes Sunday,* in which a woman who is going crazy because of a man must spiritually find her mother's mother. Only then, when she had traversed the void, can she become the kind of woman she is capable of becoming. In *After Saturday Night Comes Sunday,* as in part two of *A Blues Book,* the reader experiences an almost cinematographic sensation, as Sanchez reverses the projector, making the frames from the past flick in rapid retrogression. In much the manner of Alejo Carpentier as he envisions a "journey back to the source," the poet manipulates time and harnesses the power and magic of the rivers to give birth to herself:

> tell me. tellLLLLLL me. earth mother
> for i want to rediscover me. the secret of me
> the river of me. the morning ease of me.
> i want my body to carry my words like aqueducts.
> i want to make the world my diary
> and speak rivers.

The ritual invocation of the earth mother has its analogue in the rituals of the Orisha, the Yoruba gods. As if drawing on the Jungian collective unconscious, the poet reveals a close relationship between the riverain goddesses who reside at the bottom of the river, and Earth, whom they recognize as the pure force, the *ashe,* the power to make things happen. In *Flash of the Spirit,* Robert Farris Thompson gives a description of one of the riverain goddesses, who has an uncanny resemblance to the spirituality revealed in *A Blues Book:*

> Divination literature tells us that Oshun was once married to Ifa but fell into a more passionate involvement with the fiery thunder god, who carried her into his vast brass palace, where she ruled with him; she bore him twins and accumulated, as mothers of twins in Yorubaland are want to do, money and splendid things galore. . . . When she died, she took these things to the bottom of the river. There she reigns in glory, within the sacred depths, fully

aware that so much treasure means that she must counter inevitable waves of jealousy with witchcraft, by constant giving, constant acts of intricate generosity. Even so, she is sometimes seen crowned, in images of warlock capacity and power, brandishing a lethal sword, ready to burn and destroy immoral persons who incur her wrath, qualities vividly contrasting with her sweetness, love, and calm.

Oshun, in fact, can well be a metaphor for Sanchez's power. For in her poems, one senses a power that is feminine, and consciously so. It comes from her understanding of her connections with the universe, her connections with her ancestors, and her strong matrilineal ties with a universe that has given to its kind not only the responsibility but, indeed, the power to bear the children and nurture seed. Her power comes from a faith in continuity; seeds grow into flowers and produce their own seeds. Sanchez clearly presents the life cycle and cherishes it.

As if drawing on the Jungian collective unconscious, [Sanchez] reveals a close relationship between the riverain goddesses who reside at the bottom of the river, and Earth, whom they recognize as the pure force, the *ashe*, the power to make things happen.
— *Joanne Veal Gabbin*

Sanchez calls the phenomenon that makes sense out of these mystical connections and recurrent archetypal images "residual memory." It is her capacity to draw on this memory that deepens the implications of her poetry. And on another level, it provides a source of implications that even the poet cannot fathom. Some would call this simply—inspiration.

In speaking about how she writes, Sanchez explains a process in which one sees the art of the poet and the role of the prophet merging. In an interview that appeared in *Essence* magazine, she says that sometimes lines of poetry come and she jots them down and that sometimes a feeling comes and she will write down lines that respond to that feeling. Often for Sanchez, the inspiration comes after rereading a favorite book or the work of a poet she admires. During her best time for reflection—early in the morning, from twelve midnight until four, she reads and reworks lines, "fussing at those things that obviously don't work." However, sometimes the poet gives way to the prophet, whose voice "derives its authority, not from some inner reservoir, but from an outside . . . source." Sanchez says: "Sometimes I actually see something that moves me or makes me angry or whatever, and then line by line just pours out from God knows where. Whenever people compliment me after a reading or tell me

they enjoyed one of my books, I'll say, 'Thank you so much.' But inside I'll say to myself, 'It's not just me.' Everything that you or I could write has been written before; there's that energy there in the universe for us to pull from. Many of us just become attuned to that energy."

It was this energy that helped Sanchez begin her career as a writer. While attending New York University, she began to write seriously. At NYU, she took a course from poet Louise Bogan, a prolific writer and teacher who disliked intensely "bad writing and bad writers." Sanchez found Bogan fascinating and sincerely interested in her growth as a writer, and she did not sense in her the patronization and indifference that she had encountered at Hunter.

Encouraged by this experience, she organized a writers' workshop that met every Wednesday night in the village; there she met Amiri Baraka (LeRoi Jones) and Larry Neal, the poet-critics who became the architects of the black arts movement, and began to read with them in jazz night spots. She also joined the New York CORE and the Reform Democrats Club. At this time, she was married to Albert Sanchez, a first-generation Puerto Rican American. He did not understand her intense commitment to causes or her need to write. After four years of marriage and the birth of her first child, Sanchez found herself moving away from the narrowly defined bounds of that relationship:

> and visions came from the wall.
> bodies without heads, laughter without mouths.
> then faces crawling on the walls
> like giant spiders,
> came toward me
> and my legs buckled and
> i cried out.

And when the break was complete, she

> woke up alone
> to the middle sixties
> full of the rising wind of history . . .

In 1967, Sanchez started teaching at San Francisco State College. Her two-year tenure there was marked by student unrest, demonstrations, and the fledgling stretching of the black power movement. She found herself in the midst of the struggle to make black studies a part of the college's offerings. She, along with psychologist Nathan Hare, played a significant role in the establishment of the first black studies program in the country. She also began to document the ironies and nuances of the overall struggle for black awareness in poems that would appear in her first volume, ***Homecoming***.

Also during this time, Sanchez met poet Etheridge Knight

through Gwendolyn Brooks and Dudley Randall. While he was in prison, they began to correspond, and in 1969, they married. Twin sons, Mungu and Morani, were born to them. After little more than a year, the marriage ended in an uneasy alliance. **"Poem for Etheridge,"** "last poem i'm gonna write bout us," and other poems in *We A BadddDDD People* and *Love Poems* reveal the often poignant, sometimes tragic nature of their relationship. However, what is significant in these poems is the ability of the poet to transcend the bounds of her own experience and speak with an authority that comes from going many times to her own personal wailing wall. For example, in **"Poem No. 8,"** Sanchez brilliantly captures the sense of interminable waiting that only a woman knows intimately:

> i've been a woman
>   with my legs stretched by the wind
>   rushing the day
>   thinking i heard your voice
>   while it was only the night
>   moving over
>   making room for the dawn.

From 1967 to 1975, Sanchez was intensely involved in continuing her career as a poet and a teacher. During that time, she completed nine books and published her poems and plays in several periodicals, including *Black Scholar, Black Theatre, Black World, Journal of Black Poetry, Liberator, Massachusetts Review, Minnesota Review, New York Quarterly,* and the *Tulane Drama Review.* She also taught at the University of Pittsburgh, Rutgers University, Manhattan Community College, and Amherst College. While at Amherst, from 1972 to 1975, she taught one of the first courses on black women writers offered in an American college. For a brief period from 1972 to 1975, she was a member of the Nation of Islam, directing its cultural and educational program and writing for *Muhammad Speaks.* She resigned from the Nation of Islam in 1975 and one year later came to Philadelphia to teach at the University of Pennsylvania. After a year, Sanchez began teaching at Temple University, where she has taught Afro-American studies, English, Pan-African studies, and creative writing since then.

In 1978, Sanchez published *I've Been a Woman: New and Selected Poems.* In this volume, she concludes with a group of new poems that fall under the rubric **"Generations."** These poems attest to the significance she places on the vestiges of the past that have been gathered to bring meaning, value, direction, and inspiration to an individual's present.

In **"A Poem of Praise,"** which is dedicated to Gerald Penny, a student who died on September 23, 1973, and to the Brothers of Amherst College, Sanchez reconciles the loss of a young warrior by giving promise to the cycles of his life. The truth of the poem is that the man has been on earth and

has experienced a life that is no less beautiful, dramatic, or meaningful because it has been short. One sees the poet developing a view of the universe that holds man as a traveler, who comes from another space, walks from the morning through day, to evening, tasting "in himself the world":

> In your days made up of dreams
> in your eyes made of dawn
> you walked toward old age,
> child of the rainbow
> child of beauty
> through the broad fields
> and your eyes gained power
> and your limbs grew long like yellow corn
> an abundance of life
> an abundance of joy
> with beauty before you, you walked
> toward old age.

This traveler brings to mind another one who came "trailing clouds of glory." William Wordsworth's youth must travel from the East, farther from the splendid vision of celestial light that was his when he was born. However, consistent with the teaching of Islam (during the writing of this poem, the poet was a follower of the teachings of Elijah Muhammad), Sanchez envisions a universe in which the young man walks toward the light, wisdom, and rebirth:

> For i am man
> and i must
> run with the evening tide
> must hold up my hands
> for my life is opening
> before me.
>
> I am going to walk far to the East
> i hope to find a good morning
> somewhere.

This youth need not content himself with the memory of radiance that once was, for life moves in cycles and progresses toward endings that have, at their center, beginnings.

Sanchez's poetic kinship with Native American tribal poets is striking here. There is the same understanding of "the cyclic continuities" that make up the circle of life. There is the same respect for the generative power of language, a language that is medicinal, rooted in nature, dignified, and spare. Kenneth Lincoln, in his book *Native American Renaissance,* writes:

> Oral tribal poetry remains for the most part organic, for tribal poets see themselves as essentially keepers of the sacred word bundle. . . . They regard rhythm, vision, craft, nature, and words as gifts that

precede and continue beyond any human life. The people are born into and die out of a language that gives them being. Song-poets in this respect discover, or better rediscover, nature's poems. They never pretend to have invented a "poetic" world apart from nature, but instead believe they are permitted to husband songs as one tends growing things; they give thanks that the songs have chosen them as singers.

In a real way, Sanchez's attitude about her purpose as a poet is rooted in a way of thinking about the world that is similar to that of the poet-singers of more than five hundred Native American cultures who send out the voice. Her early Southern experience watered her sensibility—the greening of her mind—and nourished her purpose as a poet: to create positive values for her community. She writes in **"The Poet as a Creator of Social Values"** that the poet is a manipulator of symbols and language—images that have been planted by experience in the collective subconscious of a people. She believes that "the poet has the power to create new or intensified meaning and experience" and, depending on the visibility of the poet and the efficacy of the poetry itself, "create, preserve or destroy social values."

However, even more than these conditions, the poet's power depends on the clarity of her vision, her ability to interpret human nature, and her willingness to speak in tongues that will confirm her vision. For Sanchez, poetry is "subconscious conversation." She says, "When I say something on stage, I make them remember similar experiences that they have not even brought up, but I bring them up and say look remember and people say, 'Yes, I remember.'" And given this process, "poetry is as much the work of those who understand it as those who make it." Thus, when Sanchez eulogizes the Amherst student whose life ended prematurely, she is sending a voice among the people who hear and speak:

> There is nothing which does not
>   come to an end
> And to live seventeen years is good
>   in the sight of God.

The cycle-of-life theme that provides the frame for **"A Song of Praise"** gets a deeper, subtler exploration in **"Kwa mama zetu waliotuzaa."** Significantly, the poem begins with the line, "death is a five o'clock door forever changing time," which first appeared in *Sister Son/ji,* a play written in 1970. By repeating the line, the poet emphasizes the consistency, the predictability, and the weight she attributes to this theme. According to critic Joyce Ann Joyce:

> This line along with the title of the poem echoes the "In the beginning / there was no end" of *Blues Book.* Just as Sister Son/ji reaches out to the audi-

ence and asks if they will "grab the day and make it stop," **"Kwa mama zetu waliotuzaa"** illustrates how the physical, temporal, historical reality becomes an embodiment of the spiritual. For if we grab the day and make it stop, we will see that death is a concrete reality (a five o'clock door) that rules the process of life. For the death of the natural world brings forth the birth of the spiritual (forever changing time) as Sister Son/ji learns.

The lines that follow dramatically show the cyclic nature of life and ironically reveal the human attempt to still a process that is as unrelenting as waves against a shore:

>   and it was morning without sun or shadow;
> a morning already afternoon, sky, cloudy with
>   incense,
>   and it was morning male in speech;
> feminine in memory.
> but i am speaking of everyday occurrences:
> of days unrolling bandages for civilized wounds;
> of guady women chanting rituals under a waterfall
>   of stars;
> of men freezing their sperms in diamond-studded
>   wombs;
> of children abandoned to a curfew of marble.

The poem, whose title translates "for our mother who gave us birth," is at once a praise poem for the mothers (biological and spiritual) of black women and a eulogy for Shirley Graham DuBois, biographer, teacher and lecturer, whose career spanned over forty years and took her to Africa, Asia, and Europe. In the opening passages, the poet remembers her father's third wife, Geraldine Driver, a kind, caring Southern woman who was saddled with notions of her place and feared breaking loose to ride out her potential. Here, however, in memorializing her (she died of cancer in Detroit), Sanchez uses the symbolism of nature to represent continuity, growth, fruitfulness, and joy, and in effect, she undercuts the pain and unfulfillment that were hers in life:

>   mother, i call out to you
> traveling up the congo. i am preparing a place for
>   you:
>   nite made of female rain
>   i am ready to sing her song
>   prepare a place for her
>   she comes to you out of turquoise pain.
>
>   restring her eyes for me
>   restring her body for me
>   restring her peace for me
>
>   no longer full of pain, may she walk
>   bright with orange smiles, may she walk

as it was long ago, may she walk

abundant with lightning steps, may she walk
abundant with green trails, may she walk
abundant with rainbows, may she walk
as it was long ago, may she walk . . .

For Shirley Graham DuBois, who was "a bearer of roots," who taught the poet the truth of the African past, who "painted the day with palaces," Sanchez, in broad sweeps of pantheism, calls up the bells, Olokun (the goddess of the sea), the spirits of day and night. For through their persistence, their repetitiveness, their predictability, they reassure the poet of her mentor's continuity and her triumphal passage to the land of the ancestors.

At several turns in the poem, the privileged perception cuts through the eulogy:

as morning is the same as nite death and life are
one.
. . . .
at the center of death is birth
. . . .
death is coming. the whole world hears
the buffalo walk of death passing thru the
archway of new life.

From the very first metaphor, the poem is unified by the epigrams concerning death. Death is one with life and continuity; at its center is a beginning.

The dimensions of Sanchez's Southern imagination become imposing in *Homegirls & Handgrenades.* Her fascination with time and the past, her communion with nature, her reverence for the folk, her search for identity and self-actualization through meaningful relationships, and her intense spirituality born of a faith in roots and continuity predict the themes and metaphors that unify the book. With a language pregnant with the images of war, armaments, and nuclear proliferation, the poet suggests that love and the greening of the mind are the only reasonable weapons in a world dangerously toying with annihilation. In the most effective vignette in the volume, **"Just Don't Never Give Up on Love,"** the poet recounts her meeting with an eighty-four-year-old woman who inveigled her to hear her message on the power of love:

". . . C'mon over here next to me. I wants to see yo' eyes up close. You looks so uneven sittin' over there."

Did she say uneven? Did this old buddah splintering death say uneven? Couldn't she see that I had one eye shorter than the other; that my breath was

painted on porcelain; that one breast crocheted keloids under this white blouse?

I moved toward her though. I scooped up the years that had stripped me to the waist and moved toward her. And she called to me to come out, come out wherever you are young woman, playing hide and go seek with scarecrow men. I gathered myself up at the gateway of her confessionals.

As Mrs. Rosalie Johnson talks with her about her husbands and love, the young woman cries for herself and "for all the women who have ever stretched their bodies out anticipating civilization and finding ruins." Mrs. Johnson's message is cathartic; by allowing the old woman's healing words to slough off the bitterness and fear built up from past relationships, she is again open to love.

Moving the urgency of her message to global relationships, she concludes the volume with **"A Letter to Dr. Martin Luther King"** and **"MIA's."** Though very different in form, they are companion pieces that share Sanchez's urge to articulate the democratic evils (racism/apartheid/imperialism) that stunt the spiritual growth of black youth, corrupt hope by gradualism, and stall freedom. On the occasion of Martin Luther King's fifty-fourth year (the poet addresses the slain leader as a living spirit), she declares anew a faith in the regenerative power of blackness, which eschews fear and moves toward "freedom and justice for the universe." The letter ends with an explosion of feeling as the poet, remembering the chanting of black South African women at the death of Stephen Biko, adopts the chant "Ke wa rona" (he is ours) and calls the roll of black deliverers:

. . . On this your 54th year, listen and you will hear the earth delivering up curfews to the missionaries and assassins. Listen. And you will hear the tribal songs.

Ayeeee	Ayooooo	Ayeee
Ayeeee	Ayooooo	Ayeee
Malcolm . . .		Ke wa rona
Robeson . . .		Ke wa rona
Lumumba . . .		Ke wa rona
Fannie Lou . . .		Ke wa rona
Garvey . . .		Ke wa rona
Johnbrown . . .		Ke wa rona
Tubman . . .		Ke wa rona
Mandela . . .		Ke wa rona
(free Mandela		
free Mandela)		
Assata . . .		Ke wa rona

As we go with you to the sun,
as we walk in the dawn, turn our eyes

Eastward and let the prophecy come true
and let the prophecy come true
Great God, Martin, what a morning it will be!

In **"MIA's (missing in action and other atlantas),"** the datelines—Atlanta, Johannesburg, El Salvador—serve to show the world of oppression in microcosm, and the machinations that promote death (murder / assassination / "redwhiteandblue death squads"). The centerpiece of the poem is a disturbingly accurate account of the death of Biko. Here one is aware of the substantial capacity of the poet to work with the ironic voice, which gains power by the incremental repetition of "we did all we could for the man":

sept. 13:
hear ye. hear ye. hear ye.
i regret to announce that stephen
biko is dead. he has refused
food since sept. 5th. we did
all we could for the man.
he has hanged himself while sleeping
we did all we could for him.
he fell while answering our questions
we did all we could for the man.
he washed his face and hung him
self out to dry
we did all we could for him.
he drowned while drinking his supper
we did all we could for the man.
he fell
    hanged himself   starved
drowned himself
we did all we could for him.
it's hard to keep someone alive
who won't even cooperate.
hear ye.

Whether conjuring up Stephen Biko, or the "youngblood / touching and touched at random" in the killing fields of Atlanta, or the young men with "their white togas covering their / stained glass legs" in Central America, she exhorts the men and women to harvest their share of freedom.

In Sanchez's most recent volume, *Under a Soprano Sky,* she captures in the poem **"for Black history month/February 1986"** the essence of her Southern sensibility as she reflects on her visit to the Great Wall of China. As she "started to climb that long winding trail of history and survival," her thoughts turned to voices and visions that propelled history, demanded survival, and forged the cultural links of which continuity is made. Moving deeply within her culture, Sanchez "had to peel away misconceptions about Blacks." As she sang the blues, hummed the spirituals, explored the myths, and walked "a piece" down the road with Nat Turner, Douglass, Harriet Tubman, Garrison, John Brown; Martin

Delany, Malcolm X, Rosa Parks, David Walker . . . her racial memory nourished in Southern soil bears fruit. Her sense of reality, her sense of history rejected Old Black Joe, one of the plantation tradition's favorite sons, "Sambo-hood," and Jim Crow. Her sense of history embraced Lady Day's voice as she sang of strange fruit and blood on the magnolia, embraced Robeson's voice as he sang of deep rivers and the quest of the soul for peace on the other side of Jordan or the Mississippi or the Ohio. Her sense of the past, her roots, her ostensibly Southern imagination has allowed her to keep sight of her vision, a vision of peace and community that was first conceived in the green days of an Alabama childhood.

Frenzella Elaine De Lancey (essay date 1992)

SOURCE: "Refusing to be Boxed In: Sonia Sanchez's Transformation of the Haiku Form," in *Language and Literature in the African American Imagination,* edited by Carol Aisha Blackshire-Belay, Greenwood Press, 1992, pp. 21-36.

[*In the following essay, De Lancey asserts that "As [Sanchez] textualizes the form, forging her Afrocentric vision and Afrocentric structure within the discipline of the haiku form, she moves closer to a unique structure that carries her own signature."*]

One of the few titled haiku written by Sonia Sanchez, **"Walking in the rain in Guyana"** is an excellent example of both the poet's artistic vision and artistry:

watusi like trees
holding the day like green um/
brella catching rain.

Elements consistent with definitions of classical Japanese haiku as a lyric verse form in three unrhymed lines, with a 5-7-5 syllable count are evident, so, too, is the requisite emphasis on external nature. The clarifying title tells us that this haiku derives from a walk in the rain in Guyana and announces the poet's intention to "localize" the haiku in a particular manner. Sanchez uses Afrocentric motifs to textualize the haiku, making it not some universal statement about rain and tree but a particular experience, filtered through the poet's consciousness. Though Guyana is located in South America, African people are among its inhabitants; the watusi trees evoke images of the Burundi Watusi, again, images associated with Africa. Sanchez localizes this image by inserting "like" in the first line, forcing it into service as she forges an adjective-phrase, "watusi like" to describe the trees. Such techniques signal reader: this is haiku with a difference.

We recognize, however, that Sanchez's **"Walking in the rain in Guyana"** conforms to a basic concept of haiku to what haiku master Basho (1644-1694) describes as simply what is happening at this place at this moment. Equally evident is how much Sanchez's Afrocentric content textualizes the form. Forging function with ethos, she observes rules while breaking them. Sanchez's poetic practice is informed by a philosophy that utilizes function and ethos as two important distinctions in poetry. She sees poetry as form that accommodates political and personal ideas. Imamu Amiri Baraka offers a useful definition of form and content that can be applied to Sanchez's transformation of the haiku form. According to Baraka, form is "simply how a thing exists (or what a thing exists as)." Content, on the other hand, "is why a thing exists."

More than a personal poetic construction, this haiku is also an example of Sonia Sanchez's conscious decision to imbue haiku form with Afrocentric motifs, and ultimately move beyond the form as prescribed to a fusion of traditional haiku form with her own structure.
—*Frenzella Elaine de Lancey*

In her transformation of haiku Sanchez often forces the reader to ask "why." She notes that writing for her has been a "long tense road of saying what I wanted and needed to say." In **"Walking in the rain in Guyana,"** the poet fuses an unspecific, unbounded image from external nature to a particular, specific moment, filtered through her consciousness. More than a personal poetic construction, this haiku is also an example of Sonia Sanchez's conscious decision to imbue haiku form with Afrocentric motifs, and ultimately move beyond the form as prescribed to a fusion of traditional haiku form with her own structure. In other words, Sanchez is making the haiku say what she wants it to say.

Sanchez's transformation of the form is more radical than mere structural alteration, although she sometimes changes the structure of the haiku by using simile, conjunction, and metaphor. Her use of these structural markers can always be identified as functional; they are used to make the haiku speak her words, reveal her vision. In fact, Sanchez's use of the haiku form is a revolutionary textualization of both structure and form. Sometimes working within the structural strictures of classical Japanese haiku form, other times altering the form to fit her needs, and always textualizing it, Sanchez forces the form to accommodate her vision. By imbuing the haiku form with Afrocentric motifs, Sanchez textualizes the form in a specific manner, and in the instances where she must abrogate universally observed strictures, she does so to force the haiku to conform to her needs and her

vision. In her haiku, then, the effect is a movement through the uneven strictures imposed by dicta reintroduced for the English haiku. Referring specifically to her book *I've Been a Woman,* Sanchez discusses her use of haiku and tanka, and her conscious use of African themes. In *I've Been a Woman,* she points out, "I have haiku, tankas, and again, the movement towards what I call 'African' ideas and feelings and also the movement toward a black ethic and a feminine one too."

The fifth section of *I've Been a Woman* is entitled "Haikus/ Tankas & Other Love Syllables" and in it Sanchez offers haiku which focus on a number of subjects. Some are interesting fusions of nature and human elements:

> i have looked into
> my father's eyes and seen an
> african sunset.

Often these fusions of external nature and humanity emphasize one over the other. At other times, humanity and elements signifying nature are perfectly balanced in metaphorical phrases. Thus, function and form are important in the transformation Sanchez effects. For example, her use of simile and conjunction is also functional. Though she only alters the haiku 5-7-5 infrequently, her use of simile, metaphor, and other structural devices usually alert readers to important structural changes and, of course, with these changes, an unusual textualization of form. In another haiku dedicated to Gwendolyn Brooks, Sanchez signals Brooks's importance by using images from external nature to create an image of Brooks's essence as sacred:

> woman, whose color
> of life is like the sun, whose
> laughter is prayer.

We note Sanchez's use of metaphor and simile showcases Brooks. Such showcasing transforms this haiku into a compressed praise song for Gwendolyn Brooks, and external nature serves as handmaiden to Sanchez's vision. Suggesting that Brooks's vision is an exemplar, a sacred model, Sanchez clusters images for associative value within the permitted 5-7-5 syllable count and with the forbidden simile and metaphor. After establishing Brooks through metaphor, Sanchez equates Brooks's laughter with "prayer." In this final vehicle, this final image of a woman who is a sacred model, is effective in this haiku. Again, Sanchez fuses human and natural elements through clustered images and structural transformation, a woman whose essence rivals the sun becomes a sacred figure.

In the same section of *I've Been a Woman,* there are other haiku in which nature takes on the coloring of the human actors in the poetic structure. And although most of the haiku

offered below do not have discernible Afrocentric motifs,
they are examples of the poet's willingness to abrogate haiku
strictures to accommodate her vision:

> shedding my years
> earthbound now. midnite trees are
> more to my liking.

Nature becomes the clarifying element as the image of rooted
trees suggests the experience of being earthbound. Sanchez
converts this feeling into a transformative moment consonant with the speaker's perspective by playing against our
most commonly held conception of trees. Viewed at midnight, rather than in the sharply clarifying light of day, the
trees as image are subject to greater imaginative possibilities. Earthbound, the speaker continues to retain the right to
see things in her own way.

With the same ease that she subordinates external nature to
humans in some haiku, Sanchez also imbues her haiku with
highly personal moments, ignoring the stricture against the
personal in haiku.

> the rain tastes lovely
> like yo/sweat draping my body ,
> after lovemaking.

Traditional haiku conventions of nature, taste, feeling, and
present time all interact in a rather unconventional manner
here. Most noticeable, of course, is "rain" representing nature in the first line perfectly balanced against "lovemaking"
in the last. Between the first and the last line, water as in
rain has been transformed into the perspiration produced by
the efforts of the two lovers. The haiku's argument suggests
nature as human and other, and its structure effectively forges
the two. But this is also a haiku imbued with the personal
and is, therefore, a transgression of conventional practice.
In another transgression, Sanchez dares to be intensely introspective in her haiku:

> what is it about
> me that i claim all the wrong
> lives, the same endings?

Signaling metaphysical crisis, the speaker questions past
practices and centers herself in the haiku. In this profoundly
personal and introspective moment of crisis, the speaker
questions the patterns of her life, and to do so, she moves
from present to past. Her mistakes are tallied in words like
"all" and the plural "lives" and "endings." Ignoring the censure demanding external nature, Sanchez transforms the
haiku form in incisive and startling linguistic turns:

> you have pierced me so
> deeply i cannot turn a

round without bleeding.

> missing you is like
> spring standing still on a hill
> amid winter snow.

Introspective moments rarely produce epiphanies; at most,
they are moments of fragmented insight. The haiku form
complements Sanchez's poetic renderings of such moments
and is thus particularly appropriate; yet, this is a revolutionary move. In their quiet intensity, each haiku represents the
poet's vision. While not obviously Afrocentric in terms of
motifs, these haiku represent the view of an African American woman. Specifically, they represent an artist aware of
censure choosing to work against the imposed norm. Even
in those haiku that are not decidedly Afrocentric, one finds
Sanchez presenting her own vision in her own way and saying what she wants to say.

So far, I have advanced the notion of Sanchez's haiku as decidedly revolutionary, whether she is presenting introspective moments or making political statements. In changing the
form by textualizing it, Sanchez demonstrates her own considerable skill as poet. But to truly understand the imperative that informs Sanchez's transformations, one must
examine briefly the nature of certain strictures in haiku writing.

Claims about what constitutes haiku are curiously antithetical to general practices. For example, there seems to be general agreement that Japanese haiku is rimeless, its seventeen
syllables usually arranged in three lines, often following a
5-7-5 pattern. However, in *The Art and Craft of Poetry: An
Introduction,* Lawrence John Zillman writes that in haiku one
is not concerned "with metrical feet, rime, or contrived stanzas." Rather the emphasis should be on the "two basic patterns" in which "everything is to be said in either thirty-one
or seventeen syllables. The tanka, the longer structure, is
made up of five lines, of tanka 5-7-5-7-7 syllables respectively." In fact, writers of English haiku often ignore such
patterns. Rime, then, appears to mark the important difference between Japanese and English haiku. This single adjustment seems to be the only acknowledged transition from
the Japanese to the English haiku. But it is also evident that
certain strictures are deeply ingrained. Still to be considered
is the often cited constraint from Basho urging the restriction of content in haiku to what is happening in this place
and this moment.

Editors and critics frequently ignore the flexibility of Basho's
definition of haiku. Rather, they evoke the strongest strictures, insisting not only upon the "present moment" in haiku,
but also that the subject matter of haiku focus on external
nature—that the poet focus on what can be seen, heard,
smelled, tasted, or touched. In her haiku, Sanchez most of-

ten observes one stricture while transforming another. While her observation of the 5-7-5 seventeen syllable stricture is most consistent, she takes the "present moment" and imbues it with any number of Afrocentric images or her unique, sometimes introspective vision. In the intensely personal haiku about lovemaking, she reinvests the stricture of taste, taking it from conventional dicta and turning it on its head.

According to X. J. Kennedy, "Haiku is an art of few words, many suggestions. A haiku starts us thinking and feeling." Sonia Sanchez uses the haiku form in a manner that forces her readers to think, and she does it successfully because she alters the form. It would seem then that some flexibility must be offered to the poet who wants to textualize haiku; yet, a cursory examination of the *1990 Poet's Market* finds that many strictures continue to dominate in a rather monolithic manner: "Do not use metaphor/simile/" and "Do not tell your emotions."

Unlike Kennedy or Zillman, many editors are unyielding proponents of traditional strictures. They expect the content in haiku to focus on external nature; they expect haiku writers to reject simile and metaphor. And these editors exercise some control over poets by their ability to reject haiku that do not conform to strictures. This, in turn, influences the poetry community, wedding haiku writers who want to publish to traditional strictures. Apparently monolithic, this perspective seems to be based on false notions, and as in all arbitrary dicta, the contradictions serve as imperatives for poets who want to alter the form. One of the more clarifying statements about Japanese haiku is offered by Kennedy, but even his flexible comments present censures against Sanchez's transformation of the haiku form:

> Haiku poets look out upon a literal world, seldom looking inward to discuss their feelings. Japanese haiku tend to be seasonal in subject, but because they are so highly compressed, they usually just imply a season: a blossom indicates spring; a crow on a branch, autumn; snow, winter. Not just pretty little sketches of nature (as some Westerners think), haiku assumes a view of the universe in which observer and nature are not separated.

The obvious difference between the description offered by Kennedy and Sanchez's haiku is that she does not hesitate to look inward, producing introspective haiku. Yet Kennedy's statement confirms that there are still misconceptions among practitioners and editors about what constitutes haiku. Further, the obvious gap between these misconceptions and views such as Kennedy's, is a proving ground that Sanchez stakes out for herself as she redefines the haiku form. Thus, the contradictions become Sanchez's imperative for transforming haiku.

As Carolyn Rodgers, George Kent, and others point out, Sanchez has traditionally used new forms. In one of her articles "Black poetry—where it's at," Rodgers offers a comprehensive typology of black expression in poetry. She identifies Sanchez's use of the "shouting" poem as an example of her utilization of new forms. George Kent offers a more extensive analysis of Sanchez's skill, not as a poet experimenting with new forms, but as a poet who has experimented with form and mastered it. Citing her mastery of mountain-top poetry, Kent refers specifically to Sanchez's *A Blues Book for Blue Black Magical Women* as "a culmination of spiritual and poetic powers." He speaks of Sanchez's earlier experiments with language and spelling as "efforts to force the speaking voice to speak from the printed page." He applauds her "simplicity of diction" and her "careful but undistracting uses of natural and mechanically induced pauses." In textualizing haiku, Sanchez produces exciting experimental forms and verifies earlier critical assessments of her work. Indeed, she reveals herself as a poet at the top of her craft. Just as she forces the stricture concerning nature in haiku to accommodate her vision of human nature and external nature, and the relationship they share, so, too, does she push the form and herself. This fusion of form finds Sanchez offering beautiful images of external nature in harmony with man:

> the trees are laughing
> at us. positioning their
> leaves in morning smiles.

Seemingly antithetical elements of nature are made to serve, through artistic skill, a different function:

> We are sudden stars
> you and i exploding in
> our blue black skins.

In the forbidden use of metaphor Sanchez combines the external nature, represented by the "stars," with the human element, thereby creating a certain texture in the form: the "you and i" and the "blue black skins" are human elements fused with stars. One becomes the other. In another lyrical instance Sanchez combines disparate elements, including simile, to make external nature and humanity complement each other:

> O this day like an
> orange peeled against the sky
> murmurs me and you.

Sanchez uses powerful elements from external nature perfectly equipoised against the human aspect. Furthermore, we have another instance of Sanchez using the forbidden simile and conjunction to establish the harmony important in human relationships and textualizing the poem in terms of several antithetical elements: structure and form; nature and man. The love for humanity comes through in this haiku precisely because Sanchez uses simile and conjunction. The effect of "like" between the orange and the sky balances them against the "me and you" of the haiku. Aspects of nature work for the humans in the poem, and there is harmony.

In another beautiful image of harmony, nature, and man, poet and haiku strictures merge to become a Sonia Sanchez construction wholly Afrocentric in technique, becoming what Carolyn Rodgers calls a "mindblowing" poem:

> morning snow falling
> astride this carousel called
> life. i am sailing.

"Mindblowing" because it uses the haiku to demonstrate poetic skill as well as poetic vision, this haiku reveals a poet boxing her way out and away from prescriptive form. Her refusal to yield to form is a lesson in itself. The opening lines signal conventional haiku, but each line moves the haiku away from the conventional toward individual technique and vision. Internal punctuation in the last line suggests that the poet will simply settle for the injection of the word "life" to signal her experimentation with form. On this introspective note, she is, in fact, situated in the present, but as she muses about "carousel called life" we recognize this structure as both synchronic and diachronic in nature; it is, therefore, introspective. However, after the period, which makes it appear to be an afterthought, the phrase "i am sailing" alters our response to the haiku. One could argue that this is the most powerful line in the haiku. "Mindblower poems" according to Rodgers, "seek to expand our minds, to break the chains that strangle them, so that we can begin to image alternatives for black people." The artist's technical finessing thrills the reader who expects the poem to move in one direction, but finds it moving in another. This haiku, like others, not only signals Sanchez's mastery of form, it also reveals her ability to forge her own technique with those aspects of haiku that she needs. Although she forces it to accommodate Afrocentric vision, Sanchez has healthy respect for haiku form. Keenly aware of the form's possibilities, she applauds its power to discipline novice poets. Thus, she is not attempting to destroy this existing form as a reactionary response to arbitrary dicta. In fact, an examination of her haiku convinces one that though her altering of structure is revolutionary, the extent to which Sanchez imbues the content and structure of haiku, filling it with an Afrocentric texture filtered through her unique womanist vision, is even more revolutionary. This tension between form as control and form as discipline informs Sanchez's most political haiku. Political vision in her work both disrupts the structure and offers future possibilities for form:

> redlips open wide

> like a wound winding down on
> the city. clotting.

A political poem that is indeed "mindblowing," this disturbing haiku offers a poetic argument. It incorporates the poet's sense of her role as vatic poet who serves the dual function of communicating with a particular community and the wider world. A powerful vignette, its vision is prophetic and moves the poet toward a new form that is Afrocentric in both structure and form. Sanchez breaks some rules while retaining others. As noted earlier, the insistence upon the present and external nature in haiku is important in conventional dicta. In this example, Sanchez turns this stricture on its head, inverting it so sharply that we sense an urgent note. The present tense Sanchez offers is not a soothing photograph of nature, but an intrusive and disturbing vignette, beginning an ominous chapter. Inherent in this haiku is the tension between present and future that the poet observes and advises. Thus, the texture, philosophy, and structure of this poem combine to render it wholly Afrocentric. As a poet, Sanchez observes and then tells what she sees, hinting at future implications. This is her strongest forte as a poet, and the haiku's compressed form works to her advantage. Forced to be brief, she must communicate her vision quickly. This rapid closure adds to the urgency of the moment.

As she forces this form to do much more than is expected, Sanchez also forces the reader to interact with the haiku, to go beyond the three lines to the implications of the vignette, to seek and know the future the poet thinks the circumstances augur. In effect, the reader is forced to inquire as to what is beyond its frame. Even if we did not have the dedication **"for a blk/prostitute,"** we would recognize this as a political haiku. Sanchez's careful structuring also alerts us that we must become involved not only in analyzing her haiku, but in responding to the situation she describes. In effect, she is producing haiku that make us feel and respond in much the same way that X. J. Kennedy suggests. Sanchez goes beyond form, in this instance creating a personal situation between poet and community. Indeed, her technical skill moves this haiku beyond Afrocentric content to Afrocentric discourse as we recognize the required interaction between poem and reader as "call-and-response," an Afrocentric form of discourse.

From the beginning the images elicit associations bordering on the grotesque. The synecdochic image "redlips open wide" suggests the myriad functions the prostitute serves, but in the simile "like a wound" the grotesqueness is deepened with the comparison of the lips to a wound with infectious connotations. "Clotting" further suggests unnaturalness, but this impression is achieved by reversing our preconceived notion of clotting. We must shift from the impression of clotting as positive, stemming the loss of blood, to clotting as negative, cutting off the heart's circulation. As a clot, the prostitute places the entire community at risk. In the case of the African American community, she is a special risk, but because she is a member of the community, her pain becomes communal pain: "Winding down on the city" reinforces the image of veins, circumscribing blood's course through the body. This "black prostitute," then, is headed to the heart of our existence; as a clot, she presents mortal danger. Once we have the picture in focus, it becomes for us a vignette. Sanchez's message comes in her careful structuring of images. In addition to the alignment of images, she uses the end-stop powerfully. In fact, she is "bringing it on home" to the reader. "Redlips open wide" is a powerful, lingering image, etching in the mind's eye a picture of the prostitute walking down the street. But the whole of its impact is made by Sanchez's structural innovation. End-stop as used by Sanchez in this instance, provides the tension between present and future, between the poet's prescience and our own dawning awareness. The period after "city," and the final word "clotting" moves the reader from disinterested observer to worried inner-city dweller or African American member of the community.

Sanchez is perceived as a militant writer. Such a perception has as much to do with the themes she addresses in her poetry as the form she uses. Critics, however, tend to focus on her militant themes. Certainly it is understandable that critics focus on Sanchez's use of certain themes in her work, but her disruption of the haiku form is directly related to her fusion of function and ethos in poetry, and though she is consistently revolutionary, she is also a skilled artist. Ironically, because of the general perception of her as militant, Sanchez's use of the haiku puzzles some scholars who associate her militancy solely with free verse and rarely with haiku. In an interview with Herbert Leibowitz, Sanchez talks about the perception of her as militant and places her work in perspective:

> My early poetry was introspective, poetry that probably denied or ignored I was black. I wrote about trees, and birds, and whatever, and that was hard, living in Harlem, since we didn't see too many trees, though I did draw on my residual memories of the South. People kept saying to me, if you write a political poem, it will be considered propaganda— an ineffective and poor poem—but I read Neruda and saw that he didn't deny the personal. In the early Sixties I became aware that the personal was the political.

Sanchez's statement reveals her own philosophy of poetry: poetry can be both personal and political. Further, this statement accounts for her unique fusion of external elements, introspective elements, and highly personal elements in her haiku. For Sanchez, the use of nature in an artificial sense serves no useful purpose. Human concerns fuel her struc-

tures. She uses nature in a way that forces it to serve a function. As she points out, her journey from the point at which she struggled to write about trees and plants from residual memories to her own realization that she could write revolutionary poetry has been a "long, tense road."

Because of her tendency to focus on the human condition in her poetry, Sanchez is often associated with militancy. Two misconceptions account for this tendency: Sanchez's highly militant and often publicized free verse poetry, which employs tropes and themes associated with political struggle, and the conventional notion of haiku that influences both the poetry and critical community. Sanchez's insistence upon her own vision puzzles both critics and friends alike. Her account of a friend's reaction to her love poetry offers an example of how she is perceived:

> When I gave my book *Love Poems* to a friend, she said, "God, I didn't know you wrote love poems." But in every book of mine there's been a section of lyrical pieces. If you describe me, as some critics do, as a lyrical poet, I say yes I am, but I'm also a hard-hitting poet and a political poet because this is a lyrical world and a terrible world, too, and I have to talk about that.

Terrible lyricism informs and surprises in the haiku dedicated to John Brown:

> man of stained glass legs
> harvesting the blood of Nat
> in a hangman's noose.

A perfect 5-7-5 form, this praise poem for John Brown exemplifies the terrible lyricism to which Sanchez refers. This haiku does not focus on nature, but on the bravery of John Brown's stand, situating him in history with Nat Turner. But it also deconstructs history in a surprising manner. Though she concedes with the reference to "stained glass legs" that John Brown's stand deserves our respect, Sanchez is also making it clear that Nat Turner was the first to die. Ironically, John Brown, though branded as a maniac by Lincoln, receives recognition that makes him a hero in the fight for African American freedom from European slavery. Afrocentric texture is apparent in this haiku, but so is its "teaching" or "running it down" quality. Rodgers defines "teaching" or "running it down" poems as those attempting to give direction to African American people. And in this dedication to John Brown, as in the prostitute poem, Sanchez is teaching, "running it down" to those who suffer from historical amnesia.

What is most striking about this form is the reader's sense that Sanchez has almost overwhelmed the form with the weight of significance. Yet, her lyricism not only saves the haiku, but gives it a cutting edge: "stained glass legs" is an overwhelmingly beautiful image. The reader inclined toward facile sympathy for John Brown is prohibited by the clarifying images. The fragile, glass legs are placed in proper perspective by the images of Brown "harvesting" Nat Turner's blood. Nat Turner becomes the model for John Brown, as is made clear by the image of Nat in the "hangman's noose." This deliberate use of form is as shocking as the vignette of the prostitute moving down the street. In the prostitute haiku, Sanchez is poet predicting future consequences; in the haiku dedicated to John Brown, she is the poet correcting the past. In another haiku dedicated to Paul Robeson, Sanchez is the poet suggesting the importance of Afrocentric vision. Reading our figures through Afrocentric lenses moves us closer to our African roots.

> your voice unwrapping
> itself from the Congo
> contagious as shrines.

Interestingly, this haiku does not conform to the 5-7-5 haiku constraints (it is 5-6-5 in this case). In content and texture, it resembles the haiku dedicated to John Brown. Both poems were deliberately pressed into the service of the African American experience. Though both are Afrocentric in nature, in the latter example, we also see Sanchez's introduction of "African" motifs and forging connections with African as a homeland. In each case the dedication identifies the haiku as political. Most powerful is the poet's decision to connect a hero figure with the African homeland. Like the haiku that opens this essay, the haiku dedicated to John Brown and Paul Robeson are political, yet lyrical.

In *The Militant Black Writer in Africa and the United States* Stephen Henderson talks about the inevitable distortion which occurs when African Americans attempt to fit themselves into the disinterested categories America prescribes for them. Offering Phillis Wheatley as an example of an artist who experienced geometric death, Henderson maintains that Wheatley was boxed in by alien forms. He views Wheatley as a "privileged slave" or "black prodigy" unable "to come to grips honestly with her blackness." As a poet, she was "boxed in by the right angles of the heroic couplet, ... an early emblem of geometric death." Henderson sees Wheatley as a tragic African American poet subsumed by form. But even if we qualify this view by indicating the extenuating nature of Wheatley's circumstances, we must admit that African American authors frequently must renegotiate prescribed forms to offer their own vision of the world.

In transforming haiku, Sonia Sanchez declares her own "linguistic manumission," refusing to be boxed in by its form. As she textualizes the form, forging her Afrocentric vision and Afrocentric structure within the discipline of the haiku form, she moves closer to a unique structure that carries her own signature.

Regina B. Jennings (essay date 1992)

SOURCE: "The Blue/Black Poetics of Sonia Sanchez," in *Language and Literature in the African American Imagination,* edited by Carol Aisha Blackshire-Belay, Greenwood Press, 1992, pp. 119-32.

[*In the following essay, Jennings describes Sanchez's aesthetics and asserts that her work has "inscribed the humanity of black people."*]

As a poet, Sonia Sanchez has evolved since her first book *Homecoming* published in 1969 during the heart of the Black Power Movement. Back then her poetics included a strident tropology that displayed a matriarchal protection of black people. Today, after publishing twelve books of poetry, including the acclaimed *Homegirls and Handgrenades* and *Under a Soprano Sky,* one can still discover poetic conventions developed during the Black Arts Movement. The purpose of this artistic movement involved challenging the Eurocentric hegemony in art by developing a new aesthetic that represented the ethos, pathos, and expression of African Americans. These neo-renaissance artists were inspired by the rhetorical eloquence and activism of Rev. Martin Luther King, Jr. and Malcolm X. From this era of intense political activism, artists such as Sonia Sanchez wrote poems illustrating a resistance to inequality best described in "Black Art" by Imamu Amiri Baraka.

> **It is obvious that revolutionary fervor characterized some of Sanchez's work, but it is essential for understanding her poetics, as well as the neo-aesthetic of the sixties, to recognize that anarchy was not the goal.**
> —*Regina B. Jennings*

It is obvious that revolutionary fervor characterized some of Sanchez's work, but it is essential for understanding her poetics, as well as the neo-aesthetic of the sixties, to recognize that anarchy was not the goal. These poets considered themselves to be word soldiers for black people, defending their right to have equality, honor, and glory. In each of Sanchez's volumes of poetry, for example, one finds the artist handling themes that include love, harmony, race unification, myth, and history. Her poetic personas are diverse, incorporating themes from China, to Nicaragua, to Africa. Yet, there is a pattern in her figurative language that blends an

African connection. In this article, I shall examine the Afrocentric tropes that embody Sanchez's poetics. To use Afrocentricity in this regard is to examine aspects of traditional African culture not limited by geography in Sanchez's work. A body of theory that argues such an African commonality is in Kariamu Welsh's *The Concept of Nzuri: Towards Defining an Afrocentric Aesthetic.* Using her model will enable this kind of topological investigation.

Houston Baker, Jr. presents a different aesthetic in *Blues, Ideology, and Afro-American Literature.* This book is a point of departure from Africa, concentrating solely on discussions of African American art from a black American perspective. On the back cover of **Under a Soprano Sky,** Baker maintains that blue/black motif appears in selected works by Sanchez. Baker's definition of the blues constitutes a transitory motion found precisely in this motif. The blues manifests itself in Sanchez's prosody in varying degrees and in differing forms. It determines shape and category, directs the vernacular, and informs the work. To demonstrate this specific vitality in Sanchez's poetry, Baker's construct of a blues matrix is an apt qualifier.

One can identify the blues as matrix and Afrocentric tropology in Sanchez's literary vision when one understands the significance of her axiology. Her ethics informs not only her creativity but her essays and articles as well. Her focus is to inscribe the humanity of blacks to challenge the Eurocentric perspective of black inferiority. Her particular axiology emerged during the greatest period of social unrest between whites and blacks. In the sixties, African American artists deliberately fused politics and art to direct social change. That Sanchez's axiology influenced her ethics has to be considered in order to understand why her poetry inverts the tropology of "white" and "black." The artists of the Black Arts Movement were at war with America. Their tone and perspective encouraged black people to rethink their collective position and to seize control to direct their destiny. Consider this Sanchez poem entitled **"Memorial":**

> i didn't know bobby
>   hutton in fact it is
>   too hard to re
>   cord all the dying
>   young/blks.
>   in this country.
> but   this i do know
>   he was
>   part of a long/term/plan
>   for blk/people.
>   he was denmark
>   vesey.
>   malcolm
>   garvey. all the

>   dead/blk/men
>   of our now/time
>   and ago/time.
>   check it out. for
>   bobby wd be living today.
>   Panther/jacket/beret
>   and all.
>   check it out & don't let
>   it happen again.
>   we got enough
>   blk/martyrs for all the
>   yrs to come
>   that is, if they
>   still coming
>   after all the shit/
>   yrs of these
>   white/yrs   goes down

The ethics in **"Memorial"** involve the dichotomy between "white" and "blk" (black). By positioning Bobby Hutton historically in the pantheon of heroic black men who died fighting against racial oppression, Sanchez elevates him. In death, she has magnified the significance of how he lived. The conditionality of being black in this poem denotes heroism against tyranny. In fact, D. H. Melhem argues that heroism exists in Sanchez's poetry. In the ideology of black people, Panthers are resistance leaders. Thus, by capturing the humanity of heroes in the first five stanzas, the persona suggests to the reader that he or she too can incorporate Hutton's heroics.

The term "white" adjectivally expresses the racism in America responsible for all the "years" of heroic deaths. White is now an inverted symbol, the antithesis of its traditional meaning of purity and goodness. Imamu Amiri Baraka, one of the definers of the black aesthetic, along with Larry Neal, "modernized the black poem by fusing it with modernist and postmodernist forms and ideas." William Harris writes that poets such as Sanchez learned from Baraka to invert poetic techniques. "Even the most cursory reading of contemporary black poetry reveals the extent to which it was influenced by projective form and avant-garde." However, Sanchez herself states that her inversion of symbols derived directly from the Muslims and Malcolm X. The meaning of avant-garde has to be broadened to include the philosophy of Malcolm X. To adopt a projective form was crucial to the sixties poet who stood before audiences during this politically tense era. Poets such as Sanchez were in the forefront of reshaping the ideology and activism of black people. Elements of the avant-garde challenged the status quo in society and in art. Welsh writes: "the idea of art for the sake of art has firm roots in European culture. Africans, for the most part, do not believe in the concept of art for art's sake. The life force is the motivating factor in the expression and the product of art."

In **"Memorial,"** the lines "check it out & don't let it happen again" speak directly to the reader, suggesting three modes of action. First, it encourages the reader or listener to review the situation inherent in the poem. Second, it expresses the need for a defensive and offensive posture against oppression. Third, it speaks of black control. This utterance of action points to the passivity of the audience. In this matriarchal persona, using accusatory language and tone in such lines as "part of a long/term/plan," Sanchez infuses the fracture that has historically wounded African American advancement. Likewise, the concept of black annihilation is in the denotation of the final terms "goes down."

Annihilation is a seminal notion in the collective black psyche based upon African enslavement. Therefore, Sanchez's linguistic war with America comes out of the ethos of black people. Conversely, another seminal theme throughout her body of work is one of racial solidarity. Using this theme, her persona as matriarchal protector assumes mythic dimensions. The following untitled poem from *We a BaddDDD People* is an example:

> i am a blk/wooOOOOMAN
> >   my face.
> >   my brown
> >   bamboo/colored
> >   blk/berry/face
> > will spread itself over
> > this western hemisphere and
> >   be remembered.
> > be sunnnnnnnNNNGG.
> >   for i will be called
> >   QUEEN. &
> >   walk/move in
> >   blk/queenly/ways

Here one can see that the ontology of "blk" has mythological and historical advantages. Male and female deities enrich the mythology of traditional Africa. As "queen," the black woman is an avatar, possessing extraordinary powers, stretching her "face" across the continents. To be black in this archetypal voice is to be potent, omnipotent, and good. In **"Memorial"** and in the above black woman poem, a feature of deictics, (verb tenses, adverbials, pronouns, demonstratives) is similar, in particular, to the concept of time. Both poems converge the timeless present with the future. However, in this black woman poem, the power of myth determines a success that will occur in the future. This sense of continuity depicts power, harmony, and victory. Welsh writes: "It is the consciousness of victory that produces in cyclical fashion an aesthetic will. The consciousness of victory will involve redefinition and reconstruction and a fundamental understanding of the creative processes, historical factors, and cultural legacies of Africa."

In the above poem, the aesthetic will is victorious because of the "redefinition" of black that has broadened into a nationalistic "consciousness." This nationalism that challenges Eurocentricism in art and society is an utterance that welcomes its own distinctiveness. It has a concern for all black people distinguished in the gradations of hue. Pragmatics this deliberate demonstrate how deeply Sanchez's poetics emerge from the concept of race solidarity. Unlike black poets of previous decades such as Countee Cullen and Claude McKay, Sanchez finds victory in being black. The ontology of black in the poetry of Cullen and McKay, on the other hand, involves one or all of the following declensions: inferiority, shame, denial, and escape. Form is another difference in Sanchez's poetry. She does not write poems in traditional taxonomy, imitating and revising established meter, versification, and rhyme. Her poetic patterns are avant-garde.

The theme and genre of the black woman verse show a definite African connection. This is a praise poem popular in Africa since 2000 b.c. By writing the above poem, Sanchez gives honor to the power of the female principle which will not only be "remembered" but be "sunnnnnnnNNNGG." Song and its traditional significance in African culture has already been established. From the mundane to the extraordinary, it is interwoven within traditional African culture. When a child cuts its first teeth, the people sing. When a king is coronated, the people sing. Larry Neal writes: "Most contemporary black writing of the last few years has been aimed at consolidating the African American personality. And it has not been essentially a literature of protest. It has, instead, turned its attention inward to the internal problems of the group."

Pigmentation problems have plagued African Americans since their sojourn in this country. Sanchez suggests this problem by lyrically presenting the solution. Her presentation demonstrates the realism inherent in an Afrocentric aesthetic because it must be "representational of the ethos of black people." Sanchez continues:

> and the world
> >   shaken by
> >   my blkness
> will channnNNNNNNGGGGGEEEE
> >   colors. and be
> >   reborn.
> >   blk. again.

To be reborn black again is a prelude to collective self-reliance. The final two lines suggest that blacks were in power prior to whites; therefore, seeking control is in concert with past behavior. Her historical reference probably points toward the ancient Egyptians or Kemitans. This reach back to Africa for a common past is a commonality argued in *The*

Concept of Nzuri: "Numerous writers have expounded on the historical and cultural bond between continental and diasporan Africans. It is not based solely on color, but the bond exists because of a common African heritage that dates back to predynastic Egypt."

Sonia Sanchez's poetic voice is visionary and archetypal. She wrote the above black woman poem twenty-one years before scholars in a focused manner textualized the notion of a common African aesthetic. Another facet of this theoretical aesthetic is found in the staggered formation of letters in particular words. This formation is an element of the avant-garde, introduced during the 1960s. For example, consider the spelling of the sign "change." Its orthographic repetition signals a specificity in quality and energy of expression. Dona Richards defines this energy as *ntu,* a manifestation of the energy informing our ontology. By transforming the orthography of "change," Sanchez causes her listeners and readers to enter a textured relationship with the sign's denotation, connotation, and sound. To hear or read a word formulated this way gives an unsettling tension. This orthography for the effect of sound is a poetic praxis that demonstrates the Black Arts Movement's theory of audience involvement, which can be traced back to traditional Africa. David Miller writes that some of Sanchez's poetry is "in essence, communal chant performances in which [she] as poet, provides the necessary language for the performance. The perceptions in such poems are deliberately generalized, filtered through the shared consciousness of the urban black." It is here where Sanchez's style sharply contrasts the performances of other sixties poets. Houston Baker would compare this technique to that of the blues or jazz singer making and improvising the moment simultaneously. To compare Sanchez to a more traditional poet is like comparing how singers Patti LaBelle and Paul Simon hit high notes. Thus, Sanchez's "quality of expression" as defined by Welsh, produces an energy that electrifies audiences, involving them in the experience of the performance.

An Afrocentric artist does not view society impartially because "society gives visions and perspectives to the artist." This interrelationship between poet and audience can also be examined in this next poetic praxis. Sanchez prefaces her poetry in a manner that warms the audience. Before she recites, she generally talks informally to her public. By the time she actually reads a poem, they have come to know her as friend, mother, sister, or guide. The following selections demonstrate how Sanchez speaks directly to and with her audience, requesting guidance, direction, companionship, and leadership. The first short excerpt is from a poem entitled **"blk rhetoric"** and the second is from **"let us begin the real work":**

> who's gonna make all
> that beautiful blk/rhetoric

> mean something . . .

> . . .

> with our
> minds/hands/souls.
> with our blk/visions
> for blk/lives.
> let us begin
> the begin/en work now.
> while our
> children still
> remember us & loooooove.

"Blk rhetoric" begs for an answer. The reader can be silent or the listener can shout the answer. It doesn't matter; the question encourages a response. Here the poet is asking for direction and guidance. She is asking either to join or to be joined in the task of building a better future for black people. In **"let us begin the real work,"** the deictics (pronoun usage) illustrate further the nonseparation between poet and audience. The pronoun "I" is absent. Jonathan Culler writes that the artist constructs a "model of human personality and human behavior in order to construct referents for the pronouns." Sanchez's "human behavior" is represented in the possessive case pronouns throughout the work. They bind the artist not only to her creation, but also to her audience. She takes responsibility for the behavior she calls forth in the poem. The use of "our" in particular shows the respect and interrelatedness the artist has for the audience, and by extension, society. She is "with" them, representing their ethos and pathos in poetry and performance. Terminology such as "our" visions and "our children" creates a commonality of purpose and strongly indicates her position as one of the people. The pragmatics suggest that she is not a leader but an utterer and clarifier of what is already known. To paraphrase Malcolm X in a 1972 film about his life, Sanchez is only telling the people what they already know.

Similarly, the blues is a creative form indigenously American that has always been known. In selected poems from Sanchez's collection, one finds, as Houston Baker points out, a blue/black motif.

> we are sudden stars
> you and i exploding in
> our blue black skins

To the redefinition of "black" as aesthetically and mythically good, Sanchez adds the color blue. This blue motif changes meaning in different poems, but it consistently demonstrates itself as a literary engagement issuing specific denotations to expression. Houston Baker defines the blues as matrix. It is an impetus for the search for an American form of critical inquiry. The blues is, of course, best known as a musical art form removed from linguistics and semantics. Naturally when one thinks of the blues perhaps one conjures up a grits and gravy black man fingering his guitar or a whiskey brown woman moaning about her man leaving town. Baker extends these cultural metaphors. In *Blues, Ideology, and Afro-American Literature,* his theoretical blues matrix informs African American literature, giving it inventive play in symbol and myth. Its expression gives the literature an emotive of music. The blues emerges out of black vernacular expression and history. It is the motion of the enslaved American Africans bringing coherence to experience.

In the above poem entitled **"Haiku,"** Sanchez gives us the energy of the blues "exploding" inside a distinctive American couple. Being both black and blue is an American duality that symbolizes the tragic institution of European slavery and the vital energizer that reformed the tragedy. It is significant that in Sanchez's collection of poetry, she frequently writes symbolically in sharp and brilliant haiku that form a "locus of a moment of revelation." **"Haiku"** reveals the heights of cosmological love, one boundless as the universe, with energies constantly in transformation and motion. Baker writes:

> To suggest a trope for the blues as a forceful matrix in cultural understanding is to summon an image of the black blues singer at the railway junction lustily transforming experiences of durative (increasingly oppressive) landscape into the energies of rhythmic song. The railway juncture is marked by transience. Only a radically altered discursive prospect—one that dramatically dissociates itself from the "real"—can provide access to the blues artistry.

To adjectivally describe "stars" as "sudden" marks this transience. Considering that the blues is always in motion contextualizes the differing modes of exploration that Sanchez creates when this motif appears. Using "blue" to denote mythic propensities, she creates it as a healing force, not just for her own personal self, but as a remedy for the distress that disturbs humanity. Consider this excerpt from **"Story."**

> when will they touch the godhead
> and leave the verses of the rock?
> and i was dressed in blue
> blue of the savior's sky.
> soon, o soon, i would be worthy.

Notice that the voice is restrained and reverent as if in prayer. The mythical elements are obvious, giving a timeless quality to the poem, but a certain deictic movement signaled by the word *when* quietly reaches back into antiquity. For a spe-

cific effect, Sanchez's typography moves inward in the final three lines. This kind of typographic movement alerts the reader that something special is occurring in those lines. It is the persona, perhaps being either ritualized or anointed for the job of saving souls. The comparison of "blue" as the color of the garment worn with the "blue" of the "savior's sky" dramatically accentuates the healing potential of "blue" as color and as spatial covering of the universe. This blues matrix is undertoned with a subtle sadness; yet it is not the sadness normally associated with the blues singer. It is more like the melancholy of a holy person relinquishing her personal wants to be able to fulfill an ordained prophecy. Larry Neal called it the Blues God that survived the Middle Passage: "The blues god is an attempt to isolate the blues element as an ancestral force, as the major ancestral force of the Afro-American. It's like an Orisha figure."

Orisha are African deities that can interact with mortals through prayer, sacrifice, and dance. They are either male or female, each controlling specific powers that inform human existence. In traditional African culture, one of the ways people can become avatars is through ritual where those chosen dress in the colors of the god and adorn themselves or are adorned in natural objects of the diety's habitat. For example, the riverain goddess Oshun heals with water and carries a fan crafted in a fish motif because her spirit moves through fish. In **"Story,"** the persona's spirit is placated and made reverential through blue as motif. This shows a specific example of how the blues matrix influenced Sanchez's poetics. From the mythic to the commonplace, it can determine content, category, and form. A point of contrast is in the next selection where Sanchez writes a blues poem written in black vernacular expression.

> will you love me baby when the sun goes down
> i say will you love me baby when the sun goes
> down
> or you just a summer time man leaving fo winter
> comes
> round.

This poem entitled **"blues"** can be sung or recited in the style of a blues song. Its mimesis is in the melody and lyric of music. Repetition is a poetic as well as a blues convention reifying the stated question. The terms "i say" merely add stress, signifying the importance of the initial inquiry. Langston Hughes gave the concept of the "blues-singing black" prominence in poetry. As a folk poet or a poet of the folk Hughes's works have marks of orature. According to Richard Barksdale in *Black American Literature and Humanism,* Hughes poetry contains naming, enumerating, hyperbole, understatement, and street-talk rhyming. Plus, Hughes's has a recurring motif of a "sun down" image. Sanchez in a real sense is a disciple of the Hughesian school. In her repeated line is a signifying "sun down" image.

An examination of the deictics of verb tense demonstrates the converging of the present with the future. The speaker is asking a question that can only be answered in the future. Baker refers to blues translators as those who interpret the experiencing of experience. The persona is allowing the readers to partake of her knowledge of distinct circumstances that ended in grief and loss.

Metaphorically ingesting her "man" demonstrates the music in lyrical and figurative language. Cannibalistically, this man is very much a part of the persona. Yet, an irony is in the final two lines: the persona is not going to suffer grief and loss again. Larry Neal writes: "even though the blues may be about so-called hard times, people generally feel better after hearing them or seeing them. They tend to be ritually liberating in that sense."

Aware of experiencing experience, the persona, "sees" the probability of sorrow lying before her. In the seeing is the "liberating" because she is free to make choices about her life. She can choose to continue her present course, or she may redirect her situation, excluding the danger signal in front of her, or she may take some other mode of action, keeping the situation in tact but with some element of difference. This series of options in this folksy expression is heightened because of the final stanza.

This is the inventive play of the blues. Was the persona teasing us all along? Will she indeed start a brand new life? Will she continue to question the stability of her mate, or is she preparing him for the difference, the changes that life automatically brings? The answer rests in the mystery of the Blues God, always in motion, forever in productive transit.

The poetry of Sonia Sanchez continues to be in productive transit. She is a poet spanning over two decades, creating a new aesthetic that fused politics and art. She believes that the artist is the creator of social values and her legacy and artistry indicate that single purpose. As the co-founder of the Black Studies Program at San Francisco State College, in 1967 she has been the antithesis of the ivory tower scholar. Sanchez's activism is difficult to equal. Not only did she fight for a Black Studies Program, but she is the first person to develop and teach a course concerning black women in literature. Sanchez has lived and created in an Afrocentric perspective before this way of knowing became textualized. Creating a protective matriarchal persona, she has through versification, plays, and children's books inscribed the humanity of black people. Being our champion and critic, she has forged a blue motif that cleanses, heals, mystifies, and rejoices.

FURTHER READINGS

Criticism

Clark, Sebastian. "Sonia Sanchez and Her Work." *Black World* 20, No. 8 (June 1971): 41-8, 96-8.
> Discusses the main themes found in Sanchez's poetry and asserts that "her very life-style is perpetually proposed as a link to the ideals and realizations of *Blackness* which so profoundly pervades her work."

Root, William Pitt. "Anything But Over." *Poetry* 123, No. 1 (October 1973): 34-56.
> Provides an overview of Sanchez and her poetry.

Additional coverage of Sanchez's life and career is contained in the following sources published by Gale: *Black Literature Criticism; Black Writers,* **Vol. 2;** *Children's Literature Review,* **Vol. 18;** *Contemporary Authors,* **Vol. 33-36R;** *Contemporary Authors New Revision Series,* **Vols. 24, and 49;** *Dictionary of Literary Biography,* **Vol. 41;** *Dictionary of Literary Biography Documentary Series,* **Vol. 8;** *DISCovering Authors Modules: Multicultural Authors; Major Authors and Illustrators for Children and Young Adults; Major Twentieth-Century Writers; Poetry Criticism,* **Vol. 9; and** *Something About the Author,* **Vol. 22.**

William Trevor

1928-

(Full name William Trevor Cox) Irish short story writer, novelist, and dramatist.

The following entry presents an overview of Trevor's career through 1998. For further information on his life and works, see *CLC,* Volumes 7, 9, 14, 25, and 71.

INTRODUCTION

Considered one of the premier writers in English alive today, Trevor has earned the highest praise from critics who compare him to fellow Irishman James Joyce. Trevor is known for his skill in describing the lives of unhappy, unloved, self-delusional characters, and evoking sympathy and humor rather than pity or ridicule for his misfits. Although his short stories and novels are not widely known outside Britain, Trevor has consistently won numerous awards and has enjoyed a prolific career.

Biographical Information

Trevor was born in Mitchelstown, County Cork, Ireland on May 24, 1928. Born into a Protestant family in a predominantly Catholic area, Trevor moved frequently as a result of his father's job. Attending thirteen schools throughout his youth, Trevor claims that he felt like an outsider and this gave him a greater ability to observe others, a talent he would later use in his writing. He attended Sandford Park School in Dublin and St. Columbia's College in Dublin before receiving a B.A. in history from Trinity College in 1950. In the early 1950s Trevor took a number of teaching posts in Northern Ireland and England while also pursuing a successful career as a sculptor. He married Jane Ryan in 1952, with whom he had two sons, Patrick and Dominic. After becoming disillusioned with sculpting, he published his first novel, *A Standard Behaviour,* in 1958. Through the early 1960s he worked as a advertising copywriter while simultaneously pursuing his writing career. He quit the advertising job to pursue writing full time in 1965, the same year he won the Hawthornden Prize for literature for his second novel *Old Boys* (1964). Since then, he has won the Benson Medal in 1975 for *Angles at the Ritz and Other Stories* (1975), an Allied Irish Bank Prize for Literature in 1976, the Heinemann Award for fiction in 1976, the Whitbread Prize in 1978 for *The Children of Dynmouth* (1976) and again in 1983 for *Fools of Fortune* (1983), the Irish community Prize in 1979 and the *Sunday Express* Book of the Year Award in 1994 for *Felicia's Journey* (1994). In addition, he was awarded honorary doctorates of literature from University of Exeter;

Trinity College, Dublin; Queens University, Belfast, and National University of Ireland, Cork, as well as being awarded Commander of the Order of the British Empire. Many of Trevor's works have been adapted into popular and award winning television movies and radio and theater plays. He continues to live and write in England.

Major Works

Trevor is known for his short stories and novels about people on the fringe of society, living in old boarding houses and hotels, who are unhappy and lonely. Set in England, novels such as *The Boarding House* (1965), *Mrs. Eckdorf in O'Neill's Hotel* (1969), and *The Children of Dynmouth* (1976) as well as his early short story collections deal with "the theme of loneliness and hunger for love . . ." to quote Julian Gitzen. In his novels and stories his characters search for the truth, although not all of them are willing to accept it. Particularly well known, Trevor's story "The Ballroom of Romance" recounts a young woman's decision to accept her fate and marry an alcoholic bachelor rather than continue to dream of a better life. In the 1980s Trevor turned his attention to Ireland and the political turmoil there. Setting many of his works in the past, he focused on themes of retribution, forgiveness, conflict, and isolation. *Fools of Fortune* (1983) centers upon a man living in self-imposed exile in Italy after the death of his family in the Anglo-Irish war. The novel links the importance of history, both personal and national, in shaping destiny, as well as the ways in which people create their own isolation. Stories in his collections *The News from Ireland* (1986) and *Beyond the Pale, and Other Stories* (1981) such as "Attracta", "Beyond the Pale", "Another Christmas," and "The News From Ireland" explore the conflict between Catholics and Protestants, arguing that while the past cannot be forgotten, forgiveness can bring restitution. *After Rain* (1996), a collection of short stories, and *Felicia's Journey* (1994) constitute Trevor's later works. The former centers on revelations of truth in twelve stories which are thematically connected, while the latter focuses on the destruction of a young unwed pregnant Irish girl and the forces who prey upon her.

Critical Reception

Critics of Trevor's work contend that he is among the greatest short story writers of the late twentieth century. Compared with James Joyce, Evelyn Waugh, Graham Greene, Henry James, and Samuel Beckett, Trevor is praised for his dark humor, his intimate portraits of sad, delusional characters, and his skill at evoking commonplace but lonely settings. Gary Krist writes that Trevor is "arguably the English-speaking world's premier practitioner of a certain brand of artistically distanced fiction . . ." and Stephen Schiff contends that "Trevor is probably the greatest living writer of short stories in the English language. . . ." Suzanne Morrow Paulson holds that not enough attention has been paid to Trevor's novels. She and other critics assert that within his novels Trevor perfects his character development and merges the tragic and comic. However, others argue that Trevor's work is uneven. James Lasden states: "A faltering muse seems to preside over [Trevor's] work, with the habit of bestowing superb openings, then disappearing, sometimes to return at the last moment, sometimes not." Other critics of Trevor's *Collected Stories* agree that the quality of his work fluctuates and that some of his characters fail to capture Trevor's interest and falter. However, Lasden concludes that "(w)hat Trevor does have . . . is something approaching genius for conveying ordinary human unhappiness."

PRINCIPAL WORKS

A Standard of Behaviour (novel) 1958
The Old Boys (novel) 1964; (play) 1971
The Boarding House (novel) 1965
The Love Department (novel) 1966

The Day We Got Drunk on Cake and Other Stories (short stories) 1967
Mrs. Eckdorf in O'Neill's Hotel (novel) 1969
Miss Gomez and the Brethren (novel) 1971
The Ballroom of Romance and Other Stories (short stories) 1972
Going Home (play) 1972
Elizabeth Alone (novel) 1973
The Fifty-Seventh Saturday (play) 1973
A Perfect Relationship (play) 1973
Marriages (play) 1974
Angels at the Ritz and Other Stories (short stories) 1975
The Children of Dynmouth (novel) 1976
Old School Ties (short stories) 1976
Lovers of Their Time and Other Stories (short stories) 1978
The Distant Past and Other Stories (short stories) 1979
Other People's Worlds (novel) 1980
Beyond the Pale and Other Stories (short stories) 1981
Scenes from an Album (play) 1981
Fools of Fortune (novel) 1983
The Stories of William Trevor (short stories) 1983
A Writer's Ireland: Landscape in Literature (nonfiction) 1984
The News from Ireland and Other Stories (short stories) 1986
Nights at the Alexandra (short stories) 1987
The Silence in the Garden (novel) 1988
Family Sins and Other Stories (short stories) 1990
Two Lives: Reading Turgenev and My House in Umbria (novellas) 1991
The Collected Stories (short stories) 1992
Excursions in the Real World: Autobiographical Essays (autobiography) 1994
Felicia's Journey (novel) 1994
Ireland: Selected Stories (short stories) 1995
After Rain (short stories) 1996

CRITICISM

Julian Gitzen (essay date 1979)

SOURCE: "The Truth-Tellers of William Trevor," in *Critique*, Vol. 21, No. 1, 1979, pp. 59-72.

[*In the following essay, Gitzen explores the themes of loneliness and self-delusion in Trevor's work.*]

Since the appearance of his first novel, *A Standard of Behavior* (1958), William Trevor has published a total of eleven volumes of fiction. Despite the popularity of *The Old Boys* (1964), *The Boarding House* (1965), and *The Ballroom of Romance* (1972), extensive analysis of his writing is as yet in short supply. Reviewers, on the other hand, have neither ignored Trevor nor hesitated to classify him. With virtual unanimity, they have labeled him a comic writer, differing only in their terms of reference, which vary from "black comedy" to "comedy of humor" to "pathetic" or "compassionate" comedy. As a satirist, he is most frequently compared with Evelyn Waugh, although Muriel Spark, Angus Wilson, Kingsley Amis, and Ivy Compton-Burnett are also mentioned. Additional points of comparison could readily be suggested: Trevor's ear for humorously banal small talk is reminiscent of Pinter; what has been referred to as "the incredulous, stuffy exactitude . . . the fustily elegant grammar" of his language recalls Beckett; his ruthless undeviating pursuit of a grubby, shabby verisimilitude evokes the work not only of Graham Greene but of such contemporaries as Edna O'Brien, John Updike, and David Storey. In addition, his interest in psychological questions and his preference for the traditional short story and novel allies him with writers as diverse as Henry James and Saul Bellow.

If Trevor is a comic writer, however, he with Beckett is assuredly among the most melancholy, as reflected in his characters' surroundings, in their situations and activities, and particularly in the theme of loneliness and hunger for love which more than any other feature distinguishes his writing. As a preface to exploring this theme, let us review Trevor's typical locales and representative features of the people who inhabit them. Consistently, his interest has focused on the marginal setting: a gaudy pub in a seedy district being demolished for reconstruction; a threadbare boarding house, its brown wallpaper and cheap furnishings unchanged for forty years; a deteriorating and unfrequented hotel in a Dublin backstreet; a tract house enveloped in tall weeds and grass, smelling of home-brewed beer and home-grown mushrooms. These are appropriate backgrounds for the lonely and forgotten, far removed from centers of purposeful activity and social ferment. Despite feeble resorts to the public media, these characters, described as "survivors, remnants, dregs," find little to which they may attach themselves. They are unenamored of the images on their television screens and cannot or will not be gathered into the collective mindlessness of popular culture. Most typical are those at the social fringes: the timid and ineffectual middle-aged bachelor reduced to an insignificant job, the homely spinster alone with memories of dead parents, the petty criminal, ever dodging but seldom unscathed. Many are orphans in search of surrogate families; others are so old that they have outlived both family and friends. Though many are married, not a single couple is conspicuously happy or contented; indeed, distorted or frustrated sexuality abounds. With divorce almost epidemic, numerous separated characters drift into solitary middle age. The majority are more notable for weakness or failure than for strength or success, which contributes to the choice they are usually forced to make: either to recognize (and forgive) cruelty or unfaithfulness in those they love or

limitations in themselves, or to cultivate comforting illusions, ranging from harmless daydreams and fantasies to compulsive and profound convictions. According to their differing temperaments and needs, some accept the truth, while others find illusions the only bearable remedy. Indeed, furnished as they often are with active capacities for fantasy and reverie, and given to daydreaming or imagining themselves in situations contrary to actuality, Trevor's characters are peculiarly well fitted for creating and sustaining illusions.

With its constriction of form, the short story highlights Trevor's thematic concerns. Each of his three collections of stories centers on a common theme, and the themes of each are notably similar. The first, *The Day We Got Drunk on Cake* (1967), carries no epigraph, but a fitting motto would be Mrs. Fitch's: *in vino veritas*. Characteristically, the setting is the pub or cocktail party, where excessive consumption loosens the tongue of one character, causing him to make blunt statements offensive to his companion. Tension increases as the unpalatable truth emerges. Alternatively, the truth about their situations occurs spontaneously to the leading characters, although the reactions of others toward them may trigger their awareness. **"The General's Day"** is typical, especially since it involves heavy drinking as a medium for truth. At seventy-eight, General Suffolk is among the extremely old people for whom Trevor has a particular fondness, no doubt because of their conspicuous loneliness but possibly also because he considers them the least afraid of truth and, therefore, the most refreshingly blunt of speech. On the day of the story, the General is frustrated in his attempts to carry on his favorite practices of drinking congenially with friends and seducing middle-aged women. Late at night, bitterly disappointed and very drunk, he suddenly realizes that he has grown unwelcome and even repulsive to others and thinks with lucid horror, "My God Almighty, I could live for twenty years."

The Ballroom of Romance (1972) concerns love unrequited, unequally shared, or selfishly taken for granted. Again loneliness becomes a source of anxiety, bringing with it the choice between truth and illusion. The heroine of the title story is thirty-six-year-old Bridie, whose one entertainment through the laborious years on her father's farm has been the Saturday night dance in a building named **"The Ballroom of Romance."** But romance has eluded Bridie, despite her faithfulness as a customer. At sixteen she fell in love with a young man whom she met at the ballroom, only to see him marry another. Having abandoned her quest for love, Bridie now aims only for a companionable marriage, centering her current hopes on the dance-band drummer. On the evening of the story, however, Bridie becomes conscious of the desperately predatory gestures of Madge Dowding, a spinster three years older; noticing the amusement of younger women at Madge's expense, Bridie realizes that she cannot return again to the ballroom, lest she too become a figure of the fun. Surrendering all further thoughts of the drummer, she resigns herself to eventual marriage to the wastrel, Bowser Egan, whom she will accept—since, after her father's death, she will be lonely. Thus Madge's loneliness betrays her into an illusion from which Bridie escapes in the cause of self-esteem, while recognizing that loneliness will in time drive her to an unpalatable compromise.

"**The Grass Widows**" elaborates the theme by demonstrating how features of character or age may screen out sudden truth, condemning one generation to relive the mistakes of another until it, too, gradually acquires self-awareness. While on a yearly fishing trip with her husband, the headmaster of a public school, Mrs. Angusthorpe recognizes a kindred spirit in the honeymooning bride, Mrs. Jackson, whose husband is one of Mr. Angusthorpe's former head boys. Seeing the two men behaving so compatibly, Mrs. Angusthorpe realizes that they are similarly domineering, inconsiderate, and selfish. In hopes of sparing Mrs. Jackson an unhappiness like her own, she calls the bride's attention to the "cruelty, ruthlessness, and dullness" of their two husbands. Not surprisingly, Mrs. Jackson rejects Mrs. Angusthorpe's advice that she should leave her husband and loyally protests that he is loving and considerate. With resignation Mrs. Angusthorpe concludes that, just as young Mr. Jackson is the successor to his old headmaster, so Mrs. Jackson is her own heir, locked into the guileless confidence which marked her own entry upon marriage and fated to discover in her own painful way that she is the victim of an unequal love. "**An Evening with John Joe Dempsey**" and "**Office Romances**" also treat the premise that the young often repeat the mistakes of their elders.

The Ballroom of Romance is distinguished from the other volumes of stories in offering the additional illuminative device of variations played on the mirror-image. In nearly every story the central figure is confronted by another person whose situation parallels or highlights his own. The protagonist's eventual recognition of such a parallel may engender increased self-awareness; alternately, the failure to perceive a manifest parallel creates dramatic irony. Thus Bridie's sense of her impending resemblance to Madge Dowding inspires her resolution to stop attending the ballroom in a futile search for romance. On the other hand, Mrs. Angusthorpe finds similarities enough between herself and Mrs. Jackson but fails to draw the full moral, for she remains ironically oblivious that her advice to the bride to leave her husband is even more applicable to herself. A third mirror-image appears in "**An Evening with John Joe Dempsey**," where a fifteen-year-old boy with greater astuteness than Mrs. Angusthorpe draws the latent parallel between himself and Mr. Lynch, the celibate but lustful middle-aged bachelor, a regular drinker at the village pub. Mr. Lynch has never left his jealous and righteous old mother, but he has lived

with her at the price of lies and deception, knowing that she would be outraged if he were to act on or even confide to her his secret longings. Instead, he escapes from her to the pub, where he tells melancholy sexual anecdotes, intended, he insists, as a "warning" to lads of the town. Young John Joe, too, lives in the shadow of an overly protective widow-mother from whom already he must conceal his adolescent sexual fantasies and from whom, he wearily recognizes, he must continue to hide his desires so long as he remains, like Mr. Lynch, the willing hostage of a mother's possessive devotion.

> In *Angels at the Ritz* (1975), Trevor's characters continue to be subjected to unpleasant truths, with the opportunity to display strength in accepting or reconciling themselves to them.
> —*Julian Gitzen*

In *Angels at the Ritz* (1975), Trevor's characters continue to be subjected to unpleasant truths, with the opportunity to display strength in accepting or reconciling themselves to them. In the title story, Polly Dillard confronts two bitter and closely related truths: at thirty-six she can never again recapture the exuberant frivolity with which she and her friends celebrated her twenty-second birthday at the Ritz; second, what was unthinkable in those sparkling days is about to happen: her husband will soon sleep with her lifelong friend. These circumstances she accepts as the legacy of middle age. For characters with less sturdy powers of resignation than Polly's, illusions *can* offer a comforting means of alleviating loneliness and reducing suffering. But as illustrated by "**In Isfahan**," illusion lacks the "quality" of truth. Iris Smith, discontentedly married to an Indian and living in Bombay, meets the Englishman Normanton on a day-tour of Isfahan. In another instance of *in vino veritas,* she consumes enough liquor to stimulate the confession that she has no desire to return to India. Clearly, she conceives Normanton as the gallant companion who will reprieve her from an unpleasant fate. Despite her candor, Normanton remains reserved and affects to ignore her tentative advances, though he does not correct her romantic speculation that he is a married architect. After her departure, he inwardly reviews his own unhappy past—including two failed marriages which have discouraged him from trying again. He perceives that their encounter has at least provided her with the comforting illusion of having "met a sympathetic man." She will never know his personal shortcoming, "a pettiness which brought out cruelty in people." Their exchange has been unequal, for his impression of her represents what she actually is, while her memory of him is composed of imagined details. He is deprived of a vital dimension: "He was the stuff of fantasy. She had quality, he had none."

In broad structural and thematic terms, Trevor's novels bear a close resemblance to his short stories. Although loneliness and illusion in dreary circumstances remain his concerns, the greater length of the novels permits him to dispense with the obvious climactic device of the obstinate and unwelcome truth-teller. While Trevor takes the opportunity for elaborate character exploration (particularly in his four most recent novels), he prefers to people the increased space of the novel with a more representative society than can be usefully treated in a short story. Usually these figures vary notably in personality and concerns but are not often blood relatives. While a single figure may emerge as "major," approximately equal attention is ordinarily given various characters. Frequent, sudden transitions shift attention from person to person, maintaining the sense that diverse activities are occurring almost simultaneously, while institutional settings serve to bring the people together. In *A Standard of Behaviour* the chief locale is Mrs. Lamont's boarding house for artists; the title of *The Boarding House* speaks for itself; and *Mrs. Eckdorf in O'Neill's Hotel* (1969) features a Dublin hotel. In *Elizabeth Alone* (1973) the characters temporarily share the convalescent ward of a women's hospital, while a pub is the center of action in *Miss Gomez and the Brethren* (1971). Boarding houses also provide incidental settings in both *The Old Boys* and *Elizabeth Alone.* In taking for its locale a seaside resort town, *Children of Dynmouth* (1976) departs somewhat from Trevor's normal institutional focus. In terms of character, setting or situation, and theme, his four most representative and typical novels to date are: *The Boarding House, Elizabeth Alone, Mrs. Eckdorf in O'Neill's Hotel,* and *Miss Gomez and the Brethren.* Like his short stories, all four concern lonely people, most of whom dream, daydream, or fantasize. In addition, all four prominently feature his favorite age-group of the late middle-aged or elderly, while each introduces one of his most convincing and successful character-types, the petty criminal, confidence man, or blackmailer. As a means of distinguishing truth from illusion, each novel introduces a character in whom the others confide, who recognizes the truth about his companions. Like the short stories, the novels avoid easy thematic conclusions. While applauding truth, Trevor repeatedly demonstrates that acceptance of truth requires resoluteness and the power of forgiveness. For those unable to forgive or reconcile themselves to cruelty or suffering, illusion may remain a necessity. Alternately, loneliness and need for love may generate a forgiving nature inspired by religious faith, one transcending straightforward distinctions between reality and unreality.

In *The Boarding House,* the building and its inhabitants share a shabby, semi-impoverished decorum. In the main ineffectual and undistinguished, the residents have been overtaken by loneliness, as recognized by their landlord, Mr. Bird, who describes them as "solitary spirits. Alone." Their lonely distress accounts for their fantasies and daydreams and for the dreams which visit them in sleep. Very few of Trevor's characters are not dreamers—but those few are seldom commended, since those who do not dream usually scheme; the strong willed, selfish, brutal manipulators never or seldom dream. *The Boarding House* is furnished with one such unenviable figure in Nurse Clock (whose name perhaps is meant as a reminder of her maddeningly reliable and unemotional efficiency and purposefulness). Her natural enemy is the malicious but inept blackmailer, Studdy, whose name (viewed from any angle) must be ironic. All three attempts by Studdy to collect blackmail payments fail, and one ends in Studdy's being punched. Though not hostile toward the other boarders, who do not threaten him, Studdy bears Nurse Clock a good deal of ill will, which she returns with interest. Nurse Clock's specialty is caring for the aged; she enjoys being able to command their obedience, while profiting financially from their dependence on her. Geriatric work in a Trevor novel requires a thick-skinned constitution, since, despite their pathetic loneliness, his ancients are not merely crotchety but alertly and energetically frank and uncompromising. When informed by Nurse Clock that it is time for her injection, the eighty-nine-year-old Mrs. Maylam replies with spirit, "You can put it up your jumper for all I care. I can look after my frigging self, you know."

Nurse Clock's ambition is to manage a nursing home, and she comes near doing so when, on the death of Mr. Bird, she inherits a half-interest in the boarding house. Unfortunately, her partner in the inheritance is Studdy; the arrangement is, of course, intentionally perverse, reflecting the secret wish of Mr. Bird that his boarding house may not long survive him. He understood the mutual rapacity of Studdy and Nurse Clock and foresaw that their shameless struggle for single ownership would reveal their true characters to their fellow boarders while simultaneously destroying the boarding house as an institution. Though newly dead at the opening of the novel, Mr. Bird functions as the truth-teller, a diarist whose observations about his boarders are invariably profound. One entry reads, "Studdy is a species of petty criminal . . . Yet how can one not extend the hand of pity towards him? Anyone can see that poor old Studdy never had a friend in his life." Toward Nurse Clock he is less charitable, observing, "Nurse Clock has morbid interests. She is a woman I would fear were it not for my superior position."

After his death Mr. Bird survives as a presence in the minds of his boarders and kitchen staff. He appears in their dreams, a subconscious voice threatening their illusions. Those most jealous of their illusions react most vigorously to these dream-messages. Among them is the Nigerian, Mr. Tome Obd, who after twelve years of furtive courtship, has been rejected by the Englishwoman whom he adores. Mr. Obd dreams that Mr. Bird has risen from the dead and eventually envisions him as a ghost who repeats "Alas, Tome Obd" like an incantation. In a maniacally suicidal effort to eradicate his painful vision, Mr. Obd burns both himself and the boarding house. Thus Nurse Clock's ambition is thwarted, but not before she has been revealed as a ruthless schemer, intent on dispossessing her fellow boarders. As they watch the old house burning and recognize that they must separate, the boarders face once more the loneliness peculiar to those who have no families and virtually no friends.

In broad structural and thematic terms, Trevor's novels bear a close resemblance to his short stories. Although loneliness and illusion in dreary circumstances remain his concerns, the greater length of the novels permits him to dispense with the obvious climactic device of the obstinate and unwelcome truth-teller.
—*Julian Gitzen*

Elizabeth Alone introduces a change in narrative technique. While in *The Boarding House* the truth-telling is entrusted to a single person, in *Elizabeth Alone* individual characters make self-discoveries which they separately confide to another commonly recognized as reliable. The locale of *Elizabeth Alone* is the Cheltenham Street Women's Hospital; inevitably, the majority of notable characters are women, one of whom becomes the trusted confidant of her fellow patients. Like Mr. Bird, Elizabeth Aidallbery is charitable and compassionate but has put aside illusions in favor of truth. At forty-one she is recently divorced; with her mother in a nursing home and her daughter, Joanna, on the verge of joining a commune, Elizabeth is facing middle-age loneliness. While convalescing from a hysterectomy, she becomes acquainted with three fellow patients: Silvie Clapper loves an unreliable young Irishman named Declan; Lily Drucker is the devoted wife of Kenneth, who is dominated by a crudely possessive mother; and the elderly Miss Samson is devoted to the memory of Mr. Ibbs, late owner of a boarding house for religious persons. Mr. Ibbs, too, kept a diary and further resembles Mr. Bird in being outwardly charitable but secretly pessimistic. Before leaving the hospital, Silvie discovers that Declan is a liar and a thief, but her love enables her to accept his faults. Lily learns that before their marriage Kenneth frequently visited prostitutes, apparently because his mother's jealous dominance prevented him from courting normally. When Lily confides in her, Elizabeth sensibly counsels forgiveness, pointing out that Kenneth's furtive sexual affairs ended with his marriage. Of the confessions made to Elizabeth, the most extended and dramatic is Miss Samson's. After revealing that her discovery in Mr. Ibbs's diary of his atheism has rendered her incapable of prayer, Miss Samson shares with Elizabeth her more recent and surprising realization that she was in love with Mr. Ibbs. She explains that so long as God was associated for her with the

benign Mr. Ibbs, then God, too, appeared benevolent. Deprived of Mr. Ibbs's lustre, God seems unkind and unresponsive to human suffering. Unlike Silvie and Lily, Miss Samson appears unable to accept the truth.

Aside from her interest in her fellow patients, Elizabeth maintains a concern for her lifelong friend, Henry, who is the subject of the novel's most extensive psychological study. Though a success in public school, the jovial and well meaning Henry has known only failure as an adult, whether as husband, father, or employee. Naturally, he fondly envisions a salutary self-transformation, assuming that Elizabeth will agree to marry him. While politely refusing his proposal, she secretly entertains a willingness to accept, since, like Bridie of "The Ballroom of Romance," she dreads being left alone. She rejects Henry because she recognizes that he wants help, not love, but is too old to be helped. She considers Henry "still a child" but believes this "an impossible truth to reveal, too cruel and sorrowful, for no one could be a child at forty-one and properly survive." Her prophecy is fulfilled when Henry accidentally (and with childlike carelessness) kills himself, after experiencing the sudden and lucid understanding that, as Elizabeth has said, he is still a child or at least would rather be one. After his happy and successful childhood, adult concerns and enterprises have proven uniformly "dreary and grey," and, deprived of enthusiasm for them, he has gone from failure to failure. Drink has become his refuge, becoming the instrument of his death, when he drunkenly leaves a stove unlit, is overcome by gas, and confirms Elizabeth's judgment that the truth would be "too cruel" for him to bear. Like Tome Obd, Henry is "the stuff of fantasy" and must suffer the fate of fantasies; with the strength to accommodate herself to the truth about her shortcomings and those of others, Elizabeth survives.

Another person for whom the transition from childhood to adulthood proves troublesome is Ivy Eckdorf of *Mrs. Eckdorf in O'Neill's Hotel,* which differs from *The Boarding House* in focusing unmistakably on Mrs. Eckdorf, a photographer specializing in documentaries. An intuitive impulse based on an anecdote has led her to Dublin in the hope of photographically analyzing a "tragedy in O'Neill's Hotel." Among the people she meets are: Mrs. Sinnott, the ninety-two-year-old owner of the hotel; Eugene Sinnott, her fifty-eight-year-old son, addicted to liquor and horse racing; Philomena, Eugene's estranged wife; and O'Shea, the hotel porter. In general, these characters seem more interested in their illusions than in truth. For instance, the neighborhood prostitute, Agnes Quin, fantasizes about life as Olivia de Havilland, while her friend, Eugene Sinnott, meticulously reviews his dreams in search of possible racing tips. More dramatic is the engrossing daydream of O'Shea: upon Mrs. Eckdorf's appearance, he is seized by the totally unfounded conviction that she intends to buy and restore the deteriorating hotel. Encouraged by the ruthless photographer who realizes that his fantasy provides a plausible excuse for the intimate questions she must ask in uncovering her story, O'Shea blissfully constructs an elaborate and obsessive fantasy of the hotel rising "like a phoenix-bird."

One character who escapes serious illusions is Mrs. Sinnott, whose name (sin-not) reflects the saintly disposition which attracts others to her. Deaf and dumb, she keeps notebooks in which her visitors may write, notebooks which serve a revelatory purpose like the diaries of Mr. Bird and Mr. Ibbs. Encouraged by Mrs. Sinnott's benevolence and by the secrecy of silent communication, her visitors readily confide their frustrations and yearnings. Since Mrs. Eckdorf, in time, associates Mrs. Sinnott with God, since Mr. Bird freely compares himself with God, and since Miss Samson "confuses" Mr. Ibbs with God, some analogies may be in order: like the boarding-house owners, Mrs. Sinnott has created her own self-contained world, peopling it with figures of her own choosing, watching over and governing them; like Mr. Bird and Mr. Ibbs, she has shown particular charity toward lonely and helpless orphans. Second, like the two men, she is trusted by her household and is, consequently, favored with godlike intimate glimpses of their thoughts and affairs. Finally, her speech and hearing handicap causes her to seem divinely remote and inscrutable, while her distance is physically increased by living alone (like Mr. Bird) in a room on the top floor of the building. Eventually, she joins Mr. Bird and Mr. Ibbs in death and achieves the ultimate remoteness. Although Mrs. Eckdorf comes to regard Mrs. Sinnott as a "special servant" of God, her life has been marked by no conspicuously saintly incidents, nor does the wise priest, Father Hennessey, writing a book about women saints in Ireland, think to devote even a footnote to Mrs. Sinnott.

Unlike the serene old woman she admires, Mrs. Eckdorf is driven and tormented. She traces her misery to her parents' separation during her childhood, after which her mother's sexual dissipation instilled in the daughter a disgust for sex. Unwilling to consummate either of two marriages, she has instead become a cruelly voyeuristic photographer, deceptively boasting to be an apostle of truth, "the parent of understanding and love." Her efforts to establish important facts concerning the drama of O'Neill's Hotel are for some time frustrated by the desire of the Sinnotts to maintain their privacy, but at last she finds a willing accomplice in the worshipful O'Shea, who recalls enough of one incident to permit Mrs. Eckdorf's unerring intuition to sketch in the remainder. One night, after drinking heavily, Eugene forcibly seduced the maid Philomena. When she was found to be pregnant, Eugene married her on the recommendation of Mrs. Sinnott. After the pair proved incompatible, Philomena was left to rear her son alone—but under the benevolent eye of Mrs. Sinnott.

Having resolved this mystery, Mrs. Eckdorf finds it appli-

cable to herself. Like Philomena, she has been victimized by selfish and brutal sexual acts; unlike Philomena, she has not forgiven those intent on persuading her to "bear the thought of other people's flesh." In assuming that all of the participants in the drama at O'Neill's Hotel have forgiven each other, Mrs. Eckdorf is once more well served by her intuition. Indeed, "to have felt that sorrow everyday . . . would have been too much for . . . them to bear." Mrs. Eckdorf's failure to emulate the Sinnotts in learning forgiveness leads to her nervous breakdown. In a state of childlike simplicity (she has previously lamented that her happiness ended at the age of eight), she entertains an elaborate fantasy concerning the glorious revival of O'Neill's Hotel. O'Shea's vision, once preposterous to her, becomes her solace. She who once spoke of truth as the parent of understanding and love has been unable to act on her own wisdom. Since the inability to forgive is "too much . . . to bear," she can survive only by rejecting truth and welcoming illusions—and joining the hapless ranks of Henry and Mr. Obd.

Miss Gomez and the Brethren continues and thematically extends the pattern established in the previous novel. Mrs. Eckdorf and Miss Gomez share unhappy childhoods, and unpleasant sexual experiences leave both lonely and bitterly aware of human weakness. Equally gifted with intuitive powers, the women rely on them in uncovering details of "crimes" of sexual origin. The atheistic views of both suddenly give way to intense religious convictions, including the premise that "you can learn to forgive and not to condemn." Their religious attitudes cause both women to be regarded as insane, but only Mrs. Eckdorf actually becomes deranged. Finally, their common experiences testify that, although religious faith may be illusory, it generates a comforting sense of love and harmony.

The Jamaican Miss Gomez begins life in desperate need of comfort. As an infant, she is orphaned by a fire which leaves her the sole survivor of ninety-two persons. Haunted by the event, she finds life lonely and pointless. As an adult, she arrives in London, working as a stripper and prostitute until she discovers devotion-by-correspondence with the church of the Brethren of the Way. Her desire to spread the gospel of her faith brings her to Crow Street, most of whose buildings have recently been demolished. Here she gains employment as a cleaner in a pet shop belonging to Mrs. Bassett, whose assistant, Alban Roche, has served a jail term as a voyeur. The circle of acquaintances necessary to the story becomes complete when Miss Gomez agrees also to clean "The Thistle Arms," a decaying pub whose proprietors are Mr. and Mrs. Tuke. Their daughter, Prudence, is attracted to Alban, but the two young people are emotional casualties, Alban having been loved too much by his mother, Prudence having been unloved by either parent.

Sensing that a "crime" is about to overtake these people,

Miss Gomez seeks to establish the relevant facts, for she wishes to try the power of mutual prayer and is proceeding according to the instructions of her spiritual leader: "When the truth is clear before us, then only may we truly pray." She discovers several important facts, among them Alban's secret oedipal yearnings for his mother, set down in his private notebooks. She also becomes aware of Mrs. Tuke's dislike for her daughter and perceives that Mrs. Tuke is "afraid of reality: she cannot bear to see herself as she is. She lives in a mist of alcohol and fantasy." Before her investigation is complete, however, she is suddenly possessed by an alarming vision which (unknown to her) coincides with the death of Mrs. Bassett. Erroneously convinced that Alban is about to rape and murder Prudence, Miss Gomez appeals desperately to the understanding and sympathy of Mr. and Mrs. Tuke. Ignoring Miss Gomez' pleas to join her in prayer, the Tukes call the police. When questioned by a police sergeant, Miss Gomez explains excitedly that only faith can counter the apparent cruelty, disorder, and meaninglessness of existence. She has been taught by the Reverend Lloyd Patterson that "there is an order . . . of birth and life and death and glory: nothing happens by chance. All people are part of one another, no one is alone." When the temporarily missing Prudence reappears unharmed, Miss Gomez believes her prayers have been answered. Since Mrs. Bassett has willed her money and property to Alban, Miss Gomez sees the pet-shop owner's death as an instance of divine intervention. Now Alban can offer some security to Prudence instead of being frustrated by his inability to live with her. Thus, by ending Mrs. Bassett's life in such a timely manner, God has averted a crime.

Buoyed by the admittedly disputable evidence of the power of prayer, Miss Gomez returns to Jamaica, the headquarters of the Brethren of the Way. Upon arriving, she discovers that the Reverend Patterson is a fraud, who has recently fled with the tithes of the faithful. Hers has been only another illusion, no different than the dreams of Mrs. Tuke. Though posing as a truth-teller, Patterson was instead a dream-merchant who promised his correspondents a heaven where "no one was condemned and no one was looked down upon, in which . . . there was no loneliness, in which you took the hand that was next to yours." Despite her disappointment, Miss Gomez concludes that only such a dream can forestall widespread madness. Instead of being shattered, her faith is strengthened. The Brethren were an illusion, but—for her—the God of the Brethren is real.

The novel adds a further dimension to the question of truth *versus* illusion. Physical events may be established as true or false; truth of character or personality can be determined; but what of beliefs for which the demonstrable evidence is inconclusive? Is Miss Gomez' faith a potentially treacherous illusion, or is she correct in assuming that without faith we risk madness? Though intangible, emotional states such

as love and loneliness are more readily measurable than metaphysical truths. Emotion shades into faith, however, as with Miss Gomez, whose faith arises from loneliness. In such situations the question of illusion is difficult to resolve. William Trevor not only values and seeks psychological truth but recognizes the point at which it retreats into metaphysical mystery.

Robert E. Rhodes (essay date 1983)

SOURCE: "William Trevor's Stories of Trouble," in *Contemporary Irish Writing,* edited by James D. Brophy and Raymond J. Porter, Iona College Press, 1983, pp. 95-114.

[*In the essay below, Rhodes examines five of Trevor's short stories concerning the Irish troubles and finds that they share similar characters and themes.*]

William Trevor was born Trevor Cox in Mitchelstown, County Cork, in 1928, spent his boyhood in provincial Ireland, and was educated at St. Columba's and Trinity College, Dublin. Since 1958—and mostly since 1964—he has been the author of nine novels, five collections of short stories, and a number of radio and television dramas as well as plays for the stage. A member of the Irish Academy of Letters and the recipient of an honorary C.B.E., an unusual distinction for a non-British writer—although he has lived in Devon for a number of years—he has garnered several literary awards, including the Hawthornden Prize, the Royal Society of Literature Award, the Allied Irish Banks Prize for Literature, and the Whitbread Prize for Fiction. Brian Cleeve's 1967 *Dictionary of Irish Writers* observes that his works "have won Trevor a great critical reputation as well as popular success in America, Britain, and Europe"; and an August 1981 interview by Elgy Gillespie in *The Irish Times* notes that "These days he is a very famous writer indeed. . . ."

In addition to the formal honors that have come his way, it is true that Trevor's novels and short story collections have consistently enjoyed favorable reviews, that a number of his books have been reprinted, and that he now appears with regularity in such periodicals as the *New Yorker*. But it is also apparently and surprisingly true, despite declarations by Cleeve and Gillespie and a growing reputation, that thus far Trevor has been the subject of only two moderate-length critical studies: Mark Mortimer's 1975 "William Trevor in Dublin" and Julian Gitzen's 1979 "The Truth-Tellers of William Trevor."

Given the size of his canon and his putative reputation, it seems only a matter of time before Trevor receives the kind of critical examination that will test the works against the reputation. For the time being, at least, most such attention is likely to focus on Trevor's "non-Irish" fiction—most of which has its scene in England—since only one of his nine novels and nineteen of the fifty-five or so of the readily available short stories are "Irish," which may explain why he is not even listed in such relatively recent compilations as *A Bibliography of Modern Irish and Anglo-Irish Literature* and *Anglo-Irish Literature; A Review of Research.* Such omissions are perhaps reason to call attention to some aspects of Trevor's work that fall under the rubric "Irish."

Although Irish characters figure fairly prominently in *Elizabeth Alone* (1973) and *Other People's Lives* (1981), only *Mrs. Eckdorf in O'Neill's Hotel* (1969) among the novels takes Ireland—specifically Dublin—as its scene, and except in some fairly conventional ways it is difficult to think of this as an "Irish" novel. Of the short stories, four do not really qualify as "Irish." Of **"Miss Smith,"** Trevor himself has said that it "might perhaps have come out of anywhere, but in fact is set in a town in Munster. . . ." **"The Forty-Seventh Saturday"** is a rather comical story of the affair of two lovers with Irish names, but the scene is London and there is nothing to distinguish these lovers as "Irish" or, indeed, as different in nationality from many other pairs of lovers in Trevor's stories. The action of **"The Grass Widows"** takes place in Galway, but the story is about two English couples; and **"Memories of Youghal"** features a seedy private detective who recalls his Youghal boyhood, but the scene is a Mediterranean resort and the protagonist is really an elderly English schoolteacher.

The remaining fifteen Irish short stories form a moderate-sized but solid accomplishment, a body of work meriting the attention of ordinary discriminating readers and critics alike. Almost all of them deal with rural and small-town Irish life and reveal both knowledge of and sympathy with that life. It is not necessary, of course, to reduce the stories to categories, but it does seem that in them Trevor has played variations on a handful of themes that have unusual significance for those who would use the artist's insights to understand contemporary Irish life; repression, coming of age or failing to come of age, parent-child relationships, and love—usually thwarted.

Five of the readily available Irish stories that have appeared since 1975 show that Trevor has addressed himself to a subject that very few Irish writers have been able to avoid: the renewal of Ireland's ancient Troubles in Northern Ireland since the late 1960s and the impact of that violence on people in the North, in the Republic of Ireland, and in England. That Trevor's attention has been increasingly riveted by the Troubles is suggested by the fact that his first full-length stage play, *Scenes from an Album,* which opened in Dublin's Abbey Theatre in August 1981, clearly takes its motive from the history of the Troubles. Writing in *The Irish Times,* Elgy Gillespie notes of the play, "Once again . . . it will allow him to examine the interfaces between cultures, between Protestant and Catholic and English and Irish and Planter and Gael, toying [with] the ambiguities of their mingled lives," and she quotes Trevor as saying, "Because I *do* feel the countries are inextricably dependent on each other, and it's what I still want to write about." Add to these views Trevor's own Protestant background and his many years of writing about the English in England and he seems particularly suited to have written the five stories we will examine here: **"The Distant Past," "Saints," "Attracta," "Autumn Sunshine,"** and **"Another Christmas."**

On the whole, the protagonists in these stories differ markedly from those in Trevor's other Irish stories, and differ in ways that are significant both for their own lives and for the insights Trevor offers through their dramas.

First, there is a significant age difference. In the other stories, protagonists range from age seven to age thirty-seven at the time of significant action, with most of them being under twenty, two in their early twenties, and two in their early thirties. On the other hand, all of the protagonists in the Troubles stories are clearly older and generally well set on their life courses. Only the couple in **"Another Christmas"**—who also differ in other ways from most of these protagonists—are identified only as "middle-aged," the rest ranging from sixty-one to sixty-nine and in one case perhaps to the early seventies.

Essentially well set on their life courses by their ages, they are further defined by their religious backgrounds. Almost all the protagonists of Trevor's other Irish stories come from often repressive Catholic backgrounds. To the contrary, only the protagonists of **"Another Christmas"** and important characters, though not protagonists, in **"Attracta"** and **"Saints"** are Catholic. The rest are clearly identified as Anglican or Anglo-Irish; indeed, one is a Church of Ireland rector, and protagonists in two other stories define much of their position in Irish society by their Protestantism. In words that to some degree apply to most of these protagonists, Trevor writes of the titular character in **"Attracta"**: "Within the world of the town there was for Attracta a smaller, Protestant world. Behind green railings there was Mr. Ayrie's Protestant schoolroom. There was the Church of Ireland, with its dusty flags of another age, and Archdeacon Flower's prayers for the English royal family."

Furthermore, most of the protagonists of Trevor's other Irish stories belong to a socio-economic stratum somewhat lower than that of protagonists in stories about the Troubles, a condition that may be related to their Catholicism. With few exceptions and even these cannot be called unusually prosperous—the Catholic protagonists and their families are working class people: a farmer, a shop assistant, a butcher, a mechanic, for instance. Conversely, again with the exception of the protagonists of **"Another Christmas,"** the protagonists come from at least moderately affluent backgrounds that confer certain social distinctions. If the elderly brother and sister of **"The Distant Past"** are only shabby genteel relics of the Ascendancy Big House tradition, The protagonist of **"Saints"** is a wealthy and cultivated inheritor of the same tradition; and the other protagonists are a respectable teacher in a Protestant school and a Church of Ireland rector.

In short, by age, religious persuasion or probable inclination, and socio-economic status, the protagonists of these stories are insulated from the imperatives that often drive their younger, poorer, Catholic neighbors: sexual desire, the search for identity, establishing places for themselves in their communities. Furthermore, though these are indeed stories of the Troubles and therefore of lingering animosities, latent danger, and explosive violence, these protagonists when we first meet them are neither obvious perpetrators nor immediately personal victims of violence. While there may sometimes be some mild disharmony, on the whole their relationships with their Catholic countrymen have been amiable and sometimes affectionate. Despite their distinct minority position, they are people who seem to have achieved some kind of equilibrium in the business of living. Essentially impregnable in ways the young are not, even as members of minority in a troubled place and time, they seem capable of emerging unscathed from their contact with the renewed British-Irish conflict of the present. Still, they are victims of the past as much as Irish Catholics.

While the youthful protagonists of Trevor's other Irish stories characteristically inhabit two worlds, the everyday world and the world of fantasy or imagination, and sometimes seek harmony between them, Trevor's older protagonists, at the outset, typically seem to have left a conflict between two worlds behind or at least to have resolved such a conflict satisfactorily. Very often, however, this is because they have put the past to rest. What shatters the illusion of safety and impregnability and forever alters their worlds is the renewal of outright violence in the late 1960s *and* the recollection of past violence and its relationship to present violence. Sometimes it is a personal past, too, but, if so, it is bound inextricably to the violent English-Irish past that eventually and inevitably merges with today's violence. In short, the past not only repeats itself but is a continuation of what for the Irish has been "the cause that never dies" and for the protagonists results in almost every case in increased loneliness and isolation.

The title of **"The Distant Past,"** perhaps the earliest of Trevor's Troubles stories, signals what has become his continuing exploration of the ways in which apparently dead events of past conflicts obtrude on the present and shape the

future. **"The Distant Past"** and **"Saints,"** one of Trevor's most recent stories, have as protagonists survivors into the 1970s of the Anglo-Irish Ascendancy and, in particular, survivors of the burning of the Big Houses and the killing of their occupants during the 1920-1922 period.

The protagonists of **"The Distant Past"** are a brother and sister now, in the early 1970s, in their mid-sixties, the sole survivors of the Middletons of Carraveagh. Sixty miles south of the border separating the Republic of Ireland from Northern Ireland, the once splendid Carraveagh, built during the reign of George II, now barely shelters the Middletons as its roof suffers continued neglect and rust eats at its gutters, apt reminders of the straitened circumstances of brother and sister and of the dwindled importance of the tradition they represent and doggedly uphold. Reduced to a few acres, four cows, and some chickens, the Middletons believe the local story that their father had mortgaged the estate in order to maintain a Catholic Dublin woman, so that on his death in 1924 the two children inherited a vastly diminished estate. Consistent with their attitudes toward the new order in Ireland, "they blamed . . . the Catholic Dublin woman whom they'd never met and they blamed as well the new national regime, contriving in their eccentric way to relate the two. In the days of the Union Jack," they believe, "such women would have known their place: wasn't it all part and parcel?"

> The title of **"The Distant Past,"** perhaps the earliest of Trevor's Troubles stories, signals what has become his continuing exploration of the ways in which apparently dead events of past conflicts obtrude on the present and shape the future.
>
> —*Robert E. Rhodes*

Following the middle course suggested by their name, brother and sister have achieved—on their own terms—a *modus vivendi* for holding onto their version of the British presence in Ireland and for living with their neighbors, who know they are anachronisms. They achieve a delicate balance by the rituals of their Fridays and Sundays. On Fridays, they visit the town to sell eggs and to deliberately cultivate social intercourse with tradespeople in their shops and with other townsfolk over drinks in the bar of Healy's hotel. On Sundays, they attend St. Patrick's Protestant Church and say prayers for the king. What is symbolized by their Sunday ritual is borne out by their quietly voiced loyalty to pre-Treaty Ireland; their rising when B.B.C. plays "God Save the King"; their display of the Union Jack in the rear window of their car when Elizabeth II is crowned; their declaration that the revolutionary regime won't last—green postal boxes and a language no one can understand, indeed!

So successful are the Middletons in establishing an equilibrium that the townsfolk cherish them and their eccentricities. Visitors to the town are impressed that the Middletons can keep the old loyalties and still win the town's respect and affection, so much so that they and town are pointed to as an example that old wounds can heal and that here at least people can disagree without resorting to guns. The one nagging reminder that the revolutionary past has brought irrevocable change to Ireland and has done so with blood is the joking reminder by Fat Driscoll, butcher, that he and two others had stood in the hall of Carraveagh in the days when they might have burned it and slaughtered its occupants and instead waited with shotguns ready to kill British soldiers.

This delicately balanced situation continues during the post-World War II prosperity in the town created by an influx of tourists, and starts to end only in 1967, when news comes that sub-post offices in Belfast have been blown up, news that leads Fat Driscoll to say, "A bad business. We don't want that old stuff all over again," and Miss Middleton lightly to remind him, "We didn't want it in the first place." As British soldiers arrive in the North and incidents in Fermanagh and Armagh and in Border towns and villages multiply and create fear in the hearts of tourists, despite assurances that the trouble in the North has nothing to do with the Republic, the town's prosperity begins to wane and with it tolerance of the Middletons. Now Fat Driscoll wishes that people would remember that he had stood in the Middletons' house fifty years earlier ready to kill British soldiers instead of knowing that he has given them meat for their dog, and brother and sister are pointedly cut by former friends, even the local Catholic priest.

The resurgence of violence in the present brings to the surface not only an awareness by all that the present violence is a renewal of past violence but a sharp reminder that the specific event at Carraveagh fifty years earlier took place in the home of those who, in Irish Catholic eyes, were responsible for violence in the first place. In mourning for the end of their *modus vivendi* rather than in fear of their lives, the Middletons remove from the walls of Carraveagh the icons of their distant past: a portrait of their father in the uniform of the Irish Guards, the family crest, and the Cross of St. George, and prepare "to face the silence that would sourly thicken as their own two deaths came closer and death increased in another part of their island. . . . Because of the distant past they would die friendless. It was worse than being murdered in their beds."

If there is something quixotic about the Middletons' version of the proper relationship between England and Ireland and their choice to remain in a town that thinks otherwise, inhabit the crumbling Carraveagh, and patch together a relationship with their neighbors, there is also something gallant about their efforts to stave off isolation and loneliness, and it is not difficult to think that their efforts to create and sustain friendship—even on an illusory basis—are more admirable than their neighbors' denial of friendship because of the cash nexus, loss of income from the tourist trade, and that they deserve better than exile at home.

Contrary to this, it is difficult at first to rouse much compassion for the nameless sixty-nine-year-old narrator of **"Saints,"** inheritor of the Big House of Kilneagh, near Cork, and of enough revenues in Ireland to have been able to spend forty years in luxurious self-imposed exile in Italy in the Umbrian town of Sansepolcro. However muddled the Middletons may be about their national identity, they at least win our understanding and perhaps our compassion for seeking friendship, for dealing with the past as best they can in the home place, and for enduring a cheerless exile they neither choose nor deserve; whereas, this protagonist confesses without apparent regret that "In national terms, I've become a nothing person." Reluctant to visit Ireland, he has not returned to Cork for forty years, and when he does visit Ireland it is strictly on business and he is always glad to leave. Nor has Italy been a place of friendships or commitments to the living. Here, he confesses, he has indulged himself in drink, music, women, and the wonders of the Italian Renaissance, and we easily conjure up a cross between an old-time absentee landlord and a Roman sybarite, more a figure for contempt than compassion. But this is a story of how the Troubles reach from Ireland to Italy and from past to present to touch a life seemingly on a steady course.

And so the first impression is undercut at the very time it is being made because Trevor piques our curiosity about the reason for his protagonist's fierce rejection of Ireland, and he early on whets our curiosity further with at least three clues about the past. First and most obvious is his receipt from Cork of a telegram saying only "*Josephine is dying. Hospital of St. Bernadette,*" and his reactions: pleasure that he has been sent for, determination to go to Ireland on a personal affair, and immediate departure. Second is his observation that he has been lost in the world of Ghirlandaio and Bellini, "preferring its calmness to the pain of life," and third is his reflection that at sixty-nine he still indulges himself as best he can, "continuing to redress a balance."

The truth as we come to discover it is that he and the devoutly Catholic Josephine—his family's domestic-of-all-work sixty and more years ago—are the sole survivors of the burning of Kilneagh and the murder of the protagonist's father, sisters, and three domestics by die-hard republicans in 1922, and of his mother's subsequent suicide by slashing her wrists with a razor ten years to the day after the events at Kilneagh, the despairing act which finally drove him to make financial provisions for Josephine and to leave Ireland for Italy.

With Trevor's characteristic method of revelation, we do not learn all of this at once; and neither we nor the protagonist learn until later that Josephine had endured her own forty-year exile as a result of the burning and deaths. Trevor so designs his story that the journey from Italy to Josephine's bedside in Cork, which takes fully half the story, must be made by bus, train, taxi, plane, train, and taxi, with temporal cross-cuttings between the present journey to places associated with the painful past and the story of why those places and that past are painful. It is as if the narrator were delicately peeling back layer after painful layer of still tender scar tissue to fully expose to himself—as well as to us—for the first time in many years the horror that drove him from Ireland. As he sits by Josephine's deathbed, he realizes that she, too, is remembering the experience:

> Tears oozed from her eyes and I could tell from the contortion in her face that she was remembering not just my mother's suicide but my sisters and my father burnt alive and Mrs. Flynn [the cook] burnt also. The fire had started in the middle of the night and we were all trapped except O'Neill and John Paddy [the gardener and his son], who lived in the yard, though they always ate in the kitchen. They hauled us out the best they could, but only my mother and Josephine and myself survived. We had not been murdered when the men returned because we were not conscious, but O'Neill and John Paddy, faced by the men, were instantly shot. After my mother's burial, ten years later, Josephine said to me: "You and I are what's left of it now."

So completely has the narrator effaced his human Irish past that it is only now, after his forced recollection of that past, that he learns that he and Josephine have shared more than he knew—that in 1932, the year of his mother's suicide and the beginning of his exile from Ireland, Josephine began her own very different forty-year exile as an inmate of St. Fina's insane asylum, driven there by her memories of the burning and deaths. As Sister Power tells him what she knows of Josephine's years there, the starkest of contrasts with the narrator's exile emerges. Whereas he was driven to self-indulgence in a foreign land to redress, as he has put it earlier, a balance—the losses he had suffered in Ireland—Josephine has devoted her life to prayer for others and has come to be regarded as a saint by her fellow inmates, who attribute miracles to her. Unlike the protagonist, Josephine has neither forgotten nor tried to forget the massacre and suicide; indeed, in words that reveal Trevor's intention to underscore the continuity of the Irish Troubles into the present, Sister Power says, "She hardly ever ceased to pray. She was confused, of course. She confused the tragedy you spoke of and your mother's death with what is happening now: the other tragedies in the North. She prays that the survivors may be comforted in their mourning. She prays for God's word in Ireland."

After a brief visit to Kilneagh, "windowless and gaunt, a hideous place now", and Josephine's death and funeral, the narrator, glad as always to leave Ireland but in isolation and loneliness and trailing bitter introspection about his failures in human relations, rejects the claim of Josephine's sainthood and miracles on rational grounds. But irrationally and under the influence of considerable wine, he meditates on a long procession of saints and sees with certainty the story of Josephine taking its place with them in scene after scene in the work of Fra Angelico, Giotto, Lorenzo di Credi, and Ghirlandaio, a pageant culminating in

> the miracle that crowned them all: how she had moved that embittered man to find pleasure in the wisp that remained of a human relationship. On her deathbed she prayed that Ireland's murders might be forgiven, that all survivors be granted consolation, and rescued from the damage wrought by horror. Josephine of the Survivors they called her, Ghirlandaio and all the others.

> Before I fell asleep, I wept on the terrace, the first time since my mother's death. It was ridiculous to weep, so old and wrinkled like a crab, half drunk and even senile. And yet it wasn't in the least ridiculous: it was as right and fitting as the sainthood imparted by the inmates of St. Fina's. For a moment she stood in glory on my terrace and then she disappeared.

What are we to make of this conclusion, so close to sentimentality, skirting bathos with a narrator whose vision may be only alcohol-inspired? To put the worst construction on it, it is both sentimental and bathetic, an alcohol-induced and therefore unreal acceptance of the past. On the other hand, without this or a similar conclusion, the protagonist would remain essentially unchanged by his return to the past and the past's intrusion on his present and future, and Josephine's life of prayer and forgiveness would mean no more than the narrator's life of self-indulgence and denial of others—one survivor driven to nearly total isolation, the other to madness by the Irish Troubles. This grim possibility may be Trevor's intention. But to put the most hopeful construction on the ending, the conclusion, appropriately in a section of the story devoted to a litany of the saints, can also be read as an exemplum of the power of prayer and forgiveness, which may depart from the reality of the situation, but which softens the narrator's bitter self-reproaches, lessens his isolation, holds out some mild hope for regeneration, and in the larger context of the Troubles points beyond political and military solutions. That the story ends as it begins, in

Sansepolcro—Holy Sepulcher—only adds to the ambiguity of Trevor's conclusion.

"Attracta" and "Autumn Sunshine" are recent stories dramatizing the themes of betrayal, violence, revenge, guilt, forgiveness, redemption, and reconciliation in past and present.
—*Robert E. Rhodes*

"Attracta" and **"Autumn Sunshine"** are recent stories dramatizing the themes of betrayal, violence, revenge, guilt, forgiveness, redemption, and reconciliation in past and present. They are also stories in which the Anglican Protestantism of the protagonists figures more prominently than in any other of Trevor's Troubles stories, Attracta being the only teacher in the one-room Protestant school in a small town near Cork; Moran being the rector of St. Michael's Church of Ireland. Because of the authority derived from both their positions and long tenure in them, Attracta and Moran might have been but have chosen not to be aggressively Protestant in their work with their charges. Both are peaceable people who as adults have remained apart from religious and secular disputes and have no serious differences with their Catholic neighbors. But in the face of past violence renewing itself in the present, both depart from prepared teaching-preaching texts and counsel their small flocks to reconciliation in place of the revenge that has again become part of their human environment—a message their listeners find odd.

"Attracta" is Trevor's most complex examination of religious and sectarian allegiances. In present action that occurs in about 1975, Attracta, in her sixty-first year—after forty-some years of untroubled teaching and happiness—is haunted by a newspaper account of the death of a British army officer and the subsequent suicide in Belfast of his English wife of twenty-three, Penelope Vade. Attracta is strangely moved by these deaths, particularly Penelope's, for two reasons. First, this is a notably grisly tale of murder, vengeance, and suicide in contemporary Ulster:

> It was Penelope Vade's desire to make some kind of gesture, a gesture of courage and perhaps anger, that caused her to leave her parents' home in Haslemere and go to Belfast. Her husband . . . had been murdered in Belfast; he'd been decapitated as well. His head, wrapped in cotton-wool to absorb the ooze of blood, secured within a plastic bag and packed in a biscuit-tin, had been posted to Penelope Vade. Layer by layer the parcel had been opened by her in Haslemere. She hadn't known he was dead before his dead eyes stared into hers.

Her gesture was her mourning of him. She went to Belfast to join the Women's Peace Movement, to make the point that somehow neither he nor she had been defeated. But her gesture, publicly reported, had incensed the men who'd gone to the trouble of killing him. One after another, seven of them had committed acts of rape on her. It was after that that she had killed herself

by swallowing a bottle of aspirin. Second, Attracta is haunted by this story because it both parallels and differs from her own story, one with its beginnings in the Black-and-Tan phase of the English-Irish conflict nearly sixty years earlier.

When Attracta was three, her parents, nonmilitant Irish Protestants, had been killed in an ambush meant for the Black-and-Tans, British military terrorists. That the architects of these deaths were an Irish Protestant guerrilla and his adulterous Catholic mistress, Devereux and Geraldine Carey, suggests the complexity of loyalties Trevor brings to this story.

Thus, for example, Devereux and Geraldine, who had not stopped at any violence in the Irish cause against the British, are guilt-stricken at these innocent deaths. They stop their guerrilla activity and devote much of their lives to seeking redemption. For Devereux, this means unusual devotion to the child Attracta—elaborate birthday presents, spending long hours with her, visiting her at her Aunt Emmeline's house, for example—until, ironically, when Attracta kisses him good night she imagines it is what having a father is like. For her part, Geraldine remains in Devereux's home as housekeeper and undergoes a sea change from violent revolutionary and adulteress to the quietest and most devout person Attracta has ever known:

> Geraldine Carey was like a nun because of the dark clothes she wore, and she had a nun's piety. In the town it was said she couldn't go to mass often enough. "Why weren't you a nun, Geraldine?" Attracta asked her once. . . . But Geraldine Carey replied that she'd never heard God calling her. "Only the good are called," she said.

The story of her parents' death is not revealed to Attracta until she is eleven and the relationship with Devereux and Geraldine well established. Then the story is told to her by Purce, whose aggressive Protestantism and bigotry embarrass the town's few other Protestants. By telling Attracta and trying to sever her relationship with Devereux and Geraldine, Purce seeks revenge against Devereux, a Protestant who never goes to church and is thus a betrayer of his faith; a renegade for having fought against the British Black-and-Tans, for having been responsible for the deaths of two Protestants, and for endangering Attracta's Protestantism by allowing her contact with the formerly adulterous but now piously Catholic Geraldine Carey.

Because they have won redemption, Purce does not gain revenge against Devereux and Geraldine, which would have destroyed Attracta, too. Instead, she survives because of those she might have hated, develops an affection for the town and is happy there: "There'd been tragedy in her life but she considered that she had not suffered. People had been good to her."

Now, in 1975, Attracta, realizing that she has survived and been happy because of the goodness of those who had harmed her nearly sixty years earlier, realizes that Penelope Vade did not survive because of the continued violence of those who had killed her husband when she, instead of seeking revenge, sought reconciliation by joining the Women's Peace Movement. Realizing these things, she meditates on her life as a teacher, wondering if she has not taught the wrong things:

> She was thinking that nothing she might ever have said in her schoolroom could have prevented the death of a girl in a city two hundred miles away. Yet in a way it seemed ridiculous that for so long she had been relating the details of Cromwell's desecration and the laws of Pythagoras, when she should have been talking about Devereux and Geraldine Carey. And it was Mr. Purce she should have recalled instead of the Battle of the Boyne.

In a mood of black guilt, she reflects that in a lifetime she has neither learned nor taught anything and, in atonement for not having taught her pupils the lesson from the past that had led to her own happiness, she reads to them the account of Penelope Vade and her husband and asks what they think of it. Faced with their puzzlement, she tells her own story, identifying in the telling with Penelope in detail after painful detail, and explaining further that Penelope was also like Devereux and Geraldine in offering peace and friendship. But because they have grown calloused by the horrors of the new Irish Troubles, the children only stare and wonder what on earth Penelope Vade has to do with anything, and think that Attracta does not "appear to understand that almost every day there was the kind of vengeance she spoke of reported on the television. Bloodshed was wholesale, girls were tarred and feathered and left for dead, children no older than themselves were armed with guns."

At the last, then, Attracta, named for an Irish saint of the fifth or sixth century, succeeds only for herself but fails with others and so begs ironic contrast with Josephine of **"Saints,"** who in bringing an otherwise bitter and lonely old man some consolation might be said to have some sort of success. They have both suffered grievous personal losses

at about the same time in the past; but because she has never forgotten the past, Josephine brings it into the present and is able to console an old man; whereas, ironically, Attracta, who was able to forget the past because of the goodness of others, cannot bring the lessons of the past into the present for anyone but herself. Not only does she fail to teach the lesson to her pupils, but because they report her peculiar behavior to their parents she is eased into retirement—and thus loneliness and isolation—at the end of the term. Instead of defending her eccentric lesson, Attracta offers words that underscore the necessity of bringing the lessons of the past into the present: "Every day in my schoolroom I should have honoured the small, remarkable thing that happened in this town [i.e., that people *can* change for the better]. It matters that [Penelope Vade] died in despair, with no faith left in human life."

In **"Autumn Sunshine,"** Canon Moran of St. Michael's Church of Ireland is probably the oldest and most parochial protagonist of this set of stories. At the time of present action—September 1978—he lives alone in an eighteenth-century rectory, standing alone and looking lonely, two miles from the village of Boharbawn and eight miles from the town of Enniscorthy, County Wexford. Ministering to a small flock, a man abstemious and unambitious, he has for the most part been content, though the ordinary mild melancholy of the season is now deepened for him by the recent death of his wife of fifty years, Frances, and because his youngest and favorite daughter, Deirdre, has been in England for three years and did not return home or even write at her mother's death.

Not only is Moran rather isolated in his home, he has also always been insulated from even the mild conflicts of an Anglican pastor in a predominantly Catholic area. A man who has always disliked disorder, he had relied on Frances to resolve skirmishes with neighboring Catholics; for example, the ticklish situation of a girl in his parish made pregnant by a Catholic lad was settled when Frances had a chat with Father Hayes and the girl's mother.

Furthermore, Moran is largely at peace with his personal past. True, Frances's death is still difficult for him because it is not truly past and she has yet to become a ghost for him. True, too, he is troubled that Deirdre, always somewhat rebellious, had gone off to England without telling her parents, but she is too much the favorite to have alienated them by this. So on the whole Moran is not a man much troubled by his own past.

Nor does Trevor allow him to be very aware of the historical past of County Wexford, a past that perhaps should have engaged his attention more than it has; for, during the unsuccessful Irish rebellion of 1798 against the British, the Wexford rising was largely religious and animated by Catholic sentiments; Wexford held out against the British forces longer than any other section of Ireland; and Vinegar Hill, headquarters of the Wexford insurgents and scene of a famous Irish defeat, is only eight miles away in Enniscorthy. But the historical past is to be forced on Moran in a personal way and is to be the source of conflict, pain, and loss that are ultimately resolved only at the cost of denying to himself the truth of his own perceptions.

In this September, Deirdre returns, needing, she writes to her delighted father, to get back to Ireland for a while. She is soon followed by her English young man, Harold, too thin, wearing a black leather jacket; an electrician with dirty fingernails, bad manners, and a cockney accent. His face bears a birthmark, an affliction almost belligerent and that comes to symbolize his birth into England's lower orders and his rebellion against any establishment. It is Harold who forces the violent Irish past and an awareness of a violent Irish present into Moran's consciousness and compels him to connect the two.

For Harold is a radical who supports the Irish cause against England or any established social order. His pronouncements—he seldom converses, and in this and other ways Trevor has made him nearly a caricature—are largely cant: England has been "destroyed by class consciousness and the unjust distribution of wealth," "the struggle is worldwide," and "I'm not answerable to the bosses," for example, and his favorite catchcry, "the struggle of the Irish people." That Deirdre—named for the heroine of Irish legend's greatest love story, of whom it was prophesied at her birth that she would bring Ireland bloodshed and death—appears to be in love with him distresses Moran, and all the more when it seems possible that she is Harold's "Irish connection," that is, that he may have formed his liaison with her because she is Irish and possibly even because she is from Wexford.

If Moran is innocent of Irish history, Harold knows a great deal, including the story of Kinsella's Barn. There, in 1798, a Sergeant James, as an example to the countryside, burned in the barn twelve men and women accused of harboring insurgents; and Kinsella, innocent of either sheltering rebels or the executions, was murdered by his own farm workers. Returning from a visit to the site with Deirdre, Harold vents his hatred against James, a man who boasted that he had killed a thousand Irishmen and who had amassed great wealth at Irish expense, and further declares that Kinsella got what he deserved. When Moran protests gently that it was all two hundred years ago—implying that the past is past and best forgotten, certainly not to be dragged into the present—and that in any case Kinsella was innocent of any complicity, Harold automatically interjects that in two hundred years nothing has changed, that "The Irish people still share their bondage with the twelve in Kinsella's Barn," and that as for Kinsella, "if he was keeping a low profile in a

ditch, it would have been by arrangement with the imperial forces."

So virulent is Harold's hatred and so determined is he to cast his lot with Ireland's new revolutionaries that Moran is forced to connect past and present in two ways. First, when he addresses his small flock the following morning he departs from his prepared text and, in a spirit not unlike Attracta's when speaking to her uncomprehending pupils, "tried to make the point that one horror should not fuel another, that passing time contained its own forgiveness" and that Kinsella was innocent of everything. He thinks:

> Harold would have delighted in the vengeance exacted of an innocent man. Harold wanted to inflict pain, to cause suffering and destruction. The end justified the means for Harold, even if the end was an artificial one, a pettiness grandly dressed up. . . . He spoke of how evil drained people of their humor and compassion, how people pretended to themselves. It was worse than Frances's death, he thought, as his voice continued in the church: it was worse that Deirdre should be part of wickedness.

> He could tell that his parishioners found his sermon odd, and he didn't blame them. He was confused, and considerably distressed. In the rectory Deirdre and Harold would be waiting for him. They would all sit down to Sunday lunch while plans for atrocities filled Harold's mind, while Deirdre loved him.

The kinship between past and present is yet more specific that evening when Deirdre and Harold announce their departure for Dublin the next day, but Harold, reading a book about Che Guevara, is evasive about their exact movements. Certain that Harold intends to meet others like himself in Dublin and that Deirdre has turned her back on the rectory to join a man who plans to commit atrocities, Moran thinks:

> Harold was the same kind of man Sergeant James had been; it didn't matter that they were on different sides. Sergeant James had maybe borne an affliction also—a humped back or a withered arm. He had ravaged a country for its spoils, and his most celebrated crime was neatly at hand, so that another Englishman could make matters worse by attempting to make amends. In Harold's view the trouble had always been that these acts of war and murder died beneath the weight of print in history books, and were forgotten. But history could be rewritten, and for that Kinsella's Barn was an inspiration: Harold had journeyed to it as people make journeys to holy places.

Returning to the rectory the following morning from delivering Deirdre and Harold to the Dublin bus and deep in gloom because he believes Deirdre to be a befuddled girl under Harold's influence, Moran connects all that has happened with Frances, who had always resolved conflicts for him. Conjuring her up in the autumn sunshine, he hears her say, "Harold's just a talker. Not at all like Sergeant James," words that Moran clings to as truth because they take the curse off what he had clearly perceived to be so. In this mood of new hope, he hears Frances laugh,

> and for the first time since her death seemed far away, as her life did too. In the rectory the visitors had blurred her fingerprints to nothing and had made her a ghost that could come back. The sunlight warmed him as he sat there; the garden was less melancholy than it had been.

On the one hand, the conclusion of **"Autumn Sunshine"** is similar to that of **"Saints,"** with the spirit of a dead woman bringing comfort to a lonely old man who has been dispirited by an excursion into the past. On the other, while the protagonist of **"Saints"** appears, in one interpretation, to undergo a change that allows him to deal, perhaps ineptly and at a distance, with the reality of a violent Irish past, Moran's change is only to put the past firmly into the past once again and to determine not to accept and to deal with the reality he had earlier perceived: that Harold is really a contemporary Sergeant James. When he calls up Frances, it is for her to do what she has always done—resolve his problem for him, here by denying that Harold is like James. As Frances is now properly dead, so is his probably accurate discernment of Harold and Deirdre.

Although **"Another Christmas"** dramatizes similar themes and arrives at not dissimilar resolutions, it differs in several ways from other Trevor stories about the Troubles. The protagonists, Dermot and Norah, are a middle-aged Irish Catholic couple. They are working-class people, Dermot having been a gas company meter-reader for twenty-one years, during which time they have rented the same small terrace house from the same landlord, Mr. Joyce. What is most important for Trevor's purpose is that this middle-aged, working-class Irish Catholic couple have lived in London since the early days of their marriage in Waterford. Thus, Trevor here reverses a familiar pattern. Instead of giving us Anglo-Irish Protestants in a distinct minority position in predominantly Catholic Ireland, he gives us Irish Catholics in a distinct minority position in predominantly Protestant England, and wonders, perhaps, if they'll behave any differently from their counterparts when faced with the same violent past renewed in the present, in this instance, about 1976. On the whole, this is another story in which apparently firm human relations unravel under pressures from the renewed past.

Initially, at least, it appears that Dermot and Norah have achieved about the same *modus vivendi* in their community as that reached by the Middletons in **"The Distant Past."** Although there are several reminders in the opening pages that their background is Irish Catholic—two pictures of Waterford scenes and a picture of the Virgin and Child on the living-room walls, for instance—most of the opening pages are devoted to establishing that Dermot and Norah are at home here and doing what most English couples are doing at the same time: decorating the house for Christmas and drinking tea and talking about past Christmases, their five children, and the joy and peace of the present Christmas. On the other hand, as if showing that Dermot and Norah are simultaneously content and yet rather isolated, Trevor confines present action almost entirely to their living room. Later in the story, this suggestion of isolation becomes more sinister as Norah thinks of their entire situation in England as a trap,

> the trap they'd made for themselves. Their children spoke with London accents. Patrick and Brendan worked for English firms and would make their homes in England. Patrick had married an English girl. They were Catholics and they had Irish names, yet home for them was not Waterford.

At the opening of the story, too, it appears that Dermot and Norah have achieved a personal *modus vivendi* that is not simply a reflection of the warmth of the Christmas season. They have not had a serious quarrel in all their married life. She recognizes that he is "considerate and thoughtful in what he did do, teetotal, clever, full of kindness for herself and the family they'd reared, full of respect for her also", and he knows how to compliment her for managing things so well. But there are also intimations in these early pages that their equanimity has cost Norah something. She is a plump, cheerful, easygoing woman whose Catholicism is relaxed and practical, and she has always deferred to Dermot, who is her opposite in mien and manner: "thin and seeming ascetic, with more than a hint of the priest in him. . .", a man who gives much time to pondering religious matters while on his meter-reading route; a slow and deliberate man who, having arrived at a position, will not change his mind. As Norah well knows, "it was his opinion that mattered."

The catalyst for a serious rift between them and their English neighbors is an issue that has developed between Dermot and their landlord, Mr. Joyce. Ironically, despite his name, Mr. Joyce is not Irish but thoroughly English. This fact has not mattered for over twenty years because Mr. Joyce, now a frail and bent old bachelor, has established his own warm and human relationship with the couple and their children, spending every Friday evening with them, kissing the children good night, joining them every year for Christmas, bringing presents for the children and small gifts for themselves. More than his tenants, Norah and Dermot are his friends; and to judge from the evidence of the story, he seems to be the sole valued long-time friend they have in England.

When the I.R.A. first started bombings that took civilian lives in England, Mr. Joyce did not stop his Friday evenings with Norah and Dermot, believing, perhaps, that their friendship was not based on religious or political considerations. However, perhaps assuming that for Dermot and Norah the friendship also transcended such lines, Mr. Joyce had not hesitated quietly to condemn the I.R.A. bombers, and they had not contradicted him until one Friday night in August when Dermot had shaken his head in agreement with Mr. Joyce over the latest outrage and

> had added that they mustn't of course forget what the Catholics in the North had suffered. The bombs were a crime but it didn't do to forget that the crime would not be there if generations in the North had not been treated like animals. There'd been a silence then, a difficult kind of silence which she'd broken herself. All that was in the past, she'd said hastily, in a rush, nothing in the past or the present or anywhere could justify the killing of innocent people. Even so, Dermot had added, it didn't do to avoid the truth. Mr. Joyce had not said anything,

and he had stopped coming Friday evenings.

Now, in the midst of Christmas preparations, the issue of Mr. Joyce hangs unspoken between Norah and Dermot, and she delays until halfway through the story to say to Dermot that she is not counting on Mr. Joyce being with them for Christmas. Certain that he has been right in his condemnation of the treatment of the Catholics in the North and that Mr. Joyce would understand the justice of the I.R.A. bombings in England, Dermot insists that Mr. Joyce will come, that he has missed his Friday evenings because of illness, and that he wouldn't let the children down by not coming. Dermot refuses Norah's plea that he try to make it up with Mr. Joyce and instead says that he will pray that Mr. Joyce will come.

What emerges strongly in the second half of the story is what has been latent in the first. There is Dermot's deadly calm—he never displays emotion—and certitude that he is right; his conviction that they must keep faith with other Catholics; his belief that his position is God's position and that he has done his Catholic duty. Invoking the need for good will at the Christmas season, he repeats that one wrong leads to another wrong and that perhaps Mr. Joyce has seen this by now, failing on the one hand to see the bitter irony of his statements and on the other that Norah is tormented by the fact that seeming to condone what Mr. Joyce has condemned—the killing of innocent people—is to appear to condone the bombings.

For her part, Norah's conviction that Dermot is dead wrong and must be challenged is betrayed by manner and feelings never before associated with him: the increased impatience in her voice, her unusual edginess of manner, her raised voice, her feeling of wildness—as if she should rush into the streets to harangue passersby with her belief that the bombers are despicable and have earned hatred and death for themselves—and her impotent will to strength to pour out her rage at him:

> She looked at him, pale and thin, with his priestly face. For the first time since he had asked her to marry him in the Tara Ballroom she did not love him. He was cleverer than she was, yet he seemed half blind. He was good, yet he seemed hard in his goodness, as though he'd be better without it. Up to the very last minute on Christmas Day there would be the pretense that their landlord might arrive, that God would answer a prayer because his truth had been honoured. She considered it hypocrisy, unable to help herself in that opinion.

At the end of the story we know that the relationship between Dermot and Norah has changed irrevocably. Seeing him guilty of a cruelty no one would have believed of him, she knows that he will be as kind as always to the children on Christmas Day but that Mr. Joyce's absence—the seal on the end of a cherished friendship—will be another victory for the bombers. And she thinks that "whenever she looked at him she would remember the Christmases of the past. She would feel ashamed of him, and of herself."

Despite differences in characters and setting, **"Another Christmas"** does not differ significantly from the other stories in its conflicts and resolutions, except, of course, to parcel out approval and condemnation to Irish Catholics, too. Except for their nominal tags, Norah shares much with the Middletons, Attracta, and Canon Moran; and Dermot is brother under the skin with Fat Driscoll, Purce, and Harold. In simpler terms, both Dermot and Norah understand how the past renews itself in the present; but where Dermot blindly perpetuates that past, Norah is willing to break the circle of violence begetting violence by forgiveness. In even simpler terms, he wants justice; she wants mercy.

As reported in *The Irish Times,* William Trevor's first full-length stage play, *Scenes from an Album,* takes photographs, so to speak, of a Tyrone Anglo Irish family from Jacobean times to the present, and takes their home from castle to the present "decaying heap in which the occupants find themselves caught between the Orange Order and the IRA." If this is not precisely the situation of the protagonists in most of Trevor's Troubles stories, it is near to the spirit of those stories, an approximation whose meaning deepens when Trevor says that this Tyrone family is "the kind of Anglo-Irish family that I would have great respect for, not being that kind of Anglo-Irish myself . . .," that is, more Irish than the Irish themselves rather than his "own kind of small-town Protestant bank manager's background. . . ."

The Anglo-Irish protagonists of Trevor's stories, rather than being caricatures that might serve some propaganda, have his understanding and compassion, sentiments not withheld from the Irish Catholics of **"Another Christmas,"** either, though, on the whole, their problems seem less provocative. This is because the situation of the Anglo-Irish, deep-rooted in Ireland but retaining at least traces of a different heritage and withal often more Irish than the Irish themselves, is so anomalous that their dilemmas generate greater and more complex and more subtle conflicts and thus more opportunities for insights than the situation of either Irish Catholic nationalist or British imperialist. The arena for conflict in Trevor's stories thus opens up more than most Troubles fiction has human issues that time has not solved and that cannot be solved by merely partisan positions. Upon reflection, Trevor's Troubles stories sometimes seem so open-ended that one must hesitate before pronouncing judgment on their collective "meaning"; but if there is one consistent view, it seems to be that the past cannot be forgotten but that with resolution and forgiveness it need not be perpetuated.

Robert Towers (review date 17 May 1990)

SOURCE: "Short Satisfactions," in *The New York Review of Books,* Vol. XXXVII, No. 8, May 17, 1990, pp. 38-9.

[*In the following review Towers argues that while some of the stories in* Family Sins *are skillfully told, the collection does not measure up to Trevor's earlier work.*]

Readers of William Trevor's earlier story collections, six in all, will find in *Family Sins,* as before, that the Irish settings—mucky farms, shabby genteel boarding houses, schools, convents, hotel barrooms where more than a few drinks are taken—are coolly but sympathetically observed. So are his characters—foolish, blustering, guilty, touching in their various predicaments.

In **"The Third Party,"** Boland, who runs a small-town bakery, meets Lairdman, who is in the timber business, in the bar of Buswell's Hotel in Dublin. Boland recognizes him as someone who had attended the same school and remembers that Lairdman had once had his head held down in a lavatory while his hair was scrubbed with a lavatory brush. But they have met for a reason that can only be humiliating to Boland: his wife Annabella and Lairdman have fallen in love, and Lairdman wants Boland to relinquish Annabella

and, if possible, to give her a divorce. Boland, for whom the situation is no surprise, more or less agrees, but as he tosses back drink after drink of John Jameson's (while Lairdman sticks to lemonade, which he is too stingy to pay for), he can't help taunting his rival about the bullying episode at school. He also reveals something that Lairdman does not know and that Annabella would passionately deny: that she is unable to have children.

> Readers of William Trevor's earlier story collections . . . will find in *Family Sins* . . . that the Irish settings—mucky farms, shabby genteel boarding houses, schools, convents, hotel barrooms where more than a few drinks are taken—are coolly but sympathetically observed.
> —*Robert Towers*

Trevor is particularly skillful in showing the mixture of slyness, abjection, and cruelty in Boland. Driving the fifty miles back home after having sobered up a bit, Boland broods over his wife's longstanding unhappiness with him. "'Poor Annabella,' he said aloud. . . Poor girl, ever to have got herself married to the inheritor of a country-town bakery. Lucky, in all fairness, that cocky little Lairdman had turned up." Then he realizes that he has effectively prevented Lairdman from taking Annabella away from him—and wonders why he has done it.

> It hadn't mattered reminding Lairdman of the ignominy he had suffered as a boy; it hadn't mattered reminding him that she was a liar, or insulting him by calling him mean. All that abuse was conventional in the circumstances, an expected element in the man-to-man confrontation, the courage for it engendered by an intake of John Jameson. Yet something had impelled him to go further: little men like Lairdman always wanted children. "That's a total lie," she'd have said already on the telephone, and Lairdman would have soothed her. But soothing wasn't going to be enough for either of them.

"Honeymoon in Tramore" takes us several steps down the social scale. Davy Toome, an orphaned farm worker, and his pregnant bride, Kitty, who is the daughter of the farm owners, have come to spend their honeymoon at a seaside boarding house, St. Agnes's, run by a Mrs. Hurley. Kitty is pregnant by another man; she planned to have an abortion but lost her nerve in a fit of religious panic, and Davy, the poor orphan, saw his opportunity and asked Kitty to marry him. Trevor finely describes the details of high tea at the boarding house and the way in which the honeymooners spend their late afternoon in the drab resort, which offers as its leading attraction a motorcycle arena called the Wall of Death. That night Kitty, who has been brushing off Davy's physical advances, drinks a great many bottles of stout and loudly boasts to the Hurleys about the heartbreak she has caused Coddy Donnegan, the probable father of her child, by marrying the lowly Davy; she even makes up another suitor, the cousin of the local priest. But Davy doesn't mind. He doesn't even mind when, back in their bedroom, she vomits and then passes out. We again are made aware of the complex mixture of detachment and sympathy Trevor brings to the revelation of a hardly admirable person's inner life:

> Davy stood up and slowly took his clothes off. He was lucky that she had gone with Coddy Donnegan because if she hadn't she wouldn't now be sleeping on their honeymoon bed. Once more he looked down into her face: for eighteen years she had seemed like a queen to him and now, miraculously, he had the right to kiss her. . . . Slowly he pulled the bedclothes up and turned the light out; then he lay beside her and caressed her in the darkness. . . . He had been known as her father's hired man, but now he would be known as her husband. That was how people would refer to him, and in the end it wouldn't matter when she talked about Coddy Donnegan, or lowered her voice to mention the priest's cousin. It was natural that she should do so since she had gained less than he had from their marriage.

At least five of the stories in *Family Sins* confirm Trevor's mastery. But the collection as a whole strikes me as a little tired, a little too reminiscent of situations and effects that we have encountered before. The work for the most part lacks the energy of the stories in *Beyond the Pale* (in my view Trevor's strongest collection) or wonderfully sardonic vision that animates such early novels as *The Old Boys or The Boarding House.*

Max Deen Larsen (essay date 1992)

SOURCE: "Saints of the Ascendancy: William Trevor's Big-House Novels," in *Ancestral Voices: The Big House in Anglo-Irish Literature,* edited by Otto Rauchbauer, Lilliput Press, 1992, pp. 257-72.

[*In the following essay, Larsen explores shared themes in Trevor's two novels* Fools of Fortune *and* The Silence in the Garden.]

With the spatial awareness of a sometime sculptor, William Trevor has from the start shaped the physical environment in his fictional worlds as the tangible expression of intan-

gible human concerns. In his earlier writings, hotels and boarding houses acquire distinctive symbolic significance as the favored arenas for petty power struggles among petty predators: dingy interiors reflect dingy lives. Trevor's penchant for black humor is particularly at home in houses for the homeless, where lonely paralyzed souls act out illusory relationships and nurture grotesque fixations. In the course of his preoccupation with marital relationships, Trevor has gradually been led from the tragicomic space of boarding-house affairs to the more sombre symbolic space informing his two major Big-House novels: *Fools of Fortune* (1983) and *The Silence in the Garden* (1988). Always fascinated by the frigid intricacies of a passionless marriage, Trevor here exposes the relationship of Irish domestic life to that peculiar species of Irish erotic fervor known as fanatic class violence: indeed, his treatment of marriage in the Big-House novels tends to suggest a political *hieros gamos.*

> Go, go, go, said the bird: human kind
> Cannot bear very much reality.
>
>   T. S. Eliot, 1943

Having slain Tybalt to avenge Mercutio's death, Romeo exclaims as he flees into exile, "O I am Fortune's foole!" Young Willie Quinton in *Fools of Fortune* might have echoed Romeo's sentiments when a violent act of revenge sends this lover, too, into exile. Trevor's novel, like Shakespeare's play, relates the fortunes of two houses whose bonds of marital union are tried by the ancient curse of factional hatred. Reconciliation comes for the families of Romeo and Juliet through their deaths; reunion for Willie and Marianne in the fool's paradise of a reduced idyll. The title of the novel suggests a view of history that is fatalistic, again recalling the "misadventured" love of the rival houses of Verona, but the "fools of fortune" formula attributed to the elder William Quinton expresses none of the passion to be found in Shakespeare's tragic lovers; it is rather the good-humored sigh of a kind man confronted with an unkind world. For Trevor's book is not shaped by the precise ironies of malicious cosmic powers, but is rather controlled, in structure and in diction, by an enveloping sentiment of passive suffering, by an elegiac tone that laments lost wholeness. *Fools of Fortune* is a novel of sensibility, whose characters instinctively resist the personal communications that could lead to action and renewal.

Some of Trevor's fools do tend to become victims of the inevitable course of historical events, or think of themselves as such, lending the elder Quinton's tag tragic overtones he had not entertained: Marianne becomes increasingly fatalistic and Willie's mother succumbs to despair. There are, however, other kinds of fools abroad, such as those who imagine they are wise while being victims of their own fixations and lusts—namely, the professional teachers: Miss Halliwell, Professor and Mrs Gibb-Bachelor, the Scrotum and Mad Mack. Yet another kind of fool, and a different sort of teacher, is represented by the defrocked priest Father Kilgarriff, whose meek spirit and Christ-like rejection of violence make him a fool in the eyes of Christian Ireland. Finally, that most frightening form of foolishness, insanity itself, emerges ironically triumphant. Just as "the lunatic, the lover, and the poet are of imagination all compact", so does Imelda tread the lonely path created by the power of her imagination and her love for her unknown father; it is a path that leads through the valley of the shadow of destruction to a place of peace known only to saints and fools—the heart of Kilneagh. The concluding segments of the novel thus develop a kind of fool's paradise regained, in which the old order with its long shadow of carnage has been displaced by ambiguous gifts of the imagination, renewing the link to primal scenes of value.

The prologue to Trevor's tale of two houses suggests that the love story of Marianne and Willie contains an allegorical message about the historical relationship of England and Ireland. In drawing parallels between Woodcombe Park in Devon and Kilneagh in Co. Cork—the one reduced to making a noisy living from selling its past to tourists, the other sunk into economic and cultural silence, its past alive only in the elegiac voices of the narrative—Trevor anticipates the differing histories of the Big House in the two countries. The three-fold pattern of marital alliance connecting the Woodcombes and the Quintons over four generations ironically recapitulates the historic bond joining England and Ireland. The emotional focus of the relationship is provided by Kilneagh, built in 1770 as the seat of the Quinton family estate. Kilneagh is present throughout the book as the primal home or emotional center of being for the three narrative centers of consciousness—Willie Quinton, whose childhood was spent there and who inherits the estate; Marianne Woodcombe, his English cousin, who identifies Kilneagh with Willie and whose love for him holds her there in spite of pressures to leave; Imelda, their daughter, whose life at Kilneagh epitomizes the horror and the glory of its history. The predominantly elegiac tone of the narrative expresses the feeling shared by the three main characters of belonging to a disrupted house. The content of the narrative is, then, an account of three childhoods in which Kilneagh exerted a decisive formative influence.

Willie's share of the narrative is motivated by his wish that his early life might have been shared with Marianne, a wish that is identical with her imagined presence in Kilneagh.

> I wish that somehow you might have shared my childhood, for I would love to remember you in the scarlet drawing-room, so fragrant in summer with the scent of roses, warmed in winter by the wood Tim Paddy gathered. Arithmetic and grammar books

were laid out every morning on an oval table, red ink in one glass inkwell, black in the other.

Kilneagh before the raid embodies the sense of order, security, and harmony that determines Willie's character. The heart of the house is the scarlet drawing-room, warm and fragrant the year round, the room in which he begins to learn the lessons of history. The comfortable aura of a pastoral idyll reinforces his sense of belonging to an intact world in which *agricola*, his first word of Latin, reminds him of his own place in life ("'Now there's a word for you.'" In particular, the emblematic scene on the brass log-box preoccupies him with its mystery:

> On the sides of the brass log-box there were embossed scenes, and the one I liked best was of a farmhouse supper. Men sat around a table while a woman served, one of them reaching behind him to seize her hand. You could tell from the way he had twisted his arm behind him that it was a secret between them.

The intimations of wholeness in the scene—round the board, round the years, the secret love uniting servant and master—express the original indwelling spirit of Kilneagh. It is a humanistic spirit of compassion and social concern that had found its most memorable expression in the efforts of Anna Quinton to help the victims of the Great Famine of 1846, but whose continuing influence upon the history of the house was not altogether commensurate with the aims of the saintly matron Father Kilgarriff venerates so highly.

When Anna Quinton gave her life to alleviate the suffering caused by injustice and greed, her spirit remained at Kilneagh as *genius loci*, prompting her widower to carry on with her struggle.

> When she died of famine fever her dog-faced husband shut himself into Kilneagh for eleven years, not seeing anyone. It was said that she haunted him: looking from his bedroom window one morning he saw her on a distant hill—an apparition like the Virgin Mary. She told him that he must give away the greater part of his estate to those who had suffered loss and deprivation in the famine, and in his continuing love of her he did so.

Anna Quinton had tried to reduce the burden of guilt that membership in the landlord class placed on her family and was accorded a fool by her English relations for her trouble (thus a fool of "fortune" in another sense of the word). Her ghostly instructions to her widower to stop the guilt at its source was a first step in the direction of an ultimate solution to the foolishness of the Ascendancy system of fortune, namely the dissolution of the estate itself. But the curse of property ownership was to make itself felt in a different way in the course of the Troubles. The next English mistress at Kilneagh, Willie's mother, was the daughter of an English army colonel and united in her person the traditional Kilneagh support for Home Rule and Irish independence with a demand for militant action; her admiration for Michael Collins seemed to border on attraction. Even after the murder of her husband and daughters, Eva could not renounce the use of force to resolve conflicts but slowly killed herself with hatred, bitterness, and despair. Her successor at Kilneagh, her niece Marianne, similarly defended the justice of blood revenge and the need for armed violence, while fatalistically maintaining that the "shadow of destruction" was inescapable. As a visible symbol of the power and dominion of the Anglo-Irish landlords, the Big House was a just target for attack by revolutionaries during the Troubles; for a Big House to be burned by the British Black and Tans would have been unusual, in the case of Kilneagh a telling commentary on the dangers of becoming involved in any way with the use of armed force and a sad memorial to the family's betrayal of the spirit of Anna Quinton.

It is fitting that matriarchal dominion should be associated with the history of a Big House, for houses are, in fact, essentially female structures that embody the principles of order, security, and stability and create meaningful space for birth, nourishment, sleep, and death. The household of Kilneagh was directed by its women, beginning to our knowledge with Anna Quinton's dominion over her "dog-faced" husband, who planted a lane of birch trees as a memorial to her and retired in mourning for eleven years following her death. The dominion of Willie's mother over his father seems to have been not less complete. "She presided over the household with untroubled authority, over my father and myself and my sisters . . . ." After the raid, Aunt Fitzeustace assumed authority for the surviving resident household, the constellation of two single elderly sisters and a defunct priest recalling, with Joyce's "The Sisters", the archetypal Irish matriarchy. Marianne's advent strengthened the pattern: lacking a husband, she married a house. Viewed from a higher perspective, Kilneagh appeared quite beautiful to Marianne, but on closer inspection she found the harsh desolation of its ruined parts repellent. Even so, her love for the young man in the distant past remained untroubled by the constant signs of unrepaired destruction impressing themselves on the development of their child. The line of female ascendancy at Kilneagh ends appropriately with the deformed yet dominant life of Imelda, who bears a miraculous power of inner resurgence.

The men of Kilneagh lead quiet lives complaisantly devoted to the wishes of their more dynamic wives; it is Willie's father who moderates his wife's enthusiastic support of Michael Collins and it is the men's role to connect the realm of the house with that of the mill, the latter being their own domain. The story of Willie's childhood shows the boy uneasy in his dual attachment to house and mill, mother and father. In the prepubertal world of unbroken emotional security, Willie identifies positively with both spatial realms, experiencing pleasure in the prospect of one day assuming his father's position in the mill:

> I knew that one day I would inherit this mill. I liked the thought of that, of going to work there, of learning what my father had had to learn about grain and the machinery that ground it. I liked the mill itself, its grey stone softened with Virginia creeper, the doors of lofts and stores a reddish brown, paint that over the years had lost its shine due to the sun; in a central gable the green-faced clock was always a minute fast. I loved the smell of the place, the warm dry smell of corn, the cleanness even though there was dust in the air. I enjoyed watching the huge wheel turning in the mill-race, one cog engaging the next. The timber of the chutes was smooth with wear, leather flaps opening and falling back, then opening again. The sacks had *Quinton* on them, the letters of our name arranged in a circle.

In addition to Willie's sensuous attachment to his patrimony, the deep love between father and son has another objective correlative in their walks together from house to mill, in which two poles of significance, separated by a hill, are joined in an emotionally charged ritual act. Willie's innocent wish to perpetuate the unity of house and mill in his own person is disturbed by the prospect that he must first be sent off to boarding school: to assume the mantle of the father, he must pass through the puberty rites of his class. As it turns out, the time Willie spends at the boarding school strengthens his ties to his dead father: he resolves to renew the pattern of his father's life, to rebuild Kilneagh, and to take up his hereditary position at the mill. His love for Marianne, which flourishes together with his discovery of his father's school years, is the central emotional expression of his fledgling renewal of his father's truncated life. Both developments are interrupted when the innate rivalry between father and mother in Willie's sense of self comes to a climactic confrontation. Repressed bitterness towards his mother's self-willed decline explodes in a denunciation that is the negative emotional corollary to his constructive plans for Kilneagh and Marianne. His father had exemplified the conciliatory nature of kindness, capable of understanding the "difficult position" of a man like Doyle; his mother was more absolute in her judgments and demands. Her final act of suicide, perhaps partly motivated by her son's open abuse, was her most effective act of retribution, impelling Willie to commit the deed of vengeance she had so long yearned for. Willie construes his mother's suicide as a silent commission to complete a pattern: Doyle's tongue was cut out, his mother cut her wrists with a razor blade, and so Rudkin must be slaughtered with a butcher knife. Throwing over the years of preparation for the rebuilding of Kilneagh in his father's stead, turning his back on Kilneagh and Marianne, Willie follows his mother's example. To the curse of guilt and exile, he adds the self-imposed punishment of silence, cutting himself off, inwardly renouncing all ties to Kilneagh and the living connection to his own fatherhood.

Like Anna and Eva before her, Marianne initiates significant change in the life of a male Quinton—she makes a father of Willie, coming to him with a lamp in his night of despair, offering him the comfort of a light leading out of the long shadows of destruction. Thus, at the crossroads of maturity Willie is confronted with two paths and two rival goddesses—he must choose between the young messenger of new life and the dead messenger of destruction, the virgin's sacrifice for love and the mother's sacrifice for hate; forced to choose between sonship and fatherhood, Willie claims the former and rejects the latter. For her part, Marianne holds the ruins of Kilneagh in trust for Willie, and raises their daughter there in conjugal commitment as the truncated hope of their truncated heritage. The mother's razor or the lover's lamp? The former provokes the slaughter of revenge and the curse of exile, the latter engenders the inward light and final blessing of peace in the ancestral home.

> **A large part of *Fools of Fortune* is devoted to the place of schools and teachers in the lives of the protagonists. The scenes at institutions of learning—especially the pretentious boarding schools in the hills of Dublin and Lausanne—are peopled with seedy hypocrites and petty rogues reminiscent of Trevor's early grotesque novels.**
> **—*Max Deen Larsen***

The murder of Rudkin is the one active deed in a life otherwise distinguished by passivity and shyness, fearful of its own passions and constantly withdrawing into reserve and silence. So, too, Willie's love for Marianne consists of the poignant memory of an unspoiled past; it is told for the melancholy pleasure of the telling, after being repressed for some fifty years until old age has reduced it to fading echoes. Significantly, Willie's first return to Ireland and Co. Cork in 1972 does not include a visit to Kilneagh; the dying servant from his childhood is more important than his own daughter and her mother. The trip to take leave of Josephine, his mother's last companion, is an act of homage to his mother and to the painful memory of the distant past—paradisiacal and desecrated.

A large part of *Fools of Fortune* is devoted to the place of schools and teachers in the lives of the protagonists. The scenes at institutions of learning—especially the pretentious boarding schools in the hills of Dublin and Lausanne—are peopled with seedy hypocrites and petty rogues reminiscent of Trevor's early grotesque novels. Here the audacious school escapades in the middle section of the book provide comic relief from the sombre elegy of the main plot, underscoring along the way Kilneagh's more serious reality by means of numerous bathetic parallels: Willie's loving thoughts for Marianne are segmentally juxtaposed with his school friends' mockery of love; when lecherous Professor Gibb-Bachelor lectures to the girls he would like to seduce about the literary significance of landscapes, Kilneagh's despoiled space provides a tacit counterexample of erotic and poetic desolation; when a disgraced teacher takes revenge on Mad Mack by urinating on him in his sleep, the act is called a "slash", anticipating Willie's murderous slashing of Rudkin.

The schools are grotesque because they fail to initiate the three young protagonists into the strange and terrible reality in which they must live. Miss Halliwell's erotically oppressive pity for Willie is counterproductive, the nuns' professional pity for Imelda ineffectual. In a novel of education, conventional schools are a foil for the existential encounters that matter. As Marianne writes, admitting in her old age the truth of Father Kilgarriff's wisdom:

> He was right when he said that there's not much left in a life when murder has been committed. That moment when I guessed the truth in Mr Lanigan's office; that moment when she opened the secret drawer; that moment when he stood at his mother's bedroom door and saw her dead. After each brief moment there was as little chance for any one of us as there was for Kilneagh after the soldiers' wrath. Truncated lives, creatures of the shadows. Fools of fortune, as his father would have said; ghosts we became.

Reactions to existential encounters may not be as deterministic as Marianne came to believe. The heart of learning, at least for Willie, took place in the heart of Kilneagh, in the scarlet drawing-room. It was here that gentle Father Kilgarriff introduced the boy to pacific precepts; it was here that his mother challenged those precepts with stories embodying heroic ideals; and it was here that his father demonstrated his quietist response to the teachings of books and dangerous current affairs. Like Doyle and like Willie, his father was "in a difficult position", worried that Father Kilgarriff was not teaching his son enough, yet uncomfortable himself with the substance of what his son was supposed to be learning. In the end, the crucial learning experience, the crucible in which all preliminary learning is tried, is the personal experience of deadly sin. That "strange reality" Marianne refers to is entered into by breaking taboos—here committing murder. The changed state of consciousness following the epiphanies Marianne mentions imbues the space of Kilneagh with its peculiar significance.

Imelda's fate reproduces the fate of Kilneagh. Like Willie she is raised with the contending philosophies of life that have shaped the fortunes of the estate: Father Kilgarriff's Christlike compassion and Marianne's fatalistic justification of heroic violence. While her mother keeps Imelda's curiosity and expectations about her father alive (feelings tantamount to belonging to Kilneagh), Father Kilgarriff tries to protect Imelda from participating in the cursed history of the Big House. Gifted with extraordinary powers of imagination, Imelda pursues the reality of her father embodied in Kilneagh. Literally fascinated by intimations about the traumatic events connected with her own birth, Imelda burrows into the secret compartments of Kilneagh's past, ferreting out details that she experiences with uncanny intensity and empathy. As obsessive fantasies take control of her consciousness, she withdraws completely from the outside world and suffers without respite the horrors of ceaseless slaughter. Fortunately, the career of her madness moves beyond the incessant scenes of terror, coming to rest at the serene heart of the Big House. The harmonious world of the scarlet drawing-room, with its fragrant surrounding gardens and its enigmatic secret lovers forever turning and touching, grants Imelda a beatific vision of Paradise Regained. Her peace is construed by the Catholic populace as a sign of divine favor, a token of her saintly namesake, with whom she is explicitly compared. For Imelda had longed for her father's homecoming, and she was granted it in visions of his life's horrors and of his life's Edenic origins—the Sacred Host of her miraculous communion with Kilneagh. Her beatific vision is equally inspired by W. B. Yeats's idyllic lyric "The Lake Isle of Innis-free", which Trevor has elsewhere glossed as follows: "Heartache was soothed in Sligo, the world's weeping held at a distance by its waters and its wild, evenings were full of the linnet's wings." In Imelda the family's guilt is resolved through the combined power of mythic patterns: the quest for the father, the homecoming of the lord, and the peace of the blessed fool.

This positive interpretation of Imelda's final regression is anticipated, and perhaps implanted in her soul, by Father Kilgarriff's efforts to help her fly a kite on her ninth birthday. What she considers the happiest experience of her life is an exhilarating feeling of high flight and of shrinking to a point in the sky. The flying kite is an emotionally constructive symbol, ultimately triumphant, for Imelda's emotionally destructive urge toward personal reduction, repeatedly imaged by insects.

Imelda did not speak. She watched a fly on the wax

fruit in the centre of the table. How disappointing it would be, she thought, when it discovered that the fruit had no juice. . . . 'That lady thought I shouldn't have been given life.'

The wax fruit Imelda here associates with a cruel denial of life is, in the novel's affirmative closing image, displaced by a burgeoning harvest of mulberries. In the end, the mulberry orchard planted by Anna Quinton as a reminder of her English home is the only vital symbolic agency left intact in Kilneagh, just as the *orchard* wing was the only part of the building to survive the fateful raid. The mill being defunct (perhaps the loss of income was one reason for Willie's homecoming, so strangely lacking in ardor), the fruitfulness of Kilneagh has attained a purely spiritual state; here landscape has become literature, whereas in Woodcombe it has become a source of museum income. Like Imelda's visions of the scarlet drawing-room and the poetic peace dropping from linnet's wings, the fruit of the mulberry orchard embodies the quiet beauty of the primal ancestral spirit, now purged of the pain and guilt inflicted by the historical logic of violence. The last of the Quinton-Woodcombe families are happily dependent on the good graces of their neighbors, taking their meals in the kitchen as their servants had done years before. A special kind of salvation seems to be granted to the beggar and the suffering servant, as indeed the most admirable figures in the book are the servants—brave Tim Paddy, who saved Willie's life; saintly Josephine, her life consumed with selfless prayers for consolation; despised Father Kilgarriff, the true servant of God; the wise butler Fukes, the most competent councilor at the boarding school; and Anna Quinton herself, the paradigm of the mistress as suffering servant. If the remnant family at Kilneagh are by grace or good fortune permitted to enjoy their last days in peaceful communion with an ideal past, a harvest of mulberries (Gk. *moros*) is fitting praise for these blissful fools (*morias encomion*).

O see the poles are kissing as they cross.
                                    Dylan Thomas, 1934

Trevor's most ambitious Big-House novel, ***The Silence in the Garden,*** describes the decline and fall of a prominent family of Anglo-Irish landlords and their island estate off the coast of Co. Cork. Where the central love story in ***Fools of Fortune*** focuses on the suffering caused by the intrusion of political violence into an idyllic Ascendancy world, the latter novel uses a constellation of paralyzed love relationships to suggest a more extensive range of social, even mythic implication. Its chief concern is no longer stoically endured suffering, but rather self-inflicted suffering. ***The Silence in the Garden*** thus moves beyond the largely sentimental appeal of ***Fools of Fortune*** and develops with its texture of symbolic realism a more complex picture of the mystery of human guilt.

The narrator informs us that Carriglas, which means "green rock", is "a deceiving name, as the island was very fertile." It is the deceptive quality of the island and of the Rolleston estate lodged upon it which provides the novel with its primary source of suspense. We learn early on that there are bats in the cellar of the grand old house, and there are repeated allusions to a terrible secret hidden in its past, a family sin that mysteriously paralyzes the last generation of a once proud and powerful dynasty. If the text uses traditional Gothic elements to create narrative suspense, it exploits their inherent thematic tensions as well, for the book is ultimately about the intransigent paradox in the name Carriglas.

The island bears silent signs of its former lords, various stones recalling layers of the past. The oldest markers are the standing stones located at the summit wilderness, remnants of a pre-Christian culture that had made the island a burial ground for their kings. Then there are the ruins of a medieval abbey located near the remains of a saint's cell, where a holy well containing moist clay and a stone the saint had once used as a pillow are the objects of occasional pilgrimage and veneration. Finally, the stones of Rolleston manor itself were taken from the castle ruins of earlier overlords. The Big House of Carriglas is thus planted in a context of monuments to former tenants, spiritual and temporal, and the final phase in its history is tacitly traced against the background of sacred significance the island had possessed in the distant past. Inexorably, the silent stones of the past point to the silent garden of the future and the inevitable end of human affairs. After years of unbearable tension, after the crazed tumult of the human comedy and its frantic fleeting concerns, the paradoxical "green rock" of Carriglas signifies a return to the only peace possible—nature freed from human ambitions and vanities. Paradise is a bit of wilderness, not a residence.

***The Silence in the Garden* . . . moves beyond the largely sentimental appeal of *Fools of Fortune* and develops with its texture of symbolic realism a more complex picture of the mystery of human guilt.**
—Max Deen Larsen

As the Anglo-Irish heirs of Carriglas, the three Rolleston children have distinctly different areas of emotional attachment to their ancestral island. John James, the elder son, shows no particular feelings at all for the space of his home and consumes himself in vague and pretentious posturings towards the Irish mainland. The younger brother Lionel, on the other hand, is most at home working the land itself and puttering in the sheds; no Abraham, his life is a pastoral idyll spoiled by the shyness that prevents his union with Sarah.

Their sister Villana, by contrast, is the natural mistress of Carriglas: beautiful, clever, and willful, she had clearly been the dominant child and assumed a position of leadership over her two brothers. Thus it is Villana who habitually visits the ancient standing stones at the summit of the island, her affinity for them suggesting both her own regal nature and her need to comfort herself with the inevitable loss of every mortal sovereignty.

In the crucial year 1931, which marks a visible turning point in the history of Carriglas and to which the bulk of the novel is devoted, Rolleston manor is in a state of reduced splendor, the opulently appointed sitting room no longer representative of the economically deflated estate. The formative spirit of the House of Rolleston is nonetheless represented by the evergreen trees standing at either side of the main entrance way. Like emblematic badges for the genius loci, the strawberry trees and the monkey puzzle suggest that the family history is determined by the combined forces of compassion (the strawberry tree has red heart-shaped fruit, traditionally the token of martyrs and Christ's blood) and entanglement (the monkey puzzle has intricately entwined branches and stiff, sharp-pointed leaves). As we learn from the knowledgeable amateur historian Finnamore Balt, the family's economic decline began with its exercise of compassion in the years following the Great Famine: "'The Famine Rollestons were widely renowned for their compassion. A most remarkable generation, but alas disastrous in terms of the effect on the family fortunes.'" Finnamore Balt does not, however, realize that the puzzling refusal of the family he marries into to oppose their own ruin is likewise rooted in a kind of compassion: secret guilt and shame demand their self-denial in a life-long act of expiation. The emblematic trees remind us that compassion as well as cruelty lead to the downfall of the estate and its ordered world. If the strawberry trees and the monkey puzzle are outward signs for the fate of the Rolleston family—their ineluctable entrapment in compunction—the two tree species might equally suggest the poetic workings of the novel itself, whose appeal derives largely from the combined effects of sentiment and suspense.

Ancient Mrs Rolleston is the living embodiment of the conscience of Carriglas. Quietly, with irresistible moral authority, she compels her grandchildren to live out the consequences of their past deeds and to recompense the surviving victim as best they can. Despite her revulsion at what she thinks is Villana's emotional exploitation of Finnamore Balt, despite her suspicion about the legitimacy of Kathleen Quigley's requests for money, despite her anguish about the circumstantial nature of her family's guilt and victimization, Mrs Rolleston is committed to a moral order of humanitarian justice. If Mrs Rolleston speaks for the spirit of Carriglas, her last wish that the myrtle and hebes be protected in the garden suggests an unbroken desire for marriage and children that is thwarted by Villana's farcical marriage. Similarly, Mrs Rolleston's opponent at Villana's wedding, the Bishop of Killaloe, speaks as the voice of the bridge (the sight of which prompts him to "ponti-ficate", which is the symbol of sterile union, victorious over the fertile garden of Mrs Rolleston's desire. And yet, the logical end of her efforts will be the revision of the estate to the laboring native Irish and the reduction of the house to its working core:

> Alone in the kitchen's spaciousness, she would admire the windows and wallcupboards that so gracefully accommodated the faint concavity of the walls. The range and the long, scrubbed table formed a trinity with the dresser, the range the kitchen's heart, as the kitchen was the household's.

As Mrs Rolleston is the heart of the family, so is the kitchen the heart of the Big House: it contains the primal trinity of natural life that will survive the passing of the foolish "trinity" of the Children of Carriglas.

Mrs Rolleston's terse judgment about the key event of the novel, the wedding of Villana and Finnamore Balt, aptly describes the overriding theme of the novel as a whole: "This wedding is an occasion of farce." As a record of various thwarted, stunted, and frustrated marriages between individuals and between classes, *The Silence in the Garden* describes not one, but many farcical weddings. Mrs Rolleston deplores Villana's decision to marry Finnamore Balt because the union fails to fulfill the usual criteria for marriage: Villana does not love the man, who is old enough to be her father, erotically; she makes it clear to him from the start that they are to have no children; far from marrying for money—as most townspeople suppose—she suppresses his efforts to recover lost lands for the Rolleston family estate. Villana's union with Finnamore is not the act of cruelty Mrs Rolleston suspects, but rather an act of regressive self-comfort: the trustworthy companionship Villana expects from Finnamore is for her an escape into her early untroubled childhood. The space sacred to her passionate love of Hugh, the ice house, has become an empty temple of memories; but her nursery can be resurrected in its innocence as a nuptial bedroom. Together with her natural mate, Hugh, Villana sacrifices love and mutual fertility to atone for ill-fated childish cruelty; together with her marital companion, Finnamore Balt, Villana covenants a life of mutual care in a childless nursery. Theirs will be the kindness of a long death watch, repeating the pattern of Villana's care for an ailing speckled hen in the same room; one is led to suspect a mysterious blend of care and cruelty in her handling of both relationships.

For the inhabitants of Carriglas, 1931 is memorable as the year of Villana's wedding and the year of Cornelius Dowley's bridge. The coincidence of these two acts of union significantly reflects their common origin in Villana's fateful feral games. As a child she had taken the lead with Hugh and her brothers in hunting a poor native boy across the island like a rabbit, thus acting out a children's version of the great historical game of Ascendancy rule in Ireland. Villana's antagonist, the red-headed boy Cornelius Dowley, grows up to take revenge on his tormentors and, uniting in his person political and private terrorism, helps to initiate with revolutionary acts of violence the later union of Carriglas and the mainland. Villana's sadistic hunting game is a courtship ritual for a wedding of violence that is consummated by a bombing and then officially sanctified by the dedication of the bridge bearing the bridegroom's name. In the eyes of Catholic revolutionaries the bridge might symbolize the annexation of Anglo-Irish dominions by native Irish culture, but from the narrator's perspective the bridge has the character of an ugly shotgun wedding, justly reversing the pattern of Villana's cruel shotgun courtship. Aesthetically, the symbol for the marriage of two social worlds through violence, indeed, the very celebration of that uniting violence, is a sordid affair: the Cornelius Dowley Bridge is depicted as a callous violation of the landscape, the tall steel supports an ugly mockery of the inscrutable standing stones crowning the island. In the last chapter of the novel, the bridge has become a static part of a drab, bleak landscape, recalling in contrast the personally conducted movements of the discarded ferry boat with its humanly responsive rhythms and positive emotional aura.

The physical union of island and mainland is one objective correlative for social and political marriage, the physical union of John James and Mrs Moledy is another. The illicit love affair of the heir of Carriglas and the proprietress of the rose of Tralee boarding house is at once a realistic comedy of manners and a grotesque allegory illustrating the uneasy and sterile intercourse between two key segments of Irish society. John James's entanglement with Mrs Moledy is a counterpart to Villana's entanglement with Cornelius Dowley, and both relationships characterize the bedeviled entanglement of Anglo-Irish landlords with the Catholic Irish tenancy. John James is, at 35, a retired officer with a minor limp and no accomplishments. His identity is defined by his condescending relationship to his motherly mistress, an affectionately accommodating Catholic widow, and by his daunting relationship to his dead father, of whom John James feels that he is himself a lamentable parody. Like his father before him, John James is remarkably tall, an attribute suggesting nobility (again the regal standing stones of Carriglas) and virility. Mrs Moledy admires both qualities in her "soldier boy". Their sexual relationship is an extended metaphor for the political relationship of their respective classes before the revolution. Mrs Moledy explicitly refers to John James's "genitals" as her "king" (the "castle" he enters being hers, and it is the gentleman's genitals that are meant when he stands before her naked "on his honour", for John

James has the honor of primogeniture to bestow. The genital king does not, however, generate new life in Mrs Moledy, suggesting little future for the social union they represent. Like all Anglo-Irish landlords, John James wants to enjoy the vital substance of the native Catholic mother, but certainly not to unite their flesh in marriage. Sweet as the Rose of Tralee, the great Irish mother gives her body and her money to her proud lover, not in servility, but in the knowledge of her own superior strength. Benignly supportive of the Ascendancy, Mrs Moledy is a rather vigorous specimen of the Old Woman of Ireland, who gladly shares with her adored king the warm bulk of her canny flesh and presses him to use her savings to purchase a motorcar. Periodically the exclusive island had paid a visit to the common mainland; but now the connecting bridge has eliminated the privileged condition of the island and has, moreover, made the continuation of the gentleman's visits dependent on the financial help of the woman of the mainland. The ancient castle still desires the comforting glamor of its habitual lord and is willing to pay the price. Mrs Moledy puts down John James's attempt to resist the implication that he is prostituting himself by sitting up in bed and declaring there is no interest to be paid on her money—the real interest being paid is exposed in the falling of the bedclothes from her upper-body. Mrs Moledy's burlesque wedding with John James is a financial union consummated at the garden party and confirmed on the altar of her bed:

> The apologies that had been written down poured
> again from her lips. She would kneel before him if
> he required it. . . . He attempted to count the
> banknotes into her hands, so that there could be no
> argument afterwards. He tried to be exact and businesslike, but the notes dropped to the floor and he
> was obliged to go down on his hands and knees to
> retrieve them. . . . She sprinkled eau de Cologne on
> to her sheets, telling him not to be silly when he
> shook his head.

Sex, money, and politics—the triumvirate of power blend happily in the fruitless mutual bondage of John James and Mrs Moledy. Finally, Mrs Moledy's visit to the garden party—a Trollopean farce—is yet another counterpart to the erection of the bridge and to Cornelius Dowley's return visit to Carriglas: the uninvited wedding guest brings money to support her Ascendancy lover; the heroic ambusher brings a bomb to destroy his Ascendancy suitor. The connections of murder and of marriage equally wreak havoc in the social body of the ruling class.

The deeper issue informing the dominant wedding motif is the act of touching. The central figure of the novel is a boy who learns to eschew marriage and whose learning experience embodies the controlling issue of the book. Tom is taught by the Catholic establishment that he, born tragically out of wedlock, is a marginal member of society, even of the human race. Holy Mullihan repeatedly instructs Tom about the evils of carnal lust and makes Tom feel that he is the morally blighted fruit of deadly sin. Tom experiences his peculiar innate guilt primarily in terms of touching; most of the Catholic community are afraid to touch the boy, as if his flesh were contaminated with the heinous sin of his origin. When Tom happens to observe what he believes to be a near counterpart to his own conception, he adds another aspect to his understanding of the taboo of sexual touching—he sees that it includes an element of torment, even violence.

> 'God, you'd torment a man!' Briscoe, the bank porter, was there with the girl from Renehan's who'd
> told Tom she said prayers for him. They were lying
> on the grass by one of the tumbled-down walls,
> Briscoe with his jacket off. . . . All the time he was
> continuing to pull at her skirt and she was trying to
> stop him, even though she had one arm round his
> neck. . . . 'God, you have the fine legs,' he said, his
> voice thickly slurred, like Drunk Paddy's when he
> was shouting at the seagulls. 'God, you're great!'
> . . . She covered herself. She sat up on the grass,
> buttoning her blouse. . . . 'You're a right bitch,'
> Briscoe shouted at the girl. . . . 'A right little convent whore!' Briscoe's voice shouted, and in the
> same rough voice he swore at the girl, calling her
> names Tom thought only the boys at the Christian
> Brothers' used.

Briscoe's unconscious deification of the sexual tormentor passes without comment in Tom's thoughts. The inherent sadism in sexual relationships is less explicitly presented to the boy's emotional imagination in the performance of the Zodiacs. The overt thrill of the act is the titillation of playing with death, but the thrill of ritual violence is equally sexual, as the man blindly outlines the female figure with knives that must not touch her flesh. The knife-throwing act of the Zodiacs is a grim entertainment that mimes the force of destiny. Outlining the body of his wife with twelve knives, the husband performs a symbolic act of sacrifice (recalling Hugh's sacrifice of Villana) which torments without touching. Similarly, Briscoe and the girl from Renehan's torment each other sexually by not consummating their touching, and Ireland's social classes torment each other with the struggle for power and guilt; sexually and politically, everyone is tormented by contingencies. The act of touching in all its forms assumes in the political and religious world of 1931 ominous implications. For the guilt of union, whether sexual or political, stems from the inevitable violence attending it and the consequent violence it engenders. The long train of carnage in Ireland is alike a long train of carnal corruption. Touching is most often the prelude to suffering, whether as sexual torment, political violence, or the burden of ownership—and fertility itself seems to be the vanity of vanities.

The marital garden falls silent with the deaths of the three fruitless children of Carriglas, but in the long preceding generations the unsilent garden has been the scene of human intercourse fallen from grace, the living space of suffering impingement. Mrs Rolleston's dream reveals this deeper reality when she sees the multiple identity of the red-haired boy who is frantically chased across the island:

> 'That boy was killed at Passchendaele,' Finnamore Balt said, but she contradicted that, reminding him that it was Villana's father who had been killed at Passchendaele. 'Then he was killed on your avenue,' Finnamore Balt said, but she knew that was wrong also. 'Mr Balt asked me to marry him,' Brigid said, looking up from the bread she was making, her face delighted in the kitchen.

In the garden of Carriglas the players in the human comedy are interchangeable, finally identical all modes of interhuman connection—killing and marrying, crossing and touching, amount to the same breach of silence, the same suffering entanglement marked by the emblematic trees of the Irish Big House.

The central theme of touching acquires additional focus and intensity through the stylistic prominence of the word *cross* (as verb, adjective, noun) and its derivatives in the diction of the novel. The crossing motif embraces a multitude of meanings, all of which reinforce a core element in Trevor's vision of the human condition. Some examples: The expression for being angry or annoyed is invariably "cross", as when Mrs Moledy urges John James not to be "a crosspatch" or when she accuses him of being "cross about that bridge." The bridge itself is described as a "criss-cross of girders" — thus resembling the monkey puzzle — and the most illustrious exploit of the man it is named after was the ambush at Lahane crossroads. In her last moment alone before beginning married life, Villana crosses her legs while sitting on her bed, suggesting that her personal cross is to be a fruitless marriage. Throughout the novel the overall effect of the blended implications of crossing—transition, confusion, thwartedness, anger, piety, suffering, and crucifixion—is to suggest a world in need of purgation, a world in the throes of self-punishment. Tom learns from Holy Mullihan that his very existence is an act of blasphemy, as if his mother had walked up to "the Cross" and spit on the Savior. If, in consequence, people "cross a street" to avoid coming near him, Tom "crosses" to Mrs Rolleston's bedside and receives her kiss. Tom's crossed life in Catholic society, his status as an "untouchable" among his own people, is redeemed by the Rolleston cross of responsible self-sacrifice: Mrs Rolleston's kiss of moral adoption betokens Tom's inheritance of the estate.

John James's dominion over Carriglas thus devolves upon the servant king Tom. Like the Old Adam, John James has fallen from his first estate, having traded his birthright for the itinerant kingship of the Rose of Tralee. But Carriglas will be redeemed and transfigured through the humility of the New Adam, the Suffering Servant. Often called "the gatelodge boy" by the Rollestons, Tom's life represents the space of ritual passage, the sacred space of birth and death for the Big House. Tom suffers for the guilt of the House and of the country, and, gentle as a lamb, his life puts an end to the thread of carnage and carnality. Tom's story is the quest of an innocent to understand the prejudice directed against him. With a character free from resentment, bitterness, and hatred toward his tormentors, his path is a pilgrim's progress to secular hermitage; drawing more than Catholic piety from touching the holy clay of the hermit's well, Tom there communes with the symbol of his own deeper self and his own destiny. Only the passive humility of the atoning hero, who knows neither rebellion nor self-pity, can ultimately overcome the fanatic influence of the populist hero, Cornelius Dowley, whose fame is forged of cruelty, bitterness, and vengeance. For Tom it is enough to be pleased that "Lashaway", the horse he placed his money on, wins when he knew it would; the amount of the win is as unimportant as the bronze plate, dulled by time, honoring his violent antagonist.

The safest route of escape from the damning contingencies of power and sexuality is that of abstinence. Tom and the three Rolleston children choose to live in sterile relationships that lead away from the multiplication of contingencies and back to the garden that is silent. Rejection of estates, powers, and dominions—with their attendant guilt—also leads to the withdrawal of man from nature; the island that is shaped like a snail outlasts the passing gardens on its back, perhaps in time devouring them. The alternative to sinful touching that Tom finds most attractive is not the holy sacrament of matrimony but rather the safe haven of the confirmed bachelor.

> 'I'll tell you one thing,' the ferryman was saying on the ferry when Tom climbed on to it. 'Ireland was always famous for its bachelors.'

All celibates, religious and secular, prefer ferries to bridges, prefer living in a silent garden. Tom's spiritual exercises at the well and his forced education in the taboo of touching lead him to reject the prospect of wedding fertile Esmeralda Coyne (one of eleven daughters) and to affirm his own kind of no-touch "marriage" with Patty: Tom saves Carriglas from meretricious resurrection as a hotel and confirms the silencing of all sorrows' source, the peaceful end of all touching and all crossing. Having been constantly enjoined by a concerned Catholic community to touch the holy clay, Tom unites himself with the "green rock" of Ireland in a kind of contemplative hermitage that rejects commercial renewal and allows instead the garden wilderness to renew its primal silence. For Tom's "bewilderment" at the awesome self-inflicted punishment of the House of Rolleston is the soul's counterpart for the literal be-wild-erment of Carriglas, that deceptively named "green rock" of Ireland, for which fertility must be a miracle of grace, given the crossed nature of man. In his humility, the Suffering Servant is exalted by the divine paradox of grace—like "the green rock".

Richard Tillinghast (review date February 1993)

SOURCE: "'They Were as Good as We Were': The Stories of William Trevor," in *The New Criterion,* Vol. 11, No. 6, February, 1993, pp. 10-17.

[*In the following review Tillinghast examines Trevor's treatment of Irish culture in* The Collected Stories.]

American readers of William Trevor's fiction may find themselves at something of a loss to decide precisely what nationality or ethnic identity to assign to this acknowledged master of the short story. The usual epithet for Trevor is Anglo-Irish, which, particularly for readers unfamiliar with Ireland, roughly places him, because he was born and raised in Ireland, went to school there, attended Trinity, College, Dublin—and because a quarter of the eighty-odd pieces in his *Collected Stories* are set in Ireland or are peopled by Irish characters living abroad, usually in England. He himself has for many years lived and written in Devon.

The term "Anglo-Irish" usually either embraces the members and descendants of the Protestant Ascendancy like Yeats, Synge, and Lady Gregory—prime movers in the Irish Literary Revival; or it brings to mind the fiction written by that wonderful team of cousins who called themselves Somerville and Ross, authors of the "Irish R. M." stories, whose masterpiece was the novel *The Real Charlotte.* A somewhat imprecise Celtic mythologizing tendency is evoked in the one case; decrepit country houses, hunt balls, and a Faulknerian preoccupation with lineage in the other.

To associate Trevor with the *milieu* conjured up by the term "Anglo-Irish" would be a mistake. For one thing, the Anglo-Irish tradition itself has since the nineteenth century become increasingly attenuated. As early as the 1860s, Gladstone's disestablishment of the (Protestant) Church of Ireland, his Land Acts—and later those of Balfour—in response to the agitations associated with Parnell, together with Conservative adoption of land reform policies, drastically liberalized the landlord-and-tenant system that had ruled the island since Henry VIII and Elizabeth I revoked the legitimacy of the native Irish nobility, making them swear fealty to and draw their legitimacy from the Crown.

The history of Ireland after the land reform movement was one of Protestant return to England in the face of an Ireland that increasingly defined itself, especially under DeValera's Irish Republic, as Gaelic, agrarian, and Catholic. The Protestants who have remained in the Irish Republic are an isolated remnant. (For readers unfamiliar with Irish life, the terms Protestant and Catholic imply social distinctions as much as matters of faith.) Trevor's understanding of the lives of Irish Protestants hints at a broader identification with an element of humanity psychologically marginalized, passed-over, alienated. And since Trevor's characters and settings are in fact more often English than they are Irish, he might be more accurately though more long-windedly identified as "Protestant-Irish and English."

On this side of the Atlantic we are accustomed to seeing the Emerald Isle through a haze of sentimentality which Irish-Americans have led us to feel for the country which they, usually for very sound reasons, have left. The reality, of course, is that life for the majority of those who live in Ireland, particularly in the provinces, has been an unending struggle to make ends meet within a farming economy which offers little diversion. Bridie, in Trevor's early story **"The Ballroom of Romance,"** cares for her widowed father, who is handicapped with an amputated leg, on a small farm like so many in the country. The narrowness of this life, particularly back in the Forties and Fifties, is from an American point of view almost impossible to grasp.

As drab as life in the nearby town is, Bridie still fantasizes about it: "The town had a cinema called the Electric, and a fish-and-chip shop where people met at night, eating chips out of newspaper on the pavement outside. In the evenings, sitting in the farmhouse with her father, she often thought about the town, imagining the shop-windows lit up to display their goods and the sweet-shops still open so that people could purchase chocolates or fruit to take with them to the Electric cinema. But the town was eleven miles away, which was too far to cycle, there and back, for an evening's entertainment." Instead she cycles once a week to a grim little place called The Ballroom of Romance, dancing and socializing with the same crowd of bachelors and spinsters who frequent the place, trying to attract the attention of the drummer in the band, Dano Ryan. Dano is not interested, however. "Once, at the end of an evening, she'd pretended that there was a puncture in the back wheel of her bicycle and he'd concerned himself with it while Mr Maloney and Mr Swanton waited for him in Mr Maloney's car. He'd blown the tyre up with the car pump and had said he thought it would hold."

While there is plenty of humor in Trevor's writing, he seldom condescends to his characters, but pays laconic tribute to their stoicism and decency. Bridie's evening at The Ballroom of Romance is revealed, but only at the end of the story, to have been her last night there. When the dance hall closes, she allows the old bachelor Bowser Egan to accompany her and even to kiss her in a field along the way, after he has, in the reticent and even coded manner of these tradition-bound people, indicated he would marry her once his mother had died, leaving him the small farm where mother and son live. Marriage, as is often the case in these Irish stories, represents a sort of resigned acquiescence in the social realities of a very constricted way of life. After the chaste and sad little exchange in the field, Bowser and Bridie mount their bikes and part. Without any flourish of either exultation or self-pity, Bridie has set into motion a major decision in her circumscribed life. "She rode through the night as on Saturday nights for years she had ridden and never would ride again because she'd reached a certain age. She would wait now and in time Bowser Egan would seek her out because his mother would have died. Her father would probably have died also by then. She would marry Bowser Egan because it would be lonesome being by herself in the farmhouse."

In **"The Property of Colette Nervi,"** a story published some twenty years later, another rural Irish marriage of convenience—between a farmer and the daughter of a shopkeeper—is made affordable with money the farmer has stolen from a purse some French tourists have left sitting on top of their rental car. The French people have come to look at the little settlement's one touristic claim to fame, Drumgawnie Rath, "a ring of standing stones that predated history." One irony in the story is that people will come from all over Europe to see these unimpressive stones, though "a visitor who had spent the whole afternoon examining them and had afterwards returned to the shop to verify the way to the Rossaphin road has stated that they were the most extraordinary stones of their kind in the whole of Europe. 'I think he was maybe drunk,' Dolores's mother had commented, and her father had agreed." The stolen money will allow Henry Garvey, who will inherit a rundown old farm, to marry the crippled Dolores, who will inherit the shop at the crossroads, in a marriage ceremony where the arm-support of the crutch will be decorated in white lace. "Dolores thought she'd never seen a crutch look so pretty, and wondered if it was a marriage tradition for crippled brides, but did not ask." This last phrase is emblematic of so much in the repressive society that Trevor chronicles, where much is understood and little is spoken.

"An Evening with John Joe Dempsey" gives an insight into the life and mind of a character thoroughly out of sync with the pieties of his town. The story begins with John Joe's being sent by his widowed mother on an errand to the combination pub/grocery store that one still finds in rural Ireland—the kind of place where Himself drinks a pint while Herself does the shopping. "Mr Lynch, now a large, fresh-faced man of fifty-five who was never seen without a brown

hat on his head," who works as a clerk in a meal business, lives with his seventy-nine-year-old mother, and spends his evenings drinking in Keogh's public house, buys the fifteen-year-old boy his first bottle of stout and decides to give him some advice, starting off with some stories about the "glory girls" of London, where he was stationed while serving with the British Army. The preamble of Mr. Lynch's words of wisdom would capture any boy's attention:

> "If your daddy was alive today, he would be telling you a thing or two in order to prepare you for your manhood and the temptations in another country. Your mother wouldn't know how to tackle a matter like that, nor would Father Ryan, nor the Christian Brothers. Your daddy might have sat you down in this bar and given you your first bottle of stout. He might have told you about the facts of life."

John Joe knows exactly what he wants to hear about: "Did one of the glory girls entice yourself, Mr Lynch?" To John Joe's intense disappointment, though, and in one of the wry twists that William Trevor specializes in, the point of the story is that, faced with the "glory girl," Mr. Lynch has a vision of the Blessed Virgin! "As soon as the glory girl said we'd drink the beer before we got down to business I saw . . . the Holy Mother, as clear as if [she] was in front of me." "I couldn't repeat," he adds, "what the glory girl said when I walked away." But the reader can guess.

> **"An Evening with John Joe Dempsey" gives an insight into the life and mind of a character thoroughly out of sync with the pieties of his town.**
> —*Richard Tillinghast*

What a bring-down for the young man! Typical of Trevor's comic sense is Mr. Lynch's summing-up remark: "The facts of life is one thing, John Joe, but keep away from dirty women." Not to worry. John Joe has at fifteen learned to say what is expected of him.

> "You have pimples on your chin," said Mr Lynch in the end. "I hope you're living a clean life now."
>
> "A healthy life, Mr. Lynch."
>
> "It is a question your daddy would ask you. You know what I mean? There's some lads can't leave it alone."
>
> "They go mad in the end, Mr Lynch."

John Joe's mother and everyone else wonders why the lad

spends so much time in the company of the town idiot, a dwarf named Quigley. Brother Leahy questions him sharply about the dwarf: "Tell me this, young fellow-me-lad, what kind of a conversation do you have with old Quigley?" They talked, John Joe said, about trees and flowers and hedgerows. He liked to listen to Quigley, he said, because Quigley had acquired a knowledge of such matters. But not even Mr. Lynch is dumb enough to fall for that one. John Joe's private view is that "Quigley, a bachelor also, was a happier man than Mr Lynch. He lived in what amounted to a shed at the bottom of his niece's garden. Food was carried to him, but there were few, with the exception of John Joe, who lingered in his company." Like John Joe himself, Quigley spends most of his time thinking what it would be like to have sex with the ladies of the town, spying on them, and spinning fabulous tales about their intimate lives: "Quigley's voice might continue for an hour and a half, for there was hardly a man and his wife in the town whom he didn't claim to have observed in intimate circumstances. John Joe did not ever ask how, when there was no convenient shed to climb on to, the dwarf managed to make his way to so many exposed upstairs windows. Such a question would have been wholly irrelevant."

In a series of hilarious vignettes, Trevor retails John Joe's fantasies, each of which, simmering just beneath the surface of his imagination, involves being seduced by one of the married ladies of the town. When his mother gives him his father's old fountain pen as a birthday present, he finds himself writing, as a way of testing the pen, *It's hot in here. Wouldn't you take off your jersey?* "That's a funny thing to write," his mother says. "It came into my head," is his reply.

The end of **"An Evening with John Joe Dempsey"** follows the boy to his room, where he "looked with affection at his bed, for in the end there was only that." Our sympathies are with the boy, because in the face of the town's repression and compromise, his fantasy life embodies his only sanity: "He travelled alone, visiting in his way the women of the town, adored and adoring, more alive in his bed than he ever was at the Christian Brothers' School, or in the grey Coliseum [the cinema], or in the chip-shop, or Keogh's public house, or his mother's kitchen, more alive than ever he would be at the sawmills. In his bed he entered a paradise: it was grand being alone."

The closest Trevor gets in his short stories to an atmosphere that might be called, in the terms I have delineated above, "Anglo-Irish," is in a poignant piece called **"The Distant Past,"** which tells the story of an old brother and sister who live on in their dilapidated Georgian manor house, with its leaky roof and family crest and Cross of St. George displayed in the front hall—all that remains of an estate call Carraveagh. "The Middletons of Carraveagh the family had

once been known as, but now the brother and sister were just the Middletons, for Carraveagh didn't count any more, except to them." On the day of Queen Elizabeth's coronation in 1952, they drove into town with a small Union Jack displayed in the rear window of their car.

The Church of Ireland (Anglican) Middletons have always enjoyed affectionate relations with the Catholic Irish of the town, their loyalties to the imperial past being smiled on as harmless eccentricities. Of the display of the flag on coronation day: "'Bedad, you're a holy terror, Mr Middleton!' Fat Cranley laughingly exclaimed, noticing the flag as he lifted a tray of pork steaks from his display shelf." Part of the irony is that Fat Cranley, during the Irish War of Independence, actually fought against the British, showing up at Carraveagh with a shotgun in expectation of a battle with British troops, and locking up the family in an upstairs room. But as the Troubles of the Easter Rising and Civil War period faded into memory the town could laugh about those events, the Middletons amiably taking their place as "harmlessly peculiar," cobwebby museum pieces who give the town a bit of tone. Everyone has been able to accept this transition through which the Middletons have gone from being part of the ruling class to being two old relics of the past. "On Fridays, when they took seven or eight dozen eggs to the town, they dressed in pressed tweeds and were accompanied over the years by a series of red setters, the breed there had always been at Carraveagh."

As the older brother and sister have declined in the world, the new Ireland has prospered, becoming less a poor province of Britain and more a part of Europe, with a growing tourist trade: "the wife of a solicitor, a Mrs Duggan, began to give six o'clock parties once or twice a year, obliging her husband to mix gin and Martini in glass jugs and herself handing round a selection of nuts and small Japanese crackers." Trevor effortlessly sketches a three-paragraph history of the newly prosperous Irish Republic. As for the Middletons: "Dimly, but with no less loyalty, they still recalled the distant past and were listened to without ill-feeling when they spoke of it and of Carraveagh as it had been, and of the Queen whose company their careless father had known.

The trouble arises when the distant past stops being distant. "We can disagree without guns" was the gospel here, "the result of living in a Christian country." "That the Middletons bought their meat from a man who had once locked them into an upstairs room and had then waited to shoot soldiers in their hall was a fact that amazed the seasonal visitors." Then the new Troubles begin, with Protestant attacks on Catholic neighborhoods and the rebirth of the old IRA as a brutal revolutionary force; the rise of the Protestant paramilitaries—as bad or worse than the IRA; and the murders and retaliations. Since the town lies a scant sixty miles from the Ulster border, tourism falls off and the town's hard-won prosperity starts to ebb. The Middletons start being snubbed: "It was as though, going back nearly twenty years, people remembered the Union Jack in the window of their car and saw it now in a different light. It wasn't something to laugh at any more, nor were certain words that the Middletons had gently spoken, nor were they themselves just an old, peculiar couple." The humor, the affection, the very human accommodation between old antagonists—all of them caught between conflicting social forces over which they have no control—disappear now, in a past that has suddenly become present. "Because of the distant past they would die friendless. It was worse than being murdered in their beds."

Historians and political commentators, particularly on the left, like to speak of the Irish condition since Independence as "post-colonial"; and Irish society does exhibit some of the signs of a people still shaking off the shadows of foreign domination. Attitudes toward government and toward secular authority figures, for example, are strikingly ambivalent. But the English and the Scots were always too close to the Irish to be thought of as colonizers in the classic model. Trevor brings a subtlety of insight to the relations between Ireland and "the other island." Take Norah and Dermot of **"Another Christmas."** Irish by birth, they have emigrated shortly after their marriage and are now permanently settled in England. "Their children spoke with London accents. Patrick and Brendan worked for English firms and would make their homes in England. Patrick had married an English girl. They were Catholics and they had Irish names, yet home for them was not Waterford." In this they typify many Irish people who live in England.

The crisis of the story arises from the unspoken understanding that their landlord, Mr. Joyce (an Irish name, though the man seems not to have Irish sympathies), will for the first time in years not be coming to Christmas dinner. Norah is planning to deliver a present to him, sensing he won't come—though Mr. Joyce has not said no, and Dermot insists, "I'd say there was no need to go round with the tie, Norah. I'd say he'd make the effort on Christmas Day." (Trevor has a wonderful ear for the Irish conditional tense.) The estrangement has come about because of words spoken while the three were watching a television news report of "another outrage"—an IRA bombing. When Mr. Joyce said that he "couldn't understand the mentality of people like that . . . killing just anyone, destroying life for no reason," Dermot had countered that "they mustn't of course forget what the Catholics in the North had suffered. The bombs were a crime but it didn't do to forget that the crime would not be there if generations of Catholics in the North had not been treated as animals."

Can anyone who knows his history disagree with that? The story dramatizes how the lives of these London Irish are im-

pinged upon by the Troubles. Norah, caught between two nations, "felt she should be out on the streets, shouting in her Waterford accent, violently stating that the bombers were more despicable with every breath they drew, that hatred and death were all they deserved." At the same time her husband faces the possibility of losing his job as a meter-reader for North Thames Gas because men with Irish accents make people nervous these days. Still Norah resents his statement about Irish history because "[t]heir harmless elderly landlord might die in the course of that same year, a friendship he had valued lost, his last Christmas lonely." We can see how families, friendships, lives are affected by the continuing butchery in the North, a conflict that dates back over many centuries.

Politics, history, and social class engage Trevor's imagination not in and of themselves, but because of the way they affect people's lives. Though Northern Ireland or even Ireland is certainly not an obsession for him, Trevor has written other stories that get right into the belly of the beast. In **"Attracta,"** the title character, a Protestant schoolteacher, has somehow managed to put into the back of her mind the death of her own parents when she was three years old—they were shot down by mistake in an ambush the Nationalist insurgents had planned for the Black and Tans. In the aftermath the man responsible for the ambush has become Attracta's protector, and Attracta only learns of her parents' death when she is eleven, from a bitter, somewhat deranged old man in the town. She has managed somehow to repress all feelings toward the Troubles of the 1920s until by chance she reads in a newspaper of the suicide of an Englishwoman whose husband, an army officer, was murdered by the IRA, who decapitated him and sent his head to her in the mail. Then Attracta loses control of what she has repressed all these years, goes off her head a bit and begins to talk to her pupils about the horror that lies just beneath the surface of Irish history, the horror that most people successfully ignore. The next day the Protestant Archdeacon kindly convinces Attracta to take early retirement.

In **"Beyond the Pale,"** Cynthia, an Englishwoman on vacation in Northern Ireland with her husband, his mistress of many years, and her husband's best friend, becomes hysterical after hearing the story of a local Irishman's former girlfriend who has been killed in England in some obscure plot between the rival terrorist groups. The man drowns himself in the sea just outside the hotel where the foursome vacation, because this is where he and his girlfriend had come as children. This sends Cynthia off on a mad ramble about Irish history, in the course of which she spills the beans about her husband's affair. His mistress, who narrates the story, is more upset about this revelation than about the tragedies of Irish history: "Why couldn't it have been she who had gone down to the rocks and slipped on the seaweed or just walked into the sea, it didn't matter which? Her awful rigmarole hung about us as the last of the tea things were gathered up—the earls who'd fled, the famine and the people planted. The children were there too, grown up into murdering riff-raff."

The stickiest problem of Irish history is, writ large, the same impulse that Trevor worries relentlessly in many if not most of his stories—the impulse to hide, to suppress, to lie. I have dwelt on the specifically Irish and Irish-English sides of Trevor's work, but his preoccupation with repression and with loaded secrets is by no means limited to the national and ethnic context. He gives human nature a wide berth, sometimes turning an amused eye to our duplicities, but more often adopting a rather severe if not bitter tone. Disillusionment is the characteristic mode of this most acute observer of the human condition.

The seasoned reader of Trevor's work, upon opening a story called **"A Happy Family,"** braces himself for the "attitude adjustment" that is surely waiting in the wings, even at the moment when ordinary human contentment is being masterly evoked in passages like this: "I remember sitting in the number 73 bus, thinking of the day as I had spent it and thinking of the house I was about to enter. It was a fine evening, warm and mellow, the air heavy with the smell of London. The bus crossed Hammersmith Bridge, moving quite quickly towards the leafy avenues beyond." In a house in those leafy avenues lives a woman who will soon begin receiving phone calls from a Mr. Higgs, who uncannily knows all the secrets of her life: a caller who turns out to be imaginary—the midlife version of an imaginary childhood figure. When the woman has to be "put away" for her mental illness, her husband cannot help being disconcerted by the fact that their daughter also has an imaginary friend. "I stopped the car by our house," the story ends, "thinking that only death could make the house seem so empty, and thinking too that death was easier to understand. We made tea, I remember, the children and I, not saying very much more."

In the world inhabited by William Trevor's characters, the happy family is either transitory or illusory, or simply does not exist.
—*Richard Tillinghast*

In the world inhabited by William Trevor's characters, the happy family is either transitory or illusory, or simply does not exist. In one of my favorite stories, **"Mr McNamara,"** Trevor creates over the space of four pages a golden picture of childhood in an Irish town in the Midlands, content despite having come somewhat down in the world. "As a family we belonged to the past. We were Protestants in what had become Catholic Ireland. We'd once been part of an ascendancy, but now it was not so. Now there was the income from the granary and the mill, and the house we lived in: we sold grain and flour, we wielded no power. 'Proddy-woddy green-guts,' the Catholic children cried at us in Curransbridge. 'Catty, Catty, going to Mass,' we whispered back, 'riding on the devil's ass.' They were as good as we were." The family: a son and three daughters, "and Flannagan in the garden and Bridget our maid, and the avuncular spirit of Mr McNamara."

The parents are as good a pair as one could hope for: "when they disagreed or argued their voices weren't ever raised. They could be angry with us, but not with one another. They meted out punishments for us jointly, sharing disapproval or disappointment. We felt doubly ashamed when our misdemeanours were uncovered." The father is a large, "bulky" man who drinks from an extra-large teacup. And what is the significance of his having a special knife and fork, "extra-strong because my father was always breaking forks"? Throughout the narrator's childhood there are the father's visits to Dublin, a regular feature of which would be his visits in the bar of Fleming's Hotel with his friend Mr. McNamara: "The whole thing occurred once every month or so, the going away in the first place, the small packed suitcase in the hall, my father in his best tweed suit, Flannagan and the dog-cart. And the returning a few days later: breakfast with Mr McNamara, my sister Charlotte used to say"—because during breakfast the morning after he returned, the father would recount all the Dublin news, along with Mr. McNamara's views of it all, and the endlessly complicated though rather ordinary stories of Mr. McNamara's family, who lived in a house "in Palmerston Road, and the dog they had, a spaniel called Wolfe Tone, and a maid called Kate O'Shea, from Skibbereen."

Mr. McNamara even sends the boy a thirteenth-birthday present. Trevor has a delightful way of making a detail stand out: "One by one my presents were placed before me, my parents' brought from the sideboard by my mother. It was a package about two and a half feet long, a few inches in width. It felt like a bundle of twigs and was in fact the various parts of a box-kite. Charlotte had bought me a book called *Dickon the Impossible,* Amelia a kaleidoscope. 'Open mine exceedingly carefully,' Frances said. I did, and at first I thought it was a pot of jam. It was a goldfish in a jar." How much these details tell us of the care with which life was managed in this household! "Open mine exceedingly carefully" is redolent of the long-vanished rectitude and precision of language of the cloistered Anglo-Irish provincial middle class. Mr. McNamara's gift, though, is the best of all: a little dragon made of brass, with "two green eyes that Frances said were emeralds, and small pieces let into its back which she said looked like rubies." The boy is enjoined to write a thank-you note. "Give me the letter when you've done it," his father says. "I have to go up again in a fortnight."

But his father dies the next day—"a grim nightmare of a day, during all of which someone in the house was weeping, and often several of us together." Interestingly, Mr. McNamara, through the mother's intercession, is not informed: "My father and Mr McNamara had been bar-room friends, [Mother] pointed out: letters in either direction would not be in order." From then on, the boy's mission in life is to grow up and replace his father as owner of the granary and mill, and to further his education he is sent to a Protestant boarding school in the Dublin mountains. Eventually he works up his courage to make up an excuse to go into Dublin—"'An uncle,' I said to the small headmaster. 'Passing through Dublin, sir.'"—so that he can see Fleming's Hotel for himself.

The inevitable occurs. In one of the most exquisitely bittersweet scenes in fiction, the boy cycles up to Fleming's Hotel and goes in. "A tall grandfather clock ticked, the fire occasionally hissed. There was a smell of some kind of soup. It was the nicest, most comfortable hall I'd ever been in." He proceeds into the bar, empty except for the barman and "a woman sitting by the fire drinking orange-coloured liquid from a small glass. Behind the bar a man in a white jacket was reading the *Irish Independent*." The boy manages to order a bottle of ale, his first encounter with the stuff, and as he drinks it, waiting for Mr. McNamara to appear, he notices that the woman is looking at him, and he wonders in his naïve way if she might be a prostitute: "A boy at school called Yeats claimed that prostitutes hung about railway stations mostly, and on quays. But there was of course no reason why you shouldn't come across one in a bar . . . Yet she seemed too quietly dressed to be a prostitute."

Eventually the woman gets up and leaves, "and on her way from the bar she passed close to where I was sitting. She looked down and smiled at me." After she has left, the boy asks the barman who she is. And when the man says, "That's Nora McNamara," the reader finds he is really not surprised, remembering the little brass dragon—which is more a woman's gift than a man's—and the mother's insistence that Mr. McNamara not be notified of her husband's death, suggesting that she shared with him the fiction of "Mr." McNamara's identity.

What is perhaps even more absorbing for the student of human nature than this discovery is the boy's bitter reaction to it. As much as the boy resents his father's having given the other woman's gifts to his children, "yet somehow it was not as great as the sin of sharing with all of us this other woman's eccentric household, her sister and her sister's husband, her alcoholic aunt, a maid and a dog"—the violation of the family's sanctity that comes from the intrusion of another reality into their midst, introduced under false pretenses. He relives all of it at home on Christmas morning:

I hated the memory of him and how he would have been that Christmas morning; I hated him for destroying everything. It was no consolation to me then that he had tried to share with us a person he loved in a way that was different from the way he loved us. I could neither forgive nor understand. I felt only bitterness that I, who had taken his place, must now continue his deception, and keep the secret of his lies and his hypocrisy.

To be an adult is to be able to keep a tough secret. The boy has become a man.

William Trevor's keen eye illuminates the lives of the Irish, the Anglo-Irish, and also the English. The sequence of stories called **"Matilda's England"** is perhaps the best treatment of the English experience of World War II that I have ever read. But his vision transcends, as I have suggested, the various contexts within which he places his stories. Taken as a whole, his fiction makes a strong assertion about human nature, as an observer of which Trevor is unsparing, not given to the epiphanies we associate with other great Irish short-story writers such as James Joyce and Frank O'Connor. There is humor here, and certain moments that glow with the enjoyment of life, perfectly rendered into beautiful prose. But reading these stories one after the other can be a sobering and chastening experience. They have kept me awake at night. The reader is not advised to read consecutively, as I have done over the past several months, the twelve hundred pages of *The Collected Stories*. These are meant to be absorbed one at a time. But once the stories become part of one's mind and life, there's no shaking them.

Reynolds Price (review date 28 February 1993)

SOURCE: "A Lifetime of Tales from the Land of Broken Hearts," in *New York Times Book Review*, February 28, 1993, pp. 1, 25-7.

[*In the following review of* The Collected Stories, *Price argues that Trevor's short story writing is consistently strong but that his novels are better.*]

The voices of extraordinary writers like William Trevor are almost as quickly recognizable as those of great singers. Any lover of song will know a Pavarotti, a Leontyne Price, in an opening phrase—often in a single note. The genuinely sizable writers of fiction announce their presence almost as early. Some, like Conrad or Hemingway, speak in timbres distinctive enough to declare their markers in a single sentence. More often the novelist or short-story writer quietly names himself or herself, not by actual words or syntax but by an almost immediate revelation of what might be called his primal scene.

Even the voices of writers as wide-gauged as Tolstoy or Proust are grounded in a single scene, most often a lingering sight from childhood or early youth. And that scene is almost always one that a seasoned reader may well suspect lies near the start of a given writer's reason for writing—the physical moment in which a single enormous question rose before a watchful child and fueled the lifelong search for an answer.

In Tolstoy, it's the terrible moment in a bright country house when a boy barely 2 years old hears the news of his mother's death and senses that he stands alone, doomed to the orphan's endless starvation for perfect love. In Proust it's the scented and breathless young man poised at the bolted thick glass door of a salon teeming with human monsters he's powerless not to adore and struggle to capture, though he knows they'll despise him if he breaches the threshold that rightly divides them. In Virginia Woolf it's the silent instant in a high-ceilinged room when, after her first attack of madness, a beautiful, lean girl understands that in all her world no other person shares her eyes and the other senses that make the world so uniquely dazzling and awful a sight for her alone, demanding her witness.

And though William Trevor is very much alive and at work—his ***Collected Stories,*** consists of more than a thousand pages, many of them recent—it's seldom possible to move past the first page of any story from his broad array without detecting a boy, of 12 say, at the edge of a lush field or patchy lawn in a country far from the great world's noise, his gray eyes fixed in a just and merciless (though not unkind) gaze at a family in evening light some yards beyond him, thirsty faces taut with the pain of hiding their most urgent needs and the dread of losing their long-hid yearnings.

As with most large writers, that primal scene with its set of fixed eyes and its destined angle has proved to be Mr. Trevor's most valuable gift and his only impediment. Long before he sensed his profession—he spent long years as a painter and sculptor before deciding to write his first story—that half-concealed boy's eyes and mind had stored several remade worlds as rich in meaning as the actual earth. They'd likewise broken his heart too soon. For his one great lack as a writer is hope, the clear stream, however slight and easily stemmed, that runs on past private loss and ruin in the worlds of writers even as near desperation as Kafka or James Joyce, Mr. Trevor's huge predecessor.

William Trevor was born in 1928, a son of the troubled marriage of middle-class Protestant parents with roots in the farmland of Catholic Ireland. He moved restlessly in childhood about that small, cold, white-hot country, smaller than most American states. The atmosphere of a miserable home and the rootlessness of a vagabond childhood may have saved him from an ordinary career of balked melancholia. Mr. Trevor's distinctly alien qualities as a Protestant child without firm grounding in a particular village or city may have rescued him from the curse of self-loathing that might otherwise have silenced him or, worse, sent him forward as one more pale ventriloquist's doll worked by the strings of his dead ancestors—such giant figures as Shaw; Synge, the protean Yeats, O'Casey and the coiled reptilian exile Joyce, all natives of the same small room and perilously near at the time of his birth.

It was a peril of birth that Mr. Trevor shares with many of his fellows in other brands of fiction—American Southerners born in the wake of Faulkner, Porter, Welty and O'Connor; American Jewish males in the wake of Bellow, Malamud and Roth; most of the dozens of hapless souls born lately in any big Western city—the atmospheres of Paris, London, New York and Los Angeles that are now as nearly worked out as a sharecropper's cotton field in south Alabama or a beauty parlor in suburban Nashville.

But Mr. Trevor's apparently effortless triumph is to have taken a world worn nearly smooth by long and splendid handling and through pure intensity of attention and care to have found a nearly endless new set of subjects and tones. Almost as surprising, he has managed the greater part of his work in an all but total avoidance of the sourness of spirit, the meanness of outlook and the treacherous grandiloquence that has often afflicted those writers who inherit the bitter divisions of a small and brutally torn homeplace—Yeats and Joyce, even Faulkner in the wake of our Civil War, are not as free as William Trevor of that blight.

Yet Mr. Trevor has found a deeper chill, a core of defeat as pure and compelling in its ultimate sadness as that at the heart of Euripides—the unbroken spectacle of worthy men, women and children frozen by genetic inheritance and the warp of history. Among these 80-odd stories from 30 years, the most haunting, in their range of knowledge and depth of feeling, all focus on an action that with nearly invisible speed moves a small clutch of figures toward the instant when fate uncovers before their eyes in a silent rush the bleak denying future that they've either earned or been endowed with by family and home.

For me, among the stories that promise to last are the famous **"Ballroom of Romance," "An Evening With John Joe Dempsey," "O Fat White Woman," "Death in Jerusalem," "The Paradise Lounge," "Honeymoon in Tramore," "In Love With Ariadne"** and **"Kathleen's Field."** Of these best, only **"O Fat White Woman"** is set outside Ireland (in rural England); only **"In Love With**

Ariadne" is set in a city; all the others are deeply socketed in the Irish countryside of small towns and villages.

Such a hard limitation on place and type of character might, in different hands, threaten monotony and quick exhaustion. But just as a reader thinks "He's told me this more than once already; he's badly stuck," Mr. Trevor's sheer intensity of entry into the lives of his people stalls the complaint and proceeds to uncover new layers of yearning and pain, new angles of vision and credible thought—layers that most readers would never have guessed in men, women and lone unassisted children whose home and history would seem to have left them as mute as Galway ponies in the rain.

The father and daughter in **"Kathleen's Field"** have frames of reference as narrow as paleolithic man's, but the depth of their hunger for that very life eventually lends them a sturdy heroism of pain endured. In **"In Love With Ariadne,"** the medical student who falls for the daughter of his Dublin landlady is almost literally ignited by the heat of his need for union with the beautiful girl and so fails to guess how terrifying his courteous longing is for someone with a past where love has proved truly lethal; yet the texture of the student's need and Ariadne's fear are brought as close to the reader's face as deep-cut words on a stark gravestone.

"An Evening With John Joe Dempsey" comes as close as Mr. Trevor allows himself to affectionate hope for a character's life—a boy just turned 15 and trembling on the brink of sex—but by the end of a simple happy, evening, we hear again the barely audible leak of sadness assert itself and press in on him, now and for good: this boy's chances of meeting a mate to his own patient sweetness are virtually nil.

Such pain and defeat are so clearly drawn in the best of Mr. Trevor's stories, so memorably sounded in a prose as plain and natural as daylight, that reading them in quantity would take those appetite for suffering than most readers bring to a book. If, that is, Mr. Trevor weren't offering abundant parallel compensations—the invisible nearness of eyes and a mind as watchful as his own, as steadily concerned with human feeling; the lucid prose that works its aims with no obvious effort; and almost everywhere the faintly rising scent of laughter.

For like most other sizable writers who choose country life as the field of their work and whose brand of country is stocked with people—the farmers of Ireland and, say, our own South—who've endured the forces of nature firsthand, forces more exacting than the dangers of cities, Mr. Trevor's vision is deeply, though never entirely, comic. However bleak the present and future of a given human life, the salient nearness of a vital ongoing world of rocks and fields, ocean and shore, will throw an enormous inhuman yardstick

up against that one sad life and let us see the unreadable smile of time and fate that shines through even a child's unanswerable hope or need.

> **Mr. Trevor's vision is deeply, though never entirely, comic. However bleak the present and future of a given human life, the salient nearness of a vital ongoing world of rocks and fields, ocean and shore, will throw an enormous inhuman yardstick up against that one sad life and let us see the unreadable smile of time and fate that shines through even a child's unanswerable hope or need.**
> **—*Reynolds Price***

Only in his urban stories—and most of them are set in an England populated by the upper middle class—does Mr. Trevor's comic sense go savage. In a story like **"Raymond Bamber and Mrs. Fitch,"** in which he starts with a character whose beingness has a gruesome charm, the thrust of vicious laughter is turned at the final moment, and a comprehending tolerance rises. But in an awful excursion like **"The Teddy-Bears' Picnic,"** no single person from a group of young wealthy twits persuades Mr. Trevor inward for a closer look; and the story itself ends in a mocking laughter that praises itself as it executes the prose equivalent of a mass death sentence on all in sight (and none too soon).

That shallowness—Mr. Trevor's only recurrent fault but a luckily rare one—proceeds from both the vapidity of so much urban life, its hectic obsession with saving one's face in an endless string of pointless social risks, and from what seems Mr. Trevor's refusal or inability to wade as deeply into city life as he always manages when he stands on home ground. Confined as the meanness is to his English urban stories, a reader may wonder if the well-to-do English aren't the only possible resting place for Mr. Trevor's considerable powers of hate and destruction (he's lived in England for many years). With Irish countryfolk, even Anglo-Irish gentry, his perfect sense of pitch and sympathy can lay out the full implications of tragic on merely foolish choices; but a native tenderness spares them his malice.

In whatever country—and he's often written about Italy—his crafty skills never desert him, and now and then be manages a city story of airless dry brilliance to equal Maupassant or John O'Hara. In his novel ***Other People's Worlds,*** he has enough space and a big enough cast to string a web of masochism, psychopathy, eager self-delusion, and pathos (but only in the very old and young) that awaits readers with the horror of a Jacobean melodrama—but, as well as the horror, the shallowness of a well-made teaspoon precisely filled to the rim with water, then frozen hard.

The little that Mr. Trevor reveals in interviews about his life suggests that his desert years of work in England from the early 1950's on as a teacher and sculptor, then—of all things—as an advertising copywriter in a London agency may partly account for the sharp division of feeling in the fiction he finally turned to a decade later. That and perhaps a natural scorn for the people whose ancestors lorded over Ireland for more than three centuries. More crucially, I suspect, and despite the lean results they've brought him, he's continued his sporadic raids on the heartless English because he only encountered them in numbers after his childhood and because the short story permits him to do a quick turn at their expense and exit grinning.

In the hands of a writer as practiced as Mr. Trevor, occasional failures are far more likely to be the results of dangers inherent in a chosen form than of some weakness in the writer's equipment—a good writer's short stories fall, when they fall, mostly because the form is short. It can often deprive the writer of time and space in which to burrow beneath the gloss of worlds that don't lie near his old knowledge or engage his care; it goads him into quick and readily salable effects that do slim credit to him or his subjects.

Again such stories are a small minority of what Mr. Trevor offers; and a serious look at the best of his novels confirms that when he works nearer home and gives himself sufficient room, his hand will almost automatically feel its way very deeply indeed into minds and actual summoned places (towns and houses) that open at his touch and show their intricate, amazing cores—an Irish village on market day in a William Trevor story can come to life with the crowding abundance of Dickens's London: For despite the wider fame of his stories and his own recent and thoroughly wrong remark to *The New Yorker* that his novels are "a lot of linked-up short stories," it's in the later novels of the 10 he's published that Mr. Trevor stakes an unimpeachable claim for the size and very high value of his work.

No novels written in British English since the final trance-intensities of Virginia Woolf feel more likely to hold a long-term claim on human attention than William Trevor's most recent three—**Fools of Fortune, The Silence in the Garden** and **Reading Turgenev** (which he calls a novella in the volume, **"Two Lives,"** though it has both the length and weight of a novel).

Each of the three is set in Ireland; each studies an ample stretch of time, a life span at least; two of the three are grounded in the wake of the murderous rebellion of 1919-21 that expelled British power, unseated a resident English

gentry (most of them stayed on in their ample holdings) and left a vital continuing legacy of sworn vendetta by the native rebels or the loathed Black and Tans. Such arcs of history are hardly fit subjects for short fiction, though Joyce embalmed scraps of the early struggle in his "Dubliners"; but Joyce's genius, like his understanding; was for the overwhelming moment of bleak revelation or the vast tessellated mosaic in which sharp fragments form a larger scene for the reader prepared to donate a large part of life and time to dogged decipherment.

Mr. Trevor's knowledge—despite his disclaimer—proves deeper, broader and longer-winded than Joyce's, yet far less showy in its calm refusal to follow Joyce in the strangling pursuit of a handmade new tongue able to do more than language can. And the language of Mr. Trevor's best work, of whatever length, proves its modest but entire adequacy in telling us all he seems to know or means to tell us (he most frequently inhabits the mind of women, plainly because for him women possess the more complex and subtle thoughts and feelings). And in lean and audaciously elliptical prose, he makes wide leaps over years and actions that often seem too urgent to skip; then he lands in the darkened room of the present to lay out quietly all the years have failed to tell us, such awful truths as:

> Your father waited in silence for decades, then crossed the Irish Sea to England, killed the man who'd killed his own father in the time of the Troubles and now must live in anonymity, far from us. That fact explains the agony of your life till now.

> You've entered a loveless village marriage; your husband will prove to be kind but impotent; your in-laws are vicious. You'll turn to the cousin you loved in school; the two of you will flourish in secret till he dies young. Then at last you'll face a literally unlivable life. Choose long years of madness instead; then return to your changed home, peaceful at last.

> You'll live a whole life in the presence of lovers yet never know love. Many millions of humans, for thousands of years, have done just that. Expect no pity. Bear your load.

There are living writers, in the United States and Latin America (to go no farther), who possess a more complicated knowledge of a wider range of human life and of how that life enacts itself beneath the hand of individual will and the weight of a wider history. There are living writers of the short story to contend mightily with the recent claims of literary couturiers that Mr. Trevor is now the premier story writer in the language—in the United States alone we have Eudora Welty, William Maxwell, John Updike and Joyce Carol

Oates, to name an irresistible few. Each of these four has matched the breadth of Mr. Trevor's skills and, what is more, has found occasions for glimpsing feasible routes through the real world's thickets toward at least a modicum of human fulfillment.

But crowns on garlands in the world of fiction—however fervently readers and journalists fling them at this head or that—are meaningless to the point of hilarity. No two good writers have ever agreed to enter the same race. Some admittedly enter more races; some enter races that are more worth winning. Occasionally one performs with a grace that's overwhelming and momentarily blanks the field, as the thrillingly beautiful late work of Raymond Carver briefly held the local scene.

With this new immense collection, William Trevor has filed in serene self-trust the results of years of work of impeccable strength and a piercing profundity that's very seldom surpassed in short fiction. Seasoned admirers of his stories alone should know, however, that his long fiction is stronger still—not merely for length but resonance: the sound of a voice that with near-inaudible dignity earns its place in the narrow circle of excellence, that ragged secular communion of saints who watch our lives with unblinking care, then give us our human names and ranks, our just rewards.

Patricia Craig (review date 27 August 1993)

SOURCE: "Irish Drift," in *New Statesman and Society,* Vol. 6, No. 267, August 27, 1993, pp. 40-1.

[*In the review below, Craig praises* Excursions in the Real World *as an insightful social commentary, but argues that it is not reveal enough about Trevor.*]

The real world as opposed to the world of fiction, that is; these enjoyable essays by William Trevor provide a series of glimpses into the novelist's past. He was born in Mitchelstown, Co Cork, in 1928, a Protestant in a Catholic culture, and without even the eclat that ownership of a "big house" might have conferred. His father was a bank clerk, and his childhood peripatetic: after Mitchelstown came Youghal and Skibbereen, and that was only the start.

The family curtains, he notes, "were altered to fit windows" all over the place—windows, moreover, looking out on a not entirely hospitable vista. De Valera's Ireland didn't provide much sense of community for its non-Catholic inhabitants, whom it treated without animosity but without a great deal of comprehension. These small-town southern Protestants never found themselves completely assimilated. Trevor, as a writer, may have been lucky in this respect, and in his family's constant moves. Both accorded him an outsider's perspective, allowing his powerful gift for observation to flourish.

The essays in this book (snippets, really) don't by any means lay bare the writer; William Trevor is, and remains, "a very private person" to whom autobiographical disclosure doesn't come easily. They do, however, both isolate and illuminate the backgrounds to his novels and stories. Cork, Tipperary, Wexford, Dublin ... then London, the south of England, Venice, and back to famine-stricken Ireland in the 1840s. Trevor rightly disclaims nostalgia in his excursions: his cast of mind is altogether tougher.

True, these pieces have more in the way of charm, and rather less bleakness and irony, than Trevor's fiction; but they don't come without a pleasing precision and idiosyncrasy to give the charm an edge. The novelist's characteristic engagement with foibles of social behaviour is greatly in evidence, particularly in the sections on school life, which—in his experience—seems to have been abundant in boys' and masters' eccentricities. ("He had been known to sit on the ledge of the mantlepiece in the masters' common room to see if anyone would notice.")

Trevor may have been unconsciously assembling his material during these years, but it wasn't until the publication of *The Old Boys* (his second novel) in 1964 that he acquired a settled purpose. Before that, it was a matter of drifting—through 13 schools, through Trinity College, Dublin, various schoolmastering posts (calling to mind, in their seedy, throwaway comedy, *Decline and Fall*) and a stint as a copywriter with Notley's in London, in the company of some poets. Gavin Ewart, Peter Porter and Edward Lucie-Smith were earning a living in this way too; and Ted Hughes crops up later.

Towards the end of this collection, toned-down autobiography merges with some seductive travel writing and literary comment, including a piece on Somerville & Ross—which seems to me altogether too tolerant of the fox-hunting antics and amazed amusement of these ladies when confronted by the ever-thickening consonants and headlong illogicality of their social inferiors. As writers, they're at the opposite extreme from William Trevor, in whom elegance and accuracy are matched by the strongest appreciation of the social climate, in Ireland and elsewhere. We should be grateful for the selection of events and images in the real world that have elicited an inspired response from the storyteller.

John Hildebidle (essay date Fall 1993)

SOURCE: "Kilneagh and Challacombe: William Trevor's

Two Nations," in *Eire-Ireland,* Vol. XXVIII, No. 3, Fall, 1993, pp. 114-29.

[*In the following essay, Hildebidle contrasts* Fools of Fortune *to "Matilda's England" as he discusses Trevor's views on Ireland and England.*]

William Trevor has baldly asserted that "There is no such thing today as an Anglo-Irish novelist," which will, among other things, come as a great shock to Molly Keane. Of the supposedly nonexistent species, Trevor himself is an apparently unequivocal example. And the question arises: can one be an Anglo-Irish writer and not, sooner or later, address the peculiar embrace which so painfully joins Britain and Ireland? A reading of *The Stories of William Trevor* (1983) suggests that Trevor—born in County Cork, educated at Trinity College, but long resident in Dorset, a member of the Irish Academy of Letters and also a commander, Order of the British Empire—has tried for some years to resist the perhaps too automatic questions of nationality and Irish revolutionary politics. Indeed, he has insisted that although "I always call myself an Irish Writer, . . . the struggle in Ireland, and the sorrow, is a very good backdrop for a fiction writer, but I don't think, certainly not for me, that it is any sort of inspiration." As I will argue shortly, I think Trevor's resistance to national labels is more than an accident of biography. But when questions of national loyalty enter in, as for instance in the story **"Beyond the Pale"** and more recently in **"News from Ireland,"** they seem to do so with apparently tragic and violent force.

When it appeared, *Fools of Fortune* (1983) seemed to mark a shift in the world of Trevor's fiction, toward what we might for convenience call "The Modern Matter of Ireland," that complex of personal and political loyalties that leaves its essential mark on such contemporary works as Julia O'Faolain's *No Country for Young Men* (1980), Jennifer Johnston's *Railway Station Man* (1985), and Benedict Kiely's *Nothing Happens in Carmincross* (1985). But more recently, in *Two Lives* (1991), and especially **"Reading Turgenev,"** Trevor has returned to the bleak grey-green world of the Irish provincial bourgeoisie, to what John Stinson has neatly characterized as the "grindingly dull small-town atmosphere" which is the world of so many of his stories and of his longer works from *Mrs. Eckdorf in O'Neill's Hotel* (1969) to *Nights at the Alexandra* (1987). In a sense, *Fools of Fortune* presents a kind of parable, explaining why Trevor had for the most part avoided the harsh political realities of twentieth-century Ireland, and, if so, it has as a knotty precursor Trevor's much and deservedly anthologized **"Beyond the Pale,"** and a sequel in the title story of his 1986 collection *News from Ireland.*

Read one way, **"Beyond the Pale"** confronts the violent conditions to be found in contemporary Northern Ireland, and records the shocking intrusion of romantic and political passions into the almost pathologically genteel world of "Milly," or Dorothy Milson, its narrator. But the story refuses quite to resolve its own mysteries, and is it not at least possible that it records the imaginative construction of Cynthia? The story's narrator makes Cynthia seem an unlikely person to be offered the kind of deeply personal confession she says the dead Irishman has presented *only* to her. She is, as we are told by Milly, and not in a complimentary way, an "imaginative woman," and one who knows almost too much Irish history and Irish myth, or to put it more exactly, Irish historical myth. Two lovers separated by the terrorist violence of Belfast, reunited—in a sense—by the murderous, obsessive devotion of one of them, which ends in an act of self-destruction. It is an odd amalgam of the story of Diarmuid and Grania and the headlines from the *Irish Times.*

But it would seem that the apparent shift of manner and ground announced by *Fools of Fortune* is temporary, at most. The painfully complex interconnections between England and Ireland are played out in that novel in some detail, both in the plot and in the genealogies of the major characters. What I hope to do briefly here is to consider Trevor's account of the two cultures, and especially his diagnosis of the crucial role of memory in keeping England and Ireland so inextricably and so violently linked. To do so will require a look at another of his works, the set of three linked stories entitled **"Matilda's England."**

Fools of Fortune begins with the description of two houses: "the great house at Woodcombe Park" in Dorset, which "bustles with life," albeit of a touristic variety and "the more modest," indeed, largely ruined Kilneagh, in County Cork. The two places are linked by the genealogical complexities of the Quinton family, of which *Fools of Fortune* will recount the most recent and seemingly final chapter. The opening suggests that Trevor, adding one more item to the long list of "Big House" fictions, wants us to take his novel as an account of the two nations. But this is something of a deception. The Dorset house will appear almost not at all thereafter, except as Willie Quinton imagines it. He has, at best, a cursory and second-hand knowledge of the place. Kilneagh, by contrast, is the dominant setting of the book. Indeed, the novel can be read as an account of how this devastated place comes to conquer, or at least supplant, her native Woodcombe in the mind of the English Quinton, Marianne. She is the one character who comes to know both landscapes well, and yet she rarely talks about Woodcombe. If there is to be some sort of analogy drawn, one side of the parallel is oddly absent in the book.

But it may be in part deducible by way of **"Matilda's England."** Indeed, we might make the parallel more striking if we immodestly revise the title of Trevor's novel from *Fools of Fortune* to "Marianne's Ireland." The earlier story—taking it, for convenience, as one narrative rather than three—is suggestively parallel to the more recent novel. Both are built around characters whose fullest life seems to have been lived in the past, at the far side of some cataclysm. The burning of Kilneagh by the Black and Tans and Willie Quinton's act of revenge in *Fools of Fortune* thus play the same role as the Second World War in "Matilda's England." Both narratives recount lives haunted—perhaps willingly—by the past and especially by the period just after the First World War. Both are concerned with houses which die and then—albeit with mixed results—return to life. Both narratives are considerations of memory and of the power of memory to transform actual landscapes into symbolic ones and thereby at least to attempt to recreate some supposedly "happy" time.

"Matilda's England" portrays Matilda's gradual possession of and by the manor house of Challacombe. Matilda is raised on what had been the home-farm of the manor, before the estate fell into the hands of Lloyd's Bank. She meets the last of the ancestral owners, the aged Mrs. Ashburton, whose husband had been a shell-shocked "survivor" of the Great War and who connives to have Matilda and her two older siblings restore the tennis court of the estate. The first phase of Matilda's "life" at Challacombe ends at a grand tennis party which revives, but only approximately and temporarily, the social life of the manor. The party takes place in August, 1939, and is thus darkened by the approach of another war. A second phase takes Matilda through the war, and through adolescence, a period during which the manor house falls empty and into some decay, and during which time Matilda's father and then her brother are killed in battle. The third phase, which we are told is being written, as apparently have been the first two, in the drawing room of Challacombe, describes Matilda's marriage to the son and heir of the new owners of Challacombe, and thus her transformation into the new lady of the manor and into a new Mrs. Ashburton, aging and reclusive.

Matilda's increasing enclosure in the house and in the past is signaled by the titles and predominant settings of the three stories which make up the narrative: "The Tennis Court," "The Summer-house," and "The Drawing-room." Matilda is quite clearly warned, by her old teacher Miss Pritchard, that her apparent rise in the world is baneful and wrong, because it is an attempt to make the past come back. But Matilda, while acknowledging that she hates the present, insists "It'll be all right.'" The "It" in this case includes a sexless marriage and, as her husband quite credibly argues, feigned madness which drives him, her family, and indeed all living humans away. Matilda is rather bitter toward her husband Ralphie, in part because of another "odd feeling" that "he'd married [her] because [she] was part of an idea he'd fallen in love with." Ralphie himself rebuts this charge: "'I married you out of passion and devotion.'" Significantly, Matilda

never admits what Miss Pritchard knows and most of her family seems to sense: that she has married Ralphie not because of physical or emotional passion, but because of devotion to an idea, and the idea is not really *hers*. "'What memories of Challacombe can you have?'" Matilda asks, aware that Ralphie has never seen the house in its glory. The second-handedness of her dream makes the terrible isolation of her life all the more chilling. We leave her sitting at Mrs. Ashburton's desk, living out her own version of that older woman's existence.

The oddity of Matilda's memory is not only that it is, at bottom, borrowed, although it is worth remarking that Trevor has a keen sense of how we may find ourselves living out other people's dreams, even their obsessions. The power, or at least the recreative power, of Matilda's memory grows in direct proportion to the distance in time between the present and the moment being remembered. Of the events—at least a quarter-century old, by the time she sits down to write—of the summer of 1939, Matilda has an exact recollection. Of her more recent life, as wife and then as recluse, her memory is much less reliable. "The Drawing-room" is full of repetitions of the phrase "I remember," but the words are usually linked to events in the life of the long-dead Mrs. Ashburton. There are in the story a roughly equal number of things "I can't recall," especially the steps in the decay of Matilda's own marriage and the onset of her "madness."

What is left moot, and necessarily so, given Trevor's decision to present the story wholly through Matilda's voice and eye, is whether this oddity of mind is intentional or not; whether, in order words, Matilda is the unwitting but not, in her own view, unhappy victim of obsessive madness, which her family had apparently feared, or whether, as Ralphie insists, and as the cool precision of her narrative voice suggests, Matilda is feigning madness for her own icy ends. In either case, the dominant figure is Mrs. Ashburton. "'She twisted you, she filled you full of hate. Whatever you are now, that dead woman has done to you'," is the way Ralphie puts it. Whether Matilda's isolation is her conscious choice or not—and the issue of intention is one we will have to return to when we look at *Fools of Fortune*—it leaves her impossibly trapped. Her last words are "Nothing is like it was."

I am suggesting that we take Matilda not only as a case-study but as the, or at least a, soul of England trapped in nostalgia, self-isolated, and devoted to something that may never have existed in the first place, the happy, domestic, ordered, gracious, Edwardian England of the sort captured in brief in Philip Larkin's line "Never such innocence again." Part of Matilda's affection for Mrs. Ashburton arises from the sense that the older woman had, as unequivocally as her husband, been "a victim of violence." In that, of course, she resembles Matilda herself, who has never recovered from the terrible price exacted on her family by the Second World

War. England as a whole, as Paul Fussell has persuasively argued in *The Great War and Modern Memory,* may fairly be said to have the victim of the Western Front, never having recovered from the losses on the Somme.

If we read Challacombe as a symbol, we are only following the example of Matilda herself, who has invested the house with an order and significance that it may well never have had. The process at work seems to be something like this: given a landscape of which symbolic readings are likely— and is there an English region without its manor houses, shrines, cathedrals, and the like?—and given the presence of outside forces, both personal and historical, the individual imagination readily undertakes to "remember" the meaning of the place, even if that act stretches beyond the actual experience of the imagining mind. This sort of "memory" is in fact a form of imagination, not an alternative to it. Once "remembered" in this way, the symbol exerts a force which is quite actual and nearly physical. At such a point, the question of human will, or of whether the individual is mad or a victim or both, seems nearly beside the point. Matilda may well be mad, but her devotion to Challacombe seems incurable, perhaps because it is only an exaggeration of the attention which almost everyone pays to the place. Challacombe dominates the jokes of Matilda's beloved father. It is the object of the wealthy attentions of Ralphie's parents, and it is the "idea" to which Ralphie is himself devoted. His intention to reconstitute the manor by buying up farmlands round-about falls victim to Matilda's stronger and—both geographically and physically—more focused obsession.

In *Fools of Fortune,* this symbol-making memory is complicated not only by the violence of the outside forces—for death, in this novel, occurs very nearby, not on some distant battlefield—but also by the addition of human and sexual relations. Once again there is a "happy" moment, localized in the house of Kilneagh, and in the summer of 1918, a summer of agreeable lethargy, easy domesticity, and comfortable preadolescence. The novel recounts three distinct efforts to "remember" this time on the part of Willie Quinton, who at least actually experienced the interlude first-hand; of Marianne Quinton, who has only heard of that summer from Willie, and wants to relive it to make up for the absence of the actual Willie; and finally, of their daughter Imelda Quinton, whose imaginative "memory" is altogether second-hand, but so forceful and detailed as to constitute a form of hallucinatory madness. That the person furthest removed in time is the one most possessed by the "memory" parallels the peculiar way in which Matilda's memory of Challacombe becomes in the end more powerful than Mrs. Ashburton's. And it suggests as well they way in which "memory" attains a cumulative, incremental force.

Imelda is the biological heir to Kilneagh and apparently the last of the curiously mixed Quinton line, long characterized by Anglo-Irish intermarriage. She is also the heir to the common memory, Irish and Quinton. Indeed, though like all the Quintons she is herself Protestant, she is quite literally driven mad by the force of political symbolism, which made her father a hero of the struggle against the Black and Tans; by the force of Catholicism, since she is ridiculed by her classmates for being the only Protestant in her school and is told by Father Kilgarriff the story of St. Imelda, her patron, who like her experienced a vision at the age of twelve; and by the force of Irish cultural nostalgia, since her final steps into madness coincide with her attempt to memorize Yeats's "Lake Isle of Innisfree."

The first two sections of *Fools of Fortune,* told or written by Willie and Marianne respectively, emphasize the role of remembrance, as well as the limitations of memory. Willie sees Woodcombe and Kilneagh as places full of "the sense of the past." Ironically, considering the story which is to follow, he sees in Woodcombe something of an ideal: the commercialization of memory, since the house is now open to tourists, is to him a sign that this sense of the past is, in Dorset, "well preserved," while only "echoes" remain in Kilneagh, "in the voices of the cousins." Yet, as the novel will show, those echoes dominate the lives of family retainers like Father Kilgarriff and the maid Josephine, of the cousins Willie and Marianne, and of the children of cousins. What bothers Willie, for all the warmth of this recollection of the summer of 1918, is the fact that Marianne is not there. He says to her "I would love to remember you in the scarlet drawing-room" of which she will only ever see the burned ruin. But the facts will not allow it.

And of the facts Willie has a remarkably detailed recollection. Rather like Matilda's, Willie's memory seems all the stronger the further back in time he goes. Thus, his description of the scarlet drawing room is full of detail and number:

> Carved into the white marble of the mantelpiece were one hundred and eight leaves, in clusters of six. Four tall brass lamps had glass globes shaped like onions; the Chinese carpet was patterned with seven shades of blue. My great grandfather, framed in gilt above the mantelpiece, had most of his hair on the right-hand side of his head, and looked like a spaniel.

Already, however, the forces of the past—the echoes, if you will—are at work, in that family portrait. For one characteristic of the Irish world in the novel is that it is drenched in memory. The Quinton family has its own ghosts. An earlier English Quinton cousin was so moved by the Famine that she become a living ghost whose spirit lives on Haunt

Hill overlooking the house—a distinct counterpoint to the confused governess in "News from Ireland." Broadly construed, the "family" includes the defrocked Father Kilgarriff, a walking historical consciousness, full of the memory of lost battles and ever willing to recount the story of Willie's youth to the young Imelda.

What the boy Willie has no way of knowing is that he is about to begin being made into a symbol of himself, first by the violent work of the Black and Tans, who destroy his house and much of his family, then by the vengeful memory which dominates his mother's last years, then by his own acting out of vengeance on the person of a Black and Tan sergeant, and finally by those who remember him, both in the neighborhood and in his own family. He chafes a bit under the demands of the new role. He is uncomfortable, for instance, with the pity offered by his teacher Miss Halliwell, who sees in him the perfect tragic victim of the "Troubles." It seems almost impossible to disentangle the personal will, historical circumstance, and familial pressure, which work together to drive Willie to his act and to the exile which necessarily follows it. Having at last acted, Willie disappears almost entirely from the novel, to be replaced by his remembered image.

Memory is the subject of Marianne's narrative which, in its first pages, exactly parallels Willie's by summoning up Woodcombe and by similarly invoking remembrance. What can in this tale, however, be "vividly remembered" is not the blissful summer but the death some years afterwards of Willie's mother. That death might seem to release him from the grip of her sad and drunken spirit, but in fact it prompts him to take his vengeance. Like Willie's, Marianne's recollection is partial, for it includes Willie himself but it necessarily excludes Kilneagh before its destruction. Willie and Marianne meet only long enough for Willie to take her on a tour, which works as a kind of initial reading of the landscape, and for him to father her child. Marianne, returning to bear that child, will knowingly cut herself off from England, just as the earlier Anne Quinton had done during the Famine, by so wholly adopting as her own the plight of the Irish that she offended her English cousins. That lesson, in turn, she passes on to Imelda, along with the acknowledgment that it is the "reading" or symbolic reimagining of the place, not the place itself, which is so powerful:

> . . . [Marianne] suggested [to Imelda] a walk, and at the end of it she pointed at the tree the man [a Black and Tan informant] had been hanged from, as though her answer lay in that.

> 'Just an ordinary tree, Imelda. You could pass it by and not know a thing.'

Left to themselves, trees might once again be trees, not icons.

But Marianne has spent a lifetime learning the iconography of this place, and Imelda is to grow up under Marianne's tuition. The initial significance of the tree is not, of course, a matter of imagination at all; it is an act of ritual murder. Yet, insofar as that murder, a part of the Troubles, is in itself both sign and result of compounded memories, and compounding violence, of long centuries of Anglo-Irish history, there would seem to be no hope that the making and reading of symbols may stop. Certainly Marianne's effort to learn and to transmit the symbolic topography is conscious and intentional, a labor of love, in fact. Convinced when first they meet that Willie—as yet still the "victim" and not yet the avenging "hero" of the tragedy of Kilneagh—hates her because she is English, Marianne, like all the English Quinton "wives," remolds herself into the purest Irishry she can imagine. As she says to the family solicitors:

> 'You think I'm extravagant in my Irish fancies? Father Kilgarriff thinks so, and the others too. Yet I am part of all this now. I cannot help my fervour.'

Rather like Matilda, she invokes her own fancies as the inescapable force in her life.

Imelda, at first, seems not so entrapped in remembrance. Her story is not a remembrance at all. Told in the third person, it does not begin with a leap back in time. Both the prior sections of *Fools of Fortune* open with the date 1983 but then move back fifty years or more. Instead, Imelda's story opens with a present event, a birthday picnic. It is not until some five or six pages have passed that the first ominous sign appears: a nightmare, "the same nightmare as always, the children and the flames", the nightmare of the long-past destruction of Kilneagh.

Imelda's story records the ways in which the details of the Quinton history are passed along to her by her mother but, since he is in exile, not by her father Willie. Imelda, like Matilda, comes to imagine things which occurred before her time. But instead of willingly learned and consciously preserved memory, what takes over Imelda's mind are the uncontrollable forces of nightmare and hallucination. Strictly speaking, Imelda has no "memory" of the dark event of 1918, or of her father's act of vengeance some years later, but she has imagination and, in the end, madness. She is the victim, in terms of the narrative, of her family's effort to see the world as a landscape of symbolic memory.

But then, in his way, Willie too is a victim. He is driven from his home by violence, driven to vengeance in large measure by his mother's memory of that violence, and driven from Ireland by his own act of vengeance, to wander for half a century among towns which no one can quite pronounce or locate on the globe. The memory which dominates Willie's life is at least his own memory, and he cannot be accused of indulging in fancies. But Marianne, by her acts of "love," for she went unbidden to Willie's room, produces a child. And then, by the acts of love which make her Irish, she plays a large part in condemning that child to madness. She seems to realize this. A page from her diary imagines what Imelda might have been, had she not been raised at Kilneagh. It is Marianne who is at the center of the novel, and at the center of the tragedy it describes.

Like Matilda, Marianne takes another's circumstances as her own. Like Matilda's and rather like Father Kilgarriff's as well, Marianne's memory is one that creates rather than recalls. Marianne's "fortune" of which she is the "fool," her symbolic landscape within which she is entrapped, is chosen, like Matilda's, and even self-created. Marianne insists to the end that it is the ancestral history of murder which ruins all their lives:

> *Father Kilgarriff died today, no trouble in his great old age. He was right when he said there's not much left in a life when murder has been committed—After each brief moment there was little chance for any one of us as there was for Kilneagh after the soldier's wrath. Truncated lives, creatures of the shadows. Fools of Fortune, as his father would have said; ghosts we became.*

That is both true and false. True, so many lives in the novel are ghostly and truncated, and not by acts of memory, either. But it is the way in which "moments" so fix the lives of Willie and Marianne—whose affair is little more than momentary—that the possibility of delusion enters. They are "moments," often, of violence or discovery. But, in Marianne's case, the moment exerts an unpredictably determining force. What deflects our judgment, more fully than in the case of Matilda, is both the awfulness of some of these moments and the motives of love which, however imperfectly, provoke the acts of memory.

If there is a parallel between Matilda's England and Marianne's Ireland, it lies in the victimizing and imprisoning forces of the symbols which the characters themselves create out of circumstance, history, and myth. The "embrace" of England and Ireland is, thus, an embrace of similar beings—or, at least the embrace of the Irish and the Anglo-Irish is. Marianne's story, and its clear similarities to the lives of earlier English Quintons who crossed over the Irish Sea to marry, acts out the seduction, or really self-seduction, which captures and holds the "alien" English Protestant culture of Ireland. By the time the full price is known—a ghostly life, a mad daughter—it is of course much too late to learn from experience.

And it would not do to exaggerate the unpleasantness of this life. Just as Matilda is, in her way, happy at Challacombe,

Marianne shows no clear sign of regretting her choice to abandon Dorset for Kilneagh. What we see of her alternatives—primarily a seedy Swiss boarding school—suggests that Kilneagh, with all its dangers, may well be a sensible choice. *Fools of Fortune* ends with the Quintons reunited, at Kilneagh, in a sunny autumn. An "elderly couple" observed by a madwoman who does not seem to realize they are her parents—that is the final tableau. The old people can now share their memories. It is a grim ending, but for once there is talk of the future: an expedition to pick mulberries. The future, however, will be brief—"We cannot wait beyond tomorrow," Willie and Marianne agree. Years earlier, Marianne, pregnant, lost, and searching for Willie, had seen some cattle and envied their "drear complacency." It would seem that she, at last, has her wish. To our eyes it may seem far less than would justify all that has gone before, and far less than would defend these people from the accusation, leveled at Matilda, of luxuriating in a mad nostalgia. To Marianne and Willie, it may seem all that could be expected. And to William Trevor as well?

The toll exacted by imagination is considerable. The landscape is full of symbolic equivalences which, in the minds and the lives of Trevor's characters, take on the power of natural, predestinating powers. A reader can observe that it is the mind which had made these forces. No longer the healing act that it was to the Romantics—and still is so accounted, if only in the milder form of nostalgia—the act of memory here breeds violence and self-imprisonment. *Fools of Fortune* as a whole is a remembrance taking the place of an affair or even of a life. Yet, the contents of Trevor's compendious *Collected Stories* suggest that "drear complacency" is the most to be hoped for by anyone, Irish or not. Any interruption of the tedium of life, be it the Troubles; a knock at the door as in **"The Penthouse Apartment," "The Hotel of the Idle Moon,"** and **"A Happy Family"**; an invitation to dinner, as in **"Kinkies"**; a meeting with a stranger in an out-of-the-way inn, as in **"Beyond the Pale"**—no matter how apparently small, an intrusion can have vast, sometimes comic, but generally painful consequences. Consequently, the world of memory and even illusion constructed so carefully by Marianne and Matilda may be less a sign of madness and more a necessary defense against the inevitable shocks of existence.

Let me hazard a proposition: the close similarity between the Irishness of *Fools of Fortune* and the Englishness of **"Matilda's England"**—the similarities between provincial Ireland and lower-middle-class England throughout Trevor's fiction—implicitly rebuts the whole question of national labels. Trevor has no qualms about calling himself an "Irish" writer, although he is careful to define his "Irishness" further—he is, he says, a "small-town Irish Protestant" and therefore, in a way, an "outsider" on that island. "Are you an Irish writer, Mr. Trevor?" Well, by birth, surely. But his speech is hardly melodious "Irish" speech of Frank O'Connor or Benedict Kiely. Still, his grim, yet often simultaneously comic, view of the unpalatability of life seems to make Trevor a thoroughly Irish writer, a close cousin in all but style to John McGahern and Edna O'Brien, and to link him to the Joyce of *Dubliners* and to Samuel Beckett. After all, as Joyce was surely convinced, to write about Ireland is to write about the world and what more can we ask of a maker of fiction?

But the more directly political slant of **Fools of Fortune** has not been entirely forsworn by Trevor. **"The News from Ireland"** represents Trevor's only venture into the other great and tragic Irish story, that of the Famine. That story is, in one sense, a view of that cataclysm from the Anglo-Irish side—a perspective from which it makes little sense at all. But, considered in the light of some of the issues about imagination I have been trying to raise, the story works, in brief compass, as a consideration of the effects of imagination and of its absence. Emily, we are told, "imagines" readily a colorful past represented in the ruined monastery near the house, but she gains little, if anything from it. As the puzzled English governess observes, and as the rather cynical Protestant butler Fogarty demonstrates, "families and events are often seen historically in Ireland—more so, for some reason, than in England." The unprepossessing and rather bitter Fogarty is, surprisingly, full of such a vision, as we are told on the very first page of the story where he "thinks of other visitors there have been" to the estate now in the hands of the Ipswich Pulvertafts.

Fogarty's imagination—if that is the word for it—is surprising. In part, he is ready to pass off local "superstitions," like the infant with the stigmata which figures so unpleasantly in the story and, despite his staunch Protestantism, such legends as the Story of the True Cross, more often identified with Catholic lore. But he is capable of one rather astounding act of imagination: Fogarty can, by way of dream, foretell the future with eerie accuracy—a future of neglect of the estate, bitterness and violent action by the tenants, a dream which predicts the work of the Land League and the revolution of the 1920s. But, arising out of whatever mixture of motives, his effort to pass on this dream-knowledge is doomed; he cannot inform Miss Heddoes, whose bafflement is, perhaps, impenetrable, and can only shock and dismay her.

But the story suggests that the "news" is what is conveyed through Miss Heddoes. And, sadly, her imagination is utterly unable to encompass the Famine occurring around her. Perhaps the story serves to account for the way in which England, in spite of an absence of what the story calls "wickedness," and the landowning classes, in spite of such public-works projects as road-building which the Pulvertafts undertake, simply cannot understand Ireland, its ways or its

disasters, and that incomprehension, to say the least, seems to persist into the England of Margaret Thatcher and John Major. Miss Heddoes can record, in her diary, and transmit, in her letters, the "news from Ireland," but no communication results, nothing to pierce the bafflement of Pulvertafts and Heddoes or the angry credulity of the Irish tenants. If Miss Heddoes is a kind of protowriter, the story almost comes across as a rebuttal to the idea most recently reasserted by the Field Day group that writing has a political role to play.

And it is the question of imagination more than any political issue which continues to fascinate Trevor, as the recent pair of novellas **Two Lives** (1991) makes clear. There, Trevor has returned to familiar and apparently nonpolitical terrain. **"Reading Turgenev"** could almost be a sardonic sequel to **"The Ballroom of Romance."** But **"My House in Umbria"** endeavors, like **"Beyond the Pale,"** at least to confront a world in which political violence is proximate and frequent. That the story occurs in Umbria rather than in County Derry is almost beside the point, for there is, sadly, no part of the world where terrorism may not flourish, after all. And indeed, Trevor himself insists that he is "as horrified about a bomb in Bologna as I am about a bomb in Derry." Yet, in fact, **"My House in Umbria"** is a variation on **"Beyond the Pale,"** in which the impact of violence is direct, central, and present in the story, and in which the action of memory and imagination—a crucial factor, given the protagonist narrator's career as a romance novelist—are anything but consoling. It may be that her own way of reassembling the "fragments" of her life is a way she has of overcoming the trauma of an abandoned and abusive childhood and an adult life that has, to say the least, been colorful and full of betrayals. But that reassembling simply will not work and, although her memory does not make her draw monsters or scream aloud, like the child Aimée, it has a nagging way of recovering the malfeasances of the unpleasant Mr. Chubb and the truly loathsome stepfather, Mr. Trice. Indeed, the sad fact, as she discovers, is that her thoughts—compact of memory and imagination—regularly betray her. The child's illness is explicitly diagnosed as an overactive imagination, which has "consumed her."

The romance novelist retains a faith in her imagination—which, not surprisingly, can both recover a past that is not hers and predict a future for the rather mysterious Professor Riversmith, who comes to provide a home for the orphaned Aimée. Mary Louise, whose sad life is the substance of "Reading Turgenev," is apparently a much less imaginative creature, but, in fact, imagination saves her—the imagination of a love affair with her cousin Robert, sustained by the reading of the works of Turgenev, which can sustain her in a loveless marriage and long after the death of Robert. At first glance, the last view we have of her, through the eyes of an Anglo-Irish clergyman—"a fragile figure, yet prosperous in her love"—seems bitterly ironic. That the clergyman can quietly promise a funeral and a burial with her beloved Robert seems like a bleak hope indeed, but it is a chance for the lovers at last to "lie together" as they never have done, and never will do, in life. For once, imagination is not the complicating force it is elsewhere in Trevor's fiction. It is not the powerfully seductive force which draws Emily Delahunty into the lives of strangers seen for a moment on a train in **"My House in Umbria."** Rather, imagination is a force of comfort and love—rare commodities in the fictional world of William Trevor, who insists that his view of the world is "not an entirely pessimistic view . . . In fact, it's even faintly optimistic." Yet, even Trevor cannot wholly rebut the charge of "hopelessness" in the lives he portrays, although he insists he himself is not "a melancholic." Perhaps Trevor would agree with Kafka: "There is hope, but not for us." If hope remains, it is tied up somehow with imagination; but that same force may be what denies hope to us as well.

George Core (essay date October 1993)

SOURCE: "Belonging Nowhere, Seeing Everywhere: William Trevor and the Art of Distance," in *The Hollins Critic,* Vol. XXX, No. 4, October, 1993, pp. 1-11.

[*In the following essay, Core provides an overview of Trevor's work, discussing recurring themes and Trevor's critical reception.*]

> As a writer one doesn't belong anywhere. Fiction writers, I think, are even more outside the pale. Because society and people are our meat, one doesn't really belong in the midst of society. The great challenge in writing is always to find the universal in the local, the parochial. And to do that, one needs distance.
>
> —William Trevor (1993)

> No one has had a closer vision, or a hand at once more ironic and more tender, for the individual figure. He sees it with all its minutest signs and tricks—all its heredity of idiosyncrasies, all its particulars of weakness and strength, of ugliness and beauty, of oddity and charm; and yet it is of his essence that he sees it in the general flood of life, steeped in its relations and contacts, struggling or submerged.
>
> —Henry James, "Turgenev" (1897)

At the age of sixty-five William Trevor has written some twenty books of fiction that for range of effect—philosophi-

cal density, exactness of style and idiom, variety of character, comic depth, and tragic intensity—have been unequalled among contemporary writers of English fiction since the death of Patrick White. Trevor is a precise workman, as befits the sculptor that he was in early life; his fiction does not sprawl and heave and occasionally founder as does that of, say, White or Faulkner; and because he does not take huge risks and gamble his literary capital on big, ambitious, and complicated novels such as *Riders in the Chariot* and *Absalom, Absalom!,* he probably won't win a Nobel prize despite the considerable measure of his achievement. Trevor has earned continuing recognition in Ireland and England, including a C.B.E.; but he remains relatively neglected in the United States, despite having been awarded a Bennett prize by the *Hudson Review* in 1990 and having regularly appeared in the *New Yorker* and *Harper's* for some years.

In the thirty years of his publishing career Trevor has never lacked an audience. **The Old Boys** (1964), his first novel, was a Book-of-the-Month Club selection, and it won the Hawthornden prize in England. The ensuing years have brought more honors and a growing critical recognition, but it puzzles me that Trevor's star is not in a still greater ascendant. One reason is that he isn't a flashy writer, nor a self-promoter. And he hasn't reached his proper audience in this country partly because the English dramatizations of his fiction have seldom, if ever, been broadcast on PBS.

Trevor's second collected stories (1992) did make a great impression in the U.S. The *Times Book Review* ran a long and brilliant piece by Reynolds Price in February 1993. This big book, which contains about ninety stories, deserves a place on the same shelf of short fiction with Frank O'Connor and Elizabeth Bowen, Ernest Hemingway and Eudora Welty, A. E. Coppard and V. S. Pritchett. Now that Miss Welty and Sir Victor have quit publishing fiction, Trevor stands as the best writer of short fiction in the English language. ("The modern short story deals in moments and subtleties and shadows of grey," he has written. "It tells as little as it dares.")

No one in his right mind would argue that, say, John Updike is William Trevor's equal; and his countryman John McGahern, who has occasionally rivaled Trevor in such superb stories as "The Country Funeral," is much more uneven in his short fiction, which hiccoughs from sketches and anecdotes to fully realized stories. McGahern's collected stories (1992) include only a dozen or so works that measure up to Trevor's consistently higher standard and achievement.

This brings us to the matter of William Trevor's nationality. There would be little question of where his real sympathies lie, even had he not settled the matter. "I am Irish absolutely to the last vein in my body." Ireland, he continues, is "the country you put first, the country you feel strongest about, the country that you actually love." But, he adds, "If I had stayed in Ireland . . . , I certainly wouldn't have written. I needed the distance in order to write."

William Trevor began his writing career with two splendid comedies about London—*The Old Boys* (1964) and *The Boarding-House* (1965). These were struck in the vein of Jonsonian humor that runs through Dickens to the early Waugh. Trevor hasn't abandoned this mode, which in his hands never descends to caricature; but he has moved a great distance from it in the succeeding decades. The reason that his characters have grown more complex and sympathetic may be inferred from an observation he made with asperity to Stephen Schiff when Schiff was writing about Trevor for the *New Yorker* (January 4, 1993). (This piece is itself Jonsonian in its maker's delineations of Trevor's physiognomy.) "The thing I hate most of all is the pigeonholing of people. . . . I don't believe in the black-and-white; I believe in the gray shadows, the murkiness, the not quite knowing, and the fact that you can't ever say 'old spinster' or 'dirty old man.'" (What Trevor has said of Pritchett's characters applies equally well to his own: "As real people do, they resist the labels of good or bad; they are decent on their day, some experiencing more of those days than others do.") Although many figures of this kind—apparent stereotypes—appear in both *The Old Boys* and *The Boarding-House* and although they are flat characters for the most part, their portraits, limned thirty years ago, do not violate the axiom that Trevor has recently declared, for he has followed it from the beginning.

To say, for instance, that any of the unmarried women in *The Boarding-House*—Nurse Clock, Rose Cave, Gallelty, Miss Clericot—is simply or only a spinster is to do great violence to Trevor's delicate portraiture, especially the characterization of Nurse Clock. The same applies to the more numerous cast of ageing men, from Studdy, a petty blackmailer and thief; to Major Eele, whose taste for pornography far outruns his impulse for romance; to Tome Obd, a mad Nigerian; to Mr Scribbin, whose only delight is listening to records that reproduce the sounds of trains. This teeming cast of eccentrics and misfits, male and female, could comfortably and believably have appeared in Jonson's *Bartholomew Fair* or Dickens's *Bleak House*.

Trevor, like most first-rate writers, often takes risks that would stop a lesser and more finicky artist in his or her tracks. In *The Boarding-House* he has written a novel without a protagonist—unless, and mark this, that figure is the owner of the boardinghouse, William Wagner Bird, who is the presiding intelligence in this novel (through the agency of his journals—and through his ghostly presence). What is remarkable about that, you may be thinking. The oddity is that Bird dies in the opening scene of the novel. He leaves the boardinghouse to Nurse Clock and Mr Studdy, who are enemies and are completely unalike and greatly at odds. But

for a long period they are forced to become confederates to circumvent Bird's will and change the boardinghouse into a toney nursing home—after they have sacked most of the boarders. Studdy, a wretch and a parasite, is the closest figure to the novel's antagonist. After absorbing a few setbacks, he comes off nearly scot free as the action ends. Mr Obd, after being thwarted in his protracted courtship of an English woman and having experienced Blakean visions of his late landlord, kills himself and very nearly incinerates all the other boarders. The comedy turns very dark and ends in pathos, which is the way a story or novel by Trevor usually concludes, regardless of how light-hearted or hilarious its action has been earlier.

> The comedy [in *The Boarding House*] turns very dark and ends in pathos, which is the way a story or novel by Trevor usually concludes, regardless of how light-hearted or hilarious its action has been earlier.
> —*George Core*

One lingers in considering a character like Studdy because, as Trevor has said of Pritchett's similar figures, "from their modest foothold on the periphery they rarely inaugurate events, and influence their own destiny through occasional, glancing swipes." It is such people who fascinate Trevor—seemingly ordinary folk who become uncommon when he takes a long hard look at them and reveals their natures to us. The flat characters of the early novels have much in common with the more complicated and complex people who regularly populate the stories because as Trevor develops as a writer he accomplishes what he says of the good story—that it" economically peels off surfaces." He hit his natural stride by the seventies as the stories reprinted in *The Ballroom of Romance* (1972), *Angels at the Ritz* (1975), and *Lovers of Their Time* (1978) abundantly demonstrate. In such first-rate stories as **"In Isfahan," "Angels at the Ritz," "Matilda's England,"** and **"Torridge"** Trevor shows his mastery of the form. "He manages to stuff a short story with as much emotional incident as most people cram into a novel, without ever straining the tale's skin," Schiff shrewdly remarks.

The complexities and complications of Trevor's characters have tended to multiply and thicken as the years have passed. Consider, for example, *Mrs Eckdorf in O'Neill's Hotel* (1969), which naturally proceeded from *The Boarding-House* and is a darker and richer version of the same experience. Reduced to its essentials and oversimplified, that experience involves the overlapping lives of people living on the margins of society—and thrown together in the urban version of a drydocked ship of fools. In a boardinghouse or a hotel like O'Neill's the sad voyage of life for a long-term resident may not end until insanity or death has done its work.

Trevor is still more fascinated with the effects that a boarding school exerts on its masters and pupils, as *The Old Boys* makes plain. None of the old boys in that novel has grown up; and the protracted adolescence of Jaraby, Sole and Cridley, Nox, Turtle, Ponders, and the others is at first amusing but becomes pathetic. This theme regularly recurs in Trevor's fiction: sometimes, as in **"A School Story,"** **"Torridge,"** and **"Children of the Headmaster,"** it is the principal theme propelling the action; on other occasions, as in **"Going Home," "The Grass Widows,"** and **"The Third Party,"** the boarding-school theme is more nearly a leitmotif, a matter playing in the story's background, not generating its action, as the principals endeavor to struggle through the day and find a modicum of satisfaction.

Within the boarding school lurk many possibilities that illumine the complications of life in the wider—and, one might presume—the more responsible world of action and liability. But the preoccupations of boys often carry over into mature life—or what passes for it, as a story such as **"Torridge"** dazzlingly reveals. (Schools are incubators for infantilism and protracted adolescence.) Torridge, an unlikely butt but one all the same, has been endlessly patronized and satirized and belittled by three of his fellow students. Years later, when these "normal" chaps get together with their families for a regular reunion, one of them impulsively invites Torridge. It turns out that he, who volunteers that he is homosexual, is also the most nearly normal and human of the whole sorry lot of old boys. His series of revelations about the school leaves the other men and their families deeply shaken. "The silence continued as the conversation of Torridge haunted the dinner table. He haunted it himself. . . . Then Mrs Arrowsmith suddenly wept and the Wiltshire twins wept and Mrs Wiltshire comforted them. The Arrowsmith girl got up and walked away, and Mrs Mace-Hamilton turned to the three men and said they should be ashamed of themselves, allowing this to happen."

Here, as usual, the quiet understated style of Trevor secures the dramatic point better than a gaudier and more assertive prose would. It would be instructive to dwell upon Trevor's exact idioms of conversation and of description, the way that he marks his characters with conversational tics (Torridge keeps saying "As a matter of fact" as he reveals one unpalatable fact after another in rapid-fire succession), the simple but precise diction, the occasional clinching metaphor, the representative items and details. Let us consider this descriptive passage from the same story: "Mrs Arrowsmith was thin as a knife, fashionably dressed in a shade of ash-grey that reflected her ash-grey hair. She smoked perpetually. . . . Mrs Wiltshire was small. Shyness caused her to coil herself up in the presence of other people so that she resembled a ball.

Tonight she was in pink, a faded shade. Mrs Mace-Hamilton was carelessly plump, a large woman attired in a carelessly chosen dress that had begonias on it. She rather frightened Mrs Wiltshire. Mrs Arrowsmith found her trying." Note how easily and exactly the description moves into drama, which is to say that Trevor here shows us not merely three women together but a geometry of relations.

We are reminded of the old-fashioned novelists like Dickens and Hardy, but such a Victorian novelist would be much more lavish and pile up far more details. Trevor's details are those of the sculptor and painter that he once was: they are chosen to be representative, not comprehensive or exhaustive. He is so sure of himself and so practiced and easy in his execution that he can deliberately repeat such commonplace words as *ash-grey* and *carelessly*. And even here, in a passage that would seem neutral, humor creeps in, with Mrs Wiltshire's ball-like dimensions contrasting with the carefree plumpness of Mrs Mace-Hamilton upholstered in her frumpy dress patterned with begonias. It is the formidable Mrs Mace-Hamilton, not her vulnerable counterpart, who reproves the three old boys and bullies, one of whom is her husband.

Homosexuality of every stripe appears in Trevor's fiction. We are not surprised that it is especially important in the stories and novels about public schools, but it threads its way through much of his other fiction as well. For instance the old commander in *The Children of Dynmouth* (1976) is a repressed homosexual, and the antagonist of this novel, who is but an adolescent boy, realizes this fact although the commander's wife has not. This is one of Timothy Gedge's most startling revelations as he inveigles himself into the lives of the citizens of Dynmouth, including those of Commander and Mrs Abigail; and having no identity or life of his own, Timothy spies upon various families. Timothy, however, is not a reliable observer, for he thinks that he witnessed a murder which in fact was an accident—or, more probably, a suicide.

When the Anglican priest in Dynmouth, Quentin Featherston, puts together everything of significance involving Timothy's knowledge and his delusions about what he has witnessed, including the rogering of his own mother, Featherston explains to one of Timothy's victims, Kate, a younger child: "There was a pattern of greys, half-tones and shadows. People moved in the greyness and made of themselves heroes or villains, but the truth was that heroes and villains were unreal. The high drama of casting out devils would establish Timothy Gedge as a monster. . . . But Timothy Gedge couldn't be dismissed as easily as that. . . . [He] was as ordinary as anyone else, but the ill fortune of circumstances or nature made ordinary people eccentric and lent them colour in the greyness. And the colour was protection because ill fortune weakened its victims and made them vulnerable." (Timothy, who always wears yellow, is the victim of bad luck and is very vulnerable.) But Kate, the strong and intelligent little girl, does not believe the priest. Before we too dismiss Featherston as a sentimental psychologist or sociologist, we should remember that his beliefs about human nature are close to Trevor's own. Such sympathy as Featherston's enables this author to respond to every shade of humanity and inhumanity, including homosexuals, voyeurs, obsessed and demented souls, misfits and failures of every kind and station, and outright criminals (blackmailers, arsonists, thieves, murderers).

Such a figure appears in **"Gilbert's Mother"** (*Harper's,* May 1993). In our advanced times he would be called dysfunctional, but that is not the half of it. Gilbert, who has murdered several young women, could be an older version of Timothy; but Timothy is estranged from his mother while Gilbert has been cosseted by his. (Both characters have lost their fathers at an early age.) This story turns on the mother's dawning awareness of her son's criminality as he has gone from car theft to murder. Gilbert is an English version of the Son of Sam—and a thief and arsonist as well. Gilbert's nervous mother agonizes about whether she should report him to the police, but we—and she—know that she will not. "No one would ever understand the mystery of his existence," she thinks, "or the unshed tears they shared."

Murder of a different sort drives the action of both *Fools of Fortune* (1983) and *The Silence in the Garden* (1988), both of which devolve from the continuing sectarian violence in Ireland from the Easter Rising until the present day. Trevor reveals the barbarities of the Black and Tans as well as the IRA; but, far more important, he also reveals the festering psychic wounds that senseless barbarity leaves in its wake. "Vengeance breeding vengeance." Such, too, is the theme of **"Attracta,"** one of his most powerful stories: indeed Pritchett thinks it the best in *Lovers of Their Time.* Attracta, an elderly Protestant schoolmistress whose life has been all but ruined by her parents' accidental deaths in an ambush—and by her reflecting upon their deaths and those of a young English couple in Belfast—gradually but inexorably runs off the rails. The Englishman, a soldier, is decapitated by his murderers, who send his head through the post to his young bride, who, until the package arrives, knows not of his death. She, having gone to Belfast, is raped by his murderers and kills herself. As the story ends, Attracta has lost her livelihood for trying to awaken her charges' moral awareness. The story powerfully conveys "what is going on in the backs of the minds of all the people in the town, of whatever faction: of how all, except one or two bigots, are helplessly trying to evade or forget the evils that entangle them," as Pritchett perceives. Attracta, in contrast, sees in a moment of searing revelation: "In all a lifetime I learnt nothing. And I taught nothing either." The pathos is wrenching and recalls similar moments in *Fools*

of Fortune and *The Silence in the Garden,* neither of which succeeds so well as **"Attracta."**

In both novels and elsewhere (as in **"Beyond the Pale"**) Trevor seems off his form when he becomes enmeshed in the coils of the troubles endlessly unfolding in Ireland, as Bruce Allen has complained in "William Trevor and Other People's Worlds" (*Sewanee Review,* winter 1993). Although Allen overstates his case, one is inclined to agree that Trevor is at his best when he writes about "the individual at war with himself, his nearest and dearest, his community, and what, in a more innocent time, we might have called his soul."

In any event most readers will agree that William Trevor's essential country is the Irish village. "An Irish village on market day in a . . . Trevor story can come to life with the crowding abundance of Dickens's London," as Reynolds Price observes. I do not agree, however, with Price that Trevor's stories of London life tend to be shallow and vapid. He writes persuasively about London as well as Dublin and various foreign places, especially Italy. As is by now well known, Trevor grew up in a long succession of small towns and villages in Ireland, where his father worked as a bank manager; and he knows this life with minute exactness. He seems even more sympathetic to and at home with farms and farming communities than with the small town, as one of his best stories, **"The Ballroom of Romance,"** demonstrates vividly.

The irony of Bridie's situation is that she is stuck with her father, a crippled widower, when she would like to be in town. In the town she talks with old acquaintances who are married or working. "'You're lucky to be peaceful in the hills,' they said to Bridie, 'instead of stuck in a hole like this.'" But Bridie is trapped in her narrow round, just as they are. **"The Ballroom of Romance"** illustrates Pritchett's acute insight that "Trevor quietly settles into giving complete life histories, not for documentary reasons, but to show people changing and unaware of the shock they are preparing for themselves." In this situation Bridie is more self-aware than the usual figure in Trevor's fictive world. As the story closes, she sees herself marrying Bowser Egan, even though "he would always be drinking" and would be "lazy and useless" and profligate. It is a bleak revelation about a life teetering on the edge of defeat; yet we admire Bridie for her steadfast loyalty to her father and for her ability to deal with life's privations and reversals, of which she has confronted more than her share. This Saturday night will be her last at the Ballroom of Romance: now she will wait for her father to die and Bowser Egan's mother to die and Bowser himself to court her at last, not merely run into her at the dance hall on Saturday night.

In Trevor's fiction, romance is ordinarily this bleak and unrewarding. The artificiality of dance halls and the snatched moments within them, whether in the city (**"Afternoon Dancing"**) or the country, is frustrating for all concerned. Seldom does romance flower there or anywhere else in Trevor's world; and rarely does romance, no matter how urgent, have its way for more than a summer's day. That is but one moral of **"Lovers of Their Time,"** my favorite of Trevor's many splendid stories. Norman Britt and his lover, Marie, carry on their affair of some years in the grand second-floor bathroom of an opulent railroad hotel. "Romance ruled their brief sojourns, and love sanctified—or so they believed—the passion of their physical intimacy. Love excused their eccentricity." But, finally, the romance grinds to a halt: Norman returns to his promiscuous wife, and Marie marries another man after she and Norman have lived with her mother, who treats Norman as a boarder. In the background we hear the jejune songs of Elvis Presley and the Beatles "celebrating a bathroom love." The unnatural romances adumbrated in **"Office Romances"** are even harsher—and in **"Mulvihill's Memorial"** still more wretched. And in Trevor seldom does romance flicker more than occasionally in even the best marriages, as **"Mr McNamara," "Angels at the Ritz," "Mags,"** and *The Children of Dynmouth* reveal with chilling finality. The respite from the taxing realities of single life that marriage seems to promise evaporates quickly, so quickly in fact that in Trevor's fiction marriages often go unconsummated even though they may quietly continue, like so many bad habits, for years until a reversal occurs.

In **"Mags"** a middle-aged couple painfully discovers that her childhood friend Mags, who has come to help her with the children and stayed until death, has consumed their marriage, leaving little besides her own dowdy clothes. Mags, the "innocent predator," has changed their marriage forever. In *Reading Turgenev* (one of the paired novels of *Two Lives*) the young wife is driven to madness by her cold unmarried sisters-in-law and her inept husband, and romance for her is but a sad interlude with her cousin, a dreamer who dies early after living a life of fantasy. The woman herself gradually retreats into fantasy and then is institutionalized. Yet that is not the whole story: the other side is that Elmer Quarry and his sisters believe they were nearly poisoned by that young woman, Elmer's trying wife, Mary Louise—and that they, for all their failings, are far from being wicked. In the end we sympathize with them, particularly Elmer, whose many domestic frustrations have made him an alcoholic. He continues to coddle his wife as she returns to live in his attic and persists in her singular love affair with the memory of her cousin Robert. *Reading Turgenev* is Trevor's most acute study of madness, but that subject runs through much of his fiction, beginning with *The Boarding-House* and *Mrs Eckdorf* and running through **"The Raising of Elvira Tremlett"** to this new novel. Madness in Trevor's fiction could easily be the subject of a Ph.D. the-sis in English literature—or, better yet, in abnormal psychology.

The failure of romance, the theme of *Other People's Worlds,* need not always lead to madness. Julia Ferndale, a likeable widow, is bilked by Francis Tyte, a smooth confidence man, after their wedding when in middle age she foolishly risks all for love. Francis is by no means an innocent predator, even though he is another of Trevor's halfhearted villains and parasites. Julia sensibly cuts her losses and returns to her good life in a village. The startling contrasts between the village life of Julia and the seedy world of Francis, a member of the homosexual demimonde in the city, are as strongly presented as nearly anything that Trevor has published. This novel stands, with both parts of *Two Lives,* as one of his best, which is to say one of the most ambitious and fully realized. The early novels are far more limited, and some of the later ones, particularly *Fools of Fortune* and *The Silence In the Garden,* are too cramped and crowded within the narrow space that Trevor allows himself. The reader who wants to sample William Trevor's fiction might well begin with *Angels at the Ritz* and *Other People's Worlds.*

My unabashed advocacy of Trevor's fiction (which extends to his other writing, especially *A Writer's Ireland*) is seldom tinged with negative criticism such as I have just declared. I do wish that he were less casual about his titles. *Reading Turgenev* is a silly title for a novel otherwise so artful and subtle, and his editor should have said so. *Mrs Eckdorf at O'Neill's Hotel* is merely descriptive, and many of his stories bear such mechanical titles. I am bothered by his run-on sentences: save for these comma splices, his punctuation neatly registers the nuances of his insight into suffering humanity. Obviously I am not the person to carp about William Trevor but the one to celebrate his tender and ironic depiction of character caught in the vise of circumstance.

The critics of the future will investigate William Trevor's characters, situations, places, and themes; they will linger over the subtleties of his unvarnished prose, the old-fashioned and innovative techniques that he employs, including the great chances that he takes (such as sudden and jolting shifts in point of view and in time); they will wonder about his religion and politics; they will speculate about the unhappiness of his parents and wonder if that wound drove him to bend the bow of his art; they will ask themselves if his natural mode is the story or the short novel or the novel (I cannot answer this simple question); they will marvel that a traveler has learned foreign cultures and customs so well and ask how Trevor can write almost as surely about, say, Umbria as London or an Irish village; they will chronicle the use of Irish legend and history in his fiction; they will scratch their heads about the names he assigns to his figures, major and minor; they will try to discover the sources of his art and, in doing so, they will be forced to consider Henry James, F. M. Ford, Joyce Cary, and Elizabeth Bowen among many others; they will make weather almost as heavy of his use of popular culture, especially films and music; and they will have to measure his range as a man of letters—as critic, editor, and dramatist as well as fictionist.

Few, if any, of them will be so intelligently responsive as the best of his critics to this point, critics who include not only those I have cited, especially V. S. Pritchett and Reynolds Price, but Elizabeth Spencer, Graham Greene, and still others who have responded to him with great sensitivity and insight. Consider Price once more: "Trevor's vision is deeply, but though never entirely, comic. However bleak the present and future of a given human life, the salient nearness of a vital ongoing world of rocks and fields, ocean and shore, will throw an enormous inhuman yardstick up against that one sad life and let us see the unreadable smile of time and fate." Let the last word be Pritchett's: "As his master Chekhov did, William Trevor simply, patiently, truthfully allows life to present itself, without preaching; he is the master of the small moments of conscience that worry away at the human imagination and our passions."

Postscript: Since I wrote this essay in May, two books by and about William Trevor have been published. Suzanne Morrow Paulson's *William Trevor* appears in Twayne's Studies in Short Fiction series. Part 1 is devoted to her readings of various stories; and although the critic cannot resist indulging herself in such foolishness as gender codes and intersubjectivity, the commentaries are usually helpful. Part 2 contains two good interviews and a little criticism by Trevor himself; in part 3 some sound criticism of his fiction is reprinted, but such hands as V. S. Pritchett and Elizabeth Spencer are missing in action. The bibliography is solid and useful.

Trevor's **Excursions in the Real World** appeared in London bookshops in August; it will be published in the U.S. by Knopf. This collection contains some of the superb pieces that have been seen recently in the *New Yorker,* especially **"Field of Battle."** Most of these occasional essays are struck in the reminiscent mode, but there are a few critical pieces such as a wonderful celebration of Somerville and Ross. The most memorable pieces are the sketches of actual people that constitute the bulk of the book—such personal reports as **"Miss Quirke"** and **"Old Bull."** Trevor is not so good an essayist as a maker of fiction, but his essays are well worth reading and rereading, especially for the insight they afford into his fiction—and, less often, in this retiring man's own temperament and life.

Mary Fitzgerald-Hoyt (essay date 1993)

SOURCE: "De-colleenizing Ireland: William Trevor's *Family Sins,*" in *Notes on Modern Irish Literature,* Vol. 5, 1993, pp. 28-33.

[*In the essay below, Fitzgerald-Hoyt analyzes "Kathleen's Field" and "Events at Drimaghleen" to support of her argument that Trevor breaks typical stereotypes of Irish women.*]

The identification of Ireland with female icons—Hibernia, Erin, the old woman, the colleen—has for centuries been a potent and pernicious tendency. Curiously, these stereotypes historically have been embraced by Irish and English alike: the metaphor of Ireland as oppressed woman or occasionally as militant standard-bearer fueled Irish nationalist posters and political cartoons. Conversely, the image of weeping, pliant Hibernia was juxtaposed with the simian-appearing Fenian to indicate to English Victorian audiences the difference between good (i.e., tractable) Irish and bad (i.e., rebellious) ones.

As the diverse women in the 1988 documentary *Mother Ireland* point out, whether the image be of the poor old woman with her captive four green fields, the sorrowful Erin awaiting rescue from English oppression, the defiant Hibernia urging rebellion, or the sweet colleen beckoning the romantic tourist, such reductive images are false and unfair, bearing little resemblance to real Irish women. As Professor Lorna Reynolds has observed,

> . . . the women of my generation and of the preceding generation were more than able to hold their own in a man's world, and I cannot recall a single, simple colleen among them. . . . the women of Ireland, whether we look for them in legend, literature, or life, do not correspond to the stereotypes that have, so mysteriously, developed in the fertile imaginations of men.

Contemporary Irish women writers Eavan Boland, Anne Devlin, Julia O'Faolain, and many others have labored to free Irish women of restrictive stereotypes and given eloquent voice to the female experience in Ireland. But in studies of contemporary Irish literature little has been made of William Trevor's realistic, sympathetic portrayals of Irish women in his fiction of the last two decades.

In his most recent collection, **Family Sins,** Trevor offers complex and credible portraits of Irish women: Ariadne, whose self-assumed guilt about her father's shameful past drives her into a dreary, loveless life; Maura Brigid, psychologically bullied by a rigid family into rejecting the husband she loves; Grania, who daringly remedies the childlessness of an otherwise happy marriage. In these stories, as in all his fiction about Irish women, Trevor provides an often bleak account of lives constricted and thwarted by poverty, political injustice, religious intolerance, and domestic tyranny. Yet in two of the finest stories of the collection, **"Kathleen's Field"** and **"Events at Drimaghleen,"** Trevor takes a bolder step and explodes Ireland's long-cherished female icons.

In these stories, as in all his fiction about Irish women, Trevor provides an often bleak account of lives constricted and thwarted by poverty, political injustice, religious intolerance, and domestic tyranny.
—*Mary Fitzgerald-Hoyt*

As Kristin Morrison has pointed out in her review of *Family Sins,* the very title of **"Kathleen's Field"** carries strong emotional associations: one thinks of Cathleen ni Houlihan pleading for the rescue of her four green fields. Trevor's title functions ironically here, however, for as Morrison observes of the story's protagonist: " . . . this girl is not a queen or a countess in a parable where one national group or class exploits another; her oppressors are themselves Irish." More specifically, Kathleen Hagerty is doomed to an unhappy, victimized life primarily because her culture, for all its veneration of mythical women, undervalues real ones.

"Kathleen's Field" depicts a woman trapped by poverty, religion, and family loyalty. Kathleen Hagerty's father is already in debt but longs to buy another field that will ensure financial security for his family. His only collateral is Kathleen, whose services as a maid are exchanged for a loan of money. The bargain is at once monstrous and complex: Kathleen's wages will be applied to the debt, so she will have nothing to show for at least ten years of work. At the same time she is all too aware of her family's plight: seven of the ten children have emigrated, leaving herself, her retarded sister, and her brother Con, who without the additional field will be unable to marry and to support his sisters after their parents' deaths.

Kathleen's life as maid to the Shaughnessy family is miserable: not only is she homesick, she is bullied and ridiculed by Mrs. Shaughnessy, ignored by the son, and worst of all, subjected to Mr. Shaughnessy's unwelcome sexual advances. Her emotional turmoil is great: her Catholic upbringing has made her both acutely aware of sin and ashamed to talk about sexual matters, so she can neither tell her parents nor determine whether she is guilty of sin in tolerating Shaughnessy's sexual exhibitionism. Haunted by her loving father's gratitude to her and her mother's calm argument that she is fortunate to have such an employment opportunity,

Kathleen ultimately keeps silent, even though her misery will last for years. To Shaughnessy's public teasing about her possibly marrying someday, she thinks sadly that her plain looks have attracted no one except her unpleasant employer: it does not seem that Kathleen will be accorded the escape of marriage, either.

Part of what makes **"Kathleen's Field"** such a horrifying story is that the Hagertys are inherently good people, but economic constraint and worry about the future render them capable of viewing the sacrifice of their daughter's life as a boon rather than a blight. The inherent sexual inequality of their world, exacerbated by their poverty, deems their son's inheritance to be more important than their daughter's freedom.

But **"Kathleen's Field"** is more than a sympathetic portrait of a powerless woman. The mythical associations conjured up by its title assume a pointed irony here. No rescue is imminent for Kathleen Hagerty, and her plight is not the stuff of high tragedy but rather a chronicle of "quiet desperation." Though the Hagertys' poverty may be historically rooted in English injustice—the evils of colonialism—in this case the predominant evil is sexual inequality. Kathleen is exploited by an employer who assumes that because she is female and economically dependent upon him, she is by rights his sexual victim. Likewise, the Hagertys assume that because she is female, she will sacrifice her own desires for her family's sake.

In **"Events at Drimaghleen,"** Trevor undermines the very roots of Irish female stereotypes. Not only are we left in no doubt about the injustice of such reductive images, we are given female characters who defy any easy definition.

Maureen McDowd, youngest daughter of a farming couple, falls in love with the ne'er-do-well son of a possessive widow. The McDowds deplore what they see as a hopeless entanglement for Maureen, and when their daughter is missing from home overnight they assume she has eloped with Lancy Butler, a belief that causes McDowd to refer to her as "a little bitch." But when the McDowds arrive at the Butler farm they discover an almost unimaginable horror: Maureen, Lancy, and Mrs. Butler dead of gunshot wounds. Police and community alike conclude that Mrs. Butler, who "had been obsessively possessive, hiding from no one her determination that no other woman should ever take her son away from her", killed Maureen in jealous rage; her son "by accident or otherwise" then killed his mother and in despair ended his own life.

Though Maureen is dead at the story's beginning, through her parents' grief we are made acutely aware of how unnecessary, how wasteful her death was. But Trevor gives this rural tragedy another twist, for Maureen's bleak story goes beyond her death. The McDowds reluctantly agree to be interviewed by an unscrupulous journalist, trusting that she will be honest, and tempted by a much-needed payment of 3000 pounds. To their dismay, the journalist transforms their daughter's tragedy into a lurid tabloid distortion. The journalist concludes that Maureen herself was the murderer, "a saint by nature and possessing a saint's fervour, (who) on that fatal evening made up for all the sins she had ever resisted." The terrible irony is that the McDowds have unwittingly destroyed their daughter's reputation, and because they have accepted payment from the journalist must now live with a guilt that makes them wretched.

Trevor cannot resist another ironic twist, however; Hetty Fortune, the journalist, is English, and her story is colored by anti-Irish bigotry. Trevor has elsewhere provided biting accounts of English prejudice; here he likewise exposes bigotry's insidiousness. At the journalist's hands Maureen becomes a stereotypical pure Irish maiden of notable piety. Furthermore, the investigating policeman is rendered dim and inept, a bumbling "Mick"; the Drimaghleen community becomes threateningly self-protective. Fortune intimates that fear of reprisal prevented the Gardai from uncovering the truth: "The Irish do not easily forgive the purloining of their latter-day saints."

Through the collusion between her parents and Hetty Fortune, Maureen McDowd is "colleenized" into an unreal, reductive image. We bridle at the injustice of this process even as we pity the bereaved McDowds.

Robert Rhodes has pointed out that in **"Events at Drimaghleen"** Trevor deliberately withholds information: ultimately, no one will ever know the truth. Though forensic tests could probably have eliminated some of the confusion surrounding the crime, apparently no tests were performed—are the Gardai at fault, as Fortune suggests? Furthermore, Trevor is silent about such telling details as the placement of the bodies at the crime scene and the locations of the wounds—details that would surely rule out one set of conclusions about possible culprits.

Just as Trevor leaves us bewildered about the identity of the murderer at Drimaghleen, he leaves us wondering about the real characters of the dead, particularly about Mrs. Butler and Maureen McDowd, women whom others too readily explain away by stereotypes. Mrs. Butler is characterized by her neighbors as the possessive, overprotective mother of an only son, but this too is a familiar stereotype of Irish women, too easy a dismissal of a life. We are told that Mrs. Butler had miscarried frequently before giving birth to Lancy, that she was widowed when the child was only two, that their farm is located in an isolated spot. These bald statements both tease and trouble us, for they bespeak a life of pain and loneliness, a life that in death becomes grossly oversimpli-

fied. Immediately thereafter we are made privy to Garda O'Kelly's speculations about rumors that " . . . Mrs. Butler had been reputed to be strange in the head and given to furious jealousies where Lancy was concerned." He concludes, "In the kind of rage that people who'd known her were familiar with she had shot her son's sweetheart rather than suffer the theft of him."

The problem is, of course, that O'Kelly draws his conclusions from rumors, not facts. Because the possessive Irish mother is a familiar stereotype, it takes little to convince the Garda that he's reached a viable solution to the crime. Concerned as he is with the shock and suffering the killings have caused in the community, he looks no further for an explanation.

The mythologizing of Maureen McDowd is even more disturbing. Hetty Fortune's characterization of Maureen, unlike her description of Mrs. Butler, apparently has little foundation in reality, but her readers, familiar with the stereotype of the colleen, have little difficulty transferring it to a real woman. But Trevor has raised too many questions in our minds for us to be capable of accepting this characterization.

In this deliberate ambiguity Trevor deals a subtle yet critical blow to the stereotyping of Irish women. The events at Drimaghleen disturb us, rouse out perennial human hunger for the security of certainty. But certainty is precisely what Trevor withholds here: in fact, he discredits the misguided desire for certainty that finds stereotyping a comfortable means of explaining away troubling complexities in human behavior.

Ultimately, in both **"Kathleen's Field"** and **"Events at Drimaghleen"** Trevor attempts to de-colleenize Ireland by demonstrating the damage wrought by those who would deny Irish women the dignity of individuality.

Kristin Morrison (essay date 1993)

SOURCE: "Introduction," in *William Trevor*, Twayne, 1993, pp. 1-8.

[*In the following excerpt, Morrison discusses Trevor's Irish nationality and recurring themes within his works.*]

From some perspectives William Trevor might seem to be a British author: he lives in Devon, on the southwest coast of England; his publishers are two important British firms, Penguin and the Bodley Head; he has been awarded an honorary CBE by Queen Elizabeth II for his valuable services to literature. His work usually occupies a foot or two of shelf space in major bookshops throughout the United Kingdom. And his speech is accented by an urbane mix of various regions of Britain. Even so, William Trevor remains an Irish author—Irish by birth and by owned identity. That simple fact is essential to any full appreciation of his fiction.

In a 1976 interview with Jack White on Irish television (RTE), Trevor stated that Irish history is "the only academic subject I've ever been the least interested in" and described himself as a young man being "very, very nationalistic, intensely Irish." Going on to consider the transition from his early work as a sculptor (in his teens and twenties), deliberately using Irish motifs, to his early work as an author (in his thirties), wherein Irish elements are not immediately apparent, Trevor speculated that he "must have used something up": contrary, he says, to standard advice given fledgling authors, he began by writing about what he did not know—England—rather than about what he did know—Ireland. Yet it is clear, throughout this early interview and in subsequent ones, as well as throughout Trevor's fiction itself, that his fascination with Irish history, Irish motifs, and his whole Irish heritage did not actually get "used up" but rather went underground for a time, only to manifest itself later as a profoundly important component of his mature work.

Born in 1928 as William Trevor Cox, in Mitchelstown, County Cork, Trevor spent his childhood in various towns in the south of Ireland, moving frequently because of his father's work as a bank official. In his RTE interview Trevor speaks at length about his vivid memories of the towns and the countryside in which he grew up and his own youthful activities there: Youghal, Skibbereen, Enniscorthy; the seaside, the fishermen, people being drowned; his going to school for the first time; "the enclosed claustrophobia of small town life" that, he says, permeates so much of his fiction; his going often into Cork to the pictures ("Clark Gable in *Too Hot to Handle,* then tea at the Savoy"); his wandering off on his own, lost in the usual childhood fantasies; his immersion in books (all of Dickens, Edgar Wallace, Agatha Christie). Because of his living as "a migrant inside Ireland" (to use Jack White's phrase), and belonging to a minority religious group (Protestant), Trevor says he early developed the sense of being "outside looking in," so that when he came to be a writer, he took up his role "as a spy." Throughout the interview, however, Trevor gently resists White's tendency (more implicit than stated) to see him as not really rooted in Ireland, perhaps not really Irish. Yes, Trevor agrees, he lived in many separate spots in the south, but they all seemed similar to him; he had a sense of continuity. Yes, "the minority thing" of being a Protestant has stayed with him, but his schooling also included the (Roman Catholic) Christian Brothers. Yes, his early fiction did focus on England and the English, but as a people and a place quite different from his own, as oddities ("I found English people . . . their rules, laws, and obsessions very interesting"). And,

yes, as a matter of fact he does, even now, feel foreign in Devon, yet he experiences no conflict because "the Devon countryside and people are very like the south of Ireland where I grew up." The touchstone is always, ultimately, Ireland.

After a childhood of frequently interrupted and patchwork schooling—with some stability supplied by two years at Sandford Park School and two years at St. Columba's College in Dublin—Trevor attended Trinity College, Dublin (getting to know the city very well, especially, as he told Jack White, its night people), and was awarded a B.A. in history in 1950. His subsequent move to Northern Ireland and then to England (where he taught history and art at various schools between 1951 and 1955) in no way constituted a rejection of Ireland, no Joycean or Beckettian deliberate expatriation. As he explained to me after his reading at the Book Fair at the Edinburgh Festival in 1985, he left quite simply because there were no jobs available for sculptors in Ireland but there were in England.

Of his career as a visual artist Trevor told Jack White that he became seriously interested in sculpting at age 16 while at St. Columba's and remained a sculptor until 1960. He exhibited his work and earned his living as a professional sculptor in England, chiefly with work on churches, using Irish motifs taken from his intense study of the Book of Kells (he carved four saints from the Book of Kells for a church in Rugby, "which is rather nice—a piece of Imperialism I rather like"). His fascination with Irish crosses and other structural and decorative forms in Celtic art, along with his own intense nationalism and "desire for art to reflect the past," led eventually to his decision to give up sculpture because, as he explained in his RTE interview, "my sculpture had become wholly abstract" and "I just didn't like the look of it."

The "humanness" absent from his later sculpture was perhaps, he speculates, rediscovered in his writing. In 1958 he published his first novel, *A Standard of Behaviour*; in 1964 his second novel, *The Old Boys,* won the Hawthornden Prize. Since 1965 he has lived by his pen, publishing a novel or volume of short stories every year or two and winning most of the significant literary prizes.

The Irish strain in Trevor's artistry may have gone underground during the early part of his writing career but nonetheless remains discernible. Particularly interesting is the fact that Trevor himself finds Irish elements in work that on the surface seems not to be Irish at all. As Trevor talks on videotape with Jack White about characteristics of his use of language, he illustrates its Irish cast by citing one of his English characters (the fey/pathological adolescent nemesis Timothy Gedge, from the entirely English *The Children of Dynmouth*). Replying to White's question as to whether his work contains echoes of Ireland, Trevor first responds with an emphatic "Oh, yes"; he goes on to indicate that not only does he have a number of short stories with Irish characters or settings, as well as a novel that is "wholly Irish," but even his English, French, and American characters "speak in an Irish way." He amplifies this assertion by stating that he inevitably writes "Irish patterns of speech" and notes that there is something characteristic about "the way the Irish decorate a phrase, make it slightly funnier than does the more down-to-earth English person." Such language patterns are "a technical thing," he says, but not something he does for special effect; quite simply, "It's the only way I can write." Although Trevor has mitigated this "Irish speech" somewhat, even here in this mid-1970s interview he affirms that his use of the English language has a specifically Irish form to it. This, he says, accounts for some critics finding his characters' speech eccentric or odd, not realizing the Irish cast he has inevitably given to his non-Irish characters.

Climaxing this relatively long portion of the interview with his single specific example, Trevor points out that Timothy Gedge in *The Children of Dynmouth* "speaks with the ring of a Cork boy." Whether or not Timothy's unusually frequent use of personal names in direct address ("D' you ever go to funerals, Kate?" / "Funerals?" / "When a person dies, Kate"); whether or not his repetitions of key nouns ("I'm looking for a wedding-dress. I have an act planned with a wedding-dress") and his building his paragraphs incrementally using such repetitions, with key words often placed oddly in the phrase ("You didn't mind me looking in at the window, Stephen? Only I was passing at the time. Your dad was packing his gear up. He took the wedding-dress out of the trunk and put it back again. A faded kind of trunk, Stephen. Green it would be in its day"); whether or not that "only" and "green it would be" are distinctively or exclusively "Irish" is not the point: what is important is that Trevor *hears* Timothy Gedge speaking with the ring of a Cork boy, despite his English surname, origin, and milieu. Elsewhere in the interview, responding to the question as to which novel is his favorite, Trevor states, "I'm very fond of my Dublin book, *Mrs. Eckdorf in O'Neill's Hotel,*" which White agrees "has a strong smell of Dublin about it." Persistently, the strong smell, the ringing echo of Ireland—these permeate Trevor's sense of his work and his working.

Just as Trevor first wrote about England from the vantage point of an outsider, so later he began to write more and more about Ireland only after the years spent in England, Switzerland, and Italy had provided necessary distance, allowing him "to look back from someplace else." The word *back* is important in that assertion, indicating as it does an affirmation of his sense of continuity with his homeland (and not foreignness, such as he feels with England). The linguistic link was always there. Then, later, that abiding fascination with Irish history began to surface once again, prompted

perhaps by the renewed Troubles in Northern Ireland from 1968 on. Certainly Trevor's increasingly frequent use of Irish settings, characters, and political issues dates from about that time, culminating in his masterpieces of the 1980s, *Fools of Fortune,* **"The News from Ireland,"** and *The Silence in the Garden.*

The gardens featured in Trevor's latest novels provide important images for all his work and function as the chief recurrent metaphor, at once a lost Eden and a possible Paradise, a whole flourishing and blighted world. And very often that garden is Ireland. By a conceptual "system of correspondences," frequently expressed through a rhetorical strategy of "significant simultaneity," this metaphoric equation of Ireland and garden, with all its attendant images and related themes, shapes Trevor's entire body of fiction into a remarkable coherence. That polished coherence with its interesting complexity is the subject of this book. Through careful examination of Trevor's fiction, through close reading of the published texts, this study discovers the various elements of complexity and artistry that make Trevor's work such an elegant whole, centered on the metaphor of the garden and the important ethical question of whether that postlapsarian garden is essentially waste or can be reclaimed.

The intellectual framework of all Trevor's fiction is provided by his "system of correspondences." According to the concept that dominates his work, past and present are actually the same moment; apparently separate realms (the public and the private, the political and the domestic) inevitably overlap. The various elements of space and time are intrinsically interrelated, together constituting an elaborate and powerful set of relationships, a system of correspondences, that shapes his world. This conceptual system—with its chief recurrent metaphor, the garden—is well illustrated by an important short story, **"The News from Ireland,"** and by one of his most powerful novels, *Fools of Fortune.*

Trevor's system of correspondences raises a significant question: What is the origin of evil in such a world and how does it operate? Trevor invokes an ancient theory (that Adam's sin in the primal garden, Eden, taints all his descendants) but transforms it by the way his characters participate in their own wounding. In Trevor's account of the genealogy of evil, sin originates not only in the past but also continuously in the present, each man his own Adam, inheriting Original Sin and contributing to it capriciously, even unwittingly. Children are particularly interesting to him, simultaneously both victims and victimizers, making evil a game they are unwilling to relinquish, playing it into adulthood and old age. A variety of short stories and novels, spread across the whole of Trevor's career, illustrate these points, showing how personal, domestic, public, and political realms are mutually affected by any given act of cruelty or violence, however trivial.

Nationality and the violence it occasions are an important aspect of the political issues Trevor's later work regularly addresses. The linkage between political violence and personal cruelties develops gradually throughout Trevor's work, emerging finally as a concatenation of suffering that binds together all persons from all times and all places. Only in the last half of his writing career do nationality and national allegiance become an explicit issue, focused sharply on Ireland. The earliest fiction of this Anglo-Irish writer is set almost entirely in England with English characters; most of these novels and stories of the 1960s are comic in manner, grotesque in characterization and plotting, and generally apolitical. From the 1970s on, humor is softened by pathos; more Irish characters and settings are used; and political and domestic problems interconnect. In the 1980s and early 1990s all but one of the novels and most of the stories are Irish in setting, characterization, and subject matter; events and manner of presentation are usually serious, the tone often despairing. The earlier work shows Trevor perfecting his craft and developing those distinctive techniques and configurations of thought which ultimately lead to *Fools of Fortune* and *The Silence in the Garden,* an odyssey that moves through the city back to the garden, back home to Ireland, from a comic view of life to a much darker one in which the mutual correspondences between public and private realms are seen as some of the chief conduits of evil.

The philosophical problem of evil and specific political evils associated with nationality are joined in Trevor's fiction in a shocking metaphor: child murder used as an emblem of colonial exploitation. To highlight Trevor's treatment of this difficult subject, it is useful to juxtapose *The Silence in the Garden* (1988) with two other novels containing similar material, one by an American of very different background, Toni Morrison's *Beloved* (1987), and the other by a fellow Corkonian, Mary Leland's *The Killeen* (1985). Though child abuse and murder have occasionally been mentioned in fiction, they are rarely described in any detail; by contrast, these three novels, written within a few years of one another, are surprisingly horrifying in their explicitness. *Beloved* is, however, ultimately optimistic, while the two Irish novels significantly show a much more diffuse stain of guilt and responsibility, a more negative view of the future as a place necessarily scarred by present evils.

Summary statements about Trevor's often shocking subject matter and the interconnected evils he depicts can make his work seem sensational. But Trevor's writing is, to the contrary, subtle and finely crafted; he makes skillful use of a variety of rhetorical strategies to establish the workings of his system of correspondences and its chain of evil. Among the more important strategies are his persistent visual images, implied puns, literalized metaphors, incremental references, and significant names. *Persistent visual images* serve to show personal and political worlds mirroring each other, as illustrated in the story **"Attracta,"** with its parallels between the peaceful schoolteacher in County Cork and her former pupil murdered in Belfast. *Implied puns* supply a single word that ramifies from its obvious denotation in context to the analogous meanings it suggests throughout the rest of the text, as in the story **"Beyond the Pale,"** where deceptions in the plot are mirrored by deceptions in language. *Literalized metaphors* function in **Mrs. Eckdorf in O'Neill's Hotel,** for example, to indicate the reciprocal power and folly of both words and images. *Incremental references*—repeated items, such as trees, orchards, and fields—take on additional weight and meaning as they recur throughout Trevor's work, beginning initially as isolated references and then, through repetition and association, gradually acquiring the density and resonance of a symbol, suggesting various points of correspondence to other elements in Trevor's world and supporting his major metaphor of the garden. Finally, *names and naming* constitute profound indicators of identity, everything from obvious tags to inner sources of power, showing the extent to which even language participates in the sense of linked relationships that pervades Trevor's fiction.

Genre too is made to serve Trevor's system of correspondences. Trevor alters the traditional *Bildungsroman* to make it a political novel as well: the protagonist's process of maturation in both *Fools of Fortune* and *Nights at the Alexandra* is affected by political events that shift his quest away from the traditional goal of social integration and toward discovery of and reconciliation with his deepest self. Novels by John Banville and Brian Moore provide useful contrasting examples of contemporary *Bildungsroman* with similar concerns.

The question inevitably arises as to whether Trevor's view in his fictional world is optimistic because of his frequent comic elements or is pessimistic because of his focus on what seems an endlessly multiplying series of evil events—or, to put it another way, using Trevor's own metaphor, whether or not the garden can be redeemed, reclaimed. I conclude this book by considering the extent to which Trevor's work provides resolution for the intricate evil it explores originating in the Garden of Eden and permeating the many gardens found in his short stories and novels. From the beginning of his fiction to his latest stories, such as **"Lost Ground,"** Trevor has included three kinds of persons—some comic, some tragic—who in various ways both manifest evil and transcend it: children, celibates, and holy fools. In the 1976 novel *The Children of Dynmouth* the paradoxicality of Trevor's response to the problem of evil is most explicitly presented: apparent monsters are not outside the community but part of it, just as the snake was part of Eden; at every point goods and evils touch and mirror each other; loss may be gain; the same earth is both garden and wilderness. Placing this work against another contemporary Irish novel—Jennifer Johnston's *Shadows on Our Skin* (1977), set in Belfast and dealing with specific, recognizable political violence—helps highlight the paradoxicality of Trevor's view, a view that itself can provide redemption for that wilderness/garden of Ireland with which his work is preoccupied.

Suzanne Morrow Paulson (essay date 1993)

SOURCE: "Preface," in *William Trevor: A Study of the Short Fiction,* Twayne, 1993, pp. xi-xviii.

[*In the following excerpt from her* Preface, *Paulson argues that Trevor is one of the finest modern short story writers and that he is not appreciated adequately in the United States.*]

> My sense of tragedy probably comes from childhood—the source, I think, of both tragedy and comedy. The struggle in Ireland—and the sorrow—is a good backdrop for a fiction writer, but it is not for me any sort of inspiration. . . . What seems to nudge me is something that exists between two people, or three, and if their particular happiness or distress exists for some political reason, then the political reason comes into it—but the relationship between the people comes first.

William Trevor's reputation as a major modern writer is well-established in Europe but not in America. No one has yet focused attention on his short-story masterpieces—lost, as they are, in an overwhelming amount of attention paid his numerous fine novels. This Irish storyteller and ex-sculptor of nearly 17 years considers his short stories his most important art, and most critics see the short story form as best suited to Trevor's genius.

Trevor's short stories deserve much more critical attention than they have so far received. His short-story masterpieces belong on the shelf alongside those of Chekhov, Dostoyevski, Joyce, Conrad, James, Faulkner, and Flannery O'Connor. Brilliantly rendering the pain of adolescence, the agony of courtship and marriage in an emotionally barren terrain, and the narcissism of destructive parenting, Trevor continues a long tradition of British and Irish literature about men, women, and society. He writes a personal sort of fiction yet transcends the personal because his art encourages sympathy for even the most ridiculous of grotesques.

The depth of Trevor's understanding of people is rare in this age of perpetual violence between nations and regions, within cities and within the family. Reviewers have acknowledged what Richard Eder calls Trevor's "prophetic power."

V. S. Pritchett has declared Trevor "the master of the small movements of conscience that worry away at the human imagination and our passions." Ted Solotaroff points to Graham Greene's favorable comparison of Trevor and Joyce because "both Trevor and the early Joyce are geniuses at . . . the deeper realism: accurate observation turning into moral vision."

This Irish shape-shifter deftly renders the perspective of an elderly woman worried about senility, a young wife betrayed by an unfaithful husband, and a middle-aged spinster/schoolteacher distressed when terrorists in Belfast murder a British army officer, decapitate the corpse, and send the head to the officer's wife in a "biscuit tin." Focusing on the vagaries of personality and the more disturbing circumstances of modern life, Trevor, with his psychological and moral insights, individualizes his characters and dynamically depicts their struggles to endure personal hardship. He writes powerful prose because he masters the comic as well as the tragic impulse. His stories cannot be read indifferently, even when they make us laugh. Like other modernists he writes tragicomedy; his work renders the grotesque aspects of human nature under stress. R. Z. Sheppard rightly notes that Trevor "understands as well as any contemporary writer that the defeated, the shelved, and the slightly batty make [good] fiction."

Regressively willful men, women, and children in Trevor's stories disrupt the lives of everyone around them. Tricksters victimize the vulnerable. Traumatized wives, sensitive men, and psychologically abused children suffer because they are at the mercy of cruel authority figures. A rush into a personal relationship meant to console a wounded heart somehow falls into the soundless abyss of indifference, miscommunication, and short-circuited good intentions. The ridiculous, contemporary Everyman/woman cannot overcome a terrifying sense of alienation from Society and self. Yet few stories are tragic from start to finish.

The comic tales, such as **"Mulvihill's Memorial"** and **"The Day We Got Drunk on Cake,"** appear at times more funny than tragic; like Trevor's other masterpieces, however, they encourage what J. Hillis Miller, Robert Scholes, and others designate as an essential experience of "intersubjectivity"— that is, a reading experience reaffirming our humanity and expanding our understanding of others. When I interviewed Trevor in 1989, he declared that his primary interest is people, who, he said, "don't really change all that much." Later in the interview he said, "When you write about anyone—man or woman—there has to be some affection."

Trevor is at his absolute best in those stories expressing his sympathy for women, sensitive men, and adolescents who suffer from destructive stereotypes of feminine and masculine behavior. Whether set in urban England or rural Ireland, these stories depict women who seek autonomy but are forced to serve the interests of the farm, the country estate, or the commercial enterprise in communities demanding that men be aggressive, never nurturing, and that women be nurturing, never aggressively working to solve community and world problems.

There are exceptions, such as the aggressive wife Hilda in **"Lovers of Their Time,"** who is far from nurturing; the nurturing fathers found in **"Matilda's England"**; Agnes's nurturing husband/father in **"Teresa's Wedding"**; and the holy father in **"August Sunshine."** For the most part, however, Trevor's wives, mothers, daughters, and sensitive sons are terribly limited by society and oppressed by patriarchal authority—sometimes yielding to insanity. The politics of gender is an important aspect of Trevor's art.

Confrontations between men and women in love are especially poignant when lovers struggle for meaningful relationships—for example, in **"The Forty-seventh Saturday"** and **"Lovers of Their Time"**—but meaning is measured in dollars and cents. Alert readers must sort out the authorial voice from that of the unreliable narrator, whose shifting moods and fuzzy perceptions serve as a window to the world; readers must sort out moments in the text when the discourse of business-as-usual promotes the materialistic values of advertising and the mass media.

Replete with slogans and jingles from radio, television, and movies, commerce diminishes love in these stories. Usually, however, Trevor resists the comic writer's temptation to be satisfied with caricature. His short-story masterpieces in this vein treat with compassion those who struggle in the industrial wasteland. Anthony Glavin points out that Trevor makes "us care about people we don't especially care for," and Derek Mahon notes that his "severe [yet] compassionate judgments [are] handed down more in sorrow than in anger." This sorrow is conveyed by masterful manipulations of style rendering inner landscapes or surrealistic dreams such as those found in **"The Ballroom of Romance," "The Raising of Elvira Tremlett,"** and **"The Blue Dress."**

Nevertheless, the reader may feel revulsion given the vast range of human foibles so poignantly rendered in Trevor's stories. William Cole complains about what he sees as Trevor's "gloom, gloom," Robert Towers about his "gleeful misanthropy." The criticisms that Trevor represents too much suffering in his stories may suggest the reviewer's confusion between the character's outlook and Trevor's.

Trevor's short stories convey his wise bewilderment over life. He master-minds puzzles of experience that happen to be stories. Like Joyce and other modernists, he works almost entirely by indirection, understatement, and very subtle implication—sometimes relating horrific events in a deadpan tone, sometimes developing volatile perspectives that leap forward and backward in time and in and out of assorted characters' minds. While discussing reasons the Irish "have taken to our hearts the breathless gallop as opposed to the marathon," the short story rather than the novel, Trevor points to suffering owing to oppression by the British and then declares that the "ability to slip effortlessly from mood to mood [is] . . . the hallmark of the real short story writer." Trevor conveys an incredible range of moods—from tragic despair to comic hilarity.

A 1981 *Newsweek* review, however, calls Trevor a "Master of Malevolence." This is but one example of a reader equating the author's perspective with that of his less reliable narrators. These readers miss Trevor's humanity. John J. Stinson argues that critics assume compassion is lacking in the stories because they do not carefully sort out the many different "voices" in his work. Nor do they consider the modernist methods of the author's style and the modernist tendency to focus on the dark side of human nature. Stinson concludes that "Trevor's carefully controlled and deliberately understated stories are alive with implication. . . . Readers discover a slightly strange world full of eccentric personalities and small quirky events that remain, for all that, very much the world we know."

Trevor in fact reveals the mindscapes of a plethora of eccentric characters. Usually the reader can determine which character's mindscape is being represented—for example, in such first-person narratives as **"Beyond the Pale"**—because the passage focuses on that character, shown looking at a scene or pondering an idea. Maybe the reader is expected to identify who belongs to what stream of consciousness because it matches behavior established previously in the story as particular to that character. This latter case requires an extremely alert reader, especially when unreliable narrators reveal their own appalling natures.

Trevor's fiction is indeed difficult when an unreliable or omniscient third-person narrator—with shifting moods and fuzzy perceptions—serves as the only window to a complex world. No critic should fail to heed M. M. Bakhtin's argument that modern fiction is "multi-voiced," reflecting sociocultural and historical contexts. Besides being alert to differences between the narrator's and the author's voices, readers must sort out moments in the text when various community voices intrude—the voice of authority reflecting Catholic or Protestant church dogma; feminine communal voices rebelling against pub-crawling husbands and fathers; conforming voices of spinsters and bachelors; alienated schizophrenic voices of adolescents struggling for self-definition; and phallocentric voices of men training their sons to become farmers, auto mechanics, butchers, or various knights of industry (hotel proprietors, storekeepers, boarding school taskmasters, etc.). These voices invariably represent communal values determined by gender, class, and nationality—values that amount to powerful forces dramatically determining the course of a given life.

Trevor understands well the biological, psychological, and social forces that may undermine the best of human intentions—deterministic forces represented in the fiction of such English naturalists as George Eliot, Thomas Hardy, and Joseph Conrad—all writers Trevor mentions when talking about his work. To define Trevor's work as "naturalist" would not be inappropriate. Like both nineteenth-century naturalists and twentieth-century modernists, Trevor adopted a pessimistic attitude toward the industrial world, although his view is far less bleak than some critics suppose.

Modernist writers' pessimistic questioning of God and human nature is best represented in double fictions. Trevor's fiction is not unlike that of E.T.A. Hoffmann, Kafka, Dostoyevski, Dickens, Conrad, Joyce, Poe, Melville, Hawthorne, Twain, James, Faulkner, and Flannery O'Connor—all writers depicting Jekyll-Hyde sorts of double figures, mildly or outrageously schizophrenic protagonists with uncertain identities and a hypersensitivity to suffering in a seemingly godless world. The fragmented self struggles for meaning, longs to communicate with others, and feels lost because it is unable to integrate the finite and the infinite, as the Christian philosopher Kierkegaard sees it; the id and the superego, as the agnostic psychoanalyst Freud sees it; the anima and animus, as the mystic Jung sees it.

Moral judgements in the modern age demand difficult choices independent of mindless conformity to religious doctrines—difficult choices that force us to be divided within ourselves and against one another. Neither Catholics nor Protestants have managed to stop the atrocities perpetrated by both sides in Belfast. Joyce criticized the Catholic Church because of disparities between doctrine and the practices of particular Church representatives—disparities that further shake the foundations of religious faith. In Ireland, of course, a particularly dogmatic and stern form of Catholicism was associated with the Christian Brothers' schools. The teacher-brothers lack humanity as Trevor depicts them in his stories—Trevor being, like Joyce, a modernist in his critique of the Church. Trevor did, however, declare in a letter to me that he believes in God. His stories certainly acknowledge spiritual emptiness, materialism, and alienation in the modern age, but they affirm the importance of community, the importance of "connecting" in the Forsterian sense—as husbands and wives, fathers and mothers, and members of society.

Trevor, then, must be considered modernist in terms of his style, his focus on the dark aspects of human nature, and his skeptical attitude toward some representatives of the Church. He should be related to the nineteenth century, however,

when considering his emphasis on deterministic forces undermining human will and the ability to "connect." And let us hope that his compassion and humor prefigure the twenty-first century and a future when his tales will be more fully appreciated.

> **Trevor, then, must be considered modernist in terms of his style, his focus on the dark aspects of human nature, and his skeptical attitude toward some representatives of the Church.**
> **—*Suzanne Morrow Paulson***

Most of Trevor's stories convey a genuine optimism and a love of people—a love based on a profound understanding of suffering, a sympathetic acceptance of human weakness, and shrewd insights into social hierarchies. His interest in the more ludicrous aspects of human nature, alienation, identity, and insanity are best expressed by tragicomedy, and his most brilliant short stories borrow from this genre. He writes an intensely poetic, understated, and ironic fiction—the hallmarks of the modern short story.

What I mean to do here is spotlight representative masterpieces of human insight—masterpieces demanding that Trevor be recognized in America for his singular understanding of personality and his major contributions to the short-story form.

Gary Krist (review date Winter 1995)

SOURCE: "A Thunder of Hooves in the Drawing Room," in *The Hudson Review,* Vol. 47, No. 4, Winter, 1995, pp. 655-60.

[*In the following review, Krist argues that if readers give* Excursions in the Real World *a careful reading, they will learn a great deal about the author.*]

Any rich and active writing life creates by-products—reviews, essays, travel articles, profiles, and other occasional pieces—that accumulate in the odd corners of a writer's opus until they take on substantial heft. If the writer is good enough, these pieces, while perhaps not originally intended to appear between hard covers, may eventually be gathered into a collection and published. If the writer is better than good enough, the collection may even represent a significant literary achievement, the whole cohering despite the varied nature of the parts.

In his latest book, *Excursions in the Real World,* William

Trevor (certainly a writer who can safely be described as "better than good enough") has achieved this kind of organic-seeming miscellany, though one with a difference. Trevor has taken pieces written at various times and for various occasions in his life, supplemented them with new work, and fashioned them into a memoir. The result is a curious hybrid, a memoir not so much of the writer himself or of his milieu, but rather of the various bits of life and art that have somehow left a lasting impression on him. In fact, the person whose life is ostensibly being recalled in these gathered pieces, far from being an overwhelming presence, is actually discernible in them only by an act of inference.

One could have predicted, I suppose, that a writer like Trevor—arguably the English-speaking world's premier practitioner of a certain brand of artistically distanced fiction—would create this kind of elusive autobiography. His work has always seemed to me at odds with the confessional subjectivity of a lot of contemporary literature. In Trevor's fiction, one never senses the author grinding personal axes behind the scenery. A Trevor story represents, above all else, an act of sympathetic imagination, in which the author's sensibility is present only as a tool to bring to life the sensibility of his characters, who are always his true subject. What I've read of Trevor's fiction rarely if ever has the feel of autobiography, so I suppose it makes sense (though a somewhat ironic sense) that the same can be said of his memoirs.

While the book does contain several pieces of conventional autobiography—accounts of the small towns of the author's youth, portraits of his parents and tutors—the bulk of these *Excursions* would find no place in the reminiscences of a more self-involved artist. What Trevor gives us are mostly what he calls "personal fascinations and enthusiasms"—the places, people, and situations that somehow have remained "snagged in the memory." He doesn't write about how these various stimuli affected him or his work. Nor does he draw parallels or contrasts between other characters and himself. In fact, the word "I," so prominent in most literary memoirs, appears with remarkable infrequency here.

But in a chronicle like this one, as the author himself admits, "the recorder cannot remain entirely in the shadows, much as he might wish to do so." And so we do find tantalizing hints of Trevor here and there—in, for instance, the choice of writers he profiles. His selection goes beyond the obvious Irishmen (Joyce, Yeats, Sean O'Casey, and Beckett) to include Somerville and Ross—a pair of upper-class Victorian ladies who collaborated on a travel book called *Through Connemara in a Governess Cart* ("On a dull day, they embellished," he claims)—as well as William Gerhardie, a failed sort of genius who seems to have been his own best reviewer:

> He was ravenous for praise, fearful of even a hint

of criticism. Other writers of the time, sensing the considerable promise of his novels as soon as they appeared, were generous. But this generosity is noticeably most lavish when Gerhardie himself reports it. "What do I hear? Gerhardie? The very man I always wanted to meet," cooed H. G. Wells. "You're a genius," pronounced Shaw.

It's tempting, of course, to try to find hints of self-revelation in these selections. For instance, Trevor writes of Somerville and Ross that

> . . .it was isolation again—the very distance that lay between two upper-class women and the Ireland they wrote about—that permitted their talent to breathe and develop. By chance, or accident of birth, they discovered the perspective that art demands.

Reading these sentences in the venue of a memoir, one can't help wondering whether Trevor is describing himself here as much as he is Somerville and Ross. Is he hinting that his own art has been possible only as a result of a distance kept from the subjects he writes about? Knowing what we know about Trevor's fiction, the answer would seem to be yes. But it's difficult to say for sure, and Trevor is certainly not one to tip his hand in such a matter.

And really, it's only when one decides to give up trying to find the author subtly encoded in these pieces that many of them can be fully enjoyed. Trevor tells some wonderful stories—of pitiful, lost faculty members at the private schools of his youth, of car-battery salesmen trying to make merry in off-season Sussex, of lavishly eccentric toilers in the advertising industry of the early 1960s (Trevor wrote for a while in the offices of Marchant Smith, "one of the greatest copywriters of his time" and the originator of the immortal slogan "Top People Take The Times"). Trevor is as entertainingly deadpan as ever in this book, as when he reports that:

> Briefly I had received a modest weekly wage in return for calling for a designated brand of beer in selected Northside public houses, whether as an encouragement to others or in an effort to establish if the beer was being stocked I never fully ascertained; and since inebriation invariably prevented me from accurately completing the forms I was provided with by the brewery, my assistance was soon dispensed with.

But the tone of the book is by no means universally light. In **"Field of Battle,"** Trevor grapples with the unhappy marriage of his parents, the details of which can only be read between the lines of youthful memory:

The marriage of parents is almost always mysterious: the sensual elements scarcely bear thinking about, the romantic past can only be guessed at, and all such curiosity invariably comes too late. . . . The cold facts, all that is known, tell nothing: what happened, or did not happen, is private territory, a disappointment guarded in life and death.

Trevor does manage, however, to recreate the unseen elements of their marriage—extrapolating the early, innocent entry into romance, the silent discord hidden behind the noise of everyday life, the toll taken by constant moves around the Irish countryside. His parents stayed together through these years solely for the sake of the children, he concludes, and when the children were grown up, they separated, never to meet again—a sad, almost archetypal story in which Trevor finds a kind of heroism:

> [I]n retrospect there is something gallant about their efforts to hold together the family their one-time love had brought into existence. Their perseverance was full of a self-sacrifice that was not apparent while they were making it; and there was a courageous honesty in their refusal to hide from their children the plight their marriage had become. They did not cover up; there was no hypocrisy. . . .

Sometimes Trevor finds in a character from his past an expression of an entire era. **"Assia,"** for instance, begins with a flurry of pop sociology that would undoubtedly have pleased Trevor's old advertising mentor, Marchant Smith:

> The sixties in London had the flavour of a dream. After the drabness of the previous decade, in which nothing more exciting happened than Ban-the-Bomb marches, the Suez fiasco and a dog propelled into space, all of a sudden there was the razzmatazz of Carnaby Street and the E-Type Jag, and smart Mary Quant bringing fashion they could afford to shopgirls and typists. Flower people ran barefoot in the park, James Bond pushed aside the fuddy-duddy heroes who still trailed a Bulldog Drummond sense of decency and a stiff upper lip. Cannabis was in, LSD if you were daring. Sex set up its stall. *Jesus Christ is alive and well,* the graffiti said, *and working on a less ambitious project.*
>
> Fantasy arrived in London in the 1960s. "It's fantastic!" was the cry as wives were swapped at parties and there was dancing without steps. . . . In 1962 a young man in a lounge bar won a wager of a shilling by kissing on the lips a girl who was a stranger to him: she'd have slapped his face in the nineteen fifties, and taken him to court in the nineties. But in the sixties—mid-century breathing space

between the World Wars and AIDS—everybody laughed and anything went.

This is not great prose, perhaps (sometimes even excellent Homer nods, as Horace complained), but it serves as the backdrop to a character sketch of remarkable complexity and mystery. Assia, "tall and beautiful, her features reminiscent of Sophia Loren in a tranquil moment," is an elusive figure— of Russian abstraction, with hints of Israel and Canada mixed in, though no one has quite been able to pin her down about her background. She arrives on the scene married—happily, one supposes—to a poet named David Wevill. "Charming, attractive, unobtrusive, they were Scott Fitzgerald people sixties-style, their innocence brushed over with sophistication, their devotion to one another taken for granted." Assia would do spontaneous, sixties-style things like order roses to be sent to the new wife of her ex-husband (billing them, of course, to her ex). And, though not a liar, she would nevertheless fabricate bountifully: "Liars lie in order to obscure," Trevor writes; "Assia exaggerated only in the interests of what she saw as a greater veracity and, as her voice continued, doubts slipped away."

She tells him of meeting that other remarkable sixties couple—Ted Hughes and Sylvia Plath—and being invited over to tea. One thing leads to another, and soon she is the Other Woman in that famous relationship. It's a typical thing to have happened in that time, Trevor implies, but Plath is hardly a typical person for it to have happened to. She killed herself shortly thereafter—a staggering blow to Assia. And, alas, the times were already changing:

> When Lee Harvey Oswald did his thing it wasn't so good. Nor when Brady and Hindley did theirs. Steven Ward's loveliest lovely was in gaol, the osteopath himself was dead. . . . The seeds of Europe's Vietnam were germinating in Belfast and Derry. With half the decade to go yet, the fun fair was sleazy at the edges.

Much later, Trevor sees Assia again. She is divorced, the mother of a small child, talking of marrying yet again. Trevor advises against marriage—some people seem not to be made for the institution—but she still seems game, still telling her fabulous, half-believable tales. There is, however, a sense of defeat now to her storytelling. And Trevor catches a glimpse of something else underneath:

> "Actually I'm afraid," she murmured, before she smiled again and went away.
>
> A month or so later Assia killed her child and then herself.

But the most revealing portrait here—revealing, that is, of

Trevor and his work—is that of **"The Warden's Wife,"** one Mary *née* Savery (we never learn her married name), spouse of the headmaster of St. Columba's school, where Trevor was a student. "In all sorts of ways," Trevor writes, "it was at St. Columba's where I first became aware that black and white are densities of more complicated grays." And certainly the Warden's wife qualifies as a complicated shade of gray. A shadowy and inscrutable figure on the periphery of school life, shy to the point of mortification, she nonetheless acquires a reputation as a kind of sensualist:

> Tongue-tied among her husband's prefects at the lunchtime High Table, she was quoted as having once referred, out of the blue, to breast-feeding. So the rumour began that beneath an unprepossessing exterior, and perhaps related to her beauty in the past, this woman was more than a little aware of sex, her reference to her breasts as much evidence of it as her interest in "what went on" between her daughter and her followers. That she was allied to a man who was the declared enemy of the sensual life in all its aspects struck none of us as tragedy.

It's the very unlikeliness of her alliance with the headmaster—a cockney buffoon who is an object of fun among his students—that intrigues Trevor about her. She is obviously a serious, intelligent woman. So he wonders about her: "Did she, as she pondered in her flowerbeds, shuffle through her regrets, or wish she had her life over again?"

The answer—if it is an answer—comes only years later, when he reads her obituary in the *Old Columban*. In it he discovers, to his amazement, that during her years at St. Columba's she had become an expert on horse-racing, and regularly attended race-meetings. The realization comes to Trevor as sheer aesthetic delight:

> No one had ever said the Warden's wife was good for a tip; no one had ever imagined her laying an on-course bet. She did not seek inside information from Cog Chapman, whose father had a stables. . . . Yet this woman, who on the face of it had been smudged away to nothing, dwelt profitably on form among the callous prefects at High Table lunches, while her husband held forth about potatoes or recalled the day he met de Valera.

In Trevor's fascination with this woman we can trace the roots of his distinctive vision. Here we find a classic example of his extraordinary ordinary characters, with their extravagant internal lives that serve as refuge from the exterior blandness. If Mary Savery hadn't really existed, I suspect, Trevor would have created her. And it's this aspect of his sensibility—his perception of the outrageous abundance that exists beneath the most mundane surfaces of life—that, to my mind, lifts his work far beyond the limits of a safe and decorous classicism.

This is, in fact, the central irony of Trevor's work—this cosmic joke about the wild opulence lying at the heart of everyday life. And nowhere is the joke more slyly told than in the incantatory conclusion to this most unmemoirlike memoir, in which Trevor imagines Mary Savery's musings during one of her husband's dreary afternoon teas:

> Tea is poured and sponge cake cut, the teacups passed about. Deaf in her solitude, the Warden's wife muses among gaudy silks enriched with hoops and diamonds, half-moons and stars. Held-back wagers are placed, trainers offer a final word, and then the old-faced jockeys leap sprightly to the saddle. In the drawing-room the precious metal pouch is declared once more to have been the repository of holy writings. In the drawing-room there is the thunder of hooves.

Patrick McGrath (review date 8 January 1995)

SOURCE: "Never Did Spider More Hungrily Wait," in *New York Times Book Review,* January 8, 1995, pp. 1, 22.

[*In the following review of* Felicia's Journey, *McGrath praises Trevor's ability to create memorable characters and a satisfying resolution to a dramatic story.*]

William Trevor is an Irishman who lives in England and writes often about the English. He is a moral realist who possesses a deliciously dry wit, a nice sense of the macabre and a warm sympathy for the flawed and suffering characters he creates with such fine psychological precision. There is a conviction implicit in all his work that people divide into predators and prey, that the human condition is marked by secrecy, shame, deceit, blindness and cruelty, and that evil not only exists but also can be understood, and can even be vanquished by unpredictable eruptions of grace.

Human sexuality, with all its vagaries, is one of Mr. Trevor's preoccupations, as is the victimization of the weak. In his new novel, ***Felicia's Journey,*** which won the 1994 Sunday Express Book of the Year Award in Britain, he plays a deceptively simple variation on these themes. In the process he creates a subtle, plausible and infinitely pathetic portrait of a monster.

Felicia's Journey is about an unmarried Irish girl, adrift and friendless in the industrial English Midlands. Felicia has crossed the Irish Sea to search for the young man who made her pregnant before he disappeared. If ever there was a soul at risk, it is Felicia's. With her possessions stuffed into two shopping bags and her heart filled with naïve confidence in the empty promises of the rogue who seduced her, she presents an enticing prospect both for those who would save her and those who would destroy her.

With every passing day her tiny store of money diminishes, and the fetus grows in her womb. She trudges about a landscape of grim industrial parks, knowing only that the man she loves works in the storeroom of a lawn mower factory. As her hopes die, she becomes increasingly vulnerable. She is a weakling, limping lamely behind the herd; it must be only a matter of time before some hungry creature picks her off.

Enter Mr. Hilditch. William Trevor is unsurpassed at creating such characters. Mr. Hilditch is a large, genial, unmarried, middle-aged man who thinks and talks in platitudes and takes great satisfaction in his job as catering manager of a factory. His special pride is the canteen, with its hot meals and puddings for the workers. Mr. Hilditch is the type who spends his Sunday afternoons visiting stately homes and engaging strangers in the sort of mindless chat the English are so good at. He is, it appears, a man of stultifying banality, respectability and mediocrity.

What tips us off to the existence of concealed depths in his psyche—and the possibility of something rather unwholesome going on down there—is his eating. Mr. Hilditch eats constantly. He is very fat as a result. Powerful and massive energies are being sublimated.

So it is with no little alarm that we watch this enormous man begin to focus his attention on the hapless and miserable Felicia. Mr. Hilditch has obviously done this sort of thing before, since he doesn't try to befriend the girl; he is much too cautious to risk frightening her off. Instead he allows her to glimpse the possibility that he might help her, and then, secure in the knowledge that sooner or later she will come to him, he waits. Never did spider more hungrily anticipate fly.

By this stage, the reader is utterly engaged in Felicia's plight and feels frantic but helpless, wanting to cry out to the young woman not to go near this man—to go home, to go anywhere, to flee him. But of course, Felicia does not know the danger she is in. And curiously, neither do we, precisely. For although Mr. Trevor has skillfully persuaded us to believe that Mr. Hilditch is a monster who intends to do Felicia serious harm, he has not been at all specific.

This, in part, is what makes *Felicia's Journey* such a good read: its vague, tantalizing suggestion of unspeakably evil acts being hatched in the black, foul-smelling cellars of Mr. Hilditch's mind and the pleasurable frustration aroused by

the fact that we cannot know, at least not yet, the form these horrors will take.

But were the novel merely an account of Felicia's struggle to avoid the clutches of a man who means to hurt her, it would not sustain such interest. The contest would be ill matched, and Mr. Hilditch would too easily overwhelm his prey. Felicia needs a friend, an ally, if she is to put up a fight and escape being devoured—and she gets one. This ally takes the improbable form of the improbably named Miss Calligary, a black woman who goes door to door with her Bible, spreading news of the "paradise earth" and the wonderful future in store for "the one who dies."

In his fiction Mr. Trevor has always displayed an amused and somewhat ambivalent attitude toward priests and vicars and others of God's representatives on earth. Miss Calligary and her companions at the Gathering House are no exception. Like Mr. Hilditch, they want to lay hold of Felicia and gather her in. With their appearance, therefore, the drama begins to take on the classic outline of a battle for a soul, waged between the forces of good and evil. It's in his human fleshing of these conflicting forces, in his bestowal of these awesome roles to as unlikely a pair as Mr. Hilditch and Miss Calligary, that Mr. Trevor shows just how wise and wry and funny and morally astute an observer of the human comedy he is. Yet despite the absurdity of the antagonists, we never lose sight of the fact that the stakes they are fighting for could not be higher. Felicia is the prize.

At this point Mr. Trevor does something unexpected, and the story becomes much richer than a mere moral chess game, with Felicia as the white queen. Part of the great charm and pleasure of the book is the way it changes form, shaping up at the outset as a Gothic drama in which the uncertain nature of the monster—or, rather, of his projected acts—seems central, then turning into a sort of passion play, with angels squaring off against a demon, before finally settling to explore its true theme. This is the depiction of a severe and terrible personality disorder, and the question of whether one so afflicted might find, if not redemption, at least a scrap of saving grace.

Mr. Trevor does answer this difficult question, and his answer is suitably complicated and dramatic. For this is a story in which not only innocence and aggression are pitted against each other, but also terror and a sort of hope. There is much darkness here, but it is not unrelieved; nor do these characters and the bizarre string of events that entangles them strain credulity for a moment. Rather the reverse. They are frighteningly real.

The resolution the novel arrives at, the answer to its central question, is deeply right and satisfying. *Felicia's Journey* confirms the maxim that to understand all is to forgive all, and it demonstrates as well that in hands like Mr. Trevor's, fiction is a tool without equal for creating such understanding.

James Bowman (review date 6 March 1995)

SOURCE: "An Improbable Monster," in *National Review,* Vol. XLVII, No. 4, March 6, 1995, pp. 67-8.

[*In the following review, Bowman argues that despite Trevor's romantic depiction of the homeless,* Felicia's Journey *is well written.*]

In Britain, William Trevor's 13th novel and 21st book of fiction won the *Sunday Express* "Book of the Year" award and the Whitbread Prize. Now published in the U.S., *Felicia's Journey* should be taken as stating a most persuasive case on behalf of its 67-year-old Irish author, who has long lived in England but continues to write about both his native and his adoptive countries, as one of the two or three best living writers of fiction in English. If you haven't read him yet, you should read him now.

The Felicia of the tale is an Irish girl of 18 who lives with her father and three brothers. She shares a room with and looks after a centenarian great-grandmother widowed in the Easter rising of 1916. Unemployed and not remarkably bright or pretty, she is seduced by a young man called Johnny Lysaght who soon after goes off to England without leaving an address. Her Irish patriot father thinks he has joined the British army, but she believes his story that he works in a lawnmower factory in the Midlands. Learning she is pregnant, she leaves home to seek him there without telling anyone. Mr. Hilditch, the fat, middle-aged bachelor who is the catering manager in the first factory she tries, offers to help her, and it soon emerges that Felicia has more to worry about than being seduced and abandoned.

That Hilditch is an improbable monster emerges only very gradually during the course of this improbable thriller. For the most part his twisted psychopathology is invisible, and, absent the Grand Guignol accoutrements of the Hollywood serial killer, he becomes a study in the banality of evil. To Felicia he "isn't a man you can be alarmed about for long" because he is so reassuringly bland and ordinary—albeit with a kind of ordinariness that is new to her, on her first trip out of Ireland. She finds the mind-numbing clichés of the lower-middle class English demotic, for which Trevor has an incomparable ear, fresh and comforting, as he tells her about himself:

> "I've had a regimental career myself. The army's in my blood, as you might say."

> "You're not in the army now?"

> "I came out when Ada was first ailing. She needed care, more care than I could give, having regimental duties. No, I still help the regiment out, but it's office stuff now."

> "At the factory where I met you—"

> "Oh, no, no. No, not at all. I happened to call in there to see a friend. Well, as a matter of fact, to tell him Ada was going into hospital. People like to know a thing like that. No, I keep things straight for the regiment on the bookkeeping side now. Gets me out of the house, Ada says."

Again Felicia nods.

> "You'd stagnate if you didn't, Felicia. You'd stagnate in a big house, caring for an invalid wife, nursing really."

> "Your wife's an invalid?"

> "Best to think of Ada as that. Best for Ada, she says herself, best for me. It's what it amounts to, as a matter of honest fact, no good denying it, no good pulling the wool. You follow me, Felicia?"

> "Yes, I do."

> "If you face the facts you can take them in your stride. I had a sergeant-major under me said that, top-class man. You meet all sorts in a regimental career."

Everything here is a lie—Ada, the invalid wife, the nursing, the hospital, the regimental career, the friend at the factory, the sergeant-major. But somehow it is rendered retrospectively plausible by leading up to that humbly respectable moral resolve to "face the facts." That is how Trevor's characteristic irony works. When, later, Hilditch squeezes out a few tears for the imaginary death of the imaginary wife, Felicia is ashamed for being mistrustful of him. "No one else had been so concerned" for her plight, she reflects. And with a jolt we realize that she is right.

It takes a writer with the highest gifts to do things like that. Or delicately to anatomize Felicia's reminiscence of Johnny and her feeling of

> a call to account for the happiness she had so recklessly indulged in. "Don't worry about that side of things," he had reassured her once, as they hurried through the Mandeville woods. "All that's taken

care of by myself." Her face went red when he said it, but she was glad he had. "There's nothing wrong in it," he murmured, saying more, "nothing wrong in it when two people love one another." Yet the night she wrote the letter she felt that maybe, after all, there had been: the old-fashioned sin you had to confess if you went to Confession; the sin of being greedy, the sin of not being patient. And why should she have supposed that the happiness his love had given her was her due, and free?

That is magical writing. The direct quotation breaks off after Johnny is remembered to have said "There's nothing wrong in it" and the prose itself takes on the shyness of the girl as it pauses a moment ("saying more") before it can proceed to the hugely significant use of the word "love." We know at once that this is the only time the boy used it. Felicia's preoccupation with the past gives her something in common with her ga-ga great granny who lives, as Philip Larkin puts it, "not here and now but where all happened once." It helps her go on believing that "only being together, only their love, can bring redemption."

The novel can be read as an account of competing romanticisms. Besides Felicia's mooning over the worthless Johnny, there is her father's romance of the Irish revolution and the part in it taken by the now helpless old lady in her unimaginably remote girlhood. "Not much older than yourself she was," he tells Felicia, "when the lads went off, knowing the color of their duty. Three days later and she's a widow. She wasn't married a month and he was gone. Don't talk to me of some back-street romance, girl." Mr. Hilditch, too, is a romantic who listens to the love songs of the Forties and Fifties on his gramophone of an evening. His everyday sentimentalism is capable of appalling acts at the same time that it inspires trust in victims like Felicia: victims who now inhabit in his mind a macabre "Memory Lane."

The only flaw in this subtlest and most beautifully written of thrillers is that Trevor has his own streak of romanticism—particularly about the street people whose lives Felicia drops into and out of again. It seems to me a weakness in the book, a stretch to ask us to accept that Felicia, without the following wind of drugs, alcohol, or disease, should have made such haste to join those so without resources of intelligence or industry as to have identified themselves (at ages well in advance of hers) as life's big losers. They make a convenient symbolic association for poor Felicia, but they do not ring true, except as very temporary companions when she is at her lowest and unluckiest.

Perhaps their purpose is to prevent the novel from committing itself too completely to the slow but inexorable working out of a species of divine retribution for the sins of Mr.

Hilditch. With typically well-judged irony, Trevor shows him maddened by the continued importunities of the "God-botherers" among whom Felicia briefly sojourns—though it is only in his guilty imaginings that they have any ulterior motive beyond converting him to their weird cult, the Gatherers. As a tale of justice it would otherwise be too neat for modern tastes. But William Trevor is too good a writer not to make it a tale of justice as well as a compassionate, melancholy meditation on human wretchedness and the dark places in the heart.

Sara Maitland (review date 19 May 1995)

SOURCE: "A Most Improbable Beauty," in *Commonweal*, Vol. CXXII, No. 10, May 19, 1995, pp. 31-2.

[*In the following review, Maitland faults the conclusion of* Felicia's Journey, *but still finds the work powerful and engaging.*]

William Trevor is an eminent British writer, claimed—very properly—by the British literary establishment; winner of many of the most prestigious British literary awards. But importantly, Trevor is not British, but Irish—he was born in County Cork in 1928, brought up in provincial Ireland, and educated at Trinity College, Dublin. He is a member of the Irish Academy of Letters. He is a very Irish writer.

I simplify—there are, of course, many kinds of Irish writers. Ireland has produced some of the finest English prose writings and it would be ridiculous to try and claim that they all shared some profound Celtic singleness of style or intention. Nonetheless there is a strain in contemporary British writing which can fairly be called "Irish" and Trevor belongs in that tradition. It is above all a strain of an intense, lyrical emotion—a determination to make the reader *feel*; be moved by mundanity, by careful concentration on the little details of daily life.

Trevor is the most wonderful writer: the experience of actually being in the act of reading *Felicia's Journey* is extraordinary. "Page-turning" usually applies to plot but that is not what kept me utterly inside this novel—it was something about having to pay attention. *Felicia's Journey* is both demanding and exhilarating, frequently almost unbearable; sometimes even, the more intellectual part of this reader at least wanted to resist so blatant an attempt to have her heart wrung. It is more like the experience of reading poetry or the works of certain spiritual writers—a profound emotional engagement, coupled by a driving sense that something extremely important is going on.

Is that not enough? In the light of such a literary experience it may be unreasonable to mention that after you have staggered out from under this enchantment you may find yourself wondering whether it was all worth it.

Felicia's Journey is a novel about innocence. Felicia is, in the old-fashioned sense of the word, "simple." Pregnant, motherless, she leaves her small, dead-end Irish town in search of the father of her child who she faithfully believes loves her and has failed to learn of her plight only through the evil machinations of his mother. She has no address and rather inadequate clues. Her doomed journey takes her through the once industrial and now decayed heartland of northern England, where pathetic people live broken lives.

Trevor has the ability to present these lives without any tone of superiority—he neither minimizes nor sentimentalizes the individual brokenness, the structural despair and the darkness that both breed. But even here, he argues with passion, even at the extremes of human experience there is sweetness, there is kindness, generosity, and—by implication at least—grace.

Felicia comes from a background of harsh but clear values; formed and shaped by the heroic violence of Ireland. Her father's pride in his bedridden grandmother—the wife of a dead activist of the Easter Rising—strips Felicia of the ease of normal youth. Her father half-hopes her unemployment and consequent narrowness of aspiration will continue so that the old lady can be cared for properly. He hates his daughter's lover, not so much because of his morality but because of a rumor, neither denied nor proven by the story, that the man has joined the British army. Felicia's consciousness is filled with a mixture of a longing for love and life—but a life within the structures of this society—and a strange assortment of Catholic religious images.

She is thus totally ill-equipped to confront or even manage the destabilized, fragmented social reality in which she finds herself in England. The contrast here is finely managed: neither the rigidity of her Irish hometown community nor the complete loss of community, the sense that people can and do disappear forever in the wastelands, are offered to the reader as good, merely as different, contrasting sorrows. Nonetheless, everyone Felicia encounters has an agenda of manipulation and madness, while she is "pure" in her quest and in her heart.

Inevitably she enters hell, not a hell of her own making, but a hell provoked by her own simplicity (or, one might think, though Trevor would not say so, her stupidity). It is impossible to describe the harrowing—in all senses—of this hell without giving away the plot; and as Trevor almost manages not to do so himself (the unfolding is elliptical and mysterious and known only to the insane and the deluded), it would be mean of me to do so. But at the heart of the novel is a

genuine darkness, a man so truly dreadful that one is moved weirdly to compassion for him. Trevor, with a moral integrity that is quite extraordinary, manages to explain this terror without ever "explaining it away" or minimizing or excusing. It is still ghastly, yet it is not beyond compassion, beyond our recognition of the cruelty of chance, the arbitrary nature of evil.

By the end of the novel "a terrible beauty is born." Felicia has become a street person, and has found there a calm, an almost joyful serenity and acceptance of herself and of her life. Felicia's fate, or redemption, if it is a redemption, if she needed redeeming, is so profoundly unacceptable that it is deeply disturbing, moving, touching. Disturbed, moved, touched, I still wanted to protest: to protest at Trevor's apparent acceptance that this is good enough—good enough for Felicia, good enough for any young innocent person. By claiming, through the mystery-weighted intensity of the prose, that there is a deep spiritual truth here, Trevor forces himself into a corner—a solution that might just be good enough for the individual he has described, has become a universal proclamation. Political busy-bodies like me have to protest at the magical loveliness of the end. I cannot believe it. I cannot believe that the "lost" in this sense—those lost without consent, through evil and the indifference of society—are or should be contented; or that we, in the comfort of our literary sensibilities, should be allowed to find this place of desolation so beautiful.

Felicia is as a lamb to the slaughter. This may be true, it may be how the lives of too many innocent and not very bright women are, but it should not be held up as beautiful and lovely.

Trevor makes it beautiful. As reader I cannot but admire this. As moralist I must protest. Which frame of reference should I bring to such a novel? To this novel, which forces the question more powerfully than anything I have read in a long time?

Wendy Lesser (review date 20 October 1996)
SOURCE: "The Casualties of Deception," in *New York Times Book Review,* October 20, 1996, p. 15.

[*In the following review, Lesser considers the concepts of truth and self-knowledge in* After Rain.]

The great novels draw you in entirely, it seems, so that while you are reading them you forget you ever had another life. But the great short stories, in my experience, keep you balanced in midair, suspended somewhere between the world you normally inhabit and the world briefly illuminated by the author. You see them both at once and you feel them both at once: the emotions generated in you by the story carry over instantly and applicably to the life outside the book. This is why the best short stories can afford to be inconclusive. You, the reader, complete them by joining them back to your life—a life that, because it too is inconclusive, enables you to recognize the truth of the fictional pattern.

Everyone will have his own list of the best short stories. Mine includes most of Chekhov, one or two by James Joyce, a dozen or more from D. H. Lawrence and—in this same vein—a healthy selection from William Trevor. This Irishborn, English-domiciled writer, who is also an excellent novelist, gave us his *Collected Stories* a few years back. Now, as if to assure us that the well is far from dry, he offers a luminously disturbing new collection, *After Rain.*

Each of the 12 stories in this volume hinges on lying or concealment or omission of the truth. Deceptions and evasions permeate the book, from the brilliant opening story. **"The Piano Tuner's Wives"**—in which a blind man's second wife lies about reality in order to obliterate the visual memories left him by his first wife—to the final **"Marrying Damian,"** in which an elderly couple doesn't quarrel "because ours are the dog days of marriage and there aren't enough left to waste: a dangerous ground has long ago been charted and is avoided now."

Both lying and its evil twin, excessive truth-telling are linked in these stories to various acts of cruelty—little cruelties (like a grown son's failure to attend the birthday dinner planned for him by his doting parents) as well as more significant crimes, ranging from burglary and fraud to sectarian violence and random homicide. But deception's major casualty, as might be expected, is the covenant of marriage. Sprinkled among these dozen stories are seven divorces, six cases of adultery, five instances of explicit sexual jealousy, two or three enduring but loveless marriages and four children from broken homes.

Mr. Trevor, though, is no simple-minded advocate of "family values," and what he does with this material is entirely other than what an indignant sociologist or a preaching moralist would do. If these stories are mainly quite sad, lacking the dark, ironic, Graham-Greene-style wit that colors most of Mr. Trevor's novels, they are nonetheless open-ended. And that absence of closure gives them something approaching optimism—if not the optimism of hope, then at any rate that of fairness. People suffer deeply in most of these stories, and many of them suffer unjustly, but Mr. Trevor never allows us to see only the victim's viewpoint. There is always another perspective, another interpretation, and with that distance comes the possibility of release, not only for us but for the suffering character as well. In a way, these stories are like a complicated, infinitely subtle, delicately inflected rendering of the Freudian notion that self-knowledge might

bring freedom. But for this to be a Trevor truth, it must remain conditional.

The most overt example is the title story, **"After Rain,"** which follows 30-year-old Harriet (one of those four children of divorce) on her solitary vacation in Italy. The title phrase itself refers to her brief but intense moment of revelation about the failures in her emotional life: "The rain has stopped when Harriet leaves the church, the air is fresher. Too slick and glib, to use her love affairs to restore her faith in love: that thought is there mysteriously. She has cheated in her love affairs: that comes from nowhere too."

Not content with giving her this degree of insight, the author intensifies Harriet's discovery by allowing her to connect it with a painting she has just seen in the church. "While she stands alone among the dripping vines she cannot make a connection that she knows is there. There is a blankness in her thoughts, a density that feels like muddle also, until she realizes: the Annunciation was painted after rain. Its distant landscape, glimpsed through arches, has the temporary look that she is seeing now. It was after rain that the angel came."

"After Rain" is more schematic than most of Mr. Trevor's stories, and as such is not one of my favorites. But what it beautifully illustrates is his usual ability to be both inside and outside the character at once. Here he gives that gift of double perception to Harriet herself: she experiences "blankness," "muddle," and then an annunciation. Elsewhere he gives it only to us—a strategy that is less therapeutic for the characters, perhaps, but somehow more moving.

I'm thinking for instance, of the last paragraph in **"The Piano Tuner's Wives,"** where the authorial voice comes in from the outside to adjudicate between the first wife, Violet, and her jealous successor, Belle. Commenting on the second wife's lying contradiction of the first wife's descriptions of reality, Mr. Trevor calmly concludes: "Belle could not be blamed for making her claim, and claims could not be made without damage or destruction. Belle would win in the end because the living always do. And that seemed fair also, since Violet had won in the beginning and had had the better years."

This is not information that is available to any of the principal characters in the story: the piano tuner is blind and therefore cannot perceive the lies; Violet is dead and cannot dispute them; Belle is the sort of person who is incapable of stepping this far back from her situation. And yet something in the language of the observations—the past tense specificity of "that seemed fair," the colloquial formulation in "had the better years"—works directly against the all knowing voice of "claims could not be made without damage" or "Belle would win in the end." The implication is that Mr. Trevor's authorial knowledge is somehow contingent on the thoughts and expressions of his fictional creations, not self-sustaining and absolute. Like the blind piano tuner, he needs to listen to what his characters tell him: he may draw his own conclusions from their lies or truths, but he can have no direct, supervisory access to their reality.

Because of this gap, this space between author's knowledge and character's perception, William Trevor's stories have room to breathe. They are like something alive, shifting and changing each time you read them. The first time you read **"A Day,"** about an alcoholic wife and an adulterous husband, you may blame him for her condition. The next time you may listen closely to the story's last line—"He is gentle when he carries her, as he always is"—and see him as the daily victim of her routine heavy drinking. The third time you may wonder if she has imagined the infidelity, or at least the extent of it. The fourth time you may decide that his gentle, tacit encouragement of her oblivion is in fact the worst aspect of his cruelty. And so on.

To free one's characters from the wheel of determinism is the greatest gift an author can give, and one of the rarest. It can't be done with any *deus ex machina* tricks, or we wouldn't believe it. The release, when it comes, needs to be true to the tragic reality of the story—and by extension, to our own tragic reality. The emotion we are left with can contain resignation but can't be limited to it, it can include hope, but not at the risk of denying pain. William Trevor knows all this. What is more remarkable is the way he infuses this authorial knowledge into his stories, so that his own role in their creation fades to invisibility, leaving us in the presence of something very much like life.

Mary Fitzgerald-Hoyt (review date Spring 1997)

SOURCE: "Wonderment and Serenity" in *Irish Literary Supplement,* Vol. 16, No. 1, Spring, 1997, p. 4.

[*In the following review, Fitzgerald-Hoyt argues that Trevor achieves a coherency in the twelve stories about revelations contained in the collection* After Rain.]

In the title story of William Trevor's stunning new collection, *After Rain,* a young woman who has traveled to Italy to come to terms with a failed love affair as well as a troubled family past reflects upon a painting of the Annunciation in the church of Santa Fabiola:

> The Virgin looks alarmed, right hand arresting her visitor's advance. Beyond—background to the encounter—there are gracious arches, a balustrade and

then the sky and hills. There is a soundlessness about the picture, the silence of a mystery: no words are spoken in this captured moment, what's said between the two has already been spoken.

The scene is echoed on the book's dust jacket: a detail from a fifteenth-century Annunciation by Fra Bartolommeo and Mariotto Albertinelli focuses upon the angel's serious face and upraised, faintly minatory finger; the Virgin's hand seems to attempt to ward him off, to reject his message. Behind these poised figures stretches an Italian landscape of subdued beauty, the watery sunlight unable to illuminate the suppressed drama of the clustered buildings and distant hills.

Annunciation is an appropriate trope for these twelve stories, for all contain moments of revelation for reader and character alike. But, as implied in the Virgin's reluctant hand, annunciations can be wrenching experiences, their news unwelcome.

Ten of these stories previously appeared in magazines, yet the collection is nevertheless cohesive. Their varied settings—Ireland, England, Italy, Northern Ireland—and their diverse characters have in common a theme that pervades all of Trevor's fiction: people's abortive attempts to love and their success in damaging each other. The "annunciations" they undergo are often bitter and painful revelations. The eponymous **"Gilbert's Mother"** is convinced that her mentally disturbed son is a murderer, but without evidence, she is stymied. The parents in **"Marrying Damian,"** who were once amused by their philandering, manipulative friend, realize their insensitivity to his victims only after it becomes apparent that their own daughter will be his next. The physically blind husband of **"The Piano Tuner's Wives"** must depend on his wives to describe a world he cannot see, but his second wife, who becomes a bride at 59, is so resentful of and threatened by her deceased predecessor that she attempts to obliterate her husband's memories. Her descriptions of the places he has visited with his first wife are deliberate falsehoods that challenge and undermine his cherished recollections.

The displaced children, disaffected spouses, and alienated souls that inhabit so much of Trevor's world are much in evidence in *After Rain,* but this collection offers fresh perspectives, new characters. **"The Potato Dealer"** plays a new variation on such earlier stories as **"Teresa's Wedding"** and **"Kathleen's Field"**, where Irish daughters become pawns in the face of social convention and economic exigency. Yet here, Ellie, pregnant as the result of an affair with a curate and pressured into a loveless marriage by her rigid family, worsens an already bleak situation. The unromantic potato dealer who has married her in exchange for money and land comes to love her child, who believes him to be her father. Ellie's insistence that the child be told the truth is ultimately selfish, the unburdening of her mind rendering her daughter the object of gossip and wounding her husband's pride and self-esteem.

Since the 1970s, perhaps the major preoccupation of Trevor's Irish fiction has been the consequences of colonialism, including the tragedies wrought by political violence. The finest story in this collection, **"Lost Ground,"** first appeared in *The New Yorker* in 1992. Its reappearance is both an aesthetic delight and a sad commentary on contemporary Northern Irish history, for in the recent past it seemed that this harrowing tale of an Ulster Protestant family might become historical fiction rather than a installment of the current "news from Ireland". The aptly-named Milton, son of a militantly Unionist family, sees or imagines a vision of St. Rosa, and sets out to "justify the ways of God" to humanity by embarking on a peacemaking mission. But his mission embarrasses his family, who through their silence become complicit when his own brother murders him. At once a haunting tale of a gentle soul's destruction and an allegory of Northern Irish history, **"Lost Ground"** recalls such Trevor masterpieces as **"The News From Ireland"** and *The Silence in the Garden.*

On the back cover of *After Rain,* the aforementioned "Annunciation" is reproduced in its entirety, and the shift in perspective changes everything: now we see the Virgin's modest face and gentle, downcast eyes; the benedictory presence of God the Father. The landscape that loomed so large in the detail now fades into the distant background. Similarly, when Harriet, the unhappy protagonist in the title story, looks more closely at *her* painted Annunciation, her perspective shifts: "It isn't alarm in the Virgin's eyes, it's wonderment. In another moment there'll be serenity." This dual perspective is also an appropriate assessment of Trevor's artistry, for his closely observed, deeply compassionate stories winkle out the Virgin's reluctance, the myriad doubts, fears, and petty dishonesties that define our daily lives. Yet these painful annunciations burst upon us in subtle, ironic, beautifully realized prose. And therein lie both wonderment and serenity.

FURTHER READING

Criticism

Beards, Richard D. A Review of *Fools of Fortune* and *The Stories of William Trevor. World Literature Today* 58, No. 3 (Summer 1984): 416-17.
    Praises Trevor's skill as a story teller.

Bonaccorso, Richard. "Not Noticing History: Two Tales By William Trevor." *Connecticut Review* XVIII, No. 1 (Spring 1996): 21-7.
    Considers the role of history in Trevor's short stories "Beyond the Pale" and "The News from Ireland."

Coad, David. A Review of *Felicia's Journey. World Literature Today* 69, No. 3 (Summer 1995): 585.
    Praises the style and structure of *Felicia's Journey.*

Doherty, Francis. "William Trevor's 'A Meeting in Middle Age' and Romantic Irony." *Journal of the Short Story in English,* 16 (Spring 1997): 19-28.
    Compares Trevor's short story "A Meeting in Middle Age" with James Joyce's story "A Painful Case," arguing that while Joyce presents tragedy, Trevor offers comedy.

Haughey, Jim. "Joyce and Trevor's Dubliners: The Legacy of Colonialism." *Studies in Short Fiction* 32, No. 3 (Summer 1995): 355-65.
    Argues that although Trevor and James Joyce wrote during different periods in Irish history, they arrive at similar opinions concerning the source of Irish problems.

Lasdun, James. "A Genius for Misery." *Times Literary Supplement,* No. 4878 (27 September 1996): 23.
    Reviews *After Rain* and argues that while Trevor exhibits many faults as a short story writer, he is unrivaled in his portrayal of unhappiness.

Mittleman, Leslie B. A Review of *The News from Ireland and Other Stories. World Literature Today* 61, No. 2 (Spring 1987): 286.
    Compares Trevor's work with that of James Joyce.

Mona Van Duyn

1921-

American poet.

The following entry presents an overview of Van Duyn's career through 1994. For further information on her life and works, see *CLC,* Volumes 3, 7, and 63.

INTRODUCTION

Van Duyn's verse reflects intense emotions and thoughts beneath a placid surface of domestic life. In strictly metered poems that often recount such mundane events as trips to the zoo, hospital visits, and grocery shopping, Van Duyn reveals a constant struggle with time and relationships. The poet commented in an interview that "one of my major obsessive themes was the idea of time as a taking away of things and love and art as the holders and keepers of things." In her work, Van Duyn endeavors to perfect both love and art, thereby maintaining the aspects of life that time erodes. Although they often address such topics as a failing marriage and stressful interactions with one's aging parents, Van Duyn's poems remain essentially optimistic, focusing on the preservation rather than the devastation of relationships. While occasionally rendered in a colloquial voice, Van Duyn's verse is most often distinguished by references to classical and eighteenth-century poetry, long lines, and complex rhyme schemes.

Biographical Information

Van Duyn was born May 9, 1921, in Waterloo, Iowa. She attended Iowa State Teachers College, now the University of Northern Iowa, where she was awarded a B.A. in 1942 and an M.A. in 1943. The same year she completed her master's degree, Van Duyn married Jarvis A. Thurston, a professor of English. She has worked as an educator at the State University of Iowa, the University of Louisville, Washington University, and University College, and has been a poet in residence at the Breadloaf Writing Conference. In addition to numerous other awards and honors, Van Duyn was granted a National Book Award for Poetry in 1971 for *To See, To Take* (1970), received the Pulitzer Prize for *Near Changes* (1990) in 1991, and was named U.S. Poet Laureate in 1992.

Major Works

In her first collection of poetry, *Valentines to the Wide World* (1959), Van Duyn introduces many themes that she would develop throughout her career. In the title poem, which ad-

dresses a child's loss of innocence, the speaker discusses the possibility of rebuilding the child's worldview of hope and trust through art; Van Duyn suggests that an artist can recapture that which has been lost simply by re-creating it. The world of art, Van Duyn implies, can therefore justify the trials and disappointments of life. The poet also explores her recurring theme of marriage in *Valentines to the Wide World.* In the poem "Toward a Definition of Marriage," for example, she describes wedlock as a "duel of amateurs" that should endure despite hardships, emphasizing her belief that marriage is an essential component of civilized society. The title poem of Van Duyn's second volume of verse, *A Time of Bees* (1964), relates a story of bees that have died in the walls of a married couple's house. As the husband and a scientist-friend sift through the dead insects, collecting enzymes from their flight-wing muscles for an experiment, the wife watches, identifying with the few bees still fighting to live. The speaker views this episode as a clear illustration of the irreconcilable differences between men and women. Other poems in *A Time of Bees* deal with friendship, gardening, and mental illness. Considered until *A Time of Bees* as a "poet's poet," Van Duyn gained a wider audience with her next book, *To See, To Take.* The best-known poems in this collection are written in response to William Butler Yeats's sonnet "Leda and the Swan." "Leda" and "Leda Reconsidered" paint a less romantic picture of the myth than Yeats's elevated version. Van Duyn's lovers are perpetual strangers, destined to wrestle with the complexities of their relationship. Again, man and woman have little in common, but submit to love and its inherent difficulties. The title poem in *Letters From a Father and Other Poems* (1982), written in the form of six letters, describes in candid detail the physical ailments of the poet's aging parents and the symptoms that foreshadow their imminent death. A gift from their daughter, however, restores their interest in life. In *Near Changes,* Van Duyn's Pulitzer prize-winning collection, she again treats such topics as love, marriage, friendship, aging, and nature, but the poems are lighter in tone than her earlier works, aiming more at illuminating certain aspects of each topic rather than at communicating a sense of dissatisfaction or conflict. *If It Be Not I: Collected Poems, 1959-1982* (1992) contains all of Van Duyn's previously published collected works up to, but not including, *Near Changes.* *Firefall* (1992), according to William Logan, "is very much a book of elegy and farewell, a catalogue of the ills and complaints of age, the losses endured and the losses still to be faced." In this volume, Van Duyn explores familiar subjects such as love, art, and death through elegy, epistle, interpretive responses to well-known poems by W. B. Yeats, T. S. Eliot, W. H. Auden, and Robert Frost, and experiments with "minimalist" sonnets, a variation of the traditional forms.

Critical Reception

Many critics labeled *A Time of Bees,* as well as many of Van Duyn's other works, "domestic," including James Dickey, who observed: "[Van Duyn] is a master . . . of the exasperated-but-loving, intelligent-housewife tone." David Kalstone noted: "Every poem [in *To See, To Take*] staves off the executioner, like the home canning to which [Van Duyn] compares her work." *To See, To Take*'s straightforward, often wry poems prompted Thomas H. Landess to dub Van Duyn a "tough-minded" poet. He added: "I can think of no contemporary poet who looks at the world with a steadier eye than does Mona Van Duyn. Not only does she fail to flinch in the face of what is distasteful or awry, but more importantly she never has visions." *Letters From a Father,* published twelve years after *To See, To Take,* reinforced Van Duyn's reputation as a "tough-minded" poet. Robert Hass noted that the "detail [in *Letters to a Father*] is potentially gruesome, the story potentially sentimental, but there is something in the implied attitude of the daughter—her clear eye, amusement, repugnancy, fidelity—that complicates the whole poem and brings it alive, and it gets at an area of human experience that literature—outside of Samuel Beckett—has hardly touched." Alfred Corn has asserted that for Van Duyn to have maintained her affirmations of the powers of love and art

into the latter part of her career is a notable achievement. In assessing *Near Changes,* Corn declared: "To be older, tired, and still 'pleasure-hoping'; to be realistic and also subject to transcendent intuitions; to weigh the claims of love along with the claims of poetry; this is the vision informing *Near Changes.* During the past several decades Mona Van Duyn has assembled, in a language at once beautiful and exact, one of the most convincing bodies of work in our poetry, a poetry that explores, as [Wallace] Stevens put it, '. . . the metaphysical changes that occur, / Merely in living as and where we live.'"

PRINCIPAL WORKS

Valentines to the Wide World (poetry) 1959
A Time of Bees (poetry) 1964
To See, To Take (poetry) 1970
Bedtime Stories (poetry) 1972
Merciful Disguises: Poems Published and Unpublished (poetry) 1973
Letters from a Father and Other Poems (poetry) 1982
Near Changes (poetry) 1990
Black Method (poetry) 1991
**If It Be Not I: Collected Poems 1959-1982* (poetry) 1992
Firefall (poetry) 1992

*Includes the collections *Valentines to the Wide World, A Time of Bees, To See, To Take, Bedtime Stories, Merciful Disguises: Poems Published and Unpublished,* and *Letters from a Father and Other Poems.*

CRITICISM

John Woods (review date April 1960)

SOURCE: "The Teeming Catalogue," in *Poetry,* Vol. 96, No. 1, April, 1960, pp. 47-51.

[*In the following excerpt, Woods surveys some of the poems in* Valentines to the Wide World.]

Mona Van Duyn appears to be a fully-engaged poet. She is not the house organ of any special lobby, but is trying on several attitudes, several voices [in ***Valentines to the Wide World***].

About poetry she writes:

> But what I find most useful is the poem. To find
> some spot on the surface and then bear down until

the skin can't stand the tension and breaks under it
. . .

            Only the poem
is strong enough to make the initial rupture . . .
And I've never seen anything like it for making
    you think
that to spend your life on such old premises is a
privilege.

I am sure that some of her passages are mistakes. In Part Three of **"To My Godson, On His Christening,"** she writes:

Oh, we know our tongue tollings, baskets of
wellwishes, won't
keep you back from your life. Still burnt from
birth, you jump
toward that fire. Yet the pause we've programmed
here is misleading,
whips me (balky, strange to the course and the
speeding)
off, in a halter of words, to run for your meaning.

Although "Each skull encloses / trinkets, museums of rarities, whole zoos of wishes," the mind has a limited willingness to catalogue such variety.

These poems are committed, also, to love, to love of the world. "Love is that lovely play / that makes us and keeps us," the eight-year-old girl is told. In her third **"Valentine to the Wide World,"** she states that "Beauty is merciless and intemperate", but that one "against that rage slowly may learn to pit / love and art, which are compassionate".

In **"The Gentle Snorer,"** when two had "dimmed to silence" in a Maine retreat, a three-weeks cabin guest brought back the world, as he snored. He "sipped the succulent air", and "sleeping, he mentioned death / and celebrated breath".

He went back home. The water flapped the shore.
A thousand bugs drilled at the darkness. Over
the lake a loon howled. Nothing spoke up for us,
salvagers always of what we have always lost;
and we thought what the night needed was more
    of man,
he left us so partisan.

W. D. Snodgrass (review date Spring 1960)

SOURCE: "Four Gentlemen, Two Ladies," in *The Hudson Review*, Vol. 13, No. 1, Spring, 1960, pp. 120-31.

[*In the following excerpt, Snodgrass provides a favorable appraisal of* Valentines to the Wide World.]

At least in this present book, there are no large efforts comparable to Scott's "Memento" or "The U.S. Sailor with the Japanese Skull"; consequently there are no comparable major triumphs. At the same time, there are none of the failures or half-resolved poems; each of these poems seems achieved and delightful. Again, in developing her style, [Van Duyn] has not pushed (like Scott) toward a gnarled and crabbed lyricism; she moves instead toward a discursive style in which she tempers her natural awkward prosiness with a quiet and eccentric music. The result is something quite airy, peculiar and gracious. Here is the largest part of one of her poems on the christening of a godson:

I've thought that the dream of the world is to
    bring, and again bring,
out of a chaos of same, the irreplaceable thing,
so, when it dies, we may clap for that brilliant
    wasting. . . .

This black bubble eye of a pike, ringed with gold,
that neck-wattle, leaf veining, shell crimp,
    tailfeather, holds
marvel enough. But it's we who're the perfect,
    pure manifold.

Each sculp of feature is sole. Each skull encloses
trinkets, museums of rarities, whole zoos of
    wishes.
No one's repeated. We're spent; earth is dazzled
    with losses.

Farewell and farewell and farewell; yet we honor
    each going
with a feast of awareness whose richest flavor is
    knowing
our breed as snowflake, ourselves as yesterday's
    snowing.

And there's always something new under the sun
that warms toward our thaw. Look, the gifted air
    swarms
with it, falls from the weight of it, all those
    shapes, storms

of fresh possibilities. Now spindling down, we see
    one
who'll drift near us. With special pleasure we
    watch you come.

A long quotation; yet this language, so generous finally, makes so few claims for itself that shorter quotations would scarcely represent it.

Nearly all the poems in this book deal with love, marriage, children—with the common domestic problems. That is a sharp limitation upon the book. As Rilke tells us, for the poet whose aim is praise, the great test is how much of the world's misery and sorrow can be digested into that praise. It is not that Miss Van Duyn ignores the suffering in her material— it is only that her material excludes such wide realms of experience. Yet, sometimes it is good to know one's limits. . . . Miss Van Duyn, trying for so much less, always gives a sense of some significance, and (because of her range of diction, which can describe birth in paratrooper's terms, or marriage as a World's Fair landfill) of a fairly wide world of solidly realized objects. Much that is excluded from her subjects sneaks in through her style. . . .

Perhaps I am misled by the lovely job of bookmaking that Cummington has done for these poems. Or perhaps misled by my approval of what Miss Van Duyn is saying. I must confess that if someone said, concerning the relation of the poem to the world:

> . . . I've never seen anything like it for making you
> think that to spend your life on such old premises
> is a privilege. . . .

I would probably like it even in Deaf-and-Dumb. Again, I may be misled by my belief that Miss Van Duyn's imagery and diction can teach me a good deal. Yet again, perhaps I really am right—that Miss Van Duyn, neglected as she has been, has written some poems which will seem genuine for a good long while.

At any rate, it does seem just about time that somebody sent this world a valentine. And if I were a poor, old, monstrous, pragmatical pig of a world (as who shall say I'm not), I can't think of who I'd rather get one from.

David Kalstone (review date 2 August 1970)

SOURCE: "Charms to Stave Off the Executioner," in *New York Times Book Review,* August 2, 1970, pp. 5, 22.

[*In the following review, Kalstone offers a positive view of* To See, To Take.]

To See, To Take, Mona Van Duyn's title, like our first verbs, sounds innocent at the outset, fierce and telling later on. Infinitives in certain languages are imperatives as well; and so they are here, in poems where seeing and taking are urgent as well as pleasurable activities:

> And now, how much would she try
> to see, to take,

> of what was not hers, of what
> was not going to be offered?

The subject of these lines is **"Leda Reconsidered,"** the lady trying, in a reflective moment before the swangod takes her, to escape the fate of an earlier Leda in this same book who "married a smaller man with a beaky nose, / and melted away in the storm of everyday life."

Dwindling: it is as if all the poems in this not-so-slim volume were charms—successful ones—against that fate. Like Scheherazade's stories, they are accomplished, never ragged; and their restlessness, their driven quality, is apparent not in any hysteria or lapse in technique, but only in the felt necessity to continue the activity. Every poem staves off the executioner, like the home canning to which she compares her work:

> Oh I know, I know that, great or
>   humble, the arts
> in their helplessness can save
>   but a few selves
> by such disguises from Time's
>   hideous bite,
> and yet, a sweating Proust of
>   the pantry shelves,
> I cupboard these pickled peaches
>   in Time's despite.

Tart, literary, self-mocking, the lines are typical of one kind of poem in this book: verse which sees with an anthropologist's eye the strangeness of common activities and takes pleasure in our peculiar adaptations to survival. Many of the pieces, obliquely or head-on, concern marriage. They entertain with a certain toughness the notion that intimacy may cloud the vision, be "the absolute narrowing of possibilities." Hence, I think, the pressure to explore landscapes and vantage points which, like Miss Van Duyn's **"Colorado,"** open the half-desired way to "private enterprise," where the poet "washed once and for all / from my lips and eyes / the sexual grimace."

There are travel poems like **"Into Mexico"** and **"Postcards from Cape Split"** whose intense clarity allow her to be, really, at home with strangeness. In this last, one of the best pieces in the book, she and her family live "uncentered for three weeks" in a house engulfed by heliotrope and learn to get by on two buckets of water a day. They drive inland through the Blueberry Barrens:

> You almost miss it.
> Suddenly, under that empty space,
>   you notice
> the curious color of the ground.
>   Blue mile, blue mile,

and then a little bent-over group
    of Indians
creeping down string-marked
    aisles. Blue mile, blue mile . . .

These trips act as an endowment, allowing her fresh vision throughout and fresh returns to the everyday world, wary of its snares and wanting to make it count or rather tell. Among conventionally light subjects there are wild imaginings. **"In the Cold Kingdom"** describes an orgiastic afternoon with technicolor flavors in an ice cream shop (Zanzibar Cocoa, Mint Julep, Pumpkin), exorcising greed, "the Unconscious, that old hog, / being in charge here of the / creative act." If there is any flaw in these poems, it is the temptation yielded to in that amusing line, or in the book's self-conscious dedicatory page in praise of "poets"; on occasion Miss Van Duyn talks too much of poetry, tells what she has already shown so well, insists on a literary salvation which has obviously worked for her.

Still, it has worked. Verse in a sense restores her humanity. The book as a whole has a special rhythm, swinging out, exploring, detaching itself, and falling back to embrace the troubles it departed from. A final adventure, the long climactic poem **"Marriage, with Beasts"** is funniest and eeriest of all, making an unsparing tour of a menagerie of appetites and feelings: "Bringing our love to the zoo to see what species / it is, I carry my head under my arm, you cradle yours." Talking about the animals as a way of sharing unsharable instincts, unable to case aside her heady articulate manner, she has a brutal, comic moment facing the mountain lion and a welcome lapse back into the disguises of marriage:

> Now take what you've seen of me
>   home, and let's
> go on with our heady life. And
>   treat me, my pet,
> forever after as what I seem;
>   for it seems,
> and it is, impossible for me to
>   receive,
> under the cagey wedlock of your
>   eyes,
> what I make it impossible for you
>   to give.

This is Mona Van Duyn's third book and should, because of its sustained skill and wisdom, be the one which introduces her to an audience wider than the select one which has prized and praised her work for the past ten years. It is a volume which makes large, painful, powerful connections, and one in which we sense a whole life grasped, in the most urgent and rewarding senses of the word.

Arthur Oberg (review date Winter 1973)

SOURCE: "Deer, Doors, Dark," in *Southern Review,* Vol. 9, No. 1, Winter, 1973, pp. 243-56.

[*In the following excerpt, Oberg responds favorably to* To See, To Take.]

Unlike [Peter] Russell's book, [*The Golden Chain,*] Mona Van Duyn's *To See, To Take* takes notice of where modern poetry has been going as much as it succeeds in evolving a style that is unmistakably Miss Van Duyn's.

To See, To Take is full of things to admire—generosity and intelligence, wit and love. Beyond that, it is an outrageous book in ways that only major books, and major writers, can afford to be. Both Shakespeare and Yeats are prominent here, not so much as literary ghosts, but as sensibilities with whom Mona Van Duyn has much to share. The multiplicity of Shakespeare and that perfect control of tone which Yeats displayed in poems like **"Leda and the Swan," "Among School Children,"** and **"The Circus Animals' Desertion"** find their comparisons in the best poems of this book.

I had read *To See, To Take* before being invited to review it, and before the major prizes came. It has weathered all that attention in the manner that only important books somehow are able to do.

I have no preference for long poems to short poems, or large books to small ones. But one of the pleasures for me in reading Mona Van Duyn has always been a largeness, and a largesse, which defines her work and which the process and progression explicit in the title, *To See, To Take,* confirms.

> **One of the pleasures for me in reading Mona Van Duyn has always been a largeness, and a largesse, which defines her work and which the process and progression explicit in the title, *To See, To Take,* confirms.**
>
> **—Arthur Oberg**

In *A Time of Bees* (1964), there are poems, or at least parts of poems, that do not work; sometimes an inventiveness of image becomes so self-generating as to threaten a larger unity within a poem. Sometimes a poem takes in so much as to forget when it might best conclude. But these faults not only occur less frequently in *To See, To Take,* but are forgiven and forgotten in the grand successes of the strongest poems in the volume.

To See, To Take makes out of potential risks—the welter of prose-like experience, in particular—the very substance of its art. When, in the conclusion of the poem for Randall Jarrell, **"A Day in Late October,"** Mona Van Duyn resorts to prose, she insists upon the prose bone of death, Jarrell's and her eventual own:

> Before that happens, I want to say no bright
> or seasonal thing, only that there is too much
> the incorruptible poem refuses to swallow. At
> the end of each line, a clench of teeth and
> something falling away—tasteless memory,
>   irreducible
> hunk of love, unbelievably bitter
> repetition, rancid failure at feeling and
> naming. And the poem's revulsions become a
> lost world, which also contains what cannot be
> imagined: your death, my death.

And, all the while, the prose turns into a poetic prose, uniquely hers. More often, however, Miss Van Duyn is content to transform what she thinks and feels, or sees and takes, into artful verse. Conversely, she makes verse as unflinching as any prose could hope to be. In both cases, the poetry matters. I quote the poem **"Homework"** in full:

> Lest the fair cheeks begin their shrivelling
> before a keeping eye has lit on their fairness,
> I pluck from the stony world some that can't cling
> to stone, for a homely, transparent form to bless.
>
> Smothering Elbertas, if not Albertines,
> in the thick, scalding sweetness of my care,
> I add a touch of tart malice, some spicy scenes
> and stirring, and screw the lid on love's breathless
>   jar.
>
> There in a frieze they stand, and there they can
>   stay
> until, in the fickle world's or the jaded heart's
> hunger for freshness, they are consumed away.
> Oh I know, I know that, great or humble, the arts
>
> in their helplessness can save but a few selves
> by such disguises from Time's hideous bite,
> and yet, a sweating Proust of the pantry shelves,
> I cupboard these pickled peaches in Time's
>   despite.

"Homework" is typical of Mona Van Duyn at her best. **"A Sweating Proust of the Pantry Shelves":** this is Mona Van Duyn finding her own intimacies, using her own memories, breaking down the old distinctions between poetry and prose in order to form a style recognizably hers. **"Homework"** uncovers the same strengths—her own savage indignation, her loving care—obvious in the other, longer poems in the

book: **"Outlandish Agon," "First Flight,"** the Leda poems, **"The Creation," "Into Mexico," "To Poets' Worksheets in the Air-Conditioned Vault of a Library," "The Twins," "Marriage, With Beasts."**

Neither the length of the volume nor the poet's ability to work in various poetic modes can disguise the essential lyricism of the book. *To See, To Take* is lyrical in the compression of form and in the relentless variations on love—its anatomy and chemistry, its relationship to art and neurosis, its power in the face of cold death. Mona Van Duyn fears her capacity to love and knows how love can hallucinate. But she is also one of those few poets who can carry in her poems the convincing impression of a very non-abstract physicality and of that joy before love, and before words, which all important poetry learns to convey. On every count by which I would approach and arraign it, *To See, To Take* comes out as one of the finest books to appear in American poetry in recent years.

Harvey Shapiro (review date 22 September 1973)

SOURCE: "As Three Poets See Reality," in *The New York Times,* Vol. 123, September 22, 1973, p. 22.

[*In the following review, Shapiro provides a mixed review of* Merciful Disguises.]

Mona Van Duyn's poems, crammed with reality, present a curious case. She has been much honored by the academy—a National Book Award and a Bollingen—but among the poets in New York she has few readers. That has to do with the nature of her reality: She writes as a wife, indeed as a housewife, putting up poems as another good woman might put up peaches (she can begin "An Essay on Criticism" with a description of making prepared onion soup). Her poems describe vacation trips to the mountains or the shore. She writes about female friends, children, relatives. All of this is patently unfashionable. Unfashionable also is the fact that her poems have subjects. More damning than that, there is the basic assumption in her work that it is possible to elicit meaning from the world.

The early poems [in *Merciful Disguises*] sometimes wobble unsteadily (reading this book, a collection of all her work to date, is a bit like watching an ungainly girl grow into a graceful woman) because of the disparity between the prosaic, even folksy, detail and the very learned, literary and skilled mind alive in the language, propelling the poem. The effect is of the rhetoric sometimes jumping away from the detail into its own orbit. This plus excessive detail makes the poems difficult to take in. I assume some of this is intentional—modern metaphysical—but it misfires.

In the last poems of *A Time of Bees* (1964) there begins a chastening of language and detail that brings them together into a complete saying (for example, the moving **"A Garland for Christopher Smart,"** based on quotations from his Jubilate Agno). And this success is repeated throughout *To See, To Take* (1970), particularly in **"A Day in Late October." "Postcards from Cape Split," "What I Want to Say," "The Good Man."** These are not poems that begin with a lyric impulse. They are essayistic, discursive but powerful in their wisdom.

> What do you think love is, anyway?
> I'll tell you, a harrowing.
> And I stand here helpless with what I know,
> because in that Ministry
> to be understood leads straight to the room
> where understanding stops
> and a final scream is that of the self
> preserving itself.

Lorrie Goldensohn (essay date March 1978)

SOURCE: "Mona Van Duyn And The Politics of Love," in *Ploughshares*, Vol. 4, No. 3, March, 1978, pp. 31-44.

[*In the following essay, Goldensohn examines Van Duyn's treatment of love and the female domestic experience in her works.*]

A long time ago I watched Margaret Mead's film, *Four Families*, with a bunch of high school kids. While I sat there, wholly mesmerized by the dark flow of those domestic images with their latent and compelling content, the kids' responses had been quite different. "Is that all there is?" one prescient fourteen-year-old demanded: "Eating, sleeping, getting married, having kids and working?" The question is fair. Also a question that the very body of Mona Van Duyn's work tends to answer affirmatively; then, in a hundred fevers of dissatisfaction, ask again. Fortunately, question and answer are never so simple or final that we stop needing her additions and complications, or that large and eloquent garner of wit and good judgment which brings to her registration of ordinary life its extraordinary interest. A poet of both analytic and sensual intelligence, she asks for an alert reader, responsive to a leisurely, unforced diction, but with a fondness for paradigm and complex formal strategies—although her subjects rarely stray from that unhonored kingdom which, by so much, constitutes the heaviest weight of human experience, the domestic. Also, in Mona Van Duyn's care, the definitively female.

Ground clearly taken at her peril! To be firmly domestic in subject is to be seen as denying the heroic; to be concerned with an accommodating, rather than with an imperial impulse: "the earth in its aspect of / quiescence." Because domestic acts are rarely audible in a world of power: God may hear the fall of a sparrow, a peach pickling in a cupboard, or a married couple quarreling, but he does not then convey the sound to a very august audience chamber. Edging into the usual areas of female concern, however, like the "windy oratory of marriage" or "the politics of love—" also tends to neutralize the impact of any artist, male or female. As most artists who deal with the dailiness and private singularities of life discover, in the public beholding, artists belong to an effeminized occupation. They handle the subjective—something always suspiciously allied to the weakly feminine ground of feeling, unless it is clearly the ground of manipulated feeling, and hardened into a communications, or therapeutic industry.

But Mona Van Duyn risks a further de-glorification of her subject, love. Generally, not choosing to focus on the only theme of love traditionally allowed *grandezza*, the forms of illicit love, she concentrates instead on married love, with its problems of conflicting interests, its sagas of endurance and survival. With the exception of that enigmatic poem, **"The Voyeur,"** and the two Leda Poems, Van Duyn eludes the particular explosiveness, the short-term anarchic disruptions of romantic love, and focuses instead on household; on neighbors and families; and on the gains and losses that people make of long lives spent together.

This is not a world without pain. In **"What I want to Say,"** here is her representation of love:

> What do you think love is, anyway?
> I'll tell you, a harrowing.
> . . .
> To say I love you is a humiliation.
> . . .
> It is the absolute narrowing of possibilities,
> and everyone, down to the last man,
> dreads it.

In **"The Gardener to His God,"** even what she conceives as "love's spaciousness" is a dimension of sacred defeat:

> For in every place but love the imagination lies
> in its limits. Even poems draw back from images
> of that one country, on top of whose lunatic
>   stemming
> whoever finds himself there must sway and cling
> until the high cold God takes pity, and it all dies
> down, down into the great world's flowering.

Although here the conception clothes love in a limitless amplitude, rather than in a "narrowing of possibilities," the attribution is generally consistent with the other poem: "flowering" is the culmination of a great sweeping down, of that great crashing and bending of egos that come about through the union of any two loving souls.

While in these poems submission to love is viewed as a human obligation, in other poems, the gender that bends is usually feminine, because for Mona Van Duyn, the female carries most of the particulars of her message about love and endurance. The male has other errands. Although a transfigured Leda, privileged to see through to the heart of the god, glimpses

> what he had to work through
> as he took, over and over,
> the risk of love,
> the risk of being held,
> and saw to the bare heart
> of his soaring, his journeying

Leda herself, as in the earlier poem bearing her name, contracts in aspiration:

> To love with the whole imagination—
> she had never tried.
> Was there a form for that?
> Deep, in her inmost grubby
> female center
> (how could he know that,
> in his airiness?)
> lay the joy of being used,
> and its heavy peace, perhaps,
> would keep her down.
> To give: women and gods
> are alike in enjoying that ceremony,
> find its smoke filling and sweet.
> But to give up was an offering
> only she could savor,
> simply by covering
> her eyes.

Sounds like the feminine means utter passivity and denial. But, getting Leda closer to that form, "love with the whole imagination—" and, in a specifically female way—Van Duyn continues:

> He was close to some uncommitted
> part of her.
> Her thoughts dissolved and
> fell out of his body like dew
> onto the grass of the bank,
> the small wild flowers,
> as his shadow,
> the first chill of his ghostliness,
> fell on her skin.

> She waited for him so quietly that
> he came on her quietly, almost with tenderness
> not treading her.
> Her hand moved into the dense plumes
> on his breast to touch
> the utter stranger.

In the poem's concluding lines, which I quote in full, Leda's emptying out makes room for divinity; a providential loss of ego so complete that the mystery of otherness can be taken on. It is Leda's utter quietness, her suspension of restless advance, that "almost" disarms the god—neutralizing conquest and transforming submission into assent. In that "almost" lives the specifically feminine achievement, the mid-point which is "past the bird, short of the god"—a feminine celebration of wholly human powers that renounces the "airiness" of masculine sky-storming as vanity. A vanity, however, that Leda meets with the enabling and transformative powers of her submission and consent, thereby reading sexual relations as an almost Taoist, certainly quietist, order of acts and attitudes.

For Leda, there is no attempt to imagine the future as different; no attempt to gain Zeus' knowledge, or put on his power. With a refreshing absence of up-dated rhetoric about the approaching feminine heroic, which amounts, also, to a refusal to add aggressively simple-minded models of self-fulfillment to the vacuum that her dismissal of the conventional heroic has created, it still seems the deepest part of Van Duyn's retelling of the legend of male and female to leave the future, and the option of initiating action, to masculine prerogative:

> The men do it. Making a claim on the future, as
>   love
> makes a claim on the future, grasping.

Although this observation comes from one of her earlier poems, it is matched by re-statements in much later published work, like **"A View,"** and **"The Cities of the Plain."** In the latter poem, the nameless Lot's Wife declares,

> . . . My husband
> and our two adolescents kept their faces
> turned to the future, fled to the future.

The only woman who would think this way is crazy Sarah "whose life, / past menopause, into the withered nineties / was one long obsessed attempt to get pregnant, / to establish the future." There is little sympathy here for this unnatural matron's activities. As for the Wife:

> . . . I stood for nameless women
> whose sense of loss is not statistical,
> stood for a while, then vanished. Men

are always being turned to stone by something,
and loom through the ages in some stony
sense of things they were shocked into.

Once again, like Leda, like the "ungainly, ungodly" Danae,
Van Duyn's representative woman refuses a masculine imagination, that stony, power-driven sense of the future's possibilities, which in this retelling of the legend, fixes the male
in rigidity, but allows the woman her transfigured motion.
Nameless, Lot's Wife disappears into the nameless flux of
the natural scene, a mute and mutable portion of its irrepressible vitalities:

> I turned to pure mourning, which ends the
>   personal
> life, then quietly comes to its own end,
> Each time the clouds came and it rained,
> salt tears flowed from my whole being,
> and when that testimony was over
> grass began to grow on the plain.

The Wife's role is to mourn: salt of the earth as she is, death
and anonymity become her fortunate flaws, and in her end
are all of our beginnings. Like other "low" figures in post-
Christian and secularized mythologies, within the symbols
of this poetry, the female is granted her exaltation as a pinch
of salt, a small wildflower, a blade of grass, a drop of dew;
that is, as a bit of divinized nature.

Feminized and divinized as she is, however, Van Duyn's version of Dame Nature, Lot's Wife, rejects the punishment of
Sodom and Gomorrah as "blasphemous, impiety / to the
world as it is, to things as they are." She says instead:

> Don't ask me why, for the sake of a Perfect
> Idea, of Love or of Human Community,
> all the innocent-eyed, babies and beasts
> and birds, all growth, both food and flower,
> two whole cities, their fabulous bouquets
> of persons, frivolous, severe, rollicking,
> wry, witty, plain, lusty,
> provident, every single miracle of life
> on the whole plain should be exploded
> to ashes. I looked back, and that's what I saw.

Unlike those future-driven ideologues, the prophecy-ridden
men of her family, the Wife rejects the future's unforgiving
abuse of the life around her and continues to thrive in the
backward face of an ample present.

"Along the Road," another dark and rather beautiful poem
really belongs to the same schematization of values, but refines them further, as it puts the drama of the poem outside
human dress altogether. In this poem, enacting an Apocalypse in miniature, "They are burning the dump:"

> During the first days there will be
> only an interruption, gorgeous, mutual,
> of the textures and temperature of the world,
> a representation by three of its acres
> of uproar, extravagance, primitivism, seething,
> and our senses will tire from it
> as they tire from any other
> overmastering abundance, yet
> we will use memory and imagination
> to inform ourselves that it is a process
> of reduction. In its center
> something serious is happening.

In its slow, and leisurely language, the poem sketches that
"pure mourning, which ends the personal life," as backward-
turning memory and imagination; a simultaneously collecting and disbursing aesthetic that allows the transformations
of life's "processes of reduction" into these serenely "*serious*" events:

> . . . springs and bones
> have been bitten from their fat,
> barrels, cans, cars
> set free from the need to contain.
> All over the area there goes on
> a slow, entranced emergence
> of things out of the ashes of their usefulness.
> There is nothing seasonal here.
> If we have lost sight of comfort,
> of fleshy, vegetable consolations,
> still we have arrived at an entanglement
> of true weight, a landscape of certainties.

If we compare this with the mnemonic orotundities of Eliot's
The Waste Land, we may arrive at some exact sense of the
originality of this text; of the fairly delicate balance of its
ironies of acceptance and detachment; of its definitions of
powerful, or significant act. Once again the future is gingerly
held in the mind, its grander possibilities of change gently
derided:

> . . . this antic
> tin stretch, that petrified
> moment of rage when something tried
> to ooze out of its own nature,
> eyeful by eyeful the exact, extensive
> derangement.

On the one hand of this poem, "The comic keeps." On the
other, "our heavy, / drossless, dark deposit." It is this literally conservative awareness of matter and life-forces, this
steady levelling view which is also the antithesis of the romantic. In these asperities, if the human and mortal are given
amplitude, and larger significance, they are also given the
limit of that largesse as equally real. Another particular qual-

ity of the poetry is its insistence that comedy prevail; death itself must be allowed its withering force, without promotion to tragedy. Akin to Lot's Wife's salty dissolution, and Leda's raining-out in "the storm of everyday life," here is a characteristic scene from **"A Relative and an Absolute:"**

> When she died last winter, several relatives wrote
>   to say
> a kidney stone "as big as a peach pit" took her
>   away.
> Reading the letters, I thought, first of all, of the
>   irony,
>
> then, that I myself, though prepared to a certain
>   degree,
> will undoubtedly feel when I lie there, as lone
>   some in death
>   as she
> and just as surprised at its trivial, domestic
>   imagery.

Of this easy, deliberate tone, serenely above the intricacies of its rhyme, the quickest word to step to mind is *adult:* surely this must be the apotheosis of adulthood, in its cool judgments and calm skepticisms. And surely steadiness of view is the other striking characteristic of Mona Van Duyn's poetry. Having published her first collection at around 35, perhaps it is also not remarkable that the poems have changed so little in their basic account of things. This is a poet who began mature: the poems in 1959's *Valentines to the Wide World* have the same varied pace, the same ripe, sure and intelligent touch as the recent *Merciful Disguises.* An important index of change, however, registers in the new use of metaphors of flight and motion in relation to the feminine speakers of the poems, as Van Duyn wrestles successfully to keep maturity from hardening into complacency, and to keep active that dense thickness of imaginative engagement which has been one of her chief strengths.

Having published her first collection at around 35, perhaps it is also not remarkable that the poems have changed so little in their basic account of things. This is a poet who began mature: the poems in 1959's *Valentines to the Wide World* have the same varied pace, the same ripe, sure and intelligent touch as the recent *Merciful Disguises.*
—Lorrie Goldensohn

In **"Three Valentines to the Wide World,"** the necessary perspective seemed quite clear:

> I have never enjoyed those roadside overlooks
>   from which
> you can see the mountains of two states. The view
> keeps generating
> a kind of pure, meaningless exaltation
> that I can't find a use for. It drifts away from
>   things.

And, from the same book, in another meditation urging us away from distant prospects:

> When we eye it, not one bird's worth at a time
> but with eyes like zeppelins, it may be the vista
>   beats us,
> for what crowds quietly even through snowfence
>   metaphors
> is the unexamined life, shifting and lustrous,
> and lands may mellow or chill in that weight of
>   particulars.
> If our largeness of view leaks, does it let out more
> than we mean to waste, minute encounters,
>   tucking,
> tipping the day into an imperceptible contour?

Again, a little later:

> I can stand an outside view of myself, but nothing
> about a bird's eye view elevates or animates me in
>   the slightest.

Soaring views are for the "grasping," thrusting masculine intelligence, blindly greedy for the future. Our Leda, Lot's Wife, and Danae in their unfeathered adornment, don't generally take to a life in the air; even Midas' Wife is conspicuously content to be touched into staying right where she is.

Although some of the most pleasurable and quietly witty of the older poems do come from a lateral traverse of the earth—Maine, for instance, in **"The Gentle Snorer,"** and **"Postcards from Cape Split"**—other poems, with noticeably feminine speakers, nevertheless begin to make their appearance alongside the walkers and motorists, and start speaking differently about the overviews of the airborne. From 1970's *To See, To Take,* **"First Flight"** begins:

> Over forty years, and I haven't left your weather.
> Pocketed like a newborn kangaroo,
> I've sucked the dark particular.

But in spite of this, the risen speaker says to her man:

> So you live here, then, my foreigner . . .
> And now I can look. Oh Lord, why didn't you tell
>   me,
> you I guessed at, how serious, how beautiful it is,

that speechlessness below, a sleeping sea,
where, kissing its frost, endlessly, everywhere,
fallen, uttering, one angel voice, desire,
fills the air with light, the perfect blasphemy.

Blasphemous to the female whose recognition of divinities takes place in other elements: nevertheless, for this speaker, the captivation is literal and complete. Once she is up there, though, and turned loose in the visionary precincts, something else shakes loose but the view of the earth, and the view of herself adhering to it. As the poet continues to muse, death dissolves the ground:

The ghosts of night are joining us, shade by shade,
walking unscathed over a burning striation
until it is covered with their cool feet.
The faces around me turn toward me,
beaming, incomprehensible lamps
saying the stranger is the best beloved.
Oddly and without consequence, I am lighted.

If the poem were to speak without its syllables,
and love's spirit step out of its skin of need,
I would tremble like this.

As the earth clears beneath one's feet, the lines connecting one to particularities of sex, of age and of friendship also dissolve. Up here, one is vulnerable, and finally knowing, as revelation is manifest in the loss of categories; it lives in responsiveness, as the literal entering of a foreign perspective alters and deepens one's own. Neither the feminine nor the masculine are to have exclusive possession of any world, because their individual truths must not be trusted—must be twinned, to some extent at least, to be the poem's whole and human truth. In this poem, the narrator continues:

The plane, turning from spaciousness,

will be brought down by whoever believes
earth's the right place.
Don't tell me it is I.

But in conclusion:

When I touch you I know what I'm doing.
Nothing is inconsequential.
Gatsby is dead in his swimming pool.
Stupid children chart the wood with breadcrumbs.
I believe you in everything except
the smoothness of this diminishing.
. . .
I look into your hard eyes
since I am home and all is forgiven,
but liar, love, I see you against the sky.

Back home on the ground, the woman, still in the throes of her own expanded vision, has a good look at her lover's persistent strangeness. The truths of his gauzy space have had their gaveling moment: she has been forced to redefine the nature of her own level earth, not as a literal, material connection but as connection through love even throughout absence and strangeness. The ones we love keep to their own elements. For Mona Van Duyn, each vault into the Empyrean that we make to join the beloved is rewarded by a recoil into gravity; nevertheless, for such irresistible leaping, room must be made—even by the most reluctant flyers.

This is a point which continues to be made in **"The Fear of Flying."** Here the narrator's reluctance to leave familiar ground is seen not as a fear of death, but as a stubborn, persistent and irrational need to cling to the loved familiar, in the old ways of relation. As Lot's Wife again, in a sophisticated permutation of that role, the narrator rehearses with wry acrimoniousness all of the weary disguises that age and familiarity have imposed on long marriage. Here though, instead of the eternal aspirant, the husband is seen by the speaker as the master of revels, the supreme masquer who will not relinquish his right to assume endlessly and unvaryingly his limited repertoire of roles, most of them now rarely performed for his wife's pleasure of amusement. Although in this version of the Passion of Lot, futurity for the male seems little more than a need to ignore the cumulative past, and a continuous striving to enlarge the present, rather than to entertain the future, the wife's terms still stand unaltered: she remembers, and won't move. She says:

And we know, don't we, the last

of your roles? Remember, my dear, I played it for
  you
for long bountiful seasons?
We bathed, we melted down to the bone in the
blue air, the ripe suns

of ourselves, stretched and vined together all over,
it seemed, sweltered, grew
lush undergrowth, weeds, flowers, groundcover.
I played and played with you,

day after burning day, the part of our lives
truest, perhaps, best,
and still can play it briefly if someone believes
I can: the sensualist.

Once again, doubting and uncertain, Lot's Wife's refusal to move on is a crisis in the history of faith; paralyzed by nostalgia for the old religion as carried on in the old temple, her feet stall, and finally root where they are:

. . . Darling,

my world, my senses' home, familiar monster,
it would seem that I still love you,
and, like a schoolgirl deep in her first despair,
I hate to go above you.

There is an enormously moving prayer here, that death—the cooling of lust, increasing age, and time's multiplication of all our preoccupations with self—not isolate, or destroy our fidelities to the human focal points of love. I know of few other poets who write so well and fully about married love.

Similarly, about friendship: each of several elegies, including **"The Creation"** and **"A Goodbye,"** as well as the more general poem, **"Open Letter, Personal,"** trace the same complex verities, the same difficult balancing acts of perception, penetration and discovery. This fact of extending relationship is as important in the later poems of *Merciful Disguises* as the development of the flight metaphor, a development which appears to correct the potentially inert, or negatively quietist bent of earlier poems. With this metaphor, the poems literally move to make a place for the visionary and idealistic imagination in a female life, and accomplish their difficult ascent, as the emotional commitment to subject deepens and intensifies many of these increasingly personal poems of the later collections. This expansive movement, up and out, is complemented by another change in language and subject, which laterally extends the poet's range, this time temporally as well as spatially. This movement, a circling back to include a more remote past, allows her to retrieve her own relatively unexplored childhood.

In 1970's "Remedies, Maladies, Reasons," Mona Van Duyn relies on the pace of most of her other long narrative poems—there is the same unhastening novelistic inclusiveness, the same appetite for paradigmatic structures of exploration displayed in all of the objects and persons of its concern.
—*Lorrie Goldensohn*

In 1970's **"Remedies, Maladies, Reasons,"** Mona Van Duyn relies on the pace of most of her other long narrative poems—there is the same unhastening novelistic inclusiveness, the same appetite for paradigmatic structures of exploration displayed in all of the objects and persons of its concern. But the scraps of dialogue, the mother's diatribes included here, betray an interest in the actual transcription of the speech of others that is a new element. Later, that plentiful sprinkling of quotation marks which peppers the surface of **"Remedies, Maladies, Reasons,"** and also, implicitly, the surface of poems like **"Billing and Cooings from the *Berkeley Barb*,"** gives way, as orthography bows

to the creation of a new voice—manifestly neither the author's voice nor an author substitute—in a series of poems entitled ***Bedtime Stories,*** first published in 1972.

These fourteen poems, framed with a head-piece and a tail-piece in the author's own voice, are spoken by the poet's grandmother: looking back, they continue the threads of an agrarian domesticity in another, foreign-accented English, of another class, and of another generation. Anonymous, and egalitarian in style and intention, these and other poems appearing after *Merciful Disguises* take the same tack, thereby continuing what appears to be a necessary event in the larger life of these poems: the subversion of their maturities and finish into new vitalities; new ranges of feeling; new subject.

Robert Hass (review date 5 September 1982)

SOURCE: A review of *Letters from a Father, and Other Poems,* in *Washington Post Book World,* Vol. 12, No. 36, September 5, 1982, pp. 6-7.

[*In the following review, Hass commends* Letters from a Father, and Other Poems.]

Duyn was born in Iowa and lives in St. Louis. Her selected poems, ***Merciful Disguises,*** was published in 1973, and has been reissued in paperback this summer by Atheneum. ***Letters from a Father, and Other Poems*** is her first book since that gathering. How to convey the flavor of the title poem and the others about her elderly parents? A friend of mine, a pacifist, vegetarian ecologist, from Seattle who works for the Forest Service and lives on tofu, alfalfa sprouts, and the idea of wild rivers, married a woman from a Dutch farming family in Nebraska. Last summer he went back there to meet his in-laws. When he returned, he looked shellshocked. I asked him what had happened. "It was *awful,*" he said. "They ate these huge meat and potato meals starting at about two in the afternoon and then they just kicked back and set around for hours talking about goiters." This is the world that Van Duyn gives us in a suite of salty, baleful and weirdly tender poems.

"Letters from a Father" purports to be just that, six letters from a father to his daughter. The first of them begins with a front-line report from the was between time and the body. There is a tinge of self-pity in its, but also a sort of Brueghelesque gusto:

> Ulcerated tooth keeps me awake, there is
> such pain, would have to go to the hospital to have
> it pulled or would bleed to death from the blood
>   thinners,

but can't leave Mother, she falls and forgets her
   salve
and her tranquilizers, her ankles swell so and her
   bowels
are so bad, she almost had a stoppage and
   sometimes
what she passes is green as grass. . .

It continues—heart, prostate, bladder. The only diversion is his response to his daughter's expressed pleasure in her bird feeder. "I don't see why / you want to spend good money on grain for birds / and you say you have a hundred sparrows, I'd buy / poison and get rid of their diseases and turds."

The bird feeder, it turns out, is the key to the poem. The daughter gives one to her parents. It is not an immediate success:

   I used to like to hunt
and we had many a good meal from pigeons
and quail and pheasant but these birds won't
be good for nothing and are dirty to have so near
the house. Mother likes the redbirds though

But eventually this old couple, with very a few imaginative resources (and who can say just how useful imaginative resources are at incontinent 85) and nothing to think about but their bodies, begins to take an interest in the quick little creatures outside their window:

Some of them I can't identify
for sure, I guess they're females, the Latin words
I just skip over. Bet you'd never guess.
the sparrows I've got here, House Sparrows you
   wrote,
but I have Fox Sparrows, Song Sparrows, Vesper
   Sparrows,
Pine woods and Tree and Chipping and White
   Throat
and White Crowned Sparrows, I have six
   Cardinals,
three pairs, they come at early morning and
   night. . .

By the end of the poem there is very little information about physical debility, the note of self-pity is gone, and there are long reports on the birds. My favorite line comes from a report on Mother. "Has a scale she thinks is going to turn to a wart." The detail is potentially gruesome, the story potentially sentimental, but there is something in the implied attitude of the daughter—her clear eye, amusement, repugnance, fidelity—that complicates the whole poem and brings it alive, and it gets at an area of human experience that literature—outside of Samuel Beckett—has hardly touched.

Two of the poems are remarkable. In **"Photographs"** the daughter is going through boxes of them that the parents want to get rid of. The occasion permits Van Duyn to lift a whole world into view in a matter of five pages. It is the ordinariness of it, the frontal banality hewed to so closely, that fascinates. Here is a portrait of the father:

Small eyes that never saw another's pain
or point of view ("Your mother's always com
   plaining.
I've fed and clothed her all her life. What more
does she *want*?") Full lips that laid down the law
   for us.
Big feeder before his heart attack his Santa.
belly swells in the gas station uniform.
"You'll have to feed him good," his mother told
his bride. "If dinner's late just hurry and set
the table. He'll think the food is almost ready."

"The Stream" I won't attempt to represent by quotation. It deals with the mother's dwindled disoriented life in a nursing home after the father's death, and then with her death. It is in this poem that the daughter, the poet, comes to terms with her parents. The end of the poem is very affecting, but what is riveting is Van Duyn's description of a confused old woman dressing up, on the wrong day, for a lunch she is looking forward to. The whole sequence is very strong work, it is very close to the grain, and there is a kind of ferocity in its plainness.

M. L. Rosenthal (review date 13 March 1983)

SOURCE: "A Common Sadness," in *New York Times Book Review,* Vol. 88, March 13, 1983, p. 6.

[*In the following review, Rosenthal provides a laudatory assessment of* Letters from A Father, and Other Poems.]

Mona Van Duyn seems a naturally ebullient sort, a humorous love-welcomer who sturdily overbears disgust, resentment and the tears of things. Her style is anecdotal and expansive. . . .

Mona Van Duyn is such an engaging spirit a reader almost forgets the dark awareness with which she copes. Her title poem, **"Letters From a Father,"** starts her book off with an epistolary tale that has a happy ending—that is, for the time being. It consists of six successive "letters" from a small-town, country-bred, octogenarian father to his poet daughter. These highly colloquial letters, compressed and adapted to a loose line of five or six stresses and a pattern of alternating rhymes and half-rhymes, are handled masterfully. They begin as pure complaint, calculated to drive a daughter to distraction, with such details as: Ulcerated tooth keeps me awake, there is such pain, would have to go to the hospital to have it pulled or would bleed to death from the blood thinners, but can't leave Mother, she falls and forgets her salve and her tranquilizers, her ankles swell so and her bowels are so bad, she almost had a stoppage and sometimes what she passes is green as grass. . .

But they end with joy, brought on by a bird feeder the inspired daughter has given her parents. At first scorning the idea of spending "good money on grain" for the birds, the parents forget their ailments as they become absorbed in the birds' (and squirrels') doings around the feeder: "you would die laughing / to see Redbellied, he hangs on with his head / flat on the board." The poet allows herself but one line in her own voice—the last line: "So the world woos its children back for a final kiss."

The poem is so endearing, and so unusual in its plain humanity, that one is tempted to take it at sentimental face-value and ignore the death-obsession with which it begins and ends.

—M. L. Rosenthal

The poem is so endearing, and so unusual in its plain humanity, that one is tempted to take it at sentimental face-value and ignore the death-obsession with which it begins and ends. In the sequence of seven poems (called "Last") led off by **"Letters From a Father,"** the comic spirit gains a brief ascendancy, especially in the second piece, **"Lives of the Poets."** Here the poet tells how her mother once "commissioned" her to write a poem about the activities ("we bake cute cookies" and "make stuffed animals / to give poor Texas kids at Xmas") of her social club—"to be sung to the tune / of Silent Night Holy Night."

In the rest of this family-centered sequence, most of which has to do with her parents' last years, Miss Van Duyn's tone grows grimmer and what emerges is a struggle to forgive their earlier cruelties to her because "they are nobody's children now, or mine perhaps." The climax of the sequence comes in **"The Stream,"** a long account of a visit to her mother's nursing home in which, amid all the scarifyingly funny indignities and pain of such occasions, the daughter receives the endlessly deferred avowal of love she has been seeking all her life-all this not many days before the mother's death. The final poem of "Last" (**"The Case of The"**) is a drastic effort at distancing and encompassment. Here the blows of history, the fated character formation of families, and private suffering are focused within the same impersonal perspective, made vivid in the reported words of a murderer

before execution: "The sun done it, coming up every damn morning like it does!"

In a sense, Miss Van Duyn's work parallels Robert Lowell's; she takes the same confessional risks of humiliation and has a similar instinct for projecting hilarious discomfiture, as in the impossibly gross, thoroughly winning poem of married love called **"A Winter's Tale, by a Wife."** But the extreme egocentrism within which Lowell's genius discovered itself is absent from her work. She can write poems of pure joy, such as the gloriously alive **"Moose in the Morning, Northern Maine,"** and the sweetly amused, femininely sympathetic **"The Ballad of Blossom."** The former has a genial virtuosity as it mixes pastoral evocation of a morning scene (engulfed in "an immense cow-pie of mist") with a whimsical dismissal of the esthetic view of life, then shifts to the sudden appearance of a moose, "a ton of monarch," at the center of its bucolically delighted meditation. The latter, about a cow in heat, is, as it were, a long-distance companion to A. J. M. Smith's "Ballade un peu banale" and the opening of Basil Bunting's "Briggflatts." Together, these poems would make a charming trilogy of bovine erotica.

But apart from her freedom to be joyful, which is greater than Lowell's, she is also closer than he was to the most telling kind of compassion, detached from self-aggrandizement or self-laceration. See, for instance, her piercing poems **"The Hermit of Hudson Pond," "Ringling Brothers, Barnum and Bailey"** and **"Goya's 'Two Old People Eating Soup.'"** Her book holds a world of volatility in fine equilibrium.

Richard Lattimore (review date Spring 1983)

SOURCE: "Poetry Chronicle," in *The Hudson Review,* Vol. 36, No. 1, Spring, 1983, pp. 210-11.

[*In the following excerpt, Lattimore offers praise for* Letters from a Father, and Other Poems.]

In her sixth book, [*Letters from a Father, and Other Poems,*] Mona Van Duyn writes mostly blank verse more on the order of Frost than Stevens or Aiken, but the language is a lot racier. Or it may be couplets, rhymed stanzas, even a sonnet—but whatever it is, she dishes it out with practiced casual skill. The heart of this collection is a cluster of poems from family history, about photographs, with letters and memories, with the handsome father and mother (and daughter) losing their looks and strength until "They are no longer parents. Their child is old." **"Lives of the Poet"** describes how our poet, newly married and in her first year of college teaching, received a letter from her mother:

I was fortunate enough to have

a mother who on one occasion
encouraged me by commissioning
a poem. Newly married, I
was tackling my first teaching job
when a letter came which said, in part:
"As writing is so easy for you
I want you to write a poem about
the San Benito Ladies Auxiliary
that I belong to. Our club has twenty
members and we bake cute cookies
and serve them with coffee and do our sewing
at the meeting. We make stuffed animals
to give poor Texas kids at Xmas.
Tell all that in the poem."

And so on. She says she wrote the poem. There are other themes. **"A Reading of Rex Stout"** plays back and forth between the unappetizing murder exhibits investigated by Nero and his minions and the lovely gourmet fare they refresh themselves with in the intervals. Mona Van Duyn is easy to take and gives you something to bite on. You may sometimes want to spit it out, as when, for instance, there is, on the lake "an immense cow-pie of mist"; but there is no lack of vigor and sharp edge. "Farm dogs explode from porches"; "deer-mice with Disney ears"; or, in a scene from liberated Madrid:

Like bears on hind legs sharpening their claws,
men and women stand by the walls
and scratch with their fingernails
at the campaign posters they disagree with,
ripping tiny strips from the print.

A good poet to be writing, these days.

Alfred Corn (review date October 1990)

SOURCE: A review of *Near Changes,* in *Poetry,* Vol. CLVII, No. 1, October, 1990, pp. 47-50.

[*In the following review, Corn offers a possitive assesment of* Near Changes.]

You can't doubt she means it when, in a poem called **"Glad Heart at the Supermarket,"** Mona Van Duyn says, "Dear friends, dear aging hearts that are stressed by young / surges and shocks of feeling, dear minds aquiver, / their stiffening vessels bulged with the rush of fresh / insights, jokes, dreams, may you live forever!" There is in this book a generous sense of community, the recognition that friendship is one of the principal lights along the path, especially toward the end. The sense of pathos is all the more piercing, then, in poems

like the elegy mentioned earlier, **"For David Kalstone,"** and the villanelle **"Condemned Site,"** a lament for the death of five friends, one of its repeated lines, "In Love's old boardinghouse, the shades of five rooms are drawn." Life is like that: we watch as others walk the plank; and know that we are in the line to follow after them. Many of those who could have assisted us most, were they still here, have gone on ahead and cannot help. *Near Changes* is shot through with the pain of loss, and yet it isn't a sad book. The author really is capable of having "a glad heart at the supermarket," and we want to know why for more than esthetic reasons alone. Reading her books over the years, I've often been struck by Mona Van Duyn's special genius for the Good Life. The pleasures of the senses are readily hers; she is generous; has a habit of finding the amusing side to things, of enjoying life's absurdities without falling into scorn; and Lady Luck has given her—she knows the case is rare—a lifelong love with whom she need not put up a false show of perfect competence or unshakable serenity. **"Late Loving"** must be the most moving (and honest) poem ever written about marriage approaching the golden anniversary.

If in my mind I marry you every year
it is to calm an extravagance of love
with dousing custom, for it flames up fierce
and wild whenever I forget that we live
in double rooms whose temperature's controlled
by matrimony's turned-down thermostat.
I need the mnemonics, now that we are old,
of oath and law in re-memorizing that.

And she has friends. I enjoyed the peek into behind-the-scenes daily life in the midwestern Athens of Washington University, whose citizens, distinguished writers and their spouses, are decipherably nicknamed here and portrayed from an unaccustomed angle. In this scheme there are an appealing "Peggy" and "Howie," and another freefloating character known only as "the Insight Lady," subject to blinding intuitions with an absurd tinge to them. It is a world inhabited by an enlightened middle class, and Mona Van Duyn is one of the poets helping a portion of the reading public that went against its natural grain for several decades find its way back to familiar perspectives and virtues. Gone are the hash pipe, the Harley Davidson, and the crushed velvet gipsy dress. Well, we gave it a try, they can say, apparently without retrospective condemnation of self or others. The daily round between household, supermarket, library, and bed isn't, in any case, an entirely placid business, as Van Duyn well knows. The unconscious mind remains anarchic, especially for the artist who depends on its oracular powers. Van Duyn's startling metaphor for the unanticipated invasion of the irrational is worked out brilliantly in **"Falling in Love at Sixty-Five,"** where the poet, drifting toward sleep in the wild by the light of a Coleman lamp, is assaulted by swarms of nocturnal insects:

the bared part of me becoming a plan
for plates of an insect book whose specimens
rearranged themselves fiercely over and over
    again.
For as long as the lantern lasted they would have
    kept coming,
as if the great darkness had smiled at that tiny
    dawn
and had hurled them in fistfuls straight at the
    speaking light
in answer to what was being insisted on.

Van Duyn will never be entirely satisfied, though, with the vatic, if only for the reason that it doesn't sound good in verse.

Who gives up the world for words
gives creation a bad black eye
in uncoupling sense and sound.
Detective Time takes his voiceprint,
which ends up behind bars. Nature's ear
knows it was little to lose.

                  "Memoir"

A wonderful poem titled **"The Ferris Wheel"** casts the debate between mystery and realism in spatial terms. **"The Ferris Wheel"** gains by being read in tandem with **"First Flight,"** a poem written nearly twenty years ago. In both poems Van Duyn meditates on the pleasures and dangers of being off the ground, suspended at a superior vantage point above Mother Earth. With **"The Ferris Wheel"** of course each ascent is followed by a corresponding descent, though the narrator's swing sometimes pauses a while at the top before sinking down again. This is a rich metaphor for the cyclical activity of the imagination, first yearning toward transcendence and then yielding to the realism of terra firma. Yet the metaphor is qualified by several factors: the narrator has her spouse with her, as well as the bag of groceries (including root vegetables) she intends to cook for dinner. These go up with her and provide an anchor even at the pinnacle of the ascending cycle; moreover she finds herself looking down at the fair rather than up at the stars. Meditations on the rise as well as during the plunge downward are given resonance by allusions to Chaucer, Wordsworth, Yeats, and Graham Greene. And when she is at last deposited on the ground, a glow of transcendence follows her; it hasn't all been merely the brief salvo of a Roman candle.

The exit platform.
She lifts her sack to leave and in the doorglass
by some great mirroring gift of the lights,
stronger than love, stranger than love,
she sees for life upon her own shoulders and
    neckstem

an image which replaces her own wherever she
    seeks it:
another's "tired, pleasure-hoping" face.

To be older, tired, and still "pleasure-hoping"; to be realistic and also subject to transcendent intuitions; to weigh the claims of love along with the claims of poetry: this is the vision informing *Near Changes.* During the past several decades Mona Van Duyn has assembled, in a language at once beautiful and exact, one of the most convincing bodies of work in our poetry, a poetry that explores, as Stevens put it, ". . . the metaphysical changes that occur, / Merely in living as and where we live."

Edward Hirsch (review date 18 November 1990)

SOURCE: "Violent Desires," in *New York Times Book Review,* Vol. 95, November 18, 1990, p. 24.

[*In the following excerpt, Hirsh commends Van Duyn's "pathos and wit" in* Near Changes.]

Mona Van Duyn has a gift for making the ordinary appear strange and for turning a common situation into a metaphysical exploration. She is, as she says, a poet of "serious play"—extravagant, large-spirited, querulous—a John Donne of the postwar American suburbs who combines a breezy colloquial formalism with an underlying violence of feeling. Her most characteristic poems move on the wings of extended figuration, worrying metaphors into conceits and crackling with odd, humorous rhymes ("The world's perverse, / but it could be worse," she writes in **"Sonnet for Minimalists"**) that belie their darker emotional depths. Inventiveness is both sword and shield; wit is her weapon and protection. She is a poet of "merciful disguises."

> **Mona Van Duyn has a gift for making the ordinary appear strange and for turning a common situation into a metaphysical exploration. She is, as she says, a poet of "serious play"—extravagant, large-spirited, querulous—a John Donne of the postwar American suburbs who combines a breezy colloquial formalism with an underlying violence of feeling.**
> **—Edward Hirsch**

Near Changes, Ms. Van Duyn's seventh book, is a major addition to the corpus of her work. As in her previous collection *Letters from a Father* (1982), she explores the metaphorical possibilities and implications that inhere in daily life. For example, in **"Glad Heart at the Supermarket"** (a reversal of "A Sad Heart at the Supermarket" by Randall Jarrell) a regular jaunt to market becomes an investigation into questions of familiarity, abundance, exoticism and otherness. **"First Trip Through the Automatic Carwash"** provides the opportunity for a speculative meditation about immersion and strangeness, clarity and selfhood. The world condenses and blurs, but "at the last moment it lifts toward design": The heart makes its presence known, disheveled but whole, by jogging in place, lithely, at light's surprise. A hoot from behind makes her shift to self-control, and the muddle of everywhere falls on her clearing eyes.

In *Near Changes* Ms. Van Duyn is pre-eminently a poet of "married love," in her words, of wild feelings "doused" by custom, of outer calm and inner turmoil, of solitude and reconnection. "'Love' is finding the familiar dear," she declares in **"Late Loving":** and "'In love' is to be taken by surprise." She speaks of assessments and reassessments, of possibly using up "the whole human supply of warmth on you / before I could think of others and digress," of chafing from proximity by day but all night long lying "like crescents of Velcro, / turning together till we re-adhere." In poems such as **"Falling in Love at Sixty-Five," "Late Loving"** and **"The Block"**—virtually an entire novel condensed into 62 lines—she writes with poignant vibrancy about the aging of a childless couple. These poems place her new work in the emotional vicinity of Jarrell's "Lost World."

For Ms. Van Duyn poetry is "death's antonym," the means of transport from the inner to the outer realms, a bridge to the other. As she puts it in **"Memoir":** "Art fixes the world I-to-eye." In *Near Changes* she has "fixed" her world with pathos and wit.

Constance Hunting (essay date 1991)

SOURCE: "Methods of Transport," in *Parnassus,* Vol. 16, No. 2, 1991, pp. 377-89.

[*In the following excerpt, Hunting faults some elements of style and tone, but offers a generally favorable review of Near Changes.*]

Tietjens, Monroe, Bullis, Bollingen, Loines, Shelley, Crane, Lilly—what a long train of prizes and awards for the engine of poetry to pull! During a distinguished career, Mona Van Duyn has won them all. As well, she is a member of the National Institute of Arts and Letters and a chancellor of the Academy of American Poets. Then there are the fellowships and the honorary degrees. . . . A very long train indeed, trav-

eling a steady track through a reliable landscape. For thirty years we have been privileged to watch its progress. . . .

"Domestic" is an adjective frequently found in both positive and negative criticism of Mona Van Duyn's poetry. Her subjects are often grounded in the social occasions and preoccupations of the American middle class, a field of action by now considerably eroded. Such representative enterprises as cocktail parties, christenings, gardening, reading, and marriage have to an extent lost or mislaid meaning. (Death remains germane.) Over this shrinking but still recognizable terrain, Van Duyn flings a net of mythical, biblical, and classical allusion, interwoven with historical, philosophical, literary, and psychological references, the whole construct laden with metaphor and image and suggesting a vital complexity of human existence in time. The cumulative effect of such richness is uniformly impressive; the danger to the individual poem is that its unique impulse and integrity may be threatened by the weight of willed significance.

The apparatus demands long lines and long poems. (A brief poem in Van Duyn's *oeuvre* is rare, a welcome sport.) To guard against unwieldiness, Van Duyn marshals her materials into stanzas of varied accentual-syllabic meters in received or inventively combinative forms—quatrains, couplets, semi-disguised blank verse, villanelles, near-sonnets—replete when appropriate with assonance and rhyme displaying Browningesque assurance and aplomb.

Yet for all of her admirable technique, her poetry can sometimes fail to fully engage the reader's emotional attention. It is almost as though a check on too much spontaneity of feeling has been applied very early, perhaps before memory, a brake put on too much trust in her own sensibility, and a transference made of that trust to words. As a result, Van Duyn can tend to press words too hard, to use too many in an effort to justify the transference. The tendency has been evident from the beginning of her published work. A few lines from the long poem **"Toward a Definition of Marriage"** in her first collection, *Valentines to the Wide World* (1959), may serve as illustration: ". . . think of it as a duel of amateurs. /. . . / Now, too close together for the length of the foils, / wet with fear, they dodge, stumble, strike, / and if either thinks he would rather be touched / than touch, he still must listen to the clang and tick / of his own compulsive parrying." Any discomfort afforded by this representative passage derives less from its proliferation of images and its incessant onomatopoeic clatter than from its unremitting rain of words. The effect is less of poetry than of prose, less of prose than of talkiness.

The reader may resist engagement in part because of the qualities exhibited in the poem itself, but also from memory of the quite different qualities of the very first phrase of the title poem which opens this first collection: "The child disturbs our view." No arrangement of words could be simpler: subject, verb, object. The statement is voiced calmly, with the certainty of factual knowledge, and each of its elements is easily retained in the mind. Each is definite, yet resonates with connotations. Thus the statement is both satisfying and stimulating at once, to the senses by its sounds and the spaces between them, to the intelligence by the clarity of its communication and the reverberations of its content. The reader instinctively responds—and remembers. Ever after in Van Duyn's work he will seek a like experience of words that are felt on the pulse as language. Sometimes he will find it.

Near Changes appears after an eight year hiatus in Van Duyn's publishing career, a long while in the American timetable of letters. The new book represents a consolidation and an advance of her talent. The voice is not altered, is indeed instantly recognizable, but is charged with a new energy whose source perhaps lies in her earned certainty of her powers. Her subjects, not surprisingly, are familiar—marriage (probably her great theme), love, friends, aging, nature, myth; but rather than pouncing on and worrying them, she holds them lightly, looks, ponders, and releases them, allowing their essential properties to retain independence. Thus, with few exceptions, these poems move with confidence and authority through their spaces and paces, their matter and ornament in equable adjustment.

Predictably, such modulations of stance and approach bring new perspectives to bear on the work. A typical example in *Near Changes* is found in the title poem, which treats of a favorite Van Duyn subject, Leda of the myth, but from a refractive angle. In *To See, To Take,* her 1971 National Book Award volume, Van Duyn twice examines the story, each time focusing on the Leda figure. The first version, formal in structure, consists of four quatrains, mainly pentameter, in *a b a c* pattern. The poem is an answer to its epigraph, Yeats' closing question in his "Leda and the Swan," "Did she put on his knowledge with his power . . . ?" Van Duyn's opening phrase is an emphatic negative: "Not even for a moment." The rest of the poem develops the evidence for her reply, the first stanza positing Zeus as supreme male egotist ("When he saw the swan in her eyes he could let her drop"), the others characterizing Leda as ultimately too unimaginative a female to comprehend a possible conferred immortality:

> She tried for a while to understand what it was
> that had happened, and then decided to let it drop,
> She married a smaller man with a beaky nose,
> and melted away in the storm of everyday life.

The tone is not so much dismissive as wry, with its colloquial echoes of Yeats's intense diction, and seems to question the unassailability of myth even as it suggests that ordinary existence is challenge enough for human enterprise.

"Leda Reconsidered" presents a more complex version of the affair; moving on breath rather than meter, it thus tells in more intimate accents and at closer range of the advance of "the other," from the moment of his stepping "out of water / that paled from the loss of his whiteness" to the penultimate motion of her hand "into the dense plumes / on his breast to touch / the utter stranger." Although the actual verb tense is past indefinite, the sense of its state is progressive. Leda is at once subject (of the poem) and object (of its intruder), but at no time is she subject to him. She is not, as in Van Duyn's first version, passive, not simply "the consequence of his juice," but the instigator of the conjunction. Far from being unimaginative, she is fully aware of what is happening, and sufficiently curious to try to see herself through the swan-Zeus's eyes even as her gaze on him remains unwavering. This doubling of awareness increases the tensile strength of the poem's vision, so that although the narrative is given in the third person historical it seems to be in first-person immediate. And as Leda's gaze on the disguised god is unwavering, so is the poet's on her, to the extent that Van Duyn becomes, not Leda, but her gaze.

In "Near Changes," Van Duyn pulls back, amused but also thoughtful, from the myth per se, as she considers a trivia item concerning a Seattle man costumed as a mallard duck for a radio promotion who is attacked on a downtown street by a "'husky, 6-foot-tall / bearded stranger.' . . . Prescient as Leda." The poem is in three sections, the first transcribing, as it were, the news item in lines whose breaks suggest the syntactical patterns of informational prose, the second moving into commentary on how "the gods used to do it . . . be bull or swan," the third meditating on the infinite possibilities of "the human imagination, / which transforms past belief." As Van Duyn turns her attention from the bewilderment of the Zeus figure ("'I didn't flap my wings / or do anything like that.'") to the agitation of the Leda figure ("he sensed the presence / which to others was not apparent, / and was only protecting his nest") and goes on to discuss the position of myth in contemporary culture, the diction and tone gradually shift from the semi-comic to the wholly serious. While Van Duyn believes in the reality of myth and in its enduring autonomy, she regrets its debasement by the false myths of material and mechanical advancement, which use its putative marvels to discredit and to dissipate rather than to reveal and to reaffirm the true, coherent wonders of "the soundless spin of the globe." Beethoven now resides in the radio, the "nest" is "the brick and concrete of Sears and service stations," the swan has become a duck and Leda a bearded man—and "What's the difference?" the eternal question. Whereas in Van Duyn's initial treatment Leda avoids her mythic destiny and in the second reaches out to meet it, in "Near Changes" the only recourse of blunted, dwindled, and uniformed instinct is to assault the unwitting symbol of the threatening unknown. Yet instinct goes precisely to the intruder's most obvious badges of identification: "The perpetrator spun him around by one wing, / tore off his duck bill, / hit him over the head with it" before running away, presumably in fear and confusion. With her evolving perspective on the themes and subjects which she has chosen to cultivate, Van Duyn sees that myth, its surface powers diluted or subverted, for a while at least has gone underground; like Demeter, she searches for it even as she mourns its affective presence.

In her latest book, Van Duyn has not abandoned her earlier penchants or technical implementations; she still sometimes overloads her rifts, overdecorates the rooms of her stanzas, over-eggs the poetic pudding. Two examples might be **"Late Loving,"** a rather labored reworking of her marriage theme, and **"The Ferris Wheel,"** whose central metaphor carrying multiple referential freight—life, love marriage, sexual union—is clogged by so many allusions and images that its machinery is in danger of grinding to a halt. However, these lapses are proportionately less frequent in *Near Changes* than in her previous volumes, and poems such as **"Double Sonnet for Minimalists"** and its companion piece **"Sonnet for Minimalists"** show a nice sense of play in short, artfully simple lines whose precision reminds one of Bishop's or Clampitt's in this mode. And in spite of its tonally suburban title, **"To a Friend Who Threw Away Hair Dyes"** takes on in its brief eight lines of pentameter a Yeatsian authority and timelessness of expression in the sighting toward its close of "a beautiful, / brilliant head wearing its first cold crown." The reader, and the critic, can rest on and in the words.

William Logan (review date February 1992)

SOURCE: "Late Callings," in *Parnassus*, Vol. 18, No. 2, February, 1992, pp. 317-27.

[*In the following excerpt, Logan surveys Van Duyn's works, and responds negatively to* Firefall.]

However disorganized or haphazard our habits, we read poetry in the sequence of an expectation. The sequence a poet's books compose is unlike that which any later reader is likely to experience. The afterlife of most poets is in the crowded halls of the anthology (where a poet has position but little place), and once a poet is confined there no one but the moral scholar or tormented reader will begin his acquaintance with a poet's works in their original order. We read the living in expectation rather than elegy.

It is, however, a divided privilege to follow the work of our contemporaries as it is published. What we lose by not being able to comprehend the whole—the whole not being complete—is only partly recovered in our immediate, help-

less intimacy with the smaller concentrations of the art: the labored progress, the inward turnings, the abandoned passages and dead ends, the sudden and unexpected release into a larger climate. The volumes maintain their own version of an argument in which *High Windows* could no more precede *The Less Deceived* than *The Mills of the Kavanaughs* follow *Life Studies*. Our faith in the private reading of that argument lets us misread poets who deceive our expectations.

After the age of sixty, poets often write in the confines of those prior understandings and in diplomacy toward the future, tacitly accepting the decline in invention that accompanies long engagement with an art (or the distractions that attend recognition and regard—it was Eliot who said that the Nobel Prize was a ticket to your own funeral, and he might as well have meant the funeral for the art as well as the life). But a poet's old comprehensions may also be violently rejected, even when the poet has no idea how to replace them. It is hard to win any advantage over such conditions—the condition of paralyzed continuation or equally paralyzed revolt. The rare successes are a triumph not merely over time's debility but over the debility of a long habitation in the self.

> **She could make poems from table scraps and newspaper cuttings, as Auden used to do; and indeed her poems, like his, are often just intelligent talk: sociable and even chatty, never accidentally revealing, fondhearted if somewhat prickly, and inclined to tug on your lapels.**
> —*William Logan*

Mona Van Duyn's best poems are a little clumsy in their charmed matter-of-factness; the warrant of their honesty eases the slight roughness of their intellect. She could make poems from table scraps and newspaper cuttings, as Auden used to do; and indeed her poems, like his, are often just intelligent talk: sociable and even chatty, never accidentally revealing, fondhearted if somewhat prickly, and inclined to tug on your lapels. She lacks his intelligent ear: Her poems slouch off toward prose without some formal obligation to attend to, and her early experiments with rhyme sound like earnest low-paid doggerel:

> Now, in this evening land of fire and shadow,
> a swallow world, a fallow world, of lake and
>   meadow,
> where the mud turtle flops from his log, flat as our
>   fate,
> but the green-headed flies swarm up, so furious is
>   our delight. . . .

(from **"From Yellow Lake: An Interval"**)

In such vacant painterly descriptions, one sees her peculiar conjunction of the mundane (perhaps the muddy) and the metaphysical ("when the world's slippery, solemn arrangements / slide to a comic pratfall"). Van Duyn's poems have been exemplary lessons in how to conduct a poetry not of philosophical density (the Symbolists were more acquainted with the unmeaning densities of philosophy) but of philosophical texture. Few poets have found such inspiration in the ordinary domestic guilts—if there were no suburbs to feel guilty in, Mona Van Duyn would have had to invent them (a newspaper buried under a sycamore's shed bark has inspired *two* poems, one of them a sestina). Even in the suburbs, however, the contracts of the everyday are unforgiving:

> When she died last winter, several relatives wrote
>   to say
> a kidney stone "as big as a peach pit" took her
>   away.
> Reading the letters, I thought, first of all, of the
>   irony,
> then, that I myself, though prepared to a certain
>   degree,
> will undoubtedly feel, when I lie there, as lone
>   some in death as she
> and just as surprised at its trivial, domestic
>   imagery.

(from "A Relative and an Absolute")

Such a poetry has an abiding trust in the lived actions of the world. When Van Duyn writes that she has "sucked the dark particular," it is out of recognition that her poetry is more than usually dependent on the small breakages or vantages of daily affairs, and that the darkness of the world, its inevitable falling toward loss, is redeemed by the transient comedy of particulars: "we . . . pulled up over our heads / a comforter filled with batts of piney dark, / tied with crickets' chirretings and the *bork* / of frogs; we hid in a sleep of strangeness from/the human humdrum."

Her brisk, slightly wacky sense of language is the fitful and intimate counterpart of a grace achieved through awkwardness. In the beauty of their ungainliness, her poems have some of the lightness—the longing beneath the lightness—of Elizabeth Bishop's. Van Duyn's poems are doughier, more thorough and thoughtful, less injured, and finally less moving because not open to being moved without the intercession of language. Van Duyn is a poet who can't think until she writes, and can't feel until she thinks. This is not unusual for poets living through language—a poet's deliberated intentions often exist only in the dream life of critics.

Van Duyn had a long apprenticeship—her first book was not published until she was thirty-eight. All the emphasis in her early work on what a poem is or does ("A poem can stay

formally seated / till its person-to-person call, centuries later, is completed") was sly and unencumbered, the equivalent of what philosophers do when noodling around with their dead-cat-in-a-box conundrums. Her poems sidled toward their real subjects as if slightly intimidated by them: Van Duyn seemed surprised into tragedy or comedy by the domestic routine.

A poet so careless and beguiling could not believe in "working through otherness to recognition" if love were not the middle ground of tragedy and comedy (love may be the idea the suburbs were constructed to forget). In a life of common pursuits, love becomes an absorbing emotion not for its manners but its movement, its steady allowance of the passion of change, of the commerce of bodies: its passport out of the familiar into a "strange and willful country."

> I still see the mother I wanted, that I called to
>   come,
> coming. From the dark she rushes to my bedroom,
>
> switching the lamp on, armed with pills, oils,
>   drops,
> gargles, liniments, flannels, salves, syrups,
>
> waterbag, icebag. Bending over me,
> giant, ferocious, she drives my Enemy,
>
> in steamy, hot-packed, camphorated nights,
> from every sickening place where he hides and
>   waits.
>
> Do you think I don't know how love hallucinates?

("Remedies, Maladies, Reasons")

In the beautiful pregnancies of her half-rhymes, Van Duyn is our great, stinging poet of the adequacies of love, even of the worn or threadbare desires of the newspaper personals. A poet so haphazard in her practice rarely achieves such formal control; but in the rhymed poems of her middle period Van Duyn found a way to sharpen what she elsewhere calls "My capriciousness and downright perversity." All the casual losses could not conceal her mordant heart.

> Against intention, the feelings raise
> a whole heavy self, panting and clumsy, into these
> contortions. We live in waste. I don't know about
>   you,
> but I live in the feelings, they direct the
>   contortions of the day,
>
> and that is to live in waste. What we must do, we
>   do,
> don't we, and learn, in love and art, to see
> that the peony stalks are red, and learn to say this

416

in the calm voice of our famous helplessness.

(**"Peony Stalks"**)

Van Duyn is a poet more at ease in her resolutions than her premises, but no matter where her poems begin (and they often seem to begin with dogs) they end in the mute regards of love: A poem may start with the invention of horseradish, but it ends in "married love." The theme so infuses her work, lurks so readily around every corner, that its sudden appearance comes to seem a faded punch line; yet her endings have such forbearance, such hedged gratitude, that the poems have more dignity than they perhaps deserve.

Van Duyn has an unusual poetic intelligence—it is not pristine like Yeats' or Merwin's or Stevens', not an intelligence that might have been perfectly content had the world never existed, that acts as if the world does not exist outside poems (as if the world were the idea of the poem). It is an intelligence not corrupted by the everyday, only a little soiled by it: intimate with disappointment, with sultry and sour detachment, with the failing garden and the poisoned dog, full of minor joys and partial surrenders.

Her poems have faltered whenever they have strayed far from her themes or telling forms—her weakest work refuses the sophistication of voice and tone which her subtleties of language elsewhere demand. The artlessly plainspoken *Bedtime Stories* (1972), tales told in dialect by a maundering grandmother, did not pander to the sentimental impulse so much as surrender to it. Her recent poetry has been more than occasionally occasional, and though one expects that later in life a poet will write more than her share of elegies, many of her late poems have been driven by the moment rather than coming to embody it.

> *Firefall* **is very much a book of elegy and farewell, a catalogue of the ills and complaints of age, the losses endured and the losses still to be faced.**
> —*William Logan*

Firefall is very much a book of elegy and farewell, a catalogue of the ills and complaints of age, the losses endured and the losses still to be faced. Van Duyn has discarded much of her irony and bitter self-regard, and with them the technical fashioning that once established a subtle metaphysical register beneath the headlong suburban crises. Her new poems seem more desperately contrived by their occasions: a poem about a painting by Chagall, a poem about ads for lost children, a villanelle for the Duc d'Orléans' fifteenth-century villanelle contést, a poem about winning the Pulitzer, a poem about writers and their dogs, a poem about not being Richard Wilbur. A poem of apology for having given a friend a hideously ugly shirt (black with yellow stripes) attempts some eighteen goofy rhymes on "hornet," including "highernote," "hermit-/wit," "keep even the whoreneat," "undo a hueorknot," "blow a hornat," "no matter howornate," etc. There are two dozen "minimalist sonnets" and "extended minimalist sonnets," of this sort: "The Young plot / each glance / but know chance / will allot // a moonshot / of romance, / a slowdance / of pot, // not hearing / life's handcuffs / unlock // till wearing / their earmuffs / of Rock." Some translate famous anthology poems into Van Duynese. So, **"The Circus Animals' Desertion"**: "Linking / starts / in stinking / hearts. // Dung / clings, / but rung / sings. // Then / rust. / Again / one must // think / stink." So, **"Dover Beach"**: "Sweetness / seems. / Mess / screams. // Be / clone. / We / are alone // in unfaith / armed, / wrath / uncharmed, / / an ungirled / world."

It is dispiriting to have to say that the charms and the shrewd material intelligence of Van Duyn's poetry are almost entirely absent in this book. We are instead witness to what remains when the charms are stripped away: a scaffolding of artifice, forced reminiscence, labored jokes, and poems designed to do badly everything this poet once did so idiosyncratically and so well. Only a few passages remind the reader that she can be a poet of delicious, drenched language and difficult feeling:

> On the table rolled to ours a flat pan holds
> the posed trio under a fiery arbor
> of crabs, tails to a blue-black coil of conger.
> On either side, like bridesmaids, the symmetry,
> grace, sea-molded curves of mullet and loup;
> in the center, the bride ("a first-class bouillabaisse
> owes its quality to the *rascasse,* which is
> essential"), *rascasse* the hog-fish, known to folk
> and fishermen as the ugliest fish in the world.
> Round, lovely eyes of her finny attendants
> are blind to the rope of grotesque neck
> that lifts a snouted face to her clan of lovers.

(**"Rascasse"**)

To praise such passages (has anyone other than Anthony Hecht written with such furtive appetite?) is not to ignore the limitations of a poet more honored than anthologized: A world of enforced mildness has its tragedies, even if it has trouble naming them. The Poet Laureate has been—and still occasionally is—a rueful, darkly witty poet of odd emotional cadence and a fine cautious rapture.

Liz Rosenberg (review date 11 April 1993)

SOURCE: "The Collected Mona Van Duyn," in *Chicago Tribune Books,* April 11, 1993, pp. 6-7.

[*In the following review, Rosenberg applauds Van Duyn's abilities as a poet, and praises* If It Be Not I, *but declares that* Firefall *"is not up to [Van Duyn's] own best standards."*]

It's difficult to call "neglected" a poet who has won the Pulitzer Prize, the National Book Award and the Bollingen Prize and who is, currently, Poet Laureate of the United States. Yet for all that, Mona Van Duyn is perhaps more widely known than widely read, and that is a form of neglect that deprives us all. Nearly every poem in the generous collection *If It Be Not I* has at least one line of extraordinary beauty or of wisdom—often both—and what more dare one hope for from any one volume of poetry?

Van Duyn possesses both wit and passion, restraint and power, the art of composition and of marvelous storytelling. She can speak with genuine grandiloquence or in the earthy voice of an old farm woman, as in *Bedtime Stories,* an exceptional book of poems included in *If It Be Not I.* Her best work stands up to the best poets—there is a grandeur in it. Her **"Garland for Christopher Smart,"** for example, is the same size as Smart himself, if a different flavor; but to reach an equal wildness and wit is no mean feat.

Van Duyn's best poems are peopled or landscaped; she sees clearly and affectionately a rich variety of people—from a lobsterman come "to fix our oilstove. I am dazzled by the man in boots. / It is as if a heron stood in my dining-room," to a hypochondriacal mother armed with medicines:

> I still see the mother I wanted, that I called to
> come,
> coming. From the dark she rushes to my bedroom,
> switching the lamp on, armed with pills, oils,
> drops,
> gargles, linaments; salves, syrups,
> waterbag, icebag. Bending over me,
> giant, ferocious, she drives my Enemy,
> in steamy, hotpacked, camphorated nights,
> from every sickening place where he hides and
> waits.
> Do you think I don't know how love
> hallucinates?"

In grace and luminosity she often resembles the late Elizabeth Bishop and is, like Bishop, a past master at her craft. (See how deftly she works in rhymed couplets, above.) Her poems are composed. One can learn as much from her as from Robert Frost or Edna St. Vincent Millay, two other great formalists of our century. Her sense of narrative never wavers, and she is at home in metrical verse and in rhyme,

"that linguistic sunbeam/ [that] says things are, and are not, the same. . . ."

Most of all she does what she commands herself to do, "to pit love and art, which are compassionate." That is to say, love and art suffer together in her work. There is evidence of both the suffering and of hard-won wisdom—"To trust perception again is like learning to lean / on water. The water, moving over minnows, is haunted"—but always alongside great beauty of language and music: "The thunder rises like mist and the leaves like lovers enfold him / and time, rocks, rooks and roses grow from his body. . . ."

Her poetry is delicate but never dainty. In the loveliness and lightness of her work, Van Duyn makes other poets seem dull and inept the way the late Audrey Hepburn used to outshine famous beauties. It comes from elegance of the highest order—of being other-worldly and grounded at once, above capricious self-centeredness.

All of which makes me even sorrier to say that her new book, *Firefall,* issued simultaneously with the collected poems, is not up to her own best standards. One can hardly imagine Van Duyn rushing into anything poetically, but *Firefall* feels hastily put together; it may be that it simply follows too closely on the heels of her *Near Changes* (1991).

In any event, her "minimalist sonnets," as she calls them here—14-line rhymed poems with fewer feet per line than the norm—literally and figuratively fall short. The humor is frequently brittle, while her "translations" of other poets' great poems (Yeats, Eliot et al.) are particularly unsatisfying. Irony is Van Duyn's least becoming attire, and she wears it too often here, though there are a few mighty poems in this new collection, especially those that stand on the dark side of "goodbye," especially two dedicated to her friend, the late poet Howard Nemerov.

If It Be Not I includes all of Van Duyn's books of poems up to, but not including, the Pulitzer Prize-winning *Near Changes.* This is, on one hand, a shame, for readers will want to see the accomplishments of that award-winning book, but a blessing in disguise if it promises a second, future collected poems. In the meantime, we have a substantial number of poems worth revisiting from a poet of wonderful substance and spirit:

> I held up the poem's side first, and life's side
> second,
> for I believe in art's process of working through
> otherness to recognition
> and in its power that comes from acceptance, and
> not imposition—
> for people, that is; and if life is not a poem, and
> this is clear,

one can still imply that one sometimes wishes it
were.

Robyn Selman (review date 1 July 1993)

SOURCE: "Housekeeping," in *The Village Voice,* Vol. 38,
No. 22, July 1, 1993, pp. 60-1.

[*In the following review, Selman applauds Van Duyn's body
of work, and offers favorable assessments of* If It Be Not I
and Firefall.]

When married couples came to my parents' home for card-
playing afternoons, the husbands and wives parted at the
front door like two rivers. The gulf between them seemed
unnavigable—their card games were as different as their
drinks, laughs, and speech levels. Women whose identities
were usually defined by the consistency of their noodle puddings, were, until dinnertime, free. Literally: I remember my
Aunt Ida rising up from the canasta table and, in an outrageous act of independence, lifting her dress and stripping off
her girdle. My delight in Aunt Ida's act—her equivalent of
a man rolling up his sleeves to deal the hand—has lasted
over 20 years.

Women alone together can be wholly their own stories. Personas are lifted, girdles are shed, makeup isn't as thick. As
a child, I found this kitchen-realism was infinitely more interesting than my father's universe of hollered business deals
and Delta 88's. Though the women I knew in the suburbs
were not educated in the traditional sense, their lives were
full of accomplishment. One had been a Ziegfeld Girl, one
ran a lingerie store in Grand Central, one bested the mob in
a candy business, and one put her son through college on
the change she collected from her husband's pockets and
later invested. Though they remained powerless in the world,
their intelligence was abundant and their knowledge could
have filled reams.

Mona Van Duyn is their poet. Her lines are born out of that
disappearing mid-century klatsch. Though her language and
forms are flawless and her references ornately classical, the
meanings of her poems translate readily into a universal
suburbanese. It is the sound not of tongue in cheek, but of a
woman biting the inside of her cheek to keep from bursting
with what she knows. Van Duyn is the poet of the buzz beneath the fine, trimmed lawns; she's the poet of washing
machines who writes superbly of being a woman in all its
disguises, of marriage and daughterhood and all their masks;
she inhabits the mind behind the mind that stirs the soup.

Van Duyn has rolled up her sleeves for over 40 years in a
suburb of St. Louis. There she is surrounded not by opulent
homes or famous people, but by women and their children
and their husbands.

She is a poet among the ordinary. And just as one could be
fooled daily by the seemingly obedient women on my street,
Van Duyn's poetry is meant to surprise you. Surprise is her
métier, as in these lines from **"Marriage, With Beasts":**
"Bringing our love to the zoo to see what species / it is, I
carry my head under my arm, / you cradle yours; we will
hold them up to cages / or set them back on perch at the
proper moments. . . . / for what happens here is as informal
/ as disease, and we, like lust, are serious / about making
sense of a strange, entire surface." Scanning this nugget, my
eyes are drawn to the words *cages, cradle,* and *perch,* all
apt synonyms for suburbs or zoos. The major trope of Van
Duyn's work is the recurring plainness she presents again
and again, so often that it becomes elaborate and larger than
life. The seemingly ordinary women of St. Louis are mistresses of surface, adept at obedience, childlike innocence,
and complicity, but in Van Duyn's poems they are brilliantly
secretive. They hide their intelligence under cosmetic
touches of seductiveness and eccentrism, elusive and elaborate disguises. When I read Van Duyn's poetry I experience
the same exhilaration I found as a child watching Aunt Ida
strip off her girdle—the joy of uncovering the skin beneath
the painted, glossy foundation:

> I have given you paper faces
>   and they have grown lifelike,
> and you have stuck on my lips in
>   this sheep's smile.
> If I could get free of you I would
>   change, and I would choke
> this stooge to death and be proud
>   and violent for a while.
> As long as the moon hides half her
>   face we are friends of the moon.
> As long as sight reaches through
>   space we are fond of the stars.
> But there is no space and what
>   light is yours and what is mine
> is impossible to tell in this
>   monstrous Palomar
> where each pock is plain.

Looking at Van Duyn's collected poems, *If It Be Not I,*
which includes selections from each of her out-of-print books
from 1959 to 1982, I am struck by the fact that some of her
best work remains poems such as **"Leda Reconsidered,"**
revisions of women's roles in classical myths—myths she
upends. What Anne Sexton did for fairy-tale femmes
Cinderella and Gretel, Van Duyn does for Leda and Danae.
The poems included here from her third volume, *To See To
Take,* concentrate on the ordinary housewife's encounters
with Zeus, who is not only king of the gods, but king of the

hearth. In this cycle of poems, the domestic muse achieves her true station. Here are Zeus, Leda, Danae, and Eros gossiping over the back fence with Van Duyn's St. Louis kitchen goddess, the newly imagined Leda.

Van Duyn's **"Leda"** takes off with an epigraph from Yeats's "Leda and the Swan": "Did she put on his knowledge with his power / Before the indifferent beak could let her drop?" Yeats answers yes, Van Duyn definitely no: "Not even for a moment. He knew for one thing, what he was. / When he saw the swan in her eyes he could let her drop. / In the first look of love men find their great disguise, / and collecting these rare pictures of himself was his life." By examining layer after layer of the god's mask, Leda is able to see both the god and herself more clearly. Dropped by the god, she awakens a suburban housewife:

> Later, with the children in
> 　school, she opened her eyes
> and saw her own openness, and
> 　felt relief.
> In men's stories her life ended
> 　with his loss.
> She stiffened under the storm of
> 　his wings to a glassy shape,
> stricken and mysterious and
> 　immortal. But the fact is,
> she was not, for such an ending,
> 　abstract enough.
> She tried for a while to
> 　understand what it was
> that had happened, and then
> 　decided to let it drop.
> She married a smaller man with a
> 　beaky nose,
> and melted away in the storm of
> 　everyday life.

With **"Leda Reconsidered,"** Van Duyn juxtaposes gods and humans, great expectations and limited resources. Aprons, laundry, flaws, and all, the courageous lowlife of humans wins. Her Leda puts on a power that Yeats's Leda did not consider: In the companion poem, **"Outlandish Agon,"** she asks, "And now, how much would she try / to see, to take, / of what was not hers, of what / was not to be offered?"

Very little in the way of understanding or shared knowledge and power was offered to Van Duyn by critics of her early poetry. In 1965, shortly after the appearance of Van Duyn's second book, *A Time of Bees,* James Dickey wrote in *The New York Times Book Review,* "Mona Van Duyn is one of the best woman poets around. She is all woman, dealing very largely with the day-to-day domestic scene, both overemphasized in current poetry and yet hardly touched in depth at all." Believe it or not, this quick study, in which Dickey pro-

poses that men write about what is significant (wars, travels, philosophical themes of great importance, god), while women are condemned to write about their own little lives, was seen as a rave—good enough to be used on Van Duyn's dust jacket. But to my mind, Van Duyn long ago took Dickey's comment and ran with it, becoming a full-blown *domestic goddess.* Those accustomed to a more literary language might prefer her own description of herself from the poem **"Homework"**: "a sweating Proust of the pantry shelves." Still, a rose is a rose, and no matter how you say it, Van Duyn is one of the pioneers of a poetry that gives voice to the inner life of suburban women. Though what that inner life comprises is precisely what has eluded so many of her (male) readers. The delicious irony is that Van Duyn now has James Dickey's old job as Poet Laureate of the United States.

Even her loyal women readers may have something of a difficult time with Van Duyn. In numerous interviews over the years she has kept a distance, refusing to define herself as a feminist, which may have reduced her popularity among my contemporaries. To this day, she calls herself Mrs. Jarvis Thurston in author bios. "People blush for me in political discussion," she writes in **"Elementary Attitudes,"** and she's right. Maybe she loves her disguises too well. Just as Marilyn Monroe's naïveté seemed natural rather than performed, Van Duyn's disguises are too good; they disguise the disguises. To take Van Duyn at her word, accept her simply as the sweating Proust of the pantry shelves, is to miss the point of her work. The mask of the suburban woman enables her to explore perfection, reality, and the mediation between the two. An apron-wearing Daniel, she gains access to the master's den. One of the best woman poets, indeed.

The poems in *Letters from a Father* and *Near Changes* and now *Firefall,* her latest work, depart from the use of myth and disguises and move into more open, contemporary-sounding discussions of aging: her parents' illness, her 50-year marriage. To these she brings linguistic density and ease with form, wresting poems out of what is given to her—whether it's time's effects on the lover's body or actual letters from her father—and creating humorous, instructive, empathic work. Like Eavan Boland's poems about her Irish home front, Van Duyn's poems contain the intelligence of the besieged, but these women toss the unfamiliarity of the familiar instead of Molotov cocktails. Which makes Van Duyn's poems political acts (whether she sees them that way or not).

Firefall contains some especially delightful shorter pieces. But overall, its strength lies in the way that the new poems reinforce themes already familiar to readers of her work; it will also do well as an introduction of Van Duyn to new readers. The opening poem, **"A Dog Lover's Confession,"** an ars poetica in the form of a semisonnet, brings us back to

Van Duyn's omnipresent concern, that place between the ideal and the realized, which is nothing more or less than the suburb of life's great mysteries where we all live and work, amid the pocks.

> Perfect love I have known,
> whose animal eyes
> disregard all disguise,
> go beyond flesh and bone,
>
> and unshaken forever,
> heart's white purity
> any angel would envy.
> But I slightly prefer
>
> unpredictable pairing,
> pain and peace in one thing,
> unplumbable thoughts,
> the love that comes wearing,
> fall, fire, freeze or spring.
> black and white polka dots.

Rachel Hadas (review date 18 July 1993)

SOURCE: "Serious Poets," in *New York Times Book Review,* Vol. 98, July 18, 1993, p. 18.

[*In the following excerpt, Hadas reviews* If It Be Not I *and* Firefall, *and surveys Van Duyn's career.*]

Mona Van Duyn is a Midwesterner, and her poetry speaks expansively; her lines are loaded like a cornucopia with the things of this world. A wonderful early poem, **"Three Valentines to the Wide World"** (1959) posits a distrust of unwieldy generalities: I have never enjoyed those roadside overlooks from which you can see the mountains of two states. The view keeps generating a kind of pure, meaningless exaltation that I can't find a use for . . . a statement so abstract that it's tiresome.

Simply to see and say is never enough. However rich, Ms. Van Duyn's voice is never bland; particularity inflects her love of the world. *Firefall,* her new collection, varies the pace of the work with skinny "minimalist sonnets" that capture large themes (love, aging) with aphoristic slimness. But in her best and most ambitious poems, Ms. Van Duyn allows her capacious vision the space it needs to sweep the scene, taking in every detail until some kind of epiphany deepens the tone and moves the poem beyond the mundane. **"The Stream"** is one example; another is **"The Delivery,"** the final piece in *Firefall.* In familiar smells and muddle of voices, mashed potatoes, dimming light, hamburger, thick

creamed corn, the milk-white chill, a self is being born. And is swept away . . . .

The last four words signal the entrance to a figurative world of murkier feelings, deeper waters: to tributary, to river, deep and slow, whose sob-like surges quietly lift her and carry her unjudged freight clear to the mourning sea. And there they are, all of the heavy others (even Mother and Father), the floundering, floating or sinking human herd. . . .

> **A master of metaphor, Ms. Van Duyn is skilled at transforming the homely to the transcendent, defamiliarizing the utensils of our lives.**
> **—*Rachel Hadas***

A master of metaphor, Ms. Van Duyn is skilled at transforming the homely to the transcendent, defamiliarizing the utensils of our lives. A battered pasta bowl clasps a marriage (**"Mr. and Mrs. Jack Sprat in the Kitchen"**); food machines at a turnpike rest stop become hospital denizens (**"Emergency Room"**). **"Letters From a Father,"** an epistolary novella in verse, details an elderly couple's weaning from self-pity to rapt interest in the birds that flock to their feeder. **"Letters"** concludes with a single line (from the letters' recipient) whose celebratory valediction and valedictory celebration make it an apt summary of much of Ms. Van Duyn's best work: "So the world woos its children back for an evening kiss."

Utterly unsentimental love for the world turns up everywhere in Mona Van Duyn's work. Auden didn't include wisdom among his criteria, but if to be a major poet is to be wise and sustaining, then . . . Ms. Van Duyn [meets] this condition, too. . . .

Ben Howard (review date December 1993)

SOURCE: "Masters of Transience," in *Poetry,* Vol. CLXIII, No. 3, December, 1993, pp. 158-70.

[*In the following review, Howard offers praise for* Firefall.]

Over the course of her long career Mona Van Duyn has maintained two quite different allegiances. A celebrant of the world as well as the spirit, she has trafficked freely between privileged moments and domestic routines, the glories of changeless art and the pile of soiled laundry. "Forever the spirit wants to be embodied," she reminds us; but for Van Duyn the spirit's embodiments are, as often as not, ungainly and unseemly—the "spraddled fern of celery top," the "bloodclot of an over-ripe tomato." Likewise the sources of art, which give rise to beauty and pleasure, are themselves unpleasant and unbeautiful. "What fertilizes but muck?" she asks in **"Rascasse,"** a hymn of praise for the hogfish, "the ugliest fish in the world," whose prized "essence" is the indispensable ingredient for "first-class bouillabaisse." "[W]hat gives comfort, what creates, but ugliness?" Inhaling the "stench" of "some boggy burning," she kneels at the "unpraised heart of being, of essence."

Firefall is Van Duyn's tenth collection of poems. In forms, themes, and tonal values it is of a piece with her earlier work, although more than half of the forty-four poems have been cast in what the poet calls the "minimalist sonnet," by which she means a sonnet with lines much shorter than pentameter. Playful or rueful, witty or grave, Van Duyn's sonnets, elegies, and detailed descriptive poems entertain subjects as diverse as love, marriage, births, deaths, art, the creative process, and the "full splendor" of "the flowering self." Apart from its minimalist experiments the present collection breaks no new ground, but like the poet's earlier work it bespeaks a humane, forgiving spirit, rich in warmth and moral wisdom.

Those qualities enliven Van Duyn's poems on love and marriage, which balance elements of passion and pragmatism, realism and romance. In **"Eruption"** she warns that "trapped love can't stop," that it "will swell to a mountain / till time blows its top / and it scalds everyone." But in **"The Beginning,"** a minimalist sonnet, she looks with cool precision on passion and its changes:

> The end
> of passion
> may refashion
> a friend.
>
> Eyes meet
> in fear
> of such dear
> defeat.
>
> The heart's core,
> unbroken,
> cringes.
>
> The soul's door
> swings open
> on its hinges.

"For love to be real," the poet declares, "it must first be imaginary." But in a witty variation on a traditional motif, she envisions Cupid's good fortune in hitting a "mind" rather than a heart ("He had never known // so rich a rest, / an aim so blest"); and in a poem about dog-loving, she expresses

her preference for an imperfect love, a "love that comes wearing . . . black and white polka dots." A poem about her marriage takes a similar stance, portraying the poet and her husband as **"Mr. and Mrs. Jack Sprat in the Kitchen"** and contrasting his "ration / of compulsive precisions" with her own approximations, her "searchings" and "revisions." On a more solemn note (in **"The Marriage Sculptor"**), she depicts a troubled marriage as a wrecked sculpture, which the artist will remake into something "more brilliant and powerful, // a larger work." "Beauty / learns from beauty,'" the sculptor explains, "'the first costly form // lies coiled in the last.'"

The rhythms of death and birth, destruction and construction, prevail in *Firefall,* lending shape to particular poems and balance to the collection as a whole. **"Sondra"** commemorates the early death of a "young scholar, young artist, / young lover of people." **"Fallen Angel,"** a lyrical elegy, laments the loss of seven friends in a six-month period:

> Not from rebellion does the angel fall.
> The muscles of its pinions are huge from the stress
> of storms that beat against its blessedness,
> its migrations to need, whose distances are
> deceitful.

Yet, in **"For Julia Li Qiu,"** Van Duyn celebrates the birth of "a beautiful black-haired daughter," and in **"Addendum to 'The Block,'"** she welcomes the arrival of three babies in a single week, their advent announced by "pink or blue balloons and bold-faced signs."

Van Duyn brings a similar sense of balance to her reflections on art and the creative process. In an elegy for May Swenson she extols "the pride and peace of poems, their elegant play," and in a poem prompted by reading Richard Wilbur, she praises the "bodiless words" of poetry, its "perfect lightness" and "transparent form." Yet in the latter poem she acknowledges that no writer may "aspire" to "the sill where such poems tower," poets being frail and miserable creatures, whose messy lives resemble "paint pots," "open for using." And in **"Endings,"** she contrasts the shapelessness and messiness of life with the closures and meaningful forms of art. "For what is story if not relief from the pain / of the inconclusive, from dread of the meaningless?"

Cast in rhymed pentameters, **"Endings"** represents the kind of poem at which Van Duyn excels—the relaxed colloquial monologue, in which a gift for thoughtful reflection and a love of quotidian realities find their fullest expression. At their best, her "minimalist sonnets" sparkle and sing, but their very economy seems at odds with the poet's penchant for gritty particulars and her proclivity for extended rumination. "Life and more life I want!" she declares in **"Falls":** "Not *one* crop / but *thousands* in their unimaginable / abundance, shape, size, color, kind. . . ." To that end, as to her exploration of "the helpless sorrow / of being wise," her expansive reflections—mindful of heaven but grounded in flesh and soil—remain her trademark and her most enabling mode.

Judith Hall (essay date Winter 1994)

SOURCE: "Strangers May Run: The Nation's First Woman Poet Laureate," in *The Antioch Review,* Vol. 52, No. 1, Winter, 1994, pp. 141-46.

[*In the following essay, Hall comments on Van Duyn's stature as the first woman ever named poet laureate in the United States and discusses critical opinions of Van Duyn's works.*]

When the position of poetry consultant to the Library of Congress was elevated, by an act of Congress, to the more classic-or anglo-or botanical-sounding poet laureate, the U.S. Congress (or was it simply the government's library staff?) could not agree to elevate, with the office, the incumbent Gwendolyn Brooks. The consensus was no; the debate unpublicized, and who was surprised? When Robert Penn Warren's name emerged, it may have had—in those days, soon described as long ago, the late '80s—a ring more historic or laudatory, at least fugitive, white, various, and questing. "But go on," he said, "that's how men survive."

Six years later, Americans, in our love of variety and evanescence, have welcomed and discarded as many laureates. Finally, in June, 1992, for some reason, the nation could accept a woman laureate: Mona Van Duyn. Why a woman? "I heard that Merwin wouldn't do it." One historian would listen, satisfied, and leave to write it down.

Others argue on: Why a woman? No one would expect a volunteer. After all, it was a job and salaried; the figure, $35,000, was defined by one official as "about half a salary" for poets. Money, so precisely introduced, will yield saliva. And when our government announces, however indirectly, that poets should receive about $70,000, I swallow. I gasp. I pour domestic champagne and compose something almost patriotic about Toast-R-Ovens and iced tea and the enduring consolations of amber waving grain.

And yet, the official sounds apologetic. The library will offer only *half*—half of what the poet may deserve. To work for half? Any man would hesitate today, after the salary was publicized, half-cocked. Or having done it, however briefly, he would turn from Washington, D.C., concluding that the "job" was "ill-paid, ill-defined, and ultimately ill-executed." Why a woman? Why now? To work for *half*. . . "Oh, yes, I

see." Other historians would listen, unsatisfied, and leave. I see them walking to another institute, where they lean together, unobserved, and argue other reasons, more capricious or meritorious; why a woman poet laureate arrived.

But why Van Duyn? Perhaps that is easier to reckon than the timing of our first woman poet laureate. Before she was chosen, Van Duyn's books had won a Pulitzer, a Bollingen, and a National Book Award; such garlands, won together, were once considered the Triple Crown. Think of the poet strewn, at least as lavishly as Secretariat, with pink confetti and money and more domestic champagne. All this assurance, then, of merit, so consoling to American readers, may now prepare us for the poems. The poems?

Two volumes in 1993 heralded our first woman laureate: *Firefall,* new poems, and *If It Be Not I: Collected Poems 1959-1982.* These, along with *Near Changes* (1990), constitute a reminder of all that she has given us and justify her laureateship. Each of these three books includes "praise for Mona Van Duyn"; a curious redundancy; the same hoorays selected for each book. I linger for a minute on these accolades, composed by younger players, and consider their use, as praise is always used, for advertisement.

Her poetry is "beautiful and exact," "accessible and profound," with several noting how long she has been working: for "several decades"; "since 1959." The woman works, you see, and has "ambition . . . intelligence," attributes that still might disconcert those who want a poet to be natural; so rushing in behind to ease the nervous reader, the blurbette soothes with "humor . . . ease . . . original without eccentricity."

Advertisements are designed to soothe the reader, long enough to buy the book, and yet I am puzzled, then concerned, to see how such reviews of Van Duyn's work, and then a murmuring opinion in the field, resemble these bland remarks. "However rich, [her voice] is never bland," hails the *New York Times,* with earnest vacuity, and goes so far as to announce, cheerfully, her "utter unsentimental love for the world."

Beautiful, accessible, unsentimental: a woman's triple crown? Thank God, no "eccentricity" confirmed in Janson type on all three books. Now the poems are safe for public consumption, composed, in fact, by the somehow more consoling Mrs. Jarvis Thurston. Think of Mrs. Browning, the first woman mentioned for England's poet laureate. Mrs. Thurston; Mrs. Browning; safe. And yet, if I were seeking a woman's poetry that was "beautiful, accessible, unsentimental," I might choose Anne, Countess of Winchelsea, or even (must there be another quarrel?) Edna St. Vincent Millay, our "unofficial feminine laureate," as Louise Bogan wrote impatiently.

"A great many of my poems have been misread by mostly male critics—I mean, most of the critics *are* male," said Mona Van Duyn (Mrs. Jarvis Thurston) in an interview, apparently her fifty-eighth, as the first woman poet laureate. She was seventy-one. "I use domestic imagery and extend that imagery through the whole poem, but I'm not writing about that. It's simply used as a metaphor. There's nothing insulting about that. I *do* write some domestic poems. So do the male poets. But it is a limiting term when it's used over and over for a poet who, aside from the few domestic poems she *and* they do write, uses domestic metaphor to describe ideas. . . ."

Her tone is almost palpable fatigue, or is it anger? It is exasperating to defend the same ground fifty-eight times or dodge a well-meaning review that waters down a woman's work until it drifts away. Or accept a phantom surrogate, the blurb, when in it, one woman's verse resembles any other. Anne Bradstreet's, for example: "Tis the Work of a Woman, honoured and esteemed where she lives, for her gracious courteous disposition, the exact diligence in her place, and discreet mannaging of her family occasions."

The praise, "exact" and "mannaging" her family, in 1650, becomes in 1993 "exact" and "accessible"; "the searching intelligence of . . . the well-educated wife, good friend, and daughter." Van Duyn does indeed offer her American reader a persona in the guise of wife, friend, or daughter. She is complicit, to that extent, with social expectations; with the heterosexual reader in suburbia, who is comfortable and almost smug in middle-life, or later; who takes a little wit with bourbon after work.

This reader likes Van Duyn when she is decorous, self-mocking—poses she brings to **"Notes From a Suburban Heart"**: "I love you, in my dim-witted way." Her poems may end on this girlishly ironic note or with apology or certainty, but these are strategies intended to distract with consolation from the jeopardy she knows. Van Duyn offers her reader *half* of what he seeks: the compensations of suburbia; but offered with this "helpless" expectation is her own perspective:

> Peony stalks come up like red asparagus,
> I said; my friend said they look like dogs' penises.
> It was something misplaced I noticed, the color of
>   a wound,
> but she's right, it has something to do with love
>   too in my mind.

("Peony Stalks")

This is quintessential Van Duyn—narrative draped around a rumination; accentual stanzaic pattern with end rhymes, slanted and supported by internal assonance. Suburbia; a friend; a garden, but with dogs' penises in it and wounds.

Van Duyn is a poet of relationships recollected in tranquillity. Although most of our poetry is set in solitude, she hedges hers with others, usually one other figure at a time. Or when, in **"Three Valentines to the Wide World,"** the poem ends with a young woman witnessing her own "untended power," the experience is distilled in social terms; a parable in moonlight. And the rage and violation described are amplified by their mutation and the disturbing inevitability of her rhymed octaves:

> And if, in the middle of her life, some beauty falls
>   on
> a girl, who turns under its swarm to astonished
>   woman,
> them, into that miraculous buzzing, stung
> in the lips and eyes without mercy, strangers may
>   run.
> An untended power—I pity her and them.
> It is late, late; haste! says the falling moon,
> as blinded they stand and smart till the fever's
>   done
> and blindly she moves, wearing her furious
>   weapon.
>
> Beauty is merciless and intemperate.
> Who, turning this way and that, by day, by night,
> still stands in the heart-felt storm of its benefit,
> will plead in vain for mercy, or cry, "Put out
> the lovely eyes of the world, whose rise and set
> move us to death!" And never will temper it,
> but against that rage slowly may learn to pit
> love and art, which are compassionate.

Van Duyn's best work uses linguistic clarity as a response to long acquaintance with the irrational, the bereft, and the chronically beleaguered. In this way, only, her poetry resembles that of Elizabeth Bishop. This tension underneath Van Duyn's "accessibility" makes the stated goals for poetry—compassion, empathy (thus moral; Horatian)—more tenuous and provisional and moving.

> **Van Duyn's best work uses linguistic clarity as a response to long acquaintance with the irrational, the bereft, and the chronically beleaguered.**
> **—*Judith Hall***

One of her finest poems, **"Remedies, Maladies, Reasons,"** recollects the persona's relationship with her mother; the bond, defined by medical emergency, is chthonic and ecstatic:

> . . . She "hawks up big gobs

of stuff" that is almost orange. All of her tubes

are blocked. Her face turned purple. Lettuce she
   ate
was "passed" whole, "green as grass" in the toilet.

She "came within an inch" of a "stoppage," but
   mineral oil
saved her from all but "a running-off of the
   bowel."

Sniffing her mucus or sweat or urine, she marvels
anew at how "rotten" or "rank" or "sour" it smells.

There's never been any other interesting news.
Homer of her own heroic course, she rows

through the long disease of living, and celebrates
the "blood-red" throat, the yellow pus that
   "squirts"

from a swelling, the taste, always "bitter as gall,"
that's "belched up," the bumps that get "sore as a
   boil,"

the gas that makes her "blow up tight as a drum,"
the "racing heart," the "new kind of bug," the
   "same

old sinus," the "god-awful cold"—all things that
   make
her "sick as a dog" or "just a nervous wreck."

The poem wrestles this battering, recreating it (fifty-eight rhymed couplets altogether), and then resolves the presence of this other maker. With humor (Freud's aggressive wit) and the accumulating energy of drama, the persona makes her way towards catharsis:

I still see the mother I wanted, that I called to
   come,
coming. From the dark she rushes to my bedroom,

switching the lamp on, armed with pills, oils,
   drops,
gargles, liniments, flannels, salves, syrups,

waterbag, icebag. Bending over me,
giant, ferocious, she drives my Enemy,

in steamy, hot-packed, camphorated nights,
from every sickening place where he hides and
   waits.

Do you think I don't know how love hallucinates?

No other poet has described so well the horror and adoration that a child feels for the parent's body. She continues this in **"The Stream,"** an elegy for her mother, and in her epistolary novella-in-verse, **"Letters from a Father."** The daughter, then, like Van Duyn's appearance as a wife or friend, is a guise, a metaphor, a remedy she fingers, swallows, revealing to the reader not transcendence but empathy—that more difficult release from solitude.

And yet, compassion is not yet understood as a species of authority. The poet even doubts it. She doubles back; apologizes ("Women don't usually wrestle, except for a comic or grotesque effect"). She "eases" over her own authority, her own "slow, entranced emergence / of things out of the ashes of their usefulness." A poet of relationships will be of use, willing to strain and wrap her art for a **"Christmas Present for a Poet," "To My Godson, On His Christening,"** and **"Lines Written in a Guest Book."**

A charm, a generosity diminishes when rooted from its source, its passion. But who notices, within the smoky institutes and professional fraternities? "The Insight Lady" will arrive, bringing wit they understand; she sips the warm hors d'oeuvres with men. She's in; a woman made it in, but only *half*—not the half that is

    . . . a monstrous face;
  as broad as his chest, as long as he is
  from the top of his head to his heart. All her
  feeling and fleshiness is there.

    ("The Pietà, Rhenish, 14th C., The Cloisters")

That is the part her critics call "bizarre." Send that half—domestic champagne; the hiss of it like bees; a time of bees. That's how women survive.

Doris Earnshaw (review date Spring 1994)

SOURCE: A review of *If It Be Not I: Collected Poems 1959-1982*, in *World Literature Today*, Vol. 68, No. 2, Spring, 1994, p. 135.

[*In the following review, Earnshaw praises* If It Be Not I, *noting a few "shortcomings," but declaring the collected poems "rich, wise, and beautiful."*]

It is of course fascinating to hear the voice of an American woman poet, born in the same decade (1920s) as Adrienne Rich and Denise Levertov, who avoids politics altogether, including the politics of feminism and of the Vietnam War. Mona Van Duyn is a heartland poet, born in Waterloo, Iowa, and living in St. Louis, whereas Rich was raised and educated in sophisticated East Coast surroundings and Levertov was raised and educated in England by her Welsh mother and Russian-Jewish/Christian father. After decades of university teaching while publishing single poems and several collections with modest circulation, Van Duyn gained a wider audience when she received the 1991 Pulitzer Prize for *Near Changes.* In 1992 she was appointed by the Librarian of Congress as Poet Laureate Consultant in Poetry. Responding to the wide interest in her work, Knopf has now issued in one volume her six previously published books of poems: *Valentines to the Wide World* (1959), *A Time of Bees* (1964), *To See, To Take* (1970), *Bedtime Stories* (1972), *Poems (1965-1973)* (1973), and *Letters from a Father and Other Poems* (1982).

What was she writing about all those decades, if not the rousing public affairs of postwar America? Certain themes recur: thrift is valued, waste deplored; beauty is merciless, love and art are compassionate; the human animal owes much to other animals and likewise to flowers and fruit; the visceral and real outshines the abstract; surface and texture hold truth. She catches a moment with lyric and narrative intensity: **"The Voyeur"** places us with a woman undressing in an isolated cabin; she feels a large animal gazing at her; she finishes undressing slowly and contemplates seeking him in the woods for mating. Levertov's gift for metaphor is often stunning; the reader becomes breathless with the wide-stretching connections of her imagery. But her [Levertov's] style is marked by extremes: delicious humor countered by obtuse and clotted abstraction, brilliant showers of metaphor and a low-key talky tone that disguises her mastery of rhythm and rhyme. She can write a poem on canning pears that delights you, all the more as you realize by the last line that you have read a perfect sonnet.

Like Rich and Levertov (and Marianne Moore among others), Van Duyn has several memorable poems on marriage. However, in her case the poems are written from within the marriage bond—she has that rare experience for a poet, a single lifetime marriage. **"Toward a Definition of Marriage"** imagines five analogies: marriage is a landfill like a World's Fair island; an artlessly digressing poem; amateur duelists (my favorite!); a circus whose animals parade reluctantly, never completely trained; and windy oratory, because marriage is the politics of love. The poem wanders aimlessly, like the marriage she describes, but endears itself to the willing reader.

Bedtime Stories takes us via a grandmother's talk into American rural folklore in dialect, recalling James Whitcomb Riley, but darker. We hear the accents of old German settlers telling of strange events and common hardships. Speaking of hardships, there are enough poems about illness and hospitals to make the reader understand that Van Duyn has fought her own tigers. Unlike Sexton and Plath, she has no

mother-child poems, but the struggle for coherence of a highly gifted poet in an antipoet, toxic society must have had similarities. In one line she observes, "There is too much roughage."

Kenneth Burke has written in his introduction to Howard Nemerov's *New and Selected Essays* (1985) about what it is to be a "Nemerovian poet," and Mona Van Duyn belongs, I believe, to the category he describes. It concerns duplicity and the mix of three professions: teacher, scholar, poet. Some of the annoying, rather juvenile treatments of serious subjects seem better suited to classroom presentation to eighteen-year-olds, and the references to grants for travel, academic meetings, and her excessive borrowings betray the nonpoet roles of teacher and scholar. These shortcomings aside, most of the poetry here is rich, wise and beautiful. Van Duyn's "merciful disguises" reward the reader.

Doris Earnshaw (review date Spring 1994)

SOURCE: A review of *Firefall,* in *World Literature Today,* Vol. 68, No. 2, Spring, 1994, p. 376.

[*In the review below, Earnshaw provides a laudatory review of* Firefall.]

Firefall refers to the nightly bonfire that park rangers used to push over the high cliff in California's Yosemite Park to entertain tourists in the valley below. Van Duyn saw the spectacle when, as a girl, she toured the West with her family. The poem which relates this experience, **"Falls,"** contrasts the cascade of fire with the waterfalls at Niagara Falls, also seen on a family tour. She takes both fire and water as fertilizing elements in her poetic creativity. The poem is placed near the close of the collection, the poet's first since *Near Changes,* winner of the 1991 Pulitzer Prize for poetry. In addition to poems on Van Duyn topics (wisdom about life drawn from suburban Midwestern dailiness), *Firefall* contains a series of seven poems in a form she calls the "minimalist" sonnet. The traditional line length has been shortened, but other conventions are kept, except for an occasional added quatrain for a poem she calls "the extended minimalist" sonnet. Each poem responds to a classic and often-studied poem of Auden, Eliot, Yeats, Frost, Hopkins, and Arnold.

Some of the "minimalist" sonnets are intended to comment on the host poem with an interrogation or analysis. Some are "translations" into a more concise language. In commenting on these famous poems, Van Duyn is sure-footed, and the poems take on the pungent flavor of medieval Provencal or Old French forms. Two poems of Yeats are "translated": **"The Circus Animals' Desertion"** and **"A Prayer for My**

Daughter." The first restates the poem's thought in a straightforward manner, but the second extends the meaning metaphorically into another dimension not necessarily in the original, more a "comment" than a "translation." The exercise of matching the derived poem to the original exhilarates the mind. Van Duyn brings to the canon in English a game many would enjoy. The "comment" on Frost's "Mending Wall" poem, for example, takes eighteen lines from the forty-five-line original. Students from junior high school to university graduate seminars would be intrigued.

Many readers enjoy Van Duyn's lighthearted poems, such as, in this collection, **"Mr. and Mrs. Jack Sprat in the Kitchen"** or **"We Are in Your Area"** or **"Words for the Dumb,"** about styles of cooking, suburban annoyances, and the love of pets. **"Addendum to 'The Block'"** continues the poem from *Near Changes* that encapsulates decades of suburban living. More serious are the poems on art—**"Chagall's 'Les Plumes en Fleur'"**—and the death of loved ones: **"For May Swenson"** and **"Sondra."** Her devotion to birds, known from other poems, surfaces in **"Poets in Late Winter."** Reimaginings of Shakespeare's Tempest appear in two poems, **"Miranda Grows Up"** and **"Another Tempest."** In the first she feels Miranda's need to forgive Prospero for taking her from the island to a northern climate where the cold would chill her innocence. The second, more extreme, keeps everyone on the island, gives Fernando the line "Oh brave new world," and reveals Miranda, "the greedy daughter," as Caliban. An essay on this transformation, and on the myth of Leda (another obsessive topic with Van Duyn), would be most interesting.

The final poem, **"The Delivery,"** reaches a level of profound self-revelation. Its two parts demonstrate in one poem two modes of Van Duyn's poetry: realistic narrative and rich metaphor, the "merciful disguise." The opening narrative shows a childhood scene of domestic trauma: the girl's mother ridicules her daughter for feeling intensely a girlfriend's disgrace, saying "I wasn't scolding you, I was scolding Betty." The whole family picks up the joke and laughs as the daughter feels the birth of her "self" apart from the family. In the second part, this self, now carried underwater to "the mourning sea," meets the sinking people "(even Mother and Father)," whom she cannot rescue. She can go part way under into the "Omnipotent dark" that has seized them, but she cannot save them. She returns upward to the lighter water and then to the air. We feel the sadness that accompanies the experience of loneliness that follows illumination. The world "has too much roughage in it," she has said in another poem, but we feel in her poetry the joy of the lighted water and the air.

Robert B. Shaw (review date Spring 1994)

SOURCE: "Life Work," in *Shenandoah,* Vol. 44, Spring, 1994, pp. 38-48.

[*In the following review of* If It Be Not I, Near Changes, *and* Firefall, *Shaw surveys Van Duyn's career, declaring: "At the height of her powers, Mona Van Duyn continues to give fresh meaning to the fusty term 'a life work.'"*]

Among the many talents of Mona Van Duyn a gift for self-promotion is not conspicuous. She has served as Poet Laureate and won a Pulitzer Prize, and yet it seems only recently that her reputation has begun to catch up with her achievement. Her innate modesty has been one obvious reason for this, but there are other more capricious ones as well. For one thing, the long intervals between some of her books have made her an elusive figure to a public with a short attention span. Happily, the three volumes reviewed here [*If It Be Not I: Collected Poems 1959-1982, Near Changes,* and *Firefall*] offer a simple remedy by bringing all of her work at once into print. Beyond this, though, there remains the challenge of an audience's pet stereotypes, and it is here that Van Duyn's poems may even now make trouble for themselves by their refusal to flow into expected channels. She is an individualist both in her topics and her tone, always a good way to fend off easy celebrity.

Concerning topics: critics who are supple and acute in analyzing style can sound embarrassed, condescending, or simply at a loss when asked to consider content. I remember the nervous chuckles of some of my colleagues at Harvard in the '70's when Elizabeth Bishop proposed offering a course entitled "Subject Matter in Poetry." Poets are obliged to be practical in their thinking about this issue: they know they have to write about *something,* and the choice of material, for poets who are any good, is anything but random. It involves the discovery of subjects which will strike chords in the deep recesses of imagination as well as engaging the intellect's discursive powers. About such subjects the poet continually finds yet more to say, as Elizabeth Bishop did about travel and Marianne Moore did about animals. Gradually, by accretion and elaboration, it becomes clear that the fascination of such topics is not in themselves but in the underlying theme which emerges from the patterns and nuances of their repeated appearances. Any poem is "about" more than one thing, and its more vital meaning often is the less ostensible one.

Why can't readers remember this? Van Duyn's poems have in fact been sold short by those who have failed to see beyond their surfaces. Her "persona" in her writing seems to overlap largely with herself: an academic married to an academic, leading a comfortable upper-middle class life in Saint Louis. She has had the temerity to write poems about shopping, cooking, gardening, dogs, vacations. Practitioners of various brands of snobbery—social, political, intellectual—

have shied away from subject matter presumed by them to have no depth. The dread word "domestic," once uttered, slams shut many reputedly tolerant minds. When W. H. Auden turned to deliberately mundane subjects in *About the House* and other later volumes, his willingness to venture into what were for him previously unexplored areas was viewed as a slackening of ambition. Richard Wilbur is another poet who has suffered from this kind of stock response. Like Auden, like Wilbur, Van Duyn in her best work demonstrates that any subject is as deep as the poet makes it.

> **How is it that Van Duyn establishes a scale of value in her poetry, showing the quotidian to be something other (and better) than the "malady" it was for Stevens? One of her strategies is to locate esthetic significance in unlikely contexts.**
> **—*Robert B. Shaw***

Even if that were not so, it can be argued that domesticity has inherent if often unacknowledged profundities. It is, unsettlingly enough, what we all have in common, bohemian aspirations notwithstanding. Allen Ginsberg washes the dishes now and then, and for most of us such activities take up more time than we care to tabulate. Put domestic leisure together with domestic labor, and we have for our concern nothing less than what we often call daily life. It may seem at times less than stimulating, but it is not trivial, and one need not be an existentialist philosopher (or a novelist like Walker Percy) to apprehend rich possibilities mysteriously latent in everydayness. More than any other poet of her time Mona Van Duyn has made it her project to restore freshness to the familiar through close and caring attention to what most of us overlook.

She does this often with a welcome touch of civilized humor, but there is nothing apologetic in her tone, no self-consciousness like Cowper's mock-heroic "I sing the sofa." If we recall that Van Duyn's poems first appeared in quantity in the 1960's, we can see why her tone as well as her topics may have helped to marginalize her. Her writing must have seemed muted indeed compared with the piercing emotionalism of Sylvia Plath and other confessionalists, or the anti-war and subsequently anti-patriarchal anger of Adrienne Rich. It is not that Van Duyn never expresses negative feelings; rather, when she does so, she resists the starkness that results when such feelings are unreflectively allowed to dominate. Again, the parallel with Richard Wilbur is apt: until recently it was fairly common for critics to object that Wilbur didn't sound as if he had suffered enough. Having come to a historical juncture at which it is evident that there is more than enough suffering to go around, we may be readier than readers of the '60's were to appreciate poetry

that can take the measure of grief and loss without being paralyzed by them, and can assign to ordinary goodness something closer to its true weight while pondering our experience on this planet.

How is it that Van Duyn establishes a scale of value in her poetry, showing the quotidian to be something other (and better) than the "malady" it was for Stevens? One of her strategies is to locate esthetic significance in unlikely contexts. In **"Homework"** she draws an emblem from preserving peaches:

> Lest the fair cheeks begin their shrivelling
> before a keeping eye has lit on their fairness,
> I pluck from the stony world some that can't cling
> to stone, for a homely, transparent form to bless.

So the poem begins, and it ends,

> Oh I know, I know that, great or humble, the arts
>
> in their helplessness can save but a few selves
> by such disguises from Time's hideous bite,
> and yet, a sweating Proust of the pantry shelves,
> I cupboard these pickled peaches in Time's
> despite.

A later poem, **"Caring for Surfaces,"** flaunts political incorrectness by celebrating housecleaning:

> Dipped in detergent, dish and chandelier retrieve
> their glister, sopped, kitchen floor reflowers, knife
> rubbed with cork unrusts, colors of carpetweave
> cuffed with shampooer and vacuum with reblush
> . . .

The end of the poem, without belaboring the point, makes a distinction between gender roles:

> Round rooms of surfaces I move, round board,
>   books, bed.
> Men carve, dig, break, plunge as I smooth, shine,
>   spread.

For all its tart matter-of-factness, the last remark merely brings the main point of the poem into keener focus. Van Duyn is less interested in putting men down than she is in celebrating the constructive and esthetic qualities of what have traditionally been seen as women's tasks. Such receptiveness to unexpected beauty suddenly perceived is frequent as well in her outdoor scenes, as at the end of **"Postcards from Cape Split,"** a view of the blueberry barrens in Maine:

> Mile after mile, from road to the far mountains
> of furzy wasteland, flat. You almost miss it.

Suddenly, under that empty space, you notice
the curious color of the ground. Blue mile, blue
  mile,
and then a little bent-over group of Indians
creeping down string-marked aisles. Blue mile,
  blue mile,
and then more Indians, pushing their forked
  dustpans.
It looks like a race at some country picnic, but lost
in that monstrous space, under that vacant sky.

Why am I dazzled? It is only another harvest.
The world blooms and we all bend and bring
from ground and sea and mind its handsome
  harvests.

One notices the stress here is on the harvesters as much as on the harvest. However highly developed her esthetic sense is, it is not for Van Duyn the final arbiter of worth. Her outlook is more broadly humanistic; nature and art are not valued in and of themselves but for what they contribute to the common life of humanity. Human affection has proved to be her most enduring subject—the one more often than not beneath the surface of her domestic vignettes. In this regard she has attempted over the course of her career to fill some gaps. Literature offers us plenty of avowals of romantic passion, but not many good poems about marriage. Likewise, when one considers how important it is for maintaining civilization and keeping us sane, it is surprising how few good poems there are about friendship. Van Duyn has written fine poems about these relationships, as well as less intimate but still valuable ties of community.

Van Duyn's poems about her father and mother are not designed principally to express grievance—though to some extent they do that—but more to register a painfully achieved understanding. They are instruments of reconciliation.
—*Robert B. Shaw*

"**Toward a Definition of Marriage,**" "**Pot-au-Feu,**" "**Marriage, With Beasts,**" "**Late Loving,**" and many other pieces offer searching glimpses into the mystery of an enduring marriage—"love's dishevelment," she calls it in one poem, "a duel of amateurs" in another. The image at the end of "**Late Loving,**" typically intimate and unforced, plays on the paradox of familiarity which seemingly against all odds renews itself rather than growing stale:

What you try to give me is more than I want to
  receive,

yet each month when you pick up scissors for our
  appointment
and my cut hair falls and covers your feet I believe
that the house is filled again with the odor of
  ointment.

No sentimentalist, Van Duyn includes in her depictions of marriage traces of resistance, tension, volatility, as if in recognition of the part these play in keeping a relationship vital. Her views of friendship are equally persuasive and unplatitudinous. "**Open Letter, Personal**" is a wry and funny mock complaint: "Surely the jig is up. We've pinned each other down. / . . . And very soon / your smallest children will tire of naming my couch pillows, / black, white, green, lavender and brown." The arraignment, however, works its way to this spirited reversal:

We know the quickest way to hurt each other, and
we have used that knowledge. See, it is here, in
the joined strands of our weaknesses, that we are
netted together and heave together strongly like
the great catch of mackerel that ends an Italian
movie. I feel your bodies smell and shove and
shine against me in the mess of the pitching boat.
      My friends,
we do not like each other any more. We love.

Other evocations of friendship include "**The Gentle Snorer,**" "**The Block,**" and elegies like "**Sondra**" and (an especially brilliant one) "**The Creation.**" These, like the marriage pieces, emphasize the uncustomary nature of Van Duyn's stance. We are used to the Romantic notion inherited by Modernism of the poet as solitary, as the single contemplative figure in the landscape. Against this tendency Van Duyn affirms an insistent sociability. It sometimes seems that she uses her social world to define herself the way less gregarious poets use regional setting. Northern California, with little visible population, is the standard background for Robinson Jeffers; an equally underpopulated New England serves the purpose for Robert Frost. For Van Duyn it is not place but community that offers a milieu in which to situate herself. While the people concerned are most often those she knows well—her husband Jarvis Thurston and their circle of friends at Washington University—they may be in some cases totally anonymous, as in her praise of rest-room graffiti:

Nothing is banal or lowly that tells us how well
the world, whose highways proffer table and toilet
as signs and occasions of comfort for belly and
  bowel,
can comfort the heart too, somewhere in secret,
       . . . I bless
all knowledge of love, all ways of publishing it.

("Open Letter from a Constant Reader")

Such lines reveal an imagination resolutely un-Manichean, and an outlook that is unhesitatingly humane. In one of her rather infrequent dramatic monologues she makes Lot's wife her heroine, vindicated by the human impulse that led her to challenge God's justice and look back at Sodom's destruction, for which she was turned to a pillar of salt:

> I was not easily shocked, but that punishment
> was blasphemous, impiety
> to the world as it is, things as they are.
> I turned to pure mourning, which ends the
>   personal
> life, then quietly comes to its own end.
> Each time the clouds came and it rained,
> salt tears flowed from my whole being,
> and when that testimony was over
> grass began to grow on the plain.

("The Cities of the Plain")

The poet's openness to human diversity and willingness to forgive weakness and folly make her occasional glances at evil all the more powerful. I do not expect to forget a poem from her most recent book, **"'Have You Seen Me?'"** subtitled "Lost Children Ads":

> My face in your mail
> is no longer me.
> Stranger, don't fail
> to look carefully,
>
> hear the hopeless, mild
> query each day,
> "Where is the child
> that was taken away?"
>
> Imperceptibly
> the world's being taught.
>
> No one can see
> what I saw or thought.
>
> Someone wants me
> to be where I'm not.

All this should corroborate Van Duyn's sincerity in speaking of "the only life worth living, the empathic life." Anyone who wishes to trace the record of a complex feeling developing and refining itself over a lifetime should consult the series of poems about her parents, spread over several books. Narrow, unimaginative, self-interested, the parents could have offered a different sort of poet—Lowell or Plath—much scope for destructive caricature. In Van Duyn's

treatment they remain believable people with believable faults; they never metamorphose into those stylized monsters who abound in confessional literature. Van Duyn's poems about her father and mother are not designed principally to express grievance—though to some extent they do that—but more to register a painfully achieved understanding. They are instruments of reconciliation. In **"Remedies, Maladies, Reasons"** her dispassionate candor is breathtaking as she describes how her mother, a hypochondriac, kept her in valetudinarian bondage for much of her childhood:

> laying a fever-seeking hand on my forehead
> after school, incanting "Did your bowels move
>   good?
>
> Wrap up before you go out and don't play hard.
> Are you sure you're not coming down with a cold?
>   You
>   look tired,"
>
> keeping me numb on the couch for so many
>   weeks,
> if somehow a wily cough, flu or pox
>
> got through her guard, my legs world shake and
>   tingle,
> trying to find the blessed way back to school.

The chafe of confinement, the cause for resentment are vividly clear, and yet at the end of the poem the mother assumes an aspect in keeping with "a child's long-ago look," in which her obsessions are seen as rooted in love:

>   Bending over me,
> giant, ferocious, she drives my Enemy,
> in steamy, hot-packed, camphorated nights,
> from every sickening place where he hides and
>   waits.
>
> Do you think I don't know how love hallucinates?

Some related, equally impressive poems are **"Letters from a Father," "Photographs"** and **"The Stream,"** an elegy for her mother which concludes with this extended metaphor:

> What is love? Truly I do not know.
>
> Sometimes, perhaps, instead of a great sea,
> it is a narrow stream running urgently
>
> far below ground, held down by rocky layers,
> the deeds of father and mother, helpless sooth-
>   sayers
>
> of how our life is to be, weighted by clay,

the dense pressure of thwarted needs, the replay

of old misreadings; by hundreds of feet of soil,
the gifts and wounds of the genes, the short or tall

shape of our possibilities, seeking
and seeking a way to the top, while above, running

and stumbling this way and that on the clueless
    ground,
another seeker clutches a dowsing-wand

which bends, then lifts, dips, then straightens,
    everywhere,
saying to the dowser, it is there, it is not there,

and the untaught dowser believes, does not
    believe,
and finally simply stands on the ground above,

till a sliver of stream finds a crack and makes its
    way,
slowly, too slowly, through rock and earth and
    clay.

Here at my feet I see, after sixty years,
the welling water—to which I add these tears.

As these lines indicate, Van Duyn is a master of what Frost called "the discreet handling of metaphor." Lengthy passages, and sometimes entire poems, are sustained comparisons like this one, almost like Metaphysical conceits although they are not so aggressively witty in manner. Van Duyn is equally adept in her use of rhyme, often employing both full and half rhyme in a single poem. This is a difficult thing to do successfully, but she more often than not brings it off—perhaps by virtue of the naturalness of her diction. In her two most recent books she has grown more venturesome as a craftsman, including a number of the short-lined poems she calls "minimalist sonnets." "**'Have You Seen Me?'**" quoted above, is an example. In these pieces, as in general, she has moved toward greater compactness. It might once have been possible to feel that some of her poems were longer than they needed to be; but this is rarely the case with her latest work.

Van Duyn is a master of . . . "the discreet handling of metaphor." Lengthy passages, and sometimes entire poems, are sustained comparisons . . . almost like Metaphysical conceits although they are not so aggressively witty in manner.
—*Robert B. Shaw*

She has also extended her range as a writer of personal narrative. The long poem **"Falls"** in her latest book begins casually enough as an account of sightseeing trips in her father's trailer during her childhood. But it shifts into a higher register in describing the falls of the title. There is first the firefall at Yosemite, a nighttime display in which a large bonfire was pushed off a cliff in a continuous stream of flame:

> . . . What was the fire? Although it fell
> from the soul's home and braided into its strands
> of hue and heat that cool, unearthly white,
> its glory poured from earth's burning body, red,
> yellow, blue, orange, twining, twisting
> to light, to stainless light.

And later there is Niagara:

> No waterfall, it seemed, but earth's bringing
>   together
> of all its waters to make for that monstrous, open
> mouth (one lip one country, one another),
> out of a thousand long white quivering tongues
> one tongue that brought from the depths of throat
>   appalling,
> thunderous boasts of its own fertility.

In the poem's dexterous mixture of narrative and meditation, both falls become symbols of poetic inspiration: the fire from the silent heaven, the water from the clamorous earth. Such elemental images, Van Duyn believes, leave impressions which last a lifetime:

> May one who comes upon a final book
> and hunts in husks for kernel hints of me
> find Niagara's roar still sacred to dim ears,
> firefall still blazing bright in memory.

Fortunately, there is no reason to suppose that Firefall is by any means "a final book." At the height of her powers, Mona Van Duyn continues to give fresh meaning to the fusty term "a life work." By conferring upon her own life the reverence of cleareyed attention, she has managed to enhance the life that all of us share.

FURTHER READING

Criticism

Dickey, James. "Of Human Concern." *New York Times Book Review* 70 (21 November 1965): 74-5.
    Praises *A Time of Bees,* and calls Van Duyn "one of the best woman-poets around."

Graumnan, Lawrence, Jr. Review of *To See, To Take. The Antioch Review* 30, No. 1 (Spring 1970): 134.
    Brief review in which Grauman praises *To See, To Take* and declares that Van Duyn's poems "matter precisely because they transform, because they transcend the local domestic moment to speak to us as do myths."

Webster, Harvery Curtis. A review of *A Time of Bees. The Kenyon Review* 27, No. 2 (Spring 1965): 380-81.
    A highly laudatory assessment of A Time of Bees.

Further information on Van Duyn's life and career is contained in the following sources published by Gale: *Contemporary Authors,* **Vols. 9-12R;** *Contemporary Authors New Revision Series,* **Vols. 7, 38, and 60;** *Dictionary of Literary Biography,* **Vol. 5; and** *DISCovering Authors Modules: Poets.*

☐ Contemporary Literary Criticism

Indexes

Literary Criticism Series
Cumulative Author Index
Cumulative Topic Index
Cumulative Nationality Index
Title Index, Volume 116

How to Use This Index

The main references

> Camus, Albert
> 1913-1960 . . . . . . .CLC 1, 2, 4, 9, 11,
> 14, 32, 69; DA; DAB; DAC; DAM
> DRAM, MST, NOV; DC2; SSC 9;
> WLC

list all author entries in the following Gale Literary Criticism series:

BLC = *Black Literature Criticism*
BLCS = *Black Literature Criticism Supplement*
CLC = *Contemporary Literary Criticism*
CLR = *Children's Literature Review*
CMLC = *Classical and Medieval Literature Criticism*
DA = *DISCovering Authors*
DAB = *DISCovering Authors: British*
DAC = *DISCovering Authors: Canadian*
DAM = *DISCovering Authors Modules*
  DRAM = *dramatists;* *MST* = *most-studied*
  authors; *MULT* = *multicultural authors;* *NOV* =
  novelists; *POET* = *poets;* *POP* = *popular/genre*
  writers; *DC* = *Drama Criticism*
HLC = *Hispanic Literature Criticism*
LC = *Literature Criticism from 1400 to 1800*
NCLC = *Nineteenth-Century Literature Criticism*
PC = *Poetry Criticism*
SSC = *Short Story Criticism*
TCLC = *Twentieth-Century Literary Criticism*
WLC = *World Literature Criticism, 1500 to the Present*
WLCS = *World Literature Criticism Supplement*

The cross-references

> See also CA 89-92; DLB 72; MTCW

list all author entries in the following Gale biographical and literary sources:

AAYA = *Authors & Artists for Young Adults*
AITN = *Authors in the News*
BEST = *Bestsellers*
BW = *Black Writers*
CA = *Contemporary Authors*
CAAS = *Contemporary Authors Autobiography Series*
CABS = *Contemporary Authors Bibliographical Series*
CANR = *Contemporary Authors New Revision Series*
CAP = *Contemporary Authors Permanent Series*
CDALB = *Concise Dictionary of American Literary Biography*
CDBLB = *Concise Dictionary of British Literary Biography*

DLB = *Dictionary of Literary Biography*
DLBD = *Dictionary of Literary Biography Documentary Series*
DLBY = *Dictionary of Literary Biography Yearbook*
HW = *Hispanic Writers*
JRDA = *Junior DISCovering Authors*
MAICYA = *Major Authors and Illustrators for Children and Young Adults*
MTCW = *Major 20th-Century Writers*
NNAL = *Native North American Literature*
SAAS = *Something about the Author Autobiography Series*
SATA = *Something about the Author*
YABC = *Yesterday's Authors of Books for Children*

Literary Criticism Series
Cumulative Author Index

20/1631
See Upward. Allen
A/C Cross
See Lawrence. T(homas) E(dward)
Abasiyanik, Sait Faik 1906-1954
See Sait Faik
See also CA 123
Abbey, Edward 1927-1989
CLC 36, 59
See also CA 45-48; 128; CANR 2, 41
Abbott, Lee K(ittredge) 1947-
CLC 48
See also CA 124; CANR 51; DLB 130
Abe, Kobo 1924-1993
CLC 8, 22, 53, 81; DAM NOV
See also CA 65-68; 140; CANR 24, 60; DLB
182; MTCW 1
Abelard, Peter .... c. 1079-c. 1142
CMLC 11
See also DLB 115
Abell, Kjeld 1901-1961
CLC 15
See also CA 111
Abish, Walter 1931-
CLC 22
See also CA 101; CANR 37; DLB 130
Abrahams, Peter (Henry) 1919-
CLC 4
See also BW 1; CA 57-60; CANR 26; DLB 117;
MTCW 1
Abrams, M(eyer) H(oward) 1912-
CLC 24
See also CA 57-60; CANR 13, 33; DLB 67
Abse, Dannie 1923-
CLC 7, 29; DAB; DAM POET
See also CA 53-56, CAAS 1; CANR 4, 46, DLB
27
Achebe, (Albert) Chinua(lumogu) 1930-
**CLC 1, 3, 5, 7, 11, 26, 51, 75; BLC 1; DA;
DAB; DAC; DAM MST, MULT, NOV;
WLC**
See also AAYA 15; BW 2; CA 1-4R; CANR 6,
26, 47, 73; CLR 20; DLB 117; MAICYA;
MTCW 1; SATA 40; SATA-Brief 38
Acker, Kathy 1948-1997
CLC 45, 111
See also CA 117; 122; 162; CANR 55
Ackroyd, Peter 1949-
CLC 34, 52
See also CA 123; 127; CANR 51; DLB 155;
INT 127
Acorn, Milton 1923-
CLC 15; DAC
See also CA 103; DLB 53; INT 103
Adamov, Arthur 1908-1970
CLC 4, 25; DAM DRAM
See also CA 17-18; 25-28R; CAP 2; MTCW 1
Adams, Alice (Boyd) 1926-
CLC 6, 13, 46; SSC 24
See also CA 81-84; CANR 26, 53; DLBY 86;
INT CANR-26; MTCW 1
Adams, Andy 1859-1935
TCLC 56
See also YABC 1

Adams, Brooks 1848-1927
TCLC 80
See also CA 123; DLB 47
Adams, Douglas (Noel) 1952-
CLC 27, 60; DAM POP
See also AAYA 4; BEST 89:3; CA 106; CANR
34, 64; DLBY 83; JRDA
Adams, Francis 1862-1893
NCLC 33
Adams, Henry (Brooks) 1838-1918
TCLC 4, 52; DA; DAB; DAC; DAM MST
See also CA 104; 133; DLB 12, 47, 189
Adams, Richard (George) 1920-
CLC 4, 5, 18; DAM NOV
See also AAYA 16; AITN 1, 2; CA 49-52;
CANR 3, 35; CLR 20; JRDA; MAICYA;
MTCW 1; SATA 7, 69
Adamson, Joy(-Friederike Victoria) .. 1910-
1980 ....**CLC 17**
See also CA 69-72; 93-96; CANR 22; MTCW
1; SATA 11; SATA-Obit 22
Adcock, Fleur 1934-
CLC 41
See also CA 25-28R; CAAS 23; CANR 11, 34,
69; DLB 40
Addams, Charles (Samuel) 1912-1988
CLC 30
See also CA 61-64; 126; CANR 12
Addams, Jane 1860-1945
TCLC 76
Addison, Joseph 1672-1719
LC 18
See also CDBLB 1660-1789; DLB 101
Adler, Alfred (F.) 1870-1937
TCLC 61
See also CA 119; 159
Adler, C(arole) S(chwerdtfeger) 1932-
CLC 35
See also AAYA 4; CA 89-92; CANR 19, 40;
JRDA; MAICYA; SAAS 15; SATA 26, 63,
102
Adler, Renata 1938-
CLC 8, 31
See also CA 49-52; CANR 5, 22, 52; MTCW 1
Ady, Endre 1877-1919
TCLC 11
See also CA 107
A.E. 1867-1935
TCLC 3, 10
See also Russell, George William
Aeschylus .... 525B.C.-456B.C.
**CMLC 11; DA; DAB; DAC; DAM DRAM,
MST; DC 8; WLCS**
See also DLB 176
Aesop .... 620(?)B.C.-564(?)B.C.
CMLC 24
See also CLR 14; MAICYA; SATA 64
Affable Hawk
See MacCarthy, Sir(Charles Otto) Desmond
Africa, Ben
See Bosman, Herman Charles
Afton, Effie
See Harper, Frances Ellen Watkins

Agapida, Fray Antonio
See Irving, Washington
Agee, James (Rufus) 1909-1955
TCLC 1, 19; DAM NOV
See also AITN 1; CA 108; 148; CDALB 1941-
1968; DLB 2, 26, 152
Aghill, Gordon
See Silverberg, Robert
Agnon, S(hmuel) Y(osef Halevi) . 1888-1970
CLC 4, 8, 14; SSC 30
See also CA 17-18; 25-28R; CANR 60; CAP 2;
MTCW 1
Agrippa von Nettesheim, Henry Cornelius
1486-1535 .... **LC 27**
Aherne, Owen
See Cassill, R(onald) V(erlin)
Ai 1947-
CLC 4, 14, 69
See also CA 85-88; CAAS 13; CANR 70; DLB
120
Aickman, Robert (Fordyce) 1914-1981
CLC 57
See also CA 5-8R; CANR 3, 72
Aiken, Conrad (Potter) 1889-1973
**CLC 1, 3, 5, 10, 52; DAM NOV, POET; SSC
9**
See also CA 5-8R; 45-48; CANR 4, 60; CDALB
1929-1941; DLB 9, 45, 102; MTCW 1; SATA
3, 30
Aiken, Joan (Delano) 1924-
CLC 35
See also AAYA 1, 25; CA 9-12R; CANR 4, 23,
34, 64; CLR 1, 19; DLB 161; JRDA;
MAICYA; MTCW 1; SAAS 1; SATA 2, 30,
73
Ainsworth, William Harrison 1805-1882
NCLC 13
See also DLB 21; SATA 24
Aitmatov, Chingiz (Torekulovich) 1928-
CLC 71
See also CA 103; CANR 38; MTCW 1; SATA
56
Akers, Floyd
See Baum, L(yman) Frank
Akhmadulina, Bella Akhatovna 1937-
CLC 53; DAM POET
See also CA 65-68
Akhmatova, Anna 1888-1966
CLC 11, 25, 64; DAM POET; PC 2
See also CA 19-20; 25-28R; CANR 35; CAP 1;
MTCW 1
Aksakov, Sergei Timofeyvich 1791-1859
NCLC 2
See also DLB 198
Aksenov, Vassily
See Aksyonov, Vassily (Pavlovich)
Akst, Daniel 1956-
CLC 109
See also CA 161
Aksyonov, Vassily (Pavlovich) 1932-
CLC 22, 37, 101
See also CA 53-56; CANR 12, 48
Akutagawa, Ryunosuke 1892-1927

TCLC 16
See also CA 117; 154

Alain 1868-1951
TCLC 41
See also CA 163

Alain-Fournier .... TCLC 6
See also Fournier, Henri Alban
See also DLB 65

Alarcon, Pedro Antonio de 1833-1891
NCLC 1

Alas (y Urena), Leopoldo (Enrique Garcia)
1852-1901 .... TCLC 29
See also CA 113; 131; HW

Albee, Edward (Franklin III) 1928-
CLC 1, 2, 3, 5, 9, 11, 13, 25, 53, 86, 113;
DA; DAB; DAC; DAM DRAM, MST;
WLC
See also AITN 1; CA 5-8R; CABS 3; CANR 8,
54; CDALB 1941-1968; DLB 7; INT CANR-
8; MTCW 1

Alberti, Rafael 1902-
CLC 7
See also CA 85-88; DLB 108

Albert the Great .... 1200(?)-1280
CMLC 16
See also DLB 115

Alcala-Galiano, Juan Valera y
See Valera y Alcala-Galiano, Juan

Alcott, Amos Bronson 1799-1888
NCLC 1
See also DLB 1

Alcott, Louisa May 1832-1888
NCLC 6, 58; DA; DAB; DAC; DAM MST,
NOV; SSC 27; WLC
See also AAYA 20; CDALB 1865-1917; CLR
1, 38; DLB 1, 42, 79; DLBD 14; JRDA;
MAICYA; SATA 100; YABC 1

Aldanov, M. A.
See Aldanov, Mark (Alexandrovich)

Aldanov, Mark (Alexandrovich) 1886(?)-1957
TCLC 23
See also CA 118

Aldington, Richard 1892-1962
CLC 49
See also CA 85-88; CANR 45; DLB 20, 36, 100,
149

Aldiss, Brian W(ilson) 1925-
CLC 5, 14, 40; DAM NOV
See also CA 5-8R; CAAS 2; CANR 5, 28, 64;
DLB 14; MTCW 1; SATA 34

Alegria, Claribel 1924-
CLC 75; DAM MULT
See also CA 131; CAAS 15; CANR 66; DLB
145; HW

Alegria, Fernando 1918-
CLC 57
See also CA 9-12R; CANR 5, 32, 72; HW

Aleichem, Sholom .... TCLC 1, 35
See also Rabinovitch, Sholem

Aleixandre, Vicente 1898-1984
CLC 9, 36; DAM POET; PC 15
See also CA 85-88; 114; CANR 26; DLB 108;
HW; MTCW 1

Alepoudelis, Odysseus
See Elytis, Odysseus

Aleshkovsky, Joseph 1929-
See Aleshkovsky, Yuz
See also CA 121; 128

Aleshkovsky, Yuz .... CLC 44
See also Aleshkovsky, Joseph

Alexander, Lloyd (Chudley) 1924-
CLC 35
See also AAYA 1, 27; CA 1-4R; CANR 1, 24,

38, 55; CLR 1, 5, 48; DLB 52; JRDA;
MAICYA; MTCW 1; SAAS 19; SATA 3, 49,
81

Alexander, Samuel 1859-1938
TCLC 77

Alexie, Sherman (Joseph, Jr.) 1966-
CLC 96; DAM MULT
See also CA 138; CANR 65; DLB 175; NNAL

Alfau, Felipe 1902-
CLC 66
See also CA 137

Alger, Horatio, Jr. 1832-1899
NCLC 8
See also DLB 42; SATA 16

Algren, Nelson 1909-1981
CLC 4, 10, 33
See also CA 13-16R; 103; CANR 20, 61;
CDALB 1941-1968; DLB 9; DLBY 81, 82;
MTCW 1

Ali, Ahmed 1910-
CLC 69
See also CA 25-28R; CANR 15, 34

Alighieri, Dante
See Dante

Allan, John B.
See Westlake, Donald E(dwin)

Allan, Sidney
See Hartmann, Sadakichi

Allan, Sydney
See Hartmann, Sadakichi

Allen, Edward 1948-
CLC 59

Allen, Fred 1894-1956
TCLC 87

Allen, Paula Gunn 1939-
CLC 84; DAM MULT
See also CA 112; 143; CANR 63; DLB 175;
NNAL

Allen, Roland
See Ayckbourn, Alan

Allen, Sarah A.
See Hopkins, Pauline Elizabeth

Allen, Sidney H.
See Hartmann, Sadakichi

Allen, Woody 1935-
CLC 16, 52; DAM POP
See also AAYA 10; CA 33-36R; CANR 27, 38,
63; DLB 44; MTCW 1

Allende, Isabel 1942-
CLC 39, 57, 97; DAM MULT, NOV; HLC;
WLCS
See also AAYA 18; CA 125; 130; CANR 51;
DLB 145; HW; INT 130; MTCW 1

Alleyn, Ellen
See Rossetti, Christina (Georgina)

Allingham, Margery (Louise) 1904-1966
CLC 19
See also CA 5-8R; 25-28R; CANR 4, 58; DLB
77; MTCW 1

Allingham, William 1824-1889
NCLC 25
See also DLB 35

Allison, Dorothy E. 1949-
CLC 78
See also CA 140; CANR 66

Allston, Washington 1779-1843
NCLC 2
See also DLB 1

Almedingen, E. M. ....CLC 12
See also Almedingen, Martha Edith von
See also SATA 3

Almedingen, Martha Edith von .. 1898-1971
See Almedingen, E. M.

See also CA 1-4R; CANR 1

Almodovar, Pedro .... 1949(?)-
CLC 114
See also CA 133; CANR 72

Almqvist, Carl Jonas Love 1793-1866
NCLC 42

Alonso, Damaso 1898-1990
CLC 14
See also CA 110; 131; 130; CANR 72; DLB
108; HW

Alov
See Gogol, Nikolai (Vasilyevich)

Alta 1942-
CLC 19
See also CA 57-60

Alter, Robert B(ernard) 1935-
CLC 34
See also CA 49-52; CANR 1, 47

Alther, Lisa 1944-
CLC 7, 41
See also CA 65-68; CAAS 30; CANR 12, 30,
51; MTCW 1

Althusser, L.
See Althusser, Louis

Althusser, Louis 1918-1990
CLC 106
See also CA 131; 132

Altman, Robert 1925-
CLC 16, 116
See also CA 73-76; CANR 43

Alvarez, A(lfred) 1929-
CLC 5, 13
See also CA 1-4R; CANR 3, 33, 63; DLB 14,
40

Alvarez, Alejandro Rodriguez 1903-1965
See Casona, Alejandro
See also CA 131; 93-96; HW

Alvarez, Julia 1950-
CLC 93
See also AAYA 25; CA 147; CANR 69

Alvaro, Corrado 1896-1956
TCLC 60
See also CA 163

Amado, Jorge 1912-
CLC 13, 40, 106; DAM MULT, NOV; HLC
See also CA 77-80; CANR 35; DLB 113;
MTCW 1

Ambler, Eric 1909-
CLC 4, 6, 9
See also CA 9-12R; CANR 7, 38; DLB 77;
MTCW 1

Amichai, Yehuda 1924-
CLC 9, 22, 57, 116
See also CA 85-88; CANR 46, 60; MTCW 1

Amichai, Yehudah
See Amichai, Yehuda

Amiel, Henri Frederic 1821-1881
NCLC 4

Amis, Kingsley (William)............. 1922-1995
CLC 1, 2, 3, 5, 8, 13, 40, 44; DA; DAB;
DAC; DAM MST, NOV
See also AITN 2; CA 9-12R; 150; CANR 8, 28,
54; CDBLB 1945-1960; DLB 15, 27, 100,
139; DLBY 96; INT CANR-8; MTCW 1

Amis, Martin (Louis) 1949-
CLC 4, 9, 38, 62, 101
See also BEST 90:3; CA 65-68; CANR 8, 27,
54, 73; DLB 14, 194; INT CANR-27

Ammons, A(rchie) R(andolph) 1926-
CLC 2, 3, 5, 8, 9, 25, 57,108; DAM POET;
PC 16
See also AITN 1; CA 9-12R; CANR 6, 36, 51,
73; DLB 5, 165; MTCW 1

Amo, Tauraatua i
    See Adams, Henry (Brooks)
Anand, Mulk Raj 1905-
    CLC 23, 93; DAM NOV
    See also CA 65-68; CANR 32, 64; MTCW 1
Anatol
    See Schnitzler, Arthur
Anaximander .... c. 610B.C.-c. 546B.C.
    CMLC 22
Anaya, Rudolfo A(lfonso) 1937-
    CLC 23; DAM MULT, NOV; HLC
    See also AAYA 20; CA 45-48; CAAS 4; CANR
    1, 32, 51; DLB 82; HW 1; MTCW 1
Andersen, Hans Christian 1805-1875
    NCLC 7; DA; DAB; DAC; DAM MST,
    POP; SSC 6; WLC
    See also CLR 6; MAICYA; SATA 100; YABC
    1
Anderson, C. Farley
    See Mencken, H(enry) L(ouis); Nathan, George
    Jean
Anderson, Jessica (Margaret) Queale 1916-
    CLC 37
    See also CA 9-12R; CANR 4, 62
Anderson, Jon (Victor) 1940-
    CLC 9; DAM POET
    See also CA 25-28R; CANR 20
Anderson, Lindsay (Gordon) 1923-1994
    CLC 20
    See also CA 125; 128; 146
Anderson, Maxwell 1888-1959
    TCLC 2; DAM DRAM
    See also CA 105; 152; DLB 7
Anderson, Poul (William) 1926-
    CLC 15
    See also AAYA 5; CA 1-4R; CAAS 2; CANR
    2, 15, 34, 64; DLB 8; INT CANR-15; MTCW
    1; SATA 90; SATA-Brief 39
Anderson, Robert (Woodruff) 1917-
    CLC 23; DAM DRAM
    See also AITN 1; CA 21-24R; CANR 32; DLB
    7
Anderson, Sherwood 1876-1941
    TCLC 1, 10, 24; DA; DAB; DAC; DAM
    MST, NOV; SSC 1; WLC
    See also CA 104; 121; CANR 61; CDALB
    1917-1929; DLB 4, 9, 86; DLBD 1; MTCW
    1
Andier, Pierre
    See Desnos, Robert
Andouard
    See Giraudoux, (Hippolyte) Jean
Andrade, Carlos Drummond de .... **CLC 18**
    See also Drummond de Andrade, Carlos
Andrade, Mario de 1893-1945
    TCLC 43
Andreae, Johann V(alentin) 1586-1654
    LC 32
    See also DLB 164
Andreas-Salome, Lou 1861-1937
    TCLC 56
    See also DLB 66
Andress, Lesley
    See Sanders, Lawrence
Andrewes, Lancelot 1555-1626
    LC 5
    See also DLB 151, 172
Andrews, Cicily Fairfield
    See West, Rebecca
Andrews, Elton V.
    See Pohl, Frederik
Andreyev, Leonid (Nikolaevich) . 1871-1919
    TCLC 3

See also CA 104
Andric, Ivo 1892-1975
    CLC 8
    See also CA 81-84; 57-60; CANR 43, 60; DLB
    147; MTCW 1
Androvar
    See Prado (Calvo), Pedro
Angelique, Pierre
    See Bataille, Georges
Angell, Roger 1920-
    CLC 26
    See also CA 57-60; CANR 13, 44, 70; DLB 171,
    185
Angelou, Maya 1928-
    CLC 12, 35, 64, 77; BLC 1; DA; DAB;
    DAC; DAM MST, MULT, POET, POP;
    WLCS
    See also Johnson, Marguerite (Annie)
    See also AAYA 7, 20; BW 2; CA 65-68; CANR
    19, 42, 65; CLR 53; DLB 38; MTCW 1;
    SATA 49
Anna Comnena 1083-1153
    CMLC 25
Annensky, Innokenty (Fyodorovich) .. 1856-
    1909 .... **TCLC 14**
    See also CA 110; 155
Annunzio, Gabriele d'
    See D'Annunzio, Gabriele
Anodos
    See Coleridge, Mary E(lizabeth)
Anon, Charles Robert
    See Pessoa, Fernando (Antonio Nogueira)
Anouilh, Jean (Marie Lucien Pierre) . 1910-
    1987 **CLC 1, 3, 8, 13, 40, 50; DAM DRAM;**
    DC 8
    See also CA 17-20R; 123; CANR 32; MTCW 1
Anthony, Florence
    See Ai
Anthony, John
    See Ciardi, John (Anthony)
Anthony, Peter
    See Shaffer, Anthony (Joshua); Shaffer, Peter
    (Levin)
Anthony, Piers 1934-
    CLC 35; DAM POP
    See also AAYA 11; CA 21-24R; CANR 28, 56,
    73; DLB 8; MTCW 1; SAAS 22; SATA 84
Anthony, Susan B(rownell) 1916-1991
    TCLC 84
    See also CA 89-92; 134
Antoine, Marc
    See Proust, (Valentin-Louis-George-Eugene-)
    Marcel
Antoninus, Brother
    See Everson, William (Oliver)
Antonioni, Michelangelo 1912-
    CLC 20
    See also CA 73-76, CANR 45
Antschel, Paul 1920-1970
    See Celan, Paul
    See also CA 85-88; CANR 33, 61; MTCW 1
Anwar, Chairil 1922-1949
    TCLC 22
    See also CA 121
Apess, William .... 1798-1839(?)
    NCLC 73; DAM MULT
    See also DLB 175; NNAL
Apollinaire, Guillaume 1880-1918
    TCLC 3, 8, 51; DAM POET; PC 7
    See also Kostrowitzki, Wilhelm Apollinaris de
    See also CA 152
Appelfeld, Aharon 1932-
    CLC 23, 47

See also CA 112; 133
Apple, Max (Isaac) 1941-
    CLC 9, 33
    See also CA 81-84; CANR 19, 54; DLB 130
Appleman, Philip (Dean) 1926-
    CLC 51
    See also CA 13-16R; CAAS 18; CANR 6, 29,
    56
Appleton, Lawrence
    See Lovecraft, H(oward) P(hillips)
Apteryx
    See Eliot, T(homas) S(tearns)
Apuleius, (Lucius Madaurensis) 125(?)-175(?)
    CMLC 1
Aquin, Hubert 1929-1977
    CLC 15
    See also CA 105; DLB 53
Aragon, Louis 1897-1982
    CLC 3, 22; DAM NOV, POET
    See also CA 69-72; 108; CANR 28, 71; DLB
    72; MTCW 1
Arany, Janos 1817-1882
    NCLC 34
Arbuthnot, John 1667-1735
    LC 1
    See also DLB 101
Archer, Herbert Winslow
    See Mencken, H(enry) L(ouis)
Archer, Jeffrey (Howard) 1940-
    CLC 28; DAM POP
    See also AAYA 16; BEST 89:3; CA 77-80;
    CANR 22, 52; INT CANR-22
Archer, Jules 1915-
    CLC 12
    See also CA 9-12R; CANR 6, 69; SAAS 5;
    SATA 4, 85
Archer, Lee
    See Ellison, Harlan (Jay)
Arden, John 1930-
    CLC 6, 13, 15; DAM DRAM
    See also CA 13-16R; CAAS 4; CANR 31, 65,
    67; DLB 13; MTCW 1
Arenas, Reinaldo 1943-1990
    CLC 41; DAM MULT; HLC
    See also CA 124; 128; 133; CANR 73; DLB
    145; HW
Arendt, Hannah 1906-1975
    CLC 66, 98
    See also CA 17-20R; 61-64; CANR 26, 60;
    MTCW 1
Aretino, Pietro 1492-1556
    LC 12
Arghezi, Tudor 1880-1967
    CLC 80
    See also Theodorescu, Ion N.
    See also CA 167
Arguedas, Jose Maria 1911-1969
    CLC 10, 18
    See also CA 89-92; CANR 73; DLB 113; HW
Argueta, Manlio 1936-
    CLC 31
    See also CA 131; CANR 73; DLB 145; HW
Ariosto, Ludovico 1474-1533
    LC 6
Aristides
    See Epstein, Joseph
Aristophanes .... 450B.C.-385B.C.
    CMLC 4; DA; DAB; DAC; DAM DRAM,
    MST; DC 2; WLCS
    See also DLB 176
Aristotle .... 384B.C.-322B.C.
    CMLC 31; DA; DAB; DAC; DAM MST;
    WLCS

See Pessoa, Fernando (Antonio Nogueira)
Baroness Von S.
  See Zangwill, Israel
Barres, (Auguste-) Maurice 1862-1923
  TCLC 47
  See also CA 164; DLB 123
Barreto, Afonso Henrique de Lima
  See Lima Barreto, Afonso Henrique de
Barrett, (Roger) Syd 1946-
  CLC 35
Barrett, William (Christopher) ... 1913-1992
  CLC 27
  See also CA 13-16R; 139; CANR 11, 67; INT
  CANR-11
Barrie, J(ames) M(atthew) 1860-1937
  TCLC 2; DAB; DAM DRAM
  See also CA 104; 136; CDBLB 1890-1914;
  CLR 16; DLB 10, 141, 156; MAICYA; SATA
  100; YABC 1
Barrington, Michael
  See Moorcock, Michael (John)
Barrol, Grady
  See Bograd, Larry
Barry, Mike
  See Malzberg, Barry N(athaniel)
Barry, Philip 1896-1949
  TCLC 11
  See also CA 109; DLB 7
Bart, Andre Schwarz
  See Schwarz-Bart, Andre
Barth, John (Simmons) 1930-
  **CLC 1, 2, 3, 5, 7, 9, 10, 14, 27, 51, 89; DAM
  NOV; SSC 10**
  See also AITN 1, 2; CA 1-4R; CABS 1; CANR
  5, 23, 49, 64; DLB 2; MTCW 1
Barthelme, Donald 1931-1989
  **CLC 1, 2, 3, 5, 6, 8, 13, 23, 46, 59, 115; DAM
  NOV; SSC 2**
  See also CA 21-24R; 129; CANR 20, 58; DLB
  2; DLBY 80, 89; MTCW 1; SATA 7; SATA-
  Obit 62
Barthelme, Frederick 1943-
  CLC 36
  See also CA 114; 122; DLBY 85; INT 122
Barthes, Roland (Gerard) 1915-1980
  CLC 24, 83
  See also CA 130; 97-100; CANR 66; MTCW 1
Barzun, Jacques (Martin) 1907-
  CLC 51
  See also CA 61-64; CANR 22
Bashevis, Isaac
  See Singer, Isaac Bashevis
Bashkirtseff, Marie 1859-1884
  NCLC 27
Basho
  See Matsuo Basho
Bass, Kingsley B., Jr.
  See Bullins, Ed
Bass, Rick 1958-
  CLC 79
  See also CA 126; CANR 53
Bassani, Giorgio 1916-
  CLC 9
  See also CA 65-68; CANR 33; DLB 128, 177;
  MTCW 1
Bastos, Augusto (Antonio) Roa
  See Roa Bastos, Augusto (Antonio)
Bataille, Georges 1897-1962
  CLC 29
  See also CA 101; 89-92
Bates, H(erbert) E(rnest) 1905-1974
  CLC 46; DAB; DAM POP; SSC 10
  See also CA 93-96; 45-48; CANR 34; DLB 162,

191; MTCW 1
Bauchart
  See Camus, Albert
Baudelaire, Charles 1821-1867
  **NCLC 6, 29, 55; DA; DAB; DAC; DAM
  MST, POET; PC 1; SSC 18; WLC**
Baudrillard, Jean 1929-
  CLC 60
Baum, L(yman) Frank 1856-1919
  TCLC 7
  See also CA 108; 133; CLR 15; DLB 22; JRDA;
  MAICYA; MTCW 1; SATA 18, 100
Baum, Louis F.
  See Baum, L(yman) Frank
Baumbach, Jonathan 1933-
  CLC 6, 23
  See also CA 13-16R; CAAS 5; CANR 12, 66;
  DLBY 80; INT CANR-12; MTCW 1
Bausch, Richard (Carl) 1945-
  CLC 51
  See also CA 101; CAAS 14; CANR 43, 61; DLB
  130
Baxter, Charles (Morley) 1947-
  CLC 45, 78; DAM POP
  See also CA 57-60; CANR 40, 64; DLB 130
Baxter, George Owen
  See Faust, Frederick (Schiller)
Baxter, James K(eir) 1926-1972
  CLC 14
  See also CA 77-80
Baxter, John
  See Hunt, E(verette) Howard, (Jr.)
Bayer, Sylvia
  See Glassco, John
Baynton, Barbara 1857-1929
  TCLC 57
Beagle, Peter S(oyer) 1939-
  CLC 7, 104
  See also CA 9-12R; CANR 4, 51, 73; DLBY
  80; INT CANR-4; SATA 60
Bean, Normal
  See Burroughs, Edgar Rice
Beard, Charles A(ustin) 1874-1948
  TCLC 15
  See also CA 115; DLB 17; SATA 18
Beardsley, Aubrey 1872-1898
  NCLC 6
Beattie, Ann 1947-
  **CLC 8, 13, 18, 40, 63; DAM NOV, POP;
  SSC 11**
  See also BEST 90:2; CA 81-84; CANR 53, 73;
  DLBY 82; MTCW 1
Beattie, James 1735-1803
  NCLC 25
  See also DLB 109
Beauchamp, Kathleen Mansfield 1888-1923
  See Mansfield, Katherine
  See also CA 104; 134; DA; DAC; DAM MST
Beaumarchais, Pierre-Augustin Caron de
  1732-1799 .... **DC 4**
  See also DAM DRAM
Beaumont, Francis .... 1584(?)-1616
  LC 33; DC 6
  See also CDBLB Before 1660; DLB 58, 121
**Beauvoir, Simone (Lucie Ernestine Marie
  Bertrand) de** 1908-1986
  **CLC 1, 2, 4, 8, 14, 31, 44, 50, 71; DA; DAB;
  DAC; DAM MST, NOV; WLC**
  See also CA 9-12R; 118; CANR 28, 61; DLB
  72; DLBY 86; MTCW 1
Becker, Carl (Lotus) 1873-1945
  TCLC 63
  See also CA 157; DLB 17

Becker, Jurek 1937-1997
  CLC 7, 19
  See also CA 85-88; 157; CANR 60; DLB 75
Becker, Walter 1950-
  CLC 26
Beckett, Samuel (Barclay) 1906-1989
  **CLC 1, 2, 3, 4, 6, 9, 10, 11, 14, 18, 29, 57,
  59, 83; DA; DAB; DAC; DAM DRAM,
  MST, NOV; SSC 16; WLC**
  See also CA 5-8R; 130; CANR 33, 61; CDBLB
  1945-1960; DLB 13, 15; DLBY 90; MTCW
  1
Beckford, William 1760-1844
  NCLC 16
  See also DLB 39
Beckman, Gunnel 1910-
  CLC 26
  See also CA 33-36R; CANR 15; CLR 25;
  MAICYA; SAAS 9; SATA 6
Becque, Henri 1837-1899
  NCLC 3
  See also DLB 192
Beddoes, Thomas Lovell 1803-1849
  NCLC 3
  See also DLB 96
Bede .... c. 673-735
  CMLC 20
  See also DLB 146
Bedford, Donald F.
  See Fearing, Kenneth (Flexner)
Beecher, Catharine Esther 1800-1878
  NCLC 30
  See also DLB 1
Beecher, John 1904-1980
  CLC 6
  See also AITN 1; CA 5-8R; 105; CANR 8
Beer, Johann 1655-1700
  LC 5
  See also DLB 168
Beer, Patricia 1924-
  CLC 58
  See also CA 61-64; CANR 13, 46; DLB 40
Beerbohm, Max
  See Beerbohm, (Henry) Max(imilian)
Beerbohm, (Henry) Max(imilian) 1872-1956
  TCLC 1, 24
  See also CA 104; 154; DLB 34, 100
Beer-Hofmann, Richard 1866-1945
  TCLC 60
  See also CA 160; DLB 81
Begiebing, Robert J(ohn) 1946-
  CLC 70
  See also CA 122; CANR 40
Behan, Brendan 1923-1964
  CLC 1, 8, 11, 15, 79; DAM DRAM
  See also CA 73-76; CANR 33; CDBLB 1945-
  1960; DLB 13; MTCW 1
Behn, Aphra .... 1640(?)-1689
  **LC 1, 30; DA; DAB; DAC; DAM DRAM,
  MST, NOV, POET; DC 4; PC 13; WLC**
  See also DLB 39, 80, 131
Behrman, S(amuel) N(athaniel) .. 1893-1973
  CLC 40
  See also CA 13-16; 45-48; CAP 1; DLB 7, 44
Belasco, David 1853-1931
  TCLC 3
  See also CA 104; 168; DLB 7
Belcheva, Elisaveta 1893-
  CLC 10
  See also Bagryana, Elisaveta
Beldone, Phil "Cheech"
  See Ellison, Harlan (Jay)
Beleno

See Azuela, Mariano

Belinski, Vissarion Grigoryevich 1811-1848
    NCLC 5
    See also DLB 198

Belitt, Ben 1911-
    CLC 22
    See also CA 13-16R; CAAS 4; CANR 7; DLB
    5

Bell, Gertrude (Margaret Lowthian) . 1868-
    1926 .... **TCLC 67**
    See also CA 167; DLB 174

Bell, J. Freeman
    See Zangwill, Israel

Bell, James Madison 1826-1902
    TCLC 43; BLC 1; DAM MULT
    See also BW 1; CA 122; 124; DLB 50

Bell, Madison Smartt 1957-
    CLC 41, 102
    See also CA 111; CANR 28, 54, 73

Bell, Marvin (Hartley) 1937-
    CLC 8, 31; DAM POET
    See also CA 21-24R; CAAS 14; CANR 59; DLB
    5; MTCW 1

Bell, W. L. D.
    See Mencken, H(enry) L(ouis)

Bellamy, Atwood C.
    See Mencken, H(enry) L(ouis)

Bellamy, Edward 1850-1898
    NCLC 4
    See also DLB 12

Bellin, Edward J.
    See Kuttner, Henry

Belloc, (Joseph) Hilaire (Pierre Sebastien Rene
    Swanton) 1870-1953
    TCLC 7, 18; DAM POET; PC 24
    See also CA 106; 152; DLB 19, 100, 141, 174;
    YABC 1

Belloc, Joseph Peter Rene Hilaire
    See Belloc, (Joseph) Hilaire (Pierre Sebastien
    Rene Swanton)

Belloc, Joseph Pierre Hilaire
    See Belloc, (Joseph) Hilaire (Pierre Sebastien
    Rene Swanton)

Belloc, M. A.
    See Lowndes, Marie Adelaide (Belloc)

Bellow, Saul 1915-
    CLC 1, 2, 3, 6, 8, 10, 13, 15, 25, 33, 34, 63,
    79; DA; DAB; DAC; DAM MST, NOV,
    POP; SSC 14; WLC
    See also AITN 2; BEST 89:3; CA 5-8R; CABS
    1; CANR 29, 53; CDALB 1941-1968; DLB
    2, 28; DLBD 3; DLBY 82; MTCW 1

Belser, Reimond Karel Maria de 1929-
    See Ruyslinck, Ward
    See also CA 152

Bely, Andrey .... **TCLC 7; PC 11**
    See also Bugayev, Boris Nikolayevich

Belyi, Andrei
    See Bugayev, Boris Nikolayevich

Benary, Margot
    See Benary-Isbert, Margot

Benary-Isbert, Margot 1889-1979
    CLC 12
    See also CA 5-8R; 89-92; CANR 4, 72; CLR
    12; MAICYA; SATA 2; SATA-Obit 21

Benavente (y Martinez), Jacinto . 1866-1954
    TCLC 3; DAM DRAM, MULT
    See also CA 106; 131; HW; MTCW 1

Benchley, Peter (Bradford) 1940-
    CLC 4, 8; DAM NOV, POP
    See also AAYA 14; AITN 2; CA 17-20R; CANR
    12, 35, 66; MTCW 1; SATA 3, 89

Benchley, Robert (Charles) 1889-1945

    TCLC 1, 55
    See also CA 105; 153; DLB 11

Benda, Julien 1867-1956
    TCLC 60
    See also CA 120; 154

Benedict, Ruth (Fulton) 1887-1948
    TCLC 60
    See also CA 158

Benedict, Saint .... c. 480-c. 547
    CMLC 29

Benedikt, Michael 1935-
    CLC 4, 14
    See also CA 13-16R; CANR 7; DLB 5

Benet, Juan 1927-
    CLC 28
    See also CA 143

Benet, Stephen Vincent 1898-1943
    TCLC 7; DAM POET; SSC 10
    See also CA 104; 152; DLB 4, 48, 102; DLBY
    97; YABC 1

Benet, William Rose 1886-1950
    TCLC 28; DAM POET
    See also CA 118; 152; DLB 45

Benford, Gregory (Albert) 1941-
    CLC 52
    See also CA 69-72; CAAS 27; CANR 12, 24,
    49; DLBY 82

Bengtsson, Frans (Gunnar) 1894-1954
    TCLC 48

Benjamin, David
    See Slavitt, David R(ytman)

Benjamin, Lois
    See Gould, Lois

Benjamin, Walter 1892-1940
    TCLC 39
    See also CA 164

Benn, Gottfried 1886-1956
    TCLC 3
    See also CA 106; 153; DLB 56

Bennett, Alan 1934-
    CLC 45, 77; DAB; DAM MST
    See also CA 103; CANR 35, 55; MTCW 1

Bennett, (Enoch) Arnold 1867-1931
    TCLC 5, 20
    See also CA 106; 155; CDBLB 1890-1914;
    DLB 10, 34, 98, 135

Bennett, Elizabeth
    See Mitchell, Margaret (Munnerlyn)

Bennett, George Harold 1930-
    See Bennett, Hal
    See also BW 1; CA 97-100

Bennett, Hal .... **CLC 5**
    See also Bennett, George Harold
    See also DLB 33

Bennett, Jay 1912-
    CLC 35
    See also AAYA 10; CA 69-72; CANR 11, 42;
    JRDA; SAAS 4; SATA 41, 87; SATA-Brief
    27

Bennett, Louise (Simone) 1919-
    CLC 28; BLC 1; DAM MULT
    See also BW 2; CA 151; DLB 117

Benson, E(dward) F(rederic) 1867-1940
    TCLC 27
    See also CA 114; 157; DLB 135, 153

Benson, Jackson J. 1930-
    CLC 34
    See also CA 25-28R; DLB 111

Benson, Sally 1900-1972
    CLC 17
    See also CA 19-20; 37-40R; CAP 1; SATA 1,
    35; SATA-Obit 27

Benson, Stella 1892-1933

    TCLC 17
    See also CA 117; 155; DLB 36, 162

Bentham, Jeremy 1748-1832
    NCLC 38
    See also DLB 107, 158

Bentley, E(dmund) C(lerihew) 1875-1956
    TCLC 12
    See also CA 108; DLB 70

Bentley, Eric (Russell) 1916-
    CLC 24
    See also CA 5-8R; CANR 6, 67; INT CANR-6

Beranger, Pierre Jean de 1780-1857
    NCLC 34

Berdyaev, Nicolas
    See Berdyaev, Nikolai (Aleksandrovich)

Berdyaev, Nikolai (Aleksandrovich) ... 1874-
    1948 .... **TCLC 67**
    See also CA 120; 157

Berdyayev, Nikolai (Aleksandrovich)
    See Berdyaev, Nikolai (Aleksandrovich)

Berendt, John (Lawrence) 1939-
    CLC 86
    See also CA 146

Beresford, J(ohn) D(avys) 1873-1947
    TCLC 81
    See also CA 112; 155; DLB 162, 178, 197

Bergelson, David 1884-1952
    TCLC 81

Berger, Colonel
    See Malraux, (Georges-)Andre

Berger, John (Peter) 1926-
    CLC 2, 19
    See also CA 81-84; CANR 51; DLB 14

Berger, Melvin H. 1927-
    CLC 12
    See also CA 5-8R; CANR 4; CLR 32; SAAS 2;
    SATA 5, 88

Berger, Thomas (Louis) 1924-
    CLC 3, 5, 8, 11, 18, 38; DAM NOV
    See also CA 1-4R; CANR 5, 28, 51; DLB 2;
    DLBY 80; INT CANR-28; MTCW 1

Bergman, (Ernst) Ingmar 1918-
    CLC 16, 72
    See also CA 81-84; CANR 33, 70

Bergson, Henri(-Louis) 1859-1941
    TCLC 32
    See also CA 164

Bergstein, Eleanor 1938-
    CLC 4
    See also CA 53-56; CANR 5

Berkoff, Steven 1937-
    CLC 56
    See also CA 104; CANR 72

Bermant, Chaim (Icyk) 1929-
    CLC 40
    See also CA 57-60; CANR 6, 31, 57

Bern, Victoria
    See Fisher, M(ary) F(rances) K(ennedy)

Bernanos, (Paul Louis) Georges . 1888-1948
    TCLC 3
    See also CA 104; 130; DLB 72

Bernard, April 1956-
    CLC 59
    See also CA 131

Berne, Victoria
    See Fisher, M(ary) F(rances) K(ennedy)

Bernhard, Thomas 1931-1989
    CLC 3, 32, 61
    See also CA 85-88; 127; CANR 32, 57; DLB
    85, 124; MTCW 1

Bernhardt, Sarah (Henriette Rosine) . 1844-
    1923 .... **TCLC 75**
    See also CA 157

CLC 19
See also CA 127
Boyle, T. C. 1948-
See Boyle, T(homas) Coraghessan
Boyle, T(homas) Coraghessan 1948-
CLC 36, 55, 90; DAM POP; SSC 16
See also BEST 90:4; CA 120; CANR 44; DLBY
86
Boz
See Dickens, Charles (John Huffam)
Brackenridge, Hugh Henry 1748-1816
NCLC 7
See also DLB 11, 37
Bradbury, Edward P.
See Moorcock, Michael (John)
Bradbury, Malcolm (Stanley) 1932-
CLC 32, 61; DAM NOV
See also CA 1-4R; CANR 1, 33; DLB 14;
MTCW 1
Bradbury, Ray (Douglas) 1920-
CLC 1, 3, 10, 15, 42, 98; DA; DAB; DAC;
DAM MST, NOV, POP; SSC 29; WLC
See also AAYA 15; AITN 1, 2; CA 1-4R; CANR
2, 30; CDALB 1968-1988; DLB 2, 8; MTCW
1; SATA 11, 64
Bradford, Gamaliel 1863-1932
TCLC 36
See also CA 160; DLB 17
Bradley, David (Henry, Jr.) 1950-
CLC 23; BLC 1; DAM MULT
See also BW 1; CA 104; CANR 26; DLB 33
Bradley, John Ed(mund, Jr.) 1958-
CLC 55
See also CA 139
Bradley, Marion Zimmer 1930-
CLC 30; DAM POP
See also AAYA 9; CA 57-60; CAAS 10; CANR
7, 31, 51; DLB 8; MTCW 1; SATA 90
Bradstreet, Anne .... 1612(?)-1672
LC 4, 30; DA; DAC; DAM MST, POET;
PC 10
See also CDALB 1640-1865; DLB 24
Brady, Joan 1939-
CLC 86
See also CA 141
Bragg, Melvyn 1939-
CLC 10
See also BEST 89:3; CA 57-60; CANR 10, 48;
DLB 14
Brahe, Tycho 1546-1601
LC 45
Braine, John (Gerard) 1922-1986
CLC 1, 3, 41
See also CA 1-4R; 120; CANR 1, 33; CDBLB
1945-1960; DLB 15; DLBY 86; MTCW 1
Bramah, Ernest............................. 1868-1942
TCLC 72
See also CA 156; DLB 70
Brammer, William .... 1930(?)-1978
CLC 31
See also CA 77-80
Brancati, Vitaliano 1907-1954
TCLC 12
See also CA 109
Brancato, Robin F(idler) 1936-
CLC 35
See also AAYA 9; CA 69-72; CANR 11, 45;
CLR 32; JRDA; SAAS 9; SATA 97
Brand, Max
See Faust, Frederick (Schiller)
Brand, Millen 1906-1980
CLC 7
See also CA 21-24R; 97-100; CANR 72

Branden, Barbara .... CLC 44
See also CA 148
Brandes, Georg (Morris Cohen) . 1842-1927
TCLC 10
See also CA 105
Brandys, Kazimierz 1916-
CLC 62
Branley, Franklyn M(ansfield) 1915-
CLC 21
See also CA 33-36R; CANR 14, 39; CLR 13;
MAICYA; SAAS 16; SATA 4, 68
Brathwaite, Edward Kamau 1930-
CLC 11; BLCS; DAM POET
See also BW 2; CA 25-28R; CANR 11, 26, 47;
DLB 125
Brautigan, Richard (Gary) 1935-1984
CLC 1, 3, 5, 9, 12, 34, 42; DAM NOV
See also CA 53-56; 113; CANR 34; DLB 2, 5;
DLBY 80, 84; MTCW 1; SATA 56
Brave Bird, Mary 1953-
See Crow Dog, Mary (Ellen)
See also NNAL
Braverman, Kate 1950-
CLC 67
See also CA 89-92
Brecht, (Eugen) Bertolt (Friedrich) ... 1898-
1956TCLC 1, 6, 13, 35; DA; DAB; DAC;
DAM DRAM, MST; DC 3; WLC
See also CA 104; 133; CANR 62; DLB 56, 124;
MTCW 1
Brecht, Eugen Berthold Friedrich
See Brecht, (Eugen) Bertolt (Friedrich)
Bremer, Fredrika 1801-1865
NCLC 11
Brennan, Christopher John 1870-1932
TCLC 17
See also CA 117
Brennan, Maeve 1917-1993
CLC 5
See also CA 81-84; CANR 72
Brent, Linda
See Jacobs, Harriet A(nn)
Brentano, Clemens (Maria) 1778-1842
NCLC 1
See also DLB 90
Brent of Bin Bin
See Franklin, (Stella Maria Sarah) Miles
(Lampe)
Brenton, Howard 1942-
CLC 31
See also CA 69-72; CANR 33, 67; DLB 13;
MTCW 1
Breslin, James 1930-1996
See Breslin, Jimmy
See also CA 73-76; CANR 31; DAM NOV;
MTCW 1
Breslin, Jimmy .... CLC 4, 43
See also Breslin, James
See also AITN 1; DLB 185
Bresson, Robert 1901-
CLC 16
See also CA 110; CANR 49
Breton, Andre 1896-1966
CLC 2, 9, 15, 54; PC 15
See also CA 19-20; 25-28R; CANR 40, 60; CAP
2; DLB 65; MTCW 1
Breytenbach, Breyten .... 1939(?)-
CLC 23, 37; DAM POET
See also CA 113; 129; CANR 61
Bridgers, Sue Ellen 1942-
CLC 26
See also AAYA 8; CA 65-68; CANR 11, 36;
CLR 18; DLB 52; JRDA; MAICYA; SAAS

1; SATA 22, 90
Bridges, Robert (Seymour) 1844-1930
TCLC 1; DAM POET
See also CA 104; 152; CDBLB 1890-1914;
DLB 19, 98
Bridie, James .... TCLC 3
See also Mavor, Osborne Henry
See also DLB 10
Brin, David 1950-
CLC 34
See also AAYA 21; CA 102; CANR 24, 70; INT
CANR-24; SATA 65
Brink, Andre (Philippus) 1935-
CLC 18, 36, 106
See also CA 104; CANR 39, 62; INT 103;
MTCW 1
Brinsmead, H(esba) F(ay) 1922-
CLC 21
See also CA 21-24R; CANR 10; CLR 47;
MAICYA; SAAS 5; SATA 18, 78
Brittain, Vera (Mary) .... 1893(?)-1970
CLC 23
See also CA 13-16; 25-28R; CANR 58; CAP 1;
DLB 191; MTCW 1
Broch, Hermann 1886-1951
TCLC 20
See also CA 117; DLB 85, 124
Brock, Rose
See Hansen, Joseph
Brodkey, Harold (Roy) 1930-1996
CLC 56
See also CA 111; 151; CANR 71; DLB 130
Brodskii, Iosif
See Brodsky, Joseph
Brodsky, Iosif Alexandrovich 1940-1996
See Brodsky, Joseph
See also AITN 1; CA 41-44R; 151; CANR 37;
DAM POET; MTCW 1
Brodsky, Joseph 1940-1996
CLC 4, 6, 13, 36, 100; PC 9
See also Brodskii, Iosif; Brodsky, Iosif
Alexandrovich
Brodsky, Michael (Mark) 1948-
CLC 19
See also CA 102; CANR 18, 41, 58
Bromell, Henry 1947-
CLC 5
See also CA 53-56; CANR 9
Bromfield, Louis (Brucker) 1896-1956
TCLC 11
See also CA 107; 155; DLB 4, 9, 86
Broner, E(sther) M(asserman) 1930-
CLC 19
See also CA 17-20R; CANR 8, 25, 72; DLB 28
Bronk, William 1918-
CLC 10
See also CA 89-92; CANR 23; DLB 165
Bronstein, Lev Davidovich
See Trotsky, Leon
Bronte, Anne 1820-1849
NCLC 71
See also DLB 21, 199
Bronte, Charlotte.......................... 1816-1855
NCLC 3, 8, 33, 58; DA; DAB; DAC; DAM
MST, NOV; WLC
See also AAYA 17; CDBLB 1832-1890; DLB
21, 159, 199
Bronte, Emily (Jane) 1818-1848
NCLC 16, 35; DA; DAB; DAC; DAM
MST, NOV, POET; PC 8; WLC
See also AAYA 17; CDBLB 1832-1890; DLB
21, 32, 199
Brooke, Frances 1724-1789

Bulgakov, Mikhail (Afanas'evich) 1891-1940
TCLC 2, 16; DAM DRAM, NOV; SSC 18
See also CA 105; 152
Bulgya, Alexander Alexandrovich 1901-1956
TCLC 53
See also Fadeyev, Alexander
See also CA 117
Bullins, Ed 1935-
CLC 1, 5, 7; BLC 1; DAM DRAM, MULT;
DC 6
See also BW 2; CA 49-52; CAAS 16; CANR
24, 46, 73; DLB 7, 38; MTCW 1
Bulwer-Lytton, Edward (George Earle Lytton)
1803-1873 ....NCLC 1, 45
See also DLB 21
Bunin, Ivan Alexeyevich 1870-1953
TCLC 6; SSC 5
See also CA 104
Bunting, Basil 1900-1985
CLC 10, 39, 47; DAM POET
See also CA 53-56; 115; CANR 7; DLB 20
Bunuel, Luis 1900-1983
CLC 16, 80; DAM MULT; HLC
See also CA 101; 110; CANR 32; HW
Bunyan, John 1628-1688
LC 4; DA; DAB; DAC; DAM MST; WLC
See also CDBLB 1660-1789; DLB 39
Burckhardt, Jacob (Christoph)... 1818-1897
NCLC 49
Burford, Eleanor
See Hibbert, Eleanor Alice Burford
Burgess, AnthonyCLC 1, 2, 4, 5, 8, 10, 13, 15,
22, 40, 62, 81, 94; DAB
See also Wilson, John (Anthony) Burgess
See also AAYA 25; AITN 1; CDBLB 1960 to
Present; DLB 14, 194
Burke, Edmund .... 1729(?)-1797
LC 7, 36; DA; DAB; DAC; DAM MST;
WLC
See also DLB 104
Burke, Kenneth (Duva) 1897-1993
CLC 2, 24
See also CA 5-8R; 143; CANR 39; DLB 45,
63; MTCW 1
Burke, Leda
See Garnett, David
Burke, Ralph
See Silverberg, Robert
Burke, Thomas 1886-1945
TCLC 63
See also CA 113; 155; DLB 197
Burney, Fanny 1752-1840
NCLC 12, 54
See also DLB 39
Burns, Robert 1759-1796
PC 6
See also CDBLB 1789-1832; DA; DAB; DAC;
DAM MST, POET; DLB 109; WLC
Burns, Tex
See L'Amour, Louis (Dearborn)
Burnshaw, Stanley 1906-
CLC 3, 13, 44
See also CA 9-12R; DLB 48; DLBY 97
Burr, Anne 1937-
CLC 6
See also CA 25-28R
Burroughs, Edgar Rice 1875-1950
TCLC 2, 32; DAM NOV
See also AAYA 11; CA 104; 132; DLB 8;
MTCW 1; SATA 41
Burroughs, William S(eward) 1914-1997
CLC 1, 2, 5, 15, 22, 42, 75, 109; DA; DAB;
DAC; DAM MST, NOV, POP; WLC

See also AITN 2; CA 9-12R; 160; CANR 20,
52; DLB 2, 8, 16, 152; DLBY 81, 97; MTCW
1
Burton, Richard F. 1821-1890
NCLC 42
See also DLB 55, 184
Busch, Frederick 1941-
CLC 7, 10, 18, 47
See also CA 33-36R; CAAS 1; CANR 45, 73;
DLB 6
Bush, Ronald 1946-
CLC 34
See also CA 136
Bustos, F(rancisco)
See Borges, Jorge Luis
Bustos Domecq, H(onorio)
See Bioy Casares, Adolfo; Borges, Jorge Luis
Butler, Octavia E(stelle) 1947-
CLC 38; BLCS; DAM MULT, POP
See also AAYA 18; BW 2; CA 73-76; CANR
12, 24, 38, 73; DLB 33; MTCW 1; SATA 84
Butler, Robert Olen (Jr.) 1945-
CLC 81; DAM POP
See also CA 112; CANR 66; DLB 173; INT 112
Butler, Samuel 1612-1680
LC 16, 43
See also DLB 101, 126
Butler, Samuel 1835-1902
TCLC 1, 33; DA; DAB; DAC; DAM MST,
NOV; WLC
See also CA 143; CDBLB 1890-1914; DLB 18,
57, 174
Butler, Walter C.
See Faust, Frederick (Schiller)
Butor, Michel (Marie Francois) 1926-
CLC 1, 3, 8, 11, 15
See also CA 9-12R; CANR 33, 66; DLB 83;
MTCW 1
Butts, Mary .... 1892(?)-1937
TCLC 77
See also CA 148
Buzo, Alexander (John) 1944-
CLC 61
See also CA 97-100; CANR 17, 39, 69
Buzzati, Dino 1906-1972
CLC 36
See also CA 160; 33-36R; DLB 177
Byars, Betsy (Cromer) 1928-
CLC 35
See also AAYA 19; CA 33-36R; CANR 18, 36,
57; CLR 1, 16; DLB 52; INT CANR-18;
JRDA; MAICYA; MTCW 1; SAAS 1; SATA
4, 46, 80
Byatt, A(ntonia) S(usan Drabble) 1936-
CLC 19, 65; DAM NOV, POP
See also CA 13-16R; CANR 13, 33, 50; DLB
14, 194; MTCW 1
Byrne, David 1952-
CLC 26
See also CA 127
Byrne, John Keyes 1926-
See Leonard, Hugh
See also CA 102; INT 102
Byron, George Gordon (Noel) 1788-1824
NCLC 2, 12; DA; DAB; DAC; DAM MST,
POET; PC 16; WLC
See also CDBLB 1789-1832; DLB 96, 110
Byron, Robert 1905-1941
TCLC 67
See also CA 160; DLB 195
C. 3. 3.
See Wilde, Oscar (Fingal O'Flahertie Wills)
Caballero, Fernan 1796-1877

NCLC 10
Cabell, Branch
See Cabell, James Branch
Cabell, James Branch 1879-1958
TCLC 6
See also CA 105; 152; DLB 9, 78
Cable, George Washington 1844-1925
TCLC 4; SSC 4
See also CA 104; 155; DLB 12, 74; DLBD 13
Cabral de Melo Neto, Joao 1920-
CLC 76; DAM MULT
See also CA 151
Cabrera Infante, G(uillermo) 1929-
CLC 5, 25, 45; DAM MULT; HLC
See also CA 85-88; CANR 29, 65; DLB 113;
HW; MTCW 1
Cade, Toni
See Bambara, Toni Cade
Cadmus and Harmonia
See Buchan, John
Caedmon .... fl. 658-680
CMLC 7
See also DLB 146
Caeiro, Alberto
See Pessoa, Fernando (Antonio Nogueira)
Cage, John (Milton, Jr.) 1912-1992
CLC 41
See also CA 13-16R; 169; CANR 9; DLB 193;
INT CANR-9
Cahan, Abraham 1860-1951
TCLC 71
See also CA 108; 154; DLB 9, 25, 28
Cain, G.
See Cabrera Infante, G(uillermo)
Cain, Guillermo
See Cabrera Infante, G(uillermo)
Cain, James M(allahan) 1892-1977
CLC 3, 11, 28
See also AITN 1; CA 17-20R; 73-76; CANR 8,
34, 61; MTCW 1
Caine, Mark
See Raphael, Frederic (Michael)
Calasso, Roberto 1941-
CLC 81
See also CA 143
Calderon de la Barca, Pedro 1600-1681
LC 23; DC 3
Caldwell, Erskine (Preston) 1903-1987
CLC 1, 8, 14, 50, 60; DAM NOV; SSC 19
See also AITN 1; CA 1-4R; 121; CAAS 1;
CANR 2, 33; DLB 9, 86; MTCW 1
Caldwell, (Janet Miriam) Taylor (Holland)
1900-1985 . CLC 2, 28, 39; DAM NOV,
POP
See also CA 5-8R; 116; CANR 5; DLBD 17
Calhoun, John Caldwell 1782-1850
NCLC 15
See also DLB 3
Calisher, Hortense 1911-
CLC 2, 4, 8, 38; DAM NOV; SSC 15
See also CA 1-4R; CANR 1, 22, 67; DLB 2;
INT CANR-22; MTCW 1
Callaghan, Morley Edward 1903-1990
CLC 3, 14, 41, 65; DAC; DAM MST
See also CA 9-12R; 132; CANR 33, 73; DLB
68; MTCW 1
Callimachus .... c. 305B.C.-c. 240B.C.
CMLC 18
See also DLB 176
Calvin, John 1509-1564
LC 37
Calvino, Italo 1923-1985
CLC 5, 8, 11, 22, 33, 39, 73; DAM NOV;

Chatterji, Bankim Chandra 1838-1894
 NCLC 19
Chatterji, Saratchandra .... **TCLC 13**
 See also Chatterje, Sarat Chandra
Chatterton, Thomas 1752-1770
 LC 3; DAM POET
 See also DLB 109
Chatwin, (Charles) Bruce 1940-1989
 CLC 28, 57, 59; DAM POP
 See also AAYA 4; BEST 90:1; CA 85-88; 127;
 DLB 194
Chaucer, Daniel
 See Ford, Ford Madox
Chaucer, Geoffrey .... 1340(?)-1400
 **LC 17; DA; DAB; DAC; DAM MST,
 POET; PC 19; WLCS**
 See also CDBLB Before 1660; DLB 146
Chaviaras, Strates 1935-
 See Haviaras, Stratis
 See also CA 105
Chayefsky, Paddy .... **CLC 23**
 See also Chayefsky, Sidney
 See also DLB 7, 44; DLBY 81
Chayefsky, Sidney 1923-1981
 See Chayefsky, Paddy
 See also CA 9-12R; 104; CANR 18; DAM
 DRAM
Chedid, Andree 1920-
 CLC 47
 See also CA 145
Cheever, John 1912-1982
 **CLC 3, 7, 8, 11, 15, 25, 64; DA; DAB; DAC;
 DAM MST, NOV, POP; SSC 1; WLC**
 See also CA 5-8R; 106; CABS 1; CANR 5, 27;
 CDALB 1941-1968; DLB 2, 102; DLBY 80,
 82; INT CANR-5; MTCW 1
Cheever, Susan 1943-
 CLC 18, 48
 See also CA 103; CANR 27, 51; DLBY 82; INT
 CANR-27
Chekhonte, Antosha
 See Chekhov, Anton (Pavlovich)
Chekhov, Anton (Pavlovich) 1860-1904
 **TCLC 3, 10, 31, 55; DA; DAB; DAC; DAM
 DRAM, MST; DC 9; SSC 2, 28; WLC**
 See also CA 104; 124; SATA 90
Chernyshevsky, Nikolay Gavrilovich . 1828-
 1889 .... **NCLC 1**
Cherry, Carolyn Janice 1942-
 See Cherryh, C. J.
 See also CA 65-68; CANR 10
Cherryh, C. J. .... **CLC 35**
 See also Cherry, Carolyn Janice
 See also AAYA 24; DLBY 80; SATA 93
Chesnutt, Charles W(addell) 1858-1932
 TCLC 5, 39; BLC 1; DAM MULT; SSC 7
 See also BW 1; CA 106; 125; DLB 12, 50, 78;
 MTCW 1
Chester, Alfred .... 1929(?)-1971
 CLC 49
 See also CA 33-36R; DLB 130
Chesterton, G(ilbert) K(eith) 1874-1936
 TCLC 1, 6, 64; DAM NOV, POET; SSC 1
 See also CA 104; 132; CANR 73; CDBLB
 1914-1945; DLB 10, 19, 34, 70, 98, 149,
 178; MTCW 1; SATA 27
Chiang, Pin-chin 1904-1986
 See Ding Ling
 See also CA 118
Ch'ien Chung-shu 1910-
 CLC 22
 See also CA 130; CANR 73; MTCW 1
Child, L. Maria

See Child, Lydia Maria
Child, Lydia Maria 1802-1880
 NCLC 6, 73
 See also DLB 1, 74; SATA 67
Child, Mrs.
 See Child, Lydia Maria
Child, Philip 1898-1978
 CLC 19, 68
 See also CA 13-14; CAP 1; SATA 47
Childers, (Robert) Erskine 1870-1922
 TCLC 65
 See also CA 113; 153; DLB 70
Childress, Alice 1920-1994
 **CLC 12, 15, 86, 96; BLC 1; DAM DRAM,
 MULT, NOV; DC 4**
 See also AAYA 8; BW 2; CA 45-48; 146; CANR
 3, 27, 50; CLR 14; DLB 7, 38; JRDA;
 MAICYA; MTCW 1; SATA 7, 48, 81
Chin, Frank (Chew, Jr.) 1940-
 DC 7
 See also CA 33-36R; CANR 71; DAM MULT
Chislett, (Margaret) Anne 1943-
 CLC 34
 See also CA 151
Chitty, Thomas Willes 1926-
 CLC 11
 See also Hinde, Thomas
 See also CA 5-8R
Chivers, Thomas Holley 1809-1858
 NCLC 49
 See also DLB 3
Chomette, Rene Lucien 1898-1981
 See Clair, Rene
 See also CA 103
Chopin, Kate **TCLC 5, 14; DA; DAB; SSC 8;
 WLCS**
 See also Chopin, Katherine
 See also CDALB 1865-1917; DLB 12, 78
Chopin, Katherine 1851-1904
 See Chopin, Kate
 See also CA 104; 122; DAC; DAM MST, NOV
Chretien de Troyes .... c. 12th cent. -
 CMLC 10
Christie
 See Ichikawa, Kon
Christie, Agatha (Mary Clarissa) 1890-1976
 **CLC 1, 6, 8, 12, 39, 48, 110; DAB; DAC;
 DAM NOV**
 See also AAYA 9; AITN 1, 2; CA 17-20R; 61-
 64; CANR 10, 37; CDBLB 1914-1945; DLB
 13, 77; MTCW 1; SATA 36
Christie, (Ann) Philippa
 See Pearce, Philippa
 See also CA 5-8R; CANR 4
Christine de Pizan .... 1365(?)-1431(?)
 LC 9
Chubb, Elmer
 See Masters, Edgar Lee
Chulkov, Mikhail Dmitrievich 1743-1792
 LC 2
 See also DLB 150
Churchill, Caryl 1938-
 CLC 31, 55; DC 5
 See also CA 102; CANR 22, 46; DLB 13;
 MTCW 1
Churchill, Charles 1731-1764
 LC 3
 See also DLB 109
Chute, Carolyn 1947-
 CLC 39
 See also CA 123
Ciardi, John (Anthony) 1916-1986
 CLC 10, 40, 44; DAM POET

See also CA 5-8R; 118; CAAS 2; CANR 5, 33;
 CLR 19; DLB 5; DLBY 86; INT CANR-5;
 MAICYA; MTCW 1; SAAS 26; SATA 1, 65;
 SATA-Obit 46
Cicero, Marcus Tullius .... 106B.C.-43B.C.
 CMLC 3
Cimino, Michael 1943-
 CLC 16
 See also CA 105
Cioran, E(mil) M. 1911-1995
 CLC 64
 See also CA 25-28R; 149
Cisneros, Sandra 1954-
 CLC 69; DAM MULT; HLC; SSC 32
 See also AAYA 9; CA 131; CANR 64; DLB 122,
 152; HW
Cixous, Helene 1937-
 CLC 92
 See also CA 126; CANR 55; DLB 83; MTCW
 1
Clair, Rene .... **CLC 20**
 See also Chomette, Rene Lucien
Clampitt, Amy 1920-1994
 CLC 32, PC 19
 See also CA 110; 146; CANR 29; DLB 105
Clancy, Thomas L., Jr. 1947-
 See Clancy, Tom
 See also CA 125; 131; CANR 62; INT 131;
 MTCW 1
Clancy, Tom . **CLC 45, 112; DAM NOV, POP**
 See also Clancy, Thomas L., Jr.
 See also AAYA 9; BEST 89:1, 90:1
Clare, John 1793-1864
 NCLC 9; DAB; DAM POET; PC 23
 See also DLB 55, 96
Clarin
 See Alas (y Urena), Leopoldo (Enrique Garcia)
Clark, Al C.
 See Goines, Donald
Clark, (Robert) Brian 1932-
 CLC 29
 See also CA 41-44R; CANR 67
Clark, Curt
 See Westlake, Donald E(dwin)
Clark, Eleanor 1913-1996
 CLC 5, 19
 See also CA 9-12R; 151; CANR 41; DLB 6
Clark, J. P.
 See Clark, John Pepper
 See also DLB 117
Clark, John Pepper 1935-
 **CLC 38; BLC 1; DAM DRAM, MULT; DC
 5**
 See also Clark, J. P.
 See also BW 1; CA 65-68; CANR 16, 72
Clark, M. R.
 See Clark, Mavis Thorpe
Clark, Mavis Thorpe 1909-
 CLC 12
 See also CA 57-60; CANR 8, 37; CLR 30;
 MAICYA; SAAS 5; SATA 8, 74
Clark, Walter Van Tilburg 1909-1971
 CLC 28
 See also CA 9-12R; 33-36R; CANR 63; DLB
 9; SATA 8
Clark Bekederemo, J(ohnson) P(epper)
 See Clark, John Pepper
Clarke, Arthur C(harles) 1917-
 CLC 1, 4, 13, 18, 35; DAM POP; SSC 3
 See also AAYA 4; CA 1-4R; CANR 2, 28, 55;
 JRDA; MAICYA; MTCW 1; SATA 13, 70
Clarke, Austin 1896-1974
 CLC 6, 9; DAM POET

See also Boucolon, Maryse
See also BW 2
Condillac, Etienne Bonnot de 1714-1780
   LC 26
Condon, Richard (Thomas) 1915-1996
   CLC 4, 6, 8, 10, 45, 100; DAM NOV
   See also BEST 90:3; CA 1-4R; 151; CAAS 1;
   CANR 2, 23; INT CANR-23; MTCW 1
Confucius .... 551B.C.-479B.C.
   **CMLC 19; DA; DAB; DAC; DAM MST;
   WLCS**
Congreve, William 1670-1729
   **LC 5, 21; DA; DAB; DAC; DAM DRAM,
   MST, POET; DC 2; WLC**
   See also CDBLB 1660-1789; DLB 39, 84
Connell, Evan S(helby), Jr. 1924-
   CLC 4, 6, 45; DAM NOV
   See also AAYA 7; CA 1-4R; CAAS 2; CANR
   2, 39; DLB 2; DLBY 81; MTCW 1
Connelly, Marc(us Cook) 1890-1980
   CLC 7
   See also CA 85-88; 102; CANR 30; DLB 7;
   DLBY 80; SATA-Obit 25
Connor, Ralph .... TCLC 31
   See also Gordon, Charles William
   See also DLB 92
Conrad, Joseph 1857-1924
   **TCLC 1, 6, 13, 25, 43, 57; DA; DAB; DAC;
   DAM MST, NOV; SSC 9; WLC**
   See also AAYA 26; CA 104; 131; CANR 60;
   CDBLB 1890-1914; DLB 10, 34, 98, 156;
   MTCW 1; SATA 27
Conrad, Robert Arnold
   See Hart, Moss
Conroy, Pat
   See Conroy, (Donald) Pat(rick)
Conroy, (Donald) Pat(rick) 1945-
   CLC 30, 74; DAM NOV, POP
   See also AAYA 8; AITN 1; CA 85-88; CANR
   24, 53; DLB 6; MTCW 1
Constant (de Rebecque), (Henri) Benjamin
   1767-1830 .... NCLC 6
   See also DLB 119
Conybeare, Charles Augustus
   See Eliot, T(homas) S(tearns)
Cook, Michael 1933-
   CLC 58
   See also CA 93-96; CANR 68; DLB 53
Cook, Robin 1940-
   CLC 14; DAM POP
   See also BEST 90:2; CA 108; 111; CANR 41;
   INT 111
Cook, Roy
   See Silverberg, Robert
Cooke, Elizabeth 1948-
   CLC 55
   See also CA 129
Cooke, John Esten 1830-1886
   NCLC 5
   See also DLB 3
Cooke, John Estes
   See Baum, L(yman) Frank
Cooke, M. E.
   See Creasey, John
Cooke, Margaret
   See Creasey, John
Cook-Lynn, Elizabeth 1930-
   CLC 93; DAM MULT
   See also CA 133; DLB 175; NNAL
Cooney, Ray .... CLC 62
Cooper, Douglas 1960-
   CLC 86
Cooper, Henry St. John

See Creasey, John
Cooper, J(oan) California .... **CLC 56; DAM
MULT**
   See also AAYA 12; BW 1; CA 125; CANR 55
Cooper, James Fenimore 1789-1851
   NCLC 1, 27, 54
   See also AAYA 22; CDALB 1640-1865; DLB
   3; SATA 19
Coover, Robert (Lowell) 1932-
   **CLC 3, 7, 15, 32, 46, 87; DAM NOV; SSC
   15**
   See also CA 45-48; CANR 3, 37, 58; DLB 2;
   DLBY 81; MTCW 1
Copeland, Stewart (Armstrong) 1952-
   CLC 26
Copernicus, Nicolaus 1473-1543
   LC 45
Coppard, A(lfred) E(dgar) 1878-1957
   TCLC 5; SSC 21
   See also CA 114; 167; DLB 162; YABC 1
Coppee, Francois 1842-1908
   TCLC 25
Coppola, Francis Ford 1939-
   CLC 16
   See also CA 77-80; CANR 40; DLB 44
Corbiere, Tristan 1845-1875
   NCLC 43
Corcoran, Barbara 1911-
   CLC 17
   See also AAYA 14; CA 21-24R; CAAS 2;
   CANR 11, 28, 48; CLR 50; DLB 52; JRDA;
   SAAS 20; SATA 3, 77
Cordelier, Maurice
   See Giraudoux, (Hippolyte) Jean
Corelli, Marie 1855-1924
   TCLC 51
   See also Mackay, Mary
   See also DLB 34, 156
Corman, Cid 1924-
   CLC 9
   See also Corman, Sidney
   See also CAAS 2; DLB 5, 193
Corman, Sidney 1924-
   See Corman, Cid
   See also CA 85-88; CANR 44; DAM POET
Cormier, Robert (Edmund) 1925-
   **CLC 12, 30; DA; DAB; DAC; DAM MST,
   NOV**
   See also AAYA 3, 19; CA 1-4R; CANR 5, 23;
   CDALB 1968-1988; CLR 12; DLB 52; INT
   CANR-23; JRDA; MAICYA; MTCW 1;
   SATA 10, 45, 83
Corn, Alfred (DeWitt III) 1943-
   CLC 33
   See also CA 104; CAAS 25; CANR 44; DLB
   120; DLBY 80
Corneille, Pierre 1606-1684
   LC 28; DAB; DAM MST
Cornwell, David (John Moore) 1931-
   CLC 9, 15; DAM POP
   See also le Carre, John
   See also CA 5-8R; CANR 13, 33, 59; MTCW 1
Corso, (Nunzio) Gregory 1930-
   CLC 1, 11
   See also CA 5-8R; CANR 41; DLB 5, 16;
   MTCW 1
Cortazar, Julio 1914-1984
   **CLC 2, 3, 5, 10, 13, 15, 33, 34, 92; DAM
   MULT, NOV; HLC; SSC 7**
   See also CA 21-24R; CANR 12, 32; DLB 113;
   HW; MTCW 1
CORTES, HERNAN 1484-1547
   LC 31

Corvinus, Jakob
   See Raabe, Wilhelm (Karl)
Corwin, Cecil
   See Kornbluth, C(yril) M.
Cosic, Dobrica 1921-
   CLC 14
   See also CA 122; 138; DLB 181
Costain, Thomas B(ertram) 1885-1965
   CLC 30
   See also CA 5-8R; 25-28R; DLB 9
Costantini, Humberto .... 1924(?)-1987
   CLC 49
   See also CA 131; 122; HW
Costello, Elvis 1955-
   CLC 21
Cotes, Cecil V.
   See Duncan, Sara Jeannette
Cotter, Joseph Seamon Sr. 1861-1949
   TCLC 28; BLC 1; DAM MULT
   See also BW 1; CA 124; DLB 50
Couch, Arthur Thomas Quiller
   See Quiller-Couch, SirArthur (Thomas)
Coulton, James
   See Hansen, Joseph
Couperus, Louis (Marie Anne) ... 1863-1923
   TCLC 15
   See also CA 115
Coupland, Douglas 1961-
   CLC 85; DAC; DAM POP
   See also CA 142; CANR 57
Court, Wesli
   See Turco, Lewis (Putnam)
Courtenay, Bryce 1933-
   CLC 59
   See also CA 138
Courtney, Robert
   See Ellison, Harlan (Jay)
Cousteau, Jacques-Yves 1910-1997
   CLC 30
   See also CA 65-68; 159; CANR 15, 67; MTCW
   1; SATA 38, 98
Cowan, Peter (Walkinshaw) 1914-
   SSC 28
   See also CA 21-24R; CANR 9, 25, 50
Coward, Noel (Peirce) 1899-1973
   CLC 1, 9, 29, 51; DAM DRAM
   See also AITN 1; CA 17-18; 41-44R; CANR
   35; CAP 2; CDBLB 1914-1945; DLB 10;
   MTCW 1
Cowley, Abraham 1618-1667
   LC 43
   See also DLB 131, 151
Cowley, Malcolm 1898-1989
   CLC 39
   See also CA 5-8R; 128; CANR 3, 55; DLB 4,
   48; DLBY 81, 89; MTCW 1
Cowper, William 1731-1800
   NCLC 8; DAM POET
   See also DLB 104, 109
Cox, William Trevor 1928-
   CLC 9, 14, 71; DAM NOV
   See also Trevor, William
   See also CA 9-12R; CANR 4, 37, 55; DLB 14;
   INT CANR-37; MTCW 1
Coyne, P. J.
   See Masters, Hilary
Cozzens, James Gould 1903-1978
   CLC 1, 4, 11, 92
   See also CA 9-12R; 81-84; CANR 19; CDALB
   1941-1968; DLB 9; DLBD 2; DLBY 84, 97;
   MTCW 1
Crabbe, George 1754-1832
   NCLC 26

See Asimov, Isaac
Daly, Elizabeth 1878-1967
　　CLC 52
　See also CA 23-24; 25-28R; CANR 60; CAP 2
Daly, Maureen 1921-
　　CLC 17
　See also AAYA 5; CANR 37; JRDA; MAICYA;
　　SAAS 1; SATA 2
Damas, Leon-Gontran 1912-1978
　　CLC 84
　See also BW 1; CA 125; 73-76
Dana, Richard Henry Sr. 1787-1879
　　NCLC 53
Daniel, Samuel .... 1562(?)-1619
　　LC 24
　See also DLB 62
Daniels, Brett
　See Adler, Renata
Dannay, Frederic 1905-1982
　　CLC 11; DAM POP
　See also Queen, Ellery
　See also CA 1-4R; 107; CANR 1, 39; DLB 137;
　　MTCW 1
D'Annunzio, Gabriele 1863-1938
　　TCLC 6, 40
　See also CA 104; 155
Danois, N. le
　See Gourmont, Remy (-Marie-Charles) de
Dante 1265-1321
　　CMLC 3, 18; DA; DAB; DAC; DAM MST,
　　POET; PC 21; WLCS
d'Antibes, Germain
　See Simenon, Georges (Jacques Christian)
Danticat, Edwidge 1969-
　　CLC 94
　See also CA 152; CANR 73
Danvers, Dennis 1947-
　　CLC 70
Danziger, Paula 1944-
　　CLC 21
　See also AAYA 4; CA 112; 115; CANR 37; CLR
　　20; JRDA; MAICYA; SATA 36, 63, 102;
　　SATA-Brief 30
Da Ponte, Lorenzo 1749-1838
　　NCLC 50
Dario, Ruben 1867-1916
　　TCLC 4; DAM MULT; HLC; PC 15
　See also CA 131; HW; MTCW 1
Darley, George 1795-1846
　　NCLC 2
　See also DLB 96
Darrow, Clarence (Seward) 1857-1938
　　TCLC 81
　See also CA 164
Darwin, Charles 1809-1882
　　NCLC 57
　See also DLB 57, 166
Daryush, Elizabeth 1887-1977
　　CLC 6, 19
　See also CA 49-52; CANR 3; DLB 20
Dasgupta, Surendranath 1887-1952
　　TCLC 81
　See also CA 157
Dashwood, Edmee Elizabeth Monica de la Pas-
　　ture 1890-1943
　See Delafield, E. M.
　See also CA 119; 154
Daudet, (Louis Marie) Alphonse 1840-1897
　　NCLC 1
　See also DLB 123
Daumal, Rene 1908-1944
　　TCLC 14
　See also CA 114

Davenport, Guy (Mattison, Jr.) 1927-
　　CLC 6, 14, 38; SSC 16
　See also CA 33-36R; CANR 23, 73; DLB 130
Davidson, Avram 1923-
　See Queen, Ellery
　See also CA 101; CANR 26; DLB 8
Davidson, Donald (Grady) 1893-1968
　　CLC 2, 13, 19
　See also CA 5-8R; 25-28R; CANR 4; DLB 45
Davidson, Hugh
　See Hamilton, Edmond
Davidson, John 1857-1909
　　TCLC 24
　See also CA 118; DLB 19
Davidson, Sara 1943-
　　CLC 9
　See also CA 81-84; CANR 44, 68; DLB 185
Davie, Donald (Alfred) 1922-1995
　　CLC 5, 8, 10, 31
　See also CA 1-4R; 149; CAAS 3; CANR 1, 44;
　　DLB 27; MTCW 1
Davies, Ray(mond Douglas) 1944-
　　CLC 21
　See also CA 116; 146
Davies, Rhys 1901-1978
　　CLC 23
　See also CA 9-12R; 81-84; CANR 4; DLB 139,
　　191
Davies, (William) Robertson 1913-1995
　　CLC 2, 7, 13, 25, 42, 75, 91; DA; DAB;
　　DAC; DAM MST, NOV, POP; WLC
　See also BEST 89:2; CA 33-36R; 150; CANR
　　17, 42; DLB 68; INT CANR-17; MTCW 1
Davies, W(illiam) H(enry) 1871-1940
　　TCLC 5
　See also CA 104; DLB 19, 174
Davies, Walter C.
　See Kornbluth, C(yril) M.
Davis, Angela (Yvonne) 1944-
　　CLC 77; DAM MULT
　See also BW 2; CA 57-60; CANR 10
Davis, B. Lynch
　See Bioy Casares, Adolfo; Borges, Jorge Luis
Davis, Harold Lenoir 1896-1960
　　CLC 49
　See also CA 89-92; DLB 9
Davis, Rebecca (Blaine) Harding 1831-1910
　　TCLC 6
　See also CA 104; DLB 74
Davis, Richard Harding 1864-1916
　　TCLC 24
　See also CA 114; DLB 12, 23, 78, 79, 189;
　　DLBD 13
Davison, Frank Dalby 1893-1970
　　CLC 15
　See also CA 116
Davison, Lawrence H.
　See Lawrence, D(avid) H(erbert Richards)
Davison, Peter (Hubert) 1928-
　　CLC 28
　See also CA 9-12R; CAAS 4; CANR 3, 43; DLB
　　5
Davys, Mary 1674-1732
　　LC 1
　See also DLB 39
Dawson, Fielding 1930-
　　CLC 6
　See also CA 85-88; DLB 130
Dawson, Peter
　See Faust, Frederick (Schiller)
Day, Clarence (Shepard, Jr.) 1874-1935
　　TCLC 25
　See also CA 108; DLB 11

Day, Thomas 1748-1789
　　LC 1
　See also DLB 39; YABC 1
Day Lewis, C(ecil) 1904-1972
　　CLC 1, 6, 10; DAM POET; PC 11
　See also Blake, Nicholas
　See also CA 13-16; 33-36R; CANR 34; CAP 1;
　　DLB 15, 20; MTCW 1
Dazai Osamu 1909-1948
　　TCLC 11
　See also Tsushima, Shuji
　See also CA 164; DLB 182
de Andrade, Carlos Drummond
　See Drummond de Andrade, Carlos
Deane, Norman
　See Creasey, John
de Beauvoir, Simone (Lucie Ernestine Marie
　　Bertrand)
　See Beauvoir, Simone (Lucie Ernestine Marie
　　Bertrand) de
de Beer, P.
　See Bosman, Herman Charles
de Brissac, Malcolm
　See Dickinson, Peter (Malcolm)
de Chardin, Pierre Teilhard
　See Teilhard de Chardin, (Marie Joseph) Pierre
Dee, John 1527-1608
　　LC 20
Deer, Sandra 1940-
　　CLC 45
De Ferrari, Gabriella 1941-
　　CLC 65
　See also CA 146
Defoe, Daniel .... 1660(?)-1731
　　LC 1; DA; DAB; DAC; DAM MST, NOV;
　　WLC
　See also AAYA 27; CDBLB 1660-1789; DLB
　　39, 95, 101; JRDA; MAICYA; SATA 22
de Gourmont, Remy(-Marie-Charles)
　See Gourmont, Remy (-Marie-Charles) de
de Hartog, Jan 1914-
　　CLC 19
　See also CA 1-4R; CANR 1
de Hostos, E. M.
　See Hostos (y Bonilla), Eugenio Maria de
de Hostos, Eugenio M.
　See Hostos (y Bonilla), Eugenio Maria de
Deighton, Len .... CLC 4, 7, 22, 46
　See also Deighton, Leonard Cyril
　See also AAYA 6; BEST 89:2; CDBLB 1960 to
　　Present; DLB 87
Deighton, Leonard Cyril 1929-
　See Deighton, Len
　See also CA 9-12R; CANR 19, 33, 68; DAM
　　NOV, POP; MTCW 1
Dekker, Thomas .... 1572(?)-1632
　　LC 22; DAM DRAM
　See also CDBLB Before 1660; DLB 62, 172
Delafield, E. M. 1890-1943
　　TCLC 61
　See also Dashwood, Edmee Elizabeth Monica
　　de la Pasture
　See also DLB 34
de la Mare, Walter (John) 1873-1956
　　TCLC 4, 53; DAB; DAC; DAM MST,
　　POET; SSC 14; WLC
　See also CA 163; CDBLB 1914-1945; CLR 23;
　　DLB 162; SATA 16
Delaney, Franey
　See O'Hara, John (Henry)
Delaney, Shelagh 1939-
　　CLC 29; DAM DRAM
　See also CA 17-20R; CANR 30, 67; CDBLB

1960 to Present; DLB 13; MTCW 1

Delany, Mary (Granville Pendarves) . 1700-1788 .... **LC 12**

Delany, Samuel R(ay, Jr.) 1942-
CLC 8, 14, 38; BLC 1; DAM MULT
See also AAYA 24; BW 2; CA 81-84; CANR 27, 43; DLB 8, 33; MTCW 1

De La Ramee, (Marie) Louise 1839-1908
See Ouida
See also SATA 20

de la Roche, Mazo 1879-1961
CLC 14
See also CA 85-88; CANR 30; DLB 68; SATA 64

De La Salle, Innocent
See Hartmann, Sadakichi

Delbanco, Nicholas (Franklin) 1942-
CLC 6, 13
See also CA 17-20R; CAAS 2; CANR 29, 55; DLB 6

del Castillo, Michel 1933-
CLC 38
See also CA 109

Deledda, Grazia (Cosima) .... 1875(?)-1936
TCLC 23
See also CA 123

Delibes, Miguel .... **CLC 8, 18**
See also Delibes Setien, Miguel

Delibes Setien, Miguel 1920-
See Delibes, Miguel
See also CA 45-48; CANR 1, 32; HW; MTCW 1

DeLillo, Don 1936-
CLC 8, 10, 13, 27, 39, 54, 76; DAM NOV, POP
See also BEST 89:1; CA 81-84; CANR 21; DLB 6, 173; MTCW 1

de Lisser, H. G.
See De Lisser, H(erbert) G(eorge)
See also DLB 117

De Lisser, H(erbert) G(eorge) 1878-1944
TCLC 12
See also de Lisser, H. G.
See also BW 2; CA 109; 152

Deloney, Thomas .... (?)-1600
LC 41
See also DLB 167

Deloria, Vine (Victor), Jr. 1933-
CLC 21; DAM MULT
See also CA 53-56; CANR 5, 20, 48; DLB 175; MTCW 1; NNAL; SATA 21

Del Vecchio, John M(ichael) 1947-
CLC 29
See also CA 110; DLBD 9

de Man, Paul (Adolph Michel) 1919-1983
CLC 55
See also CA 128; 111; CANR 61; DLB 67; MTCW 1

De Marinis, Rick 1934-
CLC 54
See also CA 57-60; CAAS 24; CANR 9, 25, 50

Dembry, R. Emmet
See Murfree, Mary Noailles

Demby, William 1922-
CLC 53; BLC 1; DAM MULT
See also BW 1; CA 81-84; DLB 33

de Menton, Francisco
See Chin, Frank (Chew, Jr.)

Demijohn, Thom
See Disch, Thomas M(ichael)

de Montherlant, Henry (Milon)
See Montherlant, Henry (Milon) de

Demosthenes .... 384B.C.-322B.C.

CMLC 13
See also DLB 176

de Natale, Francine
See Malzberg, Barry N(athaniel)

Denby, Edwin (Orr) 1903-1983
CLC 48
See also CA 138; 110

Denis, Julio
See Cortazar, Julio

Denmark, Harrison
See Zelazny, Roger (Joseph)

Dennis, John 1658-1734
LC 11
See also DLB 101

Dennis, Nigel (Forbes) 1912-1989
CLC 8
See also CA 25-28R; 129; DLB 13, 15; MTCW 1

Dent, Lester .... 1904(?)-1959
TCLC 72
See also CA 112; 161

De Palma, Brian (Russell) 1940-
CLC 20
See also CA 109

De Quincey, Thomas 1785-1859
NCLC 4
See also CDBLB 1789-1832; DLB 110; 144

Deren, Eleanora .... 1908(?)-1961
See Deren, Maya
See also CA 111

Deren, Maya 1917-1961
CLC 16, 102
See also Deren, Eleanora

Derleth, August (William) 1909-1971
CLC 31
See also CA 1-4R; 29-32R; CANR 4; DLB 9; DLBD 17; SATA 5

Der Nister 1884-1950
TCLC 56

de Routisie, Albert
See Aragon, Louis

Derrida, Jacques 1930-
CLC 24, 87
See also CA 124; 127

Derry Down Derry
See Lear, Edward

Dersonnes, Jacques
See Simenon, Georges (Jacques Christian)

Desai, Anita 1937-
CLC 19, 37, 97; DAB; DAM NOV
See also CA 81-84; CANR 33, 53; MTCW 1; SATA 63

de Saint-Luc, Jean
See Glassco, John

de Saint Roman, Arnaud
See Aragon, Louis

Descartes, Rene 1596-1650
LC 20, 35

De Sica, Vittorio .... 1901(?)-1974
CLC 20
See also CA 117

Desnos, Robert 1900-1945
TCLC 22
See also CA 121; 151

Destouches, Louis-Ferdinand 1894-1961
CLC 9, 15
See also Celine, Louis-Ferdinand
See also CA 85-88; CANR 28; MTCW 1

de Tolignac, Gaston
See Griffith, D(avid Lewelyn) W(ark)

Deutsch, Babette 1895-1982
CLC 18
See also CA 1-4R; 108; CANR 4; DLB 45;

SATA 1; SATA-Obit 33

Devenant, William 1606-1649
LC 13

Devkota, Laxmiprasad 1909-1959
TCLC 23
See also CA 123

De Voto, Bernard (Augustine) 1897-1955
TCLC 29
See also CA 113; 160; DLB 9

De Vries, Peter 1910-1993
CLC 1, 2, 3, 7, 10, 28, 46; DAM NOV
See also CA 17-20R; 142; CANR 41; DLB 6; DLBY 82; MTCW 1

Dexter, John
See Bradley, Marion Zimmer

Dexter, Martin
See Faust, Frederick (Schiller)

Dexter, Pete 1943-
CLC 34, 55; DAM POP
See also BEST 89:2; CA 127; 131; INT 131; MTCW 1

Diamano, Silmang
See Senghor, Leopold Sedar

Diamond, Neil 1941-
CLC 30
See also CA 108

Diaz del Castillo, Bernal 1496-1584
LC 31

di Bassetto, Corno
See Shaw, George Bernard

Dick, Philip K(indred) 1928-1982
CLC 10, 30, 72; DAM NOV, POP
See also AAYA 24; CA 49-52; 106; CANR 2, 16; DLB 8; MTCW 1

Dickens, Charles (John Huffam) 1812-1870
NCLC 3, 8, 18, 26, 37, 50; DA; DAB; DAC; DAM MST, NOV; SSC 17; WLC
See also AAYA 23; CDBLB 1832-1890; DLB 21, 55, 70, 159, 166; JRDA; MAICYA; SATA 15

Dickey, James (Lafayette) 1923-1997
CLC 1, 2, 4, 7, 10, 15, 47, 109; DAM NOV, POET, POP
See also AITN 1, 2; CA 9-12R; 156; CABS 2; CANR 10, 48, 61; CDALB 1968-1988; DLB 5, 193; DLBD 7; DLBY 82, 93, 96, 97; INT CANR-10; MTCW 1

Dickey, William 1928-1994
CLC 3, 28
See also CA 9-12R; 145; CANR 24; DLB 5

Dickinson, Charles 1951-
CLC 49
See also CA 128

Dickinson, Emily (Elizabeth) 1830-1886
NCLC 21; DA; DAB; DAC; DAM MST, POET; PC 1; WLC
See also AAYA 22; CDALB 1865-1917; DLB 1; SATA 29

Dickinson, Peter (Malcolm) 1927-
CLC 12, 35
See also AAYA 9; CA 41-44R; CANR 31, 58; CLR 29; DLB 87, 161; JRDA; MAICYA; SATA 5, 62, 95

Dickson, Carr
See Carr, John Dickson

Dickson, Carter
See Carr, John Dickson

Diderot, Denis 1713-1784
LC 26

Didion, Joan 1934-
CLC 1, 3, 8, 14, 32; DAM NOV
See also AITN 1; CA 5-8R; CANR 14, 52; CDALB 1968-1988; DLB 2, 173, 185;

CLC 2, 3, 5, 8, 10, 22, 53; DAB; DAC;
DAM MST, NOV, POP
See also CA 13-16R; CANR 18, 35, 63; CDBLB
1960 to Present; DLB 14, 155; MTCW 1;
SATA 48

Drapier, M. B.
See Swift, Jonathan

Drayham, James
See Mencken, H(enry) L(ouis)

Drayton, Michael 1563-1631
LC 8; DAM POET
See also DLB 121

Dreadstone, Carl
See Campbell, (John) Ramsey

Dreiser, Theodore (Herman Albert) ... 1871-
1945 TCLC 10, 18, 35, 83; DA; DAC; DAM
MST, NOV; SSC 30; WLC
See also CA 106; 132; CDALB 1865-1917;
DLB 9, 12, 102, 137; DLBD 1; MTCW 1

Drexler, Rosalyn 1926-
CLC 2, 6
See also CA 81-84; CANR 68

Dreyer, Carl Theodor 1889-1968
CLC 16
See also CA 116

Drieu la Rochelle, Pierre(-Eugene) 1893-1945
TCLC 21
See also CA 117; DLB 72

Drinkwater, John 1882-1937
TCLC 57
See also CA 109; 149; DLB 10, 19, 149

Drop Shot
See Cable, George Washington

Droste-Hulshoff, Annette Freiin von .. 1797-
1848 .... NCLC 3
See also DLB 133

Drummond, Walter
See Silverberg, Robert

Drummond, William Henry 1854-1907
TCLC 25
See also CA 160; DLB 92

Drummond de Andrade, Carlos . 1902-1987
CLC 18
See also Andrade, Carlos Drummond de
See also CA 132; 123

Drury, Allen (Stuart) 1918-
CLC 37
See also CA 57-60; CANR 18, 52; INT CANR-
18

Dryden, John 1631-1700
LC 3, 21; DA; DAB; DAC; DAM DRAM,
MST, POET; DC 3; WLC
See also CDBLB 1660-1789; DLB 80, 101, 131

Duberman, Martin (Bauml) 1930-
CLC 8
See also CA 1-4R; CANR 2, 63

Dubie, Norman (Evans) 1945-
CLC 36
See also CA 69-72; CANR 12; DLB 120

Du Bois, W(illiam) E(dward) B(urghardt)
1868-1963 CLC 1, 2, 13, 64, 96; BLC 1;
DA; DAC; DAM MST, MULT, NOV; WLC
See also BW 1; CA 85-88; CANR 34; CDALB
1865-1917; DLB 47, 50, 91; MTCW 1; SATA
42

Dubus, Andre 1936-
CLC 13, 36, 97; SSC 15
See also CA 21-24R; CANR 17; DLB 130; INT
CANR-17

Duca Minimo
See D'Annunzio, Gabriele

Ducharme, Rejean 1941-
CLC 74

See also CA 165; DLB 60

Duclos, Charles Pinot 1704-1772
LC 1

Dudek, Louis 1918-
CLC 11, 19
See also CA 45-48; CAAS 14; CANR 1; DLB
88

Duerrenmatt, Friedrich 1921-1990
CLC 1, 4, 8, 11, 15, 43, 102; DAM DRAM
See also CA 17-20R; CANR 33; DLB 69, 124;
MTCW 1

Duffy, Bruce .... (?)-
CLC 50

Duffy, Maureen 1933-
CLC 37
See also CA 25-28R; CANR 33, 68; DLB 14;
MTCW 1

Dugan, Alan 1923-
CLC 2, 6
See also CA 81-84; DLB 5

du Gard, Roger Martin
See Martin du Gard, Roger

Duhamel, Georges 1884-1966
CLC 8
See also CA 81-84; 25-28R; CANR 35; DLB
65; MTCW 1

Dujardin, Edouard (Emile Louis) 1861-1949
TCLC 13
See also CA 109; DLB 123

Dulles, John Foster 1888-1959
TCLC 72
See also CA 115; 149

Dumas, Alexandre (pere)
See Dumas, Alexandre (Davy de la Pailleterie)

Dumas, Alexandre (Davy de la Pailleterie)
1802-1870 NCLC 11; DA; DAB; DAC;
DAM MST, NOV; WLC
See also DLB 119, 192; SATA 18

Dumas, Alexandre (fils) 1824-1895
NCLC 71; DC 1
See also AAYA 22; DLB 192

Dumas, Claudine
See Malzberg, Barry N(athaniel)

Dumas, Henry L. 1934-1968
CLC 6, 62
See also BW 1; CA 85-88; DLB 41

du Maurier, Daphne 1907-1989
CLC 6, 11, 59; DAB; DAC; DAM MST,
POP; SSC 18
See also CA 5-8R; 128; CANR 6, 55; DLB 191;
MTCW 1; SATA 27; SATA-Obit 60

Dunbar, Paul Laurence 1872-1906
TCLC 2, 12; BLC 1; DA; DAC; DAM
MST, MULT, POET; PC 5; SSC 8; WLC
See also BW 1; CA 104; 124; CDALB 1865-
1917; DLB 50, 54, 78; SATA 34

Dunbar, William .... 1460(?)-1530(?)
LC 20
See also DLB 132, 146

Duncan, Dora Angela
See Duncan, Isadora

Duncan, Isadora .... 1877(?)-1927
TCLC 68
See also CA 118; 149

Duncan, Lois 1934-
CLC 26
See also AAYA 4; CA 1-4R; CANR 2, 23, 36;
CLR 29; JRDA; MAICYA; SAAS 2; SATA
1, 36, 75

Duncan, Robert (Edward) 1919-1988
CLC 1, 2, 4, 7, 15, 41, 55; DAM POET;
PC 2
See also CA 9-12R; 124; CANR 28, 62; DLB

5, 16, 193; MTCW 1

Duncan, Sara Jeannette 1861-1922
TCLC 60
See also CA 157; DLB 92

Dunlap, William 1766-1839
NCLC 2
See also DLB 30, 37, 59

Dunn, Douglas (Eaglesham) 1942-
CLC 6, 40
See also CA 45-48; CANR 2, 33; DLB 40;
MTCW 1

Dunn, Katherine (Karen) 1945-
CLC 71
See also CA 33-36R; CANR 72

Dunn, Stephen 1939-
CLC 36
See also CA 33-36R; CANR 12, 48, 53; DLB
105

Dunne, Finley Peter 1867-1936
TCLC 28
See also CA 108; DLB 11, 23

Dunne, John Gregory 1932-
CLC 28
See also CA 25-28R; CANR 14, 50; DLBY 80

Dunsany, Edward John Moreton Drax Plunkett
1878-1957
See Dunsany, Lord
See also CA 104; 148; DLB 10

Dunsany, Lord .... TCLC 2, 59
See also Dunsany, Edward John Moreton Drax
Plunkett
See also DLB 77, 153, 156

du Perry, Jean
See Simenon, Georges (Jacques Christian)

Durang, Christopher (Ferdinand) 1949-
CLC 27, 38
See also CA 105; CANR 50

Duras, Marguerite 1914-1996
CLC 3, 6, 11, 20, 34, 40, 68, 100
See also CA 25-28R; 151; CANR 50; DLB 83;
MTCW 1

Durban, (Rosa) Pam 1947-
CLC 39
See also CA 123

Durcan, Paul 1944-
CLC 43, 70; DAM POET
See also CA 134

Durkheim, Emile 1858-1917
TCLC 55

Durrell, Lawrence (George) 1912-1990
CLC 1, 4, 6, 8, 13, 27, 41; DAM NOV
See also CA 9-12R; 132; CANR 40; CDBLB
1945-1960; DLB 15, 27; DLBY 90; MTCW
1

Durrenmatt, Friedrich
See Duerrenmatt, Friedrich

Dutt, Toru 1856-1877
NCLC 29

Dwight, Timothy 1752-1817
NCLC 13
See also DLB 37

Dworkin, Andrea 1946-
CLC 43
See also CA 77-80; CAAS 21; CANR 16, 39;
INT CANR-16; MTCW 1

Dwyer, Deanna
See Koontz, Dean R(ay)

Dwyer, K. R.
See Koontz, Dean R(ay)

Dwyer, Thomas A. 1923-
CLC 114
See also CA 115

Dye, Richard

CLC 18
See also BW 1; CA 69-72; CANR 25; DLB 33

Fairbairn, Roger
See Carr, John Dickson

Fairbairns, Zoe (Ann) 1948-
CLC 32
See also CA 103; CANR 21

Falco, Gian
See Papini, Giovanni

Falconer, James
See Kirkup, James

Falconer, Kenneth
See Kornbluth, C(yril) M.

Falkland, Samuel
See Heijermans, Herman

Fallaci, Oriana 1930-
CLC 11, 110
See also CA 77-80; CANR 15, 58; MTCW 1

Faludy, George 1913-
CLC 42
See also CA 21-24R

Faludy, Gyoergy
See Faludy, George

Fanon, Frantz 1925-1961
CLC 74; BLC 2; DAM MULT
See also BW 1; CA 116; 89-92

Fanshawe, Ann 1625-1680
LC 11

Fante, John (Thomas) 1911-1983
CLC 60
See also CA 69-72; 109; CANR 23; DLB 130;
DLBY 83

Farah, Nuruddin 1945-
CLC 53; BLC 2; DAM MULT
See also BW 2; CA 106; DLB 125

Fargue, Leon-Paul .... 1876(?)-1947
TCLC 11
See also CA 109

Farigoule, Louis
See Romains, Jules

Farina, Richard .... 1936(?)-1966
CLC 9
See also CA 81-84; 25-28R

Farley, Walter (Lorimer) 1915-1989
CLC 17
See also CA 17-20R; CANR 8, 29; DLB 22;
JRDA; MAICYA; SATA 2, 43

Farmer, Philip Jose 1918-
CLC 1, 19
See also CA 1-4R; CANR 4, 35; DLB 8; MTCW
1; SATA 93

Farquhar, George 1677-1707
LC 21; DAM DRAM
See also DLB 84

Farrell, J(ames) G(ordon) 1935-1979
CLC 6
See also CA 73-76; 89-92; CANR 36; DLB 14;
MTCW 1

Farrell, James T(homas) 1904-1979
CLC 1, 4, 8, 11, 66; SSC 28
See also CA 5-8R; 89-92; CANR 9, 61; DLB 4,
9, 86; DLBD 2; MTCW 1

Farren, Richard J.
See Betjeman, John

Farren, Richard M.
See Betjeman, John

Fassbinder, Rainer Werner 1946-1982
CLC 20
See also CA 93-96; 106; CANR 31

Fast, Howard (Melvin) 1914-
CLC 23; DAM NOV
See also AAYA 16; CA 1-4R; CAAS 18; CANR
1, 33, 54; DLB 9; INT CANR-33; SATA 7

Faulcon, Robert
See Holdstock, Robert P.

Faulkner, William (Cuthbert) 1897-1962
**CLC 1, 3, 6, 8, 9, 11, 14, 18, 28, 52, 68;
DA; DAB; DAC; DAM MST, NOV; SSC
1; WLC**
See also AAYA 7; CA 81-84; CANR 33;
CDALB 1929-1941; DLB 9, 11, 44, 102;
DLBD 2; DLBY 86, 97; MTCW 1

Fauset, Jessie Redmon .... 1884(?)-1961
CLC 19, 54; BLC 2; DAM MULT
See also BW 1; CA 109; DLB 51

Faust, Frederick (Schiller) ...... 1892-1944(?)
TCLC 49; DAM POP
See also CA 108; 152

Faust, Irvin 1924-
CLC 8
See also CA 33-36R; CANR 28, 67; DLB 2,
28; DLBY 80

Fawkes, Guy
See Benchley, Robert (Charles)

Fearing, Kenneth (Flexner) 1902-1961
CLC 51
See also CA 93-96; CANR 59; DLB 9

Fecamps, Elise
See Creasey, John

Federman, Raymond 1928-
CLC 6, 47
See also CA 17-20R; CAAS 8; CANR 10, 43;
DLBY 80

Federspiel, J(uerg) F. 1931-
CLC 42
See also CA 146

Feiffer, Jules (Ralph) 1929-
CLC 2, 8, 64; DAM DRAM
See also AAYA 3; CA 17-20R; CANR 30, 59;
DLB 7, 44; INT CANR-30; MTCW 1; SATA
8, 61

Feige, Hermann Albert Otto Maximilian
See Traven, B.

Feinberg, David B. 1956-1994
CLC 59
See also CA 135; 147

Feinstein, Elaine 1930-
CLC 36
See also CA 69-72; CAAS 1; CANR 31, 68;
DLB 14, 40; MTCW 1

Feldman, Irving (Mordecai) 1928-
CLC 7
See also CA 1-4R; CANR 1; DLB 169

Felix-Tchicaya, Gerald
See Tchicaya, Gerald Felix

Fellini, Federico 1920-1993
CLC 16, 85
See also CA 65-68; 143; CANR 33

Felsen, Henry Gregor 1916-
CLC 17
See also CA 1-4R; CANR 1; SAAS 2; SATA 1

Fenno, Jack
See Calisher, Hortense

Fenton, James Martin 1949-
CLC 32
See also CA 102; DLB 40

Ferber, Edna 1887-1968
CLC 18, 93
See also AITN 1; CA 5-8R; 25-28R; CANR 68;
DLB 9, 28, 86; MTCW 1; SATA 7

Ferguson, Helen
See Kavan, Anna

Ferguson, Samuel 1810-1886
NCLC 33
See also DLB 32

Fergusson, Robert 1750-1774

LC 29
See also DLB 109

Ferling, Lawrence
See Ferlinghetti, Lawrence (Monsanto)

Ferlinghetti, Lawrence (Monsanto) 1919(?)-
CLC 2, 6, 10, 27, 111; DAM POET; PC 1
See also CA 5-8R; CANR 3, 41, 73; CDALB
1941-1968; DLB 5, 16; MTCW 1

Fernandez, Vicente Garcia Huidobro
See Huidobro Fernandez, Vicente Garcia

Ferrer, Gabriel (Francisco Victor) Miro
See Miro (Ferrer), Gabriel (Francisco Victor)

Ferrier, Susan (Edmonstone) 1782-1854
NCLC 8
See also DLB 116

Ferrigno, Robert .... 1948(?)-
CLC 65
See also CA 140

Ferron, Jacques 1921-1985
CLC 94; DAC
See also CA 117; 129; DLB 60

Feuchtwanger, Lion 1884-1958
TCLC 3
See also CA 104; DLB 66

Feuillet, Octave 1821-1890
NCLC 45
See also DLB 192

Feydeau, Georges (Leon Jules Marie) 1862-
1921 .... **TCLC 22; DAM DRAM**
See also CA 113; 152; DLB 192

Fichte, Johann Gottlieb 1762-1814
NCLC 62
See also DLB 90

Ficino, Marsilio 1433-1499
LC 12

Fiedeler, Hans
See Doeblin, Alfred

Fiedler, Leslie A(aron) 1917-
CLC 4, 13, 24
See also CA 9-12R; CANR 7, 63; DLB 28, 67;
MTCW 1

Field, Andrew 1938-
CLC 44
See also CA 97-100; CANR 25

Field, Eugene 1850-1895
NCLC 3
See also DLB 23, 42, 140; DLBD 13; MAICYA;
SATA 16

Field, Gans T.
See Wellman, Manly Wade

Field, Michael 1915-1971
TCLC 43
See also CA 29-32R

Field, Peter
See Hobson, Laura Z(ametkin)

Fielding, Henry 1707-1754
**LC 1; DA; DAB; DAC; DAM DRAM,
MST, NOV; WLC**
See also CDBLB 1660-1789; DLB 39, 84, 101

Fielding, Sarah 1710-1768
LC 1, 44
See also DLB 39

Fields, W. C. 1880-1946
TCLC 80
See also DLB 44

Fierstein, Harvey (Forbes) 1954-
CLC 33; DAM DRAM, POP
See also CA 123; 129

Figes, Eva 1932-
CLC 31
See also CA 53-56; CANR 4, 44; DLB 14

Finch, Anne 1661-1720
LC 3; PC 21

CANR-22; MTCW 1

Gravel, Fern
See Hall, James Norman

Graver, Elizabeth 1964-
 CLC 70
 See also CA 135; CANR 71

Graves, Richard Perceval 1945-
 CLC 44
 See also CA 65-68; CANR 9, 26, 51

Graves, Robert (von Ranke) 1895-1985
 **CLC 1, 2, 6, 11, 39, 44, 45; DAB; DAC;
 DAM MST, POET; PC 6**
 See also CA 5-8R; 117; CANR 5, 36; CDBLB
 1914-1945; DLB 20, 100, 191; DLBD 18;
 DLBY 85; MTCW 1; SATA 45

Graves, Valerie
 See Bradley, Marion Zimmer

Gray, Alasdair (James) 1934-
 CLC 41
 See also CA 126; CANR 47, 69; DLB 194; INT
 126, MTCW 1

Gray, Amlin 1946-
 CLC 29
 See also CA 138

Gray, Francine du Plessix 1930-
 CLC 22; DAM NOV
 See also BEST 90:3; CA 61-64; CAAS 2;
 CANR 11, 33; INT CANR-11, MTCW 1

Gray, John (Henry) 1866-1934
 TCLC 19
 See also CA 119; 162

Gray, Simon (James Holliday) 1936-
 CLC 9, 14, 36
 See also AITN 1; CA 21-24R; CAAS 3; CANR
 32, 69; DLB 13; MTCW 1

Gray, Spalding 1941-
 CLC 49, 112; DAM POP; DC 7
 See also CA 128

Gray, Thomas 1716-1771
 **LC 4, 40; DA; DAB; DAC; DAM MST; PC
 2; WLC**
 See also CDBLB 1660-1789; DLB 109

Grayson, David
 See Baker, Ray Stannard

Grayson, Richard (A.) 1951-
 CLC 38
 See also CA 85-88; CANR 14, 31, 57

Greeley, Andrew M(oran) 1928-
 CLC 28; DAM POP
 See also CA 5-8R; CAAS 7; CANR 7, 43, 69;
 MTCW 1

Green, Anna Katharine 1846-1935
 TCLC 63
 See also CA 112; 159; DLB 202

Green, Brian
 See Card, Orson Scott

Green, Hannah
 See Greenberg, Joanne (Goldenberg)

Green, Hannah .... 1927(?)-1996
 CLC 3
 See also CA 73-76; CANR 59

Green, Henry 1905-1973
 CLC 2, 13, 97
 See also Yorke, Henry Vincent
 See also DLB 15

Green, Julian (Hartridge) 1900-1998
 See Green, Julien
 See also CA 21-24R; 169; CANR 33; DLB 4,
 72; MTCW 1

Green, Julien .... CLC 3, 11, 77
 See also Green, Julian (Hartridge)

Green, Paul (Eliot) 1894-1981
 CLC 25; DAM DRAM

See also AITN 1; CA 5-8R; 103; CANR 3; DLB
 7, 9; DLBY 81

Greenberg, Ivan 1908-1973
 See Rahv, Philip
 See also CA 85-88

Greenberg, Joanne (Goldenberg) 1932-
 CLC 7, 30
 See also AAYA 12; CA 5-8R; CANR 14, 32,
 69; SATA 25

Greenberg, Richard .... 1959(?)-
 CLC 57
 See also CA 138

Greene, Bette 1934-
 CLC 30
 See also AAYA 7; CA 53-56; CANR 4; CLR 2;
 JRDA; MAICYA; SAAS 16; SATA 8, 102

Greene, Gael .... **CLC 8**
 See also CA 13-16R; CANR 10

Greene, Graham (Henry) 1904-1991
 **CLC 1, 3, 6, 9, 14, 18, 27, 37, 70, 72; DA;
 DAB; DAC; DAM MST, NOV; SSC 29;
 WLC**
 See also AITN 2; CA 13-16R; 133; CANR 35,
 61; CDBLB 1945-1960; DLB 13, 15, 77,
 100, 162, 201; DLBY 91; MTCW 1; SATA
 20

Greene, Robert 1558-1592
 LC 41
 See also DLB 62, 167

Greer, Richard
 See Silverberg, Robert

Gregor, Arthur 1923-
 CLC 9
 See also CA 25-28R; CAAS 10; CANR 11;
 SATA 36

Gregor, Lee
 See Pohl, Frederik

Gregory, Isabella Augusta (Persse) 1852-1932
 TCLC 1
 See also CA 104; DLB 10

Gregory, J. Dennis
 See Williams, John A(lfred)

Grendon, Stephen
 See Derleth, August (William)

Grenville, Kate 1950-
 CLC 61
 See also CA 118; CANR 53

Grenville, Pelham
 See Wodehouse, P(elham) G(renville)

Greve, Felix Paul (Berthold Friedrich) 1879-
 1948
 See Grove, Frederick Philip
 See also CA 104; 141; DAC; DAM MST

Grey, Zane 1872-1939
 TCLC 6; DAM POP
 See also CA 104; 132; DLB 9; MTCW 1

Grieg, (Johan) Nordahl (Brun) ... 1902-1943
 TCLC 10
 See also CA 107

Grieve, C(hristopher) M(urray) . 1892-1978
 CLC 11, 19; DAM POET
 See also MacDiarmid, Hugh; Pteleon
 See also CA 5-8R; 85-88; CANR 33; MTCW 1

Griffin, Gerald 1803-1840
 NCLC 7
 See also DLB 159

Griffin, John Howard 1920-1980
 CLC 68
 See also AITN 1; CA 1-4R; 101; CANR 2

Griffin, Peter 1942-
 CLC 39
 See also CA 136

Griffith, D(avid Lewelyn) W(ark) .. 1875(?)-

1948 .... **TCLC 68**
 See also CA 119; 150

Griffith, Lawrence
 See Griffith, D(avid Lewelyn) W(ark)

Griffiths, Trevor 1935-
 CLC 13, 52
 See also CA 97-100; CANR 45; DLB 13

Griggs, Sutton Elbert .... 1872-1930(?)
 TCLC 77
 See also CA 123; DLB 50

Grigson, Geoffrey (Edward Harvey) . 1905-
 1985 .... **CLC 7, 39**
 See also CA 25-28R; 118; CANR 20, 33; DLB
 27; MTCW 1

Grillparzer, Franz 1791-1872
 NCLC 1
 See also DLB 133

Grimble, Reverend Charles James
 See Eliot, T(homas) S(tearns)

Grimke, Charlotte L(ottie) Forten . 1837(?)-
 1914
 See Forten, Charlotte L.
 See also BW 1; CA 117; 124; DAM MULT,
 POET

Grimm, Jacob Ludwig Karl 1785-1863
 NCLC 3
 See also DLB 90; MAICYA; SATA 22

Grimm, Wilhelm Karl 1786-1859
 NCLC 3
 See also DLB 90; MAICYA; SATA 22

Grimmelshausen, Johann Jakob Christoffel von
 1621-1676 .... **LC 6**
 See also DLB 168

Grindel, Eugene 1895-1952
 See Eluard, Paul
 See also CA 104

Grisham, John 1955-
 CLC 84; DAM POP
 See also AAYA 14; CA 138; CANR 47, 69

Grossman, David 1954-
 CLC 67
 See also CA 138

Grossman, Vasily (Semenovich) .. 1905-1964
 CLC 41
 See also CA 124; 130; MTCW 1

Grove, Frederick Philip .... **TCLC 4**
 See also Greve, Felix Paul (Berthold Friedrich)
 See also DLB 92

Grubb
 See Crumb, R(obert)

Grumbach, Doris (Isaac) 1918-
 CLC 13, 22, 64
 See also CA 5-8R; CAAS 2; CANR 9, 42, 70;
 INT CANR-9

Grundtvig, Nicolai Frederik Severin .. 1783-
 1872 .... **NCLC 1**

Grunge
 See Crumb, R(obert)

Grunwald, Lisa 1959-
 CLC 44
 See also CA 120

Guare, John 1938-
 CLC 8, 14, 29, 67; DAM DRAM
 See also CA 73-76; CANR 21, 69; DLB 7;
 MTCW 1

Gudjonsson, Halldor Kiljan 1902-1998
 See Laxness, Halldor
 See also CA 103; 164

Guenter, Erich
 See Eich, Guenter

Guest, Barbara 1920-
 CLC 34
 See also CA 25-28R; CANR 11, 44; DLB 5,

193
Guest, Judith (Ann) 1936-
CLC 8, 30; DAM NOV, POP
See also AAYA 7; CA 77-80; CANR 15; INT
CANR-15; MTCW 1
Guevara, Che .... CLC 87; HLC
See also Guevara (Serna), Ernesto
Guevara (Serna), Ernesto 1928-1967
See Guevara, Che
See also CA 127; 111; CANR 56; DAM MULT;
HW
Guild, Nicholas M. 1944-
CLC 33
See also CA 93-96
Guillemin, Jacques
See Sartre, Jean-Paul
Guillen, Jorge 1893-1984
CLC 11; DAM MULT, POET
See also CA 89-92; 112; DLB 108; HW
Guillen, Nicolas (Cristobal) 1902-1989
CLC 48, 79; BLC 2; DAM MST, MULT,
POET; HLC; PC 23
See also BW 2; CA 116; 125; 129; HW
Guillevic, (Eugene) 1907-
CLC 33
See also CA 93-96
Guillois
See Desnos, Robert
Guillois, Valentin
See Desnos, Robert
Guiney, Louise Imogen 1861-1920
TCLC 41
See also CA 160; DLB 54
Guiraldes, Ricardo (Guillermo) .. 1886-1927
TCLC 39
See also CA 131; HW; MTCW 1
Gumilev, Nikolai (Stepanovich) .. 1886-1921
TCLC 60
See also CA 165
Gunesekera, Romesh 1954-
CLC 91
See also CA 159
Gunn, Bill .... CLC 5
See also Gunn, William Harrison
See also DLB 38
Gunn, Thom(son William) 1929-
CLC 3, 6, 18, 32, 81; DAM POET
See also CA 17-20R; CANR 9, 33; CDBLB
1960 to Present; DLB 27; INT CANR-33;
MTCW 1
Gunn, William Harrison .... 1934(?)-1989
See Gunn, Bill
See also AITN 1; BW 1; CA 13-16R; 128;
CANR 12, 25
Gunnars, Kristjana 1948-
CLC 69
See also CA 113; DLB 60
Gurdjieff, G(eorgei) I(vanovich) 1877(?)-1949
TCLC 71
See also CA 157
Gurganus, Allan 1947-
CLC 70; DAM POP
See also BEST 90:1; CA 135
Gurney, A(lbert) R(amsdell), Jr. 1930-
CLC 32, 50, 54; DAM DRAM
See also CA 77-80; CANR 32, 64
Gurney, Ivor (Bertie) 1890-1937
TCLC 33
See also CA 167
Gurney, Peter
See Gurney, A(lbert) R(amsdell), Jr.
Guro, Elena 1877-1913
TCLC 56

Gustafson, James M(oody) 1925-
CLC 100
See also CA 25-28R; CANR 37
Gustafson, Ralph (Barker) 1909-
CLC 36
See also CA 21-24R; CANR 8, 45; DLB 88
Gut, Gom
See Simenon, Georges (Jacques Christian)
Guterson, David 1956-
CLC 91
See also CA 132; CANR 73
Guthrie, A(lfred) B(ertram), Jr. . 1901-1991
CLC 23
See also CA 57-60; 134; CANR 24; DLB 6;
SATA 62; SATA-Obit 67
Guthrie, Isobel
See Grieve, C(hristopher) M(urray)
Guthrie, Woodrow Wilson 1912-1967
See Guthrie, Woody
See also CA 113; 93-96
Guthrie, Woody ....CLC 35
See also Guthrie, Woodrow Wilson
Guy, Rosa (Cuthbert) 1928-
CLC 26
See also AAYA 4; BW 2; CA 17-20R; CANR
14, 34; CLR 13; DLB 33; JRDA; MAICYA;
SATA 14, 62
Gwendolyn
See Bennett, (Enoch) Arnold
H. D. .... CLC 3, 8, 14, 31, 34, 73; PC 5
See also Doolittle, Hilda
H. de V.
See Buchan, John
Haavikko, Paavo Juhani 1931-
CLC 18, 34
See also CA 106
Habbema, Koos
See Heijermans, Herman
Habermas, Juergen 1929-
CLC 104
See also CA 109
Habermas, Jurgen
See Habermas, Juergen
Hacker, Marilyn 1942-
CLC 5, 9, 23, 72, 91; DAM POET
See also CA 77-80; CANR 68; DLB 120
Haeckel, Ernst Heinrich (Philipp August)
1834-1919 .... TCLC 83
See also CA 157
Haggard, H(enry) Rider 1856-1925
TCLC 11
See also CA 108; 148; DLB 70, 156, 174, 178;
SATA 16
Hagiosy, L.
See Larbaud, Valery (Nicolas)
Hagiwara Sakutaro 1886-1942
TCLC 60; PC 18
Haig, Fenil
See Ford, Ford Madox
Haig-Brown, Roderick (Langmere) 1908-1976
CLC 21
See also CA 5-8R; 69-72; CANR 4, 38; CLR
31; DLB 88; MAICYA; SATA 12
Hailey, Arthur 1920-
CLC 5; DAM NOV, POP
See also AITN 2; BEST 90:3; CA 1-4R; CANR
2, 36; DLB 88; DLBY 82; MTCW 1
Hailey, Elizabeth Forsythe 1938-
CLC 40
See also CA 93-96; CAAS 1; CANR 15, 48;
INT CANR-15
Haines, John (Meade) 1924-
CLC 58

See also CA 17-20R; CANR 13, 34; DLB 5
Hakluyt, Richard 1552-1616
LC 31
Haldeman, Joe (William) 1943-
CLC 61
See also CA 53-56; CAAS 25; CANR 6, 70,
72; DLB 8; INT CANR-6
Haley, Alex(ander Murray Palmer) ... 1921-
1992 . CLC 8, 12, 76; BLC 2; DA; DAB;
DAC; DAM MST, MULT, POP
See also AAYA 26; BW 2; CA 77-80; 136;
CANR 61; DLB 38; MTCW 1
Haliburton, Thomas Chandler ... 1796-1865
NCLC 15
See also DLB 11, 99
Hall, Donald (Andrew, Jr.) 1928-
CLC 1, 13, 37, 59; DAM POET
See also CA 5-8R; CAAS 7; CANR 2, 44, 64;
DLB 5; SATA 23, 97
Hall, Frederic Sauser
See Sauser-Hall, Frederic
Hall, James
See Kuttner, Henry
Hall, James Norman 1887-1951
TCLC 23
See also CA 123; SATA 21
Hall, (Marguerite) Radclyffe 1886-1943
TCLC 12
See also CA 110; 150
Hall, Rodney 1935-
CLC 51
See also CA 109; CANR 69
Halleck, Fitz-Greene 1790-1867
NCLC 47
See also DLB 3
Halliday, Michael
See Creasey, John
Halpern, Daniel 1945-
CLC 14
See also CA 33-36R
Hamburger, Michael (Peter Leopold) 1924-
CLC 5, 14
See also CA 5-8R; CAAS 4; CANR 2, 47; DLB
27
Hamill, Pete 1935-
CLC 10
See also CA 25-28R; CANR 18, 71
Hamilton, Alexander .... 1755(?)-1804
NCLC 49
See also DLB 37
Hamilton, Clive
See Lewis, C(live) S(taples)
Hamilton, Edmond 1904-1977
CLC 1
See also CA 1-4R; CANR 3; DLB 8
Hamilton, Eugene (Jacob) Lee
See Lee-Hamilton, Eugene (Jacob)
Hamilton, Franklin
See Silverberg, Robert
Hamilton, Gail
See Corcoran, Barbara
Hamilton, Mollie
See Kaye, M(ary) M(argaret)
Hamilton, (Anthony Walter) Patrick . 1904-
1962 .... CLC 51
See also CA 113; DLB 10
Hamilton, Virginia 1936-
CLC 26; DAM MULT
See also AAYA 2, 21; BW 2; CA 25-28R;
CANR 20, 37, 73; CLR 1, 11, 40; DLB 33,
52; INT CANR-20; JRDA; MAICYA;
MTCW 1; SATA 4, 56, 79
Hammett, (Samuel) Dashiell 1894-1961

CLC 12, 19, 58; DAM MULT, NOV;
WLCS
See also AAYA 8; CA 69-72; CANR 13, 38;
DLB 173; DLBY 80; INT CANR-13; MTCW
1; SATA 53
Kinnell, Galway 1927-
CLC 1, 2, 3, 5, 13, 29
See also CA 9-12R; CANR 10, 34, 66; DLB 5;
DLBY 87; INT CANR-34; MTCW 1
Kinsella, Thomas 1928-
CLC 4, 19
See also CA 17-20R; CANR 15; DLB 27;
MTCW 1
Kinsella, W(illiam) P(atrick) 1935-
CLC 27, 43; DAC; DAM NOV, POP
See also AAYA 7; CA 97-100; CAAS 7; CANR
21, 35, 66; INT CANR-21; MTCW 1
Kipling, (Joseph) Rudyard 1865-1936
TCLC 8, 17; DA; DAB; DAC; DAM MST,
POET; PC 3; SSC 5; WLC
See also CA 105; 120; CANR 33; CDBLB
1890-1914; CLR 39; DLB 19, 34, 141, 156;
MAICYA; MTCW 1; SATA 100; YABC 2
Kirkup, James 1918-
CLC 1
See also CA 1-4R; CAAS 4; CANR 2; DLB 27;
SATA 12
Kirkwood, James .... 1930(?)-1989
CLC 9
See also AITN 2; CA 1-4R; 128; CANR 6, 40
Kirshner, Sidney
See Kingsley, Sidney
Kis, Danilo..................... 1935-1989
CLC 57
See also CA 109; 118; 129; CANR 61; DLB
181; MTCW 1
Kivi, Aleksis 1834-1872
NCLC 30
Kizer, Carolyn (Ashley) 1925-
CLC 15, 39, 80; DAM POET
See also CA 65-68; CAAS 5; CANR 24, 70;
DLB 5, 169
Klabund 1890-1928
TCLC 44
See also CA 162; DLB 66
Klappert, Peter 1942-
CLC 57
See also CA 33-36R; DLB 5
Klein, A(braham) M(oses) 1909-1972
CLC 19; DAB; DAC; DAM MST
See also CA 101; 37-40R; DLB 68
Klein, Norma 1938-1989
CLC 30
See also AAYA 2; CA 41-44R; 128; CANR 15,
37; CLR 2, 19; INT CANR-15; JRDA;
MAICYA; SAAS 1; SATA 7, 57
Klein, T(heodore) E(ibon) D(onald) ... 1947-
CLC 34
See also CA 119; CANR 44
Kleist, Heinrich von 1777-1811
NCLC 2, 37; DAM DRAM; SSC 22
See also DLB 90
Klima, Ivan 1931-
CLC 56; DAM NOV
See also CA 25-28R; CANR 17, 50
Klimentov, Andrei Platonovich ... 1899-1951
See Platonov, Andrei
See also CA 108
Klinger, Friedrich Maximilian von 1752-1831
NCLC 1
See also DLB 94
Klingsor the Magician
See Hartmann, Sadakichi

Klopstock, Friedrich Gottlieb 1724-1803
NCLC 11
See also DLB 97
Knapp, Caroline 1959-
CLC 99
See also CA 154
Knebel, Fletcher 1911-1993
CLC 14
See also AITN 1; CA 1-4R; 140; CAAS 3;
CANR 1, 36; SATA 36; SATA-Obit 75
Knickerbocker, Diedrich
See Irving, Washington
Knight, Etheridge 1931-1991
CLC 40; BLC 2; DAM POET; PC 14
See also BW 1; CA 21-24R; 133; CANR 23;
DLB 41
Knight, Sarah Kemble 1666-1727
LC 7
See also DLB 24, 200
Knister, Raymond 1899-1932
TCLC 56
See also DLB 68
Knowles, John 1926-
CLC 1, 4, 10, 26; DA; DAC; DAM MST,
NOV
See also AAYA 10; CA 17-20R; CANR 40;
CDALB 1968-1988; DLB 6; MTCW 1;
SATA 8, 89
Knox, Calvin M.
See Silverberg, Robert
Knox, John .... c. 1505-1572
LC 37
See also DLB 132
Knye, Cassandra
See Disch, Thomas M(ichael)
Koch, C(hristopher) J(ohn) 1932-
CLC 42
See also CA 127
Koch, Christopher
See Koch, C(hristopher) J(ohn)
Koch, Kenneth 1925-
CLC 5, 8, 44; DAM POET
See also CA 1-4R; CANR 6, 36, 57; DLB 5;
INT CANR-36; SATA 65
Kochanowski, Jan 1530-1584
LC 10
Kock, Charles Paul de 1794-1871
NCLC 16
Koda Shigeyuki 1867-1947
See Rohan, Koda
See also CA 121
Koestler, Arthur 1905-1983
CLC 1, 3, 6, 8, 15, 33
See also CA 1-4R; 109; CANR 1, 33; CDBLB
1945-1960; DLBY 83; MTCW 1
Kogawa, Joy Nozomi 1935-
CLC 78; DAC; DAM MST, MULT
See also CA 101; CANR 19, 62; SATA 99
Kohout, Pavel 1928-
CLC 13
See also CA 45-48; CANR 3
Koizumi, Yakumo
See Hearn, (Patricio) Lafcadio (Tessima Carlos)
Kolmar, Gertrud 1894-1943
TCLC 40
See also CA 167
Komunyakaa, Yusef 1947-
CLC 86, 94; BLCS
See also CA 147; DLB 120
Konrad, George
See Konrad, Gyoergy
Konrad, Gyoergy 1933-
CLC 4, 10, 73

See also CA 85-88
Konwicki, Tadeusz 1926-
CLC 8, 28, 54
See also CA 101; CAAS 9; CANR 39, 59;
MTCW 1
Koontz, Dean R(ay) 1945-
CLC 78; DAM NOV, POP
See also AAYA 9; BEST 89:3, 90:2; CA 108;
CANR 19, 36, 52; MTCW 1; SATA 92
Kopernik, Mikolaj
See Copernicus, Nicolaus
Kopit, Arthur (Lee) 1937-
CLC 1, 18, 33; DAM DRAM
See also AITN 1; CA 81-84; CABS 3; DLB 7;
MTCW 1
Kops, Bernard 1926-
CLC 4
See also CA 5-8R; DLB 13
Kornbluth, C(yril) M. 1923-1958
TCLC 8
See also CA 105; 160; DLB 8
Korolenko, V. G.
See Korolenko, Vladimir Galaktionovich
Korolenko, Vladimir
See Korolenko, Vladimir Galaktionovich
Korolenko, Vladimir G.
See Korolenko, Vladimir Galaktionovich
Korolenko, Vladimir Galaktionovich. 1853-
1921 .... TCLC 22
See also CA 121
Korzybski, Alfred (Habdank Skarbek) 1879-
1950 .... TCLC 61
See also CA 123; 160
Kosinski, Jerzy (Nikodem) 1933-1991
CLC 1, 2, 3, 6, 10, 15, 53, 70; DAM NOV
See also CA 17-20R; 134; CANR 9, 46; DLB
2; DLBY 82; MTCW 1
Kostelanetz, Richard (Cory) 1940-
CLC 28
See also CA 13-16R; CAAS 8; CANR 38
Kostrowitzki, Wilhelm Apollinaris de 1880-
1918
See Apollinaire, Guillaume
See also CA 104
Kotlowitz, Robert 1924-
CLC 4
See also CA 33-36R; CANR 36
Kotzebue, August (Friedrich Ferdinand) von
1761-1819 .... NCLC 25
See also DLB 94
Kotzwinkle, William 1938-
CLC 5, 14, 35
See also CA 45-48; CANR 3, 44; CLR 6; DLB
173; MAICYA; SATA 24, 70
Kowna, Stancy
See Szymborska, Wislawa
Kozol, Jonathan 1936-
CLC 17
See also CA 61-64; CANR 16, 45
Kozoll, Michael .... 1940(?)-
CLC 35
Kramer, Kathryn .... 19(?)-
CLC 34
Kramer, Larry 1935-
CLC 42; DAM POP; DC 8
See also CA 124; 126; CANR 60
Krasicki, Ignacy 1735-1801
NCLC 8
Krasinski, Zygmunt 1812-1859
NCLC 4
Kraus, Karl 1874-1936
TCLC 5
See also CA 104; DLB 118

See Irving, Washington

Lanier, Sidney 1842-1881
    NCLC 6; DAM POET
    See also DLB 64; DLBD 13; MAICYA; SATA
    18

Lanyer, Aemilia 1569-1645
    LC 10, 30
    See also DLB 121

Lao-Tzu
    See Lao Tzu

Lao Tzu .... fl. 6th cent. B.C.-
    CMLC 7

Lapine, James (Elliot) 1949-
    CLC 39
    See also CA 123; 130; CANR 54; INT 130

Larbaud, Valery (Nicolas) 1881-1957
    TCLC 9
    See also CA 106; 152

Lardner, Ring
    See Lardner, Ring(gold) W(ilmer)

Lardner, Ring W., Jr.
    See Lardner, Ring(gold) W(ilmer)

Lardner, Ring(gold) W(ilmer) 1885-1933
    TCLC 2, 14; SSC 32
    See also CA 104; 131; CDALB 1917-1929;
    DLB 11, 25, 86; DLBD 16; MTCW 1

Laredo, Betty
    See Codrescu, Andrei

Larkin, Maia
    See Wojciechowska, Maia (Teresa)

Larkin, Philip (Arthur) 1922-1985
    CLC 3, 5, 8, 9, 13, 18, 33, 39, 64; DAB;
    DAM MST, POET; PC 21
    See also CA 5-8R; 117; CANR 24, 62; CDBLB
    1960 to Present; DLB 27; MTCW 1

Larra (y Sanchez de Castro), Mariano Jose de
    1809-1837 .... **NCLC 17**

Larsen, Eric 1941-
    CLC 55
    See also CA 132

Larsen, Nella 1891-1964
    CLC 37; BLC 2; DAM MULT
    See also BW 1; CA 125; DLB 51

Larson, Charles R(aymond) 1938-
    CLC 31
    See also CA 53-56; CANR 4

Larson, Jonathan 1961-1996
    CLC 99
    See also CA 156

Las Casas, Bartolome de 1474-1566
    LC 31

Lasch, Christopher 1932-1994
    CLC 102
    See also CA 73-76; 144; CANR 25; MTCW 1

Lasker-Schueler, Else 1869-1945
    TCLC 57
    See also DLB 66, 124

Laski, Harold 1893-1950
    TCLC 79

Latham, Jean Lee 1902-1995
    CLC 12
    See also AITN 1; CA 5-8R; CANR 7; CLR 50;
    MAICYA; SATA 2, 68

Latham, Mavis
    See Clark, Mavis Thorpe

Lathen, Emma .... **CLC 2**
    See also Hennissart, Martha; Latsis, Mary J(ane)

Lathrop, Francis
    See Leiber, Fritz (Reuter, Jr.)

Latsis, Mary J(ane) .... 1927(?)-1997
    See Lathen, Emma
    See also CA 85-88; 162

Lattimore, Richmond (Alexander) 1906-1984

CLC 3
    See also CA 1-4R; 112; CANR 1

Laughlin, James 1914-1997
    CLC 49
    See also CA 21-24R; 162; CAAS 22; CANR 9,
    47; DLB 48; DLBY 96, 97

Laurence, (Jean) Margaret (Wemyss) 1926-
    1987 .. **CLC 3, 6, 13, 50, 62; DAC; DAM**
    MST; SSC 7
    See also CA 5-8R; 121; CANR 33; DLB 53;
    MTCW 1; SATA-Obit 50

Laurent, Antoine 1952-
    CLC 50

Lauscher, Hermann
    See Hesse, Hermann

Lautreamont, Comte de 1846-1870
    NCLC 12; SSC 14

Laverty, Donald
    See Blish, James (Benjamin)

Lavin, Mary 1912-1996
    CLC 4, 18, 99; SSC 4
    See also CA 9-12R; 151; CANR 33; DLB 15;
    MTCW 1

Lavond, Paul Dennis
    See Kornbluth, C(yril) M.; Pohl, Frederik

Lawler, Raymond Evenor 1922-
    CLC 58
    See also CA 103

Lawrence, D(avid) H(erbert Richards) 1885-
    1930**TCLC 2, 9, 16, 33, 48, 61; DA; DAB;**
    DAC; DAM MST, NOV, POET; SSC 4, 19;
    WLC
    See also CA 104; 121; CDBLB 1914-1945;
    DLB 10, 19, 36, 98, 162, 195; MTCW 1

Lawrence, T(homas) E(dward) ... 1888-1935
    TCLC 18
    See also Dale, Colin
    See also CA 115; 167; DLB 195

Lawrence of Arabia
    See Lawrence, T(homas) E(dward)

Lawson, Henry (Archibald Hertzberg) 1867-
    1922 .... **TCLC 27; SSC 18**
    See also CA 120

Lawton, Dennis
    See Faust, Frederick (Schiller)

Laxness, Halldor ....**CLC 25**
    See also Gudjonsson, Halldor Kiljan

Layamon .... fl. c. 1200-
    CMLC 10
    See also DLB 146

Laye, Camara 1928-1980
    CLC 4, 38; BLC 2; DAM MULT
    See also BW 1; CA 85-88; 97-100; CANR 25;
    MTCW 1

Layton, Irving (Peter) 1912-
    CLC 2, 15; DAC; DAM MST, POET
    See also CA 1-4R; CANR 2, 33, 43, 66; DLB
    88; MTCW 1

Lazarus, Emma 1849-1887
    NCLC 8

Lazarus, Felix
    See Cable, George Washington

Lazarus, Henry
    See Slavitt, David R(ytman)

Lea, Joan
    See Neufeld, John (Arthur)

Leacock, Stephen (Butler) 1869-1944
    TCLC 2; DAC; DAM MST
    See also CA 104; 141; DLB 92

Lear, Edward 1812-1888
    NCLC 3
    See also CLR 1; DLB 32, 163, 166; MAICYA;
    SATA 18, 100

Lear, Norman (Milton) 1922-
    CLC 12
    See also CA 73-76

Leautaud, Paul 1872-1956
    TCLC 83
    See also DLB 65

Leavis, F(rank) R(aymond) 1895-1978
    CLC 24
    See also CA 21-24R; 77-80; CANR 44; MTCW
    1

Leavitt, David 1961-
    CLC 34; DAM POP
    See also CA 116; 122; CANR 50, 62; DLB 130;
    INT 122

Leblanc, Maurice (Marie Emile) 1864-1941
    TCLC 49
    See also CA 110

Lebowitz, Fran(ces Ann) .... 1951(?)-
    CLC 11, 36
    See also CA 81-84; CANR 14, 60, 70; INT
    CANR-14; MTCW 1

Lebrecht, Peter
    See Tieck, (Johann) Ludwig

le Carre, John .... **CLC 3, 5, 9, 15, 28**
    See also Cornwell, David (John Moore)
    See also BEST 89:4; CDBLB 1960 to Present;
    DLB 87

Le Clezio, J(ean) M(arie) G(ustave) ... 1940-
    CLC 31
    See also CA 116; 128; DLB 83

Leconte de Lisle, Charles-Marie-Rene 1818-
    1894 ....**NCLC 29**

Le Coq, Monsieur
    See Simenon, Georges (Jacques Christian)

Leduc, Violette 1907-1972
    CLC 22
    See also CA 13-14; 33-36R; CANR 69; CAP 1

Ledwidge, Francis .... 1887(?)-1917
    TCLC 23
    See also CA 123; DLB 20

Lee, Andrea 1953-
    CLC 36; BLC 2; DAM MULT
    See also BW 1; CA 125

Lee, Andrew
    See Auchincloss, Louis (Stanton)

Lee, Chang-rae 1965-
    CLC 91
    See also CA 148

Lee, Don L. ....**CLC 2**
    See also Madhubuti, Haki R.

Lee, George W(ashington) 1894-1976
    CLC 52; BLC 2; DAM MULT
    See also BW 1; CA 125; DLB 51

Lee, (Nelle) Harper 1926-
    CLC 12, 60; DA; DAB; DAC; DAM MST,
    NOV; WLC
    See also AAYA 13; CA 13-16R; CANR 51;
    CDALB 1941-1968; DLB 6; MTCW 1;
    SATA 11

Lee, Helen Elaine .... 1959(?)-
    CLC 86
    See also CA 148

Lee, Julian
    See Latham, Jean Lee

Lee, Larry
    See Lee, Lawrence

Lee, Laurie 1914-1997
    CLC 90; DAB; DAM POP
    See also CA 77-80; 158; CANR 33, 73; DLB
    27; MTCW 1

Lee, Lawrence 1941-1990
    CLC 34
    See also CA 131; CANR 43

MacDonald, Anson
See Heinlein. Robert A(nson)
Macdonald, Cynthia 1928-
CLC 13, 19
See also CA 49-52: CANR 4. 44: DLB 105
MacDonald, George 1824-1905
TCLC 9
See also CA 106: 137: DLB 18. 163. 178;
MAICYA; SATA 33. 100
Macdonald, John
See Millar, Kenneth
MacDonald, John D(ann) 1916-1986
CLC 3, 27, 44; DAM NOV, POP
See also CA 1-4R; 121; CANR 1. 19. 60; DLB
8; DLBY 86; MTCW 1
Macdonald, John Ross
See Millar, Kenneth
Macdonald, Ross .... CLC 1, 2, 3, 14, 34, 41
See also Millar. Kenneth
See also DLBD 6
MacDougal, John
See Blish. James (Benjamin)
MacEwen, Gwendolyn (Margaret) 1941-1987
CLC 13, 55
See also CA 9-12R; 124; CANR 7, 22; DLB
53; SATA 50; SATA-Obit 55
Macha, Karel Hynek 1810-1846
NCLC 46
Machado (y Ruiz), Antonio 1875-1939
TCLC 3
See also CA 104; DLB 108
Machado de Assis, Joaquim Maria 1839-1908
TCLC 10; BLC 2; SSC 24
See also CA 107: 153
Machen, Arthur .... TCLC 4; SSC 20
See also Jones. Arthur Llewellyn
See also DLB 36. 156. 178
Machiavelli, Niccolo 1469-1527
LC 8, 36; DA; DAB; DAC; DAM MST;
WLCS
MacInnes, Colin 1914-1976
CLC 4, 23
See also CA 69-72; 65-68; CANR 21; DLB 14;
MTCW 1
MacInnes, Helen (Clark) 1907-1985
CLC 27, 39; DAM POP
See also CA 1-4R; 117; CANR 1, 28, 58; DLB
87; MTCW 1; SATA 22; SATA-Obit 44
Mackay, Mary 1855-1924
See Corelli. Marie
See also CA 118
Mackenzie, Compton (Edward Montague)
1883-1972 .... CLC 18
See also CA 21-22; 37-40R; CAP 2; DLB 34,
100
Mackenzie, Henry 1745-1831
NCLC 41
See also DLB 39
Mackintosh, Elizabeth .... 1896(?)-1952
See Tey, Josephine
See also CA 110
MacLaren, James
See Grieve, C(hristopher) M(urray)
Mac Laverty, Bernard 1942-
CLC 31
See also CA 116; 118; CANR 43; INT 118
MacLean, Alistair (Stuart) ...... 1922(?)-1987
CLC 3, 13, 50, 63; DAM POP
See also CA 57-60; 121; CANR 28, 61; MTCW
1; SATA 23; SATA-Obit 50
Maclean, Norman (Fitzroy) 1902-1990
CLC 78; DAM POP; SSC 13
See also CA 102; 132; CANR 49

MacLeish, Archibald 1892-1982
CLC 3, 8, 14, 68; DAM POET
See also CA 9-12R; 106; CANR 33. 63; DLB
4. 7. 45; DLBY 82; MTCW 1
MacLennan, (John) Hugh 1907-1990
CLC 2, 14, 92; DAC; DAM MST
See also CA 5-8R: 142; CANR 33; DLB 68;
MTCW 1
MacLeod, Alistair 1936-
CLC 56; DAC; DAM MST
See also CA 123; DLB 60
Macleod, Fiona
See Sharp. William
MacNeice, (Frederick) Louis 1907-1963
CLC 1, 4, 10, 53; DAB; DAM POET
See also CA 85-88; CANR 61; DLB 10, 20;
MTCW 1
MacNeill, Dand
See Fraser, George MacDonald
Macpherson, James 1736-1796
LC 29
See also Ossian
See also DLB 109
Macpherson, (Jean) Jay 1931-
CLC 14
See also CA 5-8R; DLB 53
MacShane, Frank 1927-
CLC 39
See also CA 9-12R; CANR 3, 33; DLB 111
Macumber, Mari
See Sandoz, Mari(e Susette)
Madach, Imre 1823-1864
NCLC 19
Madden, (Jerry) David 1933-
CLC 5, 15
See also CA 1-4R; CAAS 3; CANR 4, 45; DLB
6; MTCW 1
Maddern, Al(an)
See Ellison, Harlan (Jay)
Madhubuti, Haki R. 1942-
CLC 6, 73; BLC 2; DAM MULT, POET;
PC 5
See also Lee, Don L.
See also BW 2; CA 73-76; CANR 24, 51, 73;
DLB 5, 41; DLBD 8
Maepenn, Hugh
See Kuttner, Henry
Maepenn, K. H.
See Kuttner, Henry
Maeterlinck, Maurice 1862-1949
TCLC 3; DAM DRAM
See also CA 104; 136; DLB 192; SATA 66
Maginn, William 1794-1842
NCLC 8
See also DLB 110, 159
Mahapatra, Jayanta 1928-
CLC 33; DAM MULT
See also CA 73-76; CAAS 9; CANR 15, 33, 66
Mahfouz, Naguib (Abdel Aziz Al-Sabilgi)
1911(?)-
See Mahfuz, Najib
See also BEST 89:2; CA 128; CANR 55; DAM
NOV; MTCW 1
Mahfuz, Najib .... CLC 52, 55
See also Mahfouz, Naguib (Abdel Aziz Al-
Sabilgi)
See also DLBY 88
Mahon, Derek 1941-
CLC 27
See also CA 113; 128; DLB 40
Mailer, Norman 1923-
CLC 1, 2, 3, 4, 5, 8, 11, 14, 28, 39, 74, 111;
DA; DAB; DAC; DAM MST, NOV, POP

See also AITN 2; CA 9-12R; CABS 1; CANR
28; CDALB 1968-1988; DLB 2. 16, 28, 185;
DLBD 3; DLBY 80. 83; MTCW 1
Maillet, Antonine 1929-
CLC 54; DAC
See also CA 115; 120; CANR 46; DLB 60; INT
120
Mais, Roger 1905-1955
TCLC 8
See also BW 1; CA 105; 124; DLB 125; MTCW
1
Maistre, Joseph de 1753-1821
NCLC 37
Maitland, Frederic 1850-1906
TCLC 65
Maitland, Sara (Louise) 1950-
CLC 49
See also CA 69-72; CANR 13, 59
Major, Clarence 1936-
CLC 3, 19, 48; BLC 2; DAM MULT
See also BW 2; CA 21-24R; CAAS 6; CANR
13. 25. 53; DLB 33
Major, Kevin (Gerald) 1949-
CLC 26; DAC
See also AAYA 16; CA 97-100; CANR 21, 38;
CLR 11; DLB 60; INT CANR-21; JRDA;
MAICYA; SATA 32, 82
Maki, James
See Ozu, Yasujiro
Malabaila, Damiano
See Levi, Primo
Malamud, Bernard 1914-1986
CLC 1, 2, 3, 5, 8, 9, 11, 18, 27, 44, 78, 85;
DA; DAB; DAC; DAM MST, NOV, POP;
SSC 15; WLC
See also AAYA 16; CA 5-8R; 118; CABS 1;
CANR 28, 62; CDALB 1941-1968; DLB 2,
28, 152; DLBY 80, 86; MTCW 1
Malan, Herman
See Bosman. Herman Charles; Bosman, Herman
Charles
Malaparte, Curzio 1898-1957
TCLC 52
Malcolm, Dan
See Silverberg, Robert
Malcolm X .... CLC 82; BLC 2; WLCS
See also Little, Malcolm
Malherbe, Francois de 1555-1628
LC 5
Mallarme, Stephane 1842-1898
NCLC 4, 41; DAM POET; PC 4
Mallet-Joris, Francoise 1930-
CLC 11
See also CA 65-68; CANR 17; DLB 83
Malley, Ern
See McAuley, James Phillip
Mallowan, Agatha Christie
See Christie, Agatha (Mary Clarissa)
Maloff, Saul 1922-
CLC 5
See also CA 33-36R
Malone, Louis
See MacNeice, (Frederick) Louis
Malone, Michael (Christopher) 1942-
CLC 43
See also CA 77-80; CANR 14, 32, 57
Malory, (Sir) Thomas .... 1410(?)-1471(?)
LC 11; DA; DAB; DAC; DAM MST;
WLCS
See also CDBLB Before 1660; DLB 146; SATA
59; SATA-Brief 33
Malouf, (George Joseph) David 1934-
CLC 28, 86

See also CA 124; CANR 50

Malraux, (Georges-)Andre 1901-1976
CLC 1, 4, 9, 13, 15, 57; DAM NOV
See also CA 21-22; 69-72; CANR 34, 58; CAP
2; DLB 72; MTCW 1

Malzberg, Barry N(athaniel) 1939-
CLC 7
See also CA 61-64; CAAS 4; CANR 16; DLB
8

Mamet, David (Alan) 1947-
CLC 9, 15, 34, 46, 91; DAM DRAM; DC 4
See also AAYA 3; CA 81-84; CABS 3; CANR
15, 41, 67, 72; DLB 7; MTCW 1

Mamoulian, Rouben (Zachary) .. 1897-1987
CLC 16
See also CA 25-28R; 124

Mandelstam, Osip (Emilievich) ...... 1891(?)-
1938(?) .... **TCLC 2, 6; PC 14**
See also CA 104; 150

Mander, (Mary) Jane 1877-1949
TCLC 31
See also CA 162

Mandeville, John .... fl. 1350-
CMLC 19
See also DLB 146

Mandiargues, Andre Pieyre de .... **CLC 41**
See also Pieyre de Mandiargues, Andre
See also DLB 83

Mandrake, Ethel Belle
See Thurman, Wallace (Henry)

Mangan, James Clarence 1803-1849
NCLC 27

Maniere, J.-E.
See Giraudoux, (Hippolyte) Jean

Mankiewicz, Herman (Jacob) 1897-1953
TCLC 85
See also CA 120; 169; DLB 26

Manley, (Mary) Delariviere ..... 1672(?)-1724
LC 1
See also DLB 39, 80

Mann, Abel
See Creasey, John

Mann, Emily 1952-
DC 7
See also CA 130; CANR 55

Mann, (Luiz) Heinrich 1871-1950
TCLC 9
See also CA 106; 164; DLB 66

Mann, (Paul) Thomas 1875-1955
**TCLC 2, 8, 14, 21, 35, 44, 60; DA; DAB;
DAC; DAM MST, NOV; SSC 5; WLC**
See also CA 104; 128; DLB 66; MTCW 1

Mannheim, Karl 1893-1947
TCLC 65

Manning, David
See Faust, Frederick (Schiller)

Manning, Frederic .... 1887(?)-1935
TCLC 25
See also CA 124

Manning, Olivia 1915-1980
CLC 5, 19
See also CA 5-8R; 101; CANR 29; MTCW 1

Mano, D. Keith 1942-
CLC 2, 10
See also CA 25-28R; CAAS 6; CANR 26, 57;
DLB 6

Mansfield, Katherine **TCLC 2, 8, 39; DAB; SSC
9, 23; WLC**
See also Beauchamp, Kathleen Mansfield
See also DLB 162

Manso, Peter 1940-
CLC 39
See also CA 29-32R; CANR 44

Mantecon, Juan Jimenez
See Jimenez (Mantecon), Juan Ramon

Manton, Peter
See Creasey, John

Man Without a Spleen, A
See Chekhov, Anton (Pavlovich)

Manzoni, Alessandro 1785-1873
NCLC 29

Mapu, Abraham (ben Jekutiel) ... 1808-1867
NCLC 18

Mara, Sally
See Queneau, Raymond

Marat, Jean Paul 1743-1793
LC 10

Marcel, Gabriel Honore 1889-1973
CLC 15
See also CA 102; 45-48; MTCW 1

Marchbanks, Samuel
See Davies, (William) Robertson

Marchi, Giacomo
See Bassani, Giorgio

Margulies, Donald .... **CLC 76**

Marie de France .... c. 12th cent. -
CMLC 8; PC 22

Marie de l'Incarnation 1599-1672
LC 10

Marier, Captain Victor
See Griffith, D(avid Lewelyn) W(ark)

Mariner, Scott
See Pohl, Frederik

Marinetti, Filippo Tommaso 1876-1944
TCLC 10
See also CA 107; DLB 114

Marivaux, Pierre Carlet de Chamblain de
1688-1763 .... **LC 4; DC 7**

Markandaya, Kamala .... **CLC 8, 38**
See also Taylor, Kamala (Purnaiya)

Markfield, Wallace 1926-
CLC 8
See also CA 69-72; CAAS 3; DLB 2, 28

Markham, Edwin 1852-1940
TCLC 47
See also CA 160; DLB 54, 186

Markham, Robert
See Amis, Kingsley (William)

Marks, J
See Highwater, Jamake (Mamake)

Marks-Highwater, J
See Highwater, Jamake (Mamake)

Markson, David M(errill) 1927-
CLC 67
See also CA 49-52; CANR 1

Marley, Bob .... **CLC 17**
See also Marley, Robert Nesta

Marley, Robert Nesta 1945-1981
See Marley, Bob
See also CA 107; 103

Marlowe, Christopher 1564-1593
**LC 22; DA; DAB; DAC; DAM DRAM,
MST; DC 1; WLC**
See also CDBLB Before 1660; DLB 62

Marlowe, Stephen 1928-
See Queen, Ellery
See also CA 13-16R; CANR 6, 55

Marmontel, Jean-Francois 1723-1799
LC 2

Marquand, John P(hillips) 1893-1960
CLC 2, 10
See also CA 85-88; CANR 73; DLB 9, 102

Marques, Rene 1919-1979
CLC 96; DAM MULT; HLC
See also CA 97-100; 85-88; DLB 113; HW

Marquez, Gabriel (Jose) Garcia

See Garcia Marquez, Gabriel (Jose)

Marquis, Don(ald Robert Perry) 1878-1937
TCLC 7
See also CA 104; 166; DLB 11, 25

Marric, J. J.
See Creasey, John

Marryat, Frederick 1792-1848
NCLC 3
See also DLB 21, 163

Marsden, James
See Creasey, John

Marsh, (Edith) Ngaio 1899-1982
CLC 7, 53; DAM POP
See also CA 9-12R; CANR 6, 58; DLB 77;
MTCW 1

Marshall, Garry 1934-
CLC 17
See also AAYA 3; CA 111; SATA 60

Marshall, Paule 1929-
CLC 27, 72; BLC 3; DAM MULT; SSC 3
See also BW 2; CA 77-80; CANR 25, 73; DLB
157; MTCW 1

Marshallik
See Zangwill, Israel

Marsten, Richard
See Hunter, Evan

Marston, John 1576-1634
LC 33; DAM DRAM
See also DLB 58, 172

Martha, Henry
See Harris, Mark

Marti, Jose 1853-1895
NCLC 63; DAM MULT; HLC

Martial .... c. 40-c. 104
PC 10

Martin, Ken
See Hubbard, L(afayette) Ron(ald)

Martin, Richard
See Creasey, John

Martin, Steve 1945-
CLC 30
See also CA 97-100; CANR 30; MTCW 1

Martin, Valerie 1948-
CLC 89
See also BEST 90:2; CA 85-88; CANR 49

Martin, Violet Florence 1862-1915
TCLC 51

Martin, Webber
See Silverberg, Robert

Martindale, Patrick Victor
See White, Patrick (Victor Martindale)

Martin du Gard, Roger 1881-1958
TCLC 24
See also CA 118; DLB 65

Martineau, Harriet 1802-1876
NCLC 26
See also DLB 21, 55, 159, 163, 166, 190; YABC
2

Martines, Julia
See O'Faolain, Julia

Martinez, Enrique Gonzalez
See Gonzalez Martinez, Enrique

Martinez, Jacinto Benavente y
See Benavente (y Martinez), Jacinto

Martinez Ruiz, Jose 1873-1967
See Azorin; Ruiz, Jose Martinez
See also CA 93-96; HW

Martinez Sierra, Gregorio 1881-1947
TCLC 6
See also CA 115

Martinez Sierra, Maria (de la O'LeJarraga)
1874-1974 .... **TCLC 6**
See also CA 115

See also CA 108; 155; DLB 9
McCrae, John 1872-1918
   TCLC 12
   See also CA 109; DLB 92
McCreigh, James
   See Pohl, Frederik
McCullers, (Lula) Carson (Smith) 1917-1967
   **CLC 1, 4, 10, 12, 48, 100; DA; DAB; DAC;
   DAM MST, NOV; SSC 9, 24; WLC**
   See also AAYA 21; CA 5-8R; 25-28R; CABS
   1, 3; CANR 18; CDALB 1941-1968; DLB
   2, 7, 173; MTCW 1; SATA 27
McCulloch, John Tyler
   See Burroughs, Edgar Rice
McCullough, Colleen .... 1938(?)-
   CLC 27, 107; DAM NOV, POP
   See also CA 81-84; CANR 17, 46, 67; MTCW
   1
McDermott, Alice 1953-
   CLC 90
   See also CA 109; CANR 40
McElroy, Joseph 1930-
   CLC 5, 47
   See also CA 17-20R
McEwan, Ian (Russell) 1948-
   CLC 13, 66; DAM NOV
   See also BEST 90:4; CA 61-64; CANR 14, 41,
   69; DLB 14, 194; MTCW 1
McFadden, David 1940-
   CLC 48
   See also CA 104; DLB 60; INT 104
McFarland, Dennis 1950-
   CLC 65
   See also CA 165
McGahern, John 1934-
   CLC 5, 9, 48; SSC 17
   See also CA 17-20R; CANR 29, 68; DLB 14;
   MTCW 1
McGinley, Patrick (Anthony) 1937-
   CLC 41
   See also CA 120; 127; CANR 56; INT 127
McGinley, Phyllis 1905-1978
   CLC 14
   See also CA 9-12R; 77-80; CANR 19; DLB 11,
   48; SATA 2, 44; SATA-Obit 24
McGinniss, Joe 1942-
   CLC 32
   See also AITN 2; BEST 89:2; CA 25-28R;
   CANR 26, 70; DLB 185; INT CANR-26
McGivern, Maureen Daly
   See Daly, Maureen
McGrath, Patrick 1950-
   CLC 55
   See also CA 136; CANR 65
McGrath, Thomas (Matthew) 1916-1990
   CLC 28, 59; DAM POET
   See also CA 9-12R; 132; CANR 6, 33; MTCW
   1; SATA 41; SATA-Obit 66
McGuane, Thomas (Francis III) 1939-
   CLC 3, 7, 18, 45
   See also AITN 2; CA 49-52; CANR 5, 24, 49;
   DLB 2; DLBY 80; INT CANR-24; MTCW
   1
McGuckian, Medbh 1950-
   CLC 48; DAM POET
   See also CA 143; DLB 40
McHale, Tom .... 1942(?)-1982
   CLC 3, 5
   See also AITN 1; CA 77-80; 106
McIlvanney, William 1936-
   CLC 42
   See also CA 25-28R; CANR 61; DLB 14
McIlwraith, Maureen Mollie Hunter

See Hunter, Mollie
   See also SATA 2
McInerney, Jay 1955-
   CLC 34, 112; DAM POP
   See also AAYA 18; CA 116; 123; CANR 45,
   68; INT 123
McIntyre, Vonda N(eel) 1948-
   CLC 18
   See also CA 81-84; CANR 17, 34, 69; MTCW
   1
McKay, Claude TCLC 7, 41; BLC 3; DAB; PC
   2
   See also McKay, Festus Claudius
   See also DLB 4, 45, 51, 117
McKay, Festus Claudius 1889-1948
   See McKay, Claude
   See also BW 1; CA 104; 124; CANR 73; DA;
   DAC; DAM MST, MULT, NOV, POET;
   MTCW 1; WLC
McKuen, Rod 1933-
   CLC 1, 3
   See also AITN 1; CA 41-44R; CANR 40
McLoughlin, R. B.
   See Mencken, H(enry) L(ouis)
McLuhan, (Herbert) Marshall 1911-1980
   CLC 37, 83
   See also CA 9-12R; 102; CANR 12, 34, 61;
   DLB 88; INT CANR-12; MTCW 1
McMillan, Terry (L.) 1951-
   **CLC 50, 61, 112; BLCS; DAM MULT,
   NOV, POP**
   See also AAYA 21; BW 2; CA 140; CANR 60
McMurtry, Larry (Jeff) 1936-
   CLC 2, 3, 7, 11, 27, 44; DAM NOV, POP
   See also AAYA 15; AITN 2; BEST 89:2; CA 5-
   8R; CANR 19, 43, 64; CDALB 1968-1988;
   DLB 2, 143; DLBY 80, 87; MTCW 1
McNally, T. M. 1961-
   CLC 82
McNally, Terrence 1939-
   CLC 4, 7, 41, 91; DAM DRAM
   See also CA 45-48; CANR 2, 56; DLB 7
McNamer, Deirdre 1950-
   CLC 70
McNeile, Herman Cyril 1888-1937
   See Sapper
   See also DLB 77
McNickle, (William) D'Arcy 1904-1977
   CLC 89; DAM MULT
   See also CA 9-12R; 85-88; CANR 5, 45; DLB
   175; NNAL; SATA-Obit 22
McPhee, John (Angus) 1931-
   CLC 36
   See also BEST 90:1; CA 65-68; CANR 20, 46,
   64, 69; DLB 185; MTCW 1
McPherson, James Alan 1943-
   CLC 19, 77; BLCS
   See also BW 1; CA 25-28R; CAAS 17; CANR
   24; DLB 38; MTCW 1
McPherson, William (Alexander) 1933-
   CLC 34
   See also CA 69-72; CANR 28; INT CANR-28
Mead, Margaret 1901-1978
   CLC 37
   See also AITN 1; CA 1-4R; 81-84; CANR 4;
   MTCW 1; SATA-Obit 20
Meaker, Marijane (Agnes) 1927-
   See Kerr, M. E.
   See also CA 107; CANR 37, 63; INT 107;
   JRDA; MAICYA; MTCW 1; SATA 20, 61,
   99
Medoff, Mark (Howard) 1940-
   CLC 6, 23; DAM DRAM

See also AITN 1; CA 53-56; CANR 5; DLB 7;
   INT CANR-5
Medvedev, P. N.
   See Bakhtin, Mikhail Mikhailovich
Meged, Aharon
   See Megged, Aharon
Meged, Aron
   See Megged, Aharon
Megged, Aharon 1920-
   CLC 9
   See also CA 49-52; CAAS 13; CANR 1
Mehta, Ved (Parkash) 1934-
   CLC 37
   See also CA 1-4R; CANR 2, 23, 69; MTCW 1
Melanter
   See Blackmore, R(ichard) D(oddridge)
Melies, Georges 1861-1938
   TCLC 81
Melikow, Loris
   See Hofmannsthal, Hugo von
Melmoth, Sebastian
   See Wilde, Oscar (Fingal O'Flahertie Wills)
Meltzer, Milton 1915-
   CLC 26
   See also AAYA 8; CA 13-16R; CANR 38; CLR
   13; DLB 61; JRDA; MAICYA; SAAS 1;
   SATA 1, 50, 80
Melville, Herman 1819-1891
   **NCLC 3, 12, 29, 45, 49; DA; DAB; DAC;
   DAM MST, NOV; SSC 1, 17; WLC**
   See also AAYA 25; CDALB 1640-1865; DLB
   3, 74; SATA 59
Menander .... c. 342B.C.-c. 292B.C
   CMLC 9; DAM DRAM; DC 3
   See also DLB 176
Mencken, H(enry) L(ouis) 1880-1956
   TCLC 13
   See also CA 105; 125; CDALB 1917-1929;
   DLB 11, 29, 63, 137; MTCW 1
Mendelsohn, Jane .... 1965(?)-
   CLC 99
   See also CA 154
Mercer, David 1928-1980
   CLC 5; DAM DRAM
   See also CA 9-12R; 102; CANR 23; DLB 13;
   MTCW 1
Merchant, Paul
   See Ellison, Harlan (Jay)
Meredith, George 1828-1909
   TCLC 17, 43; DAM POET
   See also CA 117; 153; CDBLB 1832-1890;
   DLB 18, 35, 57, 159
Meredith, William (Morris) 1919-
   CLC 4, 13, 22, 55; DAM POET
   See also CA 9-12R; CAAS 14; CANR 6, 40;
   DLB 5
Merezhkovsky, Dmitry Sergeyevich ... 1865-
   1941 .... **TCLC 29**
   See also CA 169
Merimee, Prosper 1803-1870
   NCLC 6, 65; SSC 7
   See also DLB 119, 192
Merkin, Daphne 1954-
   CLC 44
   See also CA 123
Merlin, Arthur
   See Blish, James (Benjamin)
Merrill, James (Ingram) 1926-1995
   CLC 2, 3, 6, 8, 13, 18, 34, 91; DAM POET
   See also CA 13-16R; 147; CANR 10, 49, 63;
   DLB 5, 165; DLBY 85; INT CANR-10;
   MTCW 1
Merriman, Alex

See Silverberg, Robert

Merriman, Brian 1747-1805
  NCLC 70

Merritt, E. B.
  See Waddington, Miriam

Merton, Thomas 1915-1968
  CLC 1, 3, 11, 34, 83; PC 10
  See also CA 5-8R; 25-28R; CANR 22, 53; DLB
  48; DLBY 81; MTCW 1

Merwin, W(illiam) S(tanley) 1927-
  CLC 1, 2, 3, 5, 8, 13, 18, 45, 88; DAM
  POET
  See also CA 13-16R; CANR 15, 51; DLB 5,
  169; INT CANR-15; MTCW 1

Metcalf, John 1938-
  CLC 37
  See also CA 113; DLB 60

Metcalf, Suzanne
  See Baum, L(yman) Frank

Mew, Charlotte (Mary) 1870-1928
  TCLC 8
  See also CA 105; DLB 19, 135

Mewshaw, Michael 1943-
  CLC 9
  See also CA 53-56; CANR 7, 47; DLBY 80

Meyer, June
  See Jordan, June

Meyer, Lynn
  See Slavitt, David R(ytman)

Meyer-Meyrink, Gustav 1868-1932
  See Meyrink, Gustav
  See also CA 117

Meyers, Jeffrey 1939-
  CLC 39
  See also CA 73-76; CANR 54; DLB 111

Meynell, Alice (Christina Gertrude Thompson)
  1847-1922 .... TCLC 6
  See also CA 104; DLB 19, 98

Meyrink, Gustav .... TCLC 21
  See also Meyer-Meyrink, Gustav
  See also DLB 81

Michaels, Leonard 1933-
  CLC 6, 25; SSC 16
  See also CA 61-64; CANR 21, 62; DLB 130;
  MTCW 1

Michaux, Henri 1899-1984
  CLC 8, 19
  See also CA 85-88; 114

Micheaux, Oscar 1884-1951
  TCLC 76
  See also DLB 50

Michelangelo 1475-1564
  LC 12

Michelet, Jules 1798-1874
  NCLC 31

Michener, James A(lbert) .... 1907(?)-1997
  CLC 1, 5, 11, 29, 60, 109; DAM NOV, POP
  See also AAYA 27; AITN 1; BEST 90:1; CA 5-
  8R; 161; CANR 21, 45, 68; DLB 6; MTCW
  1

Mickiewicz, Adam 1798-1855
  NCLC 3

Middleton, Christopher 1926-
  CLC 13
  See also CA 13-16R; CANR 29, 54; DLB 40

Middleton, Richard (Barham) 1882-1911
  TCLC 56
  See also DLB 156

Middleton, Stanley 1919-
  CLC 7, 38
  See also CA 25-28R; CAAS 23; CANR 21, 46;
  DLB 14

Middleton, Thomas 1580-1627

LC 33; DAM DRAM, MST; DC 5
  See also DLB 58

Migueis, Jose Rodrigues 1901-
  CLC 10

Mikszath, Kalman 1847-1910
  TCLC 31

Miles, Jack .... CLC 100

Miles, Josephine (Louise) 1911-1985
  CLC 1, 2, 14, 34, 39; DAM POET
  See also CA 1-4R; 116; CANR 2, 55; DLB 48

Militant
  See Sandburg, Carl (August)

Mill, John Stuart 1806-1873
  NCLC 11, 58
  See also CDBLB 1832-1890; DLB 55, 190

Millar, Kenneth 1915-1983
  CLC 14; DAM POP
  See also Macdonald, Ross
  See also CA 9-12R; 110; CANR 16, 63; DLB
  2; DLBD 6; DLBY 83; MTCW 1

Millay, E. Vincent
  See Millay, Edna St. Vincent

Millay, Edna St. Vincent 1892-1950
  TCLC 4, 49; DA; DAB; DAC; DAM MST,
  POET; PC 6; WLCS
  See also CA 104; 130; CDALB 1917-1929;
  DLB 45; MTCW 1

Miller, Arthur 1915-
  CLC 1, 2, 6, 10, 15, 26, 47, 78; DA; DAB;
  DAC; DAM DRAM, MST; DC 1; WLC
  See also AAYA 15; AITN 1; CA 1-4R; CABS
  3; CANR 2, 30, 54; CDALB 1941-1968;
  DLB 7; MTCW 1

Miller, Henry (Valentine) 1891-1980
  CLC 1, 2, 4, 9, 14, 43, 84; DA; DAB; DAC;
  DAM MST, NOV; WLC
  See also CA 9-12R; 97-100; CANR 33, 64;
  CDALB 1929-1941; DLB 4, 9; DLBY 80;
  MTCW 1

Miller, Jason .... 1939(?)-
  CLC 2
  See also AITN 1; CA 73-76; DLB 7

Miller, Sue 1943-
  CLC 44; DAM POP
  See also BEST 90:3; CA 139; CANR 59; DLB
  143

Miller, Walter M(ichael, Jr.) 1923-
  CLC 4, 30
  See also CA 85-88; DLB 8

Millett, Kate 1934-
  CLC 67
  See also AITN 1; CA 73-76; CANR 32, 53;
  MTCW 1

Millhauser, Steven (Lewis) 1943-
  CLC 21, 54, 109
  See also CA 110; 111; CANR 63; DLB 2; INT
  111

Millin, Sarah Gertrude 1889-1968
  CLC 49
  See also CA 102; 93-96

Milne, A(lan) A(lexander) 1882-1956
  TCLC 6; DAB; DAC; DAM MST
  See also CA 104; 133; CLR 1, 26; DLB 10, 77,
  100, 160; MAICYA; MTCW 1; SATA 100;
  YABC 1

Milner, Ron(ald) 1938-
  CLC 56; BLC 3; DAM MULT
  See also AITN 1; BW 1; CA 73-76; CANR 24;
  DLB 38; MTCW 1

Milnes, Richard Monckton 1809-1885
  NCLC 61
  See also DLB 32, 184

Milosz, Czeslaw 1911-

CLC 5, 11, 22, 31, 56, 82; DAM MST,
  POET; PC 8; WLCS
  See also CA 81-84; CANR 23, 51; MTCW 1

Milton, John 1608-1674
  LC 9, 43; DA; DAB; DAC; DAM MST,
  POET; PC 19; WLC
  See also CDBLB 1660-1789; DLB 131, 151

Min, Anchee 1957-
  CLC 86
  See also CA 146

Minehaha, Cornelius
  See Wedekind, (Benjamin) Frank(lin)

Miner, Valerie 1947-
  CLC 40
  See also CA 97-100; CANR 59

Minimo, Duca
  See D'Annunzio, Gabriele

Minot, Susan 1956-
  CLC 44
  See also CA 134

Minus, Ed 1938-
  CLC 39

Miranda, Javier
  See Bioy Casares, Adolfo

Mirbeau, Octave 1848-1917
  TCLC 55
  See also DLB 123, 192

Miro (Ferrer), Gabriel (Francisco Victor)
  1879-1930 .... TCLC 5
  See also CA 104

Mishima, Yukio 1925-1970
  CLC 2, 4, 6, 9, 27; DC 1; SSC 4
  See also Hiraoka, Kimitake
  See also DLB 182

Mistral, Frederic 1830-1914
  TCLC 51
  See also CA 122

Mistral, Gabriela .... TCLC 2; HLC
  See also Godoy Alcayaga, Lucila

Mistry, Rohinton 1952-
  CLC 71; DAC
  See also CA 141

Mitchell, Clyde
  See Ellison, Harlan (Jay); Silverberg, Robert

Mitchell, James Leslie 1901-1935
  See Gibbon, Lewis Grassic
  See also CA 104; DLB 15

Mitchell, Joni 1943-
  CLC 12
  See also CA 112

Mitchell, Joseph (Quincy) 1908-1996
  CLC 98
  See also CA 77-80; 152; CANR 69; DLB 185;
  DLBY 96

Mitchell, Margaret (Munnerlyn) 1900-1949
  TCLC 11; DAM NOV, POP
  See also AAYA 23; CA 109; 125; CANR 55;
  DLB 9; MTCW 1

Mitchell, Peggy
  See Mitchell, Margaret (Munnerlyn)

Mitchell, S(ilas) Weir 1829-1914
  TCLC 36
  See also CA 165; DLB 202

Mitchell, W(illiam) O(rmond) 1914-1998
  CLC 25; DAC; DAM MST
  See also CA 77-80; 165; CANR 15, 43; DLB
  88

Mitchell, William 1879-1936
  TCLC 81

Mitford, Mary Russell 1787-1855
  NCLC 4
  See also DLB 110, 116

Mitford, Nancy 1904-1973

CLC 44
See also CA 9-12R; DLB 191
Miyamoto, Yuriko 1899-1951
TCLC 37
See also DLB 180
Miyazawa, Kenji 1896-1933
TCLC 76
See also CA 157
Mizoguchi, Kenji 1898-1956
TCLC 72
See also CA 167
Mo, Timothy (Peter) .... 1950(?)-
CLC 46
See also CA 117; DLB 194; MTCW 1
Modarressi, Taghi (M.) 1931-
CLC 44
See also CA 121; 134; INT 134
Modiano, Patrick (Jean) 1945-
CLC 18
See also CA 85-88; CANR 17, 40; DLB 83
Moerck, Paal
See Roelvaag, O(le) E(dvart)
Mofolo, Thomas (Mokopu) ...... 1875(?)-1948
TCLC 22; BLC 3; DAM MULT
See also CA 121; 153
Mohr, Nicholasa 1938-
CLC 12; DAM MULT; HLC
See also AAYA 8; CA 49-52; CANR 1, 32, 64;
CLR 22; DLB 145; HW; JRDA; SAAS 8;
SATA 8, 97
Mojtabai, A(nn) G(race) 1938-
CLC 5, 9, 15, 29
See also CA 85-88
Moliere 1622-1673
LC 28; DA; DAB; DAC; DAM DRAM,
MST; WLC
Molin, Charles
See Mayne, William (James Carter)
Molnar, Ferenc 1878-1952
TCLC 20; DAM DRAM
See also CA 109; 153
Momaday, N(avarre) Scott 1934-
CLC 2, 19, 85, 95; DA; DAB; DAC; DAM
MST, MULT, NOV, POP; WLCS
See also AAYA 11; CA 25-28R; CANR 14, 34,
68; DLB 143, 175; INT CANR-14; MTCW
1; NNAL; SATA 48; SATA-Brief 30
Monette, Paul 1945-1995
CLC 82
See also CA 139; 147
Monroe, Harriet 1860-1936
TCLC 12
See also CA 109; DLB 54, 91
Monroe, Lyle
See Heinlein, Robert A(nson)
Montagu, Elizabeth 1720-1800
NCLC 7
Montagu, Mary (Pierrepont) Wortley   1689-
1762 .... LC 9; PC 16
See also DLB 95, 101
Montagu, W. H.
See Coleridge, Samuel Taylor
Montague, John (Patrick) 1929-
CLC 13, 46
See also CA 9-12R; CANR 9, 69; DLB 40;
MTCW 1
Montaigne, Michel (Eyquem) de   1533-1592
LC 8; DA; DAB; DAC; DAM MST; WLC
Montale, Eugenio 1896-1981
CLC 7, 9, 18; PC 13
See also CA 17-20R; 104; CANR 30; DLB 114;
MTCW 1
Montesquieu, Charles-Louis de Secondat

1689-1755 .... LC 7
Montgomery, (Robert) Bruce 1921-1978
See Crispin, Edmund
See also CA 104
Montgomery, L(ucy) M(aud) 1874-1942
TCLC 51; DAC; DAM MST
See also AAYA 12; CA 108; 137; CLR 8, DLB
92; DLBD 14; JRDA; MAICYA; SATA 100;
YABC 1
Montgomery, Marion H., Jr. 1925-
CLC 7
See also AITN 1; CA 1-4R; CANR 3, 48; DLB
6
Montgomery, Max
See Davenport, Guy (Mattison, Jr.)
Montherlant, Henry (Milon) de .. 1896-1972
CLC 8, 19; DAM DRAM
See also CA 85-88; 37-40R; DLB 72; MTCW
1
Monty Python
See Chapman, Graham; Cleese, John
(Marwood); Gilliam, Terry (Vance); Idle,
Eric, Jones, Terence Graham Parry; Palin,
Michael (Edward)
See also AAYA 7
Moodie, Susanna (Strickland) 1803-1885
NCLC 14
See also DLB 99
Mooney, Edward 1951-
See Mooney, Ted
See also CA 130
Mooney, Ted .... CLC 25
See also Mooney, Edward
Moorcock, Michael (John) 1939-
CLC 5, 27, 58
See also AAYA 26; CA 45-48; CAAS 5; CANR
2, 17, 38, 64; DLB 14; MTCW 1; SATA 93
Moore, Brian 1921-
CLC 1, 3, 5, 7, 8, 19, 32, 90; DAB; DAC;
DAM MST
See also CA 1-4R; CANR 1, 25, 42, 63; MTCW
1
Moore, Edward
See Muir, Edwin
Moore, George Augustus 1852-1933
TCLC 7; SSC 19
See also CA 104; DLB 10, 18, 57, 135
Moore, Lorrie .... CLC 39, 45, 68
See also Moore, Marie Lorena
Moore, Marianne (Craig) 1887-1972
CLC 1, 2, 4, 8, 10, 13, 19, 47; DA; DAB;
DAC; DAM MST, POET; PC 4; WLCS
See also CA 1-4R; 33-36R; CANR 3, 61;
CDALB 1929-1941; DLB 45; DLBD 7;
MTCW 1; SATA 20
Moore, Marie Lorena 1957-
See Moore, Lorrie
See also CA 116; CANR 39
Moore, Thomas 1779-1852
NCLC 6
See also DLB 96, 144
Morand, Paul 1888-1976
CLC 41; SSC 22
See also CA 69-72; DLB 65
Morante, Elsa 1918-1985
CLC 8, 47
See also CA 85-88; 117; CANR 35; DLB 177;
MTCW 1
Moravia, Alberto 1907-1990
CLC 2, 7, 11, 27, 46; SSC 26
See also Pincherle, Alberto
See also DLB 177
More, Hannah 1745-1833

NCLC 27
See also DLB 107, 109, 116, 158
More, Henry 1614-1687
LC 9
See also DLB 126
More, Sir Thomas 1478-1535
LC 10, 32
Moreas, Jean .... TCLC 18
See also Papadiamantopoulos, Johannes
Morgan, Berry 1919-
CLC 6
See also CA 49-52; DLB 6
Morgan, Claire
See Highsmith, (Mary) Patricia
Morgan, Edwin (George) 1920-
CLC 31
See also CA 5-8R; CANR 3, 43; DLB 27
Morgan, (George) Frederick 1922-
CLC 23
See also CA 17-20R; CANR 21
Morgan, Harriet
See Mencken, H(enry) L(ouis)
Morgan, Jane
See Cooper, James Fenimore
Morgan, Janet 1945-
CLC 39
See also CA 65-68
Morgan, Lady .... 1776(?)-1859
NCLC 29
See also DLB 116, 158
Morgan, Robin (Evonne) 1941-
CLC 2
See also CA 69-72; CANR 29, 68; MTCW 1;
SATA 80
Morgan, Scott
See Kuttner, Henry
Morgan, Seth .... 1949(?)-1990
CLC 65
See also CA 132
Morgenstern, Christian 1871-1914
TCLC 8
See also CA 105
Morgenstern, S.
See Goldman, William (W.)
Moricz, Zsigmond 1879-1942
TCLC 33
See also CA 165
Morike, Eduard (Friedrich) 1804-1875
NCLC 10
See also DLB 133
Moritz, Karl Philipp 1756-1793
LC 2
See also DLB 94
Morland, Peter Henry
See Faust, Frederick (Schiller)
Morley, Christopher (Darlington) 1890-1957
TCLC 87
See also CA 112; DLB 9
Morren, Theophil
See Hofmannsthal, Hugo von
Morris, Bill 1952-
CLC 76
Morris, Julian
See West, Morris L(anglo)
Morris, Steveland Judkins .... 1950(?)-
See Wonder, Stevie
See also CA 111
Morris, William 1834-1896
NCLC 4
See also CDBLB 1832-1890; DLB 18, 35, 57,
156, 178, 184
Morris, Wright 1910-1998
CLC 1, 3, 7, 18, 37

See also CA 9-12R; 167; CANR 21; DLB 2;
DLBY 81; MTCW 1
Morrison, Arthur 1863-1945
TCLC 72
See also CA 120; 157; DLB 70, 135, 197
Morrison, Chloe Anthony Wofford
See Morrison, Toni
Morrison, James Douglas 1943-1971
See Morrison, Jim
See also CA 73-76; CANR 40
Morrison, Jim .... CLC 17
See also Morrison, James Douglas
Morrison, Toni 1931-
CLC 4, 10, 22, 55, 81, 87; BLC 3; DA;
DAB; DAC; DAM MST, MULT, NOV,
POP
See also AAYA 1, 22; BW 2; CA 29-32R;
CANR 27, 42, 67; CDALB 1968-1988; DLB
6, 33, 143; DLBY 81; MTCW 1; SATA 57
Morrison, Van 1945-
CLC 21
See also CA 116; 168
Morrissy, Mary 1958-
CLC 99
Mortimer, John (Clifford) 1923-
CLC 28, 43; DAM DRAM, POP
See also CA 13-16R; CANR 21, 69; CDBLB
1960 to Present; DLB 13; INT CANR-21;
MTCW 1
Mortimer, Penelope (Ruth) 1918-
CLC 5
See also CA 57-60; CANR 45
Morton, Anthony
See Creasey, John
Mosca, Gaetano 1858-1941
TCLC 75
Mosher, Howard Frank 1943-
CLC 62
See also CA 139; CANR 65
Mosley, Nicholas 1923-
CLC 43, 70
See also CA 69-72; CANR 41, 60; DLB 14
Mosley, Walter 1952-
CLC 97; BLCS; DAM MULT, POP
See also AAYA 17; BW 2; CA 142; CANR 57
Moss, Howard 1922-1987
CLC 7, 14, 45, 50; DAM POET
See also CA 1-4R; 123; CANR 1, 44; DLB 5
Mossgiel, Rab
See Burns, Robert
Motion, Andrew (Peter) 1952-
CLC 47
See also CA 146; DLB 40
Motley, Willard (Francis) 1909-1965
CLC 18
See also BW 1; CA 117; 106; DLB 76, 143
Motoori, Norinaga 1730-1801
NCLC 45
Mott, Michael (Charles Alston) 1930-
CLC 15, 34
See also CA 5-8R; CAAS 7; CANR 7, 29
Mountain Wolf Woman 1884-1960
CLC 92
See also CA 144; NNAL
Moure, Erin 1955-
CLC 88
See also CA 113; DLB 60
Mowat, Farley (McGill) 1921-
CLC 26; DAC; DAM MST
See also AAYA 1; CA 1-4R; CANR 4, 24, 42,
68; CLR 20; DLB 68; INT CANAR-24;
JRDA; MAICYA; MTCW 1; SATA 3, 55
Moyers, Bill 1934-

CLC 74
See also AITN 2; CA 61-64; CANR 31, 52
Mphahlele, Es'kia
See Mphahlele, Ezekiel
See also DLB 125
Mphahlele, Ezekiel 1919-1983
CLC 25; BLC 3; DAM MULT
See also Mphahlele, Es'kia
See also BW 2; CA 81-84; CANR 26
Mqhayi, S(amuel) E(dward) K(rune Loliwe)
1875-1945 ..... TCLC 25; BLC 3; DAM
MULT
See also CA 153
Mrozek, Slawomir 1930-
CLC 3, 13
See also CA 13-16R; CAAS 10; CANR 29;
MTCW 1
Mrs. Belloc-Lowndes
See Lowndes, Marie Adelaide (Belloc)
Mtwa, Percy .... (?)-
CLC 47
Mueller, Lisel 1924-
CLC 13, 51
See also CA 93-96; DLB 105
Muir, Edwin 1887-1959
TCLC 2, 87
See also CA 104; DLB 20, 100, 191
Muir, John 1838-1914
TCLC 28
See also CA 165; DLB 186
Mujica Lainez, Manuel 1910-1984
CLC 31
See also Lainez, Manuel Mujica
See also CA 81-84; 112; CANR 32; HW
Mukherjee, Bharati 1940-
CLC 53, 115; DAM NOV
See also BEST 89:2; CA 107; CANR 45, 72;
DLB 60; MTCW 1
Muldoon, Paul 1951-
CLC 32, 72; DAM POET
See also CA 113; 129; CANR 52; DLB 40; INT
129
Mulisch, Harry 1927-
CLC 42
See also CA 9-12R; CANR 6, 26, 56
Mull, Martin 1943-
CLC 17
See also CA 105
Muller, Wilhelm .... NCLC 73
Mulock, Dinah Maria
See Craik, Dinah Maria (Mulock)
Munford, Robert .... 1737(?)-1783
LC 5
See also DLB 31
Mungo, Raymond 1946-
CLC 72
See also CA 49-52; CANR 2
Munro, Alice 1931-
CLC 6, 10, 19, 50, 95; DAC; DAM MST,
NOV; SSC 3; WLCS
See also AITN 2; CA 33-36R; CANR 33, 53;
DLB 53; MTCW 1; SATA 29
Munro, H(ector) H(ugh) 1870-1916
See Saki
See also CA 104; 130; CDBLB 1890-1914; DA;
DAB; DAC; DAM MST, NOV; DLB 34, 162;
MTCW 1; WLC
Murasaki, Lady .... CMLC 1
Murdoch, (Jean) Iris 1919-
CLC 1, 2, 3, 4, 6, 8, 11, 15, 22, 31, 51; DAB;
DAC; DAM MST, NOV
See also CA 13-16R; CANR 8, 43, 68; CDBLB
1960 to Present; DLB 14, 194; INT CANR-

8; MTCW 1
Murfree, Mary Noailles 1850-1922
SSC 22
See also CA 122; DLB 12, 74
Murnau, Friedrich Wilhelm
See Plumpe, Friedrich Wilhelm
Murphy, Richard 1927-
CLC 41
See also CA 29-32R; DLB 40
Murphy, Sylvia 1937-
CLC 34
See also CA 121
Murphy, Thomas (Bernard) 1935-
CLC 51
See also CA 101
Murray, Albert L. 1916-
CLC 73
See also BW 2; CA 49-52; CANR 26, 52; DLB
38
Murray, Judith Sargent 1751-1820
NCLC 63
See also DLB 37, 200
Murray, Les(lie) A(llan) 1938-
CLC 40; DAM POET
See also CA 21-24R; CANR 11, 27, 56
Murry, J. Middleton
See Murry, John Middleton
Murry, John Middleton 1889-1957
TCLC 16
See also CA 118; DLB 149
Musgrave, Susan 1951-
CLC 13, 54
See also CA 69-72; CANR 45
Musil, Robert (Edler von) 1880-1942
TCLC 12, 68; SSC 18
See also CA 109; CANR 55; DLB 81, 124
Muske, Carol 1945-
CLC 90
See also Muske-Dukes, Carol (Anne)
Muske-Dukes, Carol (Anne) 1945-
See Muske, Carol
See also CA 65-68; CANR 32, 70
Musset, (Louis Charles) Alfred de 1810-1857
NCLC 7
See also DLB 192
My Brother's Brother
See Chekhov, Anton (Pavlovich)
Myers, L(eopold) H(amilton) 1881-1944
TCLC 59
See also CA 157; DLB 15
Myers, Walter Dean 1937-
CLC 35; BLC 3; DAM MULT, NOV
See also AAYA 4, 23; BW 2; CA 33-36R;
CANR 20, 42, 67; CLR 4, 16, 35; DLB 33;
INT CANR-20; JRDA; MAICYA; SAAS 2;
SATA 41, 71; SATA-Brief 27
Myers, Walter M.
See Myers, Walter Dean
Myles, Symon
See Follett, Ken(neth Martin)
Nabokov, Vladimir (Vladimirovich) ... 1899-
1977 CLC 1, 2, 3, 6, 8, 11, 15, 23, 44, 46,
64; DA; DAB; DAC; DAM MST, NOV;
SSC 11; WLC
See also CA 5-8R; 69-72; CANR 20; CDALB
1941-1968; DLB 2; DLBD 3; DLBY 80, 91;
MTCW 1
Nagai Kafu 1879-1959
TCLC 51
See also Nagai Sokichi
See also DLB 180
Nagai Sokichi 1879-1959
See Nagai Kafu

See also CA 117

Nagy, Laszlo 1925-1978
CLC 7
See also CA 129; 112

Naidu, Sarojini 1879-1943
TCLC 80

Naipaul, Shiva(dhar Srinivasa) .. 1945-1985
CLC 32, 39; DAM NOV
See also CA 110; 112; 116; CANR 33; DLB 157; DLBY 85; MTCW 1

Naipaul, V(idiadhar) S(urajprasad) ... 1932-
CLC 4, 7, 9, 13, 18, 37, 105; DAB; DAC; DAM MST, NOV
See also CA 1-4R; CANR 1, 33, 51; CDBLB 1960 to Present; DLB 125; DLBY 85; MTCW 1

Nakos, Lilika .... 1899(?)-
CLC 29

Narayan, R(asipuram) K(rishnaswami) 1906-
CLC 7, 28, 47; DAM NOV; SSC 25
See also CA 81-84; CANR 33, 61; MTCW 1; SATA 62

Nash, (Frediric) Ogden 1902-1971
CLC 23; DAM POET; PC 21
See also CA 13-14; 29-32R; CANR 34, 61; CAP 1; DLB 11; MAICYA; MTCW 1; SATA 2, 46

Nashe, Thomas .... 1567-1601(?)
LC 41
See also DLB 167

Nashe, Thomas 1567-1601
LC 41

Nathan, Daniel
See Dannay, Frederic

Nathan, George Jean 1882-1958
TCLC 18
See also Hatteras, Owen
See also CA 114; 169; DLB 137

Natsume, Kinnosuke 1867-1916
See Natsume, Soseki
See also CA 104

Natsume, Soseki 1867-1916
TCLC 2, 10
See also Natsume, Kinnosuke
See also DLB 180

Natti, (Mary) Lee 1919-
See Kingman, Lee
See also CA 5-8R; CANR 2

Naylor, Gloria 1950-
CLC 28, 52; BLC 3; DA; DAC; DAM MST, MULT, NOV, POP; WLCS
See also AAYA 6; BW 2; CA 107; CANR 27, 51; DLB 173; MTCW 1

Neihardt, John Gneisenau 1881-1973
CLC 32
See also CA 13-14; CANR 65; CAP 1; DLB 9, 54

Nekrasov, Nikolai Alekseevich 1821-1878
NCLC 11

Nelligan, Emile 1879-1941
TCLC 14
See also CA 114; DLB 92

Nelson, Willie 1933-
CLC 17
See also CA 107

Nemerov, Howard (Stanley) 1920-1991
CLC 2, 6, 9, 36; DAM POET; PC 24
See also CA 1-4R; 134; CABS 2; CANR 1, 27, 53; DLB 5, 6; DLBY 83; INT CANR-27; MTCW 1

Neruda, Pablo 1904-1973
CLC 1, 2, 5, 7, 9, 28, 62; DA; DAB; DAC; DAM MST, MULT, POET; HLC; PC 4;

WLC
See also CA 19-20; 45-48; CAP 2; HW; MTCW 1

Nerval, Gerard de 1808-1855
NCLC 1, 67; PC 13; SSC 18

Nervo, (Jose) Amado (Ruiz de) ... 1870-1919
TCLC 11
See also CA 109; 131; HW

Nessi, Pio Baroja y
See Baroja (y Nessi), Pio

Nestroy, Johann 1801-1862
NCLC 42
See also DLB 133

Netterville, Luke
See O'Grady, Standish (James)

Neufeld, John (Arthur) 1938-
CLC 17
See also AAYA 11; CA 25-28R; CANR 11, 37, 56; CLR 52; MAICYA; SAAS 3; SATA 6, 81

Neville, Emily Cheney 1919-
CLC 12
See also CA 5-8R; CANR 3, 37; JRDA; MAICYA; SAAS 2; SATA 1

Newbound, Bernard Slade 1930-
See Slade, Bernard
See also CA 81-84; CANR 49; DAM DRAM

Newby, P(ercy) H(oward) 1918-1997
CLC 2, 13; DAM NOV
See also CA 5-8R; 161; CANR 32, 67; DLB 15, MTCW 1

Newlove, Donald 1928-
CLC 6
See also CA 29-32R; CANR 25

Newlove, John (Herbert) 1938-
CLC 14
See also CA 21-24R; CANR 9, 25

Newman, Charles 1938-
CLC 2, 8
See also CA 21-24R

Newman, Edwin (Harold) 1919-
CLC 14
See also AITN 1; CA 69-72; CANR 5

Newman, John Henry 1801-1890
NCLC 38
See also DLB 18, 32, 55

Newton, Suzanne 1936-
CLC 35
See also CA 41-44R; CANR 14; JRDA; SATA 5, 77

Nexo, Martin Andersen 1869-1954
TCLC 43

Nezval, Vitezslav 1900-1958
TCLC 44
See also CA 123

Ng, Fae Myenne .... 1957(?)-
CLC 81
See also CA 146

Ngema, Mbongeni 1955-
CLC 57
See also BW 2; CA 143

Ngugi, James T(hiong'o) .... **CLC 3, 7, 13**
See also Ngugi wa Thiong'o

Ngugi wa Thiong'o 1938-
CLC 36; BLC 3; DAM MULT, NOV
See also Ngugi, James T(hiong'o)
See also BW 2; CA 81-84; CANR 27, 58; DLB 125; MTCW 1

Nichol, B(arrie) P(hillip) 1944-1988
CLC 18
See also CA 53-56; DLB 53; SATA 66

Nichols, John (Treadwell) 1940-
CLC 38

See also CA 9-12R; CAAS 2; CANR 6, 70; DLBY 82

Nichols, Leigh
See Koontz, Dean R(ay)

Nichols, Peter (Richard) 1927-
CLC 5, 36, 65
See also CA 104; CANR 33; DLB 13; MTCW 1

Nicolas, F. R. E.
See Freeling, Nicolas

Niedecker, Lorine 1903-1970
CLC 10, 42; DAM POET
See also CA 25-28; CAP 2; DLB 48

Nietzsche, Friedrich (Wilhelm) ... 1844-1900
TCLC 10, 18, 55
See also CA 107; 121; DLB 129

Nievo, Ippolito 1831-1861
NCLC 22

Nightingale, Anne Redmon 1943-
See Redmon, Anne
See also CA 103

Nightingale, Florence 1820-1910
TCLC 85
See also DLB 166

Nik. T. O.
See Annensky, Innokenty (Fyodorovich)

Nin, Anais 1903-1977
CLC 1, 4, 8, 11, 14, 60; DAM NOV, POP; SSC 10
See also AITN 2; CA 13-16R; 69-72; CANR 22, 53; DLB 2, 4, 152; MTCW 1

Nishida, Kitaro 1870-1945
TCLC 83

Nishiwaki, Junzaburo 1894-1982
PC 15
See also CA 107

Nissenson, Hugh 1933-
CLC 4, 9
See also CA 17-20R; CANR 27; DLB 28

Niven, Larry .... **CLC 8**
See also Niven, Laurence Van Cott
See also AAYA 27; DLB 8

Niven, Laurence Van Cott 1938-
See Niven, Larry
See also CA 21-24R; CAAS 12; CANR 14, 44, 66; DAM POP; MTCW 1; SATA 95

Nixon, Agnes Eckhardt 1927-
CLC 21
See also CA 110

Nizan, Paul 1905-1940
TCLC 40
See also CA 161; DLB 72

Nkosi, Lewis 1936-
CLC 45; BLC 3; DAM MULT
See also BW 1; CA 65-68; CANR 27; DLB 157

Nodier, (Jean) Charles (Emmanuel) ... 1780-1844 .... **NCLC 19**
See also DLB 119

Noguchi, Yone 1875-1947
TCLC 80

Nolan, Christopher 1965-
CLC 58
See also CA 111

Noon, Jeff 1957-
CLC 91
See also CA 148

Norden, Charles
See Durrell, Lawrence (George)

Nordhoff, Charles (Bernard) 1887-1947
TCLC 23
See also CA 108; DLB 9; SATA 23

Norfolk, Lawrence 1963-
CLC 76

Pereda y Porrua, Jose Maria de
See Pereda (y Sanchez de Porrua), Jose Maria de
Peregoy, George Weems
See Mencken, H(enry) L(ouis)
Perelman, S(idney) J(oseph) 1904-1979
  CLC 3, 5, 9, 15, 23, 44, 49; DAM DRAM; SSC 32
  See also AITN 1, 2; CA 73-76; 89-92; CANR 18; DLB 11, 44; MTCW 1
Peret, Benjamin 1899-1959
  TCLC 20
  See also CA 117
Peretz, Isaac Loeb .... 1851(?)-1915
  TCLC 16; SSC 26
  See also CA 109
Peretz, Yitzhok Leibush
  See Peretz, Isaac Loeb
Perez Galdos, Benito 1843-1920
  TCLC 27
  See also CA 125; 153; HW
Perrault, Charles 1628-1703
  LC 2
  See also MAICYA; SATA 25
Perry, Brighton
  See Sherwood, Robert E(mmet)
Perse, St.-John
  See Leger, (Marie-Rene Auguste) Alexis Saint-Leger
Perutz, Leo 1882-1957
  TCLC 60
  See also DLB 81
Peseenz, Tulio F.
  See Lopez y Fuentes, Gregorio
Pesetsky, Bette 1932-
  CLC 28
  See also CA 133; DLB 130
Peshkov, Alexei Maximovich 1868-1936
  See Gorky, Maxim
  See also CA 105; 141; DA; DAC; DAM DRAM, MST, NOV
Pessoa, Fernando (Antonio Nogueira) 1898-1935 .... **TCLC 27; HLC; PC20**
  See also CA 125
Peterkin, Julia Mood 1880-1961
  CLC 31
  See also CA 102; DLB 9
Peters, Joan K(aren) 1945-
  CLC 39
  See also CA 158
Peters, Robert L(ouis) 1924-
  CLC 7
  See also CA 13-16R; CAAS 8; DLB 105
Petofi, Sandor 1823-1849
  NCLC 21
Petrakis, Harry Mark 1923-
  CLC 3
  See also CA 9-12R; CANR 4, 30
Petrarch 1304-1374
  CMLC 20; DAM POET; PC 8
Petrov, Evgeny .... **TCLC 21**
  See also Kataev, Evgeny Petrovich
Petry, Ann (Lane) 1908-1997
  CLC 1, 7, 18
  See also BW 1; CA 5-8R; 157; CAAS 6; CANR 4, 46; CLR 12; DLB 76; JRDA; MAICYA; MTCW 1; SATA 5; SATA-Obit 94
Petursson, Halligrimur 1614-1674
  LC 8
Peychinovich
  See Vazov, Ivan (Minchov)
Phaedrus .... 18(?)B.C.-55(?)
  CMLC 25

Philips, Katherine 1632-1664
  LC 30
  See also DLB 131
Philipson, Morris H. 1926-
  CLC 53
  See also CA 1-4R; CANR 4
Phillips, Caryl 1958-
  CLC 96; BLCS; DAM MULT
  See also BW 2; CA 141; CANR 63; DLB 157
Phillips, David Graham 1867-1911
  TCLC 44
  See also CA 108; DLB 9, 12
Phillips, Jack
  See Sandburg, Carl (August)
Phillips, Jayne Anne 1952-
  CLC 15, 33; SSC 16
  See also CA 101; CANR 24, 50; DLBY 80; INT CANR-24; MTCW 1
Phillips, Richard
  See Dick, Philip K(indred)
Phillips, Robert (Schaeffer) 1938-
  CLC 28
  See also CA 17-20R; CAAS 13; CANR 8; DLB 105
Phillips, Ward
  See Lovecraft, H(oward) P(hillips)
Piccolo, Lucio 1901-1969
  CLC 13
  See also CA 97-100; DLB 114
Pickthall, Marjorie L(owry) C(hristie)   1883-1922 .... **TCLC 21**
  See also CA 107; DLB 92
Pico della Mirandola, Giovanni .. 1463-1494
  LC 15
Piercy, Marge 1936-
  CLC 3, 6, 14, 18, 27, 62
  See also CA 21-24R; CAAS 1; CANR 13, 43, 66; DLB 120; MTCW 1
Piers, Robert
  See Anthony, Piers
Pieyre de Mandiargues, Andre ... 1909-1991
  See Mandiargues, Andre Pieyre de
  See also CA 103; 136; CANR 22
Pilnyak, Boris .... **TCLC 23**
  See also Vogau, Boris Andreyevich
Pincherle, Alberto 1907-1990
  CLC 11, 18; DAM NOV
  See also Moravia, Alberto
  See also CA 25-28R; 132; CANR 33, 63; MTCW 1
Pinckney, Darryl 1953-
  CLC 76
  See also BW 2; CA 143
Pindar .... 518B.C.-446B.C.
  CMLC 12; PC 19
  See also DLB 176
Pineda, Cecile 1942-
  CLC 39
  See also CA 118
Pinero, Arthur Wing 1855-1934
  TCLC 32; DAM DRAM
  See also CA 110; 153; DLB 10
Pinero, Miguel (Antonio Gomez)   1946-1988
  CLC 4, 55
  See also CA 61-64; 125; CANR 29; HW
Pinget, Robert 1919-1997
  CLC 7, 13, 37
  See also CA 85-88; 160; DLB 83
Pink Floyd
  See Barrett, (Roger) Syd; Gilmour, David; Mason, Nick; Waters, Roger; Wright, Rick
Pinkney, Edward 1802-1828
  NCLC 31

Pinkwater, Daniel Manus 1941-
  CLC 35
  See also Pinkwater, Manus
  See also AAYA 1; CA 29-32R; CANR 12, 38; CLR 4; JRDA; MAICYA; SAAS 3; SATA 46, 76
Pinkwater, Manus
  See Pinkwater, Daniel Manus
  See also SATA 8
Pinsky, Robert 1940-
  CLC 9, 19, 38, 94; DAM POET
  See also CA 29-32R; CAAS 4; CANR 58; DLBY 82
Pinta, Harold
  See Pinter, Harold
Pinter, Harold 1930-
  CLC 1, 3, 6, 9, 11, 15, 27, 58, 73; DA; DAB; DAC; DAM DRAM, MST; WLC
  See also CA 5-8R; CANR 33, 65; CDBLB 1960 to Present; DLB 13; MTCW 1
Piozzi, Hester Lynch (Thrale) 1741-1821
  NCLC 57
  See also DLB 104, 142
Pirandello, Luigi 1867-1936
  TCLC 4, 29; DA; DAB; DAC; DAM DRAM, MST; DC 5; SSC 22; WLC
  See also CA 104; 153
Pirsig, Robert M(aynard) 1928-
  CLC 4, 6, 73; DAM POP
  See also CA 53-56; CANR 42; MTCW 1; SATA 39
Pisarev, Dmitry Ivanovich 1840-1868
  NCLC 25
Pix, Mary (Griffith) 1666-1709
  LC 8
  See also DLB 80
Pixerecourt, (Rene Charles) Guilbert de   1773-1844 .... **NCLC 39**
  See also DLB 192
Plaatje, Sol(omon) T(shekisho) ... 1876-1932
  TCLC 73; BLCS
  See also BW 2; CA 141
Plaidy, Jean
  See Hibbert, Eleanor Alice Burford
Planche, James Robinson 1796-1880
  NCLC 42
Plant, Robert 1948-
  CLC 12
Plante, David (Robert) 1940-
  CLC 7, 23, 38; DAM NOV
  See also CA 37-40R; CANR 12, 36, 58; DLBY 83; INT CANR-12; MTCW 1
Plath, Sylvia 1932-1963
  CLC 1, 2, 3, 5, 9, 11, 14, 17, 50, 51, 62, 111; DA; DAB; DAC; DAM MST, POET; PC 1; WLC
  See also AAYA 13; CA 19-20; CANR 34; CAP 2; CDALB 1941-1968; DLB 5, 6, 152; MTCW 1; SATA 96
Plato .... 428(?)B.C.-348(?)B.C.
  CMLC 8; DA; DAB; DAC; DAM MST; WLCS
  See also DLB 176
Platonov, Andrei .... **TCLC 14**
  See also Klimentov, Andrei Platonovich
Platt, Kin 1911-
  CLC 26
  See also AAYA 11; CA 17-20R; CANR 11; JRDA; SAAS 17; SATA 21, 86
Plautus .... c. 251B.C.-184B.C.
  CMLC 24; DC 6
Plick et Plock
  See Simenon, Georges (Jacques Christian)

Plimpton, George (Ames) 1927-
   CLC 36
   See also AITN 1; CA 21-24R; CANR 32, 70;
   DLB 185; MTCW 1; SATA 10
Pliny the Elder .... c. 23-79
   CMLC 23
Plomer, William Charles Franklin 1903-1973
   CLC 4, 8
   See also CA 21-22; CANR 34; CAP 2; DLB
   20, 162, 191; MTCW 1; SATA 24
Plowman, Piers
   See Kavanagh, Patrick (Joseph)
Plum, J.
   See Wodehouse, P(elham) G(renville)
Plumly, Stanley (Ross) 1939-
   CLC 33
   See also CA 108; 110; DLB 5, 193; INT 110
Plumpe, Friedrich Wilhelm 1888-1931
   TCLC 53
   See also CA 112
Po Chu-i 772-846
   CMLC 24
Poe, Edgar Allan 1809-1849
   NCLC 1, 16, 55; DA; DAB; DAC;
   DAMMST, POET; PC 1; SSC 1, 22; WLC
   See also AAYA 14; CDALB 1640-1865; DLB
   3, 59, 73, 74; SATA 23
Poet of Titchfield Street, The
   See Pound, Ezra (Weston Loomis)
Pohl, Frederik 1919-
   CLC 18; SSC 25
   See also AAYA 24; CA 61-64; CAAS 1; CANR
   11, 37; DLB 8; INT CANR-11; MTCW 1;
   SATA 24
Poirier, Louis 1910-
   See Gracq, Julien
   See also CA 122; 126
Poitier, Sidney 1927-
   CLC 26
   See also BW 1; CA 117
Polanski, Roman 1933-
   CLC 16
   See also CA 77-80
Poliakoff, Stephen 1952-
   CLC 38
   See also CA 106; DLB 13
Police, The
   See Copeland, Stewart (Armstrong); Summers,
   Andrew James; Sumner, Gordon Matthew
Polidori, John William 1795-1821
   NCLC 51
   See also DLB 116
Pollitt, Katha 1949-
   CLC 28
   See also CA 120; 122; CANR 66; MTCW 1
Pollock, (Mary) Sharon 1936-
   CLC 50; DAC; DAM DRAM, MST
   See also CA 141; DLB 60
Polo, Marco 1254-1324
   CMLC 15
Polonsky, Abraham (Lincoln) 1910-
   CLC 92
   See also CA 104; DLB 26; INT 104
Polybius .... c. 200B.C.-c. 118B.C.
   CMLC 17
   See also DLB 176
Pomerance, Bernard 1940-
   CLC 13; DAM DRAM
   See also CA 101; CANR 49
Ponge, Francis (Jean Gaston Alfred) . 1899-
   1988 .... CLC 6, 18; DAM POET
   See also CA 85-88; 126; CANR 40
Pontoppidan, Henrik 1857-1943

TCLC 29
Poole, Josephine ....CLC 17
   See also Helyar, Jane Penelope Josephine
   See also SAAS 2; SATA 5
Popa, Vasko 1922-1991
   CLC 19
   See also CA 112; 148; DLB 181
Pope, Alexander 1688-1744
   LC 3; DA; DAB; DAC; DAM MST, POET;
   WLC
   See also CDBLB 1660-1789; DLB 95, 101
Porter, Connie (Rose) .... 1959(?)-
   CLC 70
   See also BW 2; CA 142; SATA 81
Porter, Gene(va Grace) Stratton 1863(?)-1924
   TCLC 21
   See also CA 112
Porter, Katherine Anne 1890-1980
   CLC 1, 3, 7, 10, 13, 15, 27, 101; DA; DAB;
   DAC; DAM MST, NOV; SSC 4, 31
   See also AITN 2; CA 1-4R; 101; CANR 1, 65;
   DLB 4, 9, 102; DLBD 12; DLBY 80; MTCW
   1; SATA 39; SATA-Obit 23
Porter, Peter (Neville Frederick) 1929-
   CLC 5, 13, 33
   See also CA 85-88; DLB 40
Porter, William Sydney 1862-1910
   See Henry, O.
   See also CA 104; 131; CDALB 1865-1917; DA;
   DAB; DAC; DAM MST; DLB 12, 78, 79;
   MTCW 1; YABC 2
Portillo (y Pacheco), Jose Lopez
   See Lopez Portillo (y Pacheco), Jose
Post, Melville Davisson 1869-1930
   TCLC 39
   See also CA 110
Potok, Chaim 1929-
   CLC 2, 7, 14, 26, 112; DAM NOV
   See also AAYA 15; AITN 1, 2; CA 17-20R;
   CANR 19, 35, 64; DLB 28, 152; INT CANR-
   19; MTCW 1; SATA 33
Potter, (Helen) Beatrix 1866-1943
   See Webb, (Martha) Beatrice (Potter)
   See also MAICYA
Potter, Dennis (Christopher George) . 1935-
   1994 .... CLC 58, 86
   See also CA 107; 145; CANR 33, 61; MTCW 1
Pound, Ezra (Weston Loomis) 1885-1972
   CLC 1, 2, 3, 4, 5, 7, 10, 13, 18, 34, 48, 50,
   112; DA; DAB; DAC; DAM MST, POET;
   PC 4; WLC
   See also CA 5-8R; 37-40R; CANR 40; CDALB
   1917-1929; DLB 4, 45, 63; DLBD 15;
   MTCW 1
Povod, Reinaldo 1959-1994
   CLC 44
   See also CA 136; 146
Powell, Adam Clayton, Jr. 1908-1972
   CLC 89; BLC 3; DAM MULT
   See also BW 1; CA 102; 33-36R
Powell, Anthony (Dymoke) 1905-
   CLC 1, 3, 7, 9, 10, 31
   See also CA 1-4R; CANR 1, 32, 62; CDBLB
   1945-1960; DLB 15; MTCW 1
Powell, Dawn 1897-1965
   CLC 66
   See also CA 5-8R; DLBY 97
Powell, Padgett 1952-
   CLC 34
   See also CA 126; CANR 63
Power, Susan 1961-
   CLC 91
Powers, J(ames) F(arl) 1917-

CLC 1, 4, 8, 57; SSC 4
   See also CA 1-4R; CANR 2, 61; DLB 130;
   MTCW 1
Powers, John J(ames) 1945-
   See Powers, John R.
   See also CA 69-72
Powers, John R. .... CLC 66
   See also Powers, John J(ames)
Powers, Richard (S.) 1957-
   CLC 93
   See also CA 148
Pownall, David 1938-
   CLC 10
   See also CA 89-92; CAAS 18; CANR 49; DLB
   14
Powys, John Cowper 1872-1963
   CLC 7, 9, 15, 46
   See also CA 85-88; DLB 15; MTCW 1
Powys, T(heodore) F(rancis) 1875-1953
   TCLC 9
   See also CA 106; DLB 36, 162
Prado (Calvo), Pedro 1886-1952
   TCLC 75
   See also CA 131; HW
Prager, Emily 1952-
   CLC 56
Pratt, E(dwin) J(ohn) .... 1883(?)-1964
   CLC 19; DAC; DAM POET
   See also CA 141; 93-96; DLB 92
Premchand .... TCLC 21
   See also Srivastava, Dhanpat Rai
Preussler, Otfried 1923-
   CLC 17
   See also CA 77-80; SATA 24
Prevert, Jacques (Henri Marie) .. 1900-1977
   CLC 15
   See also CA 77-80; 69-72; CANR 29, 61;
   MTCW 1; SATA-Obit 30
Prevost, Abbe (Antoine Francois) 1697-1763
   LC 1
Price, (Edward) Reynolds 1933-
   CLC 3, 6, 13, 43, 50, 63; DAM NOV; SSC
   22
   See also CA 1-4R; CANR 1, 37, 57; DLB 2;
   INT CANR-37
Price, Richard 1949-
   CLC 6, 12
   See also CA 49-52; CANR 3; DLBY 81
Prichard, Katharine Susannah ... 1883-1969
   CLC 46
   See also CA 11-12; CANR 33; CAP 1; MTCW
   1; SATA 66
Priestley, J(ohn) B(oynton) 1894-1984
   CLC 2, 5, 9, 34; DAM DRAM, NOV
   See also CA 9-12R; 113; CANR 33; CDBLB
   1914-1945; DLB 10, 34, 77, 100, 139; DLBY
   84; MTCW 1
Prince .... 1958(?)-
   CLC 35
Prince, F(rank) T(empleton) 1912-
   CLC 22
   See also CA 101; CANR 43; DLB 20
Prince Kropotkin
   See Kropotkin, Peter (Aleksieevich)
Prior, Matthew 1664-1721
   LC 4
   See also DLB 95
Prishvin, Mikhail 1873-1954
   TCLC 75
Pritchard, William H(arrison) 1932-
   CLC 34
   See also CA 65-68; CANR 23; DLB 111
Pritchett, V(ictor) S(awdon) 1900-1997

CLC 5, 13, 15, 41; DAM NOV;SSC 14
See also CA 61-64; 157; CANR 31, 63; DLB
15, 139; MTCW 1

Private 19022
See Manning, Frederic

Probst, Mark 1925-
CLC 59
See also CA 130

Prokosch, Frederic 1908-1989
CLC 4, 48
See also CA 73-76; 128; DLB 48

Prophet, The
See Dreiser, Theodore (Herman Albert)

Prose, Francine 1947-
CLC 45
See also CA 109; 112; CANR 46; SATA 101

Proudhon
See Cunha, Euclides (Rodrigues Pimenta) da

Proulx, Annie
See Proulx, E(dna) Annie

Proulx, E(dna) Annie 1935-
CLC 81; DAM POP
See also CA 145; CANR 65

**Proust, (Valentin-Louis-George-Eugene-)
Marcel** 1871-1922
TCLC 7, 13, 33; DA; DAB; DAC; DAM
MST, NOV; WLC
See also CA 104; 120; DLB 65; MTCW 1

Prowler, Harley
See Masters, Edgar Lee

Prus, Boleslaw 1845-1912
TCLC 48

Pryor, Richard (Franklin Lenox Thomas)
1940- .... CLC 26
See also CA 122

Przybyszewski, Stanislaw 1868-1927
TCLC 36
See also CA 160; DLB 66

Pteleon
See Grieve, C(hristopher) M(urray)
See also DAM POET

Puckett, Lute
See Masters, Edgar Lee

Puig, Manuel 1932-1990
CLC 3, 5, 10, 28, 65; DAM MULT; HLC
See also CA 45-48; CANR 2, 32, 63; DLB 113;
HW; MTCW 1

Pulitzer, Joseph 1847-1911
TCLC 76
See also CA 114; DLB 23

Purdy, A(lfred) W(ellington) 1918-
CLC 3, 6, 14, 50; DAC; DAM MST, POET
See also CA 81-84; CAAS 17; CANR 42, 66;
DLB 88

Purdy, James (Amos) 1923-
CLC 2, 4, 10, 28, 52
See also CA 33-36R; CAAS 1; CANR 19, 51;
DLB 2; INT CANR-19; MTCW 1

Pure, Simon
See Swinnerton, Frank Arthur

Pushkin, Alexander (Sergeyevich) 1799-1837
NCLC 3, 27; DA; DAB;DAC; DAM
DRAM, MST, POET; PC 10; SSC 27;
WLC
See also SATA 61

P'u Sung-ling 1640-1715
LC 3; SSC 31

Putnam, Arthur Lee
See Alger, Horatio, Jr.

Puzo, Mario 1920-
CLC 1, 2, 6, 36, 107; DAM NOV, POP
See also CA 65-68; CANR 4, 42, 65; DLB 6;
MTCW 1

Pygge, Edward
See Barnes, Julian (Patrick)

Pyle, Ernest Taylor 1900-1945
See Pyle, Ernie
See also CA 115; 160

Pyle, Ernie 1900-1945
TCLC 75
See also Pyle, Ernest Taylor
See also DLB 29

Pyle, Howard 1853-1911
TCLC 81
See also CA 109; 137; CLR 22; DLB 42, 188;
DLBD 13; MAICYA; SATA 16, 100

Pym, Barbara (Mary Crampton) 1913-1980
CLC 13, 19, 37, 111
See also CA 13-14; 97-100; CANR 13, 34; CAP
1; DLB 14; DLBY 87; MTCW 1

Pynchon, Thomas (Ruggles, Jr.) 1937-
CLC 2, 3, 6, 9, 11, 18, 33, 62, 72; DA; DAB;
DAC; DAM MST, NOV, POP; SSC 14;
WLC
See also BEST 90:2; CA 17-20R; CANR 22,
46, 73; DLB 2, 173; MTCW 1

Pythagoras .... c. 570B.C.-c. 500B.C.
CMLC 22
See also DLB 176

Q
See Quiller-Couch, SirArthur (Thomas)

Qian Zhongshu
See Ch'ien Chung-shu

Qroll
See Dagerman, Stig (Halvard)

Quarrington, Paul (Lewis) 1953-
CLC 65
See also CA 129; CANR 62

Quasimodo, Salvatore 1901-1968
CLC 10
See also CA 13-16; 25-28R; CAP 1; DLB 114;
MTCW 1

Quay, Stephen 1947-
CLC 95

Quay, Timothy 1947-
CLC 95

Queen, Ellery ....CLC 3, 11
See also Dannay, Frederic; Davidson, Avram;
Lee, Manfred B(ennington); Marlowe,
Stephen; Sturgeon, Theodore (Hamilton);
Vance, John Holbrook

Queen, Ellery, Jr.
See Dannay, Frederic; Lee, Manfred
B(ennington)

Queneau, Raymond 1903-1976
CLC 2, 5, 10, 42
See also CA 77-80; 69-72; CANR 32; DLB 72;
MTCW 1

Quevedo, Francisco de 1580-1645
LC 23

Quiller-Couch, SirArthur (Thomas) .. 1863-
1944 .... TCLC 53
See also CA 118; 166; DLB 135, 153, 190

Quin, Ann (Marie) 1936-1973
CLC 6
See also CA 9-12R; 45-48; DLB 14

Quinn, Martin
See Smith, Martin Cruz

Quinn, Peter 1947-
CLC 91

Quinn, Simon
See Smith, Martin Cruz

Quiroga, Horacio (Sylvestre) 1878-1937
TCLC 20; DAM MULT; HLC
See also CA 117; 131; HW; MTCW 1

Quoirez, Francoise 1935-

CLC 9
See also Sagan, Francoise
See also CA 49-52; CANR 6, 39, 73; MTCW 1

Raabe, Wilhelm (Karl) 1831-1910
TCLC 45
See also CA 167; DLB 129

Rabe, David (William) 1940-
CLC 4, 8, 33; DAM DRAM
See also CA 85-88; CABS 3; CANR 59; DLB 7

Rabelais, Francois 1483-1553
LC 5; DA; DAB; DAC; DAM MST; WLC

Rabinovitch, Sholem 1859-1916
See Aleichem, Sholom
See also CA 104

Rachilde 1860-1953
TCLC 67
See also DLB 123, 192

Racine, Jean 1639-1699
LC 28; DAB; DAM MST

Radcliffe, Ann (Ward) 1764-1823
NCLC 6, 55
See also DLB 39, 178

Radiguet, Raymond 1903-1923
TCLC 29
See also CA 162; DLB 65

Radnoti, Miklos 1909-1944
TCLC 16
See also CA 118

Rado, James 1939-
CLC 17
See also CA 105

Radvanyi, Netty 1900-1983
See Seghers, Anna
See also CA 85-88; 110

Rae, Ben
See Griffiths, Trevor

Raeburn, John (Hay) 1941-
CLC 34
See also CA 57-60

Ragni, Gerome 1942-1991
CLC 17
See also CA 105; 134

Rahv, Philip 1908-1973
CLC 24
See also Greenberg, Ivan
See also DLB 137

Raimund, Ferdinand Jakob 1790-1836
NCLC 69
See also DLB 90

Raine, Craig 1944-
CLC 32, 103
See also CA 108; CANR 29, 51; DLB 40

Raine, Kathleen (Jessie) 1908-
CLC 7, 45
See also CA 85-88; CANR 46; DLB 20; MTCW
1

Rainis, Janis 1865-1929
TCLC 29

Rakosi, Carl 1903-
CLC 47
See also Rawley, Callman
See also CAAS 5; DLB 193

Raleigh, Richard
See Lovecraft, H(oward) P(hillips)

Raleigh, Sir Walter .... 1554(?)-1618
LC 31, 39
See also CDBLB Before 1660; DLB 172

Rallentando, H. P.
See Sayers, Dorothy L(eigh)

Ramal, Walter
See de la Mare, Walter (John)

Ramana Maharshi 1879-1950
TCLC 84

CLC 7
See also CA 21-24R; CANR 46
Ricci, Nino 1959-
CLC 70
See also CA 137
Rice, Anne 1941-
CLC 41; DAM POP
See also AAYA 9; BEST 89:2; CA 65-68; CANR
12, 36, 53
Rice, Elmer (Leopold) 1892-1967
CLC 7, 49; DAM DRAM
See also CA 21-22; 25-28R; CAP 2; DLB 4, 7;
MTCW 1
Rice, Tim(othy Miles Bindon) 1944-
CLC 21
See also CA 103; CANR 46
Rich, Adrienne (Cecile) 1929-
CLC 3, 6, 7, 11, 18, 36, 73, 76; DAM POET;
PC 5
See also CA 9-12R; CANR 20, 53; DLB 5, 67;
MTCW 1
Rich, Barbara
See Graves, Robert (von Ranke)
Rich, Robert
See Trumbo, Dalton
Richard, Keith .... CLC 17
See also Richards, Keith
Richards, David Adams 1950-
CLC 59; DAC
See also CA 93-96; CANR 60; DLB 53
Richards, I(vor) A(rmstrong) 1893-1979
CLC 14, 24
See also CA 41-44R; 89-92; CANR 34; DLB
27
Richards, Keith 1943-
See Richard, Keith
See also CA 107
Richardson, Anne
See Roiphe, Anne (Richardson)
Richardson, Dorothy Miller 1873-1957
TCLC 3
See also CA 104; DLB 36
Richardson, Ethel Florence (Lindesay) 1870-
1946
See Richardson, Henry Handel
See also CA 105
Richardson, Henry Handel .... TCLC 4
See also Richardson, Ethel Florence (Lindesay)
See also DLB 197
Richardson, John 1796-1852
NCLC 55; DAC
See also DLB 99
Richardson, Samuel 1689-1761
LC 1, 44; DA; DAB; DAC; DAM MST,
NOV; WLC
See also CDBLB 1660-1789; DLB 39
Richler, Mordecai 1931-
CLC 3, 5, 9, 13, 18, 46, 70; DAC; DAM
MST, NOV
See also AITN 1; CA 65-68; CANR 31, 62; CLR
17; DLB 53; MAICYA; MTCW 1; SATA 44,
98; SATA-Brief 27
Richter, Conrad (Michael) 1890-1968
CLC 30
See also AAYA 21; CA 5-8R; 25-28R; CANR
23; DLB 9; MTCW 1; SATA 3
Ricostranza, Tom
See Ellis, Trey
Riddell, Charlotte 1832-1906
TCLC 40
See also CA 165; DLB 156
Riding, Laura .... CLC 3, 7
See also Jackson, Laura (Riding)

Riefenstahl, Berta Helene Amalia 1902-
See Riefenstahl, Leni
See also CA 108
Riefenstahl, Leni .... CLC 16
See also Riefenstahl, Berta Helene Amalia
Riffe, Ernest
See Bergman, (Ernst) Ingmar
Riggs, (Rolla) Lynn 1899-1954
TCLC 56; DAM MULT
See also CA 144; DLB 175; NNAL
Riis, Jacob A(ugust) 1849-1914
TCLC 80
See also CA 113; 168; DLB 23
Riley, James Whitcomb 1849-1916
TCLC 51; DAM POET
See also CA 118; 137; MAICYA; SATA 17
Riley, Tex
See Creasey, John
Rilke, Rainer Maria 1875-1926
TCLC 1, 6, 19; DAM POET; PC 2
See also CA 104; 132; CANR 62; DLB 81;
MTCW 1
Rimbaud, (Jean Nicolas) Arthur   1854-1891
NCLC 4, 35; DA; DAB; DAC; DAM MST,
POET; PC 3; WLC
Rinehart, Mary Roberts 1876-1958
TCLC 52
See also CA 108; 166
Ringmaster, The
See Mencken, H(enry) L(ouis)
Ringwood, Gwen(dolyn Margaret) Pharis
1910-1984 .... CLC 48
See also CA 148; 112; DLB 88
Rio, Michel .... 19(?)-
CLC 43
Ritsos, Giannes
See Ritsos, Yannis
Ritsos, Yannis 1909-1990
CLC 6, 13, 31
See also CA 77-80; 133; CANR 39, 61; MTCW
1
Ritter, Erika .... 1948(?)-
CLC 52
Rivera, Jose Eustasio 1889-1928
TCLC 35
See also CA 162; HW
Rivers, Conrad Kent 1933-1968
CLC 1
See also BW 1; CA 85-88; DLB 41
Rivers, Elfrida
See Bradley, Marion Zimmer
Riverside, John
See Heinlein, Robert A(nson)
Rizal, Jose 1861-1896
NCLC 27
Roa Bastos, Augusto (Antonio) 1917-
CLC 45; DAM MULT; HLC
See also CA 131; DLB 113; HW
Robbe-Grillet, Alain 1922-
CLC 1, 2, 4, 6, 8, 10, 14, 43
See also CA 9-12R; CANR 33, 65; DLB 83;
MTCW 1
Robbins, Harold 1916-1997
CLC 5; DAM NOV
See also CA 73-76; 162; CANR 26, 54; MTCW
1
Robbins, Thomas Eugene 1936-
See Robbins, Tom
See also CA 81-84; CANR 29, 59; DAM NOV,
POP; MTCW 1
Robbins, Tom .... CLC 9, 32, 64
See also Robbins, Thomas Eugene
See also BEST 90:3; DLBY 80

Robbins, Trina 1938-
CLC 21
See also CA 128
Roberts, Charles G(eorge) D(ouglas) .   1860-
1943 .... TCLC 8
See also CA 105; CLR 33; DLB 92; SATA 88;
SATA-Brief 29
Roberts, Elizabeth Madox 1886-1941
TCLC 68
See also CA 111; 166; DLB 9, 54, 102; SATA
33; SATA-Brief 27
Roberts, Kate 1891-1985
CLC 15
See also CA 107; 116
Roberts, Keith (John Kingston) 1935-
CLC 14
See also CA 25-28R; CANR 46
Roberts, Kenneth (Lewis) 1885-1957
TCLC 23
See also CA 109; DLB 9
Roberts, Michele (B.) 1949-
CLC 48
See also CA 115; CANR 58
Robertson, Ellis
See Ellison, Harlan (Jay); Silverberg, Robert
Robertson, Thomas William 1829-1871
NCLC 35; DAM DRAM
Robeson, Kenneth
See Dent, Lester
Robinson, Edwin Arlington 1869-1935
TCLC 5; DA; DAC; DAM MST, POET;
PC 1
See also CA 104; 133; CDALB 1865-1917;
DLB 54; MTCW 1
Robinson, Henry Crabb 1775-1867
NCLC 15
See also DLB 107
Robinson, Jill 1936-
CLC 10
See also CA 102; INT 102
Robinson, Kim Stanley 1952-
CLC 34
See also AAYA 26; CA 126
Robinson, Lloyd
See Silverberg, Robert
Robinson, Marilynne 1944-
CLC 25
See also CA 116
Robinson, Smokey .... CLC 21
See also Robinson, William, Jr.
Robinson, William, Jr. 1940-
See Robinson, Smokey
See also CA 116
Robison, Mary 1949-
CLC 42, 98
See also CA 113; 116; DLB 130; INT 116
Rod, Edouard 1857-1910
TCLC 52
Roddenberry, Eugene Wesley 1921-1991
See Roddenberry, Gene
See also CA 110; 135; CANR 37; SATA 45;
SATA-Obit 69
Roddenberry, Gene .... CLC 17
See also Roddenberry, Eugene Wesley
See also AAYA 5; SATA-Obit 69
Rodgers, Mary 1931-
CLC 12
See also CA 49-52; CANR 8, 55; CLR 20; INT
CANR-8; JRDA; MAICYA; SATA 8
Rodgers, W(illiam) R(obert) 1909-1969
CLC 7
See also CA 85-88; DLB 20
Rodman, Eric

DLB 28, 48; MTCW 1

Schwartz, Ernst
See Ozu, Yasujiro

Schwartz, John Burnham 1965-
CLC 59
See also CA 132

Schwartz, Lynne Sharon 1939-
CLC 31
See also CA 103; CANR 44

Schwartz, Muriel A.
See Eliot, T(homas) S(tearns)

Schwarz-Bart, Andre 1928-
CLC 2, 4
See also CA 89-92

Schwarz-Bart, Simone 1938-
CLC 7; BLCS
See also BW 2; CA 97-100

Schwob, Marcel (Mayer Andre) . 1867-1905
TCLC 20
See also CA 117, 168; DLB 123

Sciascia, Leonardo 1921-1989
CLC 8, 9, 41
See also CA 85-88; 130; CANR 35; DLB 177;
MTCW 1

Scoppettone, Sandra 1936-
CLC 26
See also AAYA 11; CA 5-8R; CANR 41, 73;
SATA 9, 92

Scorsese, Martin 1942-
CLC 20, 89
See also CA 110; 114; CANR 46

Scotland, Jay
See Jakes, John (William)

Scott, Duncan Campbell 1862-1947
TCLC 6; DAC
See also CA 104; 153; DLB 92

Scott, Evelyn 1893-1963
CLC 43
See also CA 104; 112; CANR 64; DLB 9, 48

Scott, F(rancis) R(eginald) 1899-1985
CLC 22
See also CA 101; 114; DLB 88; INT 101

Scott, Frank
See Scott, F(rancis) R(eginald)

Scott, Joanna 1960-
CLC 50
See also CA 126; CANR 53

Scott, Paul (Mark) 1920-1978
CLC 9, 60
See also CA 81-84; 77-80; CANR 33; DLB 14;
MTCW 1

Scott, Sarah 1723-1795
LC 44
See also DLB 39

Scott, Walter 1771-1832
NCLC 15, 69; DA; DAB; DAC; DAM
MST, NOV, POET; PC 13; SSC 32; WLC
See also AAYA 22; CDBLB 1789-1832; DLB
93, 107, 116, 144, 159; YABC 2

Scribe, (Augustin) Eugene 1791-1861
NCLC 16; DAM DRAM; DC 5
See also DLB 192

Scrum, R.
See Crumb, R(obert)

Scudery, Madeleine de 1607-1701
LC 2

Scum
See Crumb, R(obert)

Scumbag, Little Bobby
See Crumb, R(obert)

Seabrook, John
See Hubbard, L(afayette) Ron(ald)

Sealy, I. Allan 1951-

CLC 55

Search, Alexander
See Pessoa, Fernando (Antonio Nogueira)

Sebastian, Lee
See Silverberg, Robert

Sebastian Owl
See Thompson, Hunter S(tockton)

Sebestyen, Ouida 1924-
CLC 30
See also AAYA 8; CA 107; CANR 40; CLR 17;
JRDA; MAICYA; SAAS 10; SATA 39

Secundus, H. Scriblerus
See Fielding, Henry

Sedges, John
See Buck, Pearl S(ydenstricker)

Sedgwick, Catharine Maria 1789-1867
NCLC 19
See also DLB 1, 74

Seelye, John (Douglas) 1931-
CLC 7
See also CA 97-100; CANR 70; INT 97-100

Seferiades, Giorgos Stylianou 1900-1971
See Seferis, George
See also CA 5-8R; 33-36R; CANR 5, 36;
MTCW 1

Seferis, George .... CLC 5, 11
See also Seferiades, Giorgos Stylianou

Segal, Erich (Wolf) 1937-
CLC 3, 10; DAM POP
See also BEST 89:1; CA 25-28R; CANR 20,
36, 65; DLBY 86; INT CANR-20; MTCW 1

Seger, Bob 1945-
CLC 35

Seghers, Anna .... CLC 7
See also Radvanyi, Netty
See also DLB 69

Seidel, Frederick (Lewis) 1936-
CLC 18
See also CA 13-16R; CANR 8; DLBY 84

Seifert, Jaroslav 1901-1986
CLC 34, 44, 93
See also CA 127; MTCW 1

Sei Shonagon .... c. 966-1017(?)
CMLC 6

Selby, Hubert, Jr. 1928-
CLC 1, 2, 4, 8; SSC 20
See also CA 13-16R; CANR 33; DLB 2

Selzer, Richard 1928-
CLC 74
See also CA 65-68; CANR 14

Sembene, Ousmane
See Ousmane, Sembene

Senancour, Etienne Pivert de 1770-1846
NCLC 16
See also DLB 119

Sender, Ramon (Jose) 1902-1982
CLC 8; DAM MULT; HLC
See also CA 5-8R; 105; CANR 8; HW; MTCW
1

Seneca, Lucius Annaeus 4B.C.-65
CMLC 6; DAM DRAM; DC 5

Senghor, Leopold Sedar 1906-
CLC 54; BLC 3; DAM MULT, POET
See also BW 2; CA 116; 125; CANR 47; MTCW
1

Serling, (Edward) Rod(man) 1924-1975
CLC 30
See also AAYA 14; AITN 1; CA 162; 57-60;
DLB 26

Serna, Ramon Gomez de la
See Gomez de la Serna, Ramon

Serpieres
See Guillevic, (Eugene)

Service, Robert
See Service, Robert W(illiam)
See also DAB; DLB 92

Service, Robert W(illiam) .... 1874(?)-1958
TCLC 15; DA; DAC; DAM MST, POET;
WLC
See also Service, Robert
See also CA 115; 140; SATA 20

Seth, Vikram ....: 1952-
CLC 43, 90; DAM MULT
See also CA 121; 127; CANR 50; DLB 120;
INT 127

Seton, Cynthia Propper 1926-1982
CLC 27
See also CA 5-8R; 108; CANR 7

Seton, Ernest (Evan) Thompson . 1860-1946
TCLC 31
See also CA 109; DLB 92; DLBD 13; JRDA;
SATA 18

Seton-Thompson, Ernest
See Seton, Ernest (Evan) Thompson

Settle, Mary Lee 1918-
CLC 19, 61
See also CA 89-92; CAAS 1; CANR 44; DLB
6; INT 89-92

Seuphor, Michel
See Arp, Jean

**Sevigne, Marie (de Rabutin-Chantal) Marquise
de** 1626-1696
LC 11

Sewall, Samuel 1652-1730
LC 38
See also DLB 24

Sexton, Anne (Harvey) 1928-1974
CLC 2, 4, 6, 8, 10, 15, 53; DA; DAB; DAC;
DAM MST, POET; PC 2; WLC
See also CA 1-4R; 53-56; CABS 2; CANR 3,
36; CDALB 1941-1968; DLB 5, 169;
MTCW 1; SATA 10

Shaara, Michael (Joseph, Jr.) 1929-1988
CLC 15; DAM POP
See also AITN 1; CA 102; 125; CANR 52;
DLBY 83

Shackleton, C. C.
See Aldiss, Brian W(ilson)

Shacochis, Bob .... CLC 39
See also Shacochis, Robert G.

Shacochis, Robert G. 1951-
See Shacochis, Bob
See also CA 119; 124; INT 124

Shaffer, Anthony (Joshua) 1926-
CLC 19; DAM DRAM
See also CA 110; 116; DLB 13

Shaffer, Peter (Levin) 1926-
CLC 5, 14, 18, 37, 60; DAB; DAM DRAM,
MST; DC 7
See also CA 25-28R; CANR 25, 47; CDBLB
1960 to Present; DLB 13; MTCW 1

Shakey, Bernard
See Young, Neil

Shalamov, Varlam (Tikhonovich) ... 1907(?)-
1982 ....CLC 18
See also CA 129; 105

Shamlu, Ahmad 1925-
CLC 10

Shammas, Anton 1951-
CLC 55

Shange, Ntozake 1948-
CLC 8, 25, 38, 74; BLC 3; DAM DRAM,
MULT; DC 3
See also AAYA 9; BW 2; CA 85-88; CABS 3;
CANR 27, 48; DLB 38; MTCW 1

Shanley, John Patrick 1950-

MTCW 1; SATA 13, 91

Silverstein, Alvin 1933-
CLC 17
See also CA 49-52; CANR 2; CLR 25; JRDA;
MAICYA; SATA 8, 69

Silverstein, Virginia B(arbara Opshelor)
1937- .... **CLC 17**
See also CA 49-52; CANR 2; CLR 25; JRDA;
MAICYA; SATA 8, 69

Sim, Georges
See Simenon, Georges (Jacques Christian)

Simak, Clifford D(onald) 1904-1988
CLC 1, 55
See also CA 1-4R; 125; CANR 1, 35; DLB 8;
MTCW 1; SATA-Obit 56

Simenon, Georges (Jacques Christian) 1903-
1989 .. **CLC 1, 2, 3, 8, 18, 47; DAM POP**
See also CA 85-88; 129; CANR 35; DLB 72;
DLBY 89; MTCW 1

Simic, Charles 1938-
CLC 6, 9, 22, 49, 68; DAM POET
See also CA 29-32R; CAAS 4; CANR 12, 33,
52, 61; DLB 105

Simmel, Georg 1858-1918
TCLC 64
See also CA 157

Simmons, Charles (Paul) 1924-
CLC 57
See also CA 89-92; INT 89-92

Simmons, Dan 1948-
CLC 44; DAM POP
See also AAYA 16; CA 138; CANR 53

Simmons, James (Stewart Alexander) 1933-
CLC 43
See also CA 105; CAAS 21; DLB 40

Simms, William Gilmore 1806-1870
NCLC 3
See also DLB 3, 30, 59, 73

Simon, Carly 1945-
CLC 26
See also CA 105

Simon, Claude 1913-1984
CLC 4, 9, 15, 39; DAM NOV
See also CA 89-92; CANR 33; DLB 83; MTCW
1

Simon, (Marvin) Neil 1927-
CLC 6, 11, 31, 39, 70; DAM DRAM
See also AITN 1; CA 21-24R; CANR 26, 54;
DLB 7; MTCW 1

Simon, Paul (Frederick) .... 1941(?)-
CLC 17
See also CA 116; 153

Simonon, Paul .... 1956(?)-
CLC 30

Simpson, Harriette
See Arnow, Harriette (Louisa) Simpson

Simpson, Louis (Aston Marantz) 1923-
CLC 4, 7, 9, 32; DAM POET
See also CA 1-4R; CAAS 4; CANR 1, 61; DLB
5, MTCW 1

Simpson, Mona (Elizabeth) 1957-
CLC 44
See also CA 122; 135; CANR 68

Simpson, N(orman) F(rederick) 1919-
CLC 29
See also CA 13-16R; DLB 13

Sinclair, Andrew (Annandale) 1935-
CLC 2, 14
See also CA 9-12R; CAAS 5; CANR 14, 38;
DLB 14; MTCW 1

Sinclair, Emil
See Hesse, Hermann

Sinclair, Iain 1943-

CLC 76
See also CA 132

Sinclair, Iain MacGregor
See Sinclair, Iain

Sinclair, Irene
See Griffith, D(avid Lewelyn) W(ark)

Sinclair, Mary Amelia St. Clair 1865(?)-1946
See Sinclair, May
See also CA 104

Sinclair, May 1863-1946
TCLC 3, 11
See also Sinclair, Mary Amelia St. Clair
See also CA 166; DLB 36, 135

Sinclair, Roy
See Griffith, D(avid Lewelyn) W(ark)

Sinclair, Upton (Beall) 1878-1968
**CLC 1, 11, 15, 63; DA; DAB; DAC; DAM
MST, NOV; WLC**
See also CA 5-8R; 25-28R; CANR 7; CDALB
1929-1941; DLB 9; INT CANR-7; MTCW
1; SATA 9

Singer, Isaac
See Singer, Isaac Bashevis

Singer, Isaac Bashevis 1904-1991
**CLC 1, 3, 6, 9, 11, 15, 23, 38, 69, 111; DA;
DAB; DAC; DAM MST, NOV; SSC 3;
WLC**
See also AITN 1, 2; CA 1-4R; 134; CANR 1,
39; CDALB 1941-1968; CLR 1; DLB 6, 28,
52; DLBY 91; JRDA; MAICYA; MTCW 1;
SATA 3, 27; SATA-Obit 68

Singer, Israel Joshua 1893-1944
TCLC 33
See also CA 169

Singh, Khushwant 1915-
CLC 11
See also CA 9-12R; CAAS 9; CANR 6

Singleton, Ann
See Benedict, Ruth (Fulton)

Sinjohn, John
See Galsworthy, John

Sinyavsky, Andrei (Donatevich) .. 1925-1997
CLC 8
See also CA 85-88; 159

Sirin, V.
See Nabokov, Vladimir (Vladimirovich)

Sissman, L(ouis) E(dward) 1928-1976
CLC 9, 18
See also CA 21-24R; 65-68; CANR 13; DLB 5

Sisson, C(harles) H(ubert) 1914-
CLC 8
See also CA 1-4R; CAAS 3; CANR 3, 48; DLB
27

Sitwell, Dame Edith 1887-1964
CLC 2, 9, 67; DAM POET; PC 3
See also CA 9-12R; CANR 35; CDBLB 1945-
1960; DLB 20; MTCW 1

Siwaarmill, H. P.
See Sharp, William

Sjoewall, Maj 1935-
CLC 7
See also CA 65-68; CANR 73

Sjowall, Maj
See Sjoewall, Maj

Skelton, Robin 1925-1997
CLC 13
See also AITN 2; CA 5-8R; 160; CAAS 5;
CANR 28; DLB 27, 53

Skolimowski, Jerzy 1938-
CLC 20
See also CA 128

Skram, Amalie (Bertha) 1847-1905
TCLC 25

See also CA 165

Skvorecky, Josef (Vaclav) 1924-
CLC 15, 39, 69; DAC; DAM NOV
See also CA 61-64; CAAS 1; CANR 10, 34,
63; MTCW 1

Slade, Bernard .... **CLC 11, 46**
See also Newbound, Bernard Slade
See also CAAS 9; DLB 53

Slaughter, Carolyn 1946-
CLC 56
See also CA 85-88

Slaughter, Frank G(ill) 1908-
CLC 29
See also AITN 2; CA 5-8R; CANR 5; INT
CANR-5

Slavitt, David R(ytman) 1935-
CLC 5, 14
See also CA 21-24R; CAAS 3; CANR 41; DLB
5, 6

Slesinger, Tess 1905-1945
TCLC 10
See also CA 107; DLB 102

Slessor, Kenneth 1901-1971
CLC 14
See also CA 102; 89-92

Slowacki, Juliusz 1809-1849
NCLC 15

Smart, Christopher 1722-1771
LC 3; DAM POET; PC 13
See also DLB 109

Smart, Elizabeth 1913-1986
CLC 54
See also CA 81-84; 118; DLB 88

Smiley, Jane (Graves) 1949-
CLC 53, 76; DAM POP
See also CA 104; CANR 30, 50; INT CANR-
30

Smith, A(rthur) J(ames) M(arshall) ... 1902-
1980 ,,**CLC 15; DAC**
See also CA 1-4R; 102; CANR 4; DLB 88

Smith, Adam 1723-1790
LC 36
See also DLB 104

Smith, Alexander 1829-1867
NCLC 59
See also DLB 32, 55

Smith, Anna Deavere 1950-
CLC 86
See also CA 133

Smith, Betty (Wehner) 1896-1972
CLC 19
See also CA 5-8R; 33-36R; DLBY 82; SATA 6

Smith, Charlotte (Turner) 1749-1806
NCLC 23
See also DLB 39, 109

Smith, Clark Ashton 1893-1961
CLC 43
See also CA 143

Smith, Dave .... **CLC 22, 42**
See also Smith, David (Jeddie)
See also CAAS 7; DLB 5

Smith, David (Jeddie) 1942-
See Smith, Dave
See also CA 49-52; CANR 1, 59; DAM POET

Smith, Florence Margaret 1902-1971
See Smith, Stevie
See also CA 17-18; 29-32R; CANR 35; CAP 2;
DAM POET; MTCW 1

Smith, Iain Crichton 1928-
CLC 64
See also CA 21-24R; DLB 40, 139

Smith, John .... 1580(?)-1631
LC 9

See also Spillane, Frank Morrison

Spinoza, Benedictus de 1632-1677
    LC 9

Spinrad, Norman (Richard) 1940-
    CLC 46
    See also CA 37-40R; CAAS 19; CANR 20; DLB 8; INT CANR-20

Spitteler, Carl (Friedrich Georg) 1845-1924
    TCLC 12
    See also CA 109; DLB 129

Spivack, Kathleen (Romola Drucker) 1938-
    CLC 6
    See also CA 49-52

Spoto, Donald 1941-
    CLC 39
    See also CA 65-68; CANR 11, 57

Springsteen, Bruce (F.) 1949-
    CLC 17
    See also CA 111

Spurling, Hilary 1940-
    CLC 34
    See also CA 104; CANR 25, 52

Spyker, John Howland
    See Elman, Richard (Martin)

Squires, (James) Radcliffe 1917-1993
    CLC 51
    See also CA 1-4R; 140; CANR 6, 21

Srivastava, Dhanpat Rai .... 1880(?)-1936
    See Premchand
    See also CA 118

Stacy, Donald
    See Pohl, Frederik

Stael, Germaine de 1766-1817
    See Stael-Holstein, Anne Louise Germaine Necker Baronn
    See also DLB 119

Stael-Holstein, Anne Louise Germaine Necker Baronn 1766-1817
    NCLC 3
    See also Stael, Germaine de
    See also DLB 192

Stafford, Jean 1915-1979
    CLC 4, 7, 19, 68; SSC 26
    See also CA 1-4R; 85-88; CANR 3, 65; DLB 2, 173; MTCW 1; SATA-Obit 22

Stafford, William (Edgar) 1914-1993
    CLC 4, 7, 29; DAM POET
    See also CA 5-8R; 142; CAAS 3; CANR 5, 22; DLB 5; INT CANR-22

Stagnelius, Eric Johan 1793-1823
    NCLC 61

Staines, Trevor
    See Brunner, John (Kilian Houston)

Stairs, Gordon
    See Austin, Mary (Hunter)

Stannard, Martin 1947-
    CLC 44
    See also CA 142; DLB 155

Stanton, Elizabeth Cady 1815-1902
    TCLC 73
    See also DLB 79

Stanton, Maura 1946-
    CLC 9
    See also CA 89-92; CANR 15; DLB 120

Stanton, Schuyler
    See Baum, L(yman) Frank

Stapledon, (William) Olaf 1886-1950
    TCLC 22
    See also CA 111; 162; DLB 15

Starbuck, George (Edwin) 1931-1996
    CLC 53; DAM POET
    See also CA 21-24R; 153; CANR 23

Stark, Richard

See Westlake, Donald E(dwin)

Staunton, Schuyler
    See Baum, L(yman) Frank

Stead, Christina (Ellen) 1902-1983
    CLC 2, 5, 8, 32, 80
    See also CA 13-16R; 109; CANR 33, 40; MTCW 1

Stead, William Thomas 1849-1912
    TCLC 48
    See also CA 167

Steele, Richard 1672-1729
    LC 18
    See also CDBLB 1660-1789; DLB 84, 101

Steele, Timothy (Reid) 1948-
    CLC 45
    See also CA 93-96; CANR 16, 50; DLB 120

Steffens, (Joseph) Lincoln 1866-1936
    TCLC 20
    See also CA 117

Stegner, Wallace (Earle) 1909-1993
    CLC 9, 49, 81; DAM NOV; SSC 27
    See also AITN 1; BEST 90:3; CA 1-4R; 141; CAAS 9; CANR 1, 21, 46; DLB 9; DLBY 93; MTCW 1

Stein, Gertrude 1874-1946
    TCLC 1, 6, 28, 48; DA; DAB; DAC; DAM MST, NOV, POET; PC 18; WLC
    See also CA 104; 132; CDALB 1917-1929; DLB 4, 54, 86; DLBD 15; MTCW 1

Steinbeck, John (Ernst) 1902-1968
    CLC 1, 5, 9, 13, 21, 34, 45, 75; DA; DAB; DAC; DAM DRAM, MST, NOV; SSC 11; WLC
    See also AAYA 12; CA 1-4R; 25-28R; CANR 1, 35, CDALB 1929-1941; DLB 7, 9; DLBD 2; MTCW 1; SATA 9

Steinem, Gloria 1934-
    CLC 63
    See also CA 53-56; CANR 28, 51; MTCW 1

Steiner, George 1929-
    CLC 24; DAM NOV
    See also CA 73-76, CANR 31, 67, DLB 67; MTCW 1; SATA 62

Steiner, K. Leslie
    See Delany, Samuel R(ay, Jr.)

Steiner, Rudolf 1861-1925
    TCLC 13
    See also CA 107

Stendhal 1783-1842
    NCLC 23, 46; DA; DAB; DAC; DAM MST, NOV; SSC 27; WLC
    See also DLB 119

Stephen, Adeline Virginia
    See Woolf, (Adeline) Virginia

Stephen, Sir Leslie 1832-1904
    TCLC 23
    See also CA 123; DLB 57, 144, 190

Stephen, Sir Leslie
    See Stephen, Sir Leslie

Stephen, Virginia
    See Woolf, (Adeline) Virginia

Stephens, James .... 1882(?)-1950
    TCLC 4
    See also CA 104; DLB 19, 153, 162

Stephens, Reed
    See Donaldson, Stephen R.

Steptoe, Lydia
    See Barnes, Djuna

Sterchi, Beat 1949-
    CLC 65

Sterling, Brett
    See Bradbury, Ray (Douglas); Hamilton, Edmond

Sterling, Bruce 1954-
    CLC 72
    See also CA 119; CANR 44

Sterling, George 1869-1926
    TCLC 20
    See also CA 117; 165; DLB 54

Stern, Gerald 1925-
    CLC 40, 100
    See also CA 81-84; CANR 28; DLB 105

Stern, Richard (Gustave) 1928-
    CLC 4, 39
    See also CA 1-4R; CANR 1, 25, 52; DLBY 87; INT CANR-25

Sternberg, Josef von 1894-1969
    CLC 20
    See also CA 81-84

Sterne, Laurence 1713-1768
    LC 2; DA; DAB; DAC; DAM MST, NOV; WLC
    See also CDBLB 1660-1789; DLB 39

Sternheim, (William Adolf) Carl 1878-1942
    TCLC 8
    See also CA 105; DLB 56, 118

Stevens, Mark 1951-
    CLC 34
    See also CA 122

Stevens, Wallace 1879-1955
    TCLC 3, 12, 45; DA; DAB; DAC; DAM MST, POET; PC 6; WLC
    See also CA 104; 124; CDALB 1929-1941; DLB 54; MTCW 1

Stevenson, Anne (Katharine) 1933-
    CLC 7, 33
    See also CA 17-20R; CAAS 9; CANR 9, 33; DLB 40; MTCW 1

Stevenson, Robert Louis (Balfour) 1850-1894
    NCLC 5, 14, 63; DA; DAB; DAC; DAM MST, NOV; SSC 11; WLC
    See also AAYA 24; CDBLB 1890-1914; CLR 10, 11; DLB 18, 57, 141, 156, 174; DLBD 13; JRDA; MAICYA; SATA 100; YABC 2

Stewart, J(ohn) I(nnes) M(ackintosh) 1906-1994 .... **CLC 7, 14, 32**
    See also CA 85-88; 147; CAAS 3; CANR 47; MTCW 1

Stewart, Mary (Florence Elinor) 1916-
    CLC 7, 35; DAB
    See also CA 1-4R; CANR 1, 59; SATA 12

Stewart, Mary Rainbow
    See Stewart, Mary (Florence Elinor)

Stifle, June
    See Campbell, Maria

Stifter, Adalbert 1805-1868
    NCLC 41; SSC 28
    See also DLB 133

Still, James 1906-
    CLC 49
    See also CA 65-68; CAAS 17; CANR 10, 26; DLB 9; SATA 29

Sting 1951-
    See Sumner, Gordon Matthew
    See also CA 167

Stirling, Arthur
    See Sinclair, Upton (Beall)

Stitt, Milan 1941-
    CLC 29
    See also CA 69-72

Stockton, Francis Richard 1834-1902
    See Stockton, Frank R.
    See also CA 108; 137; MAICYA; SATA 44

Stockton, Frank R. .... **TCLC 47**
    See also Stockton, Francis Richard
    See also DLB 42, 74; DLBD 13; SATA-Brief

See Lovecraft. H(oward) P(hillips)

Swift, Graham (Colin) 1949-
CLC 41, 88
See also CA 117; 122; CANR 46. 71; DLB 194

Swift, Jonathan 1667-1745
**LC 1; DA; DAB; DAC; DAM MST, NOV,
POET; PC 9; WLC**
See also CDBLB 1660-1789; CLR 53; DLB 39,
95, 101; SATA 19

Swinburne, Algernon Charles..... 1837-1909
**TCLC 8, 36; DA; DAB; DAC; DAM MST,
POET; PC 24; WLC**
See also CA 105; 140; CDBLB 1832-1890;
DLB 35, 57

Swinfen, Ann .... **CLC 34**

Swinnerton, Frank Arthur 1884-1982
CLC 31
See also CA 108; DLB 34

Swithen, John
See King, Stephen (Edwin)

Sylvia
See Ashton-Warner. Sylvia (Constance)

Symmes, Robert Edward
See Duncan. Robert (Edward)

Symonds, John Addington........... 1840-1893
NCLC 34
See also DLB 57, 144

Symons, Arthur 1865-1945
TCLC 11
See also CA 107; DLB 19, 57, 149

Symons, Julian (Gustave) 1912-1994
CLC 2, 14, 32
See also CA 49-52; 147; CAAS 3; CANR 3,
33, 59; DLB 87, 155; DLBY 92; MTCW 1

Synge, (Edmund) J(ohn) M(illington) 1871-
1909 .. **TCLC 6, 37; DAM DRAM; DC 2**
See also CA 104; 141; CDBLB 1890-1914;
DLB 10, 19

Syruc, J.
See Milosz. Czeslaw

Szirtes, George 1948-
CLC 46
See also CA 109; CANR 27, 61

Szymborska, Wislawa 1923-
CLC 99
See also CA 154; DLBY 96

T. O., Nik
See Annensky, Innokenty (Fyodorovich)

Tabori, George 1914-
CLC 19
See also CA 49-52; CANR 4, 69

Tagore, Rabindranath................. 1861-1941
TCLC 3, 53; DAM DRAM, POET; PC 8
See also CA 104; 120; MTCW 1

Taine, Hippolyte Adolphe 1828-1893
NCLC 15

Talese, Gay 1932-
CLC 37
See also AITN 1; CA 1-4R; CANR 9, 58; DLB
185; INT CANR-9; MTCW 1

Tallent, Elizabeth (Ann) 1954-
CLC 45
See also CA 117; CANR 72; DLB 130

Tally, Ted 1952-
CLC 42
See also CA 120; 124; INT 124

Talvik, Heiti 1904-1947
TCLC 87

Tamayo y Baus, Manuel 1829-1898
NCLC 1

Tammsaare, A(nton) H(ansen) 1878-1940
TCLC 27
See also CA 164

Tam'si, Tchicaya U
See Tchicaya. Gerald Felix

Tan, Amy (Ruth) 1952-
CLC 59; DAM MULT, NOV, POP
See also AAYA 9; BEST 89:3; CA 136; CANR
54; DLB 173; SATA 75

Tandem, Felix
See Spitteler. Carl (Friedrich Georg)

Tanizaki, Jun'ichiro 1886-1965
CLC 8, 14, 28; SSC 21
See also CA 93-96; 25-28R; DLB 180

Tanner, William
See Amis, Kingsley (William)

Tao Lao
See Storni, Alfonsina

Tarassoff, Lev
See Troyat, Henri

Tarbell, Ida M(inerva) 1857-1944
TCLC 40
See also CA 122; DLB 47

Tarkington, (Newton) Booth 1869-1946
TCLC 9
See also CA 110; 143; DLB 9, 102; SATA 17

Tarkovsky, Andrei (Arsenyevich) 1932-1986
CLC 75
See also CA 127

Tartt, Donna .... 1964(?)-
CLC 76
See also CA 142

Tasso, Torquato 1544-1595
LC 5

Tate, (John Orley) Allen 1899-1979
CLC 2, 4, 6, 9, 11, 14, 24
See also CA 5-8R; 85-88; CANR 32; DLB 4,
45, 63; DLBD 17; MTCW 1

Tate, Ellalice
See Hibbert, Eleanor Alice Burford

Tate, James (Vincent) 1943-
CLC 2, 6, 25
See also CA 21-24R; CANR 29, 57; DLB 5,
169

Tavel, Ronald 1940-
CLC 6
See also CA 21-24R, CANR 33

Taylor, C(ecil) P(hilip) 1929-1981
CLC 27
See also CA 25-28R; 105; CANR 47

Taylor, Edward .... 1642(?)-1729
LC 11; DA; DAB; DAC; DAM MST, POET
See also DLB 24

Taylor, Eleanor Ross 1920-
CLC 5
See also CA 81-84; CANR 70

Taylor, Elizabeth 1912-1975
CLC 2, 4, 29
See also CA 13-16R; CANR 9, 70; DLB 139;
MTCW 1; SATA 13

Taylor, Frederick Winslow 1856-1915
TCLC 76

Taylor, Henry (Splawn) 1942-
CLC 44
See also CA 33-36R; CAAS 7; CANR 31; DLB
5

Taylor, Kamala (Purnaiya) 1924-
See Markandaya, Kamala
See also CA 77-80

Taylor, Mildred D. .... **CLC 21**
See also AAYA 10; BW 1; CA 85-88; CANR
25; CLR 9; DLB 52; JRDA; MAICYA; SAAS
5; SATA 15, 70

Taylor, Peter (Hillsman) 1917-1994
CLC 1, 4, 18, 37, 44, 50, 71; SSC 10
See also CA 13-16R; 147; CANR 9, 50; DLBY

81. 94; INT CANR-9; MTCW 1

Taylor, Robert Lewis 1912-
CLC 14
See also CA 1-4R; CANR 3, 64; SATA 10

Tchekhov, Anton
See Chekhov, Anton (Pavlovich)

Tchicaya, Gerald Felix 1931-1988
CLC 101
See also CA 129; 125

Tchicaya U Tam'si
See Tchicaya, Gerald Felix

Teasdale, Sara 1884-1933
TCLC 4
See also CA 104; 163; DLB 45; SATA 32

Tegner, Esaias 1782-1846
NCLC 2

Teilhard de Chardin, (Marie Joseph) Pierre
1881-1955 .... **TCLC 9**
See also CA 105

Temple, Ann
See Mortimer. Penelope (Ruth)

Tennant, Emma (Christina)................. 1937-
CLC 13, 52
See also CA 65-68; CAAS 9; CANR 10, 38,
59; DLB 14

Tenneshaw, S. M.
See Silverberg, Robert

Tennyson, Alfred 1809-1892
**NCLC 30, 65; DA; DAB; DAC; DAM
MST, POET; PC 6; WLC**
See also CDBLB 1832-1890; DLB 32

Teran, Lisa St. Aubin de ....**CLC 36**
See also St. Aubin de Teran, Lisa

Terence .... 195(?)B.C.-159B.C.
CMLC 14; DC 7

Teresa de Jesus, St. 1515-1582
LC 18

Terkel, Louis 1912-
See Terkel, Studs
See also CA 57-60, CANR 18, 45, 67; MTCW
1

Terkel, Studs ....**CLC 38**
See also Terkel. Louis
See also AITN 1

Terry, C. V.
See Slaughter, Frank G(ill)

Terry, Megan 1932-
CLC 19
See also CA 77-80; CABS 3; CANR 43; DLB 7

Tertullian .... c. 155-c. 245
CMLC 29

Tertz, Abram
See Sinyavsky, Andrei (Donatevich)

Tesich, Steve .... 1943(?)-1996
CLC 40, 69
See also CA 105; 152; DLBY 83

Teternikov, Fyodor Kuzmich 1863-1927
See Sologub, Fyodor
See also CA 104

Tevis, Walter 1928-1984
CLC 42
See also CA 113

Tey, Josephine .... **TCLC 14**
See also Mackintosh. Elizabeth
See also DLB 77

Thackeray, William Makepeace . 1811-1863
**NCLC 5, 14, 22, 43; DA; DAB; DAC; DAM
MST, NOV; WLC**
See also CDBLB 1832-1890; DLB 21, 55, 159,
163; SATA 23

Thakura, Ravindranatha
See Tagore, Rabindranath

Tharoor, Shashi 1956-

CLC 47
See also CA 21-24R; CANR 9, 24
Uriel, Henry
See Faust, Frederick (Schiller)
Uris, Leon (Marcus) 1924-
CLC 7, 32; DAM NOV, POP
See also AITN 1, 2; BEST 89:2; CA 1-4R;
CANR 1, 40, 65; MTCW 1; SATA 49
Urmuz
See Codrescu, Andrei
Urquhart, Jane 1949-
CLC 90; DAC
See also CA 113; CANR 32, 68
Ustinov, Peter (Alexander) 1921-
CLC 1
See also AITN 1; CA 13-16R; CANR 25, 51;
DLB 13
U Tam'si, Gerald Felix Tchicaya
See Tchicaya, Gerald Felix
U Tam'si, Tchicaya
See Tchicaya, Gerald Felix
Vachss, Andrew (Henry) 1942-
CLC 106
See also CA 118; CANR 44
Vachss, Andrew H.
See Vachss, Andrew (Henry)
Vaculik, Ludvik 1926-
CLC 7
See also CA 53-56; CANR 72
Vaihinger, Hans 1852-1933
TCLC 71
See also CA 116; 166
Valdez, Luis (Miguel) 1940-
CLC 84; DAM MULT; HLC
See also CA 101; CANR 32; DLB 122; HW
Valenzuela, Luisa 1938-
CLC 31, 104; DAM MULT; SSC 14
See also CA 101; CANR 32, 65; DLB 113; HW
Valera y Alcala-Galiano, Juan 1824-1905
TCLC 10
See also CA 106
Valery, (Ambroise) Paul (Toussaint Jules)
1871-1945 TCLC 4, 15; DAM POET; PC 9
See also CA 104; 122; MTCW 1
Valle-Inclan, Ramon (Maria) del 1866-1936
TCLC 5; DAM MULT; HLC
See also CA 106; 153; DLB 134
Vallejo, Antonio Buero
See Buero Vallejo, Antonio
Vallejo, Cesar (Abraham) 1892-1938
TCLC 3, 56; DAM MULT; HLC
See also CA 105; 153; HW
Vallette, Marguerite Eymery
See Rachilde
Valle Y Pena, Ramon del
See Valle-Inclan, Ramon (Maria) del
Van Ash, Cay 1918-
CLC 34
Vanbrugh, Sir John 1664-1726
LC 21; DAM DRAM
See also DLB 80
Van Campen, Karl
See Campbell, John W(ood, Jr.)
Vance, Gerald
See Silverberg, Robert
Vance, Jack .... CLC 35
See also Kuttner, Henry; Vance, John Holbrook
See also DLB 8
Vance, John Holbrook 1916-
See Queen, Ellery; Vance, Jack
See also CA 29-32R; CANR 17, 65; MTCW 1
Van Den Bogarde, Derek Jules Gaspard Ulric

Niven 1921-
See Bogarde, Dirk
See also CA 77-80
Vandenburgh, Jane .... CLC 59
See also CA 168
Vanderhaeghe, Guy 1951-
CLC 41
See also CA 113; CANR 72
van der Post, Laurens (Jan) 1906-1996
CLC 5
See also CA 5-8R; 155; CANR 35
van de Wetering, Janwillem 1931-
CLC 47
See also CA 49-52; CANR 4, 62
Van Dine, S. S. .... TCLC 23
See also Wright, Willard Huntington
Van Doren, Carl (Clinton) 1885-1950
TCLC 18
See also CA 111; 168
Van Doren, Mark 1894-1972
CLC 6, 10
See also CA 1-4R; 37-40R; CANR 3; DLB 45;
MTCW 1
Van Druten, John (William) 1901-1957
TCLC 2
See also CA 104; 161; DLB 10
Van Duyn, Mona (Jane) 1921-
CLC 3, 7, 63, 116; DAM POET
See also CA 9-12R; CANR 7, 38, 60; DLB 5
Van Dyne, Edith
See Baum, L(yman) Frank
van Itallie, Jean-Claude 1936-
CLC 3
See also CA 45-48; CAAS 2; CANR 1, 48; DLB 7
van Ostaijen, Paul 1896-1928
TCLC 33
See also CA 163
Van Peebles, Melvin 1932-
CLC 2, 20; DAM MULT
See also BW 2; CA 85-88; CANR 27, 67
Vansittart, Peter 1920-
CLC 42
See also CA 1-4R; CANR 3, 49
Van Vechten, Carl 1880-1964
CLC 33
See also CA 89-92; DLB 4, 9, 51
Van Vogt, A(lfred) E(lton) 1912-
CLC 1
See also CA 21-24R; CANR 28; DLB 8; SATA 14
Varda, Agnes 1928-
CLC 16
See also CA 116; 122
Vargas Llosa, (Jorge) Mario (Pedro) . 1936-
CLC 3, 6, 9, 10, 15, 31, 42, 85; DA; DAB;
DAC; DAM MST, MULT, NOV; HLC
See also CA 73-76; CANR 18, 32, 42, 67; DLB
145; HW; MTCW 1
Vasiliu, Gheorghe 1881-1957
See Bacovia, George
See also CA 123
Vassa, Gustavus
See Equiano, Olaudah
Vassilikos, Vassilis 1933-
CLC 4, 8
See also CA 81-84
Vaughan, Henry 1621-1695
LC 27
See also DLB 131
Vaughn, Stephanie .... CLC 62
Vazov, Ivan (Minchov) 1850-1921
TCLC 25

See also CA 121; 167; DLB 147
Veblen, Thorstein B(unde) 1857-1929
TCLC 31
See also CA 115; 165
Vega, Lope de 1562-1635
LC 23
Venison, Alfred
See Pound, Ezra (Weston Loomis)
Verdi, Marie de
See Mencken, H(enry) L(ouis)
Verdu, Matilde
See Cela, Camilo Jose
Verga, Giovanni (Carmelo) 1840-1922
TCLC 3; SSC 21
See also CA 104; 123
Vergil .... 70B.C.-19B.C.
CMLC 9; DA; DAB; DAC; DAM MST,
POET; PC 12; WLCS
Verhaeren, Emile (Adolphe Gustave) . 1855-
1916 .... TCLC 12
See also CA 109
Verlaine, Paul (Marie) 1844-1896
NCLC 2, 51; DAM POET; PC 2
Verne, Jules (Gabriel) 1828-1905
TCLC 6, 52
See also AAYA 16; CA 110; 131; DLB 123;
JRDA; MAICYA; SATA 21
Very, Jones 1813-1880
NCLC 9
See also DLB 1
Vesaas, Tarjei 1897-1970
CLC 48
See also CA 29-32R
Vialis, Gaston
See Simenon, Georges (Jacques Christian)
Vian, Boris 1920-1959
TCLC 9
See also CA 106; 164; DLB 72
Viaud, (Louis Marie) Julien 1850-1923
See Loti, Pierre
See also CA 107
Vicar, Henry
See Felsen, Henry Gregor
Vicker, Angus
See Felsen, Henry Gregor
Vidal, Gore 1925-
CLC 2, 4, 6, 8, 10, 22, 33, 72; DAM NOV,
POP
See also AITN 1; BEST 90:2; CA 5-8R; CANR
13, 45, 65; DLB 6, 152; INT CANR-13;
MTCW 1
Viereck, Peter (Robert Edwin) 1916-
CLC 4
See also CA 1-4R; CANR 1, 47; DLB 5
Vigny, Alfred (Victor) de 1797-1863
NCLC 7; DAM POET
See also DLB 119, 192
Vilakazi, Benedict Wallet 1906-1947
TCLC 37
See also CA 168
Villa, Jose Garcia 1904-1997
PC 22
See also CA 25-28R; CANR 12
Villaurrutia, Xavier 1903-1950
TCLC 80
See also HW
**Villiers de l'Isle Adam, Jean Marie Mathias
Philippe Auguste, Comte de**
.... 1838-1889
NCLC 3; SSC 14
See also DLB 123
Villon, Francois .... 1431-1463(?)
PC 13

Vinci, Leonardo da 1452-1519
    LC 12
Vine, Barbara .... CLC 50
    See also Rendell, Ruth (Barbara)
    See also BEST 90:4
Vinge, Joan (Carol) D(ennison) 1948-
    CLC 30; SSC 24
    See also CA 93-96; CANR 72; SATA 36
Violis, G.
    See Simenon, Georges (Jacques Christian)
Virgil
    See Vergil
Visconti, Luchino 1906-1976
    CLC 16
    See also CA 81-84; 65-68; CANR 39
Vittorini, Elio 1908-1966
    CLC 6, 9, 14
    See also CA 133; 25-28R
Vizenor, Gerald Robert 1934-
    CLC 103; DAM MULT
    See also CA 13-16R; CAAS 22; CANR 5, 21,
    44, 67; DLB 175; NNAL
Vizinczey, Stephen 1933-
    CLC 40
    See also CA 128; INT 128
Vliet, R(ussell) G(ordon) 1929-1984
    CLC 22
    See also CA 37-40R; 112; CANR 18
Vogau, Boris Andreyevich .... 1894-1937(?)
    See Pilnyak, Boris
    See also CA 123
Vogel, Paula A(nne) 1951-
    CLC 76
    See also CA 108
Voigt, Cynthia 1942-
    CLC 30
    See also AAYA 3; CA 106; CANR 18, 37, 40;
    CLR 13,48; INT CANR-18; JRDA;
    MAICYA; SATA 48, 79; SATA-Brief 33
Voigt, Ellen Bryant 1943-
    CLC 54
    See also CA 69-72; CANR 11, 29, 55; DLB 120
Voinovich, Vladimir (Nikolaevich) 1932-
    CLC 10, 49
    See also CA 81-84; CAAS 12; CANR 33, 67;
    MTCW 1
Vollmann, William T. 1959-
    CLC 89; DAM NOV, POP
    See also CA 134; CANR 67
Voloshinov, V. N.
    See Bakhtin, Mikhail Mikhailovich
Voltaire 1694-1778
    LC 14; DA; DAB; DAC; DAM DRAM,
    MST; SSC 12; WLC
von Daeniken, Erich 1935-
    CLC 30
    See also AITN 1; CA 37-40R; CANR 17, 44
von Daniken, Erich
    See von Daeniken, Erich
von Heidenstam, (Carl Gustaf) Verner
    See Heidenstam, (Carl Gustaf) Verner von
von Heyse, Paul (Johann Ludwig)
    See Heyse, Paul (Johann Ludwig von)
von Hofmannsthal, Hugo
    See Hofmannsthal, Hugo von
von Horvath, Odon
    See Horvath, Oedoen von
von Horvath, Oedoen
    See Horvath, Oedoen von
von Liliencron, (Friedrich Adolf Axel) Detlev
    See Liliencron, (Friedrich Adolf Axel) Detlev
    von
Vonnegut, Kurt, Jr. 1922-

CLC 1, 2, 3, 4, 5, 8, 12, 22, 40, 60, 111;
    DA; DAB; DAC; DAM MST, NOV, POP;
    SSC 8; WLC
    See also AAYA 6; AITN 1; BEST 90:4; CA 1-
    4R; CANR 1, 25, 49; CDALB 1968-1988;
    DLB 2, 8, 152; DLBD 3; DLBY 80; MTCW
    1
Von Rachen, Kurt
    See Hubbard, L(afayette) Ron(ald)
von Rezzori (d'Arezzo), Gregor
    See Rezzori (d'Arezzo), Gregor von
von Sternberg, Josef
    See Sternberg, Josef von
Vorster, Gordon 1924-
    CLC 34
    See also CA 133
Vosce, Trudie
    See Ozick, Cynthia
Voznesensky, Andrei (Andreievich) 1933-
    CLC 1, 15, 57; DAM POET
    See also CA 89-92; CANR 37; MTCW 1
Waddington, Miriam 1917-
    CLC 28
    See also CA 21-24R; CANR 12, 30; DLB 68
Wagman, Fredrica 1937-
    CLC 7
    See also CA 97-100; INT 97-100
Wagner, Linda W.
    See Wagner-Martin, Linda (C.)
Wagner, Linda Welshimer
    See Wagner-Martin, Linda (C.)
Wagner, Richard 1813-1883
    NCLC 9
    See also DLB 129
Wagner-Martin, Linda (C.) 1936-
    CLC 50
    See also CA 159
Wagoner, David (Russell) 1926-
    CLC 3, 5, 15
    See also CA 1-4R; CAAS 3; CANR 2, 71; DLB
    5; SATA 14
Wah, Fred(erick James) 1939-
    CLC 44
    See also CA 107; 141; DLB 60
Wahloo, Per 1926-1975
    CLC 7
    See also CA 61-64; CANR 73
Wahloo, Peter
    See Wahloo, Per
Wain, John (Barrington) 1925-1994
    CLC 2, 11, 15, 46
    See also CA 5-8R; 145; CAAS 4; CANR 23,
    54; CDBLB 1960 to Present; DLB 15, 27,
    139, 155; MTCW 1
Wajda, Andrzej 1926-
    CLC 16
    See also CA 102
Wakefield, Dan 1932-
    CLC 7
    See also CA 21-24R; CAAS 7
Wakoski, Diane 1937-
    CLC 2, 4, 7, 9, 11, 40; DAM POET; PC 15
    See also CA 13-16R; CAAS 1; CANR 9, 60;
    DLB 5; INT CANR-9
Wakoski-Sherbell, Diane
    See Wakoski, Diane
Walcott, Derek (Alton) 1930-
    CLC 2, 4, 9, 14, 25, 42, 67, 76; BLC 3;
    DAB; DAC; DAM MST, MULT, POET;
    DC 7
    See also BW 2; CA 89-92; CANR 26, 47; DLB
    117; DLBY 81; MTCW 1
Waldman, Anne (Lesley) 1945-

CLC 7
    See also CA 37-40R; CAAS 17; CANR 34, 69;
    DLB 16
Waldo, E. Hunter
    See Sturgeon, Theodore (Hamilton)
Waldo, Edward Hamilton
    See Sturgeon, Theodore (Hamilton)
Walker, Alice (Malsenior) 1944-
    CLC 5, 6, 9, 19, 27, 46, 58, 103; BLC 3;
    DA; DAB; DAC; DAM MST, MULT, NOV,
    POET, POP; SSC 5; WLCS
    See also AAYA 3; BEST 89:4; BW 2; CA 37-
    40R; CANR 9, 27, 49, 66; CDALB 1968-
    1988; DLB 6, 33, 143; INT CANR-27;
    MTCW 1; SATA 31
Walker, David Harry 1911-1992
    CLC 14
    See also CA 1-4R; 137; CANR 1; SATA 8;
    SATA-Obit 71
Walker, Edward Joseph 1934-
    See Walker, Ted
    See also CA 21-24R; CANR 12, 28, 53
Walker, George F. 1947-
    CLC 44, 61; DAB; DAC; DAM MST
    See also CA 103; CANR 21, 43, 59; DLB 60
Walker, Joseph A. 1935-
    CLC 19; DAM DRAM, MST
    See also BW 1; CA 89-92; CANR 26; DLB 38
Walker, Margaret (Abigail) 1915-
    CLC 1, 6; BLC; DAM MULT; PC 20
    See also BW 2; CA 73-76; CANR 26, 54; DLB
    76, 152; MTCW 1
Walker, Ted .... CLC 13
    See also Walker, Edward Joseph
    See also DLB 40
Wallace, David Foster 1962-
    CLC 50, 114
    See also CA 132; CANR 59
Wallace, Dexter
    See Masters, Edgar Lee
Wallace, (Richard Horatio) Edgar 1875-1932
    TCLC 57
    See also CA 115; DLB 70
Wallace, Irving 1916-1990
    CLC 7, 13; DAM NOV, POP
    See also AITN 1; CA 1-4R; 132; CAAS 1;
    CANR 1, 27; INT CANR-27; MTCW 1
Wallant, Edward Lewis 1926-1962
    CLC 5, 10
    See also CA 1-4R; CANR 22; DLB 2, 28, 143;
    MTCW 1
Walley, Byron
    See Card, Orson Scott
Walpole, Horace 1717-1797
    LC 2
    See also DLB 39, 104
Walpole, Hugh (Seymour) 1884-1941
    TCLC 5
    See also CA 104; 165; DLB 34
Walser, Martin 1927-
    CLC 27
    See also CA 57-60; CANR 8, 46; DLB 75, 124
Walser, Robert 1878-1956
    TCLC 18; SSC 20
    See also CA 118; 165; DLB 66
Walsh, Jill Paton .... CLC 35
    See also Paton Walsh, Gillian
    See also AAYA 11; CLR 2; DLB 161; SAAS 3
Walter, William Christian
    See Andersen, Hans Christian
Wambaugh, Joseph (Aloysius, Jr.) 1937-
    CLC 3, 18; DAM NOV, POP
    See also AITN 1; BEST 89:3; CA 33-36R;

CANR 42, 65; DLB 6; DLBY 83; MTCW 1

Wang Wei .... 699(?)-761(?)
PC 18

Ward, Arthur Henry Sarsfield 1883-1959
See Rohmer, Sax
See also CA 108

Ward, Douglas Turner 1930-
CLC 19
See also BW 1; CA 81-84; CANR 27; DLB 7,
38

Ward, Mary Augusta
See Ward, Mrs. Humphry

Ward, Mrs. Humphry 1851-1920
TCLC 55
See also DLB 18

Ward, Peter
See Faust, Frederick (Schiller)

Warhol, Andy .... 1928(?)-1987
CLC 20
See also AAYA 12; BEST 89:4; CA 89-92; 121;
CANR 34

Warner, Francis (Robert le Plastrier) 1937-
CLC 14
See also CA 53-56; CANR 11

Warner, Marina 1946-
CLC 59
See also CA 65-68; CANR 21, 55; DLB 194

Warner, Rex (Ernest) 1905-1986
CLC 45
See also CA 89-92; 119; DLB 15

Warner, Susan (Bogert) 1819-1885
NCLC 31
See also DLB 3, 42

Warner, Sylvia (Constance) Ashton
See Ashton-Warner, Sylvia (Constance)

Warner, Sylvia Townsend 1893-1978
CLC 7, 19; SSC 23
See also CA 61-64; 77-80; CANR 16, 60; DLB
34, 139; MTCW 1

Warren, Mercy Otis 1728-1814
NCLC 13
See also DLB 31, 200

Warren, Robert Penn 1905-1989
CLC 1, 4, 6, 8, 10, 13, 18, 39, 53, 59; DA;
DAB; DAC; DAM MST, NOV, POET; SSC
4; WLC
See also AITN 1; CA 13-16R; 129; CANR 10,
47; CDALB 1968-1988; DLB 2, 48, 152;
DLBY 80, 89; INT CANR-10; MTCW 1;
SATA 46; SATA-Obit 63

Warshofsky, Isaac
See Singer, Isaac Bashevis

Warton, Thomas 1728-1790
LC 15; DAM POET
See also DLB 104, 109

Waruk, Kona
See Harris, (Theodore) Wilson

Warung, Price 1855-1911
TCLC 45

Warwick, Jarvis
See Garner, Hugh

Washington, Alex
See Harris, Mark

Washington, Booker T(aliaferro) 1856-1915
TCLC 10; BLC 3; DAM MULT
See also BW 1; CA 114; 125; SATA 28

Washington, George 1732-1799
LC 25
See also DLB 31

Wassermann, (Karl) Jakob 1873-1934
TCLC 6
See also CA 104; DLB 66

Wasserstein, Wendy 1950-

CLC 32, 59, 90; DAM DRAM; DC 4
See also CA 121; 129; CABS 3; CANR 53; INT
129; SATA 94

Waterhouse, Keith (Spencer) 1929-
CLC 47
See also CA 5-8R; CANR 38, 67; DLB 13, 15;
MTCW 1

Waters, Frank (Joseph) 1902-1995
CLC 88
See also CA 5-8R; 149; CAAS 13; CANR 3,
18, 63; DLBY 86

Waters, Roger 1944-
CLC 35

Watkins, Frances Ellen
See Harper, Frances Ellen Watkins

Watkins, Gerrold
See Malzberg, Barry N(athaniel)

Watkins, Gloria .... 1955(?)-
See hooks, bell
See also BW 2; CA 143

Watkins, Paul 1964-
CLC 55
See also CA 132; CANR 62

Watkins, Vernon Phillips 1906-1967
CLC 43
See also CA 9-10; 25-28R; CAP 1; DLB 20

Watson, Irving S.
See Mencken, H(enry) L(ouis)

Watson, John H.
See Farmer, Philip Jose

Watson, Richard F.
See Silverberg, Robert

Waugh, Auberon (Alexander) 1939-
CLC 7
See also CA 45-48; CANR 6, 22; DLB 14, 194

Waugh, Evelyn (Arthur St. John) 1903-1966
CLC 1, 3, 8, 13, 19, 27, 44, 107; DA; DAB;
DAC; DAM MST, NOV, POP; WLC
See also CA 85-88; 25-28R; CANR 22; CDBLB
1914-1945; DLB 15, 162, 195; MTCW 1

Waugh, Harriet 1944-
CLC 6
See also CA 85-88; CANR 22

Ways, C. R.
See Blount, Roy (Alton), Jr.

Waystaff, Simon
See Swift, Jonathan

Webb, (Martha) Beatrice (Potter) 1858-1943
TCLC 22
See also Potter, (Helen) Beatrix
See also CA 117

Webb, Charles (Richard) 1939-
CLC 7
See also CA 25-28R

Webb, James H(enry), Jr. 1946-
CLC 22
See also CA 81-84

Webb, Mary (Gladys Meredith) . 1881-1927
TCLC 24
See also CA 123; DLB 34

Webb, Mrs. Sidney
See Webb, (Martha) Beatrice (Potter)

Webb, Phyllis 1927-
CLC 18
See also CA 104; CANR 23; DLB 53

Webb, Sidney (James) 1859-1947
TCLC 22
See also CA 117; 163; DLB 190

Webber, Andrew Lloyd ....CLC 21
See also Lloyd Webber, Andrew

Weber, Lenora Mattingly 1895-1971
CLC 12
See also CA 19-20; 29-32R; CAP 1; SATA 2;

SATA-Obit 26

Weber, Max 1864-1920
TCLC 69
See also CA 109

Webster, John .... 1579(?)-1634(?)
LC 33; DA; DAB; DAC; DAM DRAM,
MST; DC 2; WLC
See also CDBLB Before 1660; DLB 58

Webster, Noah 1758-1843
NCLC 30

Wedekind, (Benjamin) Frank(lin) 1864-1918
TCLC 7; DAM DRAM
See also CA 104; 153; DLB 118

Weidman, Jerome 1913-
CLC 7
See also AITN 2; CA 1-4R; CANR 1; DLB 28

Weil, Simone (Adolphine) 1909-1943
TCLC 23
See also CA 117; 159

Weininger, Otto 1880-1903
TCLC 84

Weinstein, Nathan
See West, Nathanael

Weinstein, Nathan von Wallenstein
See West, Nathanael

Weir, Peter (Lindsay) 1944-
CLC 20
See also CA 113; 123

Weiss, Peter (Ulrich) 1916-1982
CLC 3, 15, 51; DAM DRAM
See also CA 45-48; 106; CANR 3; DLB 69, 124

Weiss, Theodore (Russell) 1916-
CLC 3, 8, 14
See also CA 9-12R; CAAS 2; CANR 46; DLB
5

Welch, (Maurice) Denton 1915-1948
TCLC 22
See also CA 121; 148

Welch, James 1940-
CLC 6, 14, 52; DAM MULT, POP
See also CA 85-88; CANR 42, 66; DLB 175;
NNAL

Weldon, Fay 1931-
CLC 6, 9, 11, 19, 36, 59; DAM POP
See also CA 21-24R; CANR 16, 46, 63; CDBLB
1960 to Present; DLB 14, 194; INT CANR-
16; MTCW 1

Wellek, Rene 1903-1995
CLC 28
See also CA 5-8R; 150; CAAS 7; CANR 8; DLB
63; INT CANR-8

Weller, Michael 1942-
CLC 10, 53
See also CA 85-88

Weller, Paul 1958-
CLC 26

Wellershoff, Dieter 1925-
CLC 46
See also CA 89-92; CANR 16, 37

Welles, (George) Orson 1915-1985
CLC 20, 80
See also CA 93-96; 117

Wellman, John McDowell 1945-
See Wellman, Mac
See also CA 166

Wellman, Mac 1945-
CLC 65
See also Wellman, John McDowell; Wellman,
John McDowell

Wellman, Manly Wade 1903-1986
CLC 49
See also CA 1-4R; 118; CANR 6, 16, 44; SATA
6; SATA-Obit 47

CLC 1, 2, 5, 10, 22; DAB; DAC; DAM NOV; SSC 2
See also AITN 2; CA 45-48; 57-60; CANR 3, 33; CDBLB 1914-1945; DLB 34, 162; MTCW 1; SATA 22

Woiwode, L.
See Woiwode, Larry (Alfred)

Woiwode, Larry (Alfred) 1941-
CLC 6, 10
See also CA 73-76; CANR 16; DLB 6; INT CANR-16

Wojciechowska, Maia (Teresa) 1927-
CLC 26
See also AAYA 8; CA 9-12R; CANR 4, 41; CLR 1; JRDA; MAICYA; SAAS 1; SATA 1, 28, 83

Wolf, Christa 1929-
CLC 14, 29, 58
See also CA 85-88; CANR 45; DLB 75; MTCW 1

Wolfe, Gene (Rodman) 1931-
CLC 25; DAM POP
See also CA 57-60; CAAS 9; CANR 6, 32, 60, DLB 8

Wolfe, George C. 1954-
CLC 49; BLCS
See also CA 149

Wolfe, Thomas (Clayton) 1900-1938
TCLC 4, 13, 29, 61; DA; DAB; DAC; DAM MST, NOV; WLC
See also CA 104; 132; CDALB 1929-1941; DLB 9, 102; DLBD 2, 16; DLBY 85, 97; MTCW 1

Wolfe, Thomas Kennerly, Jr. 1930-
See Wolfe, Tom
See also CA 13-16R; CANR 9, 33, 70; DAM POP; DLB 185; INT CANR-9; MTCW 1

Wolfe, Tom .... CLC 1, 2, 9, 15, 35, 51
See also Wolfe, Thomas Kennerly, Jr.
See also AAYA 8; AITN 2; BEST 89:1; DLB 152

Wolff, Geoffrey (Ansell) 1937-
CLC 41
See also CA 29-32R; CANR 29, 43

Wolff, Sonia
See Levitin, Sonia (Wolff)

Wolff, Tobias (Jonathan Ansell) 1945-
CLC 39, 64
See also AAYA 16; BEST 90:2; CA 114; 117; CAAS 22; CANR 54; DLB 130; INT 117

Wolfram von Eschenbach ..... c. 1170-c. 1220
CMLC 5
See also DLB 138

Wolitzer, Hilma 1930-
CLC 17
See also CA 65-68; CANR 18, 40; INT CANR-18; SATA 31

Wollstonecraft, Mary 1759-1797
LC 5
See also CDBLB 1789-1832; DLB 39, 104, 158

Wonder, Stevie .... CLC 12
See also Morris, Stevcland Judkins

Wong, Jade Snow 1922-
CLC 17
See also CA 109

Woodberry, George Edward 1855-1930
TCLC 73
See also CA 165; DLB 71, 103

Woodcott, Keith
See Brunner, John (Kilian Houston)

Woodruff, Robert W.
See Mencken, H(enry) L(ouis)

Woolf, (Adeline) Virginia 1882-1941

TCLC 1, 5, 20, 43, 56; DA; DAB; DAC; DAM MST, NOV; SSC 7; WLC
See also CA 104; 130; CANR 64; CDBLB 1914-1945; DLB 36, 100, 162; DLBD 10; MTCW 1

Woolf, Virginia Adeline
See Woolf, (Adeline) Virginia

Woollcott, Alexander (Humphreys) 1887-1943
TCLC 5
See also CA 105; 161; DLB 29

Woolrich, Cornell 1903-1968
CLC 77
See also Hopley-Woolrich, Cornell George

Wordsworth, Dorothy 1771-1855
NCLC 25
See also DLB 107

Wordsworth, William 1770-1850
NCLC 12, 38; DA; DAB; DAC; DAM MST, POET; PC 4; WLC
See also CDBLB 1789-1832; DLB 93, 107

Wouk, Herman 1915-
CLC 1, 9, 38; DAM NOV, POP
See also CA 5-8R; CANR 6, 33, 67; DLBY 82; INT CANR-6; MTCW 1

Wright, Charles (Penzel, Jr.) 1935-
CLC 6, 13, 28
See also CA 29-32R; CAAS 7; CANR 23, 36, 62; DLB 165; DLBY 82; MTCW 1

Wright, Charles Stevenson 1932-
CLC 49; BLC 3; DAM MULT, POET
See also BW 1; CA 9-12R; CANR 26; DLB 33

Wright, Jack R.
See Harris, Mark

Wright, James (Arlington) 1927-1980
CLC 3, 5, 10, 28; DAM POET
See also AITN 2; CA 49-52; 97-100; CANR 4, 34, 64; DLB 5, 169; MTCW 1

Wright, Judith (Arandell) 1915-
CLC 11, 53; PC 14
See also CA 13-16R; CANR 31; MTCW 1; SATA 14

Wright, L(aurali) R. 1939-
CLC 44
See also CA 138

Wright, Richard (Nathaniel) 1908-1960
CLC 1, 3, 4, 9, 14, 21, 48, 74; BLC 3; DA; DAB; DAC; DAM MST, MULT, NOV; SSC 2; WLC
See also AAYA 5; BW 1; CA 108; CANR 64; CDALB 1929-1941; DLB 76, 102; DLBD 2; MTCW 1

Wright, Richard B(ruce) 1937-
CLC 6
See also CA 85-88; DLB 53

Wright, Rick 1945-
CLC 35

Wright, Rowland
See Wells, Carolyn

Wright, Stephen 1946-
CLC 33

Wright, Willard Huntington 1888-1939
See Van Dine, S. S.
See also CA 115; DLBD 16

Wright, William 1930-
CLC 44
See also CA 53-56; CANR 7, 23

Wroth, LadyMary .... 1587-1653(?)
LC 30
See also DLB 121

Wu Ch'eng-en .... 1500(?)-1582(?)
LC 7

Wu Ching-tzu 1701-1754
LC 2

Wurlitzer, Rudolph .... 1938(?)-
CLC 2, 4, 15
See also CA 85-88; DLB 173

Wycherley, William 1641-1715
LC 8, 21; DAM DRAM
See also CDBLB 1660-1789; DLB 80

Wylie, Elinor (Morton Hoyt) 1885-1928
TCLC 8; PC 23
See also CA 105; 162; DLB 9, 45

Wylie, Philip (Gordon) 1902-1971
CLC 43
See also CA 21-22; 33-36R; CAP 2; DLB 9

Wyndham, John .... CLC 19
See also Harris, John (Wyndham Parkes Lucas) Beynon

Wyss, Johann David Von 1743-1818
NCLC 10
See also JRDA; MAICYA; SATA 29; SATA-Brief 27

Xenophon .... c. 430B.C.-c. 354B.C.
CMLC 17
See also DLB 176

Yakumo Koizumi
See Hearn, (Patricio) Lafcadio (Tessima Carlos)

Yanez, José Donoso
See Donoso (Yanez), Jose

Yanovsky, Basile S.
See Yanovsky, V(assily) S(emenovich)

Yanovsky, V(assily) S(emenovich) 1906-1989
CLC 2, 18
See also CA 97-100; 129

Yates, Richard 1926-1992
CLC 7, 8, 23
See also CA 5-8R; 139; CANR 10, 43; DLB 2; DLBY 81, 92; INT CANR-10

Yeats, W. B.
See Yeats, William Butler

Yeats, William Butler 1865-1939
TCLC 1, 11, 18, 31; DA; DAB; DAC; DAM DRAM, MST, POET; PC 20; WLC
See also CA 104; 127; CANR 45; CDBLB 1890-1914; DLB 10, 19, 98, 156; MTCW 1

Yehoshua, A(braham) B. 1936-
CLC 13, 31
See also CA 33-36R; CANR 43

Yep, Laurence Michael 1948-
CLC 35
See also AAYA 5; CA 49-52; CANR 1, 46; CLR 3, 17, 54; DLB 52; JRDA; MAICYA; SATA 7, 69

Yerby, Frank G(arvin) 1916-1991
CLC 1, 7, 22; BLC 3; DAM MULT
See also BW 1; CA 9-12R; 136; CANR 16, 52; DLB 76; INT CANR-16; MTCW 1

Yesenin, Sergei Alexandrovich
See Esenin, Sergei (Alexandrovich)

Yevtushenko, Yevgeny (Alexandrovich) 1933-
CLC 1, 3, 13, 26, 51; DAM POET
See also CA 81-84; CANR 33, 54; MTCW 1

Yezierska, Anzia .... 1885(?)-1970
CLC 46
See also CA 126; 89-92; DLB 28; MTCW 1

Yglesias, Helen 1915-
CLC 7, 22
See also CA 37-40R; CAAS 20; CANR 15, 65; INT CANR-15; MTCW 1

Yokomitsu Riichi 1898-1947
TCLC 47

Yonge, Charlotte (Mary) 1823-1901
TCLC 48
See also CA 109; 163; DLB 18, 163; SATA 17

York, Jeremy
See Creasey, John

Literary Criticism Series
Cumulative Topic Index

This index lists all topic entries in Gale's *Classical and Medieval Literature Criticism, Contemporary Literary Criticism, Literature Criticism from 1400 to 1800, Nineteenth-Century Literature Criticism,* and *Twentieth-Century Literary Criticism.*

Topic Index

Contemporary Literary Criticism
Cumulative Nationality Index

Nationality Index

Nationality Index

Nationality Index

Nationality Index

Nationality Index